Perspectives on Africa

Global Perspectives

In a time of ever increasing global phenomena, the series *Global Perspectives* offers regionally focused volumes that attempt to move beyond the standard regional studies model. Each volume includes a selection of previously published articles and an extensive introduction by the volume editor, providing an overview of the history and cultures of the region under discussion. The articles are chosen to illustrate the dynamic processes by and through which scholars have described and understood regional history and culture, and to show how profoundly the ethnography of each region has influenced the direction and development of anthropological and social theory. The *Global Perspectives* series thus furnishes readers with both an introduction to the cultures of a vast array of world regions, and a history of how those cultures have been perceived and interpreted. The contributors include anthropologists, historians, philosophers, and critics. Collectively they show the multiplicities of voice in regional studies, and reveal the interpenetration of ideas and concepts within and across disciplines, regions, and historical periods.

Published

1. *Perspectives on Africa, Second Edition: A Reader in Culture, History, and Representation*, edited and introduced by Roy Richard Grinker and Christopher B. Steiner
2. *Perspectives on Las Américas: A Reader in Culture, History, and Representation*, edited and introduced by Matthew C. Gutmann, Félix V. Matos Rodríguez, Lynn Stephen, and Patricia Zavella
3. *Perspectives on the Caribbean: A Reader in Culture, History, and Representation*, edited and introduced by Philip Scher

EDITED BY ROY RICHARD GRINKER, STEPHEN C. LUBKEMANN,
AND CHRISTOPHER B. STEINER

perspectives on
Africa

A Reader in Culture, History,
and Representation

Second Edition

WILEY-BLACKWELL

A John Wiley & Sons, Ltd., Publication

This second edition first published 2010

© 2010 Blackwell Publishing Ltd except for editorial material and organization © 2010 Roy Richard Grinker, Stephen C. Lubkemann, and Christopher B. Steiner

Edition history: Blackwell Publishing Ltd (1e, 1997)

Blackwell Publishing was acquired by John Wiley & Sons in February 2007. Blackwell's publishing program has been merged with Wiley's global Scientific, Technical, and Medical business to form Wiley-Blackwell.

Registered Office
John Wiley & Sons Ltd, The Atrium, Southern Gate, Chichester, West Sussex, PO19 8SQ, United Kingdom

Editorial Offices
350 Main Street, Malden, MA 02148-5020, USA

9600 Garsington Road, Oxford, OX4 2DQ, UK

The Atrium, Southern Gate, Chichester, West Sussex, PO19 8SQ, UK

For details of our global editorial offices, for customer services, and for information about how to apply for permission to reuse the copyright material in this book please see our website at www.wiley.com/wiley-blackwell.

The right of Roy Richard Grinker, Stephen C. Lubkemann, and Christopher B. Steiner to be identified as the authors of the editorial material in this work has been asserted in accordance with the UK Copyright, Designs and Patents Act 1988.

Library of Congress Cataloging-in-Publication Data

Perspectives on Africa : a reader in culture, history, and representation / edited by Richard Grinker, Stephen C. Lubkemann, and Christopher B. Steiner. – 2nd ed.
   p. cm. – (Global perspectives)
  Includes bibliographical references and index.
  ISBN 978-1-4443-3522-4 (hardcover : alk. paper) – ISBN 978-1-4051-9060-2 (pbk. : alk. paper) 1. Ethnology–Africa, Sub-Saharan. 2. Africa, Sub-Saharan–Politics and government. 3. Africa, Sub-Saharan–Economic conditions. 4. Africa, Sub-Saharan–Social life and customs. I. Grinker, Roy Richard, 1961– II. Lubkemann, Stephen C., 1968– III. Steiner, Christopher Burghard. IV. Title. V. Series.
  GN645.P47 2010
  306.0967–dc22

2010002108

A catalogue record for this book is available from the British Library.

Set in 9.5/11.5pt Ehrhardt by SPi Publisher Services, Pondicherry
Printed in Singapore by Ho Printing Singapore Pte Ltd

01   2010

Contents

Acknowledgments

Jean and John Comaroff, *Of Revelation and Revolution, Vol. 1* (1991), from The University of Chicago Press, pp. 86–125.

Cheikh Anta Diop, "The Meaning of Our Work", pp. xii–xvii in *The African Origins of Civilisation: Myth or Reality* (1974), from Lawrence Hill Books.

Kwame Anthony Appiah, "Racisms" in *Anatomy of Racism*, ed. David Theo Goldberg (1990), pp. 3–17, included as "Europe Upside Down: Fallacies of the New Afrocentrism", *Times Literary Supplement*, 12 February 1993, from University of Minnesota Press.

V. Y. Mudimbe, *The Invention of Africa: Gnosis, Philosophy and the Order of Knowledge*, Indiana University Press (1988), pp. 1–2, 6–11, 15–16.

E. E. Evans-Pritchard, *The Nuer* (1940), pp. 95–110, 113–17, 135–8, from Oxford University Press.

Aidan W. Southall, "The Illusion of Tribe", in *The Passing of Tribal Man in Africa*, ed. P. C. W. Gutkind, pp. 28–31, 32–5, 39–43, 44, 46–50, from E.J. Brill, Leiden, 1970.

Leroy Vail, *The Creation of Tribalism in Southern Africa*, Copyright © 1988 Leroy Vail, from University of California Press, pp. 1–19.

Mary Douglas, "The Lele: Resistance to Change", in *Markets in Africa*, pp. 211–33, ed. Paul Bohannan and George Dalton (1962), from Northwestern University Press.

Catherine Coquery-Vidrovitch, "Research on an African Mode of Production", in *Relations of Production*, pp. 261–88, ed. David Seddon (1978), from Frank Cass & Co. Ltd.

Sharon Hutchinson, "The Cattle of Money and the Cattle of Girls Among the Nuer 1930–83," *American Ethnologist* (1992), 19 (2): 294–316, reproduced with permission from AAA.

Colin Turnbull, "The Lessons of the Pygmies", *Scientific American*, 208–22 (1963), pp. 28–37. Copyright © 1963 by Scientific American, Inc. from Scientific American, Inc.

Roy Richard Grinker, *Houses in the Rainforest: Ethnicity and Inequality among Farmers and Foragers in Central Africa* (1994), pp. 73–109. Copyright © 1994 The Regents of the University of California, from the University of California Press.

Edwin Wilmsen, *Land Filled with Flies* (1989), from the University of Chicago Press, pp. 1–32.

Jacqueline S. Soloway and Richard B. Lee, "Foragers, Genuine or Spurious?: Situating the Kalahari San in History", *Current Anthropology*, 31:2 (1990), pp. 109–47.

David Livingstone, 1858, "Conversations on Rain-making," pp. 22–7. In *Missionary Travels and Researches in South Africa*. London: Murray.

E. E. Evans-Pritchard, *Witchcraft, Oracles and Magic among the Azande* (1937; abridged edition 1976), from Oxford University Press.

Peter Winch, "Understanding a Primitive Society", *American Philosophical Quarterly*, I (1964), pp. 307–24, from American Philosophical Quarterly.

Ralph A. Austen, "The Moral Economy of Witchcraft: An Essay in Comparative History", *Modernity and Its Malcontents*, ed. Jean Comaroff and John Comaroff (1993), University of Chicago Press, pp. 89–110.

M. Griaule, *Conversations with Ogotemmêli* (1948), Oxford University Press, pp. 11–32, from International African Institute.

Paulin J. Hountondji, 1983. *African Philosophy, Myth and Reality*, pp. 55–70. Reprinted with permission of Indiana University Press.

Igor Kopytoff, "Ancestors as Elders in Africa," *Africa*, 41: 2 (1971), pp. 129–42. Reproduced by permission of International African Institute.

Simon Ottenberg, "Humorous Masks and Serious Politics among the Afikpo Ibo," in *African Art and Leadership*, ed. Douglas Fraser and Herbert M. Cole (1972), pp. 99–121. Copyright © 1972 by the Board of Regents of the University of Wisconsin Press. Reprinted by permission of the University of Wisconsin Press.

Olu Oguibe, "Art, Identity, Boundaries: Postmodernism and Contemporary African Art", in *Reading the Contemporary: African Art from Theory to the Marketplace*, ed. Olu Oguibe and Okwui Enwezor, pp. 17–19, 20–1, 23–5, 27–8, Institute of International Visual Arts (INIVA), London, 1999 © Olu Oguibe and INIVA.

Kelly M. Askew, "As Plato Duly Warned: Music, Politics, and Social Change in Coastal East Africa," *Anthropological Quarterly*, 2003, 76(4): 609–37.

Bayo Holsey, *Routes of Remembrance: Refashioning the Slave Trade in Ghana*, University of Chicago Press (2008), pp. 9–14, 109–10, 112–21.

Ester Boserup, "The Economics of Polygamy," in *Women's Role in Economic Development* (1970), Allen & Unwin, pp. 37–50, from Elisabeth W. Case, Agent.

Judith Van Allen, 1982, " 'Sitting on a Man': Colonialism and the Lost Political Institutions of Igbo Women," *Canadian Journal of African Studies*, 6 (2): 165–81.

Suzanne Leclerc-Madlala, "Virginity Testing: Managing Sexuality in a Maturing HIV/AIDS Epidemic", *Medical Anthropology Quarterly* 15(4), pp. 533–53, 2001.

Frederick D. Lugard, 1922, "Methods of Ruling Native Races," pp. 193–213. *The Dual Mandate in British Tropical Africa*. London: Blackwood.

Walter Rodney, *How Europe Underdeveloped Africa* (1972), Howard University Press, pp. 223–60. Copyright © 1972 by Walter Rodney. Reprinted with the permission of Howard University Press.

Terence Ranger, "The Invention of Tradition in Colonial Africa," in *The Invention of Tradition*, ed. Eric Hobsbawm and Terence Ranger (1983), by permission of the author and Past and Present Society, from Cambridge University Press.

Ngugi wa Thiong'o, *Detained: A Writer's Prison Diary* (1981), pp. 29–38, 56–62, from Heinemann Publishers (Oxford) Ltd.

Léopold Sédar Senghor, "Negritude: A Humanism of the Twentieth Century," pp. 179–92. In Wilfred Cartey and Martin Kilson, eds, *The African Reader: Independent Africa*, Vintage Books, New York. Copyright © 1970 by Wilfred Carty and Martin Kilson.

Frantz Fanon, *The Wretched of the Earth*, trans. Constance Farrington (1968, 1982) pp. 206–19, 226–7, 236–47. Copyright © 1963 by Presence Africaine, from HarperCollins Publishers Ltd and Grove/Atlantic, Inc.

Bruce J. Berman. 1991. "Nationalism, Ethnicity, and Modernity: The Paradox of Mau Mau," *Canadian Journal of African Studies/Revue canadienne des Études africaines* 25(2): 181–206.

Christopher B. Steiner. 1992. "The Invisible Face: Masks, Ethnicity, and the State in Côte d'Ivoire, West Africa," *Museum Anthropology* 16(3): 53–7. Reproduced by permission of the American Anthropological Association.

Max Gluckman, *Order and Rebellion in Tribal Africa: Collected Essays with Autobiographical Introduction*, ed. Max Gluckman, Routledge (2004), pp. 112–35. Copyright © 2004, Routledge. Reproduced by permission of Taylor & Francis Books UK.

Paul Richards, *Fighting for the Rainforest: War, Youth, and Resources in Sierra Leone*, Heinemann (1996), Portsmouth, NH, pp. xiii–xx, xxii–xxv, 25–32, 34, 56–60.

Christopher C. Taylor, *Sacrifice as Terror: The Rwandan Genocide of 1994*, Berg Publishers (2001), pp. 101–2, 105, 110–14, 117–19, 127–37, 139–40, 142–5, 153–7, 167–8, 174–6.

Stephen Lubkemann, "Where to Be an Ancestor? Reconstituting Socio-Spiritual Worlds among Displaced Mozambicans," *Journal of Refugee Studies*, Vol. 15, No. 2, 2002, Oxford University Press (2002), pp. Lub. 3–18, Lub. 20–4.

James Ferguson, *Expectations of Modernity: Myths and Meanings of Urban Life on the Zambian Copperbelt*, 1st edition (1999), pp. 1–7, 9–13, 234–47, © 1999. Reprinted by permission of University of California Press.

Peter Uvin, "Development Aid and Structural Violence. The Case of Rwanda," *Development*, 42 (3) (September 1999), pp. 49–56.

Daniel Jordan Smith, *A Culture of Corruption: Everyday Deception and Popular Discontent in Nigeria*, Princeton University Press (2008), pp. 28–52. © Princeton University Press. Reprinted by permission of Princeton University Press.

Jean-François Bayart, *The State in Africa: The Politics of the Belly*, 1993, pp. 211–27, 231–43, 268–9. Copyright © Longman Group UK Limited 1993.

Harry G. West, " 'Govern Yourselves!' Democracy and Carnage in Northern Mozambique," in Julia Paley (ed.), *Democracy: Anthropological Approaches*. Copyright © 2008 by the School for Advanced Research, Santa Fe, pp. 97–119.

Dianna Shandy, *Nuer-American Passages: Globalizing Sudanese Migration*, University Press of Florida, 1st edition, (2007), pp.109–26. Reprinted with permission by the University Press of Florida.

List of Maps

List of Figures

List of Plates

List of Tables

Introduction

Africa in Perspective

Introduction
Africa in Perspective

Even a rapid glance at the language we commonly use will demonstrate the ubiquity of visual metaphors. If we actively focus our attention on them, vigilantly keeping an eye out for those deeply embedded as well as those on the surface, we can gain an illuminating insight into the complex mirroring of perception and language. Depending, of course, on one's outlook or point of view, the prevalence of such metaphors will be accounted an obstacle or an aid to our knowledge of reality. It is, however, no idle speculation or figment of imagination to claim that if blinded to their importance, we will damage our ability to inspect the world outside and introspect the world within. And our prospects for escaping their thrall, if indeed that is even a foreseeable goal, will be greatly dimmed. ... This opening paragraph should suggest how ineluctable the modality of the visual actually is, at least in our linguistic practice. (Martin Jay 1993. *On the ease with which twenty-one visual metaphors can be used in only six sentences.*)

French scholar Marcel Griaule, one of the first anthropologists to carry out extensive field research in West Africa, was acutely aware that anthropological observation depends upon perspective. He was known to have his field assistants hold his ankles so that he could safely peer out over the edge of high cliffs to observe from above the Dogon people, whom he studied. This practice tells us much about Griaule's anthropology, to say nothing of how much he trusted his assistants. Whether as an anthropologist, or as an avid pilot, he wanted the grand view – to see everything all at once and from above. He wrote: "Man is silly: he suspects his neighbor, never the sky ... all his great and small intentions, his sanctuaries, his garbage, his careless repairs, his ambitions for growth appear on an aerial photograph." From above, Griaule wrote, he could discern "the underlying structure both of topography and of minds" (quoted in Clifford, 1988: 68).

Now imagine that you are atop the tallest structure in your community – it could be a mountain, a rooftop, the observation deck of a skyscraper or monument, or perhaps even the "Ivory

Tower" of an academic institution. The perspective appears to offer endless possibilities for sight, encumbered by little more than the biological limitations of human vision. The power of observation can be both liberating and daunting for we may sense not only how much we can see from certain places, but how little we see when we are elsewhere. From atop the imagined tower, you may cast your gaze over a wide expanse, and in so doing assume that your view is somehow "real" or "true" and that your perception is "total" and "collective."

Yet, if we can learn anything from Griaule's efforts, it is that our views are largely determined by the structures of observation. Each view frames an object or image that negates our liberation, for when we look *at* something we always, necessarily, look *from* somewhere else: whether it be from a particular place, a cardinal direction, an above or a below. Pure vision is an illusion. "There is no vision without purpose," writes literary critic W. J. T. Mitchell, for the "world is already clothed in our systems of representation" (1986: 38).

The structures that frame our perception may be as obvious as the windows of the Empire State Building, the observation deck of the Washington Monument, or the placards reading "scenic view" that dot the highways of America indicating to tourists where to take a photograph and capture their visual memory. Sometimes these structures are much less obvious, however, as when we see things through the looking glass of our own values, assumptions, or beliefs – for example, when European explorers looked at Africa through the distorting lens of colonialism, when missionaries judged African religions in terms of Christian tenets and thought, or when anthropologists evaluated beliefs in witchcraft according to the laws and methods of Western science.

Some points of view also have masters or authors – a fact that once again negates the apparent liberation of what appears to be a privileged sight (or site): Eiffel, Hancock, and Washington, among others. Like these architects of national landscapes, the master authors of anthropology have constructed the sites (or sights) from which students of Africa have viewed the histories, societies, and cultures of the continent. Their own views, in turn, were of course heavily influenced by the values of their time – values which authorized certain perspectives and limited or prohibited others. When we critically assess these perspectives, the observers become the observed, surveyors are put under surveillance and are transformed at once into subject and object.

In an essay on the development of public exhibitions in Europe, cultural critic Tony Bennett (1994: 133) reminds us that observation can also be a form of domination or surveillance; that when we engage in survey and inspection we simultaneously become the seer and the seen. There is power with the knowledge of observation, writes Bennett, "the power to order objects and persons into a world to be known and to lay it out before a vision capable of encompassing it as a totality" (1994: 149).

Just as observation is a form of control, so too is the process of writing and representing what has been observed. In a study of language and colonialism in the former Belgian Congo, anthropologist Johannes Fabian argues that

> Colonial expeditions were not just a form of invasion; nor was their purpose inspection. They were determined efforts at *in-scription*. By putting regions on a map and native words on a list, explorers laid the first and deepest, foundations for colonial power. By giving proof of the 'scientific' nature of their enterprise they exercised power in a pure subtle form – as the power to name, to describe, to classify. (1986: 24)

To return for a moment to Griaule's station atop a cliff in the rocky escarpments of Mali, we might argue also that his position makes him something of a spy – able to look at others without being looked at by them. Griaule inspects his field site with the "imperial eyes" of the colonizer that sought to describe and, in so doing, possess "their" (dominated) others in Africa and elsewhere (Pratt, 1992). The anthropologist, in this case, is invisible while what he sees from his site of observation is rendered completely visible. This is what philosopher Michel Foucault calls "disciplinary power" – a form of authority and control which is "exercised through its invisibility" (1979: 89). In most cases, of course, the structural distance between the observer and the observed is less obvious than in the case of Griaule's panoptic vision of Africa, but the underlying principle of how power and control might be gained through observation and description is almost always present in transcultural encounters and in any system of representation. "It is the fact of being constantly seen," Foucault concludes, "that maintains the disciplined individual in his subjection" (1979: 87).

If ideas about ourselves and others derive from the ways in which we see and write, and if seeing and writing are implicated in power relations, then it would be reasonable to question critically some of the products of vision and writing. These include not only books and encyclopedias, but the concepts and ideas that have emerged from them: family, kingship, clanship, tribe, culture, ethnicity, feudality, bureaucracy, state, nation, and Africa, among others. To question these terms is not to dismiss them but rather to determine how, why, and when they appeared, and assess to what degree they are "real" concepts, with reference to an objective reality, or whether they are cultural and heuristic constructs created for particular scientific, political, economic, or other purposes. The last term mentioned – Africa – is especially curious because, at one level, Africa refers to an actual geological unity (the second largest continent after Asia), but at another level it refers to much more. The naming of a continent may seem benign or innocuous, yet in past centuries, the term "continent" implied something that holds or retains. Indeed, the delineation and naming of a particular land mass by European explorers and geographers has often led to the implication that Africa has, until recently, remained relatively isolated from the currents of world history. Africa appears in European literature and art as a static, timeless, and separated land.

From this perspective, slaves may have left Africa for the New World, but little entered Africa or crossed its paths until the era of European colonialism. Such a view is absolutely wrong, since Africans have been a powerful and fundamental force in world history long before the rise of European civilizations. Africa has also been elaborated and articulated negatively in Europe and North America in broad cultural and racial terms, as "dark," "savage," "barbarous," "heathen," "uncivilized," and "underdeveloped" – expressions that have had profound ramifications on the idea of Africa in Western thought. Again, these terms mask more about Africa than they reveal, and tell us much more about Europeans than about Africans. But recognition of these views highlights the extent to which our visions or illusions of Africa are created out of particular assumptions – biases, prejudices, fantasies, or ideologies – and how these visions take shape in the various representational forms of art, literature, and scholarship.

This book is about scholarly perspectives. It is about how some writers have looked at Africa, and how we today look back at them and see scholarship in a new light. This book, then, is not only about perspectives on Africa as attitudes or points of view, but also about perspectives in a more technical and artistic sense, as the process through which scholars render complex and multidimensional experiences and phenomena as texts. Perspective – from the Latin *perspectiva*, meaning optic and clear to the sight (Jay, 1993: 53) – refers in art to the technique of rendering spatial extension into depth on a flat surface, such as drawing a three-dimensional scene on a shallow plane. The development of perspectivist technique as artistic convention during the European Renaissance privileged the viewer as the center of vision, and with the power to order conceptions of reality through his gaze (see Jay, 1993; Berger, 1972). We are concerned here with this aspect of perspective, because we believe that, as a metaphor rooted in the visual arts, it can help us understand intellectual history. Are there parallels, for example, between the illusionist painter's visual sleight-of-hand and the representation of Africa? How are the processes of seeing and looking transformed into writing, reading, and the production of knowledge?

One of the central goals of this volume is to highlight the relationship between "perspective" as technique, position, and metaphor, and "Africa" as an objective reality. We hope to uncover Africa as a concept; and to consider Africa as a subject that has been constructed, invented, and interpreted in writing. Is there such a "thing" as Africa? How can we group hundreds of different cultures and languages into a single category called Africa? How do we learn about its peoples and cultures? How can we study Africa and still comprehend it as a process of invention, and as a constructed entity that masks its own heterogeneity?

To some extent the history of learning about culture has involved a shifting of perspectives, from the privileged position of the observer looking at (or down at) objects of scientific scrutiny, to the position of a participant engaged in a dialogue, who looks with (rather than simply at) the people with whom he or she creates and shares a fieldwork experience. Many African authors, in fact, analyze their own cultures, or study the cultures of Europe that once studied them. Africanist scholars of the past largely looked from above, while many of those in the present look from a level position or from below. Looking from below implies being sensitive to the power of observation about which Bennett spoke, recognizing the biases inherent in any one perspective, and considering how anthropologists and their assistants (usually called "informants") come to understand culture together; sometimes it also means paying special attention to the beliefs, experiences, and interests of people whose voices may be relatively absent from the historical and ethnographic record: the poor, the marginalized, the oppressed. A critical reading of many texts in this volume may elicit questions about an author's perspective. Is his or her interpretation of culture a view from afar? Is it a view from close and within? Whose voices are heard? Whose voices are silent or muted?

One of the central paradoxes of intensive anthropological fieldwork is that it necessitates multiple positions: to be close for a time, during the period of field research, and then to step back and consider from afar the world in which one participated and lived. Like a pointillist painting by Seurat, which appears as a chaotic collection of dots from up close but reveals itself as a clear and detailed image from a distance, scholarly work requires movement and dynamics. The haggling one may have observed in a local cattle market in Kenya, or the witchcraft accusation one may have listened to in Democratic Republic of Congo, may appear differently from the remove of an academic vantage point. The one is now framed in terms of "the circulation of commodities," "the construction of value" or "spheres of exchange"; the other, in terms of "social control," "belief systems," or "modes of thought." Taking the language of psychoanalyst Heinz Kohut, some anthropologists have noted the value of distinguishing between "experience near" concepts – such as the Azande's conceptions of witchcraft or a Lese boy's affinity and affection for his mother's brother – and "experience distant" concepts – such as "cosmological belief" and "matrilateral alliance" (Geertz, 1983: 57). Or, to use an American example, "best friend" and "significant other" are near, while "social relations" and "love object" are distant. Sometimes the principles of culture (experience distant concepts) emerge out of the minutiae of everyday life, as a linguist might generalize from a collection of particular sentences to a set of abstract grammatical rules that stand apart from, and yet constitute, the act of speaking any one of those sentences. Stepping back is important because it is sometimes difficult to see things that are too close to us. We take them for granted and, as the saying goes, cannot see the forest for the trees.

Another paradox of movement, from far to close and from close to far, involves the dynamic relation between the exotic and the familiar. Often what piques our interest is something that seems peculiar and unfamiliar – a ritual practice, a marriage system, a religious belief. Seen from a distance, the values and practices of different cultures may even seem irrational or bizarre. How odd it must appear to some people that the Azande of central Africa, as Evans-Pritchard represented them (see Part V), explain all misfortunes, including the death of the eldest people in their communities, as caused by witchcraft. Yet, as we begin to understand a belief or practice in the context in which it exists, and from the perspective of those to whom it belongs, the irrational or the strange begins to make sense, and is thus translated into our own logic of understanding. The authors included in Part V comprehend the logic of Azande witchcraft beliefs without judging them from their own scientific or philosophical perspectives. The central debate of Part V, however, is precisely about the relation between the exotic and the familiar. Evans-Pritchard sees the Azande as not too different from Western scientists (although he considers that they are wrong to believe in witches), while Peter Winch views the Azande as quite distinct. Winch resists strongly the impulse to view the Azande in *terms* of Western science, as merely "bad scientists," and illustrates for us the risk of making the unfamiliar familiar in the wrong terms, or to erase all difference and see everyone as essentially alike. And, therein lies the difficult paradox of simultaneously making the familiar strange and the strange familiar (Spiro, 1990).

Much of the work of addressing these challenging problems is carried out by scholars at the typewriter or, today, on the word processor. The reason why we focus our attention in this volume on the act of writing is that we learn about Africa by reading texts, and we become scholars of Africa by writing them. Most anthropologists spend months, if not years, conducting research abroad, but when they return home they are confronted with translating experience into text. Ethnography, the general term for anthropological description, literally means "writing" (-graphy) "culture" (ethno-). The writing necessarily involves not only the translation of experience, but the actual construction of an ensemble of words that must fit the conventions of scholarly discourse: the words must form grammatical sentences, then paragraphs, chapters, and books. An ethnography might involve the division of a society into distinct parts, such as kinship, economy, religion, and politics, when in everyday life these aspects of culture are inextricably bound together. Certain voices may be made more salient than others simply because they were the voices the ethnographer heard. And the writer's own interests will determine how certain topics or ideas are selected for writing. Although authors seek to represent many dimensions, writing (like filmmaking) leaves a lot of social experience on the cutting room floor. Because writing is a process of selection, making and representing, scholarship and fiction have more in common than meets the eye. They constitute forms of verbal painting (Pratt, 1992).

Our concern with these problems, and what they mean for the future of African studies, led us to focus this volume on how African history and culture have been *represented* in writing. On what authority do authors represent a whole society and its identities? This is a particularly troublesome question, when we consider that many anthropologists have worked among people who cannot represent themselves in writing because they do not have a written language or because they are otherwise unable (or unauthorized) to write and publish. The academic degrees and the requirements of publishers and reading audiences may serve to authorize only certain people to speak – hence the relation between the word author and author*ize*. How do we identify, define, and characterize someone else's culture? How can we evaluate whether some characterizations are "better" or more "accurate" than others? Critical readers of scholarly work must give special care to analyzing the concepts, and the narrative strategies and structures which authors use to give themselves the authority to represent and to be believed (Clifford, 1983).

Culture

Few concepts in contemporary social science are as abstract and imprecise, and at the same time such a central object of study, as "culture." Anthropologist Clyde Kluckhohn (1978) once compiled several hundred different definitions of the term culture. Of course, the more abstract the term the more multiple are its possible meanings, and the more useful it can be as an analytic construct. It is thus not necessarily fruitful for us to offer a unified or precise definition of culture, especially since the more than fifty authors represented in this book employ the concept in different ways. For some, culture is a public system of symbols and classifications that gives meaning to an otherwise meaningless and disordered world; for others, culture is a form of integration, through which social, economic, religious, and political institutions are linked together into a coherent whole; for others yet, culture refers to the ways in which human beings create belief systems and social practices so that they are better able to benefit from the material world in which they subsist.

We would like to stress that it is extraordinarily difficult not only to define culture, but to determine if there is a place where one culture begins and another ends. Anthropologists have long been committed to identifying the boundaries of distinct cultures (in past times called "tribes," a subject addressed in Part II), and to salvaging cultures putatively on the brink of extinction in the rapid and sometimes destructive forces of modernization and globalization.

However, anthropologists and other scholars from a variety of different disciplines have begun to question the conventional view that the non–Western world consists of "endangered authenticities" (Clifford, 1988: 5). They have begun to believe, instead, that different cultures have been in contact with one another for as long as humanity has existed, and that, in the late twentieth century, the boundaries of culture are even more permeable and fluid. Most readers of this book will be familiar with the concept of authenticity, and have at some time seen advertisements for restaurants or shops offering "authentic" goods from some "exotic" corner of the globe. At what point does something become "inauthentic"? Or are we all living within a complex matrix of inauthenticities that we try to represent as homogeneous or unique cultures?

The continent of Africa can be characterized as a collection of cultures, but it is also a place for the blending of many cultures, a process sometimes called "syncretism" (Stewart and Shaw, 1994). The term refers to the merging of different forms into one, as when the Nuer of the Sudan incorporate into their social organization rituals borrowed from the neighbouring Dinka and, in the process, may no longer view them as being of Dinka origin. Or when religious leaders in Africa combine elements of Christianity or Islam with indigenous ideas and rituals into a unified system of belief and practice.

The cover of this book highlights the blending of cultures in Africa. The image appears to depict Saint Peter's Basilica in Vatican City, Rome. But the photograph, as the figures in the foreground might indicate, was taken in Africa not Italy. During the 1980s, Félix Houphouët-Boigny, the first president of independent Côte d'Ivoire, and a devout Roman Catholic, built this variation of Saint Peter's in his natal village of Yamoussoukro. His rendition of the basilica was constructed to specifications that made it larger than the original. This post-Renaissance-style European church erected in the heart of Africa's savannah, engineered by a Lebanese architect, and built by Israeli and French workers, is the largest Christian edifice ever constructed, with a dome rising nearly forty feet higher than Saint Peter's. The Basilica of Our Lady of Peace, as it is called, incorporates 272 Greek columns, resplendent doors made of thirteenth-century stained glass from France, and a 7.4-acre esplanade of Italian marble tiles designed to hold 300,000 worshippers. Pope John Paul II consecrated the basilica in September, 1990, amid a ceremony of Baule dancers (Massaquoi, 1990: 116).

When Houphouët-Boigny was buried in Yamoussoukro in 1994, a spectacular event was held at the basilica. *The New York Times* reported at length on the dazzling assemblage of visual expressions that were present that day, while also commenting on the fascinating mix of cultural traditions:

> Two months after his death, President Félix Houphouët-Boigny of the Ivory Coast [Côte d'Ivoire], one of the last of a generation of African leaders to guide his people from colonialism, finally received a somber state funeral today in the world's largest church, which he had built in his ancestral village.... All the panoply of Western religious liturgy mixed with traditional African customs were on display here: the stirring music of Handel and Gounod; the undulating music and dance of ancient African rituals; a huge chorus dressed in bright batik dress singing "*laagoh budji gnia*," the Baoule-language words for "Lord, it is you who has made all things"; a military honor guard dressed in bright red coats and brandishing glittering swords, and hundreds of village elders, resplendent in huge multi-colored strips of kente and korhogo cloth. (Noble, 1994: A1)

This is a particularly spectacular example of cultural blending and the creative assembly of diverse traditions, but what it illustrates for us is the general condition in which so-called "distinct cultures" are actually composed of many threads, each of which emerges out of the complexities of history, and which sometimes come together to form a cultural fabric of new and seamless wholes. Other notable examples of blending include Zionism, perhaps the most popular form of Christianity in southern Africa (Sundkler, 1948; Comaroff, 1985), and the Kimbanguist church of the Democratic Republic of Congo (Martin, 1975). In Zionism, the prophet Isaiah Shembe not only brought together aspects of Christianity with Zulu culture, but also the cosmological beliefs and practices of several different southern African or "Bantu" cultures. Thus, the Zulu king becomes transformed in Zionism as the Bantu Church Father. In Kimbanguism, the prophet Simon Kimbangu articulated Christian ideas of salvation, but joined them with healing and anti-witchcraft rituals.

In addition to syncretism one also finds cultural pluralism, that is, the co-existence of alternative beliefs and practices without necessarily being merged together into new syncretic entities. For instance, in many parts of Africa there are different kinds of therapeutic alternatives, and they do not always conflict with one another; different illnesses may call for different kinds of therapies. For instance, John Janzen (1978) has shown how the Kongo of the Democratic Republic of Congo choose among a variety of techniques for healing: Western medical therapies, the art of the *banganga* or "traditional healers," kinship therapy, in which kin members become integrally involved in diagnosis and treatment, and a set of ritual healing choices that can be roughly grouped under the categories of initiation and purification. There are no clear or impermeable boundaries between these therapeutic systems – for example, kinship therapy usually involves some form of purification, and *banganga* usually try to involve kin members in therapy management – yet neither do they form a syncretic system that combines, or reconciles, all of them together.

History

The process of narrating and interpreting the African past has long been an intellectual struggle against European assumptions and prejudices about the nature of time and history in Africa. As historian David William Cohen states, "The major issue in the reconstruction of the African past is ... the question of how far voices exterior to Africa shape the presentation of Africa's past and present" (1985: 198). Many historians, especially those without any background or training in African historiography, have assumed incorrectly that prior to European contact with Africa indigenous "traditions" were ancient, permanent, and reproduced from generation to generation without change. In a now famous statement made in the early 1960s, Hugh Trevor-Roper, an eminent professor of Modern History at Oxford University, declared that "Perhaps, in the future, there will be some African history to teach. But at present there is none: there is only the history of the Europeans in Africa. The rest is darkness ... and darkness is not the subject of history" (quoted in Fage, 1981: 31).

This false image of cultural isolation and temporal stagnation has been attributed not only to African history, but to prehistory as well. Graham C. Clark, for example, could write with "scientific" authority and confidence in the 1970s that much of Africa during the Late Pleistocene "remained a kind of cultural museum in which Archaic traditions continued ... without contributing to the main course of human progress" (1971: 181). Contrary to this view, however, research in paleontology and archaeology has shown that the first microlithic technology emerged in Africa, and that cattle domestication and pottery may have been indigenous African developments. We also often forget that the earliest complex states emerged on the continent of Africa, in what is today Egypt (McIntosh and McIntosh, 1983). If we cast our sights back to the evolution of humanity, we find that human-made tools appear in Africa at least 2.6 million years ago, long before they appear in Eurasia.

Africa was indeed the birthplace of human kind. The earliest available evidence of our hominid ancestors has been unearthed in the Afar region of Ethiopia, and in the Rift Valley of northern Kenya and Ethiopia, where the remains are dated at about 4.5 million years before present (see White, Suwa, and Asfaw, 1994; Leakey, Feibel, McDougall, and Walker, 1995). The first appearance in the world of modern human behavior – people acting like contemporary humans – is at least 200,000 y.b.p. in highland Ethiopia, and the first modern human beings – people who look like contemporary humans – appear at least 100,000 y.b.p. throughout east and southern Africa in what are today Ethiopia, Kenya, Tanzania, and South Africa. From prehistory onward, Africa has remained a vital and central force in building the world we live in. Until the late 1950s, however, Africanist historical scholarship consisted almost entirely of the history of Europeans in Africa, and was taught in university courses under the rubric of "colonial history." Little or no attention was paid to indigenous African views of the past or to the role Africans played in shaping global developments, processes, and structures. Explanation in this type of historiography – exogenous rather than endogenous history – consisted of locating the external (rather than internal) causes for African events, and thus denied Africans their own historical agency.

Beginning sometime in the last several decades, a period which coincides with the dismantling of European colonialism and the rise of independent African nation-states, the study of African history has unfolded in two new, radically different, and more promising directions – both of which have shifted the gaze of the historian away from Europe, and its colonial preoccupations, and toward the continent of Africa itself. The first of these new histories of Africa has been written on a global scale, and "traces connections among discernible communities, regions, peoples, and nations that anthropologists have often separated and reified as discrete entities" (Roseberry, 1989: 125). Rather than view Africa as a set of cultural enclaves, this new historical approach looks at the place of Africa in shaping the world (Wolf, 1982). This kind of transnational focus demonstrates that precolonial, colonial, and postcolonial Africa has not simply been subjected to the progression of other peoples' histories, but has produced, directed, and contributed to the course of world events.

The second type of history that is being written in Africa today is a type of "social history" that attempts to reconstruct the past from the records of ordinary lives. Rather than recount "official" histories from above – whether it be from European colonial archives or from African chronicles of conquest or kinglists of royal successions – this new history of Africa looks instead from below to discover the place and meaning of the past in the individual and collective thought of Africans. Because many African societies chronicled the past in oral rather than written form, the challenge of this type of history is to bring together a multitude of small fragments of local knowledge, myths, epic narratives, and oral texts (Vansina, 1985). From a Western point of view, there is a tendency to perceive oral traditions as being less "accurate" or "reliable" than written histories (see Henige, 1972; Clifford, 1988: 277–346). If we take the position, however, that *all* history is in fact a highly biased and often haphazard and radical selection of only a few moments salvaged from a much denser swirl of past human activities and events, then the authority of the written word is no more credible than verbal accounts. Both are representations of reality that must be understood within the cultural context of their production and reproduction. The notion of perspective, of course, underlies all historical accounts, since "different people carry in their heads different modes and systems of arranging and simplifying the complex and mas- sive information that the past remits to the living" (Cohen, 1977: 15).

Anthropology has always had a peculiar and rather uneasy relationship to history. In trying to define the field of anthropology as a distinct and unified discipline, many anthropologists in the early to mid twentieth century dismissed the study of history as something which was irrelevant to the anthropological inquiry (Schapera, 1962). Evans-Pritchard, for example, in the days before he began to stress the importance of history to social anthropology, declared in 1950 that "a society can be understood satisfactorily without reference to its past" (1950: 120). Today it is clear that anthropology cannot ignore history. The past conditions the present, and so the present must be understood as an isolated moment or a "slice of time" in what is a much broader and more complex process of change.

There have been two central shifts in historical perspective: one concerns the unit of analysis, the other social dynamics. First, whereas most anthropologists once treated African societies as discrete cultural isolates, contemporary anthropologists now view them as historically contin- gent, with permeable and changing boundaries. Second, although anthropologists once viewed societies synchronically as systems that maintained and reproduced themselves in harmonious balance, or oscillated between a small number of organizational principles (Leach, 1954), they now tend to emphasize that societies are constantly changing and in flux. Rather than looking at societies as closed "systems" from which one must attempt to distill pervasive patterns and structural principles, many anthropologists now look for "process" – shifting trajectories and the patterns of change that emerge through time. The problem with history for anthropology is that most ethnographic fieldwork is conducted in a limited geographic region and in the course of a relatively short span of time, where change may not be apparent or observable (Moore, 1986: 7). The challenge, then, is to fit the "ethnographic present" of field research into a larger frame- work of historical development, process, and change. That framework must take into account the dynamics of life in Africa, including the realities of violence, governance, displacement, and voluntary population movements.

Representation

One of the key problems in contemporary anthropology is what George Marcus and Michael Fischer (1986) have called the "crisis of representation." By this they refer to the fact that anthro- pology, and the humanities and social sciences in general, can no longer make claims of represent- ing objective truths and mimetic reality. If postmodern theory has taught us anything, it is that knowledge and its images are constructed from individual perspectives, and therefore, by definition, can only be biased, partial, and greatly simplified reductions of more complex and nuanced wholes. All descriptions of the social world are filtered through the subjective lenses of multiple frameworks of interpretation – whether it be the perception of the observer, the language of the narrator, or the assumptions of the reader. Representations, in short, can neither posit unmediated authenticity nor make claim to universal validity (Duncan and Ley, 1993: 3–5).

Those who teach and study Africa in the 21st century must learn to problematize the issue of representation in order to locate and unpack the economic, political, personal, or other motivations that might underlie any particular image of Africa. In his seminal books, entitled *The Invention of Africa* (1988) and *The Idea of Africa* (1994), Congolese scholar and philosopher V. Y. Mudimbe has argued that since Greek times Africa has "been represented in Western scholarship by 'fantasies' and 'constructs' made up by scholars and writers" (1994: xv). What Mudimbe is arguing here is not that the continent called "Africa" is somehow detached from the globe or that it is a "geographic fiction," but rather he is saying that our knowledge of Africa has been constructed and disseminated through (mostly negative) images and theories by Europeans about Africa and Africans (Gyekye, 1995: xxiv). Such images of Africa have often been used by Western writers to "establish opposites and 'others' whose actuality is always subject to the continuous interpretation and reinterpretation of their differences from 'us'" (Said, 1995: 3). For this reason, representations of Africa generally tell us far less about those who are being represented than they do about the preoccupations and prejudices of those engaged in the act of representing.

At different moments in history, negative images of Africa have been used to endorse various Western activities on the African continent – such as the slave trade, military occupation, colonial expansionism, Christian evangelical conversion, or even the terms and conditions of international World Bank loans. The following is a clear and poignant example of how a particular representation of Africa could be used for self-interested goals and, in this case, for personal economic gain. In the late eighteenth century, Archibald Dalzel, a British adventurer and political envoy in Africa, published an historical account of the West African kingdom of Dahomey (1793). In this folio volume, illustrated (and, as it were, authenticated) by numerous copperplate engravings, Dalzel painted an especially negative image of the peoples of Dahomey, describing them variously as a "savage," "warlike," and "ferocious" nation whose rulers legitimated their authority through the frenetic exercise of large-scale human sacrifices. He argued that the practice of raiding Dahomean villages to capture men and women for export as slave labor to the Americas could be justified on the grounds that it rescued potential victims of human sacrifice who would otherwise be killed by their own people. "Whatever evils the slave-trade may be attended with," wrote Dalzel, "this we are sure of, it is mercy to the unfortunate brave, and not less to poor wretches who, for a small degree of guilt, would otherwise suffer from the butcher's knife" (1793: xxv). Research into the life and career of Dalzel reveals, however, that he was heavily invested in the slave trade and, at the time that he published his account, his business was under direct attack by the anti-slave-trade movement, whose supporters were arguing in the British parliament for the abolishment of slavery (Waldman, 1965). Thus, far from an objective representation of Dahomey and its inhabitants, Dalzel's account, like so many others before and after him, was but a veiled attempt to further the author's own interests and goals.

The problem with books such as Dalzel's is that their negative imagery lingers on long after the publication of the original account. Subsequent travellers to Dahomey, for example, relied heavily on Dalzel's report, and often copied verbatim his descriptions of Dahomean rites and customs, especially the human sacrifices which they themselves often admit not having seen. "When new generations of explorers or administrators went to Africa," notes Philip Curtin, "they went with prior impressions of what they would find" (1964: xii).

The process of transcultural representation goes both ways. Since earliest contact with foreign cultures, Africans have also represented "others" in their arts, rituals, myths, and oral narratives. Some of these representations offered satirical commentary on colonial and missionary activities, others sought to incorporate the symbolic power of the "distant" and the "foreign" into indigenous belief systems and religious practices, while yet others were intended as cultural expressions of protest and resistance.

In the 1940s, a Yoruba carver named Thomas Ona Odulate created miniature sculptures of Europeans dressed in their characteristic colonial attire. These sculptures were made for sale to travelers and colonial agents who brought them back to Europe as exotic keepsakes and souvenirs of Africa. Most of these carvings captured the elements of European demeanor that most amused the Yoruba: "the pith-helmet of the district officer (often likened to a calabash); the long moustache of the colonial governor (often compared to a cat's); the white wig of the lawyer (often likened to the head of a senile person), and the spectacles on the nose of the court-clerk (often likened to the eyes of an owl)" (Lawal, 1993: 9). While the artist is known to have told his clients that these carvings were not intended to ridicule Europeans, but were meant instead to project hierarchy and rank, Nigerian art historian Babatunde Lawal cannot help but wonder whether these carvings were not also intended as subversive images against colonial authority. Were they not satirical commentary on idiosyncratic British character? Were they not objects of ridicule which functioned to "savage" the European in an African visual art?

Representation is an issue which lies at the heart of a long-standing debate in African studies regarding the cultural composition of Africa itself. On one side of the debate are those who argue that there is indeed such a thing as an "African" identity whose deep essence transcends the surface differences which distinguish one African culture from another. On the other side are those who argue that the peoples of Africa have far less culturally in common than is usually assumed.

Anglo-Ghanaian philosopher Kwame Anthony Appiah is among those who have argued that there is no cultural unity in Africa, and that Africanist discourse has inaccurately grouped together vastly divergent cultures which have little or nothing in common. "Whatever Africans share," he writes, "we do not have a common traditional culture, common languages, a common religious or conceptual vocabulary ... we do not even belong to a common race" (1992: 26). "The central cultural fact of African life," Appiah concludes elsewhere, "remains not the sameness of Africa's cultures, but their enormous diversity" (1995: 40).

Among those who maintain that there is in fact an underlying uniformity to the cultures of Africa is anthropologist Igor Kopytoff, who has argued that in the historical diffusion of cultures across the continent, "the frontiersmen were bringing with them a basically similar kit of cultural and ideological resources" (1987: 10). Thus, according to this perspective, cultures in Africa spread through time from place to place carrying with them comparable cultural baggage and deeply rooted worldviews, which today enable us to look at the continent of Africa as a coherent cultural system and an epistemological whole. As Kopytoff concludes: "it is not surprising that Sub-Saharan Africa should exhibit to such a striking degree a fundamental cultural unity" (1987: 10).

While Kopytoff's argument is largely historical and anthropological in nature, the debate over Africa's cultural unity has also been linked at times to political arguments about the place of modern Africa in a postcolonial world. Cheikh Anta Diop, for example, a Senegalese historian and outspoken proponent of Pan-African solidarity, argued beginning in the 1950s that African cultures needed to find a common historical root which could unify the inhabitants of the continent (1978). Diop asserted that just as Europe drew much of its strength from the unity it established by tracing its ancestry to a single Greco-Latin culture, so too Africa had to locate and exploit a similar unified cultural background in order to develop its own strength through a coalescing regime of self-awareness. Thus, the present diversity of Africa was, according to this argument, "more illusion than reality" (July, 1987: 138).

Other arguments for the cultural unity of Africa, which were also largely political in character, were made, for instance, by some of the other proponents of the *négritude* movement, such as the Martiniquan poet Aimé Césaire and Senegalese intellectual Léopold Senghor; by the leader of independent Ghana, Kwame Nkrumah, in his discourse on "African Personality" (1963); and by many African philosophers, including W. E. Abraham (1962), Kwesi Wiredu (1980), and Paulin Hountondji (1983), among others. What joins all of these perspectives is a common desire to go beyond the mere political or economic freedom which was offered by African independence in the 1960s. True "independence" depended upon liberating Africa from the ethical and aesthetic standards of the West, and on a process of "intellectual decolonization" which involved a search for a common African ancestry in order to reunite a divided continent (July, 1987: 18).

The question of Africa's cultural unity remains an important and controversial topic today. In a "blockbuster" exhibition of African art held at the Royal Academy of Arts in London, for example, the issue of cultural unity emerged as a central point of contention and debate. Unlike prior exhibitions of African art, which generally have concentrated on the arts of a more delimited or particular region – one defined as broadly, for example, as West or Central Africa as a whole, or as narrowly as a single ethnic group, such as Yoruba, Dan, or Dogon – this exhibition, entitled *Africa: The Art of a Continent*, included works from the entire continent, embracing Ancient Egypt and Islamic North Africa as well.

The problem, however, is what do all these diverse cultures, separated by space and time, have in common with each other? Appiah, who commented critically on the exhibition, argued that what they have in common is merely their shared classificatory history in the Western taxonomy and representation of world art. "What unites these objects as African," he writes, "is not a shared nature, not the shared character of the cultures from which they came, but *our* ideas of Africa; ideas which ... have now come to be important for many Africans, and thus are now African ideas too" (1995: 41). In our collective imagination we have come to accept a category of objects we call African art. But can geographic contiguity alone suffice as a criterion for cultural classification? How do we define the category European art? Surely, there are more nuances to such a category than merely including all art forms that emanate from the continent of Europe. Imagine, for example, an exhibition of European art which lumped together Greek statuary, illuminated Medieval manuscripts, paintings of the Italian Renaissance, and German Expressionist prints. Does an exhibition of "African art" amount to the same degree of cultural clustering of diverse artistic expressions and distinct historical moments? Or, conversely, is there a "deep" and "unconscious" African identity which unites all artistic expressions from the continent?

Museum exhibitions reveal to the viewer things that might otherwise remain unnoticed or unseen. They spotlight certain aspects of art and culture, while simultaneously masking others in the shadow of their own illuminations. To some extent, this book is itself a kind of exhibition – a collection of pieces that comes to stand for a version of what is commonly called African studies. Like an exhibition, this book offers what art historian Svetlana Alpers (1991: 27) calls "a way of seeing" – the structuring of vision which results from isolating an object of study in order to encourage the viewer to look at the familiar in an unfamiliar way or, conversely, to see the unfamiliar in a familiar way. Like a collection of objects displayed side-by-side in a museum case, this volume assembles and binds works of scholarship that might not otherwise have come together. Their juxtaposition is meant to encourage contrast and comparison, to spin the initial threads of intertextual dialogue and debate, and to engage with each other in a contest of methodology and interpretation. But the totality of this collection is inevitably artificial or, as it were, inauthentic since the field of study is constantly changing, growing, and redefining itself. Yet like the most timeless of exhibitions, which must eventually be dismantled and packed away to make room for something new, this book offers a timely collection of perspectives on Africa – a series of essays which represent our vision of African studies past and present, and a set of perspectives which will direct and condition the future of this discipline.

References

Abraham, W. E. 1962. *The Mind of Africa*. London: Weidenfeld and Nicolson.

Alpers, Svetlana. 1991. "The Museum as a Way of Seeing." In Ivan Karp and Steven D. Lavine, eds., *Exhibiting Cultures: The Poetics and Politics of Museum Display*, pp. 25–41. Washington, DC: Smithsonian Institution Press.

Appiah, Kwame Anthony. 1992. *In My Father's House: Africa in the Philosophy Culture*. New York and Oxford: Oxford University Press.

Appiah, Kwame Anthony. 1995. "Why Africa? Why Art?" *The Royal Academy Magazine* 48 (Autumn): 40–1.

Bennet, Tony. 1994. "The Exhibitionary Complex." In Nicholas B. Dirks, Geoff Eley, and Sherry B. Ortner, eds. *Culture/Power/History: A Reader in Contemporary Social Theory*. Princeton, NJ: Princeton University Press. Reprinted from *New Formations* 4: 73–102, 1988.

Berger, John. 1972. *Ways of Seeing*. New York: Viking.

Clark, Graham C. 1971. *World Prehistory: A New Outline*. Cambridge: Cambridge University Press.

Clifford, James. 1983. "On Ethnographic Authority." *Representations* 1(2): 118–46.

Clifford, James. 1988. *The Predicament of Culture: Twentieth-Century Ethnography, Literature, and Art*. Cambridge, MA: Harvard University Press.

Cohen, David William. 1977. *Womunafu's Banafu: A Study of Authority in a Nineteenth-Century African Community*. Princeton, NJ: Princeton University Press.

Cohen, David William. 1985. "Doing Social History from *Pim*'s Doorway." In Olivier Zunz, ed., *Reliving the Past: The Worlds of Social History*, pp. 191–235. Chapel Hill: The University of North Carolina Press.

Comaroff, Jean. 1985. *Body of Power, Spirit of Resistance: The Culture and History of a South African People*. Chicago: University of Chicago Press.

Curtin, Philip D. 1964. *The Image of Africa: British Ideas and Action, 1780–1850*. 2 vols. Madison: University of Wisconsin Press.

Dalzel, Archibald. 1793. *The History of Dahomy, an Inland Kingdom of Africa, compiled from authentic memoirs; with an introduction and notes*. London: Spilsbury & Sons.

Diop, Cheikh Anta. 1978. *The Cultural Unity of Black Africa*. Chicago: Third World Press.

Duncan, James, and David Ley. 1993. "Introduction: Representing the Place of Culture." In James Duncan and David Ley, eds., *Place/Culture/Representation*, pp. 1–24. London and New York: Routledge.

Evans-Pritchard, E. E. 1960 [1950]. "Social Anthropology: Past and Present." In Evans-Pritchard, *Social Anthropology and Other Essays*, pp. 139–54. New York: The Free Press.

Fabian, Johannes. 1986. *Language and Colonial Power: The Appropriation of Swahili in the Former Belgian Congo, 1880–1938*. Cambridge: Cambridge University Press.

Fage, J. D. 1981. "The Development of African Historiography." In J. Ki-Zerbo, ed., *General History of Africa, vol. 1: Methodology and African Prehistory*, pp. 25–42. Paris: UNESCO and London: Heinemann.

Foucault, Michel. 1979. *Discipline and Punish: The Birth of the Prison*. Harmondsworth: Penguin.

Geertz, Clifford. 1983. "From the Native's Point of View: On the Nature of Anthropological Understanding." In Geertz, *Local Knowledge: Further Essays in Interpretive Anthropology*, pp. 55–72. New York: Basic Books.

Gyekye, Kwame. 1995. *An Essay on African Philosophical Thought: The Akan Conceptual Scheme*. Philadelphia: Temple University Press. First published 1987.

Henige, David. 1972. *The Chronology of Oral Tradition*. Oxford: Clarendon Press.

Hountondji, Paulin J. 1983. *African Philosophy: Myth and Reality*. Bloomington: Indiana University Press.

Janzen, John. 1978. *The Quest for Therapy: Medical Pluralism in Lower Zaire*. Berkeley and Los Angeles: University of California Press.

Jay, Martin. 1993. *Downcast Eyes: The Denigration of Vision in Twentieth-Century French Thought*. Berkeley and Los Angeles: University of California Press.

July, Robert W. 1987. *An African Voice: The Role of the Humanities in African Independence*. Durham, NC: Duke University Press.

Kluckhohn, Clyde. 1978. *Culture: A Critical Review of Concepts and Definitions*. Milwood, NJ: Kraus. First published in 1952.

Kopytoff, Igor. 1987. "The Internal African Frontier: The Making of African Political Culture." In Kopytoff, ed., *The African Frontier: The Reproduction of Traditional African Societies*, pp. 3–84. Bloomington: Indiana University Press.

Lawal, Babatunde. 1993. *Oyibo: Representations of the Colonialist Other in Yoruba Art, 1826–1960*. Discussion Papers in the African Humanities 24. Boston: African Studies Center, Boston University.

Leach, Edmund R. 1954. *Political Systems of Highland Burma*. Boston: Beacon Press.

Leakey, M. G., C. S. Feibel, I. McDougall, and A. Walker. 1995. "New Four-Million-Year-Old Hominid Species from Kanapoi and Allia Bay, Kenya." *Nature* 376(6541): 565–71.

Marcus, George E., and Michael M. J. Fischer. 1986. *Anthropology as Cultural Critique: An Experimental Moment in the Human Sciences*. Chicago: University of Chicago Press.

Martin, Marie-Louise. 1975. *Kimbangu: An African Prophet and His Church*, translated by D. M. Moore. Oxford: Basil Blackwell.

Massaquoi, Hans J. 1990. "The World's Largest Church." *Ebony* 46(2): 116–22.

McIntosh, S. K., and R. J. McIntosh. 1983. "Current Directions in West African Prehistory." *Annual Review of Anthropology* 12: 215–58.

Mitchell, W. J. T. 1986. *Iconology: Image, Text, Ideology*. Chicago: University of Chicago Press.

Moore, Sally Falk. 1986. *Social Facts and Fabrications: "Customary" Law on Kilimanjaro, 1880–1980*. Cambridge: Cambridge University Press.

Mudimbe, V. Y. 1988. *The Invention of Africa: Gnosis, Philiosophy, and the Order of Knowledge*. Bloomington: Indiana University Press.

Mudimbe, V. Y. 1994. *The Idea of Africa*. Bloomington: Indiana University Press.

Nkrumah, Kwame. 1963. *Africa Must Unite*. New York: Praeger.

Noble, Kenneth B. 1994. "For Ivory Coast's Founder, Lavish Funeral." *The New York Times*, 8 February, A1.

Pratt, Mary Louse. 1992. *Imperial Eyes: Travel Writing and Transculturation*. London and New York: Routledge.

Roseberry, William. 1989. "European History and the Construction of Anthropological Subjects." In *Anthropologies and Histories: Essays in Culture, History, and Political Economy*, pp. 125–44. New Brunswick, NJ: Rutgers University Press.

Said, Edward W. 1995. "East Isn't East: The Impending End of the Age of Orientalism." *Times Literary Supplement*, 3 February, pp. 3–6.

Schapera, I. 1962. "Should Anthropologists be Historians?" *Journal of the Royal Anthropological Institute* 92: 143–56.

Spiro, Melford. E. 1990. "On the Strange and Familiar in Recent Anthropological Thought." In J. Stigler, R. A. Shweder, and G. Herdt, eds., *Cultural Psychology*. Cambridge: Cambridge University Press.

Stewart, Charles, and Rosalind Shaw, eds. 1994. *Sycretism/Anti-syncretism: the Politics of Religious Synthesis*. London and New York: Routledge.

Sundkler, Bengt G. M. 1948. *Bantu Prophets in South Africa*. London: Lutterworth Press.

Vansina, Jan, 1985. *Oral Tradition as History*. Madison: University of Wisconsin Press.

Waldman, Loren K. 1965. "An Unnoticed Aspect of Archibald Dalzel's *The History of Dahomy*." *Journal of African History* 6(2): 185–92.

White, T. D., G. Suwa, and B. Asfaw. 1994. "*Australopithecus ramidus*, a New Species of Early Hominid from Aramis, Ethiopia." *Nature* 371(6495): 306–12.

Wiredu, Kwesi. 1980. *Philosophy and an African Culture*. Cambridge: Cambridge University Press.

Wolf, Eric. 1982. *Europe and the People Without History*. Berkeley: University of California Press.

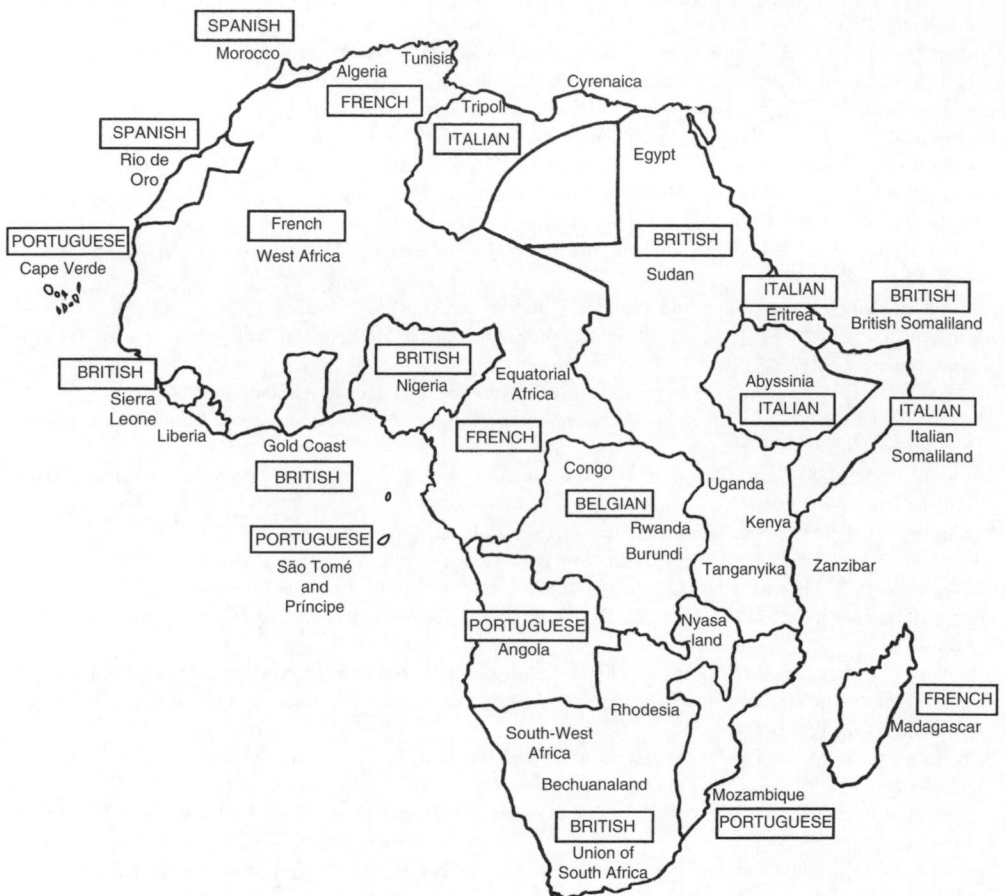

Map 1 Africa in the colonial era, *c*.1925

Map 2   Africa today, showing the ethnic groups discussed in the book

Part I

Representation and Discourse

Introduction

The essays in this part address the issue of representation, and explore how "Africa" has been imagined and constructed in both Western and African discourses (see also our General Introduction). Since earliest contact between Europe and Africa, individuals on both sides of the encounter have classified and represented the other from the perspective of their own cultural assumptions and values. Although the readings here deal largely with European images of Africa and Africans, it is important to keep in mind that from the very earliest moments of encounter Africans have also generated images of Europeans.

When European seafaring travelers first set foot on the coast of Central Africa in the late fifteenth century, for example, it is reported that the local inhabitants saw them as spirits who had returned to the living from their ancestral world somewhere far off at sea. There was no category of person in Central African thought which could account for a European, so rather than invent one they were classified according to pre-existing criteria – as dead ancestors. Describing the nature of this transcultural encounter, anthropologist Wyatt MacGaffey has written that:

> When the first Portuguese arrived in Kongo in 1485 they exhibited the principal characteristics of the dead: they were white in color, spoke an unintelligible language, and possessed technology superior even to that of the local priestly guild of smiths. ... The first Portuguese, like their successors to the present day, were regarded as visitors from the land of the dead. (1986: 199)

Representations of Europeans in African visual art first appear in the fifteenth century in ivory carvings (saltcellars, spoons, and Catholic ritual objects) which were commissioned by Portuguese merchants from artists in coastal Sierra Leone to take back as tribute to the Portuguese crown (Curnow, 1990; Blier, 1993). In the sixteenth and seventeenth centuries, Europeans were extensively depicted in bronze plaques which adorned the king's palace at the royal court of Benin. In these naturalistic representations created by highly accomplished court artists, Europeans may be identified by their military dress and accoutrements, and by their beards, moustaches, and hairstyles which were characteristic of Portuguese fashion during this period (Ezra, 1992: 128–9).

The plaques, which hung throughout the palace in Benin City, alluded to the power of the king, whose network of influence stretched as far as Europe – a remote land from where wealthy visitors came to pay their respect to the court.

As in the earlier example from the Kongo encounter with Europeans, the Portuguese were folded almost seamlessly into prior categories of Benin social structure and religious beliefs. "Because they came from across the sea, bringing with them wealth and luxury items," writes anthropologist Paula Ben-Amos, "the Portuguese travelers were readily incorporated into (or perhaps generated) the complex of ideas associated with the god Olokun, ruler of the seas and provider of earthly wealth" (1980: 28). Sadly, yet ironically, these very plaques were among the thousands of royal artifacts which were seized by the British military in 1897, during their so-called Punitive Expedition against the oba of Benin, whose agents were charged with killing six British officers in the course of a trade negotiation putatively gone awry. Many of these objects were sold shortly thereafter at auction in London, and are now held in museums and private collections throughout Europe and North America.

The British Punitive Expedition against the court of Benin took place at the height of Europe's military aggression toward Africa – an intense period of time when all European efforts were being made to secure their colonial territories and establish resolute imperial authority abroad. African resistance to European political rule was, in some areas of the continent, defiant, powerful, and often bitter (Weiskel, 1980; Ranger, 1986). Also, during the same period, African rejection of certain export commodities undermined European mercantile aspirations of economic growth and prosperity in what European entrepreneurs had hoped was a promising new consumer marketplace in the African colonies. Textile manufacturers in France, for example, could not understand why Africans would reject their latest industrial, factory-made cloth in favor of, what the French perceived to be, the more crude and rudimentary African handwoven fabrics (Steiner, 1985).

Not surprisingly, then, this was a period in European history which generated a vast amount of negative propaganda and denigratory stereotypes about Africa and Africans. It was also a time when technological developments in mass communications, especially newspapers and illustrated magazines, enabled large amounts of information to be disseminated quickly to a wide and eager audience (Schneider, 1982; Blanchard and Chatelier, 1993). Africans were depicted in the European press in a manner which was calculated to entitle and authorize colonial expansionist goals. During the late nineteenth century, for example, on the eve of France's military aggression against Dahomean resistance to colonial rule, the French press seized upon both textual and visual representations of human sacrifice in Dahomey. Most of these images had been constructed and disseminated over a century earlier by Archibald Dalzel, a British mercantile explorer who had published horrific images of human sacrifice in his *History of Dahomy* (1793) in order to rationalize European violence against Africans in the Atlantic slave trade (see the General Introduction). The "recycling" of this negative imagery by the French press was now intended to legitimate colonial rule and, once again, rationalize European actions in Africa. As historian William Schneider notes, "The mass illustrated [press] played a key role in preparing the French public for the conquest of Dahomey, which was the first episode in the French government's new policy of open colonial aggrandizement in the 1890s" (1982: 103; Campion-Vincent, 1967).

Although the colonial period produced an abundance of racist and paternalistic images of Africa in European art, literature, mass media, and scholarship, this was not always the case. European images of Africa from about the twelfth to seventeenth centuries were predominantly "positive" ones which depicted Africans either as "noble" beings living in harmony with nature, or as political allies whose vast kingdoms and empires were believed to be commensurate with the most powerful of royal monarchies which reigned in Europe. A glorified image of Africa emerged in the twelfth and thirteenth centuries when Europeans began to view Africans as potential military partners against the spread of Islam. When the Crusaders lost Jerusalem in 1244 and their strongholds in Palestine and Syria in 1291, Ethiopia became important as a possible ally against the Muslims (Debrunner, 1979: 24). A relationship of cooperation and mutual respect between Europe and Ethiopia developed throughout the ensuing four centuries. In 1634, for example, when a school for Ethiopian linguistics was established in Rome, European Christians believed that the Ethiopian language was the "original language of paradise" (Nederveen Pieterse, 1992: 28).

Although these images do not represent the "beastliness" and "barbarism" which were to be evoked later in the colonialist representation of "darkest" Africa, they are, of course, as philosopher V.Y. Mudimbe (1988: 1994) reminds us, but one of two extremes in Europe's polarized evaluation of Africa – both of which are equally based on European fantasies rather than on African realities. Mudimbe writes:

> From Herodotus onward, the West's self-representations have always included images of people situated outside of its cultural and imaginary frontiers. The paradox is that if, indeed, these outsiders were understood as localized and far away geographically, they were nonetheless imagined and rejected as the intimate and other side of the European-thinking subject. (1994: xi).

The problem of representation has been taken up by literary critic Christopher Miller in his book, *Blank Darkness: Africanist Discourse in French* (1985). In a chapter entitled "Deriving a Discourse," Miller explores the semantic and historical roots of the terms Africa and Africanist. Like Mudimbe, he argues that from the time of earliest contact, Africa has been imprinted with European constructs, such that at some moments Africans were represented as "noble," while at others they were judged "monstrous." Africa, according to Miller, was a "blank" space in Europe's collective imagination which could be populated with all sorts of invented creatures and entangled in the various products of European fears and desires.

As a professor of literature, and one who focuses on texts and their representations, Miller deals primarily with the question of language. No matter where European explorers went in Africa – whether to the most accessible regions of the continent or the most remote – they always brought back their knowledge and "discoveries" in the form of language. This language, which eventually comes to be known as Africanist discourse, is structured by its own predetermined form. That is to say, the unknown cannot be represented in language without reference to something already known. The language which was used to describe Africa was made to fit the narrative conventions of European languages and rhetoric – its models, idioms, metaphors, systems of classification, and cultural assumptions.

How different is this from the early Kongo encounter with Europeans, in which Europeans were evaluated according to pre-existing categories of thought? Does every process of transcultural representation involve locating points of intersection between the known and the unknown, the familiar and the unfamiliar, the self and the other? How would you go about describing something, say an object, to someone who had never seen anything like it before? Would you try to describe it with images or with words? Would you begin by noting what it looks like (its appearance) or what it was used for (its function)? Would you draw contrasts and comparisons between that unfamiliar object and something more commonly found in your own cultural environment?

While Miller has looked broadly at the question of representation and its discourses, Jean and John Comaroff's essay in this volume, "Africa Observed," explores the "imagined landscape" of Africa within the context of a very specific historical moment. Beginning in the late eighteenth century, they demonstrate the pervasive and profound influence of slavery in shaping European discourses about Africa. On the one hand, abolitionists argued that slavery had corrupted Africa – "deforming the normal progress of civilization" – and that Africans required emancipation and conversion to Christianity in order to be saved. On the other hand, those who opposed abolition argued that Africans were naturally incited to "savagery" and war, and that the slave trade rescued them from the fate of their own barbarism. Either way, the Comaroffs conclude, "Africa was degraded and debased."

In their attention to the European image of South Africa, in particular, the Comaroffs demonstrate how texts could be used to make specific territorial claims. Analyzing John Barrow's *Account of Travels into the Interior of Southern Africa in the Years 1797 and 1798*, for example, they argue that the author intentionally created the image of an empty landscape just waiting to be seized by British colonial rule – an "unpopulated" place inhabited only by "unregenerate natives" and "degenerate Dutchmen," both of whom fell outside British definitions of civilization and were, therefore, perceived as populations without legitimate claims to the land they happened to occupy.

The Comaroffs bring into sharp focus the relationship between gender and representation in their discussion of the portrayal of Africa as woman. Sexual metaphors of penetration abound in the literature of African exploration, where Africa was reduced "to the body of a black female yielding herself to white male discovery" (see also McClintock, 1995). During the late eighteenth century, a new political discourse surfaced in Europe which drew explicit physically derived contrasts between men and women. Rooted in the pseudo-objectivity of a newly emerging biological epistemology, (male) scientists claimed that men were the bearers of reason and rationality, while women's temperament was adversely affected by their dominant reproductive organs which were linked directly to the central nervous system. The denigration of Africa as female body was linked to this new gender ideology, such that women and Africans were equally devalued and made peripheral in contrast to the European ideal of "rational man."

The Comaroffs examine the issue of representation from the perspective of how European images of Africa are constructed and circulated. That is to say, their aim is to analyze and deconstruct the languages – textual strategies and visual grammars – that have been used to portray Africa in European narratives about other cultures. Other authors, especially those of African descent, have offered a different perspective on the issue of representation by addressing an even more fundamental question: namely, how can one hope to represent the realities and complexities of a foreign culture without possessing the full extent of language skills of an indigenous speaker? Maxwell Owusu, for example, looks less at the dissemination of knowledge about Africa in European texts, and more at the claims of authenticity and validity of the production of that very knowledge at the moment of transcultural encounter and interlocution (Owusu 1978).

Although there are some noteworthy exceptions, anthropologists in the early decades of this century rarely bothered to learn the indigenous language. Working through "native" interpreters versed to a greater or lesser degree in the language of the colonizer (such as French, English, or Portuguese), anthropologists collected data which was inevitably being filtered and corrupted through its various stages of translation. Beginning in the 1940s and 1950s, with the development of more intensive and long-term field research, anthropologists began to study the language of the people with whom they worked. Much of their knowledge was gained through dictionaries and grammars written by European and American missionaries who had become proficient in most African languages as a means to proselytize. But no matter how well versed one might become in a foreign tongue, it is arguable that unless one is raised and nurtured in the cultural environment of a linguistic group it may be hard, if not impossible, to capture all of a culture's subtleties and complexities. In building his argument, Owusu makes reference to a debate in anthropology which took place in the early 1940s between Margaret Mead and Robert Lowie on the necessity of "native languages as fieldwork tools." While Lowie believed that language competence was essential to understanding other cultures, Mead viewed language as a mere instrument of research which could be hired out through local interpreters. Although neither of these anthropologists worked in Africa, their debate raises interesting problems regarding language skills, the translation of culture, and the production of knowledge.

Owusu's argument is so compelling that one may wonder why anthropologists have not questioned language competence more seriously before. His answer to this problem forms part of his argument: throwing into doubt the issue of language proficiency in field research would undermine all anthropology except the study of one's own culture. Since historically the unit of study in anthropology has been non-Western societies (although this is now quickly changing), and since anthropology was a discipline dominated largely by Western scholars (although today this has significantly changed), the only people qualified to conduct field research in non-Western contexts would be those who had been identified as the observed – and not the observers. This dilemma explains why anthropologists have argued that what the stranger "discovers" in field research is an abstraction of "reality" which is unknowable to indigenous peoples themselves. The epistemological distance between anthropologists and the cultural data before them, the argument goes, allows them to somehow "see" things that would otherwise remain unnoticed by indigenous people who are too steeped in their own cultural traditions. The perspective championed by Owusu turns this methodological canon of anthropology on its head, and argues instead that the interpretation of culture can only come from "native" anthropologists who speak the language with sufficient competence to understand the subtleties and nuances of cultural expression.

A related debate on African languages exists, within the context of African literature, between Nigerian writer and critic Chinua Achebe and exiled Kenyan author Ngugi wa Thiong'o. Writing in the early 1960s, just a few years after Nigerian independence, Achebe argued that English ought to become the adopted language of African writers. He believed that Nigerian literature should serve to promote feelings of national solidarity, and that it could only do so by assuming the form of a "national" literature written in the national language, rather than merely an "ethnic" literature written in one of the numerous indigenous languages of Nigeria – such as Hausa, Ibo, Yoruba, and so on (Achebe, 1975: 92).

Ngugi wa Thiong'o, conversely, has argued more recently that African literature should be written in the author's mother tongue. As a child listening to stories told to him in his natal Gĩkũyũ language, he learned "to value words for their meanings and nuances. Language was not a mere string of words. It had a suggestive power well beyond the immediate and lexical meaning" (1986: 9). European languages, for Ngugi, were weapons of the colonizers – vehicles through which the African soul was held prisoner. The liberation of that expressive spirit for African authors, according to Ngugi, could only come from writing in the indigenous language of their own culture. It would seem, then, that Owusu and Ngugi are arguing from the same perspective. Both view language not simply as a tool of communication, but rather as a rich purveyor of cultural knowledge which loses its depth and meaning in the process of translation. Representation and language are thus linked in this complex matrix of culture, where they inform and predetermine one another.

Two readings in this section offer an intertextual dialogue between two African scholars regarding African cultural unity and the relationship between Europe, ancient Egypt, and sub-Saharan Africa. Beginning with Herodotus in the fifth century BC, scholars in Europe believed that the rise of civilization in ancient Greece could be attributed to the fact that it had been colonized by the peoples of ancient Egypt, and was shaped largely through its cultural borrowings from African cultures. This model, which historian Martin Bernal calls the Ancient Model, was accepted until the 1700s, when racism and "continental chauvism" overtook European historiography (1987: 1–2). To the European historians of the eighteenth and nineteenth centuries, Bernal writes, "it was simply intolerable for Greece, which was seen not merely as the epitome of Europe but also its pure childhood, to have been the result of the mixture of native Europeans and colonizing Africans" (1987: 2). In their efforts to redefine the cultural genesis of European civilization, these historians set forth an alternative model in which it was argued that the origin of ancient Greece was the product of European or Aryan influence. This model, which Bernal calls the Aryan Model, denies any cultural borrowings in ancient Greece from Africa. The shift between these two radically different theories of history can be attributed not to the discovery of new evidence or facts, but rather to changing racial attitudes in Europe during the period of the Atlantic slave trade. "After the rise of black slavery and racism," Bernal concludes on this point, "European thinkers were concerned to keep black Africans as far as possible from European civilization" (1987: 30). Thus, we see once again that the construction of history is a matter of representation, and not the cumulative growth of knowledge which leads to a higher and more objective truth. Until fairly recently, the Aryan Model was the "accepted" version of history which accounted for the rise of ancient Greek civilization.

Beginning in the mid 1940s, however, Cheikh Anta Diop, a Senegalese scholar and a strong advocate of Pan-African political unity, reversed the Aryan Model and placed conventional wisdom on its head when he argued that it was Europe that depended on Africa and not the other way around (July, 1987: 137). In scores of painstakingly researched volumes on African history and prehistory, Diop sought to demonstrate – through linguistics, archaeology, anthropology, paleontology, history, art history, chemistry, and physics – that African culture had been transmitted to Greece in ancient times across the Mediterranean, and that its influence accounted for the rise of European civilization. Europe, in other words, once again owed its existence to Africa, and in particular to the immense artistic, cultural, and technological accomplishments of ancient Egypt. At the core of Diop's argument – a point which was left somewhat ambiguous in the earlier Ancient Model – is the notion that ancient Egypt was a *black* nation, classified as a distinct African population, which had migrated north from southern Africa, rather than one associated with the ancient Near East.

Diop's work has become an important resource in the rise of the Afrocentric movement in both Europe and North America. The arguments of Afrocentrism are twofold. First it holds that most Western scholarship views the world through Eurocentric eyes (see Lambropoulos, 1993). The achievements of other cultures (especially African cultures) are subordinated to those of Europe, while racial assumptions about ancient civilizations deny that the cultural triumphs of ancient Egypt can be attributed to the accomplishments of black people. Second, Afrocentrism holds that Africa should become the center of world history. That Europe should be judged by African standards and values, and not the other way round.

In his article, "Europe Upside Down," Kwame Anthony Appiah speaks out against a rising tide of publications which embrace this new Afrocentric perspective. He argues that Afrocentrism is seriously flawed on, at least, two counts. First, he notes, by reclassifying Egypt as a black culture, Afrocentrists have accomplished nothing but simply to reverse a Eurocentric model of world history. Impressed by the presence of many of the cultural qualities with which Europeans defined civilization – a well-developed writing system, a complex political, religious, and social hierarchy, a specialized class of professional artists and artisans, and the evidence of monumental architecture – Europeans recognized ancient Egypt as the most highly (and sometimes the only) developed culture on the African continent. But, Appiah asks, what about the immense accomplishments of non-literate societies in Africa? Why should all the attention of Afrocentric discourse be focused on Egypt, when there are so many other cultures in Africa whose histories are chronicled in oral (rather than written) traditions? The attention lavished on ancient Egypt by the Afrocentric movement implies that the rest of the continent was somehow more "primitive" or "undeveloped," and thus underscores (rather than undermines) Europe's negative evaluation of Africa.

Second, Appiah remarks that Afrocentrism mistakenly tries to locate a cultural unity on the African continent (see the General Introduction). This again, he says, is a bias which grows directly out of a Eurocentric preoccupation with identifying a common core of Western culture. Appiah believes that Africa's strength derives not from its putative homogeneity but rather from its rich complexity and diversity. Elsewhere he has written that "We cannot accept … the presupposition that there is, even at quite a high level of abstraction, *an* African world view" (1992: 82; original emphasis). The Afrocentrist search for African cultural solidarity in a "fancied past of shared glories" should be replaced, he argues, by a less racially motivated quest for black unity – one that looks for universal struggles and shared experiences among a vast array of individuals, around Africa and the African diaspora, who each belong to their own distinctive communities (1992: 173–80). African culture is something which needs to be constructed in the present and future, and not something which can be retrieved from an invented past. As it now stands, however, Appiah concludes, Afrocentrism is simply Eurocentrism turned upside down.

Finally, in a chapter on "Discourse of Power and Knowledge of Otherness" the philosopher V. Y. Mudimbe explores the process of colonization as an exercise in the classification of beings and societies. Behind the brute force of Western military power and political will which enabled Europe to dominate Africa beginning in the nineteenth century lies, according to Mudimbe, a more pernicious and powerful mode of domination which is found in the way Africa and Africans were represented by Europeans in art, literature and eventually the science of Africanist discourse.

Using as his starting point a painting by sixteenth-century German artist Hans Burgkmair, Mudimbe argues that the artist represents Africans simultaneously as familiar bodies (what he calls "blackened whites") and as unfamiliar exotic beings who embody all that Europe does not. The painting, which shows a boy, a man, and a seated woman with a baby pressed to her breast, can be read at first glance as a "charming and decorative" image not untypical of the conventions of group portraiture in Europe at the time. What lie below the surface of this familiar scene, however, are the signs of exoticness that differentiate "them" from "us" – "all are naked and have either bracelets around their arms or a string around their necks, clear signs that they belong to a 'savage' universe." What Mudimbe is suggesting here in this protracted art-historical analysis is that the surface similarities draw the viewer in to suggest the possibility of resemblance and sameness to Europe, but the subtle signs of difference which emerge on closer inspection become the markers of difference which signify the exoticness of the African Other. It is these signs of difference that ultimately emerge in the nineteenth century as the distinguishing characteristics of what Europeans perceive as African inferiority and serve as the justification for colonialism and the unleashing of European hegemony in Africa. Thus, for Mudimbe, and the other authors in this section, the construction of knowledge and imagery is not merely the surface material that lies above the infrastructure of "real" political and social domination, but rather the discourse and symbol system of Europe's image of Africa is itself a form of control and colonialism that merits investigation in its own right.

References

Achebe, Chinua. 1975. *Morning Yet on Creation Day*. New York: Anchor Press and Doubleday. First published in 1964.

Appiah, Kwame Anthony. 1992. *In My Father's House: Africa in the Philosophy Culture*. New York and Oxford: Oxford University Press.

Ben-Amos, Paula. 1980. *The Art of Benin*. London: Thames and Hudson.

Bernal, Martin. 1987. *Black Athena: The Afroasiatic Roots of Classical Civilization*. Volume 1, *The Fabrication of Ancient Greece, 1785–1985*. New Brunswick, NJ: Rutgers University Press.

Blanchard, Pascal, and Armelle Chatelier, eds. 1993. *Images et Colonies*. Paris: ACHAC and SYROS.

Blier, Suzanne Preston. 1993. "Imaging Otherness in Ivory: African Portrayals of the Portuguese ca. 1492." *The Art Bulletin* 75(3): 375–96.

Campion-Vincent, Veronique. 1967. "L'image du Dahomey dans la presse française (1890–1895): les sacrifices humaines." *Cahiers d'études africaines* 7: 27–58.

Curnow, Kathy. 1990. "Alien or Accepted: African Perspectives on the Western 'Other' in 15th- and 16th-Century Art." *Visual Anthropology Review* 6(1): 38–44.

Dalzel, Archibald. 1793. *The History of Dahomy, an Inland Kingdom of Africa, compiled from authentic memoirs; with an introduction and notes*. London: Spilsbury & Sons.

Debrunner, Hans. W. 1979. *Presence and Prestige: Africans in Europe before 1918*. Basel: Basler Afrika Bibliographien.

Ezra, Kate. 1992. *Royal Art of Benin: The Perls Collection in the Metropolitan Museum of Art*. New York: The Metropolitan Museum of Art and Harry N. Abrams.

July, Robert W. 1987. *An African Voice: The Role of the Humanities in African Independence*. Durham, NC: Duke University Press.

Lambropoulos, Vassilis. 1993. *The Rise of Eurocentrism: Anatomy of Interpretation*. Princeton, NJ: Princeton University Press.

McClintock, Anne. 1995. *Imperial Leather: Race, Gender and Sexuality in the Colonial Conquest*. New York and London: Routledge.

MacGaffey, Wyatt. 1986. *Religion and Society in Central Africa: The BaKongo of Lower Zaire*. Chicago: University of Chicago Press.

Miller, Christopher L. 1985. *Blank Darkness: Africanist Discourse in French*. Chicago: University of Chicago Press.

Mudimbe, V.Y. 1988. *The Invention of Africa: Gnosis, Philosophy, and the Order of Knowledge*. Bloomington: Indiana University Press.

Mudimbe, V.Y. 1994. *The Idea of Africa*. Bloomington: Indiana University Press.

Nederveen Pieterse, Jan. 1992. *White on Black: Images of Africa and Blacks in Western Popular Culture*. New Haven and London: Yale University Press.

Ngugi wa Thiong'o. 1986. *Decolonising the Mind: The Politics of Language in African Literature*. London: James Currey.

Owusu, Maxwell. 1978. "Ethnography of Africa: The Usefulness of the Useless." *American Anthropologist* 80(1): 310–34.

Ranger, Terence. 1986. "Resistance in Africa: From Nationalist Revolt to Agrarian Protest." In Gary Y. Okihiro, ed., *Resistance: Studies in African, Caribbean, and Afro-American History*, pp. 32–52. Amherst: University of Massachusetts Press.

Schneider, William H. 1982. *An Empire for the Masses: The French Popular Image of Africa, 1870–1900*. Westport, CT: Greenwood Press.

Steiner, Christopher B. 1985. "Another Image of Africa: Toward an Ethnohistory of European Cloth Marketed in West Africa, 1873–1960." *Ethnohistory* 32(2): 91–110.

Weiskel, Timothy. 1980. *French Colonial Rule and the Baule Peoples: Resistance and Collaboration, 1889–1911*. Oxford: Clarendon Press.

Suggested Reading

Appiah, Kwame Anthony. 1991. "Is the Post in Postmodernism the Post in Postcolonial?" *Critical Inquiry* 17(2): 3–36.

Apter, Andrew. 1992. "*Que Faire?* Reconsidering Inventions of Africa." *Critical Inquiry* 19(1): 87–104.

Apter, Andrew. 2007. *Beyond Words: Discourse and Critical Agency in Africa.* Chicago: University of Chicago Press.

Campbell, Mary B. 1988. *The Witness and the Other World: Exotic European Travel Writing, 400–1600.* Ithaca: Cornell University Press.

Clinton, Jean M. 1991. *Behind the Eurocentric Veils: The Search for African Realities.* Amherst: University of Massachusetts Press.

Cohen, William B. 1980. *The French Encounter with Africans: White Response to Blacks, 1530–1880.* Bloomington: Indiana University Press.

Coombes, Annie E. 1994. *Reinventing Africa: Museums, Material Culture, and Popular Imagination.* New Haven and London: Yale University Press.

Curtin, Philip D. 1964. *The Image of Africa: British Ideas and Action, 1780–1850.* 2 vols. Madison: University of Wisconsin Press.

Diop, Cheikh Anta. 1987. *Precolonial Black Africa.* Westport, CT: L. Hill.

Diop, Cheikh Anta. 1991. *Civilization or Barbarism: An Authentic Anthropology.* New York: Lawrence Hills Books.

Ebron, Paula. 2002. *Performing Africa.* Princeton, NJ: Princeton University Press.

Edwards, Elizabeth, ed. 1992. *Anthropology and Photography, 1860–1920.* New Haven and London: Yale University Press.

Fabian, Johannes. 1983. *Time and the Other: How Anthropology Makes Its Object.* New York: Columbia University Press.

Hall, C. 2004. *Tourism and Postcolonialism: Contested Discourses, Identities and Representations* (Routledge/Contemporary Geographies of Leisure, Tourism, and Mobility). London: Routledge.

Hawk, Beverly G., ed. 1992. *Africa's Media Image.* New York: Praeger.

Kuper, Adam. 1988. *The Invention of Primitive Society: Transformations of an Illusion.* London and New York: Routledge.

Leopold, Mark. 2005. *Inside West Nile: Violence, History, and Representation on an African Frontier.* Santa Fe: School of American Research Press.

Lips, Julius E. 1937. *The Savage Hits Back.* New Haven: Yale University Press.

Lutz, Catherine A., and Jane L. Collins. 1993. *Reading National Geographic.* Chicago: University of Chicago Press.

Mackey, Eva. 1995. "Postmodernism and Cultural Politics in a Multicultural Nation: Contests over Truth in the *Into the Heart of Africa* Controversy." *Public Culture* 7: 403–31.

Miller, Christopher L. 1990. *Theories of Africans: Francophone Literature and Anthropology in Africa.* Chicago and London: The University of Chicago Press.

Nnaemeka, Obioma. 2005. *Female Circumcision and the Politics of Knowledge: African Women in Imperialist Discourses.* New York: Praeger.

Okoye, Felix N. 1971. *The American Image of Africa: Myth and Reality.* Buffalo, NY: Black Academy Press.

Onyewuenyi, Innocent C. 1993. *The African Origin of Greek Philosophy: An Exercise in Afrocentrism.* Nsukka: University of Nigeria Press.

Price, Sally. 1989. *Primitive Art in Civilized Places.* Chicago and London: University of Chicago Press.

Serequeberhan, T. 1994. *The Hermeneutics of African Philosophy: Horizon and Discourse.* New York: Routledge.

Spurlin, William J. 2006. *Imperialism within the Margins: Queer Representation and the Politics of Culture in Southern Africa.* New York: Palgrave Macmillan.

Stahl, Anne B. 2001. *Making History in Banda: Anthropological Visions of Africa's Past.* Cambridge: Cambridge University Press.

Steiner, Christopher B. 1995. "Travel Engravings and the Construction of the Primitive." In Elazar Barkan and Ronald Bush, eds., *Prehistories of the Future: The Primitivist Project and the Culture of Modernism*, pp. 202–25, 416–18. Stanford, CA: Stanford University Press.

1

Africa Observed

Discourses of the Imperial Imagination

Jean and John Comaroff

Let us ... contrast piety with atheism, the philosopher with the rude savage, the monarch with the Chief, luxury with want, philanthropy with lawless rapine: let us sct before us in one view, the lofty cathedral and the straw-hut, the flowery garden and the stony waste, the verdant meadow and the arid sands. And when our imagination shall have completed the picture, and placed it in a light which may invite contemplation, it will, I think, be impossible not to derive from it instruction of the highest class. (William Burchell 1824:2,444)

The imagined landscape of Africa was greatly elaborated in late eighteenth-century Britain, albeit less as an end in itself than as a byproduct of the making of modern European self-consciousness (cf. Said 1978; Asad 1973; Gates 1986). Its features were formed in the context of vigorous arguments about humanity, reason, and civilization – debates that were driven by the social and cultural upheavals that accompanied the rise of capitalism and that forced the nations of Europe to refashion their sense of themselves as polities on a world map. Africa became an indispensable term, a negative trope, in the language of modernity; it provided a rhetorical ground on which a new sense of heroic history could be acted out (cf. Godzich 1987).

More than anything else, perhaps, abolitionism subsumed the great debates and discourses of the age. For it raised all the crucial issues involved in the contested relationship between European and Other, savagery and civilization, free labor and servitude, man and commodity; the ideological stuff, that is, from which a liberal hegemony was being made. As Davis (1975:350) has noted, the antislavery movement replayed Adam Smith's message in another key, making of it a program for global social transformation: that all classes of society should be recognized as sharing a natural identity of interest; that the common wealth depended on the liberty of everyone to pursue their own ends in an unfettered material and moral economy.

From Jean and John Comaroff, *Of Revelation and Revolution*, vol. 1 (1991), University of Chicago Press, pp. 86–125.

Abolitionism, as some have claimed, might have been a pragmatic attempt to resolve contradictions in the culture of postenlightenment Britain. And it clearly was a dispute about the merits and morals of different modes of colonial production. But it was also an exercise in mobilizing new forms of representation and communication (see Anderson 1983) to arouse the middle and laboring classes to a passion for epic reform; the controversy was widely aired in mass-circulating pamphlets, newspapers, and religious tracts, as well as in the discriminating columns of the literary reviews. And it drew upon a number of related discourses which alike had become sites for the formulation of a coherent bourgeois awareness. These discourses arose out of a number of distinct but related fields of exploration. Each aimed to construct what Heidegger (1977:115f.; see Godzich 1987:xiv) has identified as a mechanism of mastery, an explanatory scheme capable of objectifying nature and representing it to the knowing, synthesizing human subject. Most significant among them – at least in shaping the consciousness of our evangelists – were the discoveries of the geographical mission to Africa; the investigations into human essence and difference within the emerging life sciences; and the mythology of the noble savage celebrated by the romantic movement (Curtin 1964:34), which explored otherness in a variety of aesthetic genres. Each of these discourses had its own institutional context and expressive forms. But each played off the others – often in productive discord – and conduced to an increasingly rationalized debate about the nature of civilization, the civilization of nature. And together, by virtue of *both* their form and their content, they established the dark continent as a metaphysical stage on which various white crusaders struck moral postures (Achebe 1978:9).[1]

The symbolic terrain of a rarely-seen Africa, then, was being shaped by a cascade of narratives that strung together motley "scientific facts" and poetic images – facts and images surveyed by an ever more roving European eye. As this suggests, the rhetoric of light and dark, of color and culture, was already palpable in contemporary Europe, though it had not yet taken on the full fan of connotations it was to bear in Victorian thought. Hume (1854:3,228n), after all, had argued that "there scarcely ever was a civilized nation of [Negro] complexion," and Rousseau had echoed his sentiment that blacks were mentally inferior by nature.[2] Those who opposed abolition argued that slavery was the "natural law" of Africa, as much part of the condition of savagery as the cannibalism and wanton bloodshed so luridly described by some observers (Dalzel [1793] 1799; Norris [1789] 1968). Abolitionists tended to respond by blaming the slave trade itself for deforming the normal progress of civilization (Austen and Smith 1969:79). Either way, Africa was degraded and debased.

It was also inextricably entangled in a western embrace. Romantic poets might have envisaged Africans living lives free of Europe (Brantlinger 1985:170), but the weight of public opinion at the turn of the nineteenth century suggested the opposite. So, too, did the sheer weight of evidence. Whether as purveyors or reformers of the "evil traffic," white men had written themselves into the present and future of the continent. Whatever else it might have entailed, abolitionism did not argue for European withdrawal from Africa. It made the case for the replacement of one mode of colonial extraction with another. Once emancipated, his humanity established, the savage would become a fit subject of Empire and Christendom.

In this chapter we examine each of the discourses through which Africa came to be imagined, tracing their confluence to the argument over slavery itself. In so doing, we witness the rise of a more and more elaborate model of the relationship of Europe to the "dark continent": a relationship of both complementary opposition and inequality, in which the former stood to the latter as civilization to nature, savior to victim, actor to subject. It was a relationship whose very creation implied a historical imperative, a process of intervention through which the wild would be cultivated, the suffering saved. Life would imitate the masterful gestures of art and science. The "native" would be brought into the European world, but as the recipient of a gift he could never return – except by acknowledging, gratefully, his own subordination. And in this colonizing project the Christian missionary would play a special role as agent, scribe, and moral alibi. ...

Into South Africa: Of Maps and Morals

In Britain ca. 1800, West Africa served as stereotype for the continent as a whole. The Cape of Good Hope was a secondary focus of European concern. A small colony administered since 1652 by the Dutch East India Company, it had generated little travel literature, especially in English.[3] In 1795, however, the Cape was taken over by Britain as a consequence of her war with the French, who had invaded Holland and were thought likely to seize the Dutch outpost on the sea route to the East (Harlow 1936:171f.). John Barrow, founder of the Royal Geographical Society (which was to absorb the African Association), was appointed personal secretary to Macartney, the new governor of the Colony.[4] As Macartney's protege he had accompanied the latter to China in 1792, serving officially as comptroller to the embassy but acting also as observer of Chinese civilization (Lloyd 1970:24). Now he was sent on a tour of the South African interior to represent His Majesty and to investigate the discontents of frontier farmers, whose long-standing resistance to the Dutch Company had been transferred to the new administration.[5]

Barrow's *Account of Travels into the Interior of Southern Africa in the Years 1797 and 1798* (1801–4) was self-evidently a colonial document. A legitimation of the British annexation of the Cape, it also gave eyewitness account of the degradation of the Dutch frontiersmen, who, lacking a European "spirit of improvement and experiment," had regressed to take on the qualities of their rugged and soporific surrounds (1801–4:1,67; see also Streak 1974:5f.; Coetzee 1988:29f.). The very landscape conveyed this unrefined state to Barrow's eye, schooled as he was on nicely-demarcated European vistas of private ownership (1801–4:1,57):

> As none of the [extensive lands] are enclosed there is a general appearance of nakedness in the country … which … if divided by fences, would become sufficiently beautiful, as nature in drawing the outline has performed her part.

The Dutch had not investigated the interior systematically and, perhaps most diagnostic for Barrow, had "no kind of chart or survey, save of such districts as were contiguous to the Cape" (1801–4:1,8). This was taken to indicate lax colonial control, something that the British "spirit of commerce and adventurous industry" would remedy. The frontispiece of Barrow's book has a comprehensive map of the Cape Colony, constructed from bearings, distances, and latitudes observed during his travels. The map presents this land to Britain for the taking, its virgin scapes laid tantalizingly bare, its routes of access picked out in red.

Barrow's *Account* was also a moral geography of the interior of the Cape, one which not so much emptied the landscape of its human inhabitants (Pratt 1985) as denied them any legitimate claim to it. The text cleared the ethical ground for British colonialism by depicting the territory as a polarized human universe of unregenerate natives and degenerate Dutchmen. The dualistic vision of nature in postenlightenment imagery, to which we alluded above and shall return, speaks out here. The Dutch had negated their own humanity by treating the blacks as objects, prey to be "hunted" (1801–4:1,273); they sought to validate a "monstrous" manhood (1801–4:1,145) by exterminating nature's innocents – rather than by elevating them, and all African humanity, through forceful cultivation. Their brutal bravado was founded on a myth of savagery that Barrow feels called upon to dispel (1801–4:1,196):

> It is a common idea, industriously kept up in the colony, that the Kaffers[6] are a savage, treacherous, and cruel people, a character as false as it is unmerited …

Likewise, speaking of the Khoisan, he adds that the "Hottentots" (Khoi) were "mild, quiet, and timid people, perfectly harmless, honest, faithful," their timeless customary existence destroyed by Dutch abuse (1801–04:1,151); and the "Bushmen" (San) were "like frightened children" mowed down by Boer bullets as they played with bows and arrows (1801–4:1,273).

These observations were grounded in the very real fact of genocide; there is plenty of collateral evidence to prove that a war of extermination had been waged along the frontier against the Khoisan (see e.g. Marais 1944; Marks 1972; Elphick and Malherbe 1989). Nor is there any doubt that Barrow believed himself to be writing a *historical* account of both Boer and Bushman, explaining how each had been affected by the violent encounter with the other. Nonetheless, there is in this historiography another process at work. In building his stereotypic contrasts, Barrow, intentionally or not, was also fleshing out an imaginative structure, a set of oppositions which came to be shared by many of his contemporaries (see Coetzee 1988:29f.). The Dutch farmer was European civilization grown rotten in the African sun – his "nature" made yet more degenerate, his "indolence of body and low groveling mind" corrupted yet further by being an owner and master of slaves (Barrow 1801–4 quoted by Coetzee 1988:29; see also Philip 1828,1:367f.; Moodie 1835:1,176). He was the very antithesis of Protestant enlightenment, having willfully permitted his own debasement. The "savage tribes," made so brutish by seventeenth-century Dutch reports (see Willem ten Rhyne in Schapera 1933), were really innocent and ignorant. They might dance and sing when moved by their childish passions, and slept in beds "like the nest of an ostrich" (1801–4:1,148,275). While "low on the scale of humanity," they were raw material for the civilizing project. For, notwithstanding their common predicament as "miserable savages" (1801–4:1,287) in opposition to the British, peoples such as the "Hottentots" had their own nobility. This *Account*, in short, validated the moral scheme of the first LMS and WMMS missionaries to South Africa, coloring their view of the white perverts and would-be black converts who peopled the interior.

Barrow's social position guaranteed him a wide readership among scholars, politicians, and the literate public. The natural historian Lichtenstein ([1815] 1930,2:12) noted at the time that in his native Germany the "journals and almanacks" vied to publish the British author's accounts of the "ignorance, the brutality, the filthiness" of the Dutch colonists. Lichtenstein himself had traveled in the interior of South Africa between 1803 and 1806 in the employ of the Dutch government. His own two volume narrative appeared in German in 1810 and 1812 and in English in 1812 [repr. 1928] and 1815 [repr. 1930]. It was highly critical of Barrow's portrayal of the Dutch farmers and their brutal domination of the "Caffres" (1928:1,59):

I was led almost daily to ask myself whether these were really the same African colonists which the celebrated Mr Barrow represented as such barbarians, as such more than half-savages – so much did I find the reality in contradiction to his description.

Again we are reminded that images of Africa are born of European arguments about their own essential nature.[7] Barrow was accused of betraying his own kind; of failing, as an educated European, to credit the effects of the African climate and hence to understand the "rough Cape peasantry" and their relation to the blacks (1930:2,6–13). Yet, lying beneath the surfaces of the debate, is a set of shared constructs that makes the dispute possible in the first place. Lichtenstein does not really take issue with Barrow's portrayal of Africans, although his own descriptions lack the Englishman's stress on their innocence and vulnerability. For him, "Bushmen" are miserable and voracious: "no class of savages ... lead lives so near those of brutes" or are so low on the "scale of existence" (1930:2,244). But, he adds (1930:2,65):[8]

> The rude rough man left entirely in a state of nature, is not in himself evil and wicked. ... [He] follows blindly the impulse of his passions, which lead him to acts, that to us, in the high point of civilization we have attained, appear as crimes ...

Africa might have become a moral battlefield, but its representation in late eighteenth-century Europe also reflected a conceptual order fast spreading among persons "of reason," an essential humanism in terms of which man became his own measure (Foucault 1975). No longer satisfied with a notion of himself as God's passive creature, he sought to define his "place in nature" (Thomas 1984:243 et passim); that is, to assess his position on a scale of humanity rather than on a ladder to heaven. A new narrative of human types was being written, and the African was to have a definite niche in it. As a foil to the enlightened European, he was doubly devalued: human yet ignorant of salvation to begin with, he had now lost his innocence at the hands of civilization's most depraved elements, slavers and the degenerate white men of the tropics.[9] Here, as we have said, the texts of travelers and explorers became entangled in the debate over abolition (see Barrow 1801–04:1,46). But the discourse also informed, and was informed by, arguments within the related field of natural history and the emerging science of biology.

The New Biology and the Great Chain of Being

In the early nineteenth century the life sciences were preoccupied with the "great chain of being" – and especially with its lower half. As Figlio (1976:25) observes, contemporary debates about man's place in nature hinged upon the relationship of the human species to the rest of the living world:

> There was a focusing upon the multi-faceted idea of animality, as opposed to an insistence upon a scalar, uni-dimensional hierarchy, with man at the top of the visible, and God at the top of the invisible, realm.

Rooted in the contrast between the animate and the inanimate, this focus on animality implied a concern with the properties of "life" common to all beings. And it fixed on man as the embodiment of perfection, since he alone had distinguished himself by using reason to discover his own essence. This in turn led inexorably to the concept of "generic human nature" (Stocking 1987:17), a notion that separated man from beast, people from objects, and rendered anomalous anything – like the slave trade – that confused them. But "human nature" was a highly abstract category. Once put to work in the world it was immediately subject to internal differentiation. This is where the chain of being served as a powerful metaphor, for it conjured up a hierarchy of distinct varieties within (a single) humankind.

In the epistemology of the time, then, the key to knowledge seemed to lie increasingly within man himself. The essence of life was in the unplumbed depths of organic being, to be grasped through the invasive thrust, the looking and naming, of the new biology (Foucault 1975). Its interior truth, merely signified in outer bodily form, gave rise to meaningful differences in the faculties and function of living beings.

African bodies, African nature

We have already encountered traces of this epistemology in the geographical mission, where the thrust into the African interior likened the continent to a female body. Bernhard Fabian (quoted in Nerlich 1987:179) reminds us that, in the late eighteenth century, the qualities of the scientific "spirit" were identified with the heroic "spirit" of the adventurer: the natural scientist's penetration into hitherto unknown realms had become one with the advance into regions unknown. The newly charted surfaces of the African landscape were to have a direct connection with the universe opening up within the person, for the geographical mission expanded European knowledge of the global biology of mankind. In investigating the savage, the West set up a mirror in which it might find a tangible, if inverted, self-image. Non-Europeans filled out the nether reaches of the scale of being, providing the contrast against which cultivated man might distinguish himself. On this scale, moreover, the African was assigned a particularly base position: he marked the point at which humanity gave way to animality. In treating him as the very embodiment of savagery, of deviance from a racially-defined ideal (Gould 1981:38), the travel and adventure literature gave ostensibly objective, precise descriptions of both his bodily form and his "manners and customs." In such popular accounts, in other words, African "nature" was grounded in the color, shape, and substance of the black physique.

With the rise of comparative anatomy and biology as formal sciences, the organic reduction of African society and culture took on ever greater authority. For much of the eighteenth century it had been civilization that separated savage man from his white counterpart – moral and politico-economic circumstance rather than physical endowment (Stocking 1987:18). But the vocabulary of natural science was to strengthen and legitimize the association of dark continents with black bodies and dim minds. Comparative anatomical schemes typically presented Africans as the most extreme contrast with Europeans – in the new technical argot, the "link" between man and beast (Curtin 1964:42). Linnaeus' *Systema Naturae*, first published in 1735, laid out in initial form what would soon become a convention of biological classification: a chromatic scale of white, yellow, red, and black races, each native to one of the four major continents (Gould 1981:35; Curtin 1964:37). As in the popular literature of travel and adventure, Africans were invariably placed at the bottom of the ladder of enlightenment, below such paler peoples as Asians or American Indians (Buffon 1791; Blumenbach 1775, 1795; White 1799). By 1778 Buffon, who had added such features as hair, stature, and physiognomy to his scheme, declared that white was the "real and natural colour of man" (quoted in West 1982:56).[10] Blumenbach took this yet further, to the shape of the skull, thereby introducing one of the more pervasive and enduring elements in the annals of racial taxonomy. He went on to claim, on this basis, that the Ethiopian was the lowliest deviation from the "most beautiful" Caucasian type (Street 1975:52ff.). The great chain of being, a vertical scale, had been set on its side, becoming also a linear history of human progress from the peripheral regions of the earth to its north European core. The hard facts of organic form, it seemed, could now explain and determine the place of men in the world.

Science, aesthetics, and selfhood
The life sciences, then, were part of a broader discourse about the human condition – a discourse closely tied to Europe's encounter with the non-European world. Raised to a new level of self-consciousness and authority, their "value free" knowledge found a natural validation for cultural imperialism in the inner secrets of existence. "Natural" scientists read off the degree of animality and the perfection of life from the external features of different "organisms"; for these were taken to be a function of the relative complexity, symmetry, and refinement of the faculties within. Take, for example, the influential Dutch scholar Camper, who, in a manner similar to Blumenbach, devised a scale that correlated the shape of the skull with aesthetic appearance and mental capacity: his "facial angle" measured the projection of the jaw, a protruding profile being linked with the long snouts, low brows, and sensory-bound state of animals. Applied to an eclectic array of "evidence" – including African travelers' accounts – this measurement

defined and ranked national character, giving physical shape to the current philosophical concern with the relationship of race, nationality, and civilization (cf. Hume 1854).

Camper's scale extended from dog through ape to Negro, then through the European peoples to the ideal beauty of form epitomized in Greek sculpture (1821:x; see Figlio 1976:28f.). And it was rapidly publicized well beyond the scientific community, as were his more general pronouncements. Thus the preface to an English translation of his popular lectures addressed an artistic audience on the moral and aesthetic implications of the science of comparative anatomy (1821:x):

> [The] grand object was to shew, that national differences may be reduced to rules; of which the different directions of the facial line form a fundamental norma or canon ... the knowledge of which will prevent the artist from blending the features of different nations in the same individual ...

Nationality, physical type, and aesthetic value are condensed here into an iconography that would in due course become part of the language of scientific racism. With his apartheid of the sketchpad, Camper imprinted the bodily contours of stereotypic others on the European imagination – and with them, a host of qualitative associations. His sample African profile, for instance, a distinctly bestial representation, was to become standard in nineteenth-century texts on racial difference; significantly, these texts gave prominence to images of black South Africans.

Georges Cuvier, the prestigious Swiss comparative anatomist of the early nineteenth century, took the facial angle and the biological reduction of culture to new levels of sophistication. He developed a scale to evaluate the perfection not only of the intellect but also of the introspective self, the moral core of the person. By gauging the proportion of the mid-cranial area to that of the face, he sought to reveal the degree of dependence of an organism upon external sensations; the size of the cranium itself was taken to reflect the development of reason and self-control. On this count, the "negro" stood between the "most ferocious apes" and the Europeans, who were themselves superseded by the men and deities of ancient Greek sculpture

(Figlio 1976:28). But it was the neurological dimension of Cuvier's scheme (1827:1,49f.) that raised most explicitly the spiritual and moral capacity of man. For the nervous system was the site of internal animation, and its complexity determined the higher faculties of life – intelligence and volition. The latter were expressions of a "soul or sentient principle," whose source of vitality remained, at the time, a matter of serious debate. Scientists, however, were more concerned with the physical organization of this system, which was centered on a compact inner core that reached its most perfect form in the complicated brain of man. As Figlio (1976:24) explains:

> ... this compactness [was associated] quite explicitly with the higher faculties, indeed with the sense of the "self". Just as the nervous system coalesced into a centre from which dependent nerves arose, so too was the sense of self increasingly solidified and distinct. Thus, a grading of this ... concentrating of the nervous system was simultaneously a grading of animal sentience and selfhood.

And so the bourgeois subject of the new Age of Capitalism, already secure in the Protestant ethic and rational philosophy, was given incontestable grounding in biological nature. Needless to say, the inner density and refinement associated by Cuvier with self-awareness and control were held to be underdeveloped among non-Europeans. This was especially true of blacks, who were bound by the animal reflexes of survival (1827:1,97; see Curtin 1964:231):

> The negro race is confined to the south of Mount Atlas. Its characters are, black complexion, woolly hair, compressed cranium, and flattish nose. In the prominence of the lower part of the face, and the thickness of the lips, it manifestly approaches to the monkey tribe. The hordes of which this variety is composed have always remained in a state of complete barbarism.

Cuvier's writings were summarized in the British biomedical press within months of their publication and were assiduously discussed by scientists, theologians, and men of letters (Figlio 1976:35).

In an age when specialist knowledge was not yet set apart by technical language, work such as this – and that of Camper – was rapidly directed to a receptive, almost insatiable public. Often, as in one widely read translation of Cuvier's *Animal Kingdom*, some "popular and entertaining matter" was added on the instincts and habits of animals and primitive man (1827:1,i–ii). The editors in this particular instance included a description of the "unhappy races" of South Africa, a telling bricolage of current European curiosity, with substantiating material drawn from the accounts of travelers like Barrow and Lichtenstein. Thus were the discoveries of geographical adventure converted into a scientific currency in which the universal value of man might be reckoned.

As these travel tales and salon exotica gained scientific credentials, they hardened into stereotypic representations of Africa. Their influence on the eye of subsequent European observations in South Africa was to be tangible. Cuvier's editors (1827:1,197), for example, provided an account of the "Bushmen" as pygmy "plunderers" who "lurk[ed]" in the complicit woods and bushes. This description seems to have been drawn directly from Lichtenstein (1928:1,68n), yet we encounter it, metaphor intact, in the "eyewitness" report given many years afterwards by the Rev. Edwards (1886:66). The interplay of other epithets in the *Animal Kingdom* – "Hottentots" as degraded and disgusting, or as swarthy, filthy, and greasy – may also be traced to Lichtenstein (1928:1,69).[11] They too were to flow from the pens of later writers who claimed the authority of firsthand experience.

One item among the potpourri of curiosities in the *Animal Kingdom* (1827:1,196) was a description of the "HottentotVenus," an "essential black" from the Cape Colony. This unfortunate "wild" woman of Khoi ancestry had been taken to Europe and made into a traveling exhibit, shown first in England and then, by an animal trainer, in France. She died in Paris in 1815 after European audiences had gazed in fascination at her for some five years – and promptly ended up on Cuvier's dissecting table (Gould 1985:294). His famous account of her autopsy was to be reprinted twice within a decade of its publication; it centered on the anomalies of her "organ of generation," which, in its excessive development of the *labia minora*, was held to set her kind apart from other human beings (Gilman 1985:212). Barrow, too, had written of the genital aberrations of Khoisan women, and a host of anatomical reports were to follow Cuvier in focusing on the exotic, simian qualities of black female reproductive organs. A barely suppressed infatuation with the torrid eroticism of Africa made itself respectable as biological inquiry.

The story of the Hottentot Venus reminds us that Mungo Park, albeit in somewhat different idiom, had also reduced Africa to the body of a black female yielding herself to white male discovery. This mytheme, as we shall see, was repeated in both the poetry of romantic naturalists and the sober prose of our missionary crusaders. But Cuvier's writings show particularly plainly how early nineteenth-century science actually articulated and authorized such constructions – how the various products of current European fancy sailed under the colors of biological knowledge about man, woman, and nature. Nor did the ideological message of this material remain implicit. Supplementary details on African peoples in the *Animal Kingdom* (1827:1,196) were summarized with the confident statement that "a physical obstacle to their progress seemed to be a more natural solution to [the] problem [of their lack of development] than any political or local circumstances."

The nature of gender

As all this suggests, the "signifying economy" (Godzich 1987:xi) of otherness took in gender as well as race. That "economy" has a long history, of course. But we need only break into it at the dawn of modernism. "Sometime in the late eighteenth century," Lacquer (1986:1) observes, "human sexual nature changed." It certainly did. With the reorganization of production and perception in the age of revolution, novel distinctions arose in the construction of gender. And they raised the problematic "nature of woman" to consciousness in Europe as never before.

Given the epistemology of the time, it was inevitable that this new consciousness should find the source of gender relations in the bodies of men

and women – and that biology should be invoked to explain a division of labor already established in economy and society. The ideology of the enlightened free market might celebrate equality and a generic humanity. But its material practices sanctioned the exploitation of whole categories of people, usually on the basis of "natural" distinctions like race and sex. Such stigmatizing signs often come to imply each other: in late eighteenth-century images of Africa, the feminization of the black "other" was a potent trope of devaluation. The non-European was to be made as peripheral to the global axes of reason and production as women had become at home. Both were vital to the material and imaginative order of modern Europe. Yet both were deprived of access to its highest values. Biology again provided the authoritative terms for this simultaneous process of inclusion and disqualification.

In sum, the manner in which Africa was portrayed as woman – with reference in particular to the organs of procreation – was an extension of a gender ideology fast taking root in late eighteenth-century Europe. Here "the female body in its reproductive capacity and in its distinction from that of the male, [had come] to occupy a critical place in a whole range of political discourses" (Lacquer 1986:1). As the biology of childbearing became the essence of womanhood, it also seemed to prescribe an increasingly radical, physically-derived contrast between male and female. For centuries prior to this time, both medical and commonsense knowledge appear to have assumed that women had the same reproductive organs as men; that they were "men turned outside in" (Lacquer 1986:1). Moreover, gender identity had not been vested in the anatomy of procreation alone but in more general features of moral and social disposition. In this respect too there was a continuity between male and female: far from "a total division of mental properties between the sexes," as Jordanova (1980:63) puts it, there had been "a continuum according to which reason dominated ..."

Reason and intelligence were male properties, of course; men and women had thus been arrayed along a single axis whose telos was masculine (Lacquer 1986:3). But the struggle between the two qualities had occurred within rather than between individuals, each person's temperament being the product of both. Here Foucault's insight into changing perceptions of hermaphrodites throws light on the emergence of modern gender identity. In his introduction to the memoirs of Herculine Barbin (1980:viif.), he notes that medieval canon and civil law defined them as people in whom the two sexes were juxtaposed in variable proportions. By the nineteenth century, however, it had become the task of the medical expert to "find the one true sex of the so-called hermaphrodite" (Davidson 1987), to reveal the unambiguous biological reality that underlay uncertain appearances.

The premodern language of gender had also integrated physical, mental, and social qualities, making the body an icon of moral as much as of procreative status. Jordanova (1980:49) notes that medical and philosophical writings in the eighteenth century focused on the breast as a symbol of the valued role of women in domestic nurture. The shift of attention to the uterus in nineteenth-century biology marked a retreat into the hidden recesses of gynaecological anatomy, whence female nature now seemed to emanate.

The new biology of difference and incommensurability, then, shackled women to their sexual nature as resolutely as it freed men – or at least European men – from the constraints of instinct and bodily function. "It was," one physician explained, "as if the Almighty, in creating the female sex, had taken the uterus and built up a woman around it" (Holbrook 1882; quoted in Smith-Rosenberg and Rosenberg 1973:335). Here the ideology of gender cut across contemporary models of the nervous system and became implicated in the more general definition of modern selfhood. For, by implication, women's reproductive physiology rerouted their neurological pathways, diffusing the compact density of the rational, male self. As opponents of female education were to argue, the brain and the reproductive organs simply could not develop at the same time. The uterus was assumed to be connected directly to the central nervous system, shaping its constitution and in return being affected by it (Smith-Rosenberg and Rosenberg 1973:335).

Women's sensibility was both greater and more labile than that of men, and their nervous systems lacked focus; their "fibres" were "mobile," especially "those in the uterus" (Macquart 1799; quoted in Jordanova 1980:48). Like the "low brow" non-European, the European female was played upon by strong and frequent sensations from the external environment. Her constitution was passionate and intuitive, susceptible to nervous disorders, and responsive to control by males – particularly men of science (Stocking 1987:199). A privileged relationship of sex and selfhood had been born: with the emergence of the "psyche" in later nineteenth-century thought, sexuality would become the "externalization of the hidden, inner essence of personality" (Davidson 1987:47). This development was prefigured in the vision of missionaries earlier in the century, which placed great diagnostic weight upon sexual propriety as a symptom of "moral fiber." After all, as Davidson reminds us, moral theology had once used "pervert" – a person wilfully turning to evil from good – as an antonym of "convert." There is evidence of this connotation, and of the more modern sense of "sexual deviance," in the evangelists' use of the term.

It has been pointed out (Smith-Rosenberg and Rosenberg 1973:338; Stocking 1987:199; Jordanova 1980:49) that contemporary discourses on female nature were neither unanimous nor free of contradiction. Women were held at once to be sensitive and delicate, yet hardy and longer-lived; passionate and quintessentially sexual, yet innocent and intuitively moral. Given the political load that the anatomy of woman had come to bear, such ambiguities were bound to fuel angry dispute; it is not surprising that her body soon became an ideological battleground (Lacquer 1986:24). Feminists and antifeminists both exploited these contradictions, albeit in contrasting ways – the former being no less quick than the latter to appeal to natural differences in making their case. Anna Wheeler and William Thompson (1825; quoted in Lacquer 1986:23), for example, argued that women deserved greater political participation on grounds of their innate moral aptitude and their undesiring, even passionless dispositions. And Fuller (1855), in her manifesto, *Woman in the Nineteenth Century*, described male and female as "two sides of the great radical dualism," the female system being "electrical in movement" and "intuitive in function" (quoted in Ayala 1977:263). Thus, while the debate raged over social values, its terms reinforced the hegemony of biological determinism and ineluctable gender distinction.

The new biology, in short, gave legitimacy to an idealized image of rational man. Unlike women and non-Europeans, he was a self-contained individual and was driven by inner reason, not by sensory stimuli from the social and material environment. This image of selfhood appeared simultaneously in a wide range of late eighteenth-century moral and technical discourses; biomedical science was just one voice in a richly redundant chorus, its concern with the inner body drawing attention away from man's dialectical relation with his context. But the reduction did not go unchecked. It was countered by the social reformism of mainstream enlightenment religion and philosophy, which stressed the reconstruction of persons and, through them, the world. Humanitarian and evangelical rhetoric alike had it that the possession of a soul and the capacity to reason made every human being capable of improvement. The self could be "cultured,"[12] the will strengthened by implanting spiritual truth and by "uplifting" physical and social conditions.

Thus the biological determinism of the age was usually qualified by some attention to the effects of environment; conversely, the optimism of philanthropists and evangelists was often tempered by a suspicion that nature placed limits on the ability of some human beings to develop. Nor were scientists undivided on the issues: Gould (1981:31ff.) has distinguished "hard-" from "soft-liners" among significant eighteenth and nineteenth-century thinkers on the question of the African's potential for civilization.[13] While this distinction may be too rigidly drawn, there certainly were loud and lengthy arguments about the origin and implications of racial difference. Witness the debate over the role of climate in the origin of human diversity, in which some early naturalists (e.g., Buffon 1791) and biologists (e.g., Blumenbach [1775, 1795] 1969) claimed that negro physical characteristics grew out of life in the tropics (Curtin 1964:40). Here again scientific thought evoked European notions of ecology that went back at least a hundred years – in particular, the humoral theory that "as the air is, so are the inhabitants" (cf. Hodgen 1964:283). In this legacy "southern climes" were repeatedly associated with heat and fecundity, sensuality and decay. For instance, in his defense of Cape Dutchmen against Barrow's attacks, Lichtenstein (1928:1,58) attributed their "phlegm" to the African environment. And for comparative support he quoted Goethe's similar observations of the indolent Neapolitans.

The writings of the South African missionaries suggest that they too perceived a complex connection between African bodies and landscapes. Moreover, their efforts to reform the benighted blacks were to express an unresolved conflict between the incorrigibility of natural endowment and the possibility of human improvement. Visible in the conflict, and in the entire European discourse about savagery, was an increasingly sharp – and gendered – contrast between "nature" (all that exists prior to civil society) and "civilization" or "culture" (collectively wrought existence, though not yet the modern anthropological idea of a distinct, meaningful lifeworld; see Stocking 1987:19; also note 12 above). This dichotomy was elaborated most extensively, perhaps, in the debate over the "noble savage," a chimera which relied heavily on images of Africa already in popular European circulation.

Notes

1 Notwithstanding our particular concerns here, it goes without saying that stereotypic images of "others," in Africa and elsewhere, predate the age of revolution. So does their metaphysical significance in European thought and representation. For a valuable history of medieval conceptions of the "monstrous races," see Friedman (1981).

2 On Rousseau's views in this respect, see Cook (1936); also Curtin (1964:42).

3 Three seventeenth-century accounts were published in Dutch and Latin (see Schapera 1933); two in German followed during the eighteenth century (Kolben 1731; Mentzel 1785–87).

4 Barrow's biography was notably similar to that of Park. Both were self-made sons of northern British smallholders (Lloyd 1970).

5 [...] The Cape was restored to the new Batavian Republic in 1803 under the Treaty of Amiens but

was seized again by the British in 1806, after the resumption of the Napoleonic Wars (see e.g. Davenport 1969:273f.).

6 It is clear that Barrow meant "kaffir" here to include all "aborigines." In the nineteenth century the term (also "Caffre") was often used more specifically to describe the Nguni-speaking peoples of South Africa – although it was later to become a general term of abuse for blacks, much like "nigger" in the United States of America.

7 For an account of British images of and attitudes toward the Dutch settlers, see Streak (1974), who also discusses the writings of Barrow and Lichtenstein. We are grateful to Robert Gordon for drawing our attention to this reference.

8 Lichtenstein seems to have been the first writer in this genre to make use of missionary observations of black South Africans (see the Prefatory Note to volume 1 of his *Travels* [p.vi], republished by the Van Riebeeck Society in 1928). His work in turn became an important source of European constructions of Africa.

9 See Curtin (1964:58f.) on the role of the "tropics" in this discourse.

10 We are indebted to Nahum Chandler for this reference, included in his unpublished paper, "Writing Absence: On Some Assumptions of Africanist Discourse in the West."

11 Although, as Keith Thomas (1984:42) points out, talk of Hottentots as "beasts in the skin of man" also had earlier precursors.

12 As Williams (1976:77) has noted, "culture as an independent noun, an abstract process or the product of such a process, is not important before lC18 [the late eighteenth century] not common before mC19 [the mid-nineteenth century]." Prior to this, "culture" was a noun of process, implying the "tending *of* something," usually crops or animals. From the early sixteenth century, the tending of natural growth was gradually extended by metaphor to the process of human development.

13 We are indebted to Nahum Chandler for this reference also; see n. 10 above.

References

Achebe, Chinua
1959 *Things Fall Apart*. New York: Astor-Honor Inc.
1978 An Image of Africa. *Research in African Literatures* 9:1–15.

Anderson, Benedict
1983 *Imagined Communities: Reflections on the Origin and Spread of Nationalism*. London: Verso.

Asad, Talal
1973 Two European Images of Non-European Rule. In *Anthropology and the Colonial Encounter*, ed. T. Asad. London: Ithaca Press.

Austen, Ralph A., and Woodruff D. Smith
1969 Images of Africa and British Slave-Trade Abolition: The Transition to an Imperialist Ideology. 1787–1807. *African Historical Studies* 2:69–83.

Ayala, Flavia
1977 Victorian Science and the "Genius" of Woman. *Journal of the History of Ideas* 38:261–80.

Barrow, John
1801–4 *An Account of Travels into the Interior of Southern Africa in the Years 1797 and 1798*. 2 vols. London: Cadell & Davies.
1806 *A Voyage to Cochinchina*. London: Cadell & Davies.

Blumenbach, Johann F.
1969 *On the Natural Varieties of Mankind*. Translated by T. Bendyshe from the 1775/1795 editions. New York: Bergman Publishers.

Brantlinger, Patrick
1985 Victorians and Africans: The Genealogy of the Myth of the Dark Continent. *Critical Inquiry* 12:166–203.

Buffon, George L.L.
1791 *Natural History, General and Particular*. Translated by W. Smellie. London: A. Strahan.

Burchell, William J.
1822–4 *Travels in the Interior of Southern Africa*. 2 vols. London: Longman, Hurst, Rees, Orme, Brown & Green. Reprinted 1967; Cape Town: Struik.

Camper, Petrus
1821 *The Works of the Late Professor Camper, on the Connexion between the Science of Anatomy and the Arts of Drawing, Painting, Statuary*. ... New ed., edited by T. Cogan. London: sold by J. Hearne.

Coetzee, John M.
1988 *White Writing: On the Culture of Letters in South Africa*. New Haven: Yale University Press.

Cook, Mercer
1936 Jean-Jacques Rousseau and the Negro. *Journal of Negro History* 21:294–303.

Curtin, Philip D.
1964 *The Image of Africa: British Ideas and Action, 1780–1850*. Madison: University of Wisconsin Press.

Cuvier, Georges
1827–35 *The Animal Kingdom*. ... 16 vols. London: Geo. B. Whittaker.

Dalzel, Archibald
1799 *Geschichte von Dahomy, einem Inländischen Königreich in Afrika*. Translated from *The History of Dahomey*, 1793. Leipzig: Schwickert.

Davenport, T.R.H.
1969 *The Consolidation of a New Society: The Cape Colony. In the Oxford History of South Africa*, vol. 1, ed. M. Wilson and L.M. Thompson. New York: Oxford University Press.

Davidson, Arnold I.
1987 Sex and the Emergence of Sexuality. *Critical Inquiry* 14:16–48.

Davis, Peter B.
1966 *The Problem of Slavery in Western Culture*. Ithaca: Cornell University Press.
1975 *The Problem of Slavery in the Age of Revolution 1770–1823*. Ithaca: Cornell University Press.

Edwards, John
1886 *Reminiscences of the Early Life and Missionary Labours of the Rev. John Edwards*. Edited by W.C. Holden. Grahamstown, South Africa: T.H. Grocott.

Elphick, Robert, and V.C. Malherbe
1989 The Khoisan to 1828. In *The Shaping of South African Society, 1652–1840*, ed. R. Elphick and H.B. Giliomee. Middletown, CT: Wesleyan University Press.

Figlio, Karl
1976 The Metaphor of Organization: An Historiographical Perspective on the Bio-Medical Sciences of the Early Nineteenth Century. *History of Science* 14:17–53.

Foucault, Michel
1973 *Madness and Civilization: A History of Insanity in the Age of Reason*. Translated by R. Howard. New York: Vintage Books.
1975 *The Birth of the Clinic: An Archeology of Medical Perception*. Translated by A.M. Sheridan Smith. New York: Vintage Books.
1980 *Hercule Barbin (Being the Recently Discovered Memoirs of a Nineteenth Century French Hermaphrodite)*. New York: Pantheon.

Friedman, John B.
1981 *The Monstrous Races in Medieval Art and Thought*. Cambridge: Harvard University Press.

Fuller Ossoli, Sarah M.
1855 *Woman in the Nineteenth Century*. New York: Sheldon, Lamport. Original edition, 1845.

Gates, Henry L., Jr., ed.
1986 *"Race," Writing, and Difference*. Chicago: University of Chicago Press.

Gilman, Sander L.
1985 Black Bodies, White Bodies: Toward an Iconography of Female Sexuality in Late Nineteenth Century Art, Medicine and Literature. *Critical Inquiry* 12:204–242.

Godzich, Wlad
1987 Foreword: In Quest of Modernity. In *Ideology of Adventure: Studies in Modern Consciousness, 1100–1750*, vol. 1, by Michael Nerlich. Translated by R. Crowley. Minneapolis: University of Minnesota Press.

Gould, Stephen J.
1981 *The Mismeasure of Man*. New York: W.W. Norton & Co.
1985 *The Flamingo's Smile: Reflections in Natural History*. New York: W.W. Norton & Co.

Harlow, Vincent T.
1936 The British Occupations, 1795–1806. In *The Cambridge History of the British Empire*, vol. 8, *South Africa, Rhodesia and the Protectorates*, ed. A.P. Newton and E.A. Benians. Cambridge: Cambridge University Press.

Heidegger, Martin
1977 *The Question Concerning Technology, and Other Essays*. Translated by W. Lovitt. New York: Harper & Row.

Hodgen, Margaret T.
1964 *Early Anthropology in the Sixteenth and Seventeenth Centuries*. Philadelphia: University of Pennsylvania Press.

Holbrook, Martin L.
1882 *Parturition without Pain: A Code of Directions for Escaping from the Primal Curse*. New York: Fowler & Wells.

Hume, David
1854 *The Philosophical Works*. 4 vols. Edinburgh: Adam & Charles Black; Boston: Little, Brown.

Jordanova, Ludmilla J.
1980 Natural Facts: A Historical Perspective on Science and Sexuality. In *Nature, Culture, and Gender*, ed. C.P. MacCormack and M. Strathern. Cambridge: Cambridge University Press.
1981 The History of the Family. In *Women in Society: Interdisciplinary Essays*, The Cambridge Women's Studies Group. London: Virago Press.

Kolben, Peter
1731 *The Present State of the Cape of Good Hope*. 2 vols. Translated from the German by Mr Medley. London: W. Innys.

Lacquer, Thomas
1986 Orgasm, Generation, and the Politics of Reproductive Biology. *Representations* 14:1–41.

Lichtenstein, Henry [W.H.C.]
1928–30 *Travels in Southern Africa in the Years 1803, 1804, 1805 and 1806*. 2 vols. Translated from the 1812–15 edition by A. Plumptre. Cape Town: The Van Riebeeck Society.

1973 *Foundation of the Cape* (1811) and *About the Bechuanas* (1807). Translated and edited by O.H. Spohr. Cape Town: A.A. Balkema.

Lloyd, Christopher
1970 *Mr Barrow of the Admiralty: A Life of Sir John Barrow, 1764–1848*. London: Collins.

Marais, Johannes S.
1944 *Maynier and the First Boer Republic*. Cape Town: Maskew Miller.

Marks, Shula
1972 Khoisan Resistance to the Dutch in the Seventeenth and Eighteenth Centuries. *Journal of African History* 13:55–80.

Mentzel, Otto F.
1921–5 *A Complete and Authentic Geographical and Topographical Description of the … African Cape of Good Hope. …* 2 parts. Translated from the 1785–7 original 2-vol. German edition by H.J. Mandelbrote. Cape Town: The Van Riebeeck Society.

Moodie, John W.D.
1835 *Ten Years in South Africa*. 2 vols. London: R. Bentley.

Nerlich, Michael
1987 *Ideology of Adventure: Studies in Modern Consciousness, 1100–1750*. 2 vols. Translated by R. Crowley. Minneapolis: University of Minnesota Press.

Norris, Robert
1968 *Memoirs of the Reign of Bossa Ahadee, King of Dahomey. …* Facsimile of the 1789 edition. London: Frank Cass.

Philip, John
1828 *Researches in South Africa; Illustrating the Civil, Moral, and Religious Condition of the Native Tribes*. 2 vols. London: James Duncan. Reprinted, 1969; New York: Negro Universities Press.

Pratt, Mary L.
1985 Scratches on the Face of the Country; or, What Mr. Barrow Saw in the Land of the Bushmen. *Critical Inquiry* 12:119–43.

Said, Edward W.
1978 *Orientalism*. New York: Pantheon Books.

Schapera, Isaac
1933 *The Early Cape Hottentots, Described in the Writings of Olfert Dapper (1668), Willem ten Rhyne (1686), and Johannes Gulielmus de Grevenbrock (1695)*. Original texts and translations by I. Schapera and B. Farrington. Cape Town: The Van Riebeeck Society.

Smith-Rosenberg, Carroll, and Charles Rosenberg
1973 The Female Animal: Medical and Biological Views of Woman and her Role in Nineteenth-century America. *Journal of American History* 40:323–56.

Stocking, George W.
1987 *Victorian Anthropology*. New York: The Free Press; London: Collier Macmillan.

Streak, Michael
1974 *The Afrikaner as Viewed by the English, 1795–1854*. Cape Town: Struik.

Street, Brian V.
1975 *The Savage in Literature: Representations of 'Primitive' Society in English Fiction, 1858–1920*. London and Boston: Routledge & Kegan Paul.

Thomas, Keith V.
1984 *Man and the Natural World: Changing Attitudes in England, 1500–1800*. Harmondsworth: Penguin.

West, Cornel
1982 *Prophesy Deliverance!: An Afro-American Revolutionary Christianity*. Philadelphia: Westminster Press.

White, Charles
1799 *An Account of the Regular Gradation in Man, and in Different Animals and Vegetables; and From the Former to the Latter. …* London: Printed for C. Dilly.

Williams, Raymond
1976 *Keywords: A Vocabulary of Culture and Society*. London: Oxford University.

2

The Meaning of Our Work

Cheikh Anta Diop

I began my research in September 1946; because of our colonial situation at that time, the political problem dominated all others. In 1949 the RDA[1] was undergoing a crisis. I felt that Africa should mobilize all its energy to help the movement turn the tide of repression: thus I was elected Secretary General of the RDA students in Paris and served from 1950 to 1953. On July 4–8, 1951 we held in Paris the first postwar Pan African Student Union (from London) well-represented by more than 30 delegates, including the daughter of the Oni of Ife, the late Miss Aderemi Tedju. In February 1953 the first issue of the *Voie de l'Afrique Noire* appeared; this was the organ of the RDA students. In it, I published an article entitled "Towards a Political Ideology in Black Africa."

That article contained a résumé of *Nations nègres*, the manuscript of which was already completed. All our ideas on African history, the past and future of our languages, their utilization in the most advanced scientific fields as in education generally, our concepts on the creation of a future federal state, continental or subcontinental, our thoughts on African social structures, on strategy and tactics in the struggle for national independence, and

so forth, all those ideas were clearly expressed in that article. As would subsequently be seen, with respect to the problem of the continent's political independence, the French-speaking African politicians took their own good time before admitting that this was the right political road to follow. Nevertheless, the RDA students organized themselves into a federation within France and politicized African student circles by popularizing the slogan of national independence for Africa from the Sahara to the Cape and from the Indian Ocean to the Atlantic, as our periodical attests. The archives of the FEANF (Federation of African Students in France) indicate that it did not begin to adopt anticolonialist positions until it was directed by RDA students.[2] We stressed the cultural and political content that we included in the concept of independence in order to get the latter adopted in French-speaking Africa: already forgotten is the bitter struggle that had to be waged to impose it on student circles in Paris, throughout France, and even within the ranks of RDA students.

The cultural concept especially will claim our attention here; the problem was posed in terms of restoring the collective national African personality.

From Cheikh Anta Diop, "The Meaning of our Work", pp. xii–xvii in *The African Origins of Civilisation: Myth or Reality* (1974), Lawrence Hill Books.

It was particularly necessary to avoid the pitfall of facility. It could seem too tempting to delude the masses engaged in a struggle for national independence by taking liberties with scientific truth, by unveiling a mythical, embellished past. Those who have followed us in our efforts for more than 20 years know now that this was not the case and that this fear remained groundless.

Admittedly three factors compete to form the collective personality of a people: a psychic factor, susceptible of a literary approach; this is the factor that would elsewhere be called national temperament, and that the Negritude poets have overstressed. In addition, there are the historical factor and the linguistic factor, both susceptible of being approached scientifically. These last two factors have been the subject of our studies; we have endeavored to remain strictly on scientific grounds. Have foreign intellectuals, who challenge our intentions and accuse us of all kinds of hidden motives or ridiculous ideas, proceeded any differently? When they explain their own historical past or study their languages, that seems normal. Yet, when an African does likewise to help reconstruct the national personality of his people, distorted by colonialism, that is considered backward or alarming. We contend that such a study is the point of departure for the cultural revolution properly understood. All the headlong flights of certain infantile leftists who try to bypass this effort can be explained by intellectual inertia, inhibition, or incompetence. The most brilliant pseudo-revolutionary eloquence ignores that need which must be met if our peoples are to be reborn culturally and politically. In truth, many Africans find this vision too beautiful to be true; not so long ago some of them could not break with the idea that Blacks are nonexistent culturally and historically. It was necessary to put up with the cliché that Africans had no history and try to start from there to build something modestly!

Our investigations have convinced us that the West has not been calm enough and objective enough to teach us our history correctly, without crude falsifications. Today, what interests me most is to see the formation of teams, not of passive readers, but of honest, bold research workers, allergic to complacency and busy substantiating and exploring ideas expressed in our work, such as:

1. Ancient Egypt was a Negro civilization. The history of Black Africa will remain suspended in air and cannot be written correctly until African historians dare to connect it with the history of Egypt. In particular, the study of languages, institution, and so forth, cannot be treated properly; in a word, it will be impossible to build African humanities, a body of African human sciences, so long as that relationship does not appear legitimate. The African historian who evades the problem of Egypt is neither modest nor objective, nor unruffled; he is ignorant, cowardly, and neurotic. Imagine, if you can, the uncomfortable position of a western historian who was to write the history of Europe without referring to Greco-Latin Antiquity and try to pass that off as a scientific approach.

The ancient Egyptians were Negroes. The moral fruit of their civilization is to be counted among the assets of the Black world. Instead of presenting itself to history as an insolvent debtor, that Black world is the very initiator of the "western" civilization flaunted before our eyes today. Pythagorean mathematics, the theory of the four elements of Thales of Miletus, Epicurean materialism, Platonic idealism, Judaism, Islam, and modern science are rooted in Egyptian cosmogony and science. One needs only to meditate on Osiris, the redeemer-god, who sacrifices himself, dies, and is resurrected to save mankind, a figure essentially identifiable with Christ.

A visitor to Thebes in the Valley of the Kings can view the Moslem inferno in detail (in the tomb of Seti I, of the Nineteenth Dynasty), 1700 years before the Koran. Osiris at the tribunal of the dead is indeed the "lord" of revealed religions, sitting enthroned on Judgement Day, and we know that certain Biblical passages are practically copies of Egyptian moral texts. Far be it from me to confuse this brief reminder with a demonstration. It is simply a matter of providing a few landmarks to persuade the incredulous Black African reader to bring himself to verify this. To his great surprise and satisfaction, he will discover that most of the ideas used today to domesticate, atrophy, dissolve, or steal his "soul," were conceived by his own ancestors. To become conscious of that fact is perhaps the first step toward a genuine retrieval of himself; without it, intellectual sterility is the general rule, or else the creations bear I know not what imprint of the subhuman.

In a word, we must restore the historical consciousness of the African peoples and reconquer a Promethean consciousness.

2. Anthropologically and culturally speaking, the Semitic world was born during protohistoric times from the mixture of white-skinned and black-skinned people in western Asia. This is why an understanding of the Mesopotamian Semitic world, Judaic or Arabic, requires constant reference to the underlying Black reality. If certain Biblical passages, especially in the Old Testament, seem absurd, this is because specialists, puffed up with prejudices, are unable to accept documentary evidence.

3. The triumph of the monogenetic thesis of humanity (Leakey), even at the stage of "Homo sapiens-sapiens," compels one to admit that all races descended from the Black race, according to a filiation process that science will one day explain.[3]

4. In *L'Afrique Noire précoloniale* (1960), I had two objectives: (1) to demonstrate the possibility of writing a history of Black Africa free of mere chronology of events, as the preface to that volume clearly indicates; (2) to define the laws governing the evolution of African sociopolitical structures, in order to explain the direction that historical evolution has taken in Black Africa; therefore, to try henceforth to dominate and master that historical process by knowledge, rather than simply to submit to it.

These last questions, like those about origins (Egypt), are among the key problems; once they are solved, a scholar can proceed to write the history of Africa. Consequently, it is evident why we are paying particular attention to the solution of such problems and of so many others which transcend the field of history.

The research pattern inaugurated by *L'Afrique Noire précoloniale* on the sociohistorical, not on the ethnographic, plane has since been utilized by many researchers. That, I suppose, is what has led them to describing the daily life of the Congolese or enlarging upon the various forms of political, economic, social, military, and judicial organization in Africa.

5. To define the image of a modern Africa reconciled with its past and preparing for its future.[4]

6. Once the perspectives accepted until now by official science have been reversed, the history of humanity will become clear and the history of

Africa can be written. But any undertaking in this field that adopts compromise as its point of departure as if it were possible to split the difference, or the truth, in half, would run the risk of producing nothing but alienation. Only a loyal, determined struggle to destroy cultural aggression and bring out the truth, whatever it may be, is revolutionary and consonant with real progress; it is the only approach which opens on to the universal. Humanitarian declarations are not called for and add nothing to real progress.

Similarly, it is not a matter of looking for the Negro under a magnifying glass as one scans the past; a great people has nothing to do with petty history, nor with ethnographic reflections sorely in need of renovation. It matters little that some brilliant Black individuals may have existed elsewhere. The essential factor is to retrace the history of the entire nation. The contrary is tantamount to thinking that to be or not to be depends on whether or not one is known in Europe. The effort is corrupted at the base by the presence of the very complex one hopes to eradicate. Why not study the acculturation of the white man in a Black milieu, in ancient Egypt, for example?

7. How does it happen that all modern Black literature has remained minor, in the sense that no Negro African author or artist, to my knowledge, has yet posed the problem of man's fate, the major theme of human letters?

8. In *L'Unité culturelle de l'Afrique Noire*, we tried to pinpoint the features common to Negro African civilization.

9. In the second part of *Nations nègres*, we demonstrated that African languages could express philosophic and scientific thought (mathematics, physics, and so forth)[5] and that African culture will not be taken seriously until their utilization in education becomes a reality. The events of the past few years prove that UNESCO has accepted those ideas.[6]

10. I am delighted to learn that one idea proposed in *L'Afrique Noire précoloniale* – the possibilities of pre-Columbian relations between Africa and America – has been taken up by an American scholar. Professor Harold G. Lawrence, of Oakland University, is in fact demonstrating with an abundance of proof the reality of those relationships which were merely hypothetical in my work. If the sum total of his impressive arguments stands up to

the test of chronology, if it can be proved in the final analyis that all the facts noted existed prior to the period of slavery, his research will have surely contributed solid material to the edifice of historical knowledge.

I should like to conclude by urging young American scholars of good will, both Blacks and Whites, to form university teams and to become involved, like Professor Lawrence, in the effort to confirm various ideas that I have advanced, instead of limiting themselves to a negative, sterile skepticism. They would soon be dazzled, if not blinded, by the bright light of their future discoveries. In fact, our conception of African history, as exposed here, has practically triumphed, and those who write on African history now, whether willingly or not, base themselves upon it. But the American contribution to this final phase could be decisive.

Notes

1 Rassemblement Démocratique Africain (Democratic African Rally), the RDA founded in 1946, "was the first interterritorial movement in French West Africa, created before parties in territories other than Senegal or Ivory Coast had taken root." Ruth S. Morgenthau, *Political Parties on French-speaking West Africa*. Oxford: Clarendon Press, 1964, p. 302.
2 Starting especially with the administration of Franklin, secretary general of the RDA students at Montpellier. Cf. the article by Penda Marcelle Ouegnin: "Un compte-rendu du Congrès de la FEANF organisé par les ERDA aux Sociétés savantes le 8 avril 1953," in the same bulletin cited above, May–June 1953.

   Similarly, with a few exceptions the PAI (African Independence Party) was organized by former RDA students who had returned to Africa. Various branches in France rallied to the new party which thus carried forward the RDA line and popularized the slogan of national independence that we had launched.
3 Cf. Cheikh Anta Diop, "L'Apparition de l'homosapiens," *Bulletin de l'IFAN*, XXXII, Series II, number 3, 1970. Cheikh Anta Diop, "La Pigmentation des anciens Egyptiens. Test par la mélanine," *Bulletin de l'IFAN*, XXXV, Series B, number 3, 1973.
4 Cf. Cheikh Anta Diop, *Les Fondements culturels et industriels d'un futur Etat fedéral d'Afrique Noire*.
5 In *Nations nègres*, Dr Diop translates a page of Einstein's Theory of Relativity into Wolof, the principal language of Senegal.
6 Bamako 1964 colloquium on the transcription of African languages, various measures taken to promote African languages, and so forth.

3

Europe Upside Down
Fallacies of the New Afrocentrism

Kwame Anthony Appiah

In the last few years, there has been a stream of publications, especially in the United States, aimed at establishing a new basis for the study and teaching of African and African-American culture. Whether or not they actually use the word "Afrocentric" on their packaging, these books – which differ enormously in the quality of their thought and writing, as well as in their factual reliability – have a certain common set of pre-oc-cupations, whose persistence entitles one now to speak of an Afrocentric paradigm.

This has two basic elements, one critical, the other positive, which are either argued or taken for granted. The negative thesis is that modern Western scholarship on cultural matters, high and low, is hopelessly Eurocentric. This means, to begin with, that Western scholarship understands European history, intellectual life and social institutions as an ideal type, both normatively and descriptively. But Eurocentric work also displays an inability, rooted in prejudice, to enter sympathetically into the forms of life of non-Europeans, and, especially, of black people of African descent. As a consequence, Western scholarship presupposes, so the story goes, that

Africans have produced little of much cultural worth, and that cultural works of sophistication or value (like the architecture of Great Zimbabwe or the Pyramids), even when they are in Africa, are unlikely to have been produced by black people. In support of this Eurocentric thesis, some (and occasionally a great deal of) work goes into showing that European scholars, at least since the Enlightenment, have concealed facts about the African origins of certain central elements of Western civilization; notably the Egyptian origins of the Greek "miracle" and the black African origins of the Egyptian "miracle."

This negative thesis is argued as the pro-legomenon to an alternative, positive, "Afrocentric" view, in which African cultural creativity is discov-ered to have been at the origin of Western civiliza-tion, while Western civilization, especially modern Western civilization, is either asserted or implied to be morally depraved; incapable, in particular, of living peacefully with others. We (sometimes all of us, sometimes just those of us who are black) are urged, then, to centre on African history (and par-ticularly the history of the Egypt of the Pharaohs) and return to African values.

From Kwame Anthony Appiah, "Racisms" in *Anatomy of Racism*, ed. David Theo Goldberg (1990), pp. 3–17, included as "Europe Upside Down: Fallacies of the New Afrocentrism," *Times Literary Supplement*, 12 February 1993, from University of Minnesota Press.

The Afrocentric paradigm is not just the source of a lively body of writing; it is the basis of a movement in the United States to revise the teaching of African-American children, to provide them with an Afrocentric education. Here the argument is that the Eurocentricity of what is taught in American schools, at best, fails to nurture, and at worst, actively damages the self-esteem of black children, and that what these children need instead is a diet of celebratory African history (held to begin in Egypt, and in an Egyptian civilization held to be black) and the transmission of African values.

These values are often now taught in the version developed by Maulana Karenga and associated with the invention of a feast called "Kwanzaa," designed to provide an African celebration to go with Christmas and Hanukkah. (American children are taught Swahili words, naming various allegedly African virtues, as their proper inheritance. There is something of an irony in the use of Swahili as an Afrocentric language, since hardly any of the slaves brought to the New World can have known it, and it was in fact being used in a culture in which slave-trading to the Arabian peninsula was a major element of the economy.) This particular brand of Afrocentrism goes under the label of "Kemetism" ("Kemet" being a name for ancient Egypt); and the whole package can be found in a recent book by Molefi Kete Asante, one of the intellectual leaders of the movement *Kemet: Afrocentricity and Knowledge*.

At least as important as any published work is a body of Afrocentric lore transmitted in public lectures and in discussion groups by figures who have tended in recent years to combine Afrocentrism with a peculiar anti-Semitism, which is preoccupied with attributing special responsibility for the ills of the black world to a Jewish conspiracy. Many of the leading rap stars seem to subscribe to such views, combining them with their well-known misogyny and homophobia, to produce a cultural brew as noxious as any currently available in popular culture. The diagnosis of this particular pathology is the subject of much current speculation among observers of African-American culture.

The scholarly end of the Afrocentric movement has one major hero: Cheikh Anta Diop, the Senegalese man of letters, after whom the university in Dakar is now named. Diop argued, over many years (beginning in the 1950s), for the thesis of the African origins of Greek civilization. In such works as *L'Unité culturelle de l'Afrique noire, Antériorité des civilisations nègres, Nations nègres et culture, Fondements économiques et culturels d'un état fédéral d'Afrique noir*, and *Parenté génétique de l'égyptien pharaonique et des langues négro-africaines*, he pursued a complex agenda, in which the splendours of Egypt were seen as a reason for contemporary African pride and the cultural unity derived from a common African source as the basis for modern African political unity. (For a sample of Diop's writing see Chapter 2, this volume.)

Like most cultural movements at full flood, this Afrocentrism is a composite of truth and error, insight and illusion, moral generosity and meanness. But the most striking thing about it is how thoroughly at home it is in the frameworks of nineteenth-century European thought. (One of the symptomatic features of much Afrocentric writing is that the antagonists it identifies are largely dead.) Afrocentrism, in short, seems very much to share the presuppositions of the Victorian ideologies against which it is reacting. Take, for example, the preoccupation with the ancient world. The academic curriculum of the nineteenth century traced Western civilization to roots in ancient Greece. Afrocentrists have simply challenged the old priority of the (white) Greeks, by replacing them with (black) Egyptians. There are, of course, genuine issues for discussion here about the relations between different parts of the ancient Mediterranean and the Greek "miracle." Martin Bernal (not, by my account, an Afrocentrist, because he doesn't support the positive agenda of the movement) is a hero for Afrocentrists because, in *Black Athena* (Volume One, 1987), he has taken up the challenge of refuting the modern view that the Greeks owed nothing of importance to Egypt. So far as I can see, there is now a consensus that Bernal has convincingly demonstrated the role of prejudice against blacks and Jews in classical scholarship from the Enlightenment onwards, but has not established decisively his own positive account of ancient history.

But it is not this quite genteel academic debate that has drawn Bernal to the Afrocentrists' attention. For it is essential not only to agree with

Bernal's account of ancient intellectual history but also to insist, in Diop's words, that "Ancient Egypt was a Negro civilization [and] ... the moral fruit of their civilization is to be counted among the assets of the Black world. ..." And on this matter Bernal has little to say. Fortunately he did not have to argue for this secondary thesis, since it is taken to be implicit in his title. *African Athena* (the title Bernal preferred) or *Egyptian Athena* would have left the racial issue open: *Black Athena* (his publisher's choice) does not.

This preoccupation with racial matters is very much a response to the ninteenth-century formulation of the issues, when to the classicism of the Enlightenment there was added the thought that the Western heritage was a racial possession. Which is to neglect not only Egyptian influences on the Greeks, but such minor embarrassments as the centrality of Jewish contributions to Western high culture, and the key role of the Arabs in maintaining the intellectual tradition that linked Plato to the Renaissance. It depends on a way of thinking about culture and biology which is bound to be discomfited by those scholars, black, brown and yellow, who have taken possession of Western culture in the twentieth century and mastered it, at the same time as many of the supposed racial heirs of the West have been immersed in popular culture "contaminated" by African rhythms.

But in our day racialism surely doesn't need arguing against in serious company. Do we not all know that the interconnections and interdependences of biology and culture are complex and multiple, that the old simplicities of racialism have not stood the test of exposure to the evidence? Perhaps, or, then again, perhaps not. After all, Afrocentrist interest in the colour of the ancient Egyptians presumably derives from the thought that if they were black then they were of the same race as contemporary black Africans and their New World cousins. And unless you conflate biology and culture, why should that matter?

It is hard to find in the Afrocentrist literature a clearer answer to this question than the passage from Diop I quoted earlier. Racial identity with the Egyptians makes their achievements a moral asset for contemporary blacks. (Of course, if Greece grew out of Egypt and "the West" grew out of Greece, then the West too is a moral asset of con-

temporary blacks, and its legacy of ethnocentrism presumably one of our moral liabilities. ... But I digress.) Perhaps this is why *Black Athena* and *The African Origin of Civilization* sell so well on the streets of Harlem. And if so, this is a reason that would have been entirely congenial to the nineteenth-century Eurocentrists whom Afrocentrism aims to refute.

Once we see the essentially reactive structure of Afrocentrism – that it is simply Eurocentrism turned upside-down – we can understand where its intellectual weaknesses lie. It is not surprising, for example, that in choosing to talk about Egypt and to ignore the rest of Africa and African history, Afrocentrism shares the European prejudice against cultures without writing. Eurocentrism, finding there a literate culture and a significant architecture, set about claiming that Egypt could not be black. Afrocentrism chooses Egypt because Eurocentrism had already made a claim on it.

Similarly, we should not be suprised at one of the most tiresome features of Afrocentrism, namely its persistence in what the Beninois philosopher (and current Minister of Culture) Paulin Hountondji has called "unanimism": the view that there is *an* African culture to which to appeal. (See Hountondji, Chapter 20, this volume). It is surely preposterous to suppose that there is a single African culture, shared by everyone from the civilizations of the Upper Nile thousands of years ago to the thousand or so language-zones of contemporary Africa.

In aiming to identify some common core of African civilization, the Afrocentrists seem once again to be responding to earlier attempts to identify a common core of Western culture. One can be forgiven for wondering how unitary the West really is today. But it was always a strange idea that Alexander, Alfred and Frederick the Great had something in common with each other and with the least of their subjects, which could be called Western culture. And in Africa, where whatever continuity there has been through all this time has not been mediated by even the broken textual tradition that in some sense unites "Western culture," it is not only a strange idea but a silly one.

A final irony is that Afrocentrism, which is offered in the name of black solidarity, has, by and large, entirely ignored the work of African scholars other than Diop. (This fact tends to be concealed because African–American scholars like Asante and Karenga have adopted African names.) Thus, much play has been given to another major source-book for the Afrocentrists, Janheinz Jahn's *Muntu: African cultures and the Western world*, a work that appeared in English translation in the United States with great *éclat* in the early 1960s. The book revolves around the concept of *ntu*, the stem of the Kinyaruanda-Bantu words *muntu* (person), *kintu* (thing), *hantu* (place and time) and *kuntu* (modality); "*ntu*," Jahn wrote with the *gravitas* of revelation, "is the universal force as such."

Reading this, I found myself drawn into a fantasy in which an African scholar returns to her home in Lagos or Nairobi, with the important news that she has uncovered the key to Western culture. Soon to be published: *THING: Western culture and the African world*, a work that exposes the philosophy of *ing*, written so clearly on the face of the English language. For *ing*, in the Euro-American view, is manifestly the inner dynamic essence of the world. In the structure of the terms do*ing* and mak*ing* and mean*ing*, the English (and thus, by extension all

Westerners) express their deep commitment to this conception. But the secret heart of the matter is captured in their primary ontological category of th-*ing*: every th-*ing* (or be-*ing* as their sages express the matter in the more specialized vocabulary of one of their secret societies) is not stable but ceaselessly changing. Here we see the fundamental explanation for the extraordinary neophilia of Western culture, its sense that reality is change.

The notion that there is something unitary called African culture that could thus be summarized has been subjected to devastating critique by a generation of African intellectuals. But little sign of these African accounts of African culture appears in the writings of Afrocentrism. Molefi Asante has written whole books about Akan culture without referring to the major works of such Akan philosophers as J.B. Danquah, William Abrahams, Kwasi Wiredu and Kwame Gyekye. And I am reliably informed that, on one occasion not so long ago, a distinguished Zairian intellectual was told by an African-American interlocutor that "We do not need you educated Africans coming here to tell us about African culture." ...

Resource Guide

I. Journals which specialize in African studies, and journals which frequently publish essays on Africa

Advance: The Journal of the African Development Foundation. Washington, DC: The Foundation, Superintendent of Documents, United States G. P. O. 1986–

Africa. London: International African Institute. 1928–

Africa Today. London: Africa Journal Ltd. 1981–

African Abstracts. London: International African Institute. 1950–

African Affairs. London: Royal African Society and Oxford University Press. 1901–

African Arts. Los Angeles: University of California Press.

African Historical Studies. Brookline, Mass: African Studies Center, Boston University. 1968–1971

African Insight. Pretoria: African Institute. 1980–

African Law Studies. New York: African Law Association of America. 1969–1980

African Social Research. Manchester: Manchester University Press 1966–

African Study Monographs (also called "Kyoto University African Study Mongraphs") Kyoto, Japan: Kyoto University African Studies Center. 1981–

African Studies Review. Atlanta: African Studies Association. 1970–

American Anthropologist. Washington, DC: American Anthropological Assocation. 1889–

American Ethnologist. Washington, DC: American Anthropological Association.

Anthropological Quarterly. Washington, DC: Catholic University of America Press. 1953–

Botswana Notes and Records. Gabarone: Botswana Society. 1969–

Canadian Journal of African Studies. Ottawa: Canadian Association of African Studies. 1967–

Comparative Studies in Society And History. Cambridge: Cambridge University Press. 1958–

Cultural Anthropology: Journal for the Society of Cultural Anthropology. Washington, DC: American Anthropological Association. 1986–

Cultural Survival Quarterly. Cambridge, Mass: Cultural Survival.

Current Anthropology. Chicago: University of Chicago Press. 1960–

Diaspora: A Journal of Transnational Studies. New York: Oxford University Press 1991–

East Africa Journal. Nairobi: East Africa Publishing House. 1964–

Ethos. Berkeley: University of California Press. 1973–

Harvard African Studies. Cambridge, Mass: Peabody Museum of Harvard University. 1917–

Horn of Africa. Summit, New Jersey: Horn of Africa Journal. 1978–

Human Relations Area Files (HRAF). HRAF Press.

International Journal of African Historical Studies. London: Oxford University Press. 1974–

Journal des Africanistes. Paris: Société des Africanistes. 1976–

Journal of African History. Cambridge: Cambridge University Press. 1960–

Journal of African Law. London: School of Oriental and African Studies, University of London. 1957–

Journal of African Studies. Washington, DC: Heldref. (1974–1988); Volumes 1–5, Berkeley: University of California Press; Volumes 6–15, Los Angeles: UCLA African Studies Center.

Journal of Asian and African Studies. Leiden: Brill. 1966–

Journal of Modern African Studies. Cambridge: Cambridge University Press. 1964–

Journal of Religion in Africa. Leiden: Brill. 1967–

Journal of the Royal African Society. London and New York: Macmillan. 1901–

Journal of the Royal Anthropological Institute (see also *Man*). London: Royal Anthropological Society of Great Britain and Ireland. 1907–1995 (published as *Man*) 1995–

Journal of Southern African Studies. London: Oxford University Press. 1974–

Journal of West African Language. Cambridge: Cambridge University Press in association with the Institute of African Studies, University of Ibadan, Nigeria. 1964

Man. London: Royal Anthropological Institute of Great Britain and Ireland. 1966–1995.

Mawazo. Uganda: Makerere University College. Volumes 1–4, 1967–1976.

Museum Anthropology. Washington, DC: American Anthropological Association. 1991–

Pan-African Journal. New York: Pan-African Student's Organization. 1968–1970; Westport, Connecticut: Greenwood Periodicals. 1971–

Présence Africaine. Paris: Présence Africaine. 1947–

Public Culture: Bulletin of the Project for Transnational Cultural Studies. Chicago: University of Chicago Press. 1988–

Rhodes-Livingstone Journal (also called "Human Problems in British Central Africa"). 1944–

Social Anthropology: The Journal of the European Association of Social Anthropologists. Cambridge: Cambridge University Press. 1993–

Transition. Oxford: Oxford University Press. 19**–

West African Journal of Education. Ibadan, Nigeria: Nigerian Institute of Education, University of Ibadan.

II. Bibliographies of African research materials

Africa South of the Sahara. London: Europa. 1971–

Africana Journal. New York: Africana Publishing Company. 1974–

Aguolu, Christian Chukwunedu. 1973. *Ghana in the Humanities and Social Sciences, 1900–1971: A Bibliography*. Metuchen, NJ: Scarecrow Press.

Ajayi, J. F. Ade, and Michael Crowder. 1985. *Historical Atlas of Africa*. Cambridge: Cambridge University Press.

Anafalu, Joseph C. 1981. *The Ibo-Speaking Peoples of Southern Nigeria: A Selected Annotated List of Writings, 1627–1970*. Munich: Kraus.

Anthropological Literature. Cambridge, MA: Tozzer Library, Harvard University. 1982–

Baumann, Hermann, ed. 1975–1979. *Volker afrikas und ihre traditionallen Kultern*. Wiesbaden: Franz Steiner.

Bennett, Norman Robert. 1984. *The Arab state of Zanzibar: A Bibliography*. Boston: G. K. Hall.

Bhatt, Purnima Mehta. 1980. *Scholar's Guide to Washington, DC African Studies*. Washington, DC: Smithsonian Institution Press.

Bibliographies in African Studies. Madison: African Studies Program, University of Wisconsin, Madison. 1987–

Bibliography of African Art. 1965. London: International African Institute.

Bibliography on Africa. 1989. Delhi, India: Department of African Studies, University of Delhi.

Bibliography on Africa. 1975. Warsaw: University of Warsaw, Centre of African Studies.

Blackhurst, Hector. 1996. *East and Northeast Africa Bibliography*. Lanham, MD: Scarecrow Press.

Bliss, Anne M. and J.A. Rigg. 1984. *Zambia*. Oxford and Santa Barbara: Clio Press.

Boeder, Robert B. 1979. *Malawi*, Oxford and Santa Barbara: Clio Press.

Boston University Libraries: Catalog of African Government Documents. 1976. Boston: G. K. Hall.

Brown, Clifton F. 1978. *Ethiopian Perspectives: A Bibliographic Guide to the History of Ethiopia*. Westport, CT: Greenwood Press.

Bruel, Georges. 1914. *Bibliographie de l'afrique equatoriale francaise*. Paris: E. Larose.

Bullwinkle, Davis. 1989. *African Women: A General Bibliography, 1976–1985*. New York: Greenwood.

Cambridge Encyclopedia of Africa. 1981. Roland Oliver and Michael Crowder, eds. Cambridge: Cambridge University Press.

Collison, Robert L. 1981. *Uganda*. Oxford and Santa Barbara: Clio Press.

Collison, Robert L. 1982. *Kenya*. Oxford and Santa Barbara: Clio Press.

Cook, Gillian P. 1984. *Development in Africa South of the Sahara, 1970–1980: A Select Annotated Bibliography*. Cape Town: University of Cape Town Libraries.

A Current Bibliography of African Affairs. Farmingdale, NY: Baywood Publishing Company.

Dalby, David. 1977. *Language Map of Africa and the Adjacent Islands*. London: International African Institute.

Daly, M. W. 1983. *Sudan*. Oxford and Santa Barbara: Clio Press.

Darch, Colin. 1985. *Tanzania*. Oxford and Santa Barbara: Clio Press.

Darkowska-Nidzgorska, Olenka. 1978. *Connaissance du Gabo: Guide bibliographique*. Libreville: Université Nationale el Hadj Omar Bongo.

DeLancy, Mark W. and Virginia H. DeLancey. 1975. *A Bibliography of Cameroon*. New York: Africana Publishing Company.

Der-Houssikian, Haig. 1972. *A Bibliography of African Linguistics*. Edmonton, Alberta; Champaign, IL: Linguistic Research.

Doro, Marion E. 1984. *Rhodesia/Zimbabwe: A Bibliographic Guide to the Nationalist Period*. Boston: G. K. Hall.

Duigan, Peter, ed. 1972. *Guide to Research and Reference Works on Sub-Saharan Africa*. Stanford: Hoover Institution.

Ethnographic Survey of Africa. 1950–1977. London: International African Institute and Oxford University Press.

Fage, J. D. 1987. *A Guide to Original Sources for Precolonial Western Africa Published in European Languages*. Madison: African Studies Program, University of Wisconsin, Madison.

Gamble, David P. 1979. *A General Bibliography of the Gambia*. Boston: G. K. Hall.

Gibson, Gordon D. 1969. "A Bibliography of Anthropological Bibliographies: Africa." *Current Anthropology* 10: 527–66.

Gosebrink, Jean E. Meeh. "Bibliography and Sources for African Studies." In Phyllis M. Martin and Patrick O'Meara, eds. *Africa*. pp. 381–439. Second Edition. New York: Macmillan.

Grandidier, Guillaume. 1905/06–57. *Bibliographie de Madagascar*. Paris: Comite de Madagascar.

Gary, John. 1989. *'Ashe, Traditional Religion and Healing in Sub-Saharan Africa and the Diaspora: A Classified International Bibliography*. New York: Greenwood.

Hambly, Wilfird D. 1937. *Source Book for African Anthropology. Anthropological Studies*, Volume 26. Chicago: Field Museum of Natural History.

Henderson, Francine I. and Modisakeng, Tiny. 1982. *A Guide to Periodical Articles about Botswana, 1965–1980*. Gabarone: National Institute of Development and Cultural Research.

Hartwig, Gerald W. and William M. O'Barr. 1974. *The Student Africanist's Handbook: A Guide to Resources*. Cambridge, MA: Schenkman.

International African Institute of London: Cumulative Bibliography of African Studies. 1983. Boston: G. K. Hall.

Ita, Nduntuei O. 1971. *Bibliography of Nigeria: A Survey of Anthropological and Linguistic Writings from the Earliest Times to 1966*. London: Cass.

Izard, Françoise. 1967. *Bibliographie generale de la Haute-Volta, 1956–1965*. Paris: CNRS–CVRS.

Janvier, Genevieve. 1972–1978. *Bibliographie de la Côte d'Ivoire*. Abidjan: Université d'Abidjan.

Library of Congress: Africa South of the Sahara. An Index to Periodical Literature, 1900 1970. 1981. Boston: G.K. Hall.

Liniger-Goumaz, Max. 1974. *Guinea Equatorial, bibliografia general*. Berne: Commission Nationale Suisse pour l'Unesco.

Luijik, J. N. van. 1969. *Selected Bibliography of Sociological and Anthropological Literature Relating to Modern and Traditional Medicine in Africa South of the Sahara*. Leiden: Afrika-Studiecentrum.

Mann, Michael et al. 1987. *A Thesaurus of African Languages: A Classified and Annotated Inventory of the Spoken Languages of Africa with an Appendix on their Written Representation*. London: Hans Zell for the International African Institute.

McIlwaine, John. 1993. *Africa: A Guide to Reference Material*. London and New York: Hans Zell.

Mitchell, Robert C. 1966. *A Comprehensive Bibliography of Modern African Religious Movements*. Evanston: Northwestern University Press.

Murdock, George Peter. 1959. *Africa: Its People and Their Culture History*. New York: McGraw Hill.

Murphy, John D. and Harry Goff. 1969. *A Bibliography of African Languages and Linguistics*. Washington, DC: Catholic University of America Press.

Musée de l'Homme. Bibliothèque. Paris. *Catalogue systematique de la Section Afrique* [Classified Catalog of the Africa Section]. 1970. Boston: G. K. Hall.

Musée Royale du Congo Belge. 1925/1930–1950. *Bibliographie ethnographique du Congo Belge et des regions avoisinantes*. 14 volumes. Tervuren, Belgium: Musée Royale du Congo Belge.

Musée Royale du Congo Belge. 1952–1959. *Bibliographie ethnographique du Congo Belge et des regions avoisinantes*. 10 volumes. Tervuren, Belgium: Musée Royale du Congo Belge.

Musée Royale du Congo Belge. 1962–1981. *Bibliographie enthnographique de l'Afrique sud-saharienne. sciences humaines et sociales*. 18 volumes. Tervuren, Belgium: Musée Royale du Congo Belge.

Northwestern University Catalog of the Melville Herskovits Library of African Studies, Northwestern University Library and Africana in Selected Libraries. 1978. Boston: G. K. Hall.

Nyeko, Balam. 1982. *Swaziland*. Oxford and Santa Barbara: Clio Press.

O'Connor, A.M. *Urbanization in Tropical Africa: An Annotated Bibliography*. Boston: G. K. Hall.

Ofcansky, Thomas P. 1985. *British East Africa, 1856–1963: An Annotated Bibliography*. Garland Reference Library of Social Science, Volume 158. New York: Garland.

Otchere, Freda E. 1992. *African Studies Thesaurus: Subject Headings for Library Users*. Westport, CT: Greenwood Press.

Paden, John N. and Edward W. Soja. 1970. *The African Experience*. Evanston: Northwestern University Press.

Panofsky, Hans. 1975. *A Bibliography of Africana*. Westport, CT: Greenwood Press.

Pearson, J. D. 1982. *International African Bibliography, 1973–1978*. New York: Wilson.

Porges, Laurence. 1967. *Bibliographie des regions du Senegal*. Dakar, Ministere du Plan et du Developpement.

Portugal in Africa: A Bibliography of the UCLA Collection. 1972. Los Angeles: UCLA African Studies Center.

Scheub, Harold. 1977. *African Oral Narratives, Proverbs, Riddles, Poetry, and Song*. Boston: G. K. Hall.

Scheven, Yvette, ed. 1977; 1984; 1988; 1994. *Bibliographies for African Studies*. 1994, 1988, and 1984 published by Hans Zell (London and Munich); 1977 published by Crossroads Press (Los Angeles and Waltham).

Schmidt, Nancy J. 1994. *African Studies Periodicals and Other Serials Currently on Subscription, Indiana University Libraries, Bloomington*. Bloomington: African Studies Program, Indiana University Libraries.

Schmidt, Nancy J. 1994. *Sub-Saharan African Film and Filmmakers, 1987–1992: An Annotated Bibliography*. London: Hans Zell Publishers.

Schoeman, Stanley and Elna Schoeman. 1984. *Namibia*. Oxford and Santa Barbara: Clio Press.

Stanley, Janet. 1989. *The Arts of Africa: An Annotated Bibliography*. Atlanta: African Studies Association.

Stanley, Janet. 1995. *Modern African Art: A Basic Reading List*. Washington, DC: National Museum of African Art Library, Smithsonian Institution Libraries.

Thieme, Darius L. 1964. *African Music: A Briefly Annotated Bibliography*. Washington, DC: Library of Congress.

Travis, Crole and Miriam Alam, eds. 1977. *Periodicals from Africa: A Bibliography and Union List of Periodicals Published in Africa*. Boston: G. K. Hall.

University of London. School of Oriental and African Studies. 1963; 1968–1979. *Library Catalogue*. Boston: G. K. Hall.

Van Warmelo, Nicholas J., ed. 1977. *Anthropology of Southern Africa in Periodicals to 1950: An Analysis and Index*. Johannesburg: Witwatersrand University Press.

Varley, Douglas H. 1936. *African Native Music: An Annotated Bibliography*. London: Royal Empire Society.

Webster, John B. et al. 1967. *A Bibliography on Kenya*. Syracuse: Syracuse University Program of Eastern African Studies.

Westerman, R. C. 1994. *Fieldwork in the Library: A Guide to Research in Anthropology and Related Area Studies*. Chicago: American Library Association.

Wilding, Richard. 1976. *A Bibliography of the History and Peoples of the Swahili-Speaking World: From Earliest Times to the Beginning of the Twentieth Century*. Nairobi: Lamu Society.

Wiley, David S. et al. 1982. *Africa on Film and Videotape, 1960–1981* [a guide to 7,500 films]. East Lansing: African Studies Center, Michigan State University.

Willet, Shelagh M. and David P. Ambrose. 1980. *Lesotho: A Comprehensive Bibliography*. Oxford and Santa Barbara: Clio Press.

Williams, Geoffrey J. 1967. *A Bibliography of Sierra Leone, 1925–1967*. New York: Africana Publishing Company.

Williams, Geoffrey J. 1984. *Independent Zambia: A Bibliography of the Social Sciences, 1964–1979*. Boston: G. K. Hall.

Witherall, Julian W. 1989. *Africana Resources and Collections: Three Decades of Development and Achievement*. Metuchen, NJ: Scarecrow Press.

4

Discourse of Power
and Knowledge of Otherness

V. Y. Mudimbe

[...]
The scramble for Africa, and the most active period of colonization, lasted less than a century. These events, which involved the greater part of the African continent, occurred between the late nineteenth and the mid-twentieth centuries. Although in African history the colonial experience represents but a brief moment from the perspective of today, this moment is still charged and controversial, since, to say the least, it signified a new historical form and the possibility of radically new types of discourses on African traditions and cultures. One might think that this new historical form has meant, from its origins, the negation of two contradictory myths; namely, the "Hobbesian picture of a pre-European Africa, in which there was no account of Time; no Arts; no Letters; no Society; and which is worst of all, continued fear, and danger of violent death"; and "the Rousseauian picture of an African golden age of perfect liberty, equality and fraternity" (Hodgkin, 1957:174–5).

Although generalizations are of course dangerous, *colonialism* and *colonization* basically mean organization, arrangement. The two words derive from the latin word *colère*, meaning to cultivate or

to design. Indeed the historical colonial experience does not and obviously cannot reflect the peaceful connotations of these words. But it can be admitted that the colonists (those settling a region), as well as the colonialists (those exploiting a territory by dominating a local majority) have all tended to organize and transform non-European areas into fundamentally European constructs.

I would suggest that in looking at this process, it is possible to use three main keys to account for the modulations and methods representative of colonial organization: the procedures of acquiring, distributing, and exploiting lands in colonies; the policies of domesticating natives; and the manner of managing ancient organizations and implementing new modes of production. Thus, three complementary hypotheses and actions emerge: the domination of physical space, the reformation of *natives*' minds, and the integration of local economic histories into the Western perspective. These complementary projects constitute what might be called the colonizing structure, which completely embraces the physical, human, and spiritual aspects of the colonizing experience (see, e.g., Christopher, 1984:27–87). This structure

From V. Y. Mudimbe, *The Invention of Africa: Gnosis, Philosophy and the Order of Knowledge*, Indiana University Press (1988), pp. 1–2, 6–11, 15–16.

clearly also indicates the projected metamorphosis envisioned, at great intellectual cost, by ideological and theoretical texts, which from the last quarter of the nineteenth century to the 1950s have proposed programs for "regenerating" the African space and its inhabitants.

[...]

[T]he great historical tragedy of Africa has been not so much that it was too late in making contact with the rest of the world, as the manner in which that contact was brought about; that Europe began to propagate at a time when it had fallen into the hands of the most unscrupulous financiers and captains of industry. (Césaire, 1972:23)

[...]

The colonializing structure, even in its most extreme manifestations – such as the crisis of South Africa (see, e.g., Seidman, 1985) – might not be the only explanation for Africa's present-day marginality. Perhaps this marginality could, more essentially, be understood from the perspective of wider hypotheses about the classification of beings and societies. It would be too easy to state that this condition, at least theoretically, has been a consequence of anthropological discourses. Since Turgot (who in the 1750s first classified languages and cultures according to "whether the peoples [are] hunters, shepherds, or husbandmen" [1913–23, 1:172] and ultimately defined an ascending path from savagery to commercial societies), non-Western marginality has been a sign both of a possible absolute beginning and of a primitive foundation of conventional history. Rather than retracing an already too well-known evolutionary hallucination (Duchet, 1971; Hodgen, 1971), let us take a different angle by examining both the issues derived from a fifteenth-century painting and the allocation of an "African object" to nineteenth-century anthropology.

Commenting upon *Las Meninas* of Velasquez, M. Foucault writes: "the painter is standing a little back from his canvas. He is glancing at his model: perhaps he is considering whether to add some finishing touch, though it is also possible that the first stroke has not yet been made ..." (1973:3). The painter is at one side of the canvas working or meditating on how to depict his models. Once the

painting is finished, it becomes both a given and a reflection of what made it possible. And Foucault thinks that the order of *Las Meninas* seems to be an example of "a representation [which] undertakes to represent itself ... in all its elements, with its images, the eyes to which it is offered, the faces it makes visible, the gestures that call it into being." Yet in the amazing complexity of this painting there is remarkable absence: "the person it resembles and the person in whose eyes it is only a resemblance" (Foucault, 1973:16).

Now let us consider Hans Burgkmair's painting *Exotic Tribe*. Is the painter sitting back contemplating his exotic models? How many? It is not even certain that a model is present in the room where Burgkmair is thinking about ways of subsuming particular versions of human beings. The year is 1508. Dürer is still alive. Burgkmair is by then a respected master of the new school of Augsburg he has founded. He would like to please the Fuggers and Welsers and has agreed to illustrate Bartolomäus Springer's book on his travels overseas (Kunst, 1967). He has carefully read Springer's diary, has probably studied some clumsy pencil or pen-and-ink sketches, and has decided to draw six pictures of "primitives."

The first picture of the series seems to represent a family. Let us imagine the painter at work. He has just read Springer's description of his voyage, and, possibly on the basis of some sketches, he is trying to create an image of blacks in "Gennea." Perhaps he has decided to use a model, presumably white but strongly built. The painter is staring at the pale body, imagining schemes to transform it into a black entity. The model has become a mirror through which the painter evaluates how the norms of similitude and his own creativity would impart both a human identity and a racial difference to his canvas. Perhaps the artist is already at work. Yet he has to stop regularly, walk around the model, leave the luminous space before the window, and retire into a discreet corner. His gaze addresses a point which is a question: how to superimpose the African characteristics described in Springer's narrative onto the norms of the Italian *contrapposto*? If he succeeds, the painting should be, in its originality, a celebration and a reminder of the natural link connecting human beings and, at the same time, an indication of racial or cultural differences. It should bear witness to the truth of similitudes, analogies, and possibly even the violence of antipathy. At any rate, Kunst notes that

> The nude African depicted from behind conforms to the classical rule of contraposto expressed in the compensatory balance of symmetrical parts of the body in movement: one shoulder leaning on one leg and the other, raised above the free leg. One guesses that this nude man was copied from a classic model to which the artist gave characteristics, jewelry and swords, of an exotic people still strongly attached to nature. (Kunst, 1967:19–20)

It is easy to dismiss my concern about similitude in this particular creative process. Am I not projecting a twentieth-century perspective onto the pictorial techniques of the early sixteenth century? The structure of figures is there in the first small painting, treated in a typical way. The fuss about similitude might just be, after all, only a contemporary hypothesis about the process of establishing links between beings and things from our present viewpoint. Yet it is possible to look for issues stemming from Burgkmair's representation. In effect, we can describe his artistic filiation and his dependence upon the classic ideals of the Renaissance (Kunst, 1967:20). We can also compare the principles of his technique with those apparent in some contemporary works directly or indirectly dealing with black figures, such as Erasmus Grasser's *Moor Dancers* (1480), Hieronymus Bosch's *Garden of Delights* (1500), *Katleen the Moor Woman* (1521) by Albrecht Dürer, and at the very end of the century, Cornelisz van Haarlem's *Batseba* (1594). Speculating about or analyzing the contrasts between white and black figures in these paintings, one could certainly search for a vision which refers to historically conventional explanations – for example, the sense of the characteristics and "the idea of design, that is to say, of expression by means of the pure disposition of contours and masses, and by the perfection and ordering of linear rhythm" (Fry, 1940:165). The complex play of colors in harmony and opposition, the order of shades between the white and the black, are obviously based on such intellectual and conscious references. But does not our understanding of the colorful economics of canvases refer, in a very insistent manner, to invisible traces?

The contrasts between black and white tell a story which probably duplicates a silent but powerful epistemological configuration. *Ex hypothesi* it might simply be a similitude interplay: "*Convenientia, aemulatio, analogy*, and *sympathy* tell us how the world must fold upon itself, duplicate itself, reflect itself, or form a chain with itself so that things can resemble one another. They tell us what the paths of similitude are and the directions they take; but not where it is, how one sees it, or by what mark it may be recognized" (Foucault, 1973:23–4).

Let us return to Burgkmair's finished painting. The three black figures – a boy, a man, a seated woman with a baby pressed to her breast – have the right proportions to one another and to the wider context. All are naked and have either bracelets around their arms or a string around their necks, clear signs that they belong to a "savage" universe (Kunst, 1967:20). The little boy is dancing, his oversized head turned toward the sky. At the center of the canvas, the man, presented in clear, strong lines, is staring at a faraway horizon, brandishing an arrow with his left hand and holding two other arrows in his right hand. He incarnates power, not only because he occupies the central place in the painting, but also because he is the most well-defined signifier in this scene. He is the locus defining the relationship between the boy at his left and the woman at his right, depicted with both a touch of hieratic sense and a slightly instinctual force. At the right, the woman with the baby is seated on a trunk. She seems to be staring pensively at the pelvic area of the man. The curves of her body are canonically executed.

The whole picture, in its simplicity and in the balanced rhythms of its lines, seems a truly charming and decorative painting. Yet what it really expresses is a discursive order. The structure of the figures, as well as the meaning of the nude bodies, proclaim the virtues of resemblances: in order to designate Springer's blacks, the painter has represented blackened whites. This was not rare during the sixteenth and the seventeenth centuries, as a great number of the drawings of the period reveal. That is the case for example, of the fifth picture in Filippo Pigafetta's 1591 edition of his *Relatione del Reame di Congo*, representing three Italianized African women, and that of the African king in the frontispiece of J. Ogilby's 1670 book on Africa. What is important in Burgkmair's painting, as well as in similar drawings, is their double representation.

The first, whose objective is to assimilate exotic bodies into sixteenth-century Italian painting methodology, reduces and neutralizes all differences into the sameness signified by the *white* norm, which, let us keep in mind, is more religious history than a simple cultural tradition. In concrete language this reference meant a "biblical solution to the problem of cultural differences (which) was regarded by most men as the best that reason and faith could propose" (Hodgen, 1971:254); that is, the same origin for all human beings, followed by geographical diffusion and racial and cultural diversification. And it was believed that the Bible stipulated that the African could only be the slave of his brethren.

There is another level, a more discreet one. It establishes a second representation that unites through similitude and eventually articulates distinctions and separations, thus classifying types of identities. Briefly, I can say that in Burgkmair's painting there are two representational activities: on the one hand, signs of an epistemological order which, silently but imperatively, indicate the processes of integrating and differentiating figures within the normative sameness; on the other hand, the excellence of an exotic picture that creates a cultural distance, thanks to an accumulation of accidental differences, namely, nakedness, blackness, curly hair, bracelets, and strings of pearls.

In their arrangements, these differences are pertinent signs. Because of the fundamental order which they reveal, and to which they bear witness, the virtues of resemblance erase physical and cultural variations, while maintaining and positing surface differences as meaningful of human complexity. Diego Velasquez's *Juan de Pareja* (1648) still actualizes this integrating reference, whereas major paintings such as Peter Paul Rubens's *Study of Four Blacks' Heads* (1620), Rembrandt's *Two Negroes* (1697), and Hyacinthe Rigaud's *Young Black* (1697) explicitly express and relate to

another order. A new epistemological foundation was then functioning in the West. Theories of diversification of beings, as well as classificatory tables, explain the origins of constructing taxonomies and their objectives (Foucault, 1973:125–65). The framework of Linnaeus's *Systema Naturae* (1735) is just one of the paradigmatic classifications of species and varieties of *Homo Sapiens* (*europaeus, asiaticus americanus, afer*) distinguished according to physical and temperamental characteristics (Count, 1950:355). It would be too easy to link it, *upstream*, to discursive formations about the great chain of beings and its hierarchy, and, *downstream*, first to Blumenbach's craniology and, second, to the general anti-African bias of the philosophical and scientific literature of the eighteenth and nineteenth centuries (Lyons, 1975:24–85).

Two very different discursive formations – the discovery of African art and the constitution of the object of African Studies, that is, the "invention" of Africanism as a scientific discipline – can illustrate the differentiating efficiency of such general classifying devices as pattern of reality, designation, arrangement, structure, and character. I have already suggested that resemblance has been pushed out of Rubens's, Rembrandt's, and Rigaud's perceptions of blacks. What is there, given in detailed description, might be considered as a naming and an analysis of an alterity and refers to a new epistemological ordering: a theory of understanding and looking at signs in terms of "the arrangement of identities and differences into ordered tables" (Foucault, 1973:72).

Portuguese sailors brought to Europe the first *feitiços*, African objects supposedly having mysterious powers, in the late fifteenth century. One finds them mostly in well-organized curio cabinets, along with Indian tomahawks or arrows, Egyptian artifacts, and Siamese drums. Some interpreters do consider them to be signs of a state of barbarism (Hodgen, 1971:162–203), Yet one can firmly state that more frequently they are seen as simple curiosities brought back in accordance with the tenth task of the traveler-observer in the table of Varenius's *Geographia generalis* (1650): to consider "famous Men, Artificers, and Inventions of the Natives of all countries" (Hodgen, 1971:167–8). On the whole, these objects are culturally neutral. Because of their shapes and styles, sometimes a bit terrifying, they account for the mysterious diversity of the Same (Bal, 1963:67). It is not until the eighteenth century that, as strange and "ugly" artifacts, they really enter into the frame of African art.

The black continent was still on the maps a *terra incognita*, but its peoples and their material productions were more familiar to travelers, students of the human species, merchants, and European states. From the beginning of the eighteenth century, there had been a tremendous increase in the slave trade and a profitable trans-Atlantic economy which involved most of the Western countries. In West Africa, Dahomey was a powerful commercial partner of European traders. The Ashanti empire expanded, dominating the Akans and the Oyo kingdom further to the east and increasing its power as it grew. Freed slaves and impoverished Africans were settled by European-sponsored organizations in present-day Sierra Leone. On the east coast, in 1729, Africans expelled the Portuguese from their fortresses in the northern region of Mozambique; and down south, in 1770, there was the first war between Dutch immigrants and Bantus. Two years later, James Bruce, traveling from North to Central Africa, reached the source of the White Nile in the very year that Chief Justice Mansfield declared in England that slavery was against the law (Verger, 1968).

In this atmosphere of intense and violent exchanges, *feitiços* became symbols of African art. They were viewed as primitive, simple, childish, and nonsensical. Mary H. Kingsley, at the beginning of this century, summed it up with an axiomatic evaluation: "The African has never made an even fourteenth-rate piece of cloth or pottery" (Kingsley, 1965:669). It seems to me that "a process of aesthetization" (Baudrillard, 1972) took place from the eighteenth century onward. What is called savage or primitive art covers a wide range of objects introduced by the contact between African and European during the intensified slave trade into the classifying frame of the eighteenth century. These objects, which perhaps are not art at all in their "native context," become art by being given simultaneously an aesthetic character and a potentiality for producing and reproducing other artistic forms. Taken in their initial function and significance,

might they have created a radical *mise en perspective* of the Western culture wedded to classifications (Baudrillard, 1972)? That is precisely an impossibility. Arts are based on criteria, and it is difficult to imagine that these standards can emerge from outside the "power-knowledge" field of a given culture, a field which, at a historical period, establishes its artistic bible. Therefore it is obvious that fetishes and other "primitive" pieces of art are wonderful because their structure, character, and arrangement demand a designation (Laude, 1979; Wassing, 1969). They are "savage" in terms of the evolutionary chain of being and culture, which establishes a correspondence between advancement in the civilizing process and artistic creativity, as well as intellectual achievements.

At this point, paradoxically, it is a celebration of the African craftsmanship which confirms my analysis. Admiring the beauty of a "Negro sculpture," the late R. Fry was puzzled:

> It is curious that a people who produced such great artists did not produce also a culture in our sense of the word. This shows that two factors are necessary to produce the cultures which distinguish civilised peoples. There must be, of course, the creative artist, but there must also be the power of conscious critical appreciation and comparison. (Fry, 1940:90–1)

Fry is, I am afraid, utterly wrong. The two factors do not and cannot explicate types of cultures. They only constitute a basis for the production of art and its possible modifications over time (see Laude, 1979; Delange, 1967). They cannot completely account for the internal patterns of cultures. At any rate, it is the "power-knowledge" of an epistemological field which makes possible a domineering or humbled culture. From this perspective, the point that Fry makes immediately after has great sense: "It is likely enough that the Negro artist, although capable of ... profound imaginative understanding of form, would accept our cheapest illusionist art with humble enthusiasm" (1940:91).

[...]

Explorers do not reveal otherness. They comment upon "anthropology," that is, the distance separating savagery from civilization on the diachronic line of progress (see Rotberg, 1970). R. Thornton claims that "the discovery of Africa was also a discovery *for* paper. Had the great Victorian travellers not written anything it would not be said today that they had 'discovered' anything." Strictly speaking, however, it seems difficult to prove in a convincing way that "Livingstone, Stanley, Burton, Grant, Speke and others entered into the enterprise for the sake of the text" (Thornton, 1983:509). Other students can invoke other motives such as the classical ones of curiosity, courage, generosity, contempt (Killingray, 1973:48).

At any rate, the explorer's text is not epistemologically inventive, it follows a path prescribed by a tradition. Expedition reports only establish a very concrete, vivid representation of what paintings and theories of social progress had been postulating since the Baroque period. In what the explorer's text does reveal, it brings nothing new besides visible and recent reasons to validate a discipline already remarkably defined by the Enlightenment (Lévi-Strauss, 1973: 145–56). The novelty resides in the fact that the discourse on "savages" is, for the first time, a discourse in which an explicit political power presumes the authority of a scientific knowledge and vice-versa. Colonialism becomes its project and can be thought of as a duplication and a fulfillment of the power of Western discourses on human varieties.

[...]

References

Bal, W. (1963). *Le Royaume du Congo aux XV et XVI siècles.* Documents d'histoire. Léopoldville (Kinshasa): Institut National d'Etudes Politiques.

Baudrillard, J. (1972). *Pour une critique de l'économie politique du signe.* Paris: Gallimard.

Césaire, Aimé (1972). *Discourse on Colonialism.* New York: Monthly Review Press.

Christopher, A.J. (1984). *Colonial Africa.* Lanham, MD: Rowman and Littlefield Pub. Inc.

Count, E.W., ed. (1950). *This Is Race: An Anthology Selected from the International Literature on the Races of Man.* New York: Schuman.

Delange, J. (1967). *Arts et peuples d'Afrique Noire.* Paris: Gallimard.

Duchet, M. (1971). *Anthropologie et histoire au siècle des lumières.* Paris: Maspero.

Foucault, M. (1973). *The Order of Things.* New York: Pantheon (originally *Les Mots et les Choses.* Paris: Gallimard, 1966).

Fry, R. (1940). *Vision and Design.* New York: Penguin.

Hodgen, M.T. (1971). *Early Anthropology in the Sixteenth and Seventeenth Centuries.* Philadelphia: University of Pennsylvania.

Hodgkin, Thomas (1957). *Nationalism in Africa.* New York: New York University Press, 1st edn.

Killingray, David (1973). *A Plague of Europeans: Westerners in Africa since the Fifteenth Century.* New York: Penguin.

Kingsley, M.H. (1965). *Travels in West Africa.* (Abridged version of 1900 edn.) London: Cass.

Kunst, H.J. (1967). *L'Africain dans l'art européen.* Cologne: Dumont Presse.

Laude, J. (1979). *L'Art de l'Afrique Noire.* Paris: Chêne.

Lévi-Strauss, C. (1973). *Tristes Tropiques,* trans. J. and D. Weightman. New York: Penguin.

Lyons, R.H (1975). *To Wash an Aethiop White.* New York: Teachers College Press.

Rotberg, Robert I., ed. (1970). *Africa and Its Explorers: Motives, Methods, and Impact.* Cambridge: Harvard University Press.

Seidman, A. (1985). *The Roots of Crisis in Southern Africa.* Trenton: Africa World Press.

Thornton, John K. (1983). *The Kingdom of Kongo: Civil War and Transition, 1641–1718.* Madison: University of Wisconsin Press.

Turgot, A.R.J. (1913–23). *Oeuvres de Turgot et documents le concernant, avec une bibliographie et notes.* G. Schelle, ed. Paris, 5 Vols. Vol. I, pp. 172.

Verger, P. (1968). *Flux et reflux de la traite des nègres entre le Golf du Bénin et Bahia de Todos os Santos du XV au XIX siècles.* Paris: Mouton.

Wassing, R.S. (1969). *L'Art de l'Afrique Noire.* Fribourg: Office du livre.

Part II

From Tribe to Ethnicity: Kinship and Social Organization

Introduction

Much of the history of anthropology, and of social theory in general, has been devoted to answering a central sociological question: Given that societies are made up of a multiplicity of individuals, with different interests and motivations, how do societies stay together? This is a question phrased and addressed most explicitly at the turn of the century by the French sociologist Emile Durkheim, and later, in the colonial period of the 1930s and 1940s, by anthropologists of Africa, and elsewhere, such as A.R. Radcliffe-Brown and E.E. Evans-Pritchard. They began to focus on how customs and social organizations contributed to social solidarity. The solidifying role played by a particular custom was said to be its function, and the kinship, political, and legal systems that benefited from the functions were said to constitute the social structure. These anthropologists were often referred to as "structural-functionalists." The readings in this section build upon, elaborate, and reject some of the early concepts, assumptions, and arguments.

The focus on function was the result of a movement in the discipline of anthropology away from speculative historical reconstructions and broad comparative work (such as evolutionism and diffusionism), and toward the study of how particular cultures functioned at particular historical moments. Continuing into the 1940s, many anthropologists continued to study the cultures of the world not "in their own right" (Lienhardt, 1976: 180) but to demonstrate the origins, evolution, or diffusion of cultures and culture traits in history. The new approach – sometimes called "synchronic" because of its focus on a single point in time – made anthropology more empirical and therefore more scientific. Instead of speculating about history, anthropologists wrote about what they actually observed. And instead of studying and comparing the parts of many different cultures, functionalists studied the systems of relations of particular cultures, that is, the ways in which the parts of a culture operated together to form and maintain the whole. Meyer Fortes (1953: 22–3) wrote: "A culture is a unity in so far as it is tied to a bounded social structure. In this sense I would agree that the social structure is the foundation of the whole social life of any *continuing* society" (original emphasis). Emphasizing the whole over the parts gave new life to the science of society, for anthropology now not only conformed more to the scientific method, but had in the concept "society" its own central object of study, its own raison d'être, as well as a unique theoretical perspective to orient the collection and interpretation of ethnographic data.

Functionalism offered several new directions to anthropological fieldworkers. First, the focus on society diminished the importance of individual behavior and, of course, individual variation. A major theoretical premise was that behind all individuals' actions, there had to be a social system. For example, individuals could be free to act only to the extent that there was a structure – economic, legal, political or otherwise – which permitted their acts. Second, since all societies constituted total working systems, all societies, including so-called "primitive" societies, had an understandable, rational, and valid reason for being. Thus, for example, societies without centralized states, such as the Nuer, or societies where witchcraft was the primary explanation for harm-doing, such as the Tiv or Azande, were no longer seen as backward, aberrant, or deficient, but rather as communities that operated according to a certain logic. The anthropologist's task was to identify and characterize that logic, usually analyzing one specific system at a time, such as religion, kinship, or economics, and publishing each analysis as one of a sequence of monographs (Lienhardt, 1976: 181). Third, while functionalism did not help to explain historical change, it did help to explain historical continuity and social reproduction. Various institutions, whether belief systems, economic or political systems, were analyzed to determine how they contributed to the maintenance and perpetuation of the society as a whole. Indeed, even where anthropologists wrote a good deal of history, it was synchronic history: histories that focused on reproduction rather than change.

Kinship was one of the primary mechanisms for social reproduction, especially in stateless societies. In three extraordinarily important books, all published in 1940, the contours of British social anthropology and kinship studies were established, and a productive period of fieldwork in Africa was set into motion: *African Political Systems* (1940), edited by Meyer Fortes and Edward E. Evans-Pritchard, with a foreword by A.R. Radcliffe-Brown; *The Nuer* (1940a) by Evans-Pritchard; and *The Political System of the Anuak* (1940b) by Evans-Pritchard (Kuper, 1973: 107). In the first book, Fortes and Evans-Pritchard distinguished two fundamental types of African political systems: the state society, with a centralized authority (such as the Zulu and Tswana of southern Africa), and the stateless society, a category which encompassed every society without centralized authority, from the cattle-herding Nuer of Sudan to the hunter-gatherers, the !Kung San of southern Africa and the Efe and Mbuti of central Africa. This distinction had a profound influence on the development of the anthropology of Africa (see, for example, Middleton and Tait, 1958). Evans-Pritchard's landmark book, *The Nuer*, addressed the problem of how the Nuer could live together without any apparent political structure. But there was a political structure. Indeed, the answer to the problem was that the political structure and the kinship structure were one and the same.

Before addressing the details of the relation between kinship and politics, it is necessary to put these Africanists in more historical context. It is important to note that prior to the 1940s, few anthropologists had done intensive fieldwork, learned the languages of the people they studied, or lived with them for extended periods of time. Up until the four-year field-work of Bronislaw Malinowski in the Pacific Trobriand Islands during World War I, anthropology had consisted, by and large, of the study of customs and myths collected by travelers, missionaries, and explorers, and the analysis of cultural patterns rather than the detailed workings of any one particular society. Intensive fieldwork during the late colonial period among the Nuer (Evans-Pritchard), Zulu (Max Gluckman), Tswana (Schapera), and Tallensi (Fortes), among others, demonstrated how fruitful a firsthand knowledge of language and social life could be. Other notable works based on fieldwork include Audrey Richards' *Land, Labour and Diet in Northern Rhodesia* (1939),

Melville Herskovits' *Dahomey, an African Kingdom* (1967 [1938]), Hilda Kuper's *An African Aristocracy* (1961 [1947]), and countless articles published in journals such as *Africa* (the journal of the International African Institute) and by the Rhodes-Livingstone Institute.

There were also more problematic uses of fieldwork, especially when colonial administrators funded anthropologists. Indeed, anthropology has often been called the "hand-maiden of colonialism." At an abstract level, the relationship is not difficult to see. Recent postmodernist scholarship emphasizes how intellectuals in general are complicitous in forms of domination, and anthropologists are no exception. First, administration could never be totally separated from the content and categories of *knowledge*. However much anthropologists might like to distinguish themselves, the colonists, administrators, and anthropologists emerged out of the same intellectual climate using the same intellectual apparatuses, whether we are speaking generally about the idea of encountering and mastering an "other," or more specifically of how European categories of race, gender, or class became incorporated into both scholarly analysis and colonial perspectives. And, in as much as anthropologists studied religion, they shared much with and learned much from the missionaries whose first task was often to learn the rituals and belief systems of the people with whom they would work. Second, however different they might have been, colonialism and anthropology had some similar results. For example, both introduced the concept of "tribe" to Africa, divided the world into a "West" and "others," reified "tribes" and "traditions," and ended up, often unwittingly, altering the modes of thought of many Africans so that people began to think of themselves in terms not of their own making.

However, according to two historians of African anthropology, the colonial administrators' uses of anthropologists were quite limited. In their accounts of the anthropology of Africa, both Adam Kuper (1973) and Sally Falk Moore (1994) look rather concretely at the relationship between the two professions, and point out that, despite the fact that much funding for anthropological work came from colonial administrators, and that many colonial administrators were themselves engaged in ethnographic work, seldom did the administrators listen to the anthropologists. According to Moore (1994: 19), they found, more often than not, that information on rituals, proverbs, and marriage systems was unimportant to their ability to govern, and that anthropologists often looked out for the well-being of the people with whom they lived and studied, and thus could act counter to colonial interests. Yet, there certainly were important connections to be made. Among other things, administrators were interested in anthropological work on African political systems because the methods by which Africans governed themselves impinged directly on the ability of the colony to govern. For example, the British could invest chiefs with political responsibilities in those societies with a pre-existing system of chiefs, while for other societies without chiefs, such as the hunter-gatherers and farmers of central Africa, the Belgians had to create chiefdoms and chiefs.

It is here, in the conjuncture of colonial and indigenous political systems, that we begin to see the linkage between politics and kinship. The Nuer of southern Sudan, the topic of Evans-Pritchard's chapter reprinted in this section, were scattered over an immense area of land, and without any discernible system of relationships linking them together (more than 200,000 persons over an area of more than 30,000 square miles – that is fewer than seven people per square mile). Moreover, according to seasonal changes, including availability of water during the dry season, and dangerous flooding during the rainy season, the Nuer would move often and far, in and out of villages, from inland to riverside camps. Such movement was troubling not only for ethnographers trying to understand social organization, but for the administrators who wanted to pacify, settle, and tax these communities. How could the British pacify and administer people whose order appeared only as disorder? Although there is no evidence that the British administration ever consulted Evans-Pritchard's works, or even asked for his advice, Evans-Pritchard concluded that one could make sense of the Nuer world, and that the Nuer had a well-organized political system. But it was one uniquely suited to their ecological and social needs, and one which operated according to genealogy and kinship relations.

Evans-Pritchard argued that the Nuer conceived their political relationships in terms of descent and lineage. According to this view, African societies, like the Nuer, consist of "descent groups," and these societies are organized and act according to the descent group's corporate organization. The descent group served as a legal system – a system that defined the norms and limits of behavior, and established lines of authority – as well as an economic system that governed the exchange of cattle between individuals and families. (In Part III Sharon Hutchinson highlights the tremendous importance of cattle to the Nuer.) Anthropologists used the term "lineage" to describe descent groups in which the genealogical lines were clearly drawn, and the term "clan" to describe groups in which the individuals believed, but could not fully demonstrate, that they descended from a common ancestor. The Nuer had a segmentary lineage system that consisted of a number of groups descending from the most inclusive (the tribe) to the least (say, two brothers). Each descending level consisted of groups defined by their opposition to other like segments. The segmentary lineage was thus a balance of power with no center. At any point in time, however, opposed segments could unite into a more inclusive segment to take action against another set of united segments. Brothers could be naturally opposed to one another, but if a more distantly related third party fought with one of the brothers, the two brothers would unite to form a single segment. To quote a Nuer man, "We fight against the Rengyan, but when either of us is fighting a third party, we combine with them" (Evans-Pritchard, 1940a: 143).

The system of oppositions and alliances may thus change according to social context. Evans-Pritchard (1940a: 142) says, "Each segment is itself segmented and there is opposition between its parts. The members of any segment unite for war against adjacent segments of the same order and unite with these adjacent segments against larger sections." Analogies to this system can be found in international law, where there is no official ultimate authority, and where alliances and oppositions shift according to context; for example, though Syria was diplomatically opposed to the United States, and allied with its Arab neighbor Iraq before the Gulf War, during the war Syria and the United States became allies.

One of the theoretical outcomes of Evans-Pritchard's analysis is that it helped move anthropology away from a strict empiricism and toward the study of more structural, theoretical, organizing principles. The segmentary lineage is an abstract principle, a way of conceptualizing the world. For this reason, Evans-Pritchard also focused on concepts of time and space and the degree to which these abstractions were implicated in the organization of society. The selection from *The Nuer* included in this section focuses specifically on time and space and the manner in which these ostensibly common-sense concepts are social concepts, socially constructed and socially enacted. Thus, Evans-Pritchard tells us that the Nuer words for ecological time (*tot*, village life, rainy season; *mai*, dry season) are not words for time reckoning but rather denote the cluster of social activities characteristic of the seasons. To quote Adam Kuper, "the Nuer do not say, it is *tot*, therefore we must move to the upland villages; rather they say we are in the villages, therefore it is *tot*" (1973: 89). In other words, concepts of time are determined by society and social life. In turn, social relationships could be construed in terms of time. People and cattle were more or less related in terms of the genealogical distance, that is their distance in time or generations from a common ancestor. Everyone had a measurable social or structural distance from everyone else.

The Nuer was thus not simply a book about a group of eastern Africans. It was about the future directions of anthropology. The genealogies of many major theoretical movements in structuralism, Marxism and economic anthropology, among others, can be traced back to *The Nuer* and its theoretical insights and innovations. More specifically, the work established as a central problematic the complex relations between behavior and structure, actual social inter-actions and the models for patterning them. All of this is not to say that the work is without criticism (see, for instance, Karp and Maynard, 1983; Gough, 1971; Kelly, 1985; Grinker, 1994). These criticisms suggest, in general, that Evans-Pritchard neglected social and histori-cal complexities of the Nuer in the service of his one abstract model, that he focused on line-ages when the household was also a major form of social and political organization, and that he wrongly emphasized the Nuer as a homogeneous and internally undifferentiated society, when, in fact, as subsequent work has shown, the Nuer of his time were differentiated according to rank as well as ethnicity (including aristocrats, Dinka, and other captives). Indeed, anthropolo-gists soon began questioning some of the most basic assumptions of Evans-Pritchard, and other anthropologists of his era, including the concepts of descent, lineage, and tribe. Readings by Southall and Vail speak directly to the ubiquitous concept "tribe," and illuminate its com-plexities and limitations.

"Tribe" generally referred to a group of people bound by common language, territory, and custom, and more specifically to small-scale agricultural societies considered more complex than "bands" – that is, small autonomous groups, usually hunter-gatherers and nomads, with what were sometimes called "simple" political organizations – but less complex than chiefdoms – that is, ranked societies with centralized political organizations. The segmentary lineage was, for Evans-Pritchard, a type of *tribal* organization well suited for societies that, for whatever reason, cannot sustain a fixed and centralized political system. The tribe consisted of descent groups, the basic units of collective identity and action.

The anthropologists Aidan Southall, Adam Kuper, Philip Gulliver, Morton Fried, Igor Kopytoff, June Helm, Peter Ekeh, and historian Jan Vansina, are among those who have leveled the harshest criticisms against the use of the term "tribe." These anthropologists challenged the typology that distinguished societies on the basis of authority structures, questioned the criteria used to hierarchically rank societies in terms of complexity, and pointed out the problems and limitations of the terms themselves. "Tribe" was a useful term for anthropologists, such as Evans-Pritchard, who tried to delineate the boundaries of groups with few distinct boundaries, and where ethnic identities and loyalties could shift rapidly. For the same reason, "tribe" turned out to be a useful term for administrators and local politicians because it drew the lines neces-sary for census taking, taxation, and work recruitment. Yet, as Southall and others point out, boundaries between tribes were often drawn by anthropologists or administrators quite arbi-trarily, sometimes according to language similarities and differences, and at other times accord-ing to differences in territory, religion, or dress – all, of course, as perceived by the Europeans. (Similarly, the boundaries between colonies and nations in Africa were often constructed more out of convenience than respect for local ethnic divisions, and so many societies found them-selves virtually cut in half. The Azande, for instance today live in both Sudan, a former British colony and the Democratic Republic of Congo, a former Belgian colony.)

There was another serious problem with tribe: it implied a distinction between Africa and Europe. Few Europeans of the twentieth century refer to themselves with the term tribe, yet the word continues to be used today in academic work, and especially in the mass media, to refer to Africa. When there is conflict between, say, the Flemish and the French speakers in Belgium, or between the Serbs and Bosnians of the former Yugoslavia, the international media refer to the conflict as "ethnic", yet, when the Hutu and Tutsi of Rwanda and Burundi, or the Xhosa and Zulu of South Africa, fight with one another, the media refer to the conflict as "tribal." "Tribe" is also linked to the concept "tribalism," and for this reason has a rather pejorative usage in Africa today, meaning those affiliations that pit identities against one another at the expense of unified national, political, and economic development.

In sum, "tribe" hurts more than it helps, and obscures more than it reveals. What it obscures is identities that are both malleable and dependent upon their relations with other identities. It masks our ability to see the internal diversity of African communities and to look for models other than descent and lineage to account for social and political organization. If we characterize a society in tribal terms, including the focus on descent as the key organizing principle of society, we might easily view it as a homogeneous entity. To represent the same society in ethnic terms, however, might lead us to see transformation and diversity as well as continuity and similarity. Ethnicity helps us to see how individual societies integrate individuals and groups who are not members of descent groups, who may not speak the same language, or live in the same territory.

The focus on ethnicity was a particular advantage for the study of diverse and rapidly changing communities in African cities, and urban anthropologists such as Clyde Mitchell, Max Gluckman, A.L. Epstein, and Abner Cohen made some of the most important strides in the transition from tribal to ethnic studies. Unfortunately, rural areas continued to be seen as unchanging. Moore (1994: 69) writes:

> The fact is, of course, that conditions in the countryside changed at the same time that cities grew, often in related ways. But the "tribal" *model* was not changing, since its goal was a reconstruction of a precolonial African "type," not the recording of a full, unexpurgated account of changing events and practices in the countryside at the time of fieldwork. To be sure, collective cultural differences were important then, and they have continued significance in Africa to this day. In many parts of the continent, tribal or ethnic identities have ongoing social and political salience. But this should not be mistaken for an unchanging traditionalism.

At a time, in the early twenty-first century, when African cultures are no longer bound by location, but by migration, displacement, diaspora, travel, telephone, and the internet, common territory cannot define identity. And the number of interactions between African societies, as demonstrated in ancient and modern African history, compels us to employ theoretical concepts that draw our attention to shifting identities, and to relations between groups rather than solely to relations within groups. This is, indeed, the direction in which Leroy Vail points us. We want to stress, however, that these problems in no way make the previous studies wrong or irrelevant. Critical approaches, and the development of new theoretical concepts, do not necessarily disprove; rather, they show us the limits of older approaches and concepts, open up new lines of inquiry, and lead us to see phenomena that we did not see before.

To understand the concept of ethnicity in African studies, it is necessary to outline two contrasting views of ethnicity: primordialism and instrumentalism. The former holds that ethnicity arises from similarities between individuals of a group in physical characteristics, language, and cultural features thought to be "natural" or "inherited," as distinct from particular social or historical conditions. These features have the power to impart a sense of group and individual identity, a sense of belonging to a community. In contrast, "instrumentalist" models hold that groups create ethnic identities for political and economic interests. Ethnicity, according to this view, is rationally oriented toward the fulfillment of specific goals like nationalism, access to economic power, or freedom from colonial rule. Primordialism was well suited to the synchronic tribal studies of the structural-functionalists, and instrumentalism more consonant with diachronic, historical analyses.

Most scholars today reject these simplistic alternatives and hold the position that neither is sufficient to explain ethnic group structure and sentiment. Primordialism overlooks the fact that ethnic identity is not a natural feeling that simply emerges mysteriously in all human communities, but a complex and dynamic set of symbolic meanings embedded in and patterned by history. Instrumentalists are so concerned with political and economic motivations that they sometimes ignore the question of how the particular elements or symbols of an ethnic identity are chosen. Vail stresses that some ethnic features and ties are of long standing but a great many others are of recent origin – even though people may believe they are ancient. Moreover, the meaning and definition of ethnicities change over time and differ according to historical circumstance. In other words, all ethnicities have a history. If there is anything primordial, it is not any particular ethnicity but rather the process of symbolic classification, the mechanism by which people divide the world into a "we" and a "they," and thereby give meaning to their lives (Comaroff, 1984). If we understand that process, we will better understand not only the people we study, but also the ways in which anthropologists and historians, past and present, have tried to make sense of Africa.

References

Comaroff, John L. 1984. "Of Totemism and Ethnicity: Consciousness, Practice and the Signs of Inequality." *Ethnos* 52(3–4): 301–23.

Evans-Pritchard, E.E. 1940a. *The Nuer*. Oxford: Clarendon Press.

Evans-Pritchard, E.E. 1940b. *The Political System of the Anuak of the Anglo-Egyptian Sudan*. London: P. Lund Humphries and Co. Ltd, for the LSE.

Fortes, Meyer. 1953. "The Structure of Unilineal Descent Groups." *American Anthropologist* 55: 17–41.

Fortes, Meyer and E.E. Evans-Pritchard, eds. 1940. *African Political Systems*. London: Oxford University Press, for the IAI.

Gough, Kathleen. 1971. "Nuer Kinship: A Reexamination." In T. O. Beidelman, ed., *The Translation of Culture*, pp. 79–122. London: Tavistock.

Grinker, Roy Richard. 1994. *Houses in the Rainforest: Ethnicity and Inequality among Farmers and Foragers in Central Africa*. Berkeley: University of California Press.

Herskovits, Melville. 1967 [1938]. *Dahomey: An Ancient African Kingdom*. Evanston: Northwestern University Press.

Karp, Ivan and Kent Maynard. 1983. "Reading the Nuer." *Current Anthropology* 24 (4): 481–502.

Kelly, R.C. 1985. *The Nuer Conquest: The Structure and Development of an Expansionist System*. Ann Arbor: University of Michigan Press.

Kuper, Adam. 1973. *Anthropology and Anthropologists: The Modern British School*. London: RKP.

Kuper, Hilda. 1961 [1947]. *An African Aristocracy: Rank among the Swazi*. London: Oxford University Press, for IAI.

Lienhardt, Godfrey. 1976. "Social Anthropology of Africa." In Christopher Fyfe, ed., *African Studies since 1945*, pp. 179–85. London: Longman.

Middleton, John and D. Tait, eds. 1958. *Tribes without Rulers*. London: Routledge and Kegan Paul.

Moore, Sally Falk. 1994. *Anthropology and Africa: Changing Perspectives on a Changing Scene*. Charlottesville: University of Virginia Press.

Richards, Audrey. 1939. *Land, Labour and Diet in Northern Rhodesia: An Economic Study of the Beinba Tribe*. London: International Institute of African Language and Culture.

Suggested Reading

Bates, R., V.Y. Mudimbe, and J. O'Barr, eds. 1993. *African and the Disciplines: The Contribution of Research in Africa to the Social Sciences and Humanities*. Chicago: University of Chicago Press.

Cohen, Abner, 1965. *Custom and Politics in Urban Africa: A Study of Hausa Migrants in Yoruba Towns*. Berkeley: University of California Press.

Cohen, R. 1978. "Ethnicity: Problem and Focus." *Annual Review of Anthropology* 7: 379–403.

Colson, E. 1962. *The Plateau Tonga of Northern Rhodesia: Social and Religious Studies*. Manchester: Manchester University Press.

Ekeh, Peter. 1990. "Social Anthropology and Two Contrasting Uses of Tribalism in Africa." *Comparative Studies in Society and History* 32(4): 660–700.

Fortes, Meyer. 1949. "Time and Social Structure: An Ashanti Case Study." In Meyer Fortes, ed., *Social Structure*, pp. 54–84. Oxford: Clarendon Press.

Gluckman, Max. 1958. "Analysis of a Social Situation in Modern Zululand," Rhodes–Livingstone Paper no. 28. *Bantu Studies* 14: 1–30; 147–74.

Grayburn, Nelson. 1971. *Readings in Kinship and Social Structure*. New York: Harper and Row.

Gulliver, Philip. 1971. *Neighbours and Networks*. Berkeley and Los Angeles: University of California Press.

Gutkind, Peter. 1970. *The Passing of Tribal Man in Africa*. Netherlands: Brill.

Helm, June, ed. 1968. *Essays on the Problem of Tribe*. Proceedings of the 1967 Annual Spring Meeting of the American Ethnological Society. Seattle: University of Washington Press.

Kronenfeld, David B. 2009. *Fanti Kinship and the Analysis of Kinship Terminologies*. Urbana: University of Illinois Press.

Kuper, Adam. 1982. "Lineage Theory: A Critical Retrospect." *Annual Review of Anthropology* 11: 71–95.

Lubkemann, Stephen C. 2008. *Culture in Chaos: An Anthropology of the Social Condition in War*. Chicago: University of Chicago Press.

Parkin, Robert and Linda Stone, eds. 2004. *Kinship and Family: An Anthropological Reader*. Malden: Wiley-Blackwell.

Radcliffe-Brown, A.R. 1952. *Structure and Function in Primitive Society*. New York: The Free Press.

Radcliffe-Brown, A.R. and Daryll Forde, eds. 1975 [1950]. *African Systems of Kinship and Marriage*. London: Oxford University Press for the IAI.

Sharp, J. 1980. "Can We Study Ethnicity? A Critique of Fields of Study in South African Anthropology." *Social Dynamics* 6(1): 1–16.

Shipton, Parker M. 2009. *Mortgaging the Ancestors: Ideologies of Attachment in Africa*. New Haven: Yale University Press.

Stocking, George. 1995. *After Tylor: British Social Anthropology: 1885–1951*. Madison: University of Wisconsin Press.

Sweet, James. 2006. *Recreating Africa: Culture, Kinship, and Religion in the African-Portuguese World, 1441–1770*. Chapel Hill: University of North Carolina Press.

Turner, Victor. 1957. *Schism and Continuity in an African Society: A Study of Ndembu Village Life*. Manchester: Manchester University Press.

5

The Nuer
Time and Space

E. E. Evans-Pritchard

I

In describing Nuer concepts of time we may distinguish between those that are mainly reflections of their relations to environment, which we call oecological time, and those that are reflections of their relations to one another in the social structure, which we call structural time. Both refer to successions of events which are of sufficient interest to the community for them to be noted and related to each other conceptually. The larger periods of time are almost certainly structural, because the events they relate are changes in the relationship of social groups. Moreover, time-reckoning based on changes in nature and man's response to them is limited to an annual cycle and therefore cannot be used to differentiate longer periods than seasons. Both, also, have limited and fixed notations. Seasonal and lunar changes repeat themselves year after year, so that a Nuer standing at any point of time has conceptual knowledge of what lies before him and can predict and organize his life accordingly. A man's structural future is likewise already fixed and ordered into different periods, so that the total changes in status a boy will undergo in his ordained passage through the social system, if he

lives long enough, can be foreseen. Structural time appears to an individual passing through the social system to be entirely progressive, but, as we shall see, in a sense this is an illusion. Oecological time appears to be, and is, cyclical.

The oecological cycle is a year. Its distinctive rhythm is the backwards and forwards movement from villages to camps, which is the Nuer's response to the climatic dichotomy of rains and drought. The year (*ruon*) has two main seasons, *tot* and *mai*. *Tot*, from about the middle of March to the middle of September, roughly corresponds to the rise in the curve of rainfall, though it does not cover the whole period of the rains. Rain may fall heavily at the end of September and in early October, and the country is still flooded in these months which belong, nevertheless, to the *mai* half of the year, for it commences at the decline of the rains – not at their cessation – and roughly covers the trough of the curve, from about the middle of September to the middle of March. The two seasons therefore only approximate to our division into rains and drought, and the Nuer classification aptly summarizes their way of looking at the movement of time, the direction of attention in marginal months being as significant as the actual climatic

From E. E. Evans-Pritchard, *The Nuer* (1940), pp. 95–110, 113–17, 135–8, from Oxford University Press.

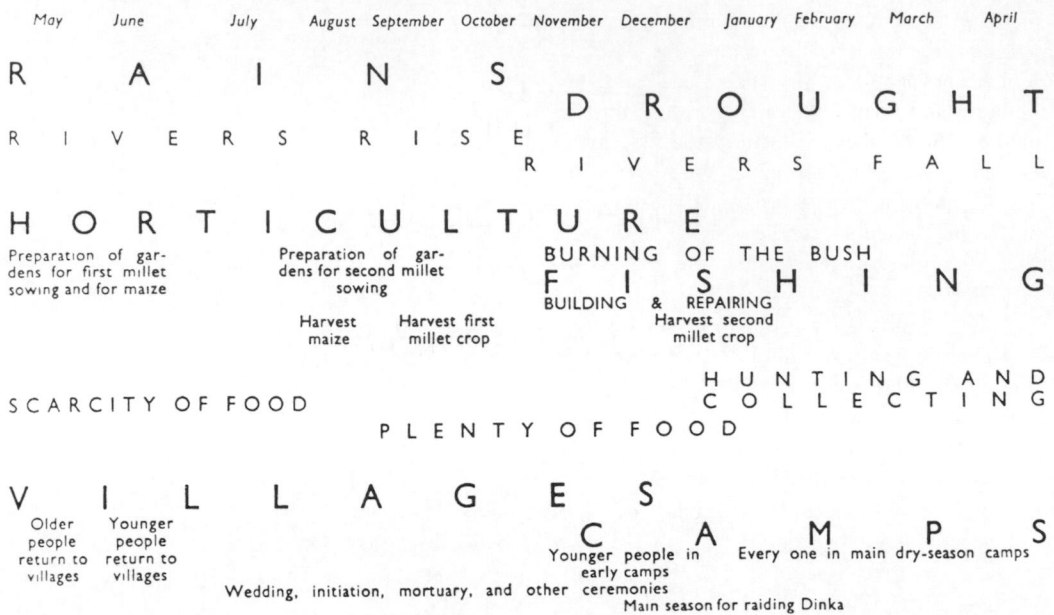

Figure 5.1

conditions. In the middle of September Nuer turn, as it were, towards the life of fishing and cattle camps and feel that village residence and horticulture lie behind them. They begin to speak of camps as though they were already in being, and long to be on the move. This restlessness is even more marked towards the end of the drought when, noting cloudy skies, people turn towards the life of villages and make preparations for striking camp. Marginal months may therefore be classed as *tot* or *mai*, since they belong to one set of activities but presage the other set, for the concept of seasons is derived from social activities rather than from the climate changes which determine them, and a year is to Nuer a period of village residence (*cieng*) and a period of camp residence (*wec*).

Seasonal variations in social activities, on which Nuer concepts of time are primarily based, have been indicated and, on the economic side, recorded at some length. The main features of these three planes of rhythm, physical, oecological, and social, are charted in Figure 5.1.

The movements of the heavenly bodies other than the sun and the moon, the direction and variation of winds, and the migration of some species of birds are observed by the Nuer, but they do not regulate their activities in relation to them nor use them as points of reference in seasonal time-reckoning. The characters by which seasons are most clearly defined are those which control the movements of the people: water, vegetation, movement of fish, &c.; it being the needs of cattle and variations in food-supply which chiefly translate oecological rhythm into the social rhythm of the year, and the contrast between modes of life at the height of the rains and at the height of the drought which provides the conceptual poles in time-reckoning.

Besides these two main seasons of *tot* and *mai* Nuer recognize two subsidiary seasons included in them, being transitional periods between them. The four seasons are not sharp divisions but overlap. Just as we reckon summer and winter as the halves of our year and speak also of spring and autumn, so Nuer reckon *tot* and *mai* as halves of their year and speak also of the seasons of *rwil* and *jiom*. *Rwil* is the time of moving from camp to village and of clearing and planting, from about the middle of March to the middle of June, before the rains have reached their peak. It counts as part of the *tot* half of the year, though it is contrasted with *tot* proper, the period of full village life and horticulture, from about the middle of June to the middle of September. *Jiom* meaning 'wind', is the period in which the persistent north wind begins to blow and people harvest, fish from dams, fire the bush, and form early camps, from about the middle of September to the middle of December. It counts as part of the *mai* half of the year, though it is contrasted with *mai* proper, from about the middle of December to the middle of March, when the main camps are formed. Roughly speaking, therefore, there are two major seasons of six months and four minor seasons of three months, but these divisions must not be regarded too rigidly since they are not so much exact units of time as rather vague conceptualizations of changes in oecological relations and social activities which pass imperceptibly from one state to another.

In [Figure 5.2] a line drawn from mid March to mid September is the axis of the year, being an approximation to a cleavage between two opposed sets of oecological relations and social activities, though not entirely corresponding to it, as may be seen in [Figure 5.3], where village life and camp life are shown in relation to the seasons of which they are the focal points. Nuer, especially the younger people, are still in camp for part of *tot* (the greater part of *rwil*) and are still in villages, especially the older people, for part of *mai* (the greater part of *jiom*), but every one is in villages during *tot* proper and in camps during *mai* proper. Since the words *tot* and *mai* are not pure units of time-reckoning but stand for the cluster of social activities characteristic of the height of the drought and of the height of the rains, one may hear a Nuer saying that he is going to '*tot*' or '*mai*' in a certain place.

The year has twelve months, six to each of the major seasons, and most adult Nuer can state them in order. In the list of months given below it has not been possible to equate each Nuer name with an English name, because our Roman months have nothing to do with the moon. It will be found, however, that a Nuer month is usually covered by the two English months equated to it in the list and generally tends to coincide with the first rather than the second.

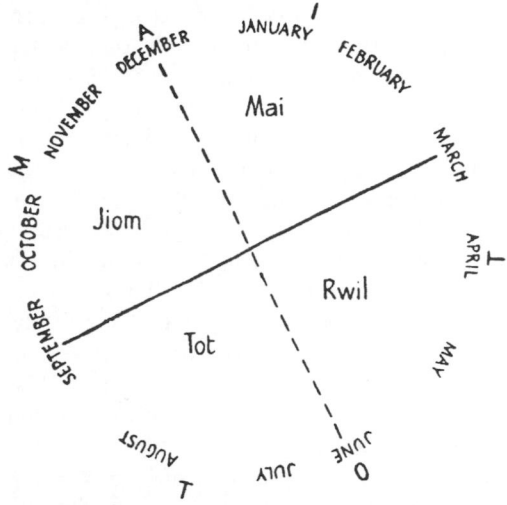

Figure 5.2

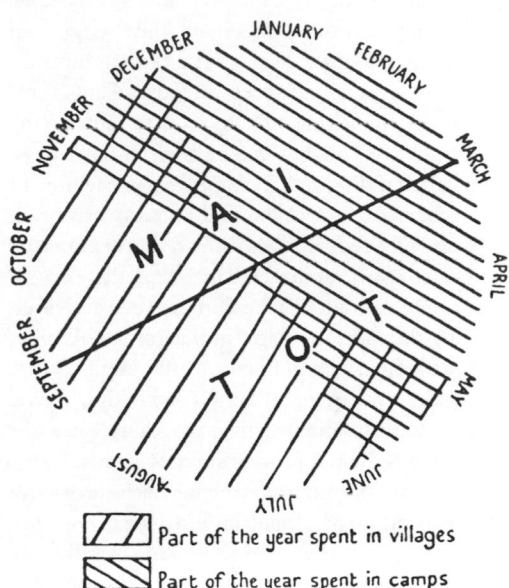

Part of the year spent in villages

Part of the year spent in camps

Figure 5.3

teer	Sept.–Oct.
lath (boor)	Oct.–Nov.
kur	Nov.–Dec.
tiop (in) dit	Dec.–Jan.

tiop (in) tot	Jan.–Feb.
pet	Feb.–Mar.
duong	Mar.–Apr.
gwaak	Apr.–May
dwat	May–June
kornyuot	June–July
paiyatni (paiyene)	July–Aug.
thoor	Aug.–Sept.

Nuer would soon be in difficulties over their lunar calendar if they consistently counted the succession of moons,[1] but there are certain activities associated with each month, the association sometimes being indicated by the name of the month. The calendar is a relation between a cycle of activities and a conceptual cycle and the two cannot fall apart, since the conceptual cycle is dependent on the cycle of activities from which it derives its meaning and function. Thus a twelve-month system does not incommode Nuer, for the calender is anchored to the cycle of oecological changes. In the month of *kur* one makes the first fishing dams and forms the first cattle camps, and since one is doing these things it must be *kur* or thereabouts. Likewise in *dwat* one breaks camp and returns to the villages, and since people are on the move it must be *dwat* or thereabouts. Consequently the calendar remains fairly stable and in any section of Nuerland there is general agreement about the name of the current month.

In my experience Nuer do not to any great extent use the name of the months to indicate the time of an event, but generally refer instead to some outstanding activity in process at the time of its occurrence, e.g. at the time of early camps, at the time of weeding, at the time of harvesting &c., and it is easily understandable that they do so, since time is to them a relation between activities. During the rains the stages in the growth of millet and the steps taken in its culture are often used as points of reference. Pastoral activities, being largely undifferentiated throughout the months and seasons, do not provide suitable points.

There are not units of time between the month and day and night. People indicate the occurrence of an event more than a day or two ago by reference to some other event which took place at the same time or by counting the number of intervening 'sleeps' or, less commonly, 'suns'. There are terms for to-day, to-morrow, yesterday, &c., but there is no precision about them. When Nuer wish to define the occurrence of an event several days in advance, such as a dance or wedding, they do so by reference to the phases of the moon: new moon, its waxing, full moon, its waning, and the brightness of its second quarter. When they wish to be precise they state on which night of the waxing or waning an event will take place, reckoning fifteen nights to

each and thirty to the moon. They say that only cattle and the Anuak can see the moon in its invisible period. The only terms applied to the nightly succession of lunar phases are those that describe its appearance just before, and in, fullness.

The course of the sun determines many points of reference, and a common way of indicating the time of events is by pointing to that part of the heavens the sun will then have reached in its course. There are also a number of expressions, varying in the degree of their precision, which describe positions of the sun in the heavens, though, in my experience, the only ones commonly employed are those that refer to its more conspicuously differentiated movements: the first stroke of dawn, sunrise, noon, and sunset. It is, perhaps, significant that there are almost as many points of reference between 4 and 6 a.m. as there are for the rest of the day. This may be chiefly due to striking contrasts caused by changes in relations of earth to sun during these two hours, but it may be noted, also, that the points of reference between them are more used in directing activities, such as starting on journeys, rising from sleep, tethering cattle in kraals, gazelle hunting, &c., than points of reference during most of the rest of the day, especially in the slack time between 1 and 3 p.m. There are also a number of terms to describe the time of night. They are to a very limited extent determined by the course of the stars. Here again, there is a richer terminology for the transition period between day and night than during the rest of the night and the same reasons may be suggested to explain this fact. There are also expressions for distinguishing night from day, forenoon from afternoon, and that part of the day which is spent from that part which lies ahead.

Except for the commonest of the terms for divisions of the day they are little used in comparison with expressions which describe routine diurnal activities. The daily timepiece is the cattle clock, the round of pastoral tasks, and the time of day and the passage of time through a day are to a Nuer primarily the succession of these tasks and their relations to one another. The better demarcated points are taking of the cattle from byre to kraal, milking, driving of the adult herd to pasture, milking of the goats and sheep, driving of the flocks and calves to pasture, cleaning of byre and kraal, bringing home of the flocks and calves, the return of the adult herd, the evening milking, and the enclosure of the beasts in byres. Nuer generally use such points of activity, rather than concrete points in the movement of the sun across the heavens, to co-ordinate events. Thus a man says, 'I shall return at milking', 'I shall start off when the calves come home', and so forth.

Oecological time-reckoning is ultimately, of course, entirely determined by the movement of the heavenly bodies, but only some of its units and notations are directly based on these movements, e.g. month, day, night, and some parts of the day and night, and such points of reference are paid attention to and selected as points only because they are significant for social activities. It is the activities themselves, chiefly of an economic kind, which are basic to the system and furnish most of its units and notations, and the passage of time is perceived in the relation of activities to one another. Since activities are dependent on the movement of the heavenly bodies and since the movement of the heavenly bodies is significant only in relation to the activities one may often refer to either in indication of the time of an event. Thus one may say, 'In the *jiom* season' or 'At early camps', 'The month of *Dwat*' or 'The return to villages', 'When the sun is warming up' or 'At milking'. The movements of the heavenly bodies permit Nuer to select natural points that are significant in relation to activities. Hence in linguistic usage nights, or rather 'sleeps', are more clearly defined units of time than days, or 'suns', because they are undifferentiated units of social activity, and months, or rather 'moons', though they are clearly differentiated units of natural time, are little employed as points of reference because they are not clearly differentiated units of activity, whereas the day, the year, and its main seasons are complete occupational units.

Certain conclusions may be drawn from this quality of time among the Nuer. Time has not the same value throughout the year. Thus in dry season camps, although daily pastoral tasks follow one another in the same order as in the rains, they do not take place at the same time. They are more a precise routine owing to the severity of seasonal conditions, especially with regard to water and pasturage, and require greater co-ordination and co-operative action. On the other hand, life in the dry season is generally uneventful, outside routine tasks, and oecological and social relations are more monotonous from month to month than in the rains when there are frequent feasts, dances, and ceremonies. When time is considered as relations between activities it will be understood that it has a different connotation in rains and drought. In the drought the daily time-reckoning is more uniform and precise while lunar reckoning receives less attention, as appears from the lesser use of names of months, less confidence in stating their order, and the common East African trait of two dry-season months with the same name (*tiop in dit* and *tiop in tot*), the order of which is often interchanged. The pace of time may vary accordingly, since perception of time is a function of systems of time-reckoning, but we can make no definite statement on this question.

Though I have spoken of time and units of time the Nuer have no expression equivalent to 'time' in our language, and they cannot, therefore, as we can, speak of time as though it were something actual, which passes, can be wasted, can be saved, and so forth. I do not think that they ever experience the same feeling of fighting against time or of having to co-ordinate activities with an abstract passage of time, because their points of reference are mainly the activities themselves, which are generally of a leisurely character. Events follow a logical order, but they are not controlled by an abstract system, there being no autonomous points of reference to which activities have to conform with precision. Nuer are fortunate.

Also they have very limited means of reckoning the relative duration of periods of time intervening between events, since they have few, and not well-defined or systematized, units of time. Having no hours or other small units of time they cannot measure the periods which intervene between positions of the sun or daily activities. It is true that the year is divided into twelve lunar units, but Nuer do not reckon in them as fractions of a unit. They may be able to state in what month an event occurred, but it is with great difficulty that they reckon the relation between events in abstract numerical symbols. They think much more easily in terms of activities and of successions of activities and in terms of social structure and of structural differences than in pure units of time.

We may conclude that the Nuer system of time-reckoning within the annual cycle and parts of the cycle is a series of conceptualizations of natural changes, and that the selection of points of reference is determined by the significance which these natural changes have for human activities.

II

In a sense all time is structural since it is a conceptualization of collateral, co-ordinated, or co-operative activities: the movements of a group. Otherwise time concepts of this kind could not exist, for they must have a like meaning for every one within a group. Milking-time and meal-times are approximately the same for all people who normally come into contact with one another, and the movement from villages to camps has approximately the same connotation everywhere in Nuerland, though it may have a special connotation for a particular group of persons. There is, however, a point at which we can say that time concepts cease to be determined by oecological factors and become more determined by structural interrelations, being no longer a reflection of man's dependence on nature, but a reflection of the interaction of social groups.

The year is the largest unit of oecological time. Nuer have words for the year before last, last year, this year, next year, and the year after next. Events which took place in the last few years are then the points of reference in time-reckoning, and these are different according to the group of persons who make use of them: joint family, village, tribal section, tribe, &c. One of the commonest ways of stating the year of an event is to mention where the people of the village made their dry season camps, or to refer to some evil that befell their cattle. A joint family may reckon time in the birth of calves of their herds. Weddings and other ceremonies, fights, and raids, may likewise give points of time, though in the absence of numerical dating no one can say without lengthy calculations how many years ago an event took place. Moreover, since time is to Nuer an order of events of outstanding significance to a group, each group has its own points of reference and time is consequently relative to structural space, locally considered. This is obvious when we examine the names given to years

by different tribes, or sometimes by adjacent tribes, for these are floods, pestilences, famines, wars, &c., experienced by the tribe. In course of time the names of years are forgotten and all events beyond the limits of this crude historical reckoning fade into the dim vista of long long ago. Historical time, in this sense of a sequence of outstanding events of significance to a tribe, goes back much farther than the historical time of smaller groups, but fifty years is probably its limit, and the farther back from the present day the sparser and vaguer become its points of reference.

However, Nuer have another way of stating roughly when events took place; not in numbers of years, but by reference to the age-set system. Distance between events ceases to be reckoned in time concepts as we understand them and is reckoned in terms of structural distance, being the relation between groups of persons. It is therefore entirely relative to the social structure. Thus a Nuer may say that an event took place after the *Thut* age-set was born or in the initiation period of the *Boiloc* age-set, but no one can say how many years ago it happened. Time is here reckoned in sets. If a man of the *Dangunga* set tells one that an event occurred in the initiation period of the *Thut* set he is saying that it happened three sets before his set, or six sets ago. Here it need only be said that we cannot accurately translate a reckoning in sets into a reckoning in years, but that we can roughly estimate a ten-year interval between the commencement of successive sets. There are six sets in existence, the names of the sets are not cyclic, and the order of extinct sets, all but the last, are soon forgotten, so that an age-set reckoning has seven units covering a period of rather under a century.

The structural system of time-reckoning is partly the selection of points of reference of significance to local groups which give these groups a common and distinctive history; partly the distance between specific sets in the age-set system; and partly distances of a kinship and lineage order. Four generation-steps (*kath*) in the kinship system are linguistically differentiated relations, grandfather, father, son, and grandson, and within a small kinship group these relationships give a time-depth to members of the group and points of reference in a line of ascent by which their relationships are determined and explained. Any

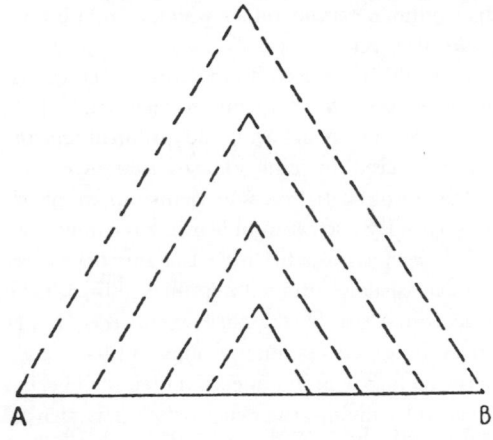

Figure 5.4

kinship relationship must have a point of reference on a line of ascent, namely a common ancestor, so that such a relationship always has a time connotation couched in structural terms. Beyond the range of the kinship system in this narrow sense the connotation is expressed in terms of the lineage system. The base line of the triangle in Figure 5.4 represents a given group of agnates and the dotted lines represent their ghostly agnatic forebears, running from this base to a point in lineage structure, the common ancestor of every member of the group. The farther we extend the range of the group (the longer becomes the base line) the farther back in lineage structure is the common ancestor (the farther from the base line is the apex of the triangle). The four triangles are thus the time depths of four extensions of agnatic relationship on an existential plane and represent minimal, minor, major, and maximal lineages of a clan. Lineage time is thus the structural distance between groups of persons on the line *AB*. Structural time therefore cannot be understood until structural distance in known, since it is a reflection of it, and we must, therefore, ask the reader to forgive a certain obscurity at this point and to reserve criticism till we have had an opportunity of explaining more clearly what is meant by structural distance.

We have restricted our discussion to Nuer systems of time-reckoning and have not considered the way in which an individual perceives time. The subject bristles with difficulties. Thus an individual may reckon the passage of time by reference to the physical appearance and status of other individuals and to changes in his own life-history, but such a method of reckoning time has no wide collective validity. We confess, however, that our observations on the matter have been slight and that a fuller analysis is beyond our powers. We have merely indicated those aspects of the problem which are directly related to the description of modes of livelihood which has gone before and to the description of political institutions which follows.

We have remarked that the movement of structural time is, in a sense, an illusion, for the structure remains fairly constant and the perception of time is no more than the movement of persons, often as groups, through the structure. Thus age-sets succeed one another forever, but there are never more than six in existence and the relative positions occupied by these six sets at any time are fixed structural points through which actual sets of persons pass in endless succession. Similarly, for reasons which we explain later, the Nuer system of lineages may be considered a fixed system, there being a constant number of steps between living persons and the founder of their clan and the lineages having a constant position relative to one another. However when many generations succeed one another the depth and range of lineages does not increase unless there has been structural change.

Beyond the limits of historical time we enter a plane of tradition in which a certain element of historical fact may be supposed to be incorporated in a complex of myth. Here the points of reference are the structural ones we have indicated. At one end this plane merges into history; at the other end into myth. Time perspective is here not a true impression of actual distances like that created by our dating technique, but a reflection of relations between lineages, so that the traditional events recorded have to be placed at the points where the lineages concerned in them converge in their lines of ascent. The events have therefore a position in structure, but no exact position in historical time as we understand it. Beyond tradition lies the horizon of pure myth which is always seen in the same time perspective. One mythological event did not precede another, for myths explain customs of general social significance rather than the interrelations of particular segments and are, therefore, not structurally stratified. Explanations of any qualities of nature or of culture are drawn from this intellectual ambient which imposes limits on the Nuer world and makes it self-contained and entirely intelligible to Nuer in the relation of its parts. The world, peoples, and cultures all existed together from the same remote past.

It will have been noted that the Nuer time dimension is shallow. Valid history ends a century ago, and tradition, generously measured, takes us back only ten to twelve generations in lineage structure, and if we are right in supposing that lineage structure never grows, it follows that the distance between the beginning of the world and the present day remains unalterable. Time is thus not a continuum, but is a constant structural relationship between two points, the first and last persons in a line of agnatic descent. How shallow is Nuer time may be judged from the fact that the tree under which mankind came into being was still standing in Western Nuerland a few years ago!

Beyond the annual cycle, time-reckoning is a conceptualization of the social structure, and the points of reference are a projection into the past of actual relations between groups of persons. It is less a means of co-ordinating events than of co-ordinating relationships, and is therefore mainly a looking-backwards, since relationships must be explained in terms of the past.

III

We have concluded that structural time is a reflection of structural distance. In the following sections we define further what we mean by structural distance, and make a formal, preliminary, classification of Nuer territorial groups of a political kind. We have classified Nuer socio-temporal categories. We now classify their socio-spatial categories.

Were a man to fly over Nuerland he would see white patches with what look like tiny fungoid growths on them. These are village sites with huts and byres. He would see that between such patches are stretches of brown and black, the brown being open grassland and the black being depressions which are swampy in the rains; and that the white patches are wider and more frequent in some parts than in others. We find Nuer give to these

distributions certain values which compose their political structure.

It would be possible to measure the exact distance between hut and hut, village and village, tribal area and tribal area, and so forth, and the space covered by each. This would give us a statement of spatial measurements in bare physical terms. By itself it would have very limited significance. Oecological space is more than mere physical distance, though it is affected by it, for it is reckoned also by the character of the country intervening between local groups and its relation to the biological requirements of their members. A broad river divides two Nuer tribes more sharply than many miles of unoccupied bush. A distance which appears small in the dry season has a different appearance when the area it covers is flooded in the rains. A village community which has permanent water near at hand is in a very different position to one which has to travel in the dry season to obtain water, pasturage, and fishing. A tsetse belt creates an impassable barrier, giving wide oecological distance between the peoples it separates, and presence or absence of cattle among neighbours of the Nuer likewise determines the oecological distance between them and the Nuer. Oecological distance, in this sense, is a relation between communities defined in terms of density and distribution, and with reference to water, vegetation, animal and insect life, and so on.

Structural distance is of a very different order, though it is always influenced and, in its political dimension, to a large extent determined by oecological conditions. By structural distance is meant, as we have already indicated in the preceding section, the distance between groups of persons in a social system, expressed in terms of values. The nature of the country determines the distribution of villages and, therefore, the distance between them, but values limit and define the distribution in structural terms and give a different set of distances. A Nuer village may be equidistant from two other villages, but if one of these belongs to a different tribe and the other to the same tribe it may be said to be structurally more distant from the first than from the second. A Nuer tribe which is separated by forty miles from another Nuer tribe is structurally nearer to it than to a Dinka tribe from which it is separated by only twenty miles. When

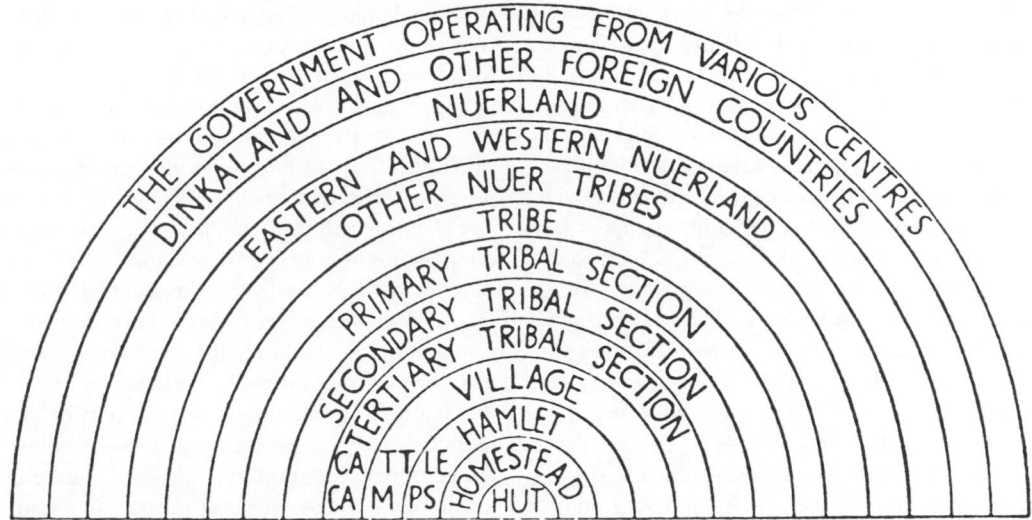

Figure 5.5   Nuer socio-spatial categories

we leave territorial values and speak of lineages and age-sets, structural space is less determined by environmental conditions. One lineage is closer to another than to a third. One age-set is closer to another than to a third. The values attached to residence, kinship, lineage, sex, and age, differentiate groups of persons by segmentation, and the relative positions of the segments to one another gives a perspective that enables us to speak of the divisions between them as divisions of structural space. Having defined what is meant by structural space we may now proceed with a description of its political divisions.

IV

We have noted that structural distance is the distance between groups of persons in social structure and may be of different kinds. Those which concern us in our present account are political distance, lineage distance, and age-set distance. The political distance between villages of a tertiary tribal section is less than the distance between tertiary segments of a secondary tribal section, and that is less than the distance between secondary segments of a primary tribal section, and so forth. The lineage distance between segments of a minor lineage is less than the distance between minor

segments of a major lineage, and that is less than the distance between major segments of a maximal lineage, and so forth. The age-set distance between segments of an age-set is less than the distance between successive age-sets and that is less than the distance between age-sets which are not successive. As we wish to develop our argument and therefore to avoid analysis which does not allow the reader to refer back to statements already made, we will give immediate consideration only to political distance and only to some characteristics of it.

Nuer give values to local distributions. It might be thought a simple matter to discover what these values are, but since they are embodied in words, one cannot understand their range of reference without considerable knowledge of the people's language and of the way they use it, for meanings vary according to the social situation and a word may refer to a variety of local groups. It is, nevertheless, possible to differentiate them and to make a crude formal classification of them, as we have done in Figure 5.5.

A single living hut (*dwil* or *ut*) is occupied by a wife and her children and, at times, by her husband. They constitute a simple residential family group. The homestead, consisting of a byre and huts, may contain a simple family group or a polygamous family and there are often one or two kinsmen living there as well. This group, which we call a household, is often referred to as the *gol*, a word which means 'hearth'. A hamlet with gardens and waste land around it is called *dhor* and each has its special name, often derived from some landmark or from the name of the senior kinsman living there. A hamlet is generally occupied by close agnatic kinsmen, often brothers, and their households, and we call this group of persons a joint family. As these groups are not treated in our account we say no more about them. It must be remembered, however, that a village is not an unsegmented unit but is a relation between a number of smaller units.

The village is a very distinct unit. It is sometimes referred to as *thur*, a ridge of high ground, but generally as *cieng*, a word which may be translated 'home', but which has such a variety of meanings that we shall devote a special section to it. A village comprises a community, linked by common residence and by a network of kinship and affinal ties, the members of which, as we have seen, form a common camp, co-operate in many activities, and eat in one another's byres and windscreens. A village is the smallest Nuer group which is not specifically of a kinship order and is the political unit of Nuerland. The people of the village have a feeling of strong solidarity against other villages and great affection for their site, and in spite of the wandering habits of Nuer, persons born and bred in a village have a nostalgia for it and are likely to return to it and make their home there, even if they have resided elsewhere for many years. Members of a village fight side by side and support each other in feuds. When the youths of a village go to dances they enter the dance in a war line (*dep*) singing their special war chant.

A cattle camp, which people of a village form in the drought and in which members of neighbouring villages participate, is known as *mec*. While this word has the meaning of 'camp' in contrast with *cieng*, 'village', both words are used in the same general sense of local community. Thus when it is said of a certain clan that they have no *mec* we are to understand that they nowhere in a tribal section or village form a dominant nucleus of the community and that, therefore, no local community takes its name from them. A large camp is called

after the dominant lineage in it or after the village community who occupy it, and small camps are sometimes named after an old person of importance who has erected his windscreen there. We have seen that the social composition of a camp varies at different times of the drought from the people of a hamlet to the people of a village, or of neighbouring villages, and that men sometimes camp with kinsmen living in camps other than those of their own villages. Consequently, while local communities of the rains tend to be also local communities in the drought their composition may be somewhat different. We again emphasize that not only are the people of a camp living in a more compact group than the people of a village, but also that in camp life there is more frequent contact between its members and greater co-ordination of their activities. The cattle are herded together, milked at the same time, and so on. In a village each household herds its own cattle, if they are herded at all, and performs its domestic and kraal tasks independently and at different times. In the drought there is increasing concentration and greater uniformity in response to the greater severity of the season.

We sometimes speak of a district to describe an aggregate of villages or camps which have easy and frequent intercommunication. The people of these villages take part in the same dances, intermarry, conduct feuds, go on joint raiding parties, share dry season camps or make camps in the same locality, and so on. This indefinite aggregate of contacts does not constitute a Nuer category or a political group, because the people do not see themselves, nor are seen by others, as a unique community, but 'district' is a term we employ to denote the sphere of a man's social contacts or of the social contacts of the people of a village and is, therefore, relative to the person or community spoken about. A district in this sense tends to correspond to a tertiary or a secondary tribal segment, according to the size of the tribe. In the smallest tribes a whole tribe is a man's district, and a district may even cut across tribal boundaries in that in a large tribe a border village may have more contacts with neighbouring villages of another tribe than with distant villages of its own tribe. The sphere of a man's social contacts may thus not entirely coincide with any structural division.

A number of adjacent villages, varying in number and total extension according to the size of the tribe, are grouped into small tribal sections and these into larger ones. In the larger tribes it is convenient to distinguish between primary, secondary, and tertiary tribal sections. These sections, of whatever size, are, like a village, spoken of as '*cieng*'. Since the next chapter is devoted to these tribal segments no more is said about them here.

V

In our account of Nuer time-reckoning we noted that in one department of time their system of reckoning is, in a broad sense, a conceptualization, in terms of activities, or of physical changes that provide convenient points of reference for activities, of those phases of the oecological rhythm which have peculiar significance for them. We further noted that in another department of time it is a conceptualization of structural relations, time units being co-ordinate with units of structural space. We have given a brief description of these units of structural space in its political or territorial dimension and have drawn attention to the influence of oecology on distribution and hence on the values given to the distribution, the interrelation between which is the political system. This system is not, however, as simple as we have presented it, for values are not simple, and we now attempt to face some of the difficulties we have so far neglected. We start this attempt by asking what it is the Nuer mean when they speak of their *cieng*.

Values are embodied in words through which they influence behaviour. When a Nuer speaks of his *cieng*, his *dhor*, his *gol*, &c., he is conceptualizing his feelings of structural distance, identifying himself with a local community, and, by so doing, cutting himself off from other communities of the same kind. An examination of the word *cieng* will teach us one of the most fundamental characteristics of Nuer local groups and, indeed, of all social groups: their structural relativity.

What does a Nuer mean when he says, 'I am a man of such-and-such a *cieng*'? *Cieng* means 'home', but its precise significance varies with the situation in which it is spoken. If one meets an Englishman in Germany and asks him where his home is, he may reply that it is England. If one

meets the same man in London and asks him the same question he will tell one that his home is in Oxfordshire, whereas if one meets him in that county he will tell one the name of the town or village in which he lives. If questioned in his town or village he will mention his particular street, and if questioned in his street he will indicate his house. So it is with the Nuer. A Nuer met outside Nuerland says that his home is *cieng Nath*, Nuerland. He may also refer to his tribal country as his *cieng*, though the more usual expression for this is *rol*. If one asks him in his tribe what is his *cieng*, he will name his village or tribal section according to the context. Generally he will name either his tertiary tribal section or his village, but he may give his primary or secondary section. If asked in his village he will mention the name of his hamlet or indicate his homestead or the end of the village in which his homestead is situated. Hence if a man says '*Wa ciengda*,' 'I am going home', outside his village he means that he is returning to it; if in his village he means that he is going to his hamlet; if in his hamlet he means that he is going to his homestead. *Cieng* thus means homestead, hamlet, village, and tribal sections of various dimensions.

The variations in the meaning of the word *cieng* are not due to the inconsistencies of language, but to the relativity of the group-values to which it refers. I emphasize this character of structural distance at an early stage because an understanding of it is necessary to follow the account of various social groups which we are about to describe. Once it is understood, the apparent contradictions in our account will be seen to be contradictions in the structure itself, being, in fact, a quality of it.

A man is a member of a political group of any kind in virtue of his non-membership of other groups of the same kind. He sees them as groups and their members see him as a member of a group, and his relations with them are controlled by the structural distance between the groups concerned. But a man does not see himself as a member of that same group in so far as his is a member of a segment of it which stands outside of and is opposed to other segments of it. Hence a man can be a member of a group and yet not a member of it. Thus a man is a member of his tribe in its relation to other tribes, but he is not a member of his tribe in the relation of his segment of it to other segments of the same kind. Likewise a man is a member of his tribal segment in its relation to other segments, but he is not a member of it in the relation of his village to other villages of the same segment. A characteristic of any political group is hence its invariable tendency towards fission and the opposition of its segments, and another characteristic is its tendency towards fusion with other groups of its own order in opposition to political segments larger than itself. Political values are thus always, structurally speaking, in conflict. One value attaches a man to his group and another to a segment of it in opposition to other segments of it, and the value which controls his action is a function of the social situation in which he finds himself. For a man sees himself as a member of a group only in opposition to other groups and he sees a member of another group as a member of a social unity however much it may be split into opposed segments.

Therefore Figure 5.5 illustrates political structure in a very crude and formal way. It cannot very easily be pictured diagrammatically, for political relations are relative and dynamic. They are best stated as tendencies to conform to certain values in certain situations, and the value is determined by the structural relationships of the persons who compose the situation. Thus whether and on which side a man fights in a dispute depends on the structural relationship of the persons engaged in it and of his own relationship to each party.

We need to refer to another important principle of Nuer political structure: the smaller the local group the stronger the sentiment uniting its members. Tribal sentiment is weaker than the sentiment of one of its segments and the sentiment of a segment is weaker than the sentiment

of a village which is part of it. Logically this might be supposed to be the case, for if unity within a group is a function of its opposition to groups of the same kind it might be surmised that the sentiment of unity within a group must be stronger than the sentiment of unity within a larger group that contains it. But it is also evident that the smaller the group the more the contacts between its members, the more varied are these contacts, and the more they are co-operative. In a big group like the tribe contacts between its members are infrequent and corporate action is limited to occasional military excursions. In a small group like the village not only are there daily residential contacts, often of a co-operative nature, but the members are united by close agnatic, cognatic, and affinal ties which can be expressed in reciprocal action. These become fewer and more distant the wider the group, and the cohesion of a political group is undoubtedly dependent on the number and strength of ties of a non-political kind.

It must also be stated that political actualities are confused and conflicting. They are confused because they are not always, even in a political context, in accord with political values, though they tend to conform to them, and because social ties of a different kind operate in the same field, sometimes strengthening them and sometimes running counter to them. They are conflicting because the values that determine them are, owing to the relativity of political structure, themselves in conflict. Consistency of political actualities can only be seen when the dynamism and relativity of political structure are understood and the relation of political structure to other social systems is taken into consideration.

Note

1 There is some evidence of an intercalary month among the Eastern Jikany, but I cannot be definite on this point, and I have not heard it mentioned in other parts of Nuerland.

6

The Illusion of Tribe

Aidan W. Southall

Introduction

Controversial though the matter is, the most generally acceptable characteristics of a tribal society are perhaps that it is a whole society, with a high degree of self-sufficency at a near subsistence level, based on a relatively simple technology without writing or literature, politically autonomous and with its own distinctive language, culture and sense of identity, tribal religion being also co-terminous with tribal society. Some would insist on further differentiation of the tribal level of social and cultural organization, on the one hand, from the very small scale band level characteristic of hunting and gathering peoples without agriculture, and on the other, from state or state-like organizations found at the upper limit of scale and complexity within the range of non-literate societies. Thus, Sahlins (1961: 323) speaks of the "tribal level, as distinguished from less-developed *bands* and more advanced *chiefdoms*." This point of view has not found much favour and can be criticised on a number of counts. At the empirical level, tribes and bands do not appear as distinct as is implied, and the concept of "chief" and "chiefdom," while

clear to some writers, is highly variable and inconsistent in the ethnographic literature as a whole. The empirical difficulties of distinguishing the tribal level in the broad sense have been considerable, and the addition of two further levels seems to make them insurmountable. It is not by multiplying global distinctions of this sort that we shall progress, but by dealing with more specialized categories of phenomena while retaining the general concept of tribe as a convenient initial descriptive label. Dozens of definitions could, of course, be quoted from authoritative anthropological writings, but for the most part, they add nothing to understanding and vary only in emphasis, one stressing language, another politics, another self-identity, and so forth.

For present purposes, to simplify the argument, we shall use tribal society in the more inclusive sense of all those societies which exhibit the first mentioned set of characteristics. On this basis, to what extent do such societies still exist? In the strict sense they cannot exist, since there are no areas of the inhabited earth unclaimed by one sovereign state or another. They can only exist in dwindling pockets so remote that such sovereign

From Aidan W. Southall, "The Illusion of Tribe," in *The Passing of Tribal Man in Africa*, ed. P. C. W. Gutkind, pp. 28–31, 32–5, 39–43, 44, 46–50, from E.J. Brill, Leiden, 1970.

claims have not yet been made effective and can be ignored. No tribal society which has lost its political autonomy can continue to be a tribal society in the full sense of this meaning, although many of its members may retain vivid and even nostalgic memories of its former full existence and may continue to be strongly influenced by the values belonging to this former state and still endeavour to act according to them in those fields where new controls and changed needs allow them to do so. It is the melancholy paradox of anthropology that effective study of such social systems dates only from a period so late that they had already ceased to exist in this full sense, so that an element of reconstruction has always entered into the study of them in these terms. But it would be foolish to deny that the end of their existence in the full sense was the beginning of a long transitional period in which their members were in varying degrees becoming incorporated into wider systems, yet continued to retain strong elements of their former state. Neglect of this has vitiated much of the work carried out supposedly in their interests by the development disciplines.

It is not only political autonomy which has been lost, though that was fundamental, and it is well to specify the changes which have generally occurred in respect of the other stated characteristics. They are no longer self sufficient, because various pressures from without and then from within have brought them to depend extensively on goods and services which they cannot produce for themselves. Even where their material well being is still little better than their former subsistence, they have none the less become involved with the wider market economy in countless seemingly irrevocable ways. By the same token, their technology is no longer simple. Even where it is little improved in efficiency, it has come to reflect in its array of tools and weapons, clothes and even foodstuffs, the vast, unseen and distant complex of the industrial world. Almost invariably some of its members have become literate, and even if they have often at the same time tended to become absentees, they none the less remain vital members of it and the very symbols of its passing. Furthermore, they have often, and necessarily, become literate in a foreign language. They have also adopted, of course under strong external persuasion if not

pressure, new religious beliefs, practices, and memberships, or at least new sets of ideas, which are incompatible with tribal society. In all these ways, the close identity of language, culture and society (if it ever existed) is now blurred and has become a series of alternatives. To say "I am a Kikuyu, a Kenyan, an African," means three very different things. The latter two identities did not exist three quarters of a century ago. What has been said here is obviously only a minimal statement of the changes that have occurred. It goes without saying that in many cases the transformation is much greater.

So far we have given a definition of what a tribal society is, conceptually, and presumably was, empirically, but have argued that it can no longer exist in this full sense, however potent many of its features may remain. The carrying over of such features into a different system is tribalism. Tribalism is usually regarded in pejorative light and the rational basis for this is that to carry over elements specific to one system into another is inappropriate. It is in the political context that tribalism is regarded with particular disfavor, and in a number of social and economic contexts also. But those who rightly stigmatise the carryover which is tribalism in these contexts would in others often favor it, especially with respect to certain family values and to aesthetic modes of expression, as for example in music, dancing and plastic arts. Thus President Julius Nyerere of Tanzania: "It has been said – and this is quite right – that Tanganyika is tribal, and we realise that we need to break up this tribal consciousness among the people and to build up a national consciousness" (Nyerere, 1966: 38–9). Yet on the other hand, "I have set up this new Ministry to help us regain our pride in our own culture. I want it to seek out the best of the traditions and customs of all our tribes and make them a part of our national culture" (op. cit. 187). "The traditional order is dying; the question which has yet to be answered is what will be built on our past, and, in consequence, what kind of society will eventually replace the traditional one" (op. cit. 6).

This is the oft discussed problem of trying to retain the good which was in the old and grafting it on to the new. But the characteristics of tribal society which we gave constitute a set of highly dependent variables. Dependent variables, whether we like it or not, constitute a functional system. We say "highly dependent" because we reject the extreme claims of total functional integration which are widely recognised as false. Tribal societies were not totally integrated. There were areas of partial integration and partial dependence in the system, allowing for the possibility of moderate change from within or without. But they were certainly quite highly integrated systems and to pick and choose among supposedly desirable and undesirable elements in them is a fatal misunderstanding of their intrinsic nature. Of course there is continuity as well as change. There are harder and softer elements in the system. But the interdependence, although partial and not total, is none the less real. There is therefore some possibility of preserving some desirable elements, but it can only be done in submission to the limitations imposed by the degree of interdependence of variables. Unfortunately, this requirement is far from being taken seriously into account by the policy makers concerned.

This is particularly relevant to those formerly tribal populations which have not lost their demographic vitality, or will to live, but rather are in many cases on the brink of, or already involved in, a dangerous population explosion, rapidly entering the modern world and usually forming the major population component of new nations, or of colonial territories in their last stages, as in most of Africa and New Guinea. The other side of the coin is the more tragic situation reported by Lévi-Strauss in "A World on the Wane" of those pathetic remnants which "had learnt from the ferocious persecutions of the previous hundred years to keep themselves entirely hidden from the outer world" – people who "were neither 'true Indians', nor, for that matter, 'true savages', but former 'savages' on whom civilization had been abruptly forced; and, as soon as they were no longer 'a danger to Society', civilization took no further interest in them" (1961: 134–5). This is the characteristic situation of aboriginal peoples throughout the Americas, except for those who have successfully made the transition into peasantries, or as individuals, become lost in industrial society. Such tragic situations are also reported sporadically from Africa where, according to Diamond (1964a: 45) the Anaguta of the Nigerian Plateau "*decided* not to join the modern world" but "move like ghosts on the outskirts of civilization ... Their culture crumbles, their population declines, their lands shrink and as an ethnic entity they change only disintegratively. They accept, they pursue their decline; for them the world ends." Or, again, the fragmentary Ik of northeastern Uganda, where, according to Turnbull (1967: 70) "social disintegration has gone to the limit" and "at the present rate the Ik are not likely to survive much longer." ...

According to Steward (1958: 44–5) "the concept of primitive or 'tribal' is based on three fundamental aspects of the behavior of members of tribal societies". These are, in brief, that it is a construct representing the ideal, normative aspect of the behaviour of "all members of a fairly small, simple, independent, self-contained and homogeneous society" ... "Tribal society is not divisible into genuine subcultural groups." Secondly, tribal culture has pattern, or configuration, some underlying unity and overall integration, and thirdly, that it is "essentially relativistic" and unique in relation to other cultures with which it contrasted. While it has been "a useful tool for analysis and comparison, especially when contrasts are sought, ... as a tool for dealing with culture change it has found little utility." To the present writer its deficiencies are more fundamental than this, for as we shall see, the cultures which lie at the lower end of the range in terms of social scale are not in fact unique and independent entities which can properly be seen as unequivocally distinct from one another. Indeed, to do so is frequently to misunderstand their essential nature. On the other hand, cultures which lie at the higher end of the scale are not as homogeneous and lacking in subcultural divisions as is implied. These divergences are much too general and glaring to be regarded as permissible deviations from a consistent core.

The ideal type or analytical model of the tribe varies a good deal in the versions of different writers, as we have seen, but it is fair to say that these variations do play round recurring common themes. However, we shall give examples to document the fact that, whichever particular choice of definition is made, empirical divergences are so gross, widespread and frequent as to render the concept of tribe as it exists in the general literature untenable. In many cases, the definitions generally current actually hinder understanding of the entities to which they are supposed to refer. The named tribes which appear in the literature frequently represent crystallizations at the wrong level, usually a level which is too large in scale because foreign observers did not initially understand the lower levels of structure or failed to correct the misrepresentations of their predecessors, or because some arbitrary and even artificial entity was chosen for the sake of easy reference, despite a realisation that it was fallacious and misleading. Furthermore, such fabrications of the foreign observer have often themselves acquired validity in the course of externally induced change and amalgamation, while the indigenous peoples concerned have also become aware of the need for larger scale as the modern world closed in upon them.

The Concept of Tribe in Africa

Since the birth of African nationalism, tribalism has always been a sore subject and for very good reasons. Some nationalists have even gone so far as to claim that tribal divisions were the deliberate creation of a Machiavellian colonial policy of divide and rule. While it is doubtful whether most colonial administrators most of the time had sufficient knowledge of the internal structure of the traditional societies they ruled and sufficient expertise in social engineering to achieve what is credited to them by this view, there is a certain element of truth in it to the extent that many of the named entities which appear as tribes in the literature appeared for the first time during the colonial period and must in this sense necessarily be considered a product of it. One of the most striking and well documented cases is that of the Luhia in Kenya.

When the German anthropologist Günter Wagner went to Kenya in 1934, Kavirondo was simply a geographical area, so named from the time of the earliest Arab, Swahili and European traders and explorers, but not so known by any of its indigenous inhabitants. Wagner notes that "owing to its constant use by Europeans, the term 'Kavirondo' has nowadays been to some extent adopted by the natives, but they use it with reference to the district rather than to themselves.

When talking to other natives – even outside the district – they always style themselves by the name of their respective sub-tribe, such as Wanga, Vugusu, Logoli, Nyole, etc. Among politically minded natives who for a number of years have been pleading for a political unification of all Bantu Kavirondo tribes under a paramount chief according to the Buganda pattern, the word *avaluhia*, meaning 'those of the same tribe', is propagated as a common designation for all Bantu Kavirondo. The term 'Kavirondo', on the other hand, is generally rejected in these quarters as being of European origin" (Wagner, 1949: 20). Many other writers have pointed out that the term Kavirondo was regarded as opprobrious for various reasons, though agreement has never been reached as to its meaning or derivation.

Wagner himself, like many another ethnographer, vacillates over his use of the term tribe, applying it sometimes to one level, sometimes to another. "In pre-European days the various sub-tribes of Bantu Kavirondo were, for their greater part, very loosely organized politically, each sub-tribe consisting of a number of more or less sovereign clans. Since British rule was established in the middle of the nineties, they have been organized into chieftaincies." However, since traditional groupings varied in size and the colonial administration aimed at uniformity and convenience in the size of administrative units, there was the usual discrepancy between the definition of groupings on the one hand and administrative chieftaincies on the other. Next Wagner distinguishes the following tribes, corresponding to what he referred to as sub-tribes in the previous passage: Vagusu, Tadjoni, Wanga, Marama, Tsotso, Tiriki, Nyala, Kabras, Hayo, Marach, Holo and Logoli, to which must also be added the Idaxo, Isuxa, Kisa, Nyole and Samia. Among such acephalous peoples the exact number of groups properly to be distinguished may be genuinely ambiguous and debatable in some instances, but the above list would generally be accepted. Bethwell Ogot (1967: 138) speaks of "the seventeen Luyia tribes." Ogot further states (1967: 139) that "the name 'Baluyia' was first adopted by the North Kavirondo Central Association in June 1935. *The elders rejected the name*, (italics mine) and it was only after the Second World War that it gained general currency." This entirely accords with the experience of the present writer, who, arriving to teach at Makerere College in 1945, found that the whole group of Bantu speaking students from North Kavirondo called themselves Abaluyia and were never known as anything else.

It may be said that the Luyia people came into existence between approximately 1935 and 1945. Before that time no such group existed either in its own or anyone else's estimation. It was clearly due to the reaction of younger and more educated men to the exigencies of the colonial situation. It arose out of previous attempts at intertribal or supratribal organization and unity such as the North Kavirondo Central Association and Bantu Kavirondo Tax-payers' Association and led to further important organizations such as the Abaluyia Union, which came to represent the Luyia away from home, especially in the big towns such as Nairobi in Kenya and Kampala in Uganda. This new supertribe was closely linked to the colonial administrative framework, being in effect based upon and in part suggested by the administrative and territorial framework of the North Kavirondo District (subsequently renamed North Nyanza District because of the already noted pejorative aura of the word Kavirondo). In language and culture the Samia were just as much Luyia as the Hayo or Marach, but the unfortunate Samia were not only cut in two by the frontier between Kenya and Uganda, but even their Kenya half was situated administratively in Central and not North Nyanza District. Consequently Samia were never considered Luyia, and Samia away from home their own separate ethnic association.

In the original conglomeration of the Luyia in the 1930s and 40s the Vugusu were the largest numerical component. This in itself favored secessionist tendencies on their part, since they occupied a compact territory on the north side of the Luyia area. During the 1950s they began to agitate for, and eventually succeeded in winning, their own administrative district, which became known as Elgon Nyanza. With this the integrity of the Luyia supertribe began to crumble and it is now arguable whether the Vugusu are Luyia or not. ...

The fact is that many tribes have come into existence in a similar way to the Luyia, through a combination of reasonable cultural similarity with colonial administrative convenience, which in more recent times has often coincided with peoples' own sense of need for wider levels of organization to enable them to exert more effective pressure on events. The Luyia never did conform to the criteria of a tribe with which we started. Indeed, by the time they first came into existence they already diverged somewhat from every criterion mentioned.

The meaning of the name Luyia is instructive. Wagner explains (1949: 55) that "the stem -hia means 'to be hot', 'to burn'" and in a concrete sense the word olu-hia means "fire place on a meadow", hence "the fire-place as the centre of public life of the clan." "It is at this oluhia that the old men of the clan community meet every morning to warm themselves and to discuss the events and news of the day as well as to settle all important matters of the clan." Despite linguistic variation between the different Luyia groups they nearly all have this term and concept. The case of the Luyia is instructive because it is comparatively rare that an adequate documentation is available to demonstrate the process of appearance of new "tribes" with reasonable completeness. But the Luyia are far from being an isolated case and the process has close counterparts in many regions of the world.

To take an example from the other side of the continent of Africa, Labouret (1931), Fortes (1945), Goody (1957) and Tait (1961) have all extensively documented the fact that in a large and populous region, including adjacent parts of Ghana, Ivory Coast and Upper Volta, any single definitive boundary drawn between one "tribe" and another was bound to be relative, arbitrary and a misrepresentation of the facts. Colson (1951: 95) has demonstrated the same point for the Plateau Tonga of Central Africa (Zambia). It was not that these peoples were an undifferentiated mass, but that they were differentiated in many subtle and complex ways for different purposes. Any idea of the Lobi, Tallensi, LoDagaba or Konkomba as clearcut, isolated, enclosed tribes is a complete travesty of the facts. Legitimate authority did not inhere to or flow from any one unequivocal level of organization, but was contingent upon the situation. ... Much the same process of the picking up, fixing and generalizing by colonial authorities of names applied to vaguely defined peoples by their neighbors or other foreigners, seems to have occurred in the case of the Yoruba. "The term Yoruba is sometimes said to have been derived from a foreign nickname, meaning cunning, given to the subjects of the Alafin of Oyo by the Fulani and Hausa. The Hausa word for the Yoruba language is *Yarbanci*. Yoruba has been commonly applied to a large group, united more by language than by culture, *whose members speak of themselves* (italics mine) as Oyo, Egba, Ijebu, Ife, Ilesha and the other names of the various tribes" (Forde, 1951: 1). However, it is debatable whether the latter named entities are any more justly designated as tribes than the Yoruba as a whole. They might just as well be called city states. Johnson seems to agree with the Hausa or Fulani derivation of the name Yoruba, suggesting that the country was first known to Europeans from the north "for in old records the Hausa and Fulani names are used for the country and its capital; thus we see in Webster's Gazetteer 'Yarriba'" (1921: xix). This he equates with Yoruba but attempts no other derivation. But he continues "this country comprises many tribes governed by their own chiefs and having their own laws. At one time they were all tributaries to one sovereign, the King of Yoruba, including Benin on the East, and Dahomey on the West, but are now independent." There appears to be no historical foundation for this title of "the King of Yoruba," except for the supposedly wider influence of the kingdom of Old Oyo before the eighteenth century, and the ritual focus of all Yoruba upon Ife. It is like the legenday crediting of former suzerainty over Buganda, Ankole and other Inter-lacustrine states to a supposed Bunyoro-Kitara "Empire." Here too there has been a persistent confusion between political and ritual relations.

Group names with an ecological referent are common all over the world and often show a very poor correlation with valid divisions between one tribe and another on the basis of political, social, cultural and linguistic facts. Madagascar is a striking case. There we have the following generally accepted names and meanings, which may none the less be apocryphal in some cases: *Antanala* (the forest people), *Antandroy* (the people of the thorny cactus forest), *Antankarana* (the people of the rocks and caves), *Antanosy* (the people of the islands),

Antefasy (the people of the sands), *Antemoro* (the people of the coast), *Antesaka* (the people who catch small fish with the hands),[1] *Antsihanaka* (the people of the lake), *Betanimena* (the people of the red land), *Bezanozano* (the bush people), and *Sakalava* (the people of the long valleys, or of the broad and long plain). A few other Malagasy peoples have acquired non-ecological designations: *Betsileo* (the many who are not conquered), *Betsimisaraka* (the many who do not separate), *Mahafaly* (those who cause joy) and *Tsimihety* (those who do not cut their hair). It is said that growing their hair long made Tsimihety men look like women and facilitated their escape from slave raiders.

Even where these ecological terms are accurate, as in the case of Antanala, they refer to people in a particular habitat rather than to people with distinct socio-cultural characteristics. Ecology can be very important, but no one now would hold it responsible for all social and cultural differences. Other terms are vague and overlapping. Many Malagasy live on the sand besides the Antefasy, very many on the coast besides the Antemoro, and very many on red earth besides the Betanimena. The Antanosy do not in fact live on islands. *Antandroy* is a fair description, but these people were neither a cultural, historical nor political unity … Another common basis of tribal naming which is in a sense more structurally genuine than many of those so far discussed is derived from the names of primal ancestors which appear in genealogies, myths and legends as founders of the people. It is obvious that this kind of eponymy is particularly to be expected in the case of segmentary lineage systems with their strong emphasis on genealogical reckoning. In such society's conception of itself and its past there is usually a series of levels which phase into one another as they proceed further back in time. The nearest level largely consists of the ancestors of specific contemporary groups, whose genealogical relationships tend to express the contemporary relations of such groups and from one or other of whom every full member of the society can trace himself directly. Beyond this there is a vaguer level of tribal heroes about whose exploits, genealogical connections and even names there are differences of opinion between different members and sections of the modern community, though these are usually recognisably common variations upon central themes. Beyond this is the yet more shadowy realm of figures who represent the origins of man and society, the differentiation of human and divine, the expression of ultimate cultural meanings in symbolic form.

In these reaches all is relative, that which is "first" is so only in relation to that which followed. "For the deeper we sound, the further down into the lower world of the past we probe and press, the more do we find that the earliest foundations of humanity, its history and culture, reveal themselves unfathomable ... Thus there may exist provisional origins, which practically and in fact form the first beginnings of the particular tradition held by a given community, folk or communion of faith; and memory, though sufficiently instructed that the depths have not actually been plumbed, yet nationally may find reassurance in some primitive point of time and, personally and historically speaking, come to rest there" (Mann, 1963: 3). Not only is the beginning thus always relative, but almost invariably there is asymmetry and contradiction associated with it.

In the case of the great Somali people, who may justifiably be called a nation as forming the basis of a new nation state, among the usual rival derivations one of the most plausible is that which traces Somali to the eponymous ancestor of most of the northern pastoral Somali. The asymmetry and contradiction lies in the fact that "the Somali nation is composed of two parts, the Somali and the Sab. Strictly, the word 'Somali' does not apply to the Sab, who say themselves that they are 'Sab' and are so described and distinguished by the 'Somali'; nor is the Sab group subsumed under the name 'Somali' in the total genealogy of the Somali nation." (Somali and Sab appear in the genealogy in the structural position of brothers, both of common descent from the Qurayshitic lineage of the Prophet Mohammed.) "The Sab stand opposed to the Somali, and are grouped with them only at a higher genealogical level, when the two ancestors Sab and Somali, are traced back to Arabian origins, in the total genealogy of the inhabitants of Somaliland" (Lewis, 1955: 15 and 1961: 12). Instances of eponymous tribal naming are very numerous among peoples with segmentary lineage organization, such as the Tiv, Gusii and others already mentioned earlier.

The difficulty of identifying one "tribe" clearly and distinctly from another is often represented as a troublesome test which the anthropologist must pass. Thus, of the Australian Tiwi, because they lived on two islands, "fuzziness on the edges of tribal territory – a chronic headache to anthropologists working with mainland tribes – did not exist" (Hart and Pilling, 1964: 11). Or again of the Tiv, "the Tiv do not present that difficulty so common in Africa: identifying the tribe" (Bohannan, 1958: 35). The difficulty is undeniable, particularly in the case of stateless societies, and meticulous exploration of the distribution, interconnections and meaning of the various elements in culture and social structure is of vital importance in such situations, but insistence on defining some global discrete entity as a tribe may simply be a refusal to recognise the fundamental characteristics of this kind of society. I have argued elsewhere (Southall, 1968) that stateless societies have the combined characteristics of: multi-polities, ritual superintegration, complementary opposition, intersecting kinship and distributive legitimacy. The contingent nature of their structure, subdivisions and boundaries is of their essence, not something to be swept away by penetrating analysis. The representation of adjacent stateless societies as a neatly discrete series of named units is to misunderstand and misrepresent them.

Despite Bohannan's categorical statement on Tiv identity, Tiv is in fact a set of contradictions, as any stateless society must be when mistakenly regarded as a discrete tribe. "A Tiv is a Tiv and can prove it" because "every Tiv can trace his descent from Tiv himself." Yet this genealogy is "not in itself a record of ancestry," nor "a portrait of political structure, for its field of relevance is greater than that of the political while, on the other hand, not all political relationships are capable of expression in its idiom." For Tiv is actually the ancestor of non-Tiv peoples also, such as the Uge and Utange, and "the name of a linguistic and cultural entity which never (prior to British Administration) acted as a political unit." As with the Nguru-Luguru-Kaguru cluster of Tanzania, the named entity is, quite characteristically, at once too large and too small.

The Tiwi also, despite the apparent clarity with which they are defined by the accident of island isolation, turn out on closer inspection to have just that fuzziness which Hart and Pilling deny. For the Tiwi "did little as a member of a tribe. Only when an outsider turned up did he need to think of himself as a Tiwi, and outsiders were very rare. For the rest of the time he thought of himself as a member of his band, thought of his band as his people, and of his band territory as his country ... The nine bands thus acted, psychologically, as small tribelets or semi-sovereign groups" (op. cit. 12–13). Thus Tiwi too turns out to be something of an illusion. Even the band was "a flexible and constantly shifting collection of individuals" (op. cit. 1, 12). "The casual way in which people left one band and joined another shows that the band was in no sense a tight political or legal group" (op. cit. 31).

The further illusion seems to be cherished that at least with language we are on safer ground with an unequivocal factor defining clearcut groups. "All Tiwi, *of course*, spoke the same language" (op. cit. 11, italics mine). Yet among the Murngin, who are not so distant from the Tiwi, either culturally or geographically, "the members of each moiety are supposed to speak different languages ... Even each clan is said to have a 'language'; and some have a different dialect, but most within a given area speak the same one. The clans claim 'languages' of their own by giving themselves linguistic names in addition to group names" (Warner, 1937: 30). Rather than assume that language always defines a cultural entity, even when most other factors fail, we should assume that language is also one of the elements which groups in an acephalous, stateless society may purposefully and almost "artificially" use as a basis of distinction and identification, even when observed empirical differences are slight. "Of course," we may add, "the tribe is almost a non-existent unit among the Murngin" (Warner, 1937: 9). "The tribes of northeastern Arnhem Land, of which Murngin is one, are very weak social units, and when measured by the ordinary definitions of what constitutes a tribe fail almost completely. The tribe is not the war-making group. On the contrary, it is usually within it that the most intensive feuds are found. Tribal membership of the clans on the borders of two tribes is uncertain and changing, or the people may sometimes insist that

they belong to both tribes. Even clans well toward the center of a tribe's territory will, under certain circumstances, range themselves with another group" (Warner, op. cit. 35). The name Murngin is little used and the moiety names are used much more commonly.

Warner's account makes it very clear that the conventional concept of tribe was quite inappropriate to what he nonetheless called his "Social Study of an Australian Tribe." He uses the name Murngin purely for convenience. "The word Murngin (fire sparks) was found as a designation only after much effort. The people do not think of themselves under this name or classification. The word has been used by me as a general term for all of the eight tribes in the area and for the groups of people located in the central part of the territory of the eight tribes. I have seized upon this name as a convenient and concise way of talking about this whole group of people; had any of the other tribes who possess the particular type of social organization found in this area been located in the center of the group, I should have used the name of that tribe rather than Murngin" (Warner, op. cit. 15). Thus, Warner constantly uses the term tribe having said that "the tribe can hardly be said to exist in this area" (ibid.). Nor, of course, was the area of Warner's eight "tribes" clearly distinguished from neighbouring areas. It was simply the area within which he was able to accomplish field work. The relativities of the Murngin and Tiwi situations are duplicated in other instances too numerous to mention, such as the Yir Yoront (Sharp, 1958), which chiefly show that the situation long ago revealed by Radcliffe-Brown and others is no peculiar anomaly, but far more prevalent than they can have realized.

It is not so unlike the case of the Amba in Western Uganda, who include two main groups, the Bulibuli and the Bwezi, who speak two entirely different languages. By an asymmetry which is also a further characteristic of stateless societies, while both Bulibuli and Bwezi are Amba, the Bulibuli are also known as the Amba proper. Each village is either Bulibuli or Bwezi, but Bulibuli and Bwezi villages are interspersed. Each village was an independent political unit and "warfare between various villages was a constant feature" (Winter, 1958: 138). But the village was not a "self-sufficient system of action" chiefly because "the men of the village must obtain wives from the outside" therefore "even the internal organization of the village can only be understood ... in terms of its interrelationship with the larger structure of which it is a part" (Winter, op. cit. 139). Each village had a maximal lineage as its core and villages based on maximal lineages belonging to the same named clan and exogamous group were linked together in important ways. Thus we have again no one categorical level of organization which can properly be picked out from the rest, but rather a number of levels, all equally important for different purposes, a number of criteria defining essentially overlapping groups and categories, so that "friends on one basis are enemies on another" and conflicts become cohesion (Gluckman, 1955: 4, 19).

Needless to say, language is even less necessarily or obviously a criterion of tribe where higher levels of political specialization have been reached and diverse groups incorporated by conquest or assimilation. Thus, Alur society contained Nilotic, Sudanic and Bantu speakers, of half a dozen different languages (Southall, 1956, passim), and such situations were common in more elaborate state systems. The Azande, Lozi and many other conquering groups incorporated numerous diverse elements, which retained considerable cultural diversity ...

An attractively precise definition of tribe was developed by Evans-Pritchard (1940: 122). Although he defines Nuer tribes by nine very concrete and culture bound criteria (loc. cit.) the essence of the definition, which was adopted and long retained by many British social anthropologists is contained in the simple sentence: "local communities have been classed as tribes or tribal segments by whether they acknowledge the obligation to pay blood-wealth or not" (ibid.). Evans-Pritchard applied the same criterion to the Kenya Luo and other Nilotic peoples, Lienhardt applied it to the Dinka, Middleton to the Lugbara, Tait to the Konkomba and so on. For a while it became an article of faith in the context of a particular approach. It was most effective in relation to the immediate matter at hand – the exposition and clarification of segmentary lineage systems. Its chief disadvantages were that there were many other varieties of socio-political structure which it

did not fit and that it further confused and outraged the commonsense of the general reader by suddenly transforming what had always been known as single "tribes," "peoples," "societies," or "cultures," into tens, dozens and even hundreds of different distinct "tribes." For example, the Dinka were divided by Lienhardt (1958: 102) into some twenty five "tribal groups," and the three of these which he happened to know well contained 27, 10 and 6 "tribes" respectively, suggesting that the total number of Dinka "tribes" would amount to many hundreds.

As the enthusiasm for segmentary lineage systems passed its peak, this precise but severely limited usage of the term tribe lost ground and eventually fell into disuse. In practice, the term sub-tribe is now substituted for it in the same context. Thus Middleton (1960: 7) refers to the Lugbara as consisting of about sixty tribes, but subsequently (1963: 82) changed this to sixty sub-tribes.

Conclusion

The problem of ethnic classification as such is a special problem which we do not attempt to cover. We can only reiterate that no unidimensional classification of socio-cultural groups can provide an adequate basis for the comparative study of specific problems, let alone for frequency distributions, because the proper units of classification and analysis will vary according to the phenomenon and the problem studied. We must expect that comparative and generalizing studies of kinship systems or specific components of them, religious, symbolic or identity systems or specific components of them, political and economic systems or their components, and so forth, will always involve a plurality of units of analysis and fields of distribution. All attempts at establishing unequivocal, all-purpose, unidemensional classifications of socio-cultural groups involve grave danger of misrepresenting the nature of societies as anthropology knows them. To hammer home the importance of interlocking, overlapping, multiple and alternative collective identities is one of the most important messages of social and cultural anthropology ... There are three sets of problems associated with the tribal concept as we have examined it: problems of definition (ambiguous, imprecise or conflicting definitions and also the failure to stick to them consistently); problems of illusion (false application of the concept to artificial or misconceived entities) and problems of transition and transformation (use of the concept of tribe unjustifiably with reference to phenomena which are a direct product of modern influences). There is a considerable overlap between the last two sets of problems. As we have seen, there are many stateless societies where inaccurate definition has simply been the product of ignorance, illusion, or inattention; but very often the "definition by illusion" has been a definition of larger scale which became permanently adopted for administrative convenience and ultimately accepted by the people themselves. We may thus say that the problems of illusion have frequently been perpetuated by those of transition and transformation …

Problems of nomenclature may seem trivial, except insofar as they breed confusion and misunderstanding among anthropologists themselves, while at the same time rendering nugatory any influence which anthropology might have upon the world of scholarship as a whole. Where unresolved problems remain, agreement upon nomenclature is unlikely. What may legitimately be demanded is that nomenclature should be clear and consistent in each discourse, so that the problems of greater moment which lie behind it can be tackled. It is simply with this in mind that we would suggest calling "tribal" that traditional form of society which we described at the beginning. Once the empirical facts are recognized there should be enough consensus for adequate communication despite many minor differences of opinion. Tribal society may be largely a phenomenon of the past, but it is still of enormous intellectual and human importance.

The distinguishing of individual tribal units is a different and perhaps misconceived problem as we have seen. The solution should be very simple. Where discrete tribal units can be empirically demonstrated – well and good, where not, the temptation to speak or write as though some unique and all embracing discrete level of organization exists when the facts belie it should be resisted. The analysis and comparative study of tribal society should proceed on the basis of more specialized categories in the fields of kinship,

ritual, politics, economics, language and so forth. Stateless societies cannot be expected to present discrete boundaries except where special geographical or historical circumstances favour it. But chiefdoms and tribal states are more likely to do so the greater the degree of their political specialization. Yet by the same token they are less homogeneous and undifferentiated than has commonly been supposed. All our social and cultural constructs are bound to encounter intermediate cases when applied to empirical data, but it must be remembered that the intermediacy is as likely as not a product of the constructs rather than of the data. Nonetheless, the distinction of tribal societies in their lack of writing and records, their simple technology and direct subsistence economy, the absence of highly differentiated consumption patterns, the importance of the domain of kinship and multiplex relationships with all the institutional implications of these characteristics holds fairly well empirically.

When we move on from tribal societies in the full sense, which must increasingly be regarded as phenomena of the past, to the transitional situations which are prevalent today, there are again two main empirical types to be distinguished. There are the tribal societies which have been transitional sometimes for long periods, in relation to the dominant influence of ancient pre-industrial states and there are those which are transitional in relation to the post-industrial states which are almost exclusively those of the western world. This distinction has been important but is now itself becoming transitory. On another dimension there is the distinction between the transitional situation of communities, necessarily usually rural, and the transitional situation of individuals derived from such communities, which may also be urban, and indeed industrial. For the reasons already stated, it seems required by consistency and also by the human situation itself that the condition of individuals and groups in all the transitional situations of the contemporary world should now be described in ethnic and not in tribal terms. While all formerly tribal peoples are becoming increasingly subject to the ubiquitous pressures of the modern industrial world, there is the paradox that the former tribal peoples are mainly to be found within the confines of the less developed nations, whose economic condition, radically transformed though it is, is being left relatively further and further behind by the developed nations, so that in this sense one dichotomy is being substituted for another at a higher level.

For anthropologists this involves a poignant dilemma. Their whole discipline has been reared upon the discovery and study of forms of culture and society which held up a contrasting mirror to their own. More recently they have been adjusting, albeit slowly, to the prospective resolution of this contrast and to joining in the further exploration of man and society with colleagues who have actually emerged from the other side of it. But although these colleagues from the other world, the *tiers monde*, can truly enter an international world of anthropological scholarship, their hands are still tied by the fact that their new world has a meaning for them and us which is in unexpected ways as contrasted to ours as was the old tribal world which has passed away. This imposes a heavy strain and responsibility of understanding and sympathy.

Anthropology claims to be a universal discipline. Committed above all things to cross-cultural perspectives and to the transcendence of the ethnocentric myopia, it is naturally embarrassed by the colonialist taint which besmirches it in so much of the *tiers monde*. If western, and especially American, anthropologists are to avoid the charge that they are prostituting the discipline to assuage their personality problems, they will have to take much more seriously the complementarity of the contribution required from the new breed of anthropologists whose fathers or grandfathers were members of non-literate societies. If this contribution is to be made, and anthropology to avoid drifting into a blind alley as a bourgeois, essentially Western culture bound pastime, western anthropologists will have to stop calling primitive and tribal the contemporary communities from which their colleagues of the new breed come. This may be a case in which human feelings have to prevail over strict logic. It is also essential if anthropologists, preeminently equipped and destined for the task as they should be, are to contribute to bridging and healing the widening economic and credibility gap between the *tiers monde* and the West.

If asked what terms then can we use, since even the most neutral and logical can so easily become contaminated (as the disheartening sequence of: undeveloped, underdeveloped, less developed, developing, has shown), I should have to answer simply for the strategic moment, for the present critical and vital generation, that for the present the word primitive should be dropped from the vocabulary of social anthropology, however much it wounds our romantic souls, that the term "tribe" should usually be applied only to the small scale societies of the past which retained their political autonomy, and that the new associations derived from them in the contemporary context should be referred to as ethnic groups as other members of the category are.

Note

1 But see Deschamps & Vianès (1959) p. 92 for another interpretation.

References

Bohannan, Laura (1958) "Political Aspects of Tiv Social Organization", in Middleton and Tait (1958).

Colson, E. (1951). "The Plateau Tonga of Northern Rhodesia", in E. Colson and M. Gluckman (eds.). *Seven Tribes of British Central Africa*, Oxford University Press, London.

Deschamps, Hubert and Suzanne Vianès (1950). *Les Malgaches du Sud-Est*, Presses Universitaires de France, Paris.

Deschamps, H., and Vianès, S. (1959). *Le Peuple Malgache. I. Les Malgaches du Sudest*, Monographies ethnologiques de Madagascar, Presses Universitaires de France, Paris.

Diamond, Stanley (1964). "What History Is", in Robert A. Manners (ed.). *Process and Pattern in Culture, Essays in Honor of Julian H. Steward*, Aldine, Chicago.

Evans-Pritchard, E. E. (1940). *The Nuer*, Oxford University Press, London.

Forde, C. Daryll (1951). *The Yoruba-Speaking Peoples of South-Western Nigeria*, International African Institute, London.

Fortes, M. (1945). *The Dynamics of Clanship among the Tallensi*, Oxford University Press, London.

Gluckman, Max (1955). *Custom and Conflict in Africa*, Blackwell, Oxford.

Goody, J. (1957). "Fields of Social Control Among the LoDagaba", *Journal of the Royal Anthropological Institute*, Vol. 87, pt. 1, p.75.

Hart, C. W. M., and Pilling, A. R. (1964). *The Tiwi of North Australia*, Holt, Rinehart and Winston, New York.

Johnson, Samuel (1921). *History of the Yorubas*, CMS, Lagos, Nigeria.

Labouret, Henri (1931). *Les tribus du rameau Lobi*, Institut d'ethnologie, Paris.

Lévi-Strauss, C. (1961). *A World on the Wane*, Criterion Books, New York.

Lewis, I. M. (1955). *Peoples of the Horn of Africa*, Ethnographic Survey of Africa, International African Institute, London.

Lewis, I.M. (1961). *A Pastoral Democracy*, Oxford University Press (for International African Institute), London.

Lienhardt, Godfrey (1958). "The Aboriginal Political Structure of Bwamba", in Middleton and Tait (1958).

Mann, Thomas (1963). *Joseph and his Brothers*, trans. H. T. Lowe-Porter, Secker and Warburg, London.

Middleton, John (1960). *Lugbara Religion*, Oxford University Press (for International African Institute), London.

Middleton, John (1963). "The Yakan or Allah Water Cult among the Lugbara", *Journal of the Royal Anthropological Institute*, Vol. 93, pt. 1.

Middleton, John, and Tait, David, eds. (1958). *Tribes without Rulers: Studies in African Segmentary Systems*, Routledge and Kegan Paul, London.

Nyerere, Julius K. (1966). *Freedom and Unity: Uhuru na Umoja*, Oxford University Press, London.

Ogot, B. A. (1967). *History of the Southern Luo*, East African Publishing House, Nairobi.

Sahlins, Marshall D. (1961). "The Segmentary Lineage: An Organization of Predatory Expansion", *American Anthropologist*, Vol. 63, No. 2, Part 1, pp. 322–345.

Sharp, Lauriston (1958). "People without Politics", in Verne F. Ray (ed.). *Systems of Political Control and Bureaucracy*, American Ethnological Society, University of Washington Press, Seattle.

Southall, A. W. (1956). *Alur Society: A Study in Processes and Types of Domination*, Heffer, Cambridge.

Southall, A. W. (1968). "Stateless Society", *Internation Encyclopaedia of the Social Sciences*, Vol. 15, Macmillan, New York, pp. 157–68.

Steward, Julian H. (1958). *Theory of Culture Change*, University of Illinois Press, Urbana.

Tait, David (Jack Goody, ed., 1961). *The Konkomba of Northern Ghana*, Oxford University Press (for International African Institute), London.

Turnbull, C. (1967). "The Ik: alias the Teuso", *Uganda Journal*, Vol. 31, No. 1, March, pp. 63–71.

Wagner, G. (1949). *The Bantu of North Kavirondo*, Vol. I, Oxford University Press, London.

Warner, W. L. (1937). *A Black Civilization: A Social Study of an Australian Tribe*, Harper, New York.

Winter, Edward (1958). "The Territorial Pattern and Lineage System of Konkomba", in Middleton and Tait (1958).

7

Ethnicity in Southern African History

Leroy Vail

> Out of the crooked timber of humanity
> no straight thing can ever be made.
> (Immanuel Kant)

Interpretations

African political leaders, experiencing it as destructive to their ideals of national unity, denounce it passionately. Commentators on the Left, recognizing it as a block to the growth of appropriate class awareness, inveigh against it as a case of "false consciousness." Apologists for South African apartheid, welcoming it as an ally of continued white dominance, encourage it. Development theorists, perceiving it as a check to economic growth, deplore it. Journalists, judging it an adequate explanation for a myriad of otherwise puzzling events, deploy it mercilessly. Political scientists, intrigued by its continuing power, probe at it endlessly. If one disapproves of the phenomenon, "it" is "tribalism"; if one is less judgmental "it" is "ethnicity."

Ethnicity's emergence as a central concern for a wide range of students of African affairs is relatively recent, and its forceful intrusion upon the dominant nationalist paradigm of the 1950s and early 1960s was both unexpected and unwelcome.[1] At that time, it was accepted that Africans were organized naturally into "tribes," but, as nationalist movements in Africa were then apparently enjoying great success, most observers believed that parochial ethnic loyalties were merely cultural ghosts lingering on into the present, weakened anomalies from a fast receding past. As such, they were destined to disappear in the face of the social, economic and political changes that were everywhere at work. People from all sectors of the political spectrum believed in this vision. For those on the Right and in the Centre, "modernization" would do the job. Greater access to education, improved communications, and the shifting of people from the slumbering "traditional" rural sector of the economy to the vibrant "modern" industrial sector by the beneficent forces of economic growth guaranteed that ethnic loyalties would fade away. In their place would grow a new, nation-oriented consciousness which would underpin progressive "nation-building," especially

From Leroy Vail, *The Creation of Tribalism in Southern Africa*, copyright © 1988 Leroy Vail, from University of California Press, pp. 1–19.

if the new nation states could make good their promises of a better life for all their citizens. Africa would be a continent of new Switzerlands in which cultural divisions would be of little political importance.

For those on the Left, too, "modernization" was the key, although it was viewed from a somewhat different perspective. The breakdown of "traditional" societies by the forces of new, state-sponsored welfare socialism, with its expanded facilities in public education, medicine and agricultural programmes, would allow newly independent African states to "skip a stage" in the evolution of their societies towards socialism and to enter directly into that blessed condition. In effect, socialism would then provide the material base for a pan-ethnic class consciousness that would transcend, if not negate, cultural differences. Africa would be a continent of new Yugoslavias.

The general paradigm of "modernization," then, appealed to almost every political viewpoint. For almost every observer nationalism seemed progressive and laudable, while ethnicity – or, as it was usually termed, "tribalism" – was retrogressive and divisive.

Ethnicity, however, failed to cooperate with its many would-be pall-bearers. It soon became clear that African nationalist movements, ideologically shaped by the basically negative sentiments of anti-colonialism and with little substantive philosophical content relevant to the day-to-day life or ordinary Africans living in post-colonial states, were simply unable to provide them with compelling intellectual, social, and political visions. Once the attainment of independence had made most of its anti-colonial message irrelevant, nationalist "thought" was transformed into a gloss for the manipulation of the institutions of the new nation-states on behalf of the interests of the ruling political parties in a succession of one party states.[2] Much state activity was devoted to the pursuit of variously defined forms of "economic development," but such development proved elusive and the much-desired economic Fruits of Independence generally failed to ripen. That growth which did occur, moreover, was usually to the benefit of the dominant political classes and possessed little popular appeal.

As a result of this quick reining in of nationalism's popular thrust within the bureaucratic structures of essentially artificial post-colonial states, ethnic or regional movements rooted in the colonial era had fresh life breathed into them and came to be seen as attractive alternatives to the dominant political parties with their demands for uncomplaining obedience from the governed. In effect, the revitalization of "tribalism" was structured into the one-party system by the very fact of that system's existence. Ethnicity became the home of the opposition in states where class consciousness was largely undeveloped. Ethnic particularism has consequently continued to bedevil efforts to "build nations" to the specifications of the ruling party for the past two decades or more. This hard political fact has called forth ever more systematic repression of dissent by those in control of the state, thus, in effect, strengthening the appeal of the ethnic alternative. Ethnicity's future, even in countries such as South Africa, where industrialization has proceeded further than anywhere else on the continent, seems secure because it is likely to provide an important focal point for whatever opposition to the dominant political classes that might exist.

With its power to divide people politically, then, and with its sturdy resistance to erosion by the ideological forces of national or class consciousness, ethnicity came to demand close – albeit often very grudging – attention after decades of neglect. Its source and appeal needed reasonable explanations, and interpretations of it have ranged widely, reflecting its multidimensional nature.

The most prominent explanation – if only because of its widespread use – is the one that, despite the great frequency with which one encounters it in media coverage of Africa, is plainly the least satisfactory. In effect, this interpretation is a restatement of the old assumption that Africans are by nature "tribal" people and that "tribalism" is little more than an irrelevant anachronism, an atavistic residue deriving from the distant past of rural Africa. It should have evaporated with the passage of time, but, inexplicably, something went wrong, and it continues to refuse to obey the laws of social and political change. It thus remains able to motivate Africans to frequent actions of conflict and violence. Ethnic consciousness is, in this view, a form of collective irrationality.

The problems with this interpretation are clear. First, it is always dangerous to assume that people consistently act out of mass irrationality. People tend to act rationally, and there is no reason on the face of it to accept that Africans are exceptions. Second, this argument is, in effect, also a tautology with no analytical power, arguing as it does that Africans act "tribalistically" because they are naturally "tribal." Third, and most tellingly, empirical evidence shows clearly that ethnic consciousness is very much a new phenomenon, an ideological construct, usually of the twentieth century, and not an anachronistic cultural artifact from the past. As an offspring of the changes associated with so-called "modernization," therefore, it is unlikely to be destroyed by the continuation of these same processes. For all these reasons, then, this interpretation must be discarded.

Other, more scholarly interpretations have been suggested to explain the origin and persistence of ethnicity in Africa. All these interpretations have two things in common. First, they derive mainly from the work of anthropologists, sociologists and, especially, political scientists, observers who have been primarily concerned with the situation in Africa at the time they actually studied it. This has meant that their interpretations have usually been concerned with ethnicity's role at the moment of observation and its potential for the future. As such, they usually give only brief attention to its history, presenting whatever history that might be uncovered as mere "background" to ethnicity's contemporary role.

Second, all these interpretations are also marked by the fact that they have evolved out of the nationalist paradigm dominant from the 1950s into the 1970s. They implicitly accept a basically evolutionary view of human history. In this view, the future ought to be better than the past, and "better" has been identified with improvements assumed to flow from an increase in political scale and the growth of national unity – in short, from "nation-building." As a consequence, most such analyses of ethnicity are concerned with the way it has traduced the promise of modernizing nationalism and are thus predisposed to negative judgments. Their emphasis, therefore, has been on ethnicity's role as a disrupter of the promising trends of secular nationalism that seemed to characterize African politics in the late 1950s and early 1960s and to promise a rosy future.

The intellectual range of these interpretations of ethnicity has been wide. One viewpoint encountered frequently – especially within Africa itself – is that ethnicity is primarily the result of a history of "divide-and-rule" tactics which colonial governments cannily employed. European anthropologists connived at such policies by specifying "tribes" culturally within the context of a uniquely colonial sociology, thereby giving the "tribe" a real, but specious, identity. The element of truth in this explanation has made it superficially attractive, especially as the South African government today actively uses both approaches in its Bantustan policies and in its stress on the uniqueness of "tribal" culture, patent efforts to promote political divisions among the country's African population.

Yet whatever its merits, it is an explanation clearly insufficient to explain the persistence of ethnic consciousness. This is so for several reasons. First, it fails to explain why, in a particular territory throughout which the colonial state employed roughly the same divide-and-rule policies, ethnic consciousness developed unevenly, strong among certain peoples but not among others, a situation common throughout Africa. Second, it tends to depict Africans as little more than either collaborating dupes or naive and gullible people, beguiled by clever colonial administrators and untrustworthy anthropologists, a situation which empirical evidence fails to corroborate. Finally, it does not explain how, three decades after the departure of the colonialists, "tribalism," or its close kin, "regionalism," lives on as strongly as ever in independent African states, the governments of which have been actively trying to suppress it, and why in some places it is growing up for the first time. The clever blandishments of subtle European administrators are clearly insufficient to explain either the origins of ethnic consciousness or its continuing appeal today.

A second interpretation, especially prominent in the 1950s and early 1960s, arose from the study of urban sociology, especially in the mining areas of Central Africa.[3] Intellectually, it was linked to the Dual Economy model of "modernization" theory, and it located its interpretation of the development of new ethnic consciousness in the experiences of rural people in industrial workplaces. As members of various cultural groups left their isolated rural areas and interacted with each other in industrial or urban locales, they formed stereotypes of themselves and others, and these stereotypes effectively highlighted and strengthened culturally defined distinctions amongst peoples. The tendency of employers to prefer certain ethnic groups for certain types of work and their conscious manipulation of ethnic differences to keep the workforce disunited resulted in competition between ethnic groups being built into the hierarchically structured workforce. In this view, ethnicity was a recent phenomenon of the modern urban workplace in which boundaries and distinctions between people had been built up. It was not a phenomenon of the rural areas, where people were assumed to live in accordance with prescriptive patterns derived from a "traditional" past and where they were largely isolated from peoples of differing cultures. As such, some scholars, as well as most African politicians of the time, assumed that the but recently formed ethnic identities were still malleable and that they would prove susceptible to an easy transformation into a national identity through processes of political mobilization associated with "nation-building," especially if the labour unions representing such workers could be coopted into the national political establishment.[4]

This interpretation is certainly valuable for its underscoring of the important point that ethnic stereotypes were indeed largely produced in work situations and in urban settings. Yet it too is unable to serve as a general explanation of ethnicity's origin or, especially, its persistence. First, by emphasizing the boundaries that the creation of ethnic stereotypes among urban Africans produced, which, in turn, created opposing notions of "them" and "us," it overlooks the more substantive intellectual content contributed by African intellectuals to the specification of concepts of ethnic self-identity within those boundaries. Positive views about one's history, the heroes of one's ethnic past, and the manifestations of one's culture, especially language, quite simply did not spring automatically from the work situation or the urban centre, yet they have all been central in defining ethnic identities and ethnic ideologies.

Second, by stressing the essentially non-rural nature of the growth of ethnic stereotypes, this interpretation implicitly accepts the notion that

rural Africa was preserved in some sort of "traditional" pickle, antithetically opposed to "modern" industrial Africa and largely untouched by the forces of change associated with capitalist expansion and urbanization. Such a view of the existence of "two Africas" with but insubstantial linkages between them has by now been convincingly discredited.[5] Quite simply, the rural areas of southern and central Africa did not remain unchanged in a brine of "tradition," with meaningful change restricted to areas of obvious economic growth. Historical change affected the rural areas as much as it did the industrial and urban areas. More to the point, empirical evidence abundantly demonstrates that it is to the rural areas that one must look for most of the intellectual content of ethnic ideologies as they developed during the twentieth century in response to such change.

A third interpretation of the growth of ethnicity is that it resulted from uneven development within African colonial territories.[6] Certain people were able to do comparatively well from the educational and employment opportunities that colonial capitalism presented unevenly, with aspirant petty bourgeois groups able to establish themselves in some areas but not in others. When it became clear that the colonial era was nearing its end, these petty bourgeois groups mobilized support along ethnic lines so that they would be in a position to maximize their opportunities for access to resources and power after independence. This situation led in turn to the continuation of specifically ethnic politics in many countries of Africa, resulting in a rash of coups d'état and civil wars as ethnic fragments of the national petty bourgeoisie competed for their own advantage. From this perspective, ethnicity tends to be seen instrumentally, as little more than an ideological mask employed by ambitious members of upwardly-aspiring groups as a way of papering over growing class divisions within their ethnic group so as to secure their own narrow interests through demagoguery and mystification. Ethnicity, then, when ordinary people embrace it, is the very epitome of "false consciousness." ...

Finally, deriving from a Durkheimian notion of the importance of the role of the "community," or Gemeinschaft, there is the "primordialist" interpretation of ethnicity, an interpretation which now appears to be in the ascendancy amongst many scholars.[7] Its attraction lies in its serious attempt to answer the crucial question as to why the ethnic message possesses such strong appeal. This interpretation seeks the explanation in the realm of psychology. Africans, it is argued, were badly affected by the disruptive socio-economic and political changes of the late nineteenth and twentieth centuries. Pre-capitalist and pre-colonial hierarchies and elements of order in social life were undermined by the growth of capitalist relations and the impact of colonialism, thereby depriving people of social and psychological security. As a result, in a hostile world they have instead sought security through the invocation of a lost past of firm values as a way of recreating a life in which they can achieve emotional and, even, perhaps, physical safety. Ethnic identity provides a comforting sense of brotherhood in a world tending towards social atomization and rootlessness. Ethnic leaders represent and embody the unity of the cultural group. In this view, ethnicity is a kind of romantic rejection of the present. Enduring rather as religious fundamentalism or faith healing do in western societies, it is a reaction to the sterility of modern positivism and has become something akin to a civil religion with great emotional appeal.

Once again, this argument is attractive, particularly as the ethnic message, once established amongst people, does appear to be a part of the natural order of the universe. It categorizes people in accordance with inevitable, largely unselfconscious ascription: people belong to tribe X because they were born in tribe X and are, regardless of personal choice, characterized by the cultural traits of tribe X. Thus one is a member of a "tribe" not by choice, but by destiny, and one thus partakes of a set of "proper" customs.

Yet there are three serious problems with this interpretation. First, the mere appeal of, or belief in, a generalized idyllic past and the presumed unity of the ethnic group seem insufficiently definite to explain the relevance to people in specific historical situations of the statements that comprise constructed ethnic ideologies. Why have vague cultural statements about language or a common history or a hero from the past succeeded in "comforting" people or mobilizing them? Does ethnicity appeal because it is intrinsically "primordial," or is it constructed as "primordial" in its discourse to render it more generally appealing? What specific messages within the ethnic ideology actually appeal the most and to whom? And why? In short, the stress upon the "primordial" aspect of ethnicity tends to overlook both the actual intellectual content of the message, which can vary from group to group, and its varying appeal among different members of the same ethnic group.

Second, by stressing the backward-looking, "primordial" aspect of ethnicity, this interpretation fails to answer the central empirical question of how the most backward-looking ethnic ideologies, with their glorification of long-dead heroes and their delight in "traditional values," have been able at the same time to contain within them a powerful acceptance of western education and skills and a willingness to "change with the times." The emphasis on the primordial past does not take into account ethnicity's forward-looking aspect which, as commentators have frequently observed, gives it a Janus-like appearance. This is so, I suggest, largely because the role of class actors in creating and shaping ethnic ideologies has been largely overlooked. It is the direct appeal of fresh ideas and institutions to certain new classes that appeared in twentieth century Africa that has been translated into the progressive face of ethnic identity. The psychological appeal of primordialism and the concern for specific present-day interests of specific classes perhaps seem unlikely bedfellows, but they are real ones nonetheless and must be explained.

Third, and directly related to the first two problems, the emphasis upon a comforting past projects upon African people's ideas an unconvincing stasis. It is simply impossible to accept that Africans, living through some of the most rapid changes that any people have lived through in all human history, have attached themselves blindly, like so many limpets, to a vision of the past that has little relevance to the present and the future just because it is "comfortable." As an interpretation, the "primordialist" explanation of ethnicity, on its own, is simply too ahistorical and non-specific to convince. In analyzing ethnicity's real appeal one must instead try to relate its actual assumptions about the past to the current historical reality of those accepting them.

A History

Thus far historians have not devoted much attention to the history of ethnicity and ethnic ideologies in southern Africa. This is somewhat puzzling, especially as many have been aware for some time that ethnicity is not a natural cultural residue but a consciously crafted ideological creation.[8] It is likely that the explanation for this relative neglect lies in the fact that historians were, like other scholars, caught up in the nationalist paradigm that dominated the entire range of African studies in the 1950s and 1960s. They thus saw studies of the growth of ethnic consciousness as parochial, misconceived, and largely irrelevant to their main concerns at that time: the recovery of Africa's precolonial past and the exploration of the growth of anti-colonial resistance and its flowering into progressive nationalism. In the optimistic nation-building mood of the time, studies of ethnicity were also extremely unpopular with African opinion-makers, embarrassing even to mention, and they exerted pressure against studies that might further divisiveness in the new nation states they thought they were "building." Thus, the history of ethnic identities largely remained to be written....

The event which served as the catalyst for the melding of diverse peoples into such a unit as southern Africa, a region extending from Namibia to Mozambique, was the discovery of gold on the Witwatersrand in 1886. This initiated the building of Africa's single most potent economic force and attracted capital investment to other, less important focuses of investment, such as the copper mines of Zaire and Zambia, the farms and ranches of Zimbabwe, and the plantations of central Mozambique and southern Malawi. The links that were rapidly constructed to weld together the various territories of the region – and their societies – included ties of finance, trade, political influence, and, especially, migrant labour.

Yet the creation of such ties was necessarily differential, and great variation is to be found from one area to another within the region. In some places, such as Lesotho, the Transkei, southern Mozambique, northern Malawi, and western Zambia, links with the Rand's mines were direct and obvious: large-scale and persistent male labour

migrancy organized through the Witwatersrand Native Labour Association demonstrated clearly the dependence of these regions. In other places, such as the Zambian and Zairian Copperbelts, central Mozambique, and southern Malawi, local capitalist interests were able to dominate and the influence of the Rand was less obvious and less direct. In still other locales, such as parts of central Malawi, southern Zambia, and parts of Zaire and Swaziland, successful peasant production permitted local Africans to avoid both long-distance labour migrancy and working for local entrepreneurs. Nonetheless, the Rand's influence was everywhere present, if only as a model of labour relations and a distant, but powerful, economic presence. Although certainly uneven, the Rand's influence knitted the region's territories together.

As a consequence of the growth of capitalist relations of production both on the Rand itself in the 1890s and in other centres of capitalist endeavour that were established throughout the region shortly afterwards, the people of virtually all its societies experienced pervasive social, economic, and political change. The range of such change was broad, and many of the changes were clearly disadvantageous to the people affected. The capitalist enterprises of the region were all highly labour-intensive, requiring large and constant supplies of cheap African labour. To push Africans into the service of these enterprises, colonial governments imposed taxes, which in many areas could be paid only through men leaving their homes to participate in labour migrancy. These taxes were imposed during, or immediately after, a series of ecological disasters during the 1890s and the early 1900s that greatly weakened the fabric of local African societies. These disasters included drought, locusts and famine, but perhaps the key one was the great rinderpest epidemic of the mid-1890s, which killed livestock through the whole of southern Africa. Because livestock was widely reckoned as the embodiment of wealth, rinderpest's impact effectively constituted a gigantic mass bankruptcy for many societies. Moreover, as the exchange of cattle for women through the system of bridewealth (*lobola*) payments was the principal way in which many of the region's societies regulated marriage and the establishment of new families, it became socially necessary to work for money, using it either to restock the herds or as a substitute for cattle in the making of bridewealth payments.

Later, widespread alienation of African land, the establishment of overcrowded "native reserves," and the entrenchment of patterns of labour migrancy resulted in both impoverished villages and strained relationships within divided families. The labour demands of mines, plantations, and industries, coupled with governmental tax and land policies and the rising needs of people to purchase discretionary goods, pressed men out of the rural areas as workers, especially after the outbreak of World War I in 1914. It should be stressed that this process of rural transformation was not restricted to black Africans. The commercialization of agriculture in large areas of South Africa also undermined an Afrikaner society that had hitherto been characterized by paternalistic relations of clientage between Afrikaner grandees and poor Afrikaner tenants. This commercialization forced from the land white Afrikaners who had long had direct access to it. They moved into the growing cities of South Africa, where, because of their lack of education or marketable skills, they came to constitute a "poor white" problem of startling dimensions.

What was common for all the region's peoples – blacks and whites alike – was that many of them were gradually losing control over their lives as control over that most basic factor of production, the land, slipped from their grasp. No longer were rural communities – whether black or white – able to exist autonomously, beyond the reach of capitalism and colonial administration. At the same time that this rural transformation was occurring, the region's mixed-race groups, such as the "Cape Coloureds" of South Africa and the Luso-Africans of Mozambique, were suffering an erosion of their positions. Earlier, through possession of language and other skills, they had enjoyed relatively secure social and economic positions as intermediaries between whites and blacks. After the 1890s, however, these positions were successfully challenged by poor Afrikaners in South Africa and immigrant Portuguese whites in Mozambique, both of which groups increasingly benefited from the support of racist state institutions. Thus they, like blacks and

some white Afrikaners, were also caught in a process of declining control over their lives and destinies.

People of all these groups fought against the erosion of their positions. For many involved in this struggle land, and access to land, came to stand at the very centre of their consciousness, being fixed there not only at the beginning of the process of the undermining of rural autonomy, but also in succeeding decades. For white Afrikaners, land ownership was also important, kept alive as the ideal Afrikaner way of life even among the poor whites of the cities and towns.

For Africans, however, access to land remained a central issue for a more pressing reason. This was because, from the very start of the industrialization process, employers and government officials alike were determined to create a system in which unskilled workers would oscillate from the rural villages to work sites and then back to the villages and in which skilled positions would be held by whites. In this way, their wives and children would remain permanently behind in the rural areas, while the men would dwell in bachelor dormitories at the work sites for the duration of their contracts. Such a system had many advantages for both capitalist entrepreneurs and European administrators. For the employers it helped keep the working class fragmented and unorganized, and it allowed them to pay wages that were less than what would have had to be paid if the whole of a worker's family migrated and settled permanently as fully proletarianized people. For the officials it assured that there would be at least some money brought into the rural areas to help sustain village life there. In some cases, moreover, the migrant labour system also enabled governments to collect capitation fees for each worker recruited.

Migrant labour had less appeal for the workers themselves, but they had little choice in the matter. The need for money and the official pressures upon the men to work as migrants on contract, coupled with the establishment of effective recruiting agencies, resulted in the rapid institutionalization of the system of oscillating migrant labour as the standard mode of labour mobilization. But because the system was one in which workers were to move back and forth, even rural areas that were little more than unproductive rural slums necessarily remained of central concern for the migrants. On the one hand, they could not remain at home to supervise life in the village and oversee their wives and children. On the other hand, they could not abandon their rural homes. Laws prevented the relocation of families to work sites and strictly regulated the length of contracts a worker could assume. Thus, it was in the rural areas that the workers' long-term interests necessarily lay, for they would eventually return there when their working life was over. Even while absent for decades from the rural areas, then, the workers' concerns typically remained sharply focused on what was occurring at home. This situation could not but produce profound apprehensions in the migrants, and the capitalist era for them was – and still is – truly an age of anxiety.

While the majority of people were affected adversely by the changes produced by industrialization and capital investment, not everyone suffered. Indeed, the establishment of capitalist enterprises and colonial administrations provided a range of opportunities that many whites and some Africans could seize. Certain people were able to respond to the growing markets for produce, becoming peasant producers or even small-scale farmers, while in South Africa, Afrikaner agriculturalists on medium-sized and large farms prospered. Others, especially those able to gain an education or useful skills, were able to take up places in the social interstices that the changing economy opened up, becoming relatively well-rewarded teachers, ministers of religion, artisans, government clerks, or even small businessmen. In effect, then, the economic changes that followed on the establishment of the Rand's gold industry and the binding together of the far-flung areas of southern and central Africa into a regional economic unit were accompanied by a rapid and increasingly sharp differentiation of the region's peoples into more favoured and less favoured societies and of the societies themselves into more favoured and less favoured classes-in-the-making.

Such rapid social and economic change eroded earlier political relationships based on clientage both within and outside of lineages, social patterns, and religious beliefs, all of which had characterized societies during the nineteenth century. This erosion in turn opened the way for new forms

of consciousness throughout the region. Worker consciousness amongst both whites and blacks appeared spasmodically in situations of localized stress on the work site. Evidence of such class solidarity was shown at times of rapid socio-economic change, appearing in such events as the Rand Rebellion of 1922, the strike of copper miners on the Zambian Copperbelt in 1935, and the African mineworkers' strike of 1946 on the Witwatersrand gold mines. But class consciousness remained exceptional for as long as the working class was weak and fragmented and difficult to infuse with a sense of community.

New types of popular religious consciousness also appeared in the form of mainline Christian churches as well as separatist churches such as Watch Tower and a myriad of Zionist sects, and these shaped their adherents' evolving new self-identities. And among the educated clerks, teachers, clerics, and businessmen who emerged in the black, "coloured" and mixed race communities a petty bourgeois consciousness, with an acceptance of Victorian notions of respectability, progress and individual uplift through hard work, gained prominence.

One of the most far-reaching and important of these new forms of consciousness was a new ethnic – or tribal – consciousness that could and did encapsulate other forms of consciousness. Ethnicity could coexist with other types of consciousness without apparent unease because it was cultural and hence based on involuntary ascription, not on personal choice. People were members of a particular ethnic group whether they liked it or not. It was simply a fact of existence. As such, ethnic identity could inhere in both petty bourgeois and worker, in both peasant farmer and striving politician.

A Model

… The creation of ethnicity as an ideological statement of popular appeal in the context of profound social, economic and political change in southern Africa was the result of the differential conjunction of various historical forces and phenomena. It is the very unevenness of their co-appearance and dynamic interaction that accounts for the unevenness of ethnic consciousness in the region. One may discern three such variables in the creation and implanting of the ethnic message. First, as was the case in the creation of such ideologies elsewhere, for example in nineteenth century European nationalism, it was essential to have a group of intellectuals involved in formulating it – a group of culture brokers. Second, there was the widespread use of African intermediaries to administer the subordinate peoples, a system usually summed up in the phrase "indirect rule," and this served to define the boundaries and texture of the new ideologies. Third, ordinary people had a real need for so-called "traditional values" at a time of rapid social change, thus opening the way for the wide acceptance of the new ideologies. What emerges perhaps most clearly from these studies is the fact that intellectuals carefully crafted their ethnic ideologies in order to define the cultural characteristics of members of various ethnic groups. ...

The role of missionaries was especially crucial in at least one – and sometimes all – of three ways, and it is evident that their influence upon the development of African history in the twentieth century has been far greater than they have been given credit for over the past two decades. First, missionaries themselves were often instrumental in providing the cultural symbols that could be organized into a cultural identity, especially a written language and a researched written history. Samuel Johnson long ago recognized that "languages are the pedigree of nations," and missionaries accepted this dictum wholeheartedly. They had the skills to reduce hitherto unwritten languages to written forms, thereby delivering the pedigrees that the new "tribes" required for acceptance. It was the missionaries who chose what the "proper" form of the language would be, thus serving both to further unity and to produce divisions by establishing firm boundaries.[9]

In addition to creating written languages, missionaries were instrumental in creating cultural identities through their specification of "custom" and "tradition" and by writing "tribal" histories. Once these elements of culture were in place and available to be used as the cultural base of a distinct new, ascriptive ethnic identity, it could replace older organizing principles that depended upon voluntary clientage and loyalty and which, as such, showed great plasticity. Thus firm, nonporous and relatively inelastic ethnic boundaries, many of which were highly arbitrary, came to be constructed and were then strengthened by the growth of stereotypes of "the other."

Second, and of considerable practical importance, European missionaries, assuming that Africans properly belonged to "tribes," incorporated into the curricula of their mission schools the lesson that the pupils had clear ethnic identities, backing up this lesson with studies of language and "tribal custom" in the vernacular. Thus, mission education socialized the young into accepting a tribal membership, and to be a member of a "tribe" became "modern" and fashionable through its close association with education.

Third, and finally, missionaries educated local Africans who then themselves served as the most important force in shaping the new ethnic ideologies. These people – usually men – were keenly aware of the forces that were pulling apart their societies and, with the examples of nationalism in Europe derived from their own mission education before them, they sought to craft similar local movements as a means of countering these problems. Despite their own western-style education, they realized that such a construct would best be understood and accepted if it were put in a cultural idiom easily accessible to the people. Thus, in formulating their new ideologies, they looked to the local area's past for possible raw material for their new intellectual bricolage.[10] Like their European predecessors during the initial stages of nineteenth century nationalism, they "rediscovered" the "true values" of their people and so defined the "ethnic soul." Their cultural strongbox was the "customs" and "traditions" of the people, identification with which they saw as giving an automatic, ascriptive cultural unity to "their" people as they confronted the challenge of colonialism and the impact of industrialization. Several studies have been made which demonstrate the role of educated people as key actors in the creation of such ideology.

In those societies where missionaries did not work, or where they did work but did not introduce education along western lines, or where African intellectuals emerged only at a late period or not at all, the development of ethnic ideologies was either stalled or never occurred. The unevenness of education in southern Africa largely determined the unevenness of the development of ethnic consciousness. In many locales it is only today, after the post-independence expansion of education and the emergence of local intellectuals, that the process of creating such ethnic ideologies and "forging traditions" has emulated what happened earlier in other societies.

It was not sufficient, however, that there should be local intellectuals – white or black – interested in the recovery of the ethnic past. A second, more instrumental factor was also required. All of southern Africa was under direct European administration of various types, and by the period after World War I, virtually all administrations were engaged in implementing systems of indirect rule, using African "traditional" authorities as intermediaries between the white administration and the ruled. Thus, if language in the form of written discourse was central in specifying the forms of culture, indirect rule provided the institutional framework for articulating these forms. Communication between the European administrators and subordinate Africans was distinctly tribal in its tone and content. Africans were talked to in terms deemed suitable, and these terms were ethnic. In the cases of the "Cape Coloureds" and the Luso-Africans of Mozambique, and, to some extent, the Afrikaners, for whom the conventions of indirect rule were not suitable, they were simply denied representation.

There were several reasons for the European policy of indirect rule. First, there was the realization that the use of so-called "traditional" African leaders could be markedly less expensive than the employment of expensive European officials. Second, administrators assumed that Africans were naturally "tribal" people. If the natural ethnic units could be strengthened, it would help ensure their continuation as discrete "tribal" groups and prevent the emergence of "de-tribalized" Africans of whom whites were deeply suspicious. This, in turn, would slow the emergence of any potentially dangerous territory-wide political consciousness that might develop. The remarks of a British War Office official in 1917 reflect these divide-and-rule tactics:

[The] spirit of nationality, or perhaps it would be more correct to say, of tribe, should be cultivated and nowhere can this be done with better chance of success than in British East Africa and Uganda, where there are numerous tribes ethnographically quite distinct from one another. It is suggested that in each ethnographically distinct district the schools should, as far as possible, form integral parts of the tribe and centres of folklore and tradition. ...

... a method may also be found whereby the efforts of missionaries may also assist in the cultivation of national spirit. This it seems might be done by allowing only one denomination to work in each demographic area and by not allowing the same denomination to work in two adjacent areas.[11]

Third, by the end of World War I it was becoming increasingly evident that the chronic absence of men from rural societies was producing great social stresses. The administrators became convinced that the rural disintegration occurring before their eyes could be slowed, if not stopped, by the encouragement of "traditional authorities" to use "traditional sanctions" in exercising control over the rural areas to counter the forces of social decay.

This acceptance of indirect rule by European administrations obviously gave opportunities to African political authorities to augment their personal power. More importantly, I suggest, it gave opportunities to the intellectuals of the areas concerned – both European missionaries and African members of the educated petty bourgeoisie – to implement their ideological programmes through alliances with the newly recognized chiefs. In this way the cultural ideals contained in their new ideologies could be at least partially actualized in the day-to-day workings of African administrations under indirect rule. Ethnic identity, thus, came to be specified not only by the written histories, grammars, and accounts of "traditional customs" produced by local culture brokers, but also – and in many respects, far more importantly – by the actual operation of the administrative mechanisms of indirect rule. This aspect of the development of ethnic identity was the consequence of the dynamic interaction of African initiative with the expectations of European administrators and forward-looking missionaries. It should be remembered, however, that the subordinate peoples did not have a free hand in their work as they had to operate within the severe constraints imposed by racist administrators who were ever alert to check initiatives deemed either unseemly or dangerous.

The presence of intellectuals, the socialization of ethnic ideas through mission schools and through the actual operation of administrative systems under indirect rule to strengthen "tribal" rule were, however, by themselves inadequate to produce a broad acceptance of an ethnic ideology. The ideology itself needed a raison d'être and an appeal, and it was this appeal that constitutes the third factor in our model of the growth of ethnicity in southern Africa.

The ideologies of nationalism have often been described as "Janus-like." They are in one aspect profoundly reactionary, looking backwards to a Golden Past: they concentrate upon its heroes, its historical successes, and its unsullied cultural purity, and are decked out with the mythic "rediscovered" social values of that past. In Africa, the explicit association of such ethnic ideologies with chiefs and headmen whose position was often firmly rooted in the past was an additional factor in accentuating the backward-looking face of ethnicity. Yet these ideologies were also clearly products of the present, concerned with current conditions, and they typically exhibited a forward-looking concern for the future. Nationalism – and tribalism – have thus appeared uncertain and ambiguous to many observers.

Yet when one looks closely at the situation in southern Africa, one comes to realize that the ethnic message's backward-looking aspects and its forward-looking concerns have been in no way contradictory. The emphases on past values, "rediscovered" traditions, and chiefly authority were truly conservative – that is, they were calculated to conserve a way of life that was in the process of being rapidly undermined by the forces of capitalism and colonialism. Forward-looking members of the petty bourgeoisie and migrant workers alike attempted to shore up their societies and their own positions in them by embracing ethnicity and accepting tribal identities.

Ethnicity appealed to the petty bourgeoisie because its forward-looking aspects ensured them a leadership role in the newly defined "tribe" as the well-informed interpreters of "tribal tradition."

Their position as allies of chiefs further legitimized their role, blunting consciousness of the class divisions that were then appearing in local societies. In this situation, it was generally accepted that they also had a duty to improve their own social and economic positions "for the good of the tribe."

Far more importantly, ethnicity appealed strongly to ordinary African men, not primarily because it gave them a sense of psychological comfort, as the primordialist interpretation argues, but because it aided them in bringing a measure of control to the difficult situations in which they found themselves in their day-to-day life. The word "control" is crucial. It was the element of control embedded in tribal ideologies that especially appealed to migrant workers, removed from their land and families and working in far distant places. The new ideologies stressed the historical integrity of the tribe and its land and, especially, the sanctity of the family and its right to land.[12] Land stood at the very centre of ethnic ideologies.

The place of women was also a central issue dealt with in ethnic ideologies. In the early decades of the century bridewealth steadily inflated in value, and women thus represented a greater "investment" by men in cattle or money. With most men absent as migrant labourers, women were also becoming more important to the day-to-day survival of the family through their work on the land. Yet such valuable women naturally often sought to act independently, even to the extent of seeking divorces or leaving the rural areas illegally to move to industrial and urban areas. This produced acute conflict between the genders. Therefore an emphasis on the need to control women and a stress on the protection of the integrity of the family came to be intrinsic to both ethnic ideologies and the actual institutional practices of indirect rule. Ethnicity's appeal was strongest for men, then, and the Tswana proverb to the effect that "women have no tribe" had a real – if unintended – element of truth in it.

Ethnic ideologies helped to provide the control necessary to minimize migrants' natural anxieties about what occurred at home. In the system of indirect rule, the chiefs were of central importance. It was they, with their new official histories, their new censuses and lists, their new courts and records, all of which employed for the first time that most fundamentally powerful invention, writing, who were now able to exercise a greatly increased degree of surveillance over both women and land in the absence of the men. It was they who brought into daily practice those "rediscovered traditions" which emphasized control in the name of "custom." The old dictum that "all politics is local" was especially valid throughout southern Africa. African men and their lineages accepted that it was in their essential interest to support the new structures of chiefs, their courts, and their educated petty bourgeois spokesmen and agents. It was also for this reason that men, when returning at the end of their contracts from the mines or farms or plantations, gave chiefs the gifts that constituted one of their most important sources of income. The good chief was a proxy who protected the interests of the migrant workers and, for that, they were ready – if not eager – to reward him materially. In effect, the bureaucratized chief of the newly constituted "tribe" had replaced the lineage head or independent patron of earlier times, and the old language of kinship came to be employed as metaphor to sustain and legitimize this new, obviously non-kinship relationship.[13]

It was for very real reasons of exercising at least a measure of control over land and women, thereby bringing at least a measure of peace to their minds, that African men welcomed the new ethnic ideologies which involved augmenting powers of chiefs in a situation of rapid social decay. Ethnicity, insofar as it was a mechanism of such control, may be interpreted, then, as a form of popular male resistance to the forces that were reshaping African lives throughout southern Africa. It was for this reason also that the appeal of ethnic ideologies was strongest amongst those who were migrant labourers. The ethnic identity that was rooted in the realities of the countryside was, rather incidentally, strengthened in the workplace, where migrants found themselves in the company of, and often in competition with, workers from other cultural groups, a situation which generated sets of largely negative ethnic stereotypes.

Men came to think of themselves as belonging to particular ethnic groups, then, not because they especially disliked their fellow workers, nor because being a member of the group made them feel good, but rather because the ethnic apparatus of the rural area – the chiefs, "traditional" courts, petty bourgeois intellectuals, and the systematized "traditional" values of the "tribe" as embodied in the ethnic ideology – all worked to preserve the very substantial interests which these men had in their home areas. Without ethnicity – or tribalism – the migrants would have been less able to exercise the control that was necessary for them to assure the continuation of their positions in rural societies and their ultimate retirement in their home areas.

In those situations in which labour migrancy was not a pressing reality (the Afrikaners, the "Cape Coloureds," the Luso-Africans of Mozambique and, to a lesser extent, contemporary Swaziland and Ciskei) … or in areas from which men did not emigrate in large numbers, such as southern Zambia and central Malawi, the ethnic message has clearly had less popular appeal, reaching no further than the petty bourgeoisie in most cases. In the case of the Afrikaners, effective class alliances between the bourgeois elements of society and the "poor whites" were brought into being only in the 1940s and afterwards. In the case of the "Cape Coloureds" and the Mozambican Luso-Africans – and possibly Swaziland and the Ciskei – the gaps between well-off and poor were too great to be easily overcome by appeals to ethnicity. In these situations, class identity – or at least class tension – has tended to overshadow ethnicity.

[…]

Notes

1　As I was preparing to write this Introduction, I was fortunate to have made available to me a preliminary version of Crawford Young's magisterial summing up of the literature on "Class, ethnicity and nationalism," which has influenced my approach considerably. Young's stimulating and valuable essay was written for the Social Science Research Council, and it will be published in a future issue of *Cahier d'études africaines*. Two other studies which influenced my writing markedly are Anthony Giddens, *A Contemporary Critique of Historical Marxism* (Berkeley and Los Angeles, 1981), and Donald L. Horowitz, *Ethnic Groups in Conflict* (Berkeley and Los Angeles, 1985). The literature on ethnicity is immense and I have decided to eschew any attempt to produce a bibliographical essay. I shall attempt to write an interpretative overview.

2 The situation is reflected in the fact that many political leaders felt the need to fabricate a "philosophy" of government in an attempt to compensate for the intellectual banality of the nationalist movements after independence. These "philosophies" generally had far greater appeal for well-intentioned non-nationals than for those dwelling within the particular countries for which they were composed.

3 Most notably, A.L. Epstein, *Politics in an Urban African Community* (Manchester, 1958), and J.C. Mitchell, *The Kalela Dance* (Manchester, 1958).

4 For example, I. Wallerstein, "Ethnicity and national integration," *Cahiers d'études africaines*, 1 (1960), pp. 129–39.

5 As in R. Palmer and N. Parsons, eds., *The Roots of Rural Poverty in South and Central Africa* (Berkeley and Los Angeles, 1977), *passim*.

6 This point was developed at an early point of study in J.S. Coleman, *Nigeria: Background to Nationalism* (Berkeley and Los Angeles, 1958) and in R. Lemarchand, *Political Awakening in the Congo* (Berkeley and Los Angeles, 1964). Interest in it has been stimulated more recently by the publication of such influential books as M. Hechter, *Internal Colonialism* (Berkeley and Los Angeles, 1975) and T. Nairn, *The Break-up of Britain: Crisis and Neo-Nationalism* (London, 1977).

7 As, for example, in Horowitz, *Ethnic Groups in Conflict, passim* and A. Giddens, *The Nation-State and Violence* (Berkeley and Los Angeles, 1985), *passim*, but especially pp. 212–221. See also J.F. Stack, Jr., ed., *The Primordial Challenge: Ethnicity in the Contemporary World* (Westport, CT, 1986).

8 Iliffe's *A Modern History of Tanganyika* (Cambridge, 1979) contains much relevant material regarding the history of ethnicity in Tanganyika. For the Afrikaners of South Africa, one should see D. Moodie, *The Rise of Afrikanerdom: Power, Apartheid and the Afrikaner Civil Religion* (Berkeley and Los Angeles, 1975); H. Adam and H. Giliomee, *Ethnic Power Mobilized* (New Haven, 1979); and D. O'Meara, *Volkskapitalisme: Class, Capital and Ideology in the Development of Afrikaner Nationalism, 1934–1938* (Cambridge, 1983). This point has been made often for European nationalism, in such important studies as Barrington Moore's *Social Origins of Dictatorship and Democracy: Lord and Peasant in the Making of the Modern World* (Harmondsworth, 1967).

9 For an interesting, although not wholly convincing, assessment of the central role of language in the building of nationalism, see B. Anderson, *Imagined Communities: Reflections on the Origin and Spread of Nationalism* (London, 1983).

10 It should be noted that intellectuals discussed in the chapters of this volume are all literate intellectuals. The nature of the evidence makes it difficult to ascertain the nature of the thought and work of non-literate intellectuals, yet it should be kept in mind that such non-literate intellectuals have indeed worked to further ethnic ideologies through oral genres. This whole topic is the subject of a forthcoming study by L. Vail and L. White.

11 Malawi National Archives, GOA 2/4/12, "Mohammadanism and Ethiopianism", Circular letter, Lt. Col. French to Gov. Smith, 7 Aug. 1917.

12 M. Chanock, *Law, Custom and Social Order: The Colonial Experience in Malawi and Zambia* (Cambridge, 1985), is an important study that goes far in exploring the role of the perceived need to control women in the development of concepts of law during the colonial period.

13 The relevance of the language of kinship ties to the development of ethnic identity is explored, within a basically primordialist interpretation, in Horowitz, *Ethnic Groups in Conflict*, pp. 55–92.

Part III

Economics as a Cultural System

Introduction

The extraordinary variety and number of studies on African economics make it virtually impossible for us to summarize them in the scope of this introduction and this volume. These studies include ethnographic analyses of households (Guyer, 1981), local and regional economic histories, including histories of the slave trade and state formation (Harms, 1981; Kopytoff and Miers, 1977; Southall, 1974), the impact of migrant labor on local community life (Murray, 1981), Marxism (Coquery-Vidrovitch, 1978; Donham, 1990; Meillassoux, 1981), migration and urbanization (Cohen, 1969; Epstein, 1958; Mayer, 1962; Mitchell, 1956; Southall, 1973; Watson, 1958), political economy (Berry, 1978, 1984; Hart, 1982), economic development and transformations in agrarian and pastoral systems (Ferguson, 1990; Fratkin et al., 1994; Little and Watts, 1994; Robertson, 1987; Werbner, 1982), and the economics of gender (Apepoju and Oppong, 1994; Boserup, 1970; Moodie and Ndatshe, 1994; Moore and Vaughan, 1994). Given the vast number of different kinds of economic studies conducted in Africa, the reader may well question whether it is possible, or fruitful, to treat economics as a distinct domain of analysis. We have therefore limited ourselves in this section to a few key texts that illustrate some central perspectives on the study of African economies, and which quite directly inform, or speak to, the readings in other parts. For example, Hutchinson (Chapter 10) and Evans-Pritchard (Chapter 5) worked in the same part of Africa, with the same population, and on similar issues, and so each of these articles contributes to a fuller understanding of the other.

In this volume, the texts that make up the chapters on social organization (Part II), hunter-gatherers (Part IV), gender (Part VIII), colonialism (Part IX), post-colonial politics (Part X), and development and globalization (Part XII) are very much concerned with economics; although the putative focus is on issues such as sex roles, ethnicity as a social boundary, or the impact of European domination upon local values, the essays are more broadly concerned with how these issues are integrated with production and material and social exchanges. All are explicit about how economics relate to other domains. Such attention to integration is, for many scholars, the hallmark of an anthropological economics, if not of the study of social organization in general, and distinguishes anthropology from the economic sciences. LeClair and Schneider thus write about the anthropologist's emphasis on social and cultural factors in economics (1968: 7):

> Economists traditionally could and did take the economic system as something of an isolate in the total social system. It could be studied in its own terms, and it was simpler to do so. By the same token, economists did not delve too much into ends in themselves; operating within a single cultural context, they could take ends as they were and felt no need for explaining them. Operating within a single social framework, they could afford to concentrate their attention on the economic system. Thus, the social and cultural systems were "given" parameters which did not need to be taken into account in the analysis.

From an anthropological viewpoint, economics must always be situated in its total sociocultural context. To illustrate how anthropologists developed such a perspective, we shall briefly outline some of the most important works and debates in the history of economic anthropology.

In a seminal work on inter-island exchange in a place far from Africa – the Trobriand Islands near Papua New Guinea – the early anthropologist Bronislaw Malinowski (1922) described a fascinating exchange system called the Kula ring. His data suggested that Western models of economic behavior were not applicable to all societies, and more specifically, that the model of the economizing individual, motivated to employ scarce means for the maximum benefit, might not be fruitfully applied to non-capitalist, non-industrial societies. Malinowski's description of the Kula ring, in which the Trobrianders move among a ring of islands to give and receive valuable armshells and necklaces, supported such a conclusion because the Trobriands expend more time and energy on the collection of the valuables than would seem economically "rational" to many Western observers. The armshells and necklaces were not, at the time of his study, convertible to cash or many other goods, nor did owning these goods translate directly into greater wealth. The meaning of the trade was symbolic and aesthetic, defined by cultural values and not by the standard sorts of maximization models one finds in American economics textbooks that, "all other things being equal," individuals will maximize their gains with an insufficiency of means. Anthropological economics thus developed as a perspective that emphasized social values and conformity over and above individual choice, utilitarianism, and "rationality."

Of course, all other things are never equal, and so such models may also not be applicable to all social and economic behavior in Western societies. We know, for example, that in the United States businesses succeed and fail on the basis of religious holidays, such as Christmas, Hannukah, Kwanzaa, and Easter, that we often spend far more on our vacations, automobiles, and children's weddings than is truly "economical," and that, indeed, the whole set of practices we call gift giving constitutes a system in which we pay for symbols and meanings, prestige, love, favor, and for the future, rather than for immediate gratifications of material goods. Economists would, no doubt, be among the first to argue that they are always concerned with the non-material questions of economics, such as how much people will pay for, or fail to maximize for, leisure, vacations, or prestige and luxury goods. Yet, conventional economic perspectives frame these questions *in terms* of maximization and choice, rather than in terms of cultural value.

For many economic anthropologists, however, there can be considerable value in applying economic theories across cultures if we search for the fit and non-fit between scientific and local models. Assessing the degree of fit can quickly bring to light how people define their economic needs differently, and we may even learn that certain economic needs are characteristic of particular kinds of societies. Marshall Sahlins (1968, 1972), for instance, has suggested that hunter-gatherer societies in general, and the !Kung San of Botswana in particular (see Part IV), do not try to maximize their economic benefits. Responding to some conventional assumptions that the subsistence economies of all hunter-gatherers, past and present, have been dismal and "poor," Sahlins calls hunter-gatherers the "original affluent society":

> This was, when you come to think of it, the original affluent society. By common understanding an affluent society is one in which all the people's wants are easily satisfied; and though we are pleased to consider this happy condition the unique achievement of industrial civilization, a better case can be made for hunters and gatherers ... For wants are "easily satisfied," either by producing much or desiring little, and there are, accordingly, two possible roads to affluence. The Galbraithean course makes assumptions peculiarly appropriate to market economies, that man's wants are great, not to say infinite, whereas his means are limited, although improvable ... But there is also a Zen solution to scarcity and affluence, beginning from premises opposite from our own, that human material ends are few and finite and technical means unchanging but on the whole adequate. (1968: 85)

Sahlins' argument is framed very much in terms of maximization models, but it is, at the same time, a powerful critique of the assumptions surrounding the concept of scarcity in the economic sciences (see Bird-David, 1992). The readings in Part IV on hunter-gatherers address this issue again in the context of a debate about the !Kung San, and present the more general problem of how and why we sometimes group culturally variable societies under single economic categories, such as "hunter-gatherer," "pastoralist," or "peasant."

We want to stress that practices which do not fit the Western model of "Economic Man" (*Homo economicus*) are therefore not irrelevant to more conventional economic analyses, and while the kinds of economic activities anthropologists sometimes describe, such as the Kula ring, or gift-giving, may seem abstract or symbolic rather than material and productive, these activities often have significant effects on material life. For example, recent research in the Trobriand Islands has shown that when Trobrianders go on trading trips, made ostensibly to obtain Kula valuables, they actually engage in a wide range of other trading activities, including trade for foodstuffs and other important materials for house and canoe building. The trade for Kula valuables functioned to reduce the variable scarcity of certain foods and other products over a wide geographical area in the Trobriand archipelago, and the trading activities themselves helped to solidify partnerships and alliances that could be exploited in the event of future crises such as natural disasters, food depletions, or war (Singh, 1962). Establishing a single determining role is, of course, a chicken and egg problem — whether the adaptive advantages of trading Kula objects determined the values attributed to them, the adaptive advantages were an unintended byproduct of the Kula system, or the consequent adaptive advantages led Trobrianders to reinforce a pre-existing Kula trade. The point to be stressed here is that economics must be seen in their total social context, not only because economic behavior is always, already, socially meaningful, but because it ramifies to all areas of social life, including those we might not assume to fall under the rubric "economy."

One of the scholars most impressed by Malinowski's Kula data was the French anthropologist Marcel Mauss, a student and nephew of Émile Durkheim. Like his uncle, Mauss focused on the society rather than the individual, and was thus interested in answering the questions we raised in the first chapter. How do societies cohere? In his book, *Essai sur le don* (translated as *The Gift*), Mauss (1954 [1925]) concluded that social solidarity is generally achieved by means of gift exchange, and therefore that gift giving and receiving are fundamental to social life. He argued that reciprocity, while seemingly a voluntary behavior, involves complex moral and social obligations because the objects that people give are never totally separated from them: gifts bind people together in social relationships, and so we are socially and morally obliged to reciprocate. If you are an anthropologist and you need to understand a society, looking at gifts is a good way to go about it. Gifts, he said, betray "all the threads of which the social fabric is composed" – religious, legal, moral, economic, aesthetic, and morphological (Mauss, 1954: 1).

Gifts may not exactly fit economists' models of "economic rationality," but they are perhaps "socially rational," to the extent that gift giving is an economic activity that is fundamental to ongoing social life. Mauss had a profound impact on anthropology, and economic anthropology in particular, because his focus on gifts led cross-cultural economics away from the study of individual rationalities and toward the study of social, collective values; moreover, he showed that exchanges can also involve persons and symbols.

Marriage, for example, is a common form of social and economic exchange, or gift exchange, in which two families join together through the "giving" of the bride and groom, the transfer of gift objects, or the establishment of bridewealth or other debt, between families. There is an old saying in many parts of the world: "marry your enemies." Thus, in Shakespeare's *Henry V*, when England and France seek to end their war, young Prince Hal of England marries Princess Catherine of France, and the result is peace and social solidarity between in-laws and also between countries. In the United States, we often think of marriage as defined by a single event – a wedding – but in many parts of the world, especially in sub-Saharan Africa, marriage is a complex political and economic process of gift giving and payment that can take many years, if not generations, to complete. Some African men and their families give marriage their highest priority, working for years to save enough money or goods for bridewealth, and subsequent payments. Among the Lese of the Democratic Republic of Congo, for example, a man must pay an initial amount of money to the bride's father or brother to set a marriage in process, another amount for rights of sexual access, and, over the years, later payments for rights in his offspring (what we might call "childwealth," and which the Lese call an "umbilical cord payment"); if the childwealth is not paid, the father cannot claim the child as his own, and the child must take his mother's clan identity. The first editor, who worked in a Lese community, could not find a single case in which all the payments had been made in full. When someone approached completion of payment, the in-laws would raise the price, justifying it on the basis of inflation, or the wife's fertility and good work. In fact, in-laws want their daughter's husband to remain in debt, fearing that if all the payments were made, the husband (and wife) might sever connections with them. Money may be spent, goats and chickens may be eaten; but debts remain. Even after all of these payments have been made, a man's in-laws may demand gifts to compensate the wife and her family for all the hard work entailed in raising small children (the Lese call this a "feces and urine payment" because the payment refers to the time of childrearing prior to toilet-training), or may require a death payment when she dies. On one occasion, a man was denied access to land and wealth he thought he had the rights to when it was determined that his grandfather (father's father) had failed to make the umbilical cord payments for genetricial rights. He and his deceased father were thus denied full membership in the clan, and rights in the clan's land.

That gift giving is a powerful institution with important social and symbolic ramifications is illustrated by an interesting variation in the sound /gift/ across some different European languages. In English, /gift/ means "present," in German, /gift/ means "poison," and in Danish and Swedish, /gift/ means both "married" and "poison." The definitions of "married" and "present" are by now clear, but what of "poison"? The poison in the gift lies in its ability to obligate; it coerces reciprocation and constitutes a relationship into which the receiver may not have wished to enter. Whether we like it or not, when someone gives us a gift, we are powerfully affected; depending on our culture's values associated with gifts, we may feel compelled to accept it, to reciprocate in some way, to define or redefine the social relationship created by the gift, to feel unworthy of the gift, to seek an escape from the relationship, interpret why the gift was given, or why a particular kind or quantity of gift was given. Gifts, like words, communicate, and they can communicate good things or bad. We may feel burdened and uncomfortable if we are given a gift larger than what we deem to be socially appropriate, or if we are given a gift from an inappropriate sphere of exchange. For example, it is generally appropriate in the United States for parents to give their children gifts of money, but money is not an appropriate gift between friends or peers. Or, as another example, when an American couple receives silverware or a toaster as a wedding gift, it is because the gift is intended to symbolize the formation of a new household; were they to receive a crate of lemons, the meaning might be entirely different. When a Lese man in the Democratic Republic of Congo receives cultivated foods from an Efe hunter-gatherer, it is a form of denigration meant to highlight the Lese man's inability to grow his own food, yet when he receives *meat* from the same man, it is a positive and welcome sign for the Lese man that he and his people are of higher social status than the Efe.

The semantics and spheres of economic exchange are highlighted in several of the articles in this volume and recognize that all economies contain the "spheres of exchange" articulated by Bohannon in his pioneering work on the Tiv. As with many anthropological developments, this concept brings us back to Malinowski. In the Trobriands, Kula exchanges constitute a realm of transaction distinct from barter or trade, which is called *gimwali*. Kula valuables, then, could not be bought, sold, or exchanged in everyday markets, but rather only in the series of exchanges of Kula goods that linked the various islands. Kula valuables, in turn, were made up of several spheres; the most important one included the armshells and necklaces, while another comprised axe-blades and lime spoons, and another involved certain foods, such as yams, bananas and taro, that could be presented or offered as gifts (Gudeman, 1986: 123). As Bohannan tells us, among the Tiv of Nigeria goods are placed in particular categories or spheres of exchange; goods within the same sphere are interchangeable, or exchangeable, but goods from different spheres are not. Chickens, goats, and everyday *subsistence goods* constitute one sphere; *prestige goods* such as cattle, rituals offices, and medicines constitute a second sphere; and *rights in people*, such as wives and children, make up the third. Although an item in any single sphere was usually exchangeable only for another item in the same sphere, some movement was possible, even desirable, because each sphere was differently valued in terms of prestige, status, and morality: the first sphere was less highly valued than the second, and the second less highly valued than the third. Many Tiv looked for opportunities to convert a first sphere good to a second sphere good, while converting a good the other way was considered quite undesirable, even shameful. Indeed, Bohannan suggests that when the Tiv invest their wealth, they invest only if it can convert to a higher category: converting subsistence wealth into prestige wealth, prestige wealth into rights in people.

The sort of culturally embedded economics we are describing here, however, does not comprise the entire field of economic anthropology, for there are many economic anthropologists who apply formal Western-derived models to other cultures, and who seek to discern economic laws, or develop economic hypotheses and theories, that help us understand, and even predict, the economic behavior of a large number of different kinds of societies (Burling, 1962; Cook, 1973; Firth, 1967). Such scholars have often been crudely labeled "formalists," while those who believe that the application of economic theory to non-industrial societies is limited, if not wrong-headed, have been called "substantivists." The concept of substantivism comes from the economic historian Karl Polanyi, who argued that organized markets in Europe are only a very recent invention, and that they have detached economics from the rest of social life. Although classical economic theories are useful for analyzing these markets, he argued, they are not useful for analyzing the economies of other societies; for Polanyi, "market" is narrowly defined as the impersonal, modern market of Europe and North America, whereas other societies engage in what he called "marketless trade," reciprocity or redistribution. He thus excludes from his definition the many complex marketplaces throughout Africa, with their various forms of production and exchange systems, indigenous currency, and artisan guilds (Bohannan and Dalton, 1962). Polanyi defined his substantivist position in opposition to formalism (1958: 243–4).

> The substantive meaning of economic derives from man's dependence for his living upon nature and his fellows. It refers to the interchange with his natural and social environment, in so far as this results in supplying him with the means of material want satisfaction.
>
> The formal meaning of economic derives from the logical character of the means–ends relationship, as apparent in such words as "economical" or "economizing." It refers to a definite situation of choice, namely, that between different uses of means induced by an insufficiency of means.
>
> ... It is our proposition that only the substantive meaning of "economic" is capable of yielding the concepts that are required by the social sciences for an investigation of all the empirical economics of the past and present.

As a named division, the debate between substantivists and formalists is now largely relegated to the history of anthropology, and most scholars today employ some mixture of the two, taking the cultural embeddedness of economy for granted, but appreciating the roles individual choice and risk play in economic practices. Still, the tension between these two perspectives continues to influence anthropological research on economics. Major questions persist about how much substantive perspectives overemphasize conformity to social values and patterns (or give too little emphasis to the choices individuals must make in selecting their economic transactions and social relationships), and how much formalist perspectives detach the individual from social context. In denying the applicability of economic theories designed for industrial societies to the analysis of non-industrial societies, do scholars with a substantivist perspective risk endorsing the existence of two separate types of societies, the industrial and non-industrial, market and non-market, "primitive" and peasant? What is the value of employing a particular definition of "market" to distinguish among different economies? There are other important questions that emerge from this debate:

- How can we use our own categories of understanding to comprehend the economies of other cultures, economies that may be constructed with categories, concepts, and symbolic schemes very different from our own?
- Is it possible that a focus on cultural values might impede some analyses of human economic behavior?
- In its emphasis on social patterns, are there aspects of economic anthropology that resemble functionalism?
- What is the relationship between individual and social economic patterns? What is the value of making a distinction between the individual and the social?
- In light of the readings included in this volume, have Africanist scholars represented the economies of Africans as distinct from industrial, market economies?
- Does European domination, colonialism, and the emergence of capitalist, class societies in Africa mean that formal Western-derived models are now applicable to African economies?

In Chapter 8, Mary Douglas addresses the problem of poverty among the Lele of the Kasai region of the Democratic Republic of Congo. In a comparative analysis of the Lele and Bushong econo- mies, she argues that economies are deeply embedded in social ideas and practices. She takes as her case two neighboring groups with starkly different levels of economic productivity: the Lele are poor, while the Bushong are rich. To some extent, their differences can be explained by the fact that the Lele have less fertile soil and less efficient technology, but they also work less at the production of goods. However, working less cannot be explained by environment, but by the social and cultural values and organization of work. She pays special attention to the interesting fact that Lele men begin working at age thirty, while the Bushong begin work at age eighteen; and whereas the Lele retire in middle-age, the Bushong retire only when they are in their sixties, or are unable to work. Douglas carefully and systematically compares the two societies' authority structures, age of mar- riage, incidence of polygyny, and importance of seniority, to show why and how they produce dif- ferent work schedules, and therefore very different levels of production, scarcity, and wealth.

In Chapter 9, Coquery-Vidrovitch's Marxist essay offers a contrasting example of economic anthropology. Marxism has had an important place in economic anthropology's move toward stud- ying regional and local economic histories. Coquery-Vidrovitch moves beyond the study of any single community to articulate a pervasive pattern of production throughout sub-Saharan Africa: an African mode of production. Coquery-Vidrovitch argues that most Africanist scholars have not taken economic inequality or class relations as central topics of study, and have instead looked pri- marily at egalitarianism and kinship organization in subsistence and stateless societies. This is where Marxism becomes relevant. One of the central features of Marxist economics is a focus on how power and wealth are unequally distributed in society. In one of the most famous works on inequality and production, for example, Claude Meillassoux (1981) describes how, among the Guro of Côte d'Ivoire, elders exploit young men by controlling the *means of reproduction* (wives), either through polygynous marriages that deplete the supply of available women, or by demanding bridewealth payments so high that young men are coerced into working for the elders. Most Marxist scholars emphasize production as the building block of other aspects of society, which then in turn support or reinforce production. While the concept of mode of production is complex, and has been subject to a wide range of interpretations and uses, Marx wrote quite clearly the following definition in the preface to *Contributions to a Critique of Political Economy*:

> The sum total of these relations of production constitutes the economic structure of society – the real foundation on which rise legal and political superstructures and to which correspond definite forms of social consciousness. The mode of production in material life determines the general character of the social, political, and spiritual processes of life (1983 [1859]: 49).

Coquery-Vidrovitch argues that the social organization of production is not defined by political organization, such as the commonly used dichotomy of state and stateless societies (see Part I), but rather by the control over long-distance trade by kinship or other groupings. Although the particular form of power that obtains in any given society is largely dependent upon the kind of groups that rise to power, the kinship system, and the general organization of labor and value, the social system is epiphenomenal, or secondary, to production. The African mode of produc- tion constitutes the basic organization of African societies.

One of Marx's most important contributions was to shed light on the social relations of pro- duction, especially through his concept "commodity fetishism." For Marx, commodity fetish- ism illustrates the tendency in a capitalist mode of production to attribute value to things (the products of labor) rather than to labor (social relations). In other words, the relationships between people appear as relationships between things. Commodity fetishism refers to the reification of capital, as in the Nuer case described by Hutchinson in Chapter 10 (see also Shipton, 1989), in which people attribute moral power and agency to money, or more generally speaking when we conceive of money as having an intrinsic value apart from the actions and beliefs of human beings. This is not to say that this conception is false, since "things" are indeed meaningfully related to one another; Marx's point is that commodity fetishism conceals the social relationships that constitute value, and masks the relations of oppression or exploitation between laborers and those who control the means of production. Precisely because it hides these relations from view, workers remain unaware of the nature of their exploitation, and commodity fetishism thus becomes an instrument of oppression.

Hutchinson elaborates upon Bohannan's work by situating the concept of spheres of exchange in the histories of the Luo and Nuer (a group historically related to the Luo) respectively, but they also bring into relief some fascinating aspects of fetishism, and the social meanings of money. She reveals the ways in which the members of these African societies classify money in cultural, moral terms. Just as religions are sometimes shaped in the image of society (see Part VI), the economy is a metaphor and model of, and for, the moral and social order. The Luo distinction between good and evil money reflects relationships between men and women, youths and elders, and is framed in terms of ancestors, lineage, and marriage payments. For Luo, an ostensibly simple good, such as a homestead rooster, should not be sold because it symbolizes masculinity, sexual potency, and the continuity of the lineage, among many other things; thus to sell a rooster for money is tantamount to selling one's masculinity and violating the integrity of the lineage, and money earned from such a sale is tainted and brings "bitter" blessings.

The Nuer distinction between good and bad uses of cattle and money turns about a distinction between blood and non-blood spheres of exchange: because the Nuer equate cattle and people, cattle represent the blood of both the animal and the lineage, and should therefore be used in exchanges that create enduring bonds between people (such as marriage), or that relate people and the supernatural (in religious ritual); money, in contrast, should be used for impersonal transactions such as paying taxes. The Nuer, like the Luo, further classify money into good and bad types. Some Nuer beer sellers, for example, separate the monies collected from Nuer and non-Nuer clients. They use money from selling beer to non-Nuer to pay taxes, and use money collected from Nuer to buy cattle. The Nuer also differentiate cattle into the "cattle of girls" (usually acquired as bridewealth) and the "cattle of money" (usually acquired through purchase), and draw a parallel between these two kinds of cattle and the blood and non-blood spheres of exchange. The former cattle ideally circulate only among kinsmen, and the latter are more freely circulated. However, Hutchinson details the complicated ways in which these distinctions are muted, or in which one kind of cattle is converted into another – from a blood sphere of exchange to a non-blood sphere exchange. The symbolic and political import of girls and women becomes central to these distinctions, as does the fact that the equation between people and cattle quite differently affected men and women. These are subjects Hutchinson takes up in great detail in a larger and more comprehensive study (Hutchinson, 1996).

For our purposes here, the larger significance of these studies is that the European introduction of certain kinds of money and modes of exchange into Africa resulted in their transformation rather than replication. Economists and evangelists have often puzzled over their inability to introduce Western concepts and practices into Africa, as if they expected them to be reproduced perfectly in all times and places. Such a perfect reproduction could occur only if economics were *isolable* from other aspects of society and history. When Islam, Christianity, European-styled nationalism and democracy, and other ideas entered into Africa, they entered into a dialogic relation with African ideas. These studies show how global phenomena, such as capital, money, taxes, and war, are given culturally specific meanings across time and space. Indeed, their historical treatments of these pastoralists contrasts with Evans-Pritchard's historical treatment of the Nuer in Chapter 5, and represent one of the important changes in intellectual perspective we outlined in the Introduction.

Hutchinson details the ways in which moral distinctions between good and bad sorts of commodities or spheres of exchange are embedded in a particular history of civil war, and other turbulence. Such distinctions serve not only as responses to history, but as history itself, shaping strategies of resistance to money and capitalism. Indeed, as Hutchinson shows, the Nuer have good reason to fear the encroachment of external political and economic forces. The attribution of life and morality to money is one way to symbolically (and unconsciously) articulate displeasure with social and cultural change. Hutchinson illustrates that the process by which people simultaneously resist and comply with economic change is marked by extraordinary ambivalence and uncertainty. It is a process in which people creatively seek ways of having a dynamic economy that still resonates with local meanings, and, in the case of the Nuer, preserves important equation between humans and cattle.

These studies, and the suggested readings, illustrate the failure of Western categories of the economy to account for economic and social behavior. Even a brief survey of the economic development studies in sub-Saharan Africa will show how little economists actually discern of the economy when they consider conventional factors such as unemployment rates and official indicators of economic growth. As Keith Hart (1973) demonstrated long ago in a study of the linkages among economic development, unemployment wage income, and rural–urban migration, a significant portion of the urban economy in Africa is made up by people who, though unemployed in the formal sector for formal wages, actually accumulate a great deal of income, and have a powerful effect on the total economy, through "legitimate" informal activities, such as farming and gardening, transport, street hawking, laundering, vehicle repair, or begging, and "illegitimate" informal activities such as theft, prostitution, gambling, smuggling, bribery, and embezzlement. In fact, these opportunities may be alluring enough that some people choose to participate in the informal sector instead of, or in addition to, the formal sector of the economy. Although economists have long argued that the central conflict (or obstacle) in African economic development is between capitalist/precapitalist, modern/traditional economic activities, such a distinction is seldom fruitful in the analysis of African economies. Many African nations have dual economies (MacGaffey, 1987, 1991) – wage earners and the self-employed – and the economies complement rather than conflict with one another (Smith, 1989: 301; Gerry, 1987; Hill, 1970). The profound economic consequences of these two co-existing sectors are not revealed in the sorts of data or statistics that form the basis of most economic work, but rather in the ethnographic studies that describe actual social and individual practices, and that illuminate the many ways in which formal and informal sectors articulate with one another. Economic anthropologists thus point the way to an especially promising area of research for anthropologists: where econometric techniques fail, the anthropologist often succeeds.

References

Adepoju, Aderanti and Christine Oppong, eds. 1994. *Gender, Work and Population in Sub-Saharan Africa*. Portsmouth, NH: Heinemann.

Berry, Sara S. 1978. *Cocoa, Custom and Socioeconomic Change in Rural West Nigeria*. Oxford: Clarendon.

Berry, Sara. 1984. *Fathers Work for their Sons: Accumulation, Mobility, and Class Formation in an Extended Yoruba Community*. Berkeley and Los Angeles: University of California Press.

Bird-David, Nurit. 1992. "Beyond the 'Original Affluent Society:' A Culturalist Reformulation." *Current Anthropology* 33(1): 25–47.

Bohannan, Paul and George Dalton, eds. 1962. *Markets in Africa*. Evanston: Northwestern University Press.

Boserup, Ester. 1970. *Women's Role in Economic Development*. London: George Allen and Unwin.

Burling, Robbins. 1962. "Maximization Theories and the Study of Economic Anthropology." *American Anthropologist* 64: 802–21.

Cohen, Abner. 1969. *Custom and Politics in Urban Africa: A Study of Hausa Migrants in Yoruba Towns*. Berkeley: University of California Press.

Cook, Scott. 1973. "Economic Anthropology: Problems in Theory, Method, and Analysis." In John J. Honigmann, ed., *Handbook of Social and Cultural Anthropology*, pp. 795–860. Chicago: Rand McNally and Company.

Coquery-Vidrovitch, Catherine. 1978. "Research on an African Mode of Production." In David Seddon, ed., *Relations of Production*. London: Cass.

Donham, Donald. 1990. *History, Power, Ideology*. Cambridge: Cambridge University Press.

Epstein, A.L. 1958. *Politics in an Urban African Community*. Manchester: Manchester University Press.

Ferguson, James. 1990. *The Anti-Politics Machine*. Cambridge: Cambridge University Press.

Firth, Raymond, ed. 1967. *Themes in Economic Anthropology*. London: Tavistock.

Fratkin, Elliot, Kathleen A. Galvin and Eric Abella Roth, eds. 1994. *African Pastoralist Systems: An Integrated Approach*. Boulder: Lynne Rienner.

Gerry, Chris. 1987. "Developing Economies and the Informal Sector in Historical Perspective." In Louis A. Ferman, Stuart Henry, and Michele Hoyman, eds. *The Informal Economy*. Special Issue of the Annals of the American Academy of Political and Social Science. Newbury Park, CA: Sage Publications.

Gudeman, Stephen. 1986. *Economics as Culture: Models and Metaphors of Livelihood*. London, Boston and Henley: Routledge and Kegan Paul.

Guyer, Jane. 1981. "Household and Community in African Studies." *African Studies Review* 24: 37–137.

Harms, Robert. 1981. *River of Wealth, River of Sorrow: The Central Zaire Basin in the Era of the Slave and Ivory Trade. 1500–1891*. New Haven: Yale University Press.

Hart, J.K. 1973. "Informal Income Opportunities and Urban Employment in Ghana." *Journal of Modern African Studies* 11(1): 61–89.

Hart, J.K. 1982. *The Political Economy of West African Agriculture*. Cambridge: Cambridge University Press.

Hill, Polly. 1970. *Studies in Rural Capitalism in West Africa*. Cambridge: Cambridge University Press.

Hutchinson, Sharon. 1996. *Nuer Dilemmas: Coping with Money, War and the State*. Berkeley and Los Angeles: University of California Press.

Kopytoff, Igor and Suzanne Miers, eds. 1977. *Slavery in Africa: Historical and Anthropological Perspectives*. Madison: University of Wisconsin Press.

LeClair, Edward E. Jr. and Harold K. Schneider, eds. 1968. *Economic Anthropology: Readings in Theory and Analysis*. New York: Holt, Rinehart and Winston.

Little, Peter D. and Michael J. Watts, eds. 1994. *Living under Contract: Contract Farming and Agrarian Transformation in Sub-Saharan Africa*. Madison: University of Wisconsin Press.

MacGaffey, Janet. 1987. *Entrepreneurs and Parasites: The Struggle for Indigenous Capitalism in Zaire*. Cambridge: Cambridge University Press.

MacGaffey, Janet. 1991. *The Real Economy of Zaire: The Contribution of Smuggling and other Unofficial Activities to National Wealth*. London: James Currey.

Malinowski, Bronislaw. 1922. *Argonauts of the Western Pacific*. New York: Dutton.

Marx, Karl. 1983 [1859]. "Mode of Production, Civil Society, and Ideology." From Karl Marx, *A Contribution to the Critique of Political Economy*, reprinted in Tom Bottomore and Patrick Goode, eds. *Readings in Marxist Sociology*, pp. 49–50. Oxford: Oxford University Press.

Mauss, Marcel. 1954 [1925]. *The Gift: Forms and Functions of Exchange in Archaic Society*, trans. Ian Cunnison. London: Cohen & West.

Mayer, Phillip. 1962. Migrancy and the Study of Africans in Town. *American Anthropologist* 64: 576–92.

Meillassoux, Claude. 1981. *Maidens, Meal and Money*. Cambridge: Cambridge University Press.

Mitchell, Clyde. 1956. "The Kalela Dance." Rhodes–Livingstone Paper, no. 27.

Moodie, T. Dunbar with Vivienne Ndatshe. 1994. *Going for God: Men, Mines and Migration*. Berkeley and Los Angeles: University of California Press.

Moore, Henrietta and Megan Vaughan. 1994. *Cutting Down Trees: Gender, Nutrition, and Agricultural Change in the Northern Province of Zambia. 1890–1990*. Portsmouth, NH: Heinemann.

Murray, Colin. 1981. *Families Divided: The Impact of Migrant Labor in Lesotho*. Johannesburg: Ravan.

Polanyi, Karl. 1958. "The Economy as Instituted Process." In Karl Polanyi, Conrad Arensberg and Harry W. Pearson, eds. *Trade and Markets in the Early Empires*, pp. 243–70. Glencoe: Free Press.

Robertson, A. F. 1987. *The Dynamics of Productive Relationships: African Share Contracts in Comparative Perspective*. Cambridge: Cambridge University Press.

Sahlins, Marshall. 1968. "Notes on the Original Affluent Society." In Richard B. Lee and Irven DeVore, eds. *Man the Hunter*, pp. 84–9. Chicago: Aldine.

Sahlins, Marshall. 1972. *Stone Age Economics*. Chicago: Aldine.

Shipton, Parker. 1989. *Bitter Money: Cultural Economy and Some African Meanings of Forbidden Commodities*. Washington, DC: American Anthropological Association.

Singh, Uberoi J. P. 1962. *Politics of the Kula Ring: An Analysis of the Findings of Bronislaw Malinowski*. Manchester: Manchester University Press.

Smith, M. Estellie. 1989. "The Informal Economy." In Stuart Plattner, ed., *Economic Anthropology*, pp. 292–317. Stanford, CA: Stanford University Press.

Southall, Aidan. 1974. "State Formation in Africa." *Annual Review of Anthropology* 3: 153–65.

Southall, Aidan, ed. 1973. *Urban Anthropology: Cross-Cultural Studies of Urbanization*. Oxford: Oxford University Press.

Watson, W. 1958. *Tribal Cohesion in a Money Economy: A Study of the Mambwe People of Northern Rhodesia*. Manchester: Manchester University, for the Rhodes-Livingstone Institute.

Werbner, Richard, ed. 1982. *Land Reforms in the Making: Tradition, Public Policy, and Ideology in Botswana*. London: Rex Collings.

Suggested Reading

Berry, Sara. 1984. "The Food Crisis and Agrarian Change in Africa: A Review Essay." *African Studies Review* 27(2): 59–112.

Bohannan, Paul and Laura Bohannan. 1968. *Tiv Economy*. London: Longman.

Chayanov, A. V. 1966 [1925]. *The Theory of Peasant Economy*. Homewood, IL: Irwin.

Chuku, Gloria. 2004. *Igbo Women and Economic Transformation in Southeastern Nigeria, 1900–1960*. New York: Routledge.

Comaroff, John L. ed. 1980. *The Meaning of Marriage Payments*. London: Academic Press.

Creevey, Lucy, ed. 1986. *Women Farmers in Africa: Rural Development in Mali and the Sahel*. Syracuse, NY: Syracuse University Press.

Curtin, Philip D. 1984. *Cross-Cultural Trade in World History*. Cambridge: Cambridge University Press.

Evans-Pritchard, E. E. 1940. *The Nuer*. Oxford: Clarendon Press.

Firth, Raymond. 1957. "The Place of Malinowski in the History of Economic Anthropology." In Raymond Firth, ed. *Man and Culture: An Evaluation of the Work of Bronislaw Malinowski*, pp. 209–28. London, Boston and Henley: Routledge and Kegan Paul.

Freund, Bill, 1984. "Labor and Labor History in Africa: A Review of the Literature." *African Studies Review* 27(2): 1–58.

Geertz, Clifford. 1963. *Agricultural Involution*. Berkeley: University of California Press.

Godelier, Maurice. 1977. *Perspectives in Marxist Anthropology*. Cambridge: Cambridge University Press.

Goody, Jack and Stanley Tambiah. 1973. *Bridewealth and Dowry*. Cambridge: Cambridge University Press.

Gras, N.S.B. 1927. "Anthropology and Economics." In W.F. Ogburn and A.A. Goldenweiser, eds., *The Social Sciences and their Inter-relations*, pp. 10–23. Boston: Houghton Mifflin.

Guyer, Jane I. 1984. "Naturalism in Models of African Production." *Man* 19: 371–88.

Guyer, Jane I. 1991. "Female Farming in Anthropology and African History." In Michaela di Leonardo, ed., *Gender at the Crossroads of Knowledge: Feminist Anthropology in the Postmodern Era*. Berkeley and Los Angeles: University of California Press.

Herskovits, Meville J. and M. Harwitz, eds. 1964. *Economic Transition in Africa*. Evanston, IL: Northwestern University Press.

Hill, Polly. 1969. "Hidden Trade in Hausaland." *Man* 4: 393–409.

Homans, George. 1958. "Social Behavior as Exchange." *American Journal of Sociology* 63: 597–606.

Leach, Jerry Wayne and Edmund Ronald Leach, eds. 1983. *The Kula: New Perspectives on Massim Exchange*. Cambridge: Cambridge University Press.

Lee, Richard B. 1979. *The !Kung San: Men, Women and Work in a Foraging Society*. Cambridge: Cambridge University Press.

Lynn, Martin. 2002. *Commerce and Economic Change in West Africa: The Palm Oil Trade in the Nineteenth Century*. Cambridge: Cambridge University Press.

Matory, J. Lorand. 1994. *Sex and the Empire that Is No More: Gender and the Politics of Metaphor in Oyo Yoruba Religion*. Minneapolis: University of Minnesota Press.

Mensah, Joseph. 2008. *Neoliberalism and Globalization in Africa: Contestations on the Embattled Continent*. New York: Palgrave.

Morgan, Lewis Henry. 1963 [1877]. *Ancient Society*. Cleveland: Meridian Books, World Publishing Co.

Ortiz, Sutti. 1983. *Economic Anthropology: Topics and Theories*. Monographs in Economic Anthropology, no. 2. Lanham, MD: University Press of America, for the Society for Economic Anthropology.

Rappaport, Roy A. 1968. *Pigs for the Ancestors*. New Haven: Yale University Press.

Rigby, Peter. 1969. *Cattle and Kinship among the Gogo*. Ithaca, NY: Cornell University Press.

Robbins, Lionel. 1935. *An Essay on the Nature and Significance of Economic Science*. New York: St Martins Press.

Salisbury, Richard F. 1962. *From Stone to Steel*. Melbourne: University of Australia Press.

Schneider, Harold K. 1964. "A Model of African Indigenous Economy and Society." *Comparative Studies in Society and History* 7: 37–55.

Shipton, Parker M. 2009. *Mortgaging the Ancestors: Ideologies of Attachment in Africa*. New Haven: Yale University Press.

Soyinka-Airewele and Rita Kiki-Edozie. 2009. *Reframing Contemporary Africa: Politics, Economics, and Culture in the Global Era*. Washington, DC: CQ Press.

Wolf, Eric. 1966. *Peasants*. Englewood Cliffs, NJ: Prentice-Hall.

8

Lele Economy Compared with the Bushong

Mary Douglas

The Lele[1] and the Bushong[2] are separated only by the Kasai River. The two tribes recognize a common origin, their houses, clothes and crafts are similar in style, their languages are closely related.[3] Yet the Lele are poor, while the Bushong are rich. The Lele produce only for subsistence, sharing their goods, or distributing them among themselves as gifts and fees. The Bushong have long been used to producing for exchange, and their native economy was noted for its use of money and its specialists and markets. Everything that the Lele have or can do, the Bushong have more and can do better. They produce more, live better, and populate their region more densely.

The first question is whether there are significant differences in the physical environment of the two peoples. Both live in the lat. 5 Degrees, in the area of forest park merging into savannah, which borders the south of the Congo rain forest. They both have a heavy annual rainfall of 1400 to 1600 mm (40 to 60 inches) per annum. The mean annual temperature is about 78 °F (25 °C). As we should expect from their proximity, the climatic conditions are much the same for both tribes.

Nonetheless, a curious discrepancy appears in their respective assessments of their climate. The Bushong, like the local Europeans, welcome the dry season of mid-May to mid-August as a cold season, whereas the Lele regard it as dangerously hot. The Bushong in the north tend to have a dry season ten days shorter (Bultot 1954) than most of the Lele (see Figure 8.1), and the Lele soils retain less moisture, and the vegetation is thinner, so that the impression of drought is more severe, but otherwise there seems no objectively measurable difference in the climate to account for their attitudes.

There are certainly important differences in the soil, drainage and vegetation. The Lele are distinctly less fortunate. Their soils belong to the most easterly extension of the Kwango plateau system, and to some extent share in the sterility characteristic of that region. On that plateau, the soils are too poor to support anything but a steppe-like vegetation in spite of the ample rainfall. The soils consist of sands, poor in assimilable minerals of any kind, lacking altogether in ferro-magnates or heavy minerals, and so permeable that they are incapable of benefiting from the heavy rainfall[4]

From Mary Douglas, "The Lele: Resistance to Change," in *Markets in Africa*, pp. 211–33, ed. Paul Bohannan and George Dalton (1962), from Northwestern University Press.

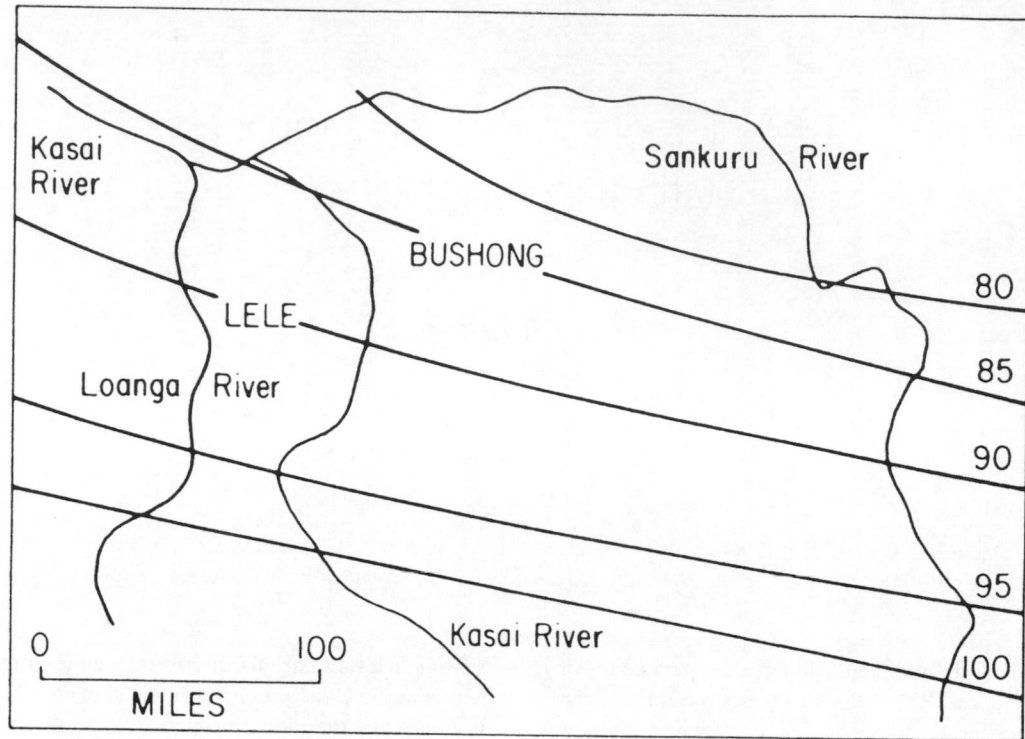

Figure 8.1   Average length of dry season expressed in days (From: F. Bultot – "Saisons et Périodes Sèches et Pluvieuses au Congo Belge." Bruxelles, 1954)

(see Figure 8.2). On the Bushong side of the Kasai River the soil is altogether richer, and mineral deposits, particularly of iron ore, occur. Whereas Lele country is characterized by rolling grasslands with forest galleries along the river banks, Bushong country is relatively well-forested, although the sketch map tends to exaggerate the forested area on their side of the Kasai.

With such important differences in their basic natural resources, we are not surprised that Lele country is poorer and more sparsely populated. But how much poverty and how low a density can be attributed to the environmental factor? Can we leave the matter here?

There is no certain method of estimating the extent to which environment itself limits the development of an area. The Pende of Gungu, immediate neighbors of the Lele, inhabit an area even poorer in soils than the Lele area, and as poor as those worked by the notoriously wretched Suku

of Kahemba and Feshi. The Lele are poor, but the Suku are known as a miserable, dispirited people, incapable of exploiting to the full such resources as their poor environment offers. The Pende are famous as energetic cultivators, well-nourished and industrious. All three peoples grow different staple crops; the Pende, millet; the Suku, manioc; the Lele, maize. There is obviously no end to the speculation one could indulge as to what the potentialities of the environment might be.

Congo geographers have been much occupied by the question of the relation between soil and population density. The whole Belgian Congo is an area of very low density. Fifty per cent of its surface has a population of less than 2.4 to the square kilometer (roughly 6 to square mile) (Gourou 1955: 4). It is generally agreed (Gourou 1955 cites Cohen; Nicolai 1952: 247) that there is a rough correlation of poor sandy soils with low densities, insofar as the small stretch of relatively more populous country

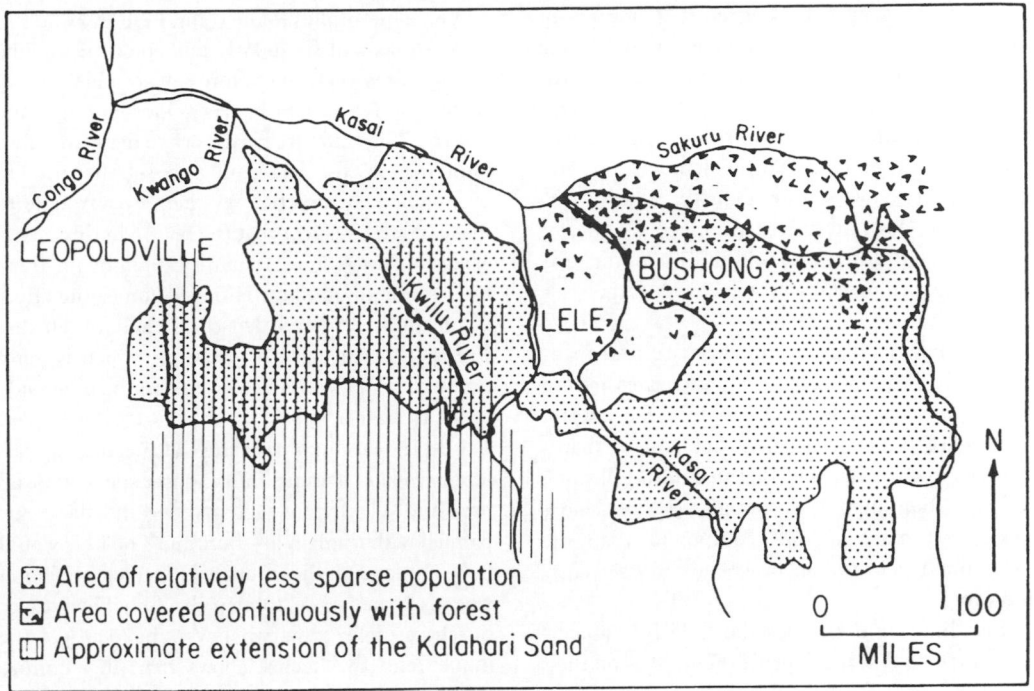

Figure 8.2 Population density and forest cover (Lele and Bushong) (From: N. Nicolai & J. Jacques – "La transformation du paysage Congolais par Chemin de Fer" 1954 p. 112)

occurs in a favored gap between the Kwango "kala-hari" plateau and sands to the north. However, it is also agreed that soil poverty in itself is not an adequate explanation of the pockets of extra low density which occur, especially on the second and fifth parallels of South latitude. Professor Gourou says emphatically and repeatedly that the sterility of the soils cannot be held to account for all the densities of less than 2 to the square kilometer (5 to the square mile) in the Belgian Congo (Gourou 1955: 52, 57, 109; Nicolai 1952). In Northern Rhodesia we have an illuminating case. The Ndembu live at an average density of 6 to the square mile, in many areas at a density of only 3, but according to a careful calculation of the capacity of their land, worked according to their own methods, the area should be capable of supporting a population of from 17 to 38 to the square mile (6.8 to 15 per square kilometer) (Turner 1957).

In short, we cannot assume, as some have done, that there is any universal tendency to maximize

food production (Harris 1959), or that the food resources of a region are the only factor limiting its population.

For the Lele and the Bushong the relative densities are as follows. The territory of Mweka, where the Bushong live, has an average density of 4–5 to the square kilometer (11 to the square mile). The BCK railway running through the area has attracted an immigrant population of Luba. If we abstract the railway zone from our figures, we find that the Bushong proper live at a density of (Gourou 1955: 109) only 3 or 4 to the square kilometer (7–10 to the square mile). The Lele[5] inhabit Basongo territory, where the average density is from 2 to 4 to the square kilometer (5–7 to the square mile), but since the Lele account for only half the population (among recent immigrants of foreign tribesmen to work in the Brabanta oil concession, refinery and port, and among Cokwe hunters), we can suppose that until recently Lele themselves used to live at a mere 1.7 to the square kilometer (4 to the square mile).

When the geographers agree that poverty of soil is not a sufficient explanation for the degree of poverty prevailing in similar areas, we are justified in looking for a sociological explanation to supplement the effect of environmental factors. For one thing, it is obvious that the demographic factor works two ways. Low density is partly the result of inferior technology, applied to inferior resources, but it may also inhibit development by hampering enterprises which need large-scale collaboration.

If we now consider technology, we find many suggestive differences. In certain processes marked superiority would be likely to increase output. Others are proof of a higher standard of living. Surveying these, we find that in hunting, fishing and housebuilding, the Bushong worker uses more specialized materials and equipment than the Lele, and in cultivation he spends more energy and time.

Take hunting first, since the Lele are passionately interested in it and pride themselves on their skill (Douglas 1954). In the eyes of their neighbors, it seems that they are notorious as inefficient hunters, particularly because they do not use nets, and only rarely make pit traps.

Hunting is the only occupation in which large numbers of Lele men regularly combine. They reckon that fifteen to twenty men and ten dogs are necessary for a good hunt. Using nets, the Bushong need a team of only ten men, and can hope to do well with five. In short, the Bushong hunter uses better capital equipment, and his hours of hunting are more productive.

Why should the Lele not have nets? The materials are present in the forest on both sides of the river, and the Lele know what nets are. Making a net is presumably a long task. In view of the local deforestation and the resulting paucity of game, it may be a case in which costly capital equipment is simply not worthwhile. Bushong nets are made by their women. Perhaps the rest of the answer lies in the different division of labor between men and women in each tribe, and the larger proportion of the total agricultural work which Lele leave to their women. Whatever the reason, we note that the absence of nets is consistent with a general Lele tendency not to invest time and labor in long-term equipment.

The same applies to pit-traps. Lele know how to make these, and frequently talk about them. The task requires a stay in the forest of several days and nights, or regular early dawn journeys and late returns. The traps are hard work to dig with only a blunt matchet for spade, and once set, they need to be watched. In practice few men ever trouble to make them. I suspect that the reason in this case is again that the amount of game caught by pit-traps tends to be disappointing in relation to the effort of making them, and that the Lele have felt discouraged when using a technique which is more productive in the thicker forests on the other side of the river.

Lest it be thought that the Lele neglect capital-intensive aids because hunting is a sport, a pleasure, and a religious activity, let me deny any parallel with English fox-hunting. The Lele would have applauded the French Brigadier of fiction who used his sabre to slay the fox. Their eager purchase of firearms whenever they can get the money and the license shows that their culture does not restrict them to inferior techniques when these do not require long-term collaboration and effort.

In fishing the Lele are also inferior. Their country is well watered by streams and rivers, and bounded on two sides by the great Kasai, and on the west by the swift-flowing Loange. Along the banks of the Kasai are fishing villages, whose men dot the river with elaborate traps and fishing platforms. These fishermen are mostly Dinga, or Bushong, and not often Lele. In one northern village, near the Kasai, Lele women used to go every two days to the nearest Dinga village where, lacking claims of kinship, they obtained fish by bartering manioc. Compared with the Bushong the Lele as a whole are not good at fishing, nor at canoe making. There is no need to describe in detail the diversity and elaborate character of Bushong fishing equipment, but it is worth noting that in some types of fishing, using several canoes trailing nets, the team may consist of twenty men or more. These skills may be a legacy from their distant past, since the Bushong claim to have entered the territory in canoes along the Kasai river, while the Lele claim to have travelled overland (Vansina 1956) and to have found the river banks already occupied by Dinga fishing villages.

If the Lele were originally landsmen, and the Bushong originally fishermen, this might account for more than the latter's present technical superiority in fishing. For primitive fishermen are necessarily more heavily equipped than are primitive hunters and cultivators. The need for fishing tackle, nets, lines, hooks, traps, curing platforms, and for watercraft as well as for weirs and dams makes quite a different balance in the allocation of time between the consumers' and producers' goods. If they started in this area with the typical balance of a fishing economy, this may have meant an initial advantage for the Bushong in the form of a habit of working for postponed consumption.

Be that as it may, Lele mostly leave fishing to their women. Their simple method is to block a slow-moving stream, so as to turn the nearest valley into a marsh. In this they make mud banks and ponds, where they set traps for fish scarcely bigger than minnows. A morning's work draining out such a pond and catching the fish floundering in the mud yields a bare pint or so of fish. In the dry season they make a two-day expedition to the Lumbundji, where they spread a saponaceous vegetable poison over the low waters, and pull out the suffocated fish by hand, or in baskets.

As to housing, Lele and Bushong huts look much alike. They are low rectangular huts, roofed with palm thatch. The walls are covered with rows of split bamboos or palm ribs, lashed onto layers of palmleaf, on a frame of strong saplings. Deceptive in appearance, Lele huts when new look much sturdier than those of the Bushong, but in practice they last less well: the Lele hut is more roughly and quickly made. A well-built one will last about six years without repair, and, as they are capable of being renewed piecemeal, by the substitution of new walls or roof thatch, they are not replaced until the whole village is moved to a new site, and the owner decides that he has neglected his hut so long that it will not stand removal. A hut in good condition is transported to a new site, with from six to eight men carrying the roof, and four at a time carrying the walls.

Bushong huts are also transportable. They are made with slightly different materials. For the roof thatch, they use the leaves of the raffia palm, as do the Lele. For the walls, they use the reputedly more waterproof leaves of a dwarf palm growing in the marshes. Over this, instead of palm ribs split in half, they sew narrow strips of bamboo, where available. Lele consider bamboo to be a tougher wood than palm, but it is rare in their region. The narrow strips are held in place by stitching in pleasing geometric patterns (Nicolai & Jacques 1954: 272ff). A rich Bushong man, who can command labor, can build a hut that will last much longer than the ordinary man's hut, up to fifteen years without major repairs. The palace of the Nyimi at Mushenge, which was still in good condition in 1956, had been originally built in 1920.

The Bushong use an ingenious technique of ventilation, a movable flap between the roof and the walls, which lets out smoke. It is impossible to say whether they do this because their building is too solid to let the smoke filter through the walls, or whether they are more fastidious and painstaking about their comfort than the Lele, whose huts do certainly retain some of the smoke of their fires.

Within the hut, the furnishings illustrate the difference in material wealth, for the Bushong have a much greater refinement of domestic goods. They sit on stools, lay their heads on carved neck rests (often necessary to accommodate an elaborate hair style). They eat from basketry plates, with iron or wooden spoons. They have a bigger range of specialized basketry or wooden containers for food, clothing, cosmetics. A man who has more than one hat needs a hat box and a place for his metal hat pins. Lele do not make fibre hats, and only a few men in the village may possess a skin hat. The beautiful Bushong caskets for cosmetics are prized objects in many European museums. When a Lele woman has prepared some cosmetic from camwood, she uses it at once, and there is rarely enough left over for it to be worth storing in a special container. Only a young mother who, being cared for by her own mother after her delivery, has nothing else to do but grind camwood for herself and the baby, stores the prepared ointment in a little hanging basket hooked into the wall, enough for a few days.

Dr Vansina was impressed with the high protein content of the Bushong diet, with the large quantities of fish and meat they ate, and the variety in their food. The Lele gave an impression of always being hungry, always dreaming of meat, often going to bed fasting because their stomach revolts at the idea of a vegetable supper. They talk a lot about hunger, and *ihiobe*, an untranslatable word for meatlessness and fishlessness. The Bushong cultivate a wider range of crops and also grow citrus fruits, pineapples, pawpaws, mangoes, sugar cane and bananas, which are either rare or completely absent in the Lele economy.

In short, the Bushong seem to be better sheltered, better fed, better supplied with goods, and with containers for storing what they do not immediately need. This is what we mean by saying that the Bushong are richer than the Lele. As to village-crafts, such as carving and smithing, the best of the Lele products can compete in quality with Bushong manufacture, but they are much scarcer. The Lele are more used to eating and drinking out of folded green leaves than from the basket plates and carved beakers common among the Bushong. Their medical instruments, too, are simpler. If, instead of cutting down a gourd top, they carve a wooden enema funnel for a baby, they make it as fine and thin as they can, but do not adorn it with the elaborate pattern found on some Bushong examples.

Before considering agriculture, we should mention the method of storing grain, for this is a rough index of output. Both Lele and Bushong houses are built with an internal grain store, suspended from the roof or supported on posts over the hearth. Here grain and even fish and meat can be preserved from the ravages of damp and of insects by the smoke of the fire. Most Lele women have no other grain store. Bushong women find this too small and use external granaries, built like little huts, raised a few feet above ground. These granaries, of which there may be one or two in a Lele village, are particularly characteristic of the southern Bushong villages, while in the north the huts which are built in the fields for a man to sleep in during the period of heaviest agricultural work are used as temporary granaries. The Lele are not in the habit of sleeping in their fields, except to shoot wild pig while the grain is ripening. This may be another indication that they do less agricultural work than the Bushong.

When we examine the techniques of cultivation, we find many contrasts. The Bushong plant five crops in succession in a system of rotation that covers two years. They grow yams, sweet potatoes, manioc, beans, and gather two and sometimes three maize harvests a year. The Lele practice no rotation and reap only one annual maize harvest. If we examine the two agricultural cycles, we see that the Bushong work continuously all the year, and that the Lele have one burst of activity, lasting about six weeks, in the height of the dry season.

Here is the probable explanation of their dread of the dry season. There is, in fact, surprisingly little range in the average monthly temperatures throughout the year. For the coldest month, July, it is only 2 °C less than the hottest month, January (Van den Plas 1947: 33–8). Nonetheless, the Europeans and the Bushong welcome the period from mid-May to mid-August as the "cold season," probably because they enjoy the cooler nights and the freedom from humidity. But the Lele, enduring the sun beating on them from a cloudless sky while they are trying to do enough agricultural work for the whole year, suffer more from the dust and impurities in the atmosphere and from the greatly increased insolation. The relatively cooler nights may make them feel the day's heat even more intensely.

Apart from the differences in crops cultivated, we may note some differences in emphasis. Lele give hunting and weaving a high priority throughout the year, while the Bushong think of them as primarily dry-season activities. Traditionally, the Lele used to burn the grassland for big hunts (in which five or six villages combined for the day) at the end of the dry season, when the bulk of their agricultural work was done. If the first rains had already broken, so much the better for the prospects of the hunt, they said, as the animals would leave their forest watering places to eat the new shoots. At the end of the dry season is the time in which the firing could do the maximum damage to the vegetation, it has been forbidden by the administration, and if permission is given at all, the firing must be over by the beginning of July. The Bushong used to burn the grassland in mid-May or early June, at the beginning of the dry season, when the sap had not altogether died down in the grass.

The cycle of work described for the Lele is largely what the old men describe as their traditional practice [Table 8.1]. It was modified by the agricultural officers of the Belgian Congo. Lele are

Table 8.1 Annual cycle of work

	Bushong		Lele
Dry Season			
Mid–May	Harvest beans, maize II, yams. Clear forest Burn grassland for hunt	Hunt, weave, draw wine	Clear forest for maize
June	Hunt, fish, weave, repair huts	" "	
Mid–July to Aug. 15	Burn forest clearings, gather bananas and pineapple. Plant hemp Hunt, fish, plant sugar cane and bananas Send tribute to capital period of plenty	" "	Women fish in low waters Burn forest clearings Sow maize
Wet Season			
Mid–August	Lift ground nuts	" "	Fire grassland for hunting
Sept.	Sow ground nut. Sow maize I Collect termites	" "	Sow voandzeia, plant manioc, bananas, peppers,
Oct.		" "	sugar cane, pineapples (occasional)
Nov.		" "	and raffia palms in
Mid–Dec.		" "	forest clearings with maize
Little Dry Season			
Mid–Dec.	Sow maize II; sow voandzeia	" "	Green maize can be plucked
Jan.	Sow tobacco, sow maize II	" "	Maize harvest
Wet Season			
Feb.	Lift ground nuts, sow beans, collect termites and grubs Reap maize I (Main crop)	" "	Lift voandzeia
March	Reap maize I. Sow tobacco, beans, yams, manioc	" "	
April to Mid–May	Gather beans, sow voandzeia and tobacco	" "	

encouraged to sow maize twice, for harvesting in November, and in April. Manioc is now mainly grown in the grassland, instead of in the forest clearings. There are some changes in the plants cultivated. Voandzeia has been replaced by ground-nuts, some hill rice is sown, and beans in some parts. These are largely treated as cash crops by the Lele, who sell them to the Europeans to earn money for tax. The other occupation which competes for their time is cutting oil-palm fruits to sell to the *Huileries du Congo Belge*, whose lorries collect weekly from the villages. Lele complain that they are now made to work harder than before, to clear more land, keep it hoed, grow more crops. They never complain that cutting oil-palm fruits interferes with their agricultural program, only that the total of extra work interferes with their hunting.

This is not the place for a detailed study of Bushong agriculture. It is enough to have shown that it is more energetically pursued and is more productive. One or two details of women's work are useful indications of a different attitude to time, work and food. Lele like to eat twice a day: in the morning at about 11 o'clock or midday, and in the evening. They complain that their wives are lazy, and only too often the morning meal consists of cold scraps from the previous night; they compare themselves unfavorably with Cokwe, who are reputed to have more industrious wives. In practice the Lele women seem to be very hardworking, but it is possible that the absence of labor-saving devices may make their timetable more arduous.

For example, one of their daily chores is to fetch water from the stream. At the same time, they carry down a heavy pile of manioc roots to soak for a few days before carrying them back to the village. Bushong women, on the other hand, are equipped with wooden troughs, filled with rain water from the roofs, so that they can soak their manioc in the village, without the labor of transporting it back and forth. Bushong women also cultivate mushrooms indoors for occasional relish, while Lele women rely on chance gathering.

Bushong women find time to do the famous raffia embroidery, perhaps because their menfolk help them more in the fields. Lele men admiring the Bushong *Velours*, were amazed to learn that women could ever be clever enough to use needle and thread, still less make this elaborate stitching. The Bushong culinary tradition is more varied than that of the Lele. This rough comparison suggests that Lele women are less skilled and industrious than Bushong women, but it is probable that a time-and-motion study of women's and men's work in the two economies would show that Lele men leave a relatively heavier burden of agricultural work to their women, for reasons which we will show later.

Another difference between Bushong and Lele techniques is in the exploitation of palms for wine. Lele use only the raffia palm for wine. Their method of drawing it kills the tree; in the process of tapping, they cut out the whole of the crown of the palm just at the time of its first flowering. During the few years before the palm has matured to this point, they take the young yellow fronds for weaving, and after drawing the sap for wine, the stump is stripped and left to rot down. Lele have no use for a tree which has once been allowed to flower, except for fuel and building purposes. The life of a palm, used in this way, is rarely more than five years, although there seems to be some range in the different times at which individual palms mature.

The Bushong also use this method on raffia palms, but they have learnt to tap oil palms by making an incision at the base of the large inflorescene, a technique which does not kill the tree. Presumably this technique could be adapted to raffia palms, since the Yakö of Cross River, Nigeria use it (Forde 1937). But neither Lele nor Bushong attempt to preserve the raffia palm in this way, and Lele do not draw any wine from oil palms, although these grow plentifully in the north of their territory. According to Lele traditions oil palms were very scarce in their country until relatively recently, and this may account for their not exploiting it for wine. But here again, consistently with other tendencies in their economy, their techniques are directed to short-term results, and do not fully use their resources.

To balance this picture of Lele inefficiency, we should mention the weaving of raffia, for here, at least, they are recognized as the better craftsmen. Their raffia cloth is of closer texture than Bushong cloth, because they use finer strands of raffia, produced by combing in three stages, whereas the Bushong only comb once. Incidentally, the fine Lele cloth is not suitable for *Velours* embroidery.

Lele take pride in producing a cloth of a regular and fine weave, and they refuse inferior cloth if it is preferred for payment. A length of woven raffia is their normal standard of value for counting debts and dues of all kinds. How little it has even now become a medium of exchange has been described elsewhere (Douglas 1958). Raffia cloth is not the medium of exchange for the Bushong, who freely used cowries, copper units, and beads before they adopted Congolese francs as an additional currency. Raffia cloth is the principal export for the Lele, whereby they obtain knives, arrowheads and camwood. This may explain why unadorned raffia cloth holds a more important place in the admittedly simpler economy of the Lele than its equivalent in the diversified economy of the Bushong.

If we ask now why one tribe is rich and the other poor, the review of technology would seem to suggest that the Lele are poorer not only because their soil is less fertile, but because they work less at the production of goods. They do not build up producer's capital, such as nets, canoes, traps and granaries. Nor do they work so long at cultivation, and their houses wear out quicker. Their reduced effort is itself partly a consequence of their poorer environment. It is probable that their soil could not be worked by the intensive methods of Bushong agriculture without starting a degenerative cycle. Hunting nets and pit-traps are less worthwhile in an area poor in forest and game. But certain other features of their economy cannot be fully explained as adaptations to the environment.

When Lele timetables of work are compared with those of the Bushong, we see no heavy schedules which suggest that there would be any shortage of labor. Yet, their economy is characterized paradoxically by an apparent shortage of hands, which confronts anyone who seeks collaborators. When a sick man wants to send a message, or needs help to clear his fields, or to repair his hut, or to draw palm wine for him, he will often be hard put to find anyone whose services he can command. "*Kwa itangu bo – No time,*" is a common reply to requests for help. His fields may lie uncleared, or his palm trees run to seed for lack of hands. This reflects the weakness of the authority structure in Lele society, and does not imply that every able-bodied man is fully employed from dawn to dusk.

Some anthropologists write as if the poorer the environment and the less efficient the techniques for exploiting it, the more the population is forced to work hard to maintain itself in existence; more productive techniques produce a surplus which enables a part of the population to be supported as a "leisure class."[6] It is not necessary to expose the fallacies of this approach, but it is worth pointing out that, poor as they are, the Lele are less fully employed than the Bushong. They do less work.

"Work," of course, is here used in a narrow sense, relevant to a comparison of material wealth. Warfare, raiding, ambushing, all planning of offensive and defensive actions, as also abductions, seductions, and reclaiming of women, making and rebutting of sorcery charges, negotiations for fines and compensations and for credit – all these absorbingly interesting and doubtless satisfying activities of Lele social life must, for this purpose of measuring comparative prosperity, be counted as alternatives to productive work. Whether we call them forms of preferred idleness, or leisure activities, or "non-productive work," no hidden judgment

of value is implied. The distinction between productive work and other activities is merely used here as rough index of material output.

If we wish to understand why the Lele work less, we need to consider whether any social factors inhibit them from exploiting their resources to the utmost. We should be prepared to find in a backward economy (no less than in our own economy) instances of decisions influenced by short-term desires which, once taken, may block the realization of long-term interests.

First, we must assess in a very general way, the attitudes shown by the Lele towards the inconveniences and rewards of work.

For the Bushong, work is the means to wealth, and wealth the means to status. They strongly emphasize the value of individual effort and achievement, and they are also prepared to collaborate in numbers over a sustained period when this is necessary to raise output. Nothing in Lele culture corresponds to the Bushong striving for riches. The Bushong talk constantly and dream about wealth, while proverbs about it being the steppingstone to high status are often on their lips. Riches, prestige, and influence at court are explicitly associated together (Vansina 1954).

On the other hand, Lele behave as if they expect the most satisfying roles of middle and old age to fall into the individual's lap in the ripeness of time, only provided that he is a real man – that is, normally virile. He will eventually marry several wives, beget children, and so enter the Begetter's cult. His infant daughters will be asked in marriage by suitors bearing gifts and ready to work for him. Later, when his cult membership is bringing in a revenue of raffia cloth from fees of new initiates, his newborn daughter's daughters can be promised in marriage to junior clansmen, who will strengthen his following in the village. His wives will look after him in his declining years. He will have stores of raffia cloths to lend or give, but he will possess this wealth because, in the natural course of events, he reached the proper status for his age. He would not be able to achieve this status through wealth.

The emphasis on seniority means that, among the Lele, work and competitiveness are not geared to their longings for prestige. Among the Bushong, largely through the mechanism of markets, through money, and through elective political office, the reverse is true. It also means that Lele society holds out its best rewards in middle life and after. Those who have reached this period of privilege have an interest in maintaining the *status quo*.

All over the world it is common for the privileged sections of a community to adopt protective policies, even against their own more long-term interests. We find traces of this attitude among old Lele men. They tend to speak and behave as if they held, collectively, a position to be defended against the encroachments of the young men. Examples of this attitude have been published everywhere (Douglas 1959a). Briefly, secrets of ritual and healing are jealously guarded, and even knowledge of the debts and marriage negotiations of their own clans are deliberately withheld from the young men, as a technique for retarding their adulthood. The old are realistic enough to know that they are dependent ultimately on the brawn and muscle of the young men, and this thought is regularly brought up in disputes, when they are pressing defense of their privileges too far: "What would happen to us, if we chased away the young men? Who would hunt with us, and carry home the game? Who would carry the European's luggage?" The young men play on this, and threaten to leave the village until eventually the dispute is settled. Although it does not directly affect the levels of production that we have been discussing, this atmosphere of jealousy between men's age-groups certainly inhibits collaboration and should probably not be underestimated in its long-term effects.

Lele also believe in restricting competition. At the beginning of the century, the Lele chief NgomaNvula tried to protect the native textile industry by threatening death for anyone who wore European cloth (Simpson 1911: 310). If a Lele man is asked why women do not weave or sew, he instantly replies: "If a woman could sew her own clothes, she might refuse to cook for the men. What could we give them instead of clothes to keep them happy?" This gives a false picture of the male contribution to the domestic economy, but it is reminiscent of some modern arguments against "equal pay" for both sexes.

Within the local section of a clan, restrictions on entry into the skilled professions are deliberately enforced. A young boy is not allowed to take up a craft practiced by a senior clansman, unless the latter agrees to retire. In the same clan, in the same village, two men rarely specialize in the same skill. If a man is a good drummer, or carver, or smith, and he sees an aptitude for the same craft in his son or nephew, he may teach the boy all he knows and work with him until he thinks the apprenticeship complete. Then, ceremonially, he hands over his own position, with his tools, and retires in favor of the younger man. This ideal is frequently practiced. The accompanying convention, that a boy must not compete with his elder kinsman, is also strong enough to stop many a would-be specialist from developing his skill. Lele openly prefer reduced output. Their specialist craftsmen are few and far between because they are expected to make matters unpleasant for rivals competing for their business. Consequently the Lele as a whole are poorer in metal or wooden objects for their own use, or for export.

Lastly, it seems that Lele old men have never been able to rely on their junior clansmen for regular assistance in the fields. As a junior work-mate, a son-in-law is more reliable than a fellow-clansman. This is so for reasons connected with the pattern of residence and the weak definition of authority within the clan (Douglas 1957). An unmarried youth has no granary of his own to fill. Work which he does to help his maternal uncles, father, or father's brothers, is counted in his favor, but he can easily use the claims of one to refuse those of another, and escape with a minimum of toil. Boys would be boys, until their middle thirties. They led the good life, of weaving, drinking, and following the manly sports of hunting and warfare, without continuous agricultural responsibilities.

The key institution in which the old men see their interests as divorced from those of the young men is polygyny. Under the old system, since the young girls were pre-empted by the older men, the age of marriage was early for girls (eleven or twelve), and late for men (in their thirties). It would be superficial to suppose that these arrangements were solely for the sexual gratification of the old men. One should see them as part of the whole economic system, and particularly as one of the parts which provide social security of the old.

The division of labor between the sexes leaves the very old men with little they can do. An old woman, by contrast, can earn her keep with many useful services. But old men use their rights over women to secure necessary services, both from women and from men. Through polygyny, the principles of male dominance and of seniority are maintained to the end. To borrow an analogy from another sphere, we could almost say that the Lele have opted for an ambitious old-age pensions scheme at the price of their general standards of living. We shall see that the whole community pays for the security in old age which polygyny represents.

In the kingdom of ends peculiar to the Lele, various institutions seem to receive their justification because they are consistent with polygyny of the old men and delayed marriage of the young. The latter were reconciled to their bachelorhood, partly by the life of sport and ease, and partly by the institution of wifesharing by age-sets. They were encouraged to turn their attention away from the young wives in their own villages by the related custom of abducting girls from rival villages (Douglas 1951). Intervillage feuding therefore appears to be an essential part of the total scheme, which furthermore commits the Lele to small-scale political life. The diversion of young men's energies to raiding and abducting from rival villages was a major cause of the low levels of production, for its effects were cumulative. The raiding gave rise to such insecurity that at some times half the able-bodied males were engaged in giving armed escort to the others. Men said that in the old days a man did not go to the forest to draw palm wine alone, but his age-mate escorted him and stood with his back to the tree, bowstring taut, watching for ambush.

Coming from Bushong country in 1907, Torday was amazed at the fortified condition of Lele villages:

> Here, too, we found enclosures, but instead of the leaf walls which are considered sufficient among the Bushongo, the separations were palisades formed by solid stakes driven into the ground. Such a wall surrounded the whole village, and the single entrance was so arranged that no more than one person was able to enter at one time. (Torday 1925: 231)

Simpson also remarked that Lele men, asked to carry his baggage from their own village to the next, armed as if going into strange country. Such insecurity is obviously inimical to trade.

We have started with polygyny as the primary value to which other habits have been adjusted, because the Lele themselves talk as if all relations between men are defined by rights to women.

The point is the more effective since the Bushong are monogamous. We know well that polygyny elsewhere does not give rise to this particular accumulation of effects. Are there any features peculiar to Lele polygyny? One is the proportion of polygynous old men, indicated by the high rate of bachelorhood. Another is in the solutions they have adopted for the problems of late marriage. In some societies with extensive polygyny, the institutions which exist for the sexual satisfaction of the young men[7] are either wholly peaceful, or directed to warfare with other tribes and not to hostilities between villages. Thirdly, where the chain of command is more sharply defined (as in patrilineal systems, or in matrilineal societies in which offices are elective or carry recognizable political responsibilities, as among the Bushong), then polygyny of older men is less likely to be accompanied by attitudes of suspicion and hostility between men's age-groups.

Having started our analysis with polygyny and the high rate of bachelorhood, tracing the various interactions, we find the Lele economy constantly pegged down to the same level of production. Something like a negative feedback appears in the relations of old to young men: the more the old reserve the girls for themselves, the more the young men are resentful and evasive; the more the young men are refractory, the more the old men insist on their prerogatives. They pick on the most unsatisfactory of the young men, refuse to allot him a wife, refuse him cult membership; the others note his punishment, and either come to heel or move off to another village. There cannot be an indefinite worsening in their relations because, inevitably, the old men will die. Then the young men inherit their widows, and, now not so young, see themselves in sight of polygynous status, to be defended by solidarity of the old.

So we find the Lele, as a result of innumerable personal choices about matters of immediate concern, committed to all the insecurity of feuding villages, and to the frustration of small-scale political life and ineffective economy.

If we prefer to start our analysis at the other end, not with polygyny but with scale of political organization, we come to the same results. For whatever reason, the Bushong developed a well organized political system (Vansina 1957), embracing 70,000 people. Authority is decentralized from the Nyimi, or paramount chief, to minor chiefs, and from these to canton heads, and from these to village heads. Judicial, legislative, and administrative powers are delegated down these channels, with decisions concerning war and peace held at the center by the Nyimi. Political office is elective or by appointment. Appropriate policing powers are attached to leaders at each point in the hierarchy. Leaders are checked by variously constituted councils, whom they must consult. The Nyimi maintains his own army to quell rebellions. Tribute of grain, salt, dried foods, and money is brought into the capitals, and redistributed to loyal subjects and officials. The chiefly courts provide well-rewarded markets for craftsmen's wares so that regional specialities are salable far from their sources. Even before the advent of Europeans there was a food-market at Musenge, the Nyimi's capital. No doubt the Kasai River, protecting them from the long arm of the Bushong Empire, is partly responsible for the Lele's never having been drawn, willy-nilly, into its orbit, and accepting its values.

The Lele village, which is their largest autonomous unit, is not so big as the smallest political unit in the Bushong system. (The Lele villages average a population of 190, and the Bushong villages 210.) True, there are Lele chiefs, who claim relationship with Bushong chiefs. Each village is, indeed, found within a chiefdom – that is, an area over which a member of the chiefly clan claims suzerainty. But in practice his rights are found to be ritual and social. Each village is completely independent. The chief has no judicial or military authority. He claims tribute, but here we have no busy palace scene in which tribute payers flock in and are lavishly fed by the special catering system which chiefly polygyny so often represents.

When a chief visited a village, he was given raffia cloths, as many as could be spared. Then the villagers asked what woman he would give them in return. He named one of his daughters, and they settled a day to fetch her. The girl became the communal wife of one of the age-sets, the whole village regarding itself as her legal husband and as son-in-law to the chief. Son-in-lawship expressed their relation to him until the day that he claimed the girl's first daughter in marriage. Then the relation became reversed, the chief being son-in-law to the village. The raffia gifts and women which went back and forth between the chief and village were not essentially different from those which linked independent villages to one another in peaceful exchange. None of this interfered with the autonomy of the village.

The simple factor of scale alone has various repercussions. There is no ladder of status up which a man may honorably climb to satisfy his competitive ambitions. There is no series of offices for which age and experience qualify a man, so that in his physical decline he can enjoy respect and influence and material rewards. The Bushong lay great emphasis on individual effort and achievement, but the Lele try to damp it down. They avoid overt roles of leadership and fear the jealousy which individual success arouses. Their truncated status system turns the Lele village in on itself, to brood on quarrels and sorcery accusations, or turns it, in hostility, against other villages, so promoting the general feeling of insecurity. The latter makes markets impossible, and renders pointless ambition to produce above home needs. The old, in such an economy, unable to save, or to acquire dignity in their declining years by occupying high political office, bolster their position by claiming the marriageable women, and building up a system of rewards reserved for those who begat in wedlock. And so we are back again to polygyny and prolonged bachelorhood.

This picture has been partly based on deductions about what Lele society must have been like twenty years before fieldwork was begun. Before 1930 they could still resort to ordeals, enslave, raid and counterraid, abduct women, and pursue blood-vengeance with barbed arrows. They still needed to fortify their villages against attacks. By 1949 the scene had changed. The young men had broken out of their restraining social environment – by becoming Christians. They enjoyed protection, from mission and government, from reprisals by pagans. They could marry young Christian girls who, similarly, were able to escape their expected lot as junior wives of elderly polygynists. Raiding was ended, age-sets were nearly finished. Old men had less authority even than before. The young Christian tended to seek employment with Europeans to escape the reproaches and suspicions which their abstention from pagan rituals engendered.[8]

It would be interesting to compare their performance as workers in the new and freer context. One might expect that, away from the influence of their old culture, Lele performance might equal or surpass that of Bushong. Unfortunately the framework for such a comparison is lacking. Neither tribe has a high reputation for industry with its respective employers, compared with immigrant Cokwe, Luba and Pende workers. This may simply be because the best reputations are earned by tribes which have longest been accustomed to wage-labor.

One is tempted to predict that, in so far as it is due to social factors, Lele are likely to change their name for idleness and lack of stamina before long. In 1949–50 they were not forthcoming in numbers for plantation labor or for cutting oil-palm nuts. By 1954, when a scattering of small shops through the territory had put trade goods within their reach, they had become eager to earn money. The restrictive influence of the old social system was already weaker.

We may now look again at the demographic factor, and distinguish some effects on it of the economy and the political system. It is obvious that in different types of economy, the active male contribution may have different time spans according to the nature of the work. If there were a modern community whose breadwinners were international skating champions, footballers, or miners at the coal-face, their period of active work would be briefer than in economies based on less physically exacting tasks. A primitive economy is, by definition, one based on rudimentary technology, and the more rudimentary, the more the work consists of purely individual physical effort. Moreover, the simpler the economy, the smaller the scope for managerial roles and ancillary sedentary work. The result, then, is that the period of full, active contribution to the economy is shorter.[9]

If we compare Lele and Bushong economies on these lines, we see that the "age of retirement" is likely to be earlier for the Lele. The typical Bushong man is able, long after he has passed his physical prime, to make a useful contribution to production, either by using his experience to direct the collaboration of others or in various administrative roles which are important in maintaining the security and order necessary for prosperity. The Lele economy, on the other hand, with its emphasis on individual work, gives less weight to experience and finds less productive work for the older man to do. We can only guess at the differences, but it is worth presenting the idea visually, as in Figure 8.3.

Furthermore, at the other end of the life span, the same trend is increased because of the late entry into agricultural work of Lele men. The young Lele is not fully employed in agriculture until he is at least thirty and married, the Bushong man when he is twenty. Figure 8.4 illustrates the idea that the active labor force in the Lele economy, as a proportion of the total population, is on both scores smaller than it is with the Bushong. The total output of the economy has to be shared among a larger population of dependants.

The comparison of the two economies has shown up something like the effects of "backwash" described by Professor Myrdal (1957). First we see that in the environment there are initial disadvantages which limit development. Secondly, we find that in the social organization itself there are further inhibiting effects which are cumulative, and which work one on another and back again on the economy, technology and population, to intensify the initial disadvantages. We have tried to present the interaction of these tendencies in a simplified form in Figure 8.5.

"Nothing succeeds like success." Somehow, sometime, the Bushong took decisions which produced a favorable turn in their fortunes and set off interactions which resulted in their political hegemony and their wealth. The Lele missed the benefits of this civilization because of their location on the other side of the Kasai River, their poorer soils, their history. The decisions they took amounted to an accommodation of their life to a lower political and economic level. Their technology was inferior, so their efforts were backed with less efficient equipment, and their economy was less productive. Their old social system barred

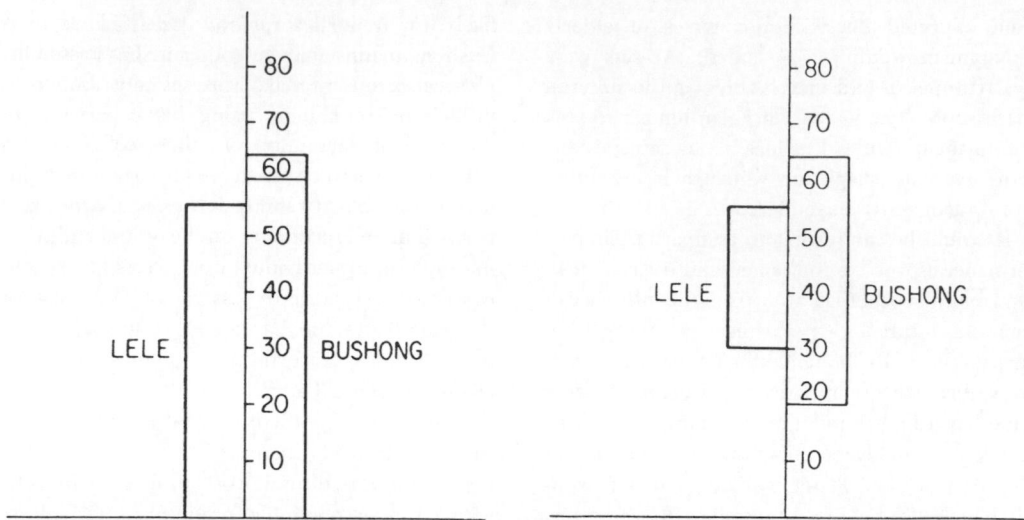

Figure 8.3 Age of retirement from work

Figure 8.4 Period of full work, showing age of entry into full agricultural responsibility

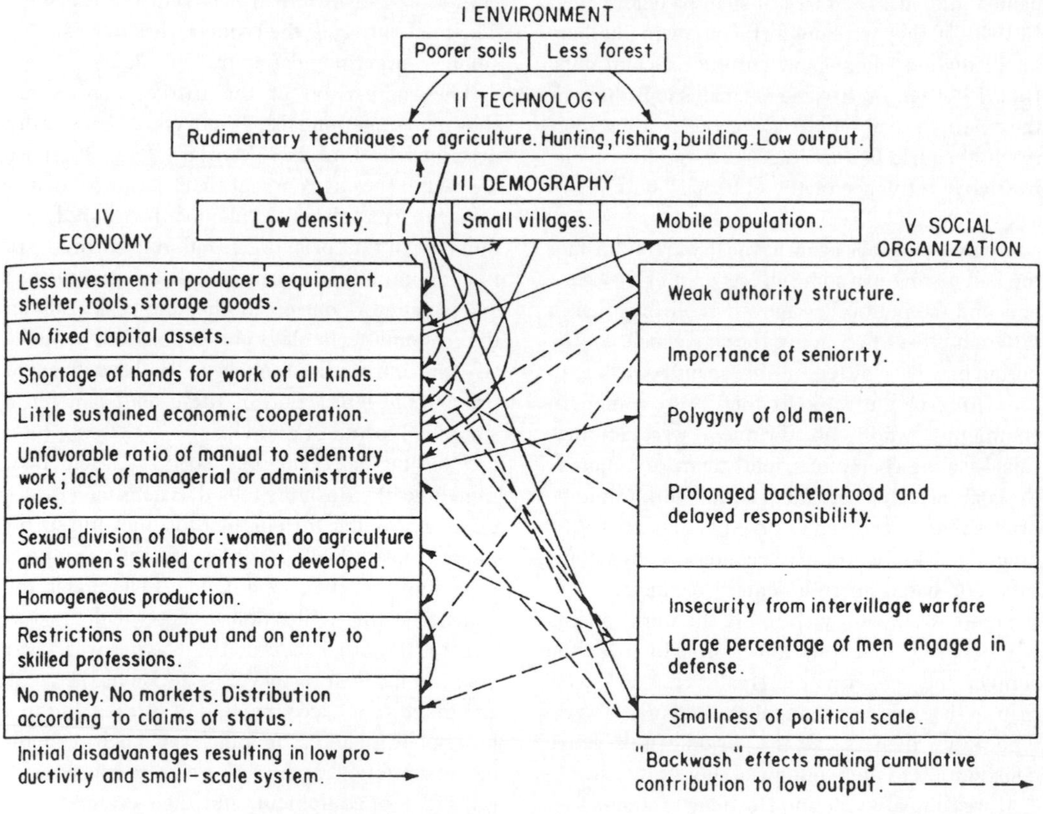

I ENVIRONMENT

| Poorer soils | Less forest |

II TECHNOLOGY

Rudimentary techniques of agriculture. Hunting, fishing, building. Low output.

III DEMOGRAPHY

| Low density. | Small villages. | Mobile population. |

IV ECONOMY

Less investment in producer's equipment, shelter, tools, storage goods.

No fixed capital assets.

Shortage of hands for work of all kinds.

Little sustained economic cooperation.

Unfavorable ratio of manual to sedentary work; lack of managerial or administrative roles.

Sexual division of labor: women do agriculture and women's skilled crafts not developed.

Homogeneous production.

Restrictions on output and on entry to skilled professions.

No money. No markets. Distribution according to claims of status.

Initial disadvantages resulting in low pro-ductivity and small-scale system. ⟶

V SOCIAL ORGANIZATION

Weak authority structure.

Importance of seniority.

Polygyny of old men.

Prolonged bachelorhood and delayed responsibility.

Insecurity from intervillage warfare

Large percentage of men engaged in defense.

Smallness of political scale.

"Backwash" effects making cumulative contribution to low output. ⟶ ⟶ ⟶

Figure 8.5 Lele economy and social organization

many of the chances which might have favored economic growth.

Anthropologists sometimes tend to discuss the adoption or rejection of new techniques in terms of a cultural mystique, as if dealing with irreducible principles, of which no analysis is feasible.[10] The Lele may be taken as a case in point. Their preference for their own inferior techniques, in spite of awareness of better methods used across the river, depend on certain institutions, and these again on their history and environment. Through economic analysis we can break down the effect of choices, each made reasonably enough in its own restricted context. By following up the interactions of these choices, one upon another, we can see how the highly idiosyncratic mold of Lele culture is related to a certain low level of production.

Notes

1   The Lele are a tribe, inhabiting the west border of the Bakuba Empire. They are divided into three chiefdoms, of which only the most westerly has been studied. The Chief of the eastern Lele, at Perominenge, apes Kuba fashions in his little capital; the men wear basketry hats held on with metal pins, the chief has some of the dress and paraphernalia of the Nyimi. How much deeper this resemblance goes, it is impossible to say, since conditions at the time of field work were not favorable for study of this chiefdom. Everything that is said here concerning the Lele refers to the western Lele, whose chief, when visits were made in 1949–50 and 1953, was Norbert Pero Mihondo. The field work was carried out under the generous auspices of the International African Institute, and of the *Institut de Recherche Scientifique en Afrique Centrale*.

2   The Bushong are the ruling tribe of the Kuba Kindom. They were studied in 1953–56 by Dr Vansina, to whom I am deeply indebted for his collaboration and for supplying unpublished information for this paper.

3   According to the Lexico-statistical survey conducted by Dr Vansina, there is an 80 per cent similarity between the two languages.

4   We are very grateful to M. L. Cahen, Director of the *Musée du Congo Belge*, Tervuren, for guidance on the physical environment of the two tribes.

5   According to P. Gourou, 1951, the average density of the population of all tribes for the Basongo–Port Francqui region, in which the Lele now account for only half, is 3 to 4 to the square kilometer. This agrees with calculations based on the total number of Lele in that area, about 26,000, and the extent of their territory, about 63 by 110 miles, which give a Lele density of roughly 4 to the square mile, or 1.7 to the sq. km.

6   For the most widely read statement of this view, see Herskovits 1952 (Part V, The Economic Surplus) and for a list of reputed subscribers to this view, see Harris 1959.

7   For example, Tiv "sister-marriage" of the "manyatta" of the Masai.

8   This process has been described in Douglas 1959b.

9   This approach was suggested by Linton 1940.

10   See Benedict (1956: 187): "Among primitive peoples, this lack of interest in 'progress' has been proverbial ... Every primitive tribe has its own cultural arrangements which ensure its survival ... They may be culturally uninterested in labor-saving devices. Often the value they put on time is extremely low, and 'wisdom' is far more valued than efficiency. Our cultural system and theirs are oriented around different ideals."

References

Benedict, Ruth
   1956 "The Growth of Culture," in *Man, Culture and Society* (H. Shapiro, ed.). New York: Oxford University Press.
Bultot, F.
   1954 "Saisons et Périodes Sèches et Pluvieuses au Congo Belge." Brussels.

Douglas, Mary
   1951 "A Form of Polyandry among the Lele," *Africa*, Vol. 21, pp. 1–12.
   1954 "The Lele of the Kasai," in *African Worlds* (D. Forde, ed.). London: Oxford University Press.
   1957 "The Pattern of Residence among the Lele," *Zaïre*, Vol. 11, pp. 818–43.

1958 "Raffia Distribution in the Lele Economy," *Africa*, Vol. 28, pp. 2 ff.

1959a "Age-Status among the Lele," *Zaïre*, Vol. 13, pp. 386–413.

1959b "The Lele of the Kasai," in *The Church and the Nations* (A. Hastings, ed.). London: Sheed & Ward.

1960 "Blood-debts among the Lele," *Journal of the Royal Anthropological Institute*, Vol. 90, No. 1, pp. 1–28.

Forde, D.

1937 "Land and Labour in a Cross River Village," *Geographical Journal*, Vol. 40, No. 1.

Gourou, P.

1951 *Atlas général du Congo: notice de la carte de la densité de la population au Congo-Belge et au Ruanda-Urundi*. Institut Royal Colonial Belge.

1955 *La Densité de la population rurale au Congo Belge, etc.* Brussels: Acad. Roy. Sci. Col. Mem. 8,1,2.

Harris, M.

1959 "The Economy Has No Surplus?" *American Anthropologist*, Vol. 61, No. 2, pp. 185–200.

Herskovits, M.

1952 *Economic Anthropology: The Economic Life of Primitive Peoples*. New York: Norton.

Linton, Ralph

1940 "A Neglected Aspect of Social Organization," *American Journal of Sociology*, Vol. 45, pp. 870–86.

Myrdal, Gunnar

1957 *Economic Theory and Underdeveloped Regions*. London: G. Duckworth.

Nicolai, H.

1952 "Problèmes du Kwango," *Bulletin de la Société Belge d'Études Géographiques*, Vol. 25, No. 2.

Nicolai, H. and Jacques, J.

1954 *La Transformation du paysage Congolais par le Chemin de Fer, L'Exemple du B.C.K.* Acad. Roy. Sci. Col. Brussels, Sect. des Sci. Natu. et Med. Mem. in 8, XXIV, L.

Simpson, H.

1911 *Land and Peoples of the Kasai*. London: Constable & Co.

Torday, E.

1925 *On the Trail of the Bushongo*. London: Seeley, Service & Co., Ltd.

Turner, V. W.

1957 *Schism and Continuity in an African Society*. Manchester: Manchester University Press.

Van den Plas, A.

1947 *La Température au Congo Belge*. Pub. Minis. Colon., pp. 33–38.

Vansina, Jan

1954 "Les Valeurs Culturelles des Bushong," *Zaïre*, No. 9, pp. 900–910, November.

1955 "Initiation Rituals of the Bushong," *Africa*, Vol. 25, pp. 138–52.

1956 "Migration dans la Province du Kasai," *Zaïre*, pp. 69–85.

1957 "L'État Kuba dans le cadre des institutions politiques Africaines," *Zaïre*, Vol. 11, pt. 1, pp. 485–92.

9

Research on an African Mode of Production*

Catherine Coquery-Vidrovitch

Until recently, African traditional societies have generally been studied in isolation and with emphasis on the particular. Economic anthropologists are only just beginning to understand the kinship structures of subsistence societies.[1] But by concentrating on the fact of subsistence, they have underestimated the importance of the organization of production and of the social hierarchy. Subsistence, which is not autarchy, does not imply the absence of a division of labour or of elementary methods of exchange, in particular, local food markets. These are not "class societies" as Marxists understand the term nowadays, and they differ from pre-capitalist Western societies in the absence of any private appropriation of the land. However, throughout Africa, they have gone beyond the stage of "primitive community." Even the economic organization of the Pygmies in the forest is based on an exchange of goods from hunting and gathering for the agricultural produce of sedentary tribes.

Thus the problem of a mode of production arises, which even Soviet historians[2] hesitate to compare to one of the stages defined for Western Europe: slavery, feudalism, and capitalism. Since Marx and Engels had outlined another mode of production, the Asiatic, Marxists naturally thought of extending to Africa this concept hitherto used for societies of the Near East (Egypt and Mesopotamia) and Far East (China).[3]

The Asiatic mode of production presupposes villages based on collective production and bound to a "higher unity" in the form of a state capable of compelling people to work. Behind this "generalized slavery," a despot "exploits these communities economically while he rules them."[4] The State becomes an entrepreneur capable of massive public works despite a limited technical capacity: irrigation systems (the river states of the Near East), military defence (the Great Wall of China), or prestige (the pyramids).[5] In this extreme form, the Asiatic mode of production is clearly not found in Black Africa. Even if we could compare certain forms of African despotism with it, we would find ourselves without the dynamic element, the "generalized slavery," which is

* Originally published as "Recherches sur un mode de production africain," *La Pensée*, 144, Editions Sociales, Paris, 1969. Translated in M.A. Klein and G.W. Johnson (eds), *Perspectives on the African Past*. Little, Brown and Company, New York, 1972.
From Catherine Coquery-Vidrovitch, "Research on an African Mode of Production", in *Relations of Production*, pp. 261–88, ed. David Seddon (1978), from Frank Cass & Co. Ltd.

found only perhaps in the massive constructions of the "Builders of Stone" in Southern Africa (Zimbabwe, eleventh to eighteenth centuries).

Conscious that some of the Asian characteristics mentioned by Marx are not found in Black Africa, researchers have been generally reluctant to push their analysis to its limits. Although they would be reluctant to admit it, their problem is an excess of respect for the master, who could not have analysed societies which were unknown in his time.

The most striking effort was Jean Suret-Canale's attempt to describe an Asiatic mode of production in pre-colonial Black Africa in terms of an evolution in three stages: the *primitive community* (which has, in fact, disappeared); the tribal or *tribo-patriarchal* structure of segmentary societies called "anarchic" or "stateless," where the basic social unit is the extended family, and which is the transition to clearly differentiated *class societies*, or *states* in which privileged aristocracies seem to have created the State above the patriarchal village.[6]

By elimination – since African societies were neither slave-based (as the term is used in ancient history) nor feudal – Suret-Canale compares their system to that of Asian societies. He has to recognize the absence of *despotism*, but is anxious to relate the African mode of production to his general plan, and hence gives a broad definition of an Asiatic mode of production: "The coexistence of an instrument of production based on the rural community ... and the exploitation of man by man in diverse forms ... which consistently use the intermediary of the community."

Suret-Canale assigns to the difference between "a stateless society" and a State an importance which is now debated for Black Africa.[7] In addition, his definition of a surplus exclusively based upon the privileged class's appropriation of the products of village labour appears to be erroneous (we shall return to this later) and his definition of an Asiatic mode of production, if not false, is too general since it omits the essential point: the motivating factor of the exploitation of man by man, that is to say the kind of these "diverse forms."

A similar problem prompted Godelier, in a study of the Asiatic mode of production,[8] to distinguish between "an Asiatic mode of production with public works" and "an Asiatic mode of production without public works." The latter seems more debatable. Once again this limited definition

omits the dynamic element from a mode of production, by leaving out its economic foundation at the level of production. In fact, public works, which surpass the means of particular communities, create the conditions of productive activity for these communities: "The State and the ruling class directly intervene in the conditions of production, and the connection between productive capacity and production lies directly with the organization of public works.[9] These public works give rise to a bureaucracy and an absolute power, which is centralized and 'despotic'."

Suret-Canale had already noted that the states of West Africa were set up differently: "they were clearly based on the union of a tribal confederation (headed by a 'king', the chief of the land), and a *market* to which the king gives security and from which he takes an important part of his revenue."[10] Godelier is also aware that the rise of empires in tropical Africa (such as mediaeval Ghana, Mali, and Songhai) was not related to the organization of public works but "to the control by tribal aristocracies of inter-tribal or inter-regional trade involving an exchange of precious products – gold, ivory, skins, etc. ... between black and white Africa."[11]

In completing his presentation, Suret-Canale unconvincingly eliminates the dynamic element in African history which stemmed from foreign contacts. He resorts to a local example rather than to scientific reasoning: his proof is the existence of the Mossi States in whose formation "trade apparently played no role whatever,"[12] – which remains to be verified. Godelier, on the other hand, accepts the consequences of his analysis. He proposes "to add a second hypothesis to that of Marx ... that there can be another path and another form for the mode of production, by which a minority dominates and exploits the community without directly interfering with their conditions of production, but by profitably taking a surplus in labour and in products."[13]

We are in complete agreement with this, and the object of this article is to show why. We take exception to the comparison between the "Asiatic mode of production" and the mode of production found in some African societies, and therefore will use the term "African mode of production." The only thing the two systems have in common is the existence of subsistence village communities. In Asia, however, it is a question of despotism and direct exploitation through generalized slavery, whereas in Africa, as we shall see, there is a superimposed bureaucracy which interferes only indirectly with the community. We do not see the necessity of examining these two types of production, which differ in so many respects, together. By considering the original features of both, and analysing the productive relationships in Africa, it will be possible to discern an "African mode of production."

Long-distance Trading

One characteristic of African societies is that they were never truly isolated. The African continent has known two major phenomena: the mobility of its people and the volume of long-distance trade. Migrations – collective movements or progressive infiltrations – came to an end only in the colonial era when colonial régimes fixed populations for more effective police control or for such administrative goals as tax collection or the allocation of lots for private property. Previously, the history of Africa was indistinguishable from the movements of its peoples. These were partly attributable to the existence of low population densities and large, relatively open areas. Nearly everywhere, except along the coasts, the land is open to movement and even the dense forest is cut by large navigable rivers such as the Congo.

Examples of movement are numerous. The most spectacular was the Bantu expansion which overflowed most earlier populations in the central and southern part of the continent.[14] The Fulbe, who took refuge in the Senegalese Tekrur after prehistoric migrations from the Sahara, moved in the opposite direction from the seventeenth century. Today they are scattered from Senegal to Lake Chad. The history of the Fang since the early nineteenth century is that of movement from Cameroon toward the Atlantic.[15] Finally, there were Nilotic movements which spread south from the Sudan throughout eastern Africa between the fifteenth and nineteenth centuries and perhaps their superior techniques reached the Lake Region, Katanga, and Rhodesia.[16] In brief, there is no ethnographic monograph which cannot present for the people studied a map of their origins marked with crisscrossing arrows, symbols of the complexity of its successive and often recent migrations.

Following these continual upheavals, African societies were at all times under foreign influence, which came from Egypt, from the Arab world, from Europe, indeed, even from Asia. The heritage of ancient Egypt spread into Nubia, to Napata and then to Meroe (the Kingdom of Kush, 600 BC to AD 300), and from there to Axum in Ethiopia. Southwest Asia looked to East Africa, which offered a reserve of manpower, a place for immigration, and numerous early ties. From the ninth century on, members of persecuted sects took refuge on the Coast. Kilwa, in Swahili country, is said to have been founded in the tenth century by a group of Iranians. Other places along the coast – Mogadiscio, Mombasa, Malindi, Pemba and, further south, Sofala (opposite Madagascar), which were great centres of Arab mercantile activity, at least until the Portuguese discovery, had a comparable origin. Indian merchants, between the eleventh and thirteenth centuries, had enough influence to introduce their system of weights and measures, and their money practices to the region, and in Kilwa, enough to even bring an adventurer of their choice (Al Hasan ibn Talut) to power in the thirteenth century. In the South, even before Islam, Malayan canoes opened the way to the Comaro Islands and Madagascar, and Malacca had regular relations with the western coasts of the Indian Ocean from the ninth and tenth centuries. Finally, the Chinese at least twice made contact with East Africa, in 1417–19 and in 1431–33, and the archaeological discoveries of Chinese and Persian pottery are numerous enough for this to have been written: "From the 10th century onwards, the buried history of Tanganyika is written in Chinese porcelain."[17]

In West Africa, contacts with the Maghreb were even earlier: in 734 an expedition from the Sous reached Sudan. Contacts were established which were never broken: in 757–58 the founding of Sijilmassa in southern Morocco opened the Sudan road for the gold caravans. As for the Europeans, they moved along the coasts from 1434 (the date when Cape Bojador, opposite the Canary Islands, was crossed) to 1487 (when they doubled the Cape of Tempests, later the Cape of Good Hope).

These contacts led to long-distance commerce across the Sahara and the Indian Ocean. This cannot be reduced to external factors: the Arab conquest, the Portuguese Exploration, or the colonial impact. They profoundly affected the interior too by encouraging the collaboration of coastal kingdoms (slave-traders, for example), and of inland tribes who acted as intermediaries. In the Congolese basin, merchandise got through long before white men did, preceding the half-breed Portuguese traders, the "pombeiros" who had been trickling toward the Pool along the caravan trails since the end of the fifteenth century. In the Gabonese back country, the people of the Ogooué had European-made textiles, pearls, and "neptunes"[18] in their possession. The Fang of Woleu-Ntem, an area barely penetrated before the twentieth century (within the borders of southern Cameroon), had guns from trading before anyone there had ever seen a white man.[19] Likewise, during his mediaeval Sudanese empires, the people of the forest regions, including the Gold Coast, whose mines were opened in the mid-fourteenth century by Mandé initiative, had received merchandise of Maghreb origin (glass beads, salt) in exchange for iron ore, ivory, or kola nuts which had been sent up North.

It was not necessary for trading to achieve a large volume in order to exercise great influence. History shows, however, that it often reached considerable proportions: gold and salt in medieval West Africa, or the gold and copper exported via the Monomotapa, rulers of an empire centred in the bend of the Zambesi river and Sofala on the Indian Ocean. In addition, there were slave traders. At least 10 to 20 million were sent to the Atlantic trade between the sixteenth and nineteenth centuries.[20] The trans-Sahara trade to the Ottoman empire was at about 10,000 a year in the nineteenth century (compared to 70,000 sent to America)[21] and in the same period, large numbers were being shipped from the Congo basin to Zanzibar and the Indian Ocean trade.

A Critique of the Traditional Contrast in Black Africa: States versus Stateless Societies

The economic life of pre-colonial African societies was characterized by the juxtaposition of two apparently contradictory levels: the local subsistence village and international, even transcontinental commerce. This economic phenomenon is paralleled by and inseparable from a political one pointed out by Balandier, the conflict between a kinship-based tribal structure and a territorial organization with centralizing tendencies.[22] Does that mean we must link (as Suret-Canale implicitly does) first subsistence to "tribo-patriarchal" or stateless society and, second, long-distance trade and the more or less despotic state? The analogy is questionable. In order to show this, we shall limit ourselves to a few examples. Let historians and anthropologists make the case which will permit us to verify what in our present state of knowledge must be considered a research hypothesis.

Anthropologists have certainly proved to what degree kinship structures are associated with the economic structures of subsistence. Segmentary societies, until recently placed in the poorly defined and poorly studied category of primitive "classless societies," show themselves on closer analysis to be rather diversified. Once again, it is Balandier who reminds us that in Black Africa "all societies are heterogeneous to varying degrees."[23] This primitive community is made up of "social strata" which are involved in "antagonism, competition and conflict."[24] In its simplest form, it is the domination of the elder over the younger, the elder controlling the means of production because they can demand that the younger "remit the product of their labour."[25] They can exclusively hoard or exchange "prestige goods," which reinforce their position – and, thus, we have a process of accumulation in the villages, capable of developing and accentuating inequalities. This is not a full outline. It is sufficient to underline the danger of denying that subsistence is "an economic, scientific, and Marxist category" because "it is only a void, the absence of a market economy and market goods."[26] Such a negative definition risks the rejection of "all pre-capitalist societies ... in the vague concept of traditional society,"[27] which would explain in part the lack of interest shown in this problem by Europocentric historians, including Marxists. We find no such strong refusal in Marx himself. On the contrary, he states that

the specific economic form in which unpaid surplus labour is exacted from the direct producers ... is the basis of *any form of economic* community ... and, at the same time, the basis of its *specific political form*. It is always necessary to seek the hidden foundation of any *social edifice*, and consequently, of any political form which draws its relationship from sovereignty and dependence in the immediate relationship between the manager of the means of production and the direct manager (a connection whose different aspects naturally correspond ... to a *certain degree* of productive social force).[28]

Is it necessary, on the contrary, to associate long-distance trading and centralized power? This seems much more dubious. To be sure, the most striking examples have been studied within states: Ghana and Mali were tied to trade with Maghreb; Benin and Dahomey experienced a similar development with the slave-trade; Zanzibar flourished in the nineteenth century with slave and ivory trading in East Africa. But recent studies prove that long-distance trade influenced the most diverse societies. Along the Congo River and its main tributaries (the Oubangui, Sangha, Likouala, Alima, to mention only the north bank), trade was the only means of existence for certain segmentary peoples. In the sixteenth century trading took place between the Portuguese and the Kongo Kingdom situated on the south of the Congo. But, by 1850, the latter no longer existed. Beyond the Bakongo of the coastal zone, trade had reached the Bateke of Stanley Pool, and, further up-river, the Bubangi who lived where the Sangha and Oubangui rivers met the Congo.[29] There, the power of the chief rarely extended beyond the village or fraction of a village. Nonetheless, these river people, isolated on knolls along a complex system of lagoons, constituted a dynamic whole; unable to earn a living from the marshy soil, they turned to trade in local food products and in slaves. On the upper Alima, the Bubangi (locally called Lakuba) set up temporary encampments for the dry season and traded about 20 tons a day of manioc from the Batekes of the plateau and the Mbochi of the river. In return they offered the fruits of their activity: mats, pottery, paddles, nets, harpoons, and dried fish which they produced in large amounts.

With these activities, which were indispensable to the maintenance of their position in this strategic, though barren area, they combined their role as agents for long-distance Congolese trading: in exchange for European merchandise, they received ivory from Likouala. Further upstream came slaves, wood, ivory and, before long, rubber from the Sangha and the Oubangui. Important markets developed around Pool and along the rivers. These products were provided by similar segmentary groups operating further upstream. The inhabitants of the forest knew that the river came from "the land of white men" armed with guns, who were certainly Arabs. This fact, amongst others, confirms the extent of Congolese trade which handled products and men over great distances.

No matter what society is examined, the permanence of trade transcends the traditional contrast between states and stateless societies. Balandier has already shown the coexistence of apparently contradictory elements at the heart of *all* African politics, state or stateless. In both, all forms of transition can be discovered. To be sure, there is a progress toward centralized organization, but the difference is qualitative rather than essential; even in the most "despotic" societies (mediaeval Sudanese kingdoms, the Kongo in the sixteenth century, and Dahomey in the nineteenth century), the authority of the sovereign never replaced the tribe-patriarchal organization. At most, it involved a superimposed bureaucracy, which respected the structures of rural life. To recognize this trait common to all African societies is, at the same time, to seek its economic basis. One of the motives of African history is to be found in the dialectical interplay, or the absence of interplay, between apparently heterogeneous socio-economic levels within the same unit (the coexistence of communal clan structures and territorial entities, the superimposition of subsistence and long-distance trade). At any given moment, their history reveals a certain stage of development in these relationships, whose contradictions were perpetually generating disequilibrium and conflict.

Toward an "African Mode of Production"?

By taking into account these specific traits it becomes possible to discern an *African mode of production* distinct from the classic model of the *Asiatic mode of production*.

Black Africa, as we have stated, never had an Asiatic type of despotism. That does not mean that there were no aristocracies or privileged classes. But the rulers who had power in various places were hastily identified as "absolute monarchs" by European observers. The demands which they made with the aid of the ruling class were neither, nor exclusively, wrought on "the hard-working peasantry, made up both of free men and captives," which was, in Africa, as elsewhere, "the fundamental exploited class."[30] To be sure, there were exceptions. In pre-colonial Senegal the families which had power also possessed rights to land and to work from the peasants (as a collectivity, however, with neither the exploiters nor the exploited considered as individuals).[31] In Burundi, property (livestock and pastures) was controlled by the *Tutsi* at the expense of the *Hutu*. This suggests a relationship of a feudal nature.[32]

However, it seems excessive to seek the only motive for this development of African societies in the productive forces of a subsistence economy. Such a statement, which seeks within African society the opposition of exploiters and the exploited reveals a lack of observation of the actual data. Black Africa is the one place in the world where agriculture was least liable to produce a surplus. Agricultural and craft techniques were particularly rudimentary (no wheel nor plow: the only tool was the hoe). The necessity of improving production with the aid of new tools or large public works was never felt. A rather sparse population was able to meet its needs without too much effort from land which was abundant, though not fertile. No ruler, in order to live, ever needed to take food from village production *in quantity*. At most, he was content to organize for his own benefit the labour of his wives (the case of Dahomey, for example), and "domestic" slaves, but this was not comparable to what has been called the "slavery mode of production." The tribute levied by the best-organized despots (the kings of the Kongo and Dahomey) does not seem to have been used as payment for services or to provide labour needed on tasks of public utility. It is not certain that tribute was regularly used to feed the people of the court, and nothing indicates that it was even used as a public aid fund to which those in need could appeal.[33] In the Kongo, the King and the nobles redistributed what they had received among vassals

who requested it.[34] In Dahomey, the "customs festival," an annual ceremony celebrated since the eighteenth century in honour of the royal ancestors, fulfilled the same function. It was an occasion for the sovereign to collect the tribute but, above all, to dazzle his assembled subjects for several weeks with the dynasty's wealth and bounty, either by the public sacrifice of hundreds of slaves,[35] or by the distribution of spirits, poured out in great quantities, or of cowries (local money) and cloth cast out from public platforms.[36] In brief, the fees demanded were, above all, of symbolic value, a guarantee of the social structure. Not that the relationship of exploiters to exploited did not exist; rather the African despot exploited his subjects less than the neighbouring tribes. In fact, it was long-distance trading which provided the major part of his surplus. From this point of view, the customs festival was not a retrograde institution which limited or paralysed European contacts – on the contrary, it stimulated the economic life of the country and encouraged the intense trading activity necessary to supply this "fair" with all sorts of products (slaves in exchange for European merchandise). Let us not be reproached here for excessively favouring the *mode of circulation of goods* at the expense of the *mode of production*; the fundamental problem was not to transport merchandise but to procure it – in a certain sense to "produce" it. It was evidently a bastardized form of production, both immediate and apparent, which was in fact ruinous, since, in the long run, it sterilized the country instead of enriching it. There were two ways of procuring goods: war (in the case of slave raids),[37] or peaceful exchanges with neighbouring peoples (the case of salt and gold in the Sudan), a type of externally oriented exchange comparable to a form of production and opposed to circulation within a given society.

Suret-Canale noted the basic role of trade in Black Africa, "the decisive element in the consolidation of the first states in tropical Africa."[38] He has not sufficiently explored its significance, however, because of his concern to establish *direct* domination of the aristocracy over the peasantry. The control of long-distance trading demanded the subordination of the bulk of the population to those who benefited from it. Yet the control exercised by the ruling class was manifested *indirectly*, by the exclusive possession of goods which were accumulated in a process analogous to the way "prestige goods" are often amassed by the elders in a subsistence society: for example, red cotton fabric from Europe which the Bateke chiefs kept for their funerals[39] and weapons accumulated in the arsenals of the Sultans of Haut-Oubangui. Furthermore, indirect domination did not exclude its corollary, direct domination, especially in the case of the gun trade, which conditioned them both. In acquiring arms, the sovereign assured himself of control of military enlistment, the payment of tributes and the work of the plantations which in turn promoted the accumulation of an exportable surplus (for example, palm oil cultivated by the king's plantations in Dahomey since the mid-nineteenth century). But, let us repeat, the major revenues came not from village communities, but from outside the territory, from the annual raids or from peaceful commercial transactions which secured products at rates much lower than their actual value. Thus, life in the kingdom of Dahomey was marked by military expeditions launched each dry season towards the Ashanti in the West or the Yoruba cities in the East, in order to bring back the slaves required by the economy. This was also true in the Kongo and probably in Benin. In central Africa, the Likouba (Bubangi) obtained manioc from the Bateke and the Mbochi "at ridiculously low prices."[40] At Stanley Pool they resold the red wood, the ivory and the slaves brought upstream at five or six times, indeed, perhaps ten times the price.[41] Even in the case of the empires founded on mineral wealth (gold from the Sudan or from southern Africa), the ruler's problem was not to impose on his subjects a collective effort to extract the ores. It was to obtain, at a low price, a metal sometimes located far from his territory. Neither the King of Ghana, nor the Emperor of Mali controlled the producers who probably operated within a hunting and gathering economy. They knew even less about them because of silent barter. This oft-described process forbade the two parties to enter into direct contact. The merchants who came from the North displayed their merchandise (salt) in a specific place and then they withdrew. The next morning, opposite each object they wanted to sell, they found an amount of gold-dust. If they thought the offer

sufficient, they took the gold; if not, they touched nothing, until a supplementary amount was added or, if their demand was too high, it was all taken away. When the Emperor of Mali had one of the traders carried off in order to discover "what kind of men did not allow themselves to be seen or to be spoken to," the only result was the suspension of trade for three years.[42] In addition, Arab writers reported absurd stories about cannibals or deformed savages who worked the veins of gold after the rains. ...[43] In southern Africa, the ore-bearing sites spread from Katanga to the Limpopo are more extensive than the ruins of the "stone builders," which testify to a political organization around Zimbabwe and Mapungubwe (South Rhodesia) and seem to corroborate an analogous hypothesis of "production" by trade rather than by direct exploitation.[44]

The African mode of production is based then upon the combination of a patriarchal–communal economy and the exclusive ascendancy of one group over long-distance trade. The form of power at any given moment depends upon the nature of this group. If political authority was in the hands of the heads of kinship groups at the village level, their preeminence was then uncontested. In the case of the Fang or the Bubangi, it was only threatened by the rivalry of small groups involved in the same trade. In the middle Congo, the system collapsed only under the pressure of external factors: the intrusion of Europeans who seized control of trade for their own profit and eliminated the traditional middlemen.

If, on the other hand, in a more differentiated political system, a privileged class succeeded in controlling long-distance trade by means of a hereditary caste or because of an accumulation of capital, the régime combined the tribo-patriarchal system and a new kind of territorial ambition. The mediaeval Sudanese empires, for example, were characterized by the utilization of traditional animist structures by an Arabized aristocracy which controlled trade. It would be an error to imagine these to be Islamic states (especially since Ghana was already declining when Islam took root). The function of these empires was to control and exploit trade between the western Sudan and North Africa. Their goal was domination for profit and this economic objective allowed them to realize their political form. The ruling class was interested in presenting a Moslem facade, through the organization of its Courts and the pilgrimages, which would favour good relations with the Maghreb, a client and supplier. However, Islamic proselytizing would have threatened internal stability. We have no evidence that Islam had a solid base outside of the large cities; on the contrary, even within monarchical institutions the descriptions left by Arab geographers show that the leaders felt the need to graft their power onto a typically pagan structure, probably of Mandé origin. Hence the pomp which surrounded the King, the rites he had to follow (not to drink in public, not to converse directly with his subjects ...), and the submissive demonstrations of his dignitaries (who prostrated themselves in the dust or performed sacramental dances in honour of the sovereign). To abandon these traditions would have provoked hostility, since the masses were attached to patriarchal forms. The evolution of the empires resulted from the equilibrium between these two antagonistic currents: in Songhai, for example, Sonni Ali (1464–92), a champion of militant paganism, aroused a Moslem reaction against himself. To be sure, he subdued the whole loop of the Niger river, but the history of the Empire became a constant competition between pagans and Moslems, which weakened the state and encouraged the Moroccan conquest in 1591. This resolved the conflict by uniting all in resistance in the name of the animist cause – but at the price of economic supremacy.[45] ...

When a privileged group or a despot lost control of long-distance trade this eventually led to the decline of his political power: this was the case in the Kingdom of the Kongo. At first it owed its cohesion to the King's monopoly of long-distance trade which probably existed within central Africa from the twelfth century: lumps of sea salt were carried inland, as well as the "zimbu" shellfish from the isle of Luanda which was used as money. On the other hand, raffia mats and ivory were received at the Pool from forest areas. When the ruler lost control of trade with Europe, he also lost control of outlying provinces. Chiefs on the coast from Loango and Soyo north of the river's mouth to Angola in the south profited by the distance from the capital to seize control of markets, with the aid of Portuguese merchants from São Tomé. From the sixteenth century on, these peripheral coastal peoples gradually freed themselves. The vassals became brokers, and from this trade they took a power which permitted them to compete with the authority they henceforth rejected.[46]

The examples presented do not in themselves claim to establish a general law. In the present state of our knowledge, they are simply an effort to explain the coexistence of contradictory political and economic elements. This coexistence was undoubtedly explained by the preference of the minorities in power to exploit their neighbours rather than their subjects. No African political régime, no matter how despotic, felt the need to eliminate communal village structures within their borders which did not interfere with their exploitation. As long as the village transmitted its tribute to the chief of the district or of the province, it ran the life of the collectivity as it pleased. The elders assured the worship of the clan's ancestors; the chief of the land allotted arable land to each family and to each generation; groups of women dominated the local food markets. There was no need to supply the ruler with a contingent of plantation labourers or porters, tasks generally performed by royal slaves seized in foreign countries. The most frequent obligations were limited to military service, or, as in Dahomey, the selection of some girls for the harem of the "Amazon" corps, the élite female warriors of the King.

To be sure, in many African societies trade played a lesser role; this was the case of the Gouro of the Ivory Coast, even though kola markets existed and played a dynamic role. Trade was a way for the younger Gouro, who controlled it, to challenge the supremacy of their elders.[47] In any case, wherever trade was limited, it seems that nothing endangered the "tribe-patriarchal" structures because nothing was capable of assuring enough of a surplus. As to the "military hegemonies" which prevailed elsewhere, were they as extraneous to a long-distance trade economy as is said? For example, it would be necessary to study further the role played by the little known merchant class in the Mossi kingdoms. Elsewhere, pastoral occupations encouraged the development of the Fulbe, by favouring the accumulation of wealth in the form of livestock. Whatever might be said of them, their prosperity first manifested itself in active cattle markets. The Fulbe States, heirs to Ousman don Fodio, especially, controlled in the nineteenth century, and no doubt before that, the slave trade which supplied all of Sudan with slaves.[48] It is not necessary, however, to require identification of everything. We admit that in Africa there were several types of ascendency by a ruling class over the rest of the population: control of long-distance trade often implied military power (for example, the slave-trade kingdoms). No doubt the latter prevailed, sometimes by itself in certain "parasitic military States" (Buganda, for example, where the State appeared to be a war machine designed to plunder slaves, cattle, and prestige objects destined for the chiefs, the military officers, and the bravest warriors, thereby making possible the mobilization of a large part of the population for two annual campaigns).[49] It would also be necessary to distinguish between West Africa and the inter-lacustrine zone. In the former, land was controlled collectively by the village community (only the King of Dahomey in the nineteenth century asserted his right of eminent domain, when he took over land for the palm plantations sought by Europeans). In the latter, phenomena akin to the appropriation of land by the ruling class are discerned quite early (the case of Ruanda, for example).

These examples prove the need for more case studies. It would be equally desirable to begin a comparison with other so-called subsistence societies, beginning with the Maghreb. There we also find this juxtaposition of two economic systems impervious to each other on the village and on the State level. Perhaps we could then also clarify the reasons for a dichotomy which has struck all African historians: the *invariability* of the communal bases of subsistence as opposed to the *instability* of the socio-political level. The second term, although inseparable from the first, could be explained by other factors. It might arise from the complex interplay of diverse elements. Among these, long-distance trade was among the most dynamic, but also the most vulnerable, since it was subject to external as well as internal factors.

We can see how much the African mode of production, which cannot be reduced to the pre-capitalist modes of production in the West, is also radically different from those of Asia, because

there is no true despotism directly exploiting a peasant class. A final problem remains: the possible evolution of this mode of production. It has often been suggested that the Asiatic mode of production was doomed to stagnation. Godelier, on the contrary, insists that the movement of a society toward an Asiatic mode of production, revealing the emergence of a fluid class structure "is the greatest advance of productive forces possible on the basis of early communal forms of production." Evolution beyond this stage (providing that it is not petrified at this stage), could only come from the working out of its internal contradictions. Class structures would progressively take precedence over communal ones, through the development of private property.[50]

Can a comparable evolution of the African mode of production be conceived? Stagnation is more frequent than elsewhere, for the productive forces are not real forces. Founded upon war or trade, production is sterile. To be sure, a surplus is guaranteed for the privileged class, but it is an apparent surplus, whose long-term price is the impoverishment of the country. The Sudanese Empires disappeared without leaving a trace, as soon as commerce was reversed, the trade to the North of gold for salt, being redirected to the Guinea area discovered by the Portuguese, where gold and then slaves were traded for European merchandise. The States founded upon the slave trade were finally overcome by that which created their prosperity: the Kongo, starting in the seventeenth century, Benin, even before the eighteenth century, and the Ashanti Confederation (Gold Coast) in the nineteenth century. Is that to say that the Africa mode of production was condemned to be engulfed, or to be disintegrated? In one case at least, that of Dahomey, it was capable of evolution: King Ghézo agreed to renounce the increasingly uncertain slave trade in the middle of the nineteenth century in favour of a "legitimate commerce," encouraged by Europeans and based upon actual production: palm oil and palm kernels.

Sufficient accumulation of capital allowed him to develop huge plantations under his direct control. It was the beginning of the passage to a mode of production having some characteristics of the *ancien régime* (most labour was servile, supplied by annual slave raids), and certain forms akin to feudalism, but with monarchy increasingly claiming the right of eminent domain over property. By the carefully maintained confusion between "lands of the kingdom" and "lands of the king," he proceeded to the private appropriation of land. The peasants were compelled to maintain trees and collect oil; the *topo* took care of applying strict regulations. Those who possessed palm groves were obligated to take care of the soil and harvest the fruit, under penalty of a fine or loss of land. They could not cut a palm tree without royal authorization. Palm oil made the king wealthy through taxes levied on trade. His subjects owed him a tax in kind on the oil sold, estimated at one-eighteenth of the harvest. Special officials, stationed in the various cities, collected the taxes which multiplied in Dahomey. In Allada, the former capital, every vessel which passed through "the large and the small," was taxed.[51]

Would this development have been possible elsewhere? It seems to be outlined, at least, in the inter-lacustrine area – a system with feudal tendencies in Ruanda, based on the capitalization of cattle. All this was shattered by the conquest, which altered relationships between the colonizers and the colonized and caused African societies to move toward a capitalist system which was "adulterated in that capitalist relationships were closely linked to more archaic forms to the greater profit of the privileged."[52] However, these examples indicate that one African society was no less capable than any other of assimilating elements from the West, and of overcoming its contradictions, provided that she could control herself the transformation of her economy. By substituting the exploitation of the palm groves for the destructive slave trade, Dahomey was integrated into a new economic system without a shattering of its equilibrium. It began by altering the mode of production.

Notes

1   Especially Claude Meillassoux "Essai d'interprétation du phénomène économique dans les sociétés traditionnelles d'autosubsistence." *Cahiers d'Études Africaines*, 4, pp. 3–67, 1960, and *Anthropologie économique des Gouro de Côte-d'Ivoire* (Paris 1964).

2   On the opening of the debate on the Asiatic mode of production in the Soviet Union, see J. Chesneaux "Où en est la discussion sur le mode de production asiatique. II," *La Pensée*, 129 (1966).

3   On this, see the synthesis of J. Chesneaux: "Le mode de production asiatique. Quelques perspectives de recherche." *La Pensée*, 114 (1964). "Où en est la discussion sur le mode de production asiatique?," *La Pensée*, 122 (1965). "Où en est … II," 129 (1966). "Où en est … III," 138 (April 1968), pp. 21–42.

4   J. Chesneaux: "Le M.P.A. quelques perspectives …," *La Pensée*, 114 (1964).

5   Ch. Parain: "Protohistoire méditerranéenne et mode de production asiatique," *La Pensée*, 127, pp. 26–27 (1966).

6   Jean Suret-Canale: "Les sociétés traditionnelles en Afrique noire et le concept du mode de production asiatique," *La Pensée*, 177, pp. 19–42 (1964).

7   Whatever type of society is considered, political institutions are based upon principles of descent and two categories of relationships – lineage and political – always appear both complementary and antagonistic. G. Balandier: *Anthropologie politique*, Paris 1967, p. 61.

8   M. Godelier: *La notion de mode de production asiatique et les schémas marxistes d'évolution des sociétés.* C.E.R.M., Paris, 1963.

9   Godelier, *op. cit.*, p. 29.

10 Suret-Canale: "Les sociétés traditionnelles …," *op. cit.*, p. 37.

11 Godelier, *op. cit.*, p. 30.

12 "This hypothesis is invalidated by the existence of the Mossi States …," Suret-Canale, *op. cit.*, p. 37.

13 Godelier, *op. cit.*, p. 37.

14 J. H. Greenberg: *Languages of Africa* (Bloomington, 1962).

15 P. Alexandre: "Proto-histoire du groupe beto-bulu-fang: essai de synthèse provisoire," *Cahiers d'Études Africaines*, V, pp. 503–60 (1965).

16 Oliver and Mathew: *History of East Africa*, chap. VI. "Discernible developments in the interior. c. 1500–1840" (London, 1962), pp. 169–211. R. Oliver and J. D. Fage, *A short history of Africa* (London, 1962), p. 52.

17 Sir Mortimer Wheeler, "Archaeology in East Africa." *Tanganyika notes and records*, 40 p. 46 (1955). G.S.P. Freeman-Grenville has done important studies of money found on the coast, which confirms commercial contacts with Yemen, Arabia

and Asia. Cf. "East African coin finds and their historical significance," *Journal of African History*, I, pp. 31–44 (1960). On the history of the contacts between East Africa and the Indian Ocean see Auguste Toussaint: *History of the Indian Ocean*. Tr. by Jane Guicharnaud (London, 1966); A. Villers, *The Indian Ocean* (London, 1952); J. M. Gray, *History of Zanzibar from the Middle Ages* (London, 1962); G.S.P. Freeman-Grenville, *The mediaeval history of the Tanganyika coast* (London, 1962); J.-L. Duyvendak, *China's discovery of Africa* (London, 1949).

18   Great plates of embossed copper which were used for money, especially for the payment of dowries (originally produced by the Portuguese, they were in use until the 20th century).

19   Catherine Coquery-Vidrovitch (ed.), *Brazza et la prise de possession du Congo* (Paris: Mouton, 1970).

20   For a long time it was estimated at 20–50 million. Philip Curtin estimates that 10 million would be the maximum. See *The Atlantic slave trade* (Madison, 1970).

21   A. Adu Boahen: *Britain, the Sahara and the Western Sudan* (London, 1965).

22   G. Balandier: *Anthropologie politique, op. cit.*

23   Ibid. p. 93.

24   Ibid. p. 93.

25   Cf. Meillassoux: *Anthropologie économique des Coure, op. cit.*, p. 217.

26   Suret-Canale: "Structure et anthropologic économique," *La Pensée*, 135, p. 99 (1967). In saying this, Suret-Canale evidently goes beyond his own line of thought, since he has devoted himself to an analysis of the "tribe-patriarchal" society and has defined the *productive forces* based on communal agriculture: "Les sociétés traditionnelles ...," *La Pensée*, 117, pp. 19–42 (1964).

27   Hence Godelier's contradiction: he reproaches Meillassoux while accusing him at the same time of over-emphasizing "the fact of inequality ... in most classless societies." "A propos de deux textes d'anthropologie économique," *L'homme* (1967), p. 86.

28   Marx: *Le capital*, III, Ed. Soc., pp. 171–2. On this subject see Parrain: "Proto-histoire méditerranéenne ...," *La pensée*, 127, p. 26 (1966).

29   G. Sautter: *De l'Atlantique au fleuve Congo* (Paris, 1965), pp. 215–325. Also see: C. Coquery-Vidrovitch (ed.), *Brazza et la prise de possession du Congo, op. cit.* and J. Vansina: "Long-distance trade routes in Central Africa," *Journal of African History*, III, 3, 375–90 (1960).

30   J. Suret-Canale: "Les sociétés traditionnelles ...," *op. cit.*, *La Pensée*, 117, p. 30 (1964). Godelier

expresses the same thing in an analogous, although less categorical, form: the aristocracy, "assures the *bases* of its class exploitation by the deduction of a part of the communities' product (in work and goods)," *La notion de M.P.A. ..., op. cit.*, p. 30.

31   Kalidou Deme: "Les classes sociales dans le Sénégal pré-colonial," *La Pensée*, 130, p. 17 (1966).

32   J.-J. Maquet: *The premise of inequality in Ruanda* (London, 1961).

33   Peter C. Lloyd: "The political structure of African kingdoms," *Political systems and the distribution of power* (London, 1965), p. 78.

34   W. G. L. Randles: *L'ancien royaume du Congo des origines à la fin du XIX* siècle, Chap. 5, "La fiscalité" (Paris, 1969).

35   About a hundred each year, and more than five hundred for the grand Customs Festival celebrated the year of the King's funeral.

36   Coquery-Vidrovitch: "La fête des coutumes au Dahomey, historique et essai d'interprétation," *Annales*, 4, pp. 696–716 (1964).

37   "War, *which is one of the forms of production*, in a characteristic fashion generates what is called 'parasitic-military States' found in Ancient times as well as in the Middle Ages." G.-A. Melckechvili: "Esclavage, féodalisme et mode de production asiatique dans l'Orient ancien," *La Pensée*, No. 132 (1967), p. 41.

38   Suret-Canale: "Les sociétés traditionnelles ...," *La Pensée*, No. 117 (1964), p. 36.

39   G. Sautter: "Le plateau congolais de Mbé," *Cahiers d'Études Africaines*, No. 2 (1960), p. 37.

40   From the testimony of European observers. C. Coquery-Vidrovitch (ed.), *Brazza et la prise de possession du Congo*.

41   A knife bought for 3 bars of copper in Ikelemba was resold for 60 bars in Bonga; a slave bought for 20 bars was resold for 400–500 bars. *Ibid.*

42   A. Ca' da Mosto: *The Voyages of Cadamosto*. Tr. and ed. G. R. Crone (London, 1937).

43   See the evidence in: Al-Bakri, 1068: *Description de L'Afrique*, trans. (Algiers, 1913), p. 381; Al-Omari, 1338: *L'Afrique moins l'Egypte*, trans. (Paris, 1927), pp. 70–1; A. Ca' da Mosto, *The Voyages ...*

44   See R. Summers: *Ancient Mining in Rhodesia* (Salisbury, 1969).

45   J. D. Fage, "Some thoughts on state formation in the Western Sudan before the 17th century," *Boston Univ. Papers in African History*, I, pp. 17–34, 1964.

46   W. G. L. Randles, Chap. IV, "L'Économic"; XI, "Les conséquences de l'ouverture de la nouvelle frontière," *op. cit.*

47   Meillassoux: *Anthropologie économique ..., op. cit.*

48 C. Coquery-Vidrovitch: "La politique française en Haute-Sangha," *Revue française d'histoire d'outre-mer*, 186, pp. 29–31 (1965).

49 D. Sperber: *Les paysans-clients au Buganda*, Communication au Colloque du Groupe de Recherche en Anthropologie et Sociologie Politique (CRASP) (Paris, 29 March 1968). However, this thesis assumes that Buganda was more independent of commercial relationships with the coast than Dahomey or Ashanti, which can be debated.

50 M. Godelier, *op. cit.*, pp. 31–33.

51 C. Coquery-Vidrovitch: "Le blocus de Whydah (1876–1877) et la rivalité franc-anglaise au Dahomey," *Cahiers d'Études Africaines*, II, p. 384 (1965).

52 Y. Lacoste: *Géographie du sens-développement*, pp. 230–31. Paris, 1965.

10

The Cattle of Money and the Cattle of Girls among the Nuer, 1930–83

Sharon Hutchinson

Money's uniqueness, Simmel suggests, lies in its ability to extend and diversify human interdependence while excluding everything personal and specific (1978[1900]:297–303). Money distances self from other and self from object, generating within the individual dissident feelings of self-sufficiency and alienation, powerlessness and personal freedom (Simmel 1978[1900]:307–11):

> In as much as interests are focused on money and to the extent that possessions consist of money, the individual will develop the tendency and feeling of independent importance in relation to the social whole. He will relate to the social whole as one power confronting another, since he is free to take up business relations and co-operation wherever he likes. (Simmel 1978[1900]:343)

The "close relationship … between a money economy, individualization, and enlargement of the circle of social relationships" enables the individual to buy himself not only out of bonds with specific others but also, Simmel notes, out of those bonds rooted in his possessions (1978[1900]:347, 403ff.). As "the embodiment of the relativity of existence," money drives a wedge between "possessing" and "being": "through money, man is no longer enslaved in things" (Simmel 1978[1900]: 409, 307, 404).

While Simmel welcomes elimination of the personal element of exchange as the gateway to "human freedom" (1978[1900]:297–303), he is acutely aware, nonetheless, of the potential instability, disorientation, and despair generated by money's perpetual wrenching of the personal values from things. The development of a money economy, he notes, encourages avarice and other socially detrimental forms of possessive individualism (Simmel 1978[1900]:247). Moreover, as money's empty and indifferent character wears away the "direction-giving significance of things," individuals strive, Simmel observes, to reinvest their possessions with "a new importance, a deeper meaning, a value of their own":

> If modern man is free – free because he can sell everything, and free because he can buy everything – then he now seeks (often in problematical vacillations) in the objects themselves that vigor, stability and inner unity which he has lost because

From Sharon Hutchinson, "The Cattle of Money and the Cattle of Girls among the Nuer 1930–83," *American Ethnologist* (1992), 19(2): 294–316, reproduced with permission from AAA.

of the changed money conditioned relationship that he has with them. (Simmel 1978[1900]:404)

For Marx, in contrast, money is a "privileged commodity" to the extent that the congelations of human labor embodied in all other commodities come to express their values in it (1967[1867]:93). The development of "a 'money-form' of commodity exchange" is thus critical, he argues, for the recognition of human labor and productive powers as an abstract totality and, concomitantly, for the creation of a universal labor market (1967[1867]:35–84). Yet in making possible the sale of human labor as a general commodity, "a 'money-form' of commodity exchange" also facilitates relations of exploitation and alienation within the production process by effectively disassociating the value of concrete labor from the value of the products it can produce (Marx 1967[1867]:167ff., 195–8). The monetization of production relations, in other words, tends to intensify the "fetishism" inherent in simpler forms of commodity exchange by further obscuring the subjective relatization of the contribution that the producer makes to the product. For it is "just this ultimate money-form of the world of commodities," Marx states, "that actually conceals, instead of disclosing, the social character of private labor, and the social relations between individual producers" (1967[1867]:76). In brief, money plays privileged symbolic as well as material roles in the transformation of "direct social relations between individuals at work" into "material relations between persons and social relations between things," a transformation that lies at the heart of Marx's analysis of capitalism (Marx 1967[1867]:73).

In this article, I draw on the theoretical perspectives of Marx and Simmel in an effort to understand how a particular cattle-raising people in Africa, the Nuer of southern Sudan, have creatively incorporated "a 'money-form' of commodity exchange" into their culture and social life over the last half century. Following Marx, I highlight social and economic processes connected with the spread of colonialism and of capitalist relations of production underlying the gradual empowerment of money in Nuer eyes. Yet I also aspire to a more phenomenological understanding – à la Simmel – of money's enigmatic qualities as variously perceived,

experienced, and evaluated by Nuer. How have these people been grappling with the allegedly "liberating" and "alienating" potentials of a rapidly expanding regional money economy?

In exploring these issues, I will concentrate on how Nuer have gradually interdefined cattle and money so as to create a unique system of wealth categories. Significantly, this system appears to exceed, both in complexity and in inner dynamism, anything previously reported in the burgeoning literature on the "commoditization" of human/cattle relations in other parts of Africa (see, for example, Comaroff and Comaroff 1990; Ferguson 1985; Murray 1981; Parkin 1980; Sansom 1976; Shipton 1989). Unlike the "one-" and "two-way barrier" systems recorded among the Basotho (Ferguson 1985) and the Luo (Shipton 1989) respectively, this system of wealth categories does not pivot on a simple opposition between "cattle" and "cash." Nor may it be characterized as an unambiguous attempt to dam the corrosive flow of cash, as appears to be the case among the southern Tswana (Comaroff and Comaroff 1990:212). Rather, Nuer attitudes toward money appear far more ambivalent and contextually differentiated. Although individuals may "resist" equating money with cattle in some contexts, they actively seek out and use money in others as a means of tempering instabilities and inequalities within the cattle economy itself. In developing these points here, I try to show how the various wealth categories collectively devised by Nuer facilitate movements of money and cattle between "market" and "non-market" spheres of exchange at the same time as they affirm the existence of an axiological boundary between these spheres. I also reflect more generally on how the increasing use of money by Nuer has contributed over the last half century to a profound reevaluation of the place of cattle in their lives. All in all, it is hoped that this article will enrich our appreciation of the myriad ways in which market and non-market forms of consciousness and sociality are empirically entwined in the world today.

On the Oneness of Cattle and People: 1930

According to Evans-Pritchard (1940, 1951, 1956), the Nuer of the early 1930s were almost totally absorbed in the care, exchange, and sacrifice of their beloved cattle. Few Nuer at that time understood the concept of currency; fewer still understood the impersonal principles of market exchange; and literally no one parted willingly with a cow for money. Wage-labor opportunities were universally spurned as being tantamount to slavery. Rather, people at that time were bound to their herds in an intimate symbiosis of survival (Evans-Pritchard 1940:16–50). Mutual "parasites" is how Evans-Pritchard characterized them (1940:36). Whereas cattle depended on human beings for protection and care, people depended on cattle as insurance against ecological hazards and as vital sources of milk, meat, leather, and dung. Yet cattle were value far beyond their material contributions to human survival: cattle were the principal means by which Nuer created and affirmed enduring bonds among themselves as well as between themselves and divinity. In sacrificial and exchange contexts, cattle were considered direct extensions of the human persona. Their vitality and fertility were continuously being equated with, and opposed to, those of human beings. This human/cattle equation was perhaps most obvious in moments of bloodwealth and bridewealth exchange. However, it permeated myriad other contexts, saturating, as it were, the whole of Nuer social life at that time.

What is perhaps less evident from Evans-Pritchard's descriptions is that something was definitely gained by Nuer communities as a whole through the cultural assertion of a fundamental identity between cattle and people. Because cattle and people were in some sense "one," individuals were able to transcend some of the profoundest of human frailties and thereby achieve a greater sense of mastery over their world: death became surmountable, infertility reversible, and illness something that could be actively defined and cured. This equation gave "life," as it were, a second chance. Were a man to die without heirs, his relatives were able – indeed obliged – to collect cattle and marry a "ghost wife" to bear children for him. Likewise, were a woman to prove infertile, she was "free" to become a social man, gather cattle, and marry a wife to produce children for her. And were it not for rites of cattle sacrifice, people would have stood condemned at that time to a passive forebearance of severe illness, environmental

crises, and countless other difficulties. But because human and bovine vitality were identified in such contexts, all these experiences of vulnerability and hardship could be lifted to a collective plane where they could be given form and meaning and actively coped with. Lastly, the ever-present possibility of translating human values into cattle values enhanced people's abilities to achieve lasting periods of peace among themselves. Although cattle were frequent subjects of dispute among kinsmen as well as non-kinsmen, there is a well-known saying that runs, "*Thilɛ duer mi baal yaŋ*" ("No [human] error exceeds the cow"). Cattle, in other words, were – and to a large extent continue to be – the conflict resolvers par excellence.

It was thus the ideological assertion of a fundamental "oneness" between cattle and people that enabled people to extend the potency of human action in tempering the perplexing vicissitudes and vulnerabilities of life. In a society where procreation, physical well-being, and communal peace were – and continue to be – among the highest cultural values, these "extensions" or "augmentations" of life" should not be underestimated. To ignore them or to gloss over them by thinking of cattle exchange and sacrifice solely in terms of "reciprocity," "compensation," and "restitution" would be to reduce, I think, the creative potency of Nuer culture as a whole at that time. [...]

The Creation of Cattle and Labor Markets in Nuerland: 1930–83

The experience of British colonial conquest (1898–1930), swiftly followed in some regions by that of famine, made the early 1930s deeply disillusioning years for many Nuer. Effectively barred from replenishing their stock through raiding, men stood idle as successive waves of rinderpest decimated their herds (see Johnson 1980:469). For the conquering Anglo-Egyptian regime, in contrast, this was a period of optimism and of rapid political and economic advances. The radical administrative measures imposed as part of the "Nuer settlement" of 1929–30, which required among other things separation of the (Lou and Gawaar) Nuer from their Dinka neighbors, appeared to herald a new era of interethnic peace. Similarly, the successful elimination or capture of all major Nuer prophets seemed to clear the way for the birth of a new breed of tractable government chiefs (Johnson 1979, 1980:403–67). Such optimism, though short-lived in most instances, also sparked off scores of government work projects – carried out with conscripted Nuer labor – which included the construction of roads, steamer stations, administrative centers, and the like (END 66.A.2, 22 February 1934, "Assistant District Commissioner to Governor"). Conditions formerly hindering the expansion of northern trade into the region also ended abruptly (cf. Evans-Pritchard 1940:87–8). Improvements in public security and transport greatly facilitated the penetration of seasonal merchants, while cattle epidemics and food shortages ensured the rapid development of a hide export/ grain import trade. ...

Although seasonal markets and local British administrative officials were frequently at odds, these two groups nevertheless shared a common economic objective: the creation and maintenance of a profitable export trade in Nuer cattle. The greatest difficulty they faced in this regard was to advise adequate ways to tempt, force, cajole, or otherwise pressure Nuer into handing over their largest and fattest oxen for sale to meat markets in the north (WND 64 B.1., 25 March 1941, "J. Wilson, Assistant District Commissioner, to Governor"). [...]

By 1933, seasonal Arab merchants had taken the lead by establishing two modes of cattle extraction, both of them circuitous. The first, a sort of cow/ox conversion racket, took advantage of interethnic cycles of trade then developing between the western Nuer and their Twic Dinka and Baggara Arab neighbors:

> The Nuer ... have no desire to sell bulls [oxen] for money but they will exchange them for cow calves. [Baggara] Arabs [bordering the Leek and Bul Nuer in the west] and Twij Dinka are willing to sell cow calves. Thus ... the merchants buy cow calves for money from the former and exchange them to the Nuer and [other] Dinka for big bulls. (WND 64 B.1., c. 1933, "Assistant District Commissioner to Governor") [...]

In eastern Nuerland, where neighboring ethnic groups were both more distant and more cattle-poor than in the west, merchants relied instead on seasonal fluctuations in local grain supplies to generate a cattle export trade:

> The agents go out to various trading posts in September and October [at harvest time] and buy grain and hides in exchange for trade goods [such as fishing hooks, beads, spears, and cloth] mostly though occasionally money is used. A second series of posts along the rivers catch the more distant tribes on their way to the dry weather camp. From February to April trade is practically at a standstill but then the reverse flow begins and grain is sold back to the improvident at enhanced prices for animals. Generally speaking, the grain bought from the Nuer is sold for Province requirements, i.e. police, Army, merkaz [town] requirements, and the grain resold to the natives is imported. This naturally depends largely upon prices but few merchants can afford to keep their capital locked up. The turnover is small but the profits are large as the grain and hides, etc., are bought cheap for trade goods acquired at trade prices and imported grain is sold at a profit for animals valued cheaply. (SAD 212/13/3, 1930, "Eastern Nuerland, Province Handbook")

Add to these extractive strategies the confiscation of cattle in annual tribute collections and in court fines and it's not surprising that the oxen export trade grew rapidly during the 1930s and 1940s.

But individual Nuer were still neither buying nor selling their cattle with money. The mutual convertibility of these two media had simply not been established for them. This situation continued, moreover, despite post-1935 administrative efforts to shift the basis of tribute collection in eastern Nuerland from cattle to cash (officials discovered early on that this "changeover ... nearly always ends in more cash for Government" [UN 1/45/332, 1939, "E. G. Coryton, Handing Over Notes"] [...] as well as to provide conscripted Nuer labor with "a small pecuniary reward." [...] Barter continued to dominate the private sector, and government wages remained far too low to permit a ready conversion of coins into cattle. [...] The situation changed dramatically, however, following the introduction during the late 1940s of government-sponsored cattle auctions for the disposal of livestock acquired through court fines. By this time, government chiefs' courts were well established throughout Nuerland and were generating increasingly vital administrative revenues. [...] More important for our purposes, government fines' cattle, unlike tribute oxen, often included a large proportion of heifers. [...] Thus, for the first time Nuer men were able to purchase what they desired most: young, fertile heifers to increase their herds. And it was this opportunity that motivated them to enter the cattle market as buyers – and as money-paying ones at that. Because these auctions were carried out strictly on a cash basis, individuals wishing to participate were normally forced to sell an ox to a private merchant before the auction in order to have the requisite cash. [...] Hence from the government's perspective, these auctions had the added benefit of stimulating the export trade in Nuer oxen. Eventually, the administration established dry-season public auctions (to which anyone could bring cattle) in various district centers of Nuerland, first on a weekly and later on a daily basis. ...

Nevertheless, the two basic extractive strategies established by itinerant merchants during the 1930s had really changed very little. Famine continued to fuel the grain import/cattle export trade, though coinage had replaced barter to some extent. The cow/ox conversion racket, in contrast, had been effectively captured by the government, with many local export merchants benefiting from this "takeover" as well. The net result was that individual Nuer were now replenishing their herds at one another's expense rather than at the expense of outlying neighbors. As far as Nuer were concerned, money remained in such contexts little more than a means of swapping cattle with the government. In other words, cattle only became money in order to become cattle again: C→M→C.

... By 1959, these schemes required an estimated 15,000 seasonal pickers in addition to permanent tenant labor (UNPAR, 1959–60). And thus each year the government would relay increasingly urgent appeals for additional "Nilotic" labor to migrate to these sites through local Dinka, Shilluk, Nuer, Atuot, and Anuak chiefs. Significantly, Nuer men were consistently singled out by scheme owners and by government administrators alike as the most desirable "backwater" recruits, for reasons made clear in the following quotation:

Nuers proved the best of the lot. They usually arrived in high spirits and spent the hours proceeding to their station, dancing and singing in the field; they show enthusiasm and interest in their work. Unlike comers from other localities who started grumbling the moment they arrived and when they are transported to the fields it needs a miracle to make them refrain from going on strike [sic]. (WND 57.A., 1959–60, "Eastern Nuer District Annual Report")

Before long, however, these unwitting strike-breakers began venturing farther and farther north, encouraged by the promise of higher wages. By 1960, scores of young Nuer men had reached Khartoum, where they commonly obtained employment as day laborers in the constructions industry. Because of these increasingly lucrative wage-labor opportunities, it actually became possible for a man to earn enough money during a dry season to purchase a cow calf or two on his return to Nuerland. Hence a new relationship between cattle and money was forged: no longer was it necessary for a man to give up a cow in order to get one. Money could yield cattle directly: M→C [...]

With the explosion of the civil war in Nuerland in 1963–64, all this economic activity ground to a sudden halt. Regional cattle and grain markets collapsed as their northern Arab controllers retreated to heavily garrisoned towns. Scores of villages were razed by rebel-seeking army battalions while local herds were plundered mercilessly by both parties to the conflict. Families living within reach of government roads and towns scattered deeper and deeper into the bush. Hundreds of young men working or studying in the north flocked back to join southern secessionist forces while others fled in the opposite direction. The eastern Jikany and Lou Nuer suffered most intensely. And thus, by the time a negotiated peace settlement was signed in 1972, some 40,000 eastern Nuer had abandoned their homes to seek refuge in Ethiopia.

As part of the Addis Ababa Agreement of 1972, thousands of southern rebels (including an unknown number of Nuer) were integrated into the national army and police forces. Hundreds of others were offered civilian posts in the newly established southern regional government, only to be laid off a few months later due to inadequate funds. These new posts, though temporary in many cases, injected large amounts of paper currency into the regional economy, currency which Nuer were increasingly willing to accept in exchange for their cattle. Bachelors hoping to replenish their war-ravaged herds and thereby achieve a quicker road to marriage adopted short-term, seasonal labor migration to northern cities on a massive scale. Following employment patterns set by their predecessors, most of these youths became day laborers in the Khartoum construction industry. [...] After working some four to 18 months, many of them returned laden with colorful clothes, mosquito nets, plastic shoes, blankets, mattresses, sunglasses, and other highly valued goods and courting paraphernalia. Indeed, failure to obtain imported display items left young men in parts of eastern Nuerland vulnerable to the coordinated insults and rejection of marriageable girls. "If he comes back from the north and his dog recognizes him, don't converse with him!" runs the famous dictum of Nyaboth Nguany Thoan, an influential Lou girl leader. Among Nuer communities west of the Bahr al-Jabal, where during the early 1980s a fat stately ox was still more likely to catch a girl's eye than the flamboyant dance leggings so avidly adopted in the east, most migrants preferred to invest their earnings in bridewealth cattle.

During the post- (or, rather inter-) civil war era between 1972 and 1983, the economic vacuum created by the hasty departure of northern merchants during the war began to suck in Nuer adventurers desiring to try their luck at trading. Although some of these would-be merchants managed to start their businesses with funds gained through wage labor or the sale of fish, grain, crocodile skins, and other local resources, most relied on a sale of family livestock. Eventually, the more prosperous of these succeeded in penetrating the long-distance grain import/cattle export trade formerly monopolized by their northern Arab counterparts. And as more and more Nuer began to appreciate the enormous profits that could be reaped by driving cattle overland to Kosti or by founding a modest "bush shop," it became easier for a young man to persuade his elders to sell a few head of cattle in order that he might become a part-time trader. This is not to say that the local customers benefited from the changeover. On the contrary, many of the newly established Nuer merchants proved to be even more rapacious than their Arab predecessors. Markups of over 200 percent on trade goods were standard in many outlying "bush" shops throughout the early 1980s. Furthermore, it was not uncommon at that time to hear ordinary people complain that the newly emerging class of Nuer merchants had begun to adopt novel attitudes toward money. As David Kek Moinydet, an eastern Gajiok Nuer, explained:

The trouble with these young [Nuer] merchants is that they treat their money like cattle. In the old days, you didn't give a cow to just anyone. An [unrelated] man might have to live and work in your homestead for years before receiving a cow. Well, now, these young merchants are taking this same attitude toward their money: if you're not close enough to be "counted" a cow [in marriage], you're not close enough to be lent money!

However, these merchants were not the only ones who began to view money in a new light. During the same inter-civil war era, scores of Nuer communities initiated, under the auspices of local chiefs, "self-help" projects, including the construction of primary schools, veterinary facilities, and medical dispensaries as well as the repair and extension of local roads. These projects were invariably funded by local cattle contributions – some being more voluntary then others. Tragically, most of the buildings later remained idle owing to the central government's failure to provide promised staff and supplies. Yet even so, these developments would seem to reflect a definite attitudinal shift. Increasingly, cattle were being viewed, in some contexts at least, as potential sources of capital to be invested in specific projects, some private and others collective: C→M.

And thus, by the time I began investigating these issues firsthand in 1980, money had become a part of everyday social life. Or as one wry old eastern Gajaak man quipped: "Today everyone wants to die with a piaster in his hand!"

The three basic stages I have identified in the gradual forging of the cattle/money equation (namely C→M→C, M→C and C→M) are helpful,

I think, in understanding the nature and limits of the mutual convertibility of cattle and money as these are revealed through a half century of archival records. They do little justice, however, to the intricacy of cattle/money ties as more recently defined by Nuer. For the various Ms and various Cs of which they consist are by no means interchangeable. Rather contemporary Nuer, as we shall see, regard neither money nor cattle as "things in themselves."

The Circulation of Blood, Cattle, and Money: 1980–83

First formulation: "money has no blood" To what extent did the increased mutual convertibility of cattle and money stimulate Nuer to reassess critically the inherent logic and general significance of the cattle/human equation so central to their culture during the early 1930s? I begin with the observation that by 1983, money (*you*) had penetrated some fields of exchange more thoroughly than others. In exchange for grain, fishing hooks, cloth, guns, and medicines, as well as in the payment of taxes, court fines, school fees, and the like, people gladly substituted money for cattle whenever they could. Indeed, the giving up of a cow in such contexts was regarded as a truly lamentable loss: ideally, Nuer reserved cattle for more important occasions such as marriage, initiation, and sacrifice, or – as I would summarize Nuer statements in this regard – for the creation and affirmation of enduring bonds among themselves as well as between themselves and divinity. In contrast, the role of cattle as sacrificial victim and as the indispensable exchange object at times of initiation, feud settlement and, to a lesser degree, marriage had scarcely been affected by the massive introduction of currency. This is not to say that people's attitudes toward these rites remained constant between 1930 and 1983. On the contrary, the significance of cattle sacrifice, for instance, was steadily undermined by mounting waves of Christian conversion, by increased Nuer acceptance of Western medicines and concepts of illness, and by growing expectations that a host would provide meat for guests. Even so, money could not replace cattle in these contexts. Nor could it replace the gift of a "personality ox" at initiation,

though the overall significance of this ox also declined in regions where increasing numbers of Nuer youths rejected scarification. Furthermore, most people actively resisted the idea that money was an adequate substitute for cattle in bridewealth and bloodwealth exchange – although small amounts of money, as I noted, had begun to infiltrate some marriage payments by the early 1980s.

I hasten to add that this characterization of the unequal penetration of money into Nuer social life – based as it is upon a distinction between "blood" and "nonblood" associated spheres of exchange – is entirely my own construction: Nuer would not use such terms. This idea developed, rather, out of numerous comments made by individual Nuer (during general discussions about cattle sacrifice, feuding, marriage, incest, pollution, and other issues) to the effect that "cattle, like people, have blood" but "money has no blood." I interpreted these comments to mean that money was an "inappropriate" medium of exchange in certain contexts because it could not bind people together like *riem*, "blood" whether that "blood" were conceived as human, bovine, or both in relation to particular types of enduring ties.

For instance, I was once asked by a highly intelligent and unusually well traveled eastern Gajaak youth, who had ventured at one point as far as Iraq in search of profitable employment, whether I knew the ultimate source of money (*you*). After remarking spontaneously to the effect that he realized different countries used different currencies, Peter Pal Jola went on to say:

> But there's something I still don't understand about money. Money's not like the cow because the cow has blood and breath and, like people, gives birth. But money does not. So, tell me, do you know whether God [*kuɔdh*] or Man [*raan*] creates money?

Widespread as these uncertainties may be or have been among Nuer, they in no way prevented people from appreciating and using money as an everyday medium of exchange. Indeed, individual musings about money's ultimate origin were in many ways extraneous to the immediate feel of the various bits of metal and paper ever passing through their hands. It was not the mystery of money's generative powers that colored the give-and-take of daily life but rather, as we shall see, money's "sterility" as compared with the self-generating capacity of cattle. Similarly, it was the immediate, not the ultimate, source of money that defined what Nuer considered to be very different sorts of money. In order to understand why this was so, we must delve into the symbolism of "blood."

Although not equated with "life" (*tëk*) itself, blood or *riem* is the substance with which each and every human life begins. Conception is understood by Nuer as a mysterious merger of male and female "blood" flows, forged by the life-creating powers of *kuɔdh* (divinity). Without the direct participation and continual support of divinity, no child could be born or survive long enough to bring forth another generation. Moreover, since procreation is the paramount goal of life for everyone and the only form of immortality valued, "blood" may be understood as that which fuses the greatest of human desires with that profound humility with which Nuer contemplate the transcendent powers of divinity. A newborn child *is* "blood" and is referred to as such during the first month or two of life. Milk, semen, sweat – these too *are* "blood." It is as if *riem* were the mutable source of all human – and hence all social – energy.

As an element of life, blood converges with two other powerful forces of vitality: *yieɣ* (breath) and *tiiy/tiei* (awareness). Blood, however, is unique among these cardinal principles of life in that it is eminently social. Unlike either "breath" or "awareness," blood passes from person to person and from generation to generation, endowing interpersonal relations with a certain substance and fluidity. Both the coming of manhood and the coming of womanhood are marked by passages of blood. For a girl, the blood that flows during her first childbirth ushers her into adulthood; for a boy, it is the blood shed during the ordeal of scarification at initiation. The perpetual expansion, union, and contraction of kin groups are likewise spoken about in terms of the creation, transferral, and loss of *riem*. And thus, by emphasizing the fact that cattle, like people, have "blood," individuals were calling attention to the fact that cattle and people are capable of a parallel extension of vitality through time. Money, of course, is not

augmentative in that sense. If anything, it appears condemned in Sudan to a continual loss of force, to a perpetual withering in the face of mounting inflation.

Now, insofar as individuals actually succeeded in restricting their use of cash to "nonblood" as opposed to "blood" associated fields of exchange, money was less a challenge than a support for the life-affirmed and life-affirming "truth" that "cattle and people are one." As Nyacuol Gaai, an elderly Leek woman, put it: "Money protects cattle" ("*Gangɛ ɣɔk piny*"; literally, "[Money] delays them on the ground"). People with money, in other words, could keep their cattle with them longer.

Yet why, one might ask, all this emphasis on "blood" when there were so many other differences between cattle and money that people could have stressed as well? Money is not only "bloodless" (and hence milkless) but also devoid of "breath," "awareness," and individualizing names, colors, temperaments, exchange histories, and so forth (cf. Comaroff and Comaroff 1990:211). Money is an utterly depersonalized medium in this sense. Moreover, unlike cattle, money can pass in relative secrecy from one locked metal footlocker to another. In my experience, nevertheless, Nuer men and women did not mention these elements of contrast when debating the nature and limits of convertibility between cattle and money. This is not to say that they did not appreciate or take advantage of them from time to time; it is to say, rather, that the symbolism of "blood" which so pervades their culture had been taken up and elaborated once again – this time, it would seem, so as to deny the possibility of a direct equation between money and people. It was as though people were attempting to reassure themselves that, though cattle and people were equated in some contexts and cattle and money in others, money and people were – and always would be – incommensurate. The gulf that divided them ran as deep and broad as Nuer images of "blood" in the generation of life and in the continuation of the social order. By stressing the unique "blood" linkage between cattle and people so as to exclude the intrusive medium of money, many Nuer, it would seem, were also rallying to the defense of those "augmentations of life" made possible by the ideological truth that "cattle and people are one."

Everything I have said thus far presumes that "cattle" and "money" are discrete units of comparison. But for Nuer, as I hinted, these were not "things in themselves." Rather, Nuer successfully crossbred the concepts of "money" and "cattle," bringing forth a generation of hybrid categories that proved exceptionally adaptable to an increasingly unstable social and economic environment. And nowhere did these hybrid categories thrive so well as in the vast field of bridewealth exchange. For it was here, in an open environment, where negotiations ranged freely and where there were no rigid rules to mar the horizon, that these categories first came into their own. It was here, too, that my initial observation regarding the differential penetration of money into "blood" and "non-blood" associated spheres of exchange could be exposed as excessively static. For in reality, money and cattle were flowing increasingly out, in, and between these opposed spheres of exchange.

Second formulation: the cattle of money and the cattle of girls I should, perhaps, first check the assumption that "money" and "cattle" were wholly interchangeable: not all money was good, I was told, for buying cattle. There was something called *you cieth* – literally, the "money of shit" – that allegedly could not be invested fruitfully in cattle. Strikingly similar in some ways to the cattle-harming money of the Kenyan Luo (Shipton 1989), the "money of shit" was, nevertheless, defined differently. [...] Whereas the "bitter money" of the Luo originates in the sale of specific resources such as land, tobacco, cannabis, and gold, *you cieth* was quite literally money people earned in local towns by collecting and dumping the waste of household bucket latrines. Following the colonial administration's introduction of bucket latrines during the 1940s, it was difficult, of course, to find people willing to empty them each day – or rather under the cover of night. Eventually, the administration came to depend on prisoners for this service. In the interim, however, it seems Nuer women and men collectively rejected this type of work by convincing one another that "a cow bought with 'shit money' cannot live" (*"yaŋ mi ci kok ke you cieth, lcɛbi tëɣ"*). What began, I suspect, as a prideful statement that "we, the people of the people, will not do such work"

soon became an accepted fact of social life. ... In this way, individuals sought to prevent the contaminating source of this money from polluting their cherished cattle, which were, after all, consumed as well as exchanged.

In addition to the "money of shit," there were five basic categories of monetary and cattle wealth prevalent during the 1980s – all of them important for understanding contemporary patterns of bridewealth circulation. [...] The first of these, *ɣɔk nyiët*, "the cattle of girls/daughters," referred to bridewealth cattle received by specific relatives of the bride on the basis of a system of "inheritable rights" (*cuɔŋ*) and "obligations" (*laad*; singular, *lat*) (cf. Evans-Pritchard 1951:74–89; Howell 1954:97–122; Hutchinson 1985). [...] Although nominally owned by the official recipient, these cows formed part of "the ancestral herd" from which close agnates ideally drew in order to marry, have sons, and thereby extend the patriline (see Evans-Pritchard 1951:83, 1956:285).

In contrast, purchased cattle, *ɣɔk youni* or "the cattle of money," were less subject to the claims of extended kinsmen. They circulated between extended kinsmen, I was told, more as a "privilege" – that is, as a *muc* (a "free gift") or a *lony* (a "free" releasing) – than as a *cuɔŋ*, or inheritable right. Their purchaser, in other words, was somewhat freer to dispose of them as he wished – especially if he acquired them after having married and established a household of his own. In contrast, it was far more difficult – though by no means impossible during the early 1980s – for an unmarried youth residing in his father's household to differentiate effectively between cattle acquired through his own labor and those gained through his sister's marriages, for the father retained formal rights of disposal over all cattle entering his household throughout his lifetime. He could, if he desired, redistribute cattle purchased by his sons among various wives' households as well as draw freely upon them in meeting cattle obligations toward extended kin. Indeed, during the 1980s it was commonly expected in some parts of Nuerland – most notably in regions west of the Bahr al-Jabal – that bachelors engaged in seasonal labor migration would reaffirm their kinship solidarity upon their return home by freely giving one of the first bull calves purchased with their wages to a favorite maternal uncle, paternal uncle, paternal cousin, or other close relative. This gesture of solidarity was often complemented with a special sacrifice, carried out by a distant patrilineal kinsman (*guan böthni*), which was intended both to bless and to integrate other cattle purchased into the familial herd. The "cattle of money," in other words, could be ritually transformed in these regions into the "cattle of girls." Significantly, these expectations and concomitant rites were not, to the best of my knowledge, prevalent among the Nuer groups east of the Bahr al-Jabal before the eruption of the second civil war (1983 to the present).

Following the father's death, there was considerably more room for negotiation and dissent among brothers – particularly paternal half brothers – over shared rights in the familial herd. Hence, when I questioned various men and women on this score, I received a wide range of opinions – each expressed with an air of uncompromised certainty. A group of middle-aged eastern Gajiok men, for instance, assured me that following the father's death, "cattle of money" passed only as a "privilege" between paternal half brothers; full brothers, they argued, would normally be more supportive of one another and would thus willingly pool all cattle wealth. In contrast, several other Gajiok and western Leek men and women argued that half brothers retained full rights to one another's cattle, however acquired, until such time as all had married. A third opinion ran that a married man could own purchased cattle individually, regardless of the marital status of his half brothers. Finally, there were some Nuer (notably several western youths in the process of collecting sufficient cattle for their own marriages) who boldly declared: "A cow of your wages is a cow of your sweat and no one has rights in it other than you." In brotherly disputes over "rights" and "obligations" held in cattle, the ability to assert one or an other of these interpretations of "cattle of money" would thus seem crucial. [...] Indeed, from this perspective it would seem that the concept of *γɔk youni* had added a new twist to what was otherwise a longstanding "zone of contestation" among patrilineal kinsmen by giving hardworking younger brothers and sons a bit

of turf from which to begin negotiating for a greater share of status and autonomy within the family fold. [...]

But not all money could be turned into the "cattle of money." Only money earned as wages or through the sale of grain, gum, fish, crocodile skins, or other goods obtained by self-exertion could become *γɔk youni*. Money acquired by these means was closely associated with *leth puany*, "human sweat," and was referred to as *you lad*, "the money of work." [...] This type of money stood opposed to that gained by the sale of collectively owned cattle: *you γɔɔk*, or "the money of cattle." Whereas the former was individually owned, the latter carried with it all of the collective rights held in the cattle sold. Being an individual possession, the "money of work" could be "requested" (*thieiɛ*) or "begged" (*liimɛ*) from its owner by persistent relatives in need of school fees or simply desirous of a refreshing bowl of beer in the marketplace. The "money of cattle" was of a different order. Ideally, it was never squandered on small requests or projects but was instead reserved to purchase younger, fertile cattle to expand and upgrade the familial herd.

It is noteworthy that this distinction often worked to the disadvantage of Nuer whose immediate livelihood depended less on cattle than on wages. As a poorly paid, junior administrative official in Bentiu lamented:

> When a man goes to sell a cow [ox] at market, we, the relatives, usually don't bother him because we know that he is going to use that money to buy [female] cattle that will increase the herd. But then that same man can come and pester me here [in Bentiu] to give him money for beer. He may have a thousand pounds in his pocket from the cattle he has just sold. But that money is different; he wouldn't think of using it for beer. Nor could it be begged from him like the money of work. That's why it is so difficult for us who now live in town.

This fifth and final wealth category was also referred to as *γɔk youni* "the cattle of money." However, these were not real cows at all but rather sums of money substituted for a usually quite small portion of bridewealth cattle requested.

There was no possibility during the early 1980s of linguistically eliding the distinction between money parading as cattle and real cattle purchased in the marketplace in such contexts, despite the fact that both could be referred to as γɔk youni, "the cattle of money." For real cattle, regardless of their exchange origins, were invariably identified during bridewealth negotiations on the basis of their sex, color, age, horn shape, and other distinguishing features. Hence any reference to "cattle of money" in such contexts was unambiguously understood to mean "money cattle" as opposed to "purchased cattle." (For clarity's sake, I will use the term "cattle of money" here to mean only purchased cattle and will use the inverse term "money cattle," when referring to cash passed in lieu of bridewealth cows.)

Now, whether or not a young man could pass money in lieu of a bridewealth cow or two depended entirely, I was told, on the will of his would-be father-in-law. The latter could always refuse, demanding that the young man take his money and buy a real cow instead. Hence only a "generous" father-in-law, I was told, would accept such a "cow." And for this reason, the number of "money cattle" transferred in Nuer marriages before the reeruption of civil war in 1983 was remarkably small.

The first thing to note about the various wealth categories outlined is that they facilitated movements of cattle and money between "blood" and "nonblood" spheres of exchange at the same time as they confirmed the presence of a conceptual boundary between these spheres. Social principles characteristic of "kinship" exchange were continuously being drawn, together with cattle and money, into the marketplace and vice versa. Consider the following hypothetical – though by no means atypical – series of cattle and money exchanges.

Imagine that an ox, originally obtained as bridewealth, is sold at market and the money so acquired is later invested in a young heifer: "cattle of girls" → "money of cattle" → "cattle of girls" (Cg→Mc→Cg). Now, in this sequence, the collective rights and privileges held in the original bridewealth ox are not lost as it is transformed into money and later back again into cattle. As a concept, then, the "money of cattle" both affirms and protects these collective cattle rights based as they are on shared "blood," as cattle pass in and out of the marketplace, a "nonblood"-associated sphere of social relations and exchange. Conversely, a successful migrant who invests his savings in cattle ("money of work" → "cattle of money" [Mw→Cm]) is able to smuggle principles of personal autonomy and private ownership associated with market exchange into the realm of kinship relations via the concepts "money of work" and "cattle of money." […] In this system, there are no absolutes: it is always a matter of specific cattle and specific sums of money, defined in terms of their immediate sources.

The relativity with which different sorts of cattle and money are classified is readily apparent in bridewealth exchange. For whether or not a particular cow is collectively defined as a "cow of money" or a "cow of girls" depends entirely on the negotiating position of the exchange partners. Whereas the groom and his party are normally quite conscious of which cows are "cattle of money" and which are "cattle of girls," from the perspective of the bride's family, all cattle received in marriage are "cattle of girls" (see Figure 10.1). …

But what interests, one might ask, has this system of cattle/money distinctions really served? What has been its role, if any, in patterning relations of autonomy and dependence between men and women, young and old, kin and non-kin, wife-takers and wifegivers, and cattle-rich and cattle-poor, wage earners and nonwage earners, and so on?

With respect to familial and extended kin ties, this system of wealth distinctions certainly enhanced individual possibilities for autonomy by weakening feelings of mutual dependence among agnates and among cognates. With the expansion of the market economy, young men became far less dependent on the good will of their fathers, older brothers, and paternal and maternal uncles in the collection of bridewealth cattle than they were, say, during the 1930s and 1940s. The abilities of senior men to amass power in the form of cattle wealth declined accordingly – though, as I noted earlier, western Nuer elders developed ritual means of muting the "cattle of money"/"cattle of girls" distinction. Although one might suspect that these developments may contribute in the

GROOM'S FAMILY   BRIDE'S FAMILY

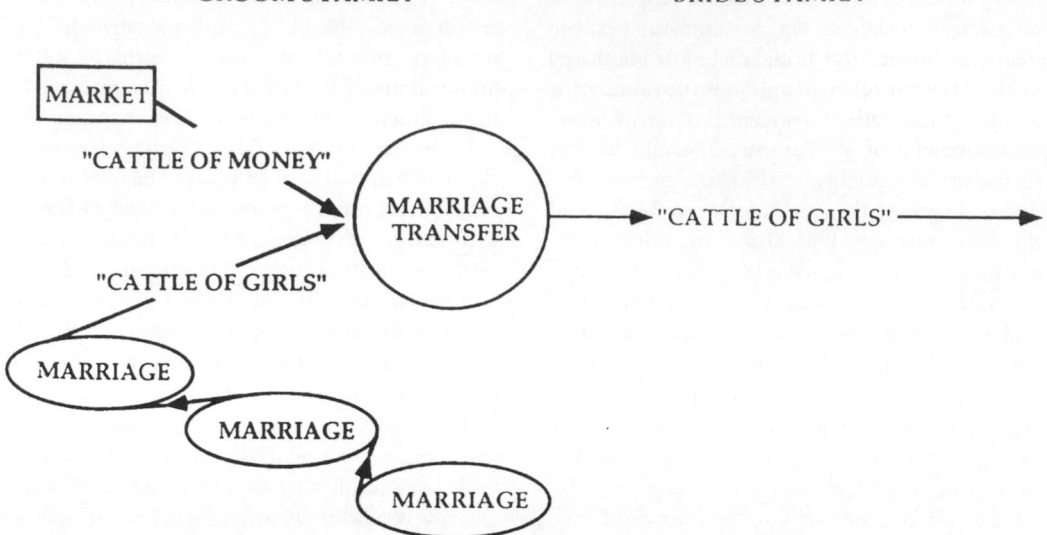

Figure 10.1 The relativity of the "cattle of money"/"cattle of girls" distinction

long run to the development of sharper inequalities of wealth among men, it would be difficult, I think, to convince many contemporary Nuer of this. In fact, several men and women argued that the introduction of money and the creation of local cattle, grain, and labor markets had significantly eased social inequalities inherent in the cattle economy itself – most notably, inequalities based on birth order and on relative family size. Whereas a sisterless man was often condemned to a bachelor's life during the 1930s and 1940s, he was "free" during the early 1980s to take up trading and wage labor in order to obtain marriage cattle. The money economy, in other words, was valued by many for having provided industrious individuals with additional opportunities to transcend poverty and misfortune. As one optimistic eastern Gajiok youth exclaimed, *Ci caan ŋɔɔk* ("Poverty [misfortune] has ended").

With regard to affinal ties, this system of wealth categories had an additional advantage, for it provided a farsighted individual with an opportunity to reduce the risk that his own marriage would someday be negatively affected by the divorce of a close female relative. When one considers the fact that divorce rates among Nuer nearly tripled between 1936 and 1983, this was not an insignificant

advantage. Indeed, for reasons described in detail elsewhere (Hutchinson 1990), Nuer men and women of the 1980s were divorcing not only more frequently than earlier generations but also at later and later points in the marriage. Whereas Evans-Pritchard claims that during the 1930s divorce was "highly unusual" after the birth of a child to the union and "impossible" after the birth of a second (1951:94), during the 1980s it was not uncommon for government courts to sever unions involving two, three, or even four children (Hutchinson 1990:402–4). Recovery of the original bridewealth cattle and their offspring was especially arduous in such cases since the cattle had usually long been dispersed through a multitude of other marriages. If they had not spread too far afield and the woman's husband knew of their whereabouts, he was likely to push in court for the return of those cows and their calves. If not, the courts maintained that substitutes be provided. Yet sometimes the family of the wife was unable to muster suitable substitutes without recalling cattle used in other marriages. Although the bride's people were not responsible for replacing cows that had died naturally in their own homestead, they were expected to replace all those that "had accomplished something" ("*mi ci duɔr laat*") for the bride's

family – that is, those that had been used to solidify a second marriage, nullify a familial debt, or
otherwise further the bride's family's objectives
before dying in other people's homesteads. As a
result of these rather stringent court-sanctioned
interpretations of the cattle obligations of the
wife's family vis-à-vis the divorcing husband, the
rupture of one marriage sometimes weakened others. If the marriage secondarily affected was a relatively recent one, it too could end in divorce. [...]

What must be realized, however, is that these
potential difficulties could be avoided by farsighted individuals through the skillful manipulation of the cattle/money categories outlined above.
A young man could attempt to reduce the risk that
his own marriage would someday be weakened by
the divorce of a female relative by including as
many "cattle of money" in his bridewealth settlement as possible. For, unlike the "cattle of girls,"
purchased cattle did not conduct shock waves created by other people's divorces. Since they came
from the market, they could only be reclaimed, in
principle, by the groom himself. During the 1980s
this marriage strategy was especially favored by
western Nuer men. [...] I often heard men advocate the advantages of marrying with "cattle of
money" as opposed to "cattle of girls" with the
expression "*Yaŋ mi ci kok ke you, thilɛ riɛk*" ("A
cow bought with money is risk-free").

For all of these reasons, many men and women
had come to regard "cattle of money" as a more
secure form of wealth than "cattle of girls." Hence,
contrary to what one might have expected, the
growth of cattle and labor markets in Nuerland
actually contributed in some ways to the stability
of marital alliances: the more rapidly "cattle of
girls" were transformed via market exchanges into
"cattle of money," the less likely it was that the
rupture of one marriage would adversely affect
others. In other ways, of course, the expanding
market economy had a profoundly negative impact
on Nuer marriages. During the 1980s, marriages
were often strained to breaking point by the
extended absences of husbands striving to earn a
bit of cash in Khartoum. [...] Age- and gender-
based asymmetries within the community were
also reduced to some extent by the continual transformation of "cattle of girls" into "cattle of
money" via the marketplace. For in principle, any-

one could earn money and purchase cattle –
although, as I have explained, the rights of
bachelors and married women were far more
circumscribed in this regard than were those of
married men and unmarried women.

At the same time, however, "cattle of money"
were continually being transformed into "cattle of
girls" via bridewealth transfers and special sacrificial offerings. As "cattle of girls," they could be
used to justify and support the same age and gender asymmetries that they would tend to undermine as "cattle of money." In this way, Nuer were
able to integrate and, in some sense, even synthe-
size practices and principles of monetary exchange
with those characteristic of more enduring
bonds of kinship and community. The synthesis
achieved, however, was based on a perpetual alternation between, rather than a definitive fusion of,
the conflicting social principles concerned.

From a slightly different perspective, one might
argue that Nuer fused the concepts of cattle and
money in such a way as to permit certain market
values to bleed into bridewealth exchange without
threatening the uniqueness of the cattle/people
equation so fundamental to their social order. One
did not actually need to use money in bridewealth
transfers in order to take advantage of principles
of private property and of limited liability associated with money: a few "cattle of money" would
do. Thus, the self-generating aspect of bridewealth
cattle, so central to Nuer images of perpetuation
of alliances, was preserved – and all those "augmentations of life" rooted in the cultural assertion
of an identity between cattle and people were
protected.

Yet money, as I noted, had begun to make some
inroads into the field of bridewealth exchange via
the concept of "money cattle." Though these
inroads were still limited during the early 1980s,
there is every reason to believe that the tremendous hardships of war, famine, and disease Nuer
are currently suffering will so decimate their herds
that more and more people will be reduced to
marrying with "money cattle" in the future. [...]
A major shift from cattle to cash as the dominant
medium of bridewealth exchange would require,
however, a radical rethinking of the nature and
logic of alliance. The notion that alliances are
founded on an equation between human and

bovine "blood" and perpetuated through a parallel extension of cattle and people through time would have to be totally reformulated in order to take account of money's "bloodless" nature. It remains to be seen whether or not the Nuer communities will transcend the overwhelming hardships they are currently experiencing to create more radical reformulations of their concepts of alliance, descent, and personhood in the future.

Conclusions

As of 1983, money had not developed into a generalized medium of exchange among Nuer. Nor had its introduction over the previous half century precipitated the emergence of a "unicentric economy" (Bohannan 1959:501). Rather, Nuer incorporated money into a weighted exchange system in which cattle remained the dominant metaphor of value. The elaborate system of cattle and money wealth categories they devised provided them with a sense of stability in the midst of change. Cattle and money were able to move freely between "market" and "kinship" spheres of exchange without threatening the cattle/human equation so fundamental to cultural concepts of personhood and transgenerational alliance. Money's powers of effacement were largely checked by an ideological elaboration of the unique "blood" links binding people and cattle. At the same time, the hybrid cattle/money categories developed greatly enhanced the abilities of young Nuer migrants, in particular, to understand and come to terms with the noncattle, "nonblood" forms of sociality increasingly binding them to the world at large.

Although the emergence of the cattle/money equation did not sunder the strong human bonds of identification with cattle, it contributed to a significant contraction of Nuer concepts of selfhood and sociality. Before the introduction of currency, the sense of self people cultivated in and through their relations with cattle invariably implied the support and participation of a collectivity of persons, including ancestors and divinities as well as numerous contemporaries. Cattle's role in creating and maintaining this socially enriched sense of self was subsequently weakened, as we have seen, by the emerging opportunities for individually acquiring and owning cattle made possible by "a

'moneyform' of commodity exchange." Although cattle could now be converted into money and vice versa, the "cattle of money" and the "money of work" could not be used to augment self and society in the same way as the "cattle of girls" because, as Nuer put it, "money has no blood."

While the wealth system that Nuer developed would appear, from this perspective, to be an ingenious compromise between market and nonmarket forms of consciousness and sociality, it also reflected, as I have shown, major socioeconomic transformations in the relative autonomy and dependence of senior men versus junior men, cattle owners versus those without cattle, full brothers versus half brothers, wage earners versus nonwage earners, men versus women, husbands versus wives, married women versus unmarried women, wife-takers versus wife-givers, and merchants versus nonmerchants. I have pointed out, for instance, how this system of categories contributed to a marked decrease in the ability of senior men to amass power in the form of cattle wealth. "Cattle of money" and "money of work" played key roles in this power shift by giving wage-earning younger brothers and sons a potential basis from which to assert greater autonomy and status within the family. With respect to patrilineal connections, this system also aggravated conflicts of interest, inherent in the very structure of agnatic descent, between the collective and the individual procreative goals of lineage members. Nevertheless, older men and women continued to maintain strong moral pressure on the younger generation to reject formal division of the family's "energy" before marriage and the establishment of an independent household. [...]

These issues, however, were far from resolved in 1983. Moreover, Nuer at that time were profoundly aware of the increasing precariousness of their social world in general and their cattle wealth in particular with respect to the widening vortex of violence then gaining momentum throughout the southern Sudan. More recently, the traumas of an increasingly brutal civil war have been exacerbated by encroaching rinderpest epidemics, slave raids, disease, and unprecedented famine. Thousands upon thousands of Nuer have been forced to seek refuge in northern cities or across the international frontier (see Hutchinson 1991). Their herds are being steadily decimated, their communities and families severed and destroyed. This continuing tragedy will undoubtedly pro- voke further reexaminations of their notions of selfhood and sociality in the years to come.

References

Archives and manuscript collections

DAK Dakhlia (Interior) Files, National Records Office, Khartoum, Sudan
END Eastern Nuer District Files, Nasir, Upper Nile Province, Sudan
SAD Sudan Archive, Oriental Library, University of Durham, England
UN Upper Nile Province Files, National Records Office, Khartoum, Sudan
UNPAR Upper Nile Province Annual Reports, Western Nuer District Files, Bentiu, Upper Nile Province, Sudan
UNPMD Upper Nile Province Monthly Diary, University of Khartoum Library, Khartoum, Sudan
WND Western Nuer District Files, Bentiu, Upper Nile Province, Sudan

Bohannan, Paul
1959 The Impact of Money on an African Subsistence Economy. *Journal of Economic History* 19:491–503.
Comaroff, Jean, and John L. Comaroff
1990 Goodly Beasts, Beastly Goods: Cattle and Commodities in a South African Context. *American Ethnologist* 17:195–216.
Evans-Pritchard, Edward E.
1940 *The Nuer*. Oxford: Clarendon Press.
1951 *Kinship and Marriage among the Nuer*. Oxford: Clarendon Press.
1956 *Nuer Religion*. Oxford: Oxford University Press.
Ferguson, James
1985 The Bovine Mystique. *Man* (n.s.) 20:647–74.
Howell, Paul P.
1954 *A Manual of Nuer Law*. London: Oxford University Press.
Hutchinson, Sharon
1980 Relations between the Sexes among the Nuer: 1930. *Africa* 50:371–87.

1985 Changing Concepts of Incest among the Nuer. *American Ethnologist* 12:625–41.
1988 *The Nuer in Crisis: Coping with Money, War, and the State*. PhD dissertation. Anthropology Department, University of Chicago.
1990 Rising Divorce among the Nuer, 1936–83. *Man* (n.s.) 25:393–411.
1991 War through the Eyes of the Dispossessed: Three Stories of Survival. *Disasters* 15:166–71.
Johnson, Douglas
1979 Colonial Policy and Prophets: The "Nuer-Settlement," 1929–1930. *Journal of the Anthropological Society of Oxford* 10:1–20.
1980 *History and Prophecy among the Nuer of Southern Sudan*. PhD dissertation. University of California, Los Angeles.
Marx, Karl
1967[1867] *Capital: A Critique of Political Economy*. Vol. 1. New York: International Publishers.
Murray, Colin
1981 *Families Divided: The Impact of Migrant Labour in Lesotho*. New York: Cambridge University Press.
Parkin, David
1980 Kind Bridewealth and Hard Cash: Eventing a Structure. In *The Meaning of Marriage Payments*. J. L. Comaroff, ed. pp. 197–200. New York: Academic Press.
Sansom, Basil
1976 A Signal Transaction and its Currency. In *Transaction and Meaning*. B. Kapferer, ed. pp. 143–61. Philadelphia: Institute for the Study of Human Issues.
Shipton, Parker
1989 *Bitter Money: Cultural Economy and Some African Meanings of Forbidden Commodities*. Washington, DC: American Anthropological Association.
Simmel, Georg
1978[1900] *Philosophy of Money*. London: Routledge and Kegan Paul.

Part IV

Hunter-Gatherers in Africa

Introduction

Because cultural anthropology is defined, in large part, by the writing of ethnographies, we tend to associate major ethnographic topics with certain authors and societies – for example, "lineage theory" with Meyer Fortes and the Tallensi, witchcraft with Edward Evans-Pritchard and the Azande, and ritual with Victor Turner and the Ndembu. When we think about the study of hunter-gatherers, the first names that come to mind are Colin Turnbull and Richard B. Lee, the Mbuti Pygmies of central Africa and the !Kung San of southern Africa.

Turnbull's accounts of the Mbuti Pygmies of the Ituri Rainforest of Zaire, and Richard B. Lee's analyses of the !Kung San of the Kalahari Desert in Botswana and Namibia, have had a profound impact upon the teaching and study of cultural anthropology. Throughout the world, Turnbull's two major publications, *The Forest People* (1961) and *Wayward Servants* (1965), have been standard reading in courses on anthropology and African cultures, and have been the basis for a significant number of comparative studies on economic, political, and gender egalitarianism. His data have been cited, analyzed, and incorporated by hundreds of authors in anthropology books and articles on subjects as varied as cultural and biological evolution, sex roles, violence, and political economy.

One reason these ethnographies can be considered among the great works in the history of anthropology is that they have stimulated dialogue and debate between anthropologists of different sub-fields. Cultural anthropologists have studied the San and the Mbuti to learn about key features of all hunter-gatherer societies: these features include egalitarianism, sharing, few exclusive rights to resources, and the absence of food surplus. Cultural anthropologists have also addressed the question of how and why these groups maintain a hunting and gathering lifestyle in the face of political, economic, and social change in Africa. Paleontologists and archaeologists have been especially interested in the San as a model for humanity's pre-agricultural past; many of these specialists argue that since 99 percent of human existence has been spent hunting and gathering (agriculture is a mere 10,000 years old), contemporary hunter-gatherers provide us with a window, albeit an imperfect one, into our past. As Sherwood Washburn writes in his foreword to Richard Lee and Irven DeVore's *Kalahari Hunter-Gatherers*:

> The importance of the San comes from the fundamental role which hunting has played in human history. Large-brained humans (Homo erectus and subsequent forms) supported themselves by hunting and gathering for at least a million years prior to the advent of agriculture ... Before the onset of agriculture man had evolved into his present form, and all the basic patterns of human behavior had appeared: language, complex social life, arts, complex technology. It was during this span of about 99 percent of the duration of the genus Homo that hunting was a major factor in the adaptation of man. If we are to understand the origin of man, we must understand man the hunter and woman the gatherer. (Washburn, 1976: xv)

As we shall see in the readings below, the use of hunter-gatherer societies as analogies for human life in the distant past is highly problematic.

Indeed, since the 1970s an enormous number of critical questions have been asked about the San and the Mbuti, and the extent to which contemporary peoples can teach us about human history:

- Can these societies tell us something meaningful about human nature and evolution?
- To what degree does the study of these societies separate hunter-gatherers from the total cultural and historical context in which they are embedded?
- Is it useful to group culturally variable societies under the single category "hunter-gatherer" simply because of their subsistence strategy?
- By defining societies in these terms, does the category itself favor certain theoretical approaches, such as Marxism, cultural evolutionism, or cultural materialism, that account for social and cultural differences in terms of technology and economy?
- Since archaeological evidence now shows that ancestors of the San have engaged in regional trade as far back as AD 500, to what extent have the San, and other hunter-gatherer groups, been embedded in regional interactions or in world political and economic systems?
- Is it possible that the people we assume to have been hunter-gatherers for hundreds or even thousands of years have long oscillated between a variety of subsistence strategies, including herding and agriculture?
- If the archaeological evidence cited by recent authors is accepted, are hunter-gatherer societies therefore misrepresented in the literature as ahistorical primitive isolates?

So-called "revisionists," such as Edwin Wilmsen and James Denbow, find these to be compelling questions and want to challenge previous representations of hunter-gatherers in general, and Lee's characterizations of the San, in particular. They claim that Lee treats the San as pure, isolated, and timeless hunter-gatherers.

The chapters by Turnbull, Grinker, Wilmsen, and Solway and Lee reveal the complexity of this debate. Turnbull describes how the Mbuti Pygmies divide their universe into two spheres: a forest world, that is completely good, and a village world that is malevolent. He analyzes the many social and economic relationships between the Mbuti Pygmies and Bila farmers in the Ituri forest, Democratic Republic of Congo, but argues that they can be viewed as autonomous societies. He also claims that, despite the many social arenas in which the two groups interact, and the ostensible dominance of the farmers over the hunter-gatherers, the Mbuti are independent actors who, in the village world, merely pretend to be subordinates so that they can exploit the farmer's foods. In Chapter 12, Grinker argues, in contrast to Turnbull, that the separation of forest and village worlds is an ethnic classification, and that the two groups are integral parts of the same but differentiated social system. Whereas Turnbull explores the hunter-gatherer/farm relationships primarily from the hunter-gatherer perspective, Grinker takes the farmer perspective. In his study of the Lese farmers and Efe (Pygmies), who live just to the north of the Mbuti with whom Turnbull worked, he finds that both groups depend upon one another for their own distinctive social and cultural identities. In addition, he argues that previous hunter-gatherer studies focus so much on economics that they often overlook the role that symbols, ideas, and social organization play in structuring relations of inequality between hunter-gatherers and farmers. Grinker elaborates the Lese house as one of the mechanisms the Lese and the Efe use to integrate themselves into an asymmetrical social system defined by both ethnicity and gender. The focus on the house stands in contrast not only to Turnbull's portrait of the Mbuti, but also to the work of other authors who have taken the clan and lineage as the central organizing principles of society and economy (see Part I, for example). The house helps us to comprehend certain kinds of relationships – ethnic and gendered relationships – that remain virtually invisible from the perspective of descent models. Elsewhere, Grinker (1994: 197–8) writes:

> It is in light of inequality that the house holds promise for a critical anthropology of Africa, a field that has relied so heavily on analyses of clans, descent groups, and other units that are, sometimes by definition, egalitarian social organizations, and often have little to do with gender or ethnic relations ... Clans tell us something very important about the ideologies framed by men about men, but they often tell us mainly about sameness and equality, egalitarianism and solidarity. It is in the context of egalitarianism, of course, that the clan, descent and lineage become so important to the Lese. The organization of descent lines into clans is especially important in times of conflict ... for collective action in the case of dispute or illness. But while the clan is essential to Lese social life, it is simply one level, one location, from which to analyze social organization. One location is not more important than the other, but an accurate anthropological picture depicts society as the product of the relationship between these two co-existing models.

Richard Lee has addressed some of the critical questions we listed above in his 1979 book *The !Kung San: Men, Women, and Work in a Foraging Society*. Lee attempts to show that the !Kung data, especially those concerning demography, mobility, food acquisition, and the division of labor, are directly relevant to the study of human evolution. One of Lee's more profound and influential conclusions is that our human ancestors, like the !Kung and other hunter-gatherers, forged a relatively peaceful collective existence in which human beings shared their resources, and suppressed antisocial individualism. He suggests, "a truly communal life is often dismissed as a utopian ideal ... but the evidence of foraging peoples tells us otherwise" (1979: 461).

The 1980s was a fertile time for hunter-gatherer studies, especially for Lee's critics. Numerous authors, such as Edwin Wilmsen and James Denbow (1990), provided their own data to challenge Lee's conclusions. Among other things, they argued aggressively that the !Kung were contemporary people who should not be compared with humans living in the Stone Age. As Wilmsen states clearly, the !Kung that we observe today are the product of a long history influenced by complex international and regional forces. Solway and Lee respond to these so-called "revisionists" by showing how problematic the concept of history can be. First, in many of the works that situate the San in regional and international systems, the history of the San has been defined as "contact," that is, as social change motivated by forces external to the group itself. Contrary to the revisionist's intentions, this view, Solway and Lee argue, perpetuates the idea of the hunter-gatherer as fragile, pristine, and unable to produce or adapt to innovation and change. Hunter-gatherers can make their own histories in a complex process that includes exogenously and endogenously produced forces. In arguing that contact between groups does not always lead to relations of domination and subordination, they also suggest that hunter-gatherers have the agency, resistance, and resilience to remain relatively autonomous even in the face of powerful outside influences.

Second, history is as variable as culture. The historical processes that affect just one area of the Kalahari desert (an area roughly the size of France) may not affect another. Following up on this point, the authors show, through oral history, archaeology, and ethnography, that the Dobe San (among whom Lee conducted most of his fieldwork) and the Western Kweneng San have had radically different historical experiences. Whereas the latter were intimately involved with Bantu pastoralists and fur traders for several hundred years, and were directly affected by both the Difaqane wars of the early 1800s, and British colonial rule, the Dobe San have remained isolated and independent of other ethnic groups even to this day. Anthropologists, they argue, cannot generalize from one San area to the other without taking into account the total historical contexts of each group.

These arguments are hotly contested by Wilmsen and by Schrire (1992), and by Wilmsen and Denbow (1992). In sharp contrast to Solway and Lee, Wilmsen and Denbow claim that the San of the Dobe region were subordinated to a dominant Early Iron Age society in the first millennium AD. The San, they claim, are Botswana's underclass. San identity is the result of a long and complicated past in which they were marginalized from the centers of economic and political power, and forced into poverty and occasional isolation. The category "San," they suggest, is an invented anthropological category that overlooks the realities of San life, and masks their true history.

The Kalahari debate draws our attention to several important methodological and theoretical issues in anthropology: as discussed above, these include the problems of (1) how to situate the local communities anthropologists often study in the larger social, economic, and historical contexts in which they exist, (2) how to conceptualize history and contact, and (3) how anthropologists interested in human and cultural evolution can find fruitful ethnographic analogies among contemporary peoples. These readings also force us to consider the problematic relationship between ethnographic cases and analytic categories. Argument over the San is in many respects an argument over the very nature of anthropological classification because the comparative categories we employ are often only as good as the individual ethnographies that constitute them. "Hunter-gatherer," as a category, is equated so often with Lee's specific presentation of the San that criticisms of Lee's ethnography may apply equally well to the general study of hunter-gatherers as a cross-cultural type. This debate thus illustrates the theoretical perils encountered when, as we noted in the opening paragraph of this introduction, certain societies become the quintessential examples of particular topics, theories, or classifications.

References

Grinker, Roy Richard. 1994. *Houses in the Rainforest: Ethnicity and Inequality among Farmers and Foragers in Central Africa*. Berkeley: University of California Press.

Lee, Richard B. 1979. *The !Kung San: Men, Women, and Work in a Foraging Society*. Cambridge: Cambridge University Press.

Washburn, S. 1976. "Foreword." In R. B. Lee and I. DeVore, eds., *Kalahari Hunter-Gatherers: Studies of the !Kung San and their Neighbors*. Cambridge, MA: Harvard University Press.

Wilmsen, E. and Denbow, J. 1990. "Paradigmatic History of San-Speaking Peoples and Current Attempts at Revision." *Current Anthropology* 31: 589–24.

Suggested Reading

Bahuchet, S. and H. Giullaume. 1982. "Aka–Farmer Relations in the Northwest Congo Basin." In Richard Lee and Eleanor Leacock, eds., *Politics and History in Band Societies*, pp. 189–212. Cambridge: Cambridge University Press.

Bailey, R.C., G. Head, M. Jenike, B. Owen, R. Rechtman, and E. Zechenter. 1989. "Hunting and Gathering in Tropical Rain Forest: Is it Possible?" *American Anthropologist* 91(1): 59–83.

Barnard, Alan. 1992. *Hunters and Herders of Southern Africa: A Comparative Ethnography of the Khoisan Peoples*. Cambridge: Cambridge University Press.

Bird-David, Nurit. 1992. "Beyond 'The Original Affluent Society': A Culturalist Reformulation." *Current Anthropology* 33(1): 25–47.

Cavalli-Sforza, L. 1987. *African Pygmies*. Orlando: Academic Press.

Hart, J. A. and T. B. Hart. 1984. "The Mbuti of Zaire: Political Change and the Opening of the Ituri Forest." *Cultural Survival Quarterly* 8(3): 18–20.

Hewlett, Barry. 1991. *Intimate Fathers: The Nature and Context of Aka Pygmy Paternal Care*. Ann Arbor: University of Michigan.

Ichikawa, M. 1978. "The Residential Groups of the Mbuti Pygmies." *Senri Ethological Studies* 1: 131–88.

Ichikawa, M. 1981. "Ecological and Sociological Importance of Honey to the Mbuti Net-Hunters, Eastern Zaire." *African Study Monographs* 1: 55–68.

Ingold, T., D. Riches, and J. Woodburn, eds. 1997. *Hunters and Gatherers*, 2 vols. New York: Berg.

Johnson, M. 1931. *Congorilla: Adventures with Pygmies and Gorillas in Africa*. New York: Bewer, Warren, and Putnam.

Johnston, Sir H.H. 1903. The Pygmies of the Great Congo Forest. *Annual Report of the Board of Regents of the Smithsonian Institution, the Year ending 1902*, pp. 479–91.

Katz, Richard. 1982. *Boiling Energy: Community Healing among the Kalahari !Kung*. Cambridge, MA: Harvard University Press.

Kuper, Adam. 1993. "Post-Modernism, Cambridge, and the Great Kalahari Debate." *Social Anthropology* 1(1): 57–71.

Lee, R.B. and I. DeVore, eds. 1968. *Man the Hunter*. Chicago: Aldine.

Lee, R.B. and E. Leacock, eds. 1982. *Politics and History in Band Societies*. Cambridge: Cambridge University Press.

Lee, Richard B. and Richard Daly. 2004. *The Cambridge Encyclopedia of Hunters and Gatherers*. Cambridge: Cambridge University Press.

Marshall, Lorna. 1976. *The !Kung of Nyae Nyae*. Cambridge: Cambridge University Press.

Panter-Brick, Catherine, Robert H. Layton, and Peter Rowley-Conwy, eds. 2001. *Hunter-Gatherers: An Interdisciplinary Perspective*. Cambridge: Cambridge University Press.

Schebesta, P. 1933. *Among Congo Pygmies*. London: Hutchinson and Co.

Schebesta, P. 1936. *My Pygmy and Negro Hosts*. London: Hutchinson and Co.

Schebesta, P. 1952. "Les Pygmées du Congo Belge." *Mem. Inst. Roy. Colonial Belge*, ser. 8, vol. 26, fasc. 2.

Schrire, C. 1984. *Past and Present in Hunter-Gatherer Studies*. Orlando: Academic Press.

Shostak, Marjorie. 1981. *Nisa: The Life of a !Kung Woman*. London: Allen Lane.

Tanno, T. 1976. "The Mbuti Net-Hunters in the Ituri Forest, Eastern Zaire: Their Hunting Activities and Band Composition." *Kyoto University African Studies* 10: 101–35.

Terashima, H. 1984. "The Structure of the Band of Mbuti Archers." In J. Itani and T. Yoneyama, eds., *Afurika Bunka no Kenkyu*, pp. 3–41. Kyoto: Academica Shuppan-kai.

Terashima, H. 1985. "Variation and Composition Principles of the Residence Group (Band) of the Mbuti Pygmies – Beyond a Typical/Atypical Dichotomy." *African Study Monographs*, Supplementary Issue, 4: 103–20.

Terashima, H. 1987. "Why Do Efe Girls Marry Farmers? The Socio-ecological Backgrounds of Inter-Ethnic Marriage in the Ituri Forest of Central Africa." *African Study Monographs* 6: 65–84.

Turnbull, Colin. 1961. *The Forest People*. New York: Simon and Schuster.

Turnbull, Colin. 1965a. *The Mbuti Pygmies: An Ethnographic Survey*. Anthropological Papers of the American Museum of Natural History 50(3): 139–282.

Turnbull, Colin. 1965b. *Wayward Servants: The Two Worlds of the African Pygmies*. New York: Natural History Press.

Turnbull, Colin. 1983. *The Mbuti Pygmies: Change and Adaptation*. New York: Holt, Rinehart and Winston.

Vansina, Jan. 1990. *Paths in the Rainforest*. Madison: University of Wisconsin Press.

Yellen, John E. "The Present and the Future of Hunter-Gatherer Studies." In C.C. Lamberg-Karlovsky, ed., *Archaeological Thought in America*. Cambridge: Cambridge University Press.

11

The Lesson of the Pygmies

Colin M. Turnbull

It has long been assumed that these inhabitants of the African rain forest had adapted to a kind of serfdom in villages. The discovery that they have not has implications for the problems of Africa today.

In the welter of change and crisis confronting the lives of the peoples of Africa it would seem difficult to work up concern for the fate of the 40,000 Pygmies who inhabit the rain forests in the northeastern corner of the Congo. The very word "pygmy" is a term of derogation. According to early explorers and contemporary anthropologists, the Pygmies have no culture of their own – not even a language. They became submerged, it is said, in the village customs and beliefs of the Bantu and Sudanic herdsmen – cultivators who occupied the periphery of the forest and reduced them to a kind of serfdom some centuries ago. By the testimony of colonial administrators and tourists they are a scurvy lot: thievish, dirty and shrouded with an aura of impish deviltry. Such reports reflect in part the sentiments of the village tribes; in many villages the Pygmies are regarded as not quite people.

To argue that the Pygmies are people – even to show that they maintain to this day the integrity of an ancient culture – will not avert or temper the fate that is in prospect for them. The opening of the rain forests of Central Africa to exploitation threatens to extinguish them as a people. The Pygmies are, in truth, *bamiki nde ndura*: children of the forest. Away from the villages they are hunters and food gatherers. The forest provides them with everything they need, generally in abundance, and enables them to lead an egalitarian, cooperative and leisured existence to which evil, in the sense of interpersonal malevolence, is so foreign that they have no word for it. After centuries of contact with the "more advanced" cultures of the villages and in spite of all appearances, their acculturation to any other mode of life remains almost nil. They have fooled the anthropologists as they have fooled the villagers. For this reason if

From Colin Turnbull, "The Lessons of the Pygmies," *Scientific American*, 208–22 (1963), pp. 28–37. Copyright © 1963 by Scientific American, Inc. from Scientific American, Inc.

for no other, the Pygmies deserve the concerned attention of the world outside. Their success should make us pause to reconsider the depth of acculturation that we have taken for granted as existing elsewhere, as industrial civilization has made its inexorable conquest of the earth.

The reason for the prevailing erroneous picture of the Pygmies is now clear. It had hitherto been generally impossible to have access to them except through the offices of the village headman, who would call the local Pygmies in from the forest to be interviewed. To all appearances they lived in some sort of symbiosis, if not serfdom, with the village people, subject to both the secular and the religious authority of the village. The fact that Pygmy boys undergo the village ritual of initiation in a relation of subservience to village boys was cited as evidence of ritual dependence, and it has been held that the Pygmies are economically dependent on the villages for metal and for plantation foods, presumably needed to supplement the meat they hunt in the forest. The few investigators who got away from the villages did not manage to do so without an escort of villagers, acting as porters or guides. Even in the forest the presence of a single villager transforms the context as far as the Pygmies are concerned; therefore all such observations were still basically of Pygmies in the village, not in their natural habitat.

My own initial impression was just as erroneous. By good fortune my contact with the Pygmies circumvented the village and was established from the outset on a basis that identified me with the world of the forest. Seeing them almost exclusively in the context of the forest, I saw a picture diametrically opposed to the one generally drawn. Instead of dependence, I saw at first independence of the village, a complete lack of acculturation – in fact, little contact of any kind. It was only after two additional stays in the Ituri Forest, the home ground of the Congo Pygmies, that I was able to put the two contradictory pictures of their life together and to see the whole. It turned out that neither is wrong; each is right in its particular context. The relation of the Pygmies to the villagers is a stroke of adaptation that has served their survival and even their convenience without apparent compromise of the integrity of their forest-nurtured culture.

The BaMbuti, as the Pygmies of the Ituri Forest are known to themselves and to their neighbors, may be the original inhabitants of the great stretch of rain forest that reaches from the Atlantic coast right across Central Africa to the open grassland country on the far side of the chain of great lakes that divides the Congo from East Africa. Their origin, along with that of Negrito peoples elsewhere in the world, is lost in the prehistoric past. Most Pygmies have unmistakable features other than height (they average less than four and a half feet) that distinguish them from Negroes. They are well muscled, usually sway-backed and have legs that are short in proportion to their torsos. Their faces, with wide-set eyes and flat, broad noses, have a characteristically alert expression, direct and unafraid, as keen as the attitude of the body, which is always poised to move with speed and agility at a moment's notice. They do not envy their neighbors, who jeer at them for their puny stature; in the enclosure of the forest, where life may depend on the ability to move swiftly and silently, the taller Negroes are as clumsy as elephants. For his part the Pygmy hunter wins his spurs by killing an elephant, which he does by running underneath the animal and piercing its bladder with a succession of quick jabs from a shortshafted spear.

A BaMbuti hunting band may consist of as many as 30 families, more than 100 men, women and children in all. On the move from one encampment to another they fill the surrounding forest with the sound of shouted chatter, laughter and song. Along with the venting of high spirits, this ensures that lurking leopards and buffaloes will be flushed into the forest well ahead of the band and not be accidentally cornered on the trail. The women, carrying or herding the infants, dart from the trail to gather food, and the men scout the forests for game on the flanks and in the van of the ragged procession. Arriving at the campsite in no particular order, all join in the task of building huts. The men usually cut the saplings to make the frames and sometimes also the giant Phrynium leaves to cover them; the women take charge of the actual building. The saplings are driven securely into the ground around a 10-foot circle, then deftly bent and intertwined to form a lattice dome; on this structure the leaves are hung like shingles, in

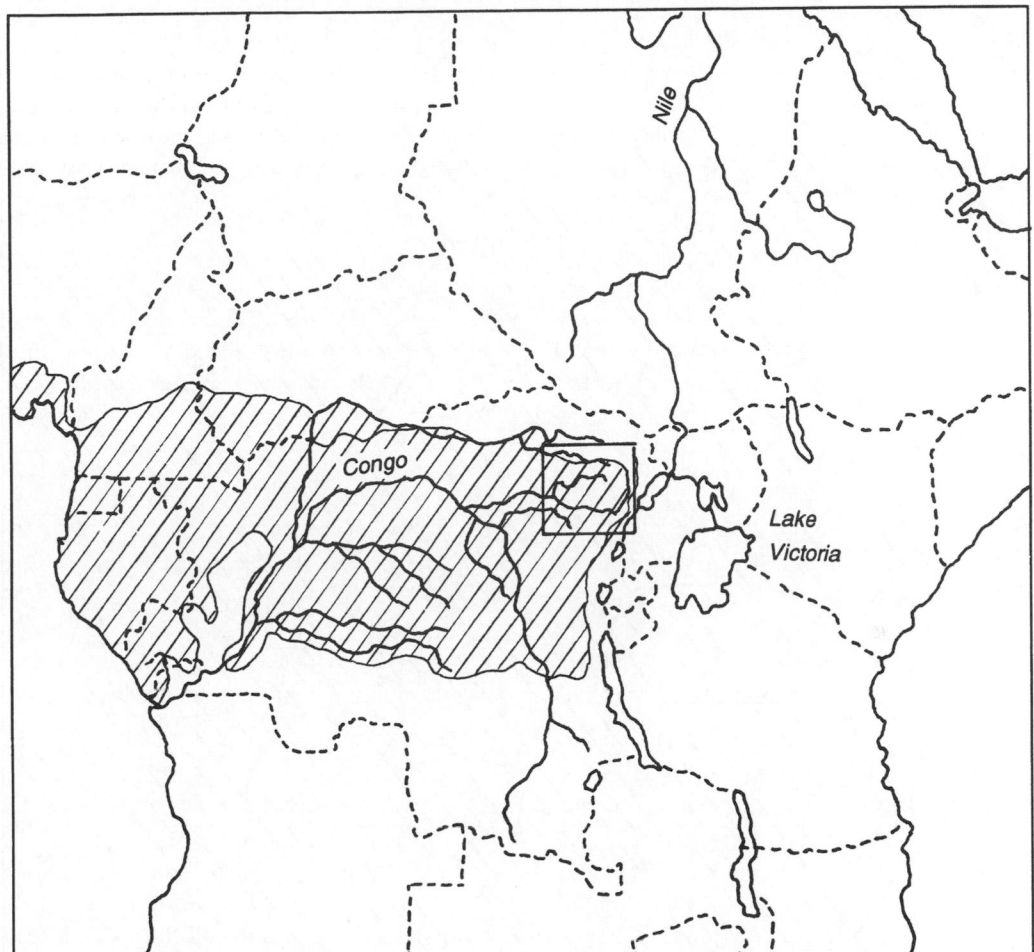

Figure 11.1 Ituri Forest inhabited by the Pygmies occupies an area of roughly 50,000 square miles in the northeastern corner of the tropical rain forest of the Congo, in Central Africa

overlapping tiers. Before nightfall, with the first arrivals helping the stragglers to complete their tasks, the camp is built and the smoke of cooking fires rises into the canopy of the forest. The entire enterprise serves to demonstrate a salient feature of BaMbuti life: everything gets done with no direction and with no apparent organization.

A morning is usually all that is needed to secure the supply of food. The women know just where to look for the wild fruits that grow in abundance in the forests, although they are hidden to outsiders. The women recognize the undistinguished *itaba* vine, which leads to a cache of nutritious, sweet-tasting roots; the kind of weather that brings mushrooms springing to the surface, the exact moment when termites swarm and must be harvested to provide an important delicacy. The men hunt with bows and poison-tipped arrows, with spears for larger game and with nets. The last involves the Pygmy genius for co-operation. Each family makes and maintains its own net, four feet high and many yards long. Together they string the nets across a strategically chosen stretch of ground. The hunters, often joined by the women and older children, beat the forest, driving the game into the nets.

By afternoon they have brought enough food into camp and sometimes a surplus that will enable

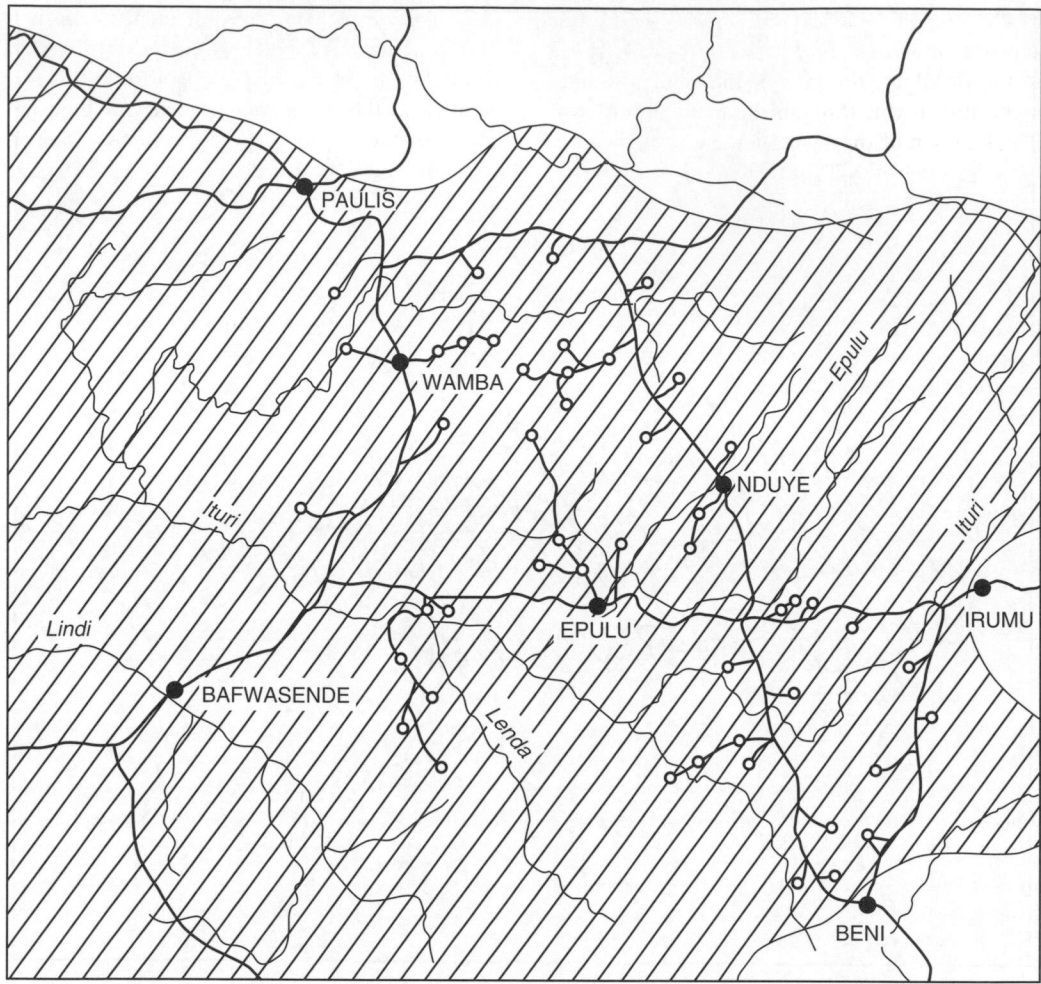

Figure 11.2 Detail map of the Ituri Forest shows the Pygmy camps visited by the author (small open circles), villages (black dots) and various rivers (thin lines). The camps are connected by forest paths (medium lines), the villages by roads (heavy lines)

them to stay in camp the next day. Time is then spent repairing the nets, making new bows and arrows, baskets and other gear and performing various other chores. This still leaves a fair amount of free time, which is spent, apart from eating and sleeping, either in playing with the children and teaching them adult activities or in gathering in impromptu groups for song and dance.

The BaMbuti have developed little talent in the graphic arts beyond the occasional daubing of a bark cloth with red or blue dye, smeared on with a finger or a twig. They do, however, have an

intricate musical culture. Their music is essentially vocal and noninstrumental. It displays a relatively complex harmonic sense and a high degree of rhythmic virtuosity. With the harmony anchored in the dominant and therefore all in one chord, the singing is often in canon form, with as many parts as there are singers and with improvisations and elaborations contributed freely by each. A song may have some general meaning, but it may also be totally devoid of words and consist simply of a succession of vowel sounds. The real meaning of the song, its importance and power, is in the sound.

In the crisis festival of the *molimo*, the closest approximation to a ritual in the unformalized life of the BaMbuti, the men of the band will sing, night after night, through the night until dawn. The function of the sound now is to "awaken the forest" so that it will learn the plight of its children or hear of their joy in its bounty.

The spirit of co-operation, seen in every activity from hunting to singing, takes the place of formal social organization in the BaMbuti hunting band. There is no headman, and individual authority and individual responsibility are shunned by all. Each member of the band can expect and demand the co-operation of others and must also give it. In essence the bonds that make two brothers hunt together and share their food are not much greater than those that obtain between a member of a band and a visiting Pygmy, even if he is totally unrelated. Any adult male is a father to any child; any woman, a mother. They expect the same help and respect from all children and they owe the same responsibilities toward them.

When the Pygmies encamp for a while near a village, the character of the band and its activities undergo profound and complete transformation. This happens even when a lone villager pays a visit to a Pygmy camp. Not only do such activities as singing and dancing and even hunting change, but so also do the complex interpersonal relations. The Pygmies then behave toward each other as they would if they were in a village. They are no longer a single, united hunting band, co-operating closely, but an aggregate of individual families, within which there may even be disunity. On periodic visits to the village with which their hunting band is associated, the Pygmies occupy their own semipermanent campsite between the village and the forest. Each family usually has a particular village family with which it maintains a loose and generally friendly exchange relation. At such times the Pygmies not only supply meat, they may also supply some labor. Their main function, as the villagers see it, is to provide such forest products as meat, honey and the leaves and saplings needed for the construction of village houses. The villagers do not like the forest and go into it as seldom as possible.

It is on these occasions that travelers have seen the Pygmies and decided that they are vassals to the villagers, with no cultural identity of their own. It is true that this is how the BaMbuti appear while they are in the villages, because in this foreign world their own code of behavior does not apply. In the village they behave with a shrewd sense of expediency. It in no way hurts them to foster the villagers' illusion of domination; it even helps to promote favorable economic relations. As far as the BaMbuti are concerned, people who are not of the forest are not people. The mixture of respect, friendship and cunning with which they treat their village neighbors corresponds to the way they treat the animals of the forest: they use them as a source of food and other goods, respecting them as such and treating them with tolerant affection when they are not needed. The Pygmies have a saying that echoes the proverb of the goose and the golden egg, to the effect that they never completely and absolutely eat the villagers, they just eat them.

In the mistaken interpretations of this peculiar relation the fact that the Pygmies seem to have lost their original language is often cited as evidence of their acculturation to the village. Linguists, on the other hand, see nothing surprising in this fact. Small, isolated hunting bands, caught up in the intertribal competition that must have attended the Bantu invasion that began half a millennium ago, could well have lost their own language in a couple of generations. It is by no means certain, however, that the Pygmy language is extinct. Certain words and usages appear to be unique to the Pygmies and do not occur in the languages and dialects of any of the numerous neighboring tribes. What is more, the Pygmies' intonation is so distinctive, no matter which of the languages they are speaking, as to render their speech almost unintelligible to the villager whose language it is supposed to be.

Some authorities maintain that the Pygmies rely on the villagers for food and metal. As for food, my own experience has shown that the BaMbuti hunting bands are perfectly capable of supporting themselves in the forest without any help from outside. The farther away from the villages they are, in fact, the better they find the hunting and gathering. If anything, it is the villagers who depend on the Pygmies, particularly for meat to supplement their protein-deficient diet.

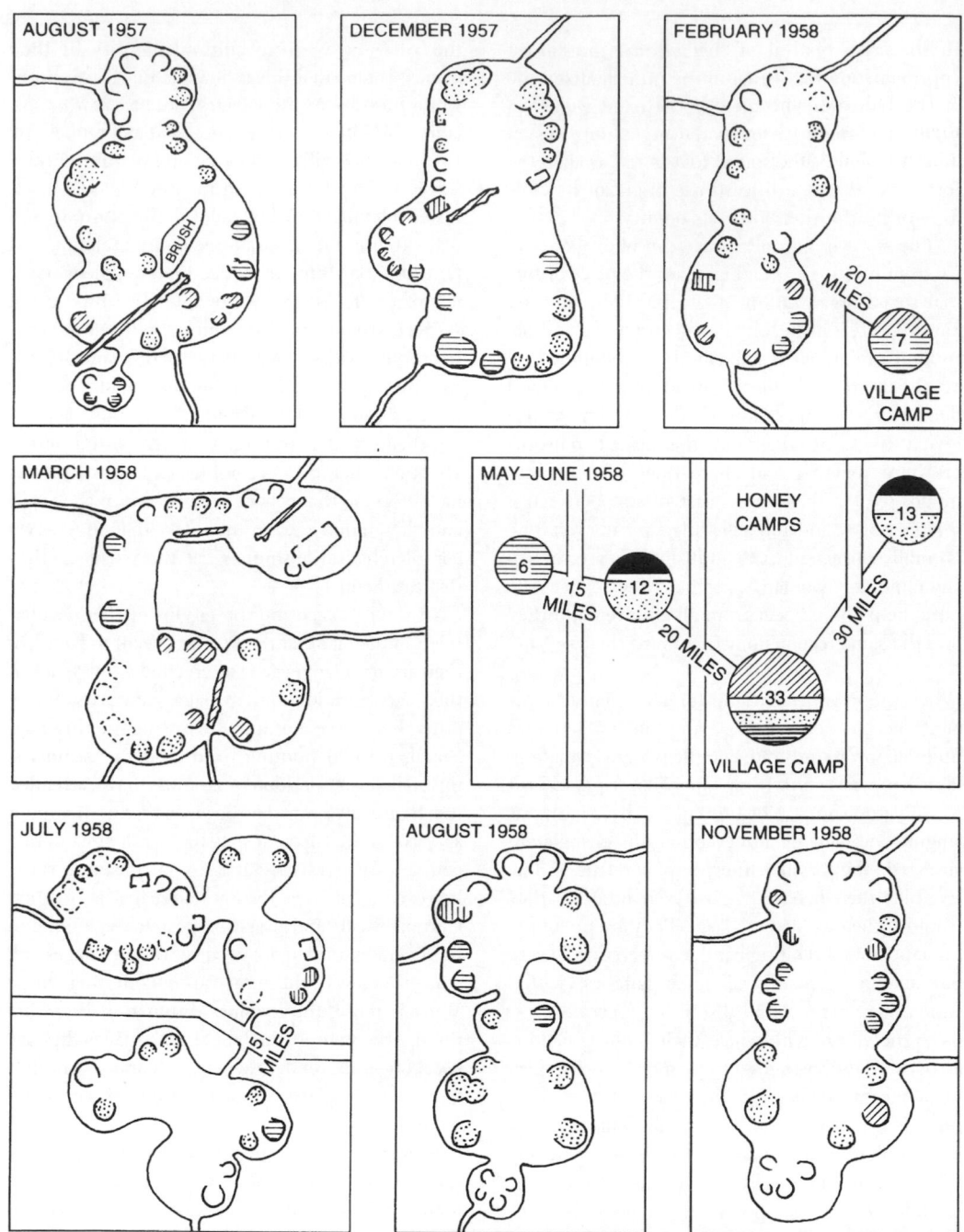

Figure 11.3 Forest camps change structure and constitution in cyclical fashion as Pygmies move from one campsite to another; they become increasingly fragmented at the approach of the honey season (May through June), break up during the season (figures show number of families) and re-form afterward. The disposition of huts, direction in which they face and their shapes are as shown; some were later abandoned (broken lines). Of the clans constituting the group with which the author stayed during the period, the main one was the Bapuemi (solid-coloured areas). A quarrel resulted in a split camp (lower left), which gradually re-formed.

It is more difficult to determine to what extent the BaMbuti are dependent on village metal. A few old men speak of hardening the points of their wooden spears in fire, and children's spears are still made in this way. Except for elephant hunting the spear is mostly a defensive weapon, and the loss of metal spear blades would not be serious. Knife and ax blades are more important; the word *machetti* – for the long, heavy-bladed brush-slashing knife – is well established in the Pygmy vocabulary. There are thorny vines, however, that can serve adequately as scrapers and others that when split give a sharp if temporary cutting edge, like that of split bamboo. When I have pressed the question, it has been stated to me that, in the absence of metal blades, "we would use stones." On the other hand, I have never succeeded in persuading a Pygmy to show me how. The answer to such a request was invariably: "Why should I go to all that trouble when it is so easy to get metal tools from the villagers?"

This is in fact the core of the Pygmies' economic relation with the villagers, and it renders the term "symbiosis" inapplicable. There is nothing they need badly enough to make them dependent on the villagers, although they use many artifacts acquired from them. Metal cooking utensils are a good example: the Pygmies can get along without these comfortably. They use them only for the cooking of village foods that require boiling, such as rice; forest foods call for no such utensils. The BaMbuti will exchange goods with the villagers and even work for them, but only as long as it suits their convenience and no longer. No amount of persuasion will hold them. If a villager attempts coercion, the Pygmy simply packs up and goes back to the forest, secure in the knowledge that he will not be followed. On the next occasion he will offer his goods in another village. Tribal records are full of disputes in which one villager has accused another of stealing "his" Pygmies.

In the absence of effective economic control the villagers attempt to assert political and religious authority. The villagers themselves are the source of the myth that they "own" the Pygmies in a form of hereditary serfdom. They appoint Pygmy headmen, each responsible for his band to the appropriate village headman. Because the bands not only shift territorially but also change as to their inner composition, however, a village headman can no more be sure which Pygmy families comprise "his" band than he can tell at any time where the band has wandered. In his appointed Pygmy headman he has a scapegoat he can blame for failure of the band to fulfill its side of some exchange transaction. But the Pygmy has no wealth with which to pay fines and can rarely be caught for the purpose of enforcing any other restitution.

The villagers nonetheless believe themselves to be the masters. They admit it is a hard battle and point out that the Pygmies are in league with the powerful and tricky spirits of the forest. The fear the villagers have of the forest goes beyond a fear of the animals; it is also a respect based on the knowledge that they are newcomers, if of several hundred years' standing. This respect is even extended to the Pygmies. Some villages make offering to the Pygmies of the first fruit, acknowledging that the Pygmies were there before them and so have certain rights over the land. This offering is also expected to placate the forest spirits. Ultimately, however, the villagers hope to subject the Pygmies to the village spirits and thereby to assume total domination.

In carrying the contest into the realm of the supernatural, the villagers invoke the full armory of witchcraft and sorcery. To the villagers these methods of social control are just as scientific and real as, say, political control through armed force. Moreover, although witchcraft and sorcery generally get their results by psychological pressure, they can sometimes be implemented by physiological poisons. There are strange tales of illness and of death due to sorcery, and no Pygmy wants to be cursed by a villager. On receiving threats of this kind the hunting band takes to the forest, secure in the belief that village magic is no more capable of following them into the forest than are the villagers themselves.

More subtly, the villagers engage the Pygmies in the various important rituals of the village culture. A Pygmy birth, marriage or death, occurring when the hunting band is bivouacked near a village, sets in motion the full village ceremonial appropriate to the occasion. The "owner" of the Pygmy in each case assumes the obligation of providing the childprotecting amulet, of negotiating the exchange of bride wealth or of paying the cost of the obsequies. Such intervention in a Pygmy marriage not only ensures that the union is regularized according to village ritual; it also gives the owners in question indissoluble rights, natural and supernatural, over the new family. The Pygmies willingly submit to the ritual because it means a three-day festival during which they will be fed by the villagers and at end of which, with luck, they will be able to make off with a portion of the bride wealth. On returning to the forest the couple may decide that it was just a flirtation and separate, leaving the villagers to litigate the expense of the transaction and the wedding feast. Although they are economically the losers, the villagers nonetheless believe that by forcing or cajoling the Pygmies through the ritual they have subjected them, at least to some extent, to the control of the village supernatural.

The same considerations on both sides apply to a funeral. The ritual places certain obligations on the family of the deceased and lays supernatural sanctions on them; death also involves, almost invariably, allegations of witchcraft or sorcery. Once again, therefore, the villagers are eager to do what is necessary to bring the Pygmies within the thrall of the local spirit world. And once again the Pygmies are willing to co-operate, knowing that the village funerary ritual prescribes a funerary feast. Even though their custom calls for quick and unceremonious disposal of the dead, they are glad to let the villagers do the disposing and even to submit to head-shaving and ritual baths in return for a banquet.

By far the most elaborate ritual by which the villagers hope to bring the Pygmies under control is the initiation of the Pygmy boys into manhood through the ordeal of circumcision, called *nkumbi*. All village boys between the ages of nine and 12 are subject to this practice, which takes place every three years. Pygmy boys of the appropriate age who happen to be in the vicinity are put through the same ceremony with the village boys. A Pygmy boy is sent first "to clean the knife," as the villagers put it, and then he is followed by a village boy. These two boys are thereafter joined by the blood they shed together in the unbreakable bond of *kare*, or blood brotherhood. Any default, particularly

on the part of the Pygmy, will invoke the wrath of the ancestors and bring all manner of curses on the offender. So once more the Pygmies are placed under the control of the village spirits and the putative bonds between the serfs and their owners are reinforced. Some villagers also see this practice as a means of securing for themselves an assured complement of Pygmy serfs to serve them in the afterworld.

As in all the other ritual relations, the BaMbuti have their own independent motivation and rationalization for submitting their sons to the pain and humiliation of *nkumbi*. For one thing, the Pygmy boys acquire the same secular adult status in the village world as their village blood brothers. The Pygmies, moreover, have the advantage of knowing that the bonds they do not consider unbreakable nonetheless tie their newly acquired village brothers; they made use of this knowledge by imposing on their *kare*. Finally, for the adult male relatives of the Pygmy initiates the ceremony means three months or so of continuous feasting at the expense of the villagers.

Once the *nkumbi* is over and the Pygmies have returned to the forest, it becomes clear that the ritual has no relevance to the inner life of the family and the hunting band. The boys who have gone to such trouble to become adults in the village sit on the laps of their mothers, signifying that they know they are really still children. In Pygmy society they will not become adults until they have proved themselves as hunters.

Back in the forest the Pygmies once again become forest people. Their counter to the villagers' efforts to bring them under domination is to keep the two worlds apart. This strategy finds formal expression in the festival of the *molimo*. The *molimo* songs are never sung when a band is making a visitation to a village or is encamped near it. Out in the forest, during the course of each night's singing, the trail leading off from the camp in the direction of the village is ceremonially blocked with branches and leaves, shutting out the profane world beyond.

The relation between Pygmy and the village cultures thus resolves itself in a standoff. Motivated as it is by economics, the relation is inherently an adversary one. The villagers seek to win the contest by domination; the Pygmies seek to perpetuate it by a kind of indigenous apartheid. Because the relation is one of mutual convenience rather than necessity, it works with reasonable success in the economic realm. The villagers ascribe the success, however, to their spiritual domination; any breakdown they cannot correct they are content to leave to rectification by the supernatural, a formula that works within their own society. The Pygmies hold, on the other hand, that the forest looks after its own, a belief that is borne out by their daily experience. In the nature of the situation, each group is able to think it has succeeded, as indeed in its own eyes it has. The very separateness of the two worlds makes this dual solution possible. But it is a solution that can work only in the present context.

A breakdown began when the Belgians insisted that the villagers plant cotton and produce a food surplus. The villagers then needed the Pygmies even more as a source of manpower. At the same time, with roads being cut through the forest, the movement of game became restricted. If the process had continued, the Pygmies would have found it increasingly difficult to follow their hunting and food-gathering way of life and would indeed have become the economic dependants of the villagers. The present political turmoil in the Congo has given the Pygmies a temporary reprieve.

In some areas, however, the Belgians had decided to pre-empt the untapped Pygmy labor force for themselves and had already set about "liberating" the Pygmies from the mythical yoke of the villagers, persuading them to set up plantations of their own. The result was disastrous. Used to the constant shade of the forest, to the purity of forest water and to the absence of germ-carrying flies and mosquitoes, the Pygmies quickly succumbed to sunstroke and to various illnesses against which the villagers have some immunity. Worse yet, with the abandoning of hunting and food gathering the entire Pygmy social structure collapsed. Forest values were necessarily left behind in the forest, and there was nothing to take their place but a pathetic and unsuccessful imitation of the new world around them, the world of villagers and of Europeans.

This whole problem was much discussed among the Pygmies just prior to the independence of the Congo. In almost every case they reached the determination that as long as the forest existed they would try to go on living as they had always lived. More than once I was told, with no little insight, that "when the forest dies, we die." So for the Pygmies, in a sense, there is no problem. They have seen enough of the outside world to feel able to make their choice, and their choice is to preserve the sanctity of their own world up to the very end. Being what they are, they will doubtless continue to play a masterful game of hide-and-seek, but they will not easily sacrifice their integrity.

It is for future administrations of the Congo that the problem will be a real one, both moral and practical. Can the vast forest area justifiably be set aside as a reservation for some 40,000 Pygmies? And if the forest is to be exploited, what can one do with its inhabitants, who are physically, temperamentally and socially so unfitted for any other form of life? If the former assessment of the Pygmy–villager relation had been correct and the Pygmies had really been as acculturated as it seemed, the problem would have resolved itself into physiological terms only, serious enough but not insuperable. As it is, seeing that the Pygmies have for several hundred years successfully rejected almost every basic element of the foreign cultures surrounding them, the prospects of adaptation are fraught with hazards.

Traditional values die hard, it would seem, and continue to thrive even when they are considered long since dead and buried. In dealing with any African peoples, I suspect, we are in grave danger if we assume too readily that they are the creatures we like to think we have made them. If the Pygmies are any indication, and if we realize it in time, it may be as well for us and for Africa that they are not.

12

Houses in the Rainforest

Gender and Ethnicity among the Lese and Efe in Zaire

Roy Richard Grinker

We [the Lese] gained our independence from the Belgians in 1960, but the Efe [Pygmies] have not gained their independence from us.

A Lese man at the funeral of his Efe partner

At night in Lese villages, men sit outside their houses in their *pasa*, the roofed meeting places in the village plaza, and tell stories. At the center of the pasa is a fire. The nights are chilly in the rain forest and children may come to warm themselves by the fire while their mothers sit on makeshift chairs on the edge of the pasa. At these times, men and women will talk about the forest, of its dangers and darkness, and of the tricksters and other spirits that harass and torment the farmers who try to enter. It seemed to me that the stories were directed toward the children and even intended to frighten them. One story tells of a man who goes to the forest and is seduced by a female forest spirit. She forces her way into his body and rips open his skin, disemboweling and killing him. Another story tells of a farmer who goes to the forest to set an animal trap. He meets a female forest spirit with leprosy who tells him that he can pass

by only if he licks the blood and pus from her lesions. Even after he agrees, she transforms herself into a knife and impales him. A third story tells of an Efe spirit named Befe who comes from the forest into the village, exhumes and rapes the corpse of a Lese girl, and then rapes the village houses by penetrating the doors with his large phallus.

This chapter is about the village and the forest. But it is more generally about the opposition between the Lese and the Efe. It is difficult to imagine oppositions that are more sharp and fundamental than those which the Lese make between themselves and the Efe: village versus forest, culture versus nature, the civilized versus the savage, male versus female, white versus red, light versus dark. The Lese hold that they are civilized and cultural, because, among other things, they live in villages, cultivate food crops, and go to school and

From Roy Richard Grinker, *Houses in the Rainforest: Ethnicity and Inequality among Farmers and Foragers in Central Africa* (1994), pp. 73–109. Copyright © 1994 The Regents of the University of California, from the University of California Press.

church, whereas the Efe are savages who live in the forest, hunt and gather, have only temporary settlements, and know nothing of God, mathematics, and the French language. Through metaphor, the Lese seek both to define themselves and to denigrate the Efe.

Gender is perhaps the most salient metaphor for characterizing the Efe; Lese men and women frequently characterize the Efe, and the forest in which the Efe live, as female.[1] The Lese, in contrast, characterize themselves, and the village in which they live, as male. In fact, the distinctions they make between themselves and the Efe, as groups, can be seen to parallel those between men and women in general, and between Lese men and their wives in particular. The Lese see the Lese–Efe relationship as part of a series of male–female oppositions, which, by implication, puts the Efe in the subordinate female position. The metaphor also implies a more specific relationship between the Efe and Lese men's wives and draws an analogic equivalence between them. In the Lese house, these two groups of people are subordinate to Lese men, and are thus culturally represented in similar ways. The central argument of this chapter is that the symbolic incorporation of the Efe into the Lese house is made possible by a particular Lese discourse about Lese–Efe differences …

The Forest and the Village

Although both the Lese and the Efe live in the Ituri forest, the Lese of Malembi with whom I lived deny that they themselves live in the forest. They say they live in the village and the Efe live in the forest. This dichotomy, repeated time and time again in Turnbull's work, is as fundamental to the Lese as was the opposition between Europe and the "dark continent," the white and the black. The forest for the Lese is analogous to the "jungle" for the European, conceived as impenetrable, dark, and dangerous. Stanley's description of the "green hell" (Vansina 1990:39) he traveled through while crossing the Ituri forest is echoed in the experience of other explorers, missionaries, and administrators in the Congo. And the Lese of Malembi, recalling the missionaries and other Europeans, are proud that they are "of the village," whereas the Efe are "of the forest." The forest is the place

where the hostile ancestral spirits of the Lese dwell, spirits the Lese call *tore*, and translate into Swahili as *shaitani* (Satan), and the attributes associated with the forest – darkness, wetness, danger, and uncertainty, among other things – are therefore also associated with the Efe. The construction of ethnic boundaries goes hand in hand with the construction of inequality, in which the village is made to represent everything good, while the forest represents everything bad. This division of the world is echoed by Bahuchet and Guillaume (1982) in their account of Aka–Bantu relations, as well as by E. Waehle (1985:392), who writes: "The Efe are savages and sub-humans (likened to chimpanzees or forest hogs); they are thieves; the forest is the contradiction to the village (almost as nature to culture)."

The two worlds are diametrically opposed, and the difference between them represents one of the most significant and basic markers of ethnic distinction. For example, when an Efe woman marries a Lese man, and moves, as she must, to the village, the Efe and the Lese say that she has married the village (*anga-ni ubo-ke*); the groom is said to have "married [a girl] of the forest" (*anga-ni meli-ba*). Lese men insult other Lese men who engage in extensive hunting with the term "forest people," and any man who behaves in a manner believed by the Lese to be stereotypical of the Efe will be referred to by the Lese, disparagingly, as either a "forest person" or an "Efe."

For both the Lese and the Efe, the forest begins and ends with areas cleared for Lese houses and pasa. The forest is where the cleared land surrounding the village becomes wild and overgrown. Even a small patch of wild foliage creeping into the village area will be called forest, and the Lese may say that the forest "is coming closer." With the exception of forest paths, any area in which trees and shrubs have not been cut down and weeds and vines have not been removed will be considered forest.… Efe camps, even when they are situated only a few hundred meters from the village, sometimes within the garden of their Lese partners, are said to be in the forest.

Even with this close proximity, there is a noticeable difference between Lese and Efe settlements. Though the Efe usually cut down some trees and vines, their camps are not cleared of all plant life, as are the Lese villages. The borders of Efe camps form a circle, or at least a highly curved and ambiguously defined domain. The huts are hemispherical, made of leaves and sticks, and the land of the camp area is black, brown, green, moist, and full of plant and insect life. Because the land is rarely weeded and so many trees are left standing, the sun cannot penetrate the canopy of the forest, and the land on which the Efe live remains damp and soft. The Lese villages, in addition to being well-defined and impeccably cleared areas of land, contain square or rectangular houses that are placed symmetrically in relation to the road and to other houses.

The Efe also find the opposition between the forest and the village to be significant. During my fieldwork, the Efe complained, in particular, about the insects in the village. Echoing Turnbull's reports of the Mbuti attitude toward the village (1965:18), Efe told me that the mosquitos are far more common in the villages, and that when Efe live in the villages for a long time they become ill. Indeed, outside the villages mosquitoes remain in the higher levels of the forest, where the trees have not been cut, and because the mosquitoes feed upon the monkeys and other arborial organisms, they are less irritating to human beings. In addition, when Efe camps become polluted with refuse and begin to attract fleas, the Efe can abandon the camp and quickly build another one nearby. The Efe would surely agree with Turnbull's characterization:

> Where in the villages, and in the plantations that surround them, the midday temperatures soar well into the nineties, and the ground is covered with a dry, choking dust that quickly turns to mud, in the shade of the forest the world is cool and fresh, with only rare places, such as along river banks or at salt licks, where sunlight reaches the ground without first being filtered through a leafy roof. Also from the point of view of comfort, and of health, where village conditions lead to gatherings of flies and mosquitoes, these disease bearers are seldom if ever seen in the depths of the forest, except at such sites as are easily avoided. The Mbuti frequently compare their lot, in these respects, with that of the villagers, who in turn grudgingly admit to some advantages of forest life. (1965:18)

Yet Lese men, women, and children asserted that they could not live in the forest, that they would be cold, hungry, wet, and prone to disease; they might be bitten by snakes or insects, or, worse, they might encounter trouble from supernatural forces. The Lese often complained about the insects of the forest, namely, fleas and other creatures that are attracted by the garbage that collects in Efe camps.

Lese Representations: Hygiene and Sexuality

For the Lese, then, Efe camps represent a whole set of ideas about dirt, health, bodily odors, and secretions. Lese children were particularly illuminating about these ideas. Once when I accompanied a Lese family through an area of forest to check on a fish trap in a river, we found ourselves in an Efe camp that had been abandoned for about a year. One hut was still standing, and I held the hand of a six-year-old boy to whom I was especially close as I went to look inside it. He pulled away from me suddenly, and when I asked him why he was afraid, he said that he did not want to go inside the hut. I told him I only wanted to look inside, and he said that he did not even want to look, that he might get lice or fleas or become sick and die. The huts, his father explained, still contain body products, "things of their bodies," as he put it. The same little boy once shrieked with disgust after he smelled the scent of my shaving cream; he said that it smelled like the Efe, and that the odor "made [his] stomach unhappy." Lese adults, especially women, spoke to me about Efe hygiene, and cited Efe body odor as one of the main reasons why they would not engage in sexual intercourse with Efe men (indeed, I know of no cases, and only a few rumors, of this). Moreover, though under special circumstances some Lese may eat food out of the same cooking pot as an Efe, they will not eat food off the same plate, or banana leaf, as the Efe. This is more than a simple display of inequality. Serving food on the same plate is considered to be an unclean and unsafe act. ...

When I asked one woman whether she "liked" Efe, her answer moved from comments about manners and habits to comments about cleanliness and dirt:

I like Efe. No problem if they steal from me. I will not beat them. I get angry just to frighten them. They are not like *muto* (people). They have no *akiri* (intelligence, in KiSwahili). Our heart is the same, but their akiri is not the same. Their thoughts are different. They forget quickly, like conflicts with other people, they forget them quickly. But their eyes are the same as the eyes of people. They have the same sweat, but it smells different. It is pungent (*ikochi*). They sleep [live] for two months sometimes without bathing, or maybe they don't bathe for two weeks. Their underarms smell and they sleep on old banana leaves, and the old banana leaves smell too. They do not like to wash; they are used to old things – it is their custom (*desturi* in KiSwahili). And their chests get very dirty, and if you give them soap, they do not wash their bodies, they will only wash their clothes.

Finally, the Lese of Malembi often spoke among themselves about how Efe defecate. Lese build outhouses, but the Efe do not, and, according to my informants, Efe will defecate anywhere in the forest. One Lese legend tells of an Efe girl who drowns in her own relative's diarrhea, and many other legends about the Efe incorporate excremental or anal themes. Two Lese men tried to help their Efe partners build outhouses, but said their attempts were in vain because the Efe are not "civilized" (*civilisé*), that they still live like "animals" (*ura*).

The excremental theme is used primarily to characterize the Efe, but it can be used by the Lese self-referentially in joking contexts. One joke concerning the physical differences between the Lese and the Efe asks: When someone defecates the feces falls and can be heard hitting the ground, but when someone urinates, the urine falls lightly onto the ground, and is silent – what am I talking about? The answer is: the Lese and the Efe. The Lese are fatter, taller, and heavier; the Efe are leaner, shorter, and lighter. But whereas height may be the most significant difference for American or European observers, the Lese pay closer attention to weight, skin color, the *shape* of the body, odor, the hair, and the eyebrows. The joke itself concerns the differences between the weight of Efe and Lese. One aspect of the joke that is not obvious is the analogy of color between the pairs,

feces–urine, and Lese–Efe. Both the Efe and urine are considered to be red in color, since Efe skin color is lighter and more reddish than Lese skin color, and urine is also red (there is no word in either the Lese or Efe dialects for yellow). Likewise, both feces and Lese skin color are considered to be black. The Lese admire the Efe's lighter skin color, find it more beautiful, and value highly reddish skin color among themselves.

Lese also note the variation in muscle tone and fatness. Whereas the Efe have little body fat and are very muscular, the Lese are fatter and appear less robust. The Efe are light-footed, an advantage for hunters, whereas the Lese are heavy-footed and make noise that frightens off the animals. In addition, the Efe are more hirsute. Their eyebrows are much fuller than those of the Lese, and the Lese say that when they travel in areas where there has been extensive intermarriage between Efe and Lese, where some of the physical distinctions are thus blurred, and where differences between the Lese and Efe dialects are not as clear, they can distinguish between Efe and Lese by looking first at the eyebrows. Moreover, Efe women have more chest hair than Lese women. Another joke told by Lese to refer to body hair as well as duplicity and shiftiness is the following: Efe have hairy chests – what am I talking about? The answer is: an *ene* animal trap, a large trap hole covered and hidden by leaves, sticks, vines, and other wild plants.

Lese men are extremely attracted to their stereotypical characterization of Efe women, specifically Efe women's body hair. Thirty-three out of forty men I interviewed (83%) on the subject of sexual attraction reported that during their lives they had engaged in sexual intercourse with an Efe woman; only five (12.5%), the youngest men in the sample, had never had sex with an Efe woman (two men did not wish to answer my question). In fact, the one physical attribute of the Efe women that the Lese men consistently reported as the most distinctive, attractive, and sexually arousing was body hair. Lese men speak among themselves of how exciting *torumbaka* (or public hair) is to them. *Torumbaka* literally means "hair from the crotch," but it is used specifically to refer to hair around the navel, or between the breasts; it is said to be unique to the Efe and is also said to have the power to produce instant erections in men.

Controlling Nature and Culture

Lese men project their own anxiety about control of their sexual desires for Efe women onto the Efe, whom they perceive to be sexually wild – like the forest in which they live. Indeed, the issue of control is central to Lese conceptions of the Efe and of themselves. From the Lese point of view, the Efe are uncontrolled, unrestrained; they act without planning or meditation, and their social organization is turbulent and disorderly and permits sexual relationships that the Lese consider incestuous. Efe men, according to Lese men, are addicted to sex and must engage in intercourse at least once a day. Lese men also say that the Efe's desire for marijuana predisposes the Efe toward violence and disorder. Lese men place a high value on their own self-control and for this reason very seldom smoke marijuana in adulthood. In addition, the Lese want to control the Efe. What Turnbull writes of the Bila and the Mbuti (1965:42, 83–4) applies somewhat to the Lese and the Efe, since the Lese do not use physical force and rarely go into the forest to control the Efe: "The villagers themselves admit their inability to exert physical force to bend the Mbuti to their will, for the Mbuti always have the ultimate escape of flight to the sanctuary of the forest. The villagers are completely unequipped to pursue the Mbuti into the forest and never attempt it" (1965:84). On one occasion when I was traveling to an Efe camp, an excited Lese villager named Filipe gave me a note he had written in Swahili ordering his Efe partner, Abdala, to come to the villages. The Efe who live near Malembi do not know how to read, so I read the note to them. Abdala then asked me to tell Filipe that he would come soon. When I returned to the village and reported Abdala's reply, Filipe became irate and asked, "But when? When will he come? I do not know where he is." In fact, Filipe knew very well where Abdala was, but he was perhaps expressing outrage at being unable to control his Efe's movements. Indeed, the desire to control the Efe seems to be not a desire for political domination so much as an expression of anxiety about Efe mobility. Lese men and women often seemed disturbed when they heard, sometimes by word of mouth, that their Efe partner had moved from one camp to another or had gone to a plantation to sign up for wage labor. They also seemed worried when they learned that their Efe were traveling or living near the Lese gardens – partly because of the unpredictability of their Efe's whereabouts, partly, too, because they were afraid the Efe would steal their cultivated food. Like the forest growth that encroaches upon the swept earth of the village, the Lese say the Efe encroach upon the village gardens and threaten to ruin the carefully tended fields of cultivated food. ...

In contrast to the Efe, the Lese consider themselves to be predictable and stable, controlled, restrained, organized, and thoughtful. They also believe that they have a greater *akiri* (intelligence) than the Efe. For the Lese, someone with akiri is educated, speaks several languages, can offer advice, can be trusted, is dependable, and is not self-destructive. At one Efe funeral, a Lese man simultaneously criticized and complimented the Efe in my presence by saying, "The Efe of before had no akiri, but now they do. Look at this white person [the author] who doesn't go to the forest everyday, but resides more often with the Lese. He has akiri. To go to the forest every day is bad and without akiri." In addition to being more sedentary, someone with akiri is also well-liked and diplomatic: "Someone with akiri doesn't say what he wants very quickly; he waits, and when he thinks that the person he is with likes him, and is calm, he will say what he wants." In contrast, the Efe are unwilling to "sooth" (*iruka*) their partners, and will let their desires be known at the start of a conversation with an exchange partner. ...

One of the most common and explicit ways that the Lese disparage the Efe is to accuse them of stealing ("like baboons") foods out of their garden and destroying (*ima-ni*) the garden, even after they have been given food by the Lese partner. Lese make a connection between the Efe, a specific kind of insect, and rainbows, all three of which are believed to damage or destroy the Lese crops. Efe are frequently called *kongu*, the name for a species of large flies that can always be seen buzzing near the prized *njeru* variety of bananas, and that, in legend, inhabits the far end of rainbows (*raba* – for the Lese, an extremely dangerous phenomenon) and helps the rainbow to enter into the village from outside and destroy cultivated foods. The Lese also speak of the Efe as gluttonous in their appetite for food, tobacco and marijuana, and sex. The Efe, the Lese say, cannot farm for themselves because they have no *sibosibo* (patience), and because they lack the capacity to engage in a productive activity that does not offer immediate gratification. ...

As noted earlier, the Efe and Lese speak differently. In addition to some differences in vocabulary, where the Lese use glottal consonants, the Efe instead place faucial gaps. But many Lese say that the difference is not so much in the words and grammar as in the organization of ideas. The Lese say that Efe speech is often incoherent and babbling, that when they speak they jump from one idea to the next, that their "ideas have no straight path" (*ide-ba todi a upu kikikiko embi-ani*). Paralleling what some Lese seem to think is an attention deficiency, Efe men are also said to have short and violent tempers and to murder without much provocation. These perceptions have their basis in the angry and sometimes violent fights that punctuate the daily life of many Efe camps, but actual murders are extremely rare. In addition, the Efe are the most fierce and frenzied actors at funerals. The fact that Efe always carry their bow and arrows and/or spear also contributes to the perception of the Efe as wild or savage. ...

In terms of the classification of living things, in both the Efe and the Lese dialects, the Lese are called *muto* and the Efe are called *Efe. Muto* means "person," as I was called a *mutotufe* (white person), and Africans are in general called *mutokosa* (black person). In terms of classification of ethnicity, the Lese are called *Lese* or *Dese*, and the Efe are called *Efe.* Thus, while the Lese have three terms, one to distinguish themselves from the Efe and animals (*muto*), one to distinguish themselves from other groups (*Lese*), and another to distinguish themselves from other Lese (*Dese*), the Efe have only one term. The term *Efe* thus denotes nothing other than the archer Pygmies and, unlike the word *muto*, has no other usage. The term *Efe* is not subsumed within the term *muto*. Linguistically, then, one might think that the *Efe* are not considered to be people. However, there is little uniformity regarding the location of the Efe in humanity; in the Lese language, Efe are under no circumstances called *muto*, nor do Efe refer to themselves as *muto*. In the KiNgwana form of Swahili, however, I was told, "yes the Efe are *watu* ['people,' in Swahili] but they are not muto ['people,' in Lese]." It is entirely possible that the Lese word for person, *muto*, also means "farmer." ...

Nonetheless, the extent to which the Lese hope to surpass the Efe in terms of status cannot be overemphasized because this ideology of inequality bears directly on the argument that the two groups must be considered as one. It is easy enough to simply record denigrations. The Lese are quick to say that they believe the Efe should be *amu-ba-ni karu-ta* (under our feet) as the Efe have always been *amu kondu-ni karu-ta* (under our ancestor's feet). The more difficult task is to analyze the various denigrations of distinct contexts for symbolic patterns and associations. Indeed, analysis of the characterizations tells us something more general, something central to the very fabric of Lese identity. What all these characterizations of inequality suggest is that the Efe are not wholly "other" to the Lese because they are such a strong component and defining characteristic of Lese representations of themselves. For example, for the Lese, the dirtiness of the Efe is paired with their own cleanliness, the wildness of the Efe is paired with their own wish for self-control. The Lese and the Efe are thus less in conflict than they are mutually constitutive. According to the Lese, Efe men and women act according to physical instincts involving food, sex, and aggression, and they are driven primarily by somatic influences. They are unable to harness their anger and are not capable of logical or rational thinking; they live with the forest rather than against it and, as represented in mythology, are closer to nature. The Lese believe themselves to be capable of mediating between their drives and the exigencies of proper and ordered social life. They represent rationality and reason, whereas the Efe stand for untamed passions. The Lese and the Efe are two interrelated organizations, and the Lese find meaning in their contrasts.

The contrast between the Lese as cultural and the Efe as natural is highlighted in a story that can serve as an introduction to the way in which the Lese establish unconscious symbolic oppositions about themselves and the Efe. This is one of many stories about the origin of Lese–Efe contact; every Lese phratry preserves a legend about the first meeting. Here, the narrator tells of how the Efe taught the Lese the difference between male and female genitals, and how to have sexual intercourse; the Lese in turn taught the Efe ingenuity and the value of tool use.

The Efe of long ago were Andisamba, my Efe. Andisamba's great grandfather was named Abeki. He was the Efe of Andali, of all the Lese-Dese. His wife's name was Matutobo. His grandmother's name was also Matutobo. Abeki went to the forest and returned. His grandmother came to wipe her anus on the top of his thigh. Abeki had many children, a boy here, a girl there. One day, Abeki took off to the forest, and arrived at a garden where there were ripe bananas. Efe ruin (deplete) our gardens, so the Efe went to take the bananas. He thought a lot about what his grandmother did to him, and so he thought a lot about the feces on his thigh. He had never seen bananas before, and he tried one, and he liked it. So he took bananas for his children. He now returned to the garden a third time. The villager left his village and saw footprints. The man saw the Efe sitting there, and then they saw each other. The man called out "ungbatue!" and the Efe said "ungbatue!" and the man asked the Efe to come to his village. "Do not be afraid! I will not hurt you." They went together.

   The man was named Aupa. The Efe said again "ungbatue! See it is stupid, the feces on my thigh, it is by the hand of my grandmother [andu]. Every day she does this." The man said, "Soon we will sharpen my knife [to kill the woman]." The man said he would rip open [ataba] the Efe's thigh and insert the knife inside it. Then her anus would rip, and the corpse would fall to the ground. The Efe returned until he reached his camp, and his grandmother said to Abeki's wife, "So your man returns?" The children said yes. Then she came to ask him to straighten out [itesi] his leg. She wiped herself, and the knife cut her. Corpse. They destroyed her house, and then the Efe moved with his wife to the villager's garden.[2]

   From there, the Efe man came to the village woman, and her man was waiting there. "She is ill my woman." The Efe asked "Where is she?" "She is lying down in the pasa." The man went to get some alcohol, and with the Efe, the two of them drank together. The Efe asked, "Am I not able to see this illness?" The man told the Efe to go and look. He said, "My wife has no penis or testicles, only a wound in her crotch, and every month she bleeds from it, and I cannot stop the bleeding for several days."[3] The Efe said, "I will teach you." So he had sex with the village woman, and she became pregnant, and a child came, the first child. Later he gave her another pregnancy. The villager got mad at the Efe and said, "You will have sex with my woman? I will try myself." From there the Efe and Lese were together.[4]

By illustrating sex between a Lese woman and an Efe man, the characters reverse the conditions of the present day, in which intercourse between Lese women and Efe men is prohibited. But the origin story dramatizes the fact that it is the Efe who symbolically contribute knowledge of the natural world, while it is the Lese who contribute knowledge of the cultural world, to the Lese–Efe relationship. The forest, and the Efe who inhabit it, represent the wild and uncontrollable aspects of humanity, while the village, and the Lese who inhabit it, represent the civilized and controlled aspects of humanity. The Lese–Efe relationship binds the Efe to the Lese village. Conceptually, the villager's power lies in his exclusive knowledge of farming technique, and in the Efe's intractable and gluttonous desire for cultivated foods. The production of these foods attracts the Efe to the village and thereby controls them.

   The nature/culture dichotomy so pronounced in this story appears to parallel the distinctions between men and women noted by S. B. Ortner (1974) in her well-known essay on the universal subordination of women. Through their social roles and reproductive functions, women are identified with the natural world, while men are identified with the cultural world. Correspondingly, sexual ideologies hold that women's creativity is expressed through childbirth while men's creativity is expressed through the development of technology. Ortner's dichotomy has been subject to criticism, primarily on the grounds that it is not universal, and that conceptions of nature and culture are Western categories whose relevance in ethnographic analysis is limited (H. Moore 1988, MacCormack and Strathern 1980; Mathieu 1978). More precise and meaningful criticisms emerge from the analysis of gender in detailed ethnographic studies (MacCormack and Strathern 1980). Do the Lese pair Efe and women together as representations of nature? If so, what is the nature of the relationship between these two categories of person? The Lese and Efe case appears to support the applicability of such a dichotomy to male–female relations in general, but it does not. For, as we shall see, the idiom of gender used to denigrate the Efe does not derive from women qua woman, but from wives. And wives are denigrated not because they are women but because they are outsiders.

To answer the questions posed in the preceding paragraph, let us now look more deeply into the construction of Lese identity to examine the symbolic organization of the images of the Efe as women. We will find not only that Lese identity is formed through the conjunction of gender and ethnicity but also that the house is a basic locus of the gender and ethnic differentiation that encompasses many of the symbolic representations. ...

Metaphor and the House

We can discern an analogy whereby Lese is to male as Efe is to Lese men's wives. But this does not mean that wives and Efe have sexual similarities. The analogy juxtaposes village insiders (Lese men) and village outsiders (wives and Efe); wives and Efe are structurally similar as village outsiders. More specifically, gender symbolism creates an analogic equivalence between the Lese men's wives and the Efe by stressing the parallels between the relationship the Efe have to the residences of their Lese partners, and the relationships wives have to their husband's residences. There is a paradoxical usage of the gender idiom by Lese women; Lese women denigrate Efe women in the same way as they denigrate Efe men – as "female." This usage highlights the point that the most culturally saline aspect of the idiom is not differentiation between male and female, but differentiation between "outsiders" and "insiders." The Lese feminization of the Efe arises not out of perceived similarities between women and Efe, but rather out of the structural similarities established by the use of gender as a metaphor of denigration.

The gender metaphor is an "external" or "analogic" metaphor which, as defined by Aristotle in the *Poetics*, is "when one thing is in the same relationship to another as a third is to a fourth" (Sapir 1977:22–3). Metaphor is ordinarily conceived as the juxtaposition of two terms from separate domains, such that they share certain features. To use Sapir's example, "George is a lion" conveys the sense that, although George is not really a lion, he and the lion are alike because they share courage or ferociousness (1977:23). Efe and women are not alike but are arranged in metonymic juxtaposition. As Sapir phrases it, "The similarity now derives from the relationship each term has to its proper domain" (1977:23). In the case of the Lese denigration of the Efe, the two terms "woman" (which we have already seen is more accurately defined as "wife") and "Efe" are linked not because they are similar but because they share a common link to a third domain: the Lese village and house.

What appears to be the characterization of the Efe as women is actually the characterization of the Efe as Lese men's wives. Both the Efe and wives are outsiders in relation to any Lese house or village. ...

Conceptually, Efe partners and wives are brought together in the Lese house. Marriage and the Lese–Efe relationship are the basic constituents of the house, and ideally they are formed at the same time. A man sets up a house only after he is married, and all married Lese men should have Efe partners that they inherited following the marriage.[5] In a man's first marriage, the arrival of his wife should be within a year or two of the inheritance and establishment of a partnership with an Efe man.[6] In fact, on a few occasions, Lese men described their relationship to their Efe partners with the term *anga-ni*, which means "marriage" but also refers to the joining together of two separate things. Marriages and houses, like husbands and wives, Lese and Efe, go hand in hand in social life. Houses are thus places for the coming together of things from the outside and things from the inside.

Marriage is considered to be in process from the earliest negotiations of bridewealth or classificatory sister exchange, but the union is not fully legitimized until the bride actually comes to the husband's village to stay in a house with him. Children born to a woman not living in the house of the father are thus frequently the subject of custody disputes between the families of the future bride and groom. The house is also the symbol of the dissolution of marriage. When a woman arrives at her husband's house she brings with her a *membo*, the collection of materials also called "things of the house" – such things as utensils for food gathering, processing, and cooking, and blankets, baskets, combs. The presence of the membo in the house represents the continuity of the union. A woman who wishes to leave her husband permanently will collect her membo and leave with it, thus "destroying" (*ima*) the house, and therefore the marriage. A woman who wishes to frighten her husband will take her membo and hide it in another place in the village, and a woman who simply wishes to separate from her husband for a short time will leave her membo intact, thus assuring her husband that the separation, even if carried out in the wake of a fight, is not permanent. Similarly, an Efe man identifies himself with a particular house by aligning himself specifically with his partner, rather than with other men in the village. Before the actual inheritance of the partnership, Efe men and women will perform services and provide goods for a number of Lese within a village, but once the Efe man is "shown," he is expected to limit his village interactions to the house of his partner. One way that the alliance is expressed is by the giving of products designated as "forest goods" to his Lese partner. These include things such as arrows designed for monkey hunting, termites, and fruits. The Lese partner may in turn give his partner the dog from the house, to be used by him when hunting. The Lese partner will also give his Efe kitchen items, such as metal pots and pans for cooking. Just as a marriage dissolves with the removal of kitchen items from the Lese house, the Lese–Efe partnership is seen to dissolve when the Efe man returns kitchen items to the Lese house. While these two actions may seem to be the opposite of one another, the difference between taking and returning the goods reflects differences in residence. Efe men are members of the house, although they do not actually live in the house. They are incorporated, in part, by possessing "goods of the house." The return of these goods separates the Efe partner from the house, just as the removal of the goods by wives separates women from the house.

The terminology used to characterize marriage parallels the terminology used at the onset of the Lese–Efe relationship. A Lese man may establish a relation with an Efe partner by inheritance or by some other sort of arrangement. But even in the case of a direct inheritance passing from father to son, the recipient must have been "shown" the Efe either by his father or by another Lese in his own village. The term for "to show" is *itadu*, a word that is used to describe personal interactions in only two other contexts: that is, the "showing" of a wife to her future husband, and the "showing" of an unmarried woman to a man as a real or classificatory sister to exchange for a wife. The person who "shows" someone either a wife, or an Efe partner, is called *lakadu*, and the use of this term in Lese–Efe society is exclusive to these two contexts. This points to an equivalence, from the Lese men's perspective, between relationships with Efe men and relationships with wives. "Showing" establishes the dominance of the Lese men in both marriage and ethnic relations. I should also add that, just as some few Lese men marry polygynously, so too is it possible (although it is rare) for a Lese man to be shown and to maintain partnerships with more than one Efe. …

Aku-Dole: The Denigration of Lese Men

Lese men who are outsiders are also frequently denigrated in the form of "feminization." Lese men, women, and children who come to villages as visitors are not explicitly denigrated, but Lese men who have come from far away to live in a particular village to which they are distantly related are often treated badly. They are asked to help wives in some of their chores, a humiliating task for most men, because, they say, they are asked to behave like Efe men and like Lese men's wives, sitting and working with women in the kitchen. These men are then criticized for doing precisely what they are asked to do and are referred to pejoratively as *aku-dole*, literally "man–woman" – that is, a man who is like a woman (or like an Efe man). Village agnates also refer to such immigrants as *meremere*, a pejorative term meaning specifically someone who has come to the village but is not a direct patrilineal descendent. Thus, outsider Lese men are denigrated with the same idiom used to denigrate Efe men and Lese men's wives.

Red and white, female and male

Having demonstrated the saliency of gender as a metaphor for relationships between insiders and outsiders, we can now explore the metaphors of "red" and "white." Both "red" and "white" are open-ended in that they have a variety of different meanings. But the meanings together constitute a specific pattern of metaphoric relationships. The colors red and white are related to one another in the same way as female and male; wives (as a gender) and the Efe (as an ethnic group) are symbolized by redness, whereas men (as a gender) and the Lese (as an ethnic group) are symbolized by whiteness. Red, white, Efe, Lese, female, male are all of a piece, as we shall see in the symbolic constitution of human bodies, the Lese–Efe partnership, and house construction.

Lese relate lack of control, wildness, anger, and violence directly to the color red (*ikomba*), and more specifically to blood (*kutu*). Someone who is angry has hot blood (*kutukemu*); he is "with blood" or his blood is "traveling fast." Anger stimulates the circulation of blood within the internal organs and promotes a loss of control. When Lese describe the internal organs, they say that the heart should ideally be without blood, that blood should remain in the stomach; a heart that is filled with blood will cause death. Blood is also a life-giving substance. The patriline, as a life-giving force, passes to its members the same blood. Long ago, opposing clans fused and became "brothers" after the leaders of the two clans made incisions in their palms and then shook their hands, thus "mixing the blood." When an elderly man was on his deathbed in 1987, members of his clan reported to me that he confessed to murdering seven Lese witches during the 1950s after he administered *sambasa* poison to them at a witchcraft ordeal. He was reported as feeling remorseful and saying, "Their blood made our clan strong, but blocked my path to God."

The colors are also related to fertility. Menstrual blood is said to be the *tisi*, or semen, of the woman. Women are thought to be most fecund during, and just after, menstruation because the blood has begun to flow and can mix with the *tisi*, or semen, of the men. The theory of conception is thus encompassed within the red (*ikomba*) – white

(*itufe*) categories. When a child is born, its white aspects, the bones, bone marrow, and brain, are attributed to the contribution of the father's *tisi*, while its red aspects, the organs and blood, are attributed to the contribution of the mother's *tisi*. The bones are said to protect the organs, as a man protects a woman, as a Lese protects his Efe partner by feeding him and raising his children within the structure of the Lese partner's house.

J. W. Fernandez (1982:122–3) notes a nearly identical theory of conception for the Fang of central Africa and similarly describes how Fang women's symbolic role in house building parallels the Fang theory of conception: "The extension and replication of corporeal experience which was involved in the older procedure [of traditional house building] lay in the Fang belief that in the creation of the infant the red drop of female blood containing the homunculus was surrounded by the protective and fostering shell of white male semen. In the adult person the male element was the skeletal structure and tissues and tendons, all white, within which the sources of vitality – the blood and bloody organs – carried on their primary activity." Turner (1967) has also written of the red–white dichotomy, stating that, for the Ndembu, red is directly related to women's blood, the blood of murdering or stabbing, the blood of circumcision, and, in general, to power, anger, and danger. White, on the other hand, relates to semen, life, goodness, fertility, health, and good fortune. In addition, Turner notes that although the colors red and white are not always sex-linked, the incorporation of the two colors in ritual contexts often stands for the opposition of the sexes. The main contrast with the Ndembu is that, for the Lese, red and white together, *as opposed to white on its own*, represent fertility.

Blood flow signifies life, but the excessive flow of blood can lead to death and must be stopped with white bark powder. In the most common Lese origin myth, the story of Hara, the creator, the deceased are brought back to life when white bark powder is placed on their bleeding sores; in the Hara story, the main character Akireche starts life by first causing a man's tongue to bleed, and then stopping the flow of blood with white bark powder, thus separating him as a human being distinct from the trees and plants of the forest; finally, in the origin myth presented above, the Lese man fears that his wife will bleed to death, and the Efe man stops the woman from menstruating by inseminating her with semen [white *tisi*].

The symbolism extends to house building. When Lese build houses, men travel into the forest, or recruit their Efe to travel there, to find the appropriate small trees and vines for building material. Lese men take the trees and build the walls (*ai-ba*) and doors (*ai-ti*) of the house (*ai*). After the walls are complete, Lese men and women and Efe men begin digging up the reddish iron-rich earth at the edge of the village, arrange barrels or pots with which to collect water, and wait for a rainy day. The water or rain turns the earth into mud, and, on the day of mudding, women and children begin to mud the walls. Mudding is considered to be women's work. Men contribute the sticks – the skeleton – while the women contribute the mud. The mud is wet and red, as opposed to the dry, hard, light-colored trees, and must be supported by the structure of the walls. The notion that one element supports the other resembles the statements of the earliest observers of the Lese and the Efe (Schweinfurth in 1918 and Schebesta in 1938–1948) that their relations were characterized by dependency (Waehle 1985:391). Indeed, the dependency relations of both conception and the construction of the house parallel the relations between the two ethnic groups. The mud and the organs depend on (*ogbi*) the structure, as the Lese say that the Efe depend on (*ogbi*) them for their subsistence.[7] The house is thus a combination of the male and the female, in which the female depends upon and is encompassed by the male, just as the Efe depend upon and are encompassed by the Lese.

The Efe are indeed described as being red in color, and their habitat is described as being dark and wet and dirty. In contrast, the sunny village is bright, dry, and clean. The goods that the Efe are supposed to give to the Lese (meat and honey) are called red; these are, of course, also wet goods – bloody, sticky, moist. Thus meat and honey are red like the Efe who acquire those goods, and wet and dark, like the forest. The village, and the Lese, represent the production and accumulation of white, dry goods – cassava, potatoes, corn – which are cultivated, cultural products. Iron, also given by the Lese to the Efe, is referred to as white. I would even suggest that the red–white dichotomy also includes

sexual relations and intermarriage between the Efe and the Lese: Lese men give white *tisi* to the Efe women, who contribute red *tisi* to the production of a child within the village context. ...

The red–white dichotomy contains within it symbolic oppositions of social relations, sexual relations, house building, and exchange relations, and constitutes a specific pattern of meaning. The Efe, as (1) red, (2) hot-blooded partners contributing (3) red and bloody goods are integrated symbolically into a pattern of Lese beliefs. Moreover, each of the oppositions presented above (Efe–Lese, fertile–infertile, dark–light, red–white, meat–cultivated foods, wet–dry, wet goods–dry goods, dirty–clean, natural–cultural) are functions of the ideas about the differences between the inside and outside of the village, and between men and women. The oppositions also bring us back to the symbolic material out of which ethnic relations are constructed. We can imagine a series of nesting structures, each encompassing and encompassed by another. Blood is encompassed by semen, organs by the skeleton, the body by the house, female and Efe by Lese and male.

European Images

The consistent use of metaphors of gender to differentiate between the two ethnic groups is striking in its similarity to the use of metaphors of gender in European constructions of Africans and Africa. In an eloquent description of the place of Africa and Africans in the European scientific and religious discourse of the eighteenth and nineteenth centuries, Comaroff and Comaroff note that the "thrust into the African interior likened the continent to a female body" (1991:98). Gender was as salient a category as race, a lens through which domination at home could be projected onto domination abroad; as the Comaroffs put it, "In late eighteenth century images of Africa, the feminization of the black 'other' was a potent trope of devaluation. The non-European was to be made as peripheral to the global axes of reason and production as women had become at home" (Comaroff and Comaroff 1991:105). Africa was imagined as female in a number of ways: as a body to be penetrated by Europe, as mysterious and erotic, deprived of power, natural rather than cultural, and irrational and labile rather than rational and stable. These characterizations grew out of fundamental changes in gender ideology in Europe; whereas in the eighteenth century, maleness and femaleness were often thought of as fluid and imprecise categories, nineteenth-century scientific discourse held that a single sex could be discovered (Comaroff and Comaroff 1991:106). The scientist's challenge was to discover the true nature of women, which, it was imagined, was embedded in the body in general, and the uterus in particular. The uterus became the center and cause of emotional and neurological disorders (Sulloway 1979:23–69), such as hysteria (from the Greek word for womb or uterus, *hystera*). Men, in contrast, were driven not by their organs or sexual nature but by reason, sensibility, and rationality. As we saw above, Lese distinctions between male and female are grounded upon distinctions in mental capacity, and between culture and nature.

I would not argue that the Lese appropriated the European metaphor; there are no data to support such an argument. But Europeans and the Lese may have formed similar characterizations because they use the same cultural material for their symbolic representations of the denigrated other. "Female," a meaningful category of domination in both local European and Lese contexts, becomes the basis for domination in other areas as well. The category served both colonists and the Lese as a way to define and maintain both difference and social boundaries (see Cooper and Stoler 1989:610).

Certainly there is some similarity between the Lese dehumanization of the Efe and the European dehumanization of all Africans and of foragers such as the Efe in particular. In an early example, the physician Edward Tyson presented the body of a chimpanzee as the body of a "Pygmy." Chimpanzees were not named until 1816, so Tyson believed that his chimp specimen was an ancient dwarf, not quite monkey and not quite human. Tyson's title placed the Pygmies squarely within the animal kingdom: *The Anatomy of a Pygmy Compared with that of a Monkey, an Ape, and a Man, with an Essay concerning the Pygmies of the Antients. Wherein it will appear that they are all either Apes or Monkies, and not Men, as formerly pretended, to which is added the Anatomy and Description of a Rattlesnake: also of the Musk-hog.*

With a Discourse upon the Jointed and Round-Worm (Tyson 1751 [1699]). But if Africans were not human, then the missionaries had their work cut out for them; they were in the business of saving souls, and only human beings had souls. However, nineteenth-century scientists appreciated the idea of a chain of being, within which a variety of different kinds of human beings were organized hierarchically (Comaroff and Comaroff 1991:98). Biologists were mapping the mind of God, and every new discovery of different, and supposedly inferior, human beings led to further knowledge of the greatness of Western civilization, and the intricacies of God's creations (DeVore 1989). Thus, even when it was concluded that Africans, including Pygmies, were human, writers continued to describe these peoples using nonhuman images. Sir Harry H. Johnston, for example, reported to the Smithsonian Institution (1903) that the "Pygmies of the Great Congo Basin" were "ape-like negroes" (p. 481) with "baboon-like adroitness" (p. 482) reminiscent of the "gnomes and fairies of German and Celtic tradition" (p. 482).

The metaphor of the Efe as children also echoes the way that Europeans denigrated Africans. Alongside the popular European image of the noble savage ran the arrogant and patronizing image of Africans as children – children who were pure and unadulterated by an existence outside the Western world, and childlike in their naïveté. The Comaroffs note of the Tswana (1991:117),

> By the time our missionaries encountered the Tswana and began to write their own texts, the infantilization of Africans was firmly established. Adult black males were the "boys" whom the civilizing mission hoped one day to usher into "moral manhood." And "boys" they would remain well into the age of apartheid, whether or not they actually became Christian. Even at their most subtle and well meaning, the various discourses on the nature of the savage pressed his immaturity upon European consciousness, adding to his race and symbolic gender yet a third trope of devaluation. This was no less true of the abolitionist movement, the most self-consciously compassionate voice of the age.

If adults were seen as children, one wonders what African children were likened to. In his report on the "dwarfs" of the Congo, Johnston described "a survival in the adult of that hair which appears in the fetus in all human races, a soft brownish down" (1903:488). Martin Johnson (1931), in his popular account of the Pygmies of the Ituri, *Congorilla: Adventures with Pygmies and Gorillas in Africa*, continued the image:

> The pygmies lead happy lives of carefree slavery in their Utopian forest homeland. They are mere children mentally as well as physically, always ready to sing, dance and make merry. They spend their days like youngsters at an endless picnic and there is nothing mean or malicious about them. They are truly unspoiled children of nature. (1931:62).[8]

Even today, the image of Africans as children runs through much of the literature on the Pygmies, such as K. Duffy's recent book, *Children of the Rainforest* (1984), and Turnbull's romantic depiction of the Mbuti as carefree, happy, and playful (1961).

Metaphors of Denigration in the Lese House

The Lese view of the Efe as children extends beyond the level of everyday discourse to the symbolic representation of Lese houses, into which the Efe are symbolically incorporated as children. This view is directly connected with Lese conceptions of the house as a reproductive domain.

Lese clans present a contradiction. One's membership in a clan depends on one's descent as reckoned patrilineally, and though every woman is a member of a clan, clans are idealized as groups of men. But social relationships reckoned through the mother are just as important to every Lese man or woman. Like clans, houses are constituted by both males and females, despite the fact that it is men who found and give identity to the house. Clans and houses are, in fact, conceived in a way that mediates the contradiction between their character and composition. They are both personified as mothers, and are said to be *ochiani*, to contain birth potential, or more literally, a uterus or womb (*ochi*). Clans and houses are reproductive organs. Marriage creates the uterus for the house and therefore also for the clan. Conflicts within

the house, from dispute to divorce, disturb the uterus and produce infertility. To increase the fertility of the uterus, the Lese bury the placentas of the live births of Lese men's wives and sometimes Efe partners' wives inside the house into which the child was born. Stillbirths, the placentas of stillbirths, and the remains of miscarriages are all buried outside the house. The house is also said to contain a specifically Efe uterus, meaning that the house can produce Efe children and eventually Efe partners for one's family.

In addition to making children from adults, houses also make adults out of children. As one informant phrased the ideal, "most people in a village are either parents or children." People are "children" until they marry and have their own house, at which time they should become parents. The few Lese men who are thirty or forty years old but still unmarried and childless are in fact considered to be children. Although Lese men refer to their Efe partners and others of his generation as *imamungu*, literally, "my mother's child," or "sister/brother," Efe partners are considered to be the "children" of a particular house and, as in the Lese kitchen, are frequently denigrated by forms of teasing reserved for children. Many Efe partners at some time during their childhood lived in their father's Lese partner's houses, and are then said to be the children of the village, and to have been "raised" (*ire*) by the Lese. Even Lese children tease Efe men. One three-year-old boy was chasing a chicken around the periphery of the kitchen when he looked up and said to a member of his father's Efe's camp, "I won't let you take care of my chicken because it would get sick and die." It was a childishly innocent remark, perhaps, but an insult nonetheless. Children also denigrate Efe children as objects for manipulation and control. In children's play, Lese girls treat Efe girls as if they were dolls, braiding their hair and adorning them with beads, earrings, and other forms of ornamentation.

Are the Europeans who came to the Ituri forests ultimately to blame for the Lese treatment of the Efe as children? The Lese were likely introduced to some of the European images of denigration, and, I would suggest, the Lese were often the ones denigrated. But where the Lese were treated like children, they in turn treated the Efe like children.

By using images provided by Europeans, the Lese may have been able to construct a more positive image of themselves. Frequently during my stay in Zaire, my Lese informants justified their denigration of the Efe by referring to their experiences with colonial administrators, and it seemed to me more than just an attempt to speak to me in a language they thought I might find meaningful; in several contexts in which I was a distant observer, I heard that the Lese had "colonized" (*colonisé*) the Efe, that the Efe were "savage" (*sauvage*) and needed to be tamed. One informant said, "We [Lese] gained our independence from the Belgians in 1960, but the Efe have not gained their independence from us." To some extent, these Lese are merely saying that the Efe cannot live without the Lese because they are culturally and materially deficient. Informants cited the fact that the Efe do not speak French and speak Swahili poorly; in situations that demand communication with state authorities, such as the settlement of disputes, the paying of taxes, and participation in state-organized work groups Lese men represent their Efe before the authorities. The Lese also say that although the Efe work for them in their gardens, they know little or nothing about horticultural techniques and cannot even feed themselves; the Efe can become independent, according to these informants, but only after they learn to govern themselves.

The Efe's inability to govern themselves is shown, my informants say, in the absence of Efe houses. While the Lese stay put in village houses, the Efe do not have houses and may move their residence many times a year. Houses, my Lese informants said, could bring the Efe into civilization, but the Efe refuse to build them. Permanent settlements, they insisted, could also "civilize" the Efe, but again the Efe refuse. The Lese themselves were, of course, very mobile until they were relocated by the Belgians, who hoped the Lese would remain in their villages at least seven years, and did their best to restrict mobility by allotting strictly delimited areas of land to each clan with a chiefdom. Today, the Lese say that the Efe need to be settled, and one of the best ways to do that is to make sure they are integrated into Lese life. If the Efe ever separate from the Lese, my informants said, the Efe would be in a situation of chaos or disorder (*ovio*). The integration into the Lese social world gives the Efe a "place" (*fazi*).

The question of independence raises two other issues: the relation between the Efe and humanity, and the relation between the Lese as the saved, and the Efe as the heathen. It is commonplace in Africa for intergroup comparisons to involve mythical representations of one group as nonhuman, or else descended from the nonhuman. Lese origin stories tell of how the Lese came from a mountainous region ravaged by wars and famine, to find the Efe already living in the forest; other stories tell of the Efe's relation to nature. The story in which the Lese free the Efe from a life in trees is a story of liberation from savage ways. The missionaries under the colonial administration, like the Lese today, argued that membership in a civilized community like a mission was dependent not only on conversion to Christianity but also on the formation of permanent houses and gardens. Savages are accepted as mobile, but the civilized are always permanent. In the Lese language, a church is "God's House" (*mungu-ba ai*): heaven is called the "giant house" (*ai-tudu*), echoing another Lese notion that in ancient times all Lese lived in one house and the men gathered under one pasa. The Efe are thus the heathen (*paien*) who have not been admitted to the house of God and therefore have little hope of attaining salvation and humanity.

Notes

1 Feminizing the subordinate or subordinating by feminizing is extremely common. Two of the most compelling examples are Jean and John Comaroff's discussion of the feminization of Africa and Africans by nineteenth-century Europeans (Comaroff and Comaroff 1991) and Jean Jackson's description of the Tukanoan denigration of the Maku in the central Northwest Amazon (1983:227–239).

2 The content of the story, in which the Efe and Lese partner collude to murder the Efe's grandmother,

deserves some attention. The term *andu*, used for the grandmother, is a term of reference and address for any woman of a given Ego's grandparents' generation reckoned either matrilineally or patrilineally (including the biological grandmothers). Here, *andu* may refer simply to an elderly woman living in the same residence as the Efe man, Abeki. We can assume coresidence, since the man and woman have frequent and intimate contact. Most of the listeners to this story believed that the woman was unmarried, or widowed. Elderly women, especially widows, are not enjoyed by the Lese, and they are rarely encouraged to remain with their children. Widows whose children have died are encouraged even more strongly to leave the affinal village and return to their natal village. They are thought to be dangerous as witches and to be needy and unproductive drains on the economy. Infertile widows are psychologically abused, and sometimes physically abused, until they pack their belongings and return to their natal village. Thus, listeners to this story did not consider Abeki and his Lese partner's murder of the grandmother to be unmotivated. She offers the Lese and Efe partners a common task: for the Efe, the removal of a nuisance and an unproductive consumer; for the Lese, the removal of someone who would be unable to reciprocate his gifts of food. The story is essentially about the ideal relationship between Lese and Efe partners, a relationship that can be enjoyed when the partners are free of intragroup burdens and responsibilities, potential competition, and the envy of others.

3 Blood is equated with being wounded, and young Lese children will often make the mistake of saying "I'm bleeded" (*be kutu*) or "the knife bleeded me" instead of using the proper verb for "to wound."

4 Joset (1949) reports a similar story among the Lese-Obi. "The origin of this friendship between the Mambuti and the WaLese is given to us by a known legend: One day, a MoLese was in the forest. On the trail, he met a Mambuti who was walking with his daughter. In honor of this meeting the Mambuti gave his daughter as a gift. However, [the MoLese] did not know what to do. For him, the sexual parts of the woman were a wound, which he tried, in vain, to cure with medicines. Some years later the Mambuti

returned and asked his son-in-law where were the children. The MoLese [sic] declared to his father-in-law that he didn't know what to do to have them. The Mambuti stopped the medication, and fornicated with the woman. Nine months later, the first child was born" (my translation from French).

5 Maurice Bloch (1991) makes a similar point for the Zafimaniry of Madagascar. "Marriage without a house is a contradiction in terms, simply because the Zafimaniry notion which I choose to translate as 'marriage' is distinguished from other forms of sexual union precisely by the existence of a house, and because the normal way of asking the question corresponding to our 'are you married?' is phrased, literally, to mean 'Have you obtain a house with a hearth?'" (p. 3).

6 All of these Lese of Malembi claimed to have Efe partners. Although most men inherit their Efe partners from their fathers, variations in demography prevent every man from inheriting in this way. A man's father's Efe may be childless, or he may have fathered girls only. Still more problematic, a Lese man may have more brothers than his father's Efe has sons. As a result, older sons inherit partners, and the other sons must try to establish partnerships elsewhere, usually by inheriting a partner from a patrilineally related man, such as a father's brother, or, as in a few cases, by reaching a partnership agreement with an Efe man who was not inherited, or whose *muto* died. These partnerships, far from the ideal, lack the trust and permanency of those that are inherited.

7 Curiously, the term *ogbi* is rarely used, and I have heard it used only with reference to contexts of dependence, including any situation in which someone cannot carry out a task without the help of someone else, on whom he/she therefore depends. It follows, then, that the symbolic meanings Lese attach to the Efe parallel those attached to the ideas of dependence inherent in conception and house building.

8 To these images one might add that of Ota Benga, the African Pygmy man, from Kasai, Congo Free State, brought to the United States in 1904 by Dr. Samuel P. Verner. Ota Benga was displayed at the 1904 St. Louis World's Fair, and later, in the Monkey House at the Bronx Zoo (Bradford and Blume 1992).

References

Bahuchet, S., and H. Guillaume. 1982. "Aka–Farmer Relations in the North-west Congo Basin." In *Politics and History in Band Societies*, ed. Richard Lee and Eleanor Leacock, pp. 189–212. Cambridge: Cambridge University Press.

Bloch, M. 1991. "The Resurrection of the House." Ms., Departmental Seminar; Dept. of Anthropology, University of California, Berkeley, Spring, 1991.

Bradford, P. V., and H. Blume. 1992. *Ota Benga: The Pygmy in the Zoo*. New York: St. Martin's Press.

Comaroff, Jean, and J. L. Comaroff. 1991. *Of Revelation and Revolution*, vol. I: *Christianity, Colonialism, And Consciousness in South Africa*. Chicago: University of Chicago Press.

Cooper, F., and A. L. Stoler. 1989. "Tensions of Empire: Colonial Control and Visions of Rule." *American Ethnologist* 16 (4):609–621.

DeVore, I. 1989. "The Human Place in Nature." *NAMTA Journal* 15 (1):35–46.

Duffy, K. 1984. *Children of the Rainforest*. New York: Dodd, Mead & Co.

Fernandez, J. W. 1976. *Fang Architectonics. Working Papers in the Traditional Arts*. Philadelphia: Institute for the Study of Human Issues.

Fernandez, J. W. 1982. *Bwiti*. Princeton, N.J.: Princeton University Press.

Jackson, J. 1983. *The Fish People: Linguistic Exogamy and Tukanoan Identity in Northwest Amazonia*. Cambridge: Cambridge University Press.

Johnson, M. 1931. *Congorilla: Adventures with Pygmies and Gorillas in Africa*. New York: Bewer, Warren & Putnam.

Johnston, H. H. 1903. "The Pygmies of the Great Congo Forest." Annual report of the Board of Regents of the Smithsonian Institution, for the year ending 1902, pp. 479–91.

Joset, P.E. 1949. "Notes ethnographique sur la sous-tribu des Walese Abfunkotou." *Bulletin de Juridictions Indigènes* 17:1–97.

MacCormack, C., and M. Strathern, eds. 1980. *Nature, Culture, and Gender*. Cambridge: Cambridge University Press.

Mathieu, N. 1978. "Man-Culture and Woman-Nature?" *Women's Studies* 1:55–65.

Moore, H. 1988. *Feminism and Anthropology*. Minneapolis: University of Minnesota Press.

Ortner, S. B. 1974. "Is Female to Male as Nature Is to Culture?" In *Woman, Culture, and Society*, ed. M. Rosaldo and L. Lamphere, pp. 67–88. Stanford, Calif.: Stanford University Press.

Sapir, J. D. 1977. "The Anatomy of Metaphor." In *The Social Uses of Metaphor*, ed. J. D. Sapir and J. C. Crocker, pp. 3–33. Philadelphia: University of Pennsylvania Press.

Schebesta, P. 1933. *Among Congo Pygmies*. London: Hutchinson & Co.

Schebesta, P. 1936. *My Pygmy and Negro Hosts*. London: Hutchinson & Co.

Schebesta, P. 1952. "Les Pygmées du Congo Belge." Mémoire de l'institut Royal Colonial Belge, ser. 8, vol. 26, fasc. 2.

Schweinfurth, G. 1874. *The Heart of Africa*, Vol. II. New York: Harper & Brothers.

Sulloway, Frank. 1979. *Freud: Biologist of the Mind*. New York: Basic Books.

Turnbull, C. 1961. *The Forest People*. New York: Simon & Schuster.

Turnbull, C. 1965. *Wayward Servants: The Two Worlds of the African Pygmies*. New York: Natural History Press.

Turner, V. 1967. *The Forest of Symbols*. Ithaca, N.Y.: Cornell University Press.

Tyson, E. 1751 [1699]. *The Anatomy of a Pygmy Compared with That of a Monkey, an Ape, and a Man*. Second ed. London: T. Osborne in Gray's Inn.

Vansina, J. 1990. *Paths in the Rainforest*. Madison: University of Wisconsin Press.

Waehle, E. 1985. "Efe (Mbuti Pygmy) Relations to Lese-Dese Villagers in the Ituri Forest, Zaire: Historical Changes during the last 150 Years." Paper presented at the International Symposium: African Hunter-Gatherers, Cologne, January.

13

Land Filled with Flies
The Evolution of Illusion

Edwin N. Wilmsen

The world of humankind constitutes a manifold, a totality of interconnected processes, and inquiries that disassemble this totality into bits and then fail to reassemble it falsify reality. Concepts like "nation," "society," and "culture" name bits and threaten to turn names into things. Only by understanding these names as bundles of relationships, and by placing them back into the field from which they were abstracted, can we hope to avoid misleading inferences and increase our share of understanding. (Eric Wolf, *Europe and the People without History*, 1982)

Man the Hunter: A Nineteenth-century Legacy

In company with many others called foragers in faraway corners of the earth, the San-speaking peoples of southern Africa have been relegated to an existential remoteness in time and space and being (fig. 13.1). This remoteness, as it is conceived to exist for the Kalahari, is represented as having been bridged only in recent decades, and that bridging itself is said to have been accomplished as often as not by social scientists seeking the wellspring of human existence. There is a basis for this perspective: unlike all other native peoples of southern Africa, among those called "Bushman" (most, but not all, of whom speak San languages)

none have been able, in this century, to accumulate sufficient capital to maintain significant cattle herds of their own. ...

At the same time, in this century in Botswana and Namibia, an overwhelming majority of peoples so labeled have pursued a substantially pastoralist way of life in symbiosis with, employed by, or enserfed to Bantu-speaking cattle owners, primarily Batswana and Ovaherero. As we shall see, this is equally true of earlier centuries, with the modification that some proportion of San-speakers themselves then owned herds of respectable size. And all "Bushmen foragers," no matter how far out into the Kalahari they may have been found at any particular moment, were in those previous centuries – and remain now – enmeshed in the dominant

From Edwin Wilmsen, *Land Filled with Flies* (1989), from the University of Chicago Press, pp. 1–32.

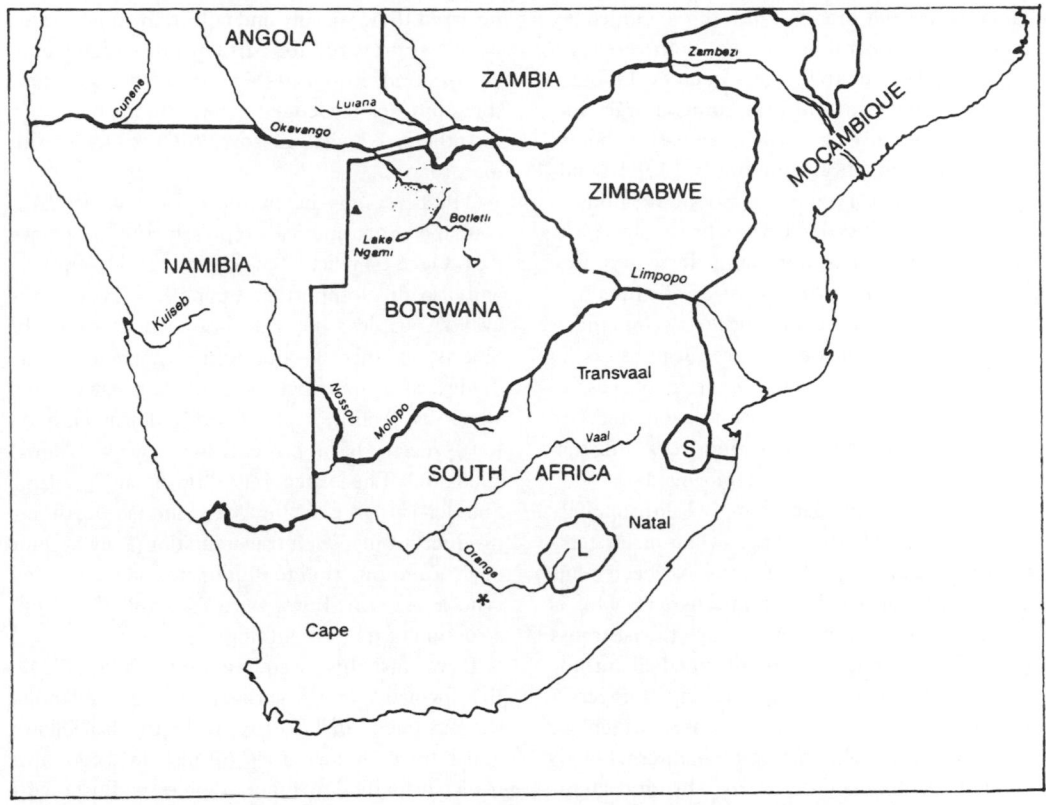

Figure 13.1   Map of southern Africa showing the countries mentioned in the text; L is Lesotho, S is Swaziland. In colonial times Botswana was known as the Bechuanaland Protectorate or simply the Protectorate; Namibia was South-West Africa to the British and Südwestafrika to the Germans. Ngamiland is the part of northwestern Botswana west of the Okavango Delta and north of Lake Ngami, in which the location of CaeCae is marked by a triangle; the asterisk marks the location of Barrow's 1797 observations

pastoralist economies of the region through kin-ship and material production networks. Despite this, during this century few contemporary San-speaking herders have been able to establish livestock-based domestic economies independent of Bantu-speaking pastoralists until this decade, when some are managing to do so. None have yet been able to enter into commodity production of cattle for readily available commercial markets now dominated by Tswana and Herero producers. What are the reasons for this state of affairs?

As we shall see, the current status of San-speaking peoples on the rural fringe of African economies can be accounted for only in terms of the social policies and economies of the colonial era

and its aftermath. Their appearance as foragers is a function of their relegations to an underclass in the playing out of historical processes that began before the current millennium and culminated in the early decades of this century. The isolation in which they are said to have been found is a creation of our view of them, not of their history as they lived it. This is as true of their indigenous material-social systems as it is of their incorporation in wider spheres of political economy in southern Africa.

A false dichotomy has crept in, a line drawn between those who produce their means of exist-ence and those who supposedly do not, between those who live on nature and those who live in it, between those whose social life is motivated primarily by self-interest and those guided by respect for reciprocal consensus. Both ecologists and materialists locate foragers in an evolutionarily prior history; we still hear contemporary forager societies spoken of as living in nature, bound together in prepolitical community. [...] An endless, aboriginal continuity of social relations is envisioned, its alterations wrenched from resistance by external impositions in the form of drastic changes in a fickle environment or of imperative direction – usually technological or economic at base – from a hostile outside world. Foragers, in this scenario, are assigned the role of passive receptor and becoming the testing laboratory for our own ideological preoccupations regarding historical transformations of social forms.

In the prevailing paradigm of anthropology applied to the Kalahari, that of evolutionary ecology, the questions posed above have been non-questions, never asked, without answers. This is because a distinction drawn by Lévi-Strauss (1967:47) has fundamentally informed all anthropological approaches to San-speaking "foragers"; that distinction is between "societies, which we might define as 'cold' in that their internal environment neighbours on the zero of historical temperature, [and] are, by their limited total manpower and their mechanical mode of functioning, distinguished from the 'hot' societies which appeared in different parts of the world following the Neolithic revolution." In fact, Lee (1979:6) goes so far as to believe that it is the very act of ethnographic fieldwork itself that "can begin to place this 'ahistorical' society into history." Ethnographers of San-speakers have assumed that these peoples were quintessential aboriginal hunters and gatherers whose way of life had changed little for millennia – those "cold" societies of Lévi-Strauss (1966:233–4), "'peoples without history' ... seeking, by the institutions they give themselves, to annul the possible effects of historical factors on their equilibrium and continuity."

Both geographic isolation and cultural conservatism were invoked to account for this static condition. It was asserted, without investigation, that neither African agropastoralists nor any other external influence had impinged significantly on their isolation until the middle third of this century. As a consequence, San-speakers were declared to be socially and culturally uninterested in and unprepared for participation in independent pastoral economies. Oddly, at the same time they were acknowledged to be seasoned herdsmen for others. We shall discover the reasons for this discordance.

These reasons lie in the epistemological discourse of Euroamerica's representation of its own past. Once established in scholarly and scientific – and of parallel importance, popular – lexicons, the events, peoples, and categories that become the objects of this discourse are transmuted into "indexical signs which perpetually point to their status as realities constituted independently of the process of representation itself" (Alonso 1988:36). The categories "Bushman," "San," "hunter-gatherer," "forager," and so forth are products of just such transmutation; they become objects and function to illuminate and legitimize a crucial area in Euroamerica's symbolic reconstruction of its own ontology.

It was just this discourse, Pratt (1985) tells us, that formed "what Mr. Barrow saw in the land of the Bushmen" in 1797 (fig. 13.1). In what follows, I shall trace the form that this discourse continues to dictate for modern ethnographies of "Bushmen." These ethnographies serve to authenticate our own subjective ontology by fitting an iconic "Bushman" into a prefigured category labeled "primitive." By displaying objectified peoples as examples of this category who exist "in a timeless present tense ... not as a particular historical event but as an instance of a pregiven custom or trait" (Pratt 1985:120), ethnography validates the epistemological program. Consequently, the intrinsic realities of these objects are, as themselves, of little or no interest to this program. What is important is that its objects conform to a discursive narrative; while any of the parts may be questioned at any time, the ontological reconstruction itself becomes increasingly unchallengeable as a whole.

Since about 1960, most students of "forager" social formations have self-consciously espoused either some form of ecological or Marxian model or some combination of such models as the foundation of their work. This may be especially true of those whose attention is on African "foragers" and their relation to "food producers"; the general formulations of Meillassoux, Terray, Dupré and Rey, and

Godelier in France, of Hindess and Hirst in England, and of Sahlins in the United States along with the particular field of studies of Lee, Silberbauer, and Tanaka in the Kalahari come readily to mind and will be examined in the course of our discussion. It is true that tenets of Marxian theory figure prominently in the presentations of the first five of these authors and infiltrate in decreasing degree those of the others. It is equally true that ecological parameters are recognized as important by all (at least to the extent that they are among the forces of production defined by Marx) and are invoked as primary explanatory factors by the last four of these writers. But the intellectual basis upon which they all construct their theoretical foundations has a far more ancient pedigree and is to be found in two corollary trajectories of nineteenth-century European thought. The first of these was an antiquarian and ethnological interest aroused by the realization that the biblical account of history could no longer accommodate accumulating empirical observations of geological, biological, and social processes made both at home and in exotic parts of the hitherto unknown world. The second was an idealist sociology that in part arose to answer questions about human society thus exposed.

It has often been remarked that these trajectories have long histories in Western thought (see, for example, Worsaae 1849:138; Sorokin 1957:vii–viii; Leacock 1972:8; Stocking 1987:9–10, passim), and this is true, with the proviso that neither their referents nor the problematic engagement with those referents has remained constant. It is nevertheless worth quoting briefly from Hesiod (Athanassakis 1983: 70–1), whose words on the subject resonate in many rationalizations of the study of "primitive foragers" today:

At first the immortals who dwell on Olympus created a golden race of mortal men.
That was when Kronos was king of the sky, and they lived like gods, carefree in their hearts,
. . . .
They knew no constraint and lived in peace and abundance as lords of their land.

Then, after recounting the second, silver, and third, bronze, races and the fourth, "divine races of heroes," Hesiod continues:

I wish I were not counted among the fifth race of men,
but rather had died before, or been born after it.
This is the race of iron. Neither day nor night will give them rest as they waste away with toil and pain
(*Works and Days*, lines 110–13, 119–20, 174–8)

These themes, of an early era of ease and equality contrasted with an ever more baneful present existence, recur regularly again in post-World War II ethnographies of African foragers, as they did in the eighteenth century. Leslie White, who helped inspire a renewed anthropological quest for human anthenticity in the evolutionary "primitive" cultures, gave voice to a common feeling when he declared that these cultures – crude and limited as they may be – were infinitely superior in meeting human needs to any other ever realized, including our own (1959:23).

In the nineteenth century, especially after about 1860, the same bi-polar eras were identified, but their attributes were reversed by evolutionists of that time, for whom foragers lived as savage brutes (Guenther 1980 assembles many of the more lurid details), a condition from which the peak of Euroamerican civilization had long ago escaped. Those who pursued a sociological search for the nature of human nature were not so sure.

Even so, two fundamental constants run through both conceptions: first, an era of pure hunters (we now say hunter-gatherers, of course) did exist separately from other eras; second, that era – although its roots lay in the prehistoric past – is represented by "hunting" peoples who live at any time, prehistoric, historic, or present. Thus, peoples living today who may be classified as foragers bear witness not only to their own lives but to those of prehistoric foragers as well. That is, not only are living peoples conceived to be fit models for the remote past, but that remote past itself is said to establish the parameters of life of these living peoples.

Lee and DeVore are unequivocal on this point. Reporting the difficulties in defining "hunters" encountered at the 1966 Man the Hunter conference, they state (1968:4): "An evolutionary definition would have been ideal; this would confine hunters to those populations with strictly Pleistocene economies – no metal, firearms, dogs, or contact with non-hunting peoples. Unfortunately such a definition would effectively eliminate most, if not all, of the peoples reported at the symposium since, as Marshall Sahlins pointed out, nowhere today do we find hunters living in a world of hunters."

The Received Past

The present without a past
The history of the Kalahari, as written, reads like a kaleidoscope of unconnected slide shows thrown up on segregated screens. That southern African savanna called a desert still functions for many as an imaginary map – almost in the tradition of medieval geographers – on which names of various exotic peoples are entered or erased in accordance with some historiographic need of the moment to segregate those peoples conceptually – more urgent than spatially – from each other. ...

Until recently, historians of the region were concerned primarily with tracing the emergence of first tribal, then modern, national states through the colonial nineteenth century and its aftermath. They did not find it necessary to elaborate the roles played by peoples considered marginal to this process. In Botswana, Tlou (1972:147) [...] began the move to broaden historical interest when he asserted that "the history of an area is more than just that of the ruling groups." He has taken his own admonition seriously and written extensively on all the Bantu-speaking peoples of Ngamiland, not just Batawana, but even he has relatively little to say about San-speakers (and Bakgalagadi) except that they were there first and live in the sandveld. Parsons (personal communication) has suggested that these peoples have been ignored because it has been too difficult to incorporate them into the narrative center of state political historiography, owing in large measure to a supposed lack of historical sources.

Recent interest in specific issues – the politics of traditional land tenure (Hitchcock 1978; Wilmsen 1982a, 1989) and a reevaluation of the nature of slavery and serfdom in the Kalahari (Tlou 1979; Miers 1983; Mautle 1986; Miers and Crowder 1988) – has stimulated research into the historical relations between San-speakers and the other peoples of the region. In Botswana, the establishment of the Bushman Development

Programme in 1975 (later the Remote Area Dwellers Programme) at a ministerial level of government led to the first significant investigations into relations among San and Bantu peoples since the League of Nations inspired investigations of the 1930s (Wily 1979). And for Namibia, Lau (1979, 1981, 1984) has begun to correct the historiographic imbalance in that country. Nonetheless, in general San-speakers are still set at the threshold of history and then effectively lost from sight. Even in as encyclopedic a work as *A New History of Southern Africa* (Parsons 1983), Khoisan peoples are discussed – uncommonly fully but nonetheless mainly in terms of Stone Age and Iron Age development – in an opening chapter and then rarely mentioned again. ...

Such remoteness from the flow of history – a remoteness in the mind, as we shall see – was felt to be necessary in order to support the professed research goals of generating new insights into cultural evolution and reconstructing the properties of societies and economies of earlier human populations. Lee and DeVore tell us they chose to work in the northern Kalahari because "the research goals required a population as isolated and traditionally oriented as possible" (Lee 1965:2). For as they will say when we examine their motivation for joining Leslie White in a renewed search for lost authenticity in human relations, "The human condition was likely to be drawn more clearly here than among other kinds of societies" (Lee and DeVore 1968:ix). I (Wilmsen 1983) have noted that most students, including myself, of Bushmen, as they were then still called, were swept into this intellectual stream and the evolutionary paradigm from which it flows. ...

It is, as a consequence, still too easy to follow Van Der Post (1958) into *The Lost World of the Kalahari* and to suppose that *The Harmless People* of Thomas (1959) are not only enchanting but factual. These authors, to be sure, wrote partly fictionalized travelers' accounts for a popular audience, but they had a serious purpose: "A search for some pure remnant of the unique and almost vanished First People of my native land, the Bushmen" (Van Der Post 1958:3); and "studying the life and customs of the people of the Kalahari, who are called the Bushmen ... the earliest human inhabitants still living in southern

Africa" (Thomas 1959:6–8). This purpose was in tune with the anthropology of their time: "To find and study Bushmen who were living in their own way ... we observed a way of life that had not changed radically in ages," as Marshall (1957:1; reprinted unchanged in 1976: 14) thought, echoing Murdock's (1959:61) influential text, which concluded that Bushmen were Paleolithic people who represented "actual remnants of that ancient population and their cultures [who] have survived into the historical period." To which Herskovitz (1962:61), in his equally praised *The Human Factor in Changing Africa*, added of the Khoisan that they had a "negligible degree of participation in influencing the course of events in the territories they inhabit." One wonders, then, if they were indeed part of the human factor.

Anthropology was itself in tune with the history of the region: "There are also the original people of the land, the Bushmen ... moving about their traditional hunting grounds from water hole to water hole. ... sometimes one may be lucky enough to come across a family group" (Sillery 1952:xii). Later historians, even those sensitive to the colonial destruction of indigenous societies, also spare little concern for San-speakers. Bley (1971:xxii) could write, "Like the Bushmen and Berg-Damara, the Saan were displaced by the arrival of later, more powerful tribes, and by 1830 none of the original inhabitants occupied a position of any importance in the territory." And this from Clarence-Smith (1979:8): "In between [agricultural and pastoralist groups] live roving bands of Khoi or Twa hunter-gatherers, who have been of little or no historic importance." ...

Ethnography and historiography, thus segregated from each other, are linked with fiction in perpetuating a conceptual isolation of San-speakers, a conceptualization that tautologically justifies its own fictitious state. Paradoxically, these peoples, who are universally considered to be the longest-term living residents of the Kalahari, are permitted antiquity while denied history.

Like the rest of southern Africa, the political and economic structures of the Kalahari in the nineteenth century were differentiated in recognizable terms. A number of diverse social groups were articulated with what appears to have been a degree of relative autonomy for each in the early

years of the century. There were Tswana agropastoral incipient states on the southern and eastern margins of the Kalahari by the mid-eighteenth century, but what the economics of the peoples they encountered may have been has not yet been made so clear. It is usually assumed that these latter were strictly foragers, or at most kept small stock, but this is poorly founded speculation. The situation was not so simple.

It is clear, however, that as the nineteenth century progressed the various Tswana groups were able to consolidate their positions and gain hegemony over the other Kalahari peoples and to appropriate an extractable surplus from them in the form of tribute. In the process, they incorporated these weakened indigenous peoples into their own social formations as a servile class. In the last quarter of the nineteenth century and the first half of the twentieth, Batswana were actively abetted in this process by a British colonial administration acting, above all, in its own interest. Gadibolae (1985; see also Wiley 1985), on the basis of previously unexamined archival records and recently acquired oral histories, reaffirms that even the minimum efforts made to control the conditions of San serfdom were initiated by the Colonial Office primarily to forestall adverse world opinion of their administration of the Protectorate.

The first question that begs to be asked, then, is to what extent these indigenous Kalahari social formations were altered, initially by African state expansion alone and later by colonial capital acting through those established states. It was, as it happened, at precisely the end of this period of hegemonic consolidation that the subjugated peoples of the Kalahari – especially those called Bushmen, San, or foragers – became the focus of anthropological attention. Consequently, a corollary question that must be asked is how this historic coincidence has led to a distortion of the ethnographic record of these peoples.

The uneven penetration of European merchant capital into the region is a second crucial factor. European traders were well established in eastern Botswana by the mid-1940s and only ten years later had saturated the farthest corners of Ngamiland in northwestern Botswana as well as adjacent Namibia (Parsons 1977: 117; Tlou 1972; Tabler 1973). These traders, however, only consolidated to themselves what had been in effect long before they arrived. Marks (1972), Clarence-Smith and Moorsom (1975), Elphick (1975, 1977), Kienetz (1977), Lau (1982), Nangati (1980), and practically all the authors in Gray and Birmingham (1970), Palmer and Parsons (1977), Marks and Atmore (1980), and Birmingham and Martin (1983) provide overwhelming evidence that European-inspired market factors were felt in every part of central and southern Africa before the actual appearance of white men in those parts. As we shall see, European trade items were received into Namibia–Ngamiland more than two hundred years before the first white man set foot there.

To be sure, the preponderance of the new wealth thus generated in the nineteenth century went directly to European traders, while the small, but still significant, remainder available to indigenous economies flowed mainly to, or at least through, chiefs and local headmen who retained the lion's share for themselves. An example encapsulates the process:

> Khama's income, now apparently freed from burdensome political reciprocities, came from his measure of monopolistic control over the market between internal and external trades at Shoshong. The income of the Ngwato king was estimated at £3,000 in 1874 and at £2,000 to £3,000 in 1877, though it is not clear whether this was in cash or cash value. The cash income was due in large measure to predominant royal ownership of the means of production – the king "owned" the land and the elephants and employed or hired out his serf hunters. He extracted a 50 per cent levy on ivory production – the "ground tusk" of every elephant shot in his domains, a common and venerable royal prerogative in Southern-Central Africa. (Parsons 1977:120)

There were exceptions, of course, but even where most rigidly true, the subjugated peoples – San-speakers and others – actually produced much of the surplus product channeled into commercial trade. This suggests that these peoples lived in societies already structured in such a way that they could organize themselves very quickly to produce an extractable surplus beyond what they

had been providing as tribute to Batswana for decades and to earlier Iron Age chiefdoms for centuries.

Thus this case echoes others in southern Africa's colonial history. San traditionalism, so called, and the cultural conservatism uniformly attributed to these people by almost all anthropologists who have worked with them until recently, is a consequence – not a cause – of the way they have been integrated into the modern capitalist economies of Botswana and Namibia. The trajectory of this integration can be traced in the written and oral records.

Setting the savage stage

In 1819, Christian Jurgensen Thomsen, secretary of the then recently established Danish National Museum of Antiquities, synthesized the work of his predecessors and arranged the museum's collections by "classifying them into three ages of Stone, Bronze, and Iron on the basis of the material used in making weapons and implements, dividing the specimens into three groups representing what he claimed were three chronologically successive ages" (Daniel 1950:41).

Contemporary, living peoples entered as models into this scheme from the beginning; J. J. A. Worsaae, Thomsen's student, wrote in his *Primeval Antiquities of Denmark* (1849) that "having read how stone implements were at present used by Pacific islanders, and knowing that the Goths made no such use of stone implements, he concluded that there must have been a Stone Age" (Daniel 1950:44). Worsaae had been anticipated by Nilsson in 1834:

> As witnesses throwing light upon ancient times I count not only antiquities, monuments, their different shapes, and the figures engraved on them, but also *popular tales*, which most frequently originate from traditions, and are therefore remnants of olden times. ... [We ought to be able, by collecting] the remains of human races long since passed away, and of the works which they have left behind, to draw a parallel between them and similar ones which still exist on earth, and thus cut out a way to the knowledge of circumstances which may have been, by comparing them with those which still exist. (Nilsson, quoted in Daniel 1950:49)

Following his own recommended procedure, Nilsson distinguished four stages in man's development. The first – naturally – was the savage stage, when man was still a hunter.

Lubbock's *Prehistoric Times* ([1865] 1913) not only gave a name to this time before history [...] but set the savage Stone Age on bedrock by separating a Paleolithic hunting stage in prehistory from its Neolithic fishing and ceramic-making successor. Lubbock devoted fully a third of his long book to "the consideration of modern savages [because] if we wish clearly to understand the antiquities of Europe, we must compare them with the rude implements and weapons still, or until lately, used by the savage races in other parts of the world" (Lubbock [1865] 1913:430–1). Lubbock not only made it clear, as in this passage, that Europe was the center of interest in all these staged scenarios, he also anticipated another modern concern that troubled Lee and DeVore in 1968 – that there were no longer any hunters living in a world peopled exclusively by hunters: "The present habits of savage races, while throwing, no doubt, much light on those of our earliest ancestors, are not to be regarded as representing them exactly, because they have been to some extent modified by external conditions, influenced by national character, which, however, is after all but the result of external conditions which have acted on previous generations" (Lubbock [1865] 1913:544).

In other words, if foragers were to be useful, it would be necessary to filter out from them what may have sifted down from the contamination of contact. Nevertheless, with suitable precautions in the employment of what we now call ethnographic analogy, "the archaeologist is free to follow the methods which have been so successfully employed in geology – the rude bone and stone implements of bygone ages being to the one what the remains of extinct animals [in relation to living species] are to the other" (Lubbock [1865] 1913:430).

The stage having been set, some action was called for. Morgan's *Ancient Society* ([1877] 1964:41–2) provided this:

Savagery was the formative period of the human race. Commencing at zero in knowledge and experience ... our savage progenitors fought the great battle, first for existence, and then for progress, until they secured safety from ferocious animals, and permanent subsistence. ... the inferiority of savage man ... is, nevertheless, substantially demonstrated by the remains of ancient art in flint stone and bone implements, by his cave life in certain areas, and by his osteological remains. It is still further illustrated by the present condition of tribes of savages in a low state of development, left in isolated sections of the earth as monuments of the past.

Tylor ([1881] 1909:24) added a mobile element: "The lowest or *savage* state is that in which man subsists on wild plants and animals, neither tilling the soil nor domesticating creatures for his food. ... [in some] regions they have to lead a wandering life in quest for the wild food which they soon exhaust in any place. In making their rude implements, the materials used by savages are what they find ready to hand, such as wood, stone, and bone, but they cannot extract metal from the ore, and therefore belong to the Stone Age."

There were confusions about just who fit where in these schemes. Worsaae's deduction from Polynesians using stone tools was one such, although this might be reconcilable with the fact that a distinction between a paleohunting and a neopotting Stone Age had not been made when he wrote. Lubbock ([1865] 1913:431) could say that "in some savage tribes we even find traces of improvement; the Bachapins, when visited by Burchell, had just introduced the art of working in iron."

These Tswana-speaking Batlhapa of southern Africa were possessors of vast herds of cattle and other domestic stock, long accustomed to iron-smithing. In the same breath, Lubbock asserts as proof of the eternal constancy of forager life that Bushmen, among others, "lived when first observed almost exactly as they do now," although it is unlikely that he was acquainted with more than the latest thirty or forty of the then three hundred years of European reporting on these peoples. These confusions are hardly to be wondered at, given the embryonic state of ethnographic reporting at the time.

Yet by 1880 the basic defining characteristics of a savage, foraging stage of human existence were in place. These will seem familiar to any survivor of a standard contemporary introductory course in anthropology: (1) the foraging way of life has its roots in a Paleolithic past that occurred long before recorded history; (2) this way of life depends exclusively on hunting and gathering wild foods regardless of when in time (Paleolithic or later) and where it is found; (3) its technology is simple and based entirely on naturally occurring raw materials; (4) social groups, limited by these constraints, are necessarily small and are virtual relicates of each other; (5) these groups are usually compelled to be highly mobile in their search for food. There was also already the caution that the effects of contact with higher cultures had to be accounted for before inferences about the evolutionary significance of any particular group of foragers could be justified. Engels ([1884] 1972:97) added some now quaint speculations on stage variations in sexuality and marriage, noting, however, that some things are just too bizarre to exist any longer, even among savages: "The primitive social stage of promiscuity, if it ever existed, belongs to such a remote epoch that we can hardly expect to prove its existence *directly* by discovering its social fossils among backward savages."

But it was Pitt-Rivers in 1875 who sounded a note whose echoes we will hear a full century later (p. 159). Borrowing from Lubbock the analogy of ethnological to paleontological materials, he asserts the by now unremarkable dogma that "amongst the arts of existing savages we find forms which, being adapted to a low condition of culture, have survived from the earliest times, and also the representatives of many successive stages through which development has taken place in times past"; he adds, however, that "two nations in very different stages of civilization may be brought side by side, as is the case in many of our colonies, but there can be no amalgamation between them. Nothing but the vices and imperfections of the superior culture can coalesce with the inferior culture without break of sequence" (Pitt-Rivers [1875] 1906:18–19).

It is in fact precisely this latter argument that is invoked by both anthropologists and administrators in decrying the present condition and future prospects of southern African San-speaking peoples. In the next chapter we shall hear it said that these San peoples are on the "threshold of the Neolithic, stripped of the accretions and complications" of later evolutionary stages, and furthermore that this condition retards their social incorporation into and economic participation in modern national states. It is taken as axiomatic that peoples in a "lower stage of evolution" will eagerly grasp at the vices of their betters while remaining ignorant of those benefits that could raise them materially and morally to new heights. Implicit in this is the notion that forager social formations are incapable of change on their own. Furthermore, change, in the event that it is stimulated by external agencies, will be gradual. Contrarily, those on a "higher plane" never wish to fall beneath themselves, although they may sometimes be compelled to do so by a capricious nature.

All of this raises a fundamental question: Before there were peoples on a higher plane, how did anyone ever become anything other than a foraging savage? The answers offered pointed to that same capricious nature, which either elevated population numbers above the sustaining capacity of resources or depressed resources below the requirements of populations. Either condition forced innovation. After "higher levels" were attained, the answer was obvious: those in a lower condition would naturally aspire to the higher once it was made known to them. But they could reach this apotheosis only through a "break in the sequence" – that is, by escaping their intrinsic primitiveness. Morgan ([1877] 1964:540) was among the few who thought that savages might sometimes rise, "for it was by this process [of imitation] constantly repeated that the most advanced tribes lifted up those below them, as fast as the latter were able to appreciate and to appropriate the means of progress."

Primitive critique of civilization

We must turn to the second intellectual trajectory of nineteenth-century Euroamerica to unravel the reasoning behind these rather odd propositions. The architects of the developing Continental sociology of the latter half of the nineteenth century shared many of the precepts of their ethnological contemporaries, although they had different agendas and were generally not preoccupied with evolution in itself. Loomis and McKinney (1957:1) point out that Tönnies ([1887] 1957), in *Gemeinschaft und Gesellschaft* (translated by them as *Community and Society*), was concerned to address the questions "What are we? Where are we? Whence did we come? Where are we going?" These are, with perhaps the exception of the last, the classic antiquarian and evolutionary questions: posing them presupposes a recognition of, if not an intent to investigate, the proposition that there are problematic historical antecedents to where it is we are.

Tönnies was aware of this and wished to merge formal and historical sociology in order to better address his questions. He is quite clear on this point ([1887] 1957:34, 42, 252), although he does not dwell on historical, let alone prehistoric, referents: "Gemeinschaft is old ... the natural relationship is, by its very essence, of earlier origin than its subject or members. ... Gemeinschaft by blood, denoting unity of being, is developed and differentiated into Gemeinschaft of locality ... a further differentiation leads to the Gemeinschaft of mind, which implies only co-operation and co-ordinated action for a common goal." That is to say, original kinship among individuals is natural and unanalyzable – either by those in it or by those observing it – but this kinship eventually becomes identified with territory and ultimately emerges as an ideology of sociality through which individuals recognize their community of interests. Or, "all three types of Gemeinschaft are closely interrelated in space as well as in time. ... the earlier type involves the later one, or the later one has developed to relative independence" (Tönnies [1887] 1957:42).

Gemeinschaft is the earlier, simpler stage of sociality when all associations of persons were replicate segments, the polar opposite of modern Gesellschaft, characterized by atomization of social forms and alienation of individuals. The crucial theme here is that small-scale, earlier, "old" Gemeinschaft is the authentic, "natural" state of human sociality, whereas large-scale, current, derivative society is artificial. The key attribute making Gemeinschaft the center of focus is this authenticity – the true state of human existence, one that may be regained by study and effort. I argue that it is this quest for authenticity that fuels the fascination with foragers – with true, untrammeled "primitives" – that exists to this day in Euroamerican thought and its authenticating agent, ethnography.

Later, in a convoluted passage – resonant of German mystical painters and architects of the time – concerning centers of development radiating toward new nuclei spawning yet others in the evolving chain, Tönnies ([1887] 1957:252) says that this "refers only to different stages and types of collective life." But the Gemeinschaft stage, at least, cannot change without external stimuli, particularly trade; it continues to exist in varying forms today. There is a vague, unstated suggestion that it cannot change because it is pure.

I am unable to find that Tönnies specifically attributed Gemeinschaft to a savage – or any other kind of – Stone Age, but the passages quoted above, along with his occasional references to the primeval core of spouses, the tents of nomads, and other then-current ethnographic attributes of that primitive stage, plus the fact that we know Tönnies was conversant with the ethnology of his day, seems to suggest that he had in mind something of the kind. He says, for example ([1887] 1957:37), that Gemeinschaft is characterized by a "perfect unity of human wills as an original or natural condition," that is, by a collective conscience. Perhaps more tellingly, he quotes copiously from Maine's *Ancient Law* ([1887] 1957:182–183) wherein the condition of the modern family is traced through reverse evolution to its simple roots in prehistory.

Durkheim too eschewed evolutionary intentions, but he called upon historical transformation processes in aboriginal societies that in the words of mid-twentieth-century anthropologists sound very familiar today. He followed Tönnies in contrasting simple, original society to complex, derived society such as he saw his contemporary Europe to be. This original, simple society was based upon mechanical solidarity, an unproblematic cultural unity. Its attributes are (1) aggregation of replicate segments composed of relatively undifferentiated individuals; (2) common beliefs and sentiments; (3) communal, collective property; (4) uninhibited mobility within the group's domain; and (5) self-sufficiency of segments. ...

Mechanically solidary societies continue to exist throughout time essentially unchanged from their initial state; indeed, they cannot change except through external stimuli. Such societies are incapable of generating any other social form from within themselves (Hirst 1975:132), for "we know that the segmental arrangement is an insurmountable obstacle to the division of labor, and must have disappeared at least partially for the division of labor to appear ... [and this is contingent upon] an exchange of movements between parts of the social mass which, until then, had no effect on one another" (Durkheim [1893] 1964:256). For such change to occur, "relationships must have formed where none previously existed, bringing erstwhile separate groups into contact ... [thus breaking down] the isolated homogeneity of each group" (Giddens 1971:78).

Before such contact went too far, one could still turn to "the simplest and most primitive" peoples to study the origins of human institutions. For Durkheim these were the Australian aborigines to whom he turned – apparently after reading English ethnologists (Giddens 1971:105) – to "discover the causes leading to the rise of the religious sentiment in humanity." Such a turn seems to contradict Durkheim's avowal that "man is a product of history. If one separates men from history, if one tries to conceive of man outside time, fixed and immobile, one takes away his nature" (quoted in Giddens 1971:106). It is a turn from which few have retraced their steps.

Earlier, with Engels in *The German Ideology* ([1846] 1977:68–69), Marx had specified the social conditions of the prior ages – conditions, moreover, that survived in the "antagonism between town and country [which] begins with the transition from barbarism to civilization, from tribe to State, from locality to nation, and runs through the whole of history to the present day." Those aboriginal conditions were (1) individuals united by bonds of family, tribe, and land; (2) human individuals as themselves instruments of production subservient to nature; (3) landed property relations those of direct natural domination and communality; (4) the premise of locality; (5) exchange chiefly that between men and nature.

In *Capital*, Marx ([1867] 1906:366–67) elaborates on this theme: "Co-operation, such as we find it at the dawn of human development, among races who live by the chase, ... is based, on the one hand, on ownership in common of the means of production, and on the other hand, on the fact

that in those cases, each individual has no more torn himself off from the navel-string of his tribe or community, than each bee has freed itself from connexion with the hive." Such individuals and such "tribes living exclusively on hunting or fishing are beyond the boundary line from which real development begins" (Marx and Engels [1846] 1977:146). ...

The invention of "Bushmen"

It fell to the nineteenth century to invent its nativity in ancient hunting savagery, which is quite a different thing from simply gaining awareness of its ancient hunting ancestors. Hobsbawm (1983:3, 8) has remarked that in the profound and rapid social transformation of the later nineteenth century, with its attendant need to accommodate the aspiring political ambitions of an expanding bourgeoisie, invented traditions served a reassuring function. In this atmosphere, constructions of evolutionary stages and sociological forms molded in imaginable configurations played important roles. To paraphrase Hobsbawm (1983:2), these stages and forms established their own past that, in contrast to the constant change and innovation of the current world, offered an unchanging, invariant structure for at least some parts of social life; they provided "sanction of precedent, social continuity and natural law as expressed in history."

"Bushmen" were inverted in this intellectual environment. They, or something like them, had to be made available to certify the ontological quest. The historical dimensions of this invention are the subject of "the past recaptured," but first we must grasp the ideological components, in extension of the foregoing discussion, that dictated the modern shape given the "Bushman" image. Gilman (1985) points out that it was physiognomy that first aroused scientific and popular interest – the black body as opposed to the white. But the mere noting of difference was not enough for "the radical empiricists of late eighteenth- and early nineteenth-century Europe. To meet their scientific standards, a paradigm was needed ... rooted in some type of unique and observable physical difference" (Gilman 1985:212). The antithetical position to the white body was found in the black, especially the Bushman-Hottentot female, with her "primitive" steatopygous physique, her "primitive" genitalia, and her "primitive" sexual appetite. Gilman (1985:229) notes that Hegel and Schopenhauer believed that all blacks remained at this most primitive stage and that their contemporary presence served to indicate how far Europeans had extricated themselves from this swamp. Bushmen were placed at the nadir of this scale of humanity. Bachofen drew on these ideas to construct this primitive promiscuous horde as the initial stage of human sociality.

But "Bushmen" as social beings rather than natural history specimens did not yet figure prominently in those formulations. Although various of these peoples were mentioned in many travelers' accounts, official reports, and dispatches from 1761 onward (even much earlier at the Cape), the first full-scale ethnographic field investigation of any "Bushmen," that by the German Siegfried Passarge among the Zhu, was conducted in the 1890s. The resulting publications did not appear until 1905 and after; though of considerable merit considering their time, they appeared too late to have much influence on theoretical constructions, which in any case were by then moving in new directions. "Bushmen" did not yet carry the ethnographical authority accorded the often-cited American Indians, Australian Aborigines, and Eskimos, among others.

That did not, however, shield "Bushmen" from being categorized along with these other colonized peoples, or from being isolated conceptually as an undifferentiated enclave among more "advanced" Africans (those at a "higher" evolutionary stage). This conceptual isolation was a prerequisite to their administrative isolation and was a major contributing factor in their deepening social and economic isolation in the emerging colonial social formation that has left its legacy in Botswana and Namibia today. This was the path to the divided present; it led from an indigenous past that was very different: "The colonial reification of rural custom produced a situation very much at variance with the precolonial situation" (Ranger 1983:254 and also Chapter 31 this volume) and had replaced prior relations among peoples with a created microcosmic society. Iliffe's (1979:324) observation that Tanganyikan natives created tribes in order to function within the colonial framework applies very

much to the Kalahari. It was also in the interests of colonial administration to codify and reify custom as a means of consolidating its control. Ethnographers were recruited to provide this codification and to help ensure that this colonial world was manageable by certifying that it was divisible.

Their own words on the matter are revealing. Radcliffe-Brown (1923:142–3), newly appointed first head of the School of African Life and Languages at the University of Cape Town, wrote in the *South African Journal of Science*, "[The study of African culture] can afford great help to the missionary or public servant who is engaged in dealing with the practical problems of the adjustment of the native civilization to the new conditions that have resulted from our occupation of the country."

Seven years later, in their "introductory Note" to *The Khoisan Peoples of South Africa*, the first volume in a series on native peoples published by that very same school, Driberg and Schapera (1930:v) reiterated Radcliffe-Brown's thesis:

> To the administrator, the missionary, the economist, and the educationist, each in his own way now moulding the life of the Native into conformity with the standards of European civilization, a thorough knowledge and understanding of the people with whom he is concerned is an indispensable preliminary to the completion of his task. It is the hope of the editors that applied anthropology no less than the academic science will in this series the groundwork upon which it may build for the future. […]

This anthropological program was designed to serve the emerging segregationist solution to the harsher effects of domination; it was a "synthesis of liberalism and 'scientific racism,'" which would hold out the prospect of evolution for individual blacks while avoiding genetic degeneration [of whites]" (Marks and Trapido 1987:8). "An intellectual organizing principle was required to validate this synthesis or compromise. The development of an anthropological notion of 'culture' came to serve this purpose admirably" (Dubrow 1987:80).

Wright (1986:105–6) draws the inescapable conclusion that this ideological context in which

anthropologists operated "served to orient their
critical faculties in a way which made for the existence of an intellectual blindspot as far as questioning the notion of tribe was concerned." He goes
on to observe that the thus reinforced continuance
of a system of administration that emphasized
"tribal" divisions was one of the major structural
reasons why collective terms – such as "Bushmen"
and later San (Wright, however, referred specifically to Nguni) – survived so long without being
called into question. ...

The need to name

In the invention of the requisite categories of tribal
administration, considerable effort was devoted to
investing names with meaning. The epistemological status of these names, as of all categorial names,
is constituted in the ideological valuation of their
predicates. For example, living in a "state of
nature" was savagery to nineteenth-century evolutionists, so much so that savagery was considered
to be the defining characteristic of the initial stage
of human existence. In the later half of the twentieth century, however, living in this same state is
again considered by some to be utopian (or at least
quasi-utopian), so much so that it could be called
the original affluent existence. In both cases the
terms are applied attributively to anyone (or any
group) who satisfies the predicate requirements of
the concept "initial stage of human life"; these are
the defining criteria mentioned several times in
the preceding discussion of nineteenth-century
evolutionary and sociological schemes. Everything
else but such individuals or groups is contingent,
both as empirical fact and as observational object;
those things that in the next chapter we shall find
Howell and Burchell avoiding are examples (cf.
Schwartz 1977:13–41). In this investment process,
language – not only the names that as labels encode
the predicates of the categories of discourse but
the specialized lexicon of the discourse itself –
carries the burden of the work of reifying those
categories and "helps to establish the authority
which re-presentations require if they are to be
seen as representative" (Alonso 1988:35).

By now it is well known that the term "Bushman"
is anglicized from Dutch/Afrikaans "Bosjesmans/
Bossiesmans" in its many spellings. The etymology
of the Dutch term is in constant and sometimes
contentious debate, revolving around the ideological investment of this term itself. It is important to
emphasize that "Bushman" came into use during
the 1680s in the Cape area only after thirty years
of Dutch applications of other "terms obviously
derived from native usage" (Parkington 1984:156).
"Within a few years it had, along with 'Bosjesman
Hottentot,' become the standard Dutch equivalent of the older [indigenous] Khoikhoi terms"
(Elphick 1977:24). Those terms were Soaqua or
Sonqua (Elphick 1977:24; Parkington 1984:151),
which some authors derive from a root common to
San of current usage; I shall take up this term in a
moment.

Parkington (1984:156) sets "Bushman" in its
original context of use. Within a few years of the
founding of the Cape settlement in 1652, local
pastoralist groups were called by their generic
self-referents or by the names of their leaders;
when explorations into the interior beyond the
Cape boundaries became frequent, unknown
peoples – many without domestic stock – were
encountered. Europeans relied on their interpreters to supply names for these peoples, and "a new
link in the chain of terminology was added. Before
the end of the seventeenth century the term
Bushmen or *Bushmen Hottentot* complemented and
replaced *Sonqua Hottentot* to describe these
peoples" (Parkington 1984:156–57). These
changes occurred at a time "when increased Dutch
interference was causing massive, and irreversible,
changes in indigenous group relations. *Bushmen*
relates more clearly to these changes" (Parkington
1984:164). Parkington suggests that Soaqua
should be understood to refer to the aboriginal
hunter-gatherer social formation of southern
Africa, whereas Bushman refers to pastoralists
and foragers whose social and material fabric had
been disrupted by Dutch intervention. As these
dispossessed groups – along with escaped slaves
and deserters from the Cape Colony, some of
whom were white Europeans – sought to establish
a mode of existence away from Dutch control,
"Bushmen," as applied to them, "became a waste-
paper basket term for all those who lived by hunting, gathering, and stealing" (Goodwin and van
Riet Lowe 1929:147). Or as Gordon (1984:196),
citing Nienaber (1952), glosses it, "'bandit.'"

Elphick (1975:23–42), however, marks the much broader indigenous use of the term "San": "KhoiKhoi themselves made no such clear and systematic distinction between peoples, their term 'San' having wide reference to both hunter and small-scale pastoral groups" (Elphick 1975:41).

Gordon contributes to the many confusions to be found in the literature of the region that perpetuate distortions in the application of this term. He says (1984:216, citing Moritz 1980:21) that the missionary Carl Hugo Hahn, in 1851 one of the first Europeans to enter the northern part of what is now Namibia, recorded in his diary that "his Herero servants referred to the Bushmen as 'Ozumbushmana' [*sic*], a term clearly derived, as he recognized, from Dutch." But Hahn recognized a great deal more; his original published account (*Petermanns* 1859:299 [reprinted in Moritz 1980:2]) reads: "Our people call the Bushmen Ozombusumana (Sing – Ombusumana), a corruption of the Dutch name. The true name, by which they have otherwise been known to the Ovaherero, is Ovaguma [Lau tells me this is written ovaguruha in Hahn's diary]. The new name will surely displace the older, and its etymology will perhaps later give philologists a headache." [...]

Gordon is eager to show that penetration by outsiders (in this case, Ovaherero) is recent; he therefore overlooks the obvious – Hahn's Herero servants were employing pidgin language forms in conversing with a European. This is an instance of the expediency with which, in the early years of their association, "Africans as a rule adopted the restricted jargon of their immediate European masters" (Fabian 1986:139).

Hahn's Herero servants no doubt did say to him that certain "Bushmen" were ozombusumana. But what were they telling him? The form of the term used provides a clue: the Otjiherero noun prefix (class 10) ozo- is applied to livestock as well as to most animals in general. The use of ozo- in this case thus carried the meaning "those Bushmen are our chattel," hardly an indication of unfamiliarity. Hahn was clearly aware of this; in his own dictionary (1857:151) he gives omu-kuna (pl. ova-kuna) as "Buschmann." The first full study of Otjiherero, that by Brincker ([1886] 1964:145), who worked among Ovaherero from 1863 to 1889, has omukuru as "einer, der verlängst gewesen ist

... die Alten, Ahnen": "one who formerly existed ... the ancients, ancestors." More recently, Katjavivi (1988:1) writes Ovakuruvehi, "the ancient (or original) ones." Irle (1917:16), in his German–Otjiherero dictionary, translates Ahne (ancestor) as "omukuru." These glosses are in keeping with Guthrie (1970, 3:310), who attaches the notions of ancestor and grandparent to his proto-Bantu root *-kúúkù. Modern ethnographers note the same term applied by Herero-speakers to specific peoples. Marshall (1976:17) says that Ovakuruha is the Herero term for Zhu. Vedder (1938:136) restricted Ovakuruha to those people he called Saan, the Heixum (Hai- ‖ 'om) of current terminology, whom he distinguished from other Bushmen.

Otjiherero has another term, ovatua, derived from the proto-Bantu root *-túá (Guthrie 1970, 4:122): "The most likely original meaning was probably either 'pygmy' or 'Bushman,' and presumably referred to the indigenous inhabitants originally encountered by the speakers of the proto-Bantu." This root also has the apparently secondarily acquired connotation "member of neighboring despised tribe." Hahn (1857:150) has the form omukoatoa, which he glosses "Eingeborener": "native." Brincker ([1886] 1964:157) has omutua, "Volker vorzukommen": "people who came before" and notes that it appears as such in many Bantu languages; these glosses reflect Guthrie's first meanings. Brincker, however, captures the derogatory connotation as well: "Die Grundbedeutung scheint 'Buschmann' im verächtlichen Sinne zu sein": "The original meaning appears to be 'Bushman' with its contemptuous connotations." Local usage conforms to these dictionary glosses. The Ovambandru people with whom I work in Botswana insist that Zhu – who are the archetypal "Bushmen" of ethnography – are not Ovatua (that is, not "Bushmen" or "member of despised tribe") but Ovakuruha (that is, "ancestral," "those who came before"). Ovatua do exist, they say, but in distant places.

Setswana elides the common Bantu root as rwa; with the plural prefix (class 1) ba-, designating the noun class pertaining to humans, this becomes Barwa. Brown ([1875] 1979:16) renders this term "Bushmen." However, the root with the locative prefix (class 7) bo- becomes "borwa": "the country of the Bushmen, hence the south to people living farther north" (Brown [1875] 1979:34); and "kwa ntlha ea Borwa" refers to the south. Digging deeper, we find "batho ba ntlha": "the first people" (Brown [1875] 1979:231); hence, except for the reference to the south, this term is cognate with other Bantu forms meaning aborigines. In practice, as we shall shortly see, it was applied to all sorts of people in particular circumstances, not only to those we today identify as San-speakers. The current form in use in Botswana is Basarwa, but this form does not occur in the nineteenth century and begins to appear only in the 1960s. A related form, Masarwa, was commonly used from the early nineteenth century or perhaps somewhat earlier to denote "Bushmen of the Bechuanaland Protectorate" (Brown [1875] 1979:183), that is, of the Kalahari; [...] this form employs the plural noun prefix (class 3) ma-, which is applied to non-Tswana and to persons of undesirable characteristics or social inferiority (Cole 1975:81). This term appears to derive from the secondary, acquired meaning of the root *-túá, "despised neighboring tribe."

Thus we find three sets of contrasting pairs: Dutch, Sonqua/Bosjesmans; Otjiherero, Ovakuru/Ovatua; Setswana, Barwa/Masarwa. In each case the first term referred to known peoples of proximate location and carried neutral or positive connotations of aboriginality in some sense. The second term referred to newly encountered frontier peoples or rumored peoples of distant location and carried negative connotations of despised foreigner. In Dutch and English these transformations in usage occurred during the period – late eighteenth and early nineteenth centuries – when those groups were rapidly expanding geographically and consolidating their gains. These changes in nomenclatural referents were ideological impositions by newly hegemonic powers upon subordinated peoples who were thus interpellated as subjects in a new order of social relations. No longer a serious threat to European power, San-speakers acquired "characteristics that the powerful commonly find in those they have subjugated: meekness, innocence, passivity, indolence coupled with physical strength and stamina, cheerfulness, absence of greed or indeed desires of any kind, internal egalitarianism, a penchant for living in the present, inability to take initiatives on

their own behalf" (Pratt 1986:46). This appears to be the first transition toward "bushmanness"; these same characteristics are attributed ethnographically to "Bushmen" today.

At the beginning of this transition the various Tswana groups were not yet dominant over other groups, but as their hegemony solidified during the course of the nineteenth century, the predicate attributes of San-speakers in Tswana ideology changed from original inhabitant to bloodthirsty marauder to childlike dependency. On the other hand, Ovaherero never established lasting hegemony in their sphere of influence; as a consequence, ovatua for them are situated somewhere over the horizon, and this term, when it is used at all, has only vague referents. Ovaherero usually refer to most local groups by their generic self-referents.

This brings us back to San. As noted already, Parkington derives this term from the same Khoikhoi root as Soaqua, which he says (1984:164) "should be referred to not as a title but as a description of a set of strategies that varied from almost complete independence [from livestock keeping] to clientship [of livestock keepers]." He says further (1984:158) that it seems certain that Soaqua was not originally meant to be capitalized "in the sense of referring to named communities" but referred to a particular and widespread life-style, which depended heavily – but apparently not exclusively – on foraging. Indeed, Vedder (1938:124) derives San from the Nama verb "sa": "to gather wild foods." Sixty-five years earlier, however, Theophilus Hahn ([1881] 1971:3) – although confessing that he was uncertain of the derivation – traced this term to the root "SA, to inhabit, to be located, to dwell, to be settled, to be quiet. Sã(n) consequently would mean Aborigines or Settlers proper. These Sã-n ... as they are styled in the Cape Records, are often called Bushmen ... a name given to indicate their abode and mode of living. ... Sã(b) has also acquired a low meaning, and is not considered to be very complimentary."

This Khoikhoi/Nama term, now written San, thus seems to be fully parallel in meaning and history to Bantu rwa/tua-kuruha, moving from proteneutral/positive to acquired negative value. As we shall see, however, Nama-speakers in northern Namibia seldom used San but usually addressed and referred to peoples by their generic self-referents, by leader names, or by borrowed terms such as Bosjesmans.

Thus, before the emergence of ethnicity as a central logic, which began toward the end of the seventeenth century at the Cape but not in the Kalahari until the nineteenth century was well begun, Khoikhoi "sa" and Bantu "tau/rwa" forms were primarily epithets of origins with economic connotations. Group identification followed the self-usage of individual social units. As a consequence of struggles to control, first, commodity production for the European mercantile market and, later, units of labor for industrializing South Africa, all of these native terms acquired negative connotations and became categorical denominations that replaced group denotations in general reference. Their origins aside, all these forms are impositions upon peoples to whom they are foreign; they retain their acquired derogatory signification and are intensely disliked by those to whom they are applied. This dislike is gaining recognition in Botswana's popular press (Leepile 1988:9), reflecting a growing awareness within the country of the pejorative connotations of Basarwa as well as of Bushman. These terms should all be relegated to archives, and the use of self-referents of self-defined social groups should be reinstated. ...

Primitive, savage, hunter-gatherer, forager, Bushman, Basarwa, San; the names have changed, their predicates and the premises from which these are drawn retain their negation of historically constructed objects. An analytical discourse that unquestioningly accepted these homogenizing categories, appropriate only to the needs of its own moment, has left us nothing but a stereotype of its subject.

References

Alonso, A.
1988 The effects of truth: Re-presentations of the past and the "imaging of community." *Journal of Historical Sociology* 1:33–57.
Athanassakis, A.
1983 *Hesiod: Theogony, Works and Days, Shield.* Baltimore: Johns Hopkins University Press.
Birmingham, D., and P. Martin, eds.
1983 *History of central Africa.* London: Longman.
Bley, H.
1971 *South-West Africa under German rule 1894–1914.* Evanston, Ill.: Northwestern University Press.
Brincker, H.
1964 *Wörterbuch und kurzgefasste Grammatik des Otji-Hérero.* Ridgewood, N.J.: Gregg Press. Fascimile reprint of 1886 original.
Brown, T.
1979 *Setswana–English dictionary.* 3d ed. Braamfontein: Pula Press. Originally published about 1875.
Clarence-Smith, W.
1979 *Slaves, peasants, and capitalists in southern Angola, 1840–1926.* Cambridge: Cambridge University Press.
Clarence-Smith, W., and R. Moorsom
1975 Underdevelopment and class formation in Ovamboland, 1845–1915. *Journal of African History* 16:365–81.
Cole, D.
1975 *An introduction to Tswana grammer.* Cape Town: Longman.

Daniel, G.
1950 *A hundred years of archaeology.* London: Duckworth.
Driberg, J., and I. Schapera
1930 Introductory note. In *The Khoisan peoples of South Africa,* by I. Schapera, pp. v–vi. London: Routledge.
Dubrow, S.
1987 Race, civilization, and culture: The elaboration of segregationist discourse in the inter-war years. In *The politics of race, class, and nationalism in twentieth-century South Africa,* ed. S. Marks and S. Trapido, pp. 71–94. London: Longman.
Durkheim, E.
1964 *The division of labour in society.* New York: Free Press. Reprint of 1893 original.
Elphick, R.
1975 *Khoikhoi and the founding of white South Africa.* New Haven: Yale University Press.
1977 *Kraal and castle.* New Haven: Yale University Press.
Engels, F.
1972 *The origin of the family, private property, and the state.* New York: International. Ed. E. Leacock from 1884 original.
Fabian, J.
1986 *Language and colonial power: The appropriation of Swahili in the former Belgian Congo, 1880–1938.* Cambridge: Cambridge University Press.

Gadibolae, M.
1985 Serfdom (Bolata) in the Nata area. *Botswana Notes and Records* 17:25–32.

Giddens, A.
1971 *Capitalism and modern social theory*. Cambridge: Cambridge University Press.

Gilman, S.
1985 Black bodies, white bodies: Toward an iconography of a female sexuality in late nineteenth-century art, medicine, and literature. In Race, writing, and difference, ed. H. Gates, Jr., pp. 204–42. *Critical Inquiry* 12.

Goodwin, A., and C. van Riet Lowe
1929 The Stone Age cultures of South Africa. *Annals of the South Africa Museum* 27:1–289.

Gordon, R.
1984 The !Kung in the Kalahari exchange: An ethnohistorical perspective. In *Past and present in hunter gatherer studies*, ed. C. Schrire, pp. 195–224. Orlando, Fla.: Academic Press.

Gray, R., and D. Birmingham
1970 *Pre-colonial African trade*. Oxford: Oxford University Press.

Guenther, M.
1980 From "brutal savages" to "harmless people": Notes on the changing Western image of the Bushmen. *Paideuma* 26:123–40.

Guthrie, M.
1970 *Comparative Bantu: An introduction to the comparative linguistics and prehistory of the Bantu languages*. Ridgewood, N.J.: Gregg.

Hahn, C.
1857 *Grundzüge einer Grammatik des Hereró nebst einem Wörterbuche*. Berlin: Wilhelm Hertz.

Hahn, T.
1895 Who are the real owners of Ghanse? C.O. 16669, Public Records Office, London.
1971 *Tsuni-||goam: The supreme being of the Khoi-Khoi*. Freeport: Books for Libraries. Reprint of 1881 original.

Herskovitz, M.
1962 *The human factor in changing Africa*. New York: Alfred Knopf.

Hirst, P.
1975 *Durkheim, Bernard and epistemology*. London: Routledge.

Hitchcock, R.
1978 *Kalahari cattle posts: A regional study of hunter-gatherers, pastoralists, and agriculturalists in the western sandveld region, Botswana*. Gaborone: Government Printer.

Hobsbawm, E.
1983 Introduction: Inventing traditions. In *The invention of tradition*, ed. E. Hobsbawm and T. Ranger, pp. 1–14. Cambridge: Cambridge University Press.

Iliffe, J.
1979 *A modern history of Tankanyika*. Cambridge: Cambridge University Press.

Irle, J.
1917 Deutsch–Herero-Wörterbuch. *Abhandlung der Hamburgischen Kolonialinstitut* 32. Hamburg: Friederichsen.

Katjavivi, P.
1988 *A history of resistance in Namibia*. London: John Currey.

Kienetz, A.
1977 The key role of the Orlam migrations in the early Europeanization of South-West Africa (Namibia). *International Journal of African Historical Studies* 10:553–72.

Lau, B.
1979 A critique of the historical sources and historiography relating to the "Damaras" in precolonial Namibia. B.A. thesis (honors), University of Cape Town.
1981 Thank God the Germans came: Vedder and Namibian historiography. In *Collected Seminar Papers*, ed. C. Saunders, pp. 24–53. Cape Town: University of Cape Town.
1982 The emergence of commando politics in Namaland, southern Namibia: 1800–1870. M.A. thesis (history), University of Cape Town.
1984 "Pre-colonial" Namibian historiography: What is to be done? Conference on Research Priorities in Namibia, Institute of Commonwealth Studies, University of London.

Leacock, E.
1972 Introduction. In *The origin of the family, private property, and the state*, by F. Engels, pp. 7–67. New York: International.

Lee, R.
1965 Subsistence ecology of !Kung Bushmen. Ph.D. diss. (anthropology), University of California, Berkeley.
1979 *The !Kung San: Men, women, and work in a foraging society*. Cambridge: Harvard University Press.

Lee, R. and I. DeVore, eds.
1968 *Man the hunter*. Chicago: Aldine.

Leepile, M.
1988 When manna falls from heaven. *Mmegi wa Dikang* 5 (18–24 June): 8–9.

Lévi-Strauss, C.
1966 *The savage mind*. Chicago: University of Chicago Press.
1967 *The scope of anthropology*. Trans. from *Leçon inaugural* (1960) by S. Ortner Paul and R. Paul. London: Jonathan Cape.

Loomis, C., and J. McKinney
1957 Introduction. In *Gemeinschaft und Gesellschaft*, by F. Tönnies, trans. C. Loomis and J. McKinney, pp. 1–29. New York: Harper and Row.

Lubbock, J.
1913 *Prehistoric times as illustrated by ancient remains and the manners and customs of modern savages.* New York: Henry Holt. Facsimile reprint of 1865 original.

Marks, S.
1972 Khoisan resistance to the Dutch in the seventeenth and eighteenth centuries. *Journal of African History* 8:55–80.

Marks, S., and A. Atmore, eds.
1980 *Economy and society in pre-industrial South Africa.* London: Longman.

Marks, S., and S. Trapido, eds.
1987 *The politics of race, class, and nationalism in twentieth century South Africa.* London: Longman.

Marshall, L.
1957 The kin terminology system of the !Kung Bushmen. *Africa* 27:1–25.
1976 *The !Kung of Nyae Nyae.* Cambridge: Harvard University Press.

Marx, K.
1906 *Capital.* New York: Kerr. Reprint of 1867 original.

Marx, K. and F. Engels
1977 *The German ideology.* New York: International. Unpublished original dated 1846.

Mautle, G.
1986 Bakgalagadi–Bakwena relationships: A case of slavery, c. 1840–c. 1930. *Botswana Notes and Records* 18:19–32.

Miers, S.
1983 Botlhanka/Bolata under colonial rule. Seminar paper, Department of History, University of Botswana.

Miers, S., and M. Crowder
1988 Botlhanka/Bolata under colonial rule. In *The end of slavery in Africa*, ed. S. Miers and R. Roberts, pp. 172–200. Madison: University of Wisconsin Press.

Morgan, L.
1964 *Ancient society.* New York: Kerr. Facsimile reprint of 1877 original.

Moritz, W.
1980 Erkundungsreise ins Ovamboland 1857: Tagebuch Carl Hugo Hahn. *Aus alten Tagen in Südwest*, 4, Schwäbisch Gmünd.

Murdock, G.
1959 *Africa: Its peoples and their culture history.* New York: McGraw-Hill.

Nangati, F.
1980 Constraints on precolonial economy: The Bakwaen state c. 1820–1885. *Pula: Botswana Journal of African Studies* 2:125–38.

Nienaber, G.
1952 Die woord "Boesman." *Theoria* 4:36–40.

Palmer, R., and N. Parsons, eds.
1977 *The roots of rural poverty in central and southern Africa.* Berkeley and Los Angeles: University of California Press.

Parkington, J.
1984 Soaqua and Bushman: Hunters and robbers. In *Past and present in hunter gatherer studies*, ed. C. Schrire, pp. 151–74. Orlando, Fla.: Academic Press.

Parsons, N.
1977 The economic history of Khama's country in Botswana, 1844–1930. In *The roots of rural poverty in central and southern Africa*, ed. R. Palmer and N. Parsons, pp. 113–43. Berkeley and Los Angeles: University of California Press.
1983 *A new history of southern Africa.* Marshalltown: Heinemann.

Pitt-Rivers, A.
1906 *The evolution of culture and other essays.* Oxford: Clarendon Press.

Pratt, M.
1985 Scratches on the face of the country; or, What Mr. Barrow saw in the land of the Bushmen. In Race, writing, and difference, ed. H. Gates, Jr., pp. 119–43. *Critical Inquiry* 12.
1986 Fieldwork in common places. In *Writing culture: The poetics and politics of ethnography*, ed. J. Clifford and G. Marcus, pp. 27–50. Berkeley and Los Angeles: University of California Press.

Radcliffe-Brown, A.
1923 The methods of ethnology and social anthropology. *South African Journal of Science* 20:142–3.

Ranger, T.
1983 The invention of tradition in colonial Africa. In *The invention of tradition*, Ed. E. Hobsbawm and T. Ranger, pp. 211–62. Cambridge: Cambridge University Press.

Schwartz, S.
1977 Introduction. In *Naming, necessity, and natural kinds*, ed. S. Schwartz, pp. 9–41. Ithaca: Cornell University Press.

Sillery, A.
1952 *The Bechuanaland Protectorate.* Oxford: Oxford University Press.

Snyman, J.
1969 *An introduction to the !Xũ language.* Cape Town: Balkema.

Sorokin, P.
1957 *Contemporary sociological theories.* New York: Harper and Row.

Stocking, G.
1987 *Victorian anthropologists.* New York: Free Press.

Tabler, E.
1973 *Pioneers of South West Africa and Ngamiland: 1738–1880.* Cape Town: Balkema.

Thomas, E.
1959 *The harmless people*. New York: Alfred Knopf.
Tlou, T.
1972 A political history of northwestern Botswana to 1906. Ph.D. diss. (history), University of Wisconsin.
1979 Servility and political control: Botlhanka among the BaTawana of northwestern Botswana, ca. 1750–1906. In *Slavery in Africa*, ed. S. Miers and I. Kopytoff, pp. 367–90. Madison: University of Wisconsin Press.
Tönnies, F.
1957 *Gemeinschaft und Gesellschaft*. Trans. C. Loomis and J. McKinney. New York: Harper and Row. Originally published 1887.
Traill, A.
1974 *The compleat guide to the Koon*. Communication 1. Johannesburg: African Studies Institute.
Tylor, E.
1909 *Anthropology*. New York: Appleton. Originally published 1881.
Van Der Post, L.
1958 *The lost world of the Kalahari*. New York: William Morrow.
Vedder, H.
1938 *South West Africa in early times: Being the story of South West Africa up to the time of Maharero's death in 1890*. London: Frank Cass.
Vossen, R.
1984 Studying the linguistic and ethno-history of the Khoe-speaking (central Khoisan) peoples of Botswana: Research in progress. *Botswana Notes and Records* 16:19–36.

White, L.
1959 *The evolution of culture*. New York: McGraw-Hill.
Wiley, D.
1985 The center cannot hold. Ph.D. diss. (history), Yale University.
Wilmsen, E.
1982a Exchange, interaction, and settlement in northwestern Botswana. In *Settlement in Botswana*, ed. R. Hitchcock and M. Smith, pp. 98–109. Marshalltown: Heinemann.
1982b Migration patterns of Remote Area Dwellers. In *Migration in Botswana: Patterns, causes, and consequences*, ed. C. Kerven, pp. 337–76. Gaborone: Central Statistics Office.
1983 The ecology of illusion: Anthropological foraging in the Kalahari. *Reviews in Anthropology* 10:9–20.
1989 Those who have each other: Land tenure of San-speaking peoples. In *We are here: Politics of aboriginal land tenure*, ed. E. Wilmsen, pp. 43–67. Berkeley and Los Angeles: University of California Press.
Wily, L.
1979 *Official policy toward San (Bushmen) hunter-gatherers in modern Botswana: 1966–1978*. Gaborone: National Institute of Development and Cultural Research.
Worsaae, P.
1849 *The primeval antiquities of Denmark*. Copenhagen: Royal Danish National Museum.
Wright, J.
1986 Politics, ideology and the invention of 'Nguni. In *Resistance and ideology in settler societies*, ed. T. Lodge, pp. 96–118. Johannesburg: Raven Press.

14

Foragers, Genuine or Spurious?
Situating the Kalahari San in History

Jacqueline S. Solway and Richard B. Lee

One of the dominant themes of critical anthropology in the 1970s and 80s has been the critique of ethnographic models that depict societies as isolated and timeless. Where an older generation of anthropologists tended to see societies as autonomous and self-regulating, the newer generation has discovered mercantilism and capitalism at work in societies hitherto portrayed as, if not pristine, then at least well beyond the reach of the "world system." Thus the Nuer (Gough 1971; Newcomer 1972; Sacks 1979; Kelly 1985), Samoans (Freeman 1983), Tallensi (Worsley 1956), Kachin (Friedman 1975, 1979; Nugent 1983), Maya (Lewis 1951; Wasserstrom 1982), and many other "classic" cases have been the subject of critical scrutiny. These studies have sought to resituate these peoples in the context of wider regional and international economies, polities, and histories (see Wolf 1982).

Studies of hunting-and-gathering peoples have been strongly influenced by this revisionism (see, e.g., Endicott 1988; Woodburn 1988; Ingold, Riches, and Woodburn 1988; Headland and Reid 1989; Howell, cited in Lewin 1989; Bower 1989; Lewin 1989). It was in the spirit of this endeavor

that we produced a critical analysis of the impact of the fur trade on the 19th-century Kalahari San (Solway and Lee 1981). A number of other scholars have focussed on the San, uncovering the early interactions between San foragers and Bantu farmers, herders, and traders within the complex historical dynamics of the Kalahari Desert (Schrire 1980, 1984a; Wilmsen 1983; Gordon 1984; Denbow 1984, 1986; Parkington 1984; Denbow and Wilmsen 1986). [...] In their zeal to discover links and to dispel myths of pristinity, however, these scholars are in danger of erecting new straw men and of doing violence of a different kind to the data – imputing links where none existed and assuming that where evidence exists for trade it implies the surrender of autonomy. What is perhaps most troubling about the Kalahari revisionism is its projection of a spurious uniformity on a vast and diverse region.

In this paper we present two case studies that demonstrate the varied nature and consequences of San contact with non-San in the Kalahari. By examining the different historical experiences of two San groups, one largely dependent on its Bantu-speaking neighbours and the other (until

From Jacqueline S. Solway and Richard B. Lee, "Foragers, Genuine or Spurious? Situating the Kalahari San in History," *Current Anthropology*, 31:2 (1990), pp. 109–47.

recently) substantially autonomous, we intend to make clear that contact may take many forms, not all of which lead to dependency, abandonment of foraging, or incorporation into "more powerful" social formations.

The attribution of dependency to societies formerly considered autonomous resonates with other themes in the culture of late capitalism. Borrowing an image from the popular film *The Gods Must Be Crazy*, we call this view the "Coke Bottle in the Kalahari Syndrome," whereby modernity falls mysteriously from the sky, setting in motion an inevitable spiral of cultural disintegration that can only be checked by the removal of the foreign element. This is clearly a caricature, but it reveals the common and unstated perception of foraging societies as so delicately balanced and fragile that they cannot accommodate innovation and change. Sahlins' (1968:2) summary law "Cultural dominance goes to technological predominance" could be the foragers' epitaph. The "Coke Bottle in the Kalahari" imagery also bears a subtext, the rueful recognition of the unlimited capacity of "advanced societies" to consume everything in their path.

We challenge the notion that contact automatically undermines foragers and that contemporary foragers are to be understood only as degraded cultural residuals created through their marginality to more powerful systems. We consider the possibility that foragers can be autonomous without being isolated and engaged without being incorporated. And we follow Marx (1977 [1887]:89–92) in proposing that exchange can occur in the absence of "exchange value." Further, our argument calls into question any model of social change that implies linearity; the historical record reveals protracted processes, with fits and starts, plateaus and reversals, and varied outcomes. While many historical foragers have assimilated to other societies, a number, such as the African Pygmies and the foragers of South and Southeast Asia, have developed stable forms of interaction with agricultural neighbours and persisted alongside them, sometimes for centuries (see, e.g., Leacock and Lee 1982; Endicott 1988; Peterson 1978). The fact that foragers have coexisted with farmers for so long is testimony to the resilience of their way of life. The position adopted here is that 20th-century foragers are nei-

ther pristine nor totally degraded and encapsulated. The historical status of African foraging peoples must be seen as the complex product of the dynamics of the foraging mode of production itself, of long interaction between foragers, farmers, and herders, and finally of dynamics growing out of their linkages with world capitalism.

The Problem

By the mid-20th century, San societies in Botswana exhibited a wide range of "adaptations." Along the Nata, Botletli, and Okavango Rivers there were "black" San who fished, owned cattle, and practiced agriculture (Cashdan 1987; Tlou 1985; Hitchcock 1987); in the Ghanzi freehold zone of western Botswana many San had become farm labourers, dependent squatters on their traditional lands (Guenther 1985, Russell 1976); in the Game Reserve areas of Khutse and the Central Kalahari, the /Gwi and other San groups lived relatively independent lives, hunting and gathering, raising small stock, and gardening (Kent 1989a; Tanaka 1980; Silberbauer 1981); and in the central sandveld many San lived clustered around Tswana cattle posts, where the men were employed as herders (Hitchcock 1978).

The historical antecedents of this diversity have been difficult to discern. Until the 1970s the available archaeological evidence indicated that the Kalahari had been a stronghold of hunter-gatherer societies and the diversity was the product of the last few hundred years (Phillipson 1977). Recent excavations, however (Denbow 1980, 1984, 1986; Wilmsen 1983, 1989b; Denbow and Wilmsen 1983, 1986), have demonstrated a much earlier Iron Age presence, in parts of the Kalahari as early as AD 500. Later Stone Age (LSA) sites, commonly associated with populations ancestral to San hunter-gatherers, are present as well and in some areas remain predominant, but a number of these sites have Iron Age materials indicating contact between farmers and foragers. Thus the time depth of contact with non-hunters has increased from a few centuries to a millennium or more, and the presence of "exotic" goods is evidence for regional trade between hunters and non-hunters.

A second line of evidence for the revisionists springs from rereadings of 19th-century accounts of exploration and trade in the Kalahari interior. Gordon (1984), for one, has argued that the interior San were so deeply involved in trade, warfare, and diplomacy that they bore little resemblance to the "autonomous" societies described by 20th-century ethnographers. A closely related issue is the question of San servitude for black overlords. Indeed, many 19th- and 20th-century sources describe the San as living in a condition close to serfdom, a perception that has coloured observations of them.

The revisionists have used these lines of evidence to call into question the claims to authenticity of a number of foraging peoples studied by Marshall (1976), Lee and DeVore (1976), Lee (1979), Silberbauer (1981), Tanaka (1980), and others. Schrire (1980, 1984b), for example, argues that the San are not hunter-gatherers at all but failed pastoralists who oscillate between herding and foraging from century to century. [...] Labelling recent ethnographies of the San "romantic accounts of Bushman isolation and independence," Denbow (1986:1) dismisses them as "an ahistorical and timeless caricature." He suggests that whatever hunters persisted through the long period of contact did so not as autonomous societies but as "part of long-standing regional systems of interaction and exchange involving neighboring peoples with quite different economic and socio-political orientations" (p. 27). Wilmsen (1983), the most outspoken critic, referencing the perspective pioneered by Wolf, challenges the idea that the flexible egalitarian sharing documented for several San groups has anything to do with the dynamics of a foraging mode of production, concluding that "it is more than merely possible that the San are classless today precisely because they are the underclass in an intrusive class structure" (p. 17). ...

The questions raised by the revisionists are challenging ones, and the claims they make go well beyond the reinterpretation of Kalahari archaeology. Yet it is an open question how much of their revision arises from the data and how much rests on unexamined inference and assumption. It will be useful to set out their claims as a series of propositions in order to clarify the boundary between fact and interpretation. They propose that (1) the Iron Age settlement of the Kalahari is earlier than previously thought, and

therefore (2) hunter-gatherers were absorbed into regional economic networks and (3) ceased to exist as independent societies well before the historic period. They go on to argue that (4) if these societies continue to exhibit characteristics associated with hunting and gathering it is because of (a) their poverty (Wilmsen) or (b) their resistance to domination by stronger societies (Schrire). Of these only Point 1 can be considered well established; Points 2 and 3 draw unwarranted conclusions from scanty data while Point 4 relies heavily on discourses that are as ideological as they are analytical.

What kinds of questions need to be asked in order to evaluate the conflicting claims of the Kalahari ethnographers and their critics? It is necessary, first, for both parties to attend to issues of regional variation. Some foragers certainly were drawn into farming and herding centuries ago, and some of these became part of regional economic systems, but, as we spell out below, both archaeology and ethnohistory contradict the view of a uniform grid of economic interdependency throughout the Kalahari. Second, we need to sensitize ourselves to the assumptions we make about the nature of "contact." For some "contact" appears to be unconsciously equated with "domination." The possibility of trade or exchange *without* some form of domination is excluded from the range of outcomes. When considering the Kalahari we need to ask further whether the conditions for domination existed there before, say, 1850. Were the societies with which the foragers came in contact after AD 500 sufficiently powerful to compel San servitude? Again the evidence shows that outcomes were variable and that in a number of areas the foraging life persisted. Third, and related, we need to examine our assumptions about the transformative power of the commodity — the view that when a society is linked to another by trade or tribute that linkage will necessarily transform social organization and create dependency. Are there other outcomes possible in which exchange relations do not undermine existing relations of production? Finally, we need to assess the evidence for San servitude; the contradictions in the literature suggest that appearances may be deceiving and in some cases San subordination may be more apparent then real. ...

Case Studies

The Western Kweneng San

Many San peoples today live on the fringes of Bantu communities or white-owned farms; [...] the Western Kweneng San are one example. In contrast to the Dobe San, whose contact with non-San has traditionally been intermittent, these Southern San have lived amongst Bantu-speaking peoples for at least 200 years. The peoples of the Dutlwe area, in the southern Kalahari 250 km west of Gaborone (fig 14.1, include three intermarrying San groups (Tshassi, Kwa, and Khute) and the Bantu-speaking Kgalagadi. The Kwena, a Tswana chiefdom, occupy the better-watered eastern edge of the desert. [...] The dominant Tswana-Kgalagadi cultural model posits a hierarchical social order in which the San and other servile peoples occupy the social and physical margins. This "Tswanacentric" model does not, however, fit everywhere with the same precision, nor has it fit equally through time. The historical record reveals a variety of linkages between San and their neighbours, with a variety of consequences. San encapsulation within the orbit of Bantu-speaking peoples and loss of autonomy have been neither automatic nor, in most instances, complete. The San of Western Kweneng have not always worked for their Bantu neighbours, nor, in spite of the pronouncements of current Kalahari residents, is there anything "natural" about the state of affairs that exists today.

The pre- and protohistoric period   Oral traditions obtained from current residents indicate that relations between Kgalagadi and San were largely symbiotic in the early period. [...] All were nomadic and lived primarily by hunting and gathering, although the Kgalagadi may have practiced some horticulture. After 1820 new waves of Kgalagadi, refugees of the wars of the turbulent period known as the Difaqane, retreated into the desert with their goats, sheep, and dogs. The Kgalagadi credit the San with having taught them desert skills, and the San made use of Kgalagadi animals, especially hunting dogs. According to the Kgalagadi, their ancestors were able to migrate to western Kweneng with their goats and sheep in the early 19th century because the animals could obtain virtually all of their moisture from melons

during the trek. These new immigrants chose a more sedentary life than their predecessors, and the pans on which they settled were also San water sources. In a Mokgalagadi's words, "The Basarwa [San] were already here. They just move around a lot. ... They were not driven away."

The fur-trade period   In the period following 1840 the Kwena, who themselves had fared badly during the Difaqane (Thompson 1975:396), were attempting to reassert and consolidate their hold on the Kalahari periphery. Threatened from the east by the Boers, they were eager to accumulate Western trade goods, particularly guns (Livingstone 1857:39). [...] To do so they needed desert products such as furs, ostrich feathers, skins, and ivory, and vast quantities of these were obtained from the peoples of the area as tribute; Livingstone writes (p. 50) that while he was living among the Kwena he observed "between twenty and thirty thousand skins ... made up into karosses; part of them were worn by the inhabitants and part sold to traders."

The San participated only indirectly in the tribute system; they and the Kgalagadi were the primary producers, hunting and preparing skins, but in most cases it was the Kgalagadi (and usually only the elite among them) who dealt with the Kwena. [...] The San hunted with dogs and occasionally with guns owned by others; they brought the hides and often some of the meat to the owners and kept a portion of the meat for themselves (see, e.g., Silberbauer and Kuper 1966; Hitchcock 1987; Schapera and van der Merwe 1945; Stow 1964 [1905]). Tobacco, grown and/or obtained by trade, was a central commodity in the system, exchanged for skins and labour. Contact between Kgalagadi and San was concentrated in the winter months, when the fur-bearing animals were most desirable and water most scarce. In this period there was little difference in the objective conditions of life of San and Kgalagadi. Their relations were less coercive than Kwena–Kgalagadi relations and resembled trade more than tribute.

Towards the end of the 19th century the Kwena's control over the periphery began to break down. The desert was difficult to police; Kwena rule was thin and maintained largely through periodic displays of force. The Kgalagadi as a result

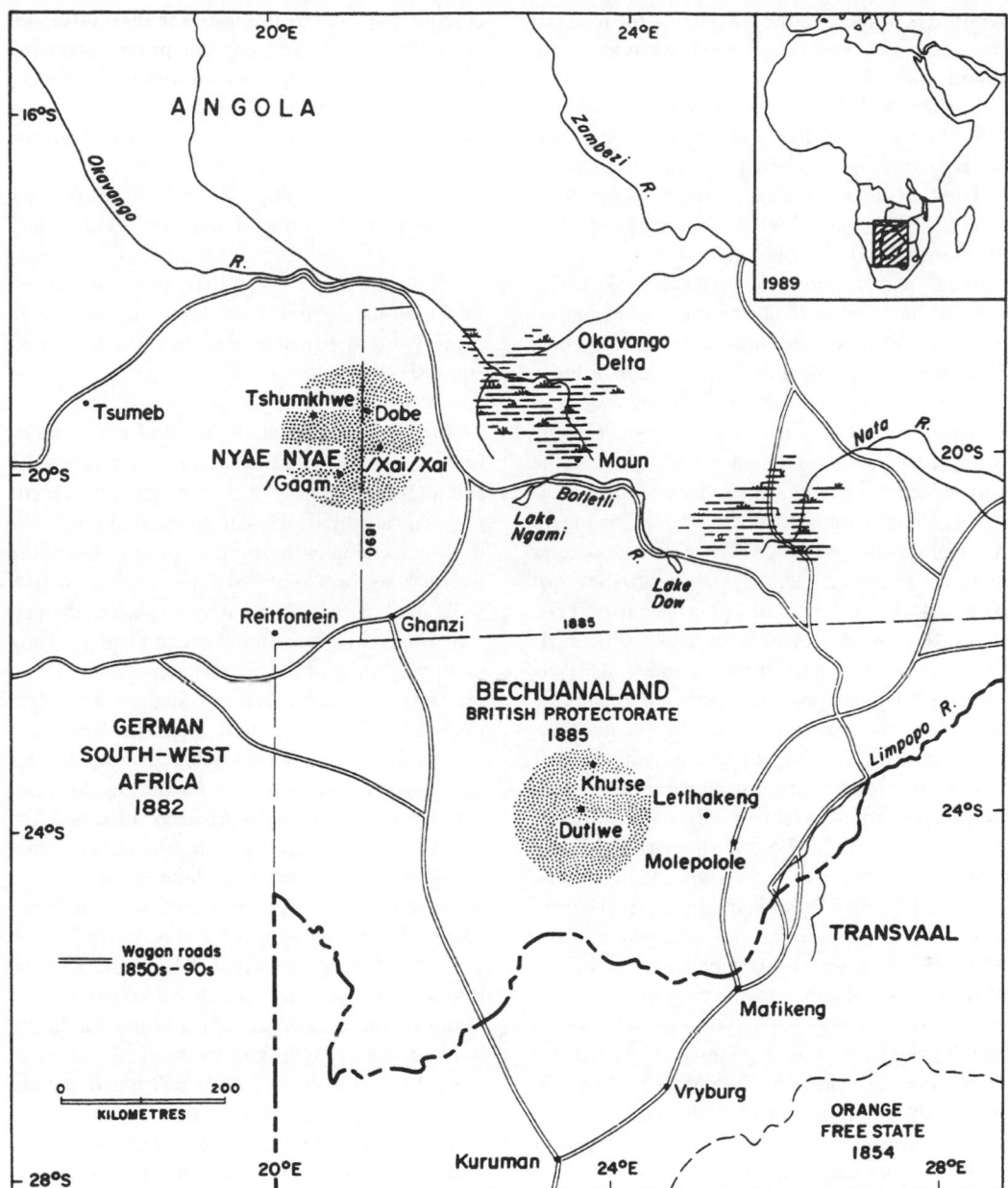

Figure 14.1   The 19th-century Kalahari, with relevant contemporary boundaries and political divisions superimposed

were able to begin to accumulate property, especially cattle (see Okihiro 1976; Schapera and van der Merwe 1945:5), thus laying the groundwork for an agro-pastoral base that did not develop

among the Kweneng San. Inequalities between the San and some Kgalagadi also began to grow. The Kgalagadi attempted to replicate in their relations with the San the Tswana hierarchical model that subordinated them to the Kwena, but the material conditions for institutionalized servitude were absent.

In 1885, with the imposition of British colonial rule, the tribute system was officially disbanded; the Kgalagadi were allowed to trade their goods, and instead of tribute a tax, of which Kwena chiefs received 10%, was collected (although in practice the transition from tribute to tax was not automatic) (Schapera and van der Merwe 1945:6). The colonial state was intrigued by the San and voiced concern over their condition, but in fact the new government had little direct impact on their life.

A colonial officer travelling through western Kweneng in 1887 considered the San the Kgalagadi's "slaves pure and simple," but at the same time he reported, "They have no fixed residence, often living miles from water and living on the melons and roots, changing their abode, as these are scarce or plentiful" (Botswana National Archives 1887a:17). (If the San had truly been slaves they would not have been following the melons but would have been working for the Kgalagadi.) This apparent contradiction emerges repeatedly; the San are described as slaves and yet as "scoundrels, snakes, and rascals" who will not stay in one place and move about as they wish (Botswana National Archives 1877b; cf. MacKenzie 1871:128–32 for the Central district). Again, an 1899 report states that the Masarwa (San) "lives a nomadic life in a wild state and hunts for the masters" (HC. 24, quoted in Schapera and van der Merwe 1945:4), thus portraying them as simultaneously enserfed and nomadic foragers. ...

Agro-pastoralism The fur trade remained for some time the primary link between San and Kgalagadi. The Kgalagadi elite who owned cattle in the early 20th century relied upon their poorer relatives rather than San for herding labour. At the same time, the development of agro-pastoral production was beginning to undermine the San's foraging base. Permanent settlement, population increase, cattle herding, and agriculture combined to reduce the environment's hunting-and-gathering potential. The desertification noted by elderly residents and by ecologists alike can be traced not simply to overhunting but to human habitation (Campbell and Child 1971; Leistner 1967). Every

bush or tree cleared to make way for cultivation, especially plowing, reduces the ground cover, disrupts root systems, facilitates erosion and reduces the soil's ability to absorb and retain moisture. It was increasingly only in the bush, away from the better water sources, that the San could maintain their autonomy. The Central Kalahari has remained (by law) free of large-scale village and livestock development and served as a "hinterland" for the San, a place where their culture and mode of subsistence have persisted and where many Western Kweneng San claim roots, refuge, and restoration. ...

The organic link By the 1940s, local agropastoralism was well established. With trading revenues and migrant labourers' wages, the Kgalagadi accumulated cattle and plows and imported new well-digging techniques that permitted expansion of the livestock sector. Cultivated water sources such as wells and boreholes came to be considered the private property of the group that dug them, [...] and eventually many of the better-watered pans (which probably had been dry-season homes of the San [Vierich 1977]) were associated with the Kgalagadi; now to obtain drinking water the San had to enter into unequal relations with the Kgalagadi. Plow agriculture and animal husbandry increased the workload at precisely the time when able-bodied young Kgalagadi men were leaving for contract work on the South African mines, and it was San labour that filled the gap (Solway 1987). By the 1950s the San had become the Kgalagadi's casual labour force. The Kgalagadi today frequently try to minimize the importance of San labour and like to think of themselves as humanitarian for "helping" them, but when pressed many will quietly admit, "We are lucky, we have Bushmen."

That the Kgalagadi's greater demand for labour occurred in concert with the growing precariousness of foraging in the area was not a result of conscious conspiracy, but neither was it a coincidence. The Kgalagadi's new productive base altered the environment; it changed their labour demands, transformed property relations over water sources, and increasingly distinguished the Kgalagadi from the San. In the 19th century differences in material conditions between the groups were small, but by the mid-20th century the hierarchical model in which the San occupy a marginal and servile position more closely matched reality than it had in the past. Hunting for the Kgalagadi had not undermined the San's foraging subsistence strategy; it is doubtful whether the Kgalagadi of the 19th century had the resources or power to compel San servitude, except in the very short term. The Kgalagadi of the 20th century, in contrast, had control of water, milk, grain, and purchased items such as tobacco, clothing, guns, and wagons, and these resources, in the face of diminishing returns from foraging, tied the San to them more thoroughly than in the past. New kinds of work that followed the rhythm of the agricultural and livestock cycle resulted in more intimate and regular association than that created by the hunting arrangements. With the expansion of Kgalagadi agriculture, San women entered the workforce in greater numbers, which meant that San social reproduction increasingly took place in the Kgalagadi's domain. Today, a few San live permanently as domestic servants with Kgalagadi; the Kgalagadi claim to "take these San as our children," but they are children who never achieve adult status. There are a number of San homesteads on the periphery of the villages, their populations waxing and waning with the seasons. The spatial marginality neatly reflects the San's social marginality and positioning somewhere between village and bush.

Although the hinterland persists and some San forage full-time in it (Kent 1989b; Silberbauer 1981), most Western Kweneng San work for the Kgalagadi at least during the agricultural season, arriving "after the flowers appear on the melon plants." Sixty years ago, coming to the village and working for the Kgalagadi was seen as a "break" from foraging in an increasingly unproductive environment. Now the village end of the cycle has taken precedence, and most San are resigned to the fact that they can make a living only by working for the Kgalagadi, begging, or accepting government aid. Foraging offers only an occasional supplement. Some San still return to the bush in the wet season. According to one woman, "We are happy to be away from the Kgalagadi. There are water roots and berries. If we come upon a tortoise or a dead animal we will eat and dance all night. We only come back because of thirst."

The Dobe San

The Dobe area, 700 km north of Dutlwe, was far from the turmoil of 19th-century colonial southern Africa. [...] The Dobe people were not affected by the Difaqane, though they had heard about it, and they were not subject to tribute. More important, the wave of black settlement did not reach them until 1925. Surrounded by a waterless belt 70–200 km in depth, the Dobe area is difficult of access even today; it would have been accessible to Iron Age peoples with livestock for only a few months in years of high rainfall, and even then only after an arduous journey. It would be risky to assume that contemporary patterns of contact (or lack of contact) were characteristic of all periods of prehistory. Fortunately, the data of archaeology can be brought to bear on this kind of question.

The pre- and protohistoric period Despite the abundant evidence of Iron Age settlement elsewhere in northwestern Botswana dating from AD 500 or earlier and despite concerted efforts to find the same in the Dobe area, there is no archaeological evidence of Iron Age occupation of the area until the 20th century (Brooks 1989; Yellen and Brooks 1988). What does exist in Later Stone Age archaeological deposits, along with a classic stone tool kit, is a few fragments of pottery and a few iron implements, items best interpreted as evidence of intermittent trade with Iron Age settlements to the east and north.

!Kung oral traditions reinforce this view. Elders speak of their ancestors' maintaining long-term trade relations with "Goba" while maintaining their territoral organization and subsistence as hunter-gatherers in the Dobe area and to the west of it. Some have gone as far as to insist that the first visitors on a large scale to their area were whites rather than blacks. According to !Xamn!a, who was born at the turn of the century, "The first outsiders to come to /Xai/Xai were /Ton [European] hunters. ... They used to shoot guns with bullets one and one-half inches thick. But this was before I was born. My wife's father, Toma!gain, worked for the /Tons." When asked which of the Tswana ruling clans had first arrived in the Dobe area in the last century, a !Goshe elder emphatically replied, "None! The !Tons

[Europeans] were first." And when asked if his "fathers" knew of blacks of any origin in the area, he replied, "No, we only knew ourselves."

The picture that emerges from the archaeological, ethnohistorical, and oral-historical evidence can be sketched as follows: The Dobe area has been occupied by hunting-and-gathering peoples for at least several thousand years. The evidence of unbroken LSA deposits 100 cm or more in depth, with ostrich eggshells and indigenous fauna from bottom to top, with a scattering of pottery and iron, and with European goods in surface levels supports a picture of relative continuity. [...] At some point between AD 500 and 1500, the interior !Kung established trade relations with "Goba" to the east and northeast and carried on trade with them in which desert products – furs, honey, and ivory – were exchanged for iron, tobacco, ceramics, and possibly agricultural products. It is unclear whether the Goba made reciprocal visits to the Dobe area or even whether the ceramics that are found are of outside origin. ...

The fur-trade period   Two kinds of economic networks were involved in the San articulation with the "world system": indirect involvement through black intermediaries – the Goba and later the Tswana – and direct contact with European hunters and traders. The indirect form resembled the precolonial African trade that the San had carried on for centuries and therefore involved no basic restructuring of relations of production. The direct European trade, while intense and disruptive, did not last very long. It was not until the 1920s and 30s, with the arrival of black settlers in the Dobe area, that basic production relations began to be modified and incorporative processes set in motion.

Several accounts exist of the lively trade that went on in the "Gaamveld" between the "Bushmen" and Afrikaner, German, and English hunter-traders in the period 1870–90 (Lee 1979:78; Solway and Lee 1981). The first European known to have visited the Dobe-Nyae/Nyae area was Hendrik van Zyl, whom Ramadjagote Harry, a Tswana born in 1903, describes as "the hunter who was responsible for killing all the elephants and rhinos in the west." Tabler (1973:114) confirms that in 1877 alone van Zyl's party killed 400 elephants in the Gaamveld and took out 8,000 lbs of ivory. !Kung recall the

period with a great deal of affection as a time of intense social activity and economic prosperity. They were provided with guns and ate enormous quantities of meat. One could find no trace of regret in these accounts for the carnage and diminution of wildlife; elephants, regarded as pests by the !Kung, are rarely hunted today. The legacy of this brief but intense irruption for the Dobe-area people can be briefly set out. One small family of !Kung, fully integrated into the Dobe community, is acknowledged to be descended from a member of van Zyl's party and a local !Kung woman. Few other impacts are evident. Even though firearms were widely distributed to African populations (Marks and Atmore 1971) and though many 19th-century-vintage weapons remained in African hands into the 1960s, only a single !Kung man, a tribal constable who had purchased his weapon with wages, possessed a gun in 1963.

A second instance of European presence, also short-lived, was the cattle drives sent by a group of Afrikaner trekkers from Angola to the Transvaal via Lewisfontein (!Kangwa), a large perennial spring in the centre of the Dobe area. The "Dorsland" Trekkers reached Angola only in 1880, and according to Clarence-Smith (1979:59–60) the trek route had fallen into disuse by 1900 (see also Gordon 1984:202).

Since most European goods – iron pots, beads, etc. – continued to be obtained through Bantu intermediaries, one would be hard put to argue that the sporadic European presence from 1870 to 1900 had transformed !Kung society. On the other hand, it is likely that the European penetration of the !Kung interior was the catalyst for incursions by Tswana and others.

!Kung call the period after the departure of the Europeans and before the arrival of permanent black settlers *koloi* (wagon), a reference to the ox-carts used by the Tswana from the 1880s to about 1925. A number of Tswana had been employed on the European hunting parties as hunters, trackers, and gun bearers. After 1880 Tswana hunter-traders with wagons began making their own trips to the Dobe area; this was part of the general expansion of the Tawana state after 1874 (Tlou 1985:49). In the !Kung oral traditions it is the !Kung and not the Tswana who are the initiators of this trade. As !Xamn!a tells it,

When the Europeans left, the Zhu/twasi were all alone. My ≠*tum* [father-in-law] said, "Let's go to the Tswana, bring their cattle here and drink their milk." So then my ≠*tum* organized the younger men and went east to collect the cattle. ... Then they chopped a brush-fence kraal under the camel thorn trees and kraaled them there. The Tswana came up to visit and hunt, then they went back leaving the San drinking the milk. Then my ≠*tum* got *shoro* [tobacco] from the Tswana and smoked it. When the *shoro* was all finished the young men collected all the steenbok skins and went east to bring back more *shoro*. The boys shouldered the tobacco and brought it back. Later they drove the cattle out to Hxore Pan where they built a kraal and ate the *tsin* beans of Hxore while the cattle drank the water. So they lived, eating *tsin*, hunting steenbok and duiker, and drinking milk. When Hxore water was dry, they loaded the pack oxen with sacks of *tsin* [for the !Kung to eat] and drove them back to /Xai/Xai. At the end of the season the cattle boys loaded the pack oxen with bales and bales of eland biltong and went east with it to collect the balls of *shoro* and sometimes bags of corn. These they would deliver to my ≠*tum*.

This account provides a good description of two forms of economic linkage: the barter system, in which desert products are exchanged for agricultural and manufactured products, and the *mafisa* system, whereby well-to-do Tswana farm out cattle to others – fellow tribesmen or members of subordinate groups. The first form of linkage does not lead to incorporation and loss of autonomy, especially when the level of trade is modest and the element of coercion is absent. *Mafisa*, by contrast, does alter the character of production at the levels of both forces and relations. Animal husbandry places foragers in a different relation to land and to predators and necessitates a shift in the patterns of labour deployment. Energy is drawn away from hunting and reallocated to herding, and in return the producers are rewarded with a more secure food source, at least in the short run. At the level of production relations, *mafisa* is a form of loan-cattle–labour exchange set in the context of a patron–client relationship.

Briefly, the *mafisa* system in northwestern Ngamiland operated as follows (see also Tlou 1985:52): The San client maintained the herd on behalf of the Tswana patron, who retained ownership of the beasts. In return San could consume all the milk the herd produced and the meat of any animal that had died of natural causes, including predation. A tally was kept of beasts lost, and all animals had to be accounted for when the patron made a periodic visit. If he was satisfied with the performance of the *mafisa* holder he might pay him a calf, but this was not obligatory. If he was not satisfied he could withdraw his animals and seek another client. Similarly, the client was free to withdraw his services – with notice – and either leave *mafisa* entirely or seek another patron and a new herd of cattle.

On the face of it, *mafisa* appears to resemble a system of agrarian dependency: ownership of the means of production, in this case cattle, is in the hands of the overlord who at his whim can withdraw the herd and thus deprive the client of his livelihood. Clients therefore existed, it would seem, in a highly vulnerable state of dependency. Only a minority of Dobe-area people became involved in *mafisa*, however, and families with cattle retained links with families fully immersed in hunting and gathering, which remained viable as an alternative economic strategy throughout the *koloi* period and beyond. Had *mafisa* been the only means of subsistence for the people of the Dobe area, then the withdrawal of the cattle would have caused a crisis in subsistence and the threat of it would have been sufficient to produce a condition of virtual serfdom. But the *mafisa* families were not peasants; they were islands of pastoralism in a sea of hunting and gathering, with benefits flowing in both directions. When cattle were withdrawn, as they often were, the bush was there to fall back on, and that same bush beckoned as an alternative if the responsibilities of keeping cattle grew too onerous.

Thus we have to consider seriously the !Kung's view of *mafisa* as something that operated in their favour. Far from having the system forced upon them or being forced into it by circumstance, !Kung who entered into it did so voluntarily, for the opportunity it provided to supplement a foraging diet with milk and occasional beef. Some of the men who went into *mafisa* did become "big men" of a sort, acting as brokers in transactions between San and black. But a large majority of !Kung remained hunter-gatherers and never relinquished their claims to foraging *n!ores*, the collectively owned hunting lands that were the foundations of their communal mode of production (see Lee 1979:333–69; 1981). In fact, many of the ranges where cattle were grazed were superimposed on these *n!ores*, and the herds were managed by members of the groups that held them. Thus the niche that had sustained the communal foraging mode of production was modified and expanded to encompass *mafisa* cattle husbandry without destroying the preexisting adaptation. [...]

Agro-pastoralism   Permanent settlement by non-San came late to the Dobe area. Starting in the mid-1920s, Herero pastoralists moved into the area at cattle posts both east and west of the Namibian border. [...] The Herero began to deepen the waterholes and dig new ones to accommodate increased numbers of cattle. ... By the late 1950s the job of herdboy had become normative for Dobe-area !Kung men between the ages of 15 and 25. ... Eventually most men returned to their camps to marry and raise families, but some married men stayed on in a semi-permanent arrangement with Herero families.

By the 1960s an alternative economy had begun to crystallize, and the Dobe !Kung were found distributed between two kinds of living groups. About 70% lived in camps – bandlike multifamily units whose members engaged in a mixed economy of foraging, *mafisa* herding, and some horticulture. The rest lived in client groups consisting of retainers and their families attached to black cattle posts. Despite the variety of economic strategies that supported them, camps continued to exhibit the characteristic patterns of collective ownership of resources and food sharing that have been documented for hunter-gatherers around the world (Lee 1979; Leacock and Lee 1982). ...

The stage was now set for the final act in the transformation of the Dobe-area !Kung from a relatively autonomous people with longstanding but non-decisive linkages to the larger regional pastoral, tributary, and mercantile economy to a people bound to the region and the world by ties of dependency. Having survived long-distance trade, contacts with European hunters, Tswana overlordship, *mafisa* herding, direct employment

on cattle posts, even forced resettlement in Namibia, the !Kung became dependent largely as a consequence of the inability of their land to support a foraging mode of production. The bush had always been the backdrop to economic change, giving the !Kung security and a degree of freedom not available to the great majority of the agrarian societies of southern Africa. Tlou (1985:54) speaks of the Tswana's difficulties in exacting tribute or service from the "BaSarwa" (San) and concludes, "The sandbelt BaSarwa rarely became serfs because they could easily escape into the Kgalagadi Desert." By 1970, however, four decades of intensive and expanding pastoralism had begun to take their toll on the capacity of the environment to support hunting and gathering. Cattle grazing and the pounding of hooves had destroyed the grass cover over many square kilometres and reduced the available niches for dozens of species of edible roots and rhizomes. Goat browsing had destroyed thousands of berry bushes and other edible plants. The reduction or removal of these food sources placed added pressure on the remaining human food sources; for example, mongongo nut harvests noticeably diminished in the 1980s. The drilling of a dozen boreholes in Bushmanland, Namibia just to the west of Dobe, in the early 1980s aggravated these trends by lowering the water table. Hunting remained viable but became subject to much stricter controls by the Game Department, and many men fearing arrest, stopped hunting. [...] The effect of these changes was seriously to undermine the foraging option and to force to Dobe-area !Kung into dependency on the cattle posts and particularly the state. The latter responded with large-scale distribution of food relief between 1980 and 1987, which further deepened dependency.

Discussion

What common and contrasting patterns of change can be discerned by a comparative analysis of the two case studies?

In the earliest period for which we have information, the pre- and protohistoric (ca. 1820), the Western Kweneng San were already sharing their land with Bantu-speaking Kgalagadi, who mediated their contact with the wider world. The Dobe

San, by contrast, were in unmediated though distant and intermittent contact with riverine peoples to their east and north. A second point of difference concerns the nature of social formations on the San peripheries after 1830. The Kwena in the south became more mobile and expansive, ranging widely in search of trade and tribute, while the neighbours of the northern !Kung were sedentary, river-orientated peoples who did not expand into the and interior.

The fur-trade period (mid-19th century) was marked by social, political, and economic turbulence, yet by the time its ripple effects reached the interior of the Kalahari the impact was often attenuated. If in Parsons's (1977:119) terms the 19th-century Tswana economies were becoming the "periphery of the periphery" of European capitalism, then surely the Kalahari must have been the "deep periphery." Driven by trade and external threat, strong chiefdoms arose in the south. The Kwena's need for guns to defend themselves against the Boers was a powerful impetus for the articulation of tributary and mercantile systems. Guns could only be obtained in exchange for desert products. The Kwena subjugated the Kgalagadi, who in turn enlisted the San to aid in primary production. While unequal exchange characterized British–Kwena and Kwena–Kgalagadi relationships, the Kgalagadi–San relationship was symbiotic if not entirely equal. In contrast, Dobe was part of a much more tenuous and extended trade network. The Ngwato occupied the pivotal position between mercantile and tributary networks. Their junior partners were the Tawana, nominal overlords of Ngamiland, who, in turn relied on Yei and Mbukushu ("Goba") intermediaries to acculumate desert products from the San, including the distant !Kung. The Tawana's power was contested by other chiefs, and they were never able to consolidate their hold on the hinterland as effectively as the Kwena (Parsons 1977; Livingstone 1857; Tlou 1985: 66–7). As a consequence there was less pressure on the !Kung to enter the system, and when they did they were able to retain more control over the terms of trade. In neither instance, however, did the fur trade have much impact on the internal organization of San societies. San exchanged their products after the completion of the productive process. Linkage was predominantly through the sphere of exchange, not production, and intervention in San society remained limited (see Bonner 1983 and Harries 1982 on similar processes elsewhere).

The expansion of herding and farming to the remoter Kalahari did not signal the end of the fur trade, but the incorporation of cattle into the desert economy shifted the priorities in the deployment of land and labour. Western Kweneng San and Dobe San entered the cattle economy under different circumstances and with different statutes. In Dutlwe, Kgalagadi acquired cattle and rendered them as *mafisa* to their poorer relatives; eventually San became their herdboys. Because cattle were kept in the village, not at distant cattle posts, San herders were in regular interaction with their employers and had their subordinate status frequently reinforced. In Dobe it was the San themselves who entered into *mafisa*, a privilege they held exclusively until the 1920s. The Tawana were absentee cattle owners; the Dobe San bore responsibility for the productive enterprise, made routine decisions, and determined their daily activities. This arrangement was much more compatible with foraging than the Western Kweneng San's situation. In neither case did even a majority of the San enter into cattle service. Many relatively independent groups remained on the peripheries of villages and cattle posts, subsisting on wild foods and continuing to provide furs for the trade. Reciprocity between foraging and non-foraging San allowed each group to enjoy the fruits of the other's labour. In lean years the foraging San would provide a safety net and alternative subsistence for their "employed" relatives, and even in good years San contact with pastoralists was largely limited to certain seasons. At all times the hinterland provided a cultural point of reference and locus of reproduction. Thus in both cases the complete incorporation, as dependants, of the San into the agro-pastoral system was delayed as long as the bush held the possibility of an alternative livelihood. [...] An important source of the continued viability of the San's foraging option was the strength of the egalitarian and reciprocal communal relations of reproduction that characterized life in the bush. As even the revisionists (e.g., Wilmsen 1989b:66) acknowledge, this way of life, while far from ideal, provides an extraordinarily rich and meaningful existence for those who practice it. Communally based societies offer their members a sense of social security, entitlement, and empowerment (Lee 1988, n.d.; Rosenberg n.d.). Aspects of this quality of life persist in both Dutlwe and Dobe even today. [...]

Several factors combined to undermine the viability of the dual subsistence economy of the Dutlwe and Dobe San. Expansion of the numbers of cattle through natural increase, purchase with wages from other areas, and migration of cattle keepers (as in Dobe after 1954), along with expanding opportunities for migrant wage labour, especially in the 1960s, created a rapidly increasing need for San labour. ...

The retreat from foraging by the San began as the agro-pastoral complex drew larger and larger numbers of labourers, male and female, into its employ. In the last analysis, however, a critical factor in moving the San into a position of dependency has been environmental degradation, which has, like an unintended scorched-earth policy, deprived them of an alternative means of livelihood. In the south, dependency increased throughout the century, and many San entered into a relationship of perpetual minor status. ...

Foragers Genuine and Spurious: The Limitations of World Systems

What kinds of socioeconomic arrangements characterized the Kalahari San in the 19th and 20th centuries, and what kinds of explanatory frameworks best account for them? These questions must be approached at two levels: the level of fact, in which the archaeological, ethnohistoric, and ethnographic evidence is set out and interrogated, and the level of discourse, in which the explanatory frameworks themselves become the focus of interrogation.

The archaeological record shows a diversity of economic adaptations in the 19th century and earlier. The interaction of Stone Age with Iron Age cultures resulted in dramatic economic shifts in some areas, while in other areas the effects were more subtle. Kalahari trade was widespread, and in many instances when tributary formations emerged in the 19th century ties of domination/subordination were superimposed on preexisting linkages. But not all

San groups experienced this pattern of early linkage and later subordination. Interrelationships were strongest on the river systems and the margins of the desert and weaker as one moved into the interior. Thus there were large areas of semi-arid southern Africa that lay outside tributary orbits, where trade was equal, non-coercive, and intermittent and where independent – but not isolated – social formations persisted into the 20th century.

In attempting to explain this situation, it is important, first, to recognize that trade and exchange cannot simply be equated with domination and loss of autonomy. Exchange is a fundamental part of human life and appears in all cultural settings (Mauss 1925; Lévi-Strauss 1949). Hunter-gatherer peoples have participated in exchange with farming and market societies for hundreds of years (in India, South-east Asia, and East Africa) while maintaining a foraging mode of production (Leacock and Lee 1982). Even with "hunters in a world of hunters," exchange was part of social life (see, e.g., Thomson 1949; Wilmsen 1974; Earle and Ericson 1977; Ericson 1977; Torrence 1986). The evidence for long-established trade relations between foragers and others has been glossed by some as evidence for the fragility of the foraging mode of production. But if it was so fragile, why did it persist?

Throughout these debates about the status of Kalahari and other foragers there has been a lack of attention to the meanings of key terms. Just what is meant by "autonomy," "dependency," "independence," "integration," and "servitude" is rarely made clear. Without consistent, agreed-upon definitions it will be difficult or impossible to resolve the issues with which we are concerned. "Autonomy," for example, has a wide range of uses. Given its currency, it is remarkable how unreflexive its anthropological uses have been. We will confine our discussion to economic autonomy, since much of the debate in hunter-gatherer studies seems to revolve around it. One of the rhetorical devices of the revisionist view of hunter-gatherers is to equate autonomy with isolation – a definition so stringent that no society can possibly satisfy it. But autonomy is not isolation and no social formation is hermetically sealed; we take it as given that all societies are involved in economic exchanges and political relations with their neighbours.

As an economic concept, autonomy refers to economic self-sufficiency, [...] and self-sufficiency in turn hinges not on the *existence* of trade – since all societies trade – but on whether that trade is indispensable for the society's survival. To demonstrate autonomy one must demonstrate self-reproduction. Dependency therefore may be defined as the inability of a society to reproduce itself without the intervention of another. [...]

Politically, two kinds of autonomy may be provisionally defined: imposed and asserted. [...] In the former, the economic autonomy of a subject group may serve the interests of the dominant group. Subordinates are encouraged to pursue their habitual activities at their own pace while providing goods or services – often on equitable terms – to the dominant group. In the latter, the autonomous group asserts its claims through its own strengths and political will. In practice these two forms may be difficult to distinguish, and which form is considered to be present will depend heavily on subjective judgements both by the peoples involved and by observers. [...] Thus the Mbuti pygmies observed by Turnbull (1962) appear to be entirely subservient to their black neighbours while they are in the villages but quite autonomous in the forest.

Autonomy is best regarded not as a thing or a property of social systems but as a relationship – between social groups and between a group and its means of production. At any given moment a society may exhibit elements of both autonomy and dependency, and it should be possible to assess the degree of each through empirical investigation.

The camp dwelling people of the Dobe area were economically self-sufficient during the 1960s. They owned the bulk of their means of production and paid no rent, tribute, or taxes in money or kind. They hunted and gathered for the large majority of their subsistence requirements and for the rest tended *mafisa* cattle or worked as herdboys for their Herero neighbours. The latter tasks provided income that was a welcome supplement but not essential to survival. How can we demonstrate its non-essentiality? First, San *mafisa* holders and herdboys were observed to leave "service" without visible detriment to their well-being. In fact, it was common for young men to work on cattle for a few years and then return to the bush at marriage (Lee

1979:58, 406–8). More compelling, in the drought of 1964, Herero crops failed and cows were dry, yet the San persevered without evident difficulty. In fact, the Herero women were observed gathering wild foods alongside their San neighbours (Lee 1979:255). Since the San carried on through this period without visible hardship (Lee 1979:437–41) despite the withdrawal of Herero resources, it is clear that the latter were not essential to their reproduction.

These lines of evidence argue for the economic autonomy of some Dobe !Kung in the 1960s. Obviously a great deal more could be said on the question of autonomy, especially from the cultural and political points of view. Even the simplest historical judgements will involve a series of mediating judgements concerning economy, polity, voluntarism and coercion. Automatically classifying second-millennium San societies as dependent, incorporated, or "peasant-like" seems no more legitimate than classifying them as "primitive isolates."

Turning to "servitude," we are confronted with a literature replete with reports of San "dependency," "serfdom," "slavery," "vassalage," and the like. [...] In contrast to the early sources cited above (and see Wilson 1975:63), which tended to portray all San as dominated, recent ones such as Silberbauer and Kuper (1966), Tlou (1977), Russell and Russell (1979), Hitchcock (1987), and Motzafi (1986) employ these terms more critically, but even here usage tends to be imprecise. Silberbauer and Kuper (1966), for example, use the term "serfdom" but note its inapplicability – the San being bound neither to the soil nor to a particular master. Guenther (1986:450) reinforces the ambiguity when he speaks of a "benignly paternalistic form of serfdom" that departs from the European pattern. Tlou (1977), Wilson (1975), and Biesele et al. (1989) use the term "clientship" to refer to a loose association between peoples with unequal access to resources that they distinguish from the classic patron–client relationship. Russell and Russell (1979:87) further qualify the term "clientship" by contrasting the rights and obligations of "employed" San with those of "client" San. The latter are said to maintain a "foot in both worlds," one in the bush and one on the farm. Thus in their terms clientship is a partial relationship from which San can disengage.

Difficulties on several levels are encountered when we try to pin down the forms and content of San servitude and dependence. First, it is obvious that terms such as serfdom and chattel slavery, developed in a specific European context, are not easily grafted onto Kalahari social relations. More specifically, the language that is used in the Kalahari itself appears to overstate the degree of dependence. Both Vierich (1982a) and Solway were struck by the exaggerated descriptions of servitude by San and black alike. The cultural vocabulary of superior/subordinate relations further illustrates the difficulty of translating words that lack cognates in the language of the observer. Silberbauer and Kuper, for example, show that the Sekgalagadi term *munyi*, used for "master" in San–black relations, is also used for the senior in asymmetrical kin relations, i.e., "elder brother." It denotes authority but falls short of our concept of mastership or ownership. Similarly, they note that the Tswana "jural model" of *bolata* (hereditary servitude) signifies something stricter than actually exists. This misunderstanding, they assert, may be the reason social commentators from 19th-century missionaries to 20th-century anthropologists have assumed that *bolata* was worse in the past and only recently has become more humane. They argue that "the practice of serfdom in Bechuanaland is much more humane than the indigenous jural model would lead one to expect: in the past some observers may have been led into assuming that the jural model represented the past, while the easy-going actuality was equated with the enlightened present" (p. 172).

At the level of concrete social relations, there is a puzzling incongruity between the exaggerated degree of inequality described by Kalahari residents and the relative ease (and frequency) with which the San "serfs" disappear into the desert for periods of time, leaving their "masters" high and dry. Vierich (1982a:282) has argued that "interdependence" more accurately describes the relationship between San and non-San and that San simply "play the beggar" to get handouts. While this may be overstating the case, clearly there is a disjunction between model and practice. In no instance in which hereditary serfdom has been asserted by Kgalagadi in theory has it been observed in practice. The Dutlwe-area San may be dependent and

have to work for someone at some time, but they retain some choice of when to work and for whom. An observer will find some San in relations of dependency and others not, but closer examination will reveal that the same individuals will move into clientship, out to the bush, and back again to clientship. Wealthy blacks will have full-time San labourers living in their compounds while their neighbours rarely or never retain San clients. [...] The full-time labourers living with blacks will be the most conspicuous to casual observers, and this may account for the prevalence of this kind of report in both the early and the more recent literature, but such reports fail to do justice to the complexity and fluidity of the situation. We certainly do not want to minimize the degree of San dependence and subjection to discrimination, but we would suggest that this is best seen as a product of underdevelopment and not a primordial condition.

Hunter-Gatherer and Agrarian Discourse: Making the Transition

We have traced in some detail the historical pathways followed by the Dutlwe and Dobe San as they changed from autonomous foragers to clients and labourers increasingly subject to and dependent upon local, national, and world economies. In order to understand these processes it is necessary to make a second transition, from discourse about hunter-gatherers to discourse about agrarian societies and the emerging world system.

In agrarian discourse structures of domination are taken as given; it is the *forms* of domination and the modes of exploitation and surplus extraction that are problematic (Amin 1972; Hindess and Hirst 1975; Shanin 1972). In the literature on the agrarian societies of the Third World, stratification, class and class struggle, patriarchy, accumulation, and immiseration constitute the basic descriptive and analytical vocabulary. In hunter-gatherer discourse it is not the forms of domination that are at issue but *whether domination is present*. This question is often side-stepped or ignored.

We are not alone in our concern about the tendency for the discourse of domination to be imposed on precapitalist societies. Beinart (1985:97), for example, dealing with the Eastern Cape – an area under far greater pressure than the Kalahari –

cautions against granting omnipotence to capitalism or the state or assuming that the migrant-labour system automatically destroys the integrity of rural societies:

> Even in so coercive an environment as South Africa, the patterns of domination were constrained – in part – by fear of the consequences of other routes and in part by the defensive responses of the dominated. Certainly, capital and the state … had only limited power to shape social relationships in those areas which were left under African occupation. … the fact that a migrant works for a wage, even for a number of years, does not necessarily determine the totality of his, much less his family's, class position and consciousness. The importance of defensive struggles in the rural areas, amongst communities which included seasoned migrants, has generally been underestimated.

Silberbauer (1989:206–7) challenges the view that hunter-gatherer contacts with other societies necessarily preclude autonomy:

> [The] concept of coexisting states, tribes, and hunter-gatherer bands can be found accurately documented in any authoritative history of the appropriate part of Africa. It does not require that any of the coexisting societies be in a state of compulsory, day-to-day mutualism with all others. Interaction can occur at sufficiently low intensity and be of such a quality as to allow hunters and gatherers (for instance) to retain cultural, social, and political, and economic autonomy (i.e., in the philosophical sense, not in that of isolated, complete independence). At least in southern Africa and Australia that state of affairs persisted only

when the hunter-gatherers were able to retain control of enough resources of sufficient variety to be largely … self-sustaining.

Perhaps the most serious consequence of imposing agrarian discourse on hunter-gatherers is that it robs the latter of their history. What is at issue here is an intellectual neo-colonialism that seeks to recreate their history in the image of our own. This revisionism trivializes these people by making their history entirely a reactive one. Even at its best revisionism grants historical animation and dignity to the San only by recasting their history as the history of oppression. But is their oppression by us the only thing, or even the main thing, that we want to know about foraging peoples? The majority of the world's foragers are, for whatever reason, people who have resisted the temptation (or threat) to become like us: to live settled lives at high densities and to accept the structural inequalities that characterize most of the world. Many former foragers – and that includes most of us – now live in stratified, entrepreneurial, bureaucratic society, but not all have followed this route, and the presence or absence of inequality and domination can be investigated empirically.

Ultimately, in understanding the histories of Third World societies or of our own, we will have to rely on the histories of specific instances and not allow preconceptions to sway us. This caveat applies equally to those who would place the hunter-gatherers in splendid isolation and those who would generalize the power relations of contemporary capitalism to most of the world's people through most of their historical experience.

References

Amin, S, 1972. Underdevelopment and dependence in black Africa: Origins and contemporary forms. *Journal of Modern African Studies* 10:503–24.

Biesele, M., M. Guenther, R. Hitchcock, R. Lee, and J. MacGregor. 1989. Hunters, clients, and squatters: The contemporary socioeconomic status of Botswana Basarwa. *African Studies Monographs* 9:109–51.

Bonner, P. 1983. *King, commoners, and concessionnaires: The evolution and dissolution of the 19th-century Swazi state.* Cambridge/New York: Cambridge University Press.

Botswana National Archives. 1887a. HC 14/2 Despatch, Administrator, British Bechuanaland to Governor, Capetown, forwarding copy of a report and a map by Captain Goold-Adams of a police patrol from Molepolole to Lehututu.

Botswana National Archives 1887b. HC 153/1 High Commission for South Africa. On Bakgalagadi and Bushmen slavery.

Brooks, A. 1989. Past subsistence and settlement patterns in the Dobe area: An archaeological perspective.

Paper presented at the 88th annual meeting of the American Anthropological Association, Washington, D.C., November.

Campbell, A., and G. Child. 1971. The impact of man on the environment of Botswana. *Botswana Notes and Records* 3:91–110.

Cashdan, Elizabeth. 1987. Trade and its origins on the Botetli River. *Journal of Anthropological Research* 43:121–38.

Clarence-Smith, W. 1979. *Slaves, peasants, and capitalists in southern Angola 1840–1926*. Cambridge and New York: Cambridge University Press.

Denbow, J. 1980. Early Iron Age remains in the Tsodilo Hills, northwestern Botswana. *South African Journal of Science* 76:474–75.

Denbow, J. 1984. "Prehistoric herders and foragers of the Kalahari: The evidence for 1500 years of interaction," in *Past and present in hunter-gatherer studies*. Edited by C. Schrire, pp. 175–93. Orlando: Academic Press.

Denbow, J. 1986. A new look at later prehistory of the Kalahari. *Journal of African History* 27:3–28.

Denbow, J., and E. Wilmsen. 1983. Iron Age pastoral settlements in Botswana. *South African Journal of Science* 79:405–8.

Denbow, J., and E. Wilmsen. 1986. Advent and the course of pastoralism in the Kalahari. *Science* 234:1509–15.

Drechsler, H. 1980. *Let us die fighting: The Nama and Herero war against Germany*. London: Zed.

Earle, T., and J. E. Ericson. Editors. 1977. *Exchange systems in prehistory*. New York: Academic Press.

Endicott, K. 1988. Can hunter-gatherers survive in the rain forest without trade? Paper presented at the University of Toronto, April.

Ericson, J. E. 1977. "Egalitarian exchange systems in California: A preliminary view," in *Exchange systems in prehistory*. Edited by T. Earle and J. E. Ericson, pp. 109–206. New York: Academic Press.

Freeman, D. 1983. *Margaret Mead in Samoa*. Cambridge: Harvard University Press.

Friedman, J. 1975. "Tribes, states, and transformations," in *Marxist analyses in social anthropology*. Edited by M. Bloch, pp. 161–202. London: Tavistock.

Friedman, J. 1979. *System, structure, and contradiction in the evolution of "Asiatic" social formations*. Copenhagen: National Museum of Denmark.

Gordon, Robert J. 1984. "The !Kung in the Kalahari exchange: An ethnohistorical perspective," in *Past and present in hunter-gatherer studies*. Edited by C. Schrire, pp. 195–224. Orlando: Academic Press.

Gough, K. 1971. "Nuer kinship: A re-examination," in *The translation of culture*. Edited by T. O. Beidelmann, pp. 79–120. London: Tavistock.

Guenther, M. 1985. "Acculturation and assimilation of the Bushmen," in *Contemporary studies on Khoisan*. Edited by I. R. Vossen and K. Keuthmann, pp. 347–73. Hamburg: Helmut Buske Verlag.

Guenther, M. 1986. *The Nhafo Bushmen of Botswana Tradition and Change*. Hamburg: H. Buske.

Harries, P. 1982. "Kinship, ideology, and the nature of pre-colonial labour migration," in *Industrialism and social change in South Africa*. Edited by S. Marks and R. Rathbone. London: Longman.

Headland, T., and L. Reid. 1989. Hunter-gatherers and their neighbors from prehistory to the present. *Current Anthropology* 30:43–66.

Hindess, B., and P. Hirst. 1975. *Pre-capitalist modes of production*. London: Routledge and Kegan Paul.

Hitchcock, Robert K. 1978. *Kalahari cattle posts: A regional study of hunter-gatherers, pastoralists, and agriculturalists in the Western Sandveld Region, Central District, Botswana*. 2 vols. Gaborone: Government Printer.

Hitchcock, Robert K., 1987. Socioeconomic change among the Basarwa in Botswana: An ethnohistorical analysis. *Ethnohistory* 34:219–55.

Kelly, R., 1985. *The Nuer conquest*. Ann Arbor: University of Michigan Press.

Kent, S. 1989a. The cycle that repeats: Shifting subsistence strategies among Kalahari Basarwa. Paper presented at the 88th annual meeting of the American Anthropological Association, Washington, D.C., November.

Kent, S. 1989b. And justice for all: The development of political centralization among newly sedentary foragers. *American Anthropologist* 91:703–11.

Leacock, E., and R. Lee. Editors 1982. *Politics and history in band societies*. Cambridge and New York: Cambridge University Press.

Lee, R. 1965. Subsistence ecology of !Kung Bushmen, PhD diss., University of California, Berkeley, Calif.

Lee, R. 1979. *The !Kung San: Men, women, and work in a foraging society*. Cambridge: Cambridge University Press.

Lee, R. 1984. *The Dobe !Kung*. New York: Holt, Rinehart and Winston.

Lee, R. 1988. "Reflections on primitive communism," in *Hunters and gatherers*, vol. 1. Edited by T. Ingold, D. Riches, and J. Woodburn, pp. 252–68. Oxford: Berg.

Lee, R. n.d. "Primitive communism and the origins of social inequality," in *The evolution of political systems*. Edited by S. Upham. Cambridge and New York: Cambridge University Press. In press.

Lee, R. B., and I. Devore. Editors. 1968. *Man the hunter*. Chicago: Aldine.

Lee, R. B. and I. Devore. 1976. *Kalahari hunter-gatherers*. Cambridge: Harvard University Press.

Leistner, O. 1967. *The plant ecology of the southern Kalahari*. Pretoria: Government Printer.

Lévi-Strauss, C. 1949. *The elementary structures of kinship*. Boston: Beacon Press.

Lewin, R. 1989. New views emerge on hunters and gatherers. *Science* 240:1146–48.

Lewis, O. 1951. *Life in a Mexican village: Tepoztlán restudied*. Urbana: University of Illinois Press.

Livingstone, David. 1857. *Missionary travels and researches in South Africa*. London: John Murray.

Mackenzie, J. 1971. (1871). *Ten years north of the Orange River: A story of everyday life and work among the South African tribes from 1859 to 1869*. Edinburgh: Edmonston and Douglas.

Marks, S., and A. Atmore. 1971. Firearms in southern Africa: A survey. *Journal of African History* 7:517–30.

Marshall, L. K. 1976. *The !Kung Bushmen of Nyae/Nyae*. Cambridge: Harvard University Press.

Marx, Karl. 1965 (1857–58). *Pre-capitalist economic formations*. New York: International Publishers. [TCP]

Marx, Karl. 1977 (1887). *Capital*. Vol. 3. New York: International Publishers.

Mauss, M. 1925. Essai sur le don. *Année Sociologique* 1:30–186.

Motzafi, P. 1986. Whither the "true Bushmen": The dynamics of perpetual marginality. *Sprache und Geschichte in Afrika* 7:295–328.

Newcomer, P. 1972. The Nuer and the Dinka: An essay on origins and environmental determinism. *Man* 7:5–11.

Nugent, D. 1983. Closed systems and contradiction in the Kachin in and out of history. *Man* 17:508–27.

Okihro, G. 1976. Hunters, herders, cultivators, and traders: Interaction and change in the Kgalagadi, nineteenth century. Ph.D. diss., University of California, Los Angeles, Calif.

Parkington, J. 1984. "Soaqua and Bushmen: Hunters and robbers," in *Past and present in hunter-gatherer studies*. Edited by C. Schrire, pp. 151–74. Orlando: Academic Press.

Parsons, N. 1977. "The economic history of Khama's country in Botswana, 1844–1930," in *The roots of rural poverty in central and southern Africa*. Edited by R. Palmer and N. Parsons, pp. 113–42. Berkeley: University of California Press.

Peterson, J.T. 1978. Hunter-gatherer/farmer exchange. *American Anthropologist* 80:335–51.

Phillipson, D. 1977. *The prehistory of southern and central Africa*. London: Heinemann.

Rosenberg, H. n.d. "Complaint discourse, aging, and caregiving among the Kung San of Botswana," in *The cultural context of aging: World-wide perspectives*. Edited by J. Sokolovsky. Boston: Bergin and Garvey. In press.

Russell, M, 1976. Slaves or workers? Relations between Bushmen, Tswana, and Boers in the Kalahari. *Journal of Southern African Studies* 2:178–97.

Russell, M. and M. Russell, 1979. *Afrikaners of the Kalahari: White minority in a black state*. Cambridge: Cambridge University Press.

Sacks, K. 1979. Causality and change on the Upper Nile. *American Ethnologist* 6:437–48.

Sahlins, M. 1968. *Tribesmen*. Englewood Cliffs: Prentice Hall.

Schapera, I., and D. F. Van Der Merwe. 1945. *Note on tribal groupings, history, and customs of the Bakgalagadi*. Communications for the School of African Studies, n.s., 13.

Schrire, Carmel. 1980. An enquiry into the evolutionary status and apparent identity of San hunter-gatherers. *Human Ecology* 8:9–32.

Schrire, Carmel. Editor. 1984a. *Past and present in hunter-gatherer studies*. Orlando: Academic Press.

Schrire, Carmel. 1984b. "Wild surmises on savage thoughts," in *Past and present in hunter-gatherer studies*. Edited by C. Schrire, pp. 1–25. Orlando: Academic Press.

Shanin, T. Editor. 1972. *Peasants and peasant societies*. New York: Penguin books.

Silberbauer, George B. 1981. *Hunter and habitat in the central Kalahari Desert*. Cambridge: Cambridge University Press.

Silberbauer, G. B., and A. Kuper. 1966. Kgalagadi masters and their Bushmen serfs. *African Studies* 25:171–79.

Solway, J. 1987. Commercialization and social differentiation in a Kalahari village. Ph.D. diss., University of Toronto, Toronto, Ont.

Solway, J., and R. B. Lee. 1981. The Kalahari fur trade. Paper presented at the 80th annual meeting of the American Anthropological Association, Los Angeles, Calif.

Stow, G. W. 1964 (1905) *The native races of South Africa*. Cape Town: C. Struik.

Tabler, E. 1973. *Pioneers of South West Africa and Ngamiland*. Cape Town: Balkema.

Tanaka, J. 1980. *The San hunter-gatherers of the Kalahari: A study in ecological anthropology*. Tokyo: University of Tokyo Press.

Thompson, B. W. 1975. *Africa: The climatic background*. Ibadan: Oxford University Press.

Thomson, D. 1949. *Economic structure and the ceremonial exchange cycle in Arnhem Land*. Melbourne: Angus and Robertson.

Tlou, T. 1977. "Servility and political control: Botlhanka among the Batawana of northwestern Botswana, ca. 1750–1906," in *Slavery in southern Africa*. Edited by

S. Miers and I. Kopytoff, pp. 367–90. Madison: University of Wisconsin Press.

Tlou, T. 1985. *A history of Ngamiland, 1750 to 1906: The formation of an African state*. Gaborone: Macmillan.

Tlou, T., and A. Campbell. 1984. *A history of Botswana*. Gaborone: Macmillan.

Torrence, R. 1986. *Production and exchange of stone tools*. Cambridge: Cambridge University Press.

Turnbull, C. 1962. *The forest people*. New York: Simon and Schuster.

Vierich, H. (Esche). 1977. *Interim report on survey of Basarwa in Kweneng*. Gaborone: Ministry of Local Government and Lands.

Vierich, H. 1982*a*. The Kua of the southeastern Kalahari: A study of the socio-ecology of dependency. Ph.D. diss., University of Toronto, Toronto, Ont.

Vierich, H. 1982*b*. "Adaptive flexibility in a multi-ethnic setting: The Basarwa of the southern Kalahari," in *Politics and history in band societies*. Edited by Eleanor Leacock and Richard Lee, pp. 213–22. Cambridge: Cambridge University Press.

Wasserstrom, R. 1982. *Class and society in Chiapas*. New York: Columbia University Press.

Wilhelm, J. 1954 (1914–19). *Die !Kung Buschleute*. Jahrbuch des Museums für Völkerkunde zu Leipzig 12.

Wilmsen, E. 1974 *Lindenmeier: A Pleistocene hunting society*. New York: Harper and Ron.

Wilmsen, E. 1983. The ecology of illusion: Anthropological foraging in the Kalahari. *Reviews in Anthropology* 10:9–20.

Wilson, M. 1975. "The hunters and herders," in *The Oxford history of South Africa*, vol. I. Edited by M. Wilson and L. Thompson, pp. 40–75. Oxford: Oxford University Press.

Wolf, E. 1982. *Europe and the people without history*. Berkeley: University of California Press.

Woodburn, J. 1988. "African hunter-gatherer social organization: Is it best understood as a product of encapsulation?" in *Hunters and gatherers*, vol. I. Edited by T. Ingold, D. Riches, and J. Woodburn, pp. 31–64. Oxford: Berg.

Worsley, P. 1956. The kinship system of the Tallensi: A reevaluation. *Journal of the Royal Anthropological Institute* 86:37–77.

Yellen, John E., and Alison S. Brooks. 1988. The Late Stone Age archaeology of the !Kangwa and /Xai/Xai Valleys, Ngamiland Botswana. *Botswana Notes and Records*. 20:5–28.

Part V

Witchcraft, Science, and Rationality: The Translation of Culture

Introduction

The readings in this section are organized around the topic of witchcraft beliefs among the Azande of southern Sudan and northern Democratic Republic of Congo. We chose these readings because, as a whole, they define the parameters and content of one of the most influential debates in the history of anthropology: a debate over the differences and similarities between European and African modes of thought.

The debate began after the publication of Evans-Pritchard's *Witchcraft, Oracles, and Magic among the Azande* (1937), a work that had a profound impact on both the cross-cultural study of modes of thought and the philosophy of science and rationality, and led many scholars to reflect critically upon some of the most important issues in the history of anthropology. Stanley J. Tambiah (1990: 3) poses the questions raised by the rationality debate:

1 How do we understand and represent the modes of thought and action of other societies, other cultures?
2 Since we have to undertake this task from a Western baseline so to say, how are we to achieve the "translation of cultures," i.e. understand other cultures as far as possible in their own terms but in our language, a task which also entails the mapping of the ideas and practices onto Western categories of understanding, and hopefully modifying these in turn to evolve a language of anthropology as a comparative science?

Evans-Pritchard was forced to address these epistemological questions because he wanted to explain one mode of thought, that of the Azande, in terms of another, that of science. In other words, Evans-Pritchard understood that the translation of culture is a fundamental task of anthropology.

In southern Africa, nearly 80 years before Evans-Pritchard published his study, the British explorer David Livingstone confronted the problem of how to understand a way of thinking radically different from his own. For the purpose of explaining the Tswana belief in rainmaking, Livingstone constructed the dialogue included in this section, a dialogue between himself (a medical doctor) and a Tswana "rain doctor." As the dialogue proceeds, we come to appreciate the intelligence, logic, and coherence of rainmaking beliefs; we also come to question the long-standing assumption that science is "rational" and reflects truth while magical beliefs are irrational and mystify reality. In Livingstone's writings, we can also discern the roots of one of Evans-Pritchard's most important arguments: that if we understand the cultural premises and social contexts of thought and action, then beliefs in supernatural causation no longer seem bizarre, irrational, or fallacious. Indeed, they may seem perfectly reasonable.

Evans-Pritchard takes the appreciation of an African mode of thought a bit further than Livingstone by analyzing in great detail the principles upon which Azande explanations are based, and by attempting to adopt for himself the Azande way of thinking. He finds that, in contrast to science, the Azande overlook certain inconsistencies in logic because they do not have an integrated theory of supernatural cause and effect. For example, the Azande believe that witchcraft substance is hereditarily transmitted down the male line. The substance predisposes people to carry out acts of witchcraft, and can be revealed through postmortem autopsy. For Evans-Pritchard, a positive finding of witchcraft substance in a person would implicate his whole clan, since the clan is a group of people biologically related through a patriline. However, despite their biological model of witchcraft inheritance, the Azande do not generalize from single cases of witchcraft to whole groups. This apparent contradiction would pose serious problems for a scientific theory, but the Azande do not formulate their beliefs as abstract and logically coherent and sustainable theories. Rather, witchcraft beliefs are produced and reproduced continuously as the Azande try to explain new misfortunes. Witchcraft is not a "thing" in and of itself, or a state of being, but rather an action (Ulin 1984: 24). Beliefs are realized through practice.

In trying to adopt Zande thinking for himself, Evans-Pritchard suggests that Zande thought can be reasonable even for the scientifically trained European. While living with the Azande, he says, "I too used to react to misfortunes in the idiom of witchcraft" (1937: 45). He realized that societies can have multiple rationalities, and that, even in England, people do not always think scientifically. Evans-Pritchard thus warns us not to characterize societies in terms of single modes of thought. As Tambiah puts it, "we should avoid caricatures of both primitive and modern mentalities, and should not represent Westerners as thinking scientifically all the time when scientific activity is a special one practiced in very circumscribed circumstances. One must compare like with like, our everyday thought with their everyday thought" (1990: 92).

Despite his apparent cultural relativism, Evans-Pritchard is unequivocal that scientific explanations of misfortune are superior to those of the Azande. He writes: "Witches, as the Azande conceive them, clearly cannot exist" (1937: 18). In other words, though witchcraft beliefs are logical, they are wrong. Because the Azande do not form hypotheses and test them against an empirical reality, their explanations are necessarily unacceptable to the Western scientist. Peter Winch claims (in Chapter 17) that Evans-Pritchard's comparison of scientific and Azande thought is a "category mistake." Winch argues that Azande and scientific thought operate according to very different rules and premises, and so cannot be used to evaluate one another. To employ the categories of science, as Evans-Pritchard does, distorts Azande thought. Not only does the scientific explanation of witchcraft reify beliefs embedded in practice, it also makes Zande thought into a reflection of science. In a remarkable passage (p. 263, this volume), Winch quotes Evans-Pritchard at length and then repeats the quotation with the words "Azande" and "mystical" transposed to "Europeans" and "scientific." The meaning and logic of both quotations are the same. The clever parody makes the Azande into scientists, thus revealing Evans-Pritchard's category mistake. Livingstone falls into the same trap as Evans-Pritchard, for his dialogue imposes onto the rainmaker the categories and logic of scientific thought. The medical doctor forces the Tswana rainmaker to debate not only as a "doctor" but in the terms of positivism, rather than in terms of his own making (Comaroff and Comaroff, 1991: 254). For Winch, both Livingstone and Evans-Pritchard are guilty of perpetuating the hegemony of science, of dictating the manner in which thought is represented. Cultural translation is possible, Winch suggests, but only if scientists are willing to modify and extend their own categories. "Since it is we who want to understand the Zande category, it appears that the onus is on us to extend our understanding so as to make room for the Zande category, rather than to insist on seeing it in terms of our own ready-made distinction between science and non-science" (Winch, 1970: 102).

Winch's argument did not go uncontested. In a provocative article in the same volume in which Winch's work was published, Robin Horton argued that what he calls "African thought" and "Western science" *can* be fruitfully compared with one another. He proposed that African societies are "closed," meaning that people do not look critically at their ideas, or search for alternative explanations, about the world. According to Horton, scientific societies, on the other hand, are "open" to the extent that they never accept, absolutely, a given theory of the world, and always look for alternatives. The former societies take their orthodox modes of explanation to the level of sacred beliefs, while the latter minimize the role of belief, faith, and certainty. Of importance to all of the chapters in this part is an implicit argument that there is such a thing as a "mode of thought." However, Horton went much further. He assumed that there are patterns and essences to be found among the modes of thought of different populations, that a multitude of different societies can share a common way of thinking, and that groups of societies can be compared to other groups of societies. Only then is it possible for Horton to juxtapose "Africa" to "western science."

Social anthropologists working on systems of belief today (Comaroff and Comaroff, 1993; Rowlands and Varnier, 1988) continue to emphasize the continued salience of idioms of witchcraft and sorcery in sub-Saharan Africa but depart somewhat from the confines of the debate begun about the Azande by exploring the ways in which the social relations of supernatural belief become implicated in local politics and economies (see both Lubkemann, Chapter 40, and West, Chapter 45, in this volume). Geschiere (1992), for example, in an important work on Cameroon, shows that markets and market behaviors do not constitute spheres of social activity distinct from spiritual beliefs, and urges us to rethink how, even in so-called "Western" economies, religion, politics, kinship, and culturally distinctive rationalities play vital and constitutive roles. (This is a point raised in many of the chapters of this volume on economics, where we discuss the issue of economic "rationality".) Another scholar, Ashforth (2005), shows that in the context of violence, chaos, and uncertainty in urban South Africa, the formation of a democratic state in South Africa is integrally related to witchcraft beliefs. And in the final chapter of this section, Ralph A. Austen compares witchcraft in Africa with the rise of witchcraft in early modern Europe in the context of different trajectories of modernity. He shows that in contemporary economic contexts, new forms of witchcraft emerge in Africa. Witchcraft in Africa today, he says, exists in ambivalent relation to the concepts of the market economy, individualism and individual accumulation. While pushing the study of witchcraft and rationality into analyses of contemporary social issues in Africa, all of these authors demonstrate the power, legacy, and usefulness of Evans-Pritchard's foundational work.

References

Ashforth, Adam. 2005. *Witchcraft, Violence, and Democracy in South Africa*. Chicago: University of Chicago Press.

Comaroff, Jean and John L. Comaroff. 1991. *Of Revelation and Revolution, Vol. 1: Christianity, Colonialism and Consciousness in South Africa*. Chicago: University of Chicago Press.

Comaroff, Jean and John L. Comaroff, eds. 1993. *Modernity & Its Malcontents: Ritual and Power in Postcolonial Africa*. Chicago: University of Chicago Press.

Geschiere, Peter. 1992. "Kinship, Witchcraft and the Market: Hybrid Patterns in Cameroonian Societies." In Roy Dilley, ed., *Contesting Markets: Analyses of Ideology, Discourse and Practice*, pp. 159–76. Edinburgh: University of Edinburgh Press.

Horton, Robin. 1970. "African Traditional Thought and Western Science," in Bryan Wilson, ed., *Rationality*, pp. 131–71. Oxford: Blackwell.

Rowlands, R. and J.P. Varnier. 1988. "Sorcery and the State in Cameroon." *Man* 23 (1): 118–32.

Tambiah, Stanley Jeyaraja. 1990. *Magic, Science, Religion and the Scope of Rationality*. Cambridge: Cambridge University Press.

Ulin, Robert C. 1984. *Understanding Cultures: Perspectives in Anthropology and Social Theory*. Austin: University of Texas Press.

Winch, Peter. 1970. "Understanding a Primitive Society," in Bryan Wilson, ed., *Rationality*, pp. 78–111. Oxford: Blackwell.

Suggested Reading

Adorno, Theodor, et al. eds. 1976. *The Positivist Dispute in German Sociology*. New York: Harper and Row.

Agassi, Joseph and Ian Charles Jarvie, eds. 1987. *Rationality: The Critical View*. Boston and Dordrecht: M. Nijhoff.

Bates, R., V.Y. Mudimbe, and J. O'Barr, eds. 1993. *Africa and the Disciplines: The Contribution of Research in Africa to the Social Sciences and Humanities*. Chicago: University of Chicago Press.

Benn, S.I. and G.W. Mortimore. 1976. *Rationality and the Social Sciences: Contributions to the Philosophy and Methodology of the Social Sciences*. London: Routledge and Kegan Paul.

Bloombill, Greta. 1962. *Witchcraft in Africa*. Capetown: H. Timmins.

Comaroff, Jean. 1984. *Body of Power, Spirit of Resistance*. Chicago: University of Chicago Press.

Devisch, Rene. 1993. *The Khita Gyn-Eco-Logical Healing Cult among the Yaka*. Chicago: University of Chicago Press.

Durkheim, Emile. 1965. *The Elementary Forms of the Religious Life*. New York: Free Press.

Evans-Pritchard, E.E. 1937. *Witchcraft, Magic and Oracles among the Azande*. Oxford: Clarendon Press.

Evans-Pritchard, E.E. 1956. *Nuer Religion*. London: Oxford University Press.

Frazer, Sir James G. 1994 [1900]. *The Golden Bough: A Study in Magic and Religion*. London: Oxford University Press.

Geertz, Clifford. 1973. *The Interpretation of Cultures*. New York: Basic Books.

Geschiere, Peter. 2009. *Magical Interpretations, Material Reality: Modernity, Witchcraft and the Occult in Postcolonial Africa*. Chicago: University of Chicago Press.

Good, Byron. 1994. *Medicine, Rationality and Experience: An Anthropological Perspective*. Cambridge: Cambridge University Press.

Harwood, Alan. 1970. *Witchcraft, Sorcery and Social Categories of the Safwa*. London: Oxford University Press for the IAI.

Heald, Suzette. 1982. "The Making of Men." *Africa* 52: 15–35.

Horton, Robin and Ruth Ferguson, eds. 1973. *Modes of Thought: Essays on Thinking in Western and Non-Western Societies*. London: Faber.

Jarvie, Ian Charles. 1984. *Rationality and Relativism: in Search of a Philosophy and History of Anthropology*. London: Routledge and Kegan Paul.

Jules-Rosette, Benetta. 1978. "The Veil of Objectivity: Prophecy, Divination and Social Inquiry." *American Anthropologist* 80: 549–71.

Karp, Ivan and Charles Bird, eds. 1980. *Explorations in African Systems of Thought*. Bloomington: Indiana University Press.

Kekes, John. 1973. "Towards a Theory of Rationality." *Philosophy of Social Science* 3(4): 275–88.

Levi-Strauss, Claude. 1966. *The Savage Mind*. Chicago: University of Chicago Press.

Macfarlane, Alan. 1970. *Witchcraft in Tudor and Stuart England: A Regional and Comparative View*. London: Routledge and Kegan Paul.

Mair, Lucy. 1970. *Witchcraft*. New York: McGraw-Hill.

Malinowski, Bronislaw. 1948. *Magic, Science and Religion*. Boston: Beacon.

Margolis, J., M. Krausz and R.M. Burian, eds. 1986. *Rationality, Relativism and the Human Sciences*. Boston and Dordrecht: M. Nijhoff.

Marwick, Max, ed. 1970. *Witchcraft and Sorcery: Selected Readings*. Middlesex: Penguin.

Mbiti, J.S. 1969. *African Religions and Philosophy*. New York: Praeger.

Middleton, John. 1963. *Witchcraft and Sorcery in East Africa*. London: Routledge and Kegan Paul.

Moore, Henrietta and Todd Sanders. 2002. *Magical Interpretations, Material Reality: Modernity, Witchcraft and the Occult in Postcolonial Africa*. New York: Routledge.

Nadel, S.F. 1952. "Witchcraft in Four African Societies." *American Anthropologist* 54: 18–29.

Packard, Randall M. 1980. "Social Change and the History of Misfortune among the Bashu of Eastern Zaire." In Ivan Karp and Charles Bird, eds., *Explorations in African Systems of Thought*, pp. 237–66. Bloomington: Indiana University Press.

Parrinder, Geoffrey. 1970. *Witchcraft: European and African*. London: Faber and Faber.

Popper, Karl. 1966. *The Open Society and its Enemies*. 5th edn. London: Hutchison.

Ranger, T. O. 1982. "The Death of Chaminuka: Spirit Mediums, Nationalism and the Guerilla War in Zimbabwe." *African Affairs*, pp. 349–69.

Riesman, Paul. 1977. *Freedom in Fulani Social Life*. Chicago: University of Chicago Press.

Sanders, Todd. 2003. "Reconsidering Witchcraft: Postcolonial Africa and Analytic (Un)Certainties." *American Anthropologist* 105(2): 338–52.

Smith, James Howard. 2008. *Bewitching Development: Witchcraft and the Reinvention of Development in Neoliberal Kenya*. Chicago: University of Chicago Press.

Tambiah, Stanley Jeyaraja. 1985. *Culture, Thought and Social Action: An Anthropological Perspective*. Cambridge, MA: Harvard University Press.

Turner, Victor. 1967. *The Forest of Symbols: Aspects of Ndembu Ritual*. Ithaca: Cornell University Press.

Turner, Victor. 1969. *The Ritual Process: Structure and Anti-Structure*. London: Routledge.

Wilson, Bryan. 1970. *Rationality*. Oxford: Blackwell.

Winch, Peter. 1958. *The Idea of a Social Science and its Relation to Philosophy*. London: Routledge and Kegan Paul.

Wittgenstein, Ludwig. 1953. *Philosophical Investigations*. New York: Macmillan.

15

Conversations on Rain-making

David Livingstone

The place where we first settled with the Bakwains is called Chonuane, and it happened to be visited, during the first year of our residence there, by one of those droughts which occur from time to time in even the most favored districts of Africa.

The belief in the gift or power of *rain-making* is one of the most deeply-rooted articles of faith in this country. The chief Sechele was himself a noted rain-doctor, and believed in it implicitly. He has often assured me that he found it more difficult to give up his faith in that than in any thing else which Christianity required him to abjure. I pointed out to him that the only feasible way of watering the gardens was to select some good, never-failing river, make a canal, and irrigate the adjacent lands. This suggestion was immediately adopted, and soon the whole tribe was on the move to the Kolobeng, a stream about forty miles distant. The experiment succeeded admirably during the first year. The Bakwains made the canal and dam in exchange for my labor in assisting to build a square house for their chief. They also built their own school under my superintendence. Our house at the River Kolobeng, which gave a name to the settlement, was the third which I had reared with

my own hands. A native smith taught me to weld iron; and having improved by scraps of information in that line from Mr Moffat, and also in carpentering and gardening, I was becoming handy at almost any trade, besides doctoring and preaching; and as my wife could make candles, soap, and clothes, we came nearly up to what may be considered as indispensable in the accomplishments of a missionary family in Central Africa, namely, the husband to be a jack-of-all-trades without doors, and the wife a maid-of-all-work within. But in our second year again no rain fell. In the third the same extraordinary drought followed. Indeed, not ten inches of water fell during these two years, and the Kolobeng ran dry; so many fish were killed that the hyenas from the whole country round collected to the feast, and were unable to finish the putrid masses. A large old alligator, which had never been known to commit any depredations, was found left high and dry in the mud among the victims. The fourth year was equally unpropitious, the fall of rain being insufficient to bring the grain to maturity. Nothing could be more trying. We dug down in the bed of the river deeper and deeper as the water receded, striving to get a little to keep the

From David Livingstone, 1858, "Conversations on Rain-Making", pp. 22–7. In *Missionary Travels and Researches in South Africa*. London: Murray.

fruit-trees alive for better times, but in vain. Needles lying out of doors for months did not rust; and a mixture of sulphuric acid and water, used in a galvanic battery, parted with all its water to the air, instead of imbibing more from it, as it would have done in England. The leaves of indigenous trees were all drooping, soft, and shriveled, though not dead; and those of the mimosæ were closed at midday, the same as they are at night. In the midst of this dreary drought, it was wonderful to see those tiny creatures, the ants, running about with their accustomed vivacity. I put the bulb of a thermometer three inches under the soil, in the sun, at midday, and found the mercury to stand at 132° to 134°; and if certain kinds of beetles were placed on the surface, they ran about a few seconds and expired. But this broiling heat only augmented the activity of the long-legged black ants: they never tire; their organs of motion seem endowed with the same power as is ascribed by physiologists to the muscles of the human heart, by which that part of the frame never becomes fatigued, and which may be imparted to all our bodily organs in that higher sphere to which we fondly hope to rise. Where do these ants get their moisture? Our house was built on a hard ferruginous conglomerate, in order to be out of the way of the white ant, but they came in despite the precaution; and not only were they, in this sultry weather, able individually to moisten the soil to the consistency of mortar for the formation of galleries, which, in their way of working, is done by night (so that they are screened from the observation of birds by day in passing and repassing toward any vegetable matter they may wish to devour), but, when their inner chambers were laid open, these were also surprisingly humid. Yet there was no dew, and, the house being placed on a rock, they could have no subterranean passage to the bed of the river, which ran about three hundred yards below the hill. Can it be that they have the power of combining the oxygen and hydrogen of their vegetable food by vital force so as to form water?

Rain, however, would not fall. The Bakwains believed that I had bound Sechele with some magic spell, and I received deputations, in the evenings, of the old counselors, entreating me to allow him to make only a few showers: "The corn will die if you refuse, and we shall become scattered. Only let him make rain this once, and we shall all,

men, women, and children, come to the school, and sing and pray as long as you please." It was in vain to protest that I wished Sechele to act just according to his own ideas of what was right, as he found the law laid down in the Bible, and it was distressing to appear hard-hearted to them. The clouds often collected promisingly over us, and rolling thunder seemed to portend refreshing showers, but next morning the sun would rise in a clear, cloudless sky; indeed, even these lowering appearances were less frequent by far than days of sunshine are in London.

The natives, finding it irksome to sit and wait helplessly until God gives them rain from heaven, entertain the more comfortable idea that they can help themselves by a variety of preparations, such as charcoal made of burned bats, inspissated renal deposit of the mountain cony – *Hyrax capensis* – (which, by the way, is used, in the form of pills, as a good antispasmodic, under the name of "stone-sweat"),[1] the internal parts of different animals – as jackals' livers, baboons' and lions' hearts, and hairy calculi from the bowels of old cows – serpents' skins and vertebrae, and every kind of tuber, bulb, root, and plant to be found in the country. Although you disbelieve their efficacy in charming the clouds to pour out their refreshing treasures, yet, conscious that civility is useful everywhere, you kindly state that you think they are mistaken as to their power. The rain-doctor selects a particular bulbous root, pounds it, and administers a cold infusion to a sheep, which in five minutes afterward expires in convulsions. Part of the same bulb is converted into smoke, and ascends toward the sky; rain follows in a day or two. The inference is obvious. Were we as much harassed by droughts, the logic would be irresistible in England in 1857.

As the Bakwains believed that there must be some connection between the presence of "God's Word" in their town and these successive and distressing droughts, they looked with no good will at the church bell, but still they invariably treated us with kindness and respect. I am not aware of ever having had an enemy in the tribe. The only avowed cause of dislike was expressed by a very influential and sensible man, the uncle of Sechele. "We like you as well as if you had been born among us; you are the only white man we can become familiar with (thoaéla); but we wish you to give up that everlasting preaching and praying; we can not become familiar with that at all. You see we never get rain, while those tribes who never pray as we do obtain abundance." This was a fact; and we often saw it raining on the hills ten miles off, while it would not look at us "even with one eye." If the Prince of the power of the air had no hand in scorching us up, I fear I often gave him the credit of doing so.

As for the rain-makers, they carried the sympathies of the people along with them, and not without reason. With the following arguments they were all acquainted, and in order to understand their force, we must place ourselves in their position, and believe, as they do, that all medicines act by a mysterious charm. The term for cure may be translated "charm" (*alaha*).

Medical Doctor. Hail, friend! How very many medicines you have about you this morning! Why, you have every medicine in the country here.

Rain Doctor. Very true, my friend; and I ought; for the whole country needs the rain which I am making.

M.D. So you really believe that you can command the clouds? I think that can be done by God alone.

R.D. We both believe the same thing. It is God that makes the rain, but I pray to him by means of these medicines, and, the rain coming, of course it is then mine. It was *I* who made it for the Bakwains for many years, when they were at Shokuane; through my wisdom, too, their women became fat and shining. Ask them; they will tell you the same as I do.

M.D. But we are distinctly told in the parting words of our Savior that we can pray to God acceptably in his name alone, and not by means of medicines.

R.D. Truly! but God told us differently. He made black men first, and did not love us as he did the white men. He made you beautiful, and gave you clothing, and guns, and gunpowder, and horses, and wagons, and many other things about which we know nothing. But towards us he had no heart. He gave us nothing except the assegai, and cattle, and rainmaking; and he did not give us hearts like yours. We never love each other. Other tribes place medicines about our country to prevent the rain, so that we may be dispersed by

hunger, and go to them, and augment their power. We must dissolve their charms by our medicines. God has given us one little thing, which you know nothing of. He has given us the knowledge of certain medicines by which we can make rain. *We* do not despise those things which you possess, though we are ignorant of them. We don't understand your book, yet we don't despise it. *You* ought not to despise our little knowledge, though you are ignorant of it.

M.D. I don't despise what I am ignorant of; I only think you are mistaken in saying that you have medicines which can influence the rain at all.

R.D. That's just the way people speak when they talk on a subject of which they have no knowledge. When we first opened our eyes, we found our forefathers making rain, and we follow in their footsteps. You, who send to Kuruman for corn, and irrigate your garden, may do without rain; *we* cannot manage in that way. If we had no rain, the cattle would have no pasture, the cows give no milk, our children become lean and die, our wives run away to other tribes who do make rain and have corn, and the whole tribe become dispersed and lost; our fire would go out.

M.D. I quite agree with you as to the value of the rain; but you can not charm the clouds by medicines. You wait till you see the clouds come, then you use your medicines, and take the credit which belongs to God only.

R.D. I use my medicines, and you employ yours; we are both doctors and doctors are not deceivers. You give a patient medicine. Sometimes God is pleased to heal him by means of your medicine; sometimes not – he dies. When he is cured, you take the credit of what God does. I do the same. Sometimes God grants us rain, sometimes not. When he does, we take the credit of the charm. When a patient dies, you don't give up trust in your medicine, neither do I when rain fails. If you wish me to leave off my medicines, why continue your own?

M.D. I give medicine to living creatures within my reach, and can see the effects, though no cure follows; you pretend to charm the clouds, which are so far above us that your medicines never reach them. The clouds usually lie in one direction, and your smoke goes in another. God alone can command the clouds. Only try and wait patiently; God will give us rain without your medicines.

R.D. Mahala–ma–kapa–a–a!! Well, I always thought white men were wise till this morning. Who ever thought of making trial of starvation? Is death pleasant, then?

M.D. Could you make it rain on one spot and not on another?

R.D. I wouldn't think of trying. I like to see the whole country green, and all the people glad; the women clapping their hands, and giving me their ornaments for thankfulness, and lullilooing for joy.

M.D. I think you deceive both them and yourself.

R.D. Well, then, there is a pair of us (meaning both are rogues).

The above is only a specimen of their way of reasoning, in which, when the language is well understood, they are perceived to be remarkably acute. These arguments are generally known, and I never succeeded in convincing a single individual of their fallacy, though I tried to do so in every way I could think of. Their faith in medicines as charms is unbounded. The general effect of argument is to produce the impression that you are not anxious for rain at all; and it is very undesirable to allow the idea to spread that you do not take a generous interest in their welfare. An angry opponent of rain-making in a tribe would be looked upon as were some Greek merchants in England during the Russian war.

Note

1 The name arises from its being always voided on one spot, in the manner practiced by others of the rhinocerontine family; and, by the action of the sun, it becomes a black, pitchy substance.

16

The Notion of Witchcraft Explains Unfortunate Events

E. E. Evans-Pritchard

I

Witches, as the Azande conceive them, clearly cannot exist. None the less, the concept of witchcraft provides them with both a natural philosophy by which the relations between men and unfortunate events are explained, and, also, a ready and stereotyped means of reacting to such events. Witchcraft beliefs also embrace a system of values which regulate human conduct.

Witchcraft is ubiquitous. It plays its part in every activity of Zande life; in agricultural, fishing, and hunting pursuits; in domestic life of homesteads as well as in communal life of district and court; it is an important theme of mental life in which it forms the background of a vast panorama of oracles and magic; its influence is plainly stamped on law and morals, etiquette and religion; it is prominent in technology and language; there is no niche or corner of Zande culture into which it does not twist itself. If blight seizes the ground-nut crop it is witchcraft; if the bush is vainly scoured for game it is witchcraft; if women laboriously bale water out of a pool and are rewarded by but a few small fish it is witchcraft; if termites do not rise when their swarming is due and a cold useless night is spent in waiting for their flight it is witchcraft; if a wife is sulky and unresponsive to her husband it is witchcraft; if a prince is cold and distant with his subject it is witchcraft; if a magical rite fails to achieve its purpose it is witchcraft; if, in fact, any failure or misfortune falls upon anyone at any time and in relation to any of the manifold activities of his life it may be due to witchcraft. The Zande attributes all these misfortunes to witchcraft unless there is strong evidence, and subsequent oracular confirmation, that sorcery or some other evil agent has been at work, or unless they are clearly to be attributed to incompetence, breach of a taboo, or failure to observe a moral rule.

To say that witchcraft has blighted the ground-nut crop, that witchcraft has scared away game, and that witchcraft has made so-and-so ill is equivalent to saying in terms of our own culture that the ground-nut crop has failed owing to blight, that game is scarce this season, and that so-and-so has caught influenza. Witchcraft participates in all misfortunes and is the idiom in which Azande speak about them and in which they explain them. To us witchcraft is something which

From E. E. Evans-Pritchard, *Witchcraft, Oracles and Magic among the Azande* (1937; abridged edition 1976), from Oxford University Press.

haunted and disgusted our credulous forefathers. But the Zande expects to come across witchcraft at any time of the day or night. He would be just as surprised if he were not brought into daily contact with it as we would be if confronted by its appearance. To him there is nothing miraculous about it. It is expected that a man's hunting will be injured by witches, and he has at his disposal means of dealing with them. When misfortunes occur he does not become awestruck at the play of supernatural forces. He is not terrified at the presence of an occult enemy. He is, on the other hand, extremely annoyed. Someone, out of spite, has ruined his ground-nuts or spoilt his hunting or given his wife a chill, and surely this is cause for anger! He has done no one harm, so what right has anyone to interfere in his affairs? It is an impertinence, an insult, a dirty, offensive trick! It is the aggressiveness and not the eeriness of these actions which Azande emphasize when speaking of them, and it is anger and not awe which we observe in their response to them.

Witchcraft is not less anticipated than adultery. It is so intertwined with everyday happenings that it is part of a Zande's ordinary world. There is nothing remarkable about a witch – you may be one yourself, and certainly many of your closest neighbours are witches. Nor is there anything awe-inspiring about witchcraft. We do not become psychologically transformed when we hear that someone is ill – we expect people to be ill – and it is the same with Zande. They expect people to be ill, i.e. to be bewitched, and it is not a matter for surprise or wonderment.

I found it strange at first to live among Azande and listen to naive explanations of misfortunes which, to our minds, have apparent causes, but after a while I learnt the idiom of their thought and applied notions of witchcraft as spontaneously as themselves in situations where the concept was relevant. A boy knocked his foot against a small stump of wood in the centre of a bush path, a frequent happening in Africa, and suffered pain and inconvenience in consequence. Owing to its position on his toe it was impossible to keep the cut free from dirt and it began to fester. He declared that witchcraft had made him knock his foot against the stump. I always argued with Azande and criticized their statements, and I did so on this

occasion. I told the boy that he had knocked his foot against the stump of wood because he had been careless, and that witchcraft had not placed it in the path, for it had grown there naturally. He agreed that witchcraft had nothing to do with the stump of wood being in his path but added that he had kept his eyes open for stumps, as indeed every Zande does most carefully, and that if he had not been bewitched he would have seen the stump. As a conclusive argument for his view he remarked that all cuts do not take days to heal but, on the contrary, close quickly, for that is the nature of cuts. Why, then, has his sore festered and remained open if there were no witchcraft behind it? This, as I discovered before long, was to be regarded as the Zande explanation of sickness.

Shortly after my arrival in Zandeland we were passing through a government settlement and noticed that a hut had been burnt to the ground on the previous night. Its owner was overcome with grief as it had contained the beer he was preparing for a mortuary feast. He told us that he had gone the previous night to examine his beer. He had lit a handful of straw and raised it above his head so that light would be cast on the pots, and in so doing he had ignited the thatch. He, and my companions also, were convinced that the disaster was caused by witchcraft.

One of my chief informants, Kisanga, was a skilled woodcarver, one of the finest carvers in the whole kingdom of Gbudwe. Occasionally the bowls and stools which he carved split during the work, as one may well imagine in such a climate. Though the hardest woods be selected they sometimes split in process of carving or on completion of the utensil even if the craftsman is careful and well acquainted with the technical rules of his craft. When this happened to the bowls and stools of this particular craftsman he attributed the misfortune to witchcraft and used to harangue me about the spite and jealousy of his neighbours. When I used to reply that I thought he was mistaken and that people were well disposed towards him he used to hold the split bowl or stool towards me as concrete evidence of his assertions. If people were not bewitching his work, how would I account for that? Likewise a potter will attribute the cracking of his pots during firing to witchcraft. An experienced potter need have no fear that his pots will crack as a result of error. He selects the proper clay, kneads it thoroughly till he has extracted all grit and pebbles, and builds it up slowly and carefully. On the night before digging out his clay he abstains from sexual intercourse. So he should have nothing to fear. Yet pots sometimes break, even when they are the handiwork of expert potters, and this can only be accounted for by witchcraft. "It is broken – there is witchcraft," says the potter simply. ...

II

In speaking to Azande about witchcraft and in observing their reactions to situations of misfortune it was obvious that they did not attempt to account for the existence of phenomena, or even the action of phenomena, by mystical causation alone. What they explained by witchcraft were the particular conditions in a chain of causation which related an individual to natural happenings in such a way that he sustained injury. The boy who knocked his foot against a stump of wood did not account for the stump by reference to witchcraft, nor did he suggest that whenever anybody knocks his foot against a stump it is necessarily due to witchcraft, nor yet again did he account for the cut by saying that it was caused by witchcraft, for he knew quite well that it was caused by the stump of wood. What he attributed to witchcraft was that on this particular occasion, when exercising his usual care, he struck his foot against a stump of wood, whereas on a hundred other occasions he did not do so, and that on this particular occasion the cut, which he expected to result from the knock, festered whereas he had dozens of cuts which had not festered. Surely these peculiar conditions demand an explanation. Again, every year hundreds of Azande go and inspect their beer by night and they always take with them a handful of straw in order to illuminate the hut in which it is fermenting. Why then should this particular man on this single occasion have ignited the thatch of his hut? Again, my friend the woodcarver had made scores of bowls and stools without mishap and he knew all there was to know about the selection of wood, use of tools, and conditions of carving. His bowls and stools did not split like the products of craftsmen who were unskilled in their

work, so why on rare occasions should his bowls and stools split when they did not split usually and when he had exercised all his usual knowledge and care? He knew the answer well enough and so, in his opinion, did his envious, back-biting neighbours. In the same way, a potter wants to know why his pots should break on an occasion when he uses the same material and technique as on other occasions; or rather he already knows, for the reason is known in advance, as it were. If the pots break it is due to witchcraft.

We shall give a false account of Zande philosophy if we say that they believe witchcraft to be the sole cause of phenomena. This proposition is not contained in Zande patterns of thought, which only assert that witchcraft brings a man into relation with events in such a way that he sustains injury.

In Zandeland sometimes an old granary collapses. There is nothing remarkable in this. Every Zande knows that termites eat the supports in course of time and that even the hardest woods decay after years of service. Now a granary is the summerhouse of a Zande homestead and people sit beneath it in the heat of the day and chat or play the African hole-game or work at some craft. Consequently it may happen that there are people sitting beneath the granary when it collapses and they are injured, for it is a heavy structure made of beams and clay and may be stored with eleusine as well. Now why should these particular people have been sitting under this particular granary at the particular moment when it collapsed? That it should collapse is easily intelligible, but why should it have collapsed at the particular moment when these particular people were sitting beneath it? Through years it might have collapsed, so why should it fall just when certain people sought its kindly shelter? We say that the granary collapsed because its supports were eaten away by termites; that is the cause that explains the collapse of the granary. We also say that people were sitting under it at the time because it was in the heat of the day and they thought that it would be a comfortable place to talk and work. This is the cause of people being under the granary at the time it collapsed. To our minds the only relationship between these two independently caused facts is their coincidence in time and space. We have no explanation of why the two chains of causation intersected at a certain time and in a certain place, for there is no interdependence between them.

Zande philosophy can supply the missing link. The Zande knows that the supports were undermined by termites and that people were sitting beneath the granary in order to escape the heat and glare of the sun. But he knows besides why these two events occurred at a precisely similar moment in time and space. It was due to the action of witchcraft. If there had been no witchcraft people would have been sitting under the granary and it would not have fallen on them, or it would have collapsed but the people would not have been sheltering under it at the time. Witchcraft explains the coincidence of these two happenings.

III

I hope I am not expected to point out that the Zande cannot analyse his doctrines as I have done for him. It is no use saying to a Zande "Now tell me what you Azande think about witchcraft" because the subject is too general and indeterminate, both too vague and too immense, to be described concisely. But it is possible to extract the principles of their thought from dozens of situations in which witchcraft is called upon to explain happenings and from dozens of other situations in which failure is attributed to some other cause. Their philosophy is explicit, but is not formally stated as a doctrine. A Zande would not say "I believe in natural causation but I do not think that that fully explains coincidences, and it seems to me that the theory of witchcraft offers a satisfactory explanation of them", but he expresses his thought in terms of actual and particular situations. He says "a buffalo charges", "a tree falls", "termites are not making their seasonal flight when they are expected to do so", and so on. Herein he is stating empirically ascertained facts. But he also says "a buffalo charged and wounded so-and-so", "a tree fell on so-and-so and killed him", "my termites refuse to make their flight in numbers worth collecting but other people are collecting theirs all right", and so on. He tells you that these things are due to witchcraft, saying in each instance, "So-and-so has been bewitched." The facts do not explain themselves or only partly explain themselves. They can only be explained fully if one takes witchcraft into consideration.

One can only obtain the full range of a Zande's ideas about causation by allowing him to fill in the gaps himself, otherwise one will be led astray by linguistic conventions. He tells you "So-and-so was bewitched and killed himself" or even simply that "So-and-so was killed by witchcraft". But he is telling you the ultimate cause of his death and not the secondary causes. You can ask him "How did he kill himself?" and he will tell you that he committed suicide by hanging himself from the branch of a tree. You can also ask "Why did he kill himself?" and he will tell you that it was because he was angry with his brothers. The cause of his death was hanging from a tree, and the cause of his hanging from a tree was his anger with his brothers. If you then ask a Zande why he should say that the man was bewitched if he committed suicide on account of his anger with his brothers, he will tell you that only crazy people commit suicide, and that if everyone who was angry with his brothers committed suicide there would soon be no people left in the world, and that if this man had not been bewitched he would not have done what he did do. If you persevere and ask why witchcraft caused the man to kill himself the Zande will reply that he supposes someone hated him, and if you ask him why someone hated him your informant will tell you that such is the nature of men.

For if Azande cannot enunciate a theory of causation in terms acceptable to us they describe happenings in an idiom that is explanatory. They are aware that it is particular circumstances of events in their relation to man, their harmfulness to a particular person, that constitutes evidence of witchcraft. Witchcraft explains *why* events are harmful to man and not *how* they happen. A Zande perceives how they happen just as we do. He does not see a witch charge a man, but an elephant. He does not see a witch push over a granary, but termites gnawing away its supports. He does not see a psychical flame igniting thatch, but an ordinary lighted bundle of straw. His perception of how events occur is as clear as our own.

IV

Zande belief in witchcraft in no way contradicts empirical knowledge of causes and effect. The world known to the senses is just as real to them as it is to us. We must not be deceived by their way of expressing causation and imagine that because they say a man was killed by witchcraft they entirely neglect the secondary causes that, as we judge them, were the true causes of his death. They are foreshortening the chain of events, and in a particular social situation are selecting the cause that is socially relevant and neglecting the rest. If a man is killed by a spear in war, or by a wild beast in hunting, or by the bite of a snake, or from sickness, witchcraft is the socially relevant cause, since it is the only one which allows intervention and determines social behaviour.

Belief in death from natural causes and belief in death from witchcraft are not mutually exclusive. On the contrary, they supplement one another, the one accounting for what the other does not account for. Besides, death is not only a natural fact but also a social fact. It is not simply that the heart ceases to beat and the lungs to pump air in an organism, but it is also the destruction of a member of a family and kin, of a community and tribe. Death leads to consultation or oracles, magic rites, and revenge. Among the causes of death witchcraft is the only one that has any significance for social behaviour. The attribution of misfortune to witchcraft does not exclude what we call its real causes but is superimposed on them and gives to social events their moral value.

Zande thought expresses the notion of natural and mystical causation quite clearly by using a hunting metaphor to define their relations. Azande always say of witchcraft that it is the *umbaga* or second spear. When Azande kill game there is a division of meat between the man who first speared the animal and the man who plunged a second spear into it. These two are considered to have killed the beast and the owner of the second spear is called the *umbaga*. Hence if a man is killed by an elephant Azande say that the elephant is the first spear and that witchcraft is the second spear and that together they killed the man. If a man spears another in war the slayer is the first spear and witchcraft is the second spear and together they killed him.

Since Azande recognize plurality of causes, and it is the social situation that indicates the relevant one, we can understand why the doctrine of witchcraft is not used to explain every failure and

misfortune. It sometimes happens that the social situation demands a commonsense, and not a mystical, judgement of cause. Thus, if you tell a lie, or commit adultery, or steal, or deceive your prince, and are found out, you cannot elude punishment by saying that you were bewitched. Zande doctrine declares emphatically "Witchcraft does not make a person tell lies"; "Witchcraft does not make a person commit adultery"; "Witchcraft does not put adultery into a man. 'Witchcraft' is in yourself (you alone are responsible), that is, your penis becomes erect. It sees the hair of a man's wife and it rises and becomes erect because the only 'witchcraft' is, itself" ("witchcraft" is here used metaphorically); "Witchcraft does not make a person steal"; "Witchcraft does not make a person disloyal." Only on one occasion have I heard a Zande plead that he was bewitched when he had committed an offence and this was when he lied to me, and even on this occasion everybody present laughed at him and told him that witchcraft does not make people tell lies.

If a man murders another tribesman with knife or spear he is put to death. It is not necessary in such a case to seek a witch, for an objective towards which vengeance may be directed is already present. If, on the other hand, it is a member of another tribe who has speared a man his relatives, or his prince, will take steps to discover the witch responsible for the event.

It would be treason to say that a man put to death on the orders of his king for an offence against authority was killed by witchcraft. If a man were to consult the oracles to discover the witch responsible for the death of a relative who had been put to death at the orders of his king he would run the risk of being put to death himself. For here the social situation excludes the notion of witchcraft as on other occasions it pays no attention to natural agents and emphasizes only witchcraft. Also, if a man were killed in vengeance because the oracles said that he was a witch and had murdered another man with his witchcraft then his relatives could not say that he had been killed by witchcraft. Zande doctrine lays it down that he died at the hand of avengers because he was a homicide. If a man were to have expressed the view that his kinsman had been killed by witchcraft and to have acted upon his opinion by consulting the poison oracle, he might have been punished for ridiculing the king's poison oracle, for it was the poison oracle of the king that had given official confirmation of the man's guilt, and it was the king himself who had permitted vengeance to take its course.

In these situations witchcraft is irrelevant and, if not totally excluded, is not indicated as the principal factor in causation. As in our own society a scientific theory of causation, if not excluded, is deemed irrelevant in questions of moral and legal responsibility, so in Zande society the doctrine of witchcraft, if not excluded, is deemed irrelevant in the same situations. We accept scientific explanations of the causes of disease, and even of the causes of insanity, but we deny them in crime and sin because here they militate against law and morals which are axiomatic. The Zande accepts a mystical explanation of the causes of misfortune, sickness, and death, but he does not allow this explanation if it conflicts with social exigencies expressed in law and morals.

For witchcraft is not indicated as a cause for failure when a taboo has been broken. If a child becomes sick, and it is known that its father and mother have had sexual relations before it was weaned, the cause of death is already indicated by breach of a ritual prohibition and the question of witchcraft does not arise. If a man develops leprosy and there is a history of incest in his case then incest is the cause of leprosy and not witchcraft. In these cases, however, a curious situation arises because when the child or the leper dies it is necessary to avenge their deaths and the Zande sees no difficulty in explaining what appears to us to be most illogical behaviour. He does so on the same principles as when a man has been killed by a wild beast, and he invokes the same metaphor of "second spear". In the cases mentioned above there are really three causes of a person's death. There is the illness from which he dies, leprosy in the case of the man, perhaps some fever in the case of the child. These sicknesses are not in themselves products of witchcraft, for they exist in their own right just as a buffalo or a granary exist in their own right. Then there is the breach of a taboo, in the one case of weaning, in the other case of incest. The child, and the man, developed fever, and leprosy, because a taboo was broken. The breach of a taboo was the cause of their sickness, but the

sickness would not have killed them if witchcraft had not also been operative. If witchcraft had not been present as "second spear" they would have developed fever and leprosy just the same, but they would not have died from them. In these instances there are two socially significant causes, breach of taboo and witchcraft, both of which are relative to different social processes, and each is emphasized by different people.

But where there has been a breach of taboo and death is not involved witchcraft will not be evoked as a cause of failure. If a man eats a forbidden food after he has made powerful punitive magic he may die, and in this case the cause of his death is known beforehand, since it is contained in the conditions of the situation in which he died even if witchcraft was also operative. But it does not follow that he will die. What does inevitably follow is that the medicine he has made will cease to operate against the person for whom it is intended and will have to be destroyed lest it turn against the magician who sent if forth. The failure of the medicine to achieve its purpose is due to breach of a taboo and not to witchcraft. If a man has had sexual relations with his wife and on the next day approaches the poison oracle it will not reveal the truth and its oracular efficacy will be permanently undermined. If he had not broken a taboo it would have been said that witchcraft had caused the oracle to lie, but the condition of the person who had attended the seance provides a reason for its failure to speak the truth without having to bring in the notion of witchcraft as an agent. No one will admit that he has broken a taboo before consulting the poison oracle, but when an oracle lies everyone is prepared to admit that a taboo may have been broken by someone.

Similarly, when a potter's creations break in firing, witchcraft is not the only possible cause of the calamity. Inexperience and bad workmanship may also be reasons for failure, or the potter may himself have had sexual relations on the preceding night. The potter himself will attribute his failure to witchcraft, but others may not be of the same opinion.

Not even all deaths are invariably and unanimously attributed to witchcraft or to the breach of some taboo. The deaths of babies from certain diseases are attributed vaguely to the Supreme Being.

Also, if a man falls suddenly and violently sick and dies, his relatives may be sure that a sorcerer has made magic against him and that it is not a witch who has killed him. A breach of the obligations of blood-brotherhood may sweep away whole groups of kin, and when one after another of brothers and cousins die it is the blood and not witchcraft to which their deaths are attributed by outsiders, though the relatives of the dead will seek to avenge them on witches. When a very old man dies, unrelated people say that he has died of old age, but they do not say this in the presence of kinsmen, who declare that witchcraft is responsible for his death.

It is also thought that adultery may cause misfortune, though it is only one participating factor, and witchcraft is also believed to be present. Thus is it said that a man may be killed in warfare or in a hunting accident as a result of his wife's infidelities. Therefore, before going to war or on a large-scale hunting expedition a man might ask his wife to divulge the names of her lovers.

Even where breaches of law and morals do not occur witchcraft is not the only reason given for failure. Incompetence, laziness, and ignorance may be selected as causes. When a girl smashes her water-pot or a boy forgets to close the door of the hen-house at night they will be admonished severely by their parents for stupidity. The mistakes of children are due to carelessness or ignorance and they are taught to avoid them while they are still young. People do not say that they are effects of witchcraft, or if they are prepared to concede the possibility of witchcraft they consider stupidity the main cause. Moreover, the Zande is not so naïve that he holds witchcraft responsible for the cracking of a pot during firing if subsequent examination shows that a pebble was left in the clay, or for an animal escaping his net if someone frightened it away by a move or a sound. People do not blame witchcraft if a woman burns her porridge nor if she presents it undercooked to her husband. And when an inexperienced craftsman makes a stool which lacks polish or which splits, this is put down to his inexperience.

In all these cases the man who suffers the misfortune is likely to say that it is due to witchcraft, but others will not say so. We must bear in mind nevertheless that a serious misfortune, especially if it results in death, is normally attributed by everyone to the action of witchcraft, especially by the sufferer and his kin, however much it may have been due to a man's incompetence or absence of self-control. If a man falls into a fire and is seriously burnt, or falls into a game-pit and breaks his neck or his leg, it would undoubtedly be attributed to witchcraft. Thus when six or seven of the sons of Prince Rikita were entrapped in a ring of fire and burnt to death when hunting cane-rats their death was undoubtedly due to witchcraft.

Hence we see that witchcraft has its own logic, its own rules of thought, and that these do not exclude natural causation. Belief in witchcraft is quite consistent with human responsibility and a rational appreciation of nature. First of all a man must carry out an activity according to traditional rules of technique, which consist of knowledge checked by trial and error in each generation. It is only if he fails in spite of adherence to these rules that people will impute his lack of success to witchcraft.

V

It is often asked whether primitive people distinguish between the natural and the supernatural, and the query may be here answered in a preliminary manner in respect to the Azande. The question as it stands may mean, do primitive peoples distinguish between the natural and the supernatural in the abstract? We have a notion of an ordered world conforming to what we call natural laws, but some people in our society believe that mysterious things can happen which cannot be accounted for by reference to natural laws and which therefore are held to transcend them, and we call these happenings supernatural. To us supernatural means very much the same as abnormal or extraordinary. Azande certainly have no such notions of reality. They have no conceptions of "natural" as we understand it, and therefore neither of the "supernatural" as we understand it. Witchcraft is to Azande an ordinary and not an extraordinary, even though it may in some circumstances be an infrequent, event. It is a normal, and not an abnormal, happening. But if they do not give to the natural and supernatural the meanings which educated Europeans give to them they nevertheless distinguish between them. For our question may be formulated, and should be formulated, in a different manner. We ought rather to ask whether primitive peoples perceive any difference between the happenings which we, the observers of their culture, class as natural and the happenings which we class as mystical. Azande undoubtedly perceive a difference between what we consider the workings of nature on the one hand and the workings of magic and ghosts and witchcraft on the other hand, though in the absence of a formulated doctrine of natural law they do not, and cannot, express the difference as we express it.

The Zande notion of witchcraft is incompatible with our ways of thought. But even to the Azande there is something peculiar about the action of witchcraft. Normally it can be perceived only in dreams. It is not an evident notion but transcends sensory experience. They do not profess to understand witchcraft entirely. They know that it exists and works evil, but they have to guess at the manner in which it works. Indeed, I have frequently been struck when discussing witchcraft with Azande by the doubt they express about the subject, not only in what they say, but even more in their manner of saying it, both of which contrast with their ready knowledge, fluently imparted, about social events and economic techniques.

They feel out of their depth in trying to describe the way in which witchcraft accomplishes its ends. That it kills people is obvious, but how it kills them cannot be known precisely. They tell you that perhaps if you were to ask an older man or a witch-doctor he might give you more information. But the older men and the witch-doctors can tell you little more than youth and laymen. They only know what the others know: that the soul of witchcraft goes by night and devours the soul of its victim. Only witches themselves understand these matters fully. In truth Azande experience feelings about witchcraft rather than ideas, for their intellectual concepts of it are weak and they know better what to do when attacked by it than how to explain it. Their response is action and not analysis.

There is no elaborate and consistent representation of witchcraft that will account in detail for its workings, nor of nature which expounds its conformity to sequences and functional interrelations. The Zande actualizes these beliefs rather than intellectualizes them, and their tenets are expressed in socially controlled behaviour rather than in doctrines. Hence the difficulty in discussing the subject of witchcraft with Azande, for their ideas are imprisoned in action and cannot be cited to explain and justify action.

17

Understanding a Primitive Society

Peter Winch

1   The Reality of Magic

An anthropologist studying a primitive people
with beliefs that we cannot possibly share and
practices we cannot comprehend wishes to make
those beliefs and practices intelligible to himself
and his readers. This means presenting an account
of them that will somehow satisfy the criteria of
rationality demanded by the culture to which he
and his readers belong: a culture whose conception of rationality is deeply affected by the achievements and methods of the sciences, and one which
treats such things as a belief in magic or the
practice of consulting oracles as almost a paradigm
of the irrational. The strains inherent in this situation are very likely to lead the anthropologist to
adopt the following posture: *We* know that Zande
beliefs in the influence of witchcraft, the efficacy
of magic medicines, the role of oracles in revealing
what is going on and what is going to happen, are
mistaken, illusory. Scientific methods of investigation have shown conclusively that there are no
relations of cause and effect such as are implied by
these beliefs and practices. All we can do then is to
show how such a system of mistaken beliefs and
inefficacious practices can maintain itself in the
face of objections that seem to us so obvious.[1]

Now although Evans-Pritchard goes a very great
deal further than most of his predecessors in trying
to present the sense of the institutions he is discussing as it presents itself to the Azande themselves, still, the last paragraph does, I believe, pretty
fairly describe the attitude he himself took at the
time of writing this book. There is more than one
remark to the effect that "obviously there are no
witches"; and he writes of the difficulty he found,
during his field work with the Azande, in shaking
off the "unreason" on which Zande life is based
and returning to a clear view of how things really
are. This attitude is not an unsophisticated one but
is based on a philosophical position ably developed
in a series of papers published in the 1930s in the
unhappily rather inaccessible *Bulletin of the Faculty
of Arts* of the University of Egypt. Arguing against
Lévy-Bruhl, Evans-Pritchard here rejects the idea
that the scientific understanding of causes and
effects which leads us to reject magical ideas is
evidence of any superior intelligence on our part.

From Peter Winch, "Understanding a Primitive Society", *American Philosophical Quarterly*, I (1964), pp. 307–24, from
American Philosophical Quarterly.

Our scientific approach, he points out, is as much a function of our culture as is the magical approach of the "savage" a function of his:

> The fact that we attribute rain to meteorological causes alone while savages believe that Gods or ghosts or magic can influence the rain-fall is no evidence that our brains function differently from their brains. It does not show that we "think more logically" than savages, at least not if this expression suggests some kind of hereditary psychic superiority. It is no sign of superior intelligence on my part that I attribute rain to physical causes. I did not come to this conclusion myself by observation and inference and have, in fact, little knowledge of the meterological process that lead to rain, I merely accept what everybody else in my society accepts, namely that rain is due to natural causes. This particular idea formed part of my culture long before I was born into it and little more was required of me than sufficient linguistic ability to learn it. Likewise a savage who believes that under suitable natural and ritual conditions the rainfall can be influenced by use of appropriate magic is not on account of this belief to be considered of inferior intelligence. He did not build up this belief from his own observations and inferences but adopted it in the same way as he adopted the rest of his cultural heritage, namely by being born into it. He and I are both thinking in patterns of thought provided for us by the societies in which we live.
>
> It would be absurd to say that the savage is thinking mystically and that we are thinking scientifically about rainfall. In either case like mental processes are involved and, moreover, the content of thought is similarly derived. But we can say that the social content of our thought about rainfall is scientific, is in accord with objective facts, whereas the social content of savage thought about rainfall is unscientific since it is not in accord with reality and may also be mystical where it assumes the existence of suprasensible forces.[2]

In a subsequent article on Pareto, Evans-Pritchard distinguishes between "logical" and "scientific."

> Scientific notions are those which accord with objective reality both with regard to the validity of their premises and to the inferences drawn from their propositions ... Logical notions are those in which according to the rules of thought inferences would be true were the premises true, the truth of the premises being irrelevant ...
>
> A pot has broken during firing. This is probably due to grit. Let us examine the pot and see if this is the cause. That is logical and scientific thought. Sickness is due to witchcraft. A man is sick. Let us consult the oracles to discover who is the witch responsible. That is logical and unscientific thought.[3]

I think that Evans-Pritchard is right in a great deal of what he says here, but wrong, and crucially wrong, in his attempt to characterize the scientific in terms of that which is "in accord with objective reality." Despite differences of emphasis and phraseology, Evans-Pritchard is in fact hereby put into the same metaphysical camp as Pareto: for both of them the conception of "reality" must be regarded as intelligible and applicable *outside* the context of scientific reasoning itself, since it is that to which scientific notions do, and unscientific notions do not, have a relation. Evans-Pritchard, although he emphasizes that a member of scientific culture has a different conception of reality from that of a Zande believer in magic, wants to go beyond merely registering this fact and making the differences explicit, and to say, finally, that the scientific conception agrees with what reality actually is like, whereas the magical conception does not.

It would be easy, at this point, to say simply that the difficulty arises from the use of the unwieldy and misleadingly comprehensive expression "agreement with reality"; and in a sense this is true. But we should not lose sight of the fact that the idea that men's ideas and beliefs must be checkable by reference to something independent – some reality – is an important one. To abandon it is to plunge straight into an extreme Protagorean relativism, with all the paradoxes that involves. On the other hand great care is certainly necessary in fixing the precise role that this conception of the independently real does play in men's thought. There are two related points that I should like to make about it at this stage.

In the first place we should notice that the check of the independently real is not peculiar to science. The trouble is that the fascination science has for us makes it easy for us to adopt its scientific form as a paradigm against which to measure the intellectual respectability of other modes of discourse. Consider what God says to Job out of the whirlwind: "Who is this that darkeneth counsel by words without knowledge? ... Where wast thou when I laid the foundations of the earth? declare, if thou hast understanding. Who hath laid the measures thereof, if thou knowest? or who hath stretched the line upon it ... Shall he that contendeth with the Almighty instruct him? he that reproveth God, let him answer it." Job is taken to task for having gone astray by having lost sight of the reality of God; this does not, of course, mean that Job has made any sort of theoretical mistake, which could be put right, perhaps, by means of an experiment.[4] God's reality is certainly independent of what any man may care to think, but what that reality amounts to can only be seen from the religious tradition in which the concept of God is used, and this use is very unlike the use of scientific concepts, say of theoretical entities. The point is that it is *within* the religious use of language that the conception of God's reality has its place, though, I repeat, this does not mean that it is at the mercy of what anyone cares to say; if this were so, God would have no reality.

My second point follows from the first. Reality is not what gives language sense. What is real and what is unreal shows itself *in* the sense that language has. Further, both the distinction between the real and the unreal and the concept of agreement with reality themselves belong to our language. I will not say that they are concepts of the language like any other, since it is clear that they occupy a commanding, and in a sense a limiting, position there. We can imagine a language with no concept, of, say, wetness, but hardly one in which there is no way of distinguishing the real from the unreal. Nevertheless we could not in fact distinguish the real from the unreal without understanding the way this distinction operates in the language. If then we wish to understand the significance of these concepts, we must examine the use they actually do have – *in* the language.

Evans-Pritchard, on the contrary, is trying to work with a conception of reality which is *not* determined by its actual use in language. He wants something against which the use can itself be appraised. But this is not possible; and no more possible in the case of scientific discourse than it is

in any other. We may ask whether a particular scientific hypothesis agrees with reality and test this by observation and experiment. Given the experimental methods, and the established use of the theoretical terms entering into the hypothesis, then the question whether it holds or not is settled by reference to something independent of what I, or anybody else, care to think. But the general nature of the data revealed by the experiment can only be specified in terms of criteria built into the methods of experiment employed and these, in turn, make sense only to someone who is conversant with the kind of scientific activity within which they are employed. A scientific illiterate, asked to describe the results of an experiment which he "observes" in an advanced physics laboratory, could not do so in terms relevant to the hypothesis being tested; and it is really only in such terms that we can sensibly speak of the "results of the experiment" at all. What Evans-Pritchard wants to be able to say is that the criteria applied in scientific experimentation constitute a true link between our ideas and an independent reality, whereas those characteristic of other systems of thought – in particular, magical methods of thought – do not. It is evident that the expressions "true link" and "independent reality" in the previous sentence cannot themselves be explained by reference to the scientific universe of discourse, as this would beg the question. We have then to ask how, by reference to what established universe of discourse, the use of those expressions *is* to be explained; and it is clear that Evans-Pritchard has not answered this question.

Two questions arise out of what I have been saying. First, is it in fact the case that a primitive system of magic, like that of the Azande, constitutes a coherent universe of discourse like science, in terms of which an intelligible conception of reality and clear ways of deciding what beliefs are and are not in agreement with this reality can be discerned! Second, what are we to make of the possibility of understanding primitive social institutions, like Zande magic, if the situation is as I have outlined? I do not claim to be able to give a satisfactory answer to the second question. It raises some very important and fundamental issues about the nature of human social life, which require conceptions different from, and harder to elucidate than, those I have hitherto introduced. I shall offer some tentative remarks about these issues in the second part of this essay. At present I shall address myself to the first question.

It ought to be remarked here that an affirmative answer to my first question would not commit me to accepting as rational all beliefs couched in magical concepts or all procedures practiced in the name of such beliefs. This is no more necessary than is the corresponding proposition that all procedures "justified" in the name of science are immune from rational criticism. A remark of Collingwood's is apposite here:

> Savages are no more exempt from human folly than civilized men, and are no doubt equally liable to the error of thinking that they, or the persons they regard as their superiors, can do what in fact cannot be done. But this error is not the essence of magic; it is a perversion of magic. And we should be careful how we attribute it to the people we call savages, who will one day rise up and testify against us.[5]

It is important to distinguish a system of magical beliefs and practices like that of the Azande, which is one of the principal foundations of their whole social life and, on the other hand, magical beliefs that might be held, and magical rites that might be practised, by persons belonging to our own culture. These have to be understood rather differently. Evans-Pritchard is himself alluding to the difference in the following passage: "When a Zande speaks of witchcraft he does not speak of it as we speak of the weird witchcraft of our own history. Witchcraft is to him a commonplace happening and he seldom passes a day without mentioning it … To us witchcraft is something which haunted and disgusted our credulous forefathers. But the Zande expects to come across witchcraft at any time of the day or night. He would be just as surprised if he were not brought into daily contact with it as we would be if confronted by its appearance. To him there is nothing miraculous about it."[6]

The difference is not merely one of degree of familiarity, however, although, perhaps, even this has more importance than might at first appear. Concepts of witchcraft and magic in our culture, at least since the advent of Christianity, have been parasitic on, and a perversion of other orthodox concepts, both religious and, increasingly, scientific. To take an obvious example, you could not understand what was involved in conducting a Black Mass, unless you were familiar with the conduct of a proper Mass and, therefore, with the whole complex of religious ideas from which the mass draws its sense. Neither would you understand the relation between these without taking account of the fact that the Black practices are rejected as *irrational* (in the sense proper to religion) in the system of beliefs on which these practices are thus parasitic. Perhaps a similar relation holds between the contemporary practice of astrology and astronomy and technology. It is impossible to keep a discussion of the rationality of Black Magic or of astrology within the bounds of concepts peculiar to them; they have an essential reference to something outside themselves. The position is like that which Socrates, in Plato's *Gorgias*, showed to be true of the Sophists' conception of rhetoric: namely, that it is parasitic on rational discourse in such a way that its irrational character can be shown in terms of this dependence. Hence, when we speak of such practices as "superstitious," "illusory," "irrational," we have the weight of our culture behind us; and this is not just a matter of being on the side of the big battalions, because those beliefs and practices belong to, and derive such sense as they seem to have, from the same culture. This enables us to show that the sense is only apparent, in terms which are culturally relevant.

It is evident that our relation to Zande magic is quite different. If we wish to understand it, we must seek a foothold elsewhere. And while there may well be room for the use of such critical expressions as "superstition" and "irrationality", the kind of rationality with which such terms might be used to point a contrast remains to be elucidated. …

Early in his book Evans-Pritchard defines certain categories in terms of which his descriptions of Zande customs are couched.

> MYSTICAL NOTIONS … are patterns of thought that attribute to phenomena suprasensible qualities which, or part of which, are not derived from observation or cannot be logically inferred from it,

and which they do not possess.[7] COMMON-SENSE NOTIONS ... attribute to phenomena only what men observe in them or what can logically be inferred from observation. So long as a notion does not assert something which has not been observed, it is not classed as mystical even though it is mistaken on account of incomplete observation ... SCIENTIFIC NOTIONS. Science has developed out of common sense but is far more methodical and has better techniques of observation and reasoning. Common sense uses experience and rules of thumb. Science uses experiment and rules of Logic ... *Our body of scientific knowledge and Logic are the sole arbiters of what are mystical, common sense, and scientific notions.* Their judgments are never absolute. RITUAL BEHAVIOUR. Any behaviour that is accounted for by mystical notions. *There is no objective nexus* between the behaviour and the event it is intended to cause. Such behaviour is usually intelligible to us only when we know the mystical notions associated with it. EMPIRICAL BEHAVIOUR. Any behaviour that is accounted for by common-sense notions.[8]

It will be seen from the phrases which I have italicized that Evans-Pritchard is doing more here than just defining certain terms for his own use. Certain metaphysical claims are embodied in the definitions: identical in substance with the claims embodied in Pareto's way of distinguishing between "logical" and "non-logical" conduct.[9] There is a very clear implication that those who use mystical notions and perform ritual behaviour are making some sort of mistake, detectable with the aid of science and logic. I shall now examine more closely some of the institutions described by Evans-Pritchard to determine how far his claims are justified.

Witchcraft is a power possessed by certain individuals to harm other individuals by "mystical" means. Its basis is an inherited organic condition, "witchcraft-substance", and it does not involve any special magical ritual or medicine. It is constantly appealed to by Azande when they are afflicted by misfortune, not so as to exclude explanation in terms of natural causes, which Azande are perfectly able to offer themselves within the limits of their not inconsiderable natural knowledge, but so as to supplement such explanations. "Witchcraft explains *why*[10] events are harmful to man and not *how*[10] they happen. A Zande perceives how they happen just as we do. He does not see a witch charge a man but an elephant. He does not see a witch push over the granary, but termites gnawing away its supports. He does not see a psychical flame igniting thatch, but an ordinary lighted bundle of straw. His perception of how events occur is as clear as our own."[11]

The most important way of detecting the influence of witchcraft and of identifying witches is by the revelations of oracles, of which in turn the most important is the "poison oracle". This name, though convenient, is significantly misleading in so far as, according to Evans-Pritchard, Azande do not have our concept of a poison and do not think of, or behave towards, *benge* – the substance administered in the consultation of the oracle – as we do of and towards poisons. The gathering, preparation, and administering of *benge* is hedged with ritual and strict taboos. At an oracular consultation *benge* is administered to a fowl, while a question is asked in a form permitting a yes or no answer. The fowl's death or survival is specified beforehand as giving the answer "yes" or "no". The answer is then checked by administering *benge* to another fowl and asking the question the other way round. "Is Prince Ndoruma responsible for placing bad medicines in the roof of my hut? The fowl DIES giving the answer 'Yes' ... Did the oracle speak truly when it said that Ndoruma was responsible? The fowl SURVIVES giving the answer 'Yes'." The poison oracle is all-pervasive in Zande life and all steps of any importance in a person's life are settled by reference to it.

A Zande would be utterly lost and bewildered without his oracle. The mainstay of his life would be lacking. It is rather as if an engineer, in our society, were to be asked to build a bridge without mathematical calculation, or a military commander to mount an extensive coordinated attack without the use of clocks. These analogies are mine, but a reader may well think that they beg the question at issue. For, he may argue, the Zande practice of consulting the oracle, unlike my technological and military examples, is completely unintelligible and rests on an obvious illusion. I shall now consider this objection.

First I must emphasize that I have so far done little more than note the *fact*, conclusively established by Evans-Pritchard, that the Azande *do* in fact conduct their affairs to their own satisfaction in this way and are at a loss when forced to abandon the practice – when, for instance, they fall into the hands of European courts. It is worth remarking too that Evans-Pritchard himself ran his household in the same way during his field researches and says: "I found this as satisfactory a way of running my home and affairs as any other I know of."

Further, I would ask in my turn: *to whom* is the practice alleged to be unintelligible? Certainly it is difficult for us to understand what the Azande are about when they consult their oracles; but it might seem just as incredible to them that the engineer's motions with his slide rule could have any connection with the stability of his bridge. But this riposte of course misses the interntion behind the objection, which was not directed to the question whether anyone in fact understands, or claims to understand, what it going on, but rather whether what is going on actually does make sense: i.e., in itself. And it may seem obvious that Zande beliefs in witchcraft and oracles cannot make any sense, however satisfied the Azande may be with them.

What criteria have we for saying that something does, or does not, make sense? A partial answer is that a set of beliefs and practices cannot make sense in so far as they involve contradictions. Now it appears that contradictions are bound to arise in at least two ways in the consultation of the oracle. On the one hand two oracular pronouncements may contradict each other; and on the other hand a self-consistent oracular pronouncement may be contradicted by future experience. I shall examine each of these apparent possibilities in turn.

Of course, it does happen often that the oracle first says "yes" and then "no" to the same question. This does not convince a Zande of the futility of the whole operation of consulting oracles: obviously, it cannot, since otherwise the practice could hardly have developed and maintained itself at all. Various explanations may be offered, whose possibility, it is important to notice, is built into the whole network of Zande beliefs and may, therefore, be regarded as belonging to the concept of an oracle. It may be said, for instance, that bad *benge* is being used; that the operator of the oracle is ritually unclean; that the oracle is being

itself influenced by witchcraft or sorcery; or it may be that the oracle is showing that the question cannot be answered straightforwardly in its present form, as with "Have you stopped beating your wife yet?" There are various ways in which the behaviour of the fowl under the influence of *benge* may be ingeniously interpreted by those wise in the ways of the poison oracle. We might compare this situation perhaps with the interpretation of dreams.

In the other type of case: where an internally consistent oracular revelation is apparently contradicted by subsequent experience, the situation may be dealt with in a similar way, by references to the influence of witchcraft, ritual uncleanliness, and so on. But there is another important consideration we must take into account here too. The chief function of oracles is to reveal the presence of "mystical" forces – I use Evans-Pritchard's term without committing myself to his denial that such forces really exist. Now though there are indeed ways of determining whether or not mystical forces are operating, these ways do not correspond to what we understand by "empirical" confirmation or refutation. This indeed is a tautology, since such differences in "confirmatory" procedures are the main criteria for classifying something as a mystical force in the first place. Here we have one reason why the possibilities of "refutation by experience" are very much fewer than might at first sight be supposed.

There is also another closely connected reason. The spirit in which oracles are consulted is very unlike that in which a scientist makes experiments. Oracular revelations are not treated as hypotheses and, since their sense derives from the way they are treated in their context, they therefore *are not* hypotheses. They are not a matter of intellectual interest but the main way in which Azande decide how they should act. If the oracle reveals that a proposed course of action is fraught with mystical dangers from witchcraft or sorcery, that course of action will not be carried out; and then the question of refutation or confirmation just does not arise. We might say that the revelation has the logical status of an unfulfilled hypothetical, were it not that the context in which this logical term is generally used may again suggest a misleadingly close analogy with scientific hypotheses.

I do not think that Evans-Pritchard would have disagreed with what I have said so far. Indeed, the following comment is on very similar lines:

Azande observe the action of the poison oracle as we observe it, but their observations are always subordinated to their beliefs and are incorporated into their beliefs and made to explain them and justify them. Let the reader consider any argument that would utterly demolish all Zande claims for the power of the oracle. If it were translated into Zande modes of thought it would serve to support their entire structure of belief. For their mystical notions are eminently coherent, being interrelated by a network of logical ties, and are so ordered that they never too crudely contradict sensory experience but, instead, experience seems to justify them. The Zande is immersed in a sea of mystical notions, and if he speaks about his poison oracle he must speak in a mystical idiom.[12]

To locate the point at which the important philosophical issue does arise, I shall offer a parody, composed by changing round one or two expression in the foregoing quotation.

Europeans observe the action of the poison oracle just as Azande observe it, but their observations are always subordinated to their beliefs and are incorporated into their beliefs and made to explain them and justify them. Let a Zande consider any argument that would utterly refute all European scepticism about the power of the oracle. If it were translated into European modes of thought it would serve to support their entire structure of belief. For their scientific notions are eminently coherent, being interrelated by a network of logical ties, and are so ordered that they never too crudely contradict mystical experience but, instead, experience seems to justify them. The European is immersed in a sea of scientific notions, and if he speaks about the Zande poison oracle he must speak in a scientific idiom.

Perhaps this too would be acceptable to Evans-Pritchard. But it is clear from other remarks in the book to which I have alluded, that at the time of writing he would have wished to add: and the European is right and the Zande wrong. This addition I regard as illegitimate and my reasons for so thinking take us to the heart of the matter.

It may be illuminating at this point to compare the disagreement between Evans-Pritchard and me to that between the Wittgenstein of the *Philosophical Investigations* and his earlier *alter ego* of the *Tractatus Logico-Philosophicus*. In the *Tractatus* Wittgenstein sought "the general form of propositions": what made propositions possible. He said that this general form is: "This is how things are"; the proposition was an articulated model, consisting of elements standing in a definite relation to each other. The proposition was true when there existed a corresponding arrangement of elements in reality. The proposition was capable of saying something because of the identity of structure, of logical form, in the proposition and in reality.

By the time Wittgenstein composed the *Investigations* he had come to reject the whole idea that there must be a general form of propositions. He emphasized the indefinite number of different uses that language may have and tried to show that these different uses neither need, nor in fact do, all have something in common, in the sense intended in the *Tractatus*. He also tried to show that what counts as "agreement or disagreement with reality" takes on as many different forms as there are different use of language and cannot, therefore, be taken as given *prior* to the detailed investigation of the use that is in question.

The *Tractatus* contains a remark strikingly like something that Evans-Pritchard says.

The limits of my language mean the limits of my world. Logic fills the world: the limits of the world are also its limits. We cannot therefore say in logic: This and this there is in the world, and that there is not.

For that would apparently presuppose that we exclude certain possibilities, and this cannot be the case since otherwise logic must get outside the limits of the world: that is, if it could consider these limits from the other side also.[13]

Evans-Pritchard discusses the phenomena of belief and scepticism, as they appear in Zande life. There *is* certainly widespread scepticism about certain things, for instance, about some of the powers claimed by witchdoctors or about the efficacy of certain magic medicines. But, he points out, such scepticism does not begin to overturn the mystical way of thinking, since it is necessarily expressed in terms belonging to that way of thinking.

> In this web of belief every strand depends on every other strand, and a Zande cannot get outside its meshes because this is the only world he knows. The web is not an external structure in which he is enclosed. It is the texture of his thought and he cannot think that his thought is wrong.[14]

Wittgenstein and Evans-Pritchard are concerned here with much the same problem, though the difference in the directions from which they approach it is important too. Wittgenstein, at the time of the *Tractatus*, spoke of "language", as if all language is fundamentally of the same kind and must have the same kind of "relation to reality"; but Evans-Pritchard is confronted by two languages which he recognizes as fundamentally different in kind, such that much of what may be expressed in the one has no possible counterpart in the other. One might, therefore, have expected this to lead to a position closer to that of the *Philosophical Investigations* than to that of the *Tractatus*. Evans-Pritchard is not content with elucidating the differences in the two concepts of reality involved; he wants to go further and say: our concept of reality is the correct one, the Azande are mistaken. But the difficulty is to see what "correct" and "mistaken" can mean in this context.

Let me return to the subject of contradictions. I have already noted that many contradictions we might expect to appear in fact do not in the context of Zande thought, where provision is made for avoiding them. But there are some situations of which this does not seem to be true, where what appear to us as obvious contradictions are left where they are, apparently unresolved. Perhaps this may be the foothold we are looking for, from which we can appraise the "correctness" of the Zande system.

Consider Zande notions about the inheritance of witchcraft. I have spoken so far only of the role of oracles in establishing whether or not someone is a witch. But there is a further and as we might think, more "direct" method of doing this, namely

by postmortem examination of a suspect's intestines for "witchcraft-substance". This may be arranged by his family after his death in an attempt to clear the family name of the imputation of witchcraft. Evans-Pritchard remarks: "To our minds it appears evident that if a man is proven a witch the whole of his clan are *ipso facto* witches, since the Zande clan is a group of persons related biologically to one another through the male line. Azande see the sense of this argument but they do not accept its conclusions, and it would involve the whole notion of witchcraft in contradiction were they to do so."[15] Contradiction would presumably arise because a few positive results of post-mortem examinations, scattered among all the clans, would very soon prove that everbody was a witch, and a few negative results, scattered among the same clans, would prove that nobody was a witch. Though, in particular situations, individual Azande may avoid personal implications arising out of the presence of witchcraft-substance in deceased relatives, by imputations of bastardy and similar devices, this would not be enough to save the generally contradictory situation I have sketched. Evans-Pritchard comments: "Azande do not perceive the contradiction as we perceive it because they have no theoretical interest in the subject, and those situations in which they express their belief in witchcraft do not force the problem upon them."[16]

It might now appear as though we had clear grounds for speaking of the superior rationality of European over Zande thought, in so far as the latter involves a contradiction which it makes no attempt to remove and does not even recognize: one, however, which is recognizable as such in the context of European ways of thinking. But does Zande thought on this matter really involve a contradiction? It appears from Evans-Pritchard's account that Azande do not press their ways of thinking about witches to a point at which they would be involved in contradictions.

Someone may now want to say that the irrationality of the Azande in relation to witchcraft shows itself in the fact that they do not press their thought about it "to its logical conclusion". To appraise this point we must consider whether the conclusion we are trying to force on them is indeed a logical one; or perhaps better, whether someone who does press this conclusion is being more rational than the Azande, who do not. Some light is thrown on this question by Wittgenstein's discussion of a game.

such that whoever begins can always win by a particular simple trick. But this has not been realized – so it is a game. Now someone draws our attention to it – and it stops being a game.

What turn can I give this, to make it clear to myself? – For I want to say: "and it stops being a game" – not: "and now we see that it wasn't a game."

That means, I want to say, it can also be taken like this: the other man did not *draw our attention* to anything; he taught us a different game in place of our own. But how can the new game have made the old one obsolete? We now see something different, and can no longer naïvely go on playing.

On the one hand the game consisted in our actions (our play) on the board; and these actions I could perform as well now as before. But on the other hand it was essential to the game that I blindly tried to win; and now I can no longer do that.[17]

There are obviously considerable analogies between Wittgenstein's example and the situation we are considering. But there is an equally important difference. Both Wittgenstein's games; the old one without the trick that enables the starter to win and the new one with the trick, are in an important sense on the same level. They are both *games*, in the form of a contest where the aim of a player is to beat his opponent by the exercise of skill. The new trick makes this situation impossible and this is why it makes the old game obsolete. To be sure, the situation could be saved in a way by introducing a new rule, forbidding the use by the starter of the trick which would ensure his victory. But our intellectual habits are such as to make us unhappy about the artificiality of such a device, rather as logicians have been unhappy about the introduction of a Theory of Types as a device for avoiding Russell's paradoxes. It is noteworthy in my last quotation from Evans-Pritchard however, that the Azande, when the possibility of this contradiction about the inheritance of witchcraft is pointed out to them, do *not* then come to regard their old beliefs about witchcraft as obsolete. "They have

no theoretical interest in the subject." This suggests strongly that the context from which the suggestion about the contradiction is made, the context of our scientific culture, is not on the same level as the context in which the beliefs about witchcraft operate. Zande notions of witchcraft do not constitute a theoretical system in terms of which Azande try to gain a quasi-scientific understanding of the world.[18] This in its turn suggests that it is the European, obsessed with pressing Zande thought where it would not naturally go – to a contradiction – who is guilty of misunderstanding, not the Zande. The European is in fact committing a category-mistake.

Something else is also suggested by this discussion: the forms in which rationality expresses itself in the culture of a human society cannot be elucidated *simply* in terms of the logical coherence of the rules according to which activities are carried out in that society. For as we have seen, there comes a point where we are not even in a position to determine what is and what is not coherent in such a context of rules, without raising questions about the point which following those rules has in the society. No doubt it was a realization of this fact which led Evans-Pritchard to appeal to a residual "correspondence with reality" in distinguishing between "mystical" and "scientific" notions. The conception of reality is indeed indispensable to any understanding of the point of a way of life. But it is not a conception which can be explicated as Evans-Pritchard tries to explicate it, in terms of what science reveals to be the case; for a form of the conception of reality must already be presupposed before we can make any sense of the expression "what science reveals to be the case."

2 Our Standards and Theirs

… In a discussion of Wittgenstein's philosophical use of language games[19] Mr Rush Rhees points out that to try to account for the meaningfulness of language solely in terms of isolated language games is to omit the important fact that ways of speaking are not insulated from each other in mutually exclusive systems of rules. What can be said in one context by the use of a certain expression depends for its sense on the uses of that expression in other contexts (different language games).

Language games are played by men who have lives to live – lives involving a wide variety of different interests, which have all kinds of different bearings on each other. Because of this, what a man says or does may make a difference not merely to the performance of the activity upon which he is at present engaged, but to his *life* and to the lives of other people. Whether a man sees point in what he is doing will then depend on whether he is able to see any unity in his multifarious interests, activities, and relations with other men; what sort of sense he sees in his life will depend on the nature of this unity. The ability to see this sort of sense in life depends not merely on the individual concerned, though this is not to say it does not depend on him at all; it depends also on the possibilities for making such sense which the culture in which he lives does, or does not, provide.

What we may learn by studying other cultures are not merely possibilities of different ways of doing things, other techniques. More importantly we may learn different possibilities of making sense of human life, different ideas about the possible importance that the carrying out of certain activities may take on for a man, trying to contemplate the sense of his life as a whole. This dimension of the matter is precisely what MacIntyre misses in his treatment of Zande magic; he can see in it only a (misguided) technique for producing consumer goods. But a Zande's crops are not just potential objects of consumption: the life he lives, his relations with his fellows, his chances for acting decently or doing evil, may all spring from his relation to his crops. Magical rites constitute a form of expression in which these possibilities and dangers may be contemplated and reflected on – and perhaps also thereby transformed and deepened. The difficulty we find in understanding this is not merely its remoteness from science, but an aspect of the general difficulty we find, illustrated by MacIntyre's procedure, of thinking about such matters at all except in terms of "efficiency of production" – production, that is, for consumption. This again is a symptom of what Marx called the "alienation" characteristic of man in industrial society, though Marx's own confusions about the relations between production and consumption are further symptoms of that same alienation. Our blindness to the point of primitive modes of life is

a corollary of the pointlessness of much of our own life.

I have now explicitly linked my discussion of the "point" of a system of conventions with conceptions of good and evil. My aim is not to engage in moralizing, but to suggest that the concept of *learning from* which is involved in the study of other cultures is closely linked with the concept of *wisdom*. We are confronted not just with different techniques, but with new possibilities of good and evil, in relation to which men may come to terms with life. An investigation into this dimension of a society may indeed require a quite detailed inquiry into alternative techniques (e.g., of production), but an inquiry conducted for the light it throws on those possibilities of good and evil. A very good example of the kind of thing I mean is Simone Weil's analysis of the techniques of modern factory production in *Oppression and Liberty*, which is not a contribution to business management, but part of an inquiry into the peculiar form which the evil of oppression takes in our culture.

In saying this, however, I may seem merely to have lifted to a new level the difficulty raised by MacIntyre of how to relate our own conceptions of rationality to those of other societies. Here the difficulty concerns the relation between our own conceptions of good and evil and those of other societies. A full investigation would thus require a discussion of ethical relativism at this point. I have tried to show some of the limitations of relativism in an earlier paper.[20] I shall close the chapter with some remarks which are supplementary to that.

I wish to point out that the very conception of human life involves certain fundamental notions – which I shall call "limiting notions" – which have an obvious ethical dimension, and which indeed in a sense determine the "ethical space", within which the possibilities of good and evil in human life can be exercised. The notions which I shall discuss very briefly here correspond closely to those which Vico made the foundation of his idea of natural law, on which he thought the possibility of understanding human history rested: birth, death, sexual relations. Their significance here is that they are inescapably involved in the life of all known human societies in a way which gives us a clue where to look, if we are puzzled about the point of an alien system of institutions. The specific forms which these concepts take, the particular institutions in which they are expressed, vary very considerably from one society to another; but their central position within a society's institutions is and must be a constant factor. In trying to understand the life of an alien society, then, it will be of the utmost importance to be clear about the way in which these notions enter into it. The actual practice of social anthropologists bears this out, although I do not know how many of them would attach the same kind of importance to them as I do.

I speak of a "limit" here because these notions, along no doubt with others, give shape to what we understand by "human life," and because a concern with questions posed in terms of them seems to me constitutive of what we understand by the "morality" of a society. In saying this, I am of course, disagreeing with those moral philosophers who have made attitudes of approval and disapproval, or something similar, fundamental in ethics, and who have held that the *objects* of such attitudes were conceptually irrelevant to the conception of morality. On that view, there might be a society where the sorts of attitude taken up in *our* society to questions about relations between the sexes were reserved, say for questions about the length people wear their hair, and *vice versa*. This seems to me incoherent. In the first place, there would be a confusion in *calling* a concern of that sort a "moral" concern, however passionately felt. The story of Samson in the Old Testament confirms rather than refutes this point, for the interdict on the cutting of Samson's hair is, of course, connected there with much else: and preeminently, it should be noted, with questions about sexual relations. But secondly, if that is thought to be merely verbal quibbling, I will say that it does not seem to me a merely conventional matter that T. S. Eliot's trinity of "birth, copulation and death" happen to be such deep objects of human concern. I do not mean that they are made such by fundamental psychological and sociological forces, though that is no doubt true. But I want to say further that the very notion of human life is limited by these conceptions.

Unlike beasts, men do not merely live but also have a conception of life. This is not something that is simply added to their life; rather, it changes the very sense which the word "life" has, when applied to men. It is no longer equivalent to "animate existence." When we are speaking of the life of man, we can ask questions about what is the right way to live, what things are most important in life, whether life has any significance, and if so what.

To have a conception of life is also to have a conception of death. But just as the "life" that is here in question is not the same as animate existence, so the "death" that is here in question is not the same as the end of animate existence. My conception of the death of an animal is of an event that will take place in the world; perhaps I shall observe it – and my life will go on. But when I speak of "my death," I am not speaking of a future event in my life;[21] I am not even speaking of an event in anyone else's life. I am speaking of the cessation of my world. That is also a cessation of my ability to do good or evil. It is not just that *as a matter of fact* I shall no longer be able to do good or evil after I am dead; the point is that my very *concept* of what it is to be able to do good or evil is deeply bound up with my concept of my life as ending in death. If ethics is a concern with the right way to live, then clearly the nature of this concern must be deeply affected by the concept of life as ending in death. One's attitude to one's life is at the same time an attitude to one's death.

This point is very well illustrated in an anthropological datum which MacIntyre confesses himself unable to make any sense of.

> According to Spencer and Gillen some aborigines carry about a stick or stone which is treated *as if* it is or embodies the soul of the individual who carries it. If the stick or stone is lost, the individual anoints himself as the dead are anointed. Does the concept of "carrying one's soul about with one" make sense? Of course we can redescribe what the aborigines are doing and transform it into sense, and perhaps Spencer and Gillen (and Durkheim who follows them) misdescribe what occurs. But if their reports are not erroneous, we confront a blank wall here, so far as meaning is concerned, although it is easy to give the rules for the use of the concept.[22]

MacIntyre does not say why he regards the concept of carrying one's soul about with one in a stick "thoroughly incoherent." He is presumably influenced by the fact that it would be hard to make sense of an action like this if performed by a twentieth-century Englishman or American; and by the fact that the soul is not a material object like a piece of paper and cannot, therefore, be carried about in a stick as a piece of paper might be. But it does not seem to me as hard to see sense in the practice, even from the little we are told about it here. Consider that a lover in our society may carry about a picture or lock of hair of the beloved; that this may symbolize for him his relation to the beloved and may, indeed, change the relation in all sorts of ways: for example, strengthening it or perverting it. Suppose that when the lover loses the locket he feels guilty and asks his beloved for her forgiveness: there might be a parallel here to the aboriginal's practice of anointing himself when he "loses his soul." And is there necessarily anything irrational about either of these practices? Why should the lover not regard his carelessness in losing the locket as a sort of betrayal of the beloved? Remember how husbands and wives may feel about the loss of a wedding ring. The aborigine is clearly expressing a concern with his life as a whole in this practice; the anointing shows the close connection between such a concern and contemplation of death. Perhaps it is precisely this practice which makes such a concern possible for him, as religious sacraments make certain sorts of concern possible. The point is that a concern with one's life as a whole, involving as it does the limiting conception of one's death, if it is to be expressed *within* a person's life, can necessarily only be expressed quasi-sacramentally. The form of the concern shows itself in the form of the sacrament.

The sense in which I spoke also of sex as a "limiting concept" again has to do with the concept of a human life. The life of a man is a man's life and the life of a woman is a woman's life: the masculinity or the femininity are not just *components* in the life, they are its *mode*. Adapting Wittgenstein's remark about death, I might say that my masculinity is not an experience in the world, but my way of experiencing the world. Now the concepts of masculinity and femininity obviously require each other. A man is a man in relation to women; and a woman is a woman in relation to men.[23] Thus the form taken by man's relation to women is of quite fundamental importance for the significance he can attach to his own life. The vulgar identification of morality with sexual morality certainly *is* vulgar; but it is a vulgarization of an important truth.

The limiting character of the concept of birth is obviously related to the points I have sketched regarding death and sex. On the one hand, my birth is no more an event in my life than is my death; and through my birth ethical limits are set for my life quite independently of my will: I am, from the outset, in specific relations to other people, from which obligations spring which cannot but be ethically fundamental.[24] On the other hand, the concept of birth is fundamentally linked to that of relations between the sexes. This remains true, however much or little may be known in a society about the contribution of males and females to procreation; for it remains true that man is born of woman, not of man. This, then, adds a new dimension to the ethical institutions in which relations between the sexes are expressed.

I have tried to do no more, in these last brief remarks, than to focus attention in a certain direction. I have wanted to indicate that forms of these limiting concepts will necessarily be an important feature of any human society and that conceptions of good and evil in human life will necessarily be connected with such concepts. In any attempt to understand the life of another society, therefore, an investigation of the forms taken by such concepts – their role in the life of the society – must always take a central place and provide a basis on which understanding may be built.

> Now since the world of nations has been made by men, let us see in what institutions men agree and always have agreed. For these institutions will be able to give us the universal and eternal principles (such as every science must have) on which all nations were founded and still preserve themselves.
>
> We observe that all nations, barbarous as well as civilized, though separately founded because remote from each other in time and space, keep these three human customs: all have some religion, all contract solemn marriages, all bury their dead. And in no nation, however savage end crude, are any human actions performed with more

elaborate ceremonies and more sacred solemnity than the rites of religion, marriage and burial. For by the axiom that "uniform ideas, born among peoples unknown to each other, must have a common ground of truth", it must have been dictated to all nations that from these institutions humanity began among them all, and therefore they must be most devoutly guarded by them all, so that the world should not again become a bestial wilderness. For this reason we have taken these three eternal and universal customs as the first principles of this Science.[25]

Notes

1 At this point the anthropologist is very likely to start speaking of the "social function" of the institution under examination. There are many important questions that should be raised about functional explanations and their relations to the issues discussed in this essay; but these questions cannot be pursued further here.

2 E. E. Evans-Pritchard, "Lévy-Bruhl's Theory of Primitive Mentality," *Bulletin of the Faculty of Arts*, University of Egypt, 1934.

3 "Science and Sentiment," *Bulletin of the Faculty of Arts*, ibid., 1935.

4 Indeed, one way of expressing the point of the story of Job is to say that in it Job is shown as going astray by being induced to make the reality and goodness of God contingent on what happens.

5 R. G. Collingwood, *Principles of Art*, Oxford (Galaxy Books), 1958, p. 67.

6 *Witchcraft, Oracles and Magic among the Azande*, p. 64.

7 The italics are mine throughout this quotation.

8 Op. cit., p. 12.

9 For further criticism of Pareto see Peter Winch, *The Idea of a Social Science*, pp. 95–111.

10 Evans-Pritchard's italics.

11 Op. cit., p. 72.

12 Ibid., p. 319.

13 Wittgenstein, *Tractatus Logico-Philosophicus*, 5. 6–5. 61.

14 Evans-Pritchard, op. cit., p. 194.

15 Ibid., p. 24.

16 Ibid., p. 25.

17 L. Wittgenstein, *Remarks on the Foundations of Mathematics*, Pt. II, Para. 77. Wittgenstein's whole discussion of "contradiction" in mathematics is directly relevant to the point I am discussing.

18 Notice that I have *not* said that Azande conceptions of witchcraft have nothing to do with understanding the world at all. The point is that a different form of the concept of understanding is involved here.

19 Rush Rhees, "Wittgenstein's Builders," *Proceedings of the Aristotelian Society*, vol. 20, 1960, pp. 171–86.

20 Peter Winch, "Nature and Convention," *Proceedings of the Aristotelian Society*, vol. 20, 1960, pp. 231–52.

21 Cf. Wittgenstein, *Tractatus Logico-Philosophicus*, 6.431–6.4311.

22 Alasdair MacIntyre, *Is Understanding Religion Compatible with Believing?* read to the Sesquicentennial Seminar of the Princeton Theological Seminar (1962).

23 These relations, however, are not simple converses. See Georg Simmel, "Das Relative und das Absolute im Geschlechter-Problem" in *Philosophische Kultur*, Leipzig, 1911.

24 For this reason, among others, I think A.I. Melden is wrong to say that present-child obligations and rights have nothing directly to do with physical genealogy. Cf. Melden, *Rights and Right Conduct* Oxford (Blackwell), 1959.

25 Giambattists Vico, *The New Science*, paras 332–3.

18

The Moral Economy of Witchcraft
An Essay in Comparative History

Ralph A. Austen[1]

In a recent study of slave trading, the Beninois historian Abiola Felix Iroko (1988:199) notes with some embarrassment an oral tradition about the provenance of cowry shells, a major currency in this commerce. According to indigenous informants, cowries were obtained by killing slaves, floating their bodies in the Atlantic Ocean, and pulling them back after cowries bad adhered to the corpses.[2]

Such local knowledge not only clashes with our empirical information on the origin of cowry shells – Iroko reminds us that they were imported to West Africa from the Indian Ocean via Europe – but also contradicts the entire body of analysis built around recent economic studies of the slave trade. Precisely by focusing on a commodity like cowries, these studies have argued for the relevance of market principles in understanding African development. First of all, it can be demonstrated that the movements of cowries and slaves across a complex international market operated according to predictable patterns of supply and demand; second, in the interior of West Africa, large-scale imports of shell currency allowed the monetization (and thus market expansion) of transactions in foodstuffs and other local consumer items (Hogendorn and Johnson 1986).

The equation of cowries with slave corpses derives from a very different view of what such commerce meant both within Africa and in African relations with the wider world. It does not take much imagination to understand why death should be the metaphor for a traffic built upon the removal of human beings from their home continent, many to a literal death but virtually all to "a bourn from which no traveller returns." The more challenging task is to consider how fully the perception embodied in such terms represents an alternative to the concept of market rationality and its encompassing discourse of modernization.

[...]

Witchcraft, as used here, is [...] an abstraction, [...] intended to represent directly the terms used by African and other societies to describe their own beliefs and practices. The introductory section of this chapter will attempt to identify an African witchcraft idiom which gives broader meaning to texts such as the Beninois oral account

From Ralph A. Austen, "The Moral Economy of Witchcraft: An Essay in Comparative History", *Modernity and Its Malcontents*, ed. Jean Comaroff and John Comaroff (1993), University of Chicago Press, pp. 89–110.

of slave–cowry transactions. The concluding section of this chapter will examine the early modern European "witch craze" in order to consider how the elaboration of common elements in European and African culture both reflects and mediates differing trajectories into the modern world.

African Witchcraft Idiom as a Discourse of History and Power

The various issues surrounding witchcraft, including the comparison of African and European cases, have long been a staple of Africanist anthropological research.[3] All these discussions share a general definition of witchcraft as the use of preternatural power by one person to damage others. Almost all have focused on beliefs about such practices and the means used to counter them rather than on the practices themselves. All assume that beliefs of this kind have important social consequences and reflect the manner in which the peoples concerned understand their broader historical experience.

For purposes of the present analysis, two issues in African witchcraft studies are to be emphasized: (1) the kinds of social relationships involved in witchcraft accusations; and (2) the role of reproduction, sexuality, and gender in these beliefs.

Virtually all existing work, at least in rural Africa, indicates that witchcraft efficacy is held to be a direct function of the intimacy between witch and victim. Thus the vast majority of accusations and rituals involve relations between peers, kin, and co-wives: the corollary being that, with greater social distance, such accusations would decline (Douglas 1970: xxx–xxxi; Marwick 1982:377ff.). Recent research, however, shows African turban elites to be afraid that those left behind in their villages are bewitching either them or the state projects with which they identify (Geschiere 1988; Ciekawy 1990 [...]). Also, while formal witchcraft accusations against the powerful and wealthy are rare, it has "become a commonplace observation in African studies" (Rowlands and Warnier 1988:121) that such ascendent individuals are perceived to be witches.

Commonplace as it may be, the equation of witchcraft with the attainment of power and wealth has been neglected in the anthropological literature, which has mainly focused on the sociology of formal witchcraft accusations. However, it is witchcraft beliefs that cross hierarchical boundaries that enter most directly into the concerns of this chapter: the contemplation of historical change by Africans, the competition of witchcraft idioms with the discourses of markets and modernization, and their comparison with early modern European antiwitchcraft beliefs.[4]

For this purpose, van Binsbergen (1981:141–2) provides a very useful distinction between "impersonal" and "anti-personal" witchcraft. The latter consists of misfortunes attributed to the ill will of peers with whom some identifiable tension already exists. It is this category which Marwick (1982:330) probably had in mind when he asserted that "increased tensions attendant upon urbanization are not necessarily expressed in the idiom of witchcraft." Impersonal witchcraft, on the other hand is defined by van Binsbergen (1981:163) in terms all too easily linked to modern situations as "the reckless manipulation of human material for strictly individual purposes."

In rural Africa the human material manipulated by witchcraft is frequently identified with control over the forces constituting the reproduction of everyday life. In the most unproblematic circumstances, these forces are contained within the domestic sphere of conjugal sexuality and food cultivation and consumption. Congenital witches are almost always described as insatiably hungry: they seek to "eat" others by imbibing their reproductive powers in the form of corpses, children, sexual fluids, and so on.

A number of studies (Goody 1970; Gottlieb 1989) have noted a distinction between female witches, who are totally stigmatized, and males who are recognized as both witches and legitimate figures of political and ritual authority. The distinctions do not lie in the activities or immediate relationships to reproduction and production which identify each category as witches: all may be guilty of killing and consuming close relatives, and the males may procure wealth only by predation upon surrounding societies. Rather it is the *public* positions held by the men in question that makes their witchcraft somehow more tolerable and even, in some cases, celebrated. This acceptance of "official" witchcraft is generally explained as a form of resignation: antiwitchcraft measures are ineffective against such concentrations of power (Rowlands and Warnier 1988:121). But it is also recognized that many Africans take the existence of witchcraft to be inevitable and ubiquitous; there is thus positive value in the fact that some figures of authority have the mystical power to ward off the malignancy of others. This need is particularly strong when the dangers come from outside the community and can only be combated by kings and diviners of one's own (Goody 1970; Austen 1986).

The conception of witchcraft as an ambiguous attribute of power within Africa is often presented in ahistorical terms, as a timeless reflection of the tension between communal values and selfish individualism and anxieties about natural threats to subsistence. Our data on witch beliefs, however, are all relatively recent; with little exception they are drawn from societies that had long been involved with either the Islamic or European outside world. It is striking that several West Central African cosmologies link witchcraft with the deployment of victims in a nocturnal and/or distant "second universe," echoing, in more or less explicit terms, the experience of the Atlantic slave trade (Hagenburcher-Sacripanti 1973:143–63; Rosny 1985:58–63; McGaffey 1986; Miller 1988:4–5).

The Beninois explanation of cowry imports should now appear more familiar, not only as a metaphorical account of the slave trade but also as the expression of a discourse equating the acquisition of wealth and power with (1) the consumption of human life and (2) links to a more powerful outside world. But if we are to assert the relevance of this discourse for understanding the wider African experience of historical change, we need to consider it in more general terms. The witchcraft idiom in Africa echoes perceptions elsewhere in the world of relationships between communal norms and externally centered market economies. The comparison of these perceptions and relationships by social scientists has produced its own metadiscourse around the concept of moral economy.

The Moral Economy Debate: Microeconomics and Culture

The central trope of the various efforts to define moral economy has been an opposition between, on the one hand, the maximizing individual and the everexpanding market of classical political economy and, on the other, a community governed by norms of collective survival and believing in a zero–sum universe – that is, a world where all profit is gained at someone else's loss. The communal/zero–sum side of this equation is broadly consistent with African beliefs identifying capitalism and witchcraft as the dangerous appropriation of limited reproductive resources by selfish individuals. The great danger of such a set of dichotomies is that it may remain trapped where it first originated, within the discourse of capitalism itself. Exotic economies thus become constructed around either a market/non-market opposition or a subsistence-based variant of market rationality. In analyzing the history of societies confronting capitalism, even from the outside of the bottom one cannot reject out of hand all references to capitalist terms. [...]

The term "moral economy" actually came into wide scholarly use through the study of early capitalist Europe, specifically with E. P. Thompson's writings on eighteenth-century Britain (Thompson 1968:225–6, 1971); its application to the Third World awaited the somewhat later book of James Scott (1976). Scott, according to his references, was indeed inspired by Thompson; yet Thompson had predecessors who were more concerned than he with non-Western economies and remain more directly relevant to the genesis of moral economy theory and its role in studying Africa.

It was the substantivist economics of Karl Polanyi[5] and his associates (1957) that initiated a sophisticated argument among anthropologists and historians about the relevance of market models to the study of economies outside of the modern West (LeClair and Schneider 1968; Hopkins 1973; Dalton 1974). The substantivists, who questioned those models ultimately lost most of the arguments. On an abstract level, their "non-market" terms (derived from a somewhat naive reading of structural-functionalist anthropology) were easily converted into "collective utilities": more concretely, what substantivists defined as uniquely Western market behavior could be documented in large portions of "primitive" and "archaic" Africa. Polanyi's explicitly Aristotelian critique of profit seeking is a perfect example of what Parry and Bloch (1989:2–3) identify as a fatal ethnocentrism in interpreting "the morality of exchange" in societies outside Europe. [...]

The more robust notion of a zero-sum universe as the basis for "traditional" economic behavior derives from the ethnographic work of George Foster (1965). Foster argued that peasants everywhere experience a world of "the limited good,"[6] but he regarded such attitudes as obstacles to both progress and true communal cohesion, much as did the more acerbic Edward Banfield (1958). Foster and Banfield are rarely cited in moral economy literature because their developmentalist outlook fits ill with the ideological stance in most of this writing; however, their vision of negative utilitarianism states most clearly its underlying premises.

Thus, in his original formulation of moral economy, Scott attributes to Third World (and even European) peasants a formal economic logic far more akin to the approach of the unnamed Foster than to the acknowledged Thompson and Polanyi. Having decided that these cultivators maintain a "subsistence ethic," Scott undertakes what he considers a sympathetic analysis of their actions by replacing the motive of profit maximization with one of risk aversion (Scott 1976:4ff.). It was thus possible for Popkin (1979) to produce a work ostensibly criticizing Scott for neglecting evidence of profit-oriented entrepreneurship in peasant communities, while actually providing a very similar picture of the calculations underlying rural Southeast Asian responses to colonial capitalism (Hunt 1988).

[...]

Nonetheless, the moral economy school has a good deal to teach those more seriously concerned with culture. Most obviously, it demands that attention be paid to the conditions of access to material resources that determine, with some degree of autonomy, the understandings of capitalism possible within any community. Furthermore, in the revised versions it provides detailed, socially sensitive accounts of political and economic strategies that illuminate any discussion of ideology.

[...]

The Moral Economy of the European Witch Craze

[...]

The comparison of African and European witchcraft studies is complicated by the fact that the former are mainly based on ethnographies of contemporary village culture, while the latter focus on the written records of now-vanished urban elites who imposed themselves upon rural society. Nonetheless, the two sets of cases share a base of rural beliefs in interpersonal witchcraft as well as a confrontation with capitalist modernization. The comparison can thus, at the very least, help to historicize further our understanding of African witchcraft and add cultural context to our understanding of European capitalism. In pursuit of these goals, my discussion of European witch-hunting will focus on three issues: the relationship between urban/elite and rural/popular culture in defining witchcraft, the role of reproduction and female sexuality within these definitions, and the process by which European witchcraft beliefs gave way to both capitalist utilitarianism and various forms of moral economy/socialist anticapitalism.

The early modern European persecutions allow us, far more easily than do the African cases, to identify two socially distinct sets of beliefs about witchcraft and the vectors of its operation. Corresponding to the Africanist notion of interpersonal witchcraft was the European term *maleficium*, literally referring to the use of preternatural powers as an expression of malice among village neighbors. At the center of the formal witch trials which resulted in the tens of thousands of public executions for witchcraft lay the elite concept of the *sabbat*, an orgiastic sacrificial ritual presided over by Satan.

Although the difference between these definitions of mystical evil is critical to understanding the persecutions in early modern Europe, it is also necessary, particularly for purposes of comparison of Africa, to recognize the ideological and practical links between them. *Maleficium* accusations, from what we know of them, seem remarkably similar to local witchcraft allegations in Africa. What we cannot easily see through existing records is the larger systems of popular beliefs within which such ideas functioned.[7]

The *sabbat*, on the other hand has no real parallel in African witchcraft belief or even "syncretistic" Christianity, because it was imagined as a specifically counter-Christian cult. Undoubtedly the content of this putative ritual, if not its structure, derived from European folk culture. Moreover, the condemnation of individuals as participants in a witches' sabbath required that they (or at least their immediate accusers) first be charged by neighbors with *maleficium*. Confessions of congress with the devil usually depended upon suggestions from the prosecutors, reinforced by torture. But there are significant cases in which villagers provided such statements spontaneously, indicating that they, too, had come to believe in the *sabbat*. As will be seen below (this chap.), this belief may have rested upon European understandings of sexuality which turn out to be critical for comparison with Africa.

The attribution of European witchcraft persecution to the rise of capitalism emerged from the study of trials in England, where both torture and *sabbat* beliefs were largely absent (Macfarlane 1970:195–97; Thomas 1971:553–67, 581–2). The argument here is that the direction of *maleficium* accusations from wealthier members toward more impoverished members of the community reflected a shift from a redistributive to an accumulative (i.e., capitalist) mode of property control. This thesis has recently been called into question: it seems not to explain the scale and timing of accusations found throughout Europe in the early modern period.[8]

However, comparison with recent African material (Geschiere 1988 [...]) suggests that such fears by newly emergent elites – and even the use of witchcraft threats by their rural neighbors or ex-neighbors – are indeed a common phenomenon in times of economic transition. But, in any case, if our aim is to understand the cultural content rather than the behavioral patterns of witchcraft accusations in these circumstances, we must give more attention to the *sabbat* than to *maleficium*.

In the *sabbat*, as in African ideas of "official" witchcraft, the deployment of preternatural malignancy against individuals is equated with concentrations of power in the public arena. The European *sabbat*, however, was formulated mainly by elites among the clergy and judiciary who accused poor and marginal individuals of allying themselves with Satan, the unambiguous antithesis of all legitimate temporal and spiritual authority. Before spelling out the contrasts with Africa, it is useful to consider the interpretations by historians of what, for them, is a puzzling similarity between

early modern Europe and primitive society. How could some of the most educated of our post-Renaissance ancestors, on the verge of the Enlightenment and the industrial revolution, have subscribed to, and worse still, acted violently upon, such "primitive superstitions"?

For Trevor-Roper (1968:90–192), who poses the question in just these terms, the answer lay in some irreducible substratum of irrational human hatred which, during the period in question, was inspired by the religious rivalries of the Reformation and counter-Reformation. Reformed religion is certainly critical to understanding the witch persecutions, but its role must be understood through a more serious social and cultural analysis than Trevor-Roper even begins to envisage. Muchembled (1987) and Ginzburg (1983) attempt such analyses by presenting the *sabbat* as a device by which the newly emerging centers of urban power stigmatized the autonomous culture of the countryside, thus promoting the establishment of a single hierarchy within each European state. This last argument, with its populist and Foucaultian overtones, has more contemporary appeal than the intellectualist approach of Trevor-Roper. But it suffers from an indifference to the content of elite witchcraft beliefs and their contradictory relationship to the rationalizing project they were apparently serving. An Africanist might further ask why in Africa, by contrast, neither indigenous intelligentsias (e.g., Iroko), mission-based churches, nor the colonial or postcolonial state have ever been very comfortable with recognizing the entire concept of witchcraft.[9] If witchcraft persecution was merely an unfortunate detour or an opportunistic strategy on the route to modernization, perhaps such discomfort is justified. But if it has some more intimate relationship with the genesis of capitalism in Europe, further questions need to be asked. One line of inquiry emerges from the obvious and discomforting links between witchcraft, gender, and sexuality.

In both Europe and Africa accusations of *maleficium* or its equivalent fall most heavily upon women. In Africa, however, the more elaborate beliefs about the use of witchcraft to attain material power tend to focus upon males or women active in the public sphere of the market place [...]. In Europe, on the other hand, women – usually with little power – still constitute the vast majority of those implicated in the most complex allegations of *sabbat* practice.

There has been no shortage of explanations for this misogynistic aspect of the European witch craze. Most commentators have stressed the vulnerability of women, particularly the older ones without husbands who were frequently charged. Yet, this is a universal condition that tells us little about the distinct situation of Europe in the sixteenth and seventeenth centuries. Muchembled (1987:67–9) provides a more historical argument that connects the rising modernism of this period with a "devalorization" of women who functioned as the main bearers of embattled rural/popular culture through their roles as healers, midwives, and purveyors of established norms and oral learning. There is much to be said for this last claim, as it suggests why specific aspects of rural culture should be so much under attack: it also helps us understand their later relegation to the realm of folklore with its gendered aura of "old wives' tales" and the nostalgic infantilization of the rural "moth erland." However, even here Muchembled (to say nothing of less nuanced feminist versions of this interpretation) reduces the specific *sabbat* charges under which women were convicted of witchcraft to mere devices of the learned urban elite for subjugating a competing source of power. The intensity with which *sabbat* ideas were apparently believed, and their high load of sexual content, suggests that they have to be taken more seriously if we want to explain the relationships between gender, witchcraft accusations, and the emergence of a modern capitalist order in Europe.[10]

From an Africanist perspective, the connection that immediately suggests itself is that of reproduction. For cases within Africa, it must be recalled, a central trope of witchcraft beliefs is the misappropriation of scarce reproductive resources from households or communities for the selfish use by accumulating individuals. Similar themes are found in European *maleficium* accusations, which frequently involve attacks on the fertility of fields, livestock, and other human beings (Briggs 1989:91; Le Roy Ladurie 1981). Such actions were sometimes attributed to the demands of Satan, and the rites of the *sabbat* regularly included the consumption of babies and fetuses. At a more abstract level, it also seems possible to identify, in both European and African representations of the sexuality of witches, a common concern with the escape of female reproductive power from the enclosed domestic space in which it serves male-dominated communal norms to the open nocturnal realms of self-contained female power (Levack 1987:126ff.).

A comparison of these representations and their historical contexts suggests, however, some important distinctions precisely around the issues of reproduction, gender politics, and accumulation. In rural Africa, reproduction (whether sexual or agricultural) and its potential misappropriation, that is, the zero-sum economy, remains a central cultural issue right through contemporary times. "Modernization" has not solved these problems; rather it has created a new category of witches in the urbanized "femmes libres," witches who literally use market control over their domestic reproductive capacities (sex, food, and even baths) for individualized accumulation (White 1990b). In the early modern European *sabbat* accounts, on the other hand, female sexuality seems to be severed from the issue of reproduction; these nightmare women are less independent of male authority than submissive to an alternative vision of masculine power, a vision opposed to the accumulative process with which the persecutors themselves identified. In short, European antiwitchcraft beliefs represent a moral economy *of*, and not opposed to, capitalism.

The frequent references to antireproductive acts in *maleficium* accusations suggest that European rural communities had concerns over maintaining the basic forces of life similar to those of Africa. As historians have regularly noted, however, the witch craze occurred in a period when population and food production capacities had recovered from earlier crises. Moreover, even in the more spontaneous rural European accounts, there is little echo of the classical African equations of witchcraft with eating and insatiable hunger. Moreover, the women accused were usually beyond reproductive age, and the striking feature of their sexuality was its continuation at this point in their lives. The many contemporary woodcut illustrations of the *sabbat* – itself a kind of licensed pornography for this era – focus on the sexual power of female witches; here they are often depicted as far younger than in the statistics of accusations, but in almost all cases they display firm breasts and buttocks, frequently being fondled in foreplay with the devil.[11]

The central role of Satan in the *sabbat* contrasts sharply with the modern African vision of witchcraft as a realm of autonomous female power. Women in the European accounts subject themselves to an alternative male authority through a conscious inversion of Christian ritual. The killing of children is a sacrificial act parodying communion (and recalling "blood libels" against Jews and other heretics) in which it is not the female witches who are nourished but rather the male anti-Christ. The sexual acts portrayed or reported sometimes include women cavorting among themselves, but more commonly concentrate on submission to Satan in acts that give no real pleasure; the devil's penis is always described as cold and pain inducing, and often it is his buttocks that are embraced.

With reference to broader social processes then, we may interpret the *sabbat* fantasy as a vision less of female reproductive power escaping male control than of male control in a mode diametrically opposed to the self-image of a reformed Christian elite. The terms of this opposition seem better understood through the categories of Max Weber than those of Muchembled. The question is not whether female sexuality, as a surrogate for rural culture, should be autonomous or subdued to an absolutist hierarchy but is, instead, whether the ethos of this subjugation should be one of orgiastic consumption or worldly asceticism. The issue of accumulation is not addressed directly in the discourse of witchcraft; however, the construction of female sexuality as a force liberated from reproductive imperatives implies a nonzero-sum universe in which both accumulation and reckless consumption of vital resources are now historical and equally "rational" possibilities. In the long-run development of European capitalism, the limitation of consumption was a critical choice, but no one could think in such terms at the time. Hence, we have the "non-rational" obsession with salvation in the afterlife – linked by Weber to capitalist accumulation – and the even more irrational premise of a satanic witch cult connected here with the repression of alternatives to such accumulation.

Unlike in Africa, therefore, the European witch in her most powerful form was the antithesis of the accumulator. If we look for a popular moral economy to oppose the reformed religious ethos of the witch hunts, we do not find it in rural witchcraft beliefs, which only fed the repression. Instead, such a counterculture expressed itself in the organizations and carnivals of misrule used during the early modern period to maintain traditional domestic order, mock the rich, and play publicly and often quite joyously with issues of sexuality and gender (Davis 1975:97–187). These practices, unlike the movements of Thompson's eighteenth century, did not directly address capitalism and could even, as Natalie Zemon Davis has noted, be channeled into the violent service of reformed religious intolerance. But in the rampant quality of even their religiosity they gave vent to energies that were culturally articulated along lines of community, reproduction, and the festive consumption of accumulated resources – thereby providing an antithesis to the spirit of witchcraft persecution.[12]

Historians of the European witch craze, who have differed so much over the analysis of its meaning and causes, disagree far less in their explanations of its demise in the late 1600s. Most scholars concur that the procedural rationality of witch-hunting finally overwhelmed the antirational premises upon which it had been based. For Trevor-Roper it was the combined destructiveness of religious warfare and the alternative worldview of the scientific revolution – previously committed to its own Neoplatonist demonology – that brought the shift. For Muchembled and some of his critics, the key was the successful erection of the absolutist state whose agents provided both a new, external enemy to rural populations and a self-critique of judicial operations based upon torture and rural folk beliefs. But again, it is Weber who provides the most useful insight into the political economy of the shift through his contention that the decline of ascetic capitalism was inevitable once its own success had made the abundance of goods so evident (Weber 1930:174ff.).

To develop this last point we must go well beyond Weber, who never himself either explicitly addressed the issue of witchcraft or explored the culture of the early eighteenth-century "consumer revolution" (McKendrick et al. 1982) which linked the era of the Protestant ethic to that of industrialization. However, if we accept the equation made above between the witch craze and the anticonsumption ethos of early capitalism, we can similarly associate the abandonment of witchcraft beliefs with Enlightenment liberalism's attacks upon European versions of zero-sum economics. The latter were expressed not through the idiom of witchcraft but rather by mercantilist trade policies, sumptuary-law restrictions on who could purchase what, and assumptions that increased wages would decrease labor incentives. From an Africanist perspective, it is more than ironic that this emergence of classical market ideology in eighteenth-century Europe depended upon the low-cost import from the Third World of commodities previously seen as luxuries – not least among them sugar produced by black slaves (Austen and Smith 1990). In Africa, it should be recalled, the export of those same slaves provides the major historical reference for the equation of capital accumulation, zero-sum economics, and witchcraft.

The decline of European witchcraft beliefs in the eighteenth century becomes more complicated if we contemplate the connections between the construction of women in witch-hunting doctrine and the cult of domesticity that accompanied nineteenth-century capitalism. The latter transformed woman from the devil's mate of the *sabbat*, a sexual force threatening both religious orthodoxy and productive enterprise, to the angel of the house, a desexualized guardian and reproducer of values endangered by the amorality of the surrounding marketplace (Cott 1977). Recent studies of rural women spinners in the protoindustrial textile industry (Medick 1984; Schneider 1989; Stone-Ferrier 1989) suggest an interesting transitional phase of revalorized female production and reproduction. Capitalists of this era explicitly calculated the benefits of women's labor both to their own factor costs and to the marriage opportunities of their employees. For their part the women, gathered together in semi-public spaces, spun not only flax but also rich and ambivalent narratives which used the idiom of witches and other preternatural forces to define the moral economy of their new situation.

This is not the place to trace such developments any further or to explore the dialectics of self-conscious domesticity in the transition to female activism in the modern public sphere. The important point for Africanists is to recognize that the middle-class domestic ideal – so heavily promoted by colonial missionaries – has its own history and moral economy; one that is not totally alien to the African idioms of reproduction and sexuality along with concerns over their relationship to market commerce.

The elite preemption and then exhaustion of the idiom of witchcraft in Europe did not – any more than the very imperfect functioning of the eighteenth-century grain markets – break down all barriers between capitalist political economy and popular moral economy. However, the latter now developed along the lines laid out by Thompson and Magagna, either negotiating the terms of capitalist expansion on the basis of existing contractual rights and obligations or converting to some version of modern socialist doctrine. In short, moral economy doctrine in Europe, even at a relatively early stage in the development of capitalism, constituted an opposing (and not always ineffectual) voice within the larger discourse that produced capitalism itself.

African efforts at socialism, on the other hand, have both aroused and deployed a continuing witchcraft idiom. To the extent that this socialism draws upon its colonial heritage and Eastern European models rather than local popular discourses, it has inspired an image of "l'état sorcier" in which public authorities exercise arbitrary control over such vital resources as medicine (Hours 1985). In one of the few tropical African cases where capitalism, both local and international, rather than the state is seen as the dominant force, the Kenyan novelist Ngugi wa Thiongo (1982) has produced a socialist vision which draws heavily upon an equation of individual wealth with the appropriation and exportation of indigenous life forces. However problematic may be Ngugi's prescriptions for cultural authenticity and socialism, his view of foreign capitalism thriving on African blood not only resembles the Beninois view of the slave trade but also draws upon long-standing Kenyan popular beliefs concerning vampirous collaboration between European technology and indigenous urban prostitutes (White 1990a).

Conclusion

This essay offers two rather opposing arguments about the relationship between culture and capitalism in Africa and Europe. On the one hand, it insists that, in both cases, there is a shared embeddedness of market rationality in a much wider discourse on moral economy, a discourse most dramatically demonstrated by the concern with witchcraft. In so doing, it seeks to subvert the hegemonic Western dichotomies between self/rational/modern and other/irrational/primitive and evoke greater empathy with African struggles to make sense of their contemporary predicament.

On the other hand, the comparison of Africa and Europe within the common terms of moral economy and witchcraft suggests some very profound differences. The African conception of the witch is tied to various forms of belief in a world where the apparent production of new wealth depends upon appropriating the scarce reproductive resources of others while collaborating with an arbitrary and destructive external power. The European vision of witchcraft is no less frightening, but it assumes an abundance rather than scarcity of the sexual energies required for reproduction. It could be, and eventually was, transcended and transformed by the same political and economic forces responsible for domestic witch hunts, industrialization, and overseas imperialism. In short, the innovative common road though witch-craft branches off into the conventional separate destinations of capitalist modernization and hegemony for Europe and marginalized domination for Africa. It is difficult, despite an Ngugi, even to depict African witchcraft idioms as a weapon of African resistance. Their immediate moral targets are other Africans while they leave the European bases of power mystified to a point where they can only be avoided, not effectively invaded.

What, finally, can be said to rescue the African vision from its subordinate position? Above all else, it represents a telling, truthful insight into the modern experience of the continent, especially at a moment when European concern for Africa becomes ever more remote and AIDS threatens local populations precisely in the realms of sexuality and reproduction. If this kind of truth is valid only for Africa, then it remains a badge of subordination. But it also may provoke a self-critique of the capitalist West (and neocapitalist Asia and Eastern Europe) in an era of massive ecological decay, of increasingly unclear links between production and the accumulation of wealth through the manipulation of stock markets, banks, and electronic media. Comparative history of this kind thus may show us not only how capitalism emerged from the unique circumstances of Europe but also how the self-proclaimed universal logic of capitalist discourse may have to subject itself to the moral and cultural interrogations of a new genre of witch finders.

Notes

1 John Comaroff and Peter Geschiere provided very helpful comments on earlier versions of this essay.

2 Following the initial presentation of this essay, colleagues have reported similar traditions from various parts of the West African coast.

3 [...] For older accounts, see Douglas 1970; Marwick 1982 [1970]. For more recent ones, Rowlands and Warnier 1988; Geschiere 1988.

4 For a comparison of African and European witchcraft concepts that stress the distinction between "primitive" and "complex" societies on the basis of what sort of malevolent behavior individuals actually confessed to, see Rowland 1990.

5 Cited by Scott (1976:6n) as "formative for my own work."

6 "Limited good" was translated into the more economistic "zero-sum" by one of Foster's commentators, but Foster accepted the term (Bennett 1966; Foster 1966).

7 I do not wish here to pursue the debate among either radical feminists (see Muchembled 1987 bibliography) or the more sober (but not entirely convincing) Carlo Ginzburg (1990, 1991) on the reconstruction of such a residual "pagan" culture.

8 Nonetheless, Muchembled (1987:175ff.), a critic of the Macfarlane/Thomas thesis relies on similar functionalist arguments (about disintegrating communal bonds) to explain the increase of *maleficium* accusations among Cambresis villagers.

9 Fiisy and Geschiere (1991) have examined recent efforts by the Cameroonian state to involve itself in

witchcraft accusations, but the practice seems restricted to one region of the country aad resembles the classic British cases of alleged *maleficium* by the poor and marginal against relatively wealthy fellow villagers.

10 What follows is perhaps the most speculative argument in this paper and can ultimately be defended only by far more empirical work than I have yet undertaken. The argument is supported, however, by the sharp contrast drawn in the work of, among others, Martin (1989) between the kinds of charges laid against witches by the Italian and Spanish Inquisition and Northern European accusations of *maleficium* and *sabbat* participation. This geographical and institutional distinction does not touch upon issues of

elite control over popular culture as represented in largely female activities; however, it does suggest a connection between the perceived sexuality of witchcraft and the centers of early modern capitalist development. On the other hand, Macfarlane (1987) argues that the precocious success of English capitalism rests precisely upon the absence of extreme witch persecution and its accompanying beliefs.

11 See examples of this iconography in Klaits (1985:54–65, 75); and Levack (1987:between 132–3).

12 Ginzburg and Muchembled have both (Le Goff and Schmitt 1981:131–40, 229–36) attempted to assimilate the history of these youth organizations to their respective arguments on witchcraft; this is not the place to pursue the debate any further.

References

Ankarloo, Bengt, and Gustav Henningsen, eds. 1990. *Early Modern Witchcraft: Centres and Peripheries.* Oxford: Clarendon.

Arnold, David. 1984*a*. Gramsci and Peasant Subalternity in India. *Journal of Peasant Studies* 11:155–77.

Arnold, David. 1984*b*. Famine in Peasant Consciousness and Peasant Action: Madras 1876–78. In *Subaltern Studies, III*, ed. R. Guha. Delhi: Oxford University Press.

Austen, Ralph A. 1986. The Criminal and the African Cultural Imagination: Normative and Deviant Heroism in Precolonial and Modern Narratives. *Africa* 56:385–98.

Austen, Ralph A., and Woodruf Smith. 1990. Private Tooth Decay as Public Economic Virtue: The Atlantic Slave-Sugar Triangle, Consumerism and European Industrialization. *Social Science History* 14:95–115.

Banfield, Edward C. 1958. *The Moral Basis of a Backward Society.* New York: Free Press.

Bennett, John W. 1966. Further Remarks on Foster's "Image of the Limited Good." *American Anthropologist* 68:206–10.

Berry, Sara. 1985. *Fathers Work for Their Sons: Accumulation, Mobility and Class Formation in an Extended Yoruba Community.* Berkeley: University of California Press.

Briggs, Robin. 1989. *Communities of Belief: Cultural and Social Tensions in Early Modern France.* Oxford: Clarendon Press.

Ciekaway, Diane. 1990. Utsai and the State: The Politics of Witchcraft Eradication in Coastal Kenya. Unpublished paper, African Studies Workshop, University of Chicago.

Cohn, Norman. 1975. *Europe's Inner Demons: an Enquiry Inspired by the Great Witch Hunt.* New York: Basic Books.

Cott, Nancy F. 1977. *The Bonds of Womanhood. Woman's Sphere in New England, 1780–1835.* New Haven: Yale University Press.

Dalton, George. 1974. Review of Hopkins (1973). *African Economic History* 1:51–101.

Davis, Natalie Zemon. 1975. *Society and Culture in Early Modern France: Eight Essays.* Stanford: Stanford University Press.

Douglas, Mary, ed. 1970. *Witchcraft Confessions and Accusations.* London: Tavistock.

Fiisy, Cyprian S., and Peter Geschiere. 1991. Judges and Witches, or How Is the State to Deal with Witchcraft? Examples from Southeastern Cameroon. *Cahiers d'Etudes Africaines* 31:135–56.

Foster, George M. 1965. Peasant Society and the Image of the Limited Good. *American Anthropologist* 67:293–315.

Foster, George M. 1966. Reply to … Bennett. *American Anthropologist* 68:210–14.

Geschiere, Peter. 1988. Sorcery and the State: Popular Modes of Action among the Maka of Southeast, Cameroon. *Critique of Anthropology* 8:35–63.

Ginzburg. Carlo. 1983. *The Night Battles: Witchcraft and Agrarian Cults in the Sixteenth and Seventeenth Centuries.* Translated by John and Anne Tedeschi. Harmondsworth: Penguin.

Ginzburg, Caro. 1990. Deciphering the Sabbath. In Ankarlo and Henningsen.

Ginzburg, Caro. 1991. *Ecstacies: Deciphering the Witches Sabbath.* Translated by Raymond Rosenthal. New York: Pantheon.

Goody, Esther. 1970. Legitimate and Illegitimate Aggression in a West African State. In Douglas.

Gottlieb, Alma. 1989. Witches, Kings and the Sacrifice of Identity among the Beng of Ivory Coast. In *Creativity of Power: Cosmology and Art in African*

Societies. ed. W. Aren and I. Karp. Washington, D.C.: Smithsonian Institution.

Guha, Ranajit, and Gayatri Chakravorty Spivak, eds. 1988. *Selected Subaltern Studies.* New York: Oxford University Press.

Hagenburcher-Sacripanti, Frank. 1973. *Les fondements spirituels du pouvoir au royaume de Loango, republique populaire du Congo.* Paris: ORSTOM.

Harris, Olivia. 1989. The Earth and the State: The ... Meanings of Money in North Potosi, Bolivia. In Parry and Bloch.

Hogendorn, Jan, and Marion Johnson. 1986. *The Shell Money of the Slave Trade.* Cambridge: Cambridge University Press.

Hopkins, A. G. 1973. *An Economic History of West Africa.* New York: Columbia University Press.

Hours, Bernard. 1985. *L'état sorcier: Sante publique et societe au Cameroun.* Paris: L'Harmattan.

Hunt, David. 1988. From the Millennial to the Everyday: James Scott's Search for the Essence of Peasant Politics. *Radical History Review* 42:155–72.

Iroko, Abiola Felix. 1988. Cauris et esclaves en Afrique occidentale entre le XVe el le XIXe siècles In *De la traite a l'esclavage, tone I: Ve–XVIIIe siècles.* ed. Serge Daget. Nantes: Centre de Recherche sur l'Histoire du Monde Atlantique.

Kahn, Joel. 1985. Peasant Ideologies in the Third World. *Annual Review of Anthropology* 14:49–75.

Klaits, Joseph. 1985. *Servants of Saten: The Age of the Witch Hunts.* Bloomington: Indiana University Press.

LeClaire, Edward E. Jr., and Harold Schneider, eds. 1968. *Economic Anthropology.* New York: Holt, Rinehart.

Le Goff, Jacques, and Jean-Claude Schmitt, eds. 1981. *Le cherivari: Actes de la table ronde organisee a Paris (25–27 avril 1977).* Paris: Ecole des Hautes Etudes en Science Sociale.

Le Roy Ladurie, Emmanuel. 1981. L'Aiguillelle: Castration by Magic. In *The Mind and Method of the Historian,* by Emmanuel Le Roy Ladurie. Translated by Ben and Sian Reynolds. Chicago: University of Chicago Press.

Levack, Brian P. 1987. *The Witch-Huat in Early Modern Europe.* London: Longman.

Macfarlane, Alan. 1970. *Witchcraft in Tudor and Stuart England.* London: Routledge & Kegan Paul.

Macfarlane, Alan. 1987. *The Culture of Capitalism.* Oxford: Blackwell.

McGaffey, Wyatt. 1986. *Religion and Society in Central Africa: The Bakongo of Lower Zaire.* Chicago: University of Chicago Press.

McKendrick, N., et al. 1982. *The Birth of a Consumer Society: The Commercialization of Eighteenth Century England.* London: Europa.

Magagna, Victor V. 1991. *Communities of Grain: Rural Rebellion in Comparative Perspective.* Ithaca: Cornell University Press.

Martin, Ruth 1989. *Witchcraft and the Inquisition in Venice.* Oxford: Blackwell.

Marwick, Max, ed. 1982 [1970]. *Witchcraft and Sorcery: Selected Readings.* Harmondsworth: Penguin.

Medick, Hans. 1984. Village Spinning Bees: Sexual Culture and Free Time among Rural Youth in Early Modern Germany. In *Interest and Emotion: Essays on the Study of Family and Kinship.* ed. H. Medick and D. Sabean. Cambridge: Cambridge University Press.

Miller, Joseph C. 1988. *Way of Death: Merchant Capitalism and the Angolan Slave Trade, 1730–1830.* Madison: Wisconsin University Press.

Muchembled, Robert. 1987. *Sorcieres: Justice et societe aux 16e et 17e siecles.* Paris: Imago.

Ngugi wa Thiongo. 1982. *Devil on the Cross.* London: Heinemann.

Parry, J., and M. Bloch, eds. 1989. *Money and the Morality of Exchange.* Cambridge: Cambridge University Press.

Polanyi, Karl, et al. 1957. *Trade and Market in the Early Empires.* Glencoe: Free Press.

Popkin, Samuel L. 1979. *The Rational Peasant: The Political Economy of Rural Society in Vietnam.* Berkeley: University of California Press.

Roeder, Philip G. 1984. Legitimacy and Peasant Revolution: An Alternative to Moral Economy. *Peasant Studies* 12:149–68.

Roseberry, William. 1989. Review of second edition of Teodor Shanin, *Peasants and Peasant Societies. Journal of Peasant Studies* 16:631–33.

Rosny, Eric de. 1985. *Healers in the Night.* Maryknoll, N.Y.: Orbis.

Rowlard, Robert. 1990. "Fantasticall and Develishe Persons": European Witchbeliefs in Comparative Perspective. In Ankarloo and Henningsen.

Rowlands, Michael, and Jean-Pierre Warnier. 1988. Sorcery, Power and the Modern State in Cameroon. *Man* 23:118–32.

Sallnow, M. J. 1989. Precious Metals in the Andean Moral Economy. In Parry and Bloch.

Schneider, Jane. 1989. Rumpelstiltskin's Bargain: Folklore and the Intensification of Linen Manufacture in Early Modern Europe. In Weiner and Schneider.

Scott, James C. 1976. *The Moral Economy of the Peasant: Rebellion and Subsistence in Southeast Asia.* New Haven: Yale University Press.

Scott, James C. 1985. *Weapons of the Weak: Everyday Forms of Peasant Resistance.* New Haven: Yale University Press.

Stone-Ferrier, Linda. 1989. Spun Virtue: The World Wound Upside Down: Seventeenth-Century Dutch Depictions of Female Handiwork. In Weiner and Schneider.

Taussig, Michael T. 1980. *The Devil and Commodity Fetishism in South America*. Chapel Hill: University of North Carolina Press.

Thomas, Keith. 1971. *Religion and the Decline of Magic*. New York: Charles Scribner's Sons.

Thompson, E. P. 1968. *The Making of the English Working Class*. Harmondsworth: Penguin.

Thompson, E. P. 1971. The Moral Economy of the Crowd in the Eighteenth Century. *Past and Present* 50:76–136.

Trevor-Roper, H. R. 1968. *The European Witch-Craze of the Sixteenth and Seventeenth Centuries and Other Essays*. New York: Harper & Row.

van Binsbergen, Wim M. J. 1981. Religions and the Problem of Evil in Western Zambia. In *Religious Change in Zambia: Exploratory Studies*, by van Binsbergen. London: Kegan Paul.

Weber, Max. 1930. *The Protestant Ethic and the Spirit of Capitalism*. Trans. Talcott Parsons. New York: Charles Scribner's Sons.

Weiner, Annette B., and Jane Schneider, eds. 1989. *Cloth and Human Experience*. Washington, D.C.: Smithsonian Institution.

White, Luise. 1990a. Bodily Fluids and Usufruct: Controlling Property in Nairobi, 1917–1939. *Canadian Journal of African Studies* 24:418–38.

White, Luise. 1990b. *The Comforts of Home: Prostitution in Colonial Nairobi*. Chicago: University of Chicago Press.

Part VI

Ancestors, Gods, and the Philosophy of Religion

Introduction

In 1931 French anthropologist Marcel Griaule, together with eight colleagues affiliated with the Musée de l'Homme in Paris, set out on a 21-month expedition, known as the Dakar–Djibouti Mission, which crossed the continent of Africa from the Atlantic Ocean to the Red Sea along the lower perimeter of the Sahara (Clifford, 1988: 55). The aim of the mission was to collect and record, as thoroughly as possible, local knowledge and material culture in order to document fully the arts, cultures, and religious beliefs of the vast territories in sub-Saharan Africa which, at the time, were under French colonial rule.

In the course of this extensive "scientific" expedition, Griaule first came in contact with the Dogon people who inhabit the rocky cliffs of the Bandiagara escarpments in what is today the Republic of Mali. Following his initial visit, Griaule returned to the Dogon region on many occasions, writing extensively on their masking and ritual traditions, on their concept of the body and soul, and on indigenous nomenclature and systems of classification and taxonomy.

Sometime in the late 1940s, Griaule was introduced to an elderly sage named Ogotemmêli who had lost his sight many years earlier in a hunting accident. This wise, blind Dogon man from the village of lower Ogol opened Griaule's eyes for the first time to the complexity and intellectual "depth" of African religious beliefs by recounting in a long series of interviews the elaborate creation myth of the Dogon universe. Written in the form of a series of object lessons, Griaule published *Conversations with Ogotemmêli* in 1948 as an attempt to present to the outside world a unified Dogon cosmology and complete philosophical system of thought (Van Beek, 1991: 139).

Griaule's writings on the Dogon were preceded just a few years earlier by the publication of a book entitled *Bantu Philosophy* (1945) written by a Belgian missionary named Placide Tempels. In this detailed and extensive volume, Tempels presented Bantu notions of magic and witchcraft as a rational and highly structured philosophy operating within a unified system of thought. Both Tempels (writing about a Bantu-speaking people) and Griaule (writing about a non-Bantu-speaking people) were battling Eurocentric stereotypes of African religious beliefs which, at the time, saw them as largely disorganized superstitions characterized by animism and ancestor-worship. Making his case for the complexity and sophistication of Dogon religion, Griaule wrote in the preface to his book that "these people live by a cosmology, a metaphysic, and a religion which put them on a par with the peoples of antiquity, and which Christian theology might indeed study with profit" (1965: 2).

Griaule's contribution to the study of Dogon cosmology came to typify French scholarship on African systems of thought. It differed from the British school – such as Evans-Pritchard's Azande ethnography for example (see Part V in this volume) – in two fundamental ways. First, Griaule argued that Dogon religion and ontology were just as complex and rigorous as any European belief system, and that therefore it should be accorded equal weight in an anthropology of world cosmologies and indigenous intellectual beliefs. Evans-Pritchard, in contrast, argued that Azande witchcraft was rational within the logic of its own universe of meaning, but that the Azande were not "rational" when judged by European values and standards of "objective" truth. The second aspect of Griaule's work which makes it typical of French writing on African systems of thought is his emphasis on intellectual coherence and narrative symbolic meaning. Unlike Evans-Pritchard and other British anthropologists of the early to mid twentieth century, the focus of Griaule's Dogon ethnography is not on ritual *behavior* or the *practice* of belief systems in the course of daily life (cf. Richards, 1966).

In his discussion of Western writings about African systems of thought, Malian philosopher Paulin J. Hountondji criticizes both Tempels and Griaule. According to Hountondji, these authors present African "philosophy" as an unarticulated intellectual system about which African people themselves are uncritical and largely unaware. Hountondji argues that Western observers of African societies have often assumed that "everybody always agrees with everybody else" (1983: 60). Griaule, for example, spins the words of a single Dogon man into the cultural fabric of an entire ethnic group's philosophy and cosmology. Contrary to this, however, men and women in African societies, like individuals everywhere, have widely divergent perspectives and contentious worldviews. Meanings are arrived at through debate and dialogue – and not simply through monolithic consent and the putative unanimity of collective opinion (Gyekye, 1995: xvii).

This false, essentialist construction of African systems of thought arises, according to Hountondji, out of a certain Western perspective which assumes that critical knowledge about Africa can only come from outside – where the Western observer somehow "sees" more than indigenous Africans can possibly see themselves. While Griaule argued that Dogon cosmology was highly complex and formed a comprehensive system of belief, he suggested at the same time that this unity was apparent only to the detached, "scientific" gaze of the outside observer. While insiders were able to recite myths and dwell upon certain isolated philosophical problems, the broader structures and implications of this universal system of thought largely eluded them.

The seminal work of Tempels and Griaule set forth a framework of investigation which was followed for years to come not only by subsequent European authors but also by an emerging group of African philosophers and scholars. Thus, in his critique of the literature on African philosophy, Hountondji takes issue not only with Tempels but also with Alexis Kagame, a Rwandan (Tutsi) historian and philosopher, whose book *La philosophie bantoue-rwandaise de l'Être* (1956) is a direct follow-up study of Tempels' work on Bantu ontology. Rather than begin from his own knowledge of Bantu culture, Kagame simply clarifies points made by Tempels, and corrects errors of fact here and there. An authentic and meaningful African philosophy, according to Hountondji, must spring from African intellectual discourse and must not simply refine and build upon Western models of Africa. But where, then, is this philosophy to be found today? According to Hountondji, this kind of African philosophy is "yet to come." In a comparison of the current dialogues on African philosophy, anthropologist Andrew Apter notes that for Hountondji, "So-called traditional African thought with its oral forms of expression and transmission may constitute a wisdom, but it lacks the power of sustained *critical reflection* that real philosophy demands" (1992: 90).

An important question, however, remains as to whether or not such a philosophy is indeed possible. What is an "authentic" African knowledge or philosophy? Who has the authority to construct or discern an African philosophy? Can African scholars, trained for the most part in European academic institutions, shed Western models of representation and intellectual precedents in order to create a pure, genuine Africanist discourse? And, furthermore, did authors like Tempels and Griaule do more harm than good in our understanding of African ontology and religion? These are difficult questions which remain at the heart of any discussion of African systems of thought.

The problem with the reproduction of European-derived models of African religious beliefs is that concepts and phrases often take on assumed meanings which are quite misleading and very different from the phenomena they are intended to describe. This point is clearly addressed in Igor Kopytoff's article "Ancestors as Elders in Africa" where the author presents a critical rethinking of the category "ancestors" in the religious beliefs of the Suku people of southwestern Democratic Republic of Congo.

Contrary to Western beliefs about life and death, Kopytoff argues that there is a continuum between the category living "elders" and that of deceased "ancestors," and that the structural relationship between elder and junior is more important to the Suku than the existential boundary which separates the living from the dead. Kopytoff argues that concepts which commonly appear in African studies literature, such as "ancestor worship" and "ancestor cults," imply a powerful spiritual and religious element which simply is not found in Suku relationships with the dead. Ancestors are considered to be the eldest members of the lineage who are appealed to in times of crisis and misfortune. The fact that they are deceased and living in the other worlds is less critical to their power of redemption than the fact that they are elders and therefore the most senior members of a particular lineage. Kopytoff's article makes clear that African religion does not operate in a realm which is separate from society, but rather religion is modeled on society itself.

This important point would subsequently be picked up by numerous other authors in the field of African studies (see the suggested readings) to show that social changes involve reorganizations of belief. Many scholars clearly echo Kopytoff, while others appear more indebted to the British anthropologist, Meyer Fortes. In a classic essay entitled *Oedipus and Job in West African Religion*, published in 1959, Fortes examines the way in which the Tallensi people of Ghana use religious concepts to order and explain key aspects of an individual's passage through the cycle of life. He identifies two sociological concepts, abstracted from African religions in general, which help explicate different types of structural relationships between humans and gods. In the first relationship, which he calls the Oedipal principle, human actions are governed by fate and destiny. Individuals are believed to take no personal responsibility for their lives, and thus place all actions and consequences in the hands of omnipotent gods and spiritual forces which are outside the realm of human influence.

In the second type of relationship, which Fortes calls the Jobian principle, individuals assume responsibility for their lives and believe that events are shaped by human actions which are only mediated in part by supernatural forces and divine justice. Throughout the course of their life, men and women can forge "contractual relationships" with the gods and, in so doing, try to subvert and overcome the elements of fate and destiny that otherwise govern the unfolding of their existence (Fortes, 1983: 4–6). Fortes argued that within every religion and system of thought there is a delicate balance between the principles of divinely imposed destiny, on the one hand, and self-determination, on the other, a point made clearly by the anthropologist Karin Barber in a well-known essay on the Yoruba of Nigeria (Barber, 1981). Barber, however, emphasizes the agency of the Yoruba, their ability to actively shape their own destinies. She shows that in their search for spiritual guidance and protection, the Yoruba did not limit themselves to gods in the Yoruba religious universe, but explored with confidence and ease the potential benefits of other religions. Because Yoruba beliefs are continually produced and reproduced through individual action, Islam and Christianity were not taken as a threat to a pre-existing or established order but were viewed as complementary systems of worship and belief. Kwame Anthony Appiah has written that "Most Africans, now, whether converted to Islam or Christianity or not, still share the beliefs of their ancestors in an ontology of invisible beings" (1992: 134). Thus, because Islam and Christianity did not overthrow existing religious beliefs, any study of Muslim and Christian religions in Africa must begin with the roots of African religious thought. Although the readings for this book do not cover specifically the emergence or presence of Islam and Christianity in Africa, bibliographic suggestions for reading in these areas are listed at the end of this introduction.

References

Appiah, Kwame Anthony. 1992. *In My Father's House: Africa in the Philosophy of Culture*. New York: Oxford University Press.

Apter, Andrew. 1992. *"Que Faire?* Reconsidering Inventions of Africa." *Critical Inquiry* 19(1): 87–104.

Barber, Karin. 1981. "How Man Makes God in West Africa: Yoruba Attitudes towards the Òrìṣà." *Africa* 51(3): 724–44.

Clifford, James. 1988. "Power and Dialogue in Ethnography: Marcel Griaule's Initiation." In *The Predicament of Culture: Twentieth-Century Ethnography, Literature, and Art*. Cambridge, MA: Harvard University Press.

Fortes, Meyer. 1983 [1959]. *Oedipus and Job in West African Religion*. Cambridge: Cambridge University Press.

Griaule, Marcel. 1965. *Conversations with Ogotemmêli: An Introduction to Dogon Religious Ideas*. London: Oxford University Press for the International African Institute.

Gyekye, Kwame. 1995 [1987]. *An Essay on African Philosophical Thought: The Akan Conceptual Scheme*. Philadelphia: Temple University Press.

Hountondji, Paulin J. 1983. *African Philosophy, Myth and Reality*. Bloomington: Indiana University Press.

Kagame, Alexis. 1956. *La philosophie bantouerwandaise de l'Être*. Brussels: Academie royale des sciences coloniales.

Richards, A. I. 1966. "African Systems of Thought: An Anglo-French Dialogue." *Man* (NS) 2: 286–98.

Tempels, Placide. 1945. *La Philosophie bantoue*. Elisabethville: Louvania. English edition 1959; *Bantu Philosophy*. Paris: Presence Africaine.

Van Beek, Walter E.A. 1991. "Dogon Restudied: A Field Evaluation of the Work of Marcel Griaule." *Current Anthropology* 32(2): 139–58.

Suggested Reading

Ashforth, Adam. 2000. *Madumo, a Man Bewitched*. Chicago: University of Chicago Press.

Blakely, Thomas D., Walter E. A. van Beek, and Dennis L. Thomson, eds. 1994. *Religion in Africa*. Portsmouth, NH: Heinemann.

Brown, Lee M. 2003. *African Philosophy: New and Traditional Perspectives*. Oxford: Oxford University Press.

Forde, Daryll, ed. 1954. *African Worlds: Studies in the Cosmological Ideas and Social Values of African Peoples*. London: Published for the International African Institute by the Oxford University Press.

Fortes, Meyer. 1987. *Religion, Morality, and the Person: The Essays on Tallensi Religion*. New York: Cambridge University Press.

Fortes, Meyer, and Germaine Dieterlen, eds. 1965. *African Systems of Thought*. London: Oxford University Press for the International African Institute.

Good, Charles M. 2004. *Steamer Parish: The Rise and Fall of Missionary Medicine on an African Frontier*. Chicago: University of Chicago Press.

Goody, Jack. 1962. *Death, Property, and the Ancestors: A Study of the Mortuary Customs of the Lodagga of West Africa*. Stanford: Stanford University Press.

Karp, Ivan, and Charles S. Bird, eds. 1980. *Explorations in African Systems of Thought*. Bloomington: Indiana University Press.

Lawal, Babatunde. 1977. "The Living Dead: Art and Immortality among the Yoruba of Nigeria." *Africa* 47(1): 50–61.

Lawson, E. Thomas. 1984. *Religions of Africa: Traditions in Transformation*. San Francisco: Harper & Row.

MacGaffey, Wyatt. 1986. *Religion and Society in Central Africa: The BaKongo of Lower Zaire*. Chicago: The University of Chicago Press.

Marshall, Ruth. 2009. *Political Spiritualities: The Pentecostal Revolution in Nigeria*. Chicago: University of Chicago Press.

Mbiti, John S. 1991. *Introduction to African Religion*. Portsmouth, NH: Heinemann.

Middleton, John. 1960. *Lugbara Religion*. London: Oxford University Press.

Oruka, H. Odera, ed. 1990. *Sage Philosophy: Indigenous Thinkers and Modern Debate on African Philosophy*. New York: E.J. Brill.

Ranger, Terence O., and Isaria N. Limambo, eds. 1972. *The Historical Study of African Religion*. London: Heinemann.

Ray, Benjamin C. 1976. *African Religions: Symbol, Ritual, and Community*. Englewood Cliffs, NJ: Prentice-Hall.

Thomas, Linda E. 2007. *Under the Canopy: Ritual Process and Spiritual Resilience in South Africa*. Columbia: University of South Carolina Press.

Twesigye, Emmanuel K. 1987. *Common Ground: Christianity, African Religion, and Philosophy*. New York: Peter Lang.

Van Binsbergen, Wim. 1981. *Religious Change in Zambia*. London: Routledge & Kegan Paul.

Further Reading on Islam and Christianity in Africa

Asante, Molefi Kete and Emeka Nwadiora. 2007. *Spear Masters: An Introduction to African Religion*. Lanham, MD: University Press of America.

Bond, George, Walton Johnson, and Sheila S. Walker, eds. 1979. *African Christianity: Patterns of Religious Continuity*. New York: Academic Press.

Bravmann, René A. 1974. *Islam and Tribal Art in West Africa*. Cambridge: Cambridge University Press.

Clarke, Peter Bernard. 1982. *West Africa and Islam: A Study of Religious Development from the 8th to the 20th Century*. London: Edward Arnold.

Clarke, Peter Bernard. 1986. *West Africa and Christianity*. London: Edward Arnold.

Cruise O'Brien, Donal B., and Christian Coulon. 1988. *Charisma and Brotherhood in African Islam*. Oxford: Clarendon Press.

Falola, Toyin, and Biodun Adediran. 1983. *Islam and Christianity in West Africa*. Ife-Ife, Nigeria: University of Ife Press.

Hanretta, Sean. 2009. *Islam and Social Change in French West Africa: History of an Emancipatory Community*. Cambridge: Cambridge University Press.

Kalu, Ogbu. 2008. *African Pentecostalism: An Introduction*. Oxford: Oxford University Press.

Katongole, Emmanuel M. 2005. *A Future for Africa: Critical Essays in Christian Social Imagination*. Chicago: University of Chicago Press.

Kritzeck, James. 1969. *Islam in Africa*. New York: Van Nostrand-Reinhold.

Lewis, I.M. 1980. *Islam in Tropical Islam*. London: International African Institute in association with Hutchinson University Library for Africa.

Nyang, Sulayman S. 1984. *Islam, Christianity, and African Industry*. Brattleboro, VT: Amara Books.

Olupona, Jacob K. and Sulayman S. Nyang, eds. 1993. *Religious Plurality in Africa: Essays in Honour of John S. Mbiti*. Berlin; New York: Mouton de Gruyter.

Phiri, Isaac. 2001. *Proclaiming Political Pluralism: Churches and Political Transitions in Africa*. New York: Praeger.

Sanneh, Lamin. 1983. *West African Christianity*. London: Allen Unwin.

Sanneh, Lamin O. 1989. *The Jakhanke Muslim Clerics: A Religious and Historical Study of Islam in Senegambia*. Lanham, MD: University Press of America.

Smith, Mary F. 1981 [1954]. *Baba of Karo: A Woman of the Muslim Hausa*. New Haven and London: Yale University Press.

Trimingham, John Spencer. 1962. *A History of Islam in West Africa*. London: Oxford University Press.

Trimingham, John Spencer. 1964. *Islam in East Africa*. Oxford: Clarendon Press.

Trimingham, John Spencer. 1968. *The Influence of Islam upon Africa*. New York: Praeger.

Zoghby, Samir M. 1978. *Islam in Sub-Saharan Africa: A Partially Annotated Guide*. Washington, DC: Library of Congress.

19

Conversations with Ogotemmêli

Marcel Griaule

First Day: Ogotemmêli

Lower Ogol, like all Dogon Villages, was a collection of houses and granaries all crowded together, flat roofs of clay alternating with cone-shaped roofs of straw. Picking one's way along its narrow streets of light and shade, between the truncated pyramids, prisms, cubes or cylinders of the granaries and houses, the rectangular porticoes, the red or white altars shaped like umbilical hernias, one felt like a dwarf lost in a maze. Everything was mottled by the rains and the heat; the mudwalls were fissured like the skins of pachyderms. Over the walls of the tiny courtyards might be seen, under the floors of the granaries, fowls, yellow dogs, and sometimes great tortoises, symbols of the patriarchs.

At a turn of the street there was a door, shaped with an axe, but, even when new, it could never have fitted the entrance built of earthen pillars with a pediment of wooden blocks. The door was as wide as a man's two shoulders; winter rains had ploughed wave-like furrows in the wood between which the knots looked like open eyes. Drought, clutching hands, and the muzzles of goats had worn it away so that it grated on its hinges and swung back against the wall with a bang like a gong, revealing a squalid courtyard, which belonged to the most remarkable man of the plains and rocks from Oropa to Nimbé, Asakarba and Tintam.

The white man stepped over the scanty midden of an old man with no family. A row of cabins, broken by a low door on the ground floor and a flat panel on the floor above, stood in the middle of the courtyard forming a façade which concealed the main building behind it. In the pediment were ten swallows' nests, and the edge of the roof was adorned by eight cones with flat stone tops. To right and left were six granaries in a row like big dice, two of them facing the neighbouring house, to which they belonged. Of the other four one was empty, another rickety, and the third split across like a half-bitten fruit. Only one of them was in use: it was half full of grain.

Opposite, between the main building and the granaries, a low house, in which there were faint sounds of life, completed the enclosure of the courtyard. On the right in a store-room open to the sky there was a perpetual whirl of down blown about by a light breeze.

From M. Griaule, *Conversations with Ogotemmêli* (1948), Oxford University Press, pp. 11–32, from International African Institute.

The man accompanying the European pronounced the usual words of greeting. Immediately a voice replied clearly and distinctly:

"God brings you! God brings you!"

"Greetings! How is your health?"

Slowly the voice drew nearer. From the shadows of the interior came the sound of hands feeling their way along walls and woodwork. A stick tapped on the floor: there was a sound of hollow earthenware: some tiny chickens made their way out one by one through the cat-hole, thrust out by the great being who was approaching.

At last there appeared a brown tunic, drawn in at the seams and frayed by long use like the standards of the warriors of old. Then a head bent beneath the lintel of the door, and the man stood up to his full height, turning towards the stranger a face that no words can describe.

"Greetings!" he said, "Greetings to those who are athirst!"

The thick lips spoke the purest Sanga language. So alive were they that one saw nothing else. All the other features seemed to be folded away, particularly as, after the first words, the head had been bent. The cheeks, the cheek-bones, the forehead and the eyelids seemed all to have suffered the same ravages; they were creased by a hundred wrinkles which had caused a painful contortion as of a face exposed to too strong a light or battered by a hail of stones. The eyes were dead.

The two visitors came from outside, and might therefore be supposed to have been working in the heat. Accordingly the old man leaning on his stick greeted them with the words:

"Welcome! Welcome after weariness! Welcome from the sun!"

The longest task of the first day was the choice of a place for the conversations. The space in front of the dwelling-house, even if the aged Ogotemmêli remained indoors, and even if the white man bent his head towards him and spoke in low tones as if in the confessional, was, according to Ogotemmêli, open to the objection that interviews there might excite the eternal curiosity of the women. The minute courtyard on the other side of the building, on the other hand, which was exposed to all the winds from the north, might be watched by children hidden in the ruined granary. There remained the courtyard itself with its wretched dung-heap, its hollow stone, its ashes and its dilapidated wall with a gap in the middle of it just high enough for curious eyes to look through.

Ogotemmêli still hesitated; he had much to say about the inconvenience of the courtyard for the purpose of conversations between men of mature years. The European for his part did not open his mouth except to agree; he even stressed the indiscreet nature of walls and the stupidity of men and, naturally, the unconscionable curiosity of women and their insatiable thirst for novelties. All these precautions interested him: they seemed so out of proportion to the simple sale of an amulet.

In the end Ogotemmêli sat down on the threshold of the lower door of the main façade; doubled up, with his face bent downwards and his hands crossed above his head, his elbows resting on his knees, he waited.

The white man was beginning to realize that the sale of the amulet was only a pretext. There was no reference to it in the subsequent conversations, and the underlying reason for the old man's action never transpired. But from various details it appeared, as time went on, that Ogotemmêli wished to pass on to the foreigner, who had first visited the country fifteen years before, and whom he trusted, the instruction which he himself had received first from his grandfather and later from his father.

But he was waiting. He was perplexed by the result of his own approaches to this man whom he could not see. Not that the man was unknown to him: for fifteen years he had been hearing about groups of Europeans, who came, under this man's guidance, to live rough and to ride about the country studying the customs of the people.

He had even followed their work since the beginning, for he had been closely associated with Ambibê Babadyé, the great dignitary of the masks and the white man's regular informant, who had only recently died. Many times in the last fifteen years Ambibê had come to Ogotemmêli for information and advice. From what Ambibê had told him, and from the reports of a number of other persons, he had formed a correct idea of the aims and objects of his interlocutor and his unwearying passion for research.

But the situation was unique. How was one to instruct a European? How could one make him understand things and rites and beliefs? Moreover this white man had already found out about the masks, and knew their secret language. He had been all over the country in every direction, and about some of its institutions he knew as much as he knew himself. How then to set about it?

The European relieved him of his embarrassment.

"When your gun exploded in your face, what were you firing at?"

"At a porcupine."

The white man was trying by an indirect approach to lead the conversation to hunting and the attitude towards the animal world, and so to totemism.

"It was an accident," said the old man. "But it was also a last warning. I knew by divination that I was to give up hunting if I wanted to protect my children. Hunting is a work of death, and it attracts death. I have had twenty-one children, and now only five are left."

All the tragedy of African mortality was in his words, and all the deep questionings of these men about death and their defencelessness in the face of it. They clung to their beliefs, as do all men everywhere, but though beliefs may console and explain, they cannot avert the experience.

It was on this plane of suffering that Ogotemmêli's personality was revealed, in itself and in its relation with supernatural powers. From the age of fifteen he had been initiated in the mysteries of religion by his grandfather. After the latter's death his father had continued the instruction. It seemed that the "lessons" had gone on for more than twenty years, and that Ogotemmêli's family was not one that took these things lightly.

Ogotemmêli himself, no doubt, had from a very early age shown signs of an eager mind and considerable shrewdness. Until he lost his sight, he was a mighty hunter who, though one-eyed from childhood as a result of smallpox, would always come back from the chase with a full bag, while the others were still toiling in the gorges. His skill as a hunter was the fruit of his profound knowledge of nature, of animals, of men and of gods. After his accident he learnt still more. Thrown back on his own resources, on his altars and on whatever he was able to hear, he had become one of the most powerful minds on the cliffs.

Indeed his name and his character were famous throughout the plateau and the hills, known (as the saying was) to the youngest boy. People came to his door for advice every day and even by night.

Phrygian caps were even now showing above the walls, and the women were making signs from a distance. It was time to go, and make room for the clients. But contact had now been made, and the conversations thereafter came about by tacit consent, according to a sort of programme and at convenient times.

Second Day: The First Word and the Fibre Skirt

Ogotemmêli, seating himself on his threshold, scraped his stiff leather snuff-box, and put a pinch of yellow powder on his tongue.

"Tobacco," he said, "makes for right thinking."

So saying, he set to work to analyse the world system, for it was essential to begin with the dawn of all things. He rejected as a detail of no interest, the popular account of how the fourteen solar systems were formed from flat circular slabs of earth one on top of the other.

He was only prepared to speak of the serviceable solar system; he agreed to consider the stars, though they only played a secondary part.

"It is quite true," he said, "that in course of time women took down the stars to give them to their children. The children put spindles through them and made them spin like fiery tops to show themselves how the world turned. But that was only a game."

The stars came from pellets of earth flung out into space by the God Amma, the one God. He had created the sun and the moon by a more complicated process, which was not the first known to man but is the first attested invention of God: the art of pottery. The sun is, in a sense, a pot raised once for all to white heat and surrounded by a spiral of red copper with eight turns. The moon is the same shape, but its copper is white. It was heated only one quarter at a time. Ogotemmêli said he would explain later the movements of these bodies. For the moment he was concerned only to indicate the main lines of the design, and from that to pass to its actors.

He was anxious, however, to give an idea of the size of the sun.

"Some," he said, "think it is as large as this encampment, which would mean thirty cubits. But it is really bigger. Its surface area is bigger than the whole of Sanga Canton."

And after some hesitation he added:

"It is perhaps even bigger than that."

He refused to linger over the dimensions of the moon, nor did he ever say anything about them. The moon's function was not important, and he would speak of it later. He said however that, while Africans were creatures of light emanating from the fullness of the sun, Europeans were creatures of the moonlight: hence their immature appearance.

He spat out his tobacco as he spoke. Ogotemmêli had nothing against Europeans. He was not even sorry for them. He left them to their destiny in the lands of the north.

The God Amma, it appeared, took a lump of clay, squeezed it in his hand and flung it from him, as he had done with the stars. The clay spread and fell on the north, which is the top, and from there stretched out to the south, which is the bottom, of the world, although the whole movement was horizontal. The earth lies flat, but the north is at the top. It extends east and west with separate members like a foetus in the womb. It is a body, that is to say, a thing with members branching out from a central mass. This body, lying flat, face upwards, in a line from north to south, is feminine. Its sexual organ is an anthill, and its clitoris a termite hill. Amma, being lonely and desirous of intercourse with this creature, approached it. That was the occasion of the first breach of the order of the universe.

Ogotemmêli ceased speaking. His hands crossed above his head, he sought to distinguish the different sounds coming from the courtyards and roofs. He had reached the point of the origin of troubles and of the primordial blunder of God.

"If they overheard me, I should be fined an ox!"

At God's approach the termite hill rose up, barring the passage and displaying its masculinity. It was as strong as the organ of the stranger, and intercourse could not take place. But God is all-powerful. He cut down the termite hill, and had intercourse with the excised earth. But the original incident was destined to affect the course of things

for ever; from this defective union there was born, instead of the intended twins, a single being, the *Thos aureus* or jackal, symbol of the difficulties of God. Ogotemmêli's voice sank lower and lower. It was no longer a question of women's ears listening to what he was saying; other, non-material, eardrums might vibrate to his important discourse. The European and his African assistant, Sergeant Koguem, were leaning towards the old man as if hatching plots of the most alarming nature.

But, when he came to the beneficent acts of God, Ogotemmêli's voice again assumed its normal tone.

God had further intercourse with his earth-wife, and this time without mishaps of any kind, the excision of the offending member having removed the cause of the former disorder. Water, which is the divine seed, was thus able to enter the womb of the earth and the normal reproductive cycle resulted in the birth of twins. Two beings were thus formed. God created them like water. They were green in colour, half human beings and half serpents. From the head to the loins they were human: below that they were serpents. Their red eyes were wide open like human eyes, and their tongues were forked like the tongues of reptiles. Their arms were flexible and without joints. Their bodies were green and sleek all over, shining like the surface of water, and covered with short green hairs, a presage of vegetation and germination.

These spirits, called Nummo, were thus two homogeneous products of God, of divine essence like himself, conceived without untoward incidents and developed normally in the womb of the earth. Their destiny took them to Heaven, where they received the instructions of their father. Not that God had to teach them speech, that indispensable necessity of all beings, as it is of the world-system; the Pair were born perfect and complete; they had eight members, and their number was eight, which is the symbol of speech.

They were also of the essence of God, since they were made of his seed, which is at once the ground, the form, and the substance of the life-force of the world, from which derives the motion and the persistence of created being. This force is water, and the Pair are present in all water: they *are* water, the water of the seas, of coasts, of torrents, of storms, and of the spoonfuls we drink.

Ogotemmêli used the terms "Water" and "Nummo" indiscriminately.

"Without Nummo," he said, "it was not even possible to create the earth, for the earth was moulded clay and it is from water (that is, from Nummo) that its life is derived."

"What life is there in the earth?" asked the European.

"The life-force of the earth is water. God moulded the earth with water. Blood too he made out of water. Even in a stone there is this force, for there is moisture in everything.

"But if Nummo is water, it also produces copper. When the sky is overcast, the sun's rays may be seen materializing on the misty horizon. These rays, excreted by the spirits, are of copper and are light. They are water too, because they uphold the earth's moisture as it rises. The Pair excrete light, because they are also light."

While he was speaking, Ogotemmêli had been searching for something in the dust. He finally collected a number of small stones. With a rapid movement he flung them into the courtyard over the heads of his two interlocutors, who had no time to bend down. The stones fell just where the Hogon's cock had been crowing a few seconds before.

"That cock is a squalling nuisance. He makes all conversation impossible."

The bird began to crow again on the other side of the wall, so Ogotemmêli sent Koguem to throw a bit of wood at him. When Koguem came back, he asked whether the cock was now outside the limits of the Tabda quarter.

"He is in the Hogon's field," said Koguem. "I have set four children to watch him."

"Good!" said Ogotemmêli with a little laugh. "Let him make the most of what remains to him of life! They tell me he is to be eaten at the next Feast of Twins."

He returned to the subject of the Nummo spirits, or (as he more usually put it, in the singular) of Nummo, for this pair of twins, he explained, represented the perfect, the ideal unit.

The Nummo, looking down from Heaven, saw their mother, the earth, naked and speechless, as a consequence no doubt of the original incident in her relations with the God Amma. It was necessary to put an end to this state of disorder. The Nummo accordingly came down to earth, bringing with them fibres pulled from plants already created in the heavenly regions. They took ten bunches of these fibres, corresponding to the number of their ten fingers, and made two strands of them, one for the front and one for behind. To this day masked men still wear these appendages hanging down to their feet in thick tendrils.

But the purpose of this garment was not merely modesty. It manifested on earth the first act in the ordering of the universe and the revelation of the helicoid sign in the form of an undulating broken line.

For the fibres fell in coils, symbol of tornadoes, of the windings of torrents, of eddies and whirlwinds, of the undulating movement of reptiles. They recall also the eight-fold spirals of the sun, which sucks up moisture. They were themselves a channel of moisture, impregnated as they were with the freshness of the celestial plants. They were full of the essence of Nummo: they *were* Nummo in motion, as shown in the undulating line, which can be prolonged to infinity.

When Nummo speaks, what comes from his mouth is a warm vapour which conveys, and itself constitutes, speech. This vapour, like all water, has sound, dies away in a helicoid line. The coiled fringes of the skirt were therefore the chosen vehicle for the words which the Spirit desired to reveal to the earth. He endued his hands with magic power by raising them to his lips while he plaited the skirt, so that the moisture of his words was imparted to the damp plaits, and the spiritual revelation was embodied in the technical instruction.

In these fibres full of water and words, placed over his mother's genitalia, Nummo is thus always present.

Thus clothed, the earth had a language, the first language of this world and the most primitive of all time. Its syntax was elementary, its verbs few, and its vocabulary without elegance. The words were breathed sounds scarcely differentiated from one another, but nevertheless vehicles. Such as it was, this ill-defined speech sufficed for the great works of the beginning of all things.

In the middle of a word Ogotemmêli gave a loud cry in answer to the hunter's halloo which the discreet Akundyo, priest of women dying in childbirth and of stillborn children, had called through the gap in the wall.

Akundyo first spat to one side, his eye riveted on the group of men. He was wearing a red Phrygian cap which covered his ears, with a raised point like a uraeus on the bridge of the nose in the fashion known as "the wind blows". His cheekbones were prominent, and his teeth shone. He uttered a formal salutation to which the old man at once replied and the exchange of courtesies became more and more fulsome.

"God's curse," exclaimed Ogotemmêli, "on any in Lower Ogol who love you not!"

With growing emotion Akundyo made shift to out-do the vigour of the imprecation.

"May God's curse rest on me," said the blind man at last, "if I love you not!"

The four men breathed again. They exchanged humorous comments on the meagreness of the game in the I valley. Eventually Akundyo took his leave of them, asserting in the slangy French of a native soldier that he was going to "look for porcupine", an animal much esteemed by these people.

The conversation reverted to the subject of speech. Its function was organization, and therefore it was good; nevertheless from the start it let loose disorder.

This was because the jackal, the deluded and deceitful son of God, desired to possess speech, and laid hands on the fibres in which language was embodied, that is to say, on his mother's skirt. His mother, the earth, resisted this incestuous action. She buried herself in her own womb, that is to say, in the anthill, disguised as an ant. But the jackal followed her. There was, it should be explained, no other woman in the world whom he could desire. The hole which the earth made in the anthill was never deep enough, and in the end she had to admit defeat. This prefigured the even-handed struggles between men and women, which, however, always end in the victory of the male.

The incestuous act was of great consequence. In the first place it endowed the jackal with the gift of speech so that ever afterwards he was able to reveal to diviners the designs of God.

It was also the cause of the flow of menstrual blood, which stained the fibres. The resulting defilement of the earth was incompatible with the reign of God. God rejected that spouse, and decided to create living beings directly. Modelling a womb in damp clay, he placed it on the earth and covered it with a pellet flung out into space from heaven. He made a male organ in the same way and having put it on the ground, he flung out a sphere which stuck to it.

The two lumps forthwith took organic shape; their life began to develop. Members separated from the central core, bodies appeared, and a human pair arose out of the lumps of earth.

At this point the Nummo Pair appeared on the scene for the purpose of further action. The Nummo foresaw that the original rule of twin births was bound to disappear, and that errors might result comparable to those of the jackal, whose birth was single. For it was because of his solitary state that the first son of God acted as he did.

"The jackal was alone from birth," said Ogotemmêli, "and because of this he did more things than can be told."

The Spirit drew two outlines on the ground, one on top of the other, one male and the other female. The man stretched himself out on these two shadows of himself, and took both of them for his own. The same thing was done for the woman. Thus it came about that each human being from the first was endowed with two souls of different sex, or rather with two principles corresponding to two distinct persons. In the man the female soul was located in the prepuce; in the woman the male soul was in the clitoris.

But the foreknowledge of the Nummo no doubt revealed to him the disadvantages of this makeshift. Man's life was not capable of supporting both beings: each person would have to merge himself in the sex for which he appeared to be best fitted.

The Nummo accordingly circumcised the man, thus removing from him all the femininity of his prepuce. The prepuce, however, changed itself into an animal which is "neither a serpent nor an insect, but is classed with serpents". This animal is called a *nay*. It is said to be a sort of lizard, black and white like the pall which covers the dead. Its name also means "four", the female number, and "Sun", which is a female being. The *nay* symbolized the pain of circumcision and the need for the man to suffer in his sex as the woman does.

The man then had intercourse with the woman, who later bore the first two children of a series of eight, who were to become the ancestors of the Dogon people. In the moment of birth the pain of parturition was concentrated in the woman's clitoris, which was excised by an invisible hand, detached itself and left her, and was changed into the form of a scorpion. The pouch and the sting symbolized the organ: the venom was the water and the blood of the pain.

The European, returning through the millet field, found himself wondering about the significance of all these actions and counteractions, all these sudden jerks in the thought of the myth.

Here, he reflected, is a Creator God spoiling his first creation; restoration is effected by the excision of the earth, and then by the birth of a pair of spirits, inventive beings who construct the world and bring to it the first spoken words; an incestuous act destroys the created order, and jeopardizes the principle of twin-births. Order is restored by the creation of a pair of human beings, and twin-births are replaced by dual souls. (But why, he asked himself, twin-births at all?)

The dual soul is a danger; a man should be male, and a woman female. Circumcision and excision are once again the remedy. (But why the *nay*? Why the scorpion?)

The answers to these questions were to come later, and to take their place in the massive structure of doctrine, which the blind old man was causing to emerge bit by bit from the mists of time.

Over the heads of the European and Koguem the dark millet clusters stood out against the leaden sky. They were passing through a field of heavy ears, stiffly erect and motionless in the breeze. When the crop is backward and thin, the ears are light and move with the slightest breath of wind. Thin crops are therefore full of sound. An abundant crop, on the other hand, is weighed down by the wind and bows itself in silence.

Third Day: The Second Word and Weaving

Anyone entering the courtyard upset its arrangements. It was so cramped that the kites, most cunning of all the acrobats of the air, could not get at the poultry. In a hollow stone there were the remains, or rather, the dregs of some millet-beer, which the poultry, cock, hen and chickens, were glad to drink. So was a yellow and white striped dog with tail erect like an Ethiopian sabre. When the door banged, all these creatures dispersed, leaving the courtyard to the humans.

Ogotemmêli, ensconced in his doorway, proceeded to enumerate the eight original ancestors born of the couple created by God. The four eldest were males: the four others were females. But by a special dispensation, permitted only to them, they were able to fertilize themselves, being dual and bisexual. From them are descended the eight Dogon families.

For humanity was organizing itself in this makeshift condition. The permanent calamity of single births was slightly mitigated by the grant of the dual soul, which the Nummo traced on the ground beside women in childbirth. Dual souls were implanted in the new-born child by holding it by the thighs above the place of the drawings with its hands and feet touching the ground. Later the superfluous soul was eliminated by circumcision, and humanity limped towards its obscure destiny.

But the divine thirst for perfection was not extinguished, and the Nummo Pair, who were gradually taking the place of God their father, had in mind projects of redemption. But, in order to improve human conditions, reforms and instruction had to be carried out on the human level. The Nummo were afraid of the terrifying effect of contact between creatures of flesh and blood on the one hand and purely spiritual beings on the other. There had to be actions that could be understood, taking place within the ambit of the beneficiaries and in their own environment. Men after regeneration must be drawn towards the ideal as a peasant is drawn to rich farmland.

The Nummo accordingly came down to earth, and entered the anthill, that is to say, the sexual part of which they were themselves the issue. Thus, they were able, among other tasks, to defend their mother against possible attempts by their elder, the incestuous jackal. At the same time, by their moist, luminous, and articulate presence, they were purging that body which was for ever defiled in the sight of God, but was nevertheless capable of acquiring in some degree the purity required for the activities of life.

In the anthill the male Nummo took the place of the masculine element, which had been eliminated by the excision of the termite-hill clitoris, while the female Nummo took the place of the female element, and her womb became part of the womb of the earth.

The Pair could then proceed to the work of regeneration, which they intended to carry out in agreement with God and in God's stead.

"Nummo in Amma's place," said Ogotemmêli, "was working the work of Amma."

In those obscure beginnings of the evolution of the world, men had no knowledge of death, and the eight ancestors, offspring of the first human couple, lived on indefinitely. They had eight separate lines of descendants, each of them being self-propagating since each was both male and female.

The four males and the four females were couples in consequence of their lower, i.e. of their sexual, parts. The four males were man and woman, and the four females were woman and man. In the case of the males it was the man, and in the case of the females it was the woman, who played the dominant role. They coupled and became pregnant each in him or herself, and so produced their offspring.

But in the fullness of time an obscure instinct led the eldest of them towards the anthill which had been occupied by the Nummo. He wore on his head as head-dress and to protect him from the sun, the wooden bowl he used for his food. He put his two feet into the opening of the anthill, that is of the earth's womb, and sank in slowly as if for a parturition *a tergo*.

The whole of him thus entered into the earth, and his head itself disappeared. But he left on the ground, as evidence of his passage into that world, the bowl which had caught on the edges of the opening. All that remained on the anthill was the round wooden bowl, still bearing traces of the food and the finger-prints of its vanished owner, symbol of his body and of his human nature, as, in the animal world, is the skin which a reptile has shed.

Liberated from his earthly condition, the ancestor was taken in charge by the regenerating Pair. The male Nummo led him into the depths of the earth, where, in the waters of the womb of his partner he curled himself up like a foetus and shrank to germinal form, and acquired the quality of water, the seed of God and the essence of the two Spirits.

And all this process was the work of the Word. The male with his voice accompanied the female Nummo who was speaking to herself and to her own sex. The spoken Word entered into her and wound itself round her womb in a spiral of eight turns. Just as the helical band of copper round the sun gives to it its daily movement, so the spiral of the Word gave to the womb its regenerative movement.

Thus perfected by water and words, the new Spirit was expelled and went up to Heaven.

All the eight ancestors in succession had to undergo this process of transformation; but, when the turn of the seventh ancestor came, the change was the occasion of a notable occurrence.

The seventh in a series, it must be remembered, represents perfection. Though equal in quality with the others, he is the sum of the feminine element, which is four, and the masculine element, which is three. He is thus the completion of the perfect series, symbol of the total union of male and female, that is to say of unity.

And to this homogeneous whole belongs especially the mastery of words, that is, of language; and the appearance on earth of such a one was bound to be the prelude to revolutionary developments of a beneficent character.

In the earth's womb he became, like the others, water and spirit, and his development, like theirs, followed the rhythm of the words uttered by the two transforming Nummo.

"The words which the female Nummo spoke to herself," Ogotemmêli explained, "turned into a spiral and entered into her sexual part. The male Nummo helped her. These are the words which the seventh ancestor learnt inside the womb."

The others equally possessed the knowledge of these words in virtue of their experiences in the same place; but they had not attained the mastery of them nor was it given to them to develop their use. What the seventh ancestor had received, therefore, was the perfect knowledge of a Word – the second Word to be heard on earth, clearer than the first and not, like the first, reserved for particular recipients, but destined for all mankind. Thus he was able to achieve progress for the world. In particular, he enabled mankind to take precedence over God's wicked son, the jackal. The latter, it is true, still possessed knowledge of the first Word, and could still therefore reveal to diviners certain heavenly purposes; but in the future order of things he was to be merely a laggard in the process of revelation.

The potent second Word developed the powers of its new possessor. Gradually he came to regard his regeneration in the womb of the earth as equivalent to the capture and occupation of that womb, and little by little he took possession of the whole organism, making such use of it as suited him for the purpose of his activities. His lips began to merge with the edges of the anthill, which widened and became a mouth. Pointed teeth made their appearance, seven for each lip, then ten, the number of the fingers, later forty, and finally eighty, that is to say, ten for each ancestor.

These numbers indicated the future rates of increase of the families; the appearance of the teeth was a sign that the time for new instruction was drawing near.

But here again the scruples of the Spirits made themselves felt. It was not directly to men, but to the ant, avatar of the earth and native to the locality, that the seventh ancestor imparted instruction.

At sunrise on the appointed day the seventh ancestor Spirit spat out eighty threads of cotton; these he distributed between his upper teeth which acted as the teeth of a weaver's reed. In this way he made the uneven threads of a warp. He did the same with the lower teeth to make the even threads. By opening and shutting his jaws the Spirit caused the threads of the warp to make the movements required in weaving. His whole face took part in the work, his nose studs serving as the block, while the stud in his lower lip was the shuttle.

As the threads crossed and uncrossed, the two tips of the Spirit's forked tongue pushed the thread of the weft to and fro, and the web took shape from his mouth in the breath of the second revealed Word.

For the Spirit was speaking while the work proceeded. As did the Nummo in the first revelation, he imparted his Word by means of a technical process, so that all men could understand. By so doing he showed the identity of material actions and spiritual forces, or rather the need for their co-operation.

The words that the Spirit uttered filled all the interstices of the stuff: they were woven in the threads, and formed part and parcel of the cloth. They were the cloth, and the cloth was the Word. That is why woven material is called *soy*, which means "It is the spoken word". *Soy* also means "seven", for the Spirit who spoke as he wove was seventh in the series of ancestors.

While the work was going on, the ant came and went on the edge in the opening in the breath of the Spirit, hearing and remembering his words. The new instruction, which she thus received, she passed on to the men who lived in those regions, and who had already followed the transformation of the sex of the earth.

Up to the time of the ancestors' descent into the anthill, men had lived in holes dug in the level soil like the lairs of animals. When their attention was drawn to the bowls which the ancestors had left behind them, they began to notice the shape of the anthill, which they thought much better than their holes. They copied the shape of the anthill accordingly, making passages and rooms as shelters from the rain, and began to store the produce of the crops for food.

They were thus advancing towards a less primitive way of life; and, when they noticed the growth of teeth round the opening, they imitated these too as a means of protection aginst wild beasts. They moulded great teeth of clay, dried them and set them up round the entrances to their dwellings.

At the moment of the second instruction, therefore, men were living in dens which were already, in some sort, a prefiguration of the place of revelation and of the womb into which each of them in due course would descend to be regenerated. And, moreover, the human anthill, with its occupants and its store-chambers for grain, was a rudimentary image of the system which, much later, was to come down to them from Heaven in the form of a marvellous granary.

These dim outlines of things to come predisposed men to take advice from the ant. The latter, after what it had seen the Spirit do, had laid in a store of cotton-fibres. These it had made into threads and, in the sight of men, drew them between the teeth of the anthill entrance as the Spirit had done. As the warp emerged, the men passed the thread of the weft, throwing it right and left in time to the opening and shutting movements of the jaws, and the resulting web was rolled round a piece of wood, fore-runner of the beam.

The ant at the same time revealed the words it had heard and the man repeated them. Thus there was recreated by human lips the concept of life in motion, of the transposition of forces, of the efficacy of the breath of the Spirit, which the seventh ancestor had created; and thus the interlacing of warp and weft enclosed the same words, the new instruction which became the heritage of mankind and was handed on from generation to generation of weavers to the accompaniment of the clapping of the shuttle and the creaking of the block, which they call the "creaking of the Word".

All these operations took place by daylight, for spinning and weaving are work for the daytime. Working at night would mean weaving webs of silence and darkness.

Fourth Day: The Third Word and the Granary of Pure Earth

Ogotemmêli had no very clear idea of what happened in Heaven after the transformation of the eight ancestors into Nummo. It is true that the eight, after leaving the earth, having completed their labours, came to the celestial region where the eldest Pair, who had transformed them, reigned. It is true also that these elders had precedence of the others, and did not fail to impose on them at once a form of organization and rules of life.

But it was never quite clear why this celestial world was disturbed to the point of disintegration, or why these disorders led to a reorganization of the terrestrial world, which had nothing to do with the celestial disputes. What is certain is that in the end the eight came down to earth again in a vast apparatus of symbols, in which was included a third and definitive Word necessary for the working of the modern world.

All that could be gathered from Ogotemmêli, by dint of patient attention to his words, was the evasive answer:

"Spirits do not fall from Heaven except in anger or because they are expelled."

It was obvious that he was conscious of the infinite complexity of the idea of God or the Spirits who took his place, and was reluctant to explain it. However an outline, slight but nevertheless adequate, of this obscure period was eventually obtained.

The Nummo Pair had received the transformed eight in Heaven. But though they were all of the same essence, the Pair had the rights of the elder generation in relation to the newcomers, on whom they imposed an organization with a network of rules, of which the most onerous was the one which separated them from one another and forbade them to visit one another.

The fact was that, like human societies in which numbers are a source of trouble, the celestial society would have been heading for disorder, if all its members had gathered together.

Though this rule was their security, the new generation of Nummo, however, proceeded to break it and thereby overthrew their destiny; and this was how it came about.

God had given the eight a collection of eight different grains intended for their food, and for these the first ancestor was responsible. Of the eight, the last was the *Digitaria*, which had been publicly rejected by the first ancestor when it was given to him, on the pretext that it was so small and so difficult to prepare. He even went so far as to swear he would never eat it.

There came, however, a critical period when all the grains were nearly exhausted except the last. The first and second ancestors, who incidentally had already broken the rule about separation, met together to eat this last food. Their action was the crowning breach of order, confirming as it did their first offence by a breach of faith. The two ancestors thereby became unclean – that is to say, of an essence incompatible with life in the celestial world. They resolved to quit that region, where they felt themselves to be strangers, and the six other ancestors threw in their lot with them and made the same decision. Moreover, they proposed to take with them when they left anything that might be of use to the men they were going to rejoin. It was then that the first ancestor, no doubt with the approval and perhaps with the help of God, began to make preparations for his own departure.

He took a woven basket with a circular opening and a square base in which to carry the earth and puddled clay required for the construction of a world-system, of which he was to be one of the counsellors. This basket served as a model for a basket-work structure of considerable size which he built upside down, as it were, with the opening, twenty cubits in diameter, on the ground, the square base, with sides eight cubits long, formed a flat roof, and the height was ten cubits. This framework he covered with puddled clay made of the earth from heaven, and in the thickness of the clay, starting from the centre of each side of the square, he made stairways of ten steps each facing towards one of the cardinal points. At the sixth step of the north staircase he put a door giving access to the interior in which were eight chambers arranged on two floors.

The symbolic significance of this structure was as follows:

The circular base represented the sun.

The square roof represented the sky.

A circle in the centre of the roof represented the moon.

The tread of each step being female and the rise of each step male, the four stairways of ten steps together prefigured the eight tens of families, offspring of the eight ancestors.

Each stairway held one kind of creature, and was associated with a constellation, as follows:

The north stairway, associated with the Pleiades, was for men and fishes.

The south stairway, associated with Orion's Belt, was for domestic animals.

The east stairway, associated with Venus, was for birds.

The west stairway, associated with the so-called "long-tailed Star", was for wild animals, vegetables, and insects.

In fact, the picture of the system was not easily or immediately grasped from Ogotemmêli's account of it.

"When the ancestor came down from Heaven," he said at first, "he was standing on a square piece of Heaven, not a very big piece, about the size of a sleeping-mat, or perhaps a bit bigger."

"How could he stand on this piece of Heaven?"

"It was a piece of celestial earth."

"A thick piece?"

"Yes! As thick as a house. It was ten cubits high with stairs on each side facing the four cardinal points."

The blind man had raised his head, which was almost always bent towards the ground. How was he to explain these geometrical forms, these steps, these exact measurements? The European had begun by thinking that what was meant was a tall prism flanked by four stairways forming a cross. He kept returning to this conception in order to get it quite clear, while the other, patiently groping in the darkness which enveloped him, sought for fresh details.

At last his ravaged face broke into a kind of smile: he had found what he wanted. Reaching into the inside of his house and lying almost flat on his back, he searched among a number of objects which grated or sounded hollow as they scraped the earth under his hand. Only his thin knees and his feet were still visible in the embrasure of the doorway; the rest disappeared in the shadows within. The front of the house looked like a great face with the mouth closed on two skinny shin-bones.

After much tugging, an object emerged from the depths and appeared framed in the doorway. It was a woven basket, black with dust and soot of the interior, with a round opening and a square base, crushed and broken, a wretched spectacle.

The thing was placed before the door, losing several strands in the process, while the whole of the blind man's body reappeared, his hand still firmly grasping the basket.

"Its only use now is to put chickens in," he said.

He passed his hands slowly over its battered remains, and proceeded to explain the world-system.

20

African Philosophy, Myth and Reality

Paulin J. Hountondji

I must emphasize that my theme is African philosophy, myth *and* reality, whereas one might have expected the conventional formula, myth *or* reality? I am not asking whether it exists, whether it is a myth *or* a reality. I observe that it does exist, by the same right and in the same mode as all the philosophies of the world: in the form of a *literature*. I shall try to account for this misunderstood reality, deliberately ignored or suppressed even by those who produce it and who, in producing it, believe that they are merely reproducing a pre-existing thought through it: through the insubstantiality of a transparent discourse, of a fluid, compliant ether whose only function is to transmit light. My working hypothesis is that such suppression cannot be innocent: this discursive self-deception serves to conceal something else, and this apparent self-obliteration of the subject aims at camouflaging its massive omnipresence, its convulsive effort to root in reality this fiction filled with itself. Tremendous censorship of a shameful text, which presents itself as impossibly transparent and almost non-existent but which also claims for its object (African pseudo-philosophy) the privilege of having always existed, outside any explicit formulation.

I therefore invert the relation: that which exists, that which is incontrovertibly given is that literature. As for the object it claims to restore, it is at most a way of speaking, a verbal invention, a *muthos*. When I speak of African philosophy I mean that literature, and I try to understand why it has so far made such strenuous efforts to hide behind the screen, all the more opaque for being imaginary, of an implicit "philosophy" conceived as an unthinking, spontaneous, collective system of thought, common to all Africans or at least to all members severally, past, present and future, of such-and-such an African ethnic group. I try to understand why most African authors, when trying to engage with philosophy, have so far thought it necessary to project the misunderstood reality of their own discourse on to such palpable fiction.

Let us therefore tackle the problem at a higher level. What is in question here, substantially, is the idea of *philosophy*, or rather, of *African philosophy*. More accurately, the problem is whether the word "philosophy," when qualified by the word "African," must retain its habitual meaning, or whether the simple addition of an adjective necessarily changes the meaning of the substantive.

From Paulin J. Hountondji, 1983. *African Philosophy, Myth and Reality*, pp. 55–70. Reprinted with permission of Indiana University Press.

What is in question, then, is the universality of the word "philosophy" throughout its possible geographical applications.

My own view is that this universality must be preserved – not because philosophy must necessarily develop the same themes or even ask the same questions from one country or continent to another, but because these differences of *content* are meaningful precisely and only as differences of *content*, which, as such, refer back to the essential unity of a single discipline, of a single style of inquiry.

The present chapter will therefore endeavour to develop the conclusions of the first two. In particular, it will attempt to show, first, that the phrase "African philosophy," in the enormous literature that has been devoted to the problem, has so far been the subject only of mythological exploitation and, second, that it is nevertheless possible to retrieve it and apply it to something else: not to the fiction of a collective system of thought, but to a set of philosophical discourses and texts.

I shall try to evince the existence of such texts and to determine both the limits and essential configurations, or general orientations, of African philosophical literature.

The Popular Concept of African Philosophy

Tempels' work will serve us as a reference.[1] More than once Tempels emphasizes that "Bantu philosophy" is experienced but not thought and that its practitioners are, at best, only dimly conscious of it:

> let us not expect the first Black in the street (especially if he is young) to give us a systematic account of his ontological system. Nevertheless, this ontology exists; it penetrates and informs all the primitive's thinking and dominates all his behaviour. Using the methods of analysis and synthesis of our own intellectual disciplines, we can and therefore must do the "primitive" the service of looking for, classifying and systematizing the elements of his ontological system.(p.15)

And further on:

> We do not claim that Bantus are capable of presenting us with a philosophical treatise complete with

an adequate vocabulary. It is our own intellectual training that enables us to effect its systematic development. It is up to us to provide them with an accurate account of their conception of entities, in such a way mat they will recognize themselves in our words and will agree, saying: "You have understood us, you know us now completely, you 'know' in the same way we 'know'."(p.24)

It is quite clear, then: the black man is here regarded, in Eboussi-Boulaga's words, as the "Monsieur Jourdain of philosophy."[2] Unwitting philosopher, he is the rival in silliness of Molière's famous character, who spoke in prose without knowing it. Ignorant of his own thoughts, he needs an interpreter to translate them for him, or rather an interpreter who, having formulated these thoughts with the white world in mind, will accidently drop a few crumbs which will inspire the Bantu, when he picks them up, with boundless gratitude.

We have already mentioned Césaire's criticism. That very necessary political critique, we said, stopped short because it failed to follow up its own theoretical implications. To aim cautious criticisms, "not at Bantu philosophy, but at the political uses to which it is being put,"[3] was to avoid questioning the genealogy of the concept itself and to treat its appearance in scientific literature as an accident, as though its only function were this very political one. It was, in fact, tantamount to shying away from an exposure of the profoundly conservative nature of the ethnophilosophical project itself.

It follows that not only *Bantu Philosophy* but the whole of ethno-philosophical literature must be subjected to an expanded and more profound version of Césaire's political criticism. For if, as a result of what might be called the ethnological division of labour (a sort of scientific equivalent of the military scramble for the Third World by the great powers), Tempels can pass for the great specialist in the Bantu area, and if, too, his reconstruction of African "philosophy" is the more sensational because of his one-to-one contrasts between this African pseudo-philosophy and an equally imaginary European philosophy,[4] similar attempts have been made by other European authors for other regions of Africa. To quote only a few, Marcel Griaule has devoted to the Dogons of the present-day Republic of Mali a book currently regarded as a classic of Dogon wisdom, *Dieu d'eau*,[5] followed by another, in collaboration with Germaine Dieterlen, entitled *Le Renard pâle*.[6] Dominique Zahan has made known to the world the religion, the spirituality and what he calls the "philosophy" of the Bambara.[7] Louis-Vincent Thomas has carried out painstaking research among the Diola of Senegal and has expatiated on their wisdom, their system of thought or, as he calls it, their "philosophy."[8]

As might have been expected, the example of these European authors has been widely followed at home. Many Africans have plunged into the same field of research, correcting on occasion – but without ever questioning its basic assumptions – the work of their Western models. Among them is the abbé Alexis Kagamé of Rwanda, with his *Philosophie bantou-rwandaise de l'être*.[9] Then there is Mgr Makarakiza of Burundi, who published in 1959 a study entitled *La Dialectique des barundi*.[10] The South African priest Antoine Mabona distinguished himself in 1960 with an article entitled "African philosophy," then in 1963 with a text on "The depths of African philosophy" and finally in 1964 with a meditation on "La spiritualité africaine."[11] In this concert Father A. Rahajarizafy has sounded the note of the Great Island by trying to define Malagasy "philosophy" in an article of 1963 on "Sagesse malgache et théologie chrétienne."[12] In 1962, François-Marie Lufuluabo, a Franciscan from the former Belgian Congo, appeared in the firmament with a booklet, *Vers une théodicée bantoue*, followed in 1963 by an article entitled "La Conception bantoue face au christianisme," signing off in 1964 with another booklet on *La Notion luba-bantoue de l'être*.[13] Then, in 1965, his compatriot, the abbé Vincent Mulago, devoted a chapter to African "philosophy" in his *Visage africain du christianisme*.[14] The former Protestant clergyman Jean-Calvin Bahoken, of Cameroun, was clearing his *Clairières métaphysiques africaines*[15] in 1967, and two years later the Kenyan pastor John Mbiti, probably fascinated by his own childhood, revealed to the world in a now classic work, *African Religions and Philosophy*, the fact that the African ignores the future, hardly knows the present and lives entirely turned towards the past.[16]

Before we go on with the catalogue, let us note that all the authors we have just quoted are churchmen, like Tempels himself. This explains their main preoccupation, which was to find a psychological and cultural basis for rooting the Christian message in the African's mind without betraying either. Of course, this is an eminently legitimate concern, up to a point. But it means that these authors are compelled to conceive of philosophy on the model of religion, as a permanent, stable system of beliefs, unaffected by evolution, impervious to time and history, ever identical to itself.

Let us now turn to the lay authors, with, here again, only a few examples. We cannot but mention Léopold Sédar Senghor, whose chatty disquisitions on "negritude" are often buttressed by an analysis of what he called, as early as 1939, the black man's "conception of the world," a phrase which he later replaced, under the influence of Tempels, with the "black metaphysic."[17] There are also the Nigerian Adesanya, author of an article published in 1958 on "Yoruba metaphysical thinking";[18] the Ghanaian William Abraham, author of a book which is remarkable in many ways, *The Mind of Africa*[19] (I believe that a book can be instructive, interesting, useful, even if it is founded on erroneous assumptions); the late-lamented Kwame Nkrumah, whose famous *Consciencism* can hardly be regarded as his best publication;[20] the Senegalese Alassane N'Daw, who devoted several articles to the subject;[21] the Camerounian Basilc-Juleat Fouda, author of a doctoral thesis defended at Lille in 1967 on "La Philosophie négro-africaine de l'existence" (unpublished);[22] the Dahomean Issiaka Prosper Laleye, also the author of a thesis, "La Conception de la personne dans la pensée traditionnelle yoruba,"[23] presented in 1970 at the Catholic University of Fribourg, in Switzerland; the Nigerian J. O. Awolalu, author of an article entitled "The Yoruba philosophy of life."[24] And there are many others.[25]

Without being motivated quite so restrictively as the church ethnophilosophers, these authors were none the less intent on locating, beneath the various manifestations of African civilization, beneath the flood of history which has swept this civilization along willy-nilly, a solid bedrock which might provide a foundation of certitudes: in other words, a system of beliefs. In this quest, we find the same preoccupation as in the negritude movement – a passionate search for the identity that was denied by the colonizer – but now there is the underlying idea that one of the elements of the cultural identity is precisely "philosophy," the idea that every culture rests on a specific, permanent, metaphysical substratum.

Let us now ask the crucial question: is this the usual meaning of the word "philosophy?" Is it the way it is understood, for instance, in the phrases "European philosophy," "nineteenth-century philosophy," etc.? Clearly not. It seems as though the word automatically changes its meaning as soon as it ceases to be applied to Europe or to America and is applied to Africa. This is a well-known phenomenon. As our Kenyan colleague Henry Odera humorously remarks:

> What may be a superstition is paraded as "African religion," and the white world is expected to endorse that it is indeed a religion but an African religion. What in all cases is a mythology is paraded as "African philosophy," and again the white culture is expected to endorse that it is indeed a philosophy but an African philosophy. What is in all cases a dictatorship is paraded as "African democracy," and the white culture is again expected to endorse that it is so. And what is early a dedevelopment or pseudo-development is described as "development," and again the white world is expected to endorse that it is development – but of course "African development."[26]

Words do indeed change their meanings miraculously as soon as they pass from the Western to the African context, and not only in the vocabulary of European or American writers but also, through faithful imitation, in that of Africans themselves. That is what happens to the word "philosophy": applied to Africa, it is supposed to designate no longer the specific discipline it evokes in its Western context but merely a collective world-view, an implicit, spontaneous, perhaps even unconscious system of beliefs to which all Africans are supposed to adhere. This is a vulgar usage of the word, justified presumably by the supposed vulgarity of the geographical context to which it is applied.

Behind this usage, then, there is a myth at work, the myth of primitive unanimity, with its suggestion

that in "primitive" societies – that is to say, non-Western societies – everybody always agrees with everybody else. It follows that in such societies there can never be individual beliefs or philosophies but only collective systems of belief. The word "philosophy" is then used to designate each belief-system of this kind, and it is tacitly agreed among well-bred people that in this context it could not mean anything else.

One can easily detect in this, one of the founding acts of the "science" (or rather the pseudoscience) called ethnology, namely, the generally tacit thesis that non-Western societies are absolutely specific, the silent postulate of a difference in *nature* (and not merely in the *evolutionary stage* attained, with regard to particular types of achievement), of a difference in *quality* (not merely in quantity or *scale*), between so-called "primitive" societies and developed ones. Cultural anthropology (another name for ethnology) owes its supposed autonomy (notably in relation to sociology) to this arbitrary division of the human community into two types of society which are taken, arbitrarily and without proof, to be fundamentally different.[27]

But let us return to the myth of unanimity. It would seem at first sight that this theoretical consensus postulated by ethnophilosophy among all members of each "primitive" community should produce a parallel consensus, at the level of results if not of methods, among all ethnophilosophers studying the same community. But, curiously enough, instead of an ideal consensus, a fine unanimity whose transparency would have revealed the spontaneous unanimity of all those "primitive philosophers," ethnophilosophical literature offers us a rich harvest of not only diverse but also sometimes frankly contradictory works.

We have noted above such divergences between Tempels and Kagamé. It would probably be easy to find similar differences between the many other works relating to the "traditional" thought of Bantus or Africans in general, if one could overcome one's understandable boredom, read all of them one by one, examine them patiently and juxtapose all the views they contain.

But I can see the objection being raised that such differences are normal, that the diversity of works is a source of wealth and not of weakness, that the internal contradictions of ethnophilosophy can be found in any science worthy of the name – physics, chemistry, mathematics, linguistics, psychoanalysis, sociology, etc. – that they are a sign of vitality, not inconsistency, a condition of progress rather than an obstacle in the path of discovery. It may be added that, as in all sciences, a reality may exist without being immediately understood, and that consequently it is not surprising if an implicit system of thought can be reconstructed only as a result of long, collective and contradictory research.

The only thing this objection overlooks is the "slight difference" between the sciences cited and ethnophilosophy that they do not postulate anything remotely comparable with the supposed unanimity of a human community; that in these sciences, moreover, a contradiction is never stagnant but always progressive, never final or absolute but indicative of an *error*, of the *falsity* of a hypothesis or thesis, which is bound to emerge from a rational investigation of the object itself, whereas a contradiction between two ethnophilosophical theses is necessarily circular, since it can never be resolved by experimentation or any other method of verification. The point is that an ethnophilosophical contradiction is necessarily *antinomal* in the Kantian sense; thesis and antithesis are equally demonstrable – in other words, equally gratuitous. In such a case contradiction does not generate synthesis but simply demonstrates the need to re-examine the very foundations of the discipline and to provide a critique of ethnophilosophical reason and perhaps of ethnological reason too.

Ethnophilosophy can now be seen in its true light. Because it has to account for an imaginary unanimity, to interpret a text which nowhere exists and has to be constantly reinvented, it is a science without an object, a "crazed language"[28] accountable to nothing, a discourse that has no referent, so that its falsity can never be demonstrated. Tempels can then maintain that for the Bantu being is power, and Kagamé can beg to differ: we have no means of settling the quarrel. It is clear, therefore, that the "Bantu philosophy" of the one is not the philosophy of the Bantu but that of Tempels, that the "Bantu-Rwandais philosophy" of the other is not that of the Rwandais but that of Kagamé. Both of them simply make use of African traditions and oral literature and project on to them their own

philosophical beliefs, hoping to enhance their credibility thereby.

That is how the functioning of this thesis of a collective African philosophy works: it is a smoke-screen behind which each author is able to manipulate his own philosophical views. It has nothing beyond this ideological function: it is an indeterminate discourse with no object.

Towards a New Concept of "African Philosophy"

Behind and beyond the ethnological pretext, philosophical views remain. The dogma of unanimism has not been completely sterile, since it has at least generated a quite distinctive philosophical literature.

Here we must note a surprising fact: while they were looking for philosophy in a place where it could never be found – in the collective unconscious of African peoples, in the silent folds of their explicit discourse – the ethnophilosophers never questioned the nature and theoretical status of their own analyses. Were these relevant to philosophy? There lay the true but undetected problem. For if we want to be scientific, we cannot apply the same word to two things as different as a spontaneous, implicit and collective world-view on the one hand and, on the other, the deliberate, explicit and individual analytic activity which takes that world-view as its object. Such an analysis should be called "philosophology" rather than "philosophy" or, to use a less barbarous term, "metaphilosophy" – but a metaphilosophy of the worst kind, an inegalitarian metaphilosophy, not a dialogue and confrontation with an existing philosophy but a reduction to silence, a denial, masquerading as the revival of an earlier philosophy.

For we know that in its highly elaborated forms philosophy is always, in a sense, a metaphilosophy, that it can develop only by reflecting on its own history, that all new thinkers must feed on the doctrines of their predecessors, even of their contemporaries, extending or refuting them, so as to enrich the philosophical heritage available in their own time. But in this case metaphilosophy does not rely on an exploitation of extra-philosophical data or on the arbitrary over-interpretation of social facts which in themselves bear no relation to philosophy. Metaphilosophy signifies, rather, a philosophical reflection on discourses which are themselves overtly and consciously philosophical. Ethnophilosophy, on the other hand, claims to be the description of an implicit, unexpressed world-view, which never existed anywhere but in the anthropologist's imagination. Ethnophilosophy is a pre-philosophy mistaking itself for a metaphilosophy, a philosophy which, instead of presenting its own rational justification, shelters lazily behind the authority of a tradition and projects its own theses and beliefs on to that tradition.

If we now return to our question, namely, whether philosophy resides in the world-view described or in the description itself, we can now assert that if it resides in either, it must be the second, the description of that vision, even if this is, in fact, a self-deluding invention that hides behind its own products. African philosophy does exist therefore, but in a new sense, as a literature produced by Africans and dealing with philosophical problems.

A contradiction? Oh no! Some may be surprised that, having patiently dismantled the ethnophilosophical machine, we should now be trying to restore it. They have simply failed to understand that we are merely recognizing the existence of that literature as *philosophical literature*, whatever may be its *value* and *credibility*. What we are acknowledging is what it *is*, not what it *says*. Having laid bare the mythological assumptions on which it is founded (these having suppressed all question of its status), we can now pay greater attention to the fact of its existence as a determinate form of philosophical literature which, however mystified and mystifying it may be (mystifying because mystified), nevertheless belongs to the history of African literature in general.

Let us be accurate: the issue here is only *African* ethnophilosophy. A work like *Bantu Philosophy* does not belong to African philosophy, since its author is not African; but Kagamé's work is an integral part of African philosophical literature. In other words, speaking of African philosophy in a new sense, we must draw a line, within ethnophilosophical literature in general, between African and non-African writers, not because one category is better than the other, or because both might not, in the last analysis, say the same thing, but because,

the subject being *African* philosophy, we cannot exclude a geographical variable, taken here as empirical, contingent, extrinsic to the content or significance of the discourse and as quite apart from any questions of *theoretical connections*. Thus Tempels' work, although it deals with an African subject and has played a decisive role in the development of African ethnophilosophy, belongs to *European* scientific literature, in the same way as anthropology in general, although it deals with non-Western societies, is an embodiment of Western science, no more and no less.

A happy consequence of this demarcation is that it emphasizes certain subtle nuances and occasional serious divergences which might otherwise have passed unnoticed and which differentiate African authors whom we initially grouped together as ethnophilosophers. It is thus possible to see the immense distance which separates, for instance, Bahoken's *Clairières métaphysiques africaines*,[29] justifiably assessed as a perfect example of ideological twaddle designed by an apparently nationalistic African to flatter the exotic tastes of the Western public from Kwame Nkrumah's *Consciencism*, written chiefly for the African public and aimed at making it aware of its new cultural identity, even though Nkrumah's book, unfortunately, partakes of the ethnological conception that there can be such a thing as a collective philosophy.

Another even more important consequence is that this African philosophical literature can now be seen to include philosophical works of those African authors who do not believe in the myth of a collective philosophy or who reject it explicitly. Let me cite a few of these. Fabien Ehoussi-Boulaga's fine article "Le Bantou problématique"[30] has already been mentioned. Another Camerounian, Marcien Towa, has given us a brilliant critique of ethnophilosophy in general, the *Essai sur la problématique philosophique dans l'Afrique actuelle*, followed by an incisive criticism of the Senghorian doctrine of negritude, *Léopold Sédar Senghor: négritude ou servitude?*[31] Henry Oruka Odera of Kenya has published a fine article entitled "Mythologies as African philosophy."[32] The Béninois (former Dahomeyan) Stanislas Spero Adotevi earned fame in 1972 with his brilliant book *Négritude et négrologues*.[33]

But more than that: African philosophical literature includes works which make no attempt whatever to broach the problem of "African philosophy," either to assert or to deny its existence. In fact, we must extend the concept to include all the research into Western philosophy carried out by Africans. This broadening of the horizon implies no contradiction: just as the writings of Western anthropologists on African societies belong to Western scientific literature, so the philosophical writings of Africans on the history of Western thought are an integral part of African philosophical literature So, obviously, African philosophical works concerning problems that are not specially related to African experience should also be included. In this sense, the articles by the Ghanaian J. E. Wiredu on Kant, on material implication and the concept of truth,[34] are an integral part of African philosophy, as are analyses of the concept of freedom or the notion of free will[35] by the Kenyan Henry Odera or the Nigerian D. E. Idoniboye. The same can be said of the research on French seventeenth-century philosophy by the Zaïrois Elungu Pere Elungu, *Etendue et connaissance dans la philosophie de Malebranche,*[36] of the epistemological introduction to *Théologie positive et théologie spéculative*[37] by his fellow countryman Tharcisse Tshibangu. The work of the Camerounian N'joh Mouelle, particularly *Jalons* and *De la médiocrité, à l'excellence: Essai sur la signification humaine du développement,*[38] may also be placed in this category, although their subjects are not only universal but also linked with the present historical situation of Africa.

By the same token we may readily claim works like those of the Ashanti scholar Anton-Wilhelm Amo, who studied and taught in German universities during the first half of the eighteenth century, as belonging to African philosophical literature, although this may be regarded as a borderline case, since Amo was trained almost entirely in the West. But is not this the case with almost every African intellectual even today?[39]

The essential point here is that we have produced a radically new definition of African philosophy, the criterion now being the geographical origin of the authors rather than an alleged specificity of content. The effect of this is to broaden the narrow horizon which has hitherto been imposed on African philosophy and to treat it, as now conceived, as a methodical inquiry with the same universal aims as those of any other philosophy in the world. In short, it destroys the dominant mythological conception of Africanness and restores the simple, obvious truth that Africa is above all a continent and the concept of Africa an empirical, geographical concept and not a metaphysical one. The purpose of this "demythologizing" of the idea of Africa and African philosophy is simply to free our faculty for theorizing from all the intellectual impediments and prejudices which have so far prevented it from getting off the ground.

Final Remarks

There can no longer be any doubt about the existence of African philosophy, although its meaning is different from that to which the anthropologists have accustomed us. It exists as a particular form of scientific literature. But, of course, once this point is established, many questions remain. For instance, how shall we distinguish philosophical literature from other forms of scientific literature, such as mathematics, physics, biology, linguistics, sociology, etc., inasmuch as these disciplines also develop as specific forms of literature? In other words, what is the particular object and area of study of philosophy? In more general terms, what relation is there between scientific literature and non-scientific literature (for instance, artistic literature), and why must we include philosophical literature in the first rather than the second?

This is not the place to answer these questions. All that we have tried to do so far has been to clear the ground for questions of this kind, since they presuppose that philosophy is recognized simply as a theoretical discipline and nothing else, a discipline which, like any other, can develop only in the form of literature.

Moreover, such questions can never receive definite and immutable answers, for the definition of a science must be revised constantly in the light of its own progress, and the articulation of theoretical discourse in general – by which we mean the demarcation of the various sciences – is itself subject to historical change. At this point, it is true, a much harder question, or series of questions, arises: how is the object of a science determined?

What conditions, economic, historical, ideological or other, contribute to fixing the frontiers of a discipline? How is a new science born? How does an old science die or cease to be considered a science?[40]

This is not the place to answer these questions either. But at least there is one thing we are in a position to affirm: no science, no branch of learning can appear except as an event in language or, more precisely, as the product of discussion. The first thing to do, then, is to organize such discussions in the midst of the society where the birth of these sciences is desired. In other words, whatever the specific object of philosophy may be, the first task of African philosophers today, if they wish to develop an authentic African philosophy, is to promote and sustain constant free discussion about all the problems concerning their discipline instead of being satisfied with a private and somewhat abstract dialogue between themselves and the Western world.[41] By reorienting their discourse in this way, they will easily overcome the permanent temptation of "folklorism" that limits their research to so-called African subjects – a temptation which has owed most of its strength to the fact that their writings have been intended for a foreign public.

It is indeed a strange paradox that in present conditions the dialogue with the West can only encourage "folklorism," a sort of collective cultural exhibitionism which compels the "Third World" intellectual to "defend and illustrate" the peculiarities of his tradition for the benefit of a Western public. This seemingly universal dialogue simply encourages the worst kind of cultural particularism, both because its supposed peculiarities are in the main purely imaginary and because the intellectual who defends them claims to speak in the name of his whole people although they have never asked him to do so and are usually unaware that such a dialogue is taking place.

On the contrary, it is to be hoped that when Africans start discussing theoretical problems among themselves, they will feel spontaneously the need to gather the broadest possible information on the scientific achievements of other continents and societies. They will take an interest in these achievements not because they will be held to be the best that can be attained but in order to assess more objectively, and if necessary improve, their own achievements in the same areas.

The paradox is therefore easily removed: interlocutors of the same origin rarely feel the need to exalt their own cultural particularities. Such a need arises only when one faces people from other countries and is forced to assert one's uniqueness by conforming to the current stereotypes of one's own society and civilization. Universality becomes accessible only when interlocutors are set free from the need to assert themselves in the face of others; and the best way to achieve this in Africa today is to organize internal discussion and exchange among all the scientists in the continent, within each discipline and – why not? – between one discipline and another, so as to create in our societies a scientific tradition worthy of the name. The difficult questions we have been asking concerning the origins, the definition, the boundaries, the evolution and the destiny of the various sciences, and more particularly the nature of philosophy and its relation to other disciplines, will then find their answers in the concrete history of our theoretical literature.

We must therefore plunge in and not be afraid of thinking new thoughts, of simply *thinking*. For every thought is new if we take the word in its active sense, even thought about past thoughts, provided we are not content simply to repeat hallowed themes, catechetically and parrot-fashion, with a pout or a purr, but on the contrary boldly rearticulate these themes, justify them, give them a new and sounder foundation. Conversely, every blustering declaration of loyalty to a so-called "modern" doctrine will be at best mere folklore – when it does not turn out to be an objective mystification – unless it is accompanied by some intellectual effort to *know*, *understand* and *think out* the doctrine by going beyond the more sensational formulations to the problematic on which it is founded. We cannot go on acting a part indefinitely. The time has come for theoretical responsibility, for taking ourselves seriously.

In Africa now the individual must liberate himself from the weight of the past as well as from the allure of ideological fashions. Amid the diverse but, deep down, so strangely similar catechisms of conventional nationalism and of equally conventional pseudo-Marxism, amid so many state ideologies functioning in the Fascist mode, deceptive alibis behind which the powers that be can quietly do the opposite of what they say and say the opposite of what they do, amid this immense confusion in which the most vulgar police state pompously declares itself to be a "dictatorship of the proletariat" and neo-Fascists mouthing pseudo-revolutionary platitudes are called "Marxist-Leninists," reducing the enormous theoretical and political subversive power of Marxism to the dimensions of a truncheon, in which, in the name of revolution, they kill, massacre, torture the workers, the trade unionists, the executives, the students; in the midst of all this intellectual and political bedlam we must all open our eyes wide and clear our own path. Nothing less will make discussions between free and intellectually responsible individuals possible. Nothing less will make a philosophy possible.

As can be seen, then, the development of African philosophical literature presupposes the removal of a number of political obstacles. In particular, it requires that democratic liberties and especially the right of free criticism, the suppression of which seems to constitute the sole aim and *raison d'être* of the official ideologies, should be acknowledged and jealously guarded. It is impossible to philosophize in Africa today without being aware of this need and of the pricelessness of freedom of expression as a necessary condition for all science, for all theoretical development and, in the last resort, for all real political and economic progress, too.

Briefly, and in conclusion, African philosophy exists, but it is not what it is believed to be. It is developing objectively in the form of a literature rather than as implicit and collective thought, but as a literature of which the output remains captive to the unanimist fallacy. Yet, happily, it is possible to detect signs of a new spirit. The liberation of this new spirit is now the necessary precondition of any progress in this field. To achieve that we must begin at the beginning; we must restore the right to criticism and free expression which are so seriously threatened by our regimes of terror and ideological confusion.

In short, it is not enough to recognize the existence of an African philosophical literature. The most important task is to transform it from the simple collection of writings aimed at non-African readers and consequently upholding the peculiarities of a so-called African "world-view" that it is today into the vehicle of a free and rigorous discussion among African philosophers themselves. Only then will this literature acquire universal value and enrich the common international heritage of human thought.

Notes

1 P. Tempels, *La Philosophie Bantoue* (Paris; Présence Africaine 1949)(AS 601). The letters AS, followed by a number, refer to the "bibliography of African thought" published by the Rev. Father Alphonse Smet, in *Cahiers philosophiques africains* no. 2 (July–December 1972), Lubumbashi. This "bibliography," despite the fact that it lumps together philosophical and non-philosophical (i.e. sociological, ethnological, even literary) texts, is nevertheless a useful instrument for any research on African literature or Western literature concerning Africa. The number following the letters AS indicates the number of the text in Smet's "Bibliography."

2 F. Eboussi-Boulaga, "Le Bantou problématique," *Présence Africaine*, no.66 (1968).

3 Aimé Césaire, *Discours sur le colonialisme* (Paris: Editions Réclame 1950)(AS 95), p.45.

4 Comparisons between the "world-view" of Third World peoples and European philosophy involve stripping the latter also of its history, its internal diversity and its richness and reducing the multiplicity of its works and doctrines to a "lowest common denominator." This common stock-in-trade of European philosophy is represented in Tempels by a vague system of thought made up of Aristotle, Christian theology and horse sense.

5 AS 214.

6 M. Griaule and G. Dieterlen, *Le Renard pâle* (Paris: Publications of the Institute of Ethnology 1965) (AS 220).

7 Dominique Zahan, *Sociétés d'initiation bambara: le n'domo, le koré* (Paris/The Hague: Mouton 1963) (AS 718); *La Dialectique du verbe chez les Bambara* (Paris/The Hague: Mouton 1963)(AS 713); *La Viande et la*

Graine, mythologie dogon (Paris: Présence Africaine 1968)(AS 719); *Religion, spiritualité el pensée africaines* (Paris: Payot 1970)(AS 716). See my review of this last book in *Les Etudes philosophiques*, no.3 (1971).

8   Louis-Vincent Thomas, *Les Diola. Essai d'analyse fonctionnelle sur une population de Basse-Casamance*, vols. I and II (Dakar; Mémoires de l'Institut Français d'Afrique Noire 1959) (not mentioned in AS); "Brève esquisse sur la pensée cosmologique du Diola", *African Systems of Thought*, prefaced by M. Fortes and G. Dieterlen (OUP 1965)(AS 620); "Un Système philosophique sénégalais: la cosmotogie des Diola," *Présence Africaine*, nos. 32–3 (1960)(AS 638); *Cinq essais sur la mort africaine*, Publications de la Faculté des Lettres et Sciences humaines (Philosophie et Sciences sociales) Dakar no. 3 (1969)(AS 621); "La Mort et la sagesse africaine. Esquisse d'une anthropologie philosophique," *Psychopathologie Africaine*, no. 3 (1967). See also other texts by the same author, cited in AS 617–39.

9   AS 294. See also, by the same author, "L'Ethnologie des Bantu," *Contemporary Philosophy. A Survey*, ed. Raymond Klibansky, vol. IV (Florence 1971) (AS 754).

10 AS 347.

11 Mongameli Antoine Mabona, "Philosophie africaine," *Présence Africaine*, no.30 (1960)(AS 342); "The Depths of African Philosophy," *Personnalité africaine et Catholicisme* (Paris: Présence Africaine 1963)(AS 343); "La Spiritualité africaine," *Présence Africaine* no. 52 (1964)(AS 344).

12 A. Rahajarizafy, "Sagesse malgache et théologie chrétienne," *Personnalité africaine et Catholicisme* (Paris: Présence Africaine 1963)(AS 504).

13 Respectively, AS 341; "La Conception bantoue face au christianisme," *Personnalité africaine et Catholicisme* (Paris: Présence Africaine 1963); AS 339.

14 AS 414. The chapter in question is the eighth, entitled "Philosophical outline"; "Dialectique existentielle des Bantous et sacramentalisme," *Aspects de la culture noire* (Paris 1958)(AS 410).

15 Jean-Calvin Bahoken, *Clairiéres métaphysiques africaines* (Paris: Présence Africaine 1967)(AS 46).

16 John Mbiti, *African Religions and Philosophy* (Heinemann 1969)(AS 372); *Concepts of God in Africa* (New York: Praeger 1970)(AS 375); *New Testament Eschatology in an African Background. A Study of the encounter between New Testament theology and African traditional concepts* (OUP 1971).

17 See in particular the texts (written between 1937 and 1963) collected in *Liberté I. Négritude et humanisme*. As a theory of "negritude," the Senghorian ethnology was always, above all, an ethnopsychology concerned essentially with defining the "Negro soul," where sociology (usually idyllic descriptions of "Negro society") and aesthetic analyses (commentaries, many of them excellent, on various works of art) are used mainly to reinforce this fantasy psychology. However, *ethnopsychology* always betrays the ambition to become an *ethnophilosophy* by accounting for the black "conception of the world" as well as for the psychological characteristics. The project is clearly formulated in the celebrated 1939 article "Ce que l'homme noir apporte" ("The black man's contribution") in which the black "conception of the world," however, still appears as a psychological quality: an animism, or rather, according to Senghor, an anthropopsychism. This is no longer so in the 1956 text "The Black African aesthetic" and the 1959 text on the "Constitutive elements of a civilization of Black African inspiration" *Liberté I*, pp. 202–17 and 252–86: apart from a few alterations, these are reprints of Senghor's reports to the First International Congress of Black Writers and Artists, Paris 1956, and to the Second Congress, Rome 1959. Explicitly referring to Tempels, but still wishing to *explain* the black's "metaphysics" in terms of black "psychophysiology," Senghor defines it rather as a system of ideas, an "existential ontology" (ibid., pp. 203–4, 264–8).

The reader will therefore readily understand that I should feel reluctant to situate ethnophilosophy "in the wake of negritude" or to treat it as a "(late) aspect of the negritude movement", as Marcien Towa does in *Essai sur la problématique philosophique dans l'Afrique actuelle* (Yaoundé: Editions Clé 1971), pp. 23, 25. If *African* ethnophilosophers are undoubtedly part of the negritude movement, they owe the philosophical pretensions of their nationalist discourse rather to the ethnophilosophy of *European* Africanists.

18 A. Adesanya, "Yoruba metaphysical thinking," *Odu*, no.5 (1958)(AS 15).

19 W. Abraham, *The Mind of Africa* (Chicago: University of Chicago Press and Weidenfeld & Nicolson 1962)(AS 5).

20 AS 436 and 438.

21 Alassane N'Daw, "Peut-on parler d'une pensée africaine?," *Présence Africaine* no. 58 (1966)(AS 420); "Pensée africaine et développement," *Problèmes sociaux congolais* (Kinshasa: CEP SI Publications 1966–7)(AS 419).

22 This unpublished thesis is mentioned here mainly because it is discussed at length by Marcien Towa

in his critique of ethnophilosophy (Towa, *Essai sur la problématique philosophique*, pp. 23–33)(AS 646).

23 Subtitled "A phenomenological approach" and prefaced by Philippe Laburthe-Tolra (Berne: Herbert Lang 1970)(AS 325).

24 The article was published in *Présence Africaine*, no. 73 (1970)(AS 39).

25 For instance, G. De Souza, *La Conception de "Vie" chez les Fon* (Cotonou: Editions du Bénin 1975): a doctoral thesis defended in 1972.

26 Henry Oruka Odera, "Mythologies as African philosophy," *East Africa Journal*, vol. IX, no. 10 (October 1972) (not mentioned in AS).

27 See, on this point, Ola Balogun, "Ethnology and its ideologies," *Consequence*, no. 1 (1974). See also my article on "Le Mythe de la philosophie spontanée," *Cahiers Philosophiques Africains*, no. 1 (1972).

28 That is, "Language gone mad." I have borrowed this phrase from the Zaïrois V. Y. Mudimbe, whose book *L'Autre Face du royaume. Une introduction à la critique des langages en folie* (Lausanne: L'Age d'homme 1973) ranks among the finest works written to this day *on* (not *of*) ethnology.

29 How revealing that this work was published in France "with the help of the Centre National de la Recherche Scientifique."

30 I have mentioned this article as the most vigorous and complete critique of Tempels to date for its rigorous analysis of the contradictions in his work. Eboussi-Balaga shows that these can ultimately be reduced to

> an interplay of value and counter-value … which characterizes the colonizer's judgements on the colonized. Bantuism is partly admirable and partly abominable. It is valuable when the colonized wish to forsake it for equality: then they are reminded that they are losing their "souls". But Bantuism becomes a vile hotchpotch of degenerate magical practices when the colonizer wishes to affirm his pre-eminence and legitimize his power. ("Le Bantou problématique," p. 32)

However, Eboussi does not totally reject the idea of an "ethnological philosophy," a philosophy which would abandon the search for an "ontological substratum for social reality," would deal with the "mythical discourse of 'native theorists'," instead of bypassing it with scorn (ibid., p.9). On this point I believe a more radical view should be taken.

31 Towa, *Essai sur la problématique philosophique; Léopold Sédar Senghor: négritude ou servitude?* (Yaoundé: Editions Cié 1971)(AS 647).

32 Odera, "Mythologies as African philosophy."

33 S.A. Adotevi, *Négritude et négrologues* (Paris: Union Générale d'Editions, Coll. 10/18 1972)(not mentioned in AS).

34 J. E. Wiredu, "Kant's synthetic *a priori* in geometry and the rise of non-Euclidean geometries," *Kantstudien*, Heft 1, Bonn (1970)(not in AS); "Material implication and 'if … then'," *International Logic Review*, no. 6, Bologna (1972) (not in AS); "Truth as opinion," *Universitas*, vol. 2, no. 3 (new series), University of Ghana (1973)(not in AS); "On an African orientation in philosophy", *Second Order*, vol. 1, no. 2, University of Ife (1972) (not in AS).

35 H. Odera, "The meaning of liberty," *Cahiers Philosophiques Africains*, no. 1, Lubumbashi (1972) (not in AS); D. E. Idoniboye, "Freewill, the linguistic philosopher's dilemma," *Cahiers Philosophiques Africains*, no. 2, Lubumbashi (1972) (not in AS).

36 E. P. Elungu, *Etendue et connaissance dans la philosophie de Malebranche* (Paris: Vrin 1973)(not in AS). One may also mention the unpublished thesis defended in Paris in 1971 by the Senegalese A. R. N'Diaye, "L'Order dans la philosophie de Malebranche."

37 T. Tshibangu, *Théologie positive et théologie spéculative* (Louvain/Paris: Béatrice-Nauwelaerts 1965) (not in AS).

38 E. N'joh Mouellé, *Falons: recherche d'une mentalité neuve* (Yaoundé: Editions Clé 1970)(AS 775); *De la médiocrité à l'excellence. Essai sur la signification humaine du développement* (Yaoundé: Editions Clé 1970)(AS 432).

39 More generally, this new definition of African philosophy opens up the possibility of a history of African philosophy, whereas the very notion of such a history was unthinkable in the ideological context of ethnophilosophy. If African philosophy is seen not as an implicit world-view but as the set of philosophical writings produced by Africans, we can at last undertake to reconstruct their chequered history, including those of Afro-Arab authors like Ibn Khaldun, Al Ghazali, etc., whatever may be the historical and theoretical distance between these texts.

40 For a consideration of these questions and some representative answers, see: L. Althusser, *For Marx* (1965), trans. B. Brewster (Allen Lane 1969); L. Althusser, *et al.*, *Reading Capital* (New Left Books 1970); G. Bachelard, *La Formation de l'esprit scientifique* (1947) (Paris: Vrin 1969); *Le Nouvel Esprit scientifique* (1934), 9th ed. (Paris: PUF 1966); G. Canguilhem,

Etudes d'histoire et de philosophie des sciences (Paris: Vrin 1968); M. Foucault, *The Birth of the Clinic* (1972), trans. A. M. Sheridan Smith (Tavistock 1973); *The Order of Things* (1966), (Tavistock 1970); *The Archaeology of Knowledge* (1969), trans. A. M. Sheridan Smith (Tavistock 1972).

41 It is worth mentioning here the part that can be played in promoting this new type of dialogue by the departments of philosophy in African universities and the philosophical associations (e.g. the Inter-African Council for Philosophy) and their respective journals.

21

Ancestors as Elders in Africa

Igor Kopytoff

Ancestor cults and ancestor worship loom large in the anthropological image of sub-Saharan Africa and few would disagree with Fortes that "comparatively viewed, African ancestor worship has a remarkably uniform structural framework" (Fortes, 1965:122). The general pattern may be quickly summarized. Ancestors are vested with mystical powers and authority. They retain a functional role in the world of the living, specifically in the life of their living kinsmen; indeed, African kin-groups are often described as communities of both the living and the dead. The relation of the ancestors to their living kinsmen has been described as ambivalent, as both punitive and benevolent and sometimes even as capricious. In general, ancestral benevolence is assured through propitiation and sacrifice; neglect is believed to bring about punishment. Ancestors are intimately involved with the welfare of their kin-group but they are not linked in the same way to every member of that group. The linkage is structured through the elders of the kin-group, and the elders' authority is related to their close link to the ancestors. In some sense the elders are the representatives of the ancestors and the mediators between diem and the kin-group.

Fortes has extended our theoretical understanding of African ancestor worship more recently by further clarifying some of its structural features (1965). Amplifying Gluckman's (1937) distinction between ancestor cults and the cults of the dead, Fortes brings out the importance of the "structural matrix of [African] ancestor worship", noting *inter alia* the relative lack of elaboration and indeed interest among the Africans in the cosmography of the afterworld in which the ancestors reside. The African emphasis is clearly not on how the dead live but on the manner in which they affect the living. Different ancestors are recognized as relevant to different structural contexts (as, for example, in groups of different genealogical levels); not all but only certain dead with particular structural positions are worshipped as ancestors; and the behaviour of ancestors reflects not their individual personalities but rather a particular legal status in the political-jural domain.

In this chapter I shall describe some activities and relationships among the Suku of south-western Congo (Kinshasa). It will be apparent that the description conforms to the generalized pattern of African ancestor cults and is congruent with

From Igor Kopytoff, "Ancestors as Elders in Africa", *Africa*, 41:2 (1971), pp. 129–42. Reproduced by permission of International African Institute.

Fortes's analysis. But, I shall show that there are difficulties in characterizing the Suku complex as an "ancestor cult" and shall bring in additional data on Suku lineage structure. I shall then contend that Fortes's analysis, while pointing in the right direction, does not go far enough because it does not take the final step of shedding the ethnocentric connotations of the very term "ancestor" – connotations that have a bearing on theory. I shall also try to show that by viewing what have been called African ancestor cults as part of the eldership complex, we can account more simply for many of Fortes's generalizations and at the same time make redundant some of the problems he raises.

The fundamental social and jural group among the Suku is the corporate matrilineage, generally consisting of some thirty-five to forty persons. Married couples live virilocally, and males live patrilocally at least until their father's death and often beyond. The membership of a matrilineage is dispersed over several villages but within an area that is not too large to preclude easy communication, consultations, and joint action in important matters. The matrilineage is a corporate unit in economic, political, jural, and religious respects. Each matrilineage is centred in a particular village which bears its name and is its administrative and ritual head-quarters, containing the formal lineage head (the oldest male member) and, usually, several other older members (Kopytoff, 1964,1965).

The dead members of the lineage, as a collectivity, are appealed to in times of crisis (such as a serious sickness or a series of misfortunes) and, more regularly, on such occasions as the marriages of women of the lineage, the breaking of sexual taboos affecting these women, the coming-out ceremony for infants, and, yearly, before the large communal hunts of the dry season. The general pattern is as follows: the head of the lineage and two or three older men of his generation go at night to the grave – any grave – of a deceased member of the lineage who was older than any of them. The Suku have no special burying places and graves are dug at random in the bush outside the lineage centre or near crossroads; the graves are not maintained and they eventually return to

bush, so that the site of a particular grave is usually forgotten in time. The location of recent graves is of course remembered, and the lineage head and the older men usually go to the grave of the last deceased man who was older than they. The other appropriate place to address the dead is at the crossing of paths.

At the grave or at the cross-roads, the old men "feed" the dead certain foods considered to be their favourite: particular kinds of forest mushroom and wild roots, palm wine, and sometimes even manioc, the Suku staple. A small hole is dug in the ground and the food is put into it. Communication with the dead takes the form of a conversational monologue, patterned but not stereotyped, and devoid of repetitive formulae. One speaks the way one speaks to living people: "You, [such and such], your junior is ill. We do not know why, we do not know who is responsible. If it is you, if you are angry, we ask your forgiveness. If we have done wrong, pardon us. Do not let him die. Other lineages are prospering and our people are dying. Why are you doing this? Why do you not look after us properly?" The words typically combine complaints, scolding, sometimes even anger, and at the same time appeals for forgiveness.

At the coming-out ceremonies for infants and at marriages, the dead members of the lineage are informed of the event; pleas are made for their approval and their efforts in insuring the success of the newborn or of the marriage and the children that will be born to it. Before the large communal hunts of the dry season, the dead members are asked to extend good luck to the enterprise. They are told that the people are hungry for meat, they are reprimanded for not granting enough meat, and they are shamed that their own people should be eating less well than other lineages. Finally, dead members of the lineage are always referred to publicly by the living elders on all ceremonial occasions involving the lineage as a unit.

These activities clearly fit the general pattern of African "ancestor cults". The ancestors are seen as retaining their role in the affairs of their kin-group and only of their kin-group. They are propitiated with "sacrifices". They are seen as dispensing both favours and misfortune; they are often accused of being capricious and of failing in their responsibilities, but, at the same time, their actions are related to possible lapses on the part of the living and are seen as legitimately punitive. The features of the "cult" emphasize the nature of the social relationship while details of the life of ancestors in the other world are de-emphasized and are, indeed, of little interest to the Suku. It is primarily the jural context that dominates the relationship with the ancestors and not the personal characteristics they may have had when they were alive.

There is, however, one immediate problem that arises in calling this an "ancestor cult": the Suku have no term that can be translated as "ancestor". These dead members of the lineage are referred to as *bambuta*. Literally, *bambuta* means the "big ones", the "old ones", those who have attained maturity, those older than oneself; collectively the term refers to the ruling elders of a lineage. A *mbuta* (singular) is literally anyone who is older than ego. The meaning is comparative. Eldership is not an absolute state of being old; being a *mbuta* is always relative to someone who is younger. Within the lineage, a *mbuta* is any older adult, older siblings as well as those of the generations above. My *bambuta* collectively are all the members of the lineage who are older than I, whether they are alive or dead. In jural contexts, where authority is vested overwhelmingly in the males, the term is effectively narrowed to all my male seniors. The lineage is thus divided into two named groups: those above me who are my *bambuta*, and those below me – my *baleke* – to whom I am an elder. By contrast, no semantic distinction is made within the lineage between those who are alive and those who are dead.

An elder – any elder – represents to a junior the entire legal and mystical authority of the lineage. The very fact of eldership confers upon a person mystical powers over the junior. He can curse his junior in the name of the lineage, thereby removing from him the mystical protection of the lineage. The curse can be formal and public, but it can also be secret and even unconscious. To use a contemporary metaphor, a Suku is under the "umbrella" of the power of his lineage; removal of this protection exposes him to the outside world, and the world is a dangerous place to be in when one is not attached to a kin-group. As the Suku phrase it, a curse "opens the road to misfortune", though it does not actively cause misfortune.

An elder's curse, always implicitly made in the name of the lineage, can only be removed by an older elder – one to whom the previous elder is a junior.

Lineage authority and the representation of the lineage to the outside world are organized on a continuum of age, that is, of relative eldership. Within this formal continuum based purely on relative age, there is also the principle of generational solidarity. Lineage members of the same generation are closer to each other and tend toward greater though never actual equality. Thus, the inequality of power and authority is most pronounced between generations. It is most presumptuous for the junior generation to question, under normal circumstances, the decisions of the senior generation and the ways in which they have been arrived at. It is the generation above me that represents to me the full authority of the lineage; generational solidarity as well as inter-generational distance means that, unless I have knowledge to the contrary, I must assume that the decision of one senior represents the decision of all seniors. This generational structure also expresses a continuum of authority. If I am middle-aged, the decision by elders of the generation above me carries for me the authority of all the senior generations above me. To a junior in the generation below me, my decision similarly carries the authority of my generation together with all the generations senior to it. To the junior, then, lineage authority is most directly embodied in the generation immediately above him, and it is presumptuous for him to go over their heads, so to speak, to yet more senior generations. Conversely, the authority of eldership is most directly exercised upon those of the generation immediately below, as they in turn properly exercise it over the generation below them. Exercising authority over the second lower generation, over the heads of the intervening one, is somewhat inappropriate. This results in muting the outward expression of authority between the alternating generations of a lineage, a pattern congruent with the relaxed etiquette between alternating generations.

In any context, the lineage is fully and legally represented by the oldest adult member of the lineage who is present. Let me give a few examples. In common with many Central African peoples, the name of the lineage is formally carried by the head of that lineage. Thus, the head of the lineage Kusu is addressed as Kusu. But this general rule expresses a more complex structure. The identification of the lineage's name with the person extends to the entire membership of the lineage; it is the lineage as a whole, *qua* corporate group, that holds the title. Cunnison (1951), writing on the Luapula peoples, has analysed this particular usage in which a person discussing his lineage and its history in the past, will refer to it by the pronoun "I." A similar usage exists among the Suku. The oldest lineage member who is present in any situation can refer to himself by the name of his lineage, and is so addressed by others. For example, an infant who is a member of the royal lineage is addressed as *Mini Kongo*, the title of the Suku king, as long as no other older member of the royal lineage is present. The moment an older member arrives on the scene, the title is shifted to him. A young man of Kusu lineage will refer to himself as Kusu and, a moment later, after an older lineage mate has arrived, he will refer to him as Kusu and will cease applying the title to himself. Ultimately, of course, if all the members of the lineage are present, the title Kusu devolves upon the oldest male member of the lineage who is also its formal head.

The continuum of eldership in representing the lineage has a jural significance in interlineage relations. Let me illustrate with an extreme example. A young man became angry with his elders and, without consulting anyone, sold to another lineage a hunting area belonging to his own. The transaction was fully legal, since he was a legitimate spokesman for his lineage in the context in which the transaction took place. His own lineage was, of course, incensed by the action; in the old days he might have been sold or even killed. But the significant point here is that the legality of the transaction was not questioned.

In short, to those on the outside, a lineage is represented by the oldest member present. Within the lineage, the lineage is represented to any one member by any older member present and, collectively, by all older members living and dead. The principle of eldership operating within the lineage corresponds, in its external relations, to its "chieftainship" (*kimfumu*). Lineage "chieftainship" is also a relative, not an absolute matter; for the

outside world, it is carried by the oldest member present. Thus, the Suku say that "everyone is a chief" – just as everyone is an elder.

Let us consider now some additional features of the ritual preceding the collective hunt of the dry season. Before the hunting season begins every Suku secures hunting luck by obtaining reassurance that the lineage wishes him well, that he continues to be under its protection. This reassurance can in principle be obtained verbally from any elder; more appropriately, it is obtained from anyone in the generation above. Young men go to the middle-aged and the middle-aged go to the old. There is a pattern in asking for luck: one beseeches, one complains, one reproves, one asks forgiveness. On his part, the older man signifies his goodwill by giving the junior some *pemba* (white clay); he also uses the occasion to remind the young man of his obligations to the old, to scold him lightly for his past misdemeanours, and to ask his forgiveness for past misfortunes. The manner of addressing the living elder is the same as the one used in addressing the dead. The Suku regard the two activities as being not merely analogous but identical, and the differences between them as incidental and contextual. Everyone goes to his elder. If I am young, I go to my elders who happen to be alive. The old people go to their elders; but since these are dead, they are to be found at the grave or at the cross-roads at night. Given the continuum of eldership, the use of any grave, as long as the dead is older than the petitioner, is understandable. Also understandable in this context is the neglect of older graves. In the light of the structure of eldership, this neglect does not represent a "weak" ancestor cult nor does it indicate shallowness of lineage structure.

If there be a "cult" here, it is a cult of *bambuta*, of elders living and dead. Every junior owes *buzitu* ("honour," "respect") to his seniors, be they "elders" or "ancestors" in Western terminology. A single set of principles regulates the relationship between senior and junior; a person deals with a single category of *bambuta* and the line dividing the living from the dead does not affect the structure of the relationship. Where the line is relevant is in the method of approaching the elder. The dead must of necessity be approached differently from the living; interaction with them necessarily appears one sided and conversations with them necessarily become monologues. Also, interaction with them is necessarily less frequent and when it occurs, it is formal – but no less formal than is the interaction with living elders on ceremonial occasions. The offer of palm wine is normal at all formal occasions when a junior approaches a senior; but dead elders, in their capacity of the dead, also have their preferred foods – the special forest mushroom and roots. Thus, it is the special methods of approach, inevitably characterizing dealings with the dead, as opposed to the living, that gives these dealings the special cast that makes us, as anthropologists and outsiders, call it a "cult." The dead *qua* dead also know more and see things that living elders do not; they are, therefore, more powerful and can sometimes be more helpful. Also, though the reasons for action by any elder are often obscure to the juniors, actions by dead elders are particularly obscure since no explanations from them are ever possible. In short, there is a difference in the manner in which the dead are approached, in contrast to the living. But the difference is related to their different physical states, even while they remain in the same structural position vis-à-vis their juniors. ...

The Western ethnocentric conviction that "ancestors" must be separated from living "elders" conditions the cognitive set with which we approach African data and theorize about them. Not only is our term "ancestor" – meaning an ascendant who is dead – denotatively ethnocentric but it is also connotatively so. Western cultural tradition (which includes ghosts) accepts that the dead can be endowed with extraordinary powers. The dead belong to what we call the "supernatural world". A Western anthropologist, working in an African society, finds it easy to accept without much further questioning that the dead, including the "ancestors," should be believed capable of extraordinary doings, that they should "mystically" confer benefits, that they should visit sickness upon the living, that they should have "supernatural" powers. Such beliefs about the dead are culturally acceptable to us, and it is appropriate that such dead should have a "cult." But living people in our cultural conceptions do not have such "mystical" powers merely because they happen to be older. If they are said

by Africans to have such powers, these must be "derived" from elsewhere; and the ancestors, being dead, are seen as an appropriate source.[1]

Our interpretations have had two opposing emphases. In the ethnographies, dealing descriptively with African beliefs, it has generally been held that Africans see the powers of the elders as derivative from the power of the ancestors. By contrast, on the theoretical level (where our cultural assumptions come to the fore and where ancestors cannot "exist" except as a symbol and an abstraction), the directionality of the explanation is exactly reversed; the powers with which ancestors are endowed become a "projection" of the palpable powers of living elders. This latter interpretation is the gist of Fortes's (1965) formulation. But what, then, of the mystical powers that elders hold directly and on their own, as among the Suku? Are they in turn to be seen as re-projections from the ancestors? When we see the powers over the juniors of both living elders and ancestors as derivative from eldership *per se*, both the above interpretations of the "sources" of power come to be beside the point. The problems they attempt to solve arise in the first place from an ethnocentric categorization of the ethnographic data.

The reformulation of the problem around the broader category of "eldership" carried other semantic implications for anthropological terminology (and consequently for the theory built on this terminology). We talk of ancestor "cults" and even of ancestor "worship." In their modern meanings[2] these English words are culturally appropriate in describing dealings with the dead and the supernatural. By contrast, we would hesitate to apply the terms "cult" and "worship" to relations with the living. Yet, if the Suku and others "worship" their dead elders, then they also "worship" their living elders. If they have a "cult" of dead elders, the same "cult" applies to the living. Obversely, if the living elders are only "respected," then so are the "ancestors," and no more than that.

These points are very well illustrated by Kenyatta (1938:265–8), with his inside view of Kikuyu culture, when he discusses "ancestors." "In this account, I shall not use that term [worship], because from practical experience I do not believe that the Gikuyu worship their ancestors. ... I shall therefore use the term 'communion with ancestors'". Kenyatta's European analogy is revealing: "There appears to be such communion with ancestors when a European family, on special occasions, has an empty chair, the seat of a dead member, at table during a meal. This custom might be closely equated with Gikuyu behaviour in this respect." "The words 'prayer' and 'worship', *gothaithaiya, goikia-mokoigoro,* are never used in dealing with the ancestors' spirits. These words are reserved for solemn rituals and sacrifices directed to the power of the unseen." As to the question of what is so often called "sacrifice": "The gifts which an elder gives to the ancestors' spirits, as when a sheep is sacrificed to them, and which perhaps seem to an outsider to be prayers directed to the ancestors, are nothing but the tributes symbolizing the gifts which the departed elders would have received had they been alive, and which the living elders now receive."

By using terms such as "cult," "worship," and "sacrifice," we introduce semantic paradoxes which we then feel compelled to explain. Thus, in the International African Institute's Salisbury seminar (Fortes and Dieterlen, 1965:18), "the view that ancestors are generally represented as punitive in character was discussed at length." The need to understand why an object of "worship" should be "punitive" arises from the semantics of the terms used. We are told in the report on the seminar that "Professor Mitchell concluded that ancestors seemed to be normally ambivalent, inflicting punishment to demonstrate the legitimate authority and exercising benevolence when appealed to. He linked this up with some remarks of Dr. Turner, who gave instances of ancestor worship being significant in group rituals of solidarity and expiation aimed at restoring amity within a community. Such rituals, Professor Mitchell suggested, would be directed towards the ancestors in their benevolent aspect, whereas in the case of misfortune the punitive aspect would be invoked in order to provide an interpretation." Such theoretical involution is unnecessary. The attitude to elders (dead or alive) is normally ambivalent; they both punish and exercise benevolence, and they necessarily participate in restoring amity within the lineage. Mitchell's complex theoretical interpretation ignores what almost every ethnography and every general descriptive statement on African

ancestor "cults" has always stressed: that African lineages are communities of both the living and the dead. Gluckman and Fortes rightly stress that "ancestor cults" are not the same thing as the cults of the dead. But this irrelevance of the "deadness" of ancestors has implications for the very idiom in which theoretical problems are cast.

Once we recognize that African "ancestors" are above all elders and to be understood in terms of the same category as living elders, we shall stop pursuing a multitude of problems of our own creation. There is nothing startling that the attitude to elders wielding authority should be ambivalent. Fortes (1965:133) makes the important point that what matters in ancestors is their jural status, that (speaking of the Tallensi) "the personality and character, the virtues or vices, success or failures, popularity or unpopularity of a person during his lifetime make no difference to his attainment of ancestorhood". But, we should add, neither do these variations make a difference in the authority invested in eldership; what matters in *formal* relations is the formal status, in dead elders as well as those alive. "It is not the whole man, but only his jural status as the parent (or parental personage, in matrilineal systems) vested with authority and responsibility, that is transmuted into ancestorhood" (ibid.). But from the point of view proposed here, what occurs is not a "transmutation" but a *retention* of status by the now dead elder. The status, that is, remains unaffected by death, while one's purely personal and idiosyncratic relationship with the elder is necessarily changed. Similarly, when Fortes states: "Ancestor worship is a representation or extension of the authority component in the jural relations of successive generations," we can restate this more simply and, I would claim, more realistically and more in keeping with African conceptions as follows: "Elders, after they die, maintain their role in the jural relations of successive generations." In Fortes's theory, people are believed to "acquire", upon death, the power to intervene in the life of their juniors. I would claim that they "continue" to have that power.

Such rephrasing simplifies the interpretation of ethnographic date. Thus, in Fortes's formulation, the son begins "officiating" in the "cult" only upon his father's death because he now becomes a jural adult (Fortes, 1965: 130–2). This succession means "ousting a predecessor", and "sacrifice" to the ancestors may be a psychologically reassuring mode of ritual reparation; the ancestor cult becomes a psychological "refuge" (Fortes, 1965:140–1, 1945:9). Without questioning the psychological dynamics specific to the Tallensi, one may suggest another formulation that would seem to be more appropriate for dealing with the general phenomenon of "sacrifice" in African "ancestor cults," since these guilt feelings and their relief cannot be shown to exist in all of these societies. We see among the Tallensi a continuum of inter-generational eldership. The power of the kin-group is represented to me (a Tale) by my father, as his father represents it to him. My father "worships" (respects) and "sacrifices" (gives tribute) to his dead father, as I respect and give tribute to him. When my father dies, my relationship with him continues (Fortes, 1959:48ff.). The chain of relationships over the generations remains unaltered, though the method of interaction with my father becomes necessarily different when he is dead. If we express this difference by speaking of "worship" and "sacrifice," in contrast to "respect" and "gift or tribute," it is because we, as Westerners, find such terms more appropriate to express dealings with the dead. And, further, "sacrifice," "expiation," and "guilt" is a comfortable semantic cluster for us. But there is surely a danger here of transmuting the semantic biases of the observer's culture into problems of the ethnology of the observed.

By treating the phrase "ancestor cults" as a rather misleading way of referring to an aspect of the relationship with elders in general, a matter that Fortes sees as a puzzle can be re-examined in a new light. The puzzle is in the fact that the Tiv and the Nuer, with genealogically based social systems not unlike those of the Tallensi, lack "ancestor worship" (Fortes, 1965:140). There is indeed a puzzle if one insists upon seeing the ancestor cult as a *symbolic projection* of the social system. In the view presented here, on the other hand, the ancestor cult is an integral *part* of the system of relationship with elders. The relationship with dead elders (that is, "ancestors") is seen as being on the same symbolic plane as that with living elders and not as secondary to it or derivative from it. From

this point of view the overall structural similarities among Tallensi, Tiv, and Nuer should not be expected to result in similar ancestor cults. Other facts would seem to be more relevant to the relationship with ancestors *qua* dead elders: the meaning and structure of eldership, the nature of the authority attributed to it, and the beliefs about the effect of death upon the elder's role.

For the Tiv, the question to be asked is: what is there in the Tiv relationship with elders that makes for relative indifference to dead elders? Pervasive Tiv egalitarianism de-emphasizes the authority of eldership and indeed exacerbates the authority problems that inhere in such segmentary systems (Bohannan, 1953:31ff.). Neither genealogical position nor age confer, of themselves, special powers on the living, while the dead are believed to have no effect on the living (ibid:83). In short, Tiv elders *qua* elders have little influence on the lives of their juniors, be the elders alive or dead. Their formal authority here is minimal and genealogically shallow. Though a relationship with the dead is not entirely lacking (Bohannan, 1969:i:35ff., and 43), it is confined to one's parents. As to the Nuer, here also elders do not carry authority and power simply by virtue of their eldership (Evans-Pritchard, 1940:179–80). The elders' passage into the other world does not change their situation in this respect.

Though "ancestor cults" should not be equated with cults of the dead, beliefs about the dead are nevertheless relevant, as illustrated by the Songye who may also be said to lack an "ancestor cult", but for rather different reasons. Here, living elders have authority; once they die, however, the relationship with them as dead elders does not last because they become reincarnated in their grandchildren.[3] To conclude,[4] the selection by anthropologists of the phrases "ancestor cult" and "ancestor worship," in dealing with African cultures, is semantically inappropriate, analytically misleading, and theortically unproductive. Fortes has rightly emphasized that the essential features of these activities are to be found not so much in the fact that the people concerned are dead as in the structural matrix in which they are placed. But he does not go far enough. By retaining the term "ancestor" (rather than use, say, "dead elders"), he continues to give undue weight in his interpretations to the fact that the persons are dead. The term "ancestor" sets up a dichotomy where there is a continuum. By conceptually separating living elder from ancestors, we unconsciously introduce Western connotations to the phenomena thus labelled and find ourselves having to deal with paradoxes of our own creation and with complex solutions to them. It is striking that African "ancestors" are more mundane and less mystical than the dead who are objects of "worship" should be in Western eyes. African elders, on the other hand, look more mystical to us than we are willing to allow the living to be. Similarly, Africans treat their living elders more "worshipfully" than the English term "respect" conveys, and they treat the ancestors with less "respect" and more contentiousness than the term "worship" should allow.

These are all paradoxes that stem from the difficulty of our vocabulary to accommodate to the fact that African living elders and dead ancestors are more similar to each other than the Western living and dead can be, that an elder's social role does not radically change when he crosses the line dividing the living from the dead, and that African "ancestorship" is but an aspect of the broader phenomenon of "eldership." The initial theoretical problem here is not so much that of uncovering deep psychological and symbolic processes as it is of probing African cultural categories and of finding adequate translations of these into the Western language used for theorizing. The terminological recasting that is proposed here (with a consequent recasting of the cognitive categories of the theorist) suggests that our understanding of variations in what we have called "ancestor cults" must begin with the analysis of eldership in particular African societies. Finally, these redefinitions also resolve the puzzle of finding "ancestor cults" to be, on the one hand, so very characteristic of Africa as a culture area and, on the other, to be inexplicably and erratically absent here and there within the area. No such problem arises when we realize that the cultural trait to be examined is not "ancestorship" but the more widely distributed African recognition of "eldership."

Notes

1   To introduce a personal note, I had no difficulty in the field in accepting the idea that the dead "ancestors" should have "supernatural" powers. But I must have driven my informants to distraction by insisting on pursuing the question of the "why" and the "where from" of the powers of the living elders. It took a kind of methodological (and cultural) leap of faith to accept as a terminal ethnographic datum that if the dead can appropriately do supernatural things, why not also the living?

2   The English word "worship" carried, to be sure, a less religious connotation in Old English, referring merely to "dignity," "honour," and "worthiness" – appropriate to one aspect of the African relationship with both elders and ancestors, but still missing its associated aspect of familiarity that, when necessary, allows scolding.

3   Personal communication from Dr. Alan P. Merriam.

4   In this paper, I have discussed only the elders/ancestors of the descent group itself, and I have made no reference to the "extra-descent group ancestor cults" discussed by McKnight (1967). Briefly summarized, McKnight's point is that the "extra-descent group ancestors" (that is, paternal ancestors in the matrilineal systems, and maternal ones in the patrilineal) are not benevolent as they should be in terms of Radcliffe-Brown's theory of extension of sentiments. McKnight shows that the relations with the kin-group of the "residual parent" need not duplicate the sentiments of the relationship with that parent. Thus, in a patrilineal society, one can be on the warmest of terms with one's mother and her brother and still have strained and even hostile relations with their kin-group as a corporate entity and with other relatives in it. And it is these latter relations that condition the relations with the "extra-descent group ancestors." McKnight's mode of analysis is consistent with the one used here. I would merely use the term "relationship with the dead elders of the extra-descent group" instead of "extra-descent group ancestor cults."

References

Bohannan, Laura and Paul. 1953. *The Tiv of Central Nigeria*. London.

Bohannan, Laura and Paul 1969. *A Source Notebook on Tiv Religion (v. I: Cosmos, Soma, Psyche and Disease)*. New Haven, Conn.

Cunnison, Ian. 1951. *History on the Luapula*, Rhodes-Livingstone Papers, 21.

Evans-Pritchard, E. 1940. *The Nuer*. Oxford.

Fortes, Meyer. 1945. *The Dynamics of Clanship among the Tallensi*. London.

Fortes, Meyer 1959. *Oedipus and Job in West African Religion*. Cambridge.

Fortes, Meyer 1965. "Some Reflections on Ancestor Worship", in *African Systems of Thought*, ed. M. Fortes and G. Dieterlen. London.

Fortes, Meyer and Dieterlen, G. (eds.). 1965. *African Systems of Thought*. London.

Gluckman, M. 1937. "Mortuary Customs and the Belief in Survival after Death among the South-Eastern Bantu", *Bantu Studies*, xi.

Homburger, L. 1941. *Les Langues négro-africaines et les peuples qui les parlent*. Paris.

Kenyatta, Jomo. 1938. *Facing Mount Kenya: The Tribal Life of the Gikuyu*. London.

Kopytoff, Igor. 1964. "Family and Lineage among the Suku of the Congo", in *The Family Estate in Africa*, ed. Robert F. Gray and P. H. Gulliver. London.

Kopytoff, Igor 1965. "The Suku of Southwestern Congo", in *Peoples of Africa*, ed. James L. Gibbs, Jr. New York.

McKnight, J. D. 1967. "Extra-Descent Group Ancestor Cults in African Societies", *Africa*, xxxvii. 1–21.

Sapir, Edward. 1921. *Language*. New York (reprinted 1949).

Wilson, Monica. 1957. *Rituals of Kinship among the Nyakyusa*. London.

For the terms for "ancestors" and "elders" in the African languages mentioned, I have used the following sources: Mary Douglas, *The Lele of the Kasai*, London, 1963; Walter Sangree, *Age, Prayer, and Politics in Tiriki, Kenya*, London, 1966; and the dictionaries of the respective languages by the following: C. W. R. Tobias and R. H. C. Turvey 1954 (Ovambo/Kwanyama), W. Holman Bentley 1887 (Kongo), R. P. A. Semain 1923 (Songye), G. Hulstaert 1952 (Nkundo/Lomongo), M. Guthrie 1935 (Ngala), M. Mamet 1955 (Ntomba), J. Whitehead 1899 (Bobangi), Edwin W. Smith 1907 and J. Torrend 1931 (Ila), C. M. Doke 1933 and 1963 (Lamba), G. M. Sanderson 1954 (Yao), C. Taylor 1959 (Ankole), Herbert W. Woodward 1882 (Bondei), C. S. Louw 1915 (Karanga), D. McJ. Malcolm 1966 and C. M. Doke and B. W. Vilakazi 1958 (Zulu), R. P. Alexandre 1953 (Mossi), B. F. and W. E. Welmers 1968 (Igbo), Charles A. Taber 1965 (Sango), A. Vekens 1928 (Mangbetu).

Part VII

Arts, Aesthetics, and Heritage

Introduction

The presence of art on the African continent stretches back to prehistory when engravings and paintings were first made on granite rock surfaces by bands of migrating hunters and gatherers, possibly as far back as 13,000 years ago. Most of these images, at least those which have survived to the present day, represent the way of life in the Later Stone Age, depicting wild animals, human figures engaged in hunting activities, and assemblages of people gathered, perhaps, for the purpose of dance or ritual (see Lewis-Williams, 1983; Garlake, 1995).

Three-dimensional sculptural art first appears in the last millennium BC, among the Nok culture, which flourished in what is today central Nigeria. The Nok produced a wide assortment of terracotta sculpture representing both animal and human figures (Fagg, 1977; Jemkur, 1992). Many of these objects, some of which have been recovered nearly intact, show remarkable attention to detail – elaborately styled hair, intricate necklace and bead ornaments, and a distinctive treatment of the head, nose, nostrils, and mouth that "clearly set these figurines apart from other prehistoric West African terracotta traditions" (Fagg, 1994: 82). To date, archaeology in sub-Saharan Africa has revealed the presence of a number of other major art-producing cultures, including, for example, ancient sites excavated at Igbo–Ukwu, Ife, Owo, and Jenne–Jeno (see Willett, 1967; Shaw, 1977; Eyo, 1980; McIntosh, 1994). From the twelfth to fifteenth centuries, royal artisans in the Kingdom of Benin produced a large corpus of exquisite bronze figures and plaques which were used as altarpieces on commemorative shrines, as well as to decorate and enhance the palace interior (see also Part I).

While much has been learned about ancient Africa through archaeology and the analysis of early artifacts, a great deal has also been learned about Africa, both past and present, through research into the vast array of contemporary arts which are produced today for use in both secular and religious contexts. While artifacts made of bronze and terracotta have survived in the archaeological record, most objects made of wood have disintegrated due to the harsh climates of tropical Africa which quickly erode wooden materials. Thus, most wooden masks and statues which still play a vital role in African life today are, for the most part, only about a hundred years old at the most.

The study of African art in Europe and America developed largely in conjunction with the discipline of anthropology at the beginning of the twentieth century. Some of the earliest works on African art were written in order to further particular claims within a broader debate between diffusionist and evolutionist schools of thought (Haddon, 1902). African art was used, in this context, either as visual evidence for the spread of cultural traits from innovative centers to imitative peripheries, or as evidence for the social evolution of cultures – from groups which were supposedly capable of only naturalistic representation to those which had presumably graduated to the mastery of geometric stylization and abstract forms (Silver, 1979).

Following in the footsteps of late Victorian anthropology, artists in Europe began to "discover" for themselves the objects of African art that were beginning to make their way into both private art collections and museums of ethnography. Writers, artists, and intellectuals, like Maurice Vlarninck, André Derain, Guillaume Apollinaire, Georges Braque, Paul Klee, Ernst Ludwig Kirchner, Emil Nolde, and Constantin Brancusi, were all impacted to some degree by the power of African aesthetics and what they perceived as the refiguring of the human form in African sculptural traditions.

Perhaps the best known example of Africa's influence on modern European art, however, is Pablo Picasso's *Les Demoiselles d'Avignon*, which was completed in 1907. Art historians have consistently noted the striking formal affinity between certain African mask styles and the "mask-like" faces of two of the five women that are the subject of this remarkable painting. Yet, only recently have scholars tried to link Picasso's interest in African art to a broader concern regarding French colonial policy in Africa. Art historian Patricia Leighten has suggested that Picasso, and many of his circle, embraced African art as a symbol of their antinationalist sentiments and, specifically, their disdain for the Colonial Party's assertion of France's national destiny and the so-called *mission civilisatrice* to the "undeveloped" peoples of Africa and Asia (Leighten, 1990: 611). *Les Demoiselles d'Avignon* was completed on the heels of stunning disclosures made to the French public in 1905–6 of European military atrocities against the indigenous populations in the French and Belgian Congos. Thus, Leighten concludes, "Far from only wanting to borrow formal motifs from African forms, Picasso purposely challenged and mocked Western artistic traditions with his allusions to black Africa, with its unavoidable associations of white cruelty and exploitation" (1990: 610).

The interest that was generated in African art by European intellectuals flowed back once again into anthropology, and became absorbed into the discipline's new theories and methods of study. As the field of anthropology altered its emphasis from diffusion to context, and from evolution to function, the study of African art followed in its path. Drawing upon the new discourse of anthropology, and in particular taking a lead from the models and theories developed by Bronislaw Malinowski and A.R. Radcliffe-Brown, the focus in the study of African art beginning sometime in the 1940s and 1950s was to become the indigenous context – which would reveal the place of art within a balanced holistic system of social and cultural functions. In this sense, art was understood simply as one of many vital organs in the proper maintenance and functioning of a stable social organism.

Simon Ottenberg's essay, "Humorous Masks and Serious Politics among the Afikpo Igbo," provides a classic example of how a functionalist approach may serve to locate the role of art (in this case masks and masking) in the maintenance of a balanced system of political power within an uncentralized or acephalous African society. Ottenberg argues that harmony and social equilibrium are maintained in Afikpo Igbo society through the regulated use of masks by junior males in a performative ritual known as the Okumkpa. Behind the relative anonymity of a wooden face mask, young men permit themselves to criticize their elders and to vent their dissatisfactions with village politics and social regulations. Without the masks, Ottenberg argues, the young men could never allow themselves such open and direct challenges to the established rule of the elders. The elders, for their part, permit the Okumkpa to take place because it allows youths to vent their frustrations without actually challenging or disrupting the established socio-political order. After the Okumkpa performance, which inverts hierarchy in a controlled context, power relations are re-established and continue to function in the same way that they did before.

Given the relatively small size of Afikpo Igbo society, where each individual knows everyone else in the village, Ottenberg's analysis of the Okumkpa raises an interesting question about the role played by masks in concealing a person's identity. Are the young men really anonymous behind their wooden face mask? Or rather do the elders recognize the masker's identity, but respect the anonymity which the mask supposedly offers? In other words, is the mask's capacity to hide individual identity simply a "structural relationship" which is acknowledged by both mask-wearer and mask-viewer? Might the mask, in this regard, be compared to the powdered wig of a British judge or barrister which marks an individual's social role and sanctifies his or her authority without actually hiding the person's true identity?

Another school of thought in anthropology which, at one point, had an impact on the study and analysis of African art is structuralism – an approach that was largely developed in France by Claude Lévi-Strauss and which became very influential in the 1950s and 1960s. Structural analysis in anthropology seeks to locate the "permutable codes" by which structural relations are transposed from one plane of reality to another (Adams, 1973: 265). In other words, structuralism attempts to identify identical, or at least similar, structural formations, such as "binary oppositions" (that is, ordering the world according to symbolic principles of dualism or structured pairs), in multiple spheres of cultural expression, including the organization of social groups, class ranking, myth, ritual, art, and collective practices (Nodelman, 1970).

Recent approaches to the study of African art have challenged what has come to be perceived as an overemphasis on local context. In so doing, the unit of analysis has been expanded not only to include contacts within and among a wide range of proximate ethnic groups (Kasfir, 1984), but also to include the impact of world religions and global travel on local art use and production. Art historian René Bravmann (1974), for example, has explored the articulation of Islam with indigenous African beliefs. Far from obliterating so-called "traditional" art forms, Bravmann has shown how the production and use of art in West Africa has adapted to the religious demands of Islam and created "syncretic" art forms which blend into a single cultural expression of Muslim and indigenous religious values (see Introduction for more on the notion of syncretism in African cultures). In another important instance of aesthetic assemblage and cultural syncretism, art historian Henry Drewal (1988, 2008) has explored the incorporation of European and Hindu beliefs about mermaids and snake-charmer goddesses into the worship and art associated with a pan-African religious cult known as Mami Wata. Drewal has shown in his research how the circulation of myths in the world system of the imagination produces a new religion and a new art form which combines indigenous beliefs about water spirits with foreign images of the "other."

Much of the research on African art today focuses on the hybridity of indigenous expressive cultures. Rather than look for "pure" aesthetic forms as anthropologists often did in the past – that is, art forms that were putatively "untouched" by European or other foreign contact – Africanist scholars today acknowledge outside influence and transcultural communication and, in their writings, often seek to demonstrate how Africans in fact celebrate artistic innovation and how artists and performers experiment with the foreign, the strange, and the new.

Those who collect African art in Europe and America often imagine that there is a "precolonial aesthetic" – an art style that originated in pristine conditions and remained unchanged for centuries until it was "contaminated" by European exploration and, later, colonialism. Although there were indeed precolonial art forms, it does not follow that these arts simply remained unchanged. Novelty and innovation have almost always played a key role in African visual and expressive cultures. People everywhere, however, tend to imagine the past as a time of "authenticity" and as a glorified moment which somehow was able to reproduce itself unchanged until outside forces caused irrevocable damage to the "ancient" practices.

This way of thinking about the relationship between the past and the present is not limited to European attitudes toward Africa, but is also manifested in African attitudes toward Europe. In a fascinating interview with West African painter Tamessir Dia, for example, art critic Thomas McEvilley captured a profound irony of postcolonial discourse about Western society. Wandering the streets of Venice in 1993, during an exhibition of contemporary art in which his work was featured, Dia contemplated the disjuncture between classical Italian art and architecture and what he perceived to be the mundane character of modern Italy:

> I keep looking at present-day Italians and try to compare them with the Italians of the past and wonder how they did such great things in the past. When I look around, not only are the architectural monuments extraordinary, but the paintings as well. I don't see any link between the relics of the past and what I see today. I keep wondering, Are these the same people? (McEvilley, 1993: 10)

In his commentary on this interview, McEvilley concludes that for "an African to exert such a judgment on the West is a profound reversal of the colonial relationship" (1993: 10).

Recent studies of African art have begun not only to question the (over) emphasis placed on local context, at the expense of a more translocal or global perspective, but they have also thrown into doubt the privileged place of pre-colonial masks and statues in the definition of what constitutes "real" art in Africa. In his research on the African art market in Côte d'Ivoire, for example, Christopher Steiner (1994) has demonstrated how the category "African art" is continually reinvented and redefined by speculators and connoisseurs in the international art market. Objects that were once classified as "curios" or "artifacts" come to be reclassified as "art." In this process, objects are given not only new monetary worth but also new cultural and political value.

Unlike art historians, who generally see the art object as their primary unit of study, anthropologists use art as a means of studying society more broadly. The study of art in this case is thus not intended as an end in itself, but rather it is a methodological tool to gain access to a wider view of social organization or to penetrate a "deeper" level of cultural knowledge. Art history and anthropology are disciplines that are clearly related to one another, but each brings a different perspective to the subject of African art (Adams, 1989; Ben-Amos, 1989). In both art history and anthropology, however, the study of African art has been heavily influenced by perspectives and trends in Western scholarship. When functionalism was in vogue, for example, many anthropologists viewed African art through the lens of functionalist theory. As functionalism waned and lost favor in the field of anthropology as a whole, so too did its application to the study of African art. The question, then, is how much of our understanding of African art emerges from Western cultural assumptions about art and aesthetics, and how much is guided by the application of models and interpretations formed in other academic domains?

Philosopher V.Y. Mudimbe has reached the conclusion in his work that the term "African art" itself, in Western academic discourse, is a constructed category which fails to address indigenous African aesthetic perceptions and sensibilities. "What is called African art," writes Mudimbe, "covers a wide range of objects introduced into a historicizing perspective of European values since the eighteenth century" (1986: 3). How can we understand African art without being guided by Western models of art and aesthetic theory?

One of the basic problems in the study of African art is the emphasis that has been placed on durable material objects. Most studies of African art begin with collections of art that have been assembled in museums in Europe and America starting in the sixteenth century. These collections of what is known in the parlance of anthropology as material culture are usually silent about the cultural context in which they were originally created and used. In some cases, what is important about the object is not its physical presence which endures in a museum collection, but rather its performative character which can only be exhibited in its indigenous cultural milieu. Art historian Robert Farris Thompson (1974) has pointed out that much African art was not meant to be experienced in the static environment of an exhibition gallery but was intended to be seen in motion. In its original context, for example, a viewer could not study the features of a wooden mask in detail but could only catch a fleeting glimpse of the object as a masked dancer swirled and spun before a gathered crowd in the village square. The aesthetic experience of seeing a mask in motion is very different from seeing a mask in a glass cabinet – artificially suspended in time and space.

Just as motion is an important component to the aesthetic dimension of an African mask, so too is sound. Most masks when danced in ritual performance are accompanied by distinct noises and otherworldly voices. These sounds, rather than any visual qualities of the wooden mask itself, are often what distinguish one mask type from another (Lifschitz, 1988). Seen in the silent realm of a museum cabinet these acoustic qualities of a mask's aesthetic configuration would be totally missed and overlooked.

Olu Oguibe's essay, "Art, Identity, Boundaries: Postmodernism and Contemporary African Art," also focuses our attention on the West's obsession with so-called traditional African art. The West's preoccupation with Africa's mythic past ripples through spheres of art collecting and museum exhibitions and creates a false dichotomy between the traditional and the modern. Oguibe's description and analysis of an encounter between art critic Thomas McEvilley and Ivoirian artist Ouattara [Watts] illustrates the complex predicament of the African artist struggling to establish his identity and mark within the framework of this peculiar world art stage. Ouattara rejects the West's strict binary opposition between "traditional" and "modern," and espouses instead a more African view on these categories which sees them as co-existing rather than mutually exclusive. Born and raised in Abidjan, Côte d'Ivoire, but trained at the Ecole des Beaux-Arts in Paris, Ouattara embraces the interplay of the modern and the traditional; he explores technology in Africa and spirituality in the West, thereby reversing the conventional dichotomy and shaking up the representational model and liberating Africa from the dominating gaze of Western classification (see Part I for further discussion of the issues surrounding the West's representation of Africa).

The control that the West exerts over the definition of authentic or legitimate African art is not only an academic debate on identity but has real consequences for African artists struggling to establish themselves and survive on the international art scene. Contemporary art making has been dominated by the West and defined largely as a Western enterprise. African artists seeking to participate in the dialogue of modern art have to somehow establish themselves on their own terms. What Oguibe identifies as Ouattara's disgust with his interlocutor McEvilley is an example of that struggle for self-definition and identity. McEvilley's question "When and where were you born?" (while seemingly innocent) provokes an inner rage in the artist who feels that his work is being judged by his geographic roots and the cultural shackles that bind him to place in Africa rather than being assessed like his Western counterparts for the objective aesthetic merits of work that ought to transcend space and time. Beyond the study of the visual arts, Africanist scholarship has also made significant contributions to our understanding of the role of music, musicians, and musical performances in African societies. The study of African music entered the academy through the field of ethnomusicology – a method of analysis that situates music in its ethnographic or cultural context. Like the early study of African art and aesthetics in anthropology, ethnomusicology treats African music as one of many determinative elements in the structuring of the cultural fabric of a society.

In recent years, this approach to the study of African music has been criticized by African scholars who view ethnomusicology (or comparative musicology) as a mode of inquiry that "marginalizes Africa in the Western musical imagination and keep[s] African scholars from entry into the scholarly conversation on African music" (Solis 2004: 108). Because the analysis of African music evaluates musical forms and performances in terms derived from Western musical practice and discourse, the scholarship tends to be largely Eurocentric. "Ethnomusicology and its cousins," writes Jean Ngoya Kidula, "can therefore be seen as systems developed by North American and European scholars to understand and 'contain' musics of rural, minority, or other cultures" (2006: 101). African scholars have been particularly critical of older ethnomusicological approaches that view colonial or Western influences on African music as detrimental forms of cultural corruption that would "overwhelm the local knowledges and practices of African culture, erasing them utterly." (Solis 2004: 107) Instead, recent scholarship on African music, that draws on postcolonial theory more broadly, insists that these transcultural influences are generative of creative cultural forms that are expressive of important, new hybrid musical genres.

Kelly Askew's article "As Plato Duly Warned: Music, Politics, and Social Change in Coast East Africa," is an excellent example of this new mode of scholarship on African music. In her essay, Askew examines the role of music in political and social change on the Swahili coast of East Africa. She analyzes two musical genres, *ngoma* and *dansi* (typically glossed as "traditional dance" and "urban jazz"), and exposes within these two genres common aesthetic principles of innovation, inventive appropriation, competitive opposition, linguistic indirection, and intertexuality.

Following the lead of James Fernandez, an anthropologist who studied the parallels in the symbolic symmetry of the visual arts and other cultural expressions among the Fang people of Gabon, Askew identifies within Swahili coast culture a continuum from choices to political and social practices. Rather than privilege political actions as "the true social reality," Askew suggests that aesthetic principles as expressed in Swahili music are determinative and not separate or less important than economic or political practice. Her analysis aims to show:

> That (1) we cannot assume that Swahili preferences for continual artistic innovation through the incorporation of foreign elements derive from Swahili economic history, and (2) that in Swahili communities political action is a key aesthetic principle.

In the end, Askew concludes (as did Fernandez) that aesthetic forms of expression are part of a cultural continuum that embraces not only the arts but also politics and economics. Music is not a mere epiphenomenon but rather a productive form of social action that has real impact on real political and economic processes.

In the final chapter of this part, "In Place of Slavery: Fashioning Coastal Identity," Bayo Holsey examines the construction of collective memory in postcolonial Ghana. The chapter explores what appears to be a contradiction in the way the inhabitants of coastal Elmina glorify the era of the Dutch-controlled slave trade (when the town was prosperous and connected to the world) and lament their present impoverished and isolated status in an independent nation state.

Holsey argues, however, that it is not the case that the residents of Elmina are nostalgic for the slave trade era, which marks the wealth of their past, but rather they reference their historic prosperity as a way of critiquing the decline of wealth and cosmopolitanism that ensued in the colonial and postcolonial periods. While the era of the Atlantic slave trade was indeed shameful and horrific, the community of Elmina was included in the global order and a player in transnational trade and affairs. Through selective memories, the people of coastal Ghana today cry out for international recognition and seek to be respected (rather than forgotten) on the world stage. Memory, like art and music, is a selectively constructed phenomenon that can be pressed into service to represent and define the collective identity of a people and nation.

References

Adams, Monni. 1973. "Structural Aspects of a Village Art." *American Anthropologist* 75(2): 265–79.

Adams, Monni. 1989. "African Visual Arts from an Art Historical Perspective." *African Studies Review* 32(2): 55–103.

Ben-Amos, Paula. 1989. "African Visual Arts from a Social Perspective." *African Studies Review* 32(2): 1–54.

Berliner, Paul. 1978. *The Soul of Mbira: Music and Traditions of the Shona People of Zimbabwe*. Berkeley: University of California Press.

Bravmann, René A. 1974. *Islam and Tribal Art in West Africa*. Cambridge: Cambridge University Press.

Drewal, Henry John. 1988. "Performing the Other: Mami Wata Worship in Africa." *The Drama Review* 32(2): 160–85.

Drewal, Henry John, ed. 2008. *Mami Wata: Arts for Water Spirits in Africa and Its Diaspora*. Los Angeles: Fowler Museum.

Eyo, Ekpo. 1980. *Treasures of Ancient Nigeria*. New York: Knopf.

Fagg, Angela. 1994. "Thoughts on Nok." *African Arts* 27(3): 79–83, 103.

Fagg, Bernard. 1977. *Nok Terracottas*. London: Ethnographica for the National Museum of Lagos.

Feld, Steven. 1995. "From Schizophonia to Schismogenisis: The Discourses and Practices of World Music and World Beat." In George E. Marcus and Fred R. Myers, eds., *The Traffic in Culture: Refiguring Art and Anthropology*, pp. 96–126. Berkeley: University of California Press.

Garlake, Peter. 1995. *The Hunter's Vision: The Prehistoric Art of Zimbabwe*. Seattle: University of Washington Press.

Haddon, Alfred C. 1902. *Evolution in Art: As Illustrated by the Life-Histories of Designs*. New York: Walter Scott.

Jemkur, J. F. 1992. *Aspects of the Nok Culture*. Zaria: Ahmadu Bello University Press.

Kasfir, Sidney Littlefield. 1984. "One Tribe, One Style? Paradigms in the Historiography of African Art." *History in Africa* 11: 163–93.

Keil, Charles. 1979. *Tiv Song*. Chicago: University of Chicago Press.

Kidula, Jean Ngoya. 2006. "Ethnomusicology, the Music Canon, and African Music: Positions, Tensions, and Resolutions in the African Academy," *Africa Today* 52(3): 99–113.

Leighten, Patricia. 1990. "The White Peril and *L'art nègre*: Picasso, Primitivism, and Anticolonialism." *The Art Bulletin* 72(4): 609–30.

Lewis-Williams, J. David. 1983. *The Rock Art of Southern Africa*. Cambridge: Cambridge University Press.

Lifschitz, Edward. 1988. "Hearing Is Believing: Acoustic Aspects of Masking in Africa." In Sidney L. Kasfir, ed., *West African Masks and Cultural Systems*, pp. 221–9. Tervuren, Belgium: Musée Royal de l'Afrique Centrale.

Meintjes, Louise. 1990. "Paul Simon's *Graceland*, South Africa, and the Mediation of Musical Meaning." *Ethnomusicology* 34(1): 34–73.

McEvilley, Thomas. 1993. *Fusion: West African Artists at the Venice Biennale*. New York: The Museum for African Art.

McIntosh, S.K. 1994. "Changing Perceptions of West Africa's Past: Archaeological Research since 1988." *Journal of Archaeological Research* 2(2): 165–98.

Mudimbe, V.Y. 1986. "African Art as a Question Mark." *African Studies Review* 29(1): 3–4.

Nodelman, Sheldon. 1970. "Structural Analysis in Art and Anthropology." In Jacques Ehermann, ed., *Structuralism*, pp. 79–93. Garden City, NJ: Anchor Books.

Poster Book Collective. 1991. *Images of Defiance: South African Resistance Posters of the 1980s*. South African History Archive. Johannesburg: Raven Press.

Price, Sally, and Richard Price. 1980. *Afro-American Arts of the Suriname Rain Forest*. Los Angeles: Museum of Cultural History, and Berkeley: University of California Press.

Shaw, Thurstan. 1977. *Unearthing Igbo-Ukwu: Archaeological Discoveries in Eastern Nigeria*. New York and Ibadan, Nigeria: Oxford University Press.

Silver, Harry R. 1979. "Ethnoart." *Annual Review of Anthropology* 8: 267–307.

Solis, Gabriel. 2004. Review of Kofi Agawu, *Representing African Music: Post-colonial Notes, Queries, Positions*. *Notes* 61(1): 106–108.

Steiner, Christopher B. 1994. *African Art in Transit*. Cambridge: Cambridge University Press.

Thompson, Robert Farris. 1974. *African Art in Motion*. Los Angeles: University of California Press.

Thompson, Robert Farris. 1984. *Flash of the Spirit: African and Afro-American Art and Philosophy*. New York: Vintage Books.

Waterman, Christopher A. 1990. *Juju: A Social History and Ethnography of an African Popular Music*. Chicago: University of Chicago Press.

Willett, Frank. 1967. *Ife in the History of West African Sculpture*. New York: McGraw-Hill.

Younge, Gavin. 1988. *Art of the South African Townships*. New York: Rizzoli.

Suggested Reading

Agawu, V. Kofi. 2003. *Representing African Music: Postcolonial Notes, Queries, Positions*. New York: Routledge.

Arnoldi, Mary Jo. 1995. *Playing with Time: Art and Performance in Central Mali*. Bloomington: Indiana University Press.

Arnoldi, Mary Jo, Christraud M. Geary, and Kris L. Hardin, eds. 1996. *African Material Culture*. Bloomington: Indiana University Press.

Barber, Karin. 1987. "Popular Arts in Africa." *African Studies Review* 30: 1–78, 113–32.

Biebuyck, Daniel, ed. 1969. *Tradition and Creativity in Tribal Art*. Berkeley: University of California Press.

Blier, Suzanne Preston. 1987. *The Anatomy of Architecture: Ontology and Metaphor in Batammaliba Architectural Expression*. Cambridge: Cambridge University Press.

Blier, Suzanne Preston. 1995. *African Vodun: Art, Psychology, and Power*. Chicago: University of Chicago Press.

Brett-Smith, Sarah. 1994. *The Making of Bamana Sculpture: Creativity and Gender*. Cambridge: Cambridge University Press.

Chernoff, John Miller. 1981. *African Rhythm and African Sensibility: Aesthetics and Social Action in African Musical Idioms*. Chicago: University of Chicago Press.

Cole, Herbert M. 1989. *Icons: Ideals and Power in the Art of Africa*. Washington, DC: Smithsonian Institution Press.

Coombes, Annie E. 1997. *Reinventing Africa: Museums, Material Culture and Popular Imagination in Late Victorian and Edwardian England*. New Haven, CT: Yale University Press.

Coombes, Annie E. 2003. *History After Apartheid: Visual Culture and Public Memory in a Democratic South Africa*. Durham, NC: Duke University Press.

Coote, Jeremy, and Anthony Shelton, eds. 1992. *Anthropology, Art, and Aesthetics*. Oxford: Oxford University Press.

Coplan, David B. 1994. *In the Time of Cannibals: The Word Music of South Africa's Basotho Migrants*. Chicago: University of Chicago Press.

Coplan, David B. 2008 (2nd ed.). *In Township Tonight! South Africa's Black City Music and Theatre*. Chicago: University of Chicago Press.

d'Azevedo, Warren L., ed. 1973. *The Traditional Artist in African Societies*. Bloomington: Indiana University Press.

Erlmann, Veit. 1996. *Nightsong: Performance, Power, and Practice in South Africa*. Chicago: University of Chicago Press.

Fernandez, James. 1977. *Fang Architectonics*. Philadelphia: Institute for the Study of Human Issues.

Forge, Anthony, ed. 1973. *Primitive Art and Society*. London: Oxford University Press.

Grossman, Wendy A. 2009. *Man Ray, African Art, and the Modernist Lens*. Minneapolis: University of Minnesota Press.

Goldwater, Robert, 1986 [1938]. *Primitivism in Modern Art*. Cambridge, MA: The Belknap Press of Harvard University Press.

Harney, Elizabeth. 2004. *In Senghor's Shadow: Art, Politics, and the Avant-Garde in Senegal, 1960–1995*. Durham, NC: Duke University Press.

Jules-Rosette, Bennetta. 1984. *The Messages of Tourist Art: An African Semiotic System in Comparative Perspective*. New York: Plenum Press.

Karp, Ivan, and Stephen D. Lavine, eds. 1991. *Exhibiting Cultures: The Poetics and Politics of Museum Display*. Washington, DC: Smithsonian Institution Press.

Kasfir, Sidney Littlefield. 2000. *Contemporary African Art*. Thames & Hudson.

Kasfir, Sidney Littlefield. 2007. *African Art and the Colonial Encounter: Inventing a Global Commodity*. Bloomington, IN: Indiana University Press.

Marcus, George E., and Fred R. Myers, eds. 1995. *The Traffic in Culture: Refiguring Art and Anthropology*. Berkeley: University of California Press.

National Museum of African Art. 1990. *African Art Studies: The State of the Discipline*. Washington, DC: Smithsonian Institution.

Oguibe, Olu, and Okwui Enwezor, eds. 1999. *Reading the Contemporary: African Art from Theory to the Marketplace*. Cambridge, MA: MIT Press.

Ottenberg, Simon. 1975. *Masked Rituals of Afikpo: The Context of an African Art*. Seattle: University of Washington Press.

Peffer, John. 2009. *Art and the End of Apartheid*. Minneapolis: University of Minnesota Press.

Price, Sally. 1989. *Primitive Art in Civilized Places*. Chicago: University of Chicago Press.

Rhodes, Colin. 1994. *Primitivism and Modern Art*. London: Thames and Hudson.

Robinson, Deanna C., Elizabeth Buck, and Marlene Cuthbert, eds. 1991. *Music at the Margins: Popular Music and Global Cultural Diversity*. Newbury Park, CA: Sage.

Rovine, Victoria. 2008. *Bogolan: Shaping Culture through Cloth in Contemporary Mali*. Bloomington: Indiana University Press.

Rubin, Arnold, ed. 1988 *Marks of Civilization: Artistic Transformations of the Human Body*. Los Angeles: Museum of Cultural History, University of California.

Schildkrout, Enid, and Curtis A. Keim. 1990. *African Reflections: Art from Northeastern Zaire*. Seattle: University of Washington Press.

Spring, Chris. 2010. *African Art in Detail*. Cambridge, MA: Harvard University Press.

Strother, Z.S. 1999. *Inventing Masks: Agency and History in the Art of the Central Pende*. Chicago: University of Chicago Press.

Thompson, Robert Farris. 2009. *Aesthetic of the Cool*. Pittsburgh: Periscope.

Visona, Monica Blackmun, Robin Poynor, and Herbert M. Cole. 2007. *History of Art in Africa*, 2nd edn. Upper Saddle River, NJ: Prentice Hall.

Vogel, Susan. 1991. *Africa Explores: 20th Century African Art*. New York: The Center for African Art.

22

Humorous Masks and Serious Politics among the Afikpo Igbo

Simon Ottenberg

Compared to their actions in ordinary life how do African men behave when they don masks and special costumes? Masking is behavior of a stylized and ritualized kind, and differs, therefore, from activity of a day-to-day nature. The question is more complex, it seems to me, than simply whether the man who puts on a goat mask is supposed to look and perhaps act like a goat or not. The same man wearing the same mask may be differently interpreted at various dances. The study of masking, then, forces us to look deeply into the specific behavior of the performers and into the relationship of their actions to crucial elements of the social structure of the society. For often the masked players symbolically represent both social tensions and political matters in their performances.

Ethnographic Background

Afikpo, the subject of this study, is a village-group composed of twenty-two villages inhabited by some 30,000 persons in southeastern Nigeria.[1] It is one of several hundred village-groups of (Igbo) who live in this portion of Nigeria and whose total population probably comprises some eight million. The Afikpo, like other Igbo, are sedentary horticulturalists with clearly delineated villages composed of well-defined social groupings. Like other Igbo, they have never formed themselves into a highly centralized political system; for many years the Afikpo village-group has had considerable autonomy in matters of traditional leadership and social control. The Afikpo are unusual for Igbo, however, in having double inilineal descent, each person belonging to corporate matrilineal groupings, which are nonresidential, dispersed, landholding descent groups, as well as to patrilineal groupings, residential groupings (associated with ancestral shrines) which form the basic units of the political system.

The typical Afikpo village is composed of several hundred to seven thousand persons and generally consists of a number of patrilineages, often unrelated, each agnatic group living in its own compound more or less at the edge of the village common. Each village also has a distinct system of male age-sets, there being some twenty sets in all.

From Simon Ottenberg, "Humorous Masks and Serious Politics among the Afikpo Ibo" in *African Art and Leadership*, ed. Douglas Fraser and Herbert M. Cole (1972), pp. 99–121. Copyright © 1972 by the Board of Regents of the University of Wisconsin. Reprinted by permission of the University of Wisconsin Press.

Each set covers about a three-year span, the men being first formed into sets in their late twenties. Sets are grouped together into grades, the oldest forming the elders' grade, which rules the village; certain younger sets perform cooperative and communal labor at the elders' discretion. These age-sets form the basis of the authority system, in which age is a primary criterion, and they also help unite men of different descent groups into a common social organization.

The male elders rule the village by common agreement amongst themselves. There are no formal village chiefs or heads; consensus is the rule. Some elders, of course, are "more equal than others," because they are outstanding speakers, have influence through their wealth and the size of their landholding, or come from influential descent groups. Fundamentally it is an egalitarian situation for persons of the same age and sex, and an authoritarian one for younger and older individuals. Too much personal power among elders, or in any Afikpo for that matter, is frowned upon.

Each village has a secret society with its own secret initiation bush, its special spirit, and a host of rituals which its members carry out in the six months following the harvest season when the society is active. All village males join the society, generally before they reach adulthood. For men it is a universal association, since without membership a man is sociologically a boy and is excluded from most adult activities. The society is thus secret only with reference to women and children.

The tripartite authority structure of the Afikpo secret society must be mentioned briefly. The first unit includes the priest and assistant priest of the society's shrine, who are aided in carrying out sacrifices and other ritual activities by a small group of interested persons.[2] These persons are generally but not necessarily elders. The second unit comprises men who have taken senior titles within the society and who have the right to settle certain village disputes which the elders themselves cannot resolve. Again, many are elders, but there are exceptions. Third, the village elders as a group have some control over the society's activities. All three of these units – and some persons are members of two or three – act cooperatively to see that the various initiations, sacrifices, dances, plays, and the other activities of the society are effectively carried out.

No highly centralized authority rules the secret society, just as there is none for the village.

Many of the society's activities are kept secret from noninitiates. These forbidden rituals include initiation ceremonies, title ceremonies of the society, the production of mysterious noises at night associated with mystical spirits, and sacrifices to the spirit of the society at its central shrine. But there is also a class of plays, dances, and musical performances carried out by society members which are open to the public; these affairs are extremely popular and well attended by men, women, and children. One of the more important types of play, consisting of a series of skits and dances, is the subject of this paper. The Okumkpa play, which lasts three to four hours or so, is performed in the village common and attended not only by local villagers but by many other Afikpo as well.

The Okumkpa Play

The Okumkpa is presented in the half of the year following the yam harvest (from about September to February), when the secret society is active in the villages. This half of the year is one in which the highly achievement-oriented Igbo of Afikpo (Simon Ottenberg 1958, 1971; LeVine 1966) turn their attention to realigning social relationships. It is the period when men take important titles by joining special title societies, thus raising their status and sometimes their power and influence. And it is the time when the elders have the opportunity to judge cases and disputes, especially in land matters. It is thus a period of productivity in social relationships. In the other half of the year attention focuses on gaining material wealth and subsistence through farming and fishing. Social ties become less a focus of concern, the manual labor of individuals and groups more so. This work period provides wealth in foodstuffs which become resources for use in the ceremonial season; during this time new social tensions arise which are attended to in the following period. The secret-society play should be seen in this context.

As is true in virtually all of the public performances, of Afikpo village secret societies, the players in the Okumkpa wear masks. They are believed to be spirits rather than people. Though most players

Plate 22.1 Igbo, Afikpo. A dancer wearing the *nne Mgbo* (mother of Mgbo) mask. The raffia backing to the mask and the method of attachment to the face are visible. Mgbom village. Ht. 9" (22.8 cm). (Photograph: author, 1960.)

are individually recognizable by their manner of dancing, walking, singing, and in other ways, the fiction is maintained that they are not really humans at all, but a general form of spirit (*mma* at Afikpo, *mmo* or *mau* elsewhere in Igbo country). If a wife sees her husband dancing in costume, she is not supposed to recognize him, nor to compliment him on his dress or dancing at a later time, though men can do so among themselves, as all are members of the secret society. But the crucial act of placing a mask on the face of a secret-society member changes his status from "mortal" to "spirit," and thus allows him to behave in certain ways with respect both to other players and to unmasked members of the audience.

The masks themselves have a characteristic Afikpo style which differs from other Igbo mask styles.[3] Masks almost invariably have a vertical orientation and are narrower than the human head. Afikpo masks project forward from the face, the projection being markedly increased by bands of raffia which are tied to the back of the mask and hold it in front of the face as seen in Plate 22.1. The masks are faces, not half or full heads, or helmets. Some are of animals – a goat, a monkey, a bird. [...] Some are stylized human faces with additional designs and projections added to them. In this second group some are male, others female, and some represent either sex or no gender at all. [...] One mask often represents a white person. A third group of masks consists of the ugly ones; they are distortions of human faces – something like the Iroquois False Face Society masks – with bulging checks, crooked noses and mouths, and ears that are out of line; these ugly masks, which often represent old men, are often dark or black in contrast to the other masks, which have brighter colors, making particular use of white. [...]

Some elements seem common to all the Okumkpa masks. Many have a human quality to

Plate 22.2 Igbo, Afikpo. The actors are playing out a skit. The main body of the performers is in the background. Mgbom village. (Photograph: author, 1960.)

them – even the animal masks – but they are almost as un-African as one could make them. The noses have a high bridge. The faces lack everted lips, and in other ways do not look like actual Igbo people, as if the Afikpo wished to produce a clearly recognizable human face, yet one as distinct from their own as possible. They appear to be saying that these faces are, after all, not really theirs, but those of some other type of being. The masks are, of course, only a part of the total costume, though perhaps the most important part, for they make the man into a spirit.

The same "non-Afikpo" appearance prevails in the costumes. With the exception of khaki shorts, which have been adopted for general use, the costumes are not in any way like the usual dress of Afikpo men. This is evident from Plate 22.2. Animal skins worn on the back, porcupine-quill hats, and raffia shoulder-hangings and skirts indicate that this is the clothing of beings who are not Afikpo men. Red plastic waist beads, normally worn by unmarried girls, are often used as part of the costume, thereby confusing the sexual identity of the dancer.

A real social distance between the players and the audience is established through the use of mask and costume in Okumkpa performances. In our society, when we watch a performance, the players are likely to be personally less well known to us and less involved in direct social relationships with us than is the case in Africa. Masks in Afikpo help to create an illusion of distance between player and audience – people who are otherwise on close social terms.

Each Okumkpa mask has a name, and its wearer is expected to dance or play, at least at times, in character with the quality of the mask. But while masks are spirits, they are not particularly powerful; they do not give the wearer the right to try disputes, to judge cases, to wield everyday political power. There are no specific shrines associated with masks. Initiates may own, commission, or rent a mask for a play, or their part in the play may be assigned by the play leaders. Thus individuals do not have a close, personal relationship with a particular *mma* spirit.

Normally, Okumkpa consists of a series of skits and songs presented annually in some of the larger Afikpo villages, but the content of the plays changes every year, somewhat as variations on a recurrent theme. The play is led by two young men who volunteer for the work and who obtain the village elders' permission to prepare it. They gather their friends, peers, and relatives in the village and other volunteers in the settlement – generally it is men in their twenties and thirties that take part. The players rehearse secretly at night in the bush for several weeks. Some older men who enjoy performing may also take part and will advise the players and judge the quality of the acts before the public performance. The play is kept secret from nonsociety members until it is given. Its two organizers lead the actual performance, wearing special masks which indicate their roles. [...] After the play is presented the songs may be sung by secret-society members of any village who choose to do so; some popular ones are heard for many years afterwards.

In general the authority relationships among the Okumpka players are voluntaristic, cooperative, and not tied directly to the authority system of these secret society. If young men do not come forward to organize a play in a given year, none will be presented; the elders do not seem to pressure strongly for it. The players are not pushed by the elders to perform in a certain way, nor is their material censored. The young men are essentially free from the usual authority of the elders. This is so even though the latter decide on what day the play is to be given and may insist that members of certain younger age-sets take part, mainly as dancers, to make the play more impressive.

An Okumkpa play may involve over a hundred actors, singers, and musicians, all masked and costumed. They sit in the center of the village common facing the section where the village elders sit; the performers move out from there to act in the skits and to dance between the scenes. [...] Only the leaders stand apart. The players wear some ten different types of masks, which constitute the whole repertory for the Afikpo, with exceptions.[4] The Okumkpa masks blend together the history

of Afikpo (Simon Ottenberg 1968a, chap. 2). Some are based on styles of the nearby Edda and Okpoha village-groups of Igbo, with which Afikpo has common historical ties; some are of Ibibio origin, an area with which the Afikpo have long had trading contacts, and some appear to be indigenous to the area, though probably of non-Ibo origin, coming from the general Cross River area of which Afikpo is a part. As we have seen, some represent animals, others male and female human-like spirits, one a white person; some are of older spirit-persons, some appear as younger beings. The masked players as a group symbolize a totality of history, man, and nature at Afikpo. They are surrounded on all sides by an audience seated in the heart of the village – the group common – which also represents the totality of human life in the community.

The skits and songs are considered humorous by the Afikpo; they are intended to evoke laughter and other pleasurable responses from the audience, and they certainly do so. None of the Afikpo masks have movable parts. They very immobility requires the careful and full use of vocal contrasts to handle subtleties, and the exaggeration of bodily movements in the skits to convey impressions of persons and indicate emotional states. These features accentuate the differences between the masked skits and songs on the one hand and everyday Afikpo behavior on the other. The masks become mobile only through the skillful use of the voice and body movement.

Although Afikpo do not distinguish sharply between the types of skits, we can group them into three basic varieties:

a   The first tells of single living individuals who have acted in foolish or greedy ways. Such persons may be men or women of any age. There are tales of men who are henpecked by their wives, who ask their wives' permission before doing things which are strictly male matters, such as taking titles. Tales tell of a man who always drinks too much at ceremonies and gets sick and vomits. As in all of these skits and songs the person is named, and specific details concerning him are often sung and acted out. The skit may tell of a man who performed an important ceremony, but was too cheap to hire a

palm-wine tapper, and so climbed the tree himself, fell down, and broke his leg. Or of a person
who became so interested in the nearby Catholic
mission that he forgot how to speak his own
tongue and now can say only English prayers –
"Our Father who art in heaven. Our Father who
art in heaven" – over and over again. Such commentaries seem to be reminders of how individuals in a wide range of social roles should behave.
They comment on the need to follow proper procedures and etiquette, to act as persons of their
particular sex and age are supposed to.

b   A second category of skits and songs concerns females, often groups of women rather than
individuals. The men may sing that women
should remember that if they wish to have children they should not sing the secret-society songs
(which they are wont to do in modified form) or
the spirit of the society will render them barren.
Or that in the old days when the women went
naked and fired their pots in the open, none
broke; but now they wear clothes and shoes and
their pots are not as good as they used to be and
break in firing. This is because the women do not
keep to custom nowadays.

The secret society is seen strictly as a male
affair. In Afikpo the sex polarity in status and
role is sharp: the economic and social activities
of the sexes are clearly separated, and they spend
little time together (Phoebe Ottenberg 1958).
Nevertheless, in a culture which emphasizes
individual achievement as this one does, and
which is today under considerable pressure for
social change, the traditional polarity is breaking
down. Men admit that it is now hard to "keep
women in their place." These songs and skits are
attempts to reaffirm role differentiation. Men
sing that women are after all women – they
should not forget their natural functions of bearing children, raising them, and cooking, or try to
change their ways. Women, for example, are not
supposed to know any of the secrets of the secret
society. If they do, it is thought that they will fail
to bear children unless cleansing rituals are performed. Nor for similar reasons are they to touch
the masked dancers. Wives of men who carve
masks are not to know that their husbands, who
do this work in secret, so occupy themselves,
even though the women may grind some of the

dyes used in decorating the masks for their men.
In short, Afikpo men see these plays, as well as
other aspects of the secret society, as reinforcing
the distinctiveness of males in contrast to
females, and as helping to maintain an authority
structure in which men dominate the government and the decision-making in village and
family affairs while females play largely domestic roles.

c   A third category of skits and songs involves
criticisms and ridicule of named leaders of the villages. These are generally elders or in some cases
enterprising middle-aged men. The skits and
songs generally involve a number of basic themes.
One is about "palaver" men, those who engage in
an argument or dispute for its own sake and so
gather bribes and personal rewards at the expense
of others, disrupting the normal tendencies toward
cooperation and peace. Another theme criticizes
the type of village leader who in a dispute sides
with the group that he expects will give him the
most money and food. One skit cites a man who
collected money from Afikpo villages ostensibly to
prosecute a court case between the Afikpo and the
Nigerian government, but who actually used the
money for himself. Or players may sing, again giving names, that certain elders are too shy to speak
in public though they have no physical defects and
can speak well, suggesting that they should come
forward and give their views. In short, these brief
dramas say that certain elders are foolish men who
make unwise decisions for their own personal
goals rather than for the whole community. They
are enjoined to listen to what is being said at the
plays, to help their own people, and to stop causing trouble, disruption, and dissension.

In a consensus society which also emphasizes individual achievement, there is always a tendency for
some elders to try to usurp power, to go too far
beyond the consensus principle. These men usually
act on their own, and for personal gain, while
appearing to represent their groups. Thus the consensus system of leadership at Afikpo makes for a
sort of contradiction: men should be personally
ambitious, but without disturbing the principle of
group control. It is hard to regulate some elders
and make them act as elders should. The contradiction at Afikpo is expressed both in the fear and in

the admiration found there for the "big palaver man." For this reason too, elders themselves (who attend the plays in large numbers and enjoy many aspects of them) often think the dances, skits, and songs extremely funny – especially if they are about other elders, and more especially other elders whom they themselves think have acted inappropriately. The plays may also serve to articulate to some elders points that other elders find difficult to express directly themselves amongst their peers. The skits and songs therefore act as a sort of authority equalizer, just as wealth-distribution ceremonies, so characteristic of Afikpo, act to prevent any individual person from obtaining economic dominance. From the point of view of the elders, therefore, the plays have ultimately desirable goals. In another skit the leaders argue endlessly and foolishly in a divorce case. This is cleverly acted out, with side comments by the play-leaders about how some men love to talk. One skit concerns some Afikpo leaders who converted to Islam allegedly for personal gains. [...] The skit goes on to say that they were foolish to change religions for personal gain, and in the long run they lost money – that they are greedy men.

Another point brought out by Okumkpa actors and singers is that when elders engage in foolish conflicts, they are liable to be killed by poison, sorcery, or other mystical means. The plays emphasize a point strongly believed in at Afikpo, namely, that disputes and conflicts by their nature kill persons, and that attempts should therefore be made to avoid them. Such disagreements kill good leaders as well as "palaver men" who stir up a dispute for personal reasons. One song, for example, tells of an argument between villages over ownership of a palm grove. The singers call upon certain named elders to give up the dispute because the grove belongs to a certain village. They sing of other prominent elders in Afikpo who died during the dispute; their deaths must be attributed to the conflict itself. This is, in fact, an old quarrel which has been going on for many years and which has cost the Afikpo a great deal of time and money without any settlement being reached. The players voice the anxiety of the public, that the elders should make peace with one another and not divert their strength into useless conflicts.

The kinds of comments these masked figures – young and middle-aged men – make concerning their leaders would be, Afikpo admit, impossible to utter, unmasked, in public. The political structure of the village is such that no young or middle-aged man would normally dare to make such statements at village councils. If he did so he would be quickly shouted down and probably fined by the elders. In fact, deferential behavior is invariably exhibited toward persons senior in age to oneself as defined by the age-set system. Younger brothers are expected to obey their older ones and not to try to outdo them in taking titles or in other political or commercial enterprises. Sons likewise may not speak up against their fathers at public meetings, nor may they take more titles than their fathers have taken while the latter are alive.

The comments about the leaders made by the Okumkpa masked dancers are therefore of an unusual nature and are so recognized by the Afikpo. This is proved by the wide interest taken in them on the part of the audience, an interest shared by the elders and other leaders present. Names of offenders are freely given, and specific situations which have occurred, or are believed to have taken place, are acted out and sung about. If the named persons are in the audience, they are not allowed to become angry, for to show annoyance or disgust is considered very bad form. They are, in fact, expected to give the actors or singers pennies or shillings to show their approval of an act well done. In practice, however, criticized leaders react in a variety of ways. Some are so happy to have their names mentioned, even if in a derogatory manner, that they are not actually angered. They may be pleased at this recognition that they have special power or influence. Others are very upset and may privately try to take revenge on the play-producers at some future time through land-case litigation or other devices; but this is considered very bad form. Thus the pattern is generally maintained that the Okumkpa plays are very funny affairs and not to be taken too seriously. It is appropriate that the masked and costumed characters are light-hearted, amusing, and sometimes ridiculous. To become overly serious is to spoil the game – to invite factionalism. Even a mask carver was referred to as "that funny man who makes masks," as one who does not have a serious or major occupation, compared, say, to iron-smithing or palm-wine tapping. It is obvious, on the other hand, that carvers' services are indispensable, for masks are of vital importance to any activities of the secret society. But a kind of make-believe about the plays establishes them as effective devices for airing tensions in the village and for getting comments across that are otherwise difficult to articulate. Because people do recognize that the carver plays a serious and important role with high status, the content of the plays is more than make-believe or play-acting. In fact, I would argue that the play does have serious underlying intent.

For the young men *do* have honest grievances against the elders. Their comments are often serious, and they have no other effective ways of getting their complaints heeded short of refusing outright to cooperate with the elders, something which they rarely do. What in effect happens is that while elders normally make moral and judicial judgments on the behavior of the young men, in the plays the situation is reversed. Here the youths say to the elders: "Look, in such and such a situation you and you and you acted poorly and unethically." The characters who act out the misbehavior of the elders often use the dark ugly masks, with gestures and voices that are exaggerated and grotesque. They make fun of a leader who has a limp or speaks in a certain manner as part of their castigation of him. It is as if they are saying that the elders being portrayed are ugly, deviating, and foolish. The point is made indirectly at other times in Okumkpa, for all of the skits are about foolish people; generally, one skit is about the most foolish man in the village, and another about the most foolish woman. The latter skit usually involves a young dancer who wears the "queen" mask, *opa nwa* (carrier-child) [...].

The spiritual forces of the Afikpo community are normally under the guidance of senior men who control and direct sacrifices and other religious rituals, in which young men play only supportive roles, supplying materials to be used in sacrifice and food for the feasts that accompany some religious activities. But in the Okumpka plays the younger men, as masked spirit dancers (*mma*), *are* the spirits and control and direct affairs. The elders, as ordinary members of the audience, sit passively, having only the secular role of reacting to the players. This is another aspect of the reversal of the leadership roles of elders and younger men that occurs through the masked plays.

Functional Analysis

A tentative functional analysis of these plays may be in order. Functional theory is not by any means well established to day, and between the earlier thinking of Emile Durkheim (1926), Alfred R. Radcliffe-Brown (1935), and Bronislaw Malinowski (1939, 1944) and the present day, it has been severely criticized (for example, Cancian 1960; Dore 1961; Erasmus 1967; Gregg and Williams 1948; Hempel 1959; Homans 1964; van den Berghe 1963) or developed in modified forms (Parsons 1951; Levy 1952; Merton 1949; Spiro 1952, 1961). Much anthropological writing on Africa has used functional analysis implicitly, and without making what was involved clear. I will try a somewhat more explicit formulation here.

First, the Okumkpa plays stress normal and expected behavior by ridiculing deviancy; a wide range of deviant acts may be dramatized. The emphasis is on maintaining traditional roles, traditional forms of sex polarity, and traditional leadership. When the players are asked why they perform such skits and songs, they answer in specific terms. The manifest function of them, intended and recognized, is to make fun of and to ridicule that which the Afikpo consider to be the foolish acts of specific individuals and sometimes of specific groups. It is the anthropologist who generalizes the totality of actions as functioning in a latent manner to attempt to reduce deviancy, to uphold traditional custom, and to attack abnormality. Curiously, the young men are those who in Afikpo press for change the most, yet simultaneously they also are the ones who emphasize tradition in their plays. Why is this so? The leaders and style-setters of the plays seem quite traditionalistic compared with some other young men; those who are considered most "progressive" do not seem to play leading roles, although they often take part. Again, the young men as a whole – whether conservative or innovative – do not wish the elders to make the judgments about new conditions, for they do not feel that the elders understand them. Nor do the youths wish women to determine for themselves what changes to implement. Men today see changes in women's behavior as a threat to themselves. The Afikpo recognize that women are more independent and self-sufficient than they were formerly when they had to go to the farms under the protection of men and when they rarely traveled to distant markets or traded extensively in their own area. Afikpo women have a saying today: "When a woman has money, what is a man!" Thus, the young men see certain aspects of social change as desirable, but others as a threat to their position; in some ways they are conservative, in others they wish to play the controlling role in change.

A second major recognized and intended aim of some of the Afikpo skits and songs is to maintain sex polarity, the dominance of men over women and the restricted social and economic role of women in the face of changing conditions. Here the function of the play is seen in general terms, as many activities of the secret society are viewed, as a way of keeping women in their traditional roles. The means of coercion is the threat of barrenness in a society in which children are highly valued and where a person's status and prestige, male or female, is partly dependent on whether or not he or she has children, especially sons. The onus for failure to have children is placed on the women in Afikpo society, as can be seen in these plays and elsewhere and is associated with the angering of supernatural spirits through some form of female misbehavior.

Yet there also seems to be a latent function involved at the psychological level which the Afikpo do not verbalize. The fact is that men are extremely anxious about their failure to produce offspring even though the women are generally blamed for this, at least at first. A man must have at least a son to have status and to perform certain ceremonies and titles. Many children bring him considerable prestige and publicly symbolize his sexuality. The plays and skits, like other aspects of Afikpo life, operate to project strong, though rarely expressed, male anxieties about childlessness upon the women, particularly upon "misbehaving" females who are identified by a male definition. Women who have passed menopause sometimes flaunt the secrecy of the society. They may say: "I am an old woman now, what can the secret-society spirit do to me. I will die anyway!" The extent to which men are somewhat annoyed and bothered by such acts may be contrasted with their real displeasure if women of childbearing age do the same. This greater annoyance suggests that male anxiety over childlessness is a serious problem in Afikpo society.

A third major function of Okumkpa plays centers around the use of the theatrical situation to air anxieties and aggressive feelings that the young men hold concerning the elders. Here again the Afikpo see as a manifest function the fact that the plays and songs ridicule the elders who do not behave as elders should, who are greedy, foolish, bribe-takers, and so on. This is quite obvious, but we have to go further to see some latent functions as well. I take it that egalitarian gerontocracy in Afikpo inevitably leads to younger men developing some resentments and hostilities toward elders. In one sense the system of political authority in these villages is a projection of the family situation. The psychological features in man which make the young rebel against their fathers in the home context also operate by extension at the village level. Criticisms of the elders' actions in the village are a very limited and ritualized working out of youths' feelings against the authority of their fathers at home. Plays provide a way of handling aggressive feelings without changing the form of village social organization. The young men apparently do not really want radically to alter this form of government, and are in fact committed to it. They see long-term rewards in the status quo, even though they are restless with it.

The question why such aggressive tendencies, such criticisms, cannot be brought out openly at public meetings in the village, except in a highly circumspect manner, is crucial to the analysis here. I suggest that such tactics would be highly disruptive. The few attempted cases that I have seen were put down with short shrift by the elders, whom the youths both respect and fear, and whose place they desire some day to take themselves. I do not think we could postulate that village unity or Afikpo society would disintegrate or disappear if direct public aggression by clearly identified youths took place, although changes would occur. The theme of "social collapse unless aggressions are strongly displaced" is an old one in functional analysis, but is also moot. The fact seems to be that the young men, on the whole, are committed to the system to which they themselves sometimes object (Simon Ottenberg 1955), and they are not interested in radically altering it. Further, they are well aware that the elders hold the ultimate sources of power – the control and regulation of supernatural forces.

Those "progressive" individuals who are not happy in this system of authority generally live outside the villages or elsewhere in Nigeria and take only a limited part in village matters.

The criticisms of the Afikpo elders also serve other latent functions, which are occasionally recognized in specific cases. One purpose is to reduce individualism among the elders and thus to maintain egalitarianism by criticizing those who draw too much power to themselves. Some elders support this view as well, for the ideal of consensus as a basis for decision-making and the fear of village domination by single individuals are both strong sentiments. In this sense the skits and songs concerned with the elders are a functional equivalent of the witchcraft accusations among the Tiv, which are directed toward powerful individuals (Bohannan 1958). Both are attempts to reduce and contain such power. Conflict among the elders seems to stir anxiety among many persons in the Afikpo village, and attempts through the plays to reduce factionalism and get the elders to pose as a cooperative group may reduce such feelings.

A further function, again one that is mainly latent and that needs little comment, is that the Okumkpa plays seem to help develop or maintain a sense of pride and accomplishment in the village as a unit, to maintain a sense of the whole, of persons acting and working together regardless of individual kinship and residential ties. Many other Afikpo come and see these plays and persons remark on which villages have produced good plays in a given year and which have not. Intervillage rivalry, which also finds expression in wrestling and whipping contests and in other secret-society plays and dances, is enhanced and maintained by this particular form of play. The theater becomes a symbolic and public statement of the state of village organization.

The use of masks and costumes as "screens" helps to facilitate the outlet of anxieties and aggressive feelings without fear either of counterattack or any reorganization of the authority structure. I take it that here, as in the case of mother-in-law jokes in our own society, the humor expressed is related to some anxiety and tension. I do not mean to imply, however, that there is a natural tendency for a society to maintain itself or for equilibrium situations automatically to assert themselves in a society

through such plays. Following Homans (1964), I suggest that individuals in the village are not anxious, in terms of their goals, to change its organization drastically at this point in time; they are interested in it as it is, and their orientation toward it is what maintains it, rather than there being any natural tendency toward equilibrium or stability.

The plays also can be looked at as dysfunctional, though I think to a relatively small degree. They may lead to anger on the part of elders and others who have been ridiculed and criticized. Such anger is often directed toward the leaders of the play, with consequent gestures of noncooperation toward the men involved (for example, pressuring to oust them from land they are using on loan). Thus every play seems to leave some residue of ill-will in the village, though this does not seriously affect the operation of the village organization and usually occurs between individuals rather than groups.

It is also worth noting that the rather free-floating authority structure of the players' group within the larger authority system of the secret society and the village is no accident. This autonomy gives players the freedom to act as they would not be able to if they were directly under the authority of the village elders, the priests' group, or the titled group of the secret society. Such functional autonomy (Gouldner 1959) is necessary for the effective preparation and performance of the plays. In order to be prepared and performed a play and its creators must be in a certain structural arrangement vis-à-vis society at large, here one of relative freedom to create, independent from the elders.

Three queries concerning this sort of analysis may now be considered. The first question is: what sort of things are *not* acted or sung about in these plays? I see two major omissions: matters having to do with the secret-society's priests (and other religious officials at Afikpo) and sexual references. Plays may criticize the priests of Afikpo's spirit shrines and diviners, but only indirectly – for example, by reminding priests in general that other priests who have failed to perform their work effectively in the past have died before their time. Beyond this, there seems to be no attack on religious leaders, probably because of their direct association with very powerful spirits. As *mma* spirits, the masked actors are free to criticize elders in their role as secular leaders, but not as religious heads. This fits well with the Afikpo view. Spirits are guardians of morality, but as a rule they are not believed to be critical or hostile to other spirits.

With regard to sexual matters, it is interesting to note that apart from an occasional reference, such matters are generally not treated in Okumkpa plays, though there is plenty of deviation from sexual norms at Afikpo which could be used as material. Rather, certain unmasked public song and dance festivals are held annually which do treat the actions and misbehavior of individuals, again giving names and details. The singers are young people – male and female – of certain ages. We have to ask why these performances can be given openly and not through the use of masked plays, and why women can take an active part in them. The answer is in a sense a test of the fitness of the analysis presented above. At this moment I cannot provide a fully satisfactory explanation, but I suggest that a primary factor is that sexual deviancy from the norm is not taken very seriously in Afikpo unless it involves a few special forms, such as sexual relationships between members of the same matrilineal clan. In fact, virtually everyone in Afikpo is involved in non-normative sexual acts, assuming it is even possible to determine accurately what normative sexuality is for this area. Further, many of these cases involve persons in different villages – which cases are therefore not purely internal matters – and also matrilineal groupings which do not have a residential base; thus the frictions that arise over these affairs often cut across villages, rather than merely affecting intravillage relationships. Hence the authority structure of the village is generally not involved, even if the violators of sexual norms are elders.

A second problem arises out of the fact that we are basing at least part of this analysis on hypotheses concerning individual anxieties and aggressive feelings. I have imputed these to the young men in terms of a general theory of father–son ties and some known facts about young men and elders at Afikpo and in other societies. But I really lack proof for Afikpo. We might learn more by using psychologically sensitive data, or, if a village in Afikpo could be found which did not carry out such plays, or did so very rarely, an examination of its authority structure and sex polarity and a careful search for functional equivalents of the masked plays might be made. A few small villages in Afikpo do not produce Okumkpa plays, but at the time they were investigated, I did not have this question in mind.

A third problem is that of evaluating what the plays really *do* to people, other than amusing and pleasing them. How are persons actually affected by them, what really is their impact on the audience – on a short-term or long-range basis? As we have seen, songs from the plays may be sung by many persons for months, even years, after the original performance, and both songs and skits are discussed in the village and elsewhere for a long time afterwards; their influence clearly extends beyond the day they are first presented, and beyond a second neighboring village where the play is sometimes given again a few days after its original performance. I have mentioned the attempt in Okumkpa plays to maintain sex polarity and egalitarian leadership. I would add that the plays seem to be primarily tension-reducing devices; they point up moral and ethical standards, they attempt to reduce individualism in leadership, they help to give a village a sense of identity and unity as against other villages, and so on. But it seems that in the analysis I have presented, and in others of like kind, we have yet to develop techniques for accurately gauging how effective the plays actually are in accomplishing these tasks. We do not, at present, have sensitive field tools to achieve this purpose. Furthermore, traditional field work techniques are inadequate in this context, so that new and more accurate tools of a different order will have to be devised. Functional analysis of the sort presented here is at a very simple and crude level operationally. It can indicate manifest intentions and latent functions, but it has few techniques for measuring actual consequences.

In any case, while the Afikpo plays themselves are humorous, popular, well attended, and very much enjoyed, much of the subject matter clearly is serious and directly tied to questions of authority and control in the village. The secrecy of the dancers, achieved through the use of masks and costume as concealing forms, is a method of publicly revealing what persons gossip about privately, or simply do not know. The masked players, through a ritual role reversal of leadership, become devices through which the secrets of the "other world" are revealed and explained. Thus masked secrecy is a mechanism to undo secrets.

Notes

1 See Phoebe Ottenberg 1958, 1965; Simon Ottenberg 1955, 1965, 1968a, 1968b, 1968c, 1970, 1971; Simon and Phoebe Ottenberg 1962.

2 In some Afikpo villages there are no formal positions of priest and assistant priest, but there is nevertheless a similar type of ritual group.

3 For other Afikpo masks and related local styles, see Bravmann 1970, pp. 65–67; Starkweather 1968, nos. 1–66; Jones 1939.

4 These exceptions include a special calabash mask worn during the initiation of a man's eldest son into the secret society, certain cloth masks, and masks that noninitiate boys make and use in play in the village.

References

Bateson, Gregory
1936 *Naven*. Cambridge, England.

Bohannan, Paul
1958 "Extra-Processual Events in Tiv Political Institutions." *American Anthropologist* 60, no. 1: 1–12.

Bravmann, René A.
1970 *West African Sculpture*. Index of Art in the Pacific Northwest, no. 1. Seattle.

Cancian, Francesca
1960 "Functional Analysis of Change." *American Sociological Review* 25, no. 6: 818–827.

Dore, Ronald P.
1961 "Function and Cause." *American Sociological Review* 26, no. 6: 843–853.

Durkheim, Emile
1926 *The Elementary Forms of the Religious Life*. 2d rev. ed. New York. Translation of *Les formes élementaires de la vie religieuse*. Paris, 1912.

Erasmus, Charles J.
1967 "Obviating the Functions of Functionalism." *Social Forces* 45, no. 3: 319–328.

Gouldner, Alvin W.
1959 "Reciprocity and Autonomy in Functional Theory." In *Symposium on Sociological Theory*, edited by L. Gross, pp. 241–270. New York.

Gregg, Dorothy, and Williams, Elgin
1948 "The Dismal Science of Functionalism." *American Anthropologist* 50, no. 4: 594–611.

Hempel, Carl G.
1959 "The Logic of Functional Analysis." In *Symposium on Sociological Theory*, edited by L. Gross, pp. 271–307. New York.

Homans, George C.
1964 "Bringing Man Back In." *American Sociological Review* 29, no. 6: 809–818.

Jones, G. I.
1939 "On the Identity of Two Masks From S. E. Nigeria in the British Museum." *Man* 39, art. 35: 33–34.

LeVine, Robert A.
1966 *Achievement Motivation in Nigeria*. Chicago.

Levy, Marion J., Jr.
1952 *The Structure of Society*. Princeton.

Malinowski, Bronislaw
1939 "The Group and the Individual in Functional Analysis." *American Journal of Sociology* 44, no. 6: 938–964.

Malinowski, Bronislaw
1944 *A Scientific Theory of Culture and Other Essays*. Chapel Hill.

Merton, Robert K.
1949 "Manifest and Latent Functions." In *Social Theory and Social Structure*, edited by R. Merton, pp. 21–81. Glencoe, Ill.

Ottenberg, Phoebe
1958 "The Changing Economic Position of Women Among the Afikpo Ibo." In *Continuity and Change in African Cultures*, edited by William R. Bascom and Melville J. Herskovits, pp. 205–223. Chicago.
1965 "The Afikpo Ibo of Eastern Nigeria." In *Peoples of Africa*, edited by James L. Gibbs, Jr., pp. 1–39. New York.

Ottenberg, Simon
1955 "Improvement Associations Among the Afikpo Ibo." *Africa* 25, no. 1: 1–28.
1958 "Ibo Receptivky to Change." In *Continuity and Change in African Cultures*, edited by William R. Bascom and Melville J. Herskovits, pp. 130–143. Chicago.
1965 "Inheritance and Succession in Afikpo." In *Studies in the Laws of Succession in Nigeria*, edited by J. Duncan M. Derrett, pp. 33–90. London.
1968a *Double Descent in an African Society: The Afikpo village-Group*. American Ethnological Society, Monograph 47. Seattle.
1968b "Statement and Reality: The Renewal of an Igbo Protective Shrine." *International Archives of Ethnography* 51: 143–162.
1968c "The Development of Credit Associations in the Changing Economy of an African Society." *Africa* 38, no. 3: 237–252.
1970 "Personal Shrines at Afikpo." *Ethnology* 9, no. 1: 26–51.

1971 *Leadership and Authority in an Africa Society: The Afikpo village-Group*. American Ethnological Society, Monograph 52. Seattle.

Ottenberg, Simon and Phoebe

1962 "Afikpo Markets: 1900–1960." In *Markets in Africa*, edited by Paul Bohannan and George Dalton, pp. 117–168. Evanston, Ill.

Parsons, Talcott

1951 *The Social System*, Glencoe, Ill.

Radcliffe-Brown, Alfred R.

1935 "On the Concept of Function in Social Science." *American Anthropologist* 37, no. 3: 394–402.

1957 *The Natural Science of Society*. Glencoe, Ill.

Spiro, Melford

1952 "Ghosts, Ifaluk and Teleological Functionalism." *American Anthropologist* 54, no. 4: 497–503.

1961 "Social Systems, Personality and Functional Analysis," In *Studying Personality Cross-Culturally*, edited by Bert Kaplan, pp. 93–127. Evanston, Ill.

Starkweather, Frank

1968 *Igbo Art: 1966*. Museum of Art, University of Michigan, Ann Arbor.

van den Berghe, Pierre L.

1963 "Dialectic and Functionalism." *American Sociological Review* 28, no. 5: 695–704.

23

Art, Identity, Boundaries

Postmodernism and Contemporary African Art

Olu Oguibe

In his rather interesting collection of interviews and plates, the postmodernist critic Thomas McEvilley[1] asks Ouattara[2] 'When and where were you born?', to which the temperamental artist responds with barely suppressed irritation. To many, this would seem an innocent and ordinary enough question, especially when the obvious intent is to present to us a, supposedly, relatively unknown artist. Asks the critic next: 'In 1957, was Abidjan a big urban centre, like today?' To which, again, Ouattara duly provides the expected answer. On the first page of the interview, there is a picture of the artist, his face is aligned against the text, his brooding countenance attesting most eloquently and visibly to his impatience with the critic's line of enquiry. One can almost sense a building tension within the artist. Reading closely, however, one also notices that McEvilley, to the contrary, is quite relaxed. For him, the chat is going well, and he is comfortable. And when He is comfortable, everyone else is comfortable. As he maps the artist with his eyes, his mind retrieves from its cabinet of tourist postcards an image of an African mammy-wagon with a line of popular wisdom inscribed on its outer board: *No Hurry in Life*. It is the way of these people, he reminds himself: generous, charitable, accommodating. They take life easy. And so his mind drafts back to Ouattara's studio, hardly taking notice of his quarry as the artist shifts uneasily on his stool, muttering under his breath. Quite predictably, the white boy fails to read the sign on the native's face. For him the gestures of the native are an invisible sign.

The critic runs his pen across his bushy face, and, as if speaking to a child on his first day at school asks: 'Would you tell me a little about your family?' There! Ouattara explodes. But only within. Like a gentleman. The ultimate signifying monkey. He understands – he is brought up to understand, everything in his history and in his experience prepares him to understand and to accept – that in dealing with the power that McEvilley represents, he is engaged in an ill-matched game of survival; a game that he must play carefully if he is to avoid profound consequences; a game he must negotiate with patience to prevent his own erasure, his own annihilation; a game that he must ultimately concede in order to live. Living in New York, Ouattara

From Olu Oguibe, "Art, Identity, Boundaries: Postmodernism and Contemporary African Art," in *Reading the Contemporary: African Art from Theory to the Marketplace*, ed. Olu Oguibe and Okwui Enwezor, pp. 17–19, 20–1, 23–5, 27–8, Institute of International Visual Arts (INIVA), London 1999 © Olu Oguibe and INIVA.

understands too well how, beyond the boundaries of colonial ethnographic displacement, the introduction of digitisation in our time has sanitised erasure and transformed it into a messless act. He understands how the mark of deletion, the ugly sites of cancellation and defacement, the crossing out, the scarred page, the marginal inscription – that which in the past testified to the processes of obliteration and through this testimonial actively subverted it – are now things of the past; and the object of the obliterative act now disappears together with the evidence of its own excision, making erasure an act without trace. This knowledge further underlines the ominousness of his location. Ouattara understands how much he needs McEvilley, how much he stands to gain by making friends with him. He recognises, albeit painfully, that the terrain he occupies, the terrain to which he is perpetually consigned, in which he is confined, is one under surveillance, where every utterance, every gesture, carries with it implications of enormous weight for himself as an African artist, and for his practice. And even more importantly, he recognises this terrain as an outpost, a location on the peripheries of the principalities that the critic represents – a border post at which McEvilley is the control official. This is the locality of the African artist dealing with the West, irrespective of her domicile. This I call the terrain of difficulty.

And so, holding his breath firmly down, gritting his teeth and silently but vigorously crossing out the dozen f-words bombing his brain while warning himself to take it all with calm, Ouattara stakes his final but ultimately futile claim, 'I prefer to talk about my work'.

Well. Not quite. The artist's polite caution does not wash with the critic. Deftly and firmly McEvilley waves Ouattara's protest aside and proceeds with his line of questioning. He feels in command; he must be seen to be in command. 'If he hollers let him go', reads an old, American plantation saying. But no. McEvilley is not fazed by the native's protests. This time, the master will have his way. Describing the women of Huxian in *About Chinese Women*, Julia Kristeva images the native as a silent presence.[3] In reading Ouattara's moment with McEvilley, we are reminded of a different silent presence, closer perhaps to the obliterated presence that Chinua Achebe identifies in

Joseph Conrad's *Heart of Darkness*, the native whose silence is an objectifying projection – what we may refer to as *significant* silence. For though this silence is not literal, it is nevertheless made real since, beyond the preferred narrative – that specified rhetoric that reiterates palatable constructs of Otherness – the native's utterances are not speech. They occupy the site of the guttural, the peripheries of sense, the space of the unintelligible where words are caught in a savage struggle and sounds turn into noise, into the surreal mirror-image of language. In this void of incoherence, utterance becomes silence because it is denied the privilege of audience. And without audience, there is no speech.

Sprawled out like Barthes in Tangier, or prowling through a market in Abidjan, the esoteric goulash of native utterance is of course the ultimate locale of Occidental desire, the last place in which to hunt for exotic pleasures. But this is not a pleasure trip. McEvilley has a book in mind and must have his story. Under the circumstances, native aspirations to desire and the dialogic ('I prefer ...'), native pretensions to power and sophistication ('to discuss my work ...'), are quickly displaced in a hegemonic withdrawal of audience that re-establishes the hierarchical location of the *Self* over the *Other*, of the white critical and artistic establishment over the African artist. On this stage of simulacral dialogue there is only one voice that counts. The Other can exist only as a projection, an echo, as the displaced sound of percussive fracture.

And so McEvilley drives his conversation with Ouattara towards the realisation of his preferred narrative, with questions not intended to reveal the artist as subject, but rather to display him as object, an object of exolicist fascination. 'How big was your family? What school did you go to? What language was spoken in your home? What religion did your family practice? Did it involve animal sacrifice?' In the end, his mission fulfilled, McEvilley finally announces to Ouattara: 'I don't have any more questions, do you have anything more to say?'

For Ouattara, though, the game is already over. It was over before it even began. It was over from the moment he was born, from the moment he was destined to be – designated as – an Other. In answer, he fumbles within for something deep and philosophical to say, something original, something in his and not the master's voice, some desperate utterance in the narrow passage of sanction accorded him, something that represents his, rather than the preferred version, the master narrative. He struggles to speechify, to repossess his body and reinvest it with humanity, with language, with articulation. He struggles at the borders of subjecthood.

Aligned to the text at this stage is another picture of the artist, as if in conclusion. But this time, the strength of determination, even defiance, which we glean from the portrait at the beginning of the text, is gone. Ouattara's countenance no longer projects a brooding tension; it no longer *projects*; that is, it no longer aspires. His disposition no longer indicates a willingness to dare, to utter with Frantz Fanon: 'Get used to me; I am not getting used to anyone'.[4] Instead, he stares into space, his face sunken and forlorn, his anger turned to despair, his attempts at the contested territory of the voice thwarted by McEvilley's hegemonic devices. Failed is his effort to displace the critic's gaze onto his work, to specify the latter as the rightful focus of contemplation, and in so doing, to claim author-ity. Clearly against his will, Outtara finds himself repositioned in the frame as the object. And though he is coerced to sketch the contours of this object, to narrate himself and to trace the ethnography of his body, he is made to do so within confines defined by another. He is forced to strip for McEvilley's pleasure.

[…]

In vetoing Ouattara's right to self-articulation, in placing a sanction against his preferred site of discourse, McEvilley effects a paradigmatic reiteration of ventriloquy as a structure of reference for Western attitudes towards African artists. This frame has its origins in colonial ethnography and the colonial desire for the faceless native, the anonym. The faceless native, displaced from individuality and coalesced into a tribe, a pack, demands and justifies representation because she stands for lack. In the event, authority is appropriated and transferred from her, and it is this authority that is subsequently exercised in constructing her for Occidental consumption. The defacement of the native consigns her to the category of the unknown.

Displaced to the befuddled corners of obscurity and rudimentary episteme, the native is made available for discovery, and this discovery transforms the discoverer into an *authority*, their supposed privileged knowledge often translating into the right to represent.

Even more specifically, the imposition of anonymity on the native, of course, deletes her claims to subjectivity and works to displace her from normativity. Not only does this conveniently underline her *Otherness*, her strangeness, her subalternity, anonymity equally magnifies the invented exoticism of her material culture, which in turn becomes a sign of her constructed exoticism. For some time, in order to emphasise the Otherness of non-Occidental cultures, ethnography applied a different rule of attribution to art from such cultures, effectively denying the identities of artists even where these were known. The figure of the individual genius, that element which more than any other defines enlightenment and modernity, was reserved for Europe while the rest of humanity was identified with the collective, anonymous production pattern that inscribes primitivism. Until recently, works of classical African art were dutifully attributed to the 'tribe', rather than to the individual artist, thus effectively erasing the latter from the narrative spaces of art history. In contemporary discourses, critics like McEvilley represent the continuation of this practice whereby novel strategies are employed to anonymise African art by either disconnecting the work from the artist, thus deleting the author-ity of the latter, or by constructing the artist away from the normativities of contemporary practice.

[…]

The effaced African artist, the faceless, anonymous native, is the correlative of Fanon's 'palatable Negro', the tolerable, consumable Other who, stripped of authority and enunciatory autonomy, is opened to the penetrative and dominatory advances of the West. The appeal of the faceless, anonymous native is in the fact that she is also a pornographic object, a docile, manipulable object of desire and pleasure. Pornography as a strategy rests on the localisation of desire and the intensification of pleasure through the effacement of the subject, the detachment of the locality of desire from the web of subjective associations and reality that impinge on the possessor's sense of social responsibility. In other words, its principal device is the objectivisation of the source of pleasure. For maximum derivative effect, the purveyor as well as the consumer of pornography must detach and frame the object, enhanced through the combined mechanisms of magnification and erasure, filling the frame with only that which satisfies the specifications of desire. Even this is further aided by positioning the object within an appropriate narrative, the right sound, the further from speech the better, all of which, by playing on the extremes of perversion and provocativeness, sufficiently hold it within the frames of the spread. Of course, the erasure of the subject, or her transfiguration into the realms of the fantastic, consolidates the purveyor's fiction of ownership, and thus of power. And power, the ability to possess unquestionably, to exercise uncontested authority and manipulate at will, is the essence of pornography.

Angela Dworkin has described the pornographic object as a colony, the terminal site of the colonised body. In Occidental discourses, African artists and African art in turn continue to occupy this site. Decoupled and anonymised, each is turned into a silent colony, a vassal enclave of pleasure and power. Each is fragmented and projected in close-up sequences and pastiches that magnify pleasure for the all-knowing critic or collector: hence the concept of the intimate outsider who is narrated into a positive relationship with these objects. Each is parcelled and packaged to suit the West's machinations and tastes, to satisfy its desires and to fit within its frames of preference.

Even the pricing of contemporary African art and artists on the international art market positions them within the frame of the cheap, pornographic object. Once, a friend who is an African art dealer received a painting by Gerard Santoni, the Ivorian artist, from one of the leading galleries in New York, with a price tag that would be considered quite modest in a degree show. Santoni is a deservedly well-regarded artist whose work has been shown at the Venice Biennale and other reputable international and contemporary art spaces. He has practised for several decades and, even with the fragmentation of values that ostentatiously characterises our age, his works would still generally be considered of the highest standard.

But Santoni is underpriced because, in the West, he and his work are consigned to the category of mere objects of pleasure and fascination, like pornography. They are positioned on those peripheries of creative genius where the aesthetic experience fails to cohere with great material value. This observation becomes particularly relevant when we consider how little collectors are willing to pay for popular art from Africa, despite the fact that it has remained the focus of Western fascination and attention over the past four decades, and has been vigorously promoted as quintessential contemporary African expression. It is to be noted that collectors spend much more money plugging the pieces in their collections and struggling to generate a discourse around them than they have expended on the artworks themselves. Across Africa, popular artists who are much touted in the West, continue to pursue their careers in conditions that bear no comparison with the affluence of their Western contemporaries.

A good illustration of this perpetual disjuncture between hype and remuneration is the Nigerian graphic artist, Middle Art, whose barber-shop signs were brought to the attention of the world by Ulli Beier and others in the early 1970s. In the 1990s, Middle Art's signs are still voraciously collected in the West, especially in Germany, where the artist continues to command critical attention and dealers continue to receive orders from collectors. But after over thirty years of selling to collections, it is remarkable to note that Middle Art has remained poor, unable to afford a proper studio or indeed, as a German dealer recently told me, to make a decent living from his work. In twenty years of narration and promotion, Middle Art's signs have not appreciated in value; nor has the artist come to be regarded as deserving better payment, which would be unimaginable in the case of a Western artist who had been so promoted and collected. Middle Art's work is cheap because the West does not consider it art 'as we know it'. As an artist, he compares to his Western contemporaries in the same way that a porn actor compares to a 'proper' stage actor. One, though highly desired, is nevertheless dispensable and cheap, while the other, identified with high culture, is appropriately valued and appreciated. Porn is recyclable and its appeal is temporary. For this reason, porn is cheap, and the object of pornographic consumption even cheaper. And both belong not in the great spaces of culture but on the supermarket shelf, on the sidewalk, in the quirky fringes of normative taste. Projected on contemporary African artists and their work, these attributes tether them to the lowest rungs of a strictly multi-tiered contemporary art market from where upward mobility is almost impossible.

The perverted desire for the pornographic manifests itself most significantly, however, in the continued preference in the West for that art from Africa that is easily imaged not as art as we know it, but as a sign of the occult, an inscription of the fantastic. The childlike paintings of the Beninois, Cyprien Toukoudagba, would not ordinarily represent great creative talent in the West, and would not, conventionally, qualify as art beyond the sixth grade. In fact, the critical acclaim enjoyed over the past few years by the fine draughtsmanship of British child artist Stephen Wiltshire testifies more accurately to contemporary Western standards of even juvenile creativity. But Toukoudagba's naïve drawings are today preferred in the West to the more sophisticated, more familiar forms that represent the cutting edge of contemporary African art precisely because his works fall below these standards, and thus inadvertently yield to dubious, perverted desires and expectations. As form, they represent a slip from normativity; they signify a coveted distance between the West and the African; they satisfy the desire for the fantastic; they are open to pornographic translation; they are strange. A few decades ago, this desire for the subnormative and pornographic was fulfilled by 'Outsider' art: the art of the blind, the autistic, the mentally disabled and clinically insane. Today, that desire is projected on Africa, and it is this perversion that locates works like Toukoudagba's within the boundaries of preference.

[…]

The issue of authenticity and its attendant anxieties are of course not matters over which contemporary African artists are likely to be found losing any sleep. On the contrary, it is those who construct authenticities and fabricate identities for them who are constantly plagued with worries. And for the precise reason that I have already indicated: such anxieties have less to do with facts of authenticity and the relevance of tradition, as with a desire to force African artists behind the confines of manufactured identities aimed to place a distance between their practice and the purloined identity of contemporary Caucasian art. In other words, the introduction of the question of authenticity is only a demand for identity, a demand for the signs of difference, a demand for cultural distance. It is a demand for the visual and formal distance without which it is impossible for contemporary Caucasian art not to reveal itself as mimic, as a culture of quotations, as a mediated translation of cultures and art traditions other than itself, as pastiche. For, having purloined its form and identity from others, it becomes relevant for Caucasian art to insist on difference in order to obliterate any traces back to the source, to E(u)rase the mimetic trail.

It is for this reason that the charge of mimicry is recurrently levelled against contemporary African artists, their work dismissed as only an imitation of Western art. By employing this device of reversal, it becomes possible for the mimic – that is contemporary Western art – to invest itself with originality and a sense of its own authenticity. In proceeding, then, to displace mimesis away from itself, and to project the same on African artists, contemporary Caucasian art is able through its narratives to reserve alterity for itself, to reserve the right to be the One and the Other at the same time and without sanction. The charge of mimicry becomes its tool for defaming and displacing those who produce from within those traditions which, in truth, it mimics; those whose existence challenges its fictions of originality.

McEvilley's seemingly innocent question to Ouattara again comes to mind: 'Where were you born?' One recognises an uncanny ring to this question, the resonance of mechanisms of surveillance and regulation employed by the West today to keep Africans outside its geographical borders. We notice a confluence of the political and the cultural. The one-sided contest for authenticity that the West insinuates, its overbearing desire to claim originality as a preserve and to dismiss others as inauthentic and mimetic, in several respects parallels its current paranoia over territory, the anxiety that it is about to be overrun by outsiders. Hence the intensification of border regulations and the redefinition of origins and identities, the recurrence of the question: 'Where were you born?'

The desire to nominalise the cutting edge of contemporary African art is a methodical mapping of territories, a project of surveillance that is one with the tradition of policing the imaginary borders of civility and progress. The implications of the above for creative practice are numerous and far-reaching. Working within the confines of distortive regulatory strategies, African artists find themselves vulnerable to potentially destructive pressures. The demand is for them to produce to specification, to affect anonymity, to concede the ability to enunciate within the sites of normativity. Even more significant is the fact that, for these artists, access to criticality in contemporary discourses is regulated by this demand for subnormativity, and here lies the importance of Thomas McEvilley's interview with Ouattara. For not only do McEvilley's devices illustrate one critic's incarcerating projections on an African artist, even more significantly, they speak to the segregationist criticality and general ambivalence of white, postmodernist contingents in the so-called discourse of Others, a criticality bounded by an interceptory demand for the identity of the Other, by the query: 'Where were you born?' They speak to the fact that within this discourse, postmodernism remains, to a remarkable extent, a mere rehash of entrenched modernist attitudes and methods, 'a continued reproduction', as Peter Hitchcock has suggested, of 'the logic of Western cultural critique that fosters the "othering" of the so-called "Third World Subject" '.[5]

These are peculiar obstacles, of course, which work outside the perimeters of limitation/transgression. The challenges they pose require of artists resistive rather than transgressive strategies. More importantly, they pose an even greater challenge for contemporary cultural theory, and for postmodernism as a critical culture. To bring its object into crisis is the duty of criticism, and postmodernism must extend this responsibility to contemporary African art, and even more so, to the logic that regulates its contemplation of non-Occidental contemporaneity. To engage meaningfully with the contemporary, a credible postmodernist criticism must place its ambivalence under crisis, and extend the borders of criticality beyond the demand for identity and subnormativity.

Notes

1 Thomas McEvilley, *Fusions: African Artists at the Venice Brinnale* (New York: Museum for African Art, 1996).
2 New York artist Ouattara was born in Ivory Coast but has lived and worked in France and the US since the 1930s.
3 See Julia Kristeva, *About Chinese Women*, trans. Anita Barrows (New York: Unzen Books, 1977: reprinted 1986).
4 Frantz Fanon after Aimé Césaire, The Fact of Blackness', in *Black Skin White Masks*, trans. C.L. Markmann (London: Pluto Press. 1986), p. 131.
5 Peter Hitchcock, 'The Othering of Cultural Studies'. *Third Text*, no. 36 (London: Winter 1993–94), pp. 11–20.

24

As Plato Duly Warned

Music, Politics, and Social Change in Coastal East Africa

Kelly M. Askew

In his classic (1971) essay "Principles of Opposition and Vitality in Fang Aesthetics," James Fernandez presents a richly textured, multi-dimensional analysis of how aesthetic preferences for balanced opposition pervade Fang social life. He argues that "when Fang assume a posture of aesthetic scrutiny the presence of skillfully related oppositions constitutes an important part of their delight and appreciation. This is so because vitality arises out of complementary opposition and for them what is aesthetically satisfying is the same as what is vitally alive" (p.370). That one can identify balanced oppositions in Fang statuary, cosmology, gender ideology, village layout, and kinship structure leads Fernandez to conclude that "[t]he Fang not only live easily with contradictions; they cannot live without them" (p.358). Given the extent to which these aesthetic principles animate and lend meaning to Fang existence, Fernandez questions the assumption that aesthetic preferences are shaped, even determined, by social structure and wonders if perhaps the inverse might not be truer: "To what extent does social structure reflect aesthetic principles? Is society aesthetic preference drawn large?" (p.373).

Fernandez's fundamental concern with the relationship between art and society remains a controversial topic today, over thirty years later. Those who argue for the primacy of material processes see economic, political, and social relations ("base") as the driving motor behind artistic production such that art ("superstructure") becomes little more than a reflection of those relations. The most extreme versions of the argument negate art altogether, as with Marx who considered both "Art" and "The State" to be "abstract determinations which in no way really ripen to true social reality" (Marx 1970:40, quoted in Graham 1997:61; see also Newcomer 1979). Those, on the other hand, who – like Fernandez – privilege aesthetic or symbolic conceptualizations of social life see the arts as vehicles through which immaterial, transcendent, even spiritual, concerns are revealed, and society as a continuing effort to attain them. And so it is that Fang villages, statues, etc. exhibit complementary oppositions so as to produce vitality in all that Fang do. Lacking vitality, life, we are told, might not be worth living.

While today's academic climate ostensibly favors the dissolution of binary oppositions such as

From Kelly M. Askew, "As Plato Duly Warned: Music, Politics, and Social Change in Coastal East Africa", *Anthropological Quarterly*, 2003, 76(4): 609–37.

art/society, symbolic/material, superstructure/ base, bias towards the material remains. This has the effect of relegating aesthetic principles and processes to the margins of economic and political matters and, moreover, perpetuates a passive view of artistic practice that I wish to contest here. Rather than viewing art forms and aesthetic principles as derived from and shaped by society/ politics/history, I argue by way of musical data from the Swahili coastal region of East Africa that economic and political practice need not be conceptualized as distinct from aesthetic principles. My goal is not to equalize the material and the aesthetic by claiming that they are mutually-determinative (a common strategy for dissolving dichotomies), nor to further the neo-Marxist position that only art employed in the service of political action and social change warrants the designation "Art" (Adorno 1970; Brecht 1964; Fischer 1963, 1969; Marcuse 1978). Instead, I intend to show through an historical and comparative analysis of two musical genres that (1) we cannot assume that Swahili preferences for continual artistic innovation through the incorporation of foreign elements derive from Swahili economic history, and (2) that in Swahili communities political action *is* a key aesthetic principle. As vitality constitutes a Fang preoccupation, so does politicking constitute a Swahili, and more generally East African, preoccupation.

Ngoma and Dansi: Two Musical Genres on the Swahili Coast

Africa's eastern littoral known to many as the "Swahili Coast" has attracted traders and travelers from inland Africa and various destinations in the Persian Gulf, India, China, and Indonesia for at least two thousand years (Middleton 1992; Horton and Middleton 2000).[1] While the nature and scale of the trade has changed significantly over time, by the late eighteenth and throughout the nineteenth centuries formal trading caravans bearing such valued commodities as ivory, gold, and slaves wended their way eastwards through the African interior to the shores of the Indian Ocean. There, Swahili middlemen living in urban settlements would purchase the cargo in exchange for goods acquired from seafaring traders come to the coast in vessels

called *dhows*. In this manner, Chinese ceramics, Indian textiles, Venetian beads, Indonesian spices, and Arabian glassware spread throughout eastern, central, and southern Africa as Swahili brokers created for themselves privileged positions in a lucrative international network.

The global cosmopolitanism of Swahili society evident in dress, technology, architecture, household decoration, language (e.g., the high percentage of loanwords in Kiswahili) and more, has invited much comment over the centuries and finds resonance in Swahili arts, especially musical performance, the focus of this essay. Such cosmopolitanism recalls the art/society debate because the reigning assumption within Swahili Studies circles is that Swahili musical forms, with their remarkable range of musical influences and fascination with foreign elements, are what they are due to this economic history. That is to say, Indian Ocean networks involved people and commodities from a variety of cultures who, in the course of trade, also exchanged musical ideas and practices (long ocean voyages were made less dull with a musician or two on board). Given that Swahili communities served as necessary intermediaries and were thereby exposed to all the many cultures – from inland and overseas – drawn to the trade, they subsequently developed aesthetic preferences for cultural borrowing and the appropriation of foreign elements.

This is not an illogical supposition, but neither is it the only one possible. While there is no such thing as a "pure" culture untainted by outside influence, preferences for innovation or adherence to existing practice do vary widely from culture to culture – even from mercantile society to mercantile society. Not all trading societies can be said to have highly syncretic arts as a result of high degrees of contact with other societies and artistic traditions. So if increased contact with foreign cultures is not a good predictor of cultural hybridity, might it not be equally plausible that Swahili merchants enjoyed tremendous economic success in decades and centuries past due to a captivation with the exotic and an aesthetic preference for constant innovation that gave them a decided competitive edge?

In this paper, I will eschew description of the most obvious example of Swahili musical hybridity – *taarab* music (an amalgamation of African, Indian, and Middle Eastern musical traits)[2] – in favor of two no less syncretic forms known as *ngoma* and *dansi*. *Ngoma* is a Bantu term found throughout equatorial and southern Africa often glossed as "traditional dance." It frequently refers to a musical event that encompasses music, dance, song, characteristic instrumentation, and a characteristic rhythm, but also translates as "drum" or "music in general" (Johnson 1989[1939]:336). *Ngoma za kienyeji* ("indigenous dances"), of which there are countless varieties, can be differentiated on the basis of ethnicity (e.g., Swahili *ngoma*, Sukuma *ngoma*, Ndendeule *ngoma*) or by context (wedding *ngoma*, initiation *ngoma*, harvest *ngoma*) or gender (women's *ngoma*, men's *ngoma*). Some *ngoma*, especially those found in large cities like Dar es Salaam (see Geiger 1997) and the famous *beni* and *lelemama ngoma* (see Ranger 1975 and Strobel 1979 respectively) that spread throughout eastern Africa, lost any links they initially may have had to a single ethnic label and developed into pan-ethnic phenomena. *Ngoma* are frequently performed during life cycle celebrations and in competitive settings. *Dansi*, on the other hand, fills the urban bar-halls of Dar es Salaam, Morogoro, Tanga, Arusha, and elsewhere with electric guitars, driving beats, and ever-changing musical technology. Derived from the English "dance," *dansi* is undifferentiated by region or ethnicity being a pan-urban phenomenon but is differentiated according to *mtindo* (sing.; pl. *mitindo*), a musical "style" unique to each well-known band (Graebner 1994b, 2000). *Dansi* bands, like soccer teams, generate large, devoted followings of fans that attend all performances and inspire onlookers to join in the dancing.

One observer of the musical scene in Tanzania cast the differences between these two musical forms as follows:

> In many ways the side by side existence of *ngoma* and the popular urban jazz form is symbolic of the peculiar paradox of contemporary African urban society – the juxtaposition of new and old. Reflecting the old, yet timeless traditions of Tanzanian society, the *ngoma* symbolizes the stabilizing force of tradition – a force which has endured the process of urbanization while still maintaining the most fundamental aspects of

African traditional life. The popular jazz band, on the other hand, is reflective of Tanzania's ability and desire to change, to be innovative, to be a part of the modern world (Martin 1982:157).

The all-too-common alignment of *ngoma* with tradition/stasis/community and *dansi* (also known as "urban jazz") with modernity/innovation/urbanism exemplified in this quote requires serious rethinking.[3] *Dansi* is too often represented as a genre of change in contradistinction from purportedly frozen-in-time *ngoma*. One ethnomusicologist allowed for the possibility of change in *ngoma* but implied that it comes at great cost and rarely succeeds: "beni ngoma groups attempted to adapt to changing circumstances … but these endeavours did not help, and new music and social changes led to the ultimate disappearance of beni ngomas" (Bender 1991:120). He describes *dansi*, on the other hand, as "modern" and prone to change, noting also that "Differing from beni ngoma, danzi were not community oriented" (*ibid*). Another author went so far as to place *ngoma* and *dansi* on opposite ends of a Marxist, historical-materialist, evolutionary schema, in which *ngoma* relate to pre-capitalist modes of production while *dansi* correlates with the experience of urban capitalism (Donner 1980).

While one can see why the heavily amplified montage of musical elements as far-ranging as Western ballroom dancing, Afro-Cuban rhythms, and Congolese guitar techniques that jointly constitute *dansi* when juxtaposed with the more acoustic, drum-heavy, ritually-oriented *ngoma might* – on initial inspection – lend itself to such interpretations, such models cannot ultimately be substantiated. As we shall see in the following analysis, the mutability, adaptability, and innovative borrowing associated with *dansi* proves just as characteristic of *ngoma* thus flatly denying such neat and tidy polar oppositions. As Karen Barber and Christopher Waterman have demonstrated in their deconstruction of a strikingly similar opposition between supposedly static, tradition-bound *oríkì* praise poetry and purportedly innovative and modern *fújì* popular music (1995), I will show how *ngoma* and *dansi* share basic aesthetic principles and represent not two poles but rather two neighboring points on a spectrum of Swahili musical practice.

But first, some qualifications are in order. Lest readers think I mistakenly confuse "Swahili" with "Tanzanian," let it be noted that while both *ngoma* and *dansi* can be found throughout Tanzania with its 120+ ethnic groups as well as in neighboring Kenya, the Swahili coastal region has issued some of the most famous of *ngoma* styles and is credited with the emergence of *dansi*. *Beni* and *lelemama* are two *ngoma* (the first male, the second female) that originated in the late 19th century on the Swahili coast near Mombasa (Kenya) and Tanga (Tanzania) before sweeping through wide swaths of East Africa. Similarly, *dansi* has been attached to specifically coastal points of origin in Dar es Salaam, Mombasa, and Tanga with the first *dansi* band so far identified being the Dar es Salaam Jazz Band, established in 1932 (Graebner 2000). So while not unique to the Swahili coast, *ngoma* and *dansi* are very much associated with the Swahili coast and Swahili history. Similarly, the aesthetic principles and historical patterns that I identify here as "Swahili" should not be understood as uniquely Swahili. Some of what I describe here applies as well to non-coastal areas of East Africa,[4] but because my research experience is with the Swahili coast, I can only apply my argument with confidence to this cultural sphere. Expanding it to assess broader East African aesthetic sensibilities – while a worthy project – is beyond the scope of this paper.

Thus, my first objective is to demonstrate that these two musical genres share aesthetic principles for continual innovation, inventive borrowing (from local as well as foreign sources), competitive opposition, figurative language, and intertextuality, which make them both as "traditional" as they are "modern." Secondly, I will highlight the similar histories they share in serving as potent resources for articulating political sentiment and enacting political activity in precolonial, colonial, and postcolonial Tanzania. Thirdly, the extent of musical politicking via both *ngoma* and *dansi* supports my claim that this constitutes yet another shared aesthetic principle. Finally, the resultant conflation of aesthetic and political domains returns us, in the conclusion, to the question with which I began, namely, how can we rethink the relationship between art and society?

Sodas, Royalty, Ships and Novel Ngoma

It was the year 1956 and the British Colonial Office had arranged for Princess Margaret to go on a five-week tour of East Africa. The royal itinerary dictated that she would depart England on September 21st and fly to Mombasa, Kenya, where she would board the royal yacht Britannia. After a day of rest, she would sail to Mauritius (to tour Port Louis and lay the foundation stone for a new Royal College School building), then on to Zanzibar (to be appointed to the Order of the Brilliant Star of Zanzibar by Sultan Khalifa, tour clove and coconut plantations, meet two women who had been delivered from slavery by British patrol boats, and receive a golden miniature dhow), and finally to Dar es Salaam where she would embark on a 10-day tour of Tanganyika with visits to Tanga, Mbeya, Tabora, Mwanza, Arusha, and Moshi. A week in Kenya, marked by the laying of more cornerstones, a royal safari in the Amboseli game reserve, and the acclaimed police nabbing of Mau Mau "terrorist" Dedan Kimathi – "A police officer said today that a special effort had been made to capture Kimathi during Princess Margaret's visit" (*The Times* 10/22/56, p.8, col. D) – would bring the royal tour to a close.

When Princess Margaret's plane landed on the humble runway at Tanga Airport, a crowd of women in identical green and yellow uniforms sang their welcome to an accompaniment of drums and syncopated rhythms beaten on cow horns with wooden sticks. Although the (London) *Times*' coverage of the royal tour included pictures and descriptions of *ngoma* dancers greeting the princess at nearly every other stop on the tour, no picture, alas, preserved her arrival in Tanga. The historical significance of this royal visit was, nonetheless, forever etched into local Tanga memory. It would be memorialized and reenacted by Swahili women's *ngoma* societies in Tanga and elsewhere along the coast, transformed into a new dance event called *kwini*, derived from "queen" (although she was but a princess). These are recalled today in juxtaposition with the memory of a giant man-o'-war (*manuwari*) plying through the streets of Tanga. Queens and miraculous amphibious ships index the climax of a furious rivalry that engrossed this coastal city for nearly a decade. *Kanada* and

Fanta, two warring women's *ngoma* societies in Tanga, were enmeshed in an intense conflict over prestige, an historic display of one-up(wo)manship. Taking their names from sister rival clubs in Kenya who, in turn, found inspiration in the recently introduced soda beverages *Canada Dry* and *Fanta Orange*, these *ngoma* societies exemplified the inventive appropriation of foreign elements characteristic of so many domains of Swahili social life.

In the 1950s, Tanganyika and Zanzibar prospered.[5] The war and its ravages were receding from memory, a process aided by an economy on the rise. The economic climate enabled the expenditure of exorbitant amounts of resources on the acquisition of prestige through *ngoma* activities.[6] By mid-century, the rage for women's *lelemama ngoma* (Strobel 1979) had already swept through the coastal region, and men's *beni ngoma* (Ranger 1975) had firmly established itself throughout the Protectorate having spread westwards from coastal Swahili points of origin. The fascination in these *ngoma* with costumes and uniforms, brass instruments, ships, railway, royalty, and military ranking was comfortably interpreted by colonial authorities as adaptation to absolute colonial power – "proof" that their attempts to foster "civilization" amongst local populations were succeeding. In fact, however, Swahili *ngoma* performance continued a long-standing aesthetic preference for exploiting and incorporating difference wherever found. In 1950s Tanga, soda beverages were the chosen rhetorical medium.

Soda beverages could be opposed in the same manner as colonial entities (*Kingi* and *Scotchi* being a major *beni ngoma* rivalry) and provide rhetorical fuel for contestation via *ngoma* performance. Anything divisive, dualistic, or contradictory could be appropriated for translation into local musical practice. *Kanada* and *Fanta*, who drew their memberships from different neighborhoods within Tanga, danced a *ngoma* called *ngoma ya ndani* ("inside dance"). Its name derives from the performance practice that identifies it, namely having to dance indoors away from male view because of the erotic and sensual dance moves that characterize the style. It was and continues to be performed in the context of weddings and female initiation ceremonies: a circle of women moving in a slow, counterclockwise rotation, each woman facing the back of the woman ahead of her, surrounding drummers seated in the circle's center. The general dance movement – a slow rotation of the hips and pelvis – is performed in synchronization to the slow 6/8 pulse of the drums – a rhythm known as *kumbwaya*.

Piecing together the story from its many variants many years later, I was told by former members of *Fanta* that it was through their organizational skill and political clout that Princess Margaret visited Tanga and, very importantly, that she did so by plane. When her plane set down at the Tanga airport, *Fanta* was there to greet her in uniform and in song. Now, however much one may doubt *Fanta*'s involvement in the royal itinerary, to the women of *Fanta*, the honor of having "brought" a real British "queen" to Tanga by plane constituted a decisive blow to their opponents *Kanada*. Former *Kanada* members, on the other hand, while conceding *Fanta*'s association with the royal visit, nevertheless claim final victory for parading an enormous man-o'-war (circa 1958) through the streets of Tanga to the shock and awe of the city's residents. In fact, it was a seven-ton Bedford lorry elaborately decorated as a man-o'-war float bearing *Kanada* members in matching uniform singing their own praises and deriding *Fanta* members for their numerous faults (the primary one, of course, being membership in the wrong group). A photo exists of the H.M.S. 1st Canada Dry Tanga[7] confirming its existence and grandeur, what with its length encompassing the frontages of some four–five houses, its erect mast resembling a giant Christian cross (quite likely, an intended visual pun), two cannons extending out from behind the mast/cross, a "captain" at the helm, and portholes and anchors painted on the sides. The significance of this feat only emerges in conjunction with a Swahili proverbial saying (*methali*), one of the many that pop up in everyday speech. *Sijaona manuwari ikipita barabarani* ("I've never seen a man-o'-war pass in the streets") is used to draw attention to limited abilities: a ship is constructed to traverse water, not land, and should be recognized for what it is (and what it is not). The H.M.S. 1st Canada Dry Tanga thus secured its victory and place in history by overturning conventional wisdom.

Not long after the passage of the famous *manuwari*, *Kanada* and *Fanta* – like *lelemama* and *beni ngoma* before – died out, eclipsed by the rise of yet another *ngoma* sensation: the *msanja ngoma*. The newness of the *msanja* dance, rhythm, and songs, however, were not matched by newness in membership since the same networks of affiliation that had supported *Kanada* and *Fanta* reconstituted themselves into *Scouti* (former *Kanada* members) and *Kenya* (former *Fanta* members). The aesthetic preferences for inventive borrowing (sodas, royalty, ships) and continual innovation (*kwini*, *msanja*) revealed in this story relate directly to another principle, that of competitive opposition (*Kanada/Fanta*, *kwini/manuwari*, *Scouti/Kenya*). If one is to best one's rival, the strategy proven most effective in coastal communities like Tanga is to appropriate and incorporate something new, be it of local or foreign origin. *Scouti* pioneers took the local membership of *Kanada* and transformed the society into something new – just as *Kenya* did with *Fanta*, and just as *Kanada* and *Fanta* had done before them. They took an "inside dance" out into the streets, in defiance of recent practice, modifying it to accommodate the more public setting by removing the hip rotation dance movement. Multiple strategies thus serve the cause of innovation, innovation, in turn, being one means of furthering and enhancing competitive opposition.

The Principle of Competitive Opposition: *Upinzani*

One need not look far to discover evidence of the aesthetic preference for competitive opposition in Swahili communities. Unlike most major American cities that channel their loyalties towards one football team, one baseball team, one basketball team, and one hockey team each, throughout East Africa cities and towns have two or more football (i.e., soccer) teams with the rivalry of one notable pair dominating the sports scene. In Tanga, for example, Coastal Union maintains a passionate rivalry with African Sports; in Zanzibar, Malindi competes with Kikwajuni while another opposition exists between Miembeni and Navy; and in Dar es Salaam, the riveting rivalry for the city – indeed the nation – is that of Simba versus Young Africans (a.k.a. "Yanga").

While the preference for multiple football clubs is not limited in East Africa to the Swahili coast, much comment has been made about Swahili town divisions into clearly defined moieties (Middleton 1992; Farrell 1980; el-Zein 1974; Lienhardt 1968; Prins 1961). The typical Swahili town is organized around a centrally located Friday mosque. The street that borders the mosque generally forms a dividing line between the two "spatially and socially opposed named halves" (Horton and Middleton 2000:130) termed *mitaa* in Kiswahili. Reminiscent of Fernandez's description of the Fang fascination with opposition, Horton and Middleton argue that "The division of towns into moieties is not merely a superficial formality. They unite by formal opposition. In some towns the members of these units fight each other, literally or not, on many occasions and especially on the New Year ... Today traditional conflict in most places no longer involves open fighting but continues in the forms of poetry competitions, football matches, 'band' competitions and the like" (*ibid*). Towns along the coast and on the islands of Zanzibar continue to display this predilection. The city of Tanga, with a population of over 200,000, has grown well beyond any clearly-defined moiety structure, yet even here people still refer to an ancient rivalry between the neighborhoods of Mkwakwani and Chumbageni.

Outside of *ngoma*, football clubs, and town structure, one can find further evidence of competitive opposition in the juxtaposition of major industries (Tanga Cement Co. versus the Tanga Port Authority, to give but one example), theatrical/musical troupes (Tanzania One Theatre versus Muungano Cultural Troupe in Dar es Salaam), and political parties (the main contest for power along the coast being between the ruling party of CCM (*Chama cha Mapinduzi* – "Party of the Revolution") and an opposition party known as CUF (Civic United Front). Not even the sacred domain of organized religion exists outside this principle. Abdin Noor Chande has analyzed in great detail the fractious and tendentious rivalry between two mosques in Tanga (Chande 1998) that invariably leads to much confusion come Ramadhan because they typically disagree (quite publicly) on when the holy month of fasting begins and ends.

Upinzani ("opposition") is the Kiswahili term for these relationships, and it can be identified in multiple domains of coastal Swahili life. As noted by ethnographer Peter Lienhardt:

> This accords with the passionate spirit of rivalry and competition prevailing so openly throughout coastal society, a part of the coastal character and of the structure of the society itself. It shows itself in traditional dances, in modern football teams and dance bands, in relations between different quarters of villages, in some agricultural customs, in political parties, and often enough in matters of religion (Lienhardt 1968:16).

Upinzani is clearly a major aesthetic tenet of Swahili society. While I would avoid essentializing it as "part of the coastal character," there is no denying the attraction it holds now, as in times past, for many Swahili individuals and groups. This generates the need to acquire a competitive advantage through continual innovation, inventive appropriation and, as will be discussed next, skilled application of figurative language.

The Swahili Turn of Phrase

Swahili styles of speech and patterns of musical construction share much in common. Musical phrases are very much tied to rhythmic structure, and the predominant preference along the coast is for some variant of a complex triple meter. Some examples are the slow 12/8 called *vugo* (also the name of a popular women's *ngoma* in Mombasa and Lamu) or another slow 12/8 called *goma* (also the name of a men's *ngoma* found from Lamu south to Tanga yet rarely performed today), a slow 6/8 called *kumbwaya* (preferred in many *ngoma* in and around Tanga), or a fast 6/8 called *chakacha* (a rhythm that has taken the entire coast over by storm). The basic triple meter allows for inexhaustible variations, each of which can spawn a new *ngoma* style and thereby accommodate the long-standing pattern for passing *ngoma* crazes. Rhythm inflects Swahili speech as well. Kiswahili phonological rules place the stress of every word on the penultimate syllable. This creates a sing-song quality that makes it very easy to bridge the oftentimes blurred boundary between speech and song. Some *ngoma* styles exploit this by constructing rhythmically symmetrical song texts with similar numbers of syllables per line, but most styles take a freer approach, allowing texts to conform to melodic requirements. Secondly, *ngoma* song texts draw on a well-established Swahili preference for figurative language. Heavily saturated in metaphor and double – even triple – entendre, *ngoma* lyrics express a Swahili passion and talent for verbal ingenuity and frequently employ the countless proverbs that Swahili-speakers pepper their speech with on a daily basis.

Take, for example, the following *msanja* song from Tanga, the *ngoma* style that immediately succeeded *Kanada* and *Fanta*. In it, the singer offers women one route out of poverty: prostitution. For the woman desirous of a better life (exemplified by high quality body oils), being "hit" by the metaphorical stick or cane, tobacco tin or paddle of undesirable men (old men or idiots) constitutes one strategy for material advancement.

Msanja Ngoma Song #1

Tanga

Kwa mafuta, mimi natumia ya uto	For body oil, I use low-grade coconut oil
Ukitaka ya uzuri, utakuja chapwa na fimbo	If you desire better quality, you will be hit with a stick
Fimbo, fimbo spesheli	A stick, a special stick
Bakora ya babu, eeh, bakora spesheli	Grandfather's cane, a special cane
Kijaluba cha babu jinga, kijaluba spesheli	The idiot's tobacco tin, a special tobacco tin
Mkwaju wa babu, eeh, mkwaju spesheli	Grandfather's tamarind paddle, a special paddle

In another *msanja* song, the singer has something she wishes to say but is restrained by the presence of someone else in the immediate vicinity (the thorn in her throat). She nevertheless continues and through deft application of metaphor describes the sweetness of her married life (characterized as a farm abundant in guava and pomegranate fruits) and her hope for a child (a harvest):

Msanja Ngoma Song #2

Tanga

Nataka nimeze	I wish to clear my throat
mate na mwiba	but a thorn is stuck[8]
umenikwama	
Siamini, eeh, kama	I can't believe that it is
unemikwama	stuck
Mwenzenu ni kilingeni	My friend is on stage,
siwezi kusema sana	I cannot speak freely
Kilichoniweka	That which attracted me
shamba mipera na	to the farm was guava
mikomamanga	and pomegranate fruits
Nayasubiri mavuno	I await the harvest and
iende nijiweke shamba	have placed myself at this farm
Siamini, eeh, kama	I can't believe that it is
unemikwama	stuck
Mwenzenu ni kilingeni	My friend is on stage,
siwezi kusema	I cannot speak
Nataka nimeze mate	I wish to clear my throat

In the following song, members of *Gita ngoma*, a mixed-gender dance society in Tanga, deride their rival society *Chera* by comparing it to a donkey. Having recently lost a competitive round to *Chera* (the metaphorical "horns"), *Gita* points out that *Chera*'s apparent success is but a façade for inherent, long-term failure. They equate themselves with a patient and resourceful farmer who is sure to succeed (or win) in the long run.

Punda wa Tanga ("Donkey of Tanga")

Gita Ngoma, Tanga

Punda wa Tanga	Donkey of Tanga
Mwaka uno waringa	You are proud of having
kuota pembe	grown horns this year
Na pembe	Yet the horns are artificial
nzakubandika	
Mkulima mwenye moyo	A determined farmer
Akikosa mwaka huno	If he suffers loss this year,
anangoja mwakani	he waits for the next year
Na jembe halitupi mtu	A hoe will not let one down
Larawarawa goma	With a slow motion the
laingia mkongwe	big dance is coming (to you), old man
Larawarawa Gita	With a slow motion Gita
laingia mkongwe naja	is coming, old man, I am coming

	CHORUS
Hazina ?uaminifu	They are not reliable
Zitaanguka njiani	They will fall along the way
Nasema punda wa	I am telling you, Donkey
Tanga	of Tanga

Thus, we have to this point identified a number of aesthetic principles that arise in Swahili *ngoma* performance: continual innovation, inventive borrowing from local and foreign sources, competitive opposition (*upinzani*), and figurative language. We shall now see how these same aesthetic attributes characterize *dansi* performance.

More Sodas, Royalty, and Ships in the Dansi Mode

Beginning in the 1930s, a new form of music was emerging in the coastal cities of Dar es Salaam, Tanga, and Mombasa: *dansi*. As historian John Iliffe describes,

> New Street followed another fashion, *dansi*, the international, individualistic ballroom dancing whose personalised sexuality shocked the elderly. Like *beni* it apparently originated around Mombasa and entered Tanganyika through Tanga, whence it was probably brought to Dar es Salaam in the early 1930s by the *avant-garde* of the Tanga Young Comrades Club and was popularised by branches of the New Generation Club formed in several towns later in the decade. With their 'kings' and 'queens' adopted from the *beni* societies, their female sections composed chiefly of nursemaids, and their insatiable thirst for tea and soft drinks, New Generation Clubs epitomised the *dansi* mode (Iliffe 1979:392).

Dansi clubs in Tanga and Dar es Salaam gave rise to major *dansi* bands whose influence would spread the genre even further afield. The Dar es Salaam Jazz Band played to enthusiastic crowds in Dar es Salaam by 1932 and spawned the birth of a host of bands that included the Morogoro Jazz Band (est. 1944 in Morogoro), Cuban Marimba Band (originally named La Paloma, est. 1948 in Dar es Salaam), Jamhuri Jazz Band (est. 1955 in Tanga), Atomic Jazz Band (est. 1956 in Tanga), and NUTA Jazz Band (organized by the National Workers Union in

Dar es Salaam in 1965) which continues to perform today under the name of OTTU (Organization of Tanzanian Trade Unions) Jazz Band – the oldest surviving band in the country.

In the 1940s and 1950s when yearnings for independence and self-rule germinated in the minds of those who would constitute the elite in an independent Tanganyika, *dansi* provided one means of appropriating symbolic power and cultural capital from colonialists to "prove their equality and ability to govern themselves along European lines" (Fair 1994:317). Not all that far removed from the appropriation of colonial imagery in *ngoma* performance, *dansi* constituted an investment in social distinction, a claim to the upper levels of a socially recognized hierarchy of the arts. Yet, if *dansi* began with the taint of colonial elite society, it certainly did not remain so for long. Current descriptions of the genre nevermore mention "fox-trots," "swing," or "waltzes." Today, *dansi* is often imputed to be a weak imitation of Congolese rumba and *soukous* (another Congolese style). Ballroom dancing as an entry into elite colonial society was not unique to Tanzania. In the Belgian Congo, "early highlife, swing and Afro-Cuban music were the staples of the first bands to play at formal dances where the few members of the elite 'evolués' could mix with Europeans (Ewens 1994:315). Afro-Cuban rhythms struck a particularly resonant chord and spawned a musical movement quickly embraced and directed by non-elites. This new movement, the Congolese rumba, created something new out of a variety of local and global elements including local melodies, French cabaret music, vocal harmonies from church hymns, and brass-band fanfares (Ewens 1994:315). Although the most famous Congolese bands (e.g., Joseph 'Le Grand Kalle' Kabasele and *African Jazz*, Franco and *OK Jazz*) formed in the 1950s, two decades after the formation of the first *dansi* bands in Tanganyika, the mass influx of Zairean musicians into Tanzania following the 1961 assassination of Prime Minister Patrice Lumumba injected the Congolese sound deep into the Tanganyikan *dansi* scene.

Yet, of equal important to us here is that *dansi* also contains elements drawn from a variety of local sources and exhibits aesthetic principles akin to those of *ngoma*. Like Congolese rumba and like the Yoruba *fújì* music described by Barber and Waterman, *dansi* constitutes a mixture of diverse traits drawn from multiple sites and multiple time periods, thus demonstrating the same tendency toward constant innovation and creative appropriation we saw in *ngoma*. Unfairly dismissed by outsiders as a weak reverberation, a poor imitation of first European ballroom music and then Zairean *soukous*, *dansi* draws on a rich local repertoire of *ngoma* rhythms, figurative language, Swahili proverbs and sayings, local dance styles, as well as the competitive opposition so prevalent in Swahili performances.

The late 1980s, early 1990s saw the emergence of a Dar es Salaam *dansi* band called *Chezimba Band*. While some of its members were drawn from the local Dar area, others hailed from Tanga, the birthplace of the band's founder and patron Paulo Muhuto.[9] Their hit song "Kijongolo" ("Tiny Millipede") included as its third verse the *msanja* song (#1) cited above.

Kijongolo ("Tiny Millipede")

Composed by Mohamedi Kisosa Mumela, c.1990
Performed by Chezimba Band, Dar es Salaam

Kijongolo sina nyumba eeeh, ntajenga barabarani	I'm a tiny millipede without a home. I'll have to build in the street
Ntajenga nyumba ya mawe ooh, gorofa ndani kwa ndani	I'll build a home of stones with different levels inside
Sijaona manuwari ikipita barabani	I've never seen a man-o'-war pass in the streets
Nikushike wapi, mpenzi wangu, wewe oh wewe?	Where shall I hold you, my love?
Mifupa mitupu. Uliona wapi nyumba ya gorofa kufugiwa kuku?	You are all bones. Where did you see a multi-storied house for raising chickens?
Ukifugia kuku ni uchafu mtupu	If you raise chickens it brings only filth
Kwa mapenzi, kwa mapenzi, mimi nakwenda Tanga	For love, for love I'm going to Tanga
Wanawake wa kiTanga ukicheka utatangatanga	The women of Tanga, laugh with them and you'll be left helpless
Hata maji ya kuoga huchangwanywa kwa hiliki, abdalasini, uwa waridi, na ka rafuu, sikia mambo	Even bathwater they infuse with cardamon, cinnamon, rose petals, and cloves – hear that!

Kama huamini nenda	If you don't believe me,
Mombasa au Unguja	go to Mombasa or Zanzibar
Kwa mafuta, kwa mafuta, mimi natumia ya uto	For body oil, I use local coconut oil
Ukitaka ya uzuri utakujachapwa na fimbo	If you desire better, you will be hit with a stick
Fimbo! Fimbo spesheli, fimbo spesheli	A stick! A special stick, special stick
Bakora ya babu, eeeh, bakora spesheli	Grandfather's cane, a special cane
Kijaluba cha babu jinga, kijaluba spesheli	The idiot's tobacco tin, a special tobacco tin
Mkwaju wa babu eeeh, mkwaju spesheli	Grandfather's tamarind paddle, a special paddle

In despairing about his poor lot in life, the singer equates himself not only with a millipede but a tiny one as indicated by the diminutive prefix *ki-*. He cites the Swahili saying already discussed above, *Sijaona manuwari ikipita barabarani* ("I've never seen a man-o'-war pass in the streets"), to indicate that he should be recognized as a poor man, nothing more. For lack of a proper plot on which to build a house, he will build his home in the streets, out of common stones not bricks. Why, he asks, does his lover demand a multi-storied home when poverty demands that the home be used for lowly, dirty economic enterprises such as raising chickens? And if his lover cannot accept his impoverished state, he suggests by way of the *msanja* verse – an example of intertextuality – that prostitution offers her one route to economic advancement.

The application of figurative speech, heterogeneous references, and intertextuality (via proverbs and *ngoma* songs) in *Kijongolo* are not unique. Examine the following song from the Tanga-based *Watangatanga Band* whose popularity peaked in the years 1992–5.

Wanipenda Visa Wanitenda ("You Love Me Yet You Mistreat Me")

Composed by Shabaan Amour and Rashidi Makunganya (c.1994) Performed by The Watangatanga Band, Tanga

Wanambia wanipenda huku visa wanitenda	You say you love me yet you mistreat me

Madamu mimi nimekushindwa mwengine hatokuweza	If I cannot bear you, no one can
Umepotea njia wendako ni porini	You have lost the way and head towards the bush
Peleleza utaona aonjae akitema hakina tamu	Investigate and you will find that what has been spit out by one is no longer good to eat
Ni kichungu raha yake ni maudhi	[Her love] is bitter. Her pleasure is vexation
Ukipenda utajiudhi	If you love her, you will only trouble yourself
Kinyuli nyulika	Beautiful one, appear!
Mwanangwa wa jumbe	The chief's daughter
Kavaa nguo mbili	Wears two dresses
Ya tatu kajifunika	With a third, she covers herself completely
Aliyejuu aondoe [repeated three times]	Remove the top one!

This song relies less on metaphor than the previous one, but figurative speech is still evident with distasteful food that has been spit out signifying a rejected lover. The singer issues a warning to other men that this woman is incapable of true love and will only cause trouble. The final verse is another example of intertextuality, in this case derived from a common children's hand game. The game is similar in style to the American children's game "Hot Potato" in which children create a line of fists piled one on top of the other and, while chanting a prescribed chant,[10] take turns removing the top one until none are left. In the Swahili version *Kinyuli*, children create a similar tower of hands piled, palm down, one on top of the other gently pinching the one below and, in singsong, chant: *"Kinyuli nyulika, mwanangwa wa jumbe, kavaa nguo mbili, ya tatu kajifunika."* After this, one child assumes the role of leader and calls out *"Aliyejuu"* to which everyone else cries out *"Aondoe!"* and the hand at the top of the pile is removed. This call and response is repeated until the last hand is removed.

Thus another aesthetic principle that has been revealed through these *dansi* lyrics is intertextuality, an extension of the principle of inventive borrowing. It is not, however, unique to *dansi*. It too appears in equal measure in *ngoma* performance with *ngoma* lyrics quoting from each other and from other musical styles including *dansi*. Once, while attending a wedding in Tanga Region, I heard performers of *mdumange ngoma* sing an excerpt from a *dansi* song that someone later identified with *Vijana Jazz Band*:[11]

Nalilia raha, mbona sipati	I cry after happiness. Why don't I get it?
Tabu na mashaka, Humu duniani	Difficulties and worries are here in the world

On another occasion, I heard performers at a Makonde initation ceremony sing as part of their *sindimba ngoma* the following excerpt from a famous *Mlimani Park Orchestra* song, "M.V. Mapenzi" ("M.V. Love"):

Duniani kuna mengi sawasawa na bahari	In this world there is much which may be likened to the sea
Kuna papa na nyangumi tena wale wa hatari	There are sharks and whales, really dangerous ones

Yet instead of continuing as the original song does: "They do not want to see our boat peacefully crossing the sea," the *ngoma* performers altered it to: "They do not want to see our *ngoma* performed in this field."[12]

One final example shows how *ngoma* songs can quote from other *ngoma* styles. The following *Gita ngoma* song interjects the lyrics to an old song that has been sung in various *ngoma* up and down the coast, including two men's *ngoma* (*ndonge* and *chama*) and one women's *ngoma* (*lele-mama*) (see Campbell 1983). The borrowed lyrics (verse 2) tell of a lion and how it does not eat its own offspring.

Mpende Akupendae

Gita Ngoma, Tanga

Mpende akupendaye uupuze moyo wako	Love the one who loves you to cool your heart
Usimpende mtu asiekupenda utaudhi moyo wako	Don't love one who doesn't love you for it will vex your heart
Si mke wala si mume ulilinde pendo lako	Women and men both you must guard your love

Penda ijapo kibaya uridhishe moyo wako	Love even one who is ugly to satisfy your heart
Usimpende huyo nduli asiekupenda waudhi nafusi yako	Don't love a hypocrite who loves you not lest it vex your soul
Yuwaunguruma wanangu iyaya ee nana	It is roaring, my children, iyaya eee
Kanguruma simba kumla mwanawe uongo	A lion roars. To eat its own? That's a lie
Akamle mwanawe simba ameukosa uganga	If the lion eats its cub, it will lose everything
Kanguruma simba hamli mwanawe uongo	It roars. The lion does not eat its cub – that's a lie
Kula vyombo	Listen to the instruments
Lipo bado	It is still here
Wanangu wa Gita Ngoma hiyo	Here they are, my children of Gita Ngoma
Haya iyangaiyanga	OK, let's celebrate
Shilingi mkononi kuitoa ina matata	To lose a shilling in the hand brings problems
Wanangu wa ngoma ni leo	My children of the ngoma lead the day
Masalam	Good-bye

As we have seen, *ngoma* and *dansi* seek inspiration and communicative potency from both local sources (proverbial wisdom, existing social networks, children's games, local rhythms and song texts) as well as from external sources (imported sodas, royalty, ships, ballroom dances, Congolese rumba). While creating quite different musical products, *ngoma* and *dansi* performers nevertheless employ shared aesthetic principles of continual innovation, inventive appropriation, figurative language, and intertextuality. Finally, *dansi*, no less than *ngoma*, is prone to the same long-standing coastal pattern of competitive opposition (*upinzani*) that evokes such appreciation and excitement in Swahili communities.

Battles of the Bands

Michael Enoch, who led the *Dar es Salaam Jazz Band* during the 1960s, explained the tendency towards competition and dueling lyrics in *dansi* performance as follows:

> To compete and dialogue in song goes back to the days of the *ngoma*, like in *mdundiko* or *tokomile*. When they dance these *ngoma*, it is like fighting. They challenge each other with songs, but then

they may really start to fight each other physically. So competition is really at the root and to provoke with song is a general characteristic of these *ngoma*. This makes up much of their charm and when you challenge each other you attract the people to prefer your group. Since the olden days this has been here with us, there was also a lot of competition back then between dance bands like Cuban Marimba and Morogoro Jazz (quoted in Graebner 2000:303–4).

One particularly infamous rivalry exists between two popular *dansi* bands in Dar es Salaam, International Orchestra Safari Sound[13] and Mlimani Park Orchestra, described at length by ethnomusicologist Werner Graebner (2000). IOSS was formed with six leading musicians who left Mlimani Park, including the charismatic singers Muhiddin Maalim and Hassani Bitchuka. While musician attrition rates are high, it causes great stirs when musicians (especially prominent ones) desert one band for another. Soon after IOSS emerged, Mlimani Park released a sequel to their earlier-cited song "M. V. Mapenzi" about the dangers of the sea, this time describing how the captains (presumably Maalim and Bitchuka) plunged themselves into the sea to be eaten by sharks and whales. IOSS countered with their song *Chatu Mkali* ("Dangerous Python") that, through metaphor and proverbial signifiers, warns listeners to beware dangerous snakes that are not to be trifled with (the snake, positively valued for its strength and cunning, self-referencing IOSS).

Competition manifests itself not only in lyrics but in dance. In both *ngoma* and *dansi*, the fundamental goal sought by musicians is to incite audience members to dance. Indeed, the success of a band or *ngoma* group in competition relates directly to how well this goal is achieved. Dance movements from *ngoma* styles frequently make their way, along with *ngoma* rhythms, into *dansi* settings, and recently several bands are self-consciously evoking *ngoma* in a "return to our roots" movement.[14]

The similarities and shared features of *ngoma* and *dansi* are many, but no one could mistake these two genres. The preceding discussion has drawn out a set of aesthetic principles that link the two genres despite immediately discernible aural, visual,

contextual and technological differences. I shift now to a discussion of how they have both played highly significant roles in political matters, so much so that it could reasonably be argued that this constitutes yet another shared aesthetic principle.

Musical Politicking

The literature on *ngoma* outlines in no uncertain terms its imbrication in regional and national-level politics. Margaret Strobel (1979) analyzed how *lelemama ngoma* societies in Mombasa, Kenya mobilized a successful campaign for women's voting rights. Terence Ranger (1975:92–6) exposed how *beni ngoma* networks in Tanga formed the nucleus of the Tanganyika Territory African Civil Servants Association (TTACSA) which, in the 1940s, evolved into the Tanganyika African Association (TAA) and a decade later would reconstitute itself as Tanganyika African National Union (TANU), established in 1954. It was TANU that led Tanganyika to independence in 1961. There is no denying the significant presence of musicians, poets, and dancers that existed within TANU during its early years, forming an essential core (see Askew 2002:95–6). Not coincidentally, TANU's first female member, Bibi Titi Mohamed, was the lead singer of a women's *ngoma* society in Dar es Salaam called *Bomba*. As Susan Geiger (1997) documented, Bibi Titi alone is credited with having increased the TANU membership of 2,000 in March 1955 by an additional 5,000 female members by September of that same year. Her success stemmed from effective recruitment of support from *ngoma* networks in Dar es Salaam.

To mobilize the women, I went to the *ngoma* groups. First of all, I went to their leaders. The leaders got together in a meeting, and after I spoke to them, they agreed to call all their people so I could come and talk to them about TANU. ... For example, I talked to Mama Swaleh Kubunju, leader of the "Tongakusema," and she called together all of the "Tongakusema" women. I met them at Livingstone Street at the corner of Kariokoo Street where Mama Kibunju stayed. She said, "Titi is calling you, and I have called you for the sake of Titi. Here she is and she will tell you what she wants."... Then I went to Mama bint Makabuli, the leader of "Rumba." She lives in Narumg'ombe Street near Lumumba Street. She is still alive, but very old. She called the "warumba." And that's how I went to "British Empire" and to "Ratu Sudan," and to the "Sahina" group – I went to all these groups (from a 1984 interview with Susan Geiger 1987:16–17).

After independence, Bibi Titi Mohamed – a woman from a modest background with a total of four years of formal primary school education – occupied a position of political prominence second only to that of Julius Nyerere himself (Geiger 1987:2).[15] Thus, Swahili *ngoma* performance proves to be a potent and effective mode of political action.

Dansi is similarly implicated in political affairs. Laura Fair documents how African political activists in pre-independence Zanzibar strategically exploited the popularity of *dansi* to attract youth to dance clubs for the underlying purpose of educating them in radical economics and politics.

> Like earlier dance traditions ... disenfranchised members of the [African] community were able to appropriate the symbolic tools of the ruling powers and to transform them into a medium which simultaneously granted power to the under-class while undermining the exclusiveness and hegemony of the ruling class. ... Dancing to fox-trots and wearing fancy gowns provided them with a cover for political education and organizing and a very effective means for attracting younger and less politically minded individuals into their organizations (Fair 1994:319).

Such covert political uses of *dansi* were not the exclusive domain of the islands, however. On the mainland, *dansi* played the same role of serving as a cover to political organization. Werner Graebner interviewed Ally Sykes, a founding member of TANU and prominent musician with the Merry Blackbirds Band, who explained:

> We often played for the "Freedom Fighters" mainly at Msimbazi Hall in Dar es Salaam. There were charities for TANU, ANC, ZANU. Many times the bands' performances acted as a cover for political meetings of TANU whose members met in the backrooms when there was a dance. The band also raised money for the political fight, for

people's travelling money or for the printing of pamphlets (Graebner 1992:228).

In addition to using musical contexts simultaneously as contexts for political discussion and organization, musicians voiced political sentiment in their songs. Sometimes they would camouflage their political messages with figurative language; other times, however, pretense and subtlety would be thrown to the wind as in the following song from the Tanganyika Boys (1960).[16]

> We want our freedom!
> The time is ripe,
> So we can get our country.
> We are not content with just anything.
> We ask God in prayer.
> All of Africa is ours!
> All of us have to get their independence,
> Especially we Tanganyikans.

Music and politics thus combine to create a powerful mix of political action and agents in Swahili history and present-day practice. Through music, Swahili individuals have appropriated European symbolic and cultural capital for themselves, voiced their political agendas in song, debated political action,[17] and used musical events as opportunities for education and organization. Moreover, the social networks that sustained musical practice – whether *dansi* or *ngoma* – have constituted ready pools of political agents implicated at various levels of political action.

If the actively pursued principles of competitive opposition (*upinzani*), inventive appropriation, or quoting from heterogeneous sources (intertextuality) can unproblematically be considered aesthetic principles, why not politicking? The regularity with which music has been the preferred mode of political action over the course of Swahili coastal history begs this question. Consider the 19th century text compiled by local Swahili ethnography Mtoro bin Mwinyi Bakari who implicates music in interpersonal politicking, "It is the custom ... if anything happens in the town, or if somebody has done something disgraceful ... to sing his disgrace in the dance" (Bakari 1981:97). This has been affirmed and reaffirmed in other sites and time periods, as on Mafia Island where

Pat Caplan noted that "women have other means of prosecuting quarrels than taking them to a forum. The singing of songs … is a customary way of scoring points off opponents" (Caplan 1995:209; also Askew 2002). Consider as well the role of *ngoma* societies in the large-scale organization of labor at the docks, for instance, in turn-of-the-century Mombasa (Cooper 1987:39–45; Willis 1993: 101). As a final example, consider the power struggles manifested through musical means between coastal elites and slave laborers associated with the caravan trade:

> Patrician control was often challenged, however, particularly at public dances. The patricians had long regarded dance ritual as an important medium for the exertion and affirmation of their community authority. But during the crisis of late 1888, aggressive armed dancers used public festivities as occasions on which to defy the patricians, repeatedly overturning decisions made by their putative leaders (Glassman 1995:7).

The overabundance of data (only a portion of which I have presented here) squarely implicates *ngoma* and *dansi* in shared histories of serving political purposes and enabling political action. This suggests that politicking itself constitutes a Swahili aesthetic principle. "To sing about" (*kumwimbia*) someone, something, some event, some process *and by so doing effect social change* is no small matter. Musicians and poets along the Swahili coast and throughout East Africa have historically accepted and served the roles of organic intellectuals (Gramsci 1971:15), actively challenging the status quo and vigorously pursuing alternatives. Musical politicking is a successful strategy, one actively and repeatedly pursued by *ngoma* and *dansi* performers alike now, in times past, and for as much as we can see of the future.

Conclusion

Although the processes that helped give rise to *dansi* (colonialism, urbanism, political turmoil in Zaire, and developments in musical technology) as compared to those that have been identified with *ngoma* (rural networks, life-cycle rituals, acoustic instrumentation, community orientation) lend superficial support to the view of one as a "modern"

phenomenon and the other "traditional," it should be clear that the mere application of these terms lends more confusion than analytic clarity. Like Barber and Waterman, I am dissatisfied with the "analytic binarisation of the field of culture, into 'indigenous' (traditional, local) and 'imported' (modern, global) elements" that too frequently results in "the simplification and reification of both halves, but especially the 'indigenous' half, which is usually taken as the baseline" (Barber and Waterman 1995:241). Close analysis reveals numerous similarities and correspondences between the two genres: a rich repertoire of Swahili proverbs, sayings, and metaphors, common rhythms, common dance movements, and in some cases, common performers. They also share a series of aesthetic principles that include continual innovation, inventive borrowing (from both internal and external sources), competitive opposition (*upinzani*), figurative language, intertextuality, and politicking (at personal, community, and national levels).

To return, then, to the ambitious question with which I began, what implications does the above analysis conflating the political, economic, and aesthetic realms of Swahili social life hold for broader debates on the relationship between art and society? Let us begin by questioning the conventional wisdom in Swahili Studies that foreign elements in Swahili musical performance (indeed, in multiple domains of coastal life) are the direct consequence of Swahili economic engagements. For more than a thousand years, Swahili merchants dominated Indian Ocean trade networks (Horton and Middleton 2000:5). They employed *innovation* in straddling two hitherto independent commercial spheres (Africa and the Indian Ocean world) and thus acquired a competitive advantage. They *appropriated* foreign elements, but at the same time reworked internally-existing elements into novel compositions. And being well accustomed to and comfortable with *competition* (with which they amused themselves when away from work), they bested potential rivals – as likely as not with their *finely-honed linguistic skills*. In other words, the aesthetic principles we identified in *ngoma* and *dansi* have clear economic utility and could help explain the economic success Swahili enjoyed for many centuries rather than be an assumed byproduct of that success.

Such a perspective restores to analyses of Swahili history and social life a sense of cultural agency that is currently missing. The ubiquity in Swahili communities of aesthetic preferences for innovation, inventive appropriation, competitive opposition, and intertextuality sheds light on the nature of Swahili cosmopolitanism. Much more than the collection of foreign surface traits, Swahili cosmopolitanism revolves around the strategic integration of foreign and local elements into art forms, economic transactions, and other domains of social life. Singular attention to the traits themselves – without thought to the motivations and mechanisms for incorporating them – supports instead the view of Swahili culture as a passive receptacle for foreign cultural influences. As with the trade networks of Senegalese Murid brotherhoods analyzed by Mamadou Diouf, we should consider how Swahili cosmopolitanism constitutes a means of "domesticating the foreign and the global by recourse to native idioms that constantly seek to assert themselves in the world and to profit from it, concretely through economic activities, and symbolically by borrowing its modes and techniques of diffusing information" (Diouf 2000:699).

And what of the relations between Swahili music and politics? Here too we find cause to doubt the conventional wisdom that musical performance is an effect of political and social processes, not an active contributor to those processes. The history of Tanganyika's ruling party, which traces its roots to *ngoma* societies, the spread of nationalist sentiment and mobilization of an independence movement via *ngoma* and *dansi* performances and networks, the training and vetting of countless political leaders through competitive performance (requiring linguistic sophistication and the ability to compose a deft response in retaliation for musically-launched attacks), and the campaign for women's suffrage in Kenya – these all position music centrally and unambiguously in political process. Art has not always been conceptualized as passive relative to society, subject to change imposed from without. Quite the contrary, it was in earlier times considered a source of worrisome power and influence. In designing the perfect state, for example, Plato wanted clear restrictions placed on musical composition. He directed that music "be preserved in [its] original form, and no innovation made ... for any musical innovation is full of danger to the whole State ... [W]hen modes of music change, the fundamental laws of the State always change with them" (*Republic* IV, 424c). The British colonial government tried to heed Plato's warning by restricting, and at times prohibiting, *ngoma* performance in Kenya, Tanganyika, and Zanzibar so as to curtail the spread of nationalism, but these efforts came too late. The present government in Tanzania has adopted a different tactic of hiring the best singers into its service (Songoyi 1988; Askew 2002) in the hope of appropriating their power for its own purposes. Art is a source of power, a mode of exercising power, and we would do well to recall Plato's warning. As stated so elegantly by Bertolt Brecht, "Art is not a mirror held up to reality, but a hammer with which to shape it."

Notes

1 The Swahili Coast proper has been identified as extending from southern Somalia through Kenya and Tanzania and into northern Mozambique. Swahili cultural influence extends further afield westwards along the interior trade routes (especially the Tanzanian cities of Tabora and Kigoma), eastwards to the Comoros Islands, and northwards to the Middle East in countries such as Oman and the United Arab Emirates.

2 For more information on *taarab* music, please consult the following: Askew 2000, 2002; Fair 1994, 2001; Fargion 1993; Farhan 1992; Graebner 1991,

1994a; Jahadhmy et al. 1966; Khatib 1992; Mgana 1991; Saleh 1980; Suleiman 1969; Topp 1992.

3 The use of the term "modern" is problematic for a variety of reasons only some of which will be analyzed here. It should not go without noting, however, that the historical baggage carried by the appellation "modern" in discussions relating to Africa – in contrast to discussion of the West where it denotes an aesthetic historical period (alongside Baroque, Classical, Romantic, Impressionistic, etc.) – evokes erroneous presuppositions of a "premodern" past.

4 The widespread East African preference for competitive musical performance spawned an edited volume on the topic – Gunderson and Barz (2000) – which includes analyses of a wide range of musical traditions. See the contributions by Pels, Kezilahabi, Ellison, Nyoni, Johansen, Cooke and Dokotum, Gilman, Hill, and Gunderson. For a study of music and political change in Uganda, see Alnaes 1969.

5 Until the 1964 formation of the United Republic of Tanzania, Tanganyika and Zanzibar (its two constituent elements) had been independent political entities.

6 For more descriptions of ngoma competitions and the great expenditure of money and resources they required, see Campbell 1983, Fair 1994, Farrell 1980, Gunderson and Barz 2000, Hartwig 1969, Lienhardt 1968, Ranger 1975, and Strobel 1979.

7 Reproduced in Askew 2002: 74.

8 The literal translation is: "I wish to swallow saliva."

9 Telephone interview with former band member Herman Kambimtoni in Durham, North Carolina, August 8, 2001.

10 "One potato, two potato, three potato, four [pause], five potato, six potato, seven potato, more."

11 *Nalilia raha. Mbona sipati? Tabu na mashaka humu duniani*, wedding, May 27, 1994, Muheza, Tanga Region.

12 Original lyrics: *Hawapendi kuiona meli yetu baharini*. Modified last line: *Hawataki kuiona ngoma yetu uwanjani*, performed at a Makonde initiation ceremony, January 16, 1993, Pande, Tanga region. Original lyrics cited in Graebner 2000: 311–12.

13 Not to be confused with the Congolese band Orchestra Safari Sound or the Kenyan band Safari Sounds.

14 *Kilimanjaro Band* of Dar es Salaam is one example. Barber and Waterman discuss this as process in which people "self-consciously valorise local practices as 'our traditional heritage' – seeing them simultaneously (as it were) from within and without, with sincerity but also with ironical self-consciousness" (1995: 243), and apply this to their deconstruction of the category "indigenous."

15 Bibi Titi Mohamed passed away on November 6, 2000. Thousands of mourners came to pay their respects at her funeral (*The Guardian*, 11/11/00).

16 Quoted in Graebner 1992: 223.

17 Glassman writes, "plebian crowds held dances to debate what to do ..." (1995: 244).

References

Adorno, Theodor. 1970. *Ästhetische Theorie*, in *Gesammelte Schriften* [Collected Writings, Vol. 7.] Frankfurt: Suhrkamp.

Alnaes, Kristen. 1969. "Songs of the Rwenzururu Rebellion: The Kongo Revolt against the Toro in Western Uganda." In P. H. Gulliver, ed. *Tradition and Transition in East Africa: Studies of the Tribal Element in the Modern Era*, pp. 243–72. London: Routledge and Kegan Paul.

Askew, Kelly M. 1999. "Female Circles and Male Lines: Gender Dynamics along the Swahili Coast," *Africa Today* 46(3/4):67–102.

Askew, Kelly M. 2000. "Following in the Tracks of *Beni*: The Diffusion of the Tanga *Taarab* Tradition." In Frank Gunderson and Gregory Barz, eds. *Mashindano! Competitive Music Performance in East Africa*, pp. 21–38. Dar es Salaam: Mkuki na Nyota Publishers.

Askew, Kelly M. 2002. *Performing the Nation: Swahili Music and Cultural Politics in Tanzania*. Chicago: University of Chicago Press.

Bakari, Mtoro bin Mwinyi. 1981. *The Customs of the Swahili People: The Desturi za Waswahili of Mtoro bin Mwinyi Bakari and Other Swahili Persons*, ed. and trans. by J.W.T. Allen. Berkeley: University of California Press.

Barber, Karin and Christopher Waterman. 1995. "Traversing the Global and the Local: Fújì Music and Praise Poetry in the Production of Contemporary Yorùbá Culture." In Daniel Miller, ed. *Worlds Apart: Modernity through the Prism of the Local*, pp. 240–262. London and New York: Routledge.

Bender, Wolfgang. 1991. *Sweet Mother: Modern African Music*. Chicago: University of Chicago Press.

Brecht, Bertolt. 1964. *Brecht on Theatre*, trans. John Willet. New York: Hill and Wang.

Campbell, Carol Ann Arneson. 1983. "Nyimbo za Kiswahili: A Socio-ethnomusicological Study of a Swahili Poetic Form." Ph.D. diss., University of Washington.

Caplan, Patricia. 1995. "'Law' and 'Custom': Marital Disputes on Northern Mafia Island, Tanzania." In Pat Caplan, ed. *Understanding Disputes: The Politics of Argument*, pp. 203–22. Oxford and Providence: Berg.

Chande, Abdin Noor. 1998. *Islam, Ulamaa and Community Development in Tanzania: A Case Study of Religious Currents in East Africa*. San Francisco: Austin & Winfield.

Cooper, Frederick. 1987. *On the African Waterfront: Urban Disorder and the Transformation of Work in Colonial Mombasa*. New Haven, CT: Yale University Press.

Diouf, Mamadou. 2000. "The Senegalese Murid Trade Diaspora and the Making of a Vernacular Cosmopolitanism," *Public Culture* 12(3):679–702.

Donner, Philip. 1980. "Music Forms in Tanzania and Their Socio-economic Base," *Jipemoyo* 3:88–98.

el-Zein, A.H.M. 1974. *The Sacred Meadows: A Structural Analysis of Religious Symbolism in an East African Town*. Evanston: Northwestern University Press.

Ewens, Graeme. 1994. "Heart of Danceness: The Music of Zaire." In Simon Broughton et al, eds. *World Music: The Rough Guide*, pp. 313–323. London: The Rough Guides.

Fair, Laura. 1994. "Pastimes and Politics: A Social History of Zanzibar's *Ng'ambo* community 1890–1950." Ph.D. diss., University of Minnesota.

Fair, Laura. 2001. *Pastimes and Politics: Culture, Community, and Identity in Post-Revolution Urban Zanzibar, 1890–1945*. Athens, OH: Ohio University Press.

Fargion, Janet Topp. 1993. "The Role of Women in *Taarab* in Zanzibar: An Historical Examination of a Process of 'Africanisation'," *The World of Music* 35(2):109–125.

Farhan, Idi. 1992. "Introduction of *Taarab* to Zanzibar in the Nineteenth Century." Paper presented to the International Conference on the History and Culture of Zanzibar, Zanzibar, December 14–16, 1992.

Farrell, Eileen Ruth. 1980. "*Ngoma ya Ushindani*: Competitive Song Exchange and the Subversion of Hierarchy in a Swahili Muslim Town on the Kenya Coast." Ph.D. diss., Harvard University.

Fernandez, James W. 1971. "Principles of Opposition and Vitality in Fang Aesthetics." In Carol F. Jopling, ed. *Art and Aesthetics in Primitive Societies*, pp.356–373. New York: E. P. Dutton.

Fischer, Ernst. 1963. *The Necessity of Art: A Marxist Approach*, trans. Anna Bostock. Middlesex, England: Penguin Books.

Fischer, Ernst. 1969. *Art against Ideology*, trans. Anna Bostock. New York: George Braziller.

Geiger, Susan. 1987. "Women in Nationalist Struggle: TANU Activists in Dar es Salaam," *International Journal of African Historical Studies* 20(1):1–26.

Fischer, Ernst. 1997. *TANU Women: Gender and Culture in the Making of Tanganyikan Nationalism, 1955–1965*. Portsmouth, NH: Heinemann.

Glassman, Jonathon. 1995. *Feasts and Riots: Revelry, Rebellion, and Popular Consciousness on the Swahili Coast, 1856–1888*. Portsmouth, NH: Heinemann.

Graebner, Werner. 1991. "Tarabu – Populäre Musik am Indischen Ozean." In Veit Erlmann, ed. *Populäre Musik in Afrika*, pp. 181–201. Berlin: Museum für Völkerkunde.

Graebner, Werner. 1992. "Music, Politics and the Media in East Africa." In *1789–1989 Musique, Histoire, Démocratie Vol. 1* Proceedings of the international conference of Vibrations (Musiques médias sociétés) and IASPM (International Association for the Studies of Popular Music), Paris, France 17–20 juillet 1989. Recherche, musique et danse 6, pp.223–233. Paris: Edition de la Maison des sciences de l'homme.

Graebner, Werner. 1994a. "Swahili Musical Party: Islamic Taarab Music of East Africa." In Simon Broughton et al, eds. *World Music: The Rough Guide*, pp.349–355. London: The Rough Guides.

Graebner, Werner. 1994b. "Marashi ya Dar es Salaam: Dance with Style: The Flavour of Dar es Salaam." In Simon Broughton et al, eds. *World Music: The Rough Guide*, pp. 355–362. London: The Rough Guides.

Graebner, Werner. 2000. "*Ngoma ya Ukae*: Competitive Social Structure in Tanzanian Dance Music Songs." In Frank Gunderson and Gregory Barz, eds. *Mashindano! Competitive Music Performance in East Africa*, pp.295–318. Dar es Salaam: Mkuki na Nyota Publishers.

Graham, Gordon. 1997. *Philosophy of the Arts: An Introduction to Aesthetics*. London and New York: Routledge.

Graham, Ronnie. 1992. *The World of African Music: Stern's Guide to Contemporary African Music, Vol.2*. London: Pluto Press.

Gramsci, Antonio. 1971. *Selections from the Prison Notebooks*, ed. and trans. Quintin Hoare and Geoffrey Nowell Smith. New York: International Publishers.

Gunderson, Frank and Gregory Barz, eds. 2000. *Mashindano! Competitive Music Performance in East Africa*. Dar es Salaam: Mkuki na Nyota Publishers.

Hartwig, G. 1969. "The Historical and Social Role of Kerebe Music," *Tanzania Notes and Records* LXX:41–56.

Horton, Mark and John Middleton. 2000. *The Swahili: The Social Landscape of a Mercantile Society*. Oxford, UK and Malden, MA: Blackwell Publishers.

Iliffe, John. 1979. *A Modern History of Tanganyika*. Cambridge: Cambridge University Press.

Jahadhmy, A. A., S. Matola, Mwalim Shabaan, and W.H. Whiteley. 1966. *Waimbaji wa Juzi*. Dar es Salaam: Chuo cha Uchunguzi wa Lugha ya Kiswahili.

Johnson, Frederick. 1989 (1939). *A Standard Swahili–English Dictionary*. Nairobi and Dar es Salaam: Oxford University Press.

Khatib, M. S. 1992. *Taarab Zanzibar*. Dar es Salaam: Tanzanian Publishing House.

Lienhardt, Peter. 1968. *The Medicine Man: "Swifa ya Nguvumali" by Hasani bin Ismael*. Oxford: Clarendon Press.

Marcuse, Herbert. 1978. *The Aesthetic Dimension: Towards a Critique of Marxist Aesthetics*. Boston: Beacon Press.

Martin, Stephen H. 1980. "Music in Urban East Africa: A Study of the Development of Urban Jazz in Dar es Salaam." Ph.D. diss., University of Washington.

Martin, Stephen H. 1982. "Music in Urban East Africa: Five Genres in Dar es Salaam," *Journal of African Studies* 9(3):155–163.

Martin, Stephen H. 1991. "Brass Bands and the *Beni* Phenomenon in Urban East Africa," *Journal of the International Library of African Music* 7(1):72–81.

Marx, Karl. 1970. *Critique of Hegel's Philosophy of Right*, trans. A. Jolin and J. O'Malley. Cambridge: Cambridge University Press.

Mgana, Issa. 1991. *Jukwaa la Taarab Zanzibar*. Helsinki: Mediafrica.

Middleton, John. 1992. *The World of the Swahili: An African Mercantile Civilization*. New Haven and London: Yale University Press.

Newcomer, Peter Jay. 1979. "The Production of Aesthetic Values." In Stanley Diamond, ed. *Toward a Marxist Anthropology: Problems and Perspectives*, pp.385–92. The Hague: Mouton.

Prins, A. H. J. 1961. *The Swahili-Speaking Peoples of Zanzibar and the East African Coast (Arabs, Shirazi, and Swahili)*. Ethnographic Survey of Africa: East-Central Africa, Part 12. London: International African Institute.

Ranger, Terence O. 1975. *Dance and Society in Eastern Africa, 1890–1970: The Beni Ngoma*. London: Heinemann.

Saleh, S. S. 1980. "Nyimbo za Taarab Unguja," *Lugha Yetu* 37: 35–46.

Songoyi, Elias Manandi. 1988. "The Artist and the State in Tanzania. A Study of Two Singers: Kalikali and Mwinamila." Ph.D. diss., University of Dar es Salaam.

Strobel, Margaret. 1979. *Muslim Women in Mombasa: 1890–1975*. New Haven and London: Yale University Press.

Suleiman, A. A. 1969. "The Swahili Singing Star Siti binti Saad and the *Tarab* Tradition in Zanzibar," *Swahili* 39:87–90.

Topp, Janet. 1992. "Women and the Africanisation of *Taarab* in Zanzibar." Ph.D. diss., School of Oriental and African Studies.

Willis, Justin. 1993. *Mombasa, the Swahili, and the Making of the Mijikenda*. Oxford: Clarendon Press.

25

In Place of Slavery
Fashioning Coastal Identity

Bayo Holsey

In April 2002, the Prince of Orange and Princess Máxima of the Netherlands traveled to Elmina as part of a state visit to commemorate three hundred years of diplomatic relations between the Netherlands and Ghana. The starting point they recognized was not the arrival of the Dutch on the coast, which had occurred a century earlier, but rather a Dutch expedition in 1701–2 from Elmina to the Asante kingdom, which would become a major supplier of slaves. While this meeting marks a key moment in the development of the slave trade, in a speech he gave to mark the event, the prince described it as a meeting "to discuss peace and prosperity." He went on to note that much of the period of the Dutch presence on the coast was marked by the slave trade, but he ultimately marginalized its significance within a larger story of a peaceful, diplomatic relationship between the Dutch and what became Ghana. In fact, he turned quickly to another favorable interpretation of this presence by noting its beneficial effects on the town of Elmina itself. Before the assembled crowd, he remarked,

> Throughout the Dutch presence on the Gold Coast, the relationship with the people of Elmina was close. The Dutch played an active part in the planning of this town and built a number of fortifications around it. The relationship is still visible in the monuments and sites in the town itself, in the Dutch family names many people from Elmina still bear and in the use of some Dutch words in the local language. We share an interest in our common past.[1]

Through these words, he described the close relationship between the Dutch and Elmina in terms of Dutch influences on architecture, families, and language.

His narrative creates an image of the "cosmopolitan" coast [that] stands in stark contrast to narratives of the "savage bush". But the prince not only constructed a cosmopolitan past, he also suggested that it could be recovered. His speech was made, after all, at the launching of a town consultation to discuss development plans for Elmina. For this reason, local residents welcomed the prince's visit, greeting him and the princess cheering and waving Dutch flags.

Their enthusiastic response to the prince's visit reflects the dire state of Elmina's economy.

From *Routes of Remembrance: Refashioning the Slave Trade in Ghana*, by Bayo Holsey, University of Chicago Press (2008), pp. 9–14, 109–10, 112–21.

Economic stagnation in the town is not only the result of the recent decline of the formerly prosperous South; Elmina's problems began long before. Its economy has in fact been in decline since the departure of the Dutch in 1872. After this time, Elmina's shipping industry remained small until its port was finally closed in 1921. Cape Coast has faced a similar situation. While it had the most important port at the turn of the century, it was soon dwarfed by Sekondi and Accra, which were connected by roads and railways to important agricultural areas (Kimble 1963).[2] Its port finally closed to international trade in 1962. In addition, in contrast to their former roles in the administration of the region, today, Elmina and Cape Coast have little role in national politics. The basis of the nation's economy has also shifted to the production of cocoa, which takes place in other regions. There are few job opportunities in these towns and high unemployment rates. Coastal residents have thus lost their political power, economic prosperity, and cultural cachet.

As a result, some of the men and women assembled to hear the prince's speech, in particular those who are familiar with the town's history, appreciated not only that he supported Elmina's economic development but also that he broached the topic of the town's past close relationship to the Dutch. Such references, they believe, provide evidence against claims of their town's inexorable marginalization. These claims, which are made through images of Africa as a dark continent and of Africans as "a race of slaves," deplete coastal residents' limited supplies of both symbolic and real capital.

Because these discourses, which were first produced by Europeans during the Atlantic and colonial eras, continue to circulate within national and international arenas today, keeping them at bay requires constant vigilance. For this reason, not only do they displace the slave trade and its attached images of savagery on to the North, many coastal residents also replace it with their own stories of their past incorporation into the Atlantic order on favorable terms. In other words, faced with their own increasing poverty, they argue that they were better off in the past than they are now, that they are in fact the heirs of a glorious past. Their past centrality within the "global ecumene" (Hannerz 1992) is in fact their rightful one, they

maintain, and one that therefore must be recovered. Their contemporary marginalization, they insist, is not the result of an inherent racial inferiority that diminishes their ability to obtain political power and economic prosperity; their power and prosperity have been confiscated. Drawn in this fashion, their images of the Atlantic era become an indictment of the present.

While coastal residents mobilize narratives about their past incorporation into the Atlantic era in order to protest their exclusion from the contemporary global economy, such descriptions are not, it is important to note, a glorification of the slave dealing that took place on the coast and was in fact the basis of its prosperity for much of the period of European settlement. They are rather, I argue, a different view of the Atlantic era altogether. Indeed, even more so than the prince, coastal residents erase the slave trade from narratives of coastal cosmopolitanism. They do so, as I discuss in the following section, by veiling histories of slave dealing that took place on the coast. These histories are for many reasons troubling, a fact which their veiled accounts indicate. Once their narratives of the Atlantic era are stripped of explicit references to the slave trade however, they are free to describe it as the golden age of the coast. Such narratives, which are the main focus of this chapter, are told then *in place* of narratives about the slave trade. These images function, furthermore, as a means of challenging arguments that naturalize their contemporary marginalization. They lend credence to their calls for greater inclusion in the global economy by providing them with a precedent.

Abjection and Atlantic Pasts

In his book, *Expectations of Modernity* (1999), James Ferguson employs the term "abjection" to refer to the experience of contemporary Copperbelt mineworkers. He explains,

> For many Zambians, then, as these details suggest, recent history has been experienced not – as the modernization plot led one to expect – as a process of moving forward or joining up with the world but as a process that has pushed them out of the place in the world that they once occupied ... *Abjection* refers to a process of being thrown aside,

expelled, or discarded ... This complex of meanings, sad to report, captures precisely the sense I
found among the Copperbelt mine-workers – a
sense that the promises of modernization had been
betrayed, and that they were being thrown out of
the circle of full humanity, thrown back into the
ranks of the "second class," cast outward and
downward into the world of rags and huts where
the color bar had always told "Africans" they
belonged (1999, 236).

Ferguson stresses that these workers' experience
of abjection was not an experience of being
excluded but rather one of being expelled (1999,
237), of losing a status that they once enjoyed.

This description well describes the experience
of today's coastal residents and particularly highly
educated ones, whose contemporary conditions
also challenge the modernization plot. While during the Atlantic era, level of education was a better
marker of economic success, today, there are few
professional jobs for the large percentage of educated men and women in Cape Coast and Elmina.
As a result, they no longer have as great an economic advantage. Because education is one of the
few fields in the region that has not declined in
significance, teachers make up a large a percentage
of the educated class (and therefore a large percentage of those mentioned in this chapter). With
their modest salaries, they illustrate the educated
class's loss of economic status with the collapse of
the economies of their towns. These men and
women are thus uniquely positioned to critique
the barriers to their social mobility. Because they
are also well acquainted with the histories of their
towns, many of these individuals do so by contrasting their contemporary conditions to the
incorporation of coastal elites into the global order
during the Atlantic era.

In many cultural contexts, groups "seek the
identity of place by laying claim to some particular
moment/location in time-space when the definition of the area and the social relations dominant
within it were to the advantage of that particular
claimant group" (Massey 1994, 169). Coastal residents' constructions of the past however define
the privileged lives of past coastal elites to be the
heritage of their entire towns, thereby painting
over past internal distinctions including those

between slaves and freepersons and between
Fantes and members of ethnic groups who settled
on the coast. Within this construction of an undifferentiated coastal population, past forms of
oppression are effectively silenced. In addition, all
contemporary coastal residents are allowed to lay
claim to this past. Their creation of a shared coastal
heritage occurs in the context of a leveling of class
differences, which has made the grounds upon
which the educated elite have traditionally asserted
their class superiority increasingly shaky.

So, what do their town histories look like? In
Elmina, many residents often stress the fact that it
was the site of the first European building in sub-
Saharan Africa and one of the first places in which
Europeans settled. In referencing the earliest
moment of the Portuguese trade, they avoid discussion of the slave trade altogether. This agenda
was apparent in Mrs Yeboah's use of the story.
A seventy-two year old teacher in Elmina,
Mrs Yeboah brought up the story in response to
my question as to what she thinks is the most
important part of history for people in her town.
She immediately responded, "How the white man
came to see them." She then explained, "They
asked for the land to build the castle, that's very
important because they [the Europeans] knew that
this was theirs [the local people's]. They came to
the chief and the chief gave them the land to build
the castle." Her assertion that Europeans viewed
the people of Elmina as citizens of a sovereign state
contrasts sharply to narratives about northerners
that suggest that Europeans saw them as nothing
more than potential slaves. In this context,
Mrs Yeboah's statement carries the subtext that the
"white man" *did not* view coastal residents as slaves
but rather as equals. But in addition to contrasting
her ancestors to slaves, she also contrasts them to
contemporary residents. By stating that this event
marks the most important moment in their history,
Mrs Yeboah suggests that such recognition by
Europeans was not forthcoming at later ones.

Residents of Cape Coast produce similar town
histories of the European presence, both orally
and in print. Because interactions with Europeans
in Cape Coast began with the slave trade, and
there is no earlier period in this encounter to
which they can refer, its residents often simply
marginalize this aspect of that relationship.

In 1994, J. Erskine Graham, Jr, a teacher at Ghana National College and a local assembly member, published a book entitled *Cape Coast in History* that traces historical developments in the town. In his description of the effects of contact with Europeans, he lists many positive effects, including the growth of the town. He quotes the Danish visitor who described Cape Coast in 1836 as "a little heaven, worthy to be reputed the most attractive citadel of the whole African coast" (1994, 23). He then writes, "Cape Coast, therefore, hitherto unimportant town, became a powerful flourishing trading centre and soon assumed a cosmopolitan outlook" (1994, 23).

In addition to constructing a glorious past, many individuals explicitly contrast it to a present decline. In an article about the history of Cape Coast, Nkunu Akyea, head of the Central Regional Development Commission, describes the desolation that has become a popular theme within accounts of both Cape Coast and Elmina:

> As far back as 1911, S.R.B. Attoh Ahuma observed ... "Cape Coast is dull and monotonous enough in all conscience". Almost a century later, the settlement presents an outward image of rusted corrugated iron-roofs with cracked and crumbling facades of the once huge clay-built imposing merchant and family home ... Undoubtedly, Cape Coast has aged: she is wrinkled, has a stooped gait with shuffling feet for steps, dim eyes and ears hard of hearing and crackling voice (2001, 38).

He explains that this decline is due to the fact that "there are no viable commercial and industrial activities in Cape Coast and its immediate environs to write home about. The town and most of the Central Region has, for about a century now, been losing its population (out-migration) to other economically more attractive adjoining areas" (2001, 38). He claims, however, that the town was not that way in the past, quoting another writer who insists, "Cape Coast has not always looked like this. The careful observer can soon see that behind its forlorn and dilapidated appearance there are indications of what was once a much more flourishing past" (2001, 38). More than a simple lament for the passing of a better time, in other words, expressions of nostalgia, these statements are highly political. They seek to provide a precedent for the coast's incorporation into the global order.

Finally, to return to my conversation with Auntie Amma, not only did she veil the trade in slaves in her story of magically reproducing beads in order to create an image of fabulous wealth, but later in the same conversation, she noted the present decline of Elmina. It began when my companion, after hearing her description of her family's past wealth, asked her, "Then you were rich, but now you are poor, why?" The question had been on my mind as well. Sitting in the courtyard in front of Auntie Amma's house, the poverty that she and her family face is undeniable. Her house, once grand, has fallen into disrepair, and the lack of job opportunities in Elmina has clearly hit her family hard. Her family's poor economic condition was made all the more startling in comparison to her description of the family's past wealth. She summed up the contrast between her family's past wealth and their present poverty saying, "*Kanka hɛn apa Edinaman ho,*" or "The Dutch boat has left Elmina."

This statement is a common saying in Elmina that is used to comment on the town's economic decline. Its original reference may be lost on members of the younger generation,[3] but it continues to function as a metaphor, like the saying "that ship has sailed," for lost opportunity. By invoking this proverb, Auntie Amma not only noted her family's situation, but also tied it into the experience of all of the residents of Elmina, and cited more generally the town's expulsion from the global economy since the departure of the Dutch and the British take over. As Elmina's long-time enemies, the British neglected the town's economy thereby marking a significant shift from the era of the Dutch presence. That residents trace their current underdevelopment to the departure of the Dutch demonstrates then their sense of abjection rather than simply a celebration of Dutch trade.

The latter interpretation easily leads to an interpretation of a blind attachment to Europeans (see Ferguson 1999; 2002), which is the diagnosis that many Ghanaians from other regions indeed provide. An extremely harsh characterization of coastal residents and Fantes in particular appeared in an editorial in December 2004 after the re-election of

President Kufuor. In response to a previous editorial that had questioned why Fantes had not supported Atta-Mills, a fellow Fante, in his bid for the presidency, the writer argues that Fantes have no sense of ethnic solidarity; rather, "the first person the Fanti owes his allegiance to is the white man." She further writes,

If one studies the history of colonial rule and the slave trade (though other coastal tribes were involved, but I will only focus on the Fante tribe), it can be said that the fantes "sold their soul to the devil" for unimportant worldly things without pausing to think of the consequences. That was the beginning of their "curse." They allowed the "white" people to plunder our gold, rape our women for pitiful remunerations such as alcohol, sweets and the chance to climb abord [sic] a ship and listen and dance to music, which was foreign to our culture. They did not stop there; they actually supplied slaves to the white men ... Fantes feel superior to the other tribes because of their affiliation with the white man. Their language is even inter-laced with the English language. They were taught to speak, eat, dress and behave like the white man.[4]

This passage demonstrates that their involvement in slave dealing is used against Fantes by others in order to vilify them. The writer also explicitly critiques coastal residents' celebration of their past affiliation with Europeans and their assimilation to European cultural practices, recalling the popular image parodied by Sekyi [...], but with much less humor. This characterization invokes Frantz Fanon's analysis of African practices of assimilation under colonialism (1967). However, while Fanon attributes this phenomenon to the effects of colonial rule on the mentality of the colonized the writer here suggests that Fante mentalities have been altered by their own greed. They chose to be traitors and have thus lost their souls.

In contrast to both interpretations, I argue not only that their practices of assimilation protected them from enslavement in the past [...] but also that today, coastal residents' do not articulate Eurocentric discourse unwittingly or unwillingly; rather, they do so out of a conscious "will to be modern" (Gable 1995) and with the intention of highlighting a fundamental contradiction, namely, that despite their past favored position, flows of

wealth and power today largely bypass them. The editorialist quoted above ignores the fact that the desire for an affiliation with "the white man" stems from a recognition of gross global inequalities and not simply from psychological damage. Her critique of this past affiliation overlooks the reality that for some, the horrors of late capitalism make the Atlantic era appear in fact desirable.

Comments like Auntie Amma's should be read, I suggest again following Ferguson (1999; 2002), not as evidence of a colonized mentality, but rather as attempts to transform an image of the coast's intrinsic outside status to an image of its past belonging followed by its unfair and unfortunate expulsion. Instead of being merely a celebration of the Atlantic era, it is actually a critique of the colonial and post-colonial eras that followed.

"Black and Proud"

Texts like *Save Elmina* provide coastal residents with narratives about their past that many readily embrace. In adopting these narratives, however, I have argued that they do not simply celebrate the European presence but rather use them to critique the present.[5] At the same time, many recognize that invocations of a glorious past are not enough to transform the conditions in which they live. This recognition reveals their skepticism with regard to the conduct of those like the prince and members of the Save Elmina Association as to whether they, despite their offers of aid, are truly committed to transforming this system of exclusion, or rather are operating in bad faith.

Kwame, for instance, expressed bitterness over the failure of the Dutch to do more for Elmina. While speaking of the Dutch, he said, "I know because the whites do a lot of research, I know that they would be aware that they have family members over here. I wish that we could unite, but you know these whites." In this way, he delivers a critique of the Dutch, suggesting that despite their awareness of their historical ties to Elmina, they have not come to its aid. The explanation for this failure, furthermore, should be obvious to me, another black person, who must "know these whites." Indeed, this statement functions on both sides of the Atlantic as a reference to anti-black racism. What he and I both know is that Elmina's marginalization is tied to the racialized nature of global exclusions in which white nations and institutions have not historically shared their wealth with others.

This critique could include the early Dutch traders as well. If they never intended that their relationship with the town be a permanent one, it is no wonder that they easily pulled up anchor when the tides turned out of their favor, leaving Elmina to its fiery fate at the hands of the British. In this context, the saying "The Dutch boat has left Elmina" takes on new meaning, alluding to not only the decline of Elmina after the Dutch departure but also to the bad faith of the Dutch throughout their occupation of Elmina. This more probing reading posits local residents' recognition that the Dutch never considered their forebears as their partners in an economic order; they rather viewed them as their pawns.

Given his critique of the Dutch, I wondered how Kwame felt about his own Dutch ancestry. A question I posed to this effect prompted the following exchange:

KWAME: I don't feel so much Dutch at this time, no I don't feel so much Dutch, though I think that I am a Ghanaian, not that I think, I am Ghanaian, I have no Dutch blood, I don't think that at all.
AUNTIE AMMA: I am proud.
KWAME: She is proud because she knows she is an indigenous Elminan –
AUNTIE AMMA: I am black and proud!
B.H. So even though your great grandfather was Dutch –
KWAME: No, we are black.

As this exchange demonstrates, while coastal residents highlight their past interactions with Europeans, they do not seek to be white; rather, their fundamental identity remains that of black people. Their desires are for inclusion in the global order that they enjoyed in the past, not for whiteness. Indeed, Auntie Amma's exclamation, "I'm black and proud," is strong evidence that she takes pride in an African identity. In making this assertion, she draws on a transnational discourse on black pride in which James Brown's 1968 anthem becomes key. Indeed, while she had been speaking primarily in Fante throughout our conversation, her sudden declaration "I'm black and proud" was made in

perfect English. Hearing Auntie Amma, an elderly woman without formal education, make this statement convinced me of just how wide the circulation of this transnational black discourse is in Ghana.

Black pride emerges not only because of the bad faith of the Dutch, but also because of the dismantling of "mixed" race privilege on the coast. In the past, while Euro-Africans were granted a special status, they retained their African identities to a large extent because of the strength of the matrilineal descent system and the persistent function of families and their larger communities as the main source of identity for local residents. Their embrace of a notion of a separate Euro-African identity was about its social and economic advantages more than a belief in their fundamental difference. With the evaporation of those advantages, being of Dutch descent has little if any meaning in Elmina today. Indeed, one can hardly speak of an "ethnoscape" to use Appadurai's term (1996) connecting Elmina and the Netherlands.

When I asked one Elmina resident if people with Dutch ancestry have any special status, he replied, "No, before they had it, but today, no. People don't respect them, especially if you don't go to school and you don't gain the wealth. Today in Elmina we know some who are illiterate, they have not been to school before, they can't say anything, but they come from [one of the Dutch families in Elmina]."

The decline of Elmina and Cape Coast more generally indicates that sites of necessary advantage have shifted geographically away from the Central Region, placing all coastal residents in the same boat. Another long-time resident of Elmina responded to my question about whether people ever talk about their Dutch ancestry, "No, they don't talk about it, they are superior? No, no, no, in fact they don't boast." As these comments demonstrate, coastal residents are less committed to claiming Dutch ancestry on an individual basis, creating, in other words, a shared ethnoscape with European nations, than they are to re-establishing "financescapes" (Appadurai 1996) with them.

In this context, it becomes clear that coastal residents' favorable constructions of the Atlantic order do not represent a colonized mentality. On the contrary, they serve to critique the global orders that followed by demonstrating that things have not always been this way. In addition, their constructions of the past often contain veiled critiques of the Atlantic order itself, serving as further evidence for the strategic use of affirmative accounts of the past. By reading statements about coastal superiority due to their proximity to Europeans as largely strategic practices, we can see Werbner's (1996) wink in play [...]. In other words, coastal residents' seeming collusion with Europeans in their celebration of their past inclusion within a Western modernity begins to reveal their experience of abjection.

In the face of contemporary national and global economies within which they occupy a marginalized position, constructing narratives about a prosperous past allows coastal residents to refute conceptualizations of their intrinsic inferiority. A notion of coastal cosmopolitanism then is an attempt to stake a claim to social and economic empowerment. Coastal residents mobilize memories of their past favored status in hopes of converting it into present symbolic capital. They submit this precedent in making their contemporary claims on state and global political economies for greater opportunities for an improved standard of living. Their narratives are similar to Sarbah's turn-of-the-century critique of colonialism as the disenfranchisement of Fantes, who had previously enjoyed a level playing field with Europeans. To stress that the Dutch boat has left Elmina is to call for an improved position within the global economy, to call, in other words, for its return. Their positive construction of the Atlantic era, furthermore, does not preclude their simultaneous critique of this era. Their relationship to the past remains, in this way, one riddled with ambivalence.

Notes

1 The full text of this speech is available at http://www.koninklijkhuis.nl/content.jsp?objectid=4172.
2 Takoradi and Tema later became Ghana's major ports.
3 In fact, when I asked a young man the literal meaning of the expression, he struggled to translate it, thinking that the reference to the Dutch must be a reference to Dutch Komenda, a neighboring coastal town.
4 Feature article of December 21, 2004 on www.ghanaweb.com.
5 Comaroff and Comaroff similarly note that "people who reject an ideological message may yet be reformed by its medium" (1992, 259).

References

Akyea, W. Nkunu. 2001. "A Touristic Dimension of the Historic and Political Role of Cape Coast in the Development of Ghana." In *Oguaaman: An Annal of History, Religion and Culture of Cape Coast*. Cape Coast: Africa Best Enterprise.

Appadurai, Arjun. 1996. *Modernity at Large: Cultural Dimensions of Globalization*. Minneapolis: University of Minnesota Press.

Comaroff, Jean, and John L. Comaroff. 1992. *Ethnography and the Historical Imagination*. Boulder: Westview Press.

Fanon, Frantz. 1967. *Black Skin, White Masks*. New York: Grove Press.

Ferguson, James. 1999. *Expectations of Modernity: Myths and Meanings of Urban Life on the Zambian Copperbelt*. Berkeley: University of California Press.

Ferguson, James. 2002. "Of Mimicry and Membership: Africans and the 'New World Society'." *Cultural Anthropology* 17(4): 551–69.

Gable, Eric. 1995. "The Decolonization of Consciousness: Local Skeptics and the 'Will to Be Modern' in a West African Village." *American Ethnologist* 22(2): 242–57.

Graham, J. Erskine. 1994. *Cape Coast in History*. Cape Coast: Anglican Printing Press.

Hannerz, Ulf. 1992. *Cultural Complexity: Studies in the Social Organization of Meaning*. New York: Columbia University Press.

Kimble, David. 1963. *A Political History of Ghana: The Rise of Gold Coast Nationalism, 1850–1928*. Oxford: Clarendon Press.

Massey, Doreen. 1994. *Space, Place, and Gender*. Minneapolis: University of Minnesota Press.

Sarbah, John Mensah. 1968a [1897]. *Fanti Customary Laws*. 3rd edn. London: Frank Cass & Co. Ltd.

Sarbah, John Mensah. 1968b [1906]. *Fanti National Constitution*. 2nd edn. London: Frank Cass & Co. Ltd.

Werbner, Richard. 1996. "Introduction: Multiple Identities, Plural Arenas." In *Postcolonial Identities in Africa*. Edited by Richard Werbner and Terence Ranger. London: Zed Books.

Part VIII

Sex and Gender Studies in Africa: Economy and Society

Introduction

The subjects of sex and gender include a wide array of theoretical issues and ethnographic topics, only some of which can be covered in a single part. Topics not addressed explicitly in this part include homosexuality, conceptions of femininity and masculinity, labor migrancy, marriage systems, health care, nutrition and fertility, among others. Of course, gender studies permeate the anthology as a whole, in works by Hutchinson, Grinker, and others. The readings in this part address the ways in which differing ideas about men and women, and their social roles, become integral parts of African political–economic and sexual life. In order to more fully contextualize these particular readings within the larger literature, however, we shall use the next few pages to outline some of the central theoretical problems in gender studies in Africa, and elsewhere.

Some anthropologists and historians working in Africa today on sex and gender concerns refer to themselves as "feminist anthropologists" (Moore, 1988), a term that deserves some critical attention. The term "feminist," as it is used in the social sciences, often characterizes specifically those works that identify the sources of women's oppression and struggles for economic and political autonomy (Cutrufelli, 1983), and that seek changes in oppressive institutions, such as female genital mutilation (usually clitoridectomy), prostitution, and marriage customs (such as polygamy and the levirate). However, anthropologist Henrietta Moore disagrees strongly that feminist works are works "about women" or about advocacy. She writes:

> The identification of feminist concerns with women's concerns has been one of the strategies employed in the social sciences to marginalize the feminist critique. This marginalization is quite unjustified. ... The basis for the feminist critique is not the study of women, but the analysis of gender relations, and of gender as a structuring principle in all human societies. (Moore, 1988: vii)

Indeed, the works of authors who characterize themselves with terms such as "feminist" or the more neutral and non-ideological sounding "gender studies" emerged together in the early 1970s, as scholars and activists began to address the invisibility of women in academic literature, and to suggest that the cultural analysis of gender categories is central, rather than a marginal specialization, to both theory and method in anthropology. Of course, women were never totally absent from ethnographies of the first part of the twentieth century, especially because anthropologists focused so much on kinship and marriage. Moreover, scholars such as Audrey Richards and Hermann Baumann took special care in the 1920s to write about the sexual division of labor in Africa, and Evans-Pritchard wrote a small, but important, case report on Azande transvestites. The problem, Moore says, "was not, therefore, one of empirical study, but rather one of *representation*" (1988: 1, our emphasis). If there is an absence, we would suggest, it is an absence of studies of men and masculinity, for men have often been taken to represent the dominant cultural patterns of society, while women have been taken as the empty category to be explained (some notable exceptions include: Hewlett, 1991; Moodie, 1994).

- How have women figured in anthropological accounts?
- Did anthropologists elicit information from them?
- Were their voices heard?
- Why did it take so long for gender to become a central focus of anthropological representation?

In the last twenty years, anthropologists have increasingly focused their attention in Africa on the study of gender, sex, and women. Anthropologists and historians, such as Caroline Bledsoe, Jane Guyer, Sara Berry, Ester Boserup, Jean Comaroff, Christine Oppong, Christine Obbo, Kristin Mann, Henrietta Moore, and Anne Whitehead, to name only a few, are among those who have helped to produce a significant body of work on African gender studies. Given that anthropologists have been studying Africa since the beginnings of the European colonization of Africa, it is reasonable to ask why it took so long for work on gender to begin. The answer lies in the fact that gender studies *anywhere* are of relatively recent origin.

"Gender" can be used generally to refer to the cultural construction of maleness and femaleness, and "sex" to refer to the division of human beings into male and female. This is a distinction that might well be called into question as a cultural construction in its own right, but the distinction has some heuristic, if not analytical, value. If one accepts that the human world is divided, naturally, into two sexes – and, it must be stressed, that until the early 1700s, Western Europeans believed that there was only one sex in the world – male (Lacqueur, 1990), and there are reasonable arguments for more than two sexes (Butler, 1990) – then the anthropological question becomes:

- What does the division between the sexes mean to people in different times and places?
- How are biological distinctions made symbolically and socially meaningful?
- How does cross-cultural analysis influence the way we think about the limits and possibilities of sex and gender categories?

Margaret Mead's early work in the Pacific islands of Oceania was perhaps the first to explicitly address the differences in sex and gender across different cultures in detail. In New Guinea, in the late 1930s, Mead studied three societies – the Arapesh, the Mundugumor, and the Tchambuli (also called the Chambri) – whose assumptions about the differences between men and women stood in stark contrast to those of Mead's social world in the United States. Arapesh held that there are no fundamental differences between men and women, that both are naturally maternal, nurturing, and non-aggressive. Mundugumor too believed that there were no fundamental differences but that men and women are both aggressive, proud, violent, and harsh. Finally, Tchambuli believed that men were, in Mead's terms, naturally feminine whereas women were naturally masculine. What this comparative study tells us is that people tend to naturalize differences between men and women, but that the form that naturalization takes is culturally variable. We must ask: Of all the ways that human beings could organize and conceptualize their worlds, why do they do it in this or that particular way? Human beings often assert that culturally constructed phenomena are really "natural" phenomena, because then they seem more real and truthful, and not subject to change.

Following Mead's research, anthropologists, in and out of Africa, have sought to explain the extraordinary diversity of beliefs about sex and gender that are taken to be so axiomatic or natural, and to explicate the complex relations between those beliefs and other aspects of culture, including art, myth, ritual, economics, and political systems. Some, such as Sherry Ortner and Michelle Rosaldo, have addressed the problem of a universal sexism: the ways in which men are frequently construed (and extolled) as "cultural" – producing and practicing technologies, and controlling a society's economic and symbolic resources – and the ways in which women are frequently construed (and denigrated) as "natural," performing sexual, reproductive, and childrearing functions. Others, such as Marilyn Strathern and Brad Shore, have noted that the "the same axes that divide and distinguish male from female (and indeed rank male over female), also cross-cut the gender categories, producing internal distinctions and gradations within them" (Ortner and Whitehead, 1981: 9; Grinker, 1994: 74–5). In other words, the categories of male–female domination become categories of domination between men. Indeed, Grinker's work in this volume on the Lese and Efe in Central Africa describes how gender categories used to distinguish men from women are used also to distinguish between whole ethnic groups. To some extent, gender becomes a free-floating set of symbols, even an artifice, applicable to myriad aspects of human existence that lie far beyond observable everyday relations between men and women.

All of these authors thus argue that the ramifications of gender concepts are complex and wide-ranging. A related argument is that we must always question the utility and validity of comparative categories, even the categories "man" and "woman." Taking aim at some recent feminist literature, Chandra Mohanty levels a harsh critique against authors who essentialize "third world women," that is, authors who create a singular, monolithic, homogeneous category of person. She contends that the process of homogenization is also, perhaps unwittingly, a process of oppression, appropriated by Western feminists as a way to characterize poor, non-Western women, as ahistorical, undifferentiated victims who can be used for Western feminist advocacy. According to Mohanty, many authors try to achieve solidarity for "women" throughout the world, but by doing so they also tend to represent women as powerless and dependent, and to reinforce ethnocentric beliefs about sex and gender. As Mohanty puts it, they risk saying that "They cannot represent themselves; they must be represented" (1991: 216).

The first reading in this part deals with polygynous marriage, a practice that appears throughout the continent of Africa, in which a man has more than one wife. This term should be distinguished from the more general term "polygamy," which refers to someone, male or female, having more than one spouse, and thus includes the specific term "polyandry," in which a woman has more than one husband. Polyandry is uncommon in Africa, having been outlawed in Nigeria and elsewhere during colonization, and occurs most frequently in north India, Tibet, and Nepal (Sangree and Levine, 1978). Throughout Africa, many men and women consider polygyny to be an ideal form of marriage, though the expense of paying bridewealth and supporting a large family often proves prohibitive for men. There are other difficulties as well. Among the Lese and Efe of northeastern Democratic Republic of Congo, for example, all men strive to have more than one wife, but even those who achieve their goal, and can support their families financially, find it difficult to keep peace in the family. Jealousies and competition between co-wives, and disputes over access to land and other resources, often make polygynous marriages more unstable than monogamous ones. In West Africa, some high-ranking men were known to have had hundreds of wives, but the most common number of spouses in polygynous marriages is two, with one woman the principal or senior wife. In Muslim marriages in Africa, and elsewhere, Qur'anic scripture dictates no more than four wives, for beyond that, the Prophet Mohammed believed, a man would not be able to attend to his family with sufficient care. Beyond two, rivalries become especially intense as alliances and factions among co-wives may emerge. In most polygynous marriages in Africa, wives commonly occupy separate huts in the same compound, may till different plots of land, and feed their children separately.

Although there are a number of important issues that arise in the study of polygamy, Boserup writes primarily about its economic logic. Drawing on data from throughout Africa, but most specifically from the Yoruba of Nigeria, Boserup outlines the relationships between polygamy, women's status, and farming.

- Why would some men want polygynous marriages?
- Why would some women want polygynous marriages?
- Is "women's" position debased in polygynous societies?
- Is the co-wife only a "guest" in her husband's house and village, with few rights of her own?

Although Boserup does not address these questions directly, it is useful to consider how ethno-centric it would be for people who live in monogamous societies to automatically assume that African polygyny has primarily negative effects on women's lives. Polygyny offers a degree of freedom not available to women in monogamous unions, allowing women to travel more frequently, engage in entrepreneurial or trade activities, or visit friends and relatives. If a woman is ill, there are others who can care for her children; if she is absent, others can care for her garden. In northeastern Democratic Republic of Congo, where women suffer from a high rate of infertility, infertile women can ensure their position within a village by bringing in an additional wife who can reproduce where she could not. Among the Lovedu of West Africa, woman–woman marriage served precisely this function, as a woman married another woman who would then have a sexual reproductive relationship with the first woman's husband. The Lovedu (Krige, 1943) are also notable in that they are one of the few African societies whose supreme ruler, the Rain Queen, was a woman. It is also difficult to extrapolate from a single custom a generalized status. As Robert Murphy notes, married women in France were allowed to have their own bank accounts only in 1968, but most West African women have always had the right to control their finances (1979: 67). Yet, polygamy is an issue on which there is little agreement, and local activists throughout Africa continue to press for the abolition of polygyny and other customs they deem harmful to women, such as circumcision and bridewealth. Depending upon one's perspective, bridewealth can appear as akin to purchase or prostitution, and polygamy as an excuse for male domination. In addition to the many women's organizations and legal advocacy groups in Africa speaking and writing on polygamy and human rights, the many perspectives on polygamy also appear in the writings of many African poets and novelists (see, for example, Mariama Ba, *So Long a Letter*, 1981). Of course this debate goes on.

Numerous authors have analyzed how male–female relations have been transformed in the context of rapid historical change in sub-Saharan Africa. In one important article, on the Baule of Côte d'Ivoire, Etienne notes that in precolonial days, Baule women controlled the production and distribution of cloth, one of the more valuable artistic and practical products in Baule life, while men controlled the staple food, yams (Etienne 1980). Although there were many male weavers, women controlled their end products because they owned the thread itself. Exchanges of cloth were vital to establishing all sorts of social relations, especially marriages, linkages between neighboring villages, and long-distance trade. Trading or selling cloth could make a man or woman wealthy, or at least help them to achieve a high level of prestige; but even more importantly, cloth gave women a significant amount of power and influence in Baule society. Women and men were equally dependent upon one another, the one for food, the other for cloth. During the French colonization of Côte d'Ivoire, however, Baule men and women were required to pay taxes, and to fulfill colonial administration quotas on agricultural production. As one result, women were sometimes forced to cultivate men's crops, such as yams, and to cultivate cotton for cash rather than for local social purposes. In addition, men, especially male weavers, could now buy thread directly from factories established by the French, thus bypassing women and alienating them from the whole production–distribution process. Consequently, women's power has decreased significantly over the years, especially within marriages, and women today sell their labor so that they can get cash. Men remunerate them as they wish because they no longer depend upon them for any essential products.

In the chapter reprinted here on the Igbo of Nigeria, Judith Van Allen also writes about women's power, and how colonialism, in this case by the British, resulted in a loss of the influence women exercised in the non-centralized political institutions of the Igbo of Nigeria. Van Allen notes that Igbo politics have always involved diffuse power relations, with status largely achieved, rather than ascribed, and the women using meetings (*mikiri*) to regulate market activity, call boycotts and strikes, and otherwise consult about women's interests that oppose men's interests. Specific actions taken against men were metaphorically referred to as "sitting on a man."

When the British colonial administration attempted to define lines of political authority among the Igbo – to produce a "native administration" consistent with the policy of "indirect rule" – they chose to ignore local political institutions of both Igbo men and women. The disastrous results of their selective blindness, and their unwillingness to include women in the new systems of local government, can be seen in Van Allen's depiction of one of the greatest demonstrations of women's power in African history: the Women's War.

Political reforms instituted by the British in 1933 did little to address women's needs, and further marginalized the women from economic and political power centers. The diffuse political system on which women's power and influence once depended was gone, as was any legitimate system of self-help, or the method of "sitting on a man." All were replaced by Native Courts, the participation in which was exclusively male, and the practice of which was geared toward men's interests. Van Allen and Etienne's articles suggest that, while colonial administrations throughout Africa consistently argued that Westernization and the introduction of modern political structures and values would expand the rights and freedoms of all individuals, women's political participation withered, giving way instead to the British ideal of the politically invisible Victorian woman.

In the final selection in this part, Suzanne LeClerc-Madlala illustrates a gendered response to a major public health concern: the HIV/AIDS epidemic in South Africa. In order to combat the spread of HIV, elderly women in the KwaZulu-Natal province, supported by political officials from numerous levels of leadership, have instituted virginity testing as a form of grassroots AIDS activism. In an article that echoes debates over one of the most salient human rights issues in sub-Saharan Africa – female circumcision – LeClerc-Madlala illustrates the complexity of values surrounding the power and influence of female sexuality. When elderly women examine girls' genitalia for evidence of sexual activity, they do so ostensibly to identify girls at risk for HIV, or who may pose a risk to others, and to punish the sexually active girl, and her family. However, the practice reveals Zulu beliefs that while female sexuality is a positive life force, it is also a source of danger and disease for men. In addition, Zulu attitudes towards female sexuality are constituted not only by conventional meanings, but also by more contemporary symbols. Girls receive Western-style school grades (A, B, or C) on the appearance of their genitalia (for example, an A for an obvious virgin, a B for someone who is possibly sexually active, and a C for a failure); fears about female sexuality are justified by a widespread concern that "modern" society promotes promiscuity; and that current female sexuality challenges the social regulation of sex vital to proper Zulu marriage and marriage payments. LeClerc-Madlala's article is fundamentally about a topic of concern to all the authors represented in this section: the ways in which sex and gender ramify to multiple areas of social life.

References

Ba, Mariama. 1981. *So Long a Letter*. Oxford: Heinemann.

Butler, Judith. 1990. *Gender Trouble: Feminism and the Subversion of Identity*. New York: Routledge.

Cutrufelli, Maria Rose, 1983. *Women of Africa: Roots of Oppression*. Nicolas Romano, trans. London: Zed Press.

Etienne, Mona. 1980. "Women and Men, Cloth and Colonization: the Transformation of Production–Distribution Relations among the Baule (Ivory Coast)." In Mona Etienne and Eleanor Leacock, eds., *Women and Colonization*, pp. 214–38. New York: Praeger.

Grinker, R.R. 1994. *Houses in the Rainforest. Ethnicity and Inequality among Farmers and Foragers in Central Africa*. Berkeley and Los Angeles: University of California Press.

Hewlett, Barry. 1991. *Intimate Fathers: The Nature and Context of Aka Pygmy Paternal Care*. Ann Arbor: University of Michigan.

Krige, Eileen. 1943. *The Realm of the Rain Queen: A Study of the Pattern of Lovedu Society*. London: Oxford University Press.

Lacqueur, Thomas. 1990. *Making Sex: Body and Gender from the Greeks to Freud*. Cambridge, MA: Harvard University Press.

Mohanty, Chandra Talpade. 1991. "Under Western Eyes: Feminist Scholarship and Colonial Discourses." In Chandra Talpade Mohantry, Ann Russo and Lourdes Torres, eds., *Third World Women and the Politics of Feminism*, pp. 51–80. Bloomington: Indiana University Press.

Moodie, T. Dunbar with Vivienne Ndatshe. 1994. *Going for Gold: Men, Mines and Migration*. Berkeley and Los Angeles: University of California Press.

Moore, Henrietta. 1988. *Feminist Anthropology*. Minneapolis: University of Minnesota Press.

Murphy, Robert. 1979. *Overture to Social Anthropology*. Princeton: Prentice-Hall.

Ortner, Sherry B. and Harriet Whitehead, eds. 1981. "Introduction: Accounting for Sexual Meanings." In *Sexual Meanings: The Cultural Construction of Gender and Sexuality*, pp. 1–28. Cambridge: Cambridge University Press.

Sangree, Walter H. and Nancy E. Levine, eds. 1978. "Women with Many Husbands: Polyandrous. Alliance and Marital Flexibility in Africa and Asia." Special Issue: *Journal of Comparative Family Studies* 11(3).

Suggested Reading

Adepoju, Aderanti and Christine Oppong, eds. 1994. *Gender, Work and Population in Sub-Saharan Africa*. Portsmouth, NH: Heinemann.

Baylies, C. 2001. *AIDS, Sexuality and Gender in Africa: Collective Strategies and Struggles in Tanzania and Zambia*. New York: Taylor and Francis.

Bledsoe, Caroline H. 1980. *Women and Marriage in Kpelle Society*. Stanford, CA: Stanford University Press.

Clark, Gracia. 1994. *Onions Are my Husband: Survival and Accumulation by West African Market Women*. Chicago: University of Chicago Press.

Creevey, Lucy, ed. 1986. *Women Farmers in Africa: Rural development in Mali and the Sahel*. Syracuse, NY: Syracuse University Press.

Crumbley, Helen. 2008. *Spirit, Structure, and Flesh: Gender and Power in Yoruba African Instituted Churches*. Madison, WI: University of Wisconsin Press.

Epprecht, Marc. 2008. *Heterosexual Africa? The History of an Idea from the Age of Exploration to the Age of AIDS.* Columbus, OH: Ohio University Press.

Gezon, Lisa. L. 2002. "Marriage, Kin, and Compensation: A Socio-political Ecology of Gender in Ankarana." *Madagascar.Anthropological Quarterly* 75 (4): 675–707.

Gouws, Amanda. 2005. *(Un)thinking Citizenship: Feminist Debates in Contemporary South Africa.* Surrey: Ashgate.

Guyer, Jane I. 1981. "Household and Community in African Studies." *African Studies Review*, 24(2/3): 87–137.

Guyer, Jane I. 1984. *Family and Farm in Southern Cameroon.* Boston: Boston University African Studies Center.

Guyer, Jane I. 1988. "The Multiplication of Labor: Historical Methods in the Study of Gender and Agricultural Change in Modern Africa. *Current Anthropology,* 29: 247–72.

Hay, Margaret Jean. 1995. *African Women South of the Sahara*, 2nd edn. New York: Longmann.

Hay, Margaret Jean and Marcia Wright, eds. 1982. *African Women and the Law: Historical Perspectives.* Boston: Boston University African Studies Center.

Heald, Suzette. 1982. "The Making of Men." *Africa* 52: 15–35.

Hodgson, Dorothy and Sheryl McCurdy. 2001. *Wicked Women and the Reconfiguration of Gender.* London: James Currey.

Issacs, Gordon and Brian McKendrick. *Male Homosexuality in South African Identity: Formation, Culture and Crisis.*

Jacobson-Widding, Anita. 1991. *Body and Space: Symbolic Models of Unity and Division in African Cosmology and Experience.* Uppsala and Stockholm, Sweden: Upsaliensis Academie.

Kalipeni, Ezekiel, Susan Craddock, Joseph R. Oppong, and Jayati Ghosh, eds. 2003. *HIV and AIDS in Africa: Beyond Epidemiology.* Malden, MA: Wiley-Blackwell.

Kratz, Corinne A. 1994. *Affecting Performance: Meaning, Movement and Experience in Okiek Women's Initiation.* Washington, DC: Smithsonian Institution Press.

Mook, Joyce Lewenger, ed. 1992. *Diversity, Farmer Knowledge and Sustainability.* Ithaca, NY: Cornell University Press.

Moore, Henrietta and Megan Vaughan. 1994. *Cutting down Trees: Gender, Nutrition, and Agricultural Change in the Northern Province of Zambia, 1890–1990.* Portsmouth, NH: Heinemann.

Murray, Colin. 1981. *Families Divided: The Impact of Migrant Labour in Lesotho.* Johannesburg: Raven.

Nattrass, Nicoli. 2004. *The Moral Economy of AIDS in South Africa.* Cambridge: Cambridge University Press.

Obbo, Christine. 1980. *African Women.* London: Zed Press.

Oppong, C. 1974. *Marriage among a Matrilineal Elite.* Cambridge: Cambridge University Press.

Parkin, David. 1975. *Town and Country in Central and Eastern Africa.* United Kingdom: IAI.

p'Bitek, Okot. 1966. *Song of Lawino.* Nairobi: East African Publishing House.

Peters, Pauline, 1994. *Dividing the Commons: Politics, Policy and Culture in Botswana.* Charlottesville: University of Virginia Press.

Rosaldo, Michelle Z. and Louise Lamphere. 1974. *Woman, Culture and Society.* Stanford, CA: Stanford University Press.

Schuster, Ilsa. 1979. *New Women of Lusaka.* New York: Mayfield.

Setel, Philip W. 2000. *A Plague of Paradoxes AIDS, Culture, and Demography in Northern Tanzania.* Chicago: University of Chicago Press.

Susser, Ida. 2009. *AIDS, Sex, and Culture: Global Politics and Survival in Southern Africa.* Malden, MA: Wiley-Blackwell.

Wojcicki, Janet Maia. 2002. "'She Drank His Money': Survival Sex and the Problem of Violence in Taverns in Gauteng Province, South Africa." *Medical Anthropology Quarterly* 16(3): 267–93.

26

The Economics of Polygamy

Ester Boserup

Some years ago, UNESCO held a seminar on the status of women in South Asia. The seminar made this concluding statement after a discussion of the problem of polygamy: "Polygamy might be due to economic reasons, that is to say, the nature of the principal source of livelihood of the social group concerned, e.g. agriculture, but data available to the Seminar would not permit any conclusions to be drawn on this point".[1]

It is understandable that such a cautious conclusion should be drawn in Asia where the incidence of polygamy is low and diminishing. In Africa, however, polygamy is widespread, and nobody seems to doubt that its occurrence is closely related to economic conditions. A report by the secretariat of the UN Economic Commission for Africa (ECA) affirms this point: "One of the strongest appeals of polygamy to men in Africa is precisely its economic aspect, for a man with several wives commands more land, can produce more food for his household and can achieve a high status due to the wealth which he can command".[2]

It is self explanatory, given women's input in African farming, that a man can get more food if he has more land and more wives to cultivate it. But why is it that the more wives he has got, the more land he can command, as the ECA statement says? The explanation lies in the fact that individual property in land is far from being the only system of land tenure in Africa. Over much of the continent, tribal rules of land tenure are still in force. This implies that members of a tribe which commands a certain territory have a native right to take land under cultivation for food production and in many cases also for the cultivation of cash crops. Under this tenure system, an additional wife is an additional economic asset which helps the family to expand its production.

In regions of shifting cultivation, where women do all or most of the work of growing food crops, the task of felling the trees in preparation of new plots is usually done by older boys and very young men, as already mentioned. An elderly cultivator with several wives is likely to have a number of such boys who can be used for this purpose. By the combined efforts of young sons and young wives he may gradually expand his cultivation and become more and more prosperous, while a man with a single wife has less help in cultivation

From Ester Boserup, "The Economics of Polygamy", in *Women's Role in Economic Development* (1970), Allen and Unwin, pp. 37–50.

and is likely to have little or no help for felling. Hence, there is a direct relationship between the size of the area cultivated by a family and the number of wives in the family. For instance, in the Bwamba region of Uganda, in East Africa, it appeared from a sample study that men with one wife cultivated an average of 1.67 acres of land, while men with two wives cultivated 2.94 acres, or nearly twice as much. The author of the study describes women in this region as "the cornerstone and the limiting factor in the sphere of agricultural production" and notes that almost all the men desire to have additional wives. A polygamic family is "the ideal family organization from the man's point of view".[3]

In female farming communities, a man with more than one wife can cultivate more land than a man with only one wife. Hence, the institution of polygamy is a significant element in the process of economic development in regions where additional land is available for cultivation under the long fallow system. There is an inverse correlation between the use of female family labour and the use of hired labour. It seems that farmers usually either have a great deal of help from their wives, or else they hire labour. Thus farmers in polygamic communities have a wider choice in this than have farmers in monogamic communities. In the former community, the use of additional female family labour is not limited to the amount of work that one wife and her children can perform; the total input of labour can be expanded by the acquisition of one or more additional wives.

This economic significance of polygamy is not restricted to the long fallow system of cultivation. In many regions, farmers have a choice between an expansion of cultivation by the use of more labour in long fallow cultivation, with a hoe, or an expansion by the transion to shorter fallow with ploughs drawn by animals.[4] In such cases, three possible ways of development present themselves to the farmer: expansion by technical change (the plough); expansion by hierarchization of the community (hired labour); or expansion by the traditional method of acquiring additional wives. In a study of economic development in Uganda, Audrey Richards pointed to this crucial role of polygamy as one of the possible ways to agricultural expansion: "It is rare to find Africans passing

out of the subsistence farm level without either the use of additional labour (read: hired labour E.B.), the introduction of the plough, which is not a practical proposition in Buganda; or by the maintenance of a large family unit, which is not a feature of Ganda social structure at the moment."[5]

In the same vein, Little's classical study of the Mende in the West African state of Sierra Leone concluded that "a plurality of wives is an agricultural asset, since a large number of women makes it unnecessary to employ much wage labour".[6] At the time of Little's study (i.e. in the 1930s), it was accepted in the more rural areas that nobody could run a proper farm unless he had at least four wives. Little found sixty-seven wives to the twenty-three cultivators included in his sample and an average of 842 households. He describes how the work of one wife enables him to acquire an additional one: "He says to his first wife, 'I like such and such a girl. Let us make a bigger farm this year.' As soon as the harvest is over for that year, he sells the rice and so acquires the fourth wife."[7]

Little's study is thirty years old, and the incidence of polygamy has declined since then. But, although households with large numbers of wives seem to have more or less disappeared in most of Africa, polygamy is still extremely widespread and is considered an economic advantage in many rural areas. The present situation can be gleaned from Table 26.1, which brings together the results of a number of sample studies about the incidence of polygamy. It is seen that none of the more recent studies shows such a high incidence of polygamic marriages as in the period of Little's old study. Most of the studies show an average number of around 1.3 wives per married man.*

In most cases over one-fifth of all married men were found to have more than one wife at the time of enquiry.†

The acquisition of an additional wife is not always used as a means of becoming richer through the expansion of cultivation. In some cases, the economic role of the additional wife enables the husband to enjoy more leisure. A village study from Gambia showed that in the village, where rice is produced by women, men who had several wives to produce rice for them produced less millet (which is a crop produced by men) than did men with only one wife.[8] Likewise, in the villages

Table 26.1   Incidence of polygamy in Africa

Country in which sample areas are located		Average number of wives per married men	Polygamic marriages as percentage of all existing marriages
Senegal	A	1.1	24
	B	1.3	23
	C	1.3	21
Sierra Leone		2.3	51
Ivory Coast		1.3	27
Nigeria	A	2.1[a]	63
	B	1.5	
Cameroon		1.0–1.3[b]	
Congo	A	1.3	11
	B	1.2	17
South Africa			14
Uganda	A	1.7	45
	B	1.2	

[a] The figures refer to male heads of families, while married sons living with these seem to be excluded.

[b] The lowest ratio refers to unskilled workers, the highest ratio to own-account workers.

Table 26.1 *Senegal: Sample A and B*, UN. ECA. Polygamy, 9–10, 70,000 persons in Dakar in 1955 and 1960. *Sample C*, Boutillier, 1962, 31, 33; 1,265 persons in the Valley of Senegal, 1957–8. Sierra Leone: Little 1948, 9–10n, 842 households in Mende Country, 1937. *Ivory Coast*: Boutillier 1960, 45, sample of 3,764 persons, 1955–6. *Nigeria: Sample A*, Galetti, 71–2; 776 families in the Yoruba region, 1950–1. *Sample B*, Mortimore, 679, sample of 5,103 persons in Kano district, 1964. *Cameroon:* Gouellain, 260, population in New-Bell, Douala, 1956. *Congo: Sample A and B*, Balandier 1955, 136. Brazzaville and Delisie, 1952. *South Africa*: Reynders 260, sample of 1,180 households in Bantu areas, 1950–1. *Uganda: Sample A*, Winter, 23, sample of seventy-one families in Bwamba, 1951. *Sample B*, Katarikawe, 8, sample of fifty-nine families in Kiga resettlement schemes, 1956–6.

in the Central African Republic men with two wives worked less than men with one wife, and they found more time for hunting, the most cherished spare time occupation for the male members of the village population.[9]

Undoubtedly, future changes in marriage patterns in rural Africa will be closely linked to future changes in farming systems which may lessen (or enhance) the economic incentive for polygamic marriages. Of course, motives other than purely economic considerations are behind a man's decision to acquire an additional wife. The desire for numerous progeny is no doubt often the main incentive. Where both the desire for children and the economic considerations are at work, the

incentives for polygamy are likely to be so powerful that religious or legal prohibition avails little.

A study of the Yoruba farmers of Nigeria has this to say: "There are no doubt other reasons why polygamy prevails in the Yoruba country as in other regions of the world; but the two which seem to be most prominent in the minds of Yoruba farmers are that wives contribute much more to the family income than the value of their keep and that the dignity and standing of the family is enhanced by an increase of progeny. While these beliefs persist the institution of polygamy will be enduring, even in families which have otherwise accepted Christian doctrine. The Yoruba farmer argues that the increased output from his farms obtainable without cash expense when he has wives to help him out-weighs the economic burden of providing more food, more clothing and larger houses."[10]

The Status of Younger Wives

It is easy to understand the point of view of the Yoruba farmers quoted above when one considers the contribution to family support which women make in this region. Economic relations between husband and wife among the Yoruba differ widely from the common practise of countries where wives are normally supported by their husbands. Only 5 per cent of the Yoruba women in the sample reproduced in Table 26.2 received from their hus-bands everything they needed – food, clothing and some cash – and only 2 per cent of them did no work other than domestic activities. A large major-ity were self-employed (in agriculture, trade or crafts) and many helped a husband on his farm in addition to their self-employment and their domes-tic duties. Most of these self-employed women had to provide at least part of the food for the family as well as clothing and cash out of their own earn-ings. Nearly one-fifth of the women received noth-ing from their husband and had to provide everything out of their own earnings; nevertheless they performed domestic duties for the husband and half of them also helped him on his farm.

There may not be many tribes in Africa where women contribute as much as the Yorubas to the upkeep of the family, but it is normal in traditional African marriages for women to support themselves and their children and to cook for the husband, often using food they produce themselves. A small sample from Bamenda in the West African Cameroons showed that the women contributed 44 per cent of the gross income of the family.[11] Many women of pastoral tribes, for instance the Fulani tribe of Northern Nigeria and Niger, are expected to provide a large part of the cash expenses of the family out of their own earnings from the sale of the milk and butter they produce. They cover the expenditure on clothing for their children and themselves as well as buying food for the family.[12] In many regions of East Africa, women are tradi-tionally expected to support themselves and many women are said to prefer to marry Moslems because a Moslem has a religious duty to support his wife.

In a family system where wives are supposed both to provide food for the family – or a large part of it – and to perform the usual domestic duties for the husband, a wife will naturally welcome one or more co-wives to share with them the burden of daily work. Therefore, educated girls in Africa who support the cause of monogamous marriage as part of a modern outlook are unable to rally the major-ity of women behind them.[13] In the Ivory Coast, an opinion study indicated that 85 per cent of the women preferred to live in polygamous rather than monogamous marriage. Most of them mentioned domestic and economic reasons for their choice.[14]

In many cases, the first wife takes the initiative in suggesting that a second wife, who can take over the most tiresome jobs in the household, should be procured. A woman marrying a man who

Table 26.2 Rights and duties of Yoruba women
Percentage of Women with the following rights and duties:

Wife receives from husband	Wife contributes to household:				
	as self-employed, family aid and housewife	as self-employed and housewife	as family aid and housewife	as housewife	Total
Nothing	8	11			19
Part of food	32	16			48
All food	15	11	1	1	28
Food, clothing and cash	1		3	1	5
Total	56	38	4	2	100

Table 26.2. Galetti 77, sample of 144 women in seventy-three families in Yoruba region, 1951–2.

already has a number of wives often joins the household more or less in the capacity of a servant for the first wife, unless it happens to be a love match.[15] It was said above that in most parts of the world there seems to be an inverse correlation between the use of female labour and the use of hired labour in agriculture, i.e. that most farmers have some help either from their wives or from hired labour. However, in some regions with widespread polygamy, hired labour is a *supplement* to the labour provided by several wives, in the sense that the tasks for which male strength is needed are done by hired labour, while the other tasks are done by wives. In such cases the husband or his adult sons act only as supervisors.

Reports from different parts of Africa, ranging from the Sudan to Nigeria and the Ivory Coast, have drawn attention to this frequent combination of male labourers and wives of polygamous cultivators working together in the fields under the supervision of one or more male family members.[16] In such cases, the availability of male labour for hire is not a factor which lessens the incentive to polygamous marriages. On the contrary, it provides an additional incentive to polygamous marriages as a means of expanding the family business without changing the customary division of labour between the two sexes. Little reported that in Sierra Leone men with several wives sometimes used them to ensnare male agricultural labourers and get them to work for them without pay.[17]

In regions where polygamy is the rule, it is likely, for obvious demographic reasons, that many males will have to postpone marriage, or even forego it. Widespread prostitution or adultery is therefore likely to accompany widespread polygamy, marriage payments are likely to be insignificant or non-existant for the bride's family and high for the bridegroom's family, sometimes amounting to several years' earnings of a seasonal labourer.[18] This will induce parents to marry off their daughters rather young, but in a period like the present, where each generation of girls is numerically larger than the previous one, the difference in age between the spouses will be narrower than it was previously.

Figures from Dakar, the capital of Senegal, shown in Table 26.3 illustrate the importance of the age difference between the spouses. Here, the

Table 26.3 Age distribution of married Moslem population of Dakar in Senegal

Age Group:	Percentages		
	First Wives	Later Wives	Husbands
Below 25 years	12	35	
25–34 years	49	44	10
35–49 years	35	19	59
50 years and over	4	2	31
All ages	100	100	100

average marriage age for women is 18 years, and the average age of first marriage for men is between 27 and 28 years. The average age difference between men and their second wives is over 15 years, and nearly all wives belong to age groups which are larger than those to which their husbands belong.[19] No less than 90 per cent of married men belong to the relatively small generations over 35, as can be seen from the table, while only 39 per cent of their first wives and 21 per cent of their second wives belong to these generations.

Economic policy during the period of colonial rule in Africa contributed to the introduction or reinforcement of the customary wide difference in marriage age of young men and girls. In order to obtain labour for road transport, construction works, mines and plantations, the Europeans recruited young villagers at an age where they might have married had they stayed on in the village. Instead they married after their return several years later. The result was an age structure in the villages with very few young men in the age group between 20 and 35 and the need to marry young girls to much older men who had returned from wage labour.

The difference between the numbers of boys and girls in villages where the custom of taking away wage labourers before marriage persists, can be seen from Figure 26.1 which gives the age distribution in Rhodesian villages as reported in a study by J. Clyde Mitchell.[20] In the age groups 20–35 nearly all the men are away and the number of women in these age groups is several times higher than that of the men. In many other parts

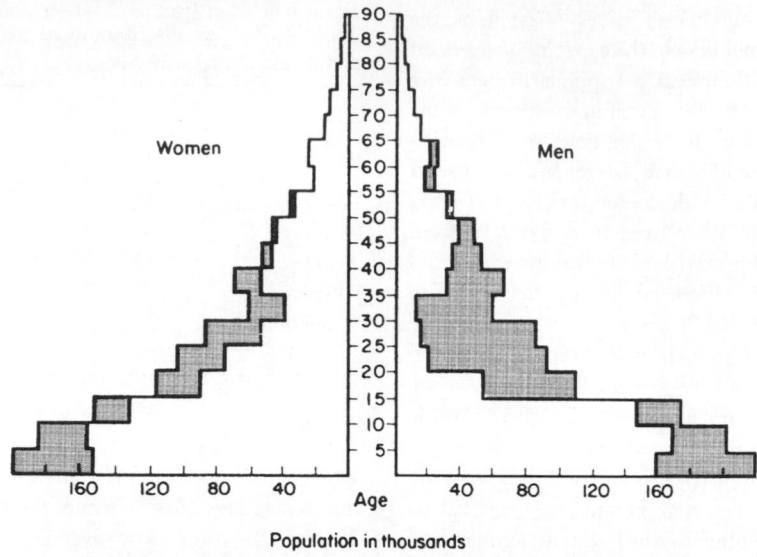

Population in thousands

Shaded portion represents persons absent from the African areas

Figure 26.1   Sex and age structure of population in African areas of South Rhodesia in 1956

of Africa, recruitment for mines, plantations and urban industries results in similarly abnormal age distributions in the villages where the labourers are recruited.

Normally, the status of the younger wife is inferior as befits the assistant or even servant to the first wife. This can be explained partly as a result of the wide age difference between husband and wife and between first and younger wife, but the historical background of the institution of polygamy must also be kept in mind. Domestic slavery survived until fairly recently in many parts of Africa, and the legal ban on slavery introduced by European colonial powers provided an incentive for men to marry girls whom otherwise they might have kept as slaves.

In a paper published as recently as 1959, it is mentioned that in the Ivory Coast women were still being pawned by husbands or fathers to work in their creditor's fields, together with his own wives and daughters and without pay until the debt was paid off, when they were free to return to their own families.[21] Today, such arrangements may be rare in Africa, but it is probable that the bride price for an additional wife is sometimes settled by the cancellation of a debt from the girl's family to the future

husband, which would come to much the same thing in terms of real economic relationships.

Embodied in Moslem law is the well-known rule that all wives must be treated equally, which implies that the younger wives must not be used as servants for the senior wives. Moreover, a limit is set to the use of wives for expansion of the family business, partly by limiting the allowable number of wives to four, and partly by making the husband responsible for the support of his wives. We have already mentioned that this serves to make Moslem men desirable marriage partners for many African girls in regions where girls married to non-Moslems are expected to support themselves and their children by hard work in the fields. Because of this principle of equal treatment, first wives in orthodox Moslem marriages may desist from making the younger wives perform the most unpleasant tasks. Often in African families – Moslem and non-Moslem – each wife has her own hut or house and cooks independently, while the husband in regular succession will live and eat with each of his wives. Even so, the wife gains by not having to feed her husband all the time, and we sometimes find that women prefer polygamy even where the wives are treated equally.

In most of Africa the rule is that a wife may leave her husband provided that she pays back the bride price. In regions where wives must do hard agricultural work, many young girls wish to find money to enable them to leave a much older husband, and many husbands fear that their young wives will be able to do so.[22] This makes older men take an interest on one hand in keeping bride prices at a level which makes it difficult for women to earn enough to pay them back and on the other hand in preventing their young wives from obtaining money incomes. Later we shall see what role these conflicting interests between men and women are playing in development policy.

Work Input and Women's Status

Polygamy offers fewer incentives in those parts of the world where, because they are more densely populated than Africa, the system of shifting cultivation has been replaced by the permanent cultivation of fields ploughed before sowing. However, in some regions where the latter system prevails, polygamy may have advantages. This is true particularly where the main crop is cotton, since women and children are of great help in the plucking season.[23] But in farming systems where men do most of the agricultural work, a second wife can be an economic burden rather than an asset. In order to feed an additional wife the husband must either work harder himself or he must hire labourers to do part of the work. In such regions, polygamy is either non-existent or is a luxury in which only a small minority of rich farmers can indulge. The proportion of polygamic marriages is reported to be below 4 per cent in Egypt, 2 per cent in Algeria, 3 per cent in Pakistan and Indonesia.[24] There is a striking contrast between this low incidence of polygamy and the fact that in many parts of Africa South of the Sahara one-third to one-fourth of all married men have more than one wife.

In regions where women do most of the agricultural work it is the bridegroom who must pay bridewealth, as already mentioned, but where women are less actively engaged in agriculture, marriage payments come usually from the girl's family. In South and East Asia the connection between the work of women and the direction of marriage payments is close and unmistakable.

For instance, in Burma, Malaya and Laos women seem to do most of the agricultural work and bride prices are customary.[25] The same is true of Indian tribal people, and of low-caste peoples whose women work. By contrast, in the Hindu communities, women are less active in agriculture, and instead of a bride price being paid by the bridegroom, a dowry has to be paid by the bride's family.[26] A dowry paid by the girl's family is a means of securing for her a good position in her husband's family. In the middle of the nineteenth century it was legal for a husband in Thailand to sell a wife for whom he had paid a bride price, but not a wife whose parents had paid a dowry to the husband.[27]

Not only the payment of a dowry but also the use of the veil is a means of distinguishing the status of the upper class wife from that of the "servant wife." In ancient Arab society, the use of the veil and the retirement into seclusion were means of distinguishing the honoured wife from the slave girl who was exposed to the public gaze in the slave market.[28] In the Sudan even today it appears to be a mark of distinction and sophistication for an educated girl to retire into seclusion when she has finished her education.[29]

In communities where girls live in seclusion, and a large dowry must be paid when they marry, parents naturally come to dread the burden of having daughters. In some of the farming communities in Northern India, where women do little work in agriculture and the parents know that a daughter will in due course cost them the payment of a dowry, it was customary in earlier times to limit the number of surviving daughters by infanticide. This practice has disappeared, in its outward forms, but nevertheless the ratio of female to male population in these districts continues to be abnormal compared to other regions of India and to tribes with working women living in the same region. A recent study of regional variations in the sex ratio of population in India[30] reached the conclusion that the small number of women in the Northern districts could not be explained either by undernumeration of females, or by migration, or by a low female birthrate. The only plausible hypothesis would be that mortality among girls was higher than among boys. The conclusion drawn was that "the persistence of socio-cultural factors are believed to be largely responsible for the excess of female mortality over the male."[31] One of these socio-cultural factors seems to be a widespread supposition that milk is not good for girls, but is good for boys. There is also a tendency to care more for sick boys than for sick girls.[32]

In a study from a district in Central India with a deficit of women, the author is very outspoken about the neglect of girls: "The Rajputs always preferred male children. ... Female infanticide, therefore, was a tolerated practise. ... Although in the past 80 years the proportion of the females to males has steadily risen yet there was always a shortage of women in the region. ... When interrogated about the possibility of existence of female infanticide, the villagers emphatically deny its existence. ... It was admitted on all hands that if a female child fell ill, then the care taken was very cursory and if she died there was little sorrow. In fact, in a nearby village a cultivator had twelve children – six sons and six daughters. All the daughters fell ill from time to time and died. The sons also fell ill but they survived. The villagers know that it was by omissions that these children had died. Perhaps there has been a transition from violence to non-violence in keeping with the spirit of the times."[33] The report adds that "no records of birth or deaths are kept. ... it was enjoined upon the Panchayat (village council) to keep these statistics, but they were never able to fulfil the task".[34] It is explicitly said in the study that the district is one where wives and daughters of cultivators take no part in field work. In some cases, the shortage of women in rural communities in North India induces the cultivators to acquire low caste women from other districts, or from other Indian States, against the payment of a bride price.[35] This need not be an infringement on caste rules. Although it is usually forbidden for a man to marry a woman of a higher caste, men of higher caste may have the right to marry women of lower castes.[36] This may then entail the payment of a bride price instead of the receipt of a dowry as would be customary in the husband's own subcaste.

To summarize the analysis of the position of women in rural communities, two broad groups may be identified: the first type is found in regions where shifting cultivation predominates and the major part of agricultural work is done by women. In such communities, we can expect to find a high incidence of polygamy, and bride wealth being paid by the future husband or his family. The women are hard working and have only a limited right of support from their husbands, but they often enjoy considerable freedom of movement and some economic independence from the sale of their own crops.

The second group is found where plough cultivation predominates and where women do less agricultural work than men. In such communities we may expect to find that only a tiny minority of marriages, if any, are polygamous; that a dowry is usually paid by the girl's family; that a wife is entirely dependent upon her husband for economic support; and that the husband has an obligation to support his wife and children, at least as long as the marriage is in force.

We find the first type of rural community in Africa South of the Sahara, in many parts of South East Asia and in tribal regions in many parts of the world. We also find this type among descendents of negro slaves in certain parts of America.[37] The second type predominates in regions influenced by Arab, Hindu and Chinese culture.

Of course, this distinction between two major types of community is a simplification, like any other generalization about social and economic matters. This must be so because many rural communities are already in transition from one type of technical and cultural system to another, and in this process of change some elements in a culture lag behind others to a varying degree. For example, some communities may continue to have a fairly high incidence of polygamy or continue to follow the custom of paying bride price long after the economic incentive for such customs has disappeared as agricultural techniques changed.

In many rural communities hired labour is replacing the work of women belonging to the cultivator family. Where this happens, the economic incentive for polygamy may disappear, since additional wives are liable to become an economic burden. This, of course, is true only if it is assumed that the women who give up farm work retire into the purely domestic sphere. It is another matter if the women substitute farming by another economic activity such as trade.

In the type of rural community where women work hard, it is a characteristic that they are valued both as workers and as mothers of the next generation and, therefore, that the men keenly desire to have more than one wife. On the other hand, in a rural community where women take little part in field work, they are valued as mothers only and the status of the barren woman is very low in comparison with that of the mother of numerous male children. There is a danger in such a community that the propaganda for birth control, if successful, may further lower the status of women both in the eyes of men and in their own eyes. This risk is less in communities where women are valued because they contribute to the well-being of the family in other ways, as well as breeding sons.

Notes

* Some of the samples were taken in urban areas, where the incidence of polygamy is often, though not always lower than in rural areas.

† To evaluate correctly this figure for the incidence of polygamy it must be taken that some of the married men, at the time of the enquiry, had one wife only because they were at an early stage of their married life, while others were older men living in monogamous marriage because they had lost other wives by death or divorce. Therefore, the figure for the incidence of polygamy would have been considerably higher if it were to show the proportion of men who have more than one wife at some stage of their married life.

1 Appadorai, 19.
2 UN. ECA., *Wom. Trad. Soc*, 5.
3 Winter, 24.
4 Simons, 79–80.
5 Richards 1952, 204.
6 Little 1951, 141–2.
7 Little 1951, 141–2, 145.
8 Haswell, 10.
9 Georges, 18, 25, 31.
10 Galetti, 77.
11 Kaberry, 141.
12 Forde, 203; Dupire 1960, 79.
13 UN. ECA., *Polygamy*, 32.
14 Boutillier 1960, 120.
15 Little 1951, 133.
16 Baumann, 307; Forde, 45; Boutillier 1960, 97; Gosselin, 521.
17 Little 1951, 141; 1948, 11.
18 Forde, 75n.
19 UN. ECA., *Polygamy*, 24.
20 Mitchell, *Soc. Backgr.*, 80.
21 d'Aby, 49.
22 Winter, 23.
23 Arnaldez, 50.
24 UN. ECA, *Wom. N. Afr.*, 41; Appadorai, 18.
25 MiMi Khaing, 109; Swift, 271; Lévy, 264.
26 Mitham, 283–4.
27 Purcell, 295.
28 Izzedin, 299.
29 Tothill, 245.
30 Visaria, 334–71.
31 Visaria, 370.
32 Karve, 103–4.
33 Bhatnagar, 61–2.
34 Bhatnagar, 65.
35 Nath, May 1965, 816.
36 Majumdar, 61.
37 Bastide, 37ff.

References

Appadurai, A., *The Status of Women in South Asia*, Bombay 1954.

Arnaldez, Roger, "Le Coran et L'emancipation de la Femme", in Mury, Gilbert (ed.) *La Femme à la Recherche d'elle-même*, Paris 1966.

Bastide, Roger, *Les Amériques Noires*, Paris 1967.

Baumann, Hermann, "The Division of Work according to Sex in African Hoe Culture", in *Africa*, Vol. I, 1928.

Bhatnagar, K. S., *Dikpatura, Village Survey*, Monographs No. 4, Madhya Pradesh, Part VI, Census of India 1961, Delhi 1964, processed.

Boutillier, J. L., *Bongouanou Côte d'Ivoire*, Paris 1960.

Boutillier, J. L., et al., *La Moyenne Vallée de Sénégal*, Paris 1962.

d'Aby, F. J. Amon, "Report on Côte d'Ivoire", in International Institute of Differing Civilizations, *Women's Role in the Development of Tropical and Sub-Tropical Countries*, Brussels 1959.

Dupire, Marguerite, "Situation de la Femme dans une Société Pastorale (Peul Wo Da Be-Nomades du Niger)" in Paulme, Denise (ed.) *Femmes d'Afrique Noire*, Paris 1960.

Forde, Daryll, "The Rural Economies" in Perham, Margery (ed.), *The Native Economies of Nigeria*, London 1946.

Galletti, R., Baldwin, K. D. S. and Dina, I. O., *Nigerian Cocoa Farmers*, London 1956.

Georges, M. M. and Guet, Gabriel, *L'emploi du Temps du Paysan dans une Zone de L'oubangui Central 1959–60*, Bureau pour le Developpement de la Production Agricole, Paris 1961, processed.

Gouellain, R., "Parenté et affinités ethniques dans l'écologie du "Grand Quartier" de New-Bell, Douala in Southall, A. (ed.), *Social Change in Modern Africa*, London 1961.

Haswell, M. R., *The Changing Pattern of Economic Activity in a Gambia Village*, HMS London 1963, processed.

Izzeddin, Nejla, *The Arab World*, Chicago 1953.

Kaberry, Phyllis M., *Women of the Grassfields. A Study of the Economic Position of Women in Bamenda, British Cameroons*. Colonial Office, Research Publication No. 14, London 1952.

Karve, Irawati, "The Indian Woman in 1975" in *Perspectives, Supplement to the Indian Journal of Public Administration*, January–March 1966.

Katarikawe, E., "Some Preliminary Results of a Survey of Kiga Resettlement Schemes in Kigezi, Ankoll and Toro Districts, Western Uganda", *Research Paper Makerere University College*, R.D.R. 31, processed.

Lévy, Banyen Phimmasone, "Yesterday and today in Laos: a Girl's Autobiographical Notes", in Ward, Barbara E. (ed.) *Women in the New Asia, The Changing Social Roles of Men and Women in South and South-East Asia*, UNESCO 1963.

Little, K. L., "The Changing Position of Women in the Sierra Leone Protectorate", in *Africa*, Vol. XVIII, 1948.

Little, K. L., *The Mende of Sierra Leone. A West African People in Transition*, London 1951.

Majumdar, D. N., "About Women in Patrilocal Societies in South Asia", in Appadorai, A. (ed), *The Status of Women in South Asia*, Bombay 1954.

Mi Mi Khaing, "Burma, Balance and Harmony", in Ward, Barbara E. (ed.), *Women in the New Asia, The Changing Social Roles of Men and Women in South and South-East Asia*, UNESCO 1963.

Mitchell, J. Clyde, "Wage Labour and African Population Movements in Central Africa", in Barbour, K. M. and Prothero, R. M. (ed.), *Essays on African Population*, London 1961.

Mitchell, J. Clyde, *Sociological Background to African Labour*, Salisbury 1961.

Nath, Kamla, "Women in the New Village", in *The Economic Weekly*. May 1965.

Purcell, V., "Report on Burma, Thailand and Malaya", in International Institute of Differing Civilizations, *Women's Role in the Development of Tropical and Sub-Tropical Countries*, Brussels 1959.

Reynders, H. J. J., "The Geographical Income of the Bantu Areas in South Africa", in Samuels, L. H.(ed.), *African Studies in Income and Wealth*, London 1963.

Richards, Audrey I., *Land, Labour and Diet in Northern Rhodesia. An Economic Study of the Bemba Tribe*, London 1939.

Richards, Audrey I., *Economic Development and Tribal Change*, Cambridge 1952.

Simons, H. J., *African Women. Their Legal Status in South Africa*, Evanston 1968.

Swift, Michael, "Men and Women in Malay Society", in Ward, Barbara E. (ed.) *Women in the New Asia. The Changing Social Roles of Men and Women in South and South-East Asia*, UNESCO 1963.

Tothill, J. D., *Agriculture in the Sudan*, London 1954.

United Nations Economic Commission for Africa, "Polygamie, Famille et Fait Urbain (Essai sur le Sénégal)," *Workshop on Urban Problems*, Addis Ababa 1963, processed.

United Nations Economic Commission for Africa, "The Employment and Socio-Economic Situation of Women in some North African Countries," *Workshop on Urban Problems*, Addis Ababa 1963, processed.

United Nations Economic Commission for Africa, "Women in the Traditional African Societies," *Workshop on Urban Problems*, Addis Ababa 1963, processed.

Visaria, Pravin M., "The Sex Ratio of the Population of India and Pakistan and Regional Variations During 1901 – 61" in Bose, Ashish (ed.) *Pattern of Population Change in India 1951–61*, Bombay 1967.

Winter, E.H., "Bwamba Economy", *East African Studies*", No. 5, Kampala 1955.

27

"Sitting on a Man"
Colonialism and the Lost Political Institutions of Igbo Women

Judith Van Allen

In the conventional wisdom, Western influence has "emancipated" African women – through the weakening of kinship bonds and the provision of "free choice" in Christian monogamous marriage, the suppression of "barbarous" practices, the opening of schools, the introduction of modern medicine and hygiene, and sometimes, of female suffrage.

But Westernization is not an unmixed blessing. The experience of Igbo women under British colonialism shows that Western influence can sometimes weaken or destroy women's traditional autonomy and power without providing modern forms of autonomy or power in exchange. Igbo women had a significant role in traditional political life. As individuals, they participated in village meetings with men. But their real political power was based on the solidarity of women, as expressed in their own political institutions – their "meetings" (*mikiri* or *mitiri*), their market networks, their kinship groups, and their right to use strikes, boycotts and force to effect their decisions.

British colonial officers and missionaries, both men and women, generally failed to see the political roles and the political power of Igbo women.

The actions of administrators weakened and in some cases destroyed women's bases of strength. Since they did not appreciate women's political institutions, they made no efforts to ensure women's participation in the modern institutions they were trying to foster.

Igbo women haven't taken leadership roles in modern local government, nationalist movements and national government and what roles they *have* played have not been investigated by scholars. The purpose in describing their *traditional* political institutions and source of power is to raise the question of *why* these women have been "invisible" historically, even though they forced the colonial authorities to pay attention to them briefly. We suggest that the dominant view among British colonial officers and missionaries was that politics was a man's concern. Socialized in Victorian England, they had internalized a set of values and attitudes about what they considered to be the natural and proper role of women that supported this belief. We suggest further that this assumption about men and politics has had a great deal to do with the fact that no one has even asked, "Whatever happened to Igbo women's organizations?" even

From Judith Van Allen, 1982, "'Sitting on a Man': Colonialism and the Lost Political Institution of Igbo women", *Canadian Journal of African Studies*, 6(2): 165–81.

though all the evidence needed to justify the question has been available for 30 years.

Igbo Traditional Political Institutions[1]

Political power in Igbo society was *diffuse*. There were no specialized bodies or offices in which legitimate power was vested, and no person, regardless of his status or ritual position, had the authority to issue *commands* which others had an obligation to obey. In line with this diffusion of authority, the right to enforce decisions was also diffuse: there was no "state" that held a monopoly of legitimate force, and the use of force to protect one's interests or to see that a group decision was carried out was considered legitimate for individuals and groups. In the simplest terms, the British tried to create specialized political institutions which commanded authority and monopolized force. In doing so they took into account, eventually, Igbo political institutions dominated by men but ignored those of the women. Thus, women were shut out from political power.

The Igbo lived traditionally in semi-autonomous villages, which consisted of the scattered compounds of 75 or so patri-kinsmen; related villages formed "village-groups" which came together for limited ritual and jural purposes. Villages commonly contained several hundred people; but size varied, and in the more densely populated areas there were "village-groups" with more than 5,000 members.[2] Disputes at all the levels above the compound were settled by group discussion until mutual agreement was reached.[3]

The main Igbo political institution seems to have been the village assembly, a gathering of all adults in the village who chose to attend. Any adult who had something to say on the matter under discussion was entitled to speak – as long as he *or she* said something the others considered worth listening to; as the Igbo say, "a case forbids no one."[4]

Matters dealt within the village assembly were those of concern to all – either common problems for which collective action was appropriate ("How can we make our market 'bigger' than the other villages' markets?") or conflicts which threatened the unity of the village.[5]

Decisions agreed on by the village assembly did not have the force of law in our terms, however.

Even after decisions had been reached, social pressure based on consensus and the ability of individuals and groups to enforce decisions in their favour played a major part in giving the force of law to decisions. As Green[6] put it:

> (O)ne had the impression ... that laws only establish themselves by degrees and then only in so far as they gain general acceptance. A law does not either exist or not exist: rather it goes through a process of establishing itself by common consent or of being shelved by a series of quiet evasions.

Persuasion about the rightness of a particular course of action in terms of tradition was of primary importance in assuring its acceptance and the leaders were people who had the ability to persuade.

The mode of political discourse was that of proverb, parable and metaphor drawn from the body of Igbo tradition.[7] The needed political knowledge was accessible to the average man or woman, since all Igbo were reared with these proverbs and parables. Influential speech was the creative and skillful use of tradition to assure others that a certain course of action was both a wise and right thing to do. The accessibility of this knowledge is indicated by an Igbo proverb: "If you tell a proverb to a fool, he will ask you its meaning."

The leaders of Igbo society were men and women who combined wealth and generosity with "mouth" – the ability to speak well. Age combined with wisdom brought respect but age alone carried little influence. The senior elders who were ritual heads of their lineages were very likely to have considerable influence, but they would not have achieved these positions in the first place if they had not been considered to have good sense and good character.[8] Wealth in itself was no guarantee of influence: a "big man" or "big woman" was not necessarily a wealthy person, but one who had shown skill and generosity in helping other individuals and, especially, the community.[9]

Men owned the most profitable crops such as palm oil, received the bulk of the money from bridewealth, and, if compound heads, presents from the members. Through the patrilineage, they controlled the land, which they could lease to non-kinsmen or to women for a good profit. Men also did most of the long-distance trading which gave higher profit than local and regional trading which was almost entirely in women's hands.[10]

Women were entitled to sell the surplus of their own crops and the palm kernels which were their share of the palm produce. They might also sell prepared foods or the products of special skills, for instance, processed salt, pots and baskets. They pocketed the entire profit, but their relatively lower profit levels kept them disadvantaged relative to the men in acquiring titles and prestige.[11]

For women as well as for men, status was largely achieved, not ascribed. A woman's status was determined more *by her own achievements* than by the achievements of her husband. The resources available to men were greater, however; so that while a woman might rank higher among women than her husband did among men, very few women could acquire the highest titles, a major source of prestige.[12]

At village assemblies men were more likely to speak than were women; women more often spoke only on matters of direct concern to them.[13] Title-holders took leading parts in discussion, and were more likely to take part in "consultation." After a case had been thoroughly discussed, a few men retired in order to come to a decision. A spokesman then announced the decision, which could be accepted or rejected by the assembly.[14]

Apparently no rule forbade women to participate in consultations but they were invited to do so only rarely. The invited women were older women, for while younger men might have the wealth to acquire the higher titles and thus make up in talent what they lacked in age, younger women could not acquire the needed wealth quickly enough to be eligible.[15]

Women, therefore, came second to men in power and influence. While status and the political influence it could bring were achieved and there were no formal limits to women's political power, men through their ascriptive status (members of the patrilineage) acquired wealth which gave them a head start and a life-long advantage over women. The Igbo say that "a child who washes his hands clean deserves to eat with his elders."[16] But at birth some children were given water and some were not.

Women's Political Institutions

Since political authority was diffuse, the settling of disputes, discussions about how to improve the village or its market, or any other problems of general concern were brought up at various gatherings such as funerals, meetings of kinsmen to discuss burial rituals, and the marketplace, gatherings whose ostensible purpose was not political discussion.[17]

The women's base of political power lay in their own gatherings. Since Igbo society was patrilocal and villages were exogamous, adult women resident in a village would almost all be wives, and others were divorced or widowed "daughters of the village" who had returned home to live. Women generally attended age-set gatherings (*ogbo*) in their natal villages, performed various ritual functions, and helped to settle disputes among their "brothers."[18] But the gatherings which performed the major role in self-rule among women and which articulated women's interests *as opposed* to those of men were the village-wide gatherings of all adult women resident in a village which under colonialism came to be called *mikiri* or *mitiri* (from "meeting").[19]

Mikiri were held whenever there was a need.[20] In *mikiri* the same processes of discussion and consultation were used as in the village assembly. There were no official leaders; as in the village, women of wealth and generosity who could speak well took leading roles. Decisions appear often to have been announced initially by wives telling their husbands. If the need arose, spokeswomen – to contact the men, or women in other villages – were chosen through general discussion. If the announcement of decisions and persuasion were not sufficient for their implementation, women could take direct action to enforce their decisions and protect their interests.[21]

Mikiri provided women with a forum in which to develop their political talents among a more egalitarian group than the village assembly. In *mikiri*, women could discuss their particular interests as traders, farmers, wives and mothers. These interests often were opposed to those of the men, and where individually women couldn't compete with men, collectively they could often hold their own.

One of the *mikiri's* most important functions was that of a market association, to promote and regulate the major activity of women: trading. At these discussions prices were set, rules established about market attendance, and fines fixed for those who violated the rules or who didn't contribute to market rituals. Rules were also made which applied to men. For instance, rowdy behavior on the part of young men was forbidden. Husbands and elders were asked to control the young men. If their requests were ignored, the women would handle the matter by launching a boycott or a strike to force the men to police themselves or they might decide to "sit on" the individual offender.[22]

"Sitting on a man" or a woman, boycotts and strikes were the women's main weapons. To "sit on" or "make war on" a man involved gathering at his compound, sometimes late at night, dancing, singing scurrilous songs which detailed the women's grievances against him and often called his manhood into question, banging on his hut with the pestles women used for pounding yams, and perhaps demolishing his hut or plastering it with mud and roughing him up a bit. A man might be sanctioned in this way for mistreating his wife, for violating the women's market rules, or for letting his cows eat the women's crops. The women would stay at his hut throughout the day, and late into the night, if necessary, until he repented and promised to mend his ways.[23] Although this could hardly have been a pleasant experience for the offending man, it was considered legitimate and no man would consider intervening.

In tackling men as a group, women used boycotts and strikes. Harris describes a case in which, after repeated request by the women for the paths to the market to be cleared (a male responsibility), all the women refused to cook for their husbands until the request was carried out.[24] For this boycott to be effective, *all* women had to cooperate so that men could not go and eat with their brothers. Another time the men of a village decided that the women should stop trading at the more distant markets from which they did not return until late at night because the men feared that the women were having sexual relations with men in those towns. The women, however, refused to comply since opportunity to buy in one market

and sell in another was basic to profit-making. Threats of collective retaliation were enough to make the men capitulate.

As farmers, women's interest conflicted with those of the men as owners of much of the larger livestock – cows, pigs, goats and sheep. The men's crop, yams, had a short season and was then dug up and stored, after which the men tended to be careless about keeping their livestock out of the women's crops. Green reports a case in which the women of a village swore an oath that if any woman killed a cow or other domestic animal on her farm the others would stand by her.[25]

A woman could also bring complaints about her husband to the *mikiri*. If most of the women agreed that the husband was at fault, they would collectively support her. They might send spokeswomen to tell the husband to apologize and to give her a present, and, if he was recalcitrant they might "sit on" him. They might also act to protect a right of wives. Harris describes a case of women's solidarity to maintain sexual freedom:

> The men … were very angry because their wives were openly having relations with their lovers. The men … met and passed a law to the effect that every woman … should renounce her lover and present a goat to her husband as a token of repentance … The women held … secret meetings and, a few mornings later, they went to a neighboring [village], leaving all but suckling children behind them … [The men] endured it for a day and a half and then they went to the women and begged their return … [T]he men gave [the women] one goat and apologized informally and formally.[26]

Thus through *mikiri* women acted to force a resolution of their individual and collective grievances.

Colonial Penetration

Into this system of diffuse authority, fluid and informal leadership, shared rights of enforcement, and a more or less stable balance of male and female power, the British tried to introduce ideas of "native administration" derived from colonial experience with chiefs and emirs in northern Nigeria. Southern Nigeria was declared a protectorate in 1900, but it was ten years before the conquest was effective. As colonial power was established in what the British perceived as a situation of "ordered anarchy," Igboland was divided into Native Court Areas which violated the autonomy of villages by lumping many unrelated villages into each court area. British District Officers were to preside over the courts, but were not always present as there were more courts than officers. The Igbo membership was formed by choosing from each village a "representative" who was given a warrant of office. These Warrant Chiefs were also constituted the Native Authority. They were required to see that the orders of the District Officers were executed in their own villages and were the only link between the colonial power and the people.[27]

It was a violation of Igbo concepts to have one man represent the village in the first place and more of a violation that he should give orders to everyone else. The people obeyed the Warrant Chief when they had to, since British power backed him up. In some places Warrant Chiefs were lineage heads or wealthy men who were already leaders in the village. But in many places they were simply ambitious, opportunistic young men who put themselves forward as friends of the conquerors. Even the relatively less corrupt Warrant Chief was still, more than anything else, an agent of the British.[28]

The people avoided using Native Courts when they could do so. But Warrant Chiefs could force cases into the Native Courts and could fine people for infractions of rules. By having the ear of the British, the Warrant Chief could himself violate traditions and even British rules, and get away with it since his version would be believed.[29]

Women suffered particularly under the arbitrary rule of Warrant Chiefs, who were reported as having taken women to marry without conforming to the customary process, which included the woman's right to refuse a particular suitor. They also helped themselves to the women's agricultural produce, and to their domestic animals.[30]

Recommendations for reform of the system were made almost from its inception both by junior officers in the field and by senior officers sent out from headquarters to investigate. But no real improvements were made.[31]

Aba and The Women's War

The Native Administration in the years before 1929 took little account of either men's or women's political institutions. In 1929, women in southern Igboland became convinced that they were to be taxed by the British. This fear on top of their resentment of the Warrant Chiefs led to what the British called the Aba Riots, and the Igbo, the Women's War. The rebellion provides perhaps the most striking example of British blindness to the political institutions of Igbo women. The women, "invisible" to the British as they laid their plans for Native Administration, suddenly became highly visible for a few months, but as soon as they quieted down, they were once again ignored, and the reforms made in Native Administration took no account of them politically.[32]

In 1925 Igbo men paid taxes, although during the census count on which the tax was based the British had denied that there was to be any taxation. Taxes were collected without too much trouble. By 1929, the prices for palm products had fallen, however, and the taxes, set at 1925 levels, were an increasingly resented burden.[33] In the midst of this resentment, an overzealous Assistant District Officer in Owerri Province decided to update the census registers by recounting households and household property, which belonged to women. Understandably, the women did not believe his assurances that new taxes were not to be invoked. They sent messages through the market and kinship networks to other villages and called a *mikiri* to decide what to do.

In the Oloko Native Court area of Owerri Province, the women decided that as long as only men were approached in a compound and asked for information, the women would do nothing. They wanted clear evidence that they were to be taxed before they acted.[34] If any woman was approached, she was to raise the alarm and they would meet to discuss retaliation.

On November 23, the agent of the Oloko Warrant Chief, Okugo, entered a compound and told a married woman, Nwanyeruwa, to count her goats and sheep. She retorted angrily, "Was your mother counted?" Thereupon "they closed, seizing each other by the throat."[35] Nwanyeruwa's report to the Oloko women convinced them that they were to be taxed. Messengers were sent to neighboring areas. Women streamed into Oloko from all over Owerri Province. They massed in protest at the district office and after several days of protest at meetings succeeded in obtaining written assurances that they were not to be taxed, and in getting Okugo arrested. Subsequently he was tried and convicted of physically assaulting women and of spreading news likely to cause alarm. He was sentenced to two years' imprisonment.[36]

News of this victory spread rapidly through the market *mikiri* network, and women in 16 Native Court areas attempted to get rid of their Warrant Chiefs as well as the Native Administration itself. Tens of thousands of women became involved, generally using the same traditional tactics, though not with the same results as in Oloko. In each Native Court area, the women marched on Native Administration centers and demanded the Warrant Chiefs' caps of office and assurances that they would not be taxed. In some areas the District Officers assured the women to their satisfaction that they were not to be taxed and the women dispersed without further incident. But the British in general stood behind the Warrant Chiefs; at that point they interpreted the women's rebellion as motivated solely by fear of taxation and Oloko was the only area in which a Warrant Chief had directly provoked the women's fears of taxation by counting their property.

Women in most areas did not get full satisfaction from the British, and, further, some British district officers simply panicked when faced by masses of angry women and acted in ways which made negotiation impossible.

In most of the Native Court areas affected, women took matters into their own hands – they "sat on" Warrant Chiefs and burned Native Court buildings, and, in some cases, released prisoners from jail. Among the buildings burned were those at Aba, a major administrative center from which the British name for the rebellion is derived. Large numbers of police and soldiers, and on one occasion Boy Scouts, were called in to quell the "disturbances." On two occasions, clashes between the women and the troops left more than 50 women dead and 50 wounded from gunfire. The lives taken were those of women only – no men, Igbo or British, were even seriously injured. The cost of

property damage – estimated at more than £60,000, was paid for by the Igbo, who were heavily taxed to pay for rebuilding the Native Administration centers.[37]

The rebellion lasted about a month. By late December, "order" was somewhat restored but sporadic disturbances and occupation by government troops continued into 1930. In all, the rebellion extended over an area of six thousand square miles, all of Owerri and Calabar Provinces, containing about two million people.[38]

The British generally saw the rebellion as "irrational" and called it a series of "riots." They discovered that the market network had been used to spread the rumor of taxation, but they did not inquire further into the concerted action of the women, the grassroots leadership, the agreement on demands, or even into the fact that thousands of women showed up at native administration centers dressed in the same unusual way: wearing short loincloths, their faces smeared with charcoal or ashes, their heads bound with young ferns, and in their hands carrying sticks wreathed with young palms.[39]

In exonerating the soldiers who fired on the women, a Commission of Enquiry spoke of the "savage passions" of the "mobs," and one military officer told the Commission that "he had never seen crowds in such a state of frenzy." Yet these "frenzied mobs" injured no one seriously, which the British found "surprising."[40]

It is not surprising if the Women's War is seen as the traditional practice of "sitting on a man," only on a larger scale. Decisions were made in *mikiri* to respond to a situation in which women were acutely wronged by the Warrant Chiefs' corruption and by the taxes they believed to be forthcoming. Spokeswomen were chosen to present their demands for the removal of the Warrant Chiefs and women followed their leadership, on several occasions sitting down to wait for negotiations or agreeing to disperse or to turn in Warrant Chiefs' caps.[41] Traditional dress, rituals and "weapons" for "sitting on" were used: the head wreathed with young ferns symbolized war, and sticks, bound with ferns or young palms, were used to invoke the powers of the female ancestors.[42] The women's behavior also followed traditional patterns: much noise, stamping, preposterous threats and a general raucous atmosphere were all part of the institution of "sitting on a man." Destroying an offender's hut – in this case the Native Court buildings – was clearly within the bounds of this sanctioning process.

The Women's War was coordinated throughout the two provinces by information sent through the market *mikiri* network. Delegates travelled from one area to another and the costs were paid by donations from the women's market profits.[43] Traditional rules were followed in that the participants were women – only a few men were involved in the demonstrations – and leadership was clearly in the hands of women.

The absence of men from the riots does not indicate lack of support. Men generally approved, and only a few older men criticized the women for not being more respectful toward the government. It is reported that both men and women shared the mistaken belief that the women, having observed certain rituals, would not be fired upon. The men had no illusions of immunity for themselves, having vivid memories of the slaughter of Igbo men during the conquest.[44] Finally, the name given the rebellion by the Igbo – the Women's War – indicates that the women saw themselves following their traditional sanctioning methods of "sitting on" or "making war on" a man.

Since the British failed to recognize the Women's War as a collective response to the abrogation of rights, they did not inquire into the kinds of structures the women had that prepared them for such action. They failed to ask, "How do the women make group decisions? How do they choose their leaders?" Since they saw only a "riot," they explained the fact that the women injured no one seriously as "luck," never even contemplating that perhaps the women's actions had traditional limits.

Because the women – and the men – regarded the inquiries as attempts to discover whom to punish, they did not volunteer any information about the women's organizations. But there is at least some question as to whether the British would have understood them if they had. The market network was discovered, but suggested no further lines of inquiry to the British. The majority of District Officers thought that the men organized the women's actions and were secretly directing them. The Bende District Officer and the Secretary of the southern Province believed that there was a secret "Ogbo Society" which exercised control over women and was responsible for fomenting the rebellion.[45] And the women's demands that they did not want the Native Court to hear cases any longer and that all white men should go to their own country, or, at least, that women should serve on the Native Courts and one be appointed District Officer – demands in line with the power of women in traditional society – were ignored.[46]

All these responses fall into a coherent pattern: *not* of purposeful discrimination against women with the intent of keeping them from playing their traditional political roles, but of a prevailing blindness to the possibility that women had *had* a significant role in traditional politics and should participate in the new system of local government. A few political officers were "of the opinion that, if the balance of society is to be kept, the women's organizations should be encouraged alongside those of the men."[47] Some commissioners even recognized "the remarkable character of organization and leadership which some of the women displayed" and recommended that "more attention be paid to the political influence of women."[48] But these men were the exception: their views did not prevail. Even in the late 1930s when the investigations of Leith-Ross and Green revealed the decreasing vitality of women's organizations under colonialism, the British still did not include women in the reformed Native Administration. When political officers warned that *young men* were being excluded, however, steps were taken to return their traditional political status.[49]

"Reforms" and Women's Loss of Power

In 1933 reforms were enacted to redress many Igbo grievances against the Native Administration. The number of Native Court Areas was greatly increased and their boundaries arranged to conform roughly to traditional divisions. Warrant Chiefs were replaced by "massed benches" – allowing large numbers of judges to sit at one time. In most cases it was left up to the villages to decide whom and how many to send.[50] This benefitted the women by eliminating the corruption of the Warrant Chiefs, and it made their persons and property more secure. But it provided no outlet for collective action, their real base of power.

As in the village assembly, the women could not compete with the men for leadership in the reformed Native Administration because as individuals they lacked the resources of the men.[51] In the various studies done on the Igbo in the 1930s, there is only one report of a woman being sent to the Native Court and her patrilineage had put up the money for her to take her titles.[52]

Since the reformed Native Administration actually took over many functions of the village assemblies, women's political participation was seriously affected. Discussions on policy no longer included any adult who wished to take part but only members of the native courts. Men who were not members were also excluded, but men's interests and point of view were represented, and, at one time or another, many men had some chance to become members; very few women ever did.[53]

The political participation and power of women had depended on the diffuseness of political power and authority within Igbo society. In attempting to create specialized political institutions on the Western model with participation on the basis of individual achievement, the British created a system in which there was no place for group solidarity, no place for what thereby became "extralegal" or simply illegal forms of group coercion, and thus very little place for women.

The British reforms undermined and weakened the power of the women by removing many political functions from *mikiri* and from village assemblies. In 1901 the British had declared all jural institutions except the Native Courts illegitimate, but it was only in the years following the 1933 reforms that Native Administration local government became effective enough to make that declaration meaningful. When this happened, the *mikiri* lost vitality.[54] Although what has happened to them since has not been reported in detail. The reports that do exist mention the functioning of market women's organizations but only as pressure groups for narrow economic interest[55] and women's participation in Igbo unions as very low in two towns.[56]

The British also weakened women's power by outlawing "self-help" – the use of force by individuals or groups to protect their own interests by punishing wrongdoers. This action – in accord with the idea that only the state may legitimately use force – made "sitting on" anyone illegal, thereby depriving women of one of their best weapons to protect wives from husbands, markets from rowdies, or coco yams from cows.[57]

The British didn't know, of course, that they were banning "sitting on a man"; they were simply banning the "illegitimate" use of force. In theory, this didn't hurt the women as wife-beaters, rowdies and owners of marauding cows could be taken to court. But courts were expensive, and the men who sat in them were likely to have different views from the women's on wife-beating, market "fun" and men's cows. By interfering with the traditional balance of power, the British effectively eliminated the women's ability to protect their own interests and made them dependent upon men for protection against men.

Since the British did not understand this, they did nothing to help women develop new ways of protecting their interest within the political system. (What the women *did* do to try to protect their interests in this situation should be a fruitful subject for study.) What women *did not* do was to participate to any significant extent in local government or, much later, in national government, and a large part of the responsibility must rest on the British, who removed legitimacy from women's traditional political institutions and did nothing to help women move into modern political institutions.

Missionary Influence

The effect of the colonial administration was reinforced by the missionaries and mission schools. Christian missions were established in Igboland in the late 19th century. They had few converts at first, but their influence by the 1930s was considered significant, generally among the young.[58] A majority of Igbo eventually "became Christians" – they had to profess Christianity in order to attend mission schools, and education was highly valued. But regardless of how nominal their membership was, they had to obey the rules to remain in good standing, and one rule was to avoid "pagan" rituals. Women were discouraged from attending *mikiri* where traditional rituals were performed or money collected for the rituals, which in effect meant all *mikiri*.[59]

Probably more significant, since *mikiri* were in the process of losing some of their political functions anyway, was mission education. English and Western education came to be seen as increasingly necessary for political leadership – needed to deal with the British and their law – and women had less access to this new knowledge than men. Boys were more often sent to school, for a variety of reasons generally related to their favored position in the patrilineage.[60] But even when girls did go, they tended not to receive the same type of education. In mission schools, and increasingly in special "training homes" which dispensed with most academic courses, the girls were taught European domestic skills and the Bible, often in the vernacular. The missionaries' avowed purpose in educating girls was to train them to be Christian wives and mothers, not for jobs or for citizenship.[61] Missionaries were not necessarily against women's participation in politics – clergy in England, as in America, could be found supporting women's suffrage. But in Africa their concern was the church, and for the church they needed Christian families. Therefore, Christian wives and mothers, not female political leaders, was the mission's aim. As Mary Slessor, the influential Calabar missionary said: "God-like motherhood is the finest sphere for women, and the way to the redemption of the world."[62]

Victorianism and Women's Invisibility

The missionaries' beliefs about woman's natural and proper role being that of a Christian helpmate and the administration's refusal to take the Igbo women seriously when they demanded political participation, are understandable in light of the colonialists having been socialized in a society dominated by Victorian values. It was during Queen Victoria's reign that the woman's-place-is-in-the-home ideology hardened into its most recent highly rigid form.[63] Although attacked by feminists, it remained the dominant mode of thought through that part of the colonial period discussed here; and it is, in fact, far from dead today, when a woman's primary identity is most often seen as that of wife and mother even when she works 40 hours a week outside the home.[64]

We are concerned here primarily with the Victorian view of women and politics which produced the expectation that men would be active in politics, but women would not. The ideal of Victorian womanhood – attainable, of course, by only the middle class, but widely believed in throughout society – was of a sensitive, morally superior being who was the hearthside guardian of Christian virtues and sentiments absent in the outside world. Her mind was not strong enough for the appropriately masculine subjects: science, business, and politics.[65] A woman who showed talent in these areas did not challenge any ideas about typical women: the exceptional woman simply "had the brain of a man," as Sir George Goldie said of Mary Kingsley.[66]

A thorough investigation of the diaries, journals, reports, and letters of colonial officers and missionaries would be needed to prove that most of them held these Victorian values. But preliminary reading of biographies, autobiographies, journals and "reminiscences," and the evidence of their own statements about Igbo women at the time of the Women's War, strongly suggest the plausibility of the hypothesis that they were deflected from any attempt to discover and protect Igbo women's political role by their assumption that politics isn't a proper, normal place for women.[67]

When Igbo women with their Women's War forced the colonial administrators to recognize their presence, their brief "visibility" was insufficient to shake these assumptions. Their behavior was simply seen as aberrant. When they returned to "normal," they were once again invisible. Although there was a feminist movement in England during that time, it had not successfully challenged basic ideas about women nor made the absence of women from public life seem to be a problem which required remedy. The movement had not succeeded in creating a "feminist" consciousness in any but a few "deviants," and such a consciousness is far from widespread today; for to have a "feminist" consciousness means that one *notices* the "invisibility" of women. One *wonders* where the women are – in life and in print.

Understanding the assumptions about women's roles prevalent in Victorian society – and still common today – helps to explain how the introduction of supposedly modern political structures and values could reduce rather than expand the political lives of Igbo women. As long as politics is presumed to be a male realm, no one wonders where the women went. The loss of Igbo women's political institutions – in life and in print – shows the need for more Western scholars to develop enough of a feminist consciousness to start wondering.

Notes

1 The Igbo-speaking peoples are heterogeneous and can only be termed a "tribe" on the basis of a common language and a contiguous territory. They were the dominant group in southeastern Nigeria, during the colonial period numbering more than three million according to the 1931 census. The Igbo in Owerri and Calabar Provinces, the two southernmost provinces, were relatively homogeneous politically, and it is their political institutions which are discussed here. Studies in depth were done of the Igbo only in the 1930s, but traditional political institutions survived "underneath" the native administration, although weakened more in some areas than in others. There were also many informants who remembered life in the precolonial days. The picture of Igbo society drawn here is based on reports by two Englishwomen, Leith-Ross and Green, who had a particular interest in Igbo women; the work of a government anthropological officer, Meek; a brief report by Harris, and the work of educated Igbo describing their own society. Uchendu and Onwuteaka. See M. M. Green, *Igbo Village Affairs* (London: Frank Cass & Co., Ltd., 1947: page citations to paperback edition. New York: Frederick A. Praeger, 1964); J.S. Harris, "The Position of Women in a Nigerian Society", *Transactions of the New York Academy of Sciences*, Series II, Vol.2, No. 5, 1940; Sylvia Leith-Ross, *African Women* (London: Faber and Faber, 1939): C. K. Meek, *Law and Authority in a Nigerian Tribe* (London: Oxford University Press, 1957, orig. publ. 1937); J. C. Onwuteaka, "The Aba Riot of 1929 and its Relation to the System of Indirect Rule". *The Nigerian Journal of Economic and Social Studies.* November 1965; Victor C. Uchendu, *The Igbo of Southeast Nigeria* (New York: Holt, Rinchart and Winston, 1965).

2 Daryll Forde and G. I. Jones, *The Ibo- and Ibibio-Speaking Peoples of South-Eastern Nigeria* (London: International African Institute, 1950), p. 39; J. S. Harris, *op. cit.*, p.141.

3 Victor C. Uchendu, *op. cit.*, pp. 41–4.

4 *Ibid.*, p. 41; M. M. Green, *op. cit.*, pp. 76–9.

5 J. S. Harris, *op. cit.*, pp. 142–3; Victor C. Uchendu, *op. cit.*, pp. 34, 42–3.

6 M. M. Green, *op. cit.*, p. 137.

7 The sources for this description are Uchendu and personal conversations with an Igbo born in Umu-Domi village of Onicha clan in Afikpo division who, however, went to mission schools from the age of seven and speaks Union Igbo rather than his village dialect.

8 Victor C. Uchendu, *op. cit.*, p. 41.

9 *Ibid.*, p. 34; C. K. Meek, *op. cit.*, p. 111.

10 M. M. Green, *op. cit.*, pp. 32–42.

11 Sylvia Leith-Ross, *op. cit.*, pp. 90–2, 138–9, 143.

12 C. K. Meek, *op. cit.*, p 203; Victor C. Uchendu, *op. cit.*, p. 86.

13 M. M. Green *op. cit.*, p. 169.

14 Victor C. Uchendu, *op. cit.*, p. 410.

15 C. K. Meek, *op. cit.*, p. 203.

16 Victor C. Uchendu, *op. cit.*, p. 19.

17 C. K. Meek, *op. cit.*, p. 125; M. M. Green, *op. cit.*, pp. 132–8.

18 M. M. Green *op. cit.*, pp. 217–320.

19 Sylvia Leith-Ross, *op. cit.*, pp. 106–8.

20 M. M. Green, *op. cit.*, pp. 178–216.

21 *Ibid.*, p. 140; Sylvia Leith-Ross, *op. cit.*, pp. 106–7.

22 J. S. Harris, *op. cit.*, pp. 146–7.

23 *Ibid.*, pp. 146–8; M. M. Green, *op. cit.*, pp. 196–7; Sylvia Leith-Ross, *op. cit.*, p. 109.

24 J.S. Harris, *op. cit.*, pp. 146–7.

25 M. M. Green, *op. cit.*, pp. 210–11.

26 J. S. Harris, *op. cit.*, 146–7.

27 Daryll Forde, "Justice and Judgment among the Southern Ibo under Colonial Rule", unpublished paper prepared for Interdisciplinary Colloquium in African Studies, University of California, Los Angeles, pp. 9–13.

28 *Ibid.*, pp. 9–13; J. C. Anene, *Southern Nigeria in Transition*, 1885–1906 (New York : The Cambridge University Press, 1967), p. 259; C. K. Meek, *op. cit.*, pp. 328–30.

29 Daryll Forde, *op. cit.*, p. 12.

30 J. C. Onwuteaka, *op. cit.*, p. 274.

31 C. K. Meek, *op. cit.*, pp. 329–30; Harry A. Gailey, *The Road to Aba* (New York: New York University Press, 1970), pp. 66–74.

32 Information on the Women's War is derived mainly from Gailey and Perham, who based their descriptions on the reports of the two Commissions of Enquiry, issued as Sessional Papers of the Nigerian Legislative Council, Nos. 12 and 28 of 1930, and the Minutes of Evidence issued with the latter. Gailey also used the early 1930s Intelligence

Reports of political officers. Meek and Afigbo also provide quotations from the reports which were not, unfortunately, available to me in full. See Margery Perham, *Native Administration in Nigeria* (London: Oxford University Press, 1937); Idem, *Lugard: The Years of Adventure, 1858–1898* (London: Collins, 1956); Idem, *Lugard: The Years of Authority, 1898–1945* (London: Collins, 1960); A. E. Afigbo, "Igbo Village Affairs", *Journal of the Historical Society of Nigeria* 4: 1, December 1967.

33 Harry A. Gailey, *op. cit.*, pp. 94–5; C. K. Meek, *op. cit.*, pp. 330–1.

34 Harry A. Gailey, *op. cit.*, pp. 107–8.

35 Margery Perham, *Native Administration in Nigeria, op. cit.*, p. 207.

36 Harry A. Gailey, *op. cit.*, pp. 108–13.

37 S. O. Esire, "The Aba Riots of 1929", *African Historian*, Vol. 1, No. 3 (1965): 13; J. S. Harris, *op. cit.*, p. 143; Margery Perham, *Native Administration in Nigeria, op. cit.*, pp. 209–12.

38 Harry A. Gailey, *op. cit.*, p. 137; Margery Perham, *Native Administration in Nigeria, op. cit.*, pp. 209–12.

39 J. S. Harris, *op. cit.*, pp. 147–8; Margery Perham, *Native Administration in Nigeria, op. cit.*, pp. 207ff; C. K. Meek, *op. cit.*, p. ix.

40 Margery Perham, *Native Administration in Nigeria, op. cit.*, pp. 212–19.

41 *Ibid.*, pp. 212ff.

42 Harris reports a curse sworn by the women on the pestles: "It is I who gave birth to you. It is I who cook for you to eat. This is the pestle I use to pound yams and coco yams for you to eat. May you soon die!" See J. S. Harris, *op. cit.*, pp. 143–5.

43 Harry A. Gailey, *op. cit.*, p. 112.

44 Margery Perham, *Native Administration in Nigeria, op. cit.*, pp. 212ff; J. C. Anene, *op. cit.*, pp. 207–24; S. O. Euke, *op. cit.*, p. 11; C. K. Meek, *op. cit.*, p. x.

45 Harry A. Gailey, *op. cit.*, pp. 130ff.

46 Sylvia Leith-Ross, *op. cit.*, p. 165; Margery Perham, *Native Administration in Nigeria, op. cit.*, pp. 165ff.

47 Margery Perham, *Native Administration in Nigeria, op. cit.*, p. 246.

48 A. E. Afigbo, *op. cit.*, p. 187.

49 C. K. Meek, *op. cit.*, p. 203.

50 Margery Perham, *Native Administration in Nigeria, op. cit.*, pp. 365ff.

51 C. K. Meek, *op. cit.*, p. 203.

52 *Ibid.*, pp. 158–9. She was divorced and had to remain unmarried as a condition of her family's paying for her title as they wanted to be sure to get their investment back when future initiates paid their fees to the established members. If she remarried, her husband's family, and not her own, would inherit her property.

53 Sylvia Leith-Ross, *op. cit.*, pp. 171–2; Lord Hailey, *Native Administration in the British African Territories, Part III, West Africa* (London: H. M. Stationary Office, 1951). pp. 160–5.

54 Sylvia Leith-Ross, *op. cit.*, pp. 110, 163, 214.

55 Henry L. Bretton, "Political Influence in Southern Nigeria", in Herbert J. Spiro (ed.), *Africa: The Primary of Politics* (New York: Random House, 1966), p. 61.

56 Audrey C. Smock, *Ibo Politics: The Role of Ethnic Unions in Eastern Nigeria* (Cambridge: The Harvard University Press, 1971), pp. 65, 137.

57 Sylvia Leith-Ross, *op. cit.*, p. 109.

58 *Ibid.*, pp. 109–18; C. K. Meek, *op. cit.*, p. xv. Maxwell states that by 1925 there were 26 mission stations and 63 missionaries (twelve of them missionary wives) in Igboland. The earliest station was established in 1857, but all but three were founded after 1900. Fifteen mission stations and 30 missionaries were among Igbo in Owerri and Calabar Provinces. See J. Lowry Maxwell, *Nigeria: The Land, the People and Christian Progress* (London: World Dominion Press, 1926), pp. 150–2.

59 Sylvia Leith-Ross, *op. cit.*, p. 110; J. F. Ade Ajayi, *Christian Missions in Nigeria, 1841–1891: The Making of a New Elite* (Evanston, Ill.. The Northwestern University Press, 1965), pp. 108–9.

60 Sylvia Leith-Ross, *op. cit.*, pp. 133, 196–7, 316.

61 *Ibid.*, pp. 189–90. According to Leith-Ross, in the "girls' training homes ... the scholastic education given was limited, in some of the smaller homes opened at a later date almost negligible, but the domestic training and the general civilizing effect were good." Evidence of these views among missionaries can be found in J. F. Ade Ajayi, *op. cit.*, pp. 65, 142–4, G. T. Basden, *Edith Warner of the Niger* (London: Seeley, Service and Co., Ltd., 1927), pp. 13, 16, 33, 55, 77, 86; Josephine C. Bulifant, *Forty Years in the African Bush* (Grand Rapids, Mich.: Zondervan Publishing House, 1950), pp. 163 and passim; W. P. Livingstone, *Mary Slessor of Calabar* (New York: George H. Doran Co., m.d.), pp. iii–vi; J. Lowry Maxwell, *op. cit.*, pp. 55, 118.

62 W. P. Livingstone, *op. cit.*, p. 328.

63 Page Smith, *Daughters of the Promised Land* (Boston: Little, Brown and Co., 1970), pp. 58–76; Doris Stenton, *The English Woman in History* (London: George Allen and Unwin, Ltd., 1957), pp. 312–44.

64 Eva Figes, *Patriarchal Attitudes* (New York: Stein and Day, 1970); Ruth E. Hartley, "Children's Concepts of Male and Female Roles", *Merrill-Palmer Quarterly*, January 1960.

65 Walter E. Houghton, *The Victorian Frame of Mind, 1830–1870* (New Haven: The Yale University Press,

1957), pp. 349–53. Numerous studies of Victorian and post-Victorian ideas about women and politics describe these patterns. In addition to Houghton, Smith and Stenton, see, for example, Kirsten Amundsen, *The Silenced Majority* (Prentice-Hall, 1971): Jessie Bernard, *Women and the Public Interst* (Aldine-Atherton, 1971): John Stuart Mill and Harriet Taylor Mill, *Essays on Sex Equality* (University of Chicago Press, 1970); Martha Vicinus (ed.), *Suffer and Be Still: Women in the Victorian Age* (Indiana University Press, 1972); Cecil Woodham-Smith, *Florence Nightingale, 1820–1910* (McGraw-Hill, 1951). It was not until 1929 that all English women could vote; women over 30 who met restrictive property qualifications got the vote in 1918.

66   Stephen Gwynn, *The Life of Mary Kingsley* (London: Macmillan and Co., Ltd., 1932), p. 252. Mary Kingsley along with other elite female "exceptions" like Flora Shaw Lugard and Margery Perham, all of whom influenced African colonial policy, held the same values as men, at least in regard to women's roles. They did not expect ordinary women to have political power any more than the men did, and they showed no particular concern for African women.

67   See, for non-missionary examples, J. C. Anene, *op. cit.*, pp. 222–34; W. R. Crocker, *Nigeria: A Critique of British Colonial Administration* (London: George Allen and Unwin, Ltd., 1936); C. K. Meek, *op. cit.*; Mary H. Kingsley, *Travels in West Africa* (London: Macmillan and Co., Ltd., 1897); Idem, *West African Studies* (London: Macmillan and Co., Ltd., 1899); Margery Perham, *op. cit.*; A.H. St. John Wood, "Nigeria: Fifty Years of Political Development among the Ibos", in Raymond Apthorpe (ed.) *From Tribal Rule to Modern Government* (Lusaka, Northern Rhodesia: Rhodes-Livingston Institute for Social Research, 1960).

28

Virginity Testing

Managing Sexuality in a Maturing HIV/AIDS Epidemic

Suzanne Leclerc-Madlala

We are the organization which does virginity testing of girls from six years old up to marriage status. Initially we started from 12 years old but by doing so we found that half of the girls tested had already lost their virginity. The reason? Because most of them have been abused by their relatives – brothers, fathers, uncles and also cousins. That's why, as *Igugu Lama Africa*, we stand up and fight against those evildoers.

We Africans must work together to prevent sexually transmitted diseases and AIDS. I don't believe in Western civilization and culture as they say we must use condoms and contraceptives, which promotes adultery. That is why I believe in African culture. The nation must be proud and join this program as we, *Igugu Lama Africa*, have started to train the young girls to plant potatoes, cabbages, peas, lettuce, etc. Because if we work together the problem will be solved.

The above views were expressed in a letter to the editor of *The Natal Witness*, a leading KwaZulu-Natal daily newspaper in July 2000. Encouraging parents to send their daughters to join *Igugu Lama Africa*, the letter appeared barely a week before a protest march took place through the main streets of the provincial capital with teenaged girls and middle aged virginity testers waving placards to demonstrate their support for the revival of this practice. The virginity testing movement has been marked by controversy from its start in the mid 1990s, yet has continued to grow as communities seek to respond to a maturing HIV/AIDS epidemic and its deepening social impact.

As the AIDS epidemic has transformed from having been an epidemic of increasing HIV infection rates during the 1980s to become an epidemic of increasing AIDS morbidity and death from the mid 1990s onwards, the call for regular virginity testing of girls has made a concurrent public appearance. Widely accepted to be primarily a heterosexually transmitted disease, current estimates

From Suzanne Leclerc-Madlala, "Virginity Testing: Managing Sexuality in a Maturing HIV/AIDS Epidemic", *Medical Anthropology Quarterly* 15(4), pp. 533–53, 2001.

are that 4.7 million of South Africa's 40 million population is seropositive for HIV. In KwaZulu-Natal province, home to the large Zulu-speaking group, HIV infection rates have consistently led the country since the first major statistics from ante-natal screening in the late 1980s became available. The start of the new millennium has brought a dramatic increase in the number of people presenting themselves at local clinics and hospitals with AIDS-related illnesses, to the point where most provincial hospitals now routinely refuse to have AIDS patients take up valuable bed-space. Provincial mortuaries are likewise reporting problems of overcrowding and an abundance of un-claimed bodies, said to be related to the problem of AIDS. Two private hospitals have recently purchased refrigerated cold-storage trucks to help cope with the overflow of corpses before they are buried with a pauper's funeral at a hospital mass burial. Also, the question of adequate land available for burials on the scale predicted by town planners, has recently become of major concern to KwaZulu-Natal provincial administrators.[1] Alongside these growing concerns and increased acknowledgements of the seriousness of the AIDS epidemic, the State President has made known his support for the views of international scholars who oppose the view that HIV is related to AIDS. Newspaper reports speak of a pervasive 'national denial' over the enormity of the AIDS problem during an era that most people expected to reflect post apartheid promises of 'the good life'. With the South African government having recently won a much celebrated court case to allow for the manufacture and importation of relatively inexpensive anti-retroviral drugs, many observers perceive a type of schizophrenia that characterizes government engagement with and official stances on the ever-growing public health crisis of HIV/AIDS.

Adding to the confusing and contradictory nature of the government's position, the State President has been increasingly referring to the need to find 'African solutions' to the African AIDS problem. This reference has been interpreted by proponents of virginity testing as a clear indication that leaders at the very highest echelons of government could be counted on to support virginity testing or at least not to obstruct its rapidly growing practice. In broad terms virginity testing refers to the practice and process of inspecting girls to determine if they are sexually chaste. This paper considers virginity testing as a response to the growing HIV/AIDS epidemic among Zulu speaking people in KwaZulu-Natal province, where this trend is most widely practiced and where it currently enjoys a high degree of public and private support.

Competing Voices

While the most visible supporters of the virginity testing movement are older, mostly uneducated women, there is also a considerable pro-virginity testing lobby that consist of well educated men who are simultaneously key advocates of an 'African renaissance' movement.[2] This group includes amongst others, government ministers at both national and provincial level, officials in the departments of education and health, non-government organizations dedicated to the re-discovery of African traditions and indigenous knowledge systems, and directors of organizations that fund AIDS awareness projects. For this group of people, virginity testing represents a way to take current debates about Africanization and cultural revival out of the elite halls of academia and demonstrate applicability at the grass-roots level. By casting the discourse on virginity testing in the idiom of African renaissance these proponents draw upon strong emotive associations that link 'lost' traditions with a long history of cultural destruction caused by the concerted onslaught of Christianity, colonialism and apartheid.

While the pro-virginity testing lobby may be a broad, powerful, and vocal one, it is not without its distracters. These come in the form of an equally vocal (mostly female) group who comprise the Human Rights and Gender Commissions, as well as many women from various social formations who advocate greater gender equity. From the point-of-view of this group virginity testing is nothing less than a new form of violation and violence against women. They argue that this practice is counter to stipulations in the national constitution that uphold rights to privacy, bodily integrity, and outlaw all forms of gender discrimination. Indeed as a result of South Africa's 1999 Human Rights Report submitted to the United Nations, it was recommended that the S.A. government take specific steps to change traditional views advocating virginity testing in those communities where it occurs.[3]

The current debate on virginity testing in South Africa remains locked in a traditional/modern paradigm, whereby culture is equated with tradition and the democratic constitution is equated with western-style modernity that, in the opinion of many rural people, espouses foreign ideas. Seldom in the debates are the two perceived to share common ground. Much of the controversy that surrounds virginity testing in South Africa recalls the ongoing debate over female circumcision in other parts of Africa (e.g. Assad 1980, Boddy 1991, Gordon 1991, Gruenbaum 1982, 1996 and Obermeyer 1999). While the two practices are very different in nature, both are viewed as socially oppressive. While virginity testing is not generally perceived to be physically harmful in the same way as circumcision, this does not preclude South African women who are opposed to virginity testing from drawing similarities between the two practices. Based on her studies of female circumcision in Sudan, Gruenbaum (1996: 456) has argued that efforts to change this practice that neglect to analyze its causes and resort to 'tradition' as the sole explanation, are problematic. The complexity of decision-making processes within a culture and the competing demands on individuals are overlooked. This is where anthropologists can make a contribution; by discovering and explaining the meaning of such practices in their various cultural contexts and by analyzing issues of causality.

In this paper, I argue that virginity testing can be understood as a 'gendered' response to a local disease experience that is fundamentally 'gendered' in nature. Examining girls to determine their chaste status is another thread reinforcing a web of meaning that places women and women's sexuality at the epicenter of blame for the current AIDS epidemic amongst the Zulu. In addition, its growing popularity highlights the gendered impact of the epidemic whereby it is also women who are shouldering the burden of care for AIDS orphans. Virginity testing is the latest clause in an on-going gendered narrative of HIV/AIDS in KwaZulu-Natal.

Methodology

This study draws upon ethnographic data gathered between 1996 and 2000 in a predominantly Zulu-speaking, peri-urban, low-income community in Durban, South Africa. Participant-observation, in-depth semi-structured interviews and focus group discussions were the primary methods used for data collection. This period encompassed formal fieldwork for my PhD dissertation on sociocultural constructions of gender, sexuality and HIV/AIDS among Zulu-speaking people in KwaZulu-Natal. A brief summary of my major findings on the gendered nature of HIV/AIDS are presented in an effort to locate the current of the virginity testing movement and support my views on the symbolic meanings attached to this practice. As the trend in virginity testing started to gain wide popularity and media exposure in the province from late 1998 onwards, I extended my research to include a post-doctoral study specifically on virginity testing. This comprised mainly interviews with key informants in the virginity testing movement as well as observations made at virginity testing events that took place between January and September 2000. In addition, interviews were conducted with members of the Gender Commission who were in the process of facilitating workshops throughout the province in an effort to understand the growing appeal of virginity testing while at the same time disseminate their views that virginity testing was an abuse of human rights and against the national constitution.

Virginity Testing: The Current Practice

With whistles blowing and balloons swaying in the wind, 85 girls are waiting in a long line while grass mats are laid in a row on the ground. They hold their panties scrunched up in their hands, and range in age from 5 to 22. The participants appear quiet and nervous. Testing time has arrived. This particular virginity testing event was one of many weekend jamborees held at various football stadiums of local townships. The event opened with speeches by self professed traditionalists, who beseeched the crowd of mostly mothers and grandmothers, virginity testers and participants, and numerous on-lookers peering through the fences, with praises for long lost African traditions and reasons why these needed to be revived. Descriptions of an ideal problem-free past characterized the first speech, made by a middle-aged male academic well known as one of the inspirations behind the current virginity testing movement. The next two speakers were women, one an academic and virginity tester herself, and the other a popular radio personality and self-styled expert on Zulu culture.

Having set the tone for this *ukuhlolwa kwezin-tombe* (virginity testing) event, the content of the speeches was no doubt aimed at convincing the girls and their mothers that they were doing the right thing. In the words of the final speaker, this was going to bring an end to 'all these new diseases and the need to worry about contraceptives and condoms'. Moreover virginity testing was going 'to save the nation'. With an end to the whistle blowing, it was time to start the proceedings. The girls lay down in groups of 10 on the grass mats. The mother (and any accompanying female relative) was asked to come forward to observe and receive the results. While one tester chatted incessantly on a cell phone, the other checked the external genitalia while wearing rubber gloves. The same pair of gloves was used for all 85 girls. At this particular proceeding, there was not much in the way of internal inspection. These particular testers, who often work as a team, believe that internal inspection is not necessary to assess virginity. They depend more on external signs such as the color and texture of the labia (very light pink and dry said to be foremost signs of virginity) and look for signs of abuse (bruises and cuts) and STIs (pimples and sores and foul smelling discharge).

Within 45 minutes all 85 girls were checked, and all but three were declared to be virgins. The three who 'failed' the test were asked to step aside, and their mothers were told to bring the girls to a clinic for further advice. Those who passed were given certificates, once the mothers paid the required five rands. A whistle blew for the girls to stand up, and the mothers started to sing and dance. As they waved their daughters' certificates to and fro, the balloons were released into the air, and the newly declared virgins were encouraged to join the celebration dance. The event thus ended as the testers left the stadium grounds, and the buses and taxis arrived to take the girls and their families home.

Defining the terrain

Contemporary virginity testing events take place in a wide variety of settings that range from the privacy of the family home, the kraal of a village chief, school halls, community centers or large public sports stadiums such as the event described above. Although provincial-wide festivals initiated in the past several years receive much local media attention, they are far from the only sites where virginity testing is taking place. Most of these public festivals such as the now yearly *Nomkhubulwane* or 'first fruits' festival, have been revived in the name of African Renaissance, by individuals who have formed the aforementioned non-government organizations aimed at fostering a 'return to tradition'. *Isivivane Samasiko* is probably the best known of these organizations. Started in 1997, the founders of *Isivivane* see the revival of dormant Zulu customs such as virginity testing as a practical way to reclaim elements of culture that may help to solve modern day problems. *Isivivane* along with *AmaGugu aseAfrika, Isiggi seSintu*, and the All Africa Cultural Group are amongst the best known of the local post-apartheid cultural organizations that conduct virginity testing in the province. With ten million rands recently set aside by the government for the study and promotion of indigenous knowledge systems, all part of the African renaissance 'project', the future of such organizations is assured well into the future.

There is no overarching cultural formation/ organization controlling or coordinating the rapidly growing practice of virginity testing in KwaZulu-Natal. This is a source of concern for the larger organizations such as *Isivivane Samasiko* that would like to act as a type of controlling 'watchdog body'. Also, the provincial health department, while not officially advocating virginity testing is actively involved in assuring that proper health measures are taken during genital inspection (by providing rubber gloves and facilitating workshops to educate testers about female reproductive anatomy). They too profess a concern for the lack of control over the virginity testing process. Amongst the better known testers in the province, there seems to be a fair degree of rivalry, jealousy and, according to some, attempts to undermine each other's reputation and limit rival practices. One tester, who is widely proclaimed to be the inspiration behind the growing movement, claims to have started her practice as early as 1993, and to have personally inspected over 60,000 girls throughout the province. This tester is in much demand, claiming that her weekends are full as she moves from one urban stadium to a rural school and on to a church hall conducting virginity tests. Although she is employed by the Department of Traditional and Environment Affairs, she conducts virginity testing in her own time, as a private practice. The fee she charges for certificates is said to help cover her transportation cost only. Other testers mark the girls with a white paint dot on the forehead as an alternative to granting a certificate. Still others ask the girls to bring their own notebooks to record the date of testing along with their pass/fail 'mark'.

Most of the girls are sent to be virginity tested by their mothers. The question of whether or not these girls are coerced or forced to be tested against their wills is of primary concern to members of the Gender and Human Rights Commissions who condemn the practice. While some girls are sent to regional centres to attend the yearly 'first fruits' *Nomkhubulwe* festivals where hundreds of girls are tested, others are tested monthly in their own communities. In some rural areas chiefs host virginity testing at their kraals, and ask all parents of un-married girls to send their children. The names of girls found to have lost their virginity are given to the chief by the appointed tester, and the chief then demands a fine from the girl's father for 'tainting' his community.

While some virginity testers are eager to maintain a sense of professionalism with the belief that they have a special knowledge and ability to conduct the tests, others relate how they would like to educate all mothers to be able to 'check' their daughters themselves. One tester firmly stated that mothers should start checking daughters as soon as possible around the age of two or three, and do so on a daily basis. She stated: 'Just as you wash her body and comb her hair, you can check if she's still "clean" down there.'

The A, B, C's of Virginity

Western educational constructs of letter grades used to mark tests in schools, have been incorporated into some virginity testing practices. An 'A' grade is given to a girl who rates highly in all assessments associated with virginity. These assessments are derived from indigenous rather than biomedical knowledge. To properly understand virginity testing among the Zulu, one must be conversant in the metaphorical language used in the folk descriptions of human bodies and human bodily processes. Here, biomedical 'reality' and scientific 'truth' are of little import. What the testers look at and look for as evidence of virginity is framed within folk constructs of human bodies and ethnomedical beliefs of health and illness. This indigenous knowledge is a knowledge that is largely articulated through metaphor and symbolic representation. Its variance with a scientific knowledge articulated through empirically established 'fact' is to be expected. This is where communication falters between the 'modern' language of the Gender Commission and the 'traditional' language of the virginity testers and their supporters. The Gender Commission may argue that hymens can be broken through horse riding and vaginal lubrication varies throughout the menstrual cycle, but this is of little relevance to the virginity testers. Rather they talk about virginity being evident if there is a visible 'white dot' somewhere deep in the vaginal canal. The thin sheath covering that they sometimes call the hymen, is described as a 'white lacy barrier'. In the metaphoric language of one tester, the barrier that signifies virginity is 'similar to the lace of a wedding veil'. So eager are girls to pass their virginity test, that some are said to resort to pushing toothpaste high up into the vagina in an attempt to mimic the white lacey veil.

According to those testers who give letter grades for virginity tests, to achieve an 'A' a girl has to meet a combination of criteria. Most important are features of the genitalia. The color of the labia should be a very light pink, the size of the vaginal opening should be very small, the vagina should be very dry and tight, and the white dot or white lacey veil should be clearly evident and intact. In addition, a girl's eyes should reflect virginity in that 'they look innocent'. Her breasts and abdomen should be firm and taut and muscles behind her knees should be tight and straight.

A 'B' grade virgin is said to be someone who may have had intercourse once or twice, or alternatively 'may have been abused'. Active complicity in the sex act may mean the difference between a

'B' and a 'C' in the virginity test, but a girl who has been abused repeatedly is likely to get a 'C' grade. Labia of a 'B' grade virgin are a deeper shade of pink, the vaginal opening slightly bigger, vagina not so tight, and vaginal walls slightly lubricated. The white dot and lacey veil are said to show evidence of 'being disturbed' but testers are reluctant to describe exactly what this looks like. Given a 'B' grade, a girl's mother will be warned to watch her daughter closely because it is possible that someone has 'touched' her in an inappropriate way. Nevertheless the girl is declared a virgin, and a certificate is given.

A 'C' grade is essentially a failure. Here, the testers describe a vagina that is 'too wide and too wet'. No evidence of a white dot or veil can be found, and the girl's eyes betray her as someone 'who knows men'. Most virginity testers say that it is useless to do anything further for these girls as 'it is too late' and 'nothing will change them'. A minority of testers claim that they would counsel these girls and impress upon them the dangers of STIs, AIDS and pregnancy. At the virginity testing events attended by the author there was little evidence of any kind of counselling for any of the girls. To be given a 'C' grade for your virginity test is to be marked with shame and disgrace. Depending on the particular tester and the host of the event, the girl's family may be asked to pay a fine. In the words of one tester, the girl is now like a 'rotten potato', she must be kept away from the virgin girls, as her presence will surely 'spoil the bunch'. As a sexually active woman, she represents a danger to the virgins. Her loss of virginity is conceived as a contagion that would cause chaste girls to lose their virginity should they remain in close company with her. In the words of one tester, her proximity would 'cause the flowers of the nation to wilt'.

The Local 'Gendering' of AIDS

To understand the symbolic value that people place on virginity testing and to shed some light on the nature of the political and cultural work being done by advocating this practice as an AIDS intervention, it is necessary to consider some of the meanings and metaphors that people attach to HIV/AIDS and the AIDS epidemic more generally. Dominant narratives of blame for the HIV/AIDS epidemic among Zulu-speaking people in KwaZulu-Natal are framed within a common discourse on female sexuality. At both a physical and behavioral level an adult woman's sexuality is metaphorically conceived as 'dirty' and potentially dangerous if not properly harnessed and contained within socially defined moral boundaries of the patrilineally linked society.[4] Folk models of human bodies reflect and support an ideology that associates female reproductive biology with both positive and negative valences. On the one hand her body is the acknowledged site of male sexual pleasure and the 'nest' within which new members of the patrilineage are nourished, grown and brought forth. On the other hand women's bodies, once they become sexually active, conjure up notions of danger, disease and the ability to weaken men and bring all manner of misfortunate to society. In the process of making meaning out of the current AIDS epidemic, the Zulu draw upon some long-established notions of pollution associated with sexually active women and their bodies. Ngubane (1977) provides us with what is possibly the most comprehensive discussion on pollution ideas among the Zulu. She states that the concept of *umnyama* that essentially means darkness and refers to a state of 'ritual' pollution that is contagious and capable of causing illness and misfortune, is primarily associated with women (1977:76).

While much of the local ethnographic literature on notions of pollution contains analyses that make use of the idiom of 'ritual' pollution (see for example Bryant 1949, Krige 1950, Berglund 1976 and Ngubane 1977), there have been recent attempts to problematize the notion of pollution and explain its utility as an expression of ill-health more generally. Work by Jewkes and Wood (1999) among mostly Xhosa-speaking women in the Eastern Cape province of South Africa (an Nguni group closely related to the Zulu) is an example of this gendre of analysis. In their descriptions of reproductive health and illness, women informants referred to 'dirty' wombs that needed to be routinely 'cleaned' in an effort to maintain reproductive health. Concurring with my research among the Zulu, Jewkes and Wood demonstrate that Xhosa notions of 'dirt' and pollution are used as an idiom of disease and extend well beyond previous ethnographic analyses of 'ritual' pollution.

'Diseased' bodies

Pollution ideology that is representative of a general idiom of disease among the Zulu is often articulated today through the use of biomedical concepts such as germs and germ theory. For example, many previous writers on the Zulu describe taboos that once functioned to restrict activities of menstruating women, or women who had recently given birth, or miscarried. Krige (1950:188) tells us that a menstruating woman was once forbidden to enter the family cattle kraal or the family gardens, as it was believed that her presence would cause 'the udders of the cow to dry up and the crops to wilt on their vines'. Most notably, intercourse with such women had to be avoided as this was (and still is to some extent) believed to 'weaken' a man and cause him to be more prone to illness or other forms of misfortunes. Today, these notions resonate in the local discourse on AIDS. A woman's 'dirty' reproductive anatomy and related secretions (menstrual blood, vaginal discharges and lubrications in general), are viewed as reservoirs of HIV 'germs'. The 'bodily secretions' of the AIDS awareness campaigns that can 'weaken' the immune system and cause men to be more prone to illnesses are new ideas that have been distilled and filtered through long-established ideas of female pollution and the peril it represented for men. The particularity of women's bodies is associated with 'nesting' qualities where not only babies grow but where potentially deadly 'germs' including HIV 'grow' and 'hide'. In descriptions of HIV/AIDS transmission patterns and sexual networks, informants consistently represent the transmission of HIV/AIDS as 'unidirectional' from woman to man. An infected man is most often represented as a passive victim of a 'dirty' woman while an infected woman is represented as the active participant in acquiring her infection, due to her own behavior.

Descriptions of the vagina by both male and female informants call forth a negative imagery of a dark, damp and mysterious passage that opens up into the body, with secretions associated with sexual excess and disease. Dry vaginas are conceptualized as 'clean' and disease-free, the imagery reflecting the moral character of its owner. The wetness of the vagina is used as an index of both the degree of a woman's sexual activity and her potential for harboring sexually transmittable 'germs'. The wetter the vagina, the more sexually active the woman and the greater the number of 'germs' likely to be found 'sticking' to the vaginal walls. Germs for STDs and HIV in particular are believed to be somehow infused within vaginal secretions that assist the germs to 'stick' to the vagina. Here the STD and HIV 'germs' are said to 'wait' and 'grow', ready to 'infect' a partner during the act of intercourse. As a dark, moist, internal orifice, the vagina is metaphorically represented as a type of natural incubator for HIV/AIDS 'germs'. Present day constructions of HIV 'germs' have, to a large extent, derived meaning from a pre-existing cognitive frameworks that inform people's ideas about female impurity and the perils associated with 'dirty' women. In the process the current HIV/AIDS epidemic is giving renewed sustenance to deeply embedded notions that help supply the rationale for gender inequity.

'Diseased' behaviour

Combining with and re-inforcing up-dated meanings attached to female impurity are perceptions of modern women conducting themselves in a manner perceived as excessive and signifying a transgression of patriarchally defined moral boundaries. Commonly held views that women today are more sexually active than in the past, often taking the initiative to attract men and commence a sexual relationship, contribute to pervasive ideas that modern women are 'out-of-control'. Mothers of young women are almost unanimous in their opinion that young women today have lost all manner of dignity and self-respect. One woman with teenage daughters, two of whom had children, reflected general opinion when she stated the following: 'Look at our girls today. They are like lost sheep, or chickens, just poking here and there. For what? They think sex is nice, boyfriends are nice. What about these babies and new diseases? Our girls are a shame and disgrace!'

Controlling Female Sexuality: Past and Present

Beyond a general agreement that virginity testing was conducted in the past, there is a high level of uncertainty today regarding the past process, its frequency and the setting for conducting the test.

Nonetheless, debates on the origins and practice of virginity testing are rooted in the common assumption that virginity before marriage was once highly regarded and a socially regulated norm. These views are well supported by previous ethnographic studies of the Zulu including accounts by Lugg (1929) Gluckman (1935, 1940), Bryant (1949) Krige (1950, 1968), Vilakazi (1965), Berglund (1976) and Ngubane (1977). Traditional bridewealth practices reflected the importance placed on a girl's virginity. Cattle were used as the foremost form of brideweath transaction known as *ilobola*. The standard ten head of cattle could be supplemented by an additional head, the 'eleventh cow' if the girl was found to be a virgin. This cow was known as *inkomo kamama*, mother's cow, and was given to the girl's mother as a sign of thanks from the in-laws for providing them with a 'pure' daughter-in-law. Significantly, female genitalia are also referred to as *inkomo kamama*. Checking the about-to-be-married young woman to establish her chaste status was said to be the job of elderly female relatives of the girl's family with the prospective mother-in-laws as a witness.

While some informants today insist that girls were once subjected to routine inspection, there is little by way of ethnographic evidence to support this assertion. Rather, the ethnography highlights other forms of social control that helped to instill the value of pre-marital chastity. Talking to girls about the importance of maintaining virginity before marriage formed part of traditional puberty rituals known as *umhlonyane* (Krige 1968). This event ideally coincided with the commencement of a girl's menses, and was marked by ritual seclusion and instruction by elderly women on how to sit properly and generally how to conduct oneself with modesty and dignity. As a fertile young woman, she would soon be deemed ready for courtship. For this, she needed to be taught ways to ensure that she would not 'expose her mother's cattle', i.e. lose her virginity.

As she matured and boys began to show an interest in her, older female relatives, the sociological 'sisters' of the clan, were the ones said to be tasked with the duty of teaching the girl about *ukusoma*. This practice referred to intracrural sexual activity that did not include penetration. By holding her thighs tightly together, a young woman

could give sexual pleasure to a man. According to Vilakazi (1965) and others, sexual activity 'between the thighs' was socially acceptable. In this way a young man would be able to achieve sexual release and a young woman would be able to avail herself of his attentions (and thus demonstrate her love) but not 'expose her mother's cattle'. Nothing, neither in the ethnographic literature nor in contemporary interviews, is ever mentioned about the type of sexual release or pleasure that a young woman would derive from *ukusoma* activity. The overwhelming impression is that *ukusoma* was about pleasing men. It was the woman's responsibility to maintain the balance between giving men pleasure through her body and guarding her virginity until marriage.

While the extent of routine virginity checking of girls or young women in the past is difficult to deduce from written accounts of past practices, these accounts make clear that even if girls did not regularly submit to genital inspection, there was a high value placed on virginity and wide social interest shown in a girl's developing body. The practice of *ukushikila*, whereby a girl was expected to raise her skirt and expose her lower abdomen, back and front, upon the command of any adult family member, is one such example. Informants today say that this was done in an effort to assess the girl's degree of physical maturity and to determine her readiness for courtship and marriage. It was a way to regularly and quickly 'inspect the goods', and also used as an index of virginity. Along with widening hips that indicated sexual maturity, flabby stomachs and 'loose' buttocks were said to be signs of lost virginity. According to one prominent virginity tester today who is also a registered nurse, 'The stomach of a virgin is tight and taut. Buttocks are held high, they do not shake much when walking. *Ukushikila* was a way to check these things.'

There is also wide agreement amongst contemporary virginity testers that taut hamstring muscles behind the knees are also an indication of virginity. Some profess that virginity can be deduced by looking 'in the eyes'. One male university professor, who is not a virginity tester himself but advocates its revival, was adamant that 'you can know a virgin by looking at her eyes. The eyes don't lie.' The current debate as to whether or not routine checking of a girl's genitalia for signs of lost virginity was 'traditional' practice' is largely a moot point. What is important is the fact that a Zulu girl's developing sexuality and her pre-marital sexual behavior has always provoked keen interest in the patrilineally structured and patriarchally dominated Zulu society. Getting girls to lie flat on the ground, knees spread wide apart and panties clutched tightly in clenched fists, is simply a most poignant contemporary reminder of a long tradition of a social preoccupation with female sexuality.

Conclusion

In this paper I have attempted to locate and analyze the phenomenon of virginity testing as a response to a maturing AIDS epidemic that is consistent with local interpretive frameworks used to understand the disease. The growing popularity of testing can be understood as a social response to an HIV/AIDS epidemic that is deeply gendered in its meaning. With women and the particularies of their modern sexuality conceptualized as the source of AIDS disease and death, inspecting girls for signs of sexual activity represents an almost inevitable development in the on-going gendered narrative of AIDS in KwaZulu-Natal. According to the 'gendered' logic of this narrative, putting a halt to the sexual activity of unmarried women will put a halt to a multiplicity of problems being thrown up by the maturing AIDS epidemic, namely the growing numbers of sick and dying people and orphaned children. A gendered epidemic requires and demands a gendered response, which virginity testing represents.

It may be argued that virginity testing provides a new site for further dividing women and entrenching gender inequality. As members of the Gender Commission argue, the current practice of virginity testing is nothing less than another form of violation and violence against women. Yet while some aspects of womanhood are being 'silenced' through virginity testing, other aspects of women's experience are given expression. It is women themselves, older and married, who are promoting, organizing, and enthusiastically facilitating these events. For some of these women, virginity testing has become a lucrative profession as their services are being sought far and wide.

Virginity testing has emerged as a new way to empower older women in a society where women's voices have historically been muted, but where women (in their roles as mothers, grandmothers and mothers-in-law) have always held power and authority over younger women. Virginity testing re-asserts that power, and, in a province where unemployment reaches 50% in some townships, having the knowledge and skills to do genital inspection are abilities that are currently highly marketable.

After more than a decade of social science research on AIDS in Africa, there is a considerable body of literature that points to the role of deeply-entrenched gender inequalities in the reproduction of 'unsafe' sexual practices that assist the spread of AIDS (see for example Green 1988, Caldwell 1989, Ankomah 1992, Schoepf 1992, Ulin 1992, McGrath et al. 1993, Obbo 1993 and 1995, Orubuloye et al. 1993, Basset and Sherman 1994, Campbell 1995, Caldwell et al. 1999). Building upon these studies there is a growing body of literature by authors such as Baylies and Bujra (2000), Bujra (2000), Foreman (1999), Kiama (1999), Leclerc-Madlala (2000), Makhaye (1998), Omvodo (1996), Redman (1996), Setel (1996) and Tallis (2000) that points to the role of male sexuality and its performance and calls for more research on notions of masculinity and their implication for the spread of AIDS in Africa. There is a need to widen our agenda for research and intervention on AIDS to examine ways to target *both men and women* for greater mutuality in sexual relations. Drawing upon Ankrah's (1991, 1997) work, Tallis (2000:259) reminds us that until gender differences and power differentials are addressed explicitly, people cannot or will not use the knowledge they have acquired to protect themselves against HIV/AIDS.

In South Africa we need to ask why virginity until marriage is, in the first instance, such a near impossibility. Culturally prescribed gender scripts that legitimate sexual violence against women have been identified as lying close to the roots of the current AIDS epidemic sweeping South Africa (Preston-Whyte et al. 1991, Leclerc-Madlala 1997, Varga 1997, Wood and Jewkes 1997, Abdool-Karim 1998). In a country that also bears the distinction of having amongst the world's highest statistics for rape (Jewkes et al. 2001), making girls responsible for maintaining virginity diverts attention away from other forces that may be driving the epidemic, i.e. the whole other half of the heterosexual equation.

At both a conceptual and practical level, virginity testing is enacting (and I would suggest further entrenching) the gender inequality that is propelling the spread of HIV/AIDS. Lining up girls for genital inspection is a contemporary social drama that reflects long existing and deeply entrenched historical anxieties about the control of female sexuality that are linked to issues of fertility and social reproduction. As part of complex political and cultural work being undertaken in the second-phase post apartheid South Africa, the public enactment (and celebratory nature) of virginity testing serves to remind us that there is much interest in ensuring that gender power differentials and patriarchal privilege remain, much like the hymen, intact.

Notes

1 These problems have consistently been reported in the local press from late 1998 onwards. More recently the enormity of the strain that the epidemic is putting on the health care system has also featured in several articles of popular magazines, with titles such as 'Swamped by Dead Bodies' (*Drum*, 23 November 2000), or 'Burials Now a Booming Business' (*Sunday Tribune*, 23 April 2001).

2 The term 'African renaissance' as used in this paper refers broadly to the philosophy of reawakening and developing all that is essentially African. In his presidential inaugural address and in his book *Africa – The Time Has Come* (1998), President Thabo Mbeki spoke eloquently and convincingly on the need to rediscover, reassert and nourish indigenous African institutions, African values, and African ways, in order to propel South Africa and the rest of the continent into the 21st century. The concept of African renaissance has been widely embraced by black intellectuals especially, and the theme has come to be associated with the current era of the Mbeki administration as a type of national guiding philosophy.

3 This statement was made by the current Chairperson of the South African Human Rights Commission speaking at a virginity testing conference held in KwaZulu-Natal in June 2000. The speaker was trying to impress upon the audience of mostly rural women that their strong support for virginity testing was against all modern trends and laws that uphold the rights of women.

4 The ideas presented in this section are a condensation of a more in-depth study and more thorough analysis of notions of gender, sexuality, and AIDS among the Zulu that formed the basis of my PhD dissertation. In this paper I briefly discuss some of my major findings and present in broad strokes my arguments on how the sociocultural construction of AIDS in KwaZulu-Natal is deeply 'gendered' in its meaning. This is included in an effort to locate the current practice of virginity testing and support my argument that virginity testing represents a further development in the on-going gendering of AIDS in South Africa.

References

Abdool-Karim, Quarraisha
    1998 Women and Aids: The Imperative for a Gendered Prognosis and Prevention Policy. *Agenda* 39: 15–35.
Ankomah, A.
    1992 Premarital Sexual Relationships in Ghana in the Era of Aids. *Health Policy and Planning* 7(2): 135–43.
Ankrah, E.M.
    1991 AIDS and the Social Side of Health. *Social Science and Medicine* 32(9).
    1997 A Transformation Process: Gender Training for Top Level Management of HIV/AIDS Prevention in USAID/AIDSCAP Women Initiative. Washington DC.
Assad, Marie
    1980 Female Circumcision in Egypt: Social Implications, Current Research, and Prospects for Change. *Studies in Family Planning* 11(I):3–16.
Bassett, Mary and J. Sherman
    1994 Female Sexual Behaviour and the Risk of HIV Infection: An Ethnographic Study in Harare, Zimbabwe. Women and AIDS Research Program, Report Series No. 9, D.C. ICRW.

Baylies, C. and J. Bujra
2000 *AIDS, Sexuality and Gender in Africa: The Struggle Continues*. London: Routledge.

Berglund, Axel-Ivor
1976 *Zulu Thought-Patterns and Symbolism*. London: Hurst & Co.

Boddy, Janice
1991 Body Politics: Continuing the Anticircumcision Crusade. *Medical Anthropology Quarterly* 5: 15–17.

Bryant, A.T.
1949 *The Zulu People*. Pietermaritzburg: Shuter and Shooter.

Bujra, Janet
2000 Targeting Men for a Change: AIDS Discourse and Activism in Africa. *Agenda* 44: 6–23.

Caldwell, John, P. Caldwell, and P. Quiggin
1989 The Sexual Context of AIDS in Sub-Saharan Africa. *Population and Development Review* 15(2): 185–234.

Caldwell, John, P. Caldwell, J. Anarf, K. Awusabo-Asare, J. Altozi, I. Orubuloye, J. Marck, W. Cosford, R. Colombo, and E. Hollings, eds.
1999 *Resistances to Behavioral Change to Reduce HIV/AIDS Infection in Predominantly Heterosexual Epidemics in the Third World Countries*. Canberra: Health Transition Centre, Australian Nat. Univ.

Campbell, Catherine
1995 Male Gender Roles and Sexuality: Implications for Women's AIDS Risk and Prevention. *Social Science and Medicine* 41(2).

Foreman, Martin ed.
1999 *AIDS and Men*. London: Panos Publ/Zed Press.

Gluckman, Max
1935 Zulu Women in Hoe Cultural Ritual. *Bantu Studies* 9: 355–6
1940 The Kingdom of the Zulu in South Africa. In *African Political Systems*. Meyers Fortes and E. E. Pritchard eds. London: Oxford University Press.

Gordon, Daniel
1991 Female Circumcision and Genital Operations in Egypt and Sudan: A Dilemma for Medical Anthropology. *Medical Anthropology Quarterly* 5: 3–14

Green, Edward
1988 AIDS in Africa: An Agenda for Behavioral Scientists In *AIDS in Africa: The Social and Policy Impact*. A. Miller and R. Rockwell eds. New York: Mellen Press.

Gruenbaum, Ellen
1982 The Movement Against Clitoridectomy and Infibulation in Sudan: Public Health Policy and the Women's Movement. *Medical Anthropology Newsletter* 13(2): 4–12.

1996 The Cultural Debate over Female Circumcision: The Sudanese are Arguing this one out for Themselves. *Medical Anthropology Quarterly* 10(4): 455–75.

Jewkes, Rachel and Kate Wood
1999 Problematizing Pollution: Dirty Wombs, Ritual Pollution and Pathological Processes. *Medical Anthropology* 18: 164–86.

Jewkes, Rachel and Naeema Abrahams
2000 Violence Against Women in South Africa: Rape and Sexual Coercion (Review Study). Medical Research Council. Johannesburg.

Jewkes, R., L. Penn-Kekana, J. Lewin, M. Ratsaka and M. Schreiber
2001 Presidence of Emotional, Physical, and Sexual Abuse of Women is Three South African Provinces. *South African Medical Journal* 91: 421–8.

Kiama, W.
1999 Men who have sex with Men in Kenya. In *AIDS and Men*. M. Foreman ed. London: Panos Publ/Zed Press.

Krige, Eileen J.
1950 *The Social System of the Zulu* (2nd ed.) London: Longmans, Green and Co.
1968 Girls' Puberty Songs and Their Relation to Fertility, Health, Morality and Religion Among the Zulu. *Africa* 38: 173–98.

Leclerc-Madlala, Suzanne
1997 Infect One, Infect All : Zulu Youth Response to the AIDS Epidemic in South Africa. *Medical Anthropology* 17: 363–80
1999 Demonizing Women in the Era of AIDS: An Analysis of the Sociocultural Construction of HIV/AIDS in KwaZulu-Natal. PhD Dissertation, University of Natal, Durban.
2000 The Silences that Nourish AIDS in Africa. *Mail and Guardian* August 11–17.

Lugg, H.
1929 Agricultural Ceremonies in Natal and Zululand. *Bantu Studies* 3: 357–383

Makhaye, G.
1998 Shosholoza's Goal: Educate Men in Soccer. *Agenda* 39

Mbeki, Thabo
1998 *Africa – The Time Has Come*. Cape Town: Tafelberg Press.

McGrath, Janet et al.
1993 Anthropology and AIDS: The Cultural Context of Sexual Risk Behavior Among Urban Women in Kampala, Uganda. *Social Science and Medicine* 36(4): 429–39.

Ngubane, Harriet
1977 *Body and Mind in Zulu Medicine*. London: Academic Press.

Obbo, Christine
1993 HIV Transmission: Men Are the Solution. *Population and Environment* 14(3): 211–43.
1995 Gender, Age and Class: Discourses on HIV Transmission and Control in Uganda. In *Culture and Sexual Risk: Anthropological Perspectives on AIDS*, H.T. Brummelhuis and G. Herdt, eds. Amsterdam: Gordon and Breach.

Obermeyer, Carol M.
1999 Female Genital Surgeries: The Known, the Unknown and the Unknowable. *Medical Anthropology Quarterly* 13(1): 79–106.

Omvodo, D.
1996 Africa Takes a More Male-Friendly Approach to Family Planning. *AIDS Analysis Africa* 6(6): 4–6.

Orubuloye, I., J. Caldwell, and P. Caldwell
1993 African Women's Control Over their Sexuality in an Era of AIDS. *Social Science and Medicine* 37(7): 859–75.

Preston-Whyte, Eleanor, Quarraisha Abdool-Karim and Maria Zondi
1991 Women and AIDS: The Triple Imperative. *Critical Health* 34: 42–7.

Redman, P.
1996 Empowering Men to Disempower Themselves: Heterosexual Masculinities, HIV and the Contradictions of Anti-oppressive Education. In *Understanding Masculinities*, M. MacanGhail ed. Buckingham: Open University Press.

Schoepf, Beth
1992 Women at Risk: Case Studies from Zaire. In *The Time of AIDS: Social Analysis, Theory and Method*, G.H. Herdt and S. Linderbaum, eds. Newbury Park, CA: Sage.

Setel, P.
1996 AIDS as a Paradox of Manhood and Development in Kilimanjaro, Tanzania. *Social Science and Medicine* 43(8): 1168–78.

Tallis, Vicci
2000 Gendering the Response to HIV/AIDS: Challenging Gender Inequality. *Agenda* 44: 58–66.

Ulin, P.
1992 African Women and AIDS: Negotiating Behavioural Change. *Social Science and Medicine* 34(1): 63–73.

Varga, Christine
1997 Sexual Decision Making and Negotiations in the midst of AIDS: Youth in KwaZulu-Natal. *Health Transition Review* 7(2): 13–40.

Vilakazi, Absolon
1965 *Zulu Transformations: A Study of the Dynamics of Social Change*. Pietermaritzburg: University of Natal Press.

Weeks, Jeffrey
1991 *Against Nature: Essays on History, Sexuality and Identity*. London: Rivers Oram.

Wood, Kate and Rachel Jewkes
1997 Violence, Rape and Sexual Coercion: Everyday Love in a South African Township. *Gender and Development* 5(2).

Part IX

Europe in Africa: Colonization

Congo Français.— La St Auguste à Loango.

Introduction

By the time of colonization, in the late 1800s, Europeans had already been in close contact with Africans for hundreds of years. For example, by the eighth century, the Islamic world included parts of north and eastern Africa, leather and bead goods arrived in southern Europe from Africa as early as the thirteenth century, and Portuguese traders opened up trade routes in central southern Africa, along the Zambezi river, in 1511. Dutch settlers, later called Afrikaners (or "Boers"), arrived in southern Africa in 1652, when the Dutch East India Company established itself there, and throughout the seventeenth, eighteenth and nineteenth centuries, following the European conquest of the New World, Dutch, French and British traders and settlers in the Americas looked to Africa as their source of slave labor.

Why did Europeans go to Africa? And once they went, why did they decide to colonize? Clearly there were economic, political and military reasons for establishing contacts, as the European empire sought to secure more and more of the world for its economic and political gains. For example, the British heavily invested in India as part of the British Empire. To get to India, where there was a rich trade in spices, and where thousands of British citizens lived and worked, one had to go around Africa past the Cape of Good Hope at the southern tip of the continent, or through the Suez Canal. Because the British wanted to protect their economic supply route, they became active in colonizing the regions that controlled the two pathways, and even intervened in military activities that affected them (for example, defending the Ottoman Empire against Russia during the late 1870s since the Ottoman Empire at that time bordered the route through the Red Sea).

When the Industrial Revolution began in Western Europe, huge amounts of capital became available for investment in Africa, and Africa became a source of new materials for Europe. During the late 1800s, for example, King Leopold II of Belgium financed his own private corporation (the Congo Free State) by exploiting rich rubber and ivory resources in what is today Democratic Republic of Congo. Colonization – permanent settlement and incorporation into the political, economic, and social system of the parent country – rather than simply exploitation, helped to secure the African lands as parts of an empire. It must be noted, however, that empire was not always profitable (Fieldhouse, 1984). Leopold, for example, lost huge sums of money when the central African rubber supply was exhausted (Grinker, 1994: 31; Jewsiewicki, 1983: 99). The growth of science during the enlightenment, including research on racial categories, was an additional motivator for travel to Africa, and was in many ways linked with missionary expedition and settlement. If the world was the creation of God, then science sought to reveal the complexity of God's world. That work necessitated categorizing and studying, as well as converting, human beings in all their physical and cultural forms. Finally, increased medical knowledge during the nineteenth century made it possible for Europeans to travel to Africa without large numbers of casualties due to tropical disease. Although Europeans may have wanted to go to Africa in greater numbers and for more lengthy periods of time, they could not do so safely until the cause of malaria was discovered in the 1840s, and it was discovered that quinine worked as a prophylactic against the malaria parasites. Still, for quite some time West Africa was known in Europe as "the white man's grave."

By 1885, a "scramble for Africa" began in which different European nations, namely, Portugal, Holland, Germany, Belgium, France and England, sought to carve up Africa as integral parts of its empires. Much like a jigsaw puzzle, Europeans at the Berlin Conference of 1884–5 made decisions on paper about which piece belonged to which nation, constructing borders in what appeared at times almost arbitrary fashion, often right through the center of particular ethnic group territories. Colonization became necessary as Europeans competed for control over the territories. Article 35 of the Berlin Act, signed during the conference (Uzoigwe, 1990: 15), stipulated that "an occupier of any such coastal possessions had also to demonstrate that it possessed sufficient 'authority' there 'to protect existing rights, and, as the case may be, freedom of trade and of transit under the conditions agreed upon'."

The social impact of the mapping on Africa and Africans was profound. The Bakongo, for example, became subjects in Portuguese, French, and Belgian colonies; and the Azande became subjects in British and Belgian colonies. Although decided by European powers more than a century ago, almost all of these borders, and the separation of ethnic groups into two or more distinct nation-states, are maintained today in independent, postcolonial, Africa. The Berlin conference thus illuminates how map-making has long been an essential part of political domination.

Although all of the colonizers participated in the Berlin conference, it would be quite misleading to think that the term "colonization" characterizes all of the activities of all Europeans in Africa during the so-called "colonial period," for there are many different kinds of colonizations, the variability determined by the culture and history of the colonizers as well as the types of societies and economies they colonized. Not only were there vast differences in how one country, such as England, colonized places as different as Nigeria and Swaziland, not to mention the differences between India and most African territories, but France, England, Portugal and Germany, among others, had distinct methods of domination. England followed Frederick Lugard's directives, some of which are included in the reading by Lugard in this part, to act paternalistically as the trustee of the colonized, and to rule *indirectly*. This meant that local African officials would mediate between the British and the people. Indirect rule was a practical alternative to direct rule, especially because in some places there were simply too few British to act as administrators, and because the British knew from previous experiences that it was impossible to abolish completely African political and social organizations, and so they needed to work with them rather than against them. With the exception of North Africa, the French and Portuguese, in contrast, sought to rule more directly over their subjects, treating local officials more as compliant subjects than as administrators.

Perhaps the most important and influential document on colonial rule, Lugard's "Dual Mandate" outlined the method of indirect rule, the legitimation of "native authority," and the system of taxation. Taxes, Lugard wrote, formed "the basis of the whole system" (1922: 201), and thus constituted the development of both colonial bureaucracies and new categories of persons – colonial elites – who stood outside the pre-existing class structures of African societies. As Betts and Asiwaju (1990: 149) note:

> The tax system was the one which most obviously encouraged the bureaucratic development of colonial rule. It assigned a common function to the administrator and the African chief, who, in assessing and collecting the tax, often in conjunction with local councils of elders or notables, reminded everyone of the regulatory power of the new system. Furthermore, after tax collectors as such, there soon appeared administrative agents who became part of the new colonial elite.

In the long history of Africa, the period of colonial rule from the 1880s to the 1960s may seem minuscule. Yet, colonialism had a profound impact on the present and future lives of all Africans – as well as on the present and future lives of the colonists. Indeed, there is a single point so obvious that it is often overlooked: colonialism not only produced the colonized, it also produced colonizers (Weiskel, 1980; Comaroff and Comaroff, 1991; Thomas, 1994). The essays included in this part highlight the complex relations between Europe and Africa during the colonial period. They also help us see that the effects of colonialism constitute a legacy that extends far beyond the historical point at which it ended, and when African nations became officially independent (Stoller, 1995). Walter Rodney's essay, for example, boldly details the oppressive effects of capitalism on African societies, but makes clear that European imperial capital was nothing *without* Africa. In a famous quotation, Frantz Fanon (1963, p. 102) says: "Europe is literally the creation of the third world." Ranger shows how Britain invented Africa, often in its own image, an argument paralleled closely in Chapter 1 by Jean and John Comaroff.

One of the common and misleading assumptions about the colonization of Africa is that it was primarily a process of conquer and rule. Certainly, that is a fair characterization as countless Africans died from European military campaigns, various other atrocities, and diseases introduced from Europe. Although these forms of domination are the easiest to see, they sometimes mask other forms of domination, exploitation, and oppression that are subtle, even elusive, and pernicious. These are the modes of power that radically change people's awareness of themselves and others, that have profound psychological implications, and forever alter the meaning of one's culture. Jean and John Comaroff (1991: 15) thus write, "The point, now commonplace, is that the essence of colonization inheres less in political overrule than in seizing and transforming 'others' by the very act of conceptualizing, inscribing, and interacting with them on terms not of their own choosing."

An example of such hegemony, used by the Comaroffs and by the editors of this volume, is the discussion between Livingstone and the rain doctor (see Chapter 15), in which the rain doctor is fashioned into a scientist of sorts, who must adopt the discourse of the colonizer, and cannot be evaluated in his own terms, according to his own worldview. Other examples can be found in the Africans' denigration of their own culture and glorification of European culture, in the abandonment of local forms of religion and the embracing of Christianity and other imported belief systems, and the priority so often given to Western forms of medicine over African medicines that have been efficacious for centuries. As additional examples, the "nation" becomes the natural unit of political organization, novelists and poets write in European languages and thus not in the languages in which they may actually think and feel, and the notions of Africa and blackness become reified as things that actually exist in the world, rather than as cultural constructions that emerged out of European contact. African history is long and ancient, but Africans have frequently been made to feel that their history began when Europeans arrived at their shores.

Along with the Comaroffs, it is useful to distinguish between two forms of power relation, "ideology" and "hegemony." The former might refer to agentive power, in which there is an identifiable instrument of power that speaks, coerces, expresses itself openly and directly. Ideologies are thus contestable, because that which is said, known, and recognized, can also be argued against. Hegemony, on the other hand, can refer to relations of power that are elusive, unrecognized, taken for granted, and therefore all the more powerful and uncontestable.

> Power also presents, or rather hides, itself in the forms of everyday life. Sometimes ascribed to transcendental, suprahistorical forces (gods or ancestors, nature or physics, biological instinct or probability), these forms are not easily questioned. Being "natural" and "ineffable," they seem to be beyond human agency, notwithstanding the fact that the interests they serve may be all too human. This kind of *nonagentive* power proliferates outside the realm of institutional politics, saturating such things as aesthetics and ethics, built form and bodily representation, medical knowledge and mundane usage. What is more, it may not be experienced as power at all, since its effects are rarely wrought by overt compulsion. They are internalized, in their negative guise, as constraints; in their neutral guise, as conventions; and, in their positive guise, as values. Yet the silent power of the sign, the unspoken authority of habit, may be as effective as the most violent coercion in shaping, directing, even dominating social thought and action. (Comaroff and Comaroff, 1991: 22)

When we say that categories and identities are constructed or invented through forms of power, it is not to say that they are false or unreal, only that they are not essential, natural, or outside of culture and history. The categories are so well constructed, in fact – so hegemonic – that they appear to be natural and true. We usually do not question that people are organized into male and female, although we know that human beings could organize the world otherwise; many English speakers do not question that the neutral pronoun in English is "he"; and few people question that the nation is the natural, or normal, unit of political organization in the world.

Truth is established often through power directed upon the body, whether through medicine, capitalism's labor, religion, or racism. These truth regimes, as Michel Foucault called them, destroy the possibility of even asking whether those truths are valid or not – because the method of evaluating validity is bound up with the forms and techniques of power that created the so-called truth. It is as if we determine the outcome of a medical malpractice case in court on the basis of what six out of ten doctors say. What is most disturbing about all of this is that, if Foucault is right, then power is capillary, everywhere moving in all directions. There is no agent to resist because we are all agents. The jailer, as he puts it, is as much a subject of surveillance, knowledge, and power as the prisoner. Ngugi wa Thiong'o leads us precisely in this direction, as he argues that many Africans – the colonial elite – unwittingly became simultaneously subjects and agents of power; that is, they became the instruments of the same hegemonic forces that constructed them. Ngugi's examples, combined with those of Ranger and Rodney, help us to see the great force of colonialism, its lasting strength and malignancy.

References

Betts, R.F. and A.I. Asiwaju. 1990. "Methods and Institutions of European Domination." In A. Adu Boahen, ed., *General History of Africa, Vol. VII: Africa under Colonial Domination, 1880–1935*, pp. 143–52. Berkeley and Los Angeles: University of California Press.

Comaroff, Jean and John Comaroff. 1991. *Of Revelation and Revolution, Vol. 1: Christianity, Colonialism, and Consciousness in South Africa*. Chicago: University of Chicago Press.

Fanon, Frantz. 1963. *The Wretched of the Earth*. New York: Grove Press.

Fieldhouse, Dennis K. 1984. *Economics and Empire, 1830–1914*. New York: Macmillan.

Grinker, Roy Richard. 1994. *Houses in the Rain Forest: Ethnicity and Inequality among Farmers and Foragers in Central Africa*. Berkeley: University of California Press.

Jewsiewicki, Bogumil. 1983. "Rural Society and the Belgian Colonial Economy". In David Birmingham and Phyllis Martin, eds., *The History of Central Africa*, vol. 2. pp. 95–125. London: Longman.

Lugard, Frederick. 1922. *The Dual Mandate in Tropical Africa*. London: Blackwood.

Stoller, Paul. 1995. *Embodying Colonial Memories: Spirit Possession, Power and the Hauka in West Africa*. New York and London: Routledge.

Thomas, Nicholas. 1994. *Colonialism's Culture: Anthropology, Travel, and Government*. Princeton: Princeton University Press.

Uzoigwe, G.N. 1990. "European Partition and Conquest of Africa: An Overview." In A. Adu Boahen, ed., *General History of Africa, Vol. VII: Africa under Colonial Domination, 1880–1935*, pp. 10–24. Berkeley and Los Angeles: University of California Press.

Weiskel, Timothy. 1980. *French Colonial Rule and the Baule Peoples: Resistance and Collaboration, 1889–1911*. Oxford: Clarendon Press.

Suggested Reading

Ajayi, J. 1968. "The Continuity of African Institutions under Colonialism." In T.O. Ranger, ed., *Emerging Themes in African History*. Proceedings of the International Congress of African Historians, Dar es Salaam, 1965. Nairobi and London: East African Publishing House. Distributed by Northwestern University Press.

Apter, Andrew. 1999. "Africa, Empire, and Anthropology: Philological Exploration of Anthropology's Heart of Darkness." *Annual Review of Anthropology* 28: 577–98.

Asad, Talal. 1975. *Anthropology and the Colonial Encounter*. London: Ithaca Press.

Atkins, Keletso. 1989. *The Moon Is Dead! Give us Money! The Cultural Origins of an African Work Ethic, Natal, South Africa, 1843–1900*. London: James Currey.

Balandier, George. "The Colonial Situation." In Pierre L. Van de Berghe, ed., *Africa: Social Problems of Change and Conflict*. San Francisco, CA: Chandler.

Blout, J.M. 1993. *The Colonizer's Model of the World: Diffusionism and Eurocentric History*. New York: Guilford.

Boahen, A. Adu. 1987. *African Perspectives on Colonialism*. Baltimore: Johns Hopkins University Press.

Buckley, Liam. 2005. "Objects of Love and Decay: Colonial Photographs in a Postcolonial Archive." *Cultural Anthropology* 20(2): 249–70.

Callaway, Helen. 1992. "Dressing for Dinner in the Bush: Rituals of Self-definition and British Imperial Authority." In Ruth Barnes and Joanne B. Eicher, eds., *Dress and Gender: Making and Meaning*. Oxford: Berg.

Cesaire, Aime. 1972 [1955]. *Discourse on Colonialism*. Trans. Joan Pinkham. New York: Monthly Review Press.

Crowder, Michael. 1968. *West Africa under Colonial Rule*. Evanston, IL: Northwestern University Press.

Crowder, Michael. 1988. *The Flogging of Phinehas McIntosh: A Tale of Colonial Folly and Injustice, Bechuanaland, 1933*. New Haven: Yale University Press.

Dirks, Nicholas, ed. 1992. *Colonialism and Culture*. Ann Arbor: University of Michigan Press.

Fernandez, James W. 1979. "Africanization, Europeanization, Christianization." *History of Religions*, 18: 284–92.

Fernandez, James W. 1982. *Bwiti: An Ethnography of the Religious Imagination in Africa*. Princeton: Princeton University Press.

Fogelman, Arianna. 2008. "Colonial Legacy in African Museology: The Case of the Ghana National Museum." *Museum Anthropology* 31(1): 19–27.

Forde, Daryll. 1939. "Government in Umor: A Study of Social Change and Problems of Indirect Rule in a Nigerian Village Community." *Africa* 12: 129–62.

Harms, Robert, ed. 1994. *Paths toward the Past: African Historical Essays in Honor of Jan Vansina*. Atlanta: African Studies Association Press.

Kuper, Adam. 1973. "Anthropology and Colonialism." In Adam Kuper, ed., *Anthropology and Anthropologists: The Modern British School*, pp. 99–120. London: RKP.

Low, D.A. 2009. *Fabrication of Empire: The British and the Uganda Kingdoms, 1890–1902*. Cambridge: Cambridge University Press.

Mannoni, O. 1990 (1948). *Prospero and Caliban: The Psychology of Colonization*. Ann Arbor: University of Michigan Press.

Memmi, Albert. 1974. *The Colonizer and the Colonized*. London: Souvenir Press.

Palmer, Robin and Neil Parsons, eds. 1977. *The Roots of Rural Poverty in Central and Southern Africa*. Berkeley: University of California Press.

Sadowsky, Jonathan. 1999. *Imperial Bedlam: Institutions of Madness in Colonial Southwest Nigeria*. Berkeley: University of California Press.

Said, Edward. 1978. *Orientalism*. New York: Vintage Books.

Said, Edward, 1989. "Representing the Colonized: Anthropology's Interlocuters." *Critical Inquiry* 15: 205–25.

Şaul, Mahir. 2004. "Money in Colonial Transition: Cowries and Francs in West Africa." *American Anthropologist* 106(1): 71–84.

Van Onselen, Charles. 1976. *Chibaro: African Mine Labour in Southern Rhodesia, 1900–1933*. London: Pluto Press.

Young, Robert J.C. 1995. *Colonial Desire: Hybridity in Theory, Culture, and Race*. London and New York: Routledge.

29

The Dual Mandate in British Tropical Africa

Methods of Ruling Native Races

Frederick D. Lugard

If continuity and decentralisation are, as I have said, the first and most important conditions in maintaining an effective administration, co-operation is the key-note of success in its application – continuous co-operation between every link in the chain, from the head of the administration to its most junior member, – co-operation between the Government and the commercial community, and, above all, between the provincial staff and the native rulers. Every individual adds his share not only to the accomplishment of the ideal, but to the ideal itself. Its principles are fashioned by his quota of experience, its results are achieved by his patient and loyal application of these principles, with as little interference as possible with native customs and modes of thought.

Principles do not change, but their mode of application may and should vary with the customs, the traditions, and the prejudices of each unit. The task of the administrative officer is to clothe his principles in the garb of evolution, not of revolution; to make it apparent alike to the educated native, the conservative Moslem, and the primitive pagan, each in his own degree, that the policy of the Government is not antagonistic but progressive – sympathetic to his aspirations and the safeguard of his natural rights. The Governor looks to the administrative staff to keep in touch with native thought and feeling, and to report fully to himself, in order that he in turn may be able to support them and recognise their work.

When describing the machinery of Government in an African dependency, I spoke of the supervision and guidance exercised by the Lieut.-Governor, the Residents, and the District Officers over the native chiefs. In this chapter I propose to discuss how those functions should be exercised.

Lord Milner's declaration that the British policy is to rule subject races through their own chiefs is generally applauded, but the manner in which the principle should be translated into practice admits of wide differences of opinion and method. Obviously the extent to which native races are capable of controlling their own affairs must vary in proportion to their degree of development and progress in social organisation, but this is a question of adaptation and not of principle. Broadly speaking, the divergent opinions in regard to the application of the principle may be found to originate in three different conceptions.

From Frederick D. Lugard, 1922, "Methods of Ruling Native Races," pp. 193–213. *The Dual Mandate in British Tropical Africa*. London: Blackwood.

The first is that the ideal of self-government can only be realised by the methods of evolution which have produced the democracies of Europe and America – viz., by representative institutions in which a comparatively small educated class shall be recognised as the natural spokesmen for the many. This method is naturally in favour with the educated African. Whether it is adapted to peoples accustomed by their own institutions to autocracy – albeit modified by a substantial expression of the popular will and circumscribed by custom – is naturally a matter on which opinions differ. The fundamental essential, however, in such a form of Government is that the educated few shall at least be representative of the feelings and desires of the many – well known to them, speaking their language, and versed in their customs and prejudices.

In present conditions in Africa the numerous separate tribes, speaking different languages, and in different stages of evolution, cannot produce representative men of education. Even were they available, the number of communities which could claim separate representation would make any central and really representative Council very unwieldy. The authority vested in the representatives would be antagonistic (as the Indian Progressives realise [...]) to that of the native rulers and their councils, – which are the product of the natural tendencies of tribal evolution, – and would run counter to the customs and institutions of the people. [...]

An attempt to adapt these principles of Western representative Government to tropical races is now being made in India. It is at present an Eastern rather than an African problem, but as a great experiment in the method of Government in tropical countries, the outcome of which "many other native races in other parts of the world are watching with strained attention," it demands at least a passing reference here.

Though the powers entrusted to the elected representatives of the people are at first restricted under the dyarchical system (which reserves certain subjects for the Central Authority), the principle of government by an educated minority, as opposed to government by native rulers, is fully accepted. It must be admitted that there is a considerable body of well-informed opinion in India and England – voiced here by the India Association,

Lord Sydenham (who speaks with the authority of an ex-Governor of Bombay), and others – which expresses much misgiving as to the wisdom of placing all political power "in the hands of a disaffected minority unrepresentative of India," and regards it as "an attempt to govern India by the narrowest of oligarchies, whose interests often conflict with those of the millions." [...]

The experiment has so far shown much promise of success, but the real test is not merely whether the native councillors show moderation and restraint as against extremists of their own class, but whether, when legislation has to be enacted which is unpopular with the illiterate masses and the martial races of India, there may be a reluctance to accept what will be called "Babu-made law," though it would have been accepted without demur as the order of "the Sirkar" – the British Raj.

It is, of course, now too late to adopt to any large extent the alternative of gradually transforming the greater part of British India into native States governed by their own hereditary dynasties, whose representatives in many cases still exist, and extending to them the principles which have so successfully guided our relations with the native States in India itself, and in Malaya in the past. It is one thing to excite an ignorant peasantry against an alien usurper, but quite another thing to challenge a native ruler.

Such a system does not exclude the educated native from participation in the government of the State to which he belongs, as a councillor to the native ruler, but it substitutes for direct British rule, not an elected oligarchy but a form of government more in accord with racial instincts and inherited traditions. It may be that while dyarchy and representative government may prove suitable to Bengal, and perhaps to some other provinces, the alternative system may be found to be best adapted to Mohamedan States, and to other of the warlike races of India, where representatives of the ancient dynasties still survive. Time alone will show. I shall recur to this subject in the next chapter.

The second conception is that every advanced community should be given the widest possible powers of self-government under its own ruler, and that these powers should be rapidly increased with the object of complete independence at the earliest possible date in the not distant future. Those who hold this view generally, I think, also consider that attempts to train primitive tribes in any form of self-government are futile, and the administration must be wholly conducted by British officials. This in the past has been the principle adopted in many dependencies. It recognised no alternative between a status of independence, like the Sultans of Malaya, or the native princes of India, and the direct rule of the district commissioner.

But the attempt to create such independent States in Africa has been full of anomalies. In the case of Egbaland, where the status had been formally recognised by treaty, the extent to which the Crown had jurisdiction was uncertain, yet, as we have seen, international conventions, including even that relating to the protection of wild animals, which was wholly opposed to native customary rights, were applied without the consent of the "Independent" State, and powers quite incompatible with independence were exercised by the Suzerain. [...]

The paramount chief might receive ceremonial visits from time to time from the Governor, and even perhaps be addressed as "Your Royal Highness," and vested with titular dignity and the tinsel insignia of office. His right to impose tolls on trade, and to exact whatever oppressive taxes he chose from his peasantry, was admitted, but his authority was subject to constant interference. The last-joined District Officer, or any other official, might issue orders, if not to him, at any rate to any of his subordinate chiefs, and the native ruler had no legal and recognised means of enforcing his commands. He was necessarily forbidden to raise armed forces – on which in the last resort the authority of the law must depend – and could not therefore maintain order.

The third conception is that of rule by native chiefs, unfettered in their control of their people as regards all those matters which are to them the most important attributes of rule, with scope for initiative and responsibility, but admittedly – so far as the visible horizon is concerned – subordinate to the control of the protecting Power in certain well-defined directions. It recognises, in the words of the Versailles Treaty, that the subject races of Africa are not yet able to stand alone, and that it would not conduce to the happiness of the vast bulk of the people – for whose welfare the

controlling Power is trustee – that the attempt should be made.

The verdict of students of history and sociology of different nationalities, such as Dr Kidd, [...] Dr Stoddard, [...] M. Beaulieu, [...] Meredith Townsend, [...] and others is unanimous that the era of complete independence is not as yet visible on the horizon of time. Practical administrators (among whom I may include my successor, Sir P. Girouard, in Northern Nigeria) have arrived at the same conclusion.

The danger of going too fast with native races is even more likely to lead to disappointment, if not to disaster, than the danger of not going fast enough. The pace can best be gauged by those who have intimate acquaintance alike with the strong points and the limitations of the native peoples and rulers with whom they have to deal.

The Fulani of Northern Nigeria are, as I have said, more capable of rule than the indigenous races, but in proportion as we consider them an alien race, we are denying self-government to the people over whom they rule, and supporting an alien caste – albeit closer and more akin to the native races than a European can be. Yet capable as they are, it requires the ceaseless vigilance of the British staff to maintain a high standard of administrative integrity, and to prevent oppression of the peasantry. We are dealing with the same generation, and in many cases with the identical rulers, who were responsible for the misrule and tyranny which we found in 1902. The subject races near the capital were then serfs, and the victims of constant extortion. Those dwelling at a distance were raided for slaves, and could not count their women, their cattle, or their crops their own. Punishments were most barbarous, and included impalement, mutilation, and burying alive. [...] Many generations have passed since British rule was established among the more intellectual people of India – the inheritors of centuries of Eastern civilisation – yet only to-day are we tentatively seeking to confer on them a measure of self-government. "Festina lente" is a motto which the Colonial Office will do well to remember in its dealings with Africa.

That the principle of ruling through the native chiefs is adopted by the different governments of British Tropical Africa can be seen from recent local pronouncements. The Governor of Sierra Leone, in his address to the Legislative Council last December (1920), remarks that "nine-tenths of the people enjoy autonomy under their own elected chiefs ... European officers are the technical advisers, and helpers of the tribal authority." The Governor of the Gold Coast on a similar occasion observed: "The chiefs are keenly appreciative of our policy of indirect rule, and of the full powers they retain under their native institutions." [...] The powers retained by the Kabaka of Uganda and his Council are very wide indeed. [...]

The system adopted in Nigeria is therefore only a particular method of the application of these principles – more especially as regards "advanced communities," – and since I am familiar with it I will use it as illustrative of the methods which in my opinion should characterise the dealings of the controlling power with subject races.

The object in view is to make each "Emir" or paramount chief, assisted by his judicial Council, an effective ruler over his own people. He presides over a "Native Administration" organised throughout as a unit of local government. The area over which he exercises jurisdiction is divided into districts under the control of "Headmen," who collect the taxes in the name of the ruler, and pay them into the "Native Treasury," conducted by a native treasurer and staff under the supervision of the chief at his capital. Here, too, is the prison for native court prisoners, and probably the school. Large cities are divided into wards for purposes of control and taxation.

The district headman, usually a territorial magnate with local connections, is the chief executive officer in the area under his charge. He controls the village headmen, and is responsible for the assessment of the tax, which he collects through their agency. He must reside in his district and not at the capital. He is not allowed to pose as a chief with a retinue of his own and duplicate officials, and is summoned from time to time to report to his chief. If, as is the case with some of the ancient Emirates, the community is a small one but independent of any other native rule, the chief may be his own district headman.

A province under a Resident may contain several separate "Native Administrations," whether they be Moslem Emirates or pagan communities.

A "division" under a British District Officer may include one or more headmen's districts, or more than one small Emirate or independent [...] pagan tribe, but as a rule no Emirate is partly in one division and partly in another. The Resident acts as sympathetic adviser and counsellor to the native chief, being careful not to interfere so as to lower his prestige, or cause him to lose interest in his work. His advice on matters of general policy must be followed, but the native ruler issues his own instructions to his subordinate chiefs and district heads – not as the orders of the Resident but as his own, – and he is encouraged to work through them, instead of centralising everything in himself – a system which in the past had produced such great abuses. The British District Officers supervise and assist the native district headmen, through whom they convey any instructions to village heads, and make any arrangements necessary for carrying on the work of the Government departments, but all important orders emanate from the Emir, whose messenger usually accompanies and acts as mouthpiece of a District Officer.

The tax – which supersedes all former "tribute," irregular imposts, and forced labour – is, in a sense, the basis of the whole system, since it supplies the means to pay the Emir and all his officials. The district and village heads are effectively supervised and assisted in its assessment by the British staff. The native treasury retains the proportion assigned to it (in advanced communities a half), and pays the remainder into Colonial Revenue.

There are fifty such treasuries in the northern provinces of Nigeria, and every independent chief, however small, is encouraged to have his own. The appropriation by the native administration of market dues, slaughter-house fees, forest licences, &c., is authorised by ordinance, and the native administration receives also the fines and fees of native courts. From these funds are paid the salaries of the Emir and his council, the native court judges, the district and village heads, police, prison warders, and other employees. The surplus is devoted to the construction and maintenance of dispensaries, leper settlements, schools, roads, courthouses, and other buildings. Such works may be carried out wholly or in part by a Government department, if the native administration requires technical assistance, the cost being borne by the native treasury.

The native treasurer keeps all accounts of receipts and expenditure, and the Emir, with the assistance of the Resident, annually prepares a budget, which is formally approved by the Lieut.-Governor.

In these advanced communities the judges of the native courts – which I shall describe in a later chapter – administer native law and custom, and exercise their jurisdiction independently of the native executive, but under the supervision of the British staff, and subject to the general control of the Emir, whose "Judicial council" consists of his principal officers of State, and is vested with executive as well as judicial powers. No punishment may be inflicted by a native authority, except through a regular tribunal. The ordinances of government are operative everywhere, but the native authority may make by-laws in modification of native custom – e.g., on matters of sanitation, &c., – and these, when approved by the Governor, are enforced by the native courts.

The authority of the Emir over his own people is absolute, and the profession of an alien creed does not absolve a native from the obligation to obey his lawful orders; but aliens – other than natives domiciled in the Emirate and accepting the jurisdiction of the native authority and courts – are under the direct control of the British staff. Townships are excluded from the native jurisdiction.

The village is the administrative unit. It is not always easy to define, since the security to life and property which has followed the British administration has caused an exodus from the cities and large villages, and the creation of innumerable hamlets, sometimes only of one or two huts, on the agricultural lands. The peasantry of the advanced communities, though ignorant, yet differs from that of the backward tribes in that they recognise the authority of the Emir, and are more ready to listen to the village head and the Council of Elders. "The development of self-government in India," says Lord Sydenham, "should begin with the *Panchayet*" (Village Council). [...] This is the base and unit of the Nigerian system.

Subject, therefore, to the limitations which I shall presently discuss, the native authority is thus *de facto* and *de jure* ruler over his own people. He appoints and dismisses his subordinate chiefs and officials. He exercises the power of allocation of lands, and with the aid of the native courts, of adjudication in land disputes and expropriation for offences against the community, these are the essential functions upon which, in the opinion of the West African Lands Committee, the prestige of the native authority depends. The lawful orders which he may give are carefully defined by ordinance, and in the last resort are enforced by Government.

Since native authority, especially if exercised by alien conquerors, is inevitably weakened by the first impact of civilised rule, it is made clear to the elements of disorder, who regard force as conferring the only right to demand obedience, that government, by the use of force if necessary, intends to support the native chief. To enable him to maintain order he employs a body of unarmed police, and if the occasion demands the display of superior force he looks to the Government – as, for instance, if a community combines to break the law or shield criminals from justice – a rare event in the advanced communities.

The native ruler derives his power from the Suzerain, and is responsible that it is not misused. He is equally with British officers amenable to the law, but his authority does not depend on the caprice of an executive officer. To intrigue against him is an offence punishable, if necessary, in a Provincial Court. Thus both British and native courts are invoked to uphold his authority.

The essential feature of the system (as I wrote at the time of its inauguration) is that the native chiefs are constituted "as an integral part of the machinery of the administration. There are not two sets of rulers – British and native – working either separately or in co-operation, but a single Government in which the native chiefs have well-defined duties and an acknowledged status equally with British officials. Their duties should never conflict and should overlap as little as possible. They should be complementary to each other, and the chief himself must understand that he has no right to place and power unless he renders his proper services to the State."

The ruling classes are no longer either demigods, or parasites preying on the community. They must work for the stipends and position they enjoy. They are the trusted delegates of the Governor, exercising in the Moslem States the well-understood powers of "Wakils" in conformity with their own Islamic system, and recognising the King's representative as their acknowledged Suzerain. ...

Pending the growth of a fuller sense of public responsibility and of an enlightened public opinion, some check may be afforded by the preparation of annual estimates of revenue and expenditure in a very simple form. These should require the approval of the Governor (or of the Lieut.-Governor), as the colonial estimates require that of the Secretary of State, and any subsequent alteration should require the like sanction. While refraining as far as possible from interference in detail, the Lieut.-Governor can, by suggestion and comparison, effect some co-ordination and uniformity where desirable, and can best discriminate between the scope which may be allowed to an individual, and the grant of extended powers of universal application. [...]

The habits of a people are not changed in a decade, and when powerful despots are deprived of the pastime of war and slaveraiding, and when even the weak begin to forget their former sufferings, to grow weary of a life without excitement and to resent the petty restrictions which have replaced the cruelties of the old despotism, it must be the aim of Government to provide new interests and rivalries in civilised progress, in education, in material prosperity and trade, and even in sport. [...]

There were indeed many who, with the picture of Fulani misrule fresh in their memory, regarded this system when it was first inaugurated with much misgiving, and believed that though the hostility of the rulers to the British might be concealed, and their vices disguised, neither could be eradicated, and they would always remain hostile at heart. They thought that the Fulani as an alien race of conquerors, who had in turn been conquered, had not the same claims for consideration as those whom they had displaced, even though they had become so identified with the people that they could no longer be called aliens.

But there can be no doubt that such races form an invaluable medium between the British staff and the native peasantry. Nor can the difficulty of finding any one capable of taking their place, or

the danger they would constitute to the State if ousted from their positions, be ignored. Their traditions of rule, their monotheistic religion, and their intelligence enable them to appreciate more readily than the negro population the wider objects of British policy while their close touch with the masses – with whom they live in daily intercourse – mark them out as destined to play an important part in the future, as they have done in the past, in the development of the tropics.

Both the Arabs in the east and the Fulani in the west are Mohamedans, and by supporting their rule we unavoidably encourage the spread of Islam, which from the purely administrative point of view has the disadvantage of being subject to waves of fanaticism, bounded by no political frontiers. In Nigeria it has been the rule that their power should not be re-established over tribes which had made good their independence, or imposed upon those who had successfully resisted domination.

On the other hand, the personal interests of the rulers must rapidly become identified with those of the controlling Power. The forces of disorder do not distinguish between them, and the rulers soon recognise that any upheaval against the British would equally make an end of them. Once this community of interest is established, the Central Government cannot be taken by surprise, for it is impossible that the native rulers should not be aware of any disaffection. [...]

This identification of the ruling class with the Government accentuates the corresponding obligation to check malpractices on their part. The task of educating them in the duties of a ruler becomes more than ever insistent; of inculcating a sense of responsibility; of convincing their intelligence of the advantages which accrue from the material prosperity of the peasantry, from free labour and initiative; of the necessity of delegating powers to trusted subordinates; of the evils of favouritism and bribery; of the importance of education, especially for the ruling class, and for the filling of lucrative posts under Government; of the benefits of sanitation, vaccination, and isolation of infection in checking mortality; and finally, of impressing upon them how greatly they may benefit their country by personal interest in such matters, and by the application of labour-saving devices and of scientific methods in agriculture.

Unintentional misuse of the system of native administration must also be guarded against. It is not, for instance, the duty of a native administration to purchase supplies for native troops, or to enlist and pay labour for public works, though its agency within carefully defined limits may be useful in making known Government requirements, and seeing that markets are well supplied. Nor should it be directed to collect licences, fees, and rents due to Government, nor should its funds be used for any purpose not solely connected with and prompted by its own needs.

I have throughout these pages continually emphasised the necessity of recognising, as a cardinal principle of British policy in dealing with native races, that institutions and methods, in order to command success and promote the happiness and welfare of the people, must be deep-rooted in their traditions and prejudices. Obviously in no sphere of administration is this more essential than in that under discussion, and a slavish adherence to any particular type, however successful it may have proved elsewhere, may, if unadapted to the local environment, be as ill-suited and as foreign to its conceptions as direct British rule would be.

The type suited to a community which has long grown accustomed to the social organisation of the Moslem State may or may not be suitable to advanced pagan communities, which have evolved a social system of their own, such as the Yorubas, the Benis, the Egbas, or the Ashantis in the West, or the Waganda, the Wanyoro, the Watoro, and others in the East. The history, the traditions, the idiosyncracies, and the prejudices of each must be studied by the Resident and his staff, in order that the form adopted shall accord with natural evolution, and shall ensure the ready co-operation of the chiefs and people.

Before passing to the discussion of methods applicable to primitive tribes, it may be of interest to note briefly some of the details – as apart from general principles – adopted in Nigeria among the advanced communities.

Chiefs who are executive rulers are graded – those of the first three classes are installed by the Governor or Lieut.–Governor, and carry a staff of office surmounted for the first class by a silver, and for the others by a brass crown. Lower grades carry a baton, and are installed by the Resident, or by the Emir, if the chief is subordinate to him. These staves of office, which are greatly prized, symbolise to the peasantry the fact that the Emir derives his power from the Government, and will be supported in its exercise. The installation of an Emir is a ceremonial witnessed by a great concourse of his people, and dignified by a parade of troops. The native insignia of office, and a parchment scroll, setting out in the vernacular the conditions of his appointment, are presented to him. The alkali (native judge) administers the following oath on the Koran: "I swear in the name of God, well and truly to serve His Majesty King George V. and his representative the Governor of Nigeria, to obey the laws of Nigeria and the lawful commands of the Governor, and of the Lieut.–Governor, provided that they are not contrary to my religion, and if they are so contrary I will at once inform the Governor through the Resident. I will cherish in my heart no treachery or disloyalty, and I will rule my people with justice and without partiality. And as I carry out this oath so may God judge me." Pagan chiefs are sworn according to their own customs on a sword.

Native etiquette and ceremonial must be carefully studied and observed in order that unintentional offence may be avoided. Great importance is attached to them, and a like observance in accordance with native custom is demanded towards British officers. Chiefs are treated with respect and courtesy. Native races alike in India and Africa are quick to discriminate between natural dignity and assumed superiority. Vulgar familiarity is no more a passport to their friendship than an assumption of self-importance is to their respect. [...] The English gentleman needs no prompting in such a matter – his instinct is never wrong. Native titles of rank are adopted, and only native dress is worn, whether by chiefs or by schoolboys. Principal chiefs accused of serious crimes are tried by a British court, and are not imprisoned before trial, unless in very exceptional circumstances. Minor chiefs and native officials appointed by an Emir may be tried by his Judicial Council. If the offence does not involve deprivation of office, the offender may be fined without public trial, if he prefers it, in order to avoid humiliation and loss of influence.

Succession is governed by native law and custom, subject in the case of important chiefs to the approval of the Governor, in order that the most capable claimant may be chosen. It is important to ascertain the customary law and to follow it when possible, for the appointment of a chief who is not the recognised heir, or who is disliked by the people, may give rise to trouble, and in any case the new chief would have much difficulty in asserting his authority, and would fear to check abuses lest he should alienate his supporters. In Moslem countries the law is fairly clearly defined, being a useful combination of the hereditary principle, tempered by selection, and in many cases in Nigeria the ingenious device is maintained of having two rival dynasties, from each of which the successor is selected alternately.

In pagan communities the method varies; but there is no rigid rule, and a margin for selection is allowed. The formal approval of the Governor after a short period of probation is a useful precaution, so that if the designated chief proves himself unsuitable, the selection may be revised without difficulty. Minor chiefs are usually selected by popular vote, subject to the approval of the paramount chief. It is a rule in Nigeria that no slave may be appointed as a chief or district headman. If one is nominated he must first be publicly freed.

Small and isolated communities, living within the jurisdiction of a chief, but owing allegiance to the chief of their place of origin – a common source of trouble in Africa – should gradually be absorbed into the territorial jurisdiction. Aliens who have settled in a district for their own purposes would be subject to the local jurisdiction.

30

How Europe Underdeveloped Africa

Walter Rodney

The black man certainly has to pay dear for carrying the white man's burden. (George Padmore (West Indian) Pan-Africanist, 1936)

In the colonial society, education is such that it serves the colonialist ... In a regime of slavery, education was but one institution for forming slaves. (Statement of FRELIMO (Mozambique Liberation Front) Department of Education and Culture, 1968)

The Supposed Benefits of Colonialism to Africa

Socio-economic services

Faced with the evidence of European exploitation of Africa, many bourgeois writers would concede at least partially that colonialism was a system which functioned well in the interests of the metropoles. However, they would then urge that another issue to be resolved is how much Europeans did for Africans, and that it is necessary to draw up a balance sheet of colonialism. On that balance sheet, they place both the credits and the debits, and quite often conclude that the good outweighed the bad. That particular conclusion can quite easily be challenged, but attention should also be drawn to the fact that the process of reasoning is itself misleading. The reasoning has some sentimental persuasiveness. It appeals to the common sentiment that "after all there must be two sides to a thing." The argument suggests that, on the one hand, there was exploitation and oppression, but, on the other hand, colonial governments did much for the benefit of Africans and they developed Africa. It is our contention that this is completely false. Colonialism had only one hand – it was a one-armed-bandit.

What did colonial governments do in the interest of Africans? Supposedly, they built railroads, schools, hospitals, and the like. The sum total of these services was amazingly small.

For the first three decades of colonialism, hardly anything was done that could remotely be termed a service to the African people. It was in fact only after the last war that social services were built as a matter of policy. How little they amounted to does not really need illustrating. After all, the statistics which show that Africa today is underdeveloped are the statistics representing the state of affairs at the end of colonialism. For that matter, the figures at the end of the first decade of African independence in spheres such as health, housing, and education are often several times higher than the figures inherited by the newly independent governments. It would be an act of the most brazen fraud to weigh the paltry social amenities provided during the colonial epoch against the exploitation, and to arrive at the conclusion that the good outweighed the bad.

Capitalism did bring social services to European workers – firstly, as a by-product of providing such services for the bourgeoisie and the middle class, and later as a deliberate act of policy. Nothing remotely comparable occurred in Africa. In 1934, long before the coming of the welfare state to Britain, expenditure for social services in the British Isles amounted to 6 pounds 15 shillings per person. In Ghana, the figure was 7 shillings 4 pence per person, and that was high by colonial standards. In Nigeria and Nyasaland, it was less that 1 shilling 9 pence per head. None of the other colonizing powers were doing any better, and some much worse.

The Portuguese stand out because they boasted the most and did the least. Portugal boasted that Angola, Guinea, and Mozambique have been their possessions for five hundred years, during which time a "civilizing mission" has been going on. At the end of five hundred years of shouldering the white man's burden of civilizing "African natives," the Portuguese has not managed to train a single African doctor in Mozambique, and the life expectancy in eastern Angola was less than thirty years. As for Guinea-Bissau, some insight into the situation there is provided by the admission of the Portuguese themselves that Guinea-Bissau was more neglected than Angola and Mozambique!

Furthermore, the limited social services within Africa during colonial times were distributed in a manner that reflected the pattern of domination and exploitation. First of all, white settlers and expatriates wanted the standards of the bourgeoisie or professional classes of the metropoles. They were all the more determined to have luxuries in Africa, because so many of them came from poverty in Europe and could not expect good services in their own homelands. In colonies like Algeria, Kenya, and South Africa, it is well known that whites created an infrastructure to afford themselves leisured and enjoyable lives. It means, therefore, that the total amenities provided in any of those colonies is no guide to what Africans got out of colonialism.

In Algeria, the figure for infant mortality was 39 per 1,000 live births among white settlers; but it jumped to 170 per 1,000 live births in the case of Algerians living in the towns. In practical terms, that meant that the medical, maternity, and sanitation services were all geared towards the well-being of the settlers. Similarly, in South Africa, all social statistics have to be broken down into at least two groups – white and black – if they are to be interpreted correctly. In British East Africa there were three groups: firstly, the Europeans, who got the most; then, the Indians, who took most of what was left; and thirdly, the Africans, who came last in their own country.

In predominantly black countries, it was also true that the bulk of the social services went to whites. The southern part of Nigeria was one of the colonial areas that was supposed to have received the most from a benevolent mother country. Ibadan, one of the most heavily populated cities in Africa, had only about 50 Europeans before the last war. For those chosen few, the British colonial government maintained a segregated hospital service of 11 beds in well-furnished surroundings. There were 34 beds for the half-million blacks. The situation was repeated in other areas, so that altogether the 4,000 Europeans in the country in the 1930s had 12 modern hospitals, while the African population of at least 40 million had 52 hospitals.

The viciousness of the colonial system with respect to the provision of social services was most dramatically brought out in the case of economic activities which made huge profits, and notably in the mining industry. Mining takes serious toll of the health of workers, and it was only recently in the metropoles that miners have had access to the kind of medical and insurance services which could safeguard their lives and health. In colonial Africa, the exploitation of miners was entirely without responsibility. In 1930, scurvy and other epidemics broke out in the Lupa gold fields of Tanganyika. Hundreds of workers died. One should not wonder that they had no facilities which would have saved some lives, because in the first place they were not being paid enough to eat properly. ...

Many Africans trekked to towns, because (bad as they were) they offered a little more than the countryside. Modern sanitation, electricity, piped water, paved roads, medical services, and schools were as foreign at the end of the colonial period as they were in the beginning – as far as most of rural Africa was concerned. Yet, it was the countryside that grew the cash crops and provided the labor that kept the system going. The peasants there knew very little of the supposed "credits" on the colonial balance sheet. ...

Within individual countries, considerable regional variations existed, depending on the degree to which different parts of a country were integrated into the capitalist money economy. Thus, the northern part of Kenya or the south of Sudan had little to offer the colonialists, and such a zone was simply ignored by the colonizing power with regard to roads, schools, hospitals, and so on. Often, at the level of the district of a given colony, there would be discrimination in providing social amenities, on the basis of contribution to exportable surplus. For instance, plantations and companies might build hospitals for their workers, because some minimum maintenance of the workers' health was an economic investment. Usually, such a hospital was exclusively for workers of that particular capitalist concern, and those Africans living in the vicinity under subsistence conditions outside the money economy were ignored altogether. ...

The financial institutions of colonial Africa were even more scandalously neglectful of indigenous African interests than was the case with the European-oriented communications system. The banks did very little lending locally. In British East Africa, credit to Africans was specifically discouraged by the Credit to Natives (Restriction) Ordinance of 1931. Insurance companies catered almost exclusively to the interests of white settlers and capitalist firms. The policy of colonial reserves in metropolitan currencies can also be cited as a "service" inimical to Africans. The Currency Boards and central banks which performed such services denied Africa access to its own funds created by exports. Instead, *the colonial reserves in Britain, France, and Belgium represented African loans to and capital investment in Europe.*

It is necessary to re-evaluate the much glorified notion of "European capital" as having been invested in colonial Africa and Asia. The money available for investment in the capitalist system was itself the consequence of the previous robbery of workers and peasants in Europe and the world at large. In Africa's case, the capital that was invested in nineteenth-century commerce was part of the capital that had been derived from the trade in slaves. The Portuguese government was the first in Europe to ship captives from Africa and the last to let go of slave trading. Much of the profit slipped out of Portuguese hands, and went instead to Britain and Germany; but the Portuguese slave trade nevertheless helped the Portuguese themselves to finance later colonial ventures, such as joint capitalist participation in agricultural and mining companies in Angola and Mozambique.

As indicated earlier, many of the entrepreneurs from the big European port towns who turned to importing African agricultural produce into Europe were formerly carrying on the trade in slaves. The same can be said of many New England firms in the United States. Some of the biggest "names" in the colonial epoch were capitalist concerns whose original capital came from the trade in slaves or from slavery itself. Lloyds, the great insurance underwriting and banking house, falls into this category, having been nourished by profits from the slave territories of the West Indies in the seventeenth and eighteenth centuries; and the ubiquitous Barclays Bank had its antecedents in slave trading. Worms et Compagnie is a French example of the same phenomenon. Back in the eighteenth century, Worms had strong links with the French slave trade, and it grew to become one of the most powerful financial houses dealing with the French empire in Africa and Asia, with particular concentration on Madagascar and the Indian Ocean.

The example of Unilever and the UAC reinforces the point that Africa was being exploited by capital produced out of African labor. When Lever Brothers took over the Niger Company in 1929, they became heirs to one of the most notorious exploiters of nineteenth-century Africa. The Niger Company was a chartered company with full governmental and police powers during the years 1885 to 1897. In that period, the company exploited Nigerians ruthlessly. Furthermore, the Niger Company was itself a monopoly that had bought up smaller firms tracing their capital directly to slave trading. Similarly, when the UAC was born out of the merger with the Eastern and African Trading Company, it was associated with some more capital that grew from a family tree rooted in the European slave trade. The capital at the disposal of the big French trading firms CFAO and SCOA can also be traced in the same way.

The process of capital accumulation and reproduction in East Africa lacks the continuity of West Africa. Firstly, Arabs as well as Europeans were participants in the slave trade from East Africa. Secondly, the Germans intervened in 1885, although they had not been previously involved; while the French (who had led the European slave trade in East Africa during the eighteenth and nineteenth centuries) concentrated on colonizing the Indian Ocean islands rather than the East African mainland. Thirdly, German colonialism did not last beyond the 1914–18 war. Even so, on the British side, the capital and profits of the colonizing East Africa Company reappeared in the trading firm of Smith Mackenzie.

The capital that was invested in colonial Africa in later years was a continuation of the nineteenth century, along with new influxes from the metropoles. If one inquired closely into the origins of the supposedly new sources, quite a few would have been connected very closely to previous exploitation of non-European peoples. However, it is not necessary to prove that every firm trading in Africa had a firsthand or secondhand connection with the European slave trade and with earlier exploitation of the continent. It is enough to remember that Europe's greatest source of primary capital accumulation was overseas, and that the profits from African ventures continually outran the capital invested in the colonies.

A conservative bourgeois writer on colonial Africa made the following remarks about the South African gold and diamond industries:

> Apart from the original capital subscribed [in the diamond industry], all capital expenditure was provided for out of profits. The industry also yielded large profits to the international firms which dealt in diamonds. These had a peculiar importance, because a considerable portion of the wealth accumulated by diamond firms was later used in the development of the [gold industry] of the Rand.

Similarly, in Angola the *Diamang* diamond company was an investment that quickly paid for itself, and was then producing capital. The combined profits of that company for the years 1954 and 1955 alone came to the total of invested capital plus 40 per cent. The excess over investment and maintenance costs was of course expatriated to Portugal, Belgium and the USA, where the shareholders of the *Diamang* were resident; and Angola was thereby investing in those countries.

In this sense, the colonies were the generators of the capital rather than the countries into which foreign capital was plowed.

Capital was constantly in motion from metropole to some part of the dependencies, from colonies to other colonies (via the metropoles), from one metropole to another, and from colony to metropole. But because of the superprofits created by non-European peoples ever since slavery, the net flow was from colony to metropole. What was called "profits" in one year came back as "capital" the next. Even progressive writers have created a wrong impression by speaking about capital "exports" from Europe to Africa and about the role of "foreign" capital. What was foreign about the capital in colonial Africa was its ownership and not its initial source.

Apologists for colonialism are quick to say that the money for schools, hospitals, and such services in Africa was provided by the British, French, or Belgian taxpayer, as the case may have been. It defies logic to admit that profits from a given colony in a given year totaled several million dollars and to affirm nevertheless that the few thousand dollars allocated to social services in that colony was the money of European taxpayers! The true situation can accurately be presented in the following terms: African workers and peasants produced for European capitalism goods and services of a certain value. A small proportion of the fruits of their efforts was retained by them in the form of wages, cash payments, and extremely limited social services, such as were essential to the maintenance of colonialism. The rest went to the various beneficiaries of the colonial system. ...

Capitalism as a system within the metropoles or epicenters had two dominant classes: firstly, the capitalists or bourgeoisie who owned the factories and banks (the major means for producing and distributing wealth); and secondly, the workers or proletariat who worked in the factories of the said bourgeoisie. Colonialism did not create a capital-owning and factory-owning class among Africans or even inside Africa; nor did it create an urbanized proletariat of any significance (particularly outside South Africa). In other words, capitalism in the form of colonialism failed to perform in Africa the tasks which it had performed in Europe in changing social relations and liberating the forces of production.

It is fairly obvious that capitalists do not set out to create other capitalists, who would be rivals. On the contrary, the tendency of capitalism in Europe from the very beginning was one of competition, elimination, and monopoly. Therefore, when the imperialist stage was reached, the metropolitan capitalists had no intention of allowing rivals to arise in the dependencies. However, in spite of what the metropoles wanted, some local capitalists did emerge in Asia and Latin America. Africa is a significant exception in the sense that, compared with other colonized peoples, far fewer Africans had access even to the middle rungs of the bourgeois ladder in terms of capital for investment.

Part of the explanation for the lack of African capitalists in Africa lies in the arrival of minority groups who had no local family ties which could stand in the way of the ruthless primary accumulation which capitalism requires. Lebanese, Syrian, Greek, and Indian businessmen rose from the ranks of petty traders to become minor and sometimes substantial capitalists. Names like Raccah and Leventis were well known in West Africa, just as names like Madhvani and Visram became well known as capitalists in East Africa.

There were clashes between the middlemen and the European colonialists, but the latter much preferred to encourage the minorities rather than see Africans build themselves up. For instance, in West Africa the businessmen from Sierra Leone were discouraged both in their own colony and in other British possessions where they chose to settle. In East Africa, there was hope among Ugandans in particular that they might acquire cotton gins and perform some capitalist functions connected with cotton growing and other activities. However, when in 1920 a Development Commission was appointed to promote commerce and industry, it favored firstly Europeans and then Indians. Africans were prohibited by legislation from owning gins.

Taking Africa as a whole, the few African businessmen who were allowed to emerge were at the bottom of the ladder and cannot be considered as "capitalists" in the true sense. They did not own sufficient capital to invest in large-scale farming, trading, mining, or industry. They were dependent both on European-owned capital and on the local capital of minority groups.

That European capitalism should have failed to create African capitalists is perhaps not so striking as its inability to create a working class and to diffuse industrial skills throughout Africa. By its very nature, colonialism was prejudiced against the establishment of industries in Africa, outside of agriculture and the extractive spheres of mining and timber felling. Whenever internal forces seemed to push in the direction of African industrialization, they were deliberately blocked by the colonial governments acting on behalf of the metropolitan industrialists. Groundnut-oil mills were set up in Senegal in 1927 and began exports to France. They were soon placed under restrictions because of protests of oil-millers in France. Similarly in Nigeria, the oil mills set up by Lebanese were discouraged. The oil was still sent to Europe as a raw material for industry, but European industrialists did not then welcome even the simple stage of processing groundnuts into oil on African soil.

Many irrational contradictions arose throughout colonial Africa as a result of the non-industrialization policy: Sudanese and Ugandans grew cotton but imported manufactured cotton goods, Ivory Coast grew cocoa and imported tinned cocoa and chocolate.

The tiny working class of colonial Africa covered jobs such as agricultural labor and domestic service. Most of it was unskilled, in contrast to the accumulating skills of capitalism proper. When it came to projects requiring technical expertise, Europeans did the supervision – standing around in their helmets and white shorts. Of course, in 1885 Africans did not have the technical know-how which had evolved in Europe during the eighteenth and nineteenth centuries. That difference was itself partly due to the kind of relations between Africa and Europe in the pre-colonial period. What is more significant, however, is the incredibly small number of Africans who were able to acquire "modern" skills during the colonial period. In a few places, such as South Africa and the Rhodesias, this was due to specific racial discrimination in employment, so as to keep the best jobs for whites. Yet, even in the absence of whites, lack of skills among Africans was an integral part of the capitalist impact on the continent.

It has already been illustrated how the presence of industry in Europe fostered and multiplied scientific techniques. The reverse side of the coin was presented in Africa: no industry meant no generation of skills. Even in the mining industry, it was arranged that the most valuable labor should be done outside Africa. It is sometimes forgotten that it is labor which adds value to commodities through the transformation of natural products. For instance, although gem diamonds have a value far above their practical usefulness, the value is not simply a question of their being rare. Work had to be done to locate the diamonds. That is the skilled task of a geologist, and the geologists were of course Europeans. Work had to be done to dig the diamonds out, which involves mainly physical labor. Only in that phase were Africans from South Africa, Namibia, Angola, Tanganyika, and Sierra Leone brought into the picture. Subsequently, work had to be done in cutting and polishing the diamonds. A small portion of this was performed by whites in South Africa, and most of it by whites in Brussels and London. It was on the desk of the skilled cutter that the rough diamond became a gem and soared in value. No Africans were allowed to come near that kind of technique in the colonial period.

Much of the dynamism of capitalism lay in the way that growth created more opportunities for further growth. Major industries had by-products,

they stimulated local raw-material usage, they expanded transport and the building industry – as was seen in the case of Unilever. In the words of the professional economists, those were the beneficial "backward and forward linkages." Given that the industries using African raw materials were located *outside* Africa, then there could be no beneficial backward and forward linkages *inside* Africa. After the Second World War, Guinea began to export bauxite. In the hands of French and American capitalists, the bauxite became aluminum. In the metropoles, it went into the making of refactory material, electrical conductors, cigarette foil, kitchen utensils, glass, jewel bearings, abrasives, lightweight structures, and aircraft. Guinean bauxite stimulated European shipping and North American hydro-electric power. In Guinea, the colonial bauxite mining left holes in the ground.

With regard to gold, the financial implications in Europe were enormous and African gold played its part in the development of the monetary system and of industry and agriculture in the metropoles. But, like bauxite and other minerals, gold is an exhaustible resource. Once it is taken out of a country's soil, that is an absolute loss that cannot be replaced. That simple fact is often obscured so long as production continues, as in South Africa; but it is dramatically brought to attention when the minerals have actually disappeared during the colonial epoch. For instance, in the south of Tanganyika, the British mined gold as fast as they could from 1933 onwards at a place called Chunya. By 1953, they had gobbled it all up and exported it abroad. By the end of the colonial period, Chunya was one of the most backward spots in the whole of Tanganyika, which was itself known as the poor Cinderella of East Africa. If that was modernization, and given the price paid in exploitation and oppression, then Africans would have been better off in the bush.

Industrialization does not only mean agriculture itself has been industrialized in capitalist and socialist countries by the intensive application of scientific principles to irrigation, fertilizers, tools, crop selection, stock breeding. (The most decisive failure of colonialism in Africa was its failure to change the technology of agricultural production.) The most convincing evidence as to the superficiality of the talk about colonialism having "modernized" Africa is the fact that the vast majority of Africans went into colonialism with a hoe and came out with a hoe. Some capitalist plantations introduced agricultural machinery, and the odd tractor found its way into the hands of African farmers; but the hoe remained the overwhelmingly dominant agricultural implement. Capitalism could revolutionize agriculture in Europe, but it could not do the same for Africa.

In some districts, capitalism brought about technological backwardness in agriculture. On the reserves of southern Africa, far too many Africans were crowded onto inadequate land, and were forced to engage in intensive farming, using techniques that were suitable only to shifting cultivation. In practice, that was a form of technical retrogression, because the land yielded less and less and became destroyed in the process. Wherever Africans were hampered in their use of their ancestral lands on a wide-ranging shifting basis, the same negative effect was to be found. Besides, some of the new cash crops like groundnuts and cotton were very demanding on the soil. In countries like Senegal, Niger, and Chad, which were already on the edge of the desert, the steady cultivation led to soil impoverishment and encroachment of the desert.

White racist notions are so deep-rooted within capitalist society that the failure of African agriculture to advance was put down to the inherent inferiority of the African. It would be much truer to say that it was due to the white intruders, although the basic explanation is to be found not in the personal ill-will of the colonialists or in their racial origin, but rather in the organized viciousness of the capitalist/colonialist system.

Failure to improve agricultural tools and methods on behalf of African peasants was not a matter of a bad decision by colonial policy-makers. It was an inescapable feature of colonialism as a whole, based on the understanding that the international division of labor aimed at skills in the metropoles and low-level manpower in the dependencies. It was also a result of the considerable use of force (including taxation) in African labor relations. People can be forced to perform simple manual labor, but very little else. This was proven when Africans were used as slaves in the West Indies and America. Slaves damaged tools and carried out sabotage, which could only be controlled by extra supervision and by keeping tools and productive processes very elementary. Slave labor was unsuitable for carrying out

industrial activity, so that in the USA the North went to war in 1861 to end slavery in the South, so as to spread true capitalist relations throughout the land. Following the same line of argument, it becomes clear why the various forms of forced agricultural labor in Africa had to be kept quite simple, and that in turn meant small earnings.

Capitalists under colonialism did not pay enough for an African to maintain himself and family. This can readily be realized by reflecting on the amounts of money earned by African peasants from cash crops. The sale of produce by an African cash-crop farmer rarely brought in 10 pounds per year and often it was less than half that amount. Out of that, a peasant had to pay for tools, seeds, and transport and he had to repay the loan to the middleman before he could call the remainder his own. Peasants producing coffee and cocoa and collecting palm produce tended to earn more than those dealing with cotton and groundnuts, but even the ordinary Akwapim cocoa farmer or Chagga coffee farmer never handled money in quantities sufficient to feed, clothe, and shelter his family. Instead, subsistence farming of yams or bananas continued as a supplement. That was how the peasant managed to eat, and the few shillings earned went to pay taxes and to buy the increasing number of things which could not be obtained without money in the middlemen's shops – salt, cloth, paraffin. If he was extremely lucky, he would have access to zinc sheets, bicycles, radios, and sewing machines, and would be able to pay school fees. It must be made quite clear that those in the last category were extremely few.

One reason why the African peasant got so little for his agricultural crops was that his labor was unskilled. That was not the whole explanation, but it is true that a product such as cotton jumped in value during the time it went through the sophisticated processes of manufacture in Europe. Karl Marx, in clarifying how capitalists appropriated part of the surplus of each worker, used the example of cotton. He explained that the value of the manufactured cotton included the value of the labor that went into growing the raw cotton, plus part of the value of the labor that made the spindles, plus the labor that went into the actual manufacture. From an African viewpoint, the first conclusion to be drawn is that the peasant working on African soil was being exploited by the industrialist who used

African raw material in Europe or America. Secondly, it is necessary to realize that the African contribution of unskilled labor was valued far less than the European contribution of skilled labor. ...

Within any social system, the oppressed find some room to maneuver through their own initiative. For instance, under the slave regime of America and the West Indies, Africans found ways and means of gaining small advantages. They would flatter and "con" the slavemasters, who were so arrogant and bigoted that they were readily fooled. Similarly, under colonialism many Africans played the game to secure what they could. Africans in positions like interpreters, police, and court officials often had their way over the ruling Europeans. However, that should not be mistaken for power or political participation or the exercise of individual freedom. Under slavery, power lay in the hands of the slave masters: under colonialism, power lay in the hands of the colonialists. The loss of power for the various African states meant a reduction in the freedom of every individual.

Colonialism was a negation of freedom from the viewpoint of the colonized. Even in quantitative terms it could not possibly bring modern political liberation to Africans comparable to the little that had been achieved by capitalism as an improvement of feudalism. In its political aspects, capitalism in the metropoles included constitutions, parliaments, freedom of the press. All of those things were limited in their application to the European working class, but they had existed in some form or fashion in the metropoles ever since the American War of Independence and the French Revolution. But Jules Ferry, a former French colonial minister, explained that the French Revolution was not fought on behalf of the blacks of Africa. Bourgeois liberty, equality, and fraternity was not for colonial subjects. Africans had to make do with bayonets, riot acts, and gunboats.

Negative Character of the Social, Political, and Economic Consequences

... During the centuries of pre-colonial trade, some control over social, political, and economic life was retained in Africa, in spite of the disadvantageous commerce with Europeans. That little control over internal matters disappeared under colonialism. Colonialism went much further than trade. It meant a tendency towards direct appropriation by Europeans of the social institutions within Africa. Africans ceased to set indigenous cultural goals and standards, and lost full command of training young members of the society. Those were undoubtedly major steps backward.

The Tunisian, Albert Memmi, puts forward the following proposition:

> The most serious blow suffered by the colonized is being removed from history and from the community. Colonization usurps any free role in either war or peace, every decision contributing to his destiny and that of the world, and all cultural and social responsibility.

Sweeping as that statement may initially appear, it is entirely true. The removal from history follows logically from the loss of power which colonialism represented. The power to act independently is the guarantee to participate actively and *consciously* in history. To be colonized is to be removed from history, except in the most passive sense. A striking illustration of the fact that colonial Africa was a passive object is seen in its attraction for white anthropologists, who came to study "primitive society." Colonialism determined that Africans were no more makers of history than were beetles – objects to be looked at under a microscope and examined for unusual features.

The negative impact of colonialism in political terms was quite dramatic. Overnight, African political states lost their power, independence, and meaning – irrespective of whether they were big empires or small polities. Certain traditional rulers were kept in office, and the formal structure of some kingdoms was partially retained, but the substance of political life was quite different. Political power had passed into the hands of foreign overlords. Of course, numerous African states in previous centuries had passed through the cycle of growth and decline. But colonial rule was different. So long as it lasted, not a single African state could flourish.

To be specific, it must be noted that colonialism crushed by force the surviving feudal states of North Africa; that the French wiped out the large Moslem state of the Western Sudan, as well as

Dahomey and kingdoms in Madagascar; that the British eliminated Egypt, the Mahdist Sudan, Asante, Benin, the Yoruba kingdoms, Swaziland, Matabeleland, the Lozi, and the East African lake kingdoms as great states. It should further be noted that a multiplicity of smaller and growing states were removed from the face of Africa by the Belgians, Portuguese, British, French, Germans, Spaniards, and Italians. Finally, those that appeared to survive were nothing but puppet creations. For instance, the Sultan of Morocco retained nominal existence under colonial rule which started in 1912; and the same applied to the Bey of Tunis; but Morocco and Tunisia were just as much under the power of French colonial administrators as neighboring Algeria, where the feudal rulers were removed altogether.

Sometimes, the African rulers who were chosen to serve as agents of foreign colonial rule were quite obviously nothing but puppets. The French and the Portuguese were in the habit of choosing their own African "chiefs"; the British went to Iboland and invented "warrant chiefs"; and all the colonial powers found it convenient to create "superior" or "paramount" rulers. Very often, the local population hated and despised such colonial stooges. There were traditional rulers such as the Sultan of Sokoto, the Kabaka of Buganda, and the Asantehene of Asante, who retained a great deal of prestige in the eyes of Africans, but they had no power to act outside the narrow boundaries laid down by colonialism, lest they find themselves in the Seychelles Islands as "guests of His Majesty's Government."

One can go so far as to say that colonial rule meant the effective eradication of African political power throughout the continent, since Liberia and Ethiopia could no longer function as independent states within the context of continent-wide colonialism. Liberia in particular had to bow before foreign political, economic, and military pressures in a way that no genuinely independent state could have accepted; and although Ethiopia held firm until 1936, most European capitalist nations were not inclined to treat Ethiopia as a sovereign state, primarily because it was African, and Africans were supposed to be colonial subjects.

The pattern of arrest of African political development has some features which can only be appreciated after careful scrutiny and the taking away of the blinkers which the colonizers put on the eyes of their subjects. An interesting case in point is that of women's role in society. Until today, capitalist society has failed to resolve the inequality between man and woman, which was entrenched in all modes of production prior to socialism. The colonialists in Africa occasionally paid lip service to women's education and emancipation, but objectively there was deterioration in the status of women owing to colonial rule.

A realistic assessment of the role of women in independent pre-colonial Africa shows two contrasting but combined tendencies. In the first place, women were exploited by men through polygamous arrangements designed to capture the labor power of women. As always, exploitation was accompanied by oppression; and there is evidence to the effect that women were sometimes treated like beasts of burden, as for instance in Moslem African societies. Nevertheless, there was a counter-tendency to insure the dignity of women to greater or lesser degree in all African societies. Mother-right was a prevalent feature of African societies, and particular women held a variety of privileges based on the fact that they were the keys to inheritance.

More important still, some women had real power in the political sense, exercised either through religion or directly within the politico-constitutional apparatus. In Mozambique, the widow of an Nguni king became the priestess in charge of the shrine set up in the burial place of her deceased husband, and the reigning king had to consult her on all important matters. In a few instances, women were actually heads of state. Among the Lovedu of Transvaal, the key figure was the Rain-Queen, combining political and religious functions. The most frequently encountered role of importance played by women was that of "Queen Mother" or "Queen Sister." In practice, that post was filled by a female of royal blood, who might be mother, sister, or aunt of the reigning king in places such as Mali, Asante, and Buganda. Her influence was considerable, and there were occasions when the "Queen Mother" was the real power and the male king a mere puppet.

What happened to African women under colonialism is that the social, religious, constitutional, and

political privileges and rights disappeared, while
the economic exploitation continued and was often
intensified. It was intensified because the division
of labor according to sex was frequently disrupted.
Traditionally, African men did the heavy labor of
felling trees, clearing land, building houses, apart
from conducting warfare and hunting. When they
were required to leave their farms to seek employment, women remained behind burdened with
every task necessary for the survival of themselves,
the children, and even the men as far as foodstuffs
were concerned. Moreover, since men entered the
money sector more easily and in greater numbers
than women, women's work became greatly inferior to that of men within the new value system of
colonialism: men's work was "modern" and wom-
en's was "traditional" and "backward." Therefore,
the deterioration in the status of African women
was bound up with the consequent loss of the right
to set indigenous standards of what work had merit
and what did not.

One of the most important manifestations of
historical arrest and stagnation in colonial Africa is
that which commonly goes under the title of "tribalism." That term, in its common journalistic setting, is understood to mean that Africans have a
basic loyalty to tribe rather than nation and that
each tribe still *retains* a fundamental hostility
towards its neighboring tribes. The examples
favored by the capitalist press and bourgeois scholarship are those of Congo and Nigeria. Their
accounts suggest that Europeans tried to make a
nation out of the Congolese and Nigerian peoples,
but they failed, because the various tribes had
their agelong hatreds; and, as soon as the colonial
power went, the natives *returned* to killing each
other. To this phenomenon, Europeans often
attach the word "atavism," to carry the notion that
Africans were returning to their primitive savagery. Even a cursory survey of the African past
shows that such assertions are the exact opposite
of the truth.

It is necessary to discuss briefly what comprises
a tribe – a term that has been avoided in this analysis, partly because it usually carries derogatory
connotations and partly because of its vagueness
and the loose ways in which it is employed in the
literature on Africa. Following the principle of
family living, Africans were organized in groups

which had common ancestors. Theoretically, the
tribe was the largest group of people claiming
descent from a common ancestor at some time in
the remote past. Generally, such a group could
therefore be said to be of the same ethnic stock,
and their language would have a great deal in common. Beyond that, members of a tribe were seldom
all members of the same political unit and very seldom indeed did they all share a common social
purpose in terms of activities, such as trade and
warfare. Instead, African states were sometimes
based entirely on part of the members of a given
ethnic group or (more usually) on an amalgamation of members of different ethnic communities.

All of the large states of nineteenth-century
Africa were multi-ethnic, and their expansion was
continually making anything like "tribal" loyalty a
thing of the past, by substituting in its place
national and class ties. However, in all parts of the
world, that substitution of national and class ties
for purely ethnic ones is a lengthy historical process; and, invariably there remains for long periods
certain regional pockets of individuals who have
their own narrow, regional loyalties, springing
from ties of kinship, language, and culture. In
Asia, the feudal states of Vietnam and Burma both
achieved a considerable degree of national homogeneity over the centuries before colonial rule. But
there were pockets of "tribes" or "minorities" who
remained outside the effective sphere of the
nationstate and the national economy and culture.

In the first place, colonialism blocked the further evolution of national solidary, because it
destroyed the particular Asian or African states
which were the principal agents for achieving the
liquidation of fragmented loyalties. In the second
place, because ethnic and regional loyalties which
go under the name of "tribalism" could not be
effectively resolved by the colonial state, they
tended to fester and grow in unhealthy forms.
Indeed, the colonial powers sometimes saw the
value of stimulating the internal tribal jealousies
so as to keep the colonized from dealing with their
principal contradiction with the European
overlords – i.e., the classic technique of divide and
rule. Certainly, the Belgians consciously fostered
that; and the racist whites in South Africa had
by the 1950s worked out a careful plan to "develop"
the oppressed African population as Zulu, as

Xhosa, and as Sotho so that the march towards broader African national and class solidarities could be stopped and turned back.

The civil war in Nigeria is generally regarded as having been a tribal affair. To accept such a contention would mean extending the definition of tribe to cover Shell Oil and Gulf Oil! But, quite apart from that, it must be pointed out that nowhere in the history of pre-colonial independent Nigeria can anyone point to the massacre of Ibos by Hausas or any incident which suggests that people up to the nineteenth century were fighting each other because of ethnic origin. Of course there were wars, but they had a rational basis in trade rivalry, religious contentions, and the clashes of political expansion. What came to be called tribalism at the beginning of the new epoch of political independence in Nigeria was itself a product of the way that people were brought together under colonialism so as to be exploited. It was a product of administrative devices, of entrenched regional separations, of differential access by particular ethnic groups into the colonial economy and culture.

31

The Invention of Tradition in Colonial Africa

Terence Ranger

Introduction

The 1870s, 1880s and 1890s were the time of a great flowering of European invented tradition – ecclesiastical, educational, military, republican, monarchical. They were also the time of the European rush into Africa. There were many and complex connections between the two processes. The concept of Empire was central to the process of inventing tradition within Europe itself, but the African empires came so late in the day that they demonstrate the effects rather than the causes of European invented tradition. Deployed in Africa, however, the new traditions took on a peculiar character, distinguishing them from both their European and Asian Imperial forms.

By contrast to India many parts of Africa became colonies of white settlement. This meant that the settlers had to define themselves as natural and undisputed masters of vast numbers of Africans. They drew upon European invented traditions both to define and to justify their roles, and also to provide models of subservience into which it was sometimes possible to draw Africans. In Africa, therefore, the whole apparatus of invented school and professional and regimental traditions became much more starkly a matter of command and control than it was within Europe itself. Moreover, in Europe these invented traditions of the new ruling classes were to some extent balanced by the invented traditions of industrial workers or by the invented "folk" cultures of peasants. In Africa, no white agriculturalist saw himself as a peasant. White workers in the mines of southern Africa certainly drew upon the invented rituals of European craft unionism but they did so partly because they were rituals of exclusiveness and could be used to prevent Africans being defined as workers.

By contrast to India, once again, Africa did not offer to its conquerors the framework of an indigenous imperial state nor existing centralized rituals of honour and degree. Ready connections between African and European systems of governance could only be made at the level of the monarchy; Africa possessed, so the colonisers thought, dozens of rudimentary kings. Hence in Africa the British made an even greater use of the idea of "Imperial Monarchy" than they did within Britain or India.

From Terence Ranger, "The Invention of Tradition in Colonial Africa", in *The Invention of Tradition*, ed. Eric Hobsbawm and Terence Ranger (1983), by permission of the author and Past and Present Society, from Cambridge University Press.

The "theology" of an omniscient, omnipotent and omnipresent monarchy became almost the sole ingredient of imperial ideology as it was presented to Africans. For the Germans, too, the Kaiser stood as the dominant symbol of German rule. The French had the more difficult task of incorporating Africans into a republican tradition.

But serviceable as the monarchical ideology was to the British, it was not enough in itself to provide the theory or justify the structures of colonial governance on the spot. Since so few connections could be made between British and African political, social and legal systems, British administrators set about inventing African traditions for Africans. Their own respect for "tradition" disposed them to look with favour upon what they took to be traditional in Africa. They set about to codify and promulgate these traditions, thereby transforming flexible custom into hard prescription.

All this is part of the history of European ideas, but it is also very much part of the history of modern Africa. These complex processes have to be understood before a historian can arrive at any understanding of the particularity of Africa before colonialism; many African scholars as well as many European Africanists have found it difficult to free themselves from the false models of colonial codified African "tradition". However, the study of these processes is not only a part of historiography but of history. The invented traditions imported from Europe not only provided whites with models of command but also offered many Africans models of "modern" behaviour. The invented traditions of African societies – whether invented by the Europeans or by Africans themselves in response – distorted the past but became in themselves realities through which a good deal of colonial encounter was expressed. ...

Bringing Africans into the Traditions of Governance

... There were two very direct ways in which Europeans sought to make use of their invented traditions to transform and modernize African thought and conduct. One was the acceptance of the idea that *some* Africans could become members of the governing class of colonial Africa, and hence the extension to such Africans of training in a neo-traditional context. The second – and more common – was an attempt to make use of what European invented traditions had to offer in terms of a redefined relationship between leader and led. The regimental tradition, after all, defined the roles of both officers and men; the great-house tradition of rural gentility defined the roles of both masters and servants; the public school tradition defined the roles of both prefects and fags. All this might be made use of to create a clearly defined hierarchical society in which Europeans commanded and Africans accepted commands, but both within a shared framework of pride and loyalty. Thus if the traditions which workers and peasants had made for themselves in Europe did not exercise much influence on Africans under colonialism, invented European traditions of subordination exercised a very considerable influence indeed.

The best illustration of the first idea – that some Africans might be turned into governors by exposure to British neo-tradition – is perhaps the famous school, King's College, Budo, in Uganda. The fullest account is by G.P. McGregor, who perceptively points out that the provision of elementary education was only just being taken seriously in Britain itself in the 1870s as part of the process of bringing the majority of the population to its place in the vocational and educational hierarchy. Hence the spread of elementary schools in Buganda at the end of the nineteenth century was a remarkably little-delayed extension of the same process to the African empire. But in Buganda, while this sort of education seemed appropriate enough to the peasant cultivator majority, the Anglican missionaries did not feel that it was suitable for the Ganda aristocracy.

So far little or nothing had been done for the children of the upper classes [wrote Bishop Tucker], who in many respects were worse off than the children of the peasants. We felt strongly that if the ruling classes of the country were to exercise in the days to come an influence for good upon their people and to have a sense of responsibility towards them, it was essential that something should be done for the education of these neglected children, on the soundest possible lines ... by the discipline of work and games in a boarding school so as to build character as to enable the

Baganda to take their proper place in the administrative, commercial and industrial life of their
own country.[1]

In short, in Buganda the missionaries aimed to
place on top of British-style elementary education
a structure of British-style secondary education
of a neo-traditional kind. They were always clear
that their aim was "the adaptation of our English
Public School method to the African scene." They
succeeded to an extraordinary extent. King's
College was built on the Coronation Hill of the
Baganda kings, so that "both Coronation Services
of this century have been held" in the college
chapel; "though some of the traditional ceremonies were observed," the service "followed many
of the features of the English coronation service."[2]
The English Public School house spirit (was)
quickly established," and the Gandan members
of Turkey House petitioned that its name be
changed to Canada House so as to go with England
House, South Africa House and Australia House –
Turkey seemed "distinctly unimperial." The
school motto, again said to have been chosen at
the request of the pupils, was a Gandan version of
Cecil Rhodes's dying words, "So little done – so
much to do."

McGregor quotes a letter from a Gandan pupil
written in the first year of the school's existence,
which enables us to see this remarkable process of
socialization through Gandan eyes.

First in the mornings when we have got up we
arrange properly our beds. If you do not arrange
it properly there is judgement or rebuke when the
Europeans make a visit … On the front of our
cups there is a likeness of a lion. That it is by
which the scholars of Budo may be known. And
no-one may eat any thing in the cubicle, nor coffee which they chew, but only in the verandah
where food is eaten. We sing one hymn and pray
and then we learn English … When we come out
at four, we go and play football, on one side eleven
and on the other side eleven, and we arrange
every man in his place, goalkeeper, and back men
and ba-half-back and ba-forward.[3]

Everyone agreed that Budo had managed to create
that intangible thing, "the spirit of the school." It
was present at Budo

at its best, as we have breathed it in England after
generations of experiment – the spirit of the
team, of discipline, of local patriotism – and very
remarkable has been the translation of it into the
heart of Africa.

Sir Phillip Mitchell thought that Budo was "one
of the few places here which has a soul." Expatriate
teachers later came to criticize "the Budonian
habit of defending worthless traditions merely on
the grounds that they have always been there."[4]

Whatever the tensions of doing so within the
imperial framework which so firmly subordinated
the Gandan ruling class to British administrative
officers, and the Gandan monarchy to the imperial
crown, there is no doubt that the missionaries created at Budo a successful complex of new traditions, which worked themselves out parallel to an
increasing ceremonialism of the role of the Kabaka
and the other Ugandan kings so as to achieve a
synthesis not unlike that accomplished in
nineteenth-century England. The Golden Jubilee
ceremonies of the college – "We had four Kings at
the high table" – were also a ritual expression of
the commitment of a large section of the Gandan
ruling class to these by now hallowed invented traditions.[5] But the Budo experiment was not to
become a general model; the British themselves
came to regret their original alliance with the
Ganda chiefs, and to believe that real modernizing
change could not be brought about through their
agency. Real modernizing change would be the
product of European commanders loyally supported by African subordinates.

Various traditions of subordination were available. One was the tradition of the hierarchy of the
great house. Part of the self-image of the European
in Africa was his prescriptive right to have black
servants – at the height of the labour crisis in the
South African mines, there were more black men
employed in Johannesburg as domestic servants
than as mine workers.[6] In 1914 Frank Weston,
bishop of Zanzibar, contrasted Islamic community
in Africa with Christian differentiation. The
African Christian, he wrote, has nothing to adhere
to but "a few Europeans who pass him in the street;
he is beneath them; they may be kind to him; he
may perhaps be a steward in their dining room, or
a butler … but Brotherhood? Well, it is not yet."[7]

There was no impulse towards "Brotherhood" in colonial Africa. For most Europeans the favoured image of their relationship with Africans was that of paternal master and loyal servant. It was an image readily transferred to industrial employment. Throughout southern Africa, African employees were not defined as workers but instead controlled and disciplined under the terms of Masters and Servants Acts.

Few whites in Africa, however, maintained domestic establishments of a size which would have allowed the full "traditional" panoply of the British servant hierarchy. A more elaborate application of European neo-traditions of subordination came with the restructuring of African armies. In Sylvanus Cookey's fascinating account of this process, the French emerge as the first and most imaginative manipulators of the military invented tradition. Faidherbe in the 1850s disbanded his demoralized pressed levies and attracted African volunteers with "seduisant" uniforms, modern arms, Koranic oaths of allegiance and crash courses in the military glory of the French tradition.

> It was even suggested from Paris, as a means of instilling at an early age a sense of the military mode in the young Africans and preparing them for a military career, that the children of the *tirailleurs* should be provided uniforms and miniature equipment similar to those of their parents.[8]

The British were slower to follow such a policy. But in the face of the French threat they also moved to regularize their African regiments. Lugard devoted his meticulous passion for detail to the transformation of his Nigerian levies from a "rabble" to a disciplined and effective fighting force. Soon he came to esteem them highly; official praise was lavished on them for their conduct in campaigns in the Gold Coast and northern Nigeria; a regimental tradition was being built up as rapidly as the spirit of Budo. Lugard's administration was largely staffed by army officers; in East Africa, too, "governments were largely military in character during these early years," and Professor George Shepperson has commented on

> the narrowness of the line between the civilian and the military ... It was through its forces as

much as its missions that European culture was brought to the indigenous inhabitants of British Central Africa.[9] ...

There was a rough periodization in all this. European invented traditions were important for Africans in a series of overlapping phases. The military neo-tradition, with its clearly visible demarcations of hierarchy and its obvious centrality to the workings of early colonialism, was the first powerful influence. Its impact reached a climax – particularly in eastern Africa – with the campaigns of the first world war. Thereafter, especially in British Africa, the military presence declined.[10] The military mode became less influential that the modes of missionary employment or the bureaucratic build-up of Africans in state and business employment. But the debate over the sequence of influence or the debate over which neo-tradition was in the end most influential – a debate that sways to and fro as African kings, surrounded by neo-traditional trappings, dominate some new African states; as bureaucratic élites triumph in others; and Mazrui's "lumpen-militariat" control yet others – is less important in the end than an assessment of the overall effect of these processes of neo-traditional socialization.

This was surely very large indeed. European invented traditions offered Africans a series of clearly defined points of entry into the colonial world, though in almost all cases it was entry into the subordinate part of a man/master relationship. They began by socializing Africans into acceptance of one or other readily available European neo-traditional modes of conduct – the historical literature is full of Africans proud of having mastered the business of being a member of a regiment or having learnt how to be an effective practitioner of the ritual of nineteenth-century Anglicanism. The process often ended with serious challenges to the colonial power, often couched in terms of the socializing neo-traditions themselves. ... This is a pattern worked out by Martin Channock for the school teacher traditionalists of Nyasaland, and in greater detail by John Iliffe for Tanganyika.[11] In its varying forms it underlay a good deal of what we call nationalism. It is distressing, but not in the least surprising, that

Kenneth Kaunda in his search for a personal ideology to help him on the road to national leadership found solace and inspiration in Arthur Mee's Books for Boys.[12]

If we return for a moment to the question of "modernization" through the use of European invented traditions, both their advantages and their limitations to the colonizers become plain. They *did* serve to separate out Africans into relatively specialized categories – the askari, the teacher, the servant and so on – and to provide a rudimentary professionalization of African workers. Embedded in the neo-traditions of governance and subordination, there were very clear-cut requirements for the observance of industrial time and work discipline – the neatly, even fanatically, prescribed segments of the schoolboys' day at Budo; the drill square as source and symbol of discipline and punctuality. On the other hand, the invented traditions which were introduced to Africans were those of governance rather than of production. Industrial workers may have been categorized as "servants", but for a very long time the true domestic servant commanded a much greater prestige and could manipulate the reciprocities contained in the master/servant relationship from which the industrial worker was cut off. Industrial workers and peasants never had access to the clear-cut and prestigious ceremonials of the soldier, the teacher, the clerk – except insofar as they assumed them for themselves in the costumes of carnival or competitive dance.[13] And as we have seen, where craft union traditions did exist Africans were specifically excluded from them. African industrial workers were left to work out for themselves a consciousness and mode of behaviour appropriate to their condition.[14]

This was one of the many reasons for the relatively high prestige among Africans in colonial Africa of non-productive employment. And at the same time, if the new traditions of subordination had begun "usefully" to define certain sorts of specializations, they gave rise later to profoundly conservative conceptualizations of these specializations, making African teachers, ministers and soldiers notoriously resistant to subsequent attempts at modernizing change. ...

Europeans and "Tradition" in Africa

The invented traditions of nineteenth-century Europe had been introduced into Africa to allow Europeans and certain Africans to combine for "modernizing" ends. But there was an inherent ambiguity in neo-traditional thought. Europeans belonging to one or other of the neo-traditions believed themselves to have a respect for the customary. They liked the idea of age-old prescriptive rights and they liked to compare the sort of title which an African chief possessed with the title to gentlemanliness which they laid claim to themselves. A profound misunderstanding was at work here. In comparing European neo-traditions with the customary in Africa the whites were certainly comparing unlike with unlike. European invented traditions were marked by their inflexibility. They involved sets of recorded rules and procedures – like the modern coronation rites. They gave reassurance because they represented what was unchanging in a period of flux. Now, when Europeans thought of the customary in Africa, they naturally ascribed to it these same characteristics. The assertion by whites that African society was profoundly conservative – living within age-old rules which did not change; living within an ideology based on the absence of change; living within a framework of clearly defined hierarchical status – was by no means always intended as an indictment of African backwardness or reluctance to modernize. Often it was intended as a compliment to the admirable qualities of tradition, even though it was a quite misconceived compliment. This attitude towards "traditional" Africa became more marked as whites came to realize in the 1920s and 1930s that rapid economic transformation was just not going to take place in Africa and that most Africans had to remain members of rural communities, or as some whites came to dislike the consequences of the changes which *had* taken place. The African collaborators, playing their role within one or other of the introduced European traditions, then came to seem less admirable than "real" Africans, still presumed to be inhabiting their own, appropriate universe of tradition.

The trouble with this approach was that it totally misunderstood the realities of pre-colonial Africa. These societies had certainly valued custom and

continuity but custom was loosely defined and infinitely flexible. Custom helped to maintain a sense of
identity but it also allowed for an adaptation so
spontaneous and natural that it was often unper-
ceived. Moreover, there rarely existed in fact the
closed corporate consensual system which came to
be accepted as characteristic of "traditional" Africa.
Almost all recent studies of nineteenth-century
pre-colonial Africa have emphasized that far from
there being a single "tribal" identity, most Africans
moved in and out of multiple identities, defining
themselves at one moment as subject to this chief, at
another moment as a member of that cult, at another
moment as part of this clan, and at yet another
moment as an initiate in that professional guild.
These overlapping networks of association and
exchange extended over wide areas. Thus the
boundaries of the "tribal" polity and the hierarchies
of authority within them did *not* define conceptual
horizons of Africans. As Wim van Binsbergen
remarks, in criticizing Africanist historians for their
acceptance of something called "Chewa identity" as
a useful organizing concept for the past:

> Modern Central Africa tribes are not so much
> survivals from a pre-colonial past but rather
> largely colonial creations by colonial officers and
> African intellectuals ... Historians fail to qualify
> the alleged Chewa homogeneity against the his-
> torical evidence of incessant assimilation and dis-
> sociation of peripheral groups ... They do not
> differentiate between a seniority system of rulers
> imposed by the colonial freezing of political
> dynamics and the pre-colonial competitive, shift-
> ing, fluid imbalance of power and influence.[15]

Similarly, nineteenth-century Africa was *not* characterized by lack of internal social and economic
competition, by the unchallenged authority of the
elders, by an acceptance of custom which gave
every person – young and old, male and female – a
place in society which was defined and protected.
Competition, movement, fluidity were as much
features of small-scale communities as they were of
larger groupings. Thus Marcia Wright has shown,
in a stimulating account of the realities of late
nineteenth-century society in the Lake Tanganyika
corridor, that economic and political competition

overrode the "customary securities" offered to
women by marriage or extended kinship relations.
Women constantly found themselves being shaken
out of the niches in which they had sought security,
and constantly tried to find new niches for themselves. Later on, of course, and in the twentieth
century, the dogmas of customary security and
immutably fixed relationships grew up in these
same societies, which came to have an appearance
of *ujamaa* style solidarity; the nineteenth-century
time of "rapid change", in which "formal structural factors" became relatively less important than
"personal resilience and powers of decision," gave
way to stablization. As Marcia Wright remarks:

> the terms of the reconstruction were dictated by
> the colonial authorities in the years after 1895,
> when pacification came to mean immobilization
> of populations, re-inforcement of ethnicity and
> greater rigidity of social definition.[16]

Hence "custom" in the Tanganyika corridor was
much more of an invention than it was a restora
tion. In other places, where the competitive
dynamic of the nineteenth century had given many
opportunities for young men to establish independent bases of economic, social and political
influence, colonialism saw an establishment of
control by elders of land allocation, marriage
transactions and political office. Small-scale
gerontocracies were a defining feature of the
twentieth rather than of the nineteenth century.

Some part of these twentieth-century processes
of "immobilization of populations, re-inforcement
of ethnicity and greater rigidity of social definition"
were the necessary and unplanned consequences of
colonial economic and political change – of the
break up of internal patterns of trade and communication, the defining of territorial boundaries, the
alienation of land, the establishment of Reserves.
But some part of them were the result of a conscious
determination on the part of the colonial authorities
to "re-establish" order and security and a sense of
community by means of defining and enforcing
"tradition". Administrators who had begun by proclaiming their support for exploited commoners
against rapacious chiefs ended by backing "traditional" chiefly authority in the interests of social

control.[17] Missionaires who had begun by taking
converts right out of their societies so as to transform their consciousness in "Christian villages"
ended by proclaiming the virtues of "traditional"
small-scale community. Everyone sought to tidy up
and make more comprehensible the infinitely complex situation which they held to be a result of the
"untraditional" chaos of the nineteenth century.
People were to be "returned" to their tribal identities; ethnicity was to be "restored" as the basis of
association and organization.[18] The new rigidities,
immobilizations and ethnic identifications, while
serving very immediate European interests, could
nevertheless be seen by the whites as fully "traditional" and hence as legitimated. The most far-
reaching inventions of tradition in colonial Africa
took place when the Europeans believed themselves
to be respecting age-old African custom. What were
called customary law, customary land-rights, customary political structure and so on, were in fact *all*
invented by colonial codification.

There is a growing anthropological and historical literature on these processes which it is not
possible to summarize here. But a few striking
statements will give an indication of the argument.
Thus John Iliffe describes the "creation of tribes"
in colonial Tanganyika:

> The notion of the tribe lay at the heart of indirect
> rule in Tanganyika. Refining the racial thinking
> common in German times, administrators believed
> that every African belonged to a tribe, just as every
> European belonged to a nation. The idea doubtless
> owed much to the Old Testament, to Tacitus and
> Caesar, to academic distinctions between tribal
> societies based on status and modern societies
> based on contract, and to the post-war anthropolo-
> gists who preferred "tribal" to the more pejorative
> word "savage." Tribes were seen as cultural units
> "possessing a common language, a single social
> system, and an established common law." Their
> political and social systems rested on kinship.
> Tribal membership was hereditary. Different
> tribes were related genealogically … As unusually
> well-informed officials knew, this stereotype bore
> little relation to Tanganyika's kaleidoscopic his-
> tory, but it was the shifting sand on which
> Cameron and his disciples erected indirect rule
> by "taking the *tribal* unit." They had the power
> and they created the political geography.[19]

Elizabeth Colson describes the evolution of "customary land law" in much the same way:

> The newly created system was described as rest-
> ing on tradition and presumably derived its legiti-
> macy from immemorial custom. The degree to
> which it was a reflection of the contemporary situ-
> ation and the joint creation of colonial officials and
> African leaders … was unlikely to be recognized.

The point is not merely that so-called custom in
fact concealed new balances of power and wealth,
since this was precisely what custom in the past
had always been able to do, but that these particular constructs of customary law became codified
and rigid and unable so readily to reflect change in
the future. Colson remarks that

> colonial officers expected the courts to enforce
> long-established custom rather than current
> opinion. Common stereotypes about African cus-
> tomary law thus came to be used by colonial offi-
> cials in assessing the legality of current decisions,
> and so came to be incorporated in "customary"
> systems of tenure.[20]

Similarly, Wyatt MacGaffey has shown how the
Bakongo peoples moved from a pre-colonial situation of "processes of dispersal and assimilation,"
of "the shunting of subordinate populations of
slaves and pawns," of "a confusion of debts, assets,
scandals and grievances," into a colonial situation
of much more precise and static definition of community and of land rights.

> In the evolution of tradition, the touchstone of
> merit was very often the presiding judge's con-
> cept of customary society, derived ultimately
> from … a lingering European image of the African
> kingdom of Prester John … Court records con-
> tain evidence of the evolution for forensic pur-
> poses away from the magical in the direction of
> the evidential and refutable … Those whose tra-
> ditions lost a case came back a year or two later
> with better traditions.

Once again, my point is not so much that "traditions" changed to accommodate new circumstances but that at a certain point they had to
stop changing; once the "traditions" relating to

community identity and land right were written down in court records and exposed to the criteria of the invented customary model, a new and unchanging body of tradition had been created.

> Eventually there resulted a synthesis of the new and the old, which is now called "custom". The main features of customary society, responding to the conditions that developed between 1908 and 1921, assumed their present form in the 1920s.[21]

Around the same time Europeans began to be more interested in and sympathetic towards the "irrational" and ritualistic aspects of "tradition". In 1917 an Anglican mission theologian suggested that for the first time missionaries in the field should "collect information with regard to the religious ideas of the black man", so that their relationship to traditional society could be understood. "In the twentieth century we are no longer contented to cut the knot, as the nineteenth century did, and say: Science has put an end to these superstitions."[22] After the first world war, Anglicans in East Africa, faced with the need to reconstruct rural society after the ravages of the fighting and the subsequent impact of the depression, began to make anthropological analyses of those aspects of "traditional" ritual which had contributed towards social stability. Out of such inquiry came the well-known policy of missionary "adaptation," which produced its most developed example in the Christianized initiation ceremonies of the Masasi diocese in south-eastern Tanganyika.[23] More generally, there emerged from this kind of thought and practice – with its emphasis upon rituals of continuity and stability – a concept of immemorial "African Traditional Religion" which did less than justice to the variety and vitality of pre-colonial African religious forms.

African Manipulation of Invented Custom

All this could not have been achieved, of course, without a good deal of African participation. As John Iliffe writes:

> The British wrongly believed that Tanganyikans belonged to tribes; Tanganyikans created tribes to function within the colonial framework ... [The] new political geography ... would have been transient had it not co-incided with similar trends among Africans. They too had to live amidst bewildering social complexity, which they ordered in kinship terms and buttressed with invented history. Moreover, Africans wanted effective units of action just as officials wanted effective units of government ... Europeans believed Africans belonged to tribes; Africans built tribes to belong to.[24]

We have already seen in the case of the Tumbuka paramountcy how African rulers and mission-educated "modernizers" could combine in an attempt to manipulate the symbols of monarchy. Iliffe shows how similar alliances helped to build up the ideas and structures of "tribal" tradition.

> During the twenty years after 1925 Tanganyika experienced a vast social reorganization in which Europeans and Africans combined to create a new political order based on mythical history ... Analysing the system [of indirect rule] one officer concluded that its main supporters were the progressive chiefs ... It is clear that they were the key figures in indirect rule. Its chief virtue was indeed to release their energies ... The native administrations employed many members of the local elite ... Even educated men without native administration posts generally acknowledged hereditary authority ... In return many chiefs welcomed educated guidance.

Iliffe describes progressive chiefs and mission-educated Africans combining in a programme of "progressive traditionalism."

> Just as later nationalists sought to create a national culture, so those who built modern tribes emphasized tribal culture. In each case educated men took the lead ... The problem was to synthesize, to "pick out what is best from (European culture) and dilute it with what we hold". In doing so, educated men naturally reformulated the past, so that their syntheses were actually new creations.[25]

One area in which African intellectuals interacted with "adaptation" missionary theory was in the invention of "Traditional Religion."

It was not until missionaries studied African religions carefully during the 1920s that most Africans dared to consider their attitudes publicly. Michel Kikurwe, a Zigua teacher and cultural tribalist, envisaged a golden age of traditional African society … Samuel Sehoza pioneered the idea that indigenous religious beliefs had prefigured Christianity.

Like the missionaries these men emphasized the function of religion in stabilizing society.

> In each district [wrote Kikurwe] men and women were busy to help one another, they taught their children the same laws and traditions. Every Chief tried as much as he could to help and please his people, and likewise his people did the same in turn, they all knew what was lawful and unlawful, and they knew that there was a powerful God in heaven.[26]

It is easy enough to see the personal advantages which these inventors of tradition stood to gain. The successful teacher or minister who stood at the right hand of a paramount was a man of very real power. The African clergy who constructed the model of "Traditional Religion" as the inspiring ideology of stable pre-colonial communities were making a claim to do the same for modern African societies by means of "adapted" Christianity.[27] Yet Iliffe concludes that

> it would be wrong to be cynical. The effort to create a Nyakyusa tribe was as honest and constructive as the essentially similar effort forty years later to create a Tanganyikan nation. Both were attempts to build societies in which men could live well in the modern world.[28]

But there was still an ambiguity in invented African tradition. However much it may have been used by the "progressive traditionalists" to inaugurate new ideas and institutions – like compulsory education under the Tumbuka paramountcy – codified tradition inevitably hardened in a way that advantaged the vested interests in possession at the time of its codification. Codified and reified custom was manipulated by such vested interests as a means of asserting or increasing control. This happened in four particular situations; though it was not restricted to them.

Elders tended to appeal to "tradition" in order to defend their dominance of the rural means of production against challenge by the young. Men tended to appeal to "tradition" in order to ensure that the increasing role which women played in production in the rural areas did not result in any diminution of male control over women as economic assets. Paramount chiefs and ruling aristocracies in polities which included numbers of ethnic and social groupings appealed to "tradition" in order to maintain or extend their control over their subjects. Indigenous populations appealed to "tradition" in order to ensure that the migrants who settled amongst them did not achieve political or economic rights.

The Use of "Tradition" by Elders against Youth

The colonial reification of rural custom produced a situation very much at variance with the pre-colonial situation. The pre-colonial movement of men and ideas was replaced by the colonial custom-bounded, microcosmic local society. It was important for the colonial authorities to limit regional interaction and thus to prevent a widening of focus on the part of Africans. For this reason they were prepared to back collaborators at the local level and to endorse their dominance. But at the same time the colonial powers wanted to extract labour from these rural societies, so that young men were being drawn to places of employment very much more distant than the range of journeying in the pre-colonial past. These young men were expected to be at one and the same time workers in a distant urban economy and acceptant citizens in the tightly defined micro-cosmic society.

This situation created many tensions. Returning migrants came back into a society tightly controlled by the elders; the elders, in turn, were alarmed at the new skills and funds possessed by the migrants. The elders stressed their customary, prescriptive rights which gave them control of land and women, and hence of patronage. MacGaffey describes the colonial Bakongo village in these terms:

> A man remains a cadet until he is about forty, perhaps longer … He is at the beck and call of his elders, whose tone towards him is often peremptory.

Young men speak of their elders as jealous and fault-finding. The status of young men is that of the client ... The control exercised over their dependants by the elders is a function of their managerial monopoly in routine public affairs.

This managerial monopoly is largely a function of the elders' control of "traditional" knowledge, on which claims to land and resources are based. MacGaffey records "the objection of elders" when "bright young men busily took notes" at a land hearing case, and thus threatened to break the elders' monopoly.[29]

The response of young men to this manipulation of "tradition" could take one of two forms. The key object was to outflank the elders and their sphere of local, but colonially invented, tradition. This could be done by adopting one or other of the European neo-traditions. Thus returning migrants often established themselves as catechists – whether recognized by the missions or not – and set up their own villages on new principles of organization, as it will be remembered was the case with the uniformed congregations of western Kenya. This was easier to do, however, in the earlier colonial period before both European church and European state began to insist on a proper subordination to custom. In MacGaffey's village, the young men, deprived of a real escape, took refuge in a fantasy one.

> For those who are young in years a degree of compensation is provided by the Dikembe, a social club catering to the unmarried men ... Dikembe culture, an interesting caricature of the serious magico-religious beliefs and principles of the older generation which it defies, contains the seeds of an anti-society ... The doors of the bachelor huts bear such inscriptions as "Palais d'Amour" in Gothic lettering ... The culture of the Dikembe is that of *billisme*, whose heroes are the stars of romantic French and American movies [and] takes its name from Buffalo Bill, "sheriff due quartier Santa Fe, metro d'amour."[30]

These light-hearted absurdities conceal a serious attempt to discredit "custom," endorsed as it is by the whites, through the subversive effects of European fantasy.

However, another path had also been open to the young in the colonial period and before the rise of the nationalist parties. This had been to outflank the reified "custom" of the elders by appeals to more dynamic and transformative aspects of the traditional. Recent commentators have increasingly seen the very widespread witchcraft eradication movements of the colonial period, with their promise of a society freed from evil, in this sort of way. MacGaffey describes how in his Bakongo village the management of witchcraft accusation by the elders caused great discontent, and led to the arrival of a "prophet" who undertook to eliminate witchcraft, an achievement which would deprive the elders of a potent form of social control. The result was "the temporary paralysis of the elders." Roy Willis has shown how in rural south-western Tanganyika in the 1950s young men tried to break the control exercised by elders over land and local "routine public affairs", by making use of a series of witchcraft eradication movements, which out-flanked invented custom by an appeal to the pre-social Golden Age.[31]

Of the many other analyses which support the argument, I will content myself with citing a particularly cogent, and as yet unpublished, account of the well-known Watch Tower sectarian movement in southern and central Africa. Sholto Cross concludes:

> The three mining belts of settler Africa ... provide the central focus of the movement and the migrant labourer was the main bearer ... The migrant system which existed in these territories ... prolonged the period in which the Africans could be regarded as bound by their tribal culture ... yet at the same time policies designed to promote labour mobility were instituted which undermined the economic basis of this tribal culture ... The rate of change in the industrial areas far outstripped that in the rural hinterlands, yet the migrant labourers continued to move between the two worlds of town and country ... The proliferation of Watch Tower villages [was caused by] the series of restraints placed upon the returning migrant. Customary authorities were jealous of the new men, whose way of life emphasized urban values ... The prevalence of women and youth in the rural Watch Tower suggests that economic cleavages were reinforced by other forms of

differentiation ... The forward looking ideas of the hoped-for liberation (promised) by millenial Watch Tower were such that customary authority itself became a major object of attack.[32]

[...]

Conclusion

African politicians, cultural nationalists and, indeed, historians are left with two ambiguous legacies from the colonial invention of traditions. One is the body of invented traditions imported from Europe which in some parts of Africa still exercises an influence on ruling class culture which it has largely lost in Europe itself. In his *Prison Diary* Ngugi wa Thiong'o (See Chapter 32, this volume) writes savagely of the contemporary Kenyan élite:

The members of a comprador bourgeoisie of a former settler colony count themselves lucky. They don't have to travel and reside abroad to know and copy the culture of the imperialist bourgeoisie: have they not learnt it all from the colonial settler representatives of metropolitan culture? Nurtured in the womb of the old colonial system, they have matured to their full compradorial heights, looking to the local Europeans as the alpha and omega of gentlemanly refinement and lady-like elegance. With racial barriers to class mobility thrown open, the deportment of a European gentleman – rosebuds and pins in coat lapels, spotless white kerchiefs in breast pockets, tail-coats, top-hats and gold-chained pocket watches – is no longer in the realm of dreams and wishes ... The most popular columns in the old settler papers ... were the social pages ... Well, the columns are now back in the glossy bourgeois monthlies ... The settler played golf and polo, went to horse-races or on the royal hunt in red-

coats and riding-breeches ... The black pupils now do the same, only with greater zeal: golf and horses have become "national" institutions.[33]

Other new states, less open to Ngugi's charges, express their national sovereignty with the national anthems, flags and rallies which Eric Hobsbawm describes for nineteenth-century Europe. Representing as they do new multi-ethnic territorial states the African nations are much less engaged in the invention of past "national cultures" than were the Scottish or Welsh Romantics.

The second ambiguous legacy is that of "traditional" African culture; the whole body of reified "tradition" invented by colonial administrators, missionaries, "progressive traditionalists," elders and anthropologists. Those like Ngugi who repudiate bourgeois élite culture face the ironic danger of embracing another set of colonial inventions instead. Ngugi himself solves the difficulty by embracing the tradition of Kenyan popular resistance to colonialism. As this chapter suggests, young men, women, immigrants – the exploited groups with whom Ngugi has sympathy – *have* sometimes been able to tap the continued vitality of the mingled continuity and innovation which resides within indigenous cultures as they have continued to develop underneath the rigidities of codified colonial custom.

As for historians, they have at least a double task. They have to free themselves from the illusion that the African custom recorded by officials or by many anthropologists is any sort of guide to the African past. But they also need to appreciate how much invented traditions of all kinds have to do with the history of Africa in the twentieth century and strive to produce better founded accounts of them than this preliminary sketch.

Notes

Terence Ranger has returned to the issues raised in this chapter in "The Invention of Tradition Revisited: The Case of Colonial Africa," in Terence Ranger and Olufemi Vaughan, eds., *Legitimacy and the State in Twentieth-Century Africa*, St Antony's/Macmillan, 1993, pp. 62–111.

1   G.P. McGregor, *Kings College, Budo: The First Sixty Years* (London, 1967), pp. 6, 16.

2   *Ibid.*, pp. 35–6.
3   *Ibid.*, pp. 17–18.
4   *Ibid.*, pp. 54, 117, 124.
5   *Ibid.*, p. 136.
6   Charles van Onselen, "The Witches of Suburbia: Domestic Service on the Witwaterstand, 1890–1914" (unpublished MS.).

7 Frank Weston, "Islam in Zanzibar Diocese," *Central Africa*, xxxii, no. 380 (Aug. 1914).

8 S.J. Cookey, "Origins and pre-1914 Character of the Colonial Armies in West Africa" (Univ. of California, Los Angeles, colloquium paper, 1972).

9 George Shepperson, "The Military History of British Central Africa: A Review Article," *Rhodes–Livingstone Journal*, no. 26 (Dec. 1959), pp. 23–33.

10 Tony Clayton, "Concepts of Power and Force in Colonial Africa, 1919–1939." Institute of Commonwealth Studies seminar (Univ. of London, Oct. 1978).

11 Martin Channock, "Ambiguities in the Malawian Political Tradition," *African Affairs*, lxxiv, no. 296 (July 1975); John Iliffe, *A Modern History of Tanganyika* (Cambridge, 1979).

12 Kenneth Kaunda, *Zambia Shall be Free* (London, 1962), p. 31.

13 Terence Ranger, *Dance and Society in Eastern Africa* (London, 1975).

14 For a discussion of recent literature on African worker consciousness see, Peter Gutkind, Jean Copans and Robin Cohen, *African Labour History* (London, 1978), introduction; John Higginson, "African Mine Workers at the Union Minière du Haut Katanga", American Historical Association (Dec. 1979).

15 Review of S.J. Ntara, *History of the Chewa*, ed. Harry Langworthy, by W.M.J. Van Binsbergen, *African Social Research* (June 1976), pp. 73–5.

16 Marcia Wright, "Women in Peril," *African Social Research* (Dec. 1975), p. 803.

17 Henry Meebelo, *Reaction to Colonialism* (Manchester, 1971).

18 Terence Ranger, "European Attitudes and African Realities: The Rise and Fall of the Matola Chiefs of South-East Tanzania," *Journal of African History*, xx, no. 1 (1979), pp. 69–82.

19 John Iliffe, *A Modern History of Tanganyika*, pp. 323–4.

20 Elizabeth Colson, "The Impact of the Colonial Period on the Definition of Land Rights," in Victor Turner (ed.), *Colonialism in Africa* (Cambridge, 1971), iii. pp. 221–51.

21 Wyatt MacGaffey, *Custom and Government in the Lower Congo* (California, 1970), pp. 207–8.

22 "The Study of African Religion," *Central Africa*, xxxv, no. 419 (Nov. 1917), p. 261.

23 Terence Ranger, "Missionary Adaptation and African Religious Institutions," in Terence Ranger and Isaria Kimambo (eds.), *The Historical Study of African Religion* (London, 1972), pp. 221–51.

24 Iliffe, *op. cit.*, p. 324.

25 *Ibid.*, pp. 327–9, 334.

26 *Ibid.*, pp. 335–6.

27 Ranger, "Missionary Adaptation and African Religious Institutions."

28 Iliffe, *op. cit.*, pp. 324–5.

29 MacGaffey, *op. cit.*, pp. 208, 222–3.

30 *Ibid.*, pp. 223–4.

31 Roy Willis, "Kamcape: An Anti-Sorcery Movement in South-West Tanzania," *Africa*, xxxi, no. 1 (1968).

32 Sholto Cross, "The Watch Tower Movement in South Central Africa, 1908–1945" (Univ. of Oxford doctoral thesis, 1973), pp. 431–8.

33 Ngugi wa Thiong'o, *Detained: A Writer's Prison Diary* (London, 1981), pp. 58–9.

32

Detained:

A Writer's Prison Diary

Ngugi wa Thiong'o

A colonial affair ... the phrase keeps on intruding into the literary flow of my mind and pen ... a colonial affair in an independent Kenya ... It is as if the phrase has followed me inside Kamĩtĩ Prison to mock at me.

In 1967, just before returning home from a three-year stay in England, I had signed a contract with William Heinemann to write a book focusing on the social life of European settlers in Kenya. The literary agent who negotiated the contract – he was also the originator of the idea – put it this way: "Theirs is a world which has forever vanished, but for that very reason, many readers will find an account of it still interesting."

The title? *A Colonial Affair!*

I had agreed to do the book because I strongly held that the settlers were part of the history of Kenya: the seventy years of this destructive alien presence could not be ignored by Kenyans.

Heaven knows, as they would say, that I tried hard to come to terms with the task. I dug up old newspapers and settlers' memoirs to get an authentic feeling of the times as the settlers lived it. A writer must be honest. But in the end I was unable to write the book. I could not quite find the right tone. The difficulty lay in more than my uncertainty as to whether or not "their world" had really vanished. An account of their social life would have to include a section on culture, and I was by then convinced that a Draculan idle class could never produce a culture.

For the settlers in Kenya were really parasites in paradise. Kenya, for them, was a huge winter home for aristocrats, which of course meant big game hunting and living it up on the backs of a million field and domestic slaves, the *Watu* as they called them. Coming ashore in Mombasa, as was clearly shown by the photographic evidence in the 1939 edition of Lord Cranworth's book, *Kenya Chronicles*, was literally on the backs of Kenyan workers. "No one coming into a new country," he writes, "could desire a more attractive welcome. We were rowed ashore in a small boat and came to land on the shoulders of sturdy Swahili natives." This was in 1906. By 1956, Sir Evelyn Baring, the governor, could still get himself photographed being carried, like a big baby, in the arms of a Kenyan worker. Thus by setting foot on Kenyan soil at Mombasa, every European was instantly transformed into a blue-blooded aristocrat. An

From Ngugi wa Thiong'o, *Detained: A Writer's Prison Diary* (1981), pp. 29–38, 56–62, from Heinemann Publishers (Oxford) Ltd.

attractive welcome: before him, stretching beyond the ken of his eyes, lay a vast valley garden of endless physical leisure and pleasure that he must have once read about in the *Arabian Nights* stories. The dream in fairy tales was now his in practice. No work, no winter, no physical or mental exertion. Here he would set up his own fiefdom. Life in these fiefdoms is well captured in Gerald Henley's novels *Consul at Sunset* and *Drinkers of Darkness*. Whoring, hunting, drinking, why worry? Work on the land was carried out by gangs of African "boys." Both *Consul at Sunset* and *Drinkers of Darkness* are fiction. Observed evidence comes from the diaries of a traveller. In her 1929–30 diaries, now brought out together under the title *East African Journey*, Margery Perham described the same life in minute detail:

> We drove out past the last scattered houses of suburban Nairobi, houses very much like their opposite numbers in England. But here ordinary people can live in sunlight; get their golf and their tennis more easily and cheaply than at home; keep three or four black servants; revel in a social freedom that often turns, by all accounts, into licence, and have the intoxicating sense of belonging to a small ruling aristocracy … certainly, on the surface, life is very charming in Nairobi, and very sociable with unlimited entertaining; all the shooting, games and bridge anyone could want. And in many houses a table loaded with drinks, upon which you can begin at any hour from 10.00am onwards, and with real concentration from 6.00pm.

And, so, beyond drinking whisky and whoring each other's wives and natives (what Margery Perham prudishly calls social freedom turned "by all accounts, into licence") and gunning natives for pleasure in this vast happy valley – oh, yes, are you married or do you live in Kenya? – the settlers produced little. No art, no literature, no culture, just the making of a little dominion marred only by niggers too many to exterminate, the way they did in New Zealand, and threatened by upstart "Gikuyu agitators."

The highest they reached in creative literature was perhaps Elspeth Huxley and she is really a scribbler of tourist guides and anaemic settler polemics blown up to the size of books. The most creative things about her writing are her titles – *The Flame Trees of Thika* and *The Mottled Lizard*, for instance – because in them she lets herself be inspired by native life and landscape. Beyond the title and the glossy covers, there is only emptiness, and emptiness as a defence of oppression has never made a great subject for literature.

Their theatre, professional and amateur, never went beyond crude imitation and desperate attempts to keep up with the West End or Broadway. This theatre never inspired a single original script or actor or critic.

In science, they could of course display Leakey. But Leakey's speciality was in digging up, dating and classifying old skulls. Like George Eliot's Casaubon, he was happier living with the dead. To the Leakeys, it often seems that the archaeological ancestors of Africans were more lovable and noble than the current ones – an apparent case of regressive evolution. Colonel Leakey, and even Lewis Leakey, hated Africans and proposed ways of killing off nationalism, while praising skulls of dead Africans as precursors of humanity. The evidence is there in black and white: L.S.B. Leakey is the author of two anti-Mau Mau books – *Mau Mau and the Kikuyu* and *Defeating Mau Mau*.

In art, their highest achievement was the mural paintings on the walls of the Lord Delamere bar in the Norfolk Hotel, Nairobi.[1] The murals stand to this day and they still attract hordes of tourists who come to enjoy racist aesthetics in art. But the murals in their artistic mediocrity possess a revealing historical realism.

On one wall are depicted scenes drawn from the English countryside: fourteen different postures for the proper deportment of an English gentleman; fox-hunting with gentlemen and ladies on horseback surrounded on all sides by well-fed hounds panting and wagging tails in anticipation of the kill to come; and of course the different pubs, from the White Hart to the Royal Oak, waiting to quench the thirst of the ladies and gentlemen after their blood sports. Kenya is England away from England, with this difference: Kenya is an England of endless summer tempered by an eternal spring of sprouting green life.

On another wall are two murals depicting aspects of settler life in that Kenya. One shows the Norfolk – the House of Lords as it was then known – in 1904.

Here again are English ladies and gentlemen – some on horseback, others sitting or standing on the verandah – but all drinking hard liquor served them by an African waiter wearing the servant's uniform of white *kanzu*, red fez, and a red band over his shoulder and front. In the foreground is an ox-wagon with two Africans: one, the driver, lashing at the dumb oxen; and the other, the pilot, pulling them along the right paths. The ribs of the "pushing boy" and the "pulling boy" are protruding, in contrast to the fully fleshed oxen and members of "the House of Lords". But the most prominent feature in this mural is "a rickshaw boy" with grinning teeth holding up this human-powered carriage for a finely dressed English lady to enter. Oxen-powered wagons for English survival goods; African powered carriages for English lords and ladies. Eleanor Cole, in her 1975 random recollections of pioneer settler life in Kenya, writes:

> Transport in Nairobi in those days was by rickshaw, one man in front between the shafts and one behind, either pushing or acting as a brake. People had their private rickshaws and put their rickshaw men in uniform. There were also public ones for hire.

The other mural depicts the same type of royal crowd at Nairobi railway station. At the forefront, is a well-fed dog wagging its tail before its lord and master. But amidst the different groups chatting or walking, stands a lone bullnecked, bull-faced settler in riding breeches with a hat covering bushy eyebrows and a grey moustache. He could have been a Colonel Grogan or a Lord Delamere or any other settler. The most representative feature about him is the *sjambok* he is firmly holding in his hands.

The rickshaw. The dog. The *sjambok*. The ubiquitous underfed, wide-eyed, uniformed native slave.

In March 1970, Colonel Grogan and four associates flogged three "rickshaw boys" outside a Nairobi court-house. The "boys" were later taken to hospital with lacerated backs and faces. Their crime? They had had the intention of alarming two white ladies by raising the rickshaw shafts an inch too high! The rhetoric of the magistrate when later Grogan, Bowkes, Gray, Fichat, and Low were summoned before him for being members of an unlawful assembly, left not the slightest doubt about the sadistic brutality of the deeds of these sons of English nobility and graduates of Cambridge:

> From the first to the last it appears to me that out of all the people present assisting at the flogging of these men, there was no one of that number who ever took the trouble to satisfy himself as to whether these natives had ever done anything deserving of punishment at all. There was no trial of any sort nor any form or pretence of trial. These boys were neither asked whether they had any defence or explanation to give, nor does it appear that they ever had any opportunity of making one. Grogan, who ordered the flogging, has himself stated that no plea or defence which they might have made would have diverted him from his purpose. This is a very unpleasant feature in the case and I consider it about as bad as it can be. Yet, in my opinion, it is further aggravated by the fact that the place selected for this unlawful act was directly in front of a courthouse.

Sweet rhetoric versus bitter reality: the culprits, all found guilty, were given prison terms ranging from seven to thirty days. Prison? Their own houses where they were free to receive and entertain guests! Elsewhere, in the plantations and estates, the "bwana" would simply have shot and buried them, or fed them to his dogs.

In 1960, Peter Harold Poole shot and killed Kamame Musunge for throwing stones at Poole's dogs in self-defence. To the settlers, dogs ranked infinitely higher than Kenyans; and Kenyans were either children (to be paternalistically loved but not appreciated, like dogs) or mindless scoundrels (to be whipped or killed). In his autobiography, *Words*, Sartre has made the apt comment that "when you love children and dogs too much, you love them instead of adults." The settlers' real love was for dogs and puppies. Thus, to hit an attacking dog was a worse crime than killing a Kenyan. And when Poole was sentenced to death, the whole colonial *Herrenvolk* cried in unison against this "miscarriage of justice." Peter Harold Poole had done what had been the daily norm since 1895.

In 1918, for instance, two British peers flogged a Kenyan to death and later burnt his body. His crime? He was suspected of having an intention to steal property. The two murderers were found guilty of a "simple hurt" and were fined two-thousand shillings each. The governor later appointed one of them a member of a district committee to dispense justice among the "natives". The gory details are there in Macgregor Ross's book *Kenya From Within*. Justice in a *sjambok*!

I thought about this in my cell at Kamĩtĩ prison and suddenly realized I had been wrong about the British settlers. I should have written that book. For the colonial system *did* produce a culture.

But it was the culture of legalized brutality, a ruling-class culture of fear, the culture of an oppressing minority desperately trying to impose total silence on a restive oppressed majority. This culture was sanctified in the colonial administration of P.C., D.C., D.O., Chiefs, right down to the askari. At Kamĩtĩ, we called it the Mbwa Kali culture.

Culture of silence and fear: the diaries and memoirs of the leading intellectual lights of the old colonial system contain full literary celebration of this settler culture. We need go no further than Colonel Meinertzhagen's *Kenya Diaries* and Baroness Blixen's *Out of Africa*.

Meinertzhagen was a commanding officer of the British forces of occupation. But he is far better known in history as the assassin of Koitalel, the otherwise unconquerable military and political leader of the Nandi people. This is what happened. Under Koitalel's inspiring leadership, the Nandi people had waged a ten-year armed struggle against the foreign army of occupation, humiliating British officers, one after the other. Enter Meinertzhagen, a gentleman. Unable to defeat the Nandi guerrilla army, the colonel invited Koitalel to a peace parley on some "neutral" ground. But only on one condition. Both men would come unarmed. Having been led to believe that the British wanted to discuss surrender terms and guarantees of safe retreat from Nandi country, Koitalel accepted. Put innocence against brutality and innocence will lose. There could be no finer illustration of this than the encounter between Koitalel and Meinertzhagen. Koitalel stretched an empty hand in greeting. Meinertzhagen stretched out a hidden gun and shot Koitalel in cold blood. The incident is recorded in *Kenya Diaries* as an act of British heroism!

Similar deeds of British colonial heroism are recorded in the same diaries.

The scene now shifts to Gĩkũyũ country, where people once again fought with tremendous courage against the better armed foreign invaders. So fierce was the struggle that in 1902 Meinertzhagen was forced to make the grudging but prophetic admission that, even if they triumphed over the people, this would only be a temporary victory: the British could never hold the country for more than fifty years. In one of several battles in Mũrang'a, a British officer was captured by the national defence army in Mũrũka and was handed to the people for justice. They killed him. Months later, Meinertzhagen stole into Mũrũka on a market day, had the whole market surrounded, and ordered a massacre of every single soul – a cold-blooded vengeance against defiant husbands and sons. Thereafter he embarked on a campaign of pillage, plunder and more murder. Meinertzhagen wrote in his diary: "Every soul was either shot or bayonetted ... we burned all huts and razed the banana plantations to the ground ... Then I went home and wept for brother officer killed."

Baroness Blixen was the separated wife of the big game hunter-cum-settler Baron von Blixen. From him she got no children but incurable syphilis. As if in compensation for unfulfilled desires and longings, the baroness turned Kenya into a vast erotic dreamland in which her several white lovers appeared as young gods and her Kenyan servants as usable curs and other animals. It is all there in her two books, *Shadows on the Grass* and *Out of Africa*. In the latter, her most famous, she celebrates a hideous colonial aesthetic in an account she entitles Kitosch's story:

Kitosch was a young native in the service of a young white settler of Molo. One Wednesday in June, the settler lent his brown mare to a friend, to ride to the station on. He sent Kitosch there to bring back the mare, and told him not to ride her, but to lead her. But Kitosch jumped on the mare, and rode her back, and on Saturday the settler, his master, was told of the offence by a man who had seen it. In punishment the settler, on Sunday afternoon, had Kitosch flogged, and afterwards tied up in his store, and here late on Sunday night Kitosch died.

The outcome of the trial in the High Court at Nakuru turned to rest solely on the intentions of the victim. It transpired by a hideous logic that Kitosch had actually wanted to die and he was therefore responsible for his death. In Anglo-Saxonland, it seems colonized natives have a fiendish desire for suicide that absolves white murderers:

> Kitosch had not much opportunity for expressing his intentions. He was locked up in the store, his message, therefore comes very simply, and in a single gesture. The night watch states that he cried all night. But it was not so, for at one o'clock he talked with toto, who was in the store with him, because the flogging had made him deaf. But at one o'clock he asked the toto to loosen his feet, and explained that in any case he could not run away. When the toto had done as he asked him, Kitosch said to him that he wanted to die. A little while after, he rocked himself from side to side, cried: "I am dead!" and died.

Medical science was even brought in to support the wish-to-die theory. This was supposed to be a psychological peculiarity of the African. He wants to die, and he dies. The irony is not Blixen's. She accepts the theory. What, of course, Kitosch said was, "Nataka kufa" which means: "I am about to die, or I am dying." But that is not the issue. It is the verdict and the conclusion. The settler was found guilty of "grievous hurt." And for a "grievous hurt" to a Kenyan, the foreign settler got two years in jail, probably on his own farm! It is not recorded how much more grievous hurt he committed later.

The fault is not Blixen's manner of telling the story – all the details are there – but her total acceptance of the hideous theory and her attempts to draw from it aesthetic conclusions meant to have universal relevance and validity:

> By this strong sense in him of what is right and decorous, the figure of Kitosch, with his firm will to die, although now removed from us by many years, stands out with a beauty of its own. In it is embodied the fugitiveness of wild things who are, in the hour of need, conscious of a refuge somewhere in existence; who go when they will; of whom we can never get hold.

The African is an animal: the settler is exonerated. Not a single word of condemnation for this practice of colonial justice. No evidence of any discomfiture. And for this, generations of western European critics from Hemingway to John Updike have showered her with praises. Some neo-colonial Africans too. But I err too in saying the African was considered an animal. In reality they loved the wild game but Africans were worse, more threatening, instinctless, unlovable, unredeemable sub-animals merely useful for brute labour. In *Out of Africa*, Karen Blixen says that her knowledge of wild game was useful in her later contact with Africans!

What of course is disgusting is the attempt by writers like Blixen to turn acts of cold-blooded murder and torture of these "black suppliers of brute labour" into deeds of heroic grandeur. It makes words lose their meaning or perhaps it is proof that the meaning of a word depends on the user. Galbraith Cole shot dead a Masai national in cold blood. The subsequent trial was a pre-arranged farce, rehearsed to the letter and gesture by all three parties, prosecutor, judge and murderer (all European of course), in such a way that on the records the Kenyan murdered would emerge guilty of unbearable armed provocation. But the settler was too arrogant to hide his murderous intentions behind a glossy mask of lies. As later reported by Karen Blixen, this is how the farce reached a climax of absurdity:

> The Judge said to Galbraith, "It's not, you know, that we don't understand that you shot only to stop the thieves." "No," Galbraith said, "I shot to kill. I said that I would do so."
>
> "Think again, Mr Cole," said the judge. "We are convinced that you only shot to stop them."
>
> "No, by God," Galbraith said, "I shot to kill."

He was acquitted. But Blixen reported Cole's admission as an act of unparalleled greatness. In a book, *Silence will Speak*, the same literary glorification of the settler culture of murder and torture is shamelessly repeated in 1977 by one Errol Trzebinksi.

Robert Ruark, in *Something of Value* and *Uhuru*, was to outdo the Huxleys, the Blixens, the Trzebinskis, in raising the reactionary settler culture of violence to the level of universality, and anybody upsetting it was seen as Hades' harbinger of doom and everlasting darkness.

Meinertzhagen, the soldier-assassin turned writer; Karen Blixen, the baroness of blighted bloom turned writer; Robert Ruark, the big-game hunter turned writer – theirs is a literary reflection of that colonial culture of silence and fear best articulated in a dispatch by an early governor, Sir A. R. Hardinge, on 5 April 1897:

> Force and the prestige which rests on a belief in force, are the only way you can do anything with those people, but once beaten and disarmed they will serve you. Temporizing is no good ... These people must learn submission by bullets – it's the only school; after that you may begin more modern and humane methods of education, and if you don't do it this year you will have to next, so why not get it over? ... In Africa to have peace you must first teach obedience, and the only tutor who impresses the lesson properly is the sword.

Thus the above acts of animal brutality were not cases of individual aberration but an integral part of colonial politics, philosophy and culture. Reactionary violence to instil fear and silence was the very essence of colonial settler culture.

Now a comprador bourgeoisie is, by its very economic base, a dependent class, a parasitic class in the *kupe*[2] sense. It is, in essence, a *mnyapala* class, a handsomely paid supervisor for the smooth operation of foreign economic interests. Its political inspiration and guidance come from outside the country. This economic and political dependency is clearly reflected in its imitative culture – excrescences of New York, Los Angeles and London. For this class, as Frantz Fanon once put it, has an extreme, incurable wish for permanent identification with the culture of the imperialist bourgeoisie. Here this class faces insurmountable difficulties and contradictions. For to truly and really become an integral part of that culture, they would have to live and grow abroad. But to do so would remove the political base of their economic constitution as a class: their control of the state of a former colony and hence their ability to mortgage a whole country and its people for a few million dollars. So this class can only admire that culture from an undesirable distance and try to ape it the best they can within the severe limitations of territory and history, but with the hope that their children will be fully uninhibited and unlimited in their Euro-Americanism.

They will order suits straight from Harrods of London or *haute couture* from Paris; buy castles and estates abroad and even build seaside and country villas there; now and then go on holidays abroad to relax and shop and bank. At home, they will meticulously groom, with the country's precious and hard-earned foreign currency reserves, a privileged elite caste of imported foreign experts and advisors, at the same time setting up a school system reproducing what they assume obtains abroad. They will send their children to the most expensive boarding schools abroad, or else approach EEC countries to build worthwhile international-class *lycées* at home for the super-elite children of the super-wealthy.

But the members of a comprador bourgeoisie of a former settler colony count themselves lucky; they don't have to travel and reside abroad to know and copy the culture of the imperialist bourgeoisie: have they not learnt it all from the colonial settler representatives of metropolitan culture? Nurtured in the womb of the old colonial system, they have matured to their full compradorial heights, looking up to the local Europeans as the alpha and omega of gentlemanly refinement and ladylike elegance. With racial barriers to class mobility thrown open, the deportment of a European gentleman – rosebuds and pins in coat lapels, spotless white kerchiefs in breast pockets, tail-coats, top-hats and gold-chained pocket watches – is no longer in the realm of dreams and wishes. Thus in a very recent book edited by Elspeth Huxley, *Pioneer's Scrapbook*, there is an approving comment about this cultural imitation:

> Henry Scott died ... on 11 April 1911 and was buried at Kikuyu. He was succeeded in the following year by Dr J. W. Arthur, who had come to Kikuyu in 1907: a man of great personal charm and driving force, who exercised a tremendous influence over the younger Kikuyu. His habit of wearing a rosebud or carnation in his lapel is perpetuated by some of the leading politicians of the present day who were small children at Kikuyu in the late twenties.

Lady Eleanor Cole, wife of the infamous Galbraith Cole, in her otherwise dry, humourless, random recollections of settler life in Kenya, writes enthusiastically about the social scene in the Nairobi of 1917:

> Nairobi was very social and people gave formal dinner parties, at which the women were dressed in long skirted low-necked gowns and men in stiff shirts and white waistcoats or in uniform. Men and women were carefully paired, and you were taken to dinner on the arm of your partner. There were strict rules of precedence, and woe betide the hostess who ignored them.

She is describing the Nairobi of 1917, but she could as easily have been describing Nairobi of the 1970s; only the latter Nairobi's wastefulness behind the feudal formality surpasses the former in sheer opulence.

The most popular columns in the old settler papers, *The Sunday Post* and *The Kenya Weekly News*, were the social pages listing who was who at this or that function at this or that club or at so and so's residence. The columns used to make hearts flutter, in tears or joy, depending of course on whether or not one was included. Those who appeared more regularly, especially at functions in exclusive clubs and residences, were regarded with envious awe and admiration by the less fortunate aspirants. After independence, the columns ceased to be, as did the two newspapers.

Well, the columns are now back in the glossy bourgeois monthlies *Viva* and *Chic* and in the Aga Khan-owned tabloid, *The Daily Nation*. They are even more popular. The columns are still a cause for joy or sorrow to many an expectant lady and gentleman. Only that this time, among the main European and Asian actors are to be found upper-crust Kenyan blacks holding, on their gentlemanly arms, ladies bedecked with gold and diamonds holding a goblet of liquor.

Lessons learnt in the Hardinge school of philosophy. First through the bullet and the sword. Then through the more "humane" and "modern" methods. The character and the behaviour of the more successful pupils would have pleased Governor Hardinge and all the other tutors, from Eliot to Malcolm Macdonald, in that famous school of colonial philosophy. First the gun, cow them; then the pen, take their minds prisoner; then filter them and pick out the top loyalists and bribe them numb with some semblance of power and wealth. And see the results.

Thus, the settler played golf and polo, went to horse-races or on the royal hunt in red-coats and riding-breeches, a herd of yapping and growling hounds on the chase. The black pupils now do the same, only with greater zeal: golf and horses have become "national" institutions.

The settler prostituted women, as when Karl Peters publicly hanged his African mistress because she preferred the company of her Kenyan brothers to his own. His pupils today have gone into the whole game with greater gusto: tourism, as practised today, can only thrive on the virtual prostitution of the whole country, becoming a sacred industry with shrines, under the name of hotels and lodges in all the cities and at the seaside. The modern-day Karl Peters need not use the gun to deter rivals. The name of the game now is money.[3]

The settler built exclusive betting clubs, drank neat whisky on the verandah of his huge mansion, or indulged in countless sundowners and cocktail parties. Their pupils continue the process: gambling casinos and strip-tease joints get full state support and legal encouragement.

The settler despised peasant languages which he termed vernacular, meaning the language of slaves, and believed that the English language was holy. Their pupils carry this contempt a stage further: some of their early educational acts on receiving the flag were to ban African languages in schools and to elevate English as the medium of instruction from primary to secondary stages. In some schools, corporal punishment is meted out to those caught speaking their mother tongues; fines are extorted for similar offences. Men at the top will fume in fury at fellow Africans who mispronounce English but will laugh with pride at their own inability to speak a single correct sentence of their own African languages. In some government departments, the ability to speak the Queen's English, exactly like an upper-class English gentleman, is the sole criterion for employment and promotion. But since few, if any, Africans can speak the language exactly like those native to it, only Englishmen get employed or promoted to critical positions of authority.

The settler loathed any intellectually challenging literature or any genuine creative expression, beyond imitations of sugary comedies from London performed by amateurs wearing robes flown from abroad to give the whole tear-jerking acrobatics a touch of the real thing. To him, African culture was a curious museum-piece or an esoteric barbaric show for the amusement of tittering ladies and gentlemen desiring glimpses of savagery. Their comprador pupils too hate books and they loathe any theatre or music that challenges their betrayal. If a certain book is in vogue, they will buy it and ask their wives or children to go through it and tell them briefly what the fuss is all about. They also loathe African culture except when it can be used to rationalize their betrayal. But they will invite a few traditional dancers to do acrobatics for visitors from abroad, later summing up the whole show with polite applause and patronizing wonder: how do these people manage such bodily contortions?

The settler built goodwill churches to thank a white God for delivering the white race from the toils of Adam and invited his African labourers to share in the joyful tidings. The settler believed in charity to passively grateful African serfs: a bit of the plunder back to the plundered? Here these dutiful pupils surpass themselves in their singular zeal to excecute the same. Charity donations and church-going become "national" imperatives and moral yardsticks for political acceptance. The cult of ostentatious godliness is raised to new ethical planes. The propertied few compete in donating money for erecting several churches in a rural village that cannot boast of a single decent primary school, much less food or water. The imperialist evangelical drive of colonial missions is now led by the state and its wealthy blacks, with the same message: trust and obey. Spiritual leaders are trotted out in a string to calm rising disgust by promising future bounty for obedient souls. There is a pathetic side to the whole exercise in apemanship exhibited by these successful pupils of Hardinge's school of philosophy.

In the 1950s a blue-blooded settler memsahib whose education never went beyond riding Arab ponies and bashing the keys of the piano, sought and found solace for her early widowhood in joining the anti-Mau Mau, anti-communist, Moral Rearmament crusade. Accompanied by a MRM team flown from its headquarters in Switzerland, paid for by the financial gnomes of Zurich, she visited schools and colleges and detention camps showing pro-imperialist religious films like *The Forgotten Factor*, *Freedom*, *The Crowning Experience* in which anti-colonial guerrillas suddenly give up their armed struggle for liberation on learning about the presumed transforming power of the four moral absolutes of honesty, unselfishness, purity and love. Her theme? Give up guns for holy kisses. Beware of godless communism.

Well? Soldierly religious words never die. In the 1970s the same words reappear in speeches by a senior cabinet minister, intellectual conqueror of universities in Africa and abroad, at fund-raising ceremonies for more and more goodwill churches. His theme? Beware of godless communism! This foreign ideology is against our African traditions. We are Christians and capitalists by birth and ancestry.

Thus far for the modern and humane features of Hardinge's school of philosophy. Playing golf and polo, gambling at modern casinos and horse-races, ogling at naked women in strip-tease clubs, creating a modern happy valley for moneyocrats from Germany and America, televising ostentatious displays of well-groomed holiness and Churchillian extravaganzas at weekends, speaking English with an upper-class English accent, all these seem harmless imitations although far reaching in their consequences. They can be fought if there's democracy. Reality is anyway more powerful than a million imitations.

Unfortunately, it is the repressive features of colonial culture – Hardinge's sword and bullet, as the only insurance of continuing their life-style – that seem to have most attracted the unqualified admiration of the compradors. The settler with the *sjambok* lording it over a mass of "pulling and pushing nigger boys", that figure so meticulously preserved on the walls of "The Lord Delamere" in the Norfolk Hotel, seems the modern ideal for the post-colonial ruling class.

How else can it be explained that the 1966 laws of detention, sedition and treason, reproduce, almost word for word, those in practice between 1951 and 1961 during the high noon of colonial culture?

Submission through the sword and the bullet! And only later is it possible to achieve the same through the modern "peaceful" methods of churches, schools, theatres, television, cinema, colonial history, junk literature – all run, supervised and approved by foreigners!

The fact is that the comprador bourgeoisie would like to resurrect the imagined grandeur and dubious dignity of colonial culture. The unilateral arbitrary arrest and detention of Kenyans opposed to imperialist culture was a major step towards reconstruction of the new colonial Jerusalem, where people would for ever sing in unison: "Trust and obey, for there is no other way, to be happy amidst us, except to trust and obey."

"Arise colonial Lazarus" is their celebratory call to divine worship at the holy shrines of imperialism:

Our father in Europe and America
Hallowed be thy name
Thy kingdom come
Thy will be done
In our wealthy Africa
Our willing and welcoming Africa
As it was done in the colonial past.
Give us this day our daily dollar
And forgive us our failures
Help us triumph over those that challenge you and us
And give us grace and aid and the power to be meek and grateful
For ever and ever, Amen.

Notes

1 On 31 December 1980 the Norfolk Hotel was bombed, reportedly by revolutionaries. But the Lord Delamere bar remained intact.

2 *Kupe*, tick; *mnyapala*, overseer.

3 I was too hasty when I wrote this. The *Standard* of 1 October 1980 carried this report: "American sailor Frank Joseph Sundstrom, who admitted killing a Kenyan, Monicah Njeri, in her Mombasa flat after an evening of sex, was yesterday discharged on the condition that he signed a bond of shs. 500 to be of good behaviour for the next two years." Sundstrom, who was with the USS *La Salle*, which was then paying a "good will" visit to Kenya, was tried before a white judge, L.G.E. Harris, and a white prosecutor, Nicholas Harwood. The government has granted military facilities to the USA, and the *La Salle* was visiting Kenya from the US Middle East fleet poised to suppress any genuine anti-imperialist nationalist uprisings in the area. The massive anger of Kenyan people at the judgement forced the retirement of Justice Harris, but a whole four months or so after the infamous judgement and even then with full benefits.

Part X

Nations and Nationalism

Introduction

It is fitting to begin this section on African nationalism with an essay by Léopold Sédar Senghor who, as founder of the Mali Federation in 1959, paved the way for national independence throughout much of Francophone West Africa. As a statesman, Senghor was instrumental, by way of skillful negotiations with French president Charles de Gaulle, in gaining independence for Senegal from French colonial rule. In 1960, Senghor was unanimously elected as the first president of the independent republic of Senegal – a nation which he successfully governed for two decades until he was succeeded by Abdou Diouf. As a poet and man of letters, Senghor was an eloquent spokesman for the intellectual philosophy and cultural movement known as négritude – a term which Senghor defined succinctly as "the sum total of cultural values of the Negro-African world."

The négritude movement began in Paris during the 1930s when francophone African and Caribbean intellectuals (bound by their common legacy as colonial subjects of France), including, in particular, Léopold Senghor and Martiniquan poet Aimé Césaire, fashioned a discourse of pan-African cultural identity which was intended as a non-violent revolt against colonialism and, in particular, as a statement of protest against France's policy of cultural assimilation in Africa (Crowder, 1962). Négritude used poetry and literature to restore the validity of African culture, and to establish a positive image of "black" consciousness – a metaphor of identity which would serve as a rallying force of nationalism in the African world (Steeves, 1973: 92). In his numerous writings on the subject, Senghor (1948, 1964) stresses the indigenous wisdom of African peoples, and argues that beneath the superficial cultural idiosyncrasies that distinguish one society from another Africans are united by a profound commonality which is expressed in their democratic social structures, their religions, their work practices, their arts, and in the rhythm of African life itself (see also our general Introduction on the notion of African cultural unity). While stressing that African cultures were united, Senghor also argued that Africa was distinct from Europe and that nation-building (as a form of anti-colonialism) could only emerge if the "African personality" was rescued from the suffocating pressure of European colonial culture. Senghor drew upon images of gender and temperament when he described Africa as "female, emotional, and rhythmic" in contrast to Europe which he characterized as "male, technical, and cold" (Lambert, 1993: 249). In his essay *Femmes Noires*, for example, Senghor constructed a female image of Africa in which he "portrays the woman Africa as a promised land from which the black person is alienated while in Europe" (Lambert, 1993: 249). How different is this image from earlier European accounts of exploration which depicted Africa as an erotic and dark female body waiting to be penetrated by European colonization (see Comaroff and Comaroff, Chapter 1)? Is it possible to construct a gendered image of a continent as both a positive and negative metaphor?

There is a central contradiction in Senghor's work which forms, at least in part, the basis of Fanon's critique of négritude. While Senghor argued that "there existed in blackness a special social quality … he expressed this outlook in French language of such skill and precision that he was admitted to the French Academy" (Manning, 1988: 165). This point not only raises the whole issue of what language should be used to establish an "authentic" voice in African national literature (see the Introduction to Part I on the debate between Chinua Achebe and Ngugi wa Thiong'o), but also throws into question the possibility of discovering "true" African identity through the framework of European scholarly discourse. How connected was Senghor to the predicament of colonial Africa when he was writing from the perspective of an elite intellectual living and studying in Paris?

Frantz Fanon was born in Martinique and became a political activist in the Algerian National Liberation Front in the 1950s. His essay, "On National Culture," was written for the Second Congress of Black Artists and Writers which was held in Rome in 1959, and was published in 1961 as a chapter in his highly acclaimed polemic *The Wretched of the Earth*. Unlike Senghor, Fanon's agenda was more political than it was academic. His essay offers a direct critique of the négritude movement, which Fanon says does not go nearly far enough in its struggle to dismantle colonialism. He argues that Senghor's vision of independent African identity is couched in European colonial racialist terms. Rather than liberate himself from the culture of the oppressor, Fanon contends that Senghor accepts the basic premise of colonial subjugation: namely, the inferiority of the colonized. Out of the indignity engendered by racist colonial rhetoric, négritude tried to rehabilitate African culture in the eyes of the West. For Fanon, however, this was neither the way to independence nor to the formation of national identity. African nationalism cannot be founded on any attempt to redress colonial discourse (a process which, through its very negation, gives credence to European stereotypes), but rather must emerge from Africa's own struggle and on its own terms (July, 1987: 215–17).

Specifically, Fanon rejects two principal tenets of the négritude movement. First, he argues that national identity cannot emerge from the (re)construction of an idealized or nostalgic past, but must be grounded on the reality of the present – a reality which, for Fanon, involves violence against the colonial authorities. "A national culture," writes Fanon, "is not a folklore, nor an abstract populism that believes it can discover the people's true nature." Second, Fanon believed that culture is national and specific to the experience of a region or local state. The emphasis in négritude on pan-African identity functioned to diffuse the struggle against colonialism. There was no "common destiny" to be shared across Africa as a whole, but there *was* a common destiny "between the Senegalese and Guinean nations which are both dominated by the same French colonialism." What Fanon largely fails to consider, however, is the question of how diverse and multiple ethnic groups can come together to form a single national culture. While the common destiny of the Senegalese may be different from that of the Guinean, what about the common destiny of the multiple ethnic groups which comprise Senegal as a nation? Are the national goals and aspirations of the Wolof, for example, the same as those of the Serer?

The problem of multi-ethnic states is the focus of the next two essays in this part. Both of the essays broach the issue of ethnicity and nationalism from a different perspective. Bruce Berman's essay "Nationalism, Ethnicity, and Modernity: The Paradox of Mau Mau" demonstrates the contested interpretation of a political/religious movement in Kenya known as Mau Mau. The Mau Mau revolt was an armed uprising by Kikuyu peasants against the colonial state in Kenya. From the early 1950s until its suppression by British authorities in 1956, a campaign of oathing (pledging allegiance to a revolutionary cause) was used to create unity among the Kikuyu people (Green, 1990). Although Mau Mau was targeted against foreign colonial rule, it was played out as a conflict between Kikuyu loyalists and Kikuyu liberationists: only a handful of the thousand deaths were "white."

During the 1950s, when Mau Mau was still active in Kenya, the colonial authorities viewed the movement as an expression of "atavistic tribalism" – a quasi-religious cult steeped in the barbarity and violence which Europeans had come to associate with Africa (see Part I). In the 1960s, following Kenya's independence from Britain, and in an era when African political science was emerging as an important field of study in the United States, writers like Carl Rosberg and John Nottingham (1966) reconsidered the colonial interpretation of Mau Mau, and concluded that to view Mau Mau as a form of atavistic tribalism was to buy into a colonial myth which was constructed out of an ideology of racism and European paranoia and fear. Mau Mau was to be understood instead as a form of "militant nationalism" whose struggle for liberation was predicated on "modern" and "rational" political motivations. Berman concludes that both interpretations of Mau Mau are flawed, and are based on identical premises about modernity, development, and nationalism. Drawing heavily on the influential work of Benedict Anderson (1983), and his concept of the nation as "an imagined community," Berman argues that Mau Mau was both a religious movement *and* a political movement. Mau Mau grew out of internal factionalism and dissent among the Kikuyu people. There was no unified front (either "ritual" or "national") but rather "a diverse and exceedingly fragmented collection of individuals, organizations and ideas, out of which no dominant concept of a Kikuyu imagined national community had emerged." By viewing nationalism as a political ideology which has more in common with kinship and religion than it does with the secularizing demands of the modern nation-state, Berman is able to account for the "passion" of Mau Mau in a way which no prior interpretation was able to do.

Finally, the problem of the multi-ethnic state is also considered by Christopher Steiner in his essay "The Invisible Face: Masks, Ethnicity, and the State in Côte d'Ivoire." Steiner asks the following question: How does the Ivoirian state bring together over sixty different ethnic groups into a single, unified vision of a nation? And, furthermore, how does the state then go about marketing this image of national identity to the rest of the world, and, specifically, to European and American tourists? The Festimask, a huge masked festival organized by the Ministry of Tourism in 1987, was an attempt to present a unified image of Côte d'Ivoire to both nationals and foreigners alike. The nation state was to be encapsulated in the image of the mask, an artform which was thought to capture the "mystical" past of the nation. Through an analysis of its huge commercial failure, Steiner uses the Festimask as an object lesson in multiethnic African nationalism, demonstrating the inherent tensions between "modern" national integration and the preservation of authentic "traditions." How different, in the end, is the Festimask from the folklore and nostalgia which Fanon criticized so heavily nearly three decades ago?

References

Anderson, Benedict. 1983. *Imagined Communities: Reflections on the Origin and Spread of Nationalism*. London and New York: Verso.

Crowder, Michael. 1962. *Senegal: A Study in French Assimilationist Policy*. London: Oxford University Press.

Green, Maia. 1990. "Mau Mau Oathing Rituals and Political Ideology in Kenya: A Re-Analysis." *Africa* 60(1): 69–87.

July, Robert W. 1987. *An African Voice: The Role of the Humanities in African Independence*. Durham, NC: Duke University Press.

Lambert, Michael C. 1993. "From Citizenship to *Négritude*: 'Making a Difference' in Elite Ideologies of Colonized Francophone West Africa." *Comparative Studies in Society and History* 35(2): 239–62.

Manning, Patrick. 1988. *Francophone Sub-Saharan Africa, 1880–1985*. Cambridge: Cambridge University Press.

Rosberg, Carl, and John Nottingham. 1966. *The Myth of Mau Mau: Nationalism in Kenya*. New York: Praeger.

Senghor, Léopold Sédar. 1948. *Anthologie de la nouvelle poésie nègre et malgache de langue française*. Paris: Presses universitaires de France. Reprinted in 1969.

Senghor, Léopold Sédar. 1964. *On African Socialism*. Translated by Mercer Cook. New York: Praeger.

Steeves, Edna L. 1973. "Négritude and the Noble Savage." *The Journal of Modern African Studies* 11(1): 91–104.

Suggested Reading

Afigbo, A.E., and S.I.O. Okita, eds. 1985. *Museums and Nation Building*. Imo State, Nigeria: New African Publishing.

Amoah, Michael. 2007. *Reconstructing the Nation in Africa: The Politics of Nationalism in Ghana*. London and New York: I.B. Tauris Academic Studies.

Bah, Abu Bakarr. 2008. *Breakdown and Reconstitution: Democracy, the Nation-State, and Ethnicity in Nigeria*. Lanham, MD: Lexington Books.

Berman, Bruce, Dickson Eyoh and Will Kymlicka, eds. 2004. *Ethnicity and Democracy in Africa*. Columbus, OH: Ohio State University Press.

Césaire, Aimé. 1969. *Return to my Native Land*. Harmondsworth: Penguin Books.

Coombes, Annie E. 1988. "Museums and the Formation of National and Cultural Identities." *The Oxford Art Journal* 11(2): 57–68.

Dia, Mamadou. 1961. *The African Nations and World Solidarity*. Translated by Mercer Cook. New York: Praeger.

Golan, Dafnah. 1994. *Inventing Shaka: Using History in the Construction of Zulu Nationalism*. Boulder, CO: Rienner.

Hodgkin, Thomas. 1957. *Nationalism in Colonial Africa*. New York: New York University Press.

Irele, Abiola. 1965. "Négritude or Black Cultural Nationalism." *The Journal of Modern African Studies* 3(3): 321–48.

July, Robert W. 1967. *The Origins of Modern African Thought*. New York: Praeger.

Kenyatta, Jomo. 1938. *Facing Mount Kenya: The Tribal Life of the Kikuyu*. London: Secker and Warburg.

Langley, J. Ayodele. 1973. *Pan-Africanism and Nationalism in West Africa, 1900–1945*. Oxford: Clarendon Press.

Malkki, Liisa H. 1995. *Purity and Exile: Violence, Memory, and National Cosmology among Hutu Refugees in Tanzania*. Chicago: University of Chicago Press.

Mark, Peter. 1994. "Art, Ritual, and Folklore: Dance and Cultural Identity among the Peoples of the Casamance." *Cahiers d'Etudes africaines* 136, 34(4): 563–84.

Neuberger, Benyamin. 1987. "History and African Concepts of Nationhood." *Canadian Review of Studies in Nationalism* 14(1): 161–79.

Simpson, Andrew. 2008. *Language and National Identity in Africa*. Oxford: Oxford University Press.

Smith, Anthony D. 1983. *State and Nation in the Third World*. Brighton: Wheatsheaf.

Straker, Jay. 2009. *Youth, Nationalism, and the Guinean Revolution*. Bloomington, IN: Indian University Press.

Verdery, Katherine. 1993. "Whither 'Nation' and 'Nationalism'?" *Daedalus* 122(3): 37–46.

Waetjen, Thembisa. 2004. *Workers and Warriors: Masculinity and the Struggle for Nation in South Africa*. Urbana: University of Illinois.

Welliver, Timothy K., ed. 1993. *African Nationalism and Independence*. New York: Garland.

33

Negritude:

A Humanism of the Twentieth Century

Léopold Sédar Senghor

During the last thirty or so years that we have been proclaiming negritude, it has become customary, especially among English-speaking critics, to accuse us of *racialism*. This is probably because the word is not of English origin. But, in the language of Shakespeare, is it not in good company with the words humanism and socialism? Mphahleles[1] have been sent about the world saying: "Negritude is an inferiority complex"; but the same word cannot mean both "racialism" and "inferiority complex" without contradiction. The most recent attack comes from Ghana, where the government has commissioned a poem entitled "I Hate Negritude" – as if one could hate oneself, hate one's being, without ceasing to be.

No, negritude is none of these things. It is neither racialism nor self-negation. Yet it is not just affirmation; it is rooting oneself in oneself, and self-confirmation: confirmation of one's *being*. Negritude is nothing more or less than what some English-speaking Africans have called the *African personality*. It is no different from the "black personality" discovered and proclaimed by the American New Negro movement. As the American

Negro poet, Langston Hughes, wrote after the first world war: "We, the creators of the new generation, want to give expression to our *black personality* without shame or fear ... We know we are handsome. Ugly as well. The drums weep and the drums laugh." Perhaps our only originality, since it was the West Indian poet, Aimé Césaire, who coined the word negritude, is to have attempted to define the concept a little more closely; to have developed it as a weapon, as an instrument of liberation and as a contribution to the humanism of the twentieth century.

But, once again, what is negritude? Ethnologists and sociologists today speak of "different civilizations." It is obvious that peoples differ in their ideas and their languages, in their philosophies and their religions, in their customs and their institutions, in their literature and their art. Who would deny that Africans, too, have a certain way of conceiving life and of living it? A certain way of speaking, singing, and dancing; of painting and sculpturing, and even of laughing and crying? Nobody, probably; for otherwise we would not have been talking about "Negro art" for the last sixty years and Africa

From Léopold Sédar Senghor, "Negritude: A Humanism of the Twentieth Century", pp. 179–92. In Wilfred Carty and Martin Kilson, eds, *The African Reader: Independent Africa*, Vintage Books, New York. Copyright © 1970 by Wilfred Carty and Martin Kilson.

would be the only continent today without its ethnologists and sociologists. What, then, is negritude?
It is – as you can guess from what precedes – *the
sum of the cultural values of the black world*; that is, a
certain active presence in the world, or better, in
the universe. It is, as John Reed and Clive Wake call
it, a certain "way of relating oneself to the world
and to others."[2] Yes, it is essentially relations with
others, an opening out to the world, contact and
participation with others. Because of what it is,
negritude is necessary in the world today: it is a
humanism of the twentieth century.

"The Revolution of 1889"

But let us go back to 1885 and the morrow of the
Berlin Conference. The European nations had just
finished, with Africa, their division of the planet.
Including the United States of America, they were
five or six at the height of their power who dominated the world. Without any complexes, they
were proud of their material strength; prouder
even of their science, and paradoxically, of their
race. It is true that at that time this was not a paradox. Gobineau, the nineteenth-century philosopher of racial supremacy, had, by a process of
osmosis, even influenced Marx, and Disraeli was
the great theoretician of that "*English race*, proud,
tenacious, confident in itself, that no climate, no
change can undermine." (The italics are mine.)
Leo Frobenius, the German ethnologist, one
of the first to apprehend the rich complexity of
African culture, writes in *The Destiny of
Civilizations*: "Each of the great nations that considers itself personally responsible for the 'destiny
of the world' believes it possesses the key to the
understanding of the whole and the other nations.
It is an attitude raised from the past."

In fact, this attitude "raised from the past" had
begun to be discredited toward the end of the nineteenth century by books like Bergson's *Time and
Free Will*, which was published in 1889. Since the
Renaissance, the values of European civilization
had rested essentially on discursive reason and
facts, on logic and matter. Bergson, with an eminently dialectical subtlety, answered the expectation of a public weary of scientism and naturalism.
He showed that facts and matter, which are the
objects of discursive reason, were only the outer

surface that had to be transcended by *intuition* in
order to achieve a *vision in depth of reality*.

But the "Revolution of 1889" – as we shall call
it – did not only affect art and literature, it completely upset the sciences. In 1880, only a year before
the invention of the word electron, a distinction was
still being drawn between matter and energy. The
former was inert and unchangeable, the latter was
not. But what characterized both of them was their
permanence and their continuity. They were both
subject to a strict mechanical determinism. Matter
and energy had, so to speak, existed from the beginning of time; they could change their shape, but not
their substance. All we lacked in order to know them
objectively in space and time were sufficiently accurate instruments of investigation and measurement.

Well, in less than fifty years, all these principles
were to be outmoded and even rejected. Thirty years
ago already, the new discoveries of science – quanta,
relativity, wave mechanics, the uncertainty principle,
electron spin – had upset the nineteenth-century
notion of determinism, which denied man's free
will, along with the concepts of matter and energy.
The French physicist, Broglie, revealed to us the
duality of matter and energy, or the wave-particle
principle that underlies things; the German physicist, Heisenberg, showed us that objectivity was
an illusion and that we could not observe facts
without modifying them; others showed that, on
the scale of the infinitely small as on that of the
immensely great, particles act on one another.
Since then, the physico-chemical laws, like matter
itself, could no longer appear unchangeable. Even
in the field, and on the scale, where they were
valid, they were only rough approximations, no
more than probabilities. It was enough to scrape
the surface of things and of facts to realize just
how much instability there is, defying our measuring instruments, probably because they are only
mechanical: *material*.

It was on the basis of these discoveries, through
a combination of logical coherence and amazing
intuition, of scientific experiment and inner experience, that Pierre Teilhard de Chardin was able to
transcend the traditional dichotomies with a new
dialectic, to reveal to us the living, throbbing unity
of the universe. On the basis, then, of the
new scientific discoveries, Teilhard de Chardin
transcends the old dualism of the philosophers

and the scientists, which Marx and Engels had perpetuated by giving matter precedence over the spirit. He advanced the theory that the stuff of the universe is not composed of two realities, but of a single reality in the shape of two phenomena; that there is not matter and energy, not even matter and spirit, but spirit–matter, just as there is space–time. Matter and spirit become a "network of relations," as the French philosopher, Bachelard, called it: energy, defined as a network of forces. In matter–spirit there is, therefore, only one energy, which has two aspects. The first, *tangential energy*, which is external, is material and quantitative. It links together the corpuscles, or particles, that make up matter. The other, *radial energy*, which is internal, is psychic and qualitative. It is centripetal force. It organizes into a complex the center-to-center relations of the internal particles of a corpuscle. Since energy is force, it follows that radial energy is the creative force, the "primary stuff of things," and tangential energy is only a residual product "caused by the interreactions of the elementary 'centers' of the consciousness, imperceptible where life has not yet occurred, but clearly apprehensible by our experience at a sufficiently advanced stage in the development of matter" (Teilhard de Chardin). It follows that where life has not yet occurred the physico–chemical laws remain valid within the limitations we have defined above, while in the living world, as we rise from plant to animal and from animal to Man, the psyche increases in consciousness until it makes and expresses itself in freedom. "Makes itself": that is, *realizes* itself, by means of – yet by transcending – material well-being through an increase of spiritual life. "Realizes itself": by that I mean it develops in harmonious fashion the two complementary elements of the soul: the heart and the mind.

The Philosophy of Being

The paradox is only apparent when I say that negritude, by its ontology (that is, its philosophy of being), its moral law and its aesthetic, is a response to the modern humanism that European philosophers and scientists have been preparing since the end of the nineteenth century, and as Teilhard de Chardin and the writers and artists of the mid-twentieth century present it.

Firstly, African ontology. Far back as one may go into his past, from the northern Sudanese to the southern Bantu, the African has always and everywhere presented a concept of the world which is diametrically opposed to the traditional philosophy of Europe. The latter is essentially *static, objective, dichotomic*; it is, in fact, dualistic, in that it makes an absolute distinction between body and soul, matter and spirit. It is founded on separation and opposition: on analysis and conflict. The African, on the other hand, conceives the world, beyond the diversity of its forms, as a fundamentally mobile, yet unique, reality that seeks synthesis. This needs development.

It is significant that in Wolof, the main language of Senegal, there are at least three words to translate the word "spirit": *xel, sago*, or *degal*, whereas images have to be used for the word "matter": *lef* (thing) or *yaram* (body). The African is, of course, sensitive to the external world, to the material aspect of beings and things. It is precisely because he is more so than the white European, because he is sensitive to the tangible qualities of things – shape, color, smell, weight, etc. – that the African considers these things merely as signs that have to be interpreted and transcended in order to reach the reality of human beings. Like others, more than others, he distinguishes the pebble from the plant, the plant from the animal, the animal from Man; but, once again, the accidents and appearances that differentiate these kingdoms only illustrate different aspects of the same reality. This reality is *being* in the ontological sense of the word, and it is life force. For the African, matter in the sense the Europeans understand it, is only a system of signs which translates the single reality of the universe: being, which is spirit, which is life force. Thus, the whole universe appears as an infinitely small, and at the same time an infinitely large, network of life forces which emanate from God and end in God, who is the source of all life forces. It is He who vitalizes and devitalizes all other beings, all the other life forces.

I have not wandered as far as might be thought from modern ontology. European ethnologists, Africanists and artists use the same words and the same expressions to designate the ultimate reality of the universe they are trying to know and to express: "spider's web," "network of forces," "communicating vessels," "system of canals," etc. This is not very different, either, from what the scientists and chemists say. As far as African ontology is concerned, too, there is no such thing as dead matter: every being, every thing – be it only a grain of sand – radiates a life force, a sort of wave-particle; and sages, priests, kings, doctors, and artists all use it to help bring the universe to its fulfilment.

For the African, contrary to popular belief, is not passive in face of the order – or disorder – of the world. His attitude is fundamentally ethical. If the moral law of the African has remained unknown for so long, it is because it derives, naturally, from his conception of the world: from his ontology – so naturally, that both have remained unknown, denied even, by Europeans, because they have not been brought to their attention by being re-examined by each new generation of Africans.

So God tired of all the possibilities that remained confined within Him, unexpressed, dormant, and as if dead. And God opened His mouth, and He spoke at length a word that was harmonious and rhythmical. All these possibilities expressed by the mouth of God *existed* and had the vocation *to live:* to express God in their turn, by establishing the link with God and all the forces deriving from Him.

In order to explain this *morality in action* of negritude, I must go back a little. Each of the identifiable life forces of the universe – from the grain of sand to the ancestor[3] – is, itself and in its turn, a network of life forces – as modern physical chemistry confirms: a network of elements that are contradictory in appearance but really *complementary.* Thus, for the African, Man is composed, of course, of matter and spirit, of body and soul; but at the same time he is also composed of a virile and a feminine element: indeed of several "souls." Man is therefore a composition of mobile life forces which interlock: a world of solidarities that seek to knit themselves together. Because he exists, he is at once end and beginning: end of the three orders of the mineral, the vegetable, and the animal, but beginning of the human order.

Let us ignore for the moment the first three orders and examine the human order. Above Man and based on him, lies this fourth world of concentric circles, bigger and bigger, higher and higher,

until they reach God along with the whole of the universe. Each circle – family, village, province, nation, humanity – is, in the image of Man and by vocation, a close-knit society.

So, for the African, living according to the moral law means living according to his nature, composed as it is of contradictory elements but complementary life forces. Thus he gives stuff to the stuff of the universe and tightens the threads of the tissue of life. Thus he transcends the contradictions of the elements and works toward making the life forces complementary to one another: in himself first of all, as Man, but also in the whole of human society. It is by bringing the complementary life forces together in this way that Man reinforces them in their movement towards God and, in reinforcing them, he reinforces himself: that is, he passes from *existing* to *being.* He cannot reach the highest form of being, for in fact only God has this quality; and He has it all the more fully as creation, and all that exists, fulfil themselves and express themselves in Him.

Dialogue

Ethnologists have often praised the unity, the balance, and the harmony of African civilization, of black society, which was based both on the *community* and on the *person*, and in which, because it was founded on dialogue and reciprocity, the group had priority over the individual without crushing him, but allowing him to blossom as a person. I would like to emphasize at this point how much these characteristics of negritude enable it to find its place in contemporary humanism, thereby permitting black Africa to make its contribution to the "Civilization of the Universal" which is so necessary in our divided but interdependent world of the second half of the twentieth century. A contribution, first of all, to international cooperation, which must be and which shall be the cornerstone of that civilization. It is through these virtues of negritude that decolonization has been accomplished without too much bloodshed or hatred and that a positive form of cooperation based on "dialogue and reciprocity" has been established between former colonizers and colonized. It is through these virtues that there has been a new spirit at the United Nations, where the "no" and the bang of the fist on the table are no longer signs of strength. It is through these virtues that peace through cooperation could extend to South Africa, Rhodesia, and the Portuguese colonies, if only the dualistic spirit of the whites would open itself to dialogue.

In fact, the contribution of negritude to the "Civilization of the Universal" is not of recent origin. In the fields of literature and art, it is contemporary with the "Revolution of 1889." The French poet, Arthur Rimbaud (1854–91), had already associated himself with negritude. But in this article I want to concentrate on the "Negro revolution" – the expression belongs to Emmanuel Berl – which helped to stir European plastic art at the beginning of this century.

Art, like literature, is always the expression of a certain conception of the world and of life; the expression of a certain philosophy and, above all, of a certain ontology. Corresponding to the philosophical and scientific movement of 1889 there was not only a literary evolution – symbolism then surrealism – but another revolution, or rather revolutions, in art, which were called, taking only the plastic arts, nabism, expressionism, fauvism, and cubism. A world of life forces that have to be *tamed* is substituted for a closed world of permanent and continuous substances that have to be *reproduced*.

Since the Greek *kouroi* (the term used for the statues of young men in classical Greek sculpture), the art of the European West had always been based on realism; the work of art had always been an imitation of the object: a *physeôs mimêsis*, to use Aristotle's expression: a corrected imitation, "improved," "idealized" by the requirements of rationality, but imitation all the same. The interlude of the Christian Middle Ages is significant insofar as Christianity is itself of Asian origin and strongly influenced by the African, St. Augustine. To what will the artist then give expression? No longer to purely objective matter, but to his spiritual self: that is, to his inner self, his spirituality, and beyond himself to the spirituality of his age and of mankind. No longer by means of perspective, relief, and chiaroscuro, but, as the French painter, Bazaine, writes, "by the most hidden workings of instinct and the sensibility." Another French painter, André Masson, makes it more explicit when he writes: "By a simple interplay of

shapes and colors legibly ordered." This interplay of shapes and colors is that of the life forces and which has been illustrated in particular by a painter like Soulages.

"Interplay of life forces": and so we come back to – negritude. As the French painter, Soulages, in fact, once told me, the African aesthetic is "that of contemporary art." I find indirect proof of this in the fact that, while the consecration and spread of the new aesthetic revolution have occurred in France, the majority of its promoters were of Slav and Germanic origin; people who, like the Africans, belong to the mystical civilizations of the senses. Of course, without the discovery of African art, the revolution would still have taken place, but probably without such vigor and assurance and such a deepening of the knowledge of Man. The fact that an art of the subject and of the spirit should have germinated outside Europe, in Africa – to which ethnologists had not yet given its true place in world culture – was proof of the human value of the message of the new European art.

Over and above its aesthetic lesson – to which we shall return later – what Picasso, Braque and the other artists and early explorers of African art were seeking was, in the first place, just this: its human value. For in black Africa art is not a separate activity, in itself or for itself: it is a social activity, a technique of living, a handicraft in fact. But it is a major activity that brings all other activities to their fulfilment, like prayer in the Christian Middle Ages: birth and education, marriage and death, sport, even war. All human activities down to the least daily act must be integrated into the subtle interplay of life forces – family, tribal, national, world, and universal forces. This harmonious interplay of life forces must be helped by *subordinating* the lower forces – mineral, vegetable, and animal – to their relations with Man, and the forces of human society to its relations with the Divine Being through the intermediary of the Ancestral Beings.

A year or two ago I attended, on the cliffs of Bandiagara in the Mali Republic, an entertainment which was a microcosm of Dogon art.[4] Even though it was but a pale reflection of the splendors of the past, this "play-concert" was an extremely significant expression of the Dogon vision of the universe. It was declaimed, sung, and danced;

sculptured and presented in costume. The whole of the Dogon universe was portrayed in this symbiosis of the arts, as is the custom in black Africa. The universe – heaven and earth – was therefore *represented* through the intermediary of Man, whose ideogram is the same as that of the universe. Then the world was *re-presented* by means of masks, each of which portrayed, at one and the same time, a totemic animal, an ancestor and a spirit. Others portrayed the foreign peoples: nomadic Fulani[5] and white Europeans. The aim of the entertainment was, by means of the symbiosis of the arts – poetry, song, dance, sculpture, and painting, used as techniques of integration – to *re-create* the universe and the contemporary world, but in a more harmonious way by making use of African humor, which corrects distortions at the expense of the foreign Fulani and the white conquerors. But this ontological vision was an entertainment – that is, an artistic demonstration – as well: a joy for the soul because a joy for the eyes and ears.

It was perhaps – indeed, it was certainly – this last aspect of the African aesthetic lesson that first attracted Picasso and Braque when, toward 1906, they discovered African art and were inspired by it. For my part, what struck me from the start of the Dogon "play-concert," even before I tried to understand its meaning, was the harmony of form and movement, of color and rhythm, that characterized it. It is this harmony by which, as a spectator, I was moved; which, in the re-creation of reality, acts on the invisible forces whose appearances are only signs, subordinates them in a complementary fashion to one another and establishes the link between them and God through the intermediary of Man. By appearances I mean the attributes of matter that strike our senses: shape and color, timbre and tone, movement and rhythm.

I have said that these appearances are signs. They are more than that: they are meaningful signs, the "lines of force" of the life forces, insofar as they are used in their pure state, with only their characteristics of shape, color, sound, movement, and rhythm. Recently M. Lods, who teaches at the National School of Art of Senegal, was showing me the pictures his students intend exhibiting at the projected Festival of African Arts. I was immediately struck by the noble and elegant interplay of shape and color. When I discovered that the pictures were not completely abstract, that they portrayed ladies, princes, and noble animals, I was almost disappointed. There was no need for me to be: the very interplay of colored shapes perfectly expressed that elegant nobility that characterizes the art of the northern Sudan.

This, then, is Africa's lesson in aesthetics: art does not consist in photographing nature but in taming it, like the hunter when he reproduces the call of the hunted animal, like a separated couple, or two lovers, calling to each other in their desire to be reunited. The call is not the simple reproduction of the cry of the Other; it is a call of complementarity, a *song*: a call of harmony to the harmony of union that enriches by increasing *Being*. We call it pure harmony. Once more, Africa teaches that art is not photography; if there are images they are rhythmical. I can suggest or create anything – a man, a moon, a fruit, a smile, a tear – simply by assembling shapes and colors (painting sculpture), shapes and movement (dance), timbre and tones (music), provided that this assembling is not an aggregation, but that it is ordered and, in short, rhythmical. For it is rhythm – the main virtue, in fact, of negritude – that gives the work of art its beauty. Rhythm is simply the movement of attraction or repulsion that expresses the life of the cosmic forces; symmetry and asymmetry, repetition or opposition: in short, the lines of force that link the meaningful signs that shapes and colors, timbre and tones, are.

Before concluding, I should like to pause for a moment on the apparent contradiction that must have been noticed between contemporary European art (which places the emphasis on the subject) and African art (which places it on the object). This is because the "Revolution of 1889" began by reacting, of necessity, against the superstition of the *object*; and the existentialist ontology of the African, while it is based on the being-subject, has God as its pole-object; God who is the fullness of Being. What was noticed, then, was simply a nuance. For the contemporary European, and the African, the work of art, like the act of knowing, expresses the confrontation, the embrace, of subject and object: "That penetration," wrote

Bazaine, "that great common structure, that deep resemblance between Man and the world, without which there is no living form."

We have seen what constitutes for the African the "deep resemblance between Man and the world." For him, then, the act of restoring the order of the world by re-creating it through art is the reinforcement of the life forces in the universe and, consequently, of God, the source of all life forces – or, in other words, the Being of the universe. In this way, we reinforce ourselves at the same time, both as interdependent forces and as beings whose being consists in revitalizing ourselves in the re-creation of art.

Notes

1 The South African writer, Ezekiel Mphahlele, author, among other books, of *The African Image*, strongly disagrees with the concept of negritude.

2 *Léopold Sédar Senghor: Selected Poems*, introduced and translated by John Reed and Clive Wake. See also: *Léopold Sédar Senghor: Prose and Poetry*, by the same authors.

3 In African religion, the ancestors are the essential link between the living and God. This is why they are surrounded by a complex ritual so as to ensure the maintenance of this link.

4 The Dogon are a West African tribe among whom wood sculpture has achieved a very remarkable degree of excellence.

5 The Fulani are a nomadic pastoral people found throughout West Africa.

34

On National Culture

Frantz Fanon

... In this chapter we shall analyze the problem, which is felt to be fundamental, of the legitimacy of the claims of a nation. It must be recognized that the political party which mobilizes the people hardly touches on this problem of legitimacy. The political parties start from living reality and it is in the name of this reality, in the name of the stark facts which weigh down the present and the future of men and women, that they fix their line of action. The political party may well speak in moving terms of the nation, but what it is concerned with is that the people who are listening understand the need to take part in the fight if, quite simply, they wish to continue to exist.

Today we know that in the first phase of the national struggle colonialism tries to disarm national demands by putting forward economic doctrines. As soon as the first demands are set out, colonialism pretends to consider them, recognizing with ostentatious humility that the territory is suffering from serious underdevelopment which necessitates a great economic and social effort. And, in fact, it so happens that certain spectacular measures (centers of work for the unemployed which are opened here and there, for example) delay the crystallization of national consciousness for a few years. But, sooner or later, colonialism sees that it is not within its powers to put into practice a project of economic and social reforms which will satisfy the aspirations of the colonized people. Even where food supplies are concerned, colonialism gives proof of its inherent incapability. The colonialist state quickly discovers that if it wishes to disarm the nationalist parties on strictly economic questions then it will have to do in the colonies exactly what it has refused to do in its own country. ...

Inside the political parties, and most often in offshoots from these parties, cultured individuals of the colonized race make their appearance. For these individuals, the demand for a national culture and the affirmation of the existence of such a culture represent a special battlefield. While the politicians situate their action in actual present-day events, men of culture take their stand in the field of history. Confronted with the native intellectual who decides to make an aggressive response to the colonialist theory of pre-colonial barbarism, colonialism will react only slightly, and still less because the ideas developed by the young colonized

From Frantz Fanon, *The Wretched of the Earth*, trans. Constance Farrington (1968, 1982), pp. 206–19, 226–7, 236–47. Copyright © 1963 by Presence Africaine, from HarperCollins Publishers Ltd and Grove/Atlantic, Inc.

intelligentsia are widely professed by specialists in the mother country. It is in fact a commonplace to state that for several decades large numbers of research workers have, in the main, rehabilitated the African, Mexican, and Peruvian civilizations. The passion with which native intellectuals defend the existence of their national culture may be a source of amazement; but those who condemn this exaggerated passion are strangely apt to forget that their own psyche and their own selves are conveniently sheltered behind a French or German culture which has given full proof of its existence and which is uncontested.

I am ready to concede that on the plane of factual being the past existence of an Aztec civilization does not change anything very much in the diet of the Mexican peasant of today. I admit that all the proofs of a wonderful Songhai civilization will not change the fact that today the Songhais are underfed and illiterate, thrown between sky and water with empty heads and empty eyes. But it has been remarked several times that this passionate search for a national culture which existed before the colonial era finds its legitimate reason in the anxiety shared by native intellectuals to shrink away from that Western culture in which they all risk being swamped. Because they realize they are in danger of losing their lives and thus becoming lost to their people, these men, hotheaded and with anger in their hearts, relentlessly determine to renew contact once more with the oldest and most pre-colonial springs of life of their people.

Let us go further. Perhaps this passionate research and this anger are kept up or at least directed by the secret hope of discovering beyond the misery of today, beyond self-contempt, resignation, and abjuration, some very beautiful and splendid era whose existence rehabilitates us both in regard to ourselves and in regard to others. I have said that I have decided to go further. Perhaps unconsciously, the native intellectuals, since they could not stand wonderstruck before the history of today's barbarity, decided to back further and to delve deeper down; and, let us make no mistake, it was with the greatest delight that they discovered that there was nothing to be ashamed of in the past, but rather dignity, glory, and solemnity. The claim to a national culture in the past does not only rehabilitate that nation and serve as a justification for the hope of a future national culture. In the sphere of psycho-affective equilibrium it is responsible for an important change in the native. Perhaps we have not sufficiently demonstrated that colonialism is not simply content to impose its rule upon the present and the future of a dominated country. Colonialism is not satisfied merely with holding a people in its grip and emptying the native's brain of all form and content. By a kind of perverted logic, it turns to the past of the oppressed people, and distorts, disfigures, and destroys it. This work of devaluing pre-colonial history takes on a dialectical significance today.

When we consider the efforts made to carry out the cultural estrangement so characteristic of the colonial epoch, we realize that nothing has been left to chance and that the total result looked for by colonial domination was indeed to convince the natives that colonialism came to lighten their darkness. The effect consciously sought by colonialism was to drive into the natives' heads the idea that if the settlers were to leave, they would at once fall back into barbarism, degradation, and bestiality.

On the unconscious plane, colonialism therefore did not seek to be considered by the native as a gentle, loving mother who protects her child from a hostile environment, but rather as a mother who unceasingly restrains her fundamentally perverse offspring from managing to commit suicide and from giving free rein to its evil instincts. The colonial mother protects her child from itself, from its ego, and from its physiology, its biology, and its own unhappiness which is its very essence.

In such a situation the claims of the native intellectual are not a luxury but a necessity in any coherent program. The native intellectual who takes up arms to defend his nation's legitimacy and who wants to bring proofs to bear out that legitimacy, who is willing to strip himself naked to study the history of his body, is obliged to dissect the heart of his people.

Such an examination is not specifically national. The native intellectual who decides to give battle to colonial lies fights on the field of the whole continent. The past is given back its value. Culture, extracted from the past to be displayed in all its splendor, is not necessarily that of his own country. Colonialism, which has not bothered to put too fine a point on its efforts, has never ceased to maintain that the Negro is a savage; and for the colonist, the Negro was neither an Angolan nor a Nigerian, for he simply spoke of "the Negro." For colonialism, this vast continent was the haunt of savages, a country riddled with superstitions and fanaticism, destined for contempt, weighed down by the curse of God, a country of cannibals – in short, the Negro's country. Colonialism's condemnation is continental in its scope. The contention by colonialism that the darkest night of humanity lay over pre-colonial history concerns the whole of the African continent. The efforts of the native to rehabilitate himself and to escape from the claws of colonialism are logically inscribed from the same point of view as that of colonialism. The native intellectual who has gone far beyond the domains of Western culture and who has got it into his head to proclaim the existence of another culture never does so in the name of Angola or of Dahomey. The culture which is affirmed is African culture. The Negro, never so much a Negro as since he has been dominated by the whites, when he decides to prove that he has a culture and to behave like a cultured person, comes to realize that history points out a well-defined path to him: he must demonstrate that a Negro culture exists.

And it is only too true that those who are most responsible for this racialization of thought, or at least for the first movement toward that thought, are and remain those Europeans who have never ceased to set up white culture to fill the gap left by the absence of other cultures. Colonialism did not dream of wasting its time in denying the existence of one national culture after another. Therefore the reply of the colonized peoples will be straight away continental in its breadth. In Africa, the native literature of the last twenty years is not a national literature but a Negro literature. The concept of negritude, for example, was the emotional if not the logical antithesis of that insult which the white man flung at humanity. This rush of negritude against the white man's contempt showed itself in certain spheres to be the one idea capable of lifting interdictions and anathemas. Because the New Guinean or Kenyan intellectuals found themselves above all up against a general ostracism and delivered to the combined contempt of their overlords their reaction was to sing praises in admiration of each other. The unconditional

affirmation of African culture has succeeded the unconditional affirmation of European culture. On the whole, the poets of negritude oppose the idea of an old Europe to a young Africa, tiresome reasoning to lyricism, oppressive logic to high-stepping nature, and on one side stiffness, ceremony, etiquette, and scepticism, while on the other frankness, liveliness, liberty, and – why not – luxuriance: but also irresponsibility.

The poets of negritude will not stop at the limits of the continent. From America, black voices will take up the hymn with fuller unison. The "black world" will see the light and Busia from Ghana, Birago Diop from Senegal, Hampaté Ba from the Soudan, and Saint-Clair Drake from Chicago will not hesitate to assert the existence of common ties and a motive power that is identical. ...

This historical necessity in which the men of African culture find themselves to racialize their claims and to speak more of African culture than of national culture will tend to lead them up a blind alley. Let us take for example the case of the African Cultural Society. This society had been created by African intellectuals who wished to get to know each other and to compare their experiences and the results of their respective research work. The aim of this society was therefore to affirm the existence of an African culture, to evaluate this culture on the plane of distinct nations, and to reveal the internal motive forces of each of their national cultures. But at the same time this society fulfilled another need: the need to exist side by side with the European Cultural Society, which threatened to transform itself into a Universal Cultural Society. There was therefore at the bottom of this decision the anxiety to be present at the universal trysting place fully armed, with a culture springing from the very heart of the African continent. Now, this Society will very quickly show its inability to shoulder these different tasks, and will limit itself to exhibitionist demonstrations, while the habitual behavior of the members of this Society will be confined to showing Europeans that such a thing as African culture exists, and opposing their ideas to those of ostentatious and narcissistic Europeans. We have shown that such an attitude is normal and draws its legitimacy from the lies propagated by men of Western culture, but the degradation of the aims of this Society will become more marked with the elaboration of the concept of negritude. The African Society will become the cultural society of the black world and will come to include the Negro dispersion, that is to say the tens of thousands of black people spread over the American continents.

The Negroes who live in the United States and in Central or Latin America in fact experience the need to attach themselves to a cultural matrix. Their problem is not fundamentally different from that of the Africans. The whites of America did not mete out to them any different treatment from that of the whites who ruled over the Africans. We have seen that the whites were used to putting all Negroes in the same bag. During the first congress of the African Cultural Society which was held in Paris in 1956, the American Negroes of their own accord considered their problems from the same standpoint as those of their African brothers. Cultured Africans, speaking of African civilizations, decreed that there should be a reasonable status within the state for those who had formerly been slaves. But little by little the American Negroes realized that the essential problems confronting them were not the same as those that confronted the African Negroes. The Negroes of Chicago only resemble the Nigerians or the Tanganyikans in so far as they were all defined in relation to the whites. But once the first comparisons had been made and subjective feelings were assuaged, the American Negroes realized that the objective problems were fundamentally heterogeneous. The test cases of civil liberty whereby both whites and blacks in America try to drive back racial discrimination have very little in common in their principles and objectives with the heroic fight of the Angolan people against the detestable Portuguese colonialism. Thus, during the second congress of the African Cultural Society the American Negroes decided to create an American society for people of black cultures.

Negritude therefore finds its first limitation in the phenomena which take account of the formation of the historical character of men. Negro and African–Negro culture broke up into different entities because the men who wished to incarnate these cultures realized that every culture is first

and foremost national, and that the problems which kept Richard Wright or Langston Hughes on the alert were fundamentally different from those which might confront Leopold Senghor or Jomo Kenyatta. In the same way certain Arab states, though they had chanted the marvelous hymn of Arab renaissance, had nevertheless to realize that their geographical position and the economic ties of their region were stronger even than the past that they wished to revive. Thus we find today the Arab states organically linked once more with societies which are Mediterranean in their culture. The fact is that these states are submitted to modern pressure and to new channels of trade while the network of trade relations which was dominant during the great period of Arab history has disappeared. But above all there is the fact that the political regimes of certain Arab states are so different, and so far away from each other in their conceptions, that even a cultural meeting between these states is meaningless.

Thus we see that the cultural problem as it sometimes exists in colonized countries runs the risk of giving rise to serious ambiguities. The lack of culture of the Negroes, as proclaimed by colonialism, and the inherent barbarity of the Arabs ought logically to lead to the exaltation of cultural manifestations which are not simply national but continental, and extremely racial. In Africa, the movement of men of culture is a movement toward the Negro-African culture or the Arab-Moslem culture. It is not specifically toward a national culture. Culture is becoming more and more cut off from the events of today. It finds its refuge beside a hearth that glows with passionate emotion, and from there makes its way by realistic paths which are the only means by which it may be made fruitful, homogeneous, and consistent.

If the action of the native intellectual is limited historically, there remains nevertheless the fact that it contributes greatly to upholding and justifying the action of politicians. It is true that the attitude of the native intellectual sometimes takes on the aspect of a cult or of a religion. But if we really wish to analyze this attitude correctly we will come to see that it is symptomatic of the intellectual's realization of the danger that he is running in cutting his last moorings and of breaking adrift from his people. This stated belief in a national culture is in fact an ardent, despairing turning toward anything that will afford him secure anchorage. In order to ensure his salvation and to escape from the supremacy of the white man's culture the native feels the need to turn backward toward his unknown roots and to lose himself at whatever cost in his own barbarous people. Because he feels he is becoming estranged, that is to say because he feels that he is the living haunt of contradictions which run the risk of becoming insurmountable, the native tears himself away from the swamp that may suck him down and accepts everything, decides to take all for granted and confirms everything even though he may lose body and soul. The native finds that he is expected to answer for everything, and to all comers. He not only turns himself into the defender of his people's past; he is willing to be counted as one of them, and henceforward he is even capable of laughing at his past cowardice.

This tearing away, painful and difficult though it may be, is however necessary. If it is not accomplished there will be serious psycho–affective injuries and the result will be individuals without an anchor, without a horizon, colorless, stateless, rootless – a race of angels. It will be also quite normal to hear certain natives declare, "I speak as a Senegalese and as a Frenchman ..." "I speak as an Algerian and as a Frenchman ..." The intellectual who is Arab and French, or Nigerian and English, when he comes up against the need to take on two nationalities, chooses, if he wants to remain true to himself, the negation of one of these determinations. But most often, since they cannot or will not make a choice, such intellectuals gather together all the historical determining factors which have conditioned them and take up a fundamentally "universal standpoint."

This is because the native intellectual has thrown himself greedily upon Western culture. Like adopted children who only stop investigating the new family framework at the moment when a minimum nucleus of security crystallizes in their psyche, the native intellectual will try to make European culture his own. He will not be content to get to know Rabelais and Diderot, Shakespeare and Edgar Allen Poe; he will bind them to his intelligence as closely as possible. ...

But at the moment when the nationalist parties are mobilizing the people in the name of national independence, the native intellectual sometimes spurns these acquisitions which he suddenly feels make him a stranger in his own land. It is always easier to proclaim rejection than actually to reject. The intellectual who through the medium of culture has filtered into Western civilization, who has managed to become part of the body of European culture – in other words who has exchanged his own culture for another – will come to realize that the cultural matrix, which now he wishes to assume since he is anxious to appear original, can hardly supply any figureheads which will bear comparison with those, so many in number and so great in prestige, of the occupying power's civilization. History, of course, though nevertheless written by the Westerners and to serve their purposes, will be able to evaluate from time to time certain periods of the African past. But, standing face to face with his country at the present time, and observing clearly and objectively the events of today throughout the continent which he wants to make his own, the intellectual is terrified by the void, the degradation, and the savagery he sees there. Now he feels that he must get away from the white culture. He must seek his culture elsewhere, anywhere at all; and if he fails to find the substance of culture of the same grandeur and scope as displayed by the ruling power, the native intellectual will very often fall back upon emotional attitudes and will develop a psychology which is dominated by exceptional sensitivity and susceptibility. This withdrawal, which is due in the first instance to a begging of the question in his internal behavior mechanism and his own character, brings out, above all, a reflex and contradiction which is muscular.

This is sufficient explanation of the style of those native intellectuals who decide to give expression to this phase of consciousness which is in the process of being liberated. It is a harsh style, full of images, for the image is the drawbridge which allows unconscious energies to be scattered on the surrounding meadows. It is a vigorous style, alive with rhythms, struck through and through with bursting life; it is full of color, too, bronzed, sunbaked, and violent. This style, which in its time astonished the peoples of the West, has nothing racial about it, in spite of frequent statements to the contrary; it expresses above all a hand-to-hand struggle and it reveals the need that man has to liberate himself from a part of his being which already contained the seeds of decay. Whether the fight is painful, quick, or inevitable, muscular action must substitute itself for concepts.

If in the world of poetry this movement reaches unaccustomed heights, the fact remains that in the real world the intellectual often follows up a blind alley. When at the height of his intercourse with his people, whatever they were or whatever they are, the intellectual decides to come down into the common paths of real life, he only brings back from his adventuring formulas which are sterile in the extreme. He sets a high value on the customs, traditions, and the appearances of his people; but his inevitable, painful experience only seems to be a banal search for exoticism. The sari becomes sacred, and shoes that come from Paris or Italy are left off in favor of pampooties, while suddenly the language of the ruling power is felt to burn your lips. Finding your fellow countrymen sometimes means in this phase to will to be a nigger, not a nigger like all other niggers but a real nigger, a Negro cur, just the sort of nigger that the white man wants you to be. Going back to your own people means to become a dirty wog, to go native as much as you can, to become unrecognizable, and to cut off those wings that before you had allowed to grow.

The native intellectual decides to make an inventory of the bad habits drawn from the colonial world, and hastens to remind everyone of the good old customs of the people, that people which he has decided contains all truth and goodness. The scandalized attitude with which the settlers who live in the colonial territory greet this new departure only serves to strengthen the native's decision. When the colonialists, who had tasted the sweets of their victory over these assimilated people, realize that these men whom they considered as saved souls are beginning to fall back into the ways of niggers, the whole system totters. Every native won over, every native who had taken the pledge not only marks a failure for the colonial structure when he decides to lose himself and to go back to his own side, but also stands as a symbol for the uselessness and the shallowness of all the work that has been accomplished. Each native who goes back over the line is a radical condemnation of the methods and of the regime; and the native intellectual finds in the scandal he gives rise to a justification and an encouragement to persevere in the path he has chosen.

If we wanted to trace in the works of native writers the different phases which characterize this evolution we would find spread out before us a panorama on three levels. In the first phase, the native intellectual gives proof that he has assimilated the culture of the occupying power. His writings correspond point by point with those of his opposite numbers in the mother country. His inspiration is European and we can easily link up these works with definite trends in the literature of the mother country. This is the period of unqualified assimilation. We find in this literature coming from the colonies the Parnassians, the Symbolists, and the Surrealists.

In the second phase we find the native is disturbed; he decides to remember what he is. This period of creative work approximately corresponds to that immersion which we have just described. But since the native is not a part of his people, since he only has exterior relations with his people, he is content to recall their life only. Past happenings of the byegone days of his childhood will be brought up out of the depths of his memory; old legends will be reinterpreted in the light of a borrowed estheticism and of a conception of the world which was discovered under other skies.

Sometimes this literature of just-before-the-battle is dominated by humor and by allegory; but often too it is symptomatic of a period of distress and difficulty, where death is experienced, and disgust too. We spew ourselves up; but already underneath laughter can be heard.

Finally in the third phase, which is called the fighting phase, the native, after having tried to lose himself in the people and with the people, will on the contrary shake the people. Instead of according the people's lethargy an honored place in his esteem, he turns himself into an awakener of the people; hence comes a fighting literature, a revolutionary literature, and a national literature. During this phase a great many men and women who up till then would never have thought of producing a literary work, now that they find themselves in exceptional circumstances – in prison, with the Maquis, or on the eve of their execution – feel the need to speak to their nation, to compose the sentence which expresses the heart of the people, and to become the mouth-piece of a new reality in action.

The native intellectual nevertheless sooner or later will realize that you do not show proof of your nation from its culture but that you substantiate its existence in the fight which the people wage against the forces of occupation. No colonial system draws its justification from the fact that the territories it dominates are culturally non-existent. You will never make colonialism blush for shame by spreading out little-known cultural treasures under its eyes. At the very moment when the native intellectual is anxiously trying to create a cultural work he fails to realize that he is utilizing techniques and language which are borrowed from the stranger in his country. He contents himself with stamping these instruments with a hallmark which he wishes to be national, but which is strangely reminiscent of exoticism. The native intellectual who comes back to his people by way of cultural achievements behaves in fact like a foreigner. Sometimes he has no hesitation in using a dialect in order to show his will to be as near as possible to the people; but the ideas that he expresses and the preoccupations he is taken up with have no common yardstick to measure the real situation which the men and the women of his country know. The culture that the intellectual leans toward is often no more than a stock of particularisms. He wishes to attach himself to the people; but instead he only catches hold of their outer garments. And these outer garments are merely the reflection of a hidden life, teeming and perpetually in motion. That extremely obvious objectivity which seems to characterize a people is in fact only the inert, already forsaken result of frequent, and not always very coherent, adaptations of a much more fundamental substance which itself is continually being renewed. The man of culture, instead of setting out to find this substance, will let himself be hypnotized by these mummified fragments which because they are static are in fact symbols of negation and outworn contrivances. Culture has never the translucidity of custom; it abhors all simplification. In its essence it is opposed to custom, for custom is always the deterioration of culture. The desire to attach oneself to tradition or bring abandoned traditions to life again does not only mean going against the current of history but also

opposing one's own people. When a people undertakes an armed struggle or even a political struggle against a relentless colonialism, the significance of tradition changes. All that has made up the technique of passive resistance in the past may, during this phase, be radically condemned. In an underdeveloped country during the period of struggle traditions are fundamentally unstable and are shot through by centrifugal tendencies. This is why the intellectual often runs the risk of being out of date. The peoples who have carried on the struggle are more and more impervious to demagogy; and those who wish to follow them reveal themselves as nothing more than common opportunists, in other words, latecomers.

In the sphere of plastic arts, for example, the native artist who wishes at whatever cost to create a national work of art shuts himself up in a stereotyped reproduction of details. These artists who have nevertheless thoroughly studied modern techniques and who have taken part in the main trends of contemporary painting and architecture, turn their backs on foreign culture, deny it, and set out to look for a true national culture, setting great store on what they consider to be the constant principles of national art. But these people forget that the forms of thought and what it feeds on, together with modern techniques of information, language, and dress have dialectically reorganized the people's intelligences and that the constant principles which acted as safeguards during the colonial period are now undergoing extremely radical changes.

The artist who has decided to illustrate the truths of the nation turns paradoxically toward the past and away from actual events. What he ultimately intends to embrace are in fact the castoffs of thought, its shells and corpses, a knowledge which has been stabilized once and for all. But the native intellectual who wishes to create an authentic work of art must realize that the truths of a nation are in the first place its realities. He must go on until he has found the seething pot out of which the learning of the future will emerge.

Before independence, the native painter was insensible to the national scene. He set a high value on non-figurative art, or more often specialized in still lifes. After independence his anxiety to rejoin his people will confine him to the most detailed representation of reality. This is representative art which has no internal rhythms, an art which is screne and immobile, evocative not of life but of death. Enlightened circles are in ecstasies when confronted with this "inner truth" which is so well expressed; but we have the right to ask if this truth is in fact a reality, and if it is not already outworn and denied, called in question by the epoch through which the people are treading out their path toward history.

In the realm of poetry we may establish the same facts. After the period of assimilation characterized by rhyming poetry, the poetic tom-tom's rhythms break through. This is a poetry of revolt; but it is also descriptive and analytical poetry. The poet ought however to understand that nothing can replace the reasoned, irrevocable taking up of arms on the people's side. Let us quote Depestre:

> The lady was not alone;
> She had a husband,
> A husband who knew everything,
> But to tell the truth knew nothing,
> For you can't have culture without making concessions.
> You concede your flesh and blood to it,
> You concede your own self to others,
> By conceding you gain
> Classicism and Romanticism,
> And all that our souls are steeped in.[1]

The native poet who is preoccupied with creating a national work of art and who is determined to describe his people fails in his aim, for he is not yet ready to make that fundamental concession that Depestre speaks of. The French poet René Char shows his understanding of the difficulty when he reminds us that "the poem emerges out of a subjective imposition and an objective choice. A poem is the assembling and moving together of determining original values, in contemporary relation with someone that these circumstances bring to the front."[2]

Yes, the first duty of the native poet is to see clearly the people he has chosen as the subject of his work of art. He cannot go forward resolutely unless he first realizes the extent of his estrangement from them. We have taken everything from the other side; and the other side gives us nothing unless by a thousand detours we swing finally round in their direction, unless by ten thousand wiles and a hundred thousand tricks they manage to draw us toward them, to seduce us, and to imprison us. Taking means in nearly every case being taken: thus it is not enough to try to free oneself by repeating proclamations and denials. It is not enough to try to get back to the people in that past out of which they have already emerged; rather we must join them in that fluctuating movement which they are just giving a shape to, and which, as soon as it has started, will be the signal for everything to be called in question. Let there be no mistake about it; it is to this zone of occult instability where the people dwell that we must come; and it is there that our souls are crystallized and that our perceptions and our lives are transfused with light. ...

The responsibility of the native man of culture is not a responsibility vis-à-vis his national culture, but a global responsibility with regard to the totality of the nation, whose culture merely, after all, represents one aspect of that nation. The cultured native should not concern himself with choosing the level on which he wishes to fight or the sector where he decides to give battle for his nation. To fight for national culture means in the first place to fight for the liberation of the nation, that material keystone which makes the building of a culture possible. There is no other fight for culture which can develop apart from the popular struggle. To take an example: all those men and women who are fighting with their bare hands against French colonialism in Algeria are not by any means strangers to the national culture of Algeria. The national Algerian culture is taking on form and content as the battles are being fought out, in prisons, under the guillotine, and in every French outpost which is captured or destroyed.

We must not therefore be content with delving into the past of a people in order to find coherent elements which will counteract colonialism's attempts to falsify and harm. We must work and fight with the same rhythm as the people to construct the future and to prepare the ground where vigorous shoots are already springing up. A national culture is not a folklore, nor an abstract populism that believes it can discover the people's true nature. It is not made up of the inert dregs of gratuitous actions, that is to say actions which are less and less attached to the ever-present reality of the people. A national culture is the whole body of efforts made by a people in the sphere of thought to describe, justify, and praise the action through which that people has created itself and keeps itself in existence. A national culture in underdeveloped countries should therefore take its place at the very heart of the struggle for freedom which these countries are carrying on. Men of African cultures who are still fighting in the name of African-Negro culture and who have called many congresses in the name of the unity of that culture should today realize that all their efforts amount to is to make comparisons between coins and sarcophagi.

There is no common destiny to be shared between the national cultures of Senegal and Guinea; but there *is* a common destiny between the Senegalese and Guinean nations which are both dominated by the same French colonialism. If it is wished that the national culture of Senegal should come to resemble the national culture of Guinea, it is not enough for the rulers of the two peoples to decide to consider their problems – whether the problem of liberation is concerned, or the trade-union question, or economic difficulties – from similar viewpoints. And even here there does not seem to be complete identity, for the rhythm of the people and that of their rulers are not the same. There can be no two cultures which are completely identical. To believe that it is possible to create a black culture is to forget that niggers are disappearing, just as those people who brought them into being are seeing the breakup of their economic and cultural supremacy.[3] There will never be such a thing as black culture because there is not a single politician who feels he has a vocation to bring black republics into being. The problem is to get to know the place that these men mean to give their people, the kind of social relations that they decide to set up, and the conception that they have of the future of humanity. It is this that counts; everything else is mystification, signifying nothing.

In 1959, the cultured Africans who met at Rome never stopped talking about unity. But one of the people who was loudest in the praise of this cultural unity, Jacques Rabemananjara, is today a minister in the Madagascan government, and as such has decided, with his government, to oppose the Algerian people in the General Assembly of the United Nations. Rabemananjara, if he had been true to himself, ought to have resigned from the government and denounced those men who claim to incarnate the will of the Madagascan people. The ninety thousand dead of Madagascar have not given Rabemananjara authority to oppose the aspirations of the Algerian people in the General Assembly of the United Nations.

It is around the peoples' struggles that African-Negro culture takes on substance, and not around songs, poems, or folklore. Senghor, who is also a member of the Society of African Culture and who has worked with us on the question of African culture, is not afraid for his part either to give the order to his delegation to support French proposals on Algeria. Adherence to African-Negro culture and to the cultural unity of Africa is arrived at in the first place by upholding unconditionally the peoples' struggle for freedom. No one can truly wish for the spread of African culture if he does not give practical support to the creation of the conditions necessary to the existence of that culture; in other words, to the liberation of the whole continent.

I say again that no speech-making and no proclamation concerning culture will turn us from our fundamental tasks: the liberation of the national territory; a continual struggle against colonialism in its new forms; and an obstinate refusal to enter the charmed circle of mutual admiration at the summit.

Reciprocal Bases of National Culture and the Fight for Freedom

Colonial domination, because it is total and tends to oversimplify, very soon manages to disrupt in spectacular fashion the cultural life of a conquered people. This cultural obliteration is made possible by the negation of national reality, by new legal relations introduced by the occupying power, by the banishment of the natives and their customs to outlying districts by colonial society, by expropriation, and by the systematic enslaving of men and women.

Three years ago at our first congress I showed that, in the colonial situation, dynamism is replaced fairly quickly by a substantification of the attitudes of the colonizing power. The area of culture is then marked off by fences and signposts. These are in fact so many defense mechanisms of the most elementary type, comparable for more than one good reason to the simple instinct for preservation. The interest of this period for us is that the oppressor does not manage to convince himself of the objective non-existence of the oppressed nation and its culture. Every effort is made to bring the colonized person to admit the inferiority of his culture which has been transformed into instinctive patterns of behavior, to recognize the unreality of his "nation," and, in the last extreme, the confused and imperfect character of his own biological structure.

Vis-à-vis this state of affairs, the native's reactions are not unanimous. While the mass of the people maintain intact traditions which are completely different from those of the colonial situation, and the artisanal style solidifies into a formalism which is more and more stereotyped, the intellectual throws himself in frenzied fashion into the frantic acquisition of the culture of the occupying power and takes every opportunity of unfavorably criticizing his own national culture, or else takes refuge in setting out and substantiating the claims of that culture in a way that is passionate but rapidly becomes unproductive.

The common nature of these two reactions lies in the fact that they both lead to impossible contradictions. Whether a turncoat or a substantialist, the native is ineffectual precisely because the analysis of the colonial situation is not carried out on strict lines. The colonial situation calls a halt to national culture in almost every field. Within the framework of colonial domination there is not and there will never be such phenomena as new cultural departures or changes in the national culture. Here and there valiant attempts are sometimes made to reanimate the cultural dynamic and to give fresh impulses to its themes, its forms, and its tonalities. The immediate, palpable, and obvious interest of such leaps ahead is nil. But if we follow up the consequences to the very end we see that preparations are being thus made to brush the cobwebs off national consciousness, to question oppression, and to open up the struggle for freedom.

A national culture under colonial domination is a contested culture whose destruction is sought in systematic fashion. It very quickly becomes a culture condemned to secrecy. This idea of a clandestine culture is immediately seen in the reactions of the occupying power which interprets attachment to traditions as faithfulness to the spirit of the nation and as a refusal to submit. This persistence in following forms of cultures which are already condemned to extinction is already a demonstration of nationality; but it is a demonstration which is a throwback to the laws of inertia. There is no taking of the offensive and no redefining of relationships. There is simply a concentration on a hard core of culture which is becoming more and more shrivelled up, inert, and empty.

By the time a century or two of exploitation has passed there comes about a veritable emaciation of the stock of national culture. It becomes a set of automatic habits, some traditions of dress, and a few broken-down institutions. Little movement can be discerned in such remnants of culture; there is no real creativity and no overflowing life. The poverty of the people, national oppression, and the inhibition of culture are one and the same thing. After a century of colonial domination we find a culture which is rigid in the extreme, or rather what we find are the dregs of culture, its mineral strata. The withering away of the reality of the nation and the death pangs of the national culture are linked to each other in mutual dependence. This is why it is of capital importance to follow the evolution of these relations during the struggle for national freedom. The negation of the native's culture, the contempt for any manifestation of culture whether active or emotional, and the placing outside the pale of all specialized branches of organization contribute to breed aggressive patterns of conduct in the native. But these patterns of conduct are of the reflexive type; they are poorly differentiated, anarchic, and ineffective. Colonial exploitation, poverty, and endemic famine drive the native more and more to open, organized revolt. The necessity for an open and decisive breach is formed progressively and imperceptibly, and comes to be felt by the great majority of the people. Those tensions which hitherto were non-existent come into being. International events, the collapse of whole sections of colonial empires and the contradictions inherent in the colonial system strengthen and uphold the native's combativity while promoting and giving support to national consciousness.

These new-found tensions which are present at all stages in the real nature of colonialism have their repercussions on the cultural plane. In literature, for example, there is relative overproduction. From being a reply on a minor scale to the dominating power, the literature produced by natives becomes differentiated and makes itself into a will to particularism. The intelligentsia, which during the period of repression was essentially a consuming public, now themselves become producers. This literature at first chooses to confine itself to the tragic and poetic style; but later on novels, short stories, and essays are attempted. It is as if a kind of internal organization or law of expression existed which wills that poetic expression become less frequent in proportion as the objectives and the methods of the struggle for liberation become more precise. Themes are completely altered; in fact, we find less and less of bitter, hopeless recrimination and less also of that violent, resounding, florid writing which on the whole serves to reassure the occupying power. The colonialists have in former times encouraged these modes of expression and made their existence possible. Stinging denunciations, the exposing of distressing conditions and passions which find their outlet in expression are in fact assimilated by the occupying power in a cathartic process. To aid such processes is in a certain sense to avoid their dramatization and to clear the atmosphere.

But such a situation can only be transitory. In fact, the progress of national consciousness among the people modifies and gives precision to the literary utterances of the native intellectual. The continued cohesion of the people constitutes for the intellectual an invitation to go further than his cry of protest. The lament first makes the indictment; and then it makes an appeal. In the period that follows, the words of command are heard. The crystallization of the national consciousness will both disrupt literary styles and themes, and also create a completely new public. While at the beginning the native intellectual used to produce his work to be read exclusively by the oppressor, whether with the intention of charming him or of denouncing him through ethnic or subjectivist means, now the native writer progressively takes on the habit of addressing his own people.

It is only from that moment that we can speak of a national literature. Here there is, at the level of literary creation, the taking up and clarification of themes which are typically nationalist. This

may be properly called a literature of combat, in the sense that it calls on the whole people to fight for their existence as a nation. It is a literature of combat, because it molds the national consciousness, giving it form and contours and flinging open before it new and boundless horizons; it is a literature of combat because it assumes responsibility, and because it is the will to liberty expressed in terms of time and space.

On another level, the oral tradition – stories, epics, and songs of the people – which formerly were filed away as set pieces are now beginning to change. The storytellers who used to relate inert episodes now bring them alive and introduce into them modifications which are increasingly fundamental. There is a tendency to bring conflicts up to date and to modernize the kinds of struggle which the stories evoke, together with the names of heroes and the types of weapons. The method of allusion is more and more widely used. The formula "This all happened long ago" is substituted with that of "What we are going to speak of happened somewhere else, but it might well have happened here today, and it might happen tomorrow." The example of Algeria is significant in this context. From 1952–3 on, the storytellers, who were before that time stereotyped and tedious to listen to, completely overturned their traditional methods of storytelling and the contents of their tales. Their public, which was formerly scattered, became compact. The epic, with its typified categories, reappeared; it became an authentic form of entertainment which took on once more a cultural value. Colonialism made no mistake when from 1955 on it proceeded to arrest these storytellers systematically.

The contact of the people with the new movement gives rise to a new rhythm of life and to forgotten muscular tensions, and develops the imagination. Every time the storyteller relates a fresh episode to his public, he presides over a real invocation. The existence of a new type of man is revealed to the public. The present is no longer turned in upon itself but spread out for all to see. The storyteller once more gives free rein to his imagination; he makes innovations and he creates a work of art. It even happens that the characters, which are barely ready for such a transformation – highway robbers or more or less anti-social vagabonds – are taken up and remodeled. The emergence of the imagination and of the creative urge in the songs and epic stories of a colonized country is worth following. The storyteller replies to the expectant people by successive approximations, and makes his way, apparently alone but in fact helped on by his public, toward the seeking out of new patterns, that is to say national patterns. Comedy and farce disappear, or lose their attraction. As for dramatization, it is no longer placed on the plane of the troubled intellectual and his tormented conscience. By losing its characteristics of despair and revolt, the drama becomes part of the common lot of the people and forms part of an action in preparation or already in progress.

Where handicrafts are concerned, the forms of expression which formerly were the dregs of art, surviving as if in a daze, now begin to reach out. Woodwork, for example, which formerly turned out certain faces and attitudes by the million, begins to be differentiated. The inexpressive or overwrought mask comes to life and the arms tend to be raised from the body as if to sketch an action. Compositions containing two, three or five figures appear. The traditional schools are led on to creative efforts by the rising avalanche of amateurs or of critics. This new vigor in this sector of cultural life very often passes unseen; and yet its contribution to the national effort is of capital importance. By carving figures and faces which are full of life, and by taking as his theme a group fixed on the same pedestal, the artist invites participation in an organized movement.

If we study the repercussions of the awakening of national consciousness in the domains of ceramics and pottery-making, the same observations may be drawn. Formalism is abandoned in the craftsman's work. Jugs, jars, and trays are modified, at first imperceptibly, then almost savagely. The colors, of which formerly there were but few and which obeyed the traditional rules of harmony, increase in number and are influenced by the repercussion of the rising revolution. Certain ochres and blues, which seemed forbidden to all eternity in a given cultural area, now assert themselves without giving rise to scandal. In the same way the stylization of the human face, which according to sociologists is typical of very clearly defined regions, becomes suddenly completely relative. The specialist coming from the home country and the ethnologist are quick to note these changes. On the whole such changes are condemned in the name of a rigid code of artistic style and of a cultural life which grows up at the heart of the colonial system. The colonialist specialists do not recognize these new forms and rush to the help of the traditions of the indigenous society. It is the colonialists who become the defenders of the native style. We remember perfectly, and the example took on a certain measure of importance since the real nature of colonialism was not involved, the reactions of the white jazz specialists when after the Second World War new styles such as the be-bop took definite shape. The fact is that in their eyes jazz should only be the despairing, broken-down nostalgia of an old Negro who is trapped between five glasses of whiskey, the curse of his race, and the racial hatred of the white men. As soon as the Negro comes to an understanding of himself, and understands the rest of the world differently, when he gives birth to hope and forces back the racist universe, it is clear that his trumpet sounds more clearly and his voice less hoarsely. The new fashions in jazz are not simply born of economic competition. We must without any doubt see in them one of the consequences of the defeat, slow but sure, of the southern world of the United States. And it is not utopian to suppose that in fifty years' time the type of jazz howl hiccuped by a poor misfortunate Negro will be upheld only by the whites who believe in it as an expression of negritude, and who are faithful to this arrested image of a type of relationship.

We might in the same way seek and find in dancing, singing, and traditional rites and ceremonies the same upward-springing trend, and make out the same changes and the same impatience in this field. Well before the political or fighting phase of the national movement, an attentive spectator can thus feel and see the manifestation of new vigor and feel the approaching conflict. He will note unusual forms of expression and themes which are fresh and imbued with a power which is no longer that of invocation but rather of the assembling of the people, a summoning together for a precise purpose. Everything works together to awaken the native's sensibility and to make unreal and inacceptable the contemplative attitude, or the acceptance of defeat. The native rebuilds his perceptions because he renews the purpose and dynamism of the craftsmen, of dancing and music, and of literature and the oral tradition. His world comes to lose its accursed character. The conditions necessary for the inevitable conflict are brought together.

We have noted the appearance of the movement in cultural forms and we have seen that this movement and these new forms are linked to the state of maturity of the national consciousness. Now, this movement tends more and more to express itself objectively, in institutions. From thence comes the need for a national existence, whatever the cost.

A frequent mistake, and one which is moreover hardly justifiable, is to try to find cultural expressions for and to give new values to native culture within the framework of colonial domination. This is why we arrive at a proposition which at first sight seems paradoxical: the fact that in a colonized country the most elementary, most savage, and the most undifferentiated nationalism is the most fervent and efficient means of defending national culture. For culture is first the expression of a nation, the expression of its preferences, of its taboos and of its patterns. It is at every stage of the whole of society that other taboos, values, and patterns are formed. A national culture is the sum total of all these appraisals; it is the result of internal and external tensions exerted over society as a whole and also at every level of that society. In the colonial situation, culture, which is doubly deprived of the support of the nation and of the state, falls away and dies. The condition for its existence is therefore national liberation and the renaissance of the state.

The nation is not only the condition of culture, its fruitfulness, its continuous renewal, and its deepening. It is also a necessity. It is the fight for national existence which sets culture moving and opens to it the doors of creation. Later on it is the nation which will ensure the conditions and framework necessary to culture. The nation gathers together the various indispensable elements necessary for the creation of a culture, those elements which alone can give it credibility, validity, life, and creative power. In the same way it is its national character that will make such a culture open to other cultures and which will enable it to influence and permeate other cultures. A non-existent culture can hardly be expected to have bearing on reality, or to influence reality. The first necessity is the re-establishment of the nation in order to give life to national culture in the strictly biological sense of the phrase.

Thus we have followed the breakup of the old strata of culture, a shattering which becomes increasingly fundamental; and we have noticed, on the eve of the decisive conflict for national freedom, the renewing of forms of expression and the rebirth of the imagination. There remains one essential question: what are the relations between the struggle – whether political or military – and culture? Is there a suspension of culture during the conflict? Is the national struggle an expression of a culture? Finally, ought one to say that the battle for freedom however fertile *a posteriori* with regard to culture is in itself a negation of culture? In short, is the struggle for liberation a cultural phenomenon or not?

We believe that the conscious and organized undertaking by a colonized people to re-establish the sovereignty of that nation constitutes the most complete and obvious cultural manifestation that exists. It is not alone the success of the struggle which afterward gives validity and vigor to culture; culture is not put into cold storage during the conflict. The struggle itself in its development and in its internal progression sends culture along different paths and traces out entirely new ones for it. The struggle for freedom does not give back to the national culture its former value and shapes; this struggle which aims at a fundamentally different set of relations between men cannot leave intact either the form or the content of the people's culture. After the conflict there is not only the disappearance of colonialism but also the disappearance of the colonized man.

This new humanity cannot do otherwise than define a new humanism both for itself and for others. It is prefigured in the objectives and methods of the conflict. A struggle which mobilizes all classes of the people and which expresses their aims and their impatience, which is not afraid to count almost exclusively on the people's support, will of necessity triumph. The value of this type of conflict is that it supplies the maximum of conditions necessary for the development and aims of culture. After national freedom has been obtained in these conditions, there is no such painful cultural indecision which is found in certain countries which are newly independent, because the nation by its manner of coming into being and in the terms of its existence exerts a fundamental influence over culture. A nation which is born of the people's concerted action and which embodies the real aspirations of the people while changing the state cannot exist save in the expression of exceptionally rich forms of culture.

The natives who are anxious for the culture of their country and who wish to give to it a universal dimension ought not therefore to place their confidence in the single principle of inevitable, undifferentiated independence written into the consciousness of the people in order to achieve their task. The liberation of the nation is one thing; the methods and popular content of the fight are another. It seems to us that the future of national culture and its riches are equally also part and parcel of the values which have ordained the struggle for freedom.

And now it is time to denounce certain pharisees. National claims, it is here and there stated, are a phase that humanity has left behind. It is the day of great concerted actions, and retarded nationalists ought in consequence to set their mistakes aright. We however consider that the mistake, which may have very serious consequences, lies in wishing to skip the national period. If culture is the expression of national consciousness, I will not hesitate to affirm that in the case with which we are dealing it is the national consciousness which is the most elaborate form of culture.

The consciousness of self is not the closing of a door to communication. Philosophic thought teaches us, on the contrary, that it is its guarantee. National consciousness, which is not nationalism, is the only thing that will give us an international dimension. This problem of national consciousness and of national culture takes on in Africa a special dimension. The birth of national consciousness in Africa has a strictly contemporaneous connection with the African consciousness. The responsibility of the African as regards national culture is also a responsibility with regard to African Negro culture. This joint responsibility is not the fact of a metaphysical principle but the awareness of a simple rule which wills that every independent nation in an Africa where colonialism is still entrenched is an encircled nation, a nation which is fragile and in permanent danger.

If man is known by his acts, then we will say that the most urgent thing today for the intellectual is to build up his nation. If this building up is true, that is to say if it interprets the manifest will of the people and reveals the eager African peoples, then the building of a nation is of necessity accompanied by the discovery and encouragement of universalizing values. Far from keeping aloof from other nations, therefore, it is national liberation which leads the nation to play its part on the stage of history. It is at the heart of national consciousness that international consciousness lives and grows. And this two-fold emerging is ultimately only the source of all culture.

Notes

1 René Depestre: "Face à la Nuit."
2 René Char, *Partage Formel*.
3 At the last school prize giving in Dakar, the president of the Senegalese Republic, Léopold Senghor, decided to include the study of the idea of negritude in the curriculum. If this decision was due to a desire to study historical causes, no one can criticize it. But if on the other hand it was taken in order to create black self-consciousness, it is simply a turning of his back upon history which has already taken cognizance of the disappearance of the majority of Negroes.

35

Nationalism, Ethnicity, and Modernity
The Paradox of Mau Mau

Bruce J. Berman

Introduction: The Continuing Fascination of Mau Mau

What was Mau Mau? What was its significance in the history of Kenya or, more broadly, the history of colonial Africa? What can an understanding of Mau Mau tell us about the colonial confrontation of African "tradition" and Western "modernity"? Almost forty years after the colonial authorities in Nairobi declared a state of emergency to crush what they insisted was a savage and wholly evil secret cult, conclusive answers to these questions remain elusive. "The horror story of the Empire in the 1950s," as John Lonsdale calls it, continues to be a source of political and intellectual controversy.[1] During the 1970s and again in the mid-1980s, Kenyan intellectuals and political figures clashed over conflicting interpretations of Mau Mau, with many aging ex-Mau Mau fighters also jumping into the fray (Odhiambo, 1988; Maughan-Brown, 1985, 20–2). The historical and fictional writings on Mau Mau of Kenya's leading intellectual dissidents, Ngugi wa Thiong'o and Maina wa Kinyatti, were factors in their detention and exile (Thiong'o and Mugo 1976; Thiong'o 1983; Kinyatti 1985,

1987). Academic interest in Mau Mau has surged once more, with a whole series of monographs and papers appearing since 1986 which explore yet again its nature and place in the politics of colonial and post-colonial Kenya (Kanogo 1987; Throup 1987; Edgerton 1989; Furedi 1989; Presley 1988; Gordon 1986; Berman 1990).

Central to the debates over Mau Mau is the nature of its relationship to nationalism in Kenya. Was it a parochial tribal uprising or the central episode of Kenya's national liberation struggle? Were the Mau Mau forest fighters tribal traditionalists or nationalist patriots? Despite its military defeat by Imperial forces, did Mau Mau force the British into social and political reforms which led to independence under an African government? If Mau Mau fought for national liberation, why was it unable to articulate a trans-ethnic national ideology? This article addresses these questions through a critical examination of the conflicting interpretations of Mau Mau's relationship with nationalism, followed by a plausible reconstruction of the relationship suggested by an understanding of the internal conflicts in Kikuyu society in the first decade after World War II.

From Bruce J. Berman, 1991, "Nationalism, Ethnicity, and Modernity: The Paradox of Mau Mau," *Canadian Journal of African Studies / Revue canadienne des Études africaines* 25(2): 181–206.

Mau Mau: Anti-Nationalism or Militant Nationalism?

In the late 1940s colonial officials first became aware of what they believed was a secret organization among African farm labourers on the European estates of the Rift Valley which they named "Mau Mau." Through the years of the Emergency from 1952 to 1960, and into the first years of Kenya's independence after 1963, the dominant interpretation of this phenomenon focused on its essentially tribal and religious character. This view, with variations, comprised the conventional wisdom about Mau Mau shared not only by colonial officials in Nairobi and London, white settlers, and missionaries but also by journalists and academic commentators from Britain and several other countries.

In the most coherent official version,[2] Mau Mau was depicted as a savage, violent, and depraved tribal cult, an expression of unrestrained emotion rather than reason. It sought to turn the Kikuyu people back to "the bad old days" before enlightened British rule had brought the blessings of modern civilization and development. When the first reports of something called "Mau Mau" reached the Provincial Administration and the Kenya Police in 1948–9, it was immediately identified as a "dini" or religious cult. As late as February 1953, the Commissioner of Police was passing on reports that linked Mau Mau with the Dini ya Msambwa, which had violently clashed with government forces a few years before.[3] The government also claimed that Mau Mau had emerged among a particularly unstable people who had difficulty adjusting to the strains of rapid social change and modernization. Playing upon their morbid fears and superstitions, Mau Mau turned the Kikuyu into savage and maniacal killers. Government intelligence reports dwelt on the "insane frenzy" and "fanatical discipline" of Mau Mau adherents.[4] It had been deliberately organized, according to the government, by cynical and unprincipled leaders, seeking only to satisfy their own lust for power. Furthermore, officials repeatedly insisted that Mau Mau was not a response to economic deprivation and material grievances arising out of colonialism, but rather was an irrational rejection of the benefits of development.

This view led them to stress repeatedly the essentially atavistic character of Mau Mau. As the British parliamentary delegation which visited Kenya in 1954 put it, "Mau Mau intentionally and deliberately seeks to lead the Africans of Kenya back to the bush and savagery, not forward into progress" (*Report to the Secretary of State*, 4). Depraved, murderous, and wholly evil, Mau Mau had to be totally destroyed.

This characterization of Mau Mau, repeated almost daily for several years in press conferences, news briefs, and interviews from government information agencies in Nairobi and London, and widely disseminated in print and broadcasts by the press throughout the world, became and remains, especially in English-speaking countries, the image of the phenomenon in popular culture. Until the mid-1960s it received powerful support in numerous studies by academic social scientists which claimed for it the status of objective scientific knowledge. The most important of these were by Louis Leakey, Kenya's leading scholar and intellectual at the time, whose interpretive authority was reinforced by his being born and raised among the Kikuyu and being one of the few whites in Kenya who spoke their language fluently. His two books (1952 and 1954) gave definitive expression to the analysis of Mau Mau as a perverted religious cult manipulated by cynical and evil leaders, and were widely disseminated by the Kenya Government, which supplied copies to all of its administrative and police officers.[5] This explanation was quickly taken up by scholars in other countries, especially amongst American anthropologists, among whom Mau Mau was readily assimilated to existing concepts of "nativistic sects," "tribal revival movements," and "crisis cults" developed in the analysis of native American responses to white colonial expansion. Its definitive expression was a 1965 article by Gilbert Kushner in the German anthropological journal *Anthropos*, which relied primarily on Leakey for empirical evidence and fixed Mau Mau firmly within the theoretical paradigm of atavistic, violent, despairing movements among peoples being overwhelmed by the advance of modern civilization (Kushner 1965; see also Rosenstiel 1953).[6] These movements were seen as nostalgic attempts to escape the rigours of modernity; not efforts to relieve the inequities of colonial development, but its utter rejection.

Thus, Mau Mau's atavistic mind and tribal scale made it the enemy, the very antithesis, of nationalism. Mau Mau could not be an expression of nationalism because it led away from everything the latter represented as an essential part of the modernization process.

> No Western observer, not even those on the anticolonial left, saw Mau Mau as the political expression of national integration … The movement's symbols had nothing "Kenyan" about them. Mau Mau, uniquely, seemed to be a core radicalism which rejected the nation. (Lonsdale 1989, 7)

By the mid-1960s this interpretation began to be challenged by a revisionist version of Mau Mau which depicted it as an essential, if radical, component of African nationalism in Kenya. First, memoirs of the Emergency by some of those active in Mau Mau began to be published, notably by J.M. Kariuki (1963), a politician who spent years in detention, and Waruhiu Itote (1967), who as "General China" had commanded the guerrilla forces in the forests of Mount Kenya until his capture in 1954. Both insisted that Mau Mau was a modern, rational, and nationalist political movement, not tribalist reaction, and that the fighters of the Land and Freedom Army had fought a glorious struggle for national liberation. Second, and more important for shaping a significant shift in academic opinion about Mau Mau, were two substantial works which brought together participants on opposite sides of the struggle with American social scientists. The first, *Mau Mau from Within*, is the autobiography of Karari Njama, a man of some education who had served as secretary to the guerrilla forces in the Aberdares and to its leader Dedan Kimathi, edited with extensive commentary by the radical anthropologist Donald Barnett. This text is an extended elaboration of the depiction of Mau Mau as a rational struggle for national liberation, substantially downplaying the Kikuyu cultural content and symbolism it employed. This is evident right at the beginning of the book in a preface signed by several prominent political figures, including Fred Kubai, Bildad Kaggia, and Achieng Oneko, who had been charged with Jomo

Kenyatta with "organizing Mau Mau." They criticized previous accounts of it:

> There is obsessive preoccupation in these works with the sinister and the awesome. The very name "Mau Mau" is an illustration of how successful propaganda can damn an entire movement to which thousands sacrificed everything, including their lives, by attaching to it an appellation that conjures up all the clichés of the "dark continent" which still crowd the European mind. (Barnett and Njama 1966, 9)

The second challenge to the interpretation of Mau Mau as atavism is a thoroughly academic monograph, based on extensive documentary analysis and numerous interviews with African political figures, composed by John Nottingham, a maverick colonial administrator who had rejected the official version of Mau Mau, and Carl Rosberg, a political scientist from the University of California at Berkeley. They state their revisionist purpose right at the outset:

> "Mau Mau" is identified with the militant nationalism and the violence which characterized the politics of central Kenya before and during the early years of the Emergency … This book presents an alternative interpretation of "Mau Mau," in which we will be concerned with the modern origins of African politics and their pattern of development, with particular emphasis on the politicization and mobilization of the Kikuyu people … In our view, the outbreak of open violence in Kenya in 1952 occurred primarily because of a European failure rather than an African one; it was not so much a failure of the Kikuyu people to adapt to a modern institutional setting as it was a failure of the European policy-makers to recognize the need for significant social and political reform. (Rosberg and Nottingham 1966, xvi–xvii)

Not only is Mau Mau identified as modern and nationalist but also the focus of the analysis is on the development of African anti-colonial nationalist opposition in Kenya in response to the concrete inequities and material grievances of colonial domination. African politics in Kenya is shown to be essentially instrumental and rational and grounded in material causes for which the British were largely responsible. The treatment of the specifically Kikuyu cultural forms and content which characterized Mau Mau is muted, with the Mau Mau oath, the central evidence for its supposed savage obscenity, depicted as a rational "instrument for achieving unity." The earlier interpretation of Mau Mau as savage and atavistic tribalism is subject to penetrating analysis as a "myth of Mau Mau" grounded in European racism and ethnocentrism. Only on the very last page do Rosberg and Nottingham conclude:

> Although oathing strengthened the Kikuyu organizational ability to challenge the colonial state, it nonetheless had the additional effect of limiting the institutional spread of the national movement to non-Kikuyu groups. This dilemma was not unrecognized by the Kikuyu leadership, for they envisaged the creation of other tribal oaths which would serve to mobilize and commit non-Kikuyu people to their style of militant nationalism. Lack of sufficient time and the Administration's success in compartmentalizing and controlling African political activity were two important factors that prevented this from occurring in any extensive manner. Thus, the pattern of nationalism as it unfolded stemmed from a rationally conceived strategy in search of political power within a context of structural conditions which severely inhibited the growth of a colony-wide national organizational movement. (1966, 354)[7]

Nationalism and Development: The Common Foundation of Divergent Explanations

How could such divergent, indeed contradictory, characterizations of Mau Mau develop as successive influential explanations of the phenomenon, with the "militant nationalism" model largely supplanting the "atavistic tribalism" model among Africanists by the end of the 1960s? The matter becomes even more compelling when one examines the explanations more closely and finds that they are in fact based on essentially identical premises about modernity, development, and nationalism. This paradox reveals some of the crucial difficulties involved not only in understanding Mau Mau, but in understanding the phenomenon called African nationalism. ...

It has been clear for many years that the concept of "traditional society," and its particular expression in Africa, "tribal society," represent idealized constructs which very imperfectly reflect what is now understood about the character of pre-colonial African societies. In particular, the dominant image of traditional society as highly integrated, stable, relatively unchanging, and largely free of disruptive internal conflict has been challenged by increasing evidence of the fluidity of political boundaries and ethnic identities and the significant levels of internal conflict revealed in contemporary historical research. The concept of traditional society was not in any case based on substantial and systematically collected empirical evidence. The pre-colonial history of African societies had barely begun to be written before the late 1960s; and the knowledge available in the late 1940s and early 1950s – largely from the haphazard and unsystematic efforts of colonial administrators and missionaries, and, for a very few African peoples, more methodical ethnographic studies by a handful of professional anthropologists – referred mostly to contemporary conditions in societies already subject to colonial rule for a generation or more. "Traditional society" represented instead the coming together of a set of seemingly incongruous assumptions and interests from a number of sources.

First, colonial administrators expressed an ideology of paternalistic authoritarianism grounded in a concept of society as an organic community, each of whose constituent parts had a specific role to play in the larger whole. Harmony and order were the basic characteristics of the organic community. While African tribal society was ignorant, impoverished, and superstition-ridden, it was also an organic community. Administrators came to see the conservation of the integrity of its institutions as instrumental for the maintenance of effective control (Berman 1990, 104–15).

While administrative ideology and its construction of tradition was imbued with a substantial element of conservative romantic irrationalism and of pastoral nostalgia for the rural community of some ill-defined golden past, it nevertheless dovetailed neatly with the far more rationalist model of traditional society of British social anthropology. The latter discipline was dominated from the 1930s until

the end of colonial rule by the functionalist paradigms of Bronislaw Malinowski and A.R. Radcliffe-
Brown, which emphasized the analysis of traditional
societies as functionally integrated homeostatic systems in which any feature of the society was to be
explained by the contribution it made to the maintenance of the whole. Despite mutual professional
jealousy and hostility, anthropological ideas became
increasingly familiar to colonial officials as anthropology was incorporated into Colonial Office training programmes, and after 1945 a growing number
of social anthropologists made their way to Kenya
and other colonies to conduct field research under
the auspices of the Colonial Social Science Research
Council. Furthermore, much anthropological work
contained significant elements of an "ethnographic
pastoral" (see Rosaldo 1986; Clifford 1986), comple-
menting that of colonial officials, which idealized the
harmony and order of functionally integrated traditional societies (Kuper 1983, chapters 3 and 4).

Finally, the vision of traditional society of
anthropologists and colonial officials was also significantly influenced by the interests and perspectives of African chiefs and elders, recognized in
British Africa as "native authorities," who were
the primary source of information about indigenous institutions and culture and sought to bolster
their legitimacy by accounts that stressed their
authoritative role in the maintenance of the order
and harmony of pre-colonial society. In Kenya,
and for the Kikuyu, all three of these elements
came together in the work of Leakey, himself an
initiated Kikuyu elder, who shared the images of
traditional society of both colonial officials and
anthropologists. ...

This construction of traditional society was also
essentially the same, if expressed in a different
idiom, as that developed by American social scientists from Parsonian structural-functionalism and
depicted in the now familiar dichotomies of the
"pattern variables": particularism *versus* universalism, ascription *versus* achievement, affectivity
versus neutrality, and diffuseness *versus* specificity
(Leys 1982, 333–4). "Modern" societies were simply constructed as the polar opposite of traditional
society on these characteristics and on numerous
empirical "indicators." The distance between traditional and modern society was traversed by a
universal and unilinear process of development,

"from tradition to modernity." All existing societies could be ranged according to their position
along this metaphorical road of social progress.

Both colonial officials and social scientists shared
to a striking degree a conception of the normal
course and sequence of this process of modernization. The political, economic, and cultural demands
of colonialism stimulated social change by driving
people out of the old "tribal" ways of doing things
and pulling them into wider social arenas. As the
networks of African societies increased in scale, the
dependence on the small tribal community would
decline, local loyalties and ethnic identities would
diminish, and wider ones would develop. Under
the impact of a monetary economy spread by wage
labour and cash crop production, traditional social
relations decline and are replaced by more instrumentally efficient modern forms.[8] The ascriptive
particularism of small-scale societies would be
increasingly replaced by the achievement-oriented
universalism of modern secular society. Not even
the most conservative district commissioner, who
rued the demise of the communal solidarities of
organic traditional societies, denied that the process led to a society based less on emotion and superstition and more on rationality and science. ...

Paternalistic authoritarianism shaped the process of political progress towards the nation-state
into a gradual tutelary procedure under the control of the colonial administration whereby local
elites through experience in local government and
administration would learn to rule and gradually
be given access to more inclusive national institutions. The implicit model was of a class stratified
national society led by an indigenous ruling elite
sharing the outlook of their colonial rulers. As
Michael Lee put it,

> Good government meant that the official classes
> accepted full responsibility for development
> schemes, neither more nor less. It was expected
> that local politicians and local civil servants would
> eventually arise to take over full responsibility,
> and therefore reconstitute the official classes.
> This process was often described as creating "a
> political class," which meant envisaging the crea-
> tion of a native elite capable of running the
> machinery required to join the society of states in
> the international order. (1967, 13–14)[9]

A former Secretary of State for the Colonies put it more bluntly and colourfully in an interview when he observed that "you can't have the institutions without a political class and you can't have a political class without the institutions" (Berman 1990, 106). This logic applied with particular force in a colony such as Kenya, with its substantial European and Asian immigrant populations. Political development for Africans was conceivable in the first instance only as ultimately part of a multiracial dominant class in which Europeans would continue to play a preponderant role for an indefinite period (Berman 1990, 301–7). ...

While nationalist organizations and leaders could be assimilated to the rationalist social engineering of nation-building, nationalist passions could not. Colonial officials and political scientists alike shared an aversion to the fervent emotions, deep personal identification, and self-sacrificial commitment also identified with nationalism. In the aftermath of World War II, these sentiments seemed not only irrational but pernicious and destructive. According to Walker Conner, scholars presumed that the war had convinced the peoples of Western Europe that nationalism was dangerous and outmoded, and the implementation of Marxism–Leninism in Eastern Europe had made it superfluous in modern socialist societies, while in studying the Third World "ethnic heterogeneity tended to be ignored or to be cavalierly dismissed as an ephemeral phenomenon," and they "offered few if any suggestions as to how a single national consciousness was to be forged among disparate ethnic elements" (1987, 196–7). Political aversion was reinforced by intellectual disdain in the face of the theoretical incoherence and historical mystification characteristic of nationalist writing and the almost total lack of nationalist thinkers who could be recognized as great by anyone outside of the particular nation they addressed. Ernest Gellner notes: "their precise doctrines are hardly worth analyzing ... nationalist ideology suffers from pervasive false consciousness" (1983, 124); and Benedict Anderson points to a central paradox when he notes the contrast between the "political power of nationalisms vs their philosophical poverty" (Anderson 1983, 14). But while nationalist ideology holds no candle to liberalism or Marxism as intellectual doctrine, it has elicited far more intense and widespread commitment. The cenotaphs and tombs of unknown soldiers, one of the most powerful and common of nationalist symbols, are not matched, as Anderson wittily reminds us, by "a Tomb of the Unknown Marxist or a cenotaph for fallen Liberals" (Anderson 1983, 17–18).

Thus, the theory and the project of national development envisioned by either British colonial officials or American social scientists had little to say about or room for nationalism as doctrine and sentiment rooted in common history, culture, and language. Indeed, in the context of Africa, it seemed improbable that any one of the numerous "tribes" contained in each colony could provide the basis for a national consciousness in the new nation-state they were creating. The growth of such ethno-cultural identities appeared to be disintegrative and to recall traditional tribalism in a way that threatened both modernization and nation-building. Moreover, in Kenya, the presence of Asians and Europeans as distinctive cultural communities demanding protection of their communal rights made it inconceivable that any African cultural forms or identities could be part of the process of political development. The participation of Africans in a multi-racial dominant class had to be on the basis of their being essentially European in education, culture, and lifestyle. Officials assumed that assimilation to a dominant European culture was the natural goal for Africans and the pre-condition for the emergence of a common Kenyan nationality. As Rosberg and Nottingham note: "The Leviathan of the colonial state represented the enlightened self-interests of the African in which the new educated man could remove himself completely from the darkness of his barbaric origins into the sun of the white man's culture" (1966, 322). Multi-racialism could not mean multi-culturalism.

The difficulty of dealing with the passions of nationalist ideology and identity within the rationalist structural and materialist model of national development provided the basis for interpreting Mau Mau as either atavistic tribalism or radical nationalism. As I suggested earlier, the difference between these interpretations was vividly expressed in the readings given to the emotive ideological and cultural content of Mau Mau as contained largely in the oaths given to its recruits.

During the Emergency, texts of oaths were the only evidence about Mau Mau presented to sustain the official version of its character. Colonial officials, white settlers and the British and international press were obsessed with the deviant weirdness and bestiality of the oaths as proving that Mau Mau was atavistic, savage, and evil.[10] Conversely, Njama and Barnett, Rosberg and Nottingham, and the various Mau Mau memoirists were equally intent on proving that it was a modern movement for national liberation and did so by stressing the politically instrumental character of the mass oaths and setting them within the context of a long history of African anti-colonial struggle and of accumulating grievances against the inequities of the colonial order. While this does show how divergent explanations were constructed within the common premises about tradition, modernity and national development, it does not explain why they were produced. To answer the latter question one must examine them within the particular historical contexts in which they appeared.

During the Emergency, particularly in its early phases, the British authorities in Nairobi and London had a desperate need for an explanation of Mau Mau which would accomplish several objectives, effectively achieved by characterizing it, as Cohen put it, as "a reversion to tribalism in a perverted and brutal form" (1959, 55). First, by convincing the cadres of the colonial state that Mau Mau in all its mystical and murderous obscenity was wholly evil, it enabled them to fight a nasty guerrilla war in good conscience. A strong predisposition to this view already existed in the racist stereotypes of African brutishness, irrationality, and bloodthirsty violence which, in their most extreme form, kept the settler population of Kenya on a constant edge of hysterical fear of the Africans they so callously exploited, and, in more moderate form, left colonial officials uneasy about unpredictable and dangerous reactions from their African wards (Berman and Lonsdale 1991b, 6–14; Kennedy 1987, chapters 8 and 9; Maughan–Brown 1985, 81–93). Second, by stigmatizing Mau Mau as the enemy of modernizing development and nationalism, the authorities were able both to insist that it had nothing to do with African grievances and, with no sense of contradiction, to continue

the project of national development through a massive programme of socio-economic reforms intended to increase substantially the incomes of both African peasants and urban workers, and also to expand rapidly education and social services in the urban locations and rural reserves. This programme was combined with a series of constitutional and political reforms which rapidly expanded African access to the central institutions of the colonial state, including the civil service.[11] Third, this characterization of Mau Mau also blunted the edge of left-wing critics of colonialism in Britain who tried to depict it as an anti-colonial liberation struggle.[12] Fourth, characterizing Mau Mau as atavistic and colonialism as progressive also helped to moderate the potential reaction by both the United States and the Soviet Union to the use of force in the colony. In the former, it blunted deep-seated American anti-colonialism and helped sustain support for the British project of national development and gradual decolonization. As far as the Soviet Union was concerned, despite the fevered claims of extreme right-wing anti-communists in Britain and among the Kenya settlers, who saw a Russian agent behind every thorn tree, the colonial authorities well knew that there was no Soviet support or encouragement for Mau Mau, but in the Cold War deep freeze of the critical 1952–6 period, they sought to deny them any possible practical or propaganda advantage by stressing the primitive and retrogressive character of the movement.[13]

By the early 1960s the political context had changed significantly. Mau Mau had been defeated, but Kenya was rapidly moving towards independence under an African majority government. While Kenyatta was lionized as still the only real national leader, new nationalist organizations in Kenya contained an uneasy blend of old leaders, mostly Kikuyu, many of whom had spent the Emergency in detention, and a new generation of largely non-Kikuyu politicians. Externally, the crucial issue was in the development of relations between the new national government and the United States and the international agencies it dominated, which collectively controlled most of the sources of aid and investment that would sustain the project of national development. Meanwhile, research on Africa, especially in the United States, had been rapidly expanded and professionalized into "African studies" dominated largely by political scientists. While this research was instrumental in persuading policy-makers in Britain that "territorial nationalism was a force for good, or at least a force to be reckoned with" (Lee 1967, 285),[14] Kenyan nationalism and many of its most important African political figures were tainted by the image of Mau Mau constructed during the Emergency. In the changed circumstances of this period, the former detainees and forest fighters sought to claim political legitimacy by insisting on a Mau Mau connection with nationalism and the independence struggle. ...

The Relationship between Mau Mau and Nationalism

The question remains as to whether there is a more effective way of understanding the passions of nationalism that will help analyze the character of Mau Mau and its relationship with nationalism in Kenya. The necessary conceptual tools can be found, I believe, in Benedict Anderson's *Imagined Communities* (1983), one of the most important theoretical essays on nationalism in recent years. In both those attributes which conform to and those which diverge from Anderson's construction of nationalism, one can understand the distinctive character of Mau Mau and its ambiguous relationship to the more typical forms of what he calls "anti-colonial nationalism."

Anderson stresses the importance of historical sequence and precedent for understanding the development of the successive forms of nationalism and the nation-state, which is its institutional container. Rather than originating in the primordial past, both are seen as the product of little more than two hundred years of development. He identifies the origins of nationalism and the modern state in the "creole nationalisms" of the Americas, North and South, and their movements for independence from 1775 to 1830. These revolutionary new nations provided a model that was widely discussed in Europe and available for emulation:

> Out of the American welter came these imagined realities: nation-states, republican institutions, common citizenships, popular sovereignty, national flags and anthems, etc., and the liquida-

tion of their conceptual opposites: dynastic empires, monarchical institutions, absolutisms, subjecthoods, inherited nobilities, serfdoms, ghettos, and so forth. ... In effect, by the second decade of the nineteenth century, if not earlier, a "model" of the independent national state was available for pirating. (Anderson 1983, 78)

This model was employed by the "populist nationalisms" of Europe, which transformed diverse and fragmented ethnic groups into "nations" based on the print-languages and written records of their history and culture, and established the precedent that for each nation an independent and sovereign state was the essential condition of its legitimate existence and survival (Anderson 1983, 66–73, 78–9). In central and eastern Europe, this populist nationalism challenged the older polyglot and multi-ethnic dynastic empires of Czarist Russia, Hapsburg Austria, and Ottoman Turkey, and ignited the struggles for national self-determination which marked the 1850–1920 period. These set off the defensive and reactionary "official nationalisms," such as Romanov Russification, which attempted a "willed merger of nation and dynastic empire" through conscious policies "adapted from the model of the largely spontaneous popular nationalisms which preceded them" (Anderson 1983, 83, 102).

The most recent variant of nationalism, according to Anderson, is the anti-colonial nationalisms of the twentieth century, for which all of the previous forms have provided accessible models of nationalism, nation-ness and the state in an international environment in which the sovereign nation-state is the dominant, indeed, unchallenged norm. This nationalism is grounded in the experience of literate and bilingual indigenous intelligentsias fluent in the language of the imperial power, schooled in its "national" history, and staffing the colonial administrative cadres up to but not including its highest levels. These new nations have been essentially isomorphic with previous imperial administrative units (Anderson 1983, 104–9, 127–8; Kitching 1985, 111–13). This perspective allows us to understand how the senior imperial administrators from the metropole were able to conceive the project of modernization and nation-building to transform colonies into nation–states, even in advance of the demands of indigenous nationalist movements.

To deal with the critical problem of the passions of nationalism, Anderson stresses the importance of understanding the nation as an imagined community:

> It is imagined because the members of even the smallest nation will never know most of their fellow-members, meet them, or even hear of them, yet in the minds of each lives the image of their communion. … it is imagined as a community, because, regardless of the actual inequality and exploitation that may prevail in each, the nation is always conceived as a deep, horizontal comradeship. Ultimately it is this fraternity that makes it possible, over the past two centuries, for so many millions of people, not so much to kill, as to willingly die for such limited imaginings. (Anderson 1983, 15–16)

Unlike the rationalism of liberalism and Marxism, nationalism is much concerned with ultimate meanings, death and immorality. Rather than a political ideology, it has more in common with kinship and religion. It replaces the religious vision of immortality with a secular one based on the nation.

> If nation–states are widely conceded to be "new" and "historical," the nations to which they give political expression always loom out of an immemorial past, and, still more important, glide into a limitless future. It is the magic of nationalism to turn chance into destiny. (Anderson 1983, 19)

Language plays the central role in the creation of the imagined community in so far as it is printed and related to the spread of mass literacy. "Print language is what invents nationalism, not a particular language per se" (Anderson 1983, 122). In the European experience a diversity of dialects was reduced to a much smaller number of standardized print vernaculars, while in the creole nations of the Americas and the colonial empires of the twentieth century, the print language was primarily that of the imperial metropole. In all of these instances, the growing number of readers formed the embryo of the nationally imagined community, with the production and consumption of novels and newspapers being particularly important in making possible the imagining of the nation (Anderson 1983, 30–9, 47–9, 61–3).

The role of print language in the development of nationalism is closely linked to the development of what Anderson calls "print capitalism." Printing and book production was one of the key industries of early capitalism. The principal consumers of literature were the growing middle classes, with the bourgeoisie being the first class to achieve solidarity on a largely imagined basis rooted in universal literacy. Finally, print language is also crucially connected to the development of the modern state. The schools and universities run by the state not only spread universal literacy, but also create the studies of history, literature, and folklore through which the nation takes on concrete and permanent existence, and can systematically reproduce itself from generation to generation. The use of the language as a language of administration shapes the consciousness of the imagined national community within the state cadres (Anderson 1983, 66–9, 74, 106–9, 127). The linkage of print language and the state transforms ethnicity into nationalism and makes the possession of a sovereign state the universally demanded norm for every imagined community.

To employ Anderson's approach to nationalism in analyzing Mau Mau, it is first necessary to note the shift in the understanding of the latter that occurred during the 1970s. In the context of studies of the political economy of colonial Kenya by Marxist and neo-Marxist historians and social scientists, which focused on the incorporation of Africans into capitalist production and exchange, and the consequent processes of class formation, the view of Mau Mau shifted again; and it came to be seen as a peasant war emerging out of the growing class struggles among the Kikuyu. While the British often called the Emergency a civil war between the mass of Kikuyu who had taken the Mau Mau oath of unity, on the one hand, and a small band of "Loyalists," on the other, and Rosberg and Nottingham had analyzed at some length the major internal political conflicts among the Kikuyu, more recent research has revealed with far greater subtlety and detail the complexity of internal differentiation and class formation among the Kikuyu not only during colonialism but also before the beginning of colonial rule.[15] In contrast to the

constructed image of a stable and harmonious tradition, the Kikuyu in the nineteenth century were
actively expanding and colonizing new territory
and already internally divided between wealthy
land-owning families and landless families attached
to them in a variety of forms of dependence. The
highest status and civic virtue

> ... lay in the labour of agrarian civilization
> directed by household heads. Honour lay in
> wealth, the proud fruit of burning back the forest
> and taming the wild, clearing a cultivated space in
> which industrious dependents might establish
> themselves in self-respecting independence; the
> possibility of working one's own salvation was the
> subject of more Kikuyu proverbs than any other.
> (Lonsdale 1990, 417)

The impact of colonial capitalism and the colonial
state hit the Kikuyu with greater force and effect
than any other of Kenya's peoples, setting off new
processes of differentiation and class formation.
Anderson stresses that in the development of
colonial nationalism "to an unprecedented extent
the key early spokesman ... were lonely, bilingual
intelligentsias unattached to sturdy local bour-
geoisies," whose pilgrimage among administrative
posts ending in the colonial capital was critical to
their imagining of a nation (1983, 127–8). This
was not true, however, for the Kikuyu or for Kenya
as a whole through most of the colonial period.
The intelligentsia and administrative cadres
among the Kikuyu were intimately connected
with the development of a petty bourgeoisie. In
the particular circumstances of Kenya as a colony
of white settlement, the Kikuyu servants of the
colonial state consisted of local chiefs and headmen, who never served outside of their original
areas, and literate clerks and artisans, who encountered their counterparts from other peoples in
Kenya only when they worked in the urban crucible of Nairobi and a few of the other major towns.
The pilgrimage for both the Kikuyu new wealthy
and new poor was a more restricted circuit between
the reserves established by the colonial state, the
white settler estates and towns of the Rift Valley,
and the capital. From the 1920s, however, the
developing elite of accumulators was internally
split by a cleavage between the collaborationist

chiefs and their families and supporters and a
younger and more populist element organized in
the Kikuyu Central Association and willing to
confront colonial authority over the issue of the
"stolen" lands alienated to white settlers and the
missionary attack on the Kikuyu custom of female
circumcision. At the other pole of the class structure, growing numbers of impoverished Kikuyu
were leaving the home territories, now increasingly crowded within their fixed boundaries, to
seek land and work as squatters or wage labourers
on settler estates or as largely unskilled workers in
the towns.

The increasing disparities of wealth and property and developing conflicts within and between
the developing social classes in Kikuyu society were
expressed in a vigorous internal debate, largely
invisible to the British in Kenya and only now being
reconstructed, over the meaning of Kikuyu-ness,
the nature of the community, the value of tradition,
the involvement in new forms of production and
exchange, and the degree of acceptance of and
assimilation to European culture.[16] Thus, the chiefs
and their supporters opposed the more militant
Kikuyu Central Association through the pointedly
named "Kikuyu Loyal Patriots." Meanwhile, in the
aftermath of the breach with the mission societies
over the custom of female circumcision, two independent school associations were formed calling
themselves the Kikuyu Independent Schools
Association and the Kikuyu Karing'a (pure or
authentic) Schools.

From the beginning, print-language and literacy
in both English and Kikuyu played a crucial role in
defining the terms and content of the debate. The
developing petty bourgeoisie was commonly
referred to as the athomi (literally, "the readers").
In 1928 the KCA began publishing a Kikuyu
language journal called Muigwithania ("The
Reconciler"), with Kenyatta as its first editor. An
article in an early issue on the word "association"
told the readers not to say "that you do not belong
to that Association. You are members of the
Association since you are all Kikuyu Karing'a (real
Kikuyu)" (Rosberg and Nottingham 1966, 100). In
1938 Kenyatta published in English his ethnography of the Kikuyu, written during his studies at
the London School of Economics with Bronislaw
Malinowski, which provided a vigorous defence of

Kikuyu custom against European criticism and provided in permanent printed form his version of a pre-colonial pastoral. In this key text of an emerging Kikuyu imagined community, as well as in other writings of the period, there is a strong element of "redemptive criticism," a "present employment of the past in the hopes of reshaping the future" (Kenyatta 1938; Clark 1989, 396).[17]

By the late 1940s the Kikuyu were a deeply divided people, increasingly in conflict among themselves as well as with the colonial political and economic order. In three centres of growing unrest, a growing mass of the dispossessed and impoverished confronted the leadership of the chiefs and the athomi. In the Rift Valley, an increasing number of squatters were expelled from settler estates for refusing to accept ever-tighter restrictions on their herds and use of settler land. In the overcrowded reserves, small peasants desperately clung to fragmented and eroded holdings no longer capable of supporting a family, while wealthy landowners sought to expel tenants and dependents to regain land for more profitable uses. In Nairobi, a largely Kikuyu labour force struggled with growing impoverishment, inflation, and unemployment. The struggle over authentic Kikuyu-ness, over the character of the imagined community, continued unabated. At this point, however, the conceptions of propertied civic virtue

> ... began to mock the majority rather than to inspire ... those who had the most cause to fight colonial rule had the least chance to merit responsibility. Those whose deeds might deliver power would have no chance to enjoy it. That was the Kikuyu tragedy, a struggle over the moralities of class formation, not mental derangement". (Lonsdale 1990, 417)

The situation was complicated by the emergence of the Kenya African Union, the first attempt at a pan-ethnic "national" political organization. In this organization we do find an expression of a more typical anti-colonial nationalism. KAU had a multi-ethinic, although largely Kikuyu, leadership of bilingual literates of the type upon which Anderson focuses. It was committed to a very different vision of the imagined community, a multi-ethnic Kenya, and to moderate constitutional politics which accepted the premises of the colonial state's version of modernization and nation-building. ...

Kikuyu struggle continued to take place in print. The dominant journal was the weekly *Mumenyereri*, edited by Henry Muoria.

> Considered the paper of Kikuyu patriotism, it published a mixture of real and imagined grievances. As tension grew in 1951 and 1952, it became uncompromising in its nationalism. Invitations to political meetings, called under the guise of "tea parties" (which usually included oathing ceremonies) at the Kikuyu Club in Nairobi's Pumwani Location, became a regular feature of the paper. (Rosberg and Nottingham 1966, 212)

There was also a considerable vernacular pamphlet literature, the most remarkable available example of which is Gakaara wa Wanjau's *Mageria no mo Mahota (The Spirit of Manhood and Perseverance for Africans)*, published in April 1952, which appeals for unity across the cleavages of "the regime of division that the white man has established over us and the bitter and destructive conflicts between ourselves this regime creates," lists all of the classes and segments of the Kikuyu and their just grievances, proclaims universal acceptance of the goals of modernization and development, enjoins the rich to "get actively involved in the people's movement," and includes this extraordinary evocation of the imagined community and the passions of nationalism:

> ... it is vital that every African plays his own role in the struggle for African freedom. To fight for freedom does not only mean making political speeches and writing political tracts. More than that, to struggle for freedom is to be imbued with a patriotic love for your country and its people, so that you become part and parcel of its suffering and its triumphs, so that, in your spiritual unity with your people, you weep with them when they weep, and you share with them their moments of joy. It is a deep and all consuming involvement with your people. It motivates you to seek to know what is happening all the time to your people; it motivates you to always seek to further the cause of freedom and independence. (Wanjau 1988, 227–43)

Wanjau speaks here of Africans and African freedom, but the language and cultural symbolism he employs are Kikuyu, and this suggests the contradictory notions of the imagined community of the nation existing during this period. For the colonial authorities, however, it was sufficiently clear to merit Wanjau's arrest at the beginning of the Emergency and his subsequent detention for ten years.

While Mau Mau was clearly not a tribal atavism seeking a return to the past, the answer to the question of "was it nationalism?" must be yes and no. What the British called Mau Mau, and by constant repetition imposed on the consciousness of both Kenya and the outside world, was no single thing, but rather a diverse and exceedingly fragmented collection of individuals, organizations and ideas, out of which no dominant concept of a Kikuyu imagined national community had emerged. At the same time, if Mau Mau was not a nativistic revival or atavistic revitalization movement, it did emerge out of a bitterly contested process of reinterpreting and reconstructing tradition that embraced the colonial authorities as well as Kikuyu factions, Leakey as well as Kenyatta; and in which cultural beliefs and symbols were profoundly important. Mau Mau was part of a struggle over the dimensions and meaning of Kikuyu ethnicity and its problematic relationship with both the internal cleavages of class and the wider solidarities of a Kenyan nation.[18]

The colonial authorities' version of Mau Mau as a conspiratorial secret cult attached to it an illusory unity of organization and ideology. The official version also played loosely with the historical sequence of events, focusing on the limited degree of organization and unity achieved by the forest fighters under Dedan Kimathi and General China, adding the connections to the Nairobi "Central Committee," combining both with the "evidence" of oaths often extracted from detainees under torture, and then projecting all of this backward to characterize "Mau Mau" before the Emergency. What the accumulated evidence records, instead, are largely failed efforts to define a Kikuyu nationality linked to a militant populist politics of the poor. How this was to relate to the other imagined communities in Kenya in an independent nation state was not clearly thought through. What is interesting is that the ideological cleavages of

contrasting visions of the Kikuyu and Kenyan nations were reproduced within the structure of the Land and Freedom Army itself in conflicts between the literate leaders like Kimathi and Karari Njama and many of the primarily illiterate rank and file of peasants and dispossessed squatters led by men like Stanley Mathenge. "This boiled down, in essence, to the rejection by the non-literate leaders of the state-building, parliamentarist 'Freedom' component, in favour of the peasant/land component, in the forest fighters' 'nationalism'" (Maughan-Brown 1985, 47). The forest fighters' own name for their movement, *ithaka na wiathi*, is perhaps better translated, according to Lonsdale, as "freedom through land" or "land and moral responsibility," which invokes "the highest civic virtue of Kikuyu elderhood, rather than the more common 'land and freedom' which invites the retrospective connotation of 'land and national independence'" (Lonsdale 1990, 416 note 118), and thus expresses the distinctive cultural content of Kikuyu internal conflicts as much as an anti-colonial liberation struggle.

The paradoxes of Mau Mau are also revealed tellingly in the career and words of Kenyatta. He both outraged and terrified the British officialdom because, in their eyes, he was the obvious charismatic nationalist leader of Kenya's Africans, but used the force of his personality and his elite education to deliberately lead the Kikuyu back to the mystical witchcraft of tribal reaction rather than unite the Africans with whites in the project of national development. They convicted him of organizing Mau Mau in a flagrantly rigged trial which threw him together with men like Kubai and Kaggia who actually had organized the mass oathings. But Kenyatta, and his colleagues in the KCA, spoke for the new generation of athomi who, even in opposing the chiefs and elders, always laid claim to the leadership of the Kikuyu in traditional terms as men of property and virtue. In the internal struggles among the Kikuyu before the Emergency, he stood on the opposite side from the leaders of the Kikuyu dispossessed, the squatters, urban workers and landless peasants; while as the leader of the KAU he struggled to hold together its multi-ethnic coalition. His denunciations of Mau Mau in 1952, when he equated it with poverty, irresponsibility and criminality, led its leaders to consider his assassination.[19]

Ironically, it was the Emergency which secured the victory of the very different nationalism of the multi-ethnic dominant class that came to power with independence, while Kenyatta's conviction and imprisonment for organizing Mau Mau probably saved his position as the national leader. The elite nationalism of this class was definitively formed during the Emergency itself among the Kikuyu loyalists and the educated elites from other ethnic communities, who shared literacy in English and who travelled their national pilgrimage in less than a decade through increasing access to the bureaucracy of the colonial state and to the expanding "national" political institutions at the centre, created by repeated rounds of constitutional reform. Simultaneously, with the detention or confinement in the reserves of the bulk of the Kikuyu labour force in the colony, replacements were found among other ethnic groups, while economic reforms both raised wages and increased peasant access to cash crop markets – all of which provided a substantially widened base of support for "nationalist" goals when African political organizations were again permitted after 1957. The pressure of this multi-ethnic elite forced the pace of British withdrawal, undermined the political position of white settlers and ultimately made independence under a "multi-racial" regime impossible (Berman 1990, chapter 9). In them, the British found, rather unexpectedly, the "political class" to whom they could safely turn over power, and belatedly discovered in Kenyatta the moderate modernizing national leader.

It is hardly surprising that the attitude of the government of independent Kenya has been ambivalent about the recognition of the contributions of Mau Mau "freedom fighters," or that the divergent post-independence interpretations of Mau Mau, as the central element in the epic of national liberation or as an isolated tribal uprising, reflect a continuing cleavage between radical populist elements among the Kikuyu and the "national" dominant class (Maughan-Brown, 1985, 57–8, 258–61).[20] Kenyatta himself, after his release from prison and political rehabilitation in the early 1960s and later as President of Kenya, continued to denounce Mau Mau and equate it with criminality and disease, repeating the very type of metaphor which the British had used to describe it. Meanwhile, his government proclaimed: "we all fought for Uhuru" and refused any special recognition of the achievements of Mau Mau or the claims of the ex-forest fighters and detainees, although it permitted some local memorials in Kikuyuland to them and to Kimathi.[21] In 1988 the monument to the "freedom fighters," which contains no explicit reference to *ithaka na wiathi* sat forlorn and graffiti-defaced at an intersection in Nyeri town, a material expression of the continuing paradoxes of Mau Mau.

Notes

1 This article is derived from a joint research project entitled "Explaining Mau Mau: A Study in the Politics of Knowledge," in which John Lonsdale and I have been engaged since 1987. While many of the ideas expressed in this article are the joint product of our work, I remain responsible for the particular interpretation offered here.

2 It is the official version developed by the authorities of the colonial state that is of primary interest in the present context. For an analysis of other variants of the explanation of Mau Mau among both Europeans and Africans during the Emergency, see Lonsdale (1990).

3 The first papers on Mau Mau received by the Provincial Commissioner of Central Province (the main Kikuyu area) were filed with previous correspondence on religious sects found in the colony. See Kenya National Archives (hereafter, KNA) PC/CP8/7/4 (covering the period 1934–53); and Public Record Office, London (hereafter, PRO)/PC822/447, Commissioner of Police, "Secret Situation Report for 11 February, 1953."

4 PRO/CO822/447, Commissioner of Police, "Secret Intelligence Report for 27 November, 1952."

5 Leakey's role as both an interpreter and actor is a major part of the story of Mau Mau that has yet to be fully appreciated. We have attempted to rectify this omission in Berman and Lonsdale (1991a).

6 So characterized, Mau Mau became a useful example for use in the comparative analysis of cults and religious movements. See, for example, Fernandez (1964) and La Barre (1971).

7   The relationship between African grievances and African politics is the dominant theme of chapters II to VI, especially pages 220–33; the "Mau Mau" oath is analyzed on pages 241–62; while the European "myth of Mau Mau" is treated on pages 320–34.

8   One of the earliest expressions of these ideas was found in the first chapters of Wilson and Wilson (1945).

9   The principal Colonial Office statement of political development policy in the immediate post-war period came in the "Despatch from the Secretary of State to the Governors of the African Territories," 25 February 1947 (Kenya Government Library, Nairobi).

10 John Lonsdale has noted the manner in which Mau Mau's "rituals of recruitment" were exploited at the time: "British war propaganda had no difficulty in portraying these as utterly repugnant, debased, and by intention, debasing. ... The paraphernalia of Mau Mau recruiting officers certainly made good copy which the press did not hesitate to exploit, if with the coy reserve which titillates as much as it repels. ... For it was reported that the oaths became ever more deviant and bestial as the war dragged on and the insurgents became more desperate or fanatic. Many accounts left the details unsaid, allowing the readers' imaginations free to wander in fascinated self-disgust. ... A visiting parliamentary delegation thought the recruitment rituals too dreadful to lay before the British electorate. The relevant appendix to the report was never published. It was deposited in the library of the House of Commons instead, where minds were apparently thought to be already sufficiently depraved" (1989, 2).

11 This programme was called "the second prong" against Mau Mau, the first being the military campaign. The various reports, memoranda, and notes relating to it are a major source of information on official thinking during the Emergency and are found in KNA/GH4/795. For fuller analysis of the reform programme in the context of the politics of the Emergency see Berman (1990, 347–71).

12 The activities of the British left and various anti-colonial associations in Britain drew the particular ire of the colonial authorities, who felt that they did not understand what Mau Mau was "really" like and that their ill-informed efforts threatened to undermine the metropolitan political and economic support necessary to crush it. The first draft of the official history of Mau Mau, circulated among senior officials in Nairobi, contained a particularly virulent attack on the left-wing "friends" of Mau Mau, which was excised from the published version (KNA/GO3/2/72).

13 The sensitivity of the Colonial Office to reactions to Mau Mau in other countries, especially the US, is indicated in the papers contained in PRO/CO822/448 *External Repercussions on the Mau Mau Situation in Kenya*; while the concern with Soviet reactions and evaluation of possible Communist involvement is discussed in PRO/CO822/461 *Communist Aspects of the Mau Mau Situation in Kenya*.

14 Lee also shows that by 1956, while in all other social sciences the majority of researchers working in British Africa were either British or citizens of the "white" Commonwealth, in political science thirteen of seventeen were Americans.

15 See, in particular, the careful synthesis and analysis of the evidence in Kitching (1980).

16 These themes are explored more fully in Lonsdale, "Wealth, Poverty and Civic Virtue in Kikuyu Political Thought" in Berman and Lonsdale (1992).

17 Clark's remarks concern Leakey's ethnography, but they apply equally well to Kenyatta's. The rivalry between Kenyatta and Leakey for the intellectual leadership of the Kikuyu and its expression in the ethnographic politics of establishing the "right" version of Kikuyu society and culture is analyzed in "Louis Leakey's Mau Mau" (Berman and Lonsdale 1991a).

18 Mau Mau can thus be usefully examined in the comparative context of the processes of constructing ethnicity and tradition discussed in Hobsbawn and Ranger (1983) (See Ranger, Chapter 31, this volume) and Vail (1989).

19 As revealed by Fred Kubai in an interview with Alan Segal broadcast in part in Granada Television's program on Kenya in its series "The End of Empire" in July 1985.

20 Ngugi wa Thiong'o has recently analyzed the split in Kenyan intellectual life between the English-speaking, neo-colonial petty-bourgeoisie which, he claims, hi-jacked independence and the "true" nationalism represented by Mau Mau. He explicitly denounces the dominant class both for its exploitation of ethnic chauvinism and its reliance on the old imperial language while praising Mau Mau, and the work of Gakaara wa Wanjau in particular, for encouraging the emergence of a genuine indigenous African-language literature, as well as expressing "the mass political movements of an awakened peasantry and working class" (1986, 23–4, 44–5, 102–4).

21 Some of Kenyatta's statements denouncing "hooliganism" and oath-taking can be found in Kenyatta (1968, 147, 154, 167, 183, 189, and 204). See also Buijtenhuijs (1973, 49–53, 61–72) and Lonsdale (1990, 418–20).

References

Anderson, Benedict. 1983. *Imagined Communities: Reflections on the Origin and Spread of Nationalism*. London: Verso.

Barnett, Donald and Karari Njama. 1966. *Mau Mau from Within: Autobiography and Analysis of Kenya's Peasant Revolt*. London: Macgibbon and Kee.

Berman, Bruce. 1990. *Control and Crisis in Colonial Kenya: The Dialectic of Domination*. London: James Currey and Athens, Ohio: Ohio University Press.

Berman, Bruce and John Lonsdale. 1991a. "Louis Leakey's Mau Mau: A Study in the Politics of Knowledge." *History and Anthropology* 5, no.2:143–204.

Berman, Bruce and John Lonsdale. 1991b. "The Shadow of Mau Mau: the Politics of Terror in Kenya." Conference on Colonialism and the Construction of Terror. Trinity College, Cambridge. March.

Berman, Bruce and John Lonsdale. 1992. *Unhappy Valley: Class, Class and State in Colonial Kenya*. London: James Currey.

Buijtenhuijs, Robert. 1973. *Mau Mau Twenty Years After: The Myth and the Survivors*. The Hague: Mouton.

Clark, Carolyn. 1989. "Louis Leakey as Ethnographer: On *The Southern Kikuyu Before 1900*. *Canadian Journal of African Studies* 23, no. 3:380–98.

Clifford, James. 1986. "On Ethnographic Allegory." In Clifford and Marcus, 98–121.

Clifford, James and George E. Marcus, eds. 1986. *Writing Culture: The Poetics and Politics of Ethnography*. Berkeley, CA: University of California Press.

Cohen, Sir Andrew. 1959. *British Policy in Changing Africa*. London: Routledge and Kegan Paul.

Conner, Walter. 1987. "Ethnonationalism." In Myron Weiner and Samuel Huntington, eds., *Understanding Political Development*. Boston: Little Brown.

Edgerton, Robert. 1989. *Mau Mau: An African Crucible*. New York: Free Press.

Fernandez, James. 1964. "African Religious Movements: Types and Dynamics." *Journal of Modern African Studies* 2, no. 4:531–49.

Furedi, Frank. 1989. *The Mau Mau War in Perspective*. London: James Currey.

Gellner, Ernest. 1983. *Nations and Nationalism. New Perspectives on the Past*. Cornell University Press.

Gordon, David. 1986. *Decolonization and the State in Kenya*. Boulder: Westview.

Hobsbawm, Eric and Terence Ranger. 1983. *The Invention of Tradition*. Cambridge: Cambridge University Press.

Itote, Waruhiu. 1967 *"Mau Mau" General*. Nairobi: East African Publishing House.

Kanogo, Tabitha. 1987. *Squatters and the Roots of Mau Mau*. London: James Currey.

Kariuki, J.M. 1963. *Mau Mau Detainee*. London: Penguin.

Kennedy, Dane. 1987. *Islands of White: Settler Society and Culture in Kenya and Southern Rhodesia 1890–1939*. Durham: Duke University Press.

Kenyatta, Jomo. 1938. *Facing Mount Kenya: The Tribal Life of the Kikuyu*. London: Secker and Warburg.

Kenyatta, Jomo. 1968. *Suffering without Bitterness: The Founding of the Kenya Nation*. Nairobi: East African Publishing House.

Kinyatti, Maina wa. 1987. *Kenya's Freedom Struggle: The Dedan Kimathi Papers*. London: Zed Press.

Kinyatti, Maina wa. 1985. *Thunder From the Mountains: Mau Mau Patriotic Songs*. London: Zed Press.

Kitching, Gavin, 1980. *Class and Economic Change in Kenya*. New Haven: Yale University Press.

Kitching, Gavin. 1985 "Nationalism: The Instrumental Passion." *Capital and Class* 25:98–116.

Kuper, Adam. 1983. *Anthropology and Anthropologists: the Modern British School*. London: Routledge and Kegan Paul.

Kushner, Gilbert. 1965. "An African Revitalization Movement: Mau Mau." *Anthropes* 60, nos. 1–6:763–802.

La Barre, Weston. 1971. "Materials for the Study of Crisis Cults: A Bibliographic Essay." *Current Anthropology* 12, no. 1:3–64.

Leakey, Louis S.B. 1952. *Mau Mau and the Kikuyu*. London: Methuen.

Leakey, Louis S.B. 1954. *Defeating Mau Mau*. London: Methuen.

Lee, Michael. 1967. *Colonial Development and Good Government*. London: Oxford University Press.

Leys, Colin. 1982. "Samuel Huntington and the End of Classical Modernization Theory." In *Introduction to the Sociology of "Developing Societies,"* edited by Hamza Alavi and Teodor Shanin. 332–349. New York and London: Monthly Review Press.

Lonsdale, John. 1989. "The Constructions of Mau Mau." Royal Historical Society, London. December.

Lonsdale, John. 1990. "Mau Maus of the Mind: Making Mau Mau and Remaking Kenya." *Journal of African History* 31, no. 4:393–421.

Maughan-Brown, David. 1985. *Land, Freedom and Fiction*. London: Zed Press.

Odhiambo, E.S. Atieno. 1988. "The Construction of History in Kenya." Canadian Association of African Studies, Kingston Ontario, May.

Presley, Cora Ann. 1988. "The Mau Mau Rebellion, Kikuyu Women, and Social Change." *Canadian Journal of African Studies*, 22:502–27.

Rosaldo, Renato. 1986. "From the Door of His Tent: The Fieldworker and the Inquisitor." In Clifford and Marcus.

Rosberg, Karl and John Nottingham. 1966. *The Myth of Mau Mau: Nationalism in Kenya*. New York: Frederick Praeger.

Rosenstiel, Annette. 1953. "An Anthropological Approach to the Mau Mau Problem." *Political Science Quarterly* 68:419–432.

Thiong'o, Ngugi wa. 1983 *Barrel of a Pen: Resistance to Repression in Neo-Colonial Kenya*. Trenton, New Jersey: Africa World Press.

Thiong'o, Ngugi wa. 1986. *Decolonizing the Mind: The Politics of Language in African Literature*. Nairobi: Heinemann Kenya.

Thiong'o, Ngugi wa and Micere Mugo. 1976. *The Trial of Dedan Kimathi*. London.

Throup, David. 1987. *The Economic and Social Origins of Mau Mau*. London: James Currey.

Vail, Leroy, ed. 1989. *The Creation of Tribalism in Southern Africa*. London: James Currey.

Wanjau, Gakaara wa. 1988. *Mau Mau Author in Detention: An Author's Detention Diary*. Nairobi: Heinemann Kenya.

Wilson, Godfrey and Monica Wilson. 1945. *The Analysis of Social Change, Based on Observations in Central Africa*. Cambridge: Cambridge University Press.

36

The Invisible Face
Masks, Ethnicity, and the State in Côte d'Ivoire

Christopher B. Steiner

This chapter examines the critical role of masks and masked performances in the Côte d'Ivoire[1] government's dual projects of (1) promoting international tourism in light of the country's most severe economic recession, and (2) fostering national unity in the face of growing ethnic factionalism and tension. Although, as I will argue, the ideological frameworks underlying these two goals are in many ways diametrically opposed to one another, I will demonstrate that the use of masks and masked dancing is an attempt on the part of the Ivoirian state to bridge the differences between these two nation-stabilizing strategies and mute their potential contradictions.

Masks and masking in Côte d'Ivoire are found in different forms in a variety of coastal and inland communities. Many of the estimated sixty ethnic groups in the country have their own style of mask carving and their own repertoire of masked dancing and performances. Although some aspects of masking are shrouded under a veil of secrecy and used only in the context of secret society activities, many forms consist largely of public displays intended purely for general entertainment. While these secular forms of masking are often carried out at the local village level, they are sometimes incorporated into public events organized by members of both regional and national government. A meeting of town mayors, a visit to a village by a district (*préfecture*) administrator, or a national tour by a high-ranking minister or diplomat are all events that would call for the performance of a masked festival. Although certain forms of secular masking probably found expression at the village level in pre-colonial times, I would argue that most public displays of masking became associated with political and bureaucratic events during colonial rule. Huge masked festivals, for example, were organized each summer by the French to celebrate Bastille Day; while smaller masked festivals were often held at the ground-breaking reception for the construction of administrative buildings, at official ceremonies for the naming of city streets, or at the unveiling of colonial monuments (see Gorer 1935:322–8).

Together with their function in national politics, masks and masking in post-colonial Côte

From Christopher B. Steiner, "The Invisible Face: Masks, Ethnicity, and the State in Côte d'Ivoire, West Africa," *Museum Anthropology* 16(3), 1992, pp. 53–7. Reproduced by permission of the American Anthropological Association.

d'Ivoire have, in recent years at least, played a critical role in the promotion of international tourism and the marketing of African art (Steiner 1994). In any one of the major marketplaces in Côte d'Ivoire, art traders line their stalls with row upon row of carved wooden masks. The major styles are attributed to the Baule, Guro, Senufo, and Dan ethnic groups. Miniature masks, called "passports," are available to tourists who do not have the room in their luggage to carry home a full-size mask.

Within the last decade, the mask has been appropriated by the Ivoirian state as a symbol of national identity or character.[2] As Duon Sadia, the Ivoirian Minister of Tourism, noted in a 1987 interview: "Because Côte d'Ivoire does not possess pyramids or grand ancient monuments like Egypt or Mexico, and because it does not have an abundance of wildlife like some of the countries in East Africa, Côte d'Ivoire has chosen to promote itself through its only indigenous product, Ivoirian man himself – with his culture and his traditions, of which masks and masking are an integral part" (Bouabré 1987:8).[3] In another interview, the Minister of Tourism further clarified the specific function of masks in the development of the modern Ivoirian polity by noting that, "We now declare that the trademark [of Côte d'Ivoire] will be the mask, for it is representative [of this country], rather pleasing to observe, and enshrouded in an air of mystery. The mask could arouse the curiosity of foreign tourists and lead them to visit our country. We have [therefore] chosen the mask for we believe that it integrates several aspects of our culture and our civilization. The mask encapsulates the traditional arts of Côte d'Ivoire, and represents the strength and history of our nation" (Philmon 1982:13).

The promotion of tourism through the marketing of the image of the mask represents, in point of fact, a radical departure in the rhetoric of the Ivoirian state. Less than a decade before this recent campaign, for example, Félix Houphouët-Boigny, President of the Republic and founder of independent Côte d'Ivoire, declared to a congress of the National Democratic Party: "We are fed up with having Africa relegated, through the futile gaze of the observer, to a land of sunshine, rhythms, and innocuous folklore" (quoted in Boutillier, Fiéloux and Ormiéres 1978:5). For Houphouët-Boigny, in his first years of power after independence, both national integration and international economic success were to be found in the promotion of modern industrial technologies rather than in a return to traditionalism or the re-creation of a "primitivist" aesthetic.

Hence, in light of this philosophy, how can one explain the state's recent shift toward traditional cultural resources and, in particular, its appropriation of the wooden mask as a symbol of national, multi-ethnic pride? I would argue that this return to traditionalism is a direct result of the nation's financial collapse following the failure of its cash-crop export economy – beginning sometime in 1980 (Brooke 1988). That is to say, as long as Côte d'Ivoire enjoyed economic prosperity through its production and export of cacao and coffee, the state used its success in the international economy as a device for rallying nationalist sentiment. It needed nothing else. Following the dramatic collapse of the price of cacao and coffee in the world market, however, politicians scrambled to find not only a new source of foreign income but also a new gathering point for nationalist sentiment. The mask was thought to be capable of achieving both. On the one hand, it fueled the Western imagination through its mystery and exotic appeal. On the other hand, it reconciled growing ethnic divisions by elevating the symbolism of the mask – with its plethora of ethnic styles and interpretations – to a single, national icon.

The first attempt by the government of Côte d'Ivoire to promote tourism and national solidarity through the use of wooden masks was the festival of masks held on April 14–15, 1979 in the town of Man, near the Liberian border in the western part of the country [Plate 36.1]. The festival was organized by Bernard Dadié, the Minister of Cultural Affairs. On the whole, the festival was poorly attended, and it received very little coverage from the Ivoirian press (only three short articles in the semi-official daily newspaper *Fraternité Matin*).

The second masked festival was organized by the Minister of Tourism, Duon Sadia. It too was held in the town of Man from February 11–15, 1983. In the second festival at Man, there was a more overt effort on behalf of the government organizers to use the mask as a symbol of Côte d'Ivoire and as a mechanism for attracting the

Plate 36.1   Masked dancer with musicians performing at the festival of masks in Man, ca. 1979.
Photographer unknown

financial benefits of tourism. The masked festival at Man, Duon Sadia noted at a press conference held at the luxurious Hotel Ivoire in Abidjan, "will be the equivalent of Carnival in Rio, with an added element of the profound soul and mystery of 'non-commercialised' Africa" (Anonymous 1983:10).[4] The 1983 festival of the masks at Man was again reported by the press to be an overall failure. Very few tourists went to the festival, and the mask-bearers, who felt they were being treated without sufficient respect, boycotted their appearance. A delegation, consisting of three ministers and a representative of the national government, had to plead in public with the masked dancers to come out and perform on the stage (Djidji 1983:11).

The Ivoirian state's appropriation of the mask reached its epitome in the summer of 1988, when the Ministries of Tourism and Culture jointly organized a national masked festival. Promoted under the name "Festimask," the festival was funded by the state at an estimated cost of $500,000. Unlike previous state-sponsored masked festivals

which were organized by district administrations with the exclusive participation of local ethnic groups, the Festimask attempted to bring all the ethnic groups of Côte d'Ivoire into a single event which, not surprisingly, was held in the President's home town of Yamoussoukro, in the center of the country. The official reason reported in the national newspaper for holding the festival in Yamoussoukro, rather than Man, was because of its proximity to the economic capital and port city of Abidjan – thereby, the argument went, encouraging more expatriates and more tourists to attend the festival of masks. However, the unstated reason for the site of the event, I would argue, was to link the festival of masks and, more generally, the symbolism of masks and masking to the national government through its association with Houphouët-Boigny's natal village and place of retreat.

When the masked festival was moved to Yamoussoukro in 1988, it became not only a vehicle for promoting international tourism, it was also used as a means of stressing national unity. Since the end of the colonial period, many burgeoning African nations have had to push for national unity in the face of internal ethnic factionalism. Although cultural pluralism may be profitable within the realm of the international art market, it is often perceived as a major obstacle in the domain of centralized state politics. As Wallerstein noted in 1960, "The dysfunctional aspects of ethnicity for national integration are obvious. The first is that ethnic groups are still particularistic in their orientation and diffuse in their obligations. ... The second problem, and one which worries African political leaders more, is separatism, which in various guises is a pervasive tendency in West Africa today" (1960:137–8). Until recently, post-colonial Côte d'Ivoire had a history of successful national integration. In a country made up of approximately sixty different ethnic groups, this record of success is an impressive triumph. One of the reasons which accounts for successful integration of ethnic groups in Côte d'Ivoire is the rapid growth and expansion of the Ivoirian economy – the so-called Ivoirian "miracle" which took place from 1960 to 1980. Since a majority of Ivoirian nationals were reaping the benefits of favorable transnational trade, it was to their (economic) advantage to remain united under a national economic cause (Dozon 1985:53–4). Since the economy has weakened, however, in the past several years, it could be argued that ethnic factionalism has become an increasing concern to the representatives of the centralized Ivoirian state. Viewed in this context, then, the masked festival at Yamoussoukro was yet another way of promoting nationalist sentiment in the face of growing ethnic factionalism. The Festimask respected ethnic heterogeneity – i.e., each masked performance was associated with a different and unique ethnic style – while, at the same time, it brought disparate ethnic groups together into a single, united cause.

The Festimask stresses national unity in at least two ways. First, it aims to bring the ethnic distinctions embedded in styles of art into a single "folkloric" category. There are no longer individual ethnic masks. All masks, said the organizers of the festival, are to be thought of as members of the PDCI (Partie Democratique de Côte d'Ivoire). All masks are to be considered Ivoirian patriots struggling for the good of the modern nation-state

(Gnangnan 1987). Secondly, the festival of masks strives to bring the concerns of the older generation (the so-called "*mentalitées traditionelles*" of the rural population) into step with national concerns, such as the promotion of international tourism and the President's long-standing campaign for West African regional peace. In the context of Festimask, the mask is a tool of the modern nation-state that serves "rational" political goals while being presented to both nationals and foreigners as a kind of "traditionalizing instrument" (Moore and Myerhoff 1977:8). At a press conference held to clarify the role of the mask in the nationalist party, the Ivoirian Minister of Tourism, Duon Sadia, said:

> When we say that the mask must become militant, we mean to signal that the mask must no longer transmit the knowledge of the ancestors in a mechanical way without any explanations. The mask must become a spokesman – communicating in the common language of our culture – for the message of peace. The performance [of Festimask] is not intended to caricature our traditional values, but rather it is aimed to preserve these traditions by adapting them to the exigencies of the modern world. (Bouabré 1987:8)

The Festimask was thus intended to collapse divisions in *both* space (i.e., ethnic geography) and time (i.e., generational differences).

According to Ernest Gellner, there are at least three pre-conditions for the flourishment of state nationalism: (1) that a population be culturally homogenous without internal ethnic sub-groupings, (2) that a population be literate and capable of authoring and propagating its own history, and (3) that a population be anonymous, fluid, mobile, and unmediated in its loyalty to the state (1983:138). International tourism in most of the developing world hinges on the exact opposite criteria from those which underlie the foundation of state nationalism. First, international tourism demands that a population be as culturally and ethnically diverse as possible. In Côte d'Ivoire, for example, the tourist art market is driven by the production of a large variety of supposedly autochthonous and stereotyped ethnic arts (cf. Graburn 1984:413). Second, international tourism seeks to discover a population that is *i*lliterate, and without a sense of historical knowledge or a proper understanding of its geographic place within the world system. And third, international tourism calls for the existence of small-scale populations in which there is no anonymity, in which whole societies recognize each and every one of its members, and in which long-distance communication is not possible among putatively isolated groups. In essence, therefore, the demands of state nationalism and the demands of international tourism are situated at opposite poles in the realm of possibilities concerning the individual's relationship to society.

The organization of Festimask was an attempt by the Ivoirian government to satisfy *simultaneously* both the monolithic requirements of effective state nationalism and the polymorphic demands of successful international tourism. By elevating the mask to a national icon, the state was attempting (1) to subvert ethnic differences, (2) to emphasize an indigenous form of national literacy and ethnohistorical consciousness, and (3) to create a national category of aesthetic identity through the hidden and anonymous face of the mask. At the same time, however, the state was also trying to encourage international tourism by stressing both the visual diversity in ethnic material productions and the exoticism of the masked dance itself.

Although the aims of the Festimask were both complex and diverse, its results were unambiguous.

Both tourists *and* nationals judged the event as a complete failure. Tourists, on the one hand, stayed away from the Festimask because, I was told by one, they anticipated a large, staged, "tourist" event. Nationals, on the other hand, were disgusted with the Festimask because they felt they had been treated without respect – like pawns in a commercial venture. As one of the elders who attended the Festimask put it to a reporter for the national press, "My son, we went to Yamoussoukro, and we were happy for we had been invited to the village of our President. ... But you should know that nobody took care of us; nobody even provided us with food, and that just isn't normal. Not only were we not greeted by the organizers of the festival, as is the custom, but when we [finally did get some food] it was their leftovers that we were sent to eat" (Anonymous 1987).

In conclusion, I would argue, the masked festival failed in the eyes of both Ivoirian nationals and foreign tourists for the same reason. In both instances, the Festimask was viewed as an inauthentic event because it had been, as it were, too "modern" in its tactics and too insensitive to the demands of "custom." The appropriation of the hidden face by the hidden hand resulted in a particular form of the commodification of ethnicity, in which neither the producers nor the consumers were willing to strike a bargain.

Notes

1   In order to respect the decree of 14 October 1985 by President Félix Houphouët-Boigny, the country name "Côte d'Ivoire" will not be translated into English.
2   The process is also reflected in the use of "traditional" symbols on West African bank notes (Francs CFA) used jointly by nations of former Afrique Occidentale Française (cf. Vogel 1991:233).

3   All translations from the French are by the author.
4   The link between an African festival and the Carnival in Rio was first made by the government of Senegal in 1974 when they tried (without success) to launch a series of "ethnic" dances which "would become as famous as the Carnival of Rio or of Nice" (Copans 1978:119).

References

Anonymous
    1983 Festivale de masques à Man. *Fraternité Matin*, 7 February, p.11.
    1987 Communiqué from the Ministry of Information to the Ministry of Tourism. Archives of the Ministry of Tourism, Abidjan.

Bouabré, Paul
    1987 Festimask 1987: Le masque doit servir à la paix. *Fraternité Matin*, 16 July, p.8.
Boutillier, J-L, Michèle Fiéloux, and J-L Ormières
    1978 Le tourisme en Afrique de l'ouest. In *Le tourisme en Afrique de l'ouest*, edited by Jean-Louis Boutillier,

Jean Copans, Michèle Fiéloux, Suzanne Lallemeand, and Jean-Louis Ormières. pp.5–83. Paris: François Maspero.

Brooke, James
1988 Ivory Coast Gambles to Prop up Cacao Prices. *The New York Times*, 21 November, section D, p.10.

Copans, Jean
1978 Idéologies et idéologues du tourisme au Sénégal: Fabrications et contenus d'une image de marque. In *Le tourisme en Afrique de l'ouest*, edited by Jean-Louis Boutillier, Jean Copans, Michèle Fiéloux, Suzanne Lallemand, and Jean-Louis Ormières. pp.108–40. Paris: François Maspero.

Djidji, Ambroise
1983 Réflexion sur le festival des masques. *Fraternité Matin*, 22 February, p.10.

Dozon, Jean-Pierre
1985 Les Bété: Une création coloniale. In *Au coeur de l'ethnie*, edited by Jean-Louis Amselle and Elikia M'Bokolo. pp.49–85. Paris: Editions la Decouverte.

Gellner, Ernest
1983 *Nations and Nationalism*. Ithaca: Cornell University Press.

Gnangan, Desiré
1987 Festivale de masque 1987. *Fraternité Matin*, 4 May, p.10.

Gorer, Geoffrey
1935 *Africa Dances*. New York: Alfred A. Knopf.

Graburn, Nelson H.H.
1984 The Evolution of Tourist Arts. *Annals of Tourism Research* 11:393–419.

Moore, Sally Falk, and Barbara Myerhoff (eds.)
1977 *Secular Ritual*. Assen, The Netherlands: Van Gorcum.

Philmon, Thierry O.
1982 Conference du Ministre Duon Sadia. *Fraternité Matin*, 2 December, pp.13–16.

Steiner, Christopher B.
1994 *African Art in Transit*. Cambridge: Cambridge University Press.

Vogel, Susan (ed.)
1991 *Africa Explores: 20th Century African Art*. New York: The Center for African Art.

Wallerstein, Immanuel
1960 Ethnicity and National Integration in West Africa. *Cahiers d'Etudes Africaines* 3:129–39.

Part XI

Violent Transformations:
Conflict and Displacement

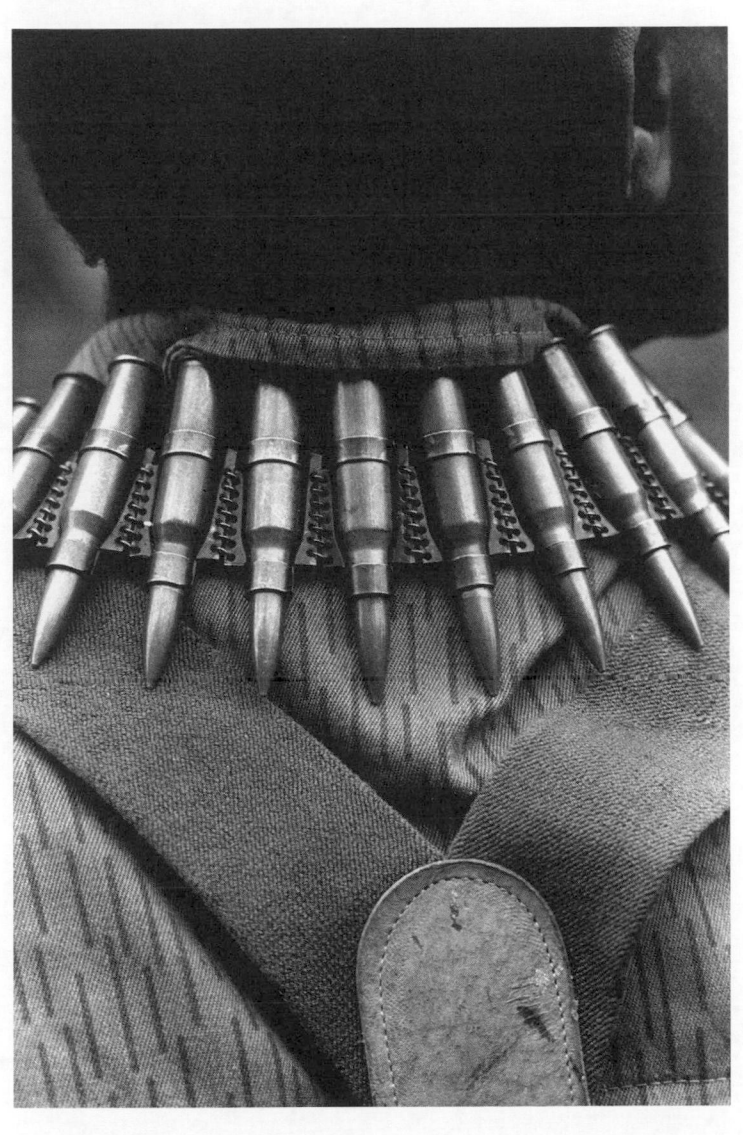

Introduction

War has become a tragic signifier for postcolonial Africa. Shortly after the turn of the millennium over 40 percent of the globe's 45 significant armed conflicts were occurring on the continent of Africa (Gurr et al., 2001). Many recent or ongoing African wars have persisted for two,[1] three,[2] or even four[3] decades, often spanning multiple generations. Thus, far from being an exceptional state of affairs, prolonged or chronically resurgent war has become a normative backdrop for the lives of many millions of Africa's inhabitants throughout the last half century (Richards, 2005a; Laband, 2007; Lubkemann, 2008).

Wherever war occurs, it is destructive and disorganizing, but as we noted in the introduction to this book, European and North American representations of conflict and violence differ depending on the location being described. The media, in particular, depict violence in Europe as "ethno-nationalist", but violence in Africa as "tribal" – with all the primeval connotations this term implies. Indeed, Africa's contemporary conflicts have tended to be cast by analysts from outside the continent as hyper-chaotic and randomly – even incomprehensively – barbaric. As Paul Richards notes, the images that predominate in media and even many scholarly depictions of these so-called "new wars" draw upon "epidemiological" metaphors that equate the spread of mass violence with the mindless irrationality of a viral contagion capable of "infesting" entire regions (2005a: 2–3). To many outside observers these conflagrations thus appear to be imprecisely located, spilling back and forth across borders, the lines between combatants and non-combatants blurred. In such representations, the objectives of warring factions in Africa seem driven less by "political" motives or ideologies than by privateering and pillage.

However, against this view of "meaningless and arbitrary violence" Richards and others (see Behrend, 1999; Besteman, 1999; Ellis, 2001; Finnstrom, 2008; Hutchinson, 1996; Lubkemann, 2008; Moran, 2006; Taylor, 1999; Wilson, 1992) convincingly argue that these "new wars" – like all wars – should be understood as long-term struggles for political ends conceived of and pursued in locally relevant terms – and thus as simply one form of social project among many that

This Introduction includes significantly adapted material from pp. 103–109 of *Culture in Chaos: An Anthropology of the Social Condition in War* (Chicago, 2008), by Stephen C. Lubkemann.

are organized by social agents embedded in specific cultural contexts. Ethnography is well-suited to the task of analyzing Africa's many violent political struggles because it is capable of rendering visible the terms of the political game, as seen and understood by those who are engaged in it.

Notably, however, for most of the twentieth century anthropologists paid little attention to the contemporary violent contests for political dominance and state power that so profoundly marked the ascension of the nation as the globe's hegemonic political form. Until rather recently most anthropological studies of organized violence tended to (1) focus on the role of violence in maintaining order in, and organizing, so-called "stateless societies," sometimes erroneously conceived of as a stage of social and political evolution or (2) debate the relative weight of biological, socio-cultural, and economic-material factors in fostering organized violence.

The failure to focus on armed struggles in which state power was at stake did not mean such conflicts were irrelevant to the social processes or settings in which cultural anthropologists were studying. In fact, de-facto colonial rule throughout most of Africa was only achieved over the last quarter of the nineteenth century and the first quarter of the twentieth through intense and brutal military campaigns that sought to give substance to the territorial claims made by European powers in the Berlin Congress of 1884–5. Thus, for example, as late as 1921 the Portuguese were still struggling to militarily subdue the independent kingdom of Barue, in what later became Mozambique, while the previous two decades witnessed numerous and brutal "pacification campaigns" such as those by the Belgians in the Congo, the British in Sudan, by African-American colonists in Liberia, and by the Germans in Namibia. Nor did it take much more than a generation or two before Africans began to violently resist the degradations of colonial rule such as occurred in the Mau Mau movement in Kenya (see Berman, Chapter 35 in this volume).

In fact, throughout most of the twentieth century many ethnographers of Africa lived with and studied African societies that had been profoundly transformed by successive dispensations of violent political struggle in the colonial age and were, at the time of the ethnographic research, being shaken by postcolonial civil wars. However, until less than three decades ago, most scholars of African societies – and mid twentieth-century anthropologists in particular – bracketed out such conflagrations from their analysis, viewing them as aberrations in the "normal" course of the everyday life that they took to be their scientific object of study. E. Evans-Pritchard published ethnographies that have been widely accepted as paragons of holistic analysis (see Evans-Pritchard in this volume), and yet he ignored how recent colonial conquest and then-ongoing military "pacification" campaigns had profoundly affected the social practices and organization of the groups that he was studying. As anthropologist Sharon Hutchinson (Chaper 10 in this volume) has noted, the irony in his case was all the greater because it was actually the "problem" of pacifying and administering the Nuer that led to his being hired by the British colonial regime to undertake this research in the first place.

Flux and destabilization presented problems to the ahistorical structural-functionalist theoretical framework (see Part II in this volume on tribe and ethnicity) that described and treated all social practices in terms of their contribution to the maintenance and reproduction of social order. Thus, even though leading social theorists of African society such as Victor Turner (1957) and Max Gluckman (Chapter 37 in this volume) would eventually draw anthropological attention to social conflict they would nevertheless still emphasize its role in reproducing structural continuity rather than in effecting social change. Even when anthropologists wrote social history, it was almost always a history of sameness and order – in other words, a synchronic rather than a diachronic history.

Anthropological interest in more sustained forms of organized political violence in which state power and the socio-political order itself were at stake is thus a rather more recent phenomenon – one related both to the dramatic decolonization struggles that erupted in the post World War II years in so many of the African societies in which anthropologists worked, and to the discipline's growing preoccupation with theorizing social change. David Lan's landmark ethnographic study of the armed struggle against the racist settler regime in Southern Rhodesia[4] was one of the first – and remains one of the few – anthropological efforts to analyze a contemporary decolonization struggle in Africa (Lan, 1985). Against a tide of analysts and political leaders who sought to portray many of the anti-colonial struggles as emancipations from culture and the past, Lan insisted on analyzing armed resistance as a project that was as culturally informed as any other. He highlighted the pivotal role that spirit mediums played in securing social legitimacy for the freedom fighters. The mediums portrayed avowedly "Marxist" guerillas as the legitimate heirs and descendants of the original ancestral spirit owners of the land. The mediums' recasting of the war in turn shaped the practice of military violence itself, as ZANLA guerrillas obeyed ritual prescriptions that mediums placed on their use of violence and carried out violent tasks the mediums assigned to them – such as ferreting out and punishing witches (Lan, 1985: 166–9). As one result, the fighters confronted "threats" that would not have otherwise been identified in Marxist precepts. Local ritual specialists thus mediated the violence of the guerrillas, the population, and the agents of the colonial state in ways that allowed vernacular understandings of power and politics to restructure the dynamics of wartime violence.

As violent political upheaval has regrettably become an almost paradigmatic feature of the African postcolonial condition it has elicited an ever more robust accounting from the anthropologists and other social scientists who work in the shadow of its persistent, pervasive, and profoundly consequential presence. These scholars include Paul Richards (1996, 2005a, 2005b) working in Sierra Leone, Donald Donham (1999) in Ethiopia, Heike Behrend (1999) and Sverker Finnstrom (2008) in Uganda, Stephen Ellis (2001) and Mats Utas (2005) in Liberia, Christian Geffray (1989), Ken Wilson (1992), Carolyn Nordstrom (1997), Alcinda Honwana (2002), Harri Englund (2002) and Stephen Lubkemann (2008) in Mozambique, Catherine Besteman (1999) in Somalia, Peter Uvin (1998) and Christopher Taylor (1999) in Rwanda, Jocelyn Alexander, JoAnn McGregor, and Terence Ranger (2000) in Zimbabwe and Sharon Hutchinson (1996) in Sudan. Arguing that dramatic acts of wartime violence are more than just a strategy for minimizing local dissent through terrorist tactics, these ethnographers of contemporary African political violence have all tended to focus on the expressive dimensions of violence in African warzones – often pursuing a meaning-centered approach that highlights topics such as language (for example, testimony, confession, and legal discourse), the interactions among different religious systems, and globalization.

Several of the newer ethnographies reveal wartime violence as not only a dramaturgical means for contending for – or with – state power but also as a means of expressing culturally specific understandings of the landscape of power itself. In her analysis of the genesis of the Holy Spirit Movement in northern Uganda (the precursor to the infamous Lord's Resistance Army) Heike Behrend demonstrates how specific local histories and culturally scripted interpretations shaped what both the organizers and armed participants in this violent insurgency understood the war "to be about." She argues that the genocidal state violence, famine, economic destitution, and even the explosion of AIDS, that were experienced under successive postcolonial regimes (Idi Amin, Obote, and Museveni) were, in the view of the Acholi of northern Uganda, all interrelated. They were all understood to be products of the rapid growth and spread of witchcraft. The movement's leader, Alice Lakwena, derived much of her power from her promise to eradicate this scourge. Consequently, her armed insurgency's agenda was cast as far more than simply a war against the government, but as a cosmic struggle against spiritual malfeasance (Behrend, 1999).

From this more recent theoretical perspective, contemporary African warfare is not merely "ethnic" or primarily "local", much less is it rooted in aspirations that hark back to a "premodern past" or that remain unaware of, or uninfluenced by the global ecumene. Rather violent action should be positioned within a broader repertoire of culturally informed tactics for countering the insecurity, volatility, and dashed expectations that ultimately result from the forms of subordinate articulation within global political-economic relations that generate sentiments of "abjection" (Ferguson, Chapter 41 in this volume) and the experience of "structural violence" (Uvin, Chapter 42 in this volume). Some of the imaginative tactics developed and deployed to cope with socio-economic vulnerability and the frustrations of the unrealized promises of development (see Part XII in this volume) have not been violent – such as the proliferating forms of charismatic Christianity that promise to harness the power of the greater force of the Holy Spirit against the perils of invisible power let loose by uncontrolled capitalism (Sommers, 2001; Ashforth, 2000; West, Chapter 45 in this volume) or the inventive internet scams that Nigerian youth deploy in an effort to get a bite at the elusive global pie (Smith, Chapter 43 in this volume). However, other tactics have proven dramatically more violent – as in the case of the well-subscribed witch-finding cults that have come to thrive throughout urban Africa (Geschiere, 1997; Comaroff and Comaroff, 1999; Smith, 2004; Ashforth, 2000), and the violent insurgencies that ultimately take to the national stage itself (Richards, Chaper 38 in this volume). Ultimately, in situating the various forms and degrees of organized political violence in Africa within this continuum, ethnographers and social historians have sought to place Africa's contemporary wars and political conflicts back within a range of social action that does not require exceptional explanation but rather explores conflict as an outcome of the stark and consequential contradictions of the everyday life of so many Africans (Richards, 2005b).

Recognizing that prolonged warfare has become the backdrop for the everyday life of many of Africa's inhabitants, rather than an exceptional social state, anthropologists and other social sciences have also increasingly placed a premium on tracing the dynamic development of social relations in African societies throughout conflict and displacement, rather than treating war as an interruption that suspends social process. Anthropologists such as Mallki (1995), Besteman (1999), Hutchinson (Chapter 10 in this volume), Lubkemann (Chapter 40 in this volume), Shandy (Chapter 46 in this volume), and Finnstrom (2008) have thus sought to investigate how gendered, generational, intra-communal, and other forms of social relations and identities can be and are profoundly transformed by the wartime reconfiguration of social and economic opportunity structures. Harrell-Bond (1986), Honwana (2002), Lubkemann (this volume), Shandy (this volume), Mallki (1995), Hutchinson (this volume) and many others have demonstrated that wartime displacement is particularly socially transformative because of its tendency to fragment social networks, to contribute to massive urbanization, to polarize and politicize identities, and to reconfigure economic activity and interdependencies.

The first chapter in this part, by Max Gluckman, introduces the reader to the functionalist argument that conflict contributes to structural continuity. In this famous essay on "rituals of rebellion," Gluckman develops the structural-functionalist logic to its extreme, arguing that instances of cathartic but ultimately socially controlled expressions of resentment against specific social power holders were actually vital for ensuring social unity. When channeled through ritual, conflict performed a vital social function: enabling systems of social power and hierarchy to persist, rather than transforming them in indeterminate ways. From this theoretical perspective, socio-political conflict was thus always a matter of rebellion rather than revolution, in which existing principles of political and social order were reaffirmed rather than overthrown.

In the second chapter in this part, on Sierra Leone, Paul Richards (1996, 2005b) formulates a particularly influential approach to war as a dramatic form of public communication. This "public dramaturgy" is as much a part of the arsenal deployed by opposing military factions as are the more obviously lethal weapons they wield in their hands. In Richards' view, violent actors often achieve their objective less through the evisceration and disempowerment of victims, and more through the messages that such bodily inscriptions communicate to a broader public about what might transpire in the future and why. Victims of violence are thus not always the primary intended audience for the messages so painfully inscribed upon their bodies. Thus, the Revolutionary United Front's (RUF) cutting off of the hands of civilians in Sierra Leone (Richards, 1996), the meticulous brick-by-brick razing of every vestige of physical infrastructure in the Mozambiquan National Resistance (RENAMO) "destruction zones" in Mozambique (Wilson, 1992), or the hobbling by machete of already immobilized victims by the *genocidaire* in Rwanda (Uvin, Chapter 42 and Taylor, Chapter 39 in this volume) – all acts that to outsiders have evidenced wanton and meaningless brutality – are revealed through ethnographic contextualization as sophisticated forms of political discourse. While his analysis does not in any way justify these acts, Richards seeks to interpret violence as a form of tragically consequential communication that renders messages with dramatic clarity within particular social contexts and in the terms of specific cultural idioms.

Thus in the intertwined Sierra Leonean and Liberian conflicts, the violent images drawn upon to convey "locally meaningful" messages include not only those culled from the centuries old Poro and Sande initiation societies, but also Rambo (Richards, this volume), Lara Croft (Utas, 2005), and the gangsta rapper Tupac Shakur (Hoffman, 2005). Similarly, in the Holy Spirit Movement in Uganda insurgents not only invoked the "Christian" spirit "Lakwena" but also appealed to that of the action hero superstar "Bruce Lee" (Behrend, 1999: 7). In short, the narratives that fundamentally shape "local" expectations may be as much derived from Hollywood's distorted depictions of life in America (Utas, 2005), the similarly gilded tales of expatriate diasporas (MacGaffey and Bazenguissa-Ganga, 2000; Matsuoka and Sorenson, 2001; Shandy, this volume), or the disproportionately privileged lives of expatriate aid workers who live, work and play in the compound just down the road (Uvin, this volume), as they are from the more "self-evidently local" realities.

In the chapter by Taylor, on the specific forms of violence perpetrated in the Rwandan genocide, we find that local notions of national political power draw on culturally specific metaphors for the body and biological reproduction. In Rwanda, terms used to conceptualize social reproduction serve as the basis for how social order and disorder are themselves understood at various levels – including that of the "national body" itself. As a result, military tactics that might strike outside observers as "irrational" – such as the proliferation of dozens of roadblocks within sight of each other – appear less arbitrary and senseless when understood as stagings of strength that draw upon local understandings of power as the capacity to both block and enable flows. Taylor's analysis of the cultural grammar of genocidal violence is particularly important because of his insights into its gendered dimensions. His explanation of the link between cultural notions of bodily purity and ideologies of ethnic national purity explains the virulence with which Hutu extremists reacted to and focused upon the "polluting" effects of cross-ethnic marriages, and the particularly gruesome gender edge that shaped their genocidal violence (Taylor, this volume).

In his chapter on central Mozambique, Lubkemann documents the ways in which the violence wielded by military factions was diverted in service to other forms of highly localized social conflict that had little, if anything, to do with the war's master political narrative. Local beliefs about the socio-spiritual consequences of not seeking redress for those wrongfully and violently killed also fed a deadly intensification of wartime violence. In this context both wartime violence and migratory strategies for coping with it were thus shaped by the local belief that meaningful social relations spanned a continuum in which the dead and the living were in continuous and highly consequential interaction (see also Kopytoff, Chapter 21 in this volume).

Lubkemann also describes the inadvertent but profound social effects of prolonged wartime spousal separation on the structure of marriage and the dramatically different transformations in this institution's meaning for men and women as a result of the transnationalization of polygyny. Moreover, he documents a moment of creative and fundamental epistemological shift that emerges as migrant men sought to renegotiate their own socio-spiritual relationships and status in ways that would allow them to pursue new transnational strategies that empowered them vis-à-vis both the state and their spouses. As his study and those of others (including Shandy, Chapter 46 and Hutchinson, Chapter 10 in this volume) illustrate, contemporary conflict and violence in Africa has ultimately underwritten a bewildering array of processes (migration, displacement, global diasporization, urbanization, involuntary immobilization in refugee camps, social network fragmentation, inflammation of local social tensions) whose transformative effects on social relations and the very terms of cultural expression have been profound and complex. The need to study social transformation throughout war is all the more pressing in the growing number of Africa's societies where armed conflicts have insisted on spanning generations, or at least on periodically punctuating their social existence.

Works such as those in this section suggest that wartime violence in Africa should not be viewed as capable of eradicating or overwriting cultural meanings (Nordstrom, 1997: 141–2; 165–73), nor as somehow qualitatively more mindless, meaningless, and "primitive" (Kaplan, 1994) than organized violence elsewhere. Rather, these studies reveal armed conflict and the violence within as forms of behavioral expression as deeply infused with already existing cultural meaning as any other, and whose "performance [of violence] cannot be amputated from that wider body of cultural performance" (Whitehead, 2004: 10).

Viewed together, the recent body of ethnographies and social histories of postcolonial African conflicts vividly demonstrate how contemporary armed insurgencies creatively draw upon culturally specific idioms and tools of resistance that are all rooted in very specific histories, and yet are far from being merely "traditionalist" in their objectives or driven by "primordial sentiments" (as Africa's "new wars" are often depicted). Rather these violent movements mobilize a creative fusion of symbols – some of contemporary and even "global" provenance and others from a more idiomatic past – in order to endorse drastic solutions to the pressing problems of the present, including historically structured social and political exclusion, thwarted expectations, and shrinking economic opportunities.

Notes

1 Mozambique, Liberia, Namibia, DRC, Algeria, Uganda.
2 Sudan, Chad, Somalia.
3 Angola, Rwanda, Burundi, Western Sahara,.
4 Renamed Zimbabwe since independence in 1980.

References

Alexander, Jocelyn, Joann McGregor and Terence Ranger, 2000. *Violence and Memory: One Hundred Years in the "Dark Forests" of Matabeleland, Zimbabwe*. Oxford: James Currey.
Ashforth, Adam. 2000. *Madumo: A Man Bewitched*. Chicago: University of Chicago Press.
Behrend, Heike. 1999. *Alice Lakwena and the Holy Spirits: War in Northern Uganda 1985–97*. Oxford: James Currey.

Besteman, Catherine. 1999. *Unraveling Somalia: Race, Violence, and the Legacy of Slavery*. Philadelphia: University of Pennsylvania Press.

Comaroff, Jean, and John L. Comaroff, eds. 1999. "Introduction." In *Modernity and Its Malcontents*. Chicago: University of Chicago Press.

Donham, Donald, L. 1999. *Marxist Modern: An Ethnographic History of the Ethiopian Revolution*. Berkeley: University of California Press.

Ellis, Stephen. 2001. *The Mask of Anarchy: The Destruction of Liberia and the Religious Dimension of an African Civil War*. New York: New York University Press.

Englund, Harri. 2002. *From War to Peace on the Mozambique-Malawi Borderland*. Edinburgh: Edinburgh University Press.

Finnstrom, Sverker. 2008. *Living with Bad Surroundings: War, History, and Everyday Moments in Northern Uganda*. Durham: Duke University Press.

Geffray, Christiaan. 1989. *A Causa das Armas: Antropologia da Guerra Contemporanea em Mocambique.[The Cause of Arms: Anthropology of the Contemporary War in Mozambique.]* Lisbon: Afrontamento.

Geschiere, Peter. 1997. *The Modernity of Witchcraft: Politics and the Occult in Postcolonial Africa*. Charlottesville, VA: University of Virginia Press.

Gurr, Ted R., M. Marshall and Deepa Khosla. 2001. *Peace and Conflict 2001: A Global Survey of Armed Conflicts, Self-Determination Movements, and Democracy*. College Park, MD: University of Maryland Center for International Development and Conflict Management.

Harrell-Bond, Barbara E. 1986. *Imposing Aid: Emergency Assistance to Refugees*. Oxford: Oxford University Press.

Hoffman, D. 2005. "Violent Events as Narrative Blocs: The Disarmament at Bo, Sierra Leone." *Anthropological Quarterly* 78(2): 329–54.

Honwana, Alicinda M. 2002. *Espiritos Vivos, Tradicoes Modernas: Possessão de Espiritos e Reintegrão Social Pós-Guerra no Sul de Moçambique*. [*Living Spirits, Modern Traditions: Spirit Possession and Social Reintegration in Post-Conflict Southern Mozambique*.] Maputo, Mozambique: Promedia.

Hutchinson, Sharon. 1996. *Nuer Dilemmas: Coping With Money, War, and the State*. Berkeley: University of California Press.

Kaplan, Robert. 1994. "The Coming Anarchy: How Scarcity, Crime, Overpopulation and Disease Are Rapidly Destroying the Social Fabric of our Planet."*Atlantic Monthly*, February: 44–76.

Laband, John, ed. 2007. *Daily Lives of Civilians in Wartime Africa: From Slavery Days to the Rwandan Genocide*. Scottsville, South Africa: University of KwaZulu-Natal Press.

Lan, David. 1985. *Guns and Rain: Guerillas and Spirit Mediums in Zimbabwe*. Berkeley: University of California Press.

Lubkemann, Stephen, 2008. *Culture in Chaos: An Anthropology of the Social Condition in War*. Chicago: University of Chicago Press.

MacGaffey, Janet, and Remy Bazenguissa-Ganga, 2000. *Congo-Paris: Transnational Traders on the Margins of the Law*. Bloomington, IN: Indiana University Press.

Mallki, Liisa. 1995. *Purity and Exile: Violence, Memory and National Cosmology among Hutu Refugees in Tanzania*. Chicago: University of Chicago Press.

Matsuoka, Atsuoko, and John Sorenson. 2001. *Ghosts and Shadows: Construction of Identity and Community in an African Diaspora*. Toronto: University of Toronto Press.

Moran, Mary. 2006. *Liberia: The Violence of Democracy*. Philadelphia, PA: University of Pennsylvania Press.

Nordstrom, Carolyn. 1997. *A Different Kind of War Story*. Philadelphia: University of Pennsylvania.

Richards, Paul. 1996. *Fighting for the Rainforest: War, Youth and Resources in Sierra Leone*. Portsmouth, NH: Heinemann.

Richards, Paul. 2005a. "New War: An Ethnographic Approach." In P. Richards, ed., *No Peace, No War: An Anthropology of Contemporary Armed Conflicts*. Athens: Ohio University Press.

Richards, Paul. 2005b. "War as Smoke and Mirrors: Sierra Leone 1991–2, 1994–5, 1995–6." *Anthropological Quarterly*, 78(2): 377–402.

Smith, Daniel J. 2004. "The Bakassi Boys: Vigilantism, Violence and the Political Imagination in Nigeria". *Cultural Anthropology* 19(3): 429–55.

Sommers, Marc. 2001. *Fear in Bongoland: Burundi Refugees in Urban Tanzania*. New York: Berghahn.

Taylor, Christopher. 1999. *Sacrifice as Terror: The Rwandan Genocide of 1994*. Oxford: Berg.

Turner, Victor. 1957. *Schism and Continuity in an African Society*. Manchester: Manchester University Press.

Utas, Mats. 2005. "Victimcy, Girlfriending, Soldiering: Tactic Agency in a Young Woman's Social Navigation of the Liberian War Zone." *Anthropological Quarterly* 78(2): 403–30.

Uvin, Peter. 1998. *Aiding Violence: The Development Enterprise in Rwanda*. New York: Kumarian Press.

Whitehead, Neil. 2004. "Introduction: Cultures, Conflicts and the Poetics of Violent Practice." In N. Whitehead, ed., *Violence*. Santa Fe: School of American Research Press.

Wilson, Ken. 1992. "Cults of Violence and Counter-Violence in Mozambique." *Journal of Southern African Studies* 18(1): 527–82.

37

Rituals of Rebellion in South-East Africa

Max Gluckman

I shall [...] consider the social components of ceremonies, [...] among the South-Eastern Bantu of Zululand, Swaziland, and Mozambique. Here there are (in some cases, were) performed, as elsewhere in Africa, national and local ceremonies at the break of the rains, sowing, first-fruits, and harvest. In one ceremony the idea of a goddess who is propitiated by the rites is clearly expressed; usually the ceremonies are directed to the ancestral spirits of the tribal chiefs or the kinship groups concerned. But whatever the ostensible purpose of the ceremonies, a most striking feature of their organization is the way in which they openly express social tensions: women have to assert licence and dominance as against their formal subordination to men, princes have to behave to the king as if they covet the throne, and subjects openly state their resentment of authority. Hence I call them rituals of rebellion. I shall argue that these ritual rebellions proceed within an established and sacred traditional system, in which there is dispute about particular distributions of power, and not about the structure of the system

itself. This allows for instituted protest, and in complex ways renews the unity of the system.

The Zulu had no developed pantheon. Their ideas of the High God were vague and there was no ritual address to him. *Heaven* was believed to be responsible for certain devastating phenomena, such as lightning. It was controlled by special magicians. The only developed deity in their religion was *Nomkubulwana*, the Princess of Heaven, who was honoured by the women and girls of local districts in Zululand and Natal, when the crops had begun to grow. The performance of these agricultural rituals by women on a local scale contrasts with great national sowing and first-fruits rites, which were mainly the responsibility of men as warriors serving the king on whom the ritual centred.

The women no longer perform their ritual to honour the goddess *Nomkubulwana*, so I did not observe it during my own work in Zululand. [...] But the goddess herself still visits that pleasant land. She moves in the mists which mark the end of the dry season and which presage the beginning of the rains. From their homes on the hills the Zulu look over these mists, which lie in the valleys touched by the light of the rising sun, and they comment on the Princess of Heaven's beauty. A missionary in Zululand wrote:

> She is described as being robed with light as a garment and having come down from heaven to teach people to make beer, to plant, to harvest, and all the useful arts. … She is a maiden and she makes her visit to the earth in the Spring of the year. She is also described as presenting the appearance of a beautiful landscape with verdant forests on some parts of her body, grass-covered slopes on others and cultivated slopes on others. She is said to be the maker of rain.[1]

According to Father Bryant, a Catholic missionary who has been the foremost student of Zulu history and culture,

> she is supposed to have first given man form. The Zulu say she moves with the mist, on one side a human being, on one side a river, on one side overgrown with grass. If no rites were performed for her, she was offended and blighted the grain. From time to time she appeared in white to women and gave them new laws or told them what would happen in the future. The rainbow is the rafter of her hut – she dwells in the sky and is connected with rain.[2]

Nomkubulwana is thus clearly a goddess of the same kind as the corn-goddesses and corn-gods of the ancient world. Father Bryant explicitly compares her with these deities and draws parallels between their respective rites. The most important of these rites among the Zulu required obscene behaviour by the women and girls. The girls donned men's garments, and herded and milked the cattle, which were normally taboo to them. Their mothers planted a garden for the goddess far out in the veld, and poured a libation of beer to her. Thereafter this garden was neglected. At various stages of the ceremonies women and girls went naked, and sang lewd songs. Men and boys hid and might not go near.

[…]

[… All] I wish to stress here is that […] a dominant rôle was ascribed to the women, and a subordinate rôle to the men […] These elements appear in ceremonies throughout the South-Eastern Bantu tribes. Thus we are told of a ceremony to drive away crop-pests among the Tsonga of Mozambique:

> Woe to the man who walks along the paths! He is pitilessly attacked by these viragos, who push him to one side, or even maltreat him, and none of his fellows will go to his assistance. They all keep out of the way, for they well know what would be in store for them, should they meet the savage crowd![3]

This temporary dominant role of the women – a dominant rôle that was publicly instituted, indeed approved, and not exercised tactfully in the background – contrasted strongly with the mores of these patriarchal peoples. Hence it is my first example of a ritual of rebellion, an instituted protest demanded by sacred tradition, which is seemingly against the established order, yet which aims to bless that order to achieve prosperity. To understand how this rebellion worked we must contrast the women's behaviour here with their accustomed behaviour.

In the first place, it is important to grasp that the men did not merely abstain from participation in the ceremonial, and regard it as a women's affair. The men were convinced that the ceremony would help produce bountiful crops: old Zulu men complained to me in 1937 that the neglect of the ceremony accounted for the poor crops of today. The men wished the ritual to be performed, and their own positive role in the ceremony was to hide, […] and to allow the girls to wear their garments and do their work while elder women behaved with Bacchantic lewdness as against the usual demand that they be modest.

Secondly, the ceremonies were performed by the women and girls of local districts, while the men as warriors in the king's regiments joined in great sowing and first-fruits ceremonies for national strength and prosperity. The direct interests of women and girls were confined to their home districts, and here they took action to get local prosperity. Their ceremonial actions, marked by dominance and lewdness, were effective in contrast to their usual subordination and modesty. I cannot here describe this contrast in detail, [...] but state briefly that they were in every respect formally under the tutelage of men. Legally women were always minors, in the care of father, brother, or husband. They could not in general become politically powerful. They were married out of their own kin-group into the homes of strangers where they were subject to many restraints and taboos. In ritual their role was not only subordinate, but also highly ambivalent and usually evil. They could perform good magic, as when a pregnant woman burnt medicines whose smoke benefited the crops. But they could not become magicians; indeed, if a woman stepped over a fireplace where magic had been prepared, she fell ill. Though the menses were the source of children, so that the menses could be beneficial, usually during their menstrual periods women were a constant threat of danger. In this condition they could spoil magic, blight crops, kill cattle, and rob the warrior of his strength and the hunter of his skill. Terrible ills afflicted a man who had intercourse with a menstruating woman. In religion women were equally suppressed and as potentially evil. They moved to reside under the protection of their husbands' stranger ancestors, whom they could not approach directly. They did not, like men, become ancestral spirits doing good for their children in return for sacrifices. For as spirits women were capriciously evil: male ancestors did not normally continue to afflict their descendants after sacrifice had been made, but female spirits might continue to cause malicious ill. The Zulu vaguely personify the power of Heaven in storms, and they distinguish two kinds of Heaven. The first, marked by sheet-lightning, is good, and male; the second, marked by forked-lightning, is female, and dangerous. Finally, as men could learn to become good magicians, so they could learn to be malignant sorcerers, deliberately choosing to be wicked. But women's inherent wickedness attracted to them sexual familiars who turned them into witches and demanded the lives of their relatives. In Zulu myths it was Eves who introduced killing by sorcery into Paradise. Most Zulu charges of witchcraft were made against women – against sisters-in-law and daughters-in-law, and between the fellow-wives of one man or the wives of brothers.

One path to good ritual action was open to women. They could be possessed by spirits and become diviners: 90 per cent of this kind of diviners were women. However, this possession was an extremely painful illness which might endure for years, and often killed the patient. The symbol of a successful initiation was the right to carry shield and spear, those badges of manhood.

Thus the standardized beliefs and practices of the Zulu stressed the social subordination and the inherent ambivalent position of women. Women potentially threatened evil by ritual means. Yet in practice they not only were useful, as the main cultivators of gardens, but also they were essential for the procreation of society. The agnatic lineage – a group of males descended through males from a male founding ancestor – was the dominant enduring group in Zulu kinship and familial life. Women of the lineage were married elsewhere to produce children for other lineages. [...] But the men who as a group were socially fertile in that their children perpetuated their existence, were on the other hand physically sterile. Under the rules which forbade men to marry their kinswomen, they had to obtain wives elsewhere in order to get children. [...] Thus the male group depended on stranger women for its perpetuation. When these women married into the group they were hedged with taboos and restraints. For while the group's continuity and strength depended on its offspring by these women, its very increase in numbers threatened that strength and continuity. A man who has two sons by his wife produces two rivals for a single position and property; and his wife is responsible for this dangerous proliferation of his personality. If he has two wives, each with sons, the cleavage, like the proliferation, is greater. Hence the role of women in producing children both strengthens and threatens to disrupt the group, and this ambivalence is expressed in the manifold beliefs I have recited. Since struggles between men over property and position, which threatened to disrupt the group, were fought in terms of their attachment to the agnatic group through stranger-women [...] it is not surprising that charges of witchcraft were brought frequently by fellow-wives, jealous not only of their husbands' favours but also for their sons, and by both men and women against sisters-in-law and daughters-in-law. Moreover, the men of the group, because of their unity, could not attack each other directly with accusations of witchcraft, but one could attack another indirectly by accusing his wife.

Cattle come into this series of conflicts, firstly as the main property, beside position, over which men fought. Land was then plentiful. Another potent source of quarrels was women. However, women and cattle were in a sense identified, though – and perhaps therefore – taboo to each other, since a man required cattle to give as marriage-payment for his wife. Cattle, the herding of which formed, with warriorhood, the admired Zulu roles, were thus not only taboo to women, but also the apparent symbol for their transfer from the security of their natal home to the uncertainties of a strange village and to the vicissitudes of conjugal life. Though marriage was the goal of all women, in the years of courtship Zulu girls were liable to suffer from hysterical attacks, which were blamed on the love-magic of their suitors. When a girl married, cattle moved into her home to replace her, and her brother used these cattle to get his own bride. The stability of her brother's marriage, established with these cattle, depended on the stability of her marriage and on her having children; for theoretically if she were divorced – though in practice divorce was extremely rare among the Zulu [...] – or if she were barren, her husband could claim the cattle with which his brother-in-law had married. The cattle thus came to symbolize not only the manner in which a girl became a wife, but also the conflict between brothers and sisters, with the brother heir to his sister's marriage as well as to the group's cattle. From this position the sister was excluded by virtue of her sex. For had her brother's and her sexes been reversed, she would have been heir to cattle and social predominance, and he destined to perpetuate a group of strangers and not his and her own natal group.

This is part of the social background in which we must try to understand the *Nomkubulwana* ceremonies with their protest of women's rebellion. They took place when women had embarked on the arduous and uncertain agricultural tasks of the year and promised a good harvest from the one

goddess in the array of virile 'gods' and ancestors. The young girls, still in their natal homes, acted as if they were their brothers: they donned male clothing, carried weapons (like the possessed diviners), and herded the beloved cattle. Their brothers remained in the huts, like women. The younger married women, [...] with lewd behaviour, planted the goddess's field: as men at the capital ceremonially sowed a field for the king. A dropping of normal restraints, and inverted and transvestite behaviour, in which women were dominant and men suppressed, *somehow* were believed to achieve good for the community – an abundant harvest. Clearly a wealth of psychological and sociological – even physiological – mechanisms are contained in that '*somehow* were believed to achieve good'. I have not time to enter into these mechanisms, of which indeed as yet we understand little. Here I stress only that the ceremonial operates seemingly by an act of rebellion, by an open and privileged assertion of obscenity, [...] by the patent acting of fundamental conflicts both in the social structure and in individual psyches.

[...]

The *Nomkubulwana* ceremony is one of many domestic rituals which exhibit these processes [...]. Other domestic ceremonies also exhibit the theme of rebellion. [...] However, I turn now to analyse a great national ceremony connected with crops and kingship, in which the theme of rebellion in the *political* process is made manifest.

The Zulu kingship was broken after the Anglo-Zulu war of 1879; but happily the kindred Swazi still perform national ceremonies which are very similar to those the Zulu used to perform. Dr Hilda Kuper [...] has given us a brilliant description of them.[4]

The Swazi *incwala* ceremony has been taken by most observers to be a typical first-fruits ceremony, and indeed no one should eat of some of the crops before it has been performed. In most South African tribes a breach of this taboo threatened ritual danger not to the transgressor, but to the leader whose right of precedence 'was stolen'. There is evidence that many broke the taboo: if caught, they were punished by the chiefs. The sanction on this taboo itself states the main theme of rebellious conflict with which we are here concerned. The king had thus to race his subjects 'to bite the new year', the passage into which was marked by the sun's turn at the tropic. But the king must also 'race the sun' and begin the ceremony before the solstice itself. This requires some calculation as the king must go into his retirement when the moon is on the wane, and symbolizes that man's powers are declining. The nation resides on the land and is dependent on the cosmic forces, but it must utilize and even subdue them. Here too the king is concerned to prevent other nations stealing a march on him.

The ceremonies vary according to the age of the king: they are reduced to a few rites if he succeeds as a boy and blossom in his maturity. But only the king among the royal clan can stage the ritual. When two princes organized their own ceremonies this led, in Swazi historical thought, to great disasters: national armies were sent to punish them for this treason. Certain immigrant provincial chiefs of other clans retain their own first-fruits ceremonies, which they stage later, but they keep away from the king's *incwala*.

Two calabashes are prepared for the ceremony. Each calabash is known as 'Princess' (*inkosatana*), and seems to be connected with the Princess *Inkosatana*, who, according to Dr Kuper, is 'a sky deity whose footprint is the rainbow, and of whose mood lightning is the expression'. This suggests further some relationship with *Nomkubulwana*. The calabashes are prepared by hereditary ritual experts known as 'The People [Priests – M. G.] of the Sea'. A pitch black bull is stolen from the herd of a subject not of the royal clan. 'He is angry and proud', and these conflicting emotions are said to impregnate the ingredients for the ritual. The bull is slain and strips of its skin are twined about the 'princess' calabashes. Then in the evening 'the Priests of the Sea' set off under the royal ancestors' blessing to get the waters of the sea and the great bordering rivers, and plants from the tangled forests of the Lebombo Mountains. This was formerly a hazardous journey into enemy lands but 'the waters of the world [were required] to give strength and purity to the king'. As they go through the country the grave priests practise licensed robbery on the people.

On the day of the night when the moon will be dark, the calabashes are placed in a sacred enclosure in the royal cattle-kraal. Some of the priests pillage the capital. The 'little ceremony' has begun.

The age-regiments of veterans from the capital of the king's dead father's queen-mother assemble in the kraal as the crescent of the weak moon. Amid the lowing of the cattle they slowly chant the sacred royal song:

> You hate the child king,
> You hate the child king (*repeated*).
> I would depart with my Father (the king),
> I fear we would be recalled.
> They put him on the stone:
> – sleeps with his sister:
> – sleeps with Lozithupa ([the] Princess):
> You hate the child king.

The words are repeated in varying order over and over again. During the chanting the regiments from the capitals of the king and his queen-mother enter the kraal and the army forms a crescent. Queens and princesses, and commoner women and children, stand in separate ranks, distant according to status. All chant a second sacred song:

> You hate him,
> Mother, the enemies are the people,
> You hate him,
> The people are wizards.
> Admit the treason of Mabedla –
> You hate him,
> You have wronged,
> bend great neck,
> those and those they hate him,
> they hate the king.

This song too is sung again, and is followed by songs 'rich in historical allusions and moral precepts', but which may be sung on secular occasions. Dr Kuper cites one: it too speaks of the king's enemies among the people for it urges revenge on those who were believed to have killed his father, King Bunu, by sorcery.

> Come let us arm, men of the capital,
> the harem is burnt,
> the shield of the lion has disappeared
> (*repeated*).

Meanwhile the king is in the sacred enclosure. The Priests of the Sea come with medicines to treat him, and women avert their eyes for 'to look on the medicines of the king can drive one mad'. A pitch black bull is killed in the enclosure, and the army moves from the crescent shape to that of the full moon against the enclosure, while a young regiment goes behind it. While the king is treated with powerful magic he is surrounded by his subjects. The army chants a royal song which is sung at all important episodes in the king's life:

> King, alas for your fate,
> King, they reject thee,
> King, they hate thee.

The chant is silenced; foreigners who do not owe allegiance to the king, and men and women of the royal clan and women pregnant by these men, are ordered away. Dr Kuper considers 'that the king at the height of his ritual treatment must be surrounded only by his loyal and unrelated subjects'. The leader of the Sea Priests shouts: 'He stabs it with both horns. Our Bull'; and the people know that the king has spat medicine to break the old year and prepare for the new. The crowd applauds, for the king 'has triumphed and is strengthening the earth'. The people chant the national anthem, now full not of hate and rejection, but of triumph:

> Here is the Inexplicable.
> Our Bull! Lion! Descend.
> Descend, Being of Heaven,
> Unconquerable.
> Play like tides of the sea,
> You Inexplicable, Great Mountain.
> Our Bull.

They disperse. Fire burns all night in the enclosure.

Before the sun rises the men assemble again in the kraal and chant the songs of rejection. They shout, 'Come, Lion, awake, the sun is leaving you,' 'They hate him, the son of Bunu,' and other insults to stir the king to activity. With the rising sun the king enters the enclosure, and it is encircled by the army. Again they sing,

> King, alas for your fate,
> King, they reject thee,
> King, they hate thee.

Foreigners and those of the royal clan are expelled and the spitting ceremony is again performed. The ritual is over.

There remains an essential 'work of the people for kingship'. The warriors weed the queen-mother's gardens, but their work is described by a term for working with little energy, with play and dawdling. The regimental leaders urge the warriors to strenuous effort and scold slackers, but, still, it is called working without energy – I suspect it is at least an unconscious protest against work for the state. The army dances; and then the people are feasted according to rank. This ends the little ceremony, and during the ensuing fortnight the people practise the songs and dances for the great ceremony which is performed when the moon is full, and man's powers with it rise to a new status. People from all over the country assemble for these days of national celebration.

The themes I am analysing have emerged in the little ceremony, so for lack of time I summarize the great ceremony, which Dr Kuper has described with unsurpassed artistry. On the first day young warriors, pure and undefiled by sexual relations, make an arduous journey to get green everlasting and quick-growing shrubs. Then they dance with the king. After they have rested, on the third day the king is treated with powerful medicines. Another stolen bull, whose theft has made its commoner owner 'angry', is killed by the youths with their bare hands: and he who was not pure is liable to be injured. Magically powerful parts of the bull are taken to treat the king. The fourth day is the great day, when, to quote Dr Kuper, 'the king appears in all his splendour, and the ambivalent attitude of love and hate felt by his brothers and his non-related subjects to him and to each other is dramatized'. The king goes naked save for a glowing ivory prepuce-cover to the sacred enclosure through his people, as they chant the songs of hate and rejection. His mothers weep and pity him. He spits medicines so that his strength goes through and awakens his people. Now he bites the new crops; and next day the various status groups of the nation do so in order of precedence. In the afternoon, the king, surrounded by men of the royal clan, dances at the head of the army. They change their song:

We shall leave them with their country,
Whose travellers are like distant thunder,
Do you hear, Dlambula, do you hear?

And the women reply,

Do you hear?
Let us go, let us go.

The words and the tune are wild and sad [say the Swazi] like the sea 'when the sea is angry and the birds of the sea are tossed on the waves'. The royal women move backwards and forwards in small, desperate groups. ... Many weep. The men's feet stamp the ground vigorously and slowly, the black plumes wave and flutter, the princes come closer, driving the king in their midst. Nearer and nearer they bring him to his sanctuary. The crowd grows frenzied, the singing louder, the bodies sway and press against the enclosure, and the king is forced within.

Dr Kuper was given two apparently conflicting interpretations of this rite. The first was that the royal clan wants to migrate again. 'They want their king to come with them, they want to leave the people whom they distrust in the country where they stayed a little while.' The second interpretation was: 'The [royal clan] show their hatred of the king. They denounce him and force him from their midst.' I think both interpretations are correct, for both are stressed in the next act. [...] The song changes:

Come, come, King of Kings,
Come, father, come,
Come king, oh come here, king.

The princes lunge with their sticks against the small doorway and beat their shields in agitation, draw back slowly and beseechingly, try to lure him out, beg him with praises: 'Come from your sanctuary. The sun is leaving you, You the High One.'

The king emerges as a wild monster, his head covered with black plumes, his body with bright green, razor-edged grass and everlasting shoots. These and other accoutrements have ritual associations. He 'appears reluctant to return to the nation. He executes a crazy elusive dance.' Then he returns to the sanctuary, and again the princes

cry to him to come out, 'king of kings'. 'They draw back, pause, sway forward. At last he responds. At his approach they retire, enticing him to follow, but after a few steps he turns back and they close behind him again.' The warriors dance vigorously, beating their shields, for 'they keep their king alive and healthy by their own movements. The mime goes on with increasing tension ... [the king] is terrifying, and as the knife-edged grass cuts into his skin he tosses his body furiously in pain and rage.'

The pure youths at last come to the front: they carry special large black shields. The song changes to triumph:

Thunder deep,
That they hear the thundrous beat.

The youths pummel their shields as the king dances towards them, but they retreat from him. He retires two or three times more to the sanctuary, and then emerges carrying a gourd, which though plucked the previous year is still green. Foreigners and royalty again leave the amphitheatre. The king again retreats, tantalizing the men: then suddenly he lurches forward, and casts the gourd on to a shield. The men stamp their feet, hiss, and thump their shields: and all disperse.

Some informants told Dr Kuper that in the times of wars the recipient of the gourd, who thus received the powerful vessel symbolizing the past, would have been killed when he went to battle; and she suggests that he may be a national scapegoat, 'a sacrifice to the future'.

The king is full of dangerous magical power. That night he cohabits with his ritual wife, made blood-sister to him, so that commoner and royal blood meet in her to make her sister-wife to the king. All the population on the next day is in a tabooed state and subject to restraints, while the king sits naked and still among his powerful councillors. 'On this day the identification of the people with the king is very marked.' For example, people who break the taboo on sleeping late are reprimanded, 'You cause the king to sleep', and are fined. The queen-mother is also treated with medicines.

On the final day certain things that were used in the ceremony are burnt on a great pyre, and the people dance and sing, but the sad songs of rejection are now taboo for a year. Rain should fall – and usually does – to quench the flames. There is feasting and revelry at the expense of the rulers, and gay love-making. The warriors weed the royal fields, and then disperse to their homes.

The ceremonies themselves exhibit their main symbolism in Dr Kuper's vivid account. One can feel the acting out of the powerful tensions which make up national life – king and state against people, and people against king and state; king allied with commoners against his rival brother-princes, commoners allied with princes against the king; the relation of the king to his mother and his own queens; and the nation united against internal enemies and external foes, and in a struggle for a living with nature. This ceremony is not a simple mass assertion of unity, but a stressing of conflict, a statement of rebellion and rivalry against the king, with periodical affirmations of unity with the king, and the drawing of power from the king. The political structure, as the source of prosperity and strength which safeguards the nation internally and externally, is made sacred in the person of the king. He is associated with his ancestors, for the political structure endures through the generations, though kings and people are born and die. The queen-mother links him with past kings, his queens with future kings. Many other elements are present, but again we see that the dramatic, symbolic acting of social relations in their ambivalence is believed to achieve unity and prosperity.

[...]

We are here confronted with a cultural mechanism which challenges study by sociologists, psychologists, and biologists: the analysis in detail of the processes by which this acting of conflict achieves a blessing – social unity. [...] Clearly we are dealing with the general problem of *catharsis* set by Aristotle in his *Politics* and his *Tragedy* – the purging of emotion through 'pity, fear and inspiration'. Here I attempt only to analyse the sociological setting of the process.

I would chiefly stress that the rebellious ritual occurs within an established and unchallenged social order. In the past the South-Eastern Bantu people may have criticized and rebelled against particular authorities and individuals, but they did not question the system of institutions.

Zulu women undoubtedly suffered severe psychical pressure in their social subordination and their transference by marriage to stranger-groups, but they desired marriage, children, well-cultivated and fertile fields to feed their husbands and families. In the *Nomkubulwana* ritual they became temporarily lewd viragoes, and their daughters martial herdsmen; but they accepted the social order and did not form a party of suffragettes. Here I think is an obvious pointer – and it is not necessarily wrong because it is obvious – to one set of social reasons why these African ceremonies could express, freely and openly, fundamental social conflicts. They possessed, not suffragettes aiming at altering the existing social and political order, but women seeking for good husbands to give them children.

Similarly, in African political life men were rebels and never revolutionaries. King and rival prince and subject all accepted the existing order and its institutions as right. Contenders for power against established authority sought only to acquire the same positions of authority for themselves. Professor Frankfort describes a similar structure in Ancient Egypt. Pharaoh 'maintains an established order (in which justice is an essential element) against the onslaught of the powers of chaos'. This order was *maat* – usually translated as 'truth', but 'which really means "right order" – the inherent structure of creation, of which justice is an integral part'. It was so 'effectively recognized by the people, that in the whole of Egypt's long history there is no evidence of any popular rising', though there were many palace intrigues.[5]

The acceptance of the established order as right and good, and even sacred, seems to allow unbridled excess, very rituals of rebellion, for the order itself keeps this rebellion within bounds. Hence to act the conflicts, whether directly or by inversion or in other symbolical form, emphasizes the social cohesion within which the conflicts exist. Every social system is a field of tension, full of ambivalence, of co-operation and contrasting struggle. This is true of relatively stationary – what I like to call *repetitive*[6] – social systems as well as of systems which are changing and developing. In a repetitive system particular conflicts are settled not by alterations in the order of offices, but by changes in the persons occupying those offices. The passage of time with its growth and change of population produces over long periods realignments, but not radical change of pattern. And as the social order always contains a division of rights and duties, and of privileges and powers as against liabilities, the ceremonial enactment of this order states the nature of the order in all its rightness. The ceremony states that in virtue of their social position princes and people hate the king, but nevertheless they support him. Indeed, they support him in virtue of, and despite, the conflicts between them. The critically important point is that even if Swazi princes do not actually hate the king, their social position may rally malcontents to them. Indeed, in a comparatively small-scale society princes by their very existence have power which threatens the king. Hence in their prescribed, compelled, ritual behaviour they exhibit opposition to as well as support for the king, but mainly support for the kingship. This is the social setting for rituals of rebellion. [...]

Here is one answer to Dr Kuper's discussion of the songs of hate and rejection with which the Swazi *support* their king:

The words of the *Incwala* songs are surprising to the European, accustomed at national celebrations, to hear royalty blatantly extolled, the virtues of the nation magnified, and the country glorified. The theme of the *Incwala* songs is hatred of the king and his rejection by the people. [A Swazi wrote]: 'The [one] song or hymn is an indirect allusion to the king's enemies not necessarily from outside, but may be from members of the royal family, or among the tribesmen. The line, 'he hates him! ahoshi ahoshi ahoshi' – is intended as a thrust against all who may not join in the *Incwala*, whose non-participation is regarded as an act of rebellion, hostility and personal hatred to the king.' Of the [rejection song he wrote]: 'It is a national expression of sympathy for the king, who, by reason of the manner of his choice, necessarily provokes enemies within the royal family. ... The songs show the hatred evoked by the king, but they also demonstrate the loyalty of his supporters. The people who sing the songs sing with pain and suffering, they hate his enemies and denounce them.' [Another Swazi] said: 'I think these songs are magical preventives against harm coming to the king.'

When the king walks naked to the sanctuary through his people,

the women weep and the song of hate rings out with penetrating melancholy. Later, when [Dr Kuper] asked the women why they had wept, the queen-mother said: 'It is pain to see him a king. My child goes alone through the people', the queens said: 'We pity him. There is no other man who could walk naked in front of everybody,' and an old man added: 'The work of a king is indeed heavy.'

It is the particular king who is hated and rejected by some that has to be pitied and supported by those who are loyal. People may hate the kingship in resenting its authority, but they do not aim to subvert it. For, 'it is the kingship and not the king who is divine'.[7]

[...]

Swazi polity was a system in which there were rebels, not revolutionaries. Should a particular king be a tyrant, his people's redress was not to seek to establish a republic, but to find some good prince whom they could establish as king. They were constrained both by belief and custom, and by the structure of groups in which they united for rebellion, to seek for their saviour leader in the royal family. For it was firmly believed that only a member of the royal family could become king. In these circumstances of a rebellion against a bad king for not observing the value of kingship, the rebellion is in fact waged to defend the kingship against the king. The people have an interest in the values of kingship and fight for them. In short, since the rebellion is to put a prince, who it is hoped will observe these values, in the king's place with the same powers, a rebellion paradoxically supports the kingship. Further, as the leader of a rebellion is a member of the royal family, rebellion confirms that family's title to the kingship. Therefore a prince can invite commoners to rebel and attack his kinsman king without invalidating his family's title. In this situation rulers fear rivals from their own ranks, and not revolutionaries of lower status: and each ruler, in fear of his rivals, has a great interest in conforming to the norms of kingship. Every rebellion therefore is a fight in defence of royalty and kingship: and in this process the hostility of commoners against aristocrats is directed to maintain the rule of the aristocrats, some of whom lead the commoners in revolt.[8]

All these alignments are dramatized in the ritual of rebellion, together with unity against nature and external foes. The king is strengthened as king: and the kingship is strengthened in his person, through association with kingly ancestors, with the queen–mother, and with inherited regalia which symbolize the throne's endurance. But his personal isolation, and the conflicts that centre on him as an individual incumbent of the throne, dramatically express the real alignments of struggles for power in the system, and intensify actions and emotions expressing loyalty. While the king is a minor few ceremonies are performed; the men do not assemble and the songs of hate are not sung. The king's personal position is too weak to allow conflict to express dramatic unity in complementary opposition.

The rebellious structure of this type of stationary society has long been noted by historians.[9] But this ritual of rebellion suggests that we may push the analysis further. The great ceremony which was believed by the Swazi to strengthen and unite their nation achieved these ends not only by massed dances and songs, abstentions and festivities, but also by emphasizing potential rebellion. If this emphasis on potential rebellion in practice made the nation feel united, is it not possible that civil rebellion itself was a source of strength to these systems? I cannot here present all the evidence that supports this bold statement. These were states based on a comparatively simple technology with limited trade connections. They had not goods to raise standards of living and the rich used their wealth largely to feed their dependents and increase their followings. Hence the societies were basically egalitarian. They also lacked a complex integrating economic system to hold them together and their system of communications was poor. Each territorial segment was on the whole economically autonomous and lightly controlled from the centre. The territorial segments therefore developed, on the basis of local loyalties and cohesion, strong tendencies to break out of the national system and set up as independent. But in practice the leaders of these territorial segments often tended to struggle for the kingship, or for power around it, rather than for independence. Periodic civil wars thus strengthened the system by canalizing tendencies

to segment, and by stating that the main goal of leaders was the sacred kingship itself. Hence when a good Zulu king had reigned long and happily two of his sons fought for his heirship during his lifetime. In other nations (e.g. Ankole) there was a free-for-all civil war between potential heirs. In others (e.g. Zulu) a peaceful king would be attacked by someone claiming he was a usurper. Frequently segments of the nation would put forward their own pretenders to the throne, each segment ready to die behind its true prince.

This suggestion is strengthened by the fact that rarely in Africa do we find clear and simple rules indicating a single prince as the true heir. Frequently the rules of succession are in themselves contradictory in that they support different heirs (e.g. Bemba), and more often still they operate uncertainly in practice (e.g. Swazi and Zulu). Almost every succession may raise rival claimants. Or the heir is selected from the royal family (Lozi). Or else the kingship rotates between different houses of the royal dynasty which represent different territorial segments (e.g. Shilluk and Nupe). Another device is the dual monarchy with rule split between two capitals, one of which may be ruled by the king's mother or sister (e.g. Swazi and Lozi). [...] The very structure of kingship thrusts struggles between rival houses, and even civil war, on the nation; and it is an historical fact that these struggles kept component groups of the nation united in conflicting allegiance around the sacred kingship. When a kingdom becomes integrated by a complex economy and rapid communication system, palace intrigues may continue, but the comparatively simple processes of segmentation and rebellion are complicated by class-struggles and tendencies to revolution. The ritual of rebellion ceases to be appropriate or possible.

Certain points remain to tie up our argument. First, why should these ceremonies take place at first-fruits and harvest? I suggest that there are real socially disruptive forces working at this season, which require physiological and psychological study. In all these tribes the first-fruits come after a period of hunger. Quarrels may arise because of the sudden access of energy from the new food, for it is after harvest that wars are waged and internecine fighting breaks out. Even before that the expectation of plenty, especially of beer, undoubtedly leads to a violent outburst of energy in the men, who are quarrelsome at this time. Some people in fact eat the new food before the ceremony is performed. There is, if crops are good – and many South African tribes held no ceremony if they were bad – the jubilant ending of uncertainty. In this background difficulties arise where one family's crops are ripe while another family lives still in hunger. The taboo on early eating allows each family to move into plenty at roughly the same time. The very move into plenty observably produces a charge of emotion in the society. As food supplies are drawn on in these subsistence economies, each household tends to withdraw into itself. After first-fruits and harvest wider social activities are resumed: weddings, dances, beer-drinks, become daily occurrences and attract whole neighbourhoods. This great change in the tempo of social life is accompanied by relief because another year has been passed successfully, while the heavy demands of the ritual, and its slow and ordered release of conflicting emotions and pent-up energy, control behaviour by the programme of ceremonies and dances, stressing unity. All are performed under the sanction of deities or royal ancestors. The Lozi have no hunger period and no great ceremonies. [...]

The women's ceremony, and the king's ceremonies at sowing and first-fruits, are clearly agricultural rituals. Some of the social and psychical tensions they cope with are associated with stages of the agricultural cycle, and the food which it is hoped to produce or which has been produced. But these tensions are related through the ritual actors to the social relationships involved in food production. Agricultural success depends on more than the fickleness of nature, though fickle nature is personified in all the ceremonies. The goddess *Nomkubulwana* is a nature-spirit who may grant good crops or not. She is a nature-spirit for women not only because she is connected with crops, but also because women act as a body in neighbourhoods. These neighbourhoods contain women from many different kinship-groups of diverse ancestral origin, and in any case women cannot approach the ancestors who are primarily held responsible for prosperity. The *Nomkubulwana* ritual is thus a land-cult, and her garden is planted far out in the veld. Like this garden, *Nomkubulwana* herself remains outside the ring of society: she does not enter the ceremony. She is propitiated when the crops begin to grow and when they are attacked by pests, so that the women and their goddess are associated with the most uncertain [...] stages of agriculture, when the women's work is heaviest. Here celebrants reverse their role drastically. This suggests for psychological study the possibility that the marital situation of women produces great strains and that these are never well subdued. They show in women's liability to nervous disorders, hysteria in fear of magical courting by men, and spirit-possession.[10] Sociologically, the ritual and the nature-spirit seem to be related to the potential instability of domestic life and groups.

The first-fruits ceremony is a political ritual organized by the state which is an enduring group: hence it exhibits different beliefs and processes. The Bantu believe that the ancestral spirits of the king are in the end primarily responsible for the weather, and for good crops. These spirits have been in life part of the society, and they are always about certain sacred spots inside men's habitations. They may be wayward in their actions, but they are inside society. The ruling king is their earthly representative who supplicates them in a small-scale ceremony at sowing; and again the first-fruits ceremony to celebrate a successful season (the Zulu called the ceremony 'playing with the king') involves the king and his ancestors. The ritual is organized to exhibit the co-operation and conflict which make up the political system. After this ceremony there follows a series of separate offerings of the first-fruits by the heads of all political groups, down to the homestead, to their own ancestors. But the women make no offering from the harvest to *Nomkubulwana*, who, by another set of beliefs, granted fertility. The period of agricultural certainty – first-fruits and harvest – is thus associated with the king and the political system, for despite the conflicts it contains, from year to year the political system is ordered and stable, beyond the stability of domestic units. However, the uncertainty and wildness of nature may enter into the king's ceremony, though it is the king who personifies these. This happens when, at the climax of the ceremony, he appears dressed in rushes and animal skins – a monster or wild thing (*Silo*) – executing a frenzied inspired dance, since he is not taught it. But even as a nature-spirit, the king is enticed into society by his allied enemies, the princes, until he throws away the past year in a last act of aggression, the casting of a gourd on to the shield of a warrior who will die. Then he becomes king again, but in tabooed seclusion which marks his subordination to the political order. The king is the servant of his subjects. Nature is subdued by the political system, in a ritual which is timed by the surest of natural phenomena – the movements of sun and moon.

Professors Fortes and Evans-Pritchard have suggested a more specifically sociological hypothesis, to explain how social cohesion in the political ceremony is associated with the new crops.[11] If the community is to achieve any of the things it values – good fellowship, children, many cattle, victory, in short, prosperity – it must have food. This is trite and obvious enough. But it is perhaps less obvious to point out that communal interests in the procuring of food may conflict with the interests of particular individuals. For to obtain food, men need land and hoes, and cattle; they need wives to cultivate their gardens. Particular individuals or groups may come into conflict over items of land, or implements, or cattle, or women. Hence individual interests in the food that is so essential stand in a sense in opposition to the community's interests that all its people be prosperous and have plenty of food. Thus elements of conflict arise over the very food that is so desired. These conflicts are settled because in holding and cultivating land, in herding cattle, and in marrying wives, men are involved not only in technical activities, but also in actions which have a legal and moral aspect in associating them with their fellows. They must on the whole fulfil their obligations and respect the rights of others 'or else the material needs of existence could no longer be satisfied. Productive labour would come to a standstill and the society disintegrate.' The greatest common interest is thus in peace and good order, and the observance of Law. Since the political structure guarantees this order and peace, which will allow food to be produced, the political structure becomes associated with food for the community at large. At the ceremony the new food is opened to all the nation, though some subjects may steal it. Thus the political order of interconnected rights and duties is made sacred: and the king who represents that order enters the divine kingship. Perhaps we may now go further, and add that conflicts between individuals and the political order as a whole are demonstrated in the ritual of rebellion. Everyone, including the king himself, is restrained by the order's authority against his individual gratification [...] Even the king approaches the kingship with care: restraints on the Swazi king are very heavy on the day when he is associated most closely with his people. His personal inadequacy and his liability to desecrate the values of kingship are exhibited in the insults he suffers.

Notes

1 Samuelson, R. C. A., *Long, Long Ago* (1929), p. 303.

2 Bryant, A. T., *The Zulu People as they were before the White Man Came* (1949), pp. 662 f.

3 Junod, H. A., *The Life of a South African Tribe* (1927), ii, p. 441.

4 In Chapter XIII, 'The Drama of Kingship', of *An African Aristocracy: Rank among the Swazi* (1947).

5 *Kingship and the Gods*, op. cit., pp. 9 and 51–2 et passim.

6 'Analysis of a Social Situation in Modern Zululand', *Bantu Studies*, xiv, 1 and 2 (March and June, 1940), (reprinted as Rhodes-Livingstone Paper No. 28, 1958).

7 Evans-Pritchard in his Frazer Lecture, 1948, *The Divine Kingship of the Shilluk*, op. cit., at p. 36, has discussed this situation.

8 See my essay 'The Kingdom of the Zulu of South Africa' in *African Political Systems*, and the Editors' *Introduction* at p. 13. See also my 'The Lozi of Barotseland in North-Western Rhodesia', in *Seven Tribes of British Central Africa* (1951).

9 See e.g., Kern, F., *Kingship and Law in the Middle Ages* (1948), translated from the German by S. B. Chrimes.

10 Dr S. Kark, who ran a Health Centre in Southern Natal, reports this in unpublished manuscripts; Lee, S. G., 'Some Zulu Concepts of Psychogenic Disorder', *South African Journal for Social Research* (1951), pp. 9–16; Kohler, M., *The Izangoma Diviners*, Ethnological Publications of the South African Department of Native Affairs, Pretoria: No. 9. (1941); Laubscher, B. J. F., *Sex Custom, and Psychopathology* (1937).

11 'Introduction' to *African Political Systems*.

38

Fighting for the Rainforest
War, Youth and Resources in Sierra Leone

Paul Richards

Small Wars in a Post-Cold War World

As the Cold War nightmare fades more attention is paid to small wars, fought with conventional weapons and for complex local reasons. Africa is scarred by a rash of small wars. Factors internal to the continent are now being offered as explanations for this troublesome rise in modern low-level insurgency. Episodes of apparently bizarre violence in Liberia, Somalia, Rwanda seem to fit a pattern. Surely this is evidence that Africa is, inherently, a wild and dangerous place? Here is violence driven by environmental and cultural imperatives which the West has had no hand in shaping, and now has no responsibility to try and contain. These violent urges are politically meaningless and beyond the scope of conventional diplomacy or conciliation. They are best understood as natural forces – the cultural consequences of a biological tendency by Africans to populate their countries to the point of environmental collapse.

Arguments linking environmental determinism and cultural essentialism are hardly new. They have been regularly refuted by Africanists. Just as quickly they spring up again. The fear of the revenge of the enslaved and dispossessed is hard to quell. Recent versions of the argument offer a new twist by adding modern weapons and the spread of drug culture. Most journalistic reportage and not a little academic writing reflects this view, which is becoming more, not less, influential, obliging their dissenters to return to the fray.

Are these proponents of Malthus-with-guns saying anything new about war and Africa? It is time to submit the environmentalist argument to re-examination, but taking the cheap AK-47s and crack cocaine fully into account. To distinguish this post-Cold War argument from earlier Malthusian visions of African dystopia[1] I propose the label 'New Barbarism'. [This] is a critique of the New Barbarism thesis.

Malthus-with-guns: The New Barbarism Thesis

Three central ideas underpin the New Barbarism thesis [...] in Africa and more widely.

First, cultural identity is an essential and durable, rather than context-dependent, feature of social

From Paul Richards, *Fighting for the Rainforest: War, Youth and Resources in Sierra Leone*, Heinemann (1996), Portsmouth, NH, pp. xiii–xx, xxii–xxv, 25–32, 34, 56–60.

systems. Different cultures and civilizations are thereby prone to clash (Huntington 1993).

Second, war in the post-Cold War world has changed. States have lost the monopoly of military violence once underwritten by nuclear balance of terror. The equipment is cheap, and widely available to religious, cultural and criminal organizations prepared to pursue armed conflict independently of sovereign states and without reference to international opinion [...]

Third, culture clash, resource competition and environmental breakdown provoke a rash of small, localized and essentially uncontrollable armed conflicts. Many are anarchic disputes – i.e. apolitical events indistinguishable from banditry and crime. Insulation rather than intervention is the rational response of the major powers.

This potent mix of ideas was brought together in a book on the Balkan conflict by American journalist Robert Kaplan (Kaplan 1993). [...] When the Yugoslavian state broke up suppressed ethnic and religious animosity broke out like a disease. Kaplan then extended the argument to Africa in an influential essay ('The coming anarchy', *Atlantic Monthly*, February 1994).[2] Violence in Liberia, Rwanda, Somalia is not war in any ordinary political sense of the term (a continuation of diplomacy by other means, as Clausewitz viewed it [...]). Far from fully understood even by the participants themselves, these conflicts, in Kaplan's eyes, were clear evidence of Africa's gathering environmental crisis. Maintaining peace in such conditions is beyond the scope of regular diplomacy or peace-keeping intervention. [...]

New Barbarism in Sierra Leone?

Kaplan's thesis has proved extraordinarily influential in the U.S. His article was faxed to every American embassy in Africa, and has undoubtedly influenced U.S. policy. This is less because of the cogency of thought and quality of evidence, than because of the way Kaplan tapped into broader currents of thinking.

Kaplan's essay begins and ends in the small West African country of Sierra Leone. Arguably the oldest modern state in West Africa (with a constitutional history dating back to 1787) Sierra Leone first experienced war in 1991 when a small

rebellion took shape on the eastern border with Liberia, launched from territory controlled by one of the factions fighting the Liberian civil war. Lacking any Cold War roots, or evident religious or ethnic dimensions, but possessing a high quotient of apparently bizarre and random acts of violence, many perpetrated by children, this conflict is cited by Kaplan as a prime instance of the New Barbarism.

By the time Kaplan visited Sierra Leone (in late 1993) government troops maintained only tenuous control of large parts of forested eastern and southern Sierra Leone. What had caused anarchy to spread so quickly through these West African forests? According to Kaplan, the war was a product of social breakdown caused by population pressure and environmental collapse.

Throughout West Africa, drought and land hunger (he argues) had driven young people to the teeming and only superficially modernized shanty-town suburbs of the coastal cities. Spun off from a failing traditional society, these criminally-inclined young migrants were 'loose molecules in a very unstable social fluid' (Kaplan 1994). The perpetrators of the violence in eastern and southern Sierra Leone lacked any clear political purpose. They were better pictured as criminals and bandits. Reverting to old, superstition-riddled, forms of violence, these gangs of youngsters, roaming the Sierra Leone countryside, armed with AK-47s and killing for scraps, are likened by Kaplan to the hungry mercenary hordes ravaging seventeenth-century Germany prior to the ending of the Thirty Years War.

Testing New Barbarism

[...] New Barbarism's essential propositions are found wanting in several major respects.

Although the local history of resource acquisition is relevant to understanding the war there is no run-away environmental crisis in Sierra Leone. Young people caught up in the dispute specifically point to political failures as a cause of the war, and deny the relevance of Malthusian factors. The data on population trends and land resources confirm the essential soundness of this point of view.

Whereas it is true that the war in Sierra Leone is a terror war, and involves horrifying acts of brutality against defenceless civilians, this sad fact cannot in any way be taken to prove a reversion to some kind of essential African savagery. Terror is *supposed* to unsettle its victims. The confused accounts of terrorized victims of violence do not constitute evidence of the irrationality of violence. Rather they show the opposite – that the tactics have been fully effective in disorientating, traumatizing and demoralizing victims of violence. In short, they are devilishly well-calculated. [...]

Lacking heavy weapons, both rebels and government forces have made extensive use of cultural resources in their campaigns. In particular, the rebels deploy forest knowledge in both practical and symbolic ways to make converts to their cause and demoralize opponents. By those cultural plays they manifest a distinctly 'post-modern' awareness of modern media and the propaganda opportunities they provide. The skills on view are those of the hybrid and globalized world of Atlantic commerce rather than the 'traditional' subsistence worlds of the African bush.

New Barbarism pays scant regard to the insurgents' own claims concerning the purpose of their movement (that they took up arms to fight for multi-party democracy and against state corruption). Kaplan (1994) prefers instead to endorse a view widespread among capital city elites and in diplomatic circles at the time of his visit, but now known to be incorrect, that the rebel movement had been destroyed and the violence was exclusively the work of bandits and military splinter groups. [...] In fact the war has a clear political context, and the belligerents have perfectly rational political aims, however difficult it may be to justify the levels of violence they employ in pursuit of these aims. The rebel leadership has a clear political vision of a reformed and accountable state. Failure to communicate that vision owes more to the poverty, incompetence, and sectarian isolation of the movement than to any inherent trend towards anarchy in today's devastated West African forests.

As in any war opportunist individuals and groups muddy the waters with atrocities and looting. But these opportunist acts by themselves are insufficient to explain the continuation of the conflict. The war in Sierra Leone drags on essentially because there are social factors feeding the conflict, and

because the main rebel group feels it has not yet had a chance to get its political point of view across, and that it needs to do so to honour activists who died in its cause.

Contra New Barbarism the violence of the Sierra Leone conflict is shown to be moored, culturally, in the hybrid Atlantic world of international commerce in which, over many years, Europeans and Americans have played a prominent and often violent part. Although a small and highly localized conflict, the war has a global range of symbolic and dramaturgical reference. It deserves to be regarded as one of the world's first truly post-Cold War conflicts, since it owes little if anything to Super Power rivalry, and everything to the media flows and cultural hybridizations that make up globalized modernity (cf. Waters 1995). The challenge is to understand that 'we' and 'they' have made this bungled world of Atlantic-edge rain-forest-cloaked violence together. In a world of globalization disengagement from Africa's violence is no longer an option.

Fighting for the Rain Forest: A Crisis of the Patrimonial State

If we reject New Barbarism what better explanations of the war in Sierra Leone might be offered?

Long-term patterns of 'primitive accumulation' of forest and mineral resources in Sierra Leone have fed a modern politics dominated by patrimonial redistribution (Rono 1995, Kpundeh 1995). The political elite builds support through distributing resources on a personal basis to followers. Relatively few resources are distributed according to principles of bureaucratic rationality or accountability. In the 1980s, through a combination of circumstances, the resources available for patrimonial redistribution in Sierra Leone went into sharp decline, a decline exacerbated by the ending of the Cold War and a general reduction and tightening up of overseas aid budgets. This crisis has tested the loyalty of the younger generation in particular. Meanwhile, as a result of political machinations and resource shortages the state's capacity to control some of its peripheral regions was weakened. The Liberian border region was a particular casualty of this aspect of state recession, allowing dissidents to enter the country from Liberia and deploy methods of violent social destabilization invented in the course of the Liberian civil war (1989–96). The Sierra Leone war [...] is a product of this protracted, post-colonial, crisis of patrimonialism.

[...]

A War More Barbaric Than Most?

The Sierra Leone insurgency began on 23 March 1991 (Musa and Musa 1993), Seeking to overthrow the patrimonial rule of President Joseph Saidu Momoh and the All People's Congress (APC) a small and lightly armed rebel force fought for a year in the forested districts of eastern and southern Sierra Leone before Momoh and the APC were ousted in a coup by junior officers disenchanted by government lack of support for their efforts in confronting the rebels.

Rebel violence in the first phase of the war fell mainly upon unarmed villagers, and civilian support for the young officers' regime, the National Provisional Ruling Council (NPRC), was based on a promise to the victims of the violence to bring the war to a brisk conclusion.

After the NPRC coup fighting between government troops and rebels resumed. The rebels suffered major losses but vowed to fight on. Dissension within the army gave them the chance to counter-attack. Having initially taken up arms to oust the APC, the rebels justified further extension of the long-drawn-out bush war with the claim that the NPRC regime, after a bright start, had reverted to the patrimonial politics of the APC. By January 1995 the insurgents were within sight of the capital Freetown. Suffering subsequent reverses they declared an interest in peace negotiations. The first tentative contacts concerning a peace process took place during the latter half of 1995, but without any obvious reduction in the intensity of the fighting.

The rebel group appears to be remarkably small. It is run by a War Council of 21 people, and has several thousand young members. It has little if any territorial base, and few settlements of any size under its firm control, apart from its forest camps. It obtains resources by mining diamonds in the forest and capturing food and weapons, mainly from NPRC sources. It builds membership by conscription of young people it judges amenable to its political message.

Most of these youngsters, in fact, have little option about whether or not they join. Terrorized in the process of capture they are later treated generously by the rebels and the secrets of the movement are revealed. This process amounts to a type of initiation, for several centuries a near-universal feature of forest society in the western half of West Africa. Initiation separates young people from their immediate family and builds adult loyalties to a wider society.[3]

In a country of c. 4 million, an estimated 15,000 civilians have been killed and more than 40 per cent of the total population displaced during five years of war. Local communities are still ruled by widely-respected Paramount Chiefs. It is some measure of the dislocation caused by the conflict that half the country's Paramount Chiefs are displaced, living in Freetown or one of the three main provincial towns (Bo, Kenema and Makeni). Manifestly not an ethnic conflict, and therefore failing to fit the main international media 'slot' reserved for the reporting of African war, the Sierra Leone insurgency has had little coverage apart from incidents involving the capture of foreign hostages by the rebels.

Superficially, some of the facts of the war seem to fit the theory of New Barbarism. Fighting takes place mainly by means of hit-and-run raids and ambushes in thickly forested country. With little hardware, the rebels have to rely upon bushcraft, misinformation and terror tactics to control villagers and demoralize the better-armed government troops. This leads them into actions (beheading chiefs, cutting the hands and fingers off villagers) that cause outsiders to assume a wanton and mindless violence. Further reflection shows it to be nothing of the sort.

Take, for instance, a spate of incidents in villages between Bo and Moyamba in September–October 1995 in which rebels cut off the hands of village women. What clearer instance could there be of a reversion to primitive barbarity? Images flood into the mind of hands cut off for the manufacture of magic potions.

But behind this savage series of incidents lay, in fact, a set of simple strategic calculations. The insurgent movement spreads by capturing young people. Short of food in the pre-harvest period, some captives, irrespective of the risks, sought to defy the movement and return to their villages where the early harvest was about to commence. How could the rebels prevent such defections? By stopping the harvest. When the news of rebel amputations spread in central Sierra Leone (the rice granary of the war-affected region) few women were prepared to venture out into the fields. The harvest ceased. [...]

Conflict in Sierra Leone is no exception to the generalization that modern warfare targets civilians as well as enlisted troops. Whether the rebels in Sierra Leone were in any way justified in their decision to take up violence is highly debatable. The consequences have been tragic. But their actions are not the actions of madmen or mindless savages. Once a decision to resort to violence had been taken, hand cutting, throat slitting and other acts of terror became rational ways of achieving intended strategic outcomes. There is little if any analytical value, it seems to me, in distinguishing between cheap war based on killing with knives and cutlasses, and expensive wars in which civilians are maimed or destroyed with sophisticated laser-guided weapons. All war is terrible. It makes no sense to call one kind of war 'barbaric' when all that is meant is that it is cheap.

Some Theoretical Considerations

[...]

War as performance
War, and coping with war, are matters of performance. The apparently pointless bitterness of a 'rebellion without cause' (Bradbury 1995) makes considerable sense as a drama of state recession, renewal and revenge. Performance theory concerns itself with the stage management of events. Applied to war, performance theory tries to understand how people make power through managing violence and terror as expressive resources.

A dramaturgical emphasis in analysis makes it possible, for example, to consider the Sierra Leone insurgents in terms of a rationalistic framework proposed by Lipsedge and Littlewood (1996) for the study of domestic sieges – violent events also commonly seen as crazy or incomprehensible.

Sieges typically involve an estranged father, distraught at being separated from children he loves, seizing them and threatening to kill them. This apparent contradiction generally leads to the conclusion that hostage takers are 'mad'. Lipsedge and Littlewood propose, however, that the rationality of the domestic siege lies in its coherence as drama. Sieges are events 'staged' in such a way as to attract wider media interest. Once media exposure is gained, the event then demands of onlookers that they ponder the question 'what external events have driven me, a reasonable person, to such despair, that I am prepared to behave like a lunatic, and threaten to kill my own children?'

The Sierra Leone rebels indulged in a spate of (international) hostage taking in 1994–5. Possession of the hostages got the rebel movement TV exposure internationally. Releasing the hostages, rebel leader Foday Sankoh, a professional photographer as well as ex-soldier, and skilled, therefore, in *representation*, as well as trained in the practicalities of violence, explained that they had been seized 'for their own protection', since Sierra Leone was now such a dangerous place. This sounds like poor logic, since the rebels were the ones making the country so dangerous, but makes dramaturgical sense. Sankoh was, it seems, 'posing' his struggle in siege-like terms to bring out the extent to which 'reasonable people' had turned to desperate measures, faced with the social dereliction caused by the extensive engagement, over many years, of patrimonial politicians and business elites in international commerce in gold, slaves, diamonds and tropical forest products.

Insurgents in Sierra Leone also draw upon more local dramaturgical resources, especially those associated with initiation. In Sierra Leone, the masked 'devil' is an expression of the secret energy of societies gathered together in this way. The young initiates captured by the rebels return to the countryside which they lay waste as 'bush devils'. Their terror campaign is more than *representation* of a crisis, therefore. It is an attempt *to mobilize power* through the expression of 'war as masquerade'. Theories of performance provide clues to the essential dramaturgical coherence, and powerfulness, of what it is the insurgents are trying to achieve.

War as discourse

Globalization Theory argues that the modern world is constructed as much from symbolic exchanges as from material transactions (Waters 1995). The worlds beyond the periphery of a patrimonial state in crisis are cut off, to greater or lesser extent, from regular material transactions the rest of us take for granted. In practical terms 'state collapse' means collapse of roads and other communications leading into these marginal regions. For regions 'beyond the pale' symbolic transactions assume a larger than normal significance in the attempt to re-establish contact with the wider world.

When insurgents entered Sierra Leone in 1991 they demanded an international press conference to talk to an international audience. They lacked sponsors and equipment, and the world ignored them. Once they had seized their first international hostages, outsiders were forced to try and locate the rebels and find out what they wanted. When negotiations opened, one demand of the insurgents (though not met) was for an international satellite phone link, to make up for lost time in promoting their cause. Subsequently (as noted) the rebels received TV coverage as part of a deal to recover the hostages. [...]

War itself is a type of text – a violent attempt to 'tell a story' or to 'cut in on the conversation' of others from whose company the belligerents feel excluded. [...]

Culture theory

Far from isolating countries like Liberia and Sierra Leone from the wider world, as the New Barbarism literature attempts, we should be actively exploring [...] in what ways such national tragedies can be understood from a comparative sociological perspective. Here, it may pay to ponder possible similarities of cultural response to social exclusion evident in the thinking of forest rebels in Sierra Leone and anti-Federal forest survivalists in the United States. Structural position as 'excluded intellectuals' may be the common thread in the hostile response of both groups to perceived corruption at the federal or patrimonial (i.e. hierarchical) metropollion core.

'Radical scepticism', Douglas writes, 'may flourish (and prove highly destructive) where an elite, educated and privileged, is faced with unacceptable arbitrary power, and is helpless to challenge it' (Douglas 1986, p. 80). Excluded intellectuals are irresponsibly destructive. Where hierarchs look to their ancestors, sectarians need martyrs. Sometimes, as in Sierra Leone or Oklahoma City, these mutually reinforcing processes lead to real violence and tragic consequences.

[...] I consider it plausible, and useful, to think of the rebel movement in Sierra Leone as a sectarian intellectual response to the perceived corruption of a metropolitan patrimonial elite. Far from random, the violence is an expression of the social exclusion of a group of educated exiles determined to force patrons 'in town' to imagine what life is like for the young minds stranded 'in the bush'. [...]

Understanding the RUF: Excluded Intellectuals?

[...]

The RUF when it first appeared was a small group of exiles, with a common experience of being driven to the margins of Sierra Leonean society and beyond by experiences under the All People's Congress government of Siaka Stevens (1968–85). Living as exiles in Liberia when the civil war started, several preferred to accept the chance to fight their way back home than remain in Liberia as refugees. [...]

RUF leader Foday Sabana Sankoh, a native of Magburaka in Tonkolili District, was once a corporal in the signals section in the Sierra Leone army. Cashiered and jailed for seven years under suspicion of involvement in a coup plot against Siaka Stevens in 1971, Sankoh set up, on release, a photographic business run from a shed in front of the Public Works Compound in Bo. He later shifted to the diamond districts, basing himself in Segbwema, Kailahun District, for several years.

During his Segbwema period Sankoh was noted for trekking the back paths leading from bush-mining camp to camp, rather than using the roads and public transport. Living the reality of state recession in Kailahun he would have acquired a good working knowledge of both the forested terrain and the lifestyle and political sentiments of the diamond tributors of this border region so crucial to the economic fortunes of the state. Senior figures in government, army and civil service had interests in small diamond mining operations and logging operations in the border zone. Sponsorship ties linking the diamond diggers of the region to the Freetown political elite, smuggling, and arbitrary acts of the 'anti-smuggling' services are hardly likely to have escaped the notice of this itinerant recorder of day-to-day life as he scoured the nooks and crannies of the border zone in embittered internal exile.

Other figures in the RUF share Sankoh's background (rustication from a state institution under the APC). Philip Palmer, a combatant in the Pujohun sector in 1991, identified himself to eye-witnesses as a Liberian-based exile radicalized by the APC response to student protests against Siaka Stevens. One of the RUF's senior military figures, ex-Lieutenant James Massally, was jailed for his alleged involvement in the 1971 coup plot. Some RUF recruits worked as rural teachers prior to the rebellion. Some graduates enter teaching only for lack of other preferment and see a rural secondary school as a punishment posting. Other recruits were rusticated student protesters or workers living on, unemployed, in the environs of the institutions from which they had been sacked. Early attacks on the Teachers' College at Bunumbu in Kailahun District may have provided a small 'crop' of such disgruntled educators. Later raids on Njala University College and the Sierra Rutile mine at Mobimbi (both in southern Sierra Leone) seem to have been spurred by plans to 'liberate' other 'internal' exiles.

Once rescued, activists seemingly plan revenge against the institution that has shamed them. One attack on Njala in 1995 targeted only the university records for destruction. Leaders of the attack identified themselves as sent-down former students. They may have been seeking to disguise the fact that they never graduated. The university authorities were warned not to try to re-open the institution while 'the war of liberation' continued.

Only at first sight do these revenge-inspired attacks seem pointless. An attack on the rutile mine at Mobimbi in October 1995 left many buildings burnt. The rutile and bauxite mines, among the very few large-scale solvent ventures in the Sierra Leone countryside, were frequently milked on an *ad hoc* basis by government ministers, unable to persuade the government to negotiate proper mining agreements, fair to all parties.[4] In periods of economic crisis mine managements sometimes provided the then APC regime with the foreign exchange or fuel oil necessary to keep the country running on a week-to-week basis. Such deals frequently turned out to have been to the private advantage of the politicians in question.[5]

The NPRC had promised democracy, but a democratically elected leader would be no guarantee that such patrimonial abuses might not return. The attack on the mine was prefaced by a message to the NPRC government that there would be no mine left for any incoming, democratically elected, president 'to enjoy'.

The abuses thus being flagged are real. It is the rebel response that provokes amazement. Why destroy? Why not take over the facilities and run them in the insurgent interest? Multinational miners in Africa are political realists and would soon come to terms.

What I want to suggest is that these dramatic gestures of protest are a typical academic response. They serve to illuminate (in flames, as it were) widespread patrimonial abuses linked to mining and other forms of resource appropriation in the Sierra Leone countryside in which national political elites and international interests appear to have connived. The point about such protest is that it makes satisfying sense on paper, or in the mind. It is the lack of regard for the practical consequences in a country of such great poverty that is so shocking. It is not at all clear how the RUF would propose running the country without mining revenues, or do they believe in their heart-of-hearts that they will never come to power? This is why it seems Mary Douglas (1986) may be right. The irresponsible destructiveness of excluded intellectual elites can be very great. What could be a more perfect illustration of her point than to attack a university, not for loot, but to destroy its record system?

According to the New Barbarism thesis, the attacks just described are evidence that a mindless or criminal element is at work in Sierra Leone; just the opposite interpretation is offered here. This is not barbarism, but the product of the intellectual anger of an excluded educated elite. [...]

Capture: Why the Rebellion Expands

The RUF has expanded through capturing the kind of young people it considers potential recruits to its cause. There is a calculated judgement that dislocated youths in mining-wrecked countryside will come to see the world like the RUF, even when forced to join the movement against their will. But how is this loyalty induced?

In the short term fear must be a factor – especially fear of what government forces will do to any young person suspected of association with the movement, if re-captured. Certainly, summary execution of rebel suspects (as carefully documented by Amnesty international since 1992) has served as a powerful aid to the RUF's retention of its captive youngsters (Amnesty International 1992, 1993).

But the rebels have more positive inducements to loyalty as well. Some are straightforwardly material. One young girl, asked why she came to identify with the people who had seized her from her home, answered frankly: 'they offered me a choice of shoes and dresses – I never had decent shoes before.'

It is also important to realize that the rebels consider their business camps an alternative to the failed schooling found in the wider society. State recession means dysfunctional schooling. Teachers' salaries, pittances at best, were paid late or not at all. Conditions worsened under the financial austerity programmes imposed on the country by the IMF and World Bank from 1977 onwards. Rural teachers' salaries were paid last of all. I have vivid memories of the time and money rural teachers in schools around Gola Forest wasted in journeys to the provincial headquarters in Kenema to enquire whether long back-dated pay had yet arrived. Sometimes they could only obtain amounts 'on account' by paying heavy 'interest' to the authorities ('bribes' by any other name).[6]

For many seized youngsters in the diamond districts functional schooling had broken down long before the RUF arrived. The rebellion was a chance to resume their education. Captives report being schooled in RUF camps, using fragments and scraps of revolutionary texts for books, and receiving a good basic training in the arts of bush warfare. Many captive children adapt quickly,[7]

and exult in new-found skills, and the chance, perhaps for the first time in their lives, to show what they can do. Stood-down boy soldiers in Liberia have spoken longingly of their guns not as weapons of destruction but as being the first piece of modern kit they have ever known how to handle (Hodges 1992).

The RUF is clearly limited in the weapons at its command (being restricted mainly to supplies obtained through ambush of, or deals with, government troops or troops in neighbouring countries) and, boy-scout-like, the youngsters in the movement carve wooden replicas to create the impression of greater strength than they actually possess. [...]

Cultural Resonances:
Camps and Initiation

The RUF knows how to manipulate to its advantage the cultural 'infrastructure' of rural life in Sierra Leone. Two aspects require brief introduction here – forest camps and initiation.

The RUF believes it is fighting to save Sierra Leonean society from itself. Cut off from that society by exile, and five years of forest-based combat, the leadership sees devastation all around it. This vision, reinforced by 'sobels' and bandits, is a self-fulfilling prophecy. Attacks on civilians and atrocities against women 'prove' that wider society is as the RUF believes it to be – dangerous and corrupt. The burning of villages and the killing of villagers make concrete the assertion that captives have no home to return to, at least until larger victory is won. Even the international hostages were told that their capture was necessary 'for their safety'. As in the chaotic days of the overseas slave trade, security is to be found in isolated camps deep inside the forest.

The main idiom of transition from childhood to adulthood in forest society is that of initiation, followed by instruction in adult ways in the 'bush school'. The Poro Society 'devil' comes to town to seize young boys from their mothers. In the colonial period, before the value of Western education was fully appreciated, the state, in effect, did the same thing when seeking to fill its schools. But now the educational 'devil' no longer calls. In a state near to collapse, with teachers no longer regularly paid, the RUF 'devil' steps into the breach.

With initiation already deeply etched in the lives of many young people in the Upper Guinean forests, capture may serve to recapitulate aspects of the experience. Villagers apply an initiation 'model' to the disaster that has befallen them; they perceive that their children have been taken from them by force (as in initiation) and turned into alien creatures by the power of rebel magic. Offered rudimentary schooling in the bush, and instruction in skills of guerrilla warfare, many captives quickly readjust to their lot.

[...]

The Leopard Has Come to Town: The Dramaturgy of Forest War

Sierra Leone is a compact ring of forested or once-forested territory gathered around a coastal primate city, Freetown, containing today about 20–25 per cent of the country's total population. [...] The country has a long history of violent opposition between 'bush' (the forest) and 'town' (established patrimonial authority linked to overseas trade).

Spreading from a heavily forested periphery from which a weakened patrimonial state was seen to be withdrawing, the present war [...] is seen by protagonists [...] as a crisis of 'bush' come to 'town' (or as a saying puts it, *lepet don kam na ton* – 'the leopard has entered the city'). The leopard is a long-standing and powerful symbol of malign, and illegitimate, political agency in Sierra Leonean life. According to one local theory it is the animal form assumed by weakened political elites seeking, by stealth, to rebuild their political fortunes (Richards 1993). The rebel leadership stalks the enfeebled patrimonial state to reverse and revenge its earlier banishment from political light into outer forested darkness.

But the crisis of bush come to town has international resonances as well. Sierra Leone was one of the first places where the Western world came into exploitative contact with the great African rain forest.

[...] The Sierra Leone river was an early, and late, centre for the slave trade, based on the fort at Bunce Island. [...] A tradition of meeting Atlantic maritime service needs survived until very recently. Freetown harbour was a major staging post for

Allied forces fighting in North Africa during the Second World War. [...] In a last gasp of empire, Freetown harbour was used for bunkering purposes by the British Falklands fleet.

Shaped by its involvement in the violence-laden Atlantic world, Sierra Leone has also felt the impress of comparably violent attacks on local forest resources. [...]

By their actions the rebels make a rhetorical point deeply rooted in this troubled history of resource extraction. First you used our harbour and took us as slaves, and then you took our timber, ivory and valuable mineral resources. But now we have been dumped in the darkness of the bush. This darkness comprises both reduction in the educational opportunity for which the country has long been famous, and the physical darkness that frequently afflicted the two rural higher educational establishments from which some of the rebel leadership comes.

The insurgents use the forest, then, as a stage on which to enact a drama of state recession. But with their stage opening directly onto the Atlantic world the rebels hoped that this might make the drama visible even to the international community as far away as New York and London. [...]

The Political Culture of Patrimonial Decline

Youth culture in Sierra Leone reflects some of these dilemmas of state recession. This is seen especially clearly in interpretations of the Rambo film *First Blood*, viewed locally as a charter for self-empowerment under conditions of patrimonial decline. The rebels have tried to build on this legacy. [...]

Journalistic comment on Sierra Leone, and more so on Liberia, has regularly drawn attention to the carnival-like elements of insurgency in the region, implicitly contrasting, so Mary Moran (1994) has argued, the bizarre battle costumes of young fighters in Liberia (Kung Fu kit, horror comic masks, young men setting off for battle in women's dresses and underwear) with the clean, orderly, rationalistic uniforms and battle order of the allied forces in the Gulf War, the media-oriented show-case for modern combat.

Moran interprets these odd costumes, convincingly, as youthful *jeux d'ésprit* intended to 'attack' the values of the Liberian regime of Samuel Doe. Doe was seen by his opponents, she argues, as the epitome of the ignorant, brutal rank-and-file soldiery whose day-to-day petty brutality served to keep many African post-colonial regimes in power. The crossdressing, horror-comic-helmeted, young teenage rebel fighter was, by contrast, brilliantly recapitualting an inventive pre-colonial tradition, where dress served to disguise and protect, rather than express, the true character of the warrior. But here we have no simple reversion to the African past. These are post-modern costumes, straight from Hong Kong or an American joke shop catalogue, made mainly from that deeply traditional African raw material – plastic.

As Kellie Conteh's remarks suggest, the carnival element is not without tactical purpose. But perhaps at the same time the costumes are also close in spirit to the international Saturday Night finery of the diamond digger 'on the town' (flares and platform-soled shoes were especial 1970s favourites). The imprecatory graffiti the RUF leave behind in sacked villages relate to the rich stock of slogans adorning the shutters and lintels of the village rooms of school-educated young people throughout rural Sierra Leone. These graffiti are often ironic commentary on the strange juxtapositions of the local and global, as experienced by those at the bottom of the social pile.

[…]

All warfare has its expressive dimensions. In low-intensity warfare, in poor countries like Sierra Leone, this expressive dimension may be highly visible, for want of more practically functional kit. It deserves proper exegesis, not the 'isn't this bizarre' dismissal it receives in the international media.

[…] The complaint that the Sierra Leone rebels have never articulated their political demands is true only to the extent that the intended audience continues to ignore the expressive poses they strike through their destructive actions.

One of these poses seems to grow out of a widespread interpretation young people in Sierra Leone have made of the 1982 Rambo film, *First Blood*.

[…]

Video has had a wide impact in the forested diamond districts of Sierra Leone, and this little drama of the social exclusion of the miseducated is often cited by young people as one of their favourite films, or the film they found most enlightening (significantly, the word they most often use in this context is 'educative'). *First Blood* has several times been compared, by informants, to the impact of studying Shakespeare's *Macbeth* at school. *Macbeth* strips the mask of public service from politics to reveal naked personal ambition beneath. The point that strikes home about Rambo is social exclusion. Ejected from town by the corrupt and comfortable forces of law and order, with only his wits for protection, Rambo is on his own in the forest. The *result* of social exclusion, the film seems to say, is unconstrained violence. That violence is cathartic, since it serves to wake up society at large to the neglected cleverness of youth. The film speaks eloquently to young people in Sierra Leone fearing a collapse of patrimonial support in an era of state recession.

Western media critics see little in Rambo beyond 'American Cold War militarism' under the Reagan presidency. […] To Toffler and Toffler (1994) Rambo symbolizes a passing era in which war was based on brawn and bravery not brains. Young Sierra Leoneans […] draw an exactly opposite conclusion from *First Blood*. Rambo suggests that someone young, clever and strong always has a chance to outsmart the well-armod but slow-witted opponent. It is curious to see prophet and disciples at odds over this point. The Tofflers focus on the computer software in 'smart war'; young Sierra Leoneans prefer to note the unbounded potential of the human software.

Rebels in both Liberia and Sierra Leone were alert to the political potential of the Rambo message for their young captives from the beginning. An eye-witness in Gbarnga in the early days of the NPFL reported five generator-powered video parlours running night and day to show such material to young fighters. A young combatant interviewed attests that all factions in Liberia and Sierra Leone have routinely used *First Blood* and similar videos to inspire, to entertain, and perhaps to orient their young captives towards the ambush skills that are the staple fare of this kind of low-level jungle warfare. The Rambo figure frequently appeared in the murals depicting the war painted by urban youths in Sierra Leone following the NPRC coup. Rebels frequently affected Rambo-style headbands. Some adopted the name. One RUF commando in Kailahun – summing up the war in two words – was known as 'Nasty Rambo'.

[…]

Rambo is a trickster figure in classic West African mould. His exploits are close in spirit to those of Musa Wo, the youth trickster of Mende tradition (Cosentino 1989). Musa Wo stories serve to remind Mende elders not to neglect the energy and cunning of the young. Rather the challenge is to harness these skills for the greater social good. The RUF rebellion seems at first to indicate patrimonialism at the end of its tether about to be replaced by the violence of youthful self-empowerment. This would suggest that the RUF's ultimate aim is to replace the patrimonial system with a revolutionary egalitarian system of its own devising. But another interpretation is also possible. The *Schadenfreude* of the young rebels may be equivalent to 'wrecking the police station'. The main aim of the destruction may not be to clear away the old system entirely, but to establish a national debate about a new and fairer patrimonialism. Year Zero or an African Welfare State? – this remains the major unresolved question concerning the war aims of the insurgents in Sierra Leone.

Conclusion

Baffled international reaction to the war in Sierra Leone suggests little understanding of the socio-economic and forest-bound conditions under which the RUF has expanded, or why the movement could continue to survive more or less indefinitely beyond the recession-shrunk edges of a weak state. According to outside assumptions, 'proper' rebellions in Africa should have 'people' (an ethnic identity), contiguous territory under unambiguous control of the rebels, and an announced programme that the world at large can understand. In short, they should be Biafra-like 'mini-states' in waiting. None of these criteria apply to the rebel movement in Sierra Leone, so doubts were entertained about whether it existed at all. External views are still dominated by the notion that African states are arbitrary colonial creations, and that political progress will depend on the emergence of more 'natural' units. Although the RUF might not be out of place as a survivalist movement in Montana, say, there is no place for any such Rambo-style social movement in the mental schemes outsiders have laid down for Africa. If the category does not exist then neither can the phenomenon.

Here, however, a different argument has been proposed. The RUF is much more readily understandable, it is suggested, if the background of state recession is put in place. The movement is a creature of the unresolved contradictions of the post-colonial state. Cold War aid kept alive a façade of international respectability – the official state. Donor pressure in the post-Cold War period has demanded deep reforms – but the reformers are leaning not on a real set of institutions, but on a façade. The real state, much reduced but still fed in significant measure by diamond wealth, remains patrimonial in character. Donors cannot reach that state, and Sierra Leoneans have not yet developed any firm consensus about what they want in its place or how to achieve it.

Notes

1 A word signifying the opposite of Utopia.

2 Tim Wirth, Under-Secretary at the US Department of Global Affairs, faxed Kaplan's article to every US embassy around the world (Bradshaw 1996). According to the same source the article 'so rattled top officials at the United Nations that they called a confidential meeting to discuss its implications'.

3 Capture by the rebels, by contrast, seems to induce the apparently paradoxical loyalties between hostage and captor known in Western psychiatric models as the Stockholm Syndrome.

4 The management of the rutile mine had been anxious that government should replace these informal arrangements with an up-dated mining act and transparent

royalty agreements fair both to government and mining interests. There was much foot-dragging on the government side, since the existing *ad hoc* arrangements were advantageously opaque.

5   A documentary made for BBC TV in 1991 on the environmental consequences of mining found plenty of local voices ready to testify against the companies. But the programme makers failed to press the question of the government's role in such abuses. The documentary was seen on video throughout the country.

6   One of the leading figures in the RUF in 1995, Fayia Musa, a Njala graduate in agriculture and participant in student protests against Siaka Stevens in 1977, was recruited in 1991 while working as a secondary school teacher under these kinds of conditions in isolated Kallahun District.

7   It is relevant to note what psychiatrists term the Stockholm Syndrome. This is the condition in which terrified captives subsequently identify with their captors – perhaps because to their surprise they are treated with respect, even kindness – and become loyal supporters of the hostage-takers' cause. A famous example was the case of an American newspaper heiress seized by an urban guerrilla group, the Symbionese Liberation Army; the young woman later became an apparently willing participant in the group's armed operations.

References

Amnesty International
1992 *The extrajudicial execution of suspected rebels and collaborators*. London: International Secretariat of Amnesty International, Index AFR 51/02/92.
1993 *Sierra Leone. Prisoners of war? Children detained in barracks and prison*. London: International Secretariat of Amnesty International, Index AFR 51/06/93.

Bradbury, M.
1995 *Rebels without a cause: an exploratory report for CARE Britain on the conflict of Sierra Leone*. London: unpublished mimeo.

Cosentino, D.
1989 'Midnight charters: Musa Wo and the Mende myths of chaos.' In W. Arens & I. Karp, eds., *The creativity of power*. Washington DC: Smithsonian Institution Press.

Douglas, M.
1986 'The social preconditions of radical skepticism'. In J. Law, ed., *Power, action and belief: a new sociology of knowledge*. London: Routledge and Kegan Paul.

Hodges, R.K.
1992 'A view of psychological problems resulting from the Liberian civil conflict and recommendations for counselling and other corrective activities.' Appendix V, in *A Report of the Roundtable Conference on Strategies and Direction for the Reconstruction and Development of Liberia*. The New African Research & Development Agency, Monrovia.

Huntington, S.P.
1993 'The clash of civilizations?' *Foreign Affairs*, 72 (Summer).

Kaplan, R.D.
1993 *Balkan ghosts: a journey through history*. London: Macmillan.

Kaplan, R.D.
1994 'The coming anarchy: how scarcity, crime, overpopulation, and disease are rapidly destroying the social fabric of our planet.' *Atlantic Monthly*, February pp. 44–76.

Kpundeh, S.J.
1995 *Politics and corruption in Africa: a case study of Sierra Leone*. Lanham MD: University Press of America.

Lipsedge, M. and Littlewood, R.
1996 'Psychopathology and its public models: a provisional typology and a dramaturgy of domestic sieges', submitted to *British Journal of Medical Psychology*.

Moran, Mary
1994 'Warriors or soldiers: masculinity and ritual transvestism in the Liberian civil war.' In Constance R. Sutton, ed., *Feminism, nationalism and militarism*, Arlington VA: American Anthropological Association/ Association for Feminist Anthropology.

Musa, S. and Musa, J. Lansana
1993 *The invasion of Sierra Leone: a chronicle of events of a nation under siege*. Washington DC: Sierra Leone Institute for Policy Studies.

Richards, P.
1993 'Natural symbols and natural history: chimpanzees, elephants and experiments in Mende thought.' In K. Milton, ed., *Environmentalism: the view from anthropology*, ASA Monograph 32, London: Routledge.

Toffler, A. and Toffler, H.
1994 *War and anti-war: survival at the dawn of the 21st century*. London: Little, Brown & Co.

Waters, J.
1995 *Globalization*. London: Routledge.

39

Sacrifice as Terror

The Rwandan Genocide of 1994

Christopher C. Taylor

Although much of what I will concern myself with in this paper involves the politics of ethnicity in Rwanda, my major point is that we cannot make sense of the Rwandan tragedy through political and historical analysis alone, although these are certainly necessary. Indeed, something political and historical happened in Rwanda in 1994, but something cultural happened as well. The violence which occurred there, and which continues to a lesser extent today, was not merely symptomatic of a fragmented social order succumbing to externally and internally generated tensions. Beneath the aspect of disorder there lay an eerie order to the violence of 1994 Rwanda. Many of the actions followed a cultural patterning, a structured and structuring logic, as individual Rwandans lashed out against a perceived internal other that threatened in their imaginations both their personal integrity and the cosmic order of the state. It was overwhelmingly Tutsi who were the sacrificial victims in what in many respects was a massive ritual of purification, a ritual intended to purge the nation of 'obstructing beings' as the threat of obstruction was imagined through a Rwandan

ontology that situates the body politic in analogous relation to the individual human body.

As I will attempt to show […], many of the representations concerning bodily integrity that I encountered in popular medicine during fieldwork in Rwanda in 1983–5, 1987, and 1993–4, emerged in the techniques of physical cruelty employed by Hutu extremists during the genocide. But there was no simple cultural determinism to the Rwandan genocide. I do not advance the argument that the political events of 1994 were in any way caused by these symbols nor by Rwandan 'culture', conceived of in a simplistic and culturalist way in the manner of Goldhagen's controversial analysis of the Nazi genocide (1996). These representations operated as much during times of peace as at times of war. The 'generative schemes' – the logical substrate of oppositions, analogies, and homologies – upon which the representations were based constituted for many Rwandans, a practical, everyday sense of body, self, and others. Because these 'generative schemes' were internalized during early socialization, they took on a nearly unconscious or 'goes without saying' quality

From Christopher C. Taylor, *Sacrifice as Terror: The Rwandan Genocide of 1994*, Berg Publishers (2001), pp. 101–2, 105, 110–14, 117–19, 127–37, 139–40, 142–5, 153–7, 167–8, 174–6.

(Bourdieu, 1990: 67–79). Although many Rwandan social actors embodied this knowledge, they never explicitly verbalized it. It could not, therefore, be ideological in any direct or simple way, despite the fact that Hutu extremists made use of political symbols that bore the imprint of the generative schemes.

The symbolic system I describe here takes root in representations that go back at least to the nineteenth century and elements of it can be discerned in the rituals of Rwandan sacred kingship practised during pre-colonial and early colonial times. In that sense much of this symbolism is relatively old. It must be emphasized, however, that neither the symbolic nor the normative structures of early Rwanda were faithfully and mechanically reproduced during the events of 1994. Clearly both manifest continuity with and divergence from the past. The context in which the symbols appeared was quite contemporary, for the discourse of Hutu ethnic nationalism with its accompanying characteristics of primordialism, biological determinism, essentialism, and racism are nothing if not modern. [...]

Many [...] techniques of cruelty were encountered in Rwanda during the 1994 genocide: impaling, evisceration of pregnant women, forced incest, forced cannibalism of family members. There were also other forms of torture and terror in Rwanda that may or may not have occurred in Burundi: the widespread killing of victims at roadblocks erected on highways, roads, streets, or even on small footpaths; the severing of the Achilles' tendons of human and cattle victims; emasculation of men; and breast oblation of women.

In order to make these forms of violence comprehensible in terms of the local symbolism, It is first necessary to understand, as Pierre Clastres instructs us, that social systems inscribe 'law' onto the bodies of their subjects (1974). Occasionally physical torture is an integral part of the ritual process intended to inculcate society's norms and values. Using *The Penal Colony* by way of illustration Clastres states, 'Here Kafka designates the body as a writing surface, a surface able to receive the law's readable text'. [...] Clastres expands upon this by considering the cognitive role of the body in ritual, 'The body mediates in the acquisition of knowledge; this knowledge inscribes itself upon the body'

[1974: 154]. And ritual, Clastres emphasizes, involves the mnemonics of ordeal and pain, '[...] society prints its mark on the body of its youth. [...] The mark acts as an obstacle to forgetting; the body carries the traces of a memory printed upon it; *the body is a memory*' [1974: 156].

[...]

Rwandan Symbolism and the Body

[...] The Rwandan body is, following Clastres, an imprinted body – imprinted with the condensed memories of history. Following Kapferer, it is only through myth and symbol that we can grasp the logic of these condensed memories and their significance to Rwandan Hutu nationalism because the latter derived much of its passionate force from a mythic logic constitutive of being and personhood:

> Broadly, the legitimating and emotional force of myth is not in the events as such but in the logic that conditions their significance. This is so when the logic is also vital in the way human actors are culturally given to constituting a self in the everyday routine world and move out toward others in that world. Mythic reality is mediated by human beings into the worlds in which they live. Where human beings recognize the argument of mythic reality as corresponding to their own personal constitutions – their orientation within and movement through reality – so myth gathers force and can come to be seen as embodying ultimate truth. Myth so enlivened, I suggest, can become imbued with commanding power, binding human actors to the logical movement of its scheme. In this sense, myth is not subordinated to the interests of the individual or group but can itself have motive force. It comes to define significant experience in the world, experience which in its significance is also conceived of as intrinsic to the constitution of the person. By virtue of the fact that myth engages a reasoning which is also integral to everyday realities, part of the taken-for-granted or 'habitus' [Bourdieu, 1977] of the mundane world, myth can charge the emotions and fire the passions. (Kapferer, 1988: 46–7)

Nevertheless, in order to understand these mythic and pre-reflective dimensions of ontology, we need to move beyond Kapferer's and Dumont's categories of 'egalitarian and individualistic' versus 'hierarchical and encompassing'. We need to shift analysis to an almost 'molecular' level and to consider the structures of thought that underlie the construction of the moral person in Rwanda and that constitute a specific practical logic of being in the world. These structures must be seen both in their formalist dimension and in specific instances of their use and enactment in everyday social life. Proceeding in this fashion we may then be able to appreciate that, lurking beneath the extraordinary events and violence of the genocide, one perceives the logic of ordinary sociality.

Much of this ordinary, practical logic can be discerned in Rwandan practices related to the body and aimed at maintaining it or restoring it to health and integrity. From Rwandan popular medical practices that I observed during the 1980s, I have advanced the hypothesis elsewhere that a root metaphor underlies conceptualizations of the body (Taylor, 1992). Basically these conceptualizations are characterized by an opposition between orderly states of humoral and other flows to disorderly ones. [...] Analogies are constructed that take this opposition as their base and then relate bodily processes to those of social and natural life. In the unfolding of human and natural events, flow/blockage symbolism mediates between physiological, sociological, and cosmological levels of causality. Popular healing aims at restoring bodily flows that have been perturbed by human negligence and malevolence. Bodily fluids such as blood, semen, breast milk, and menstrual blood are a recurrent concern as is the passage of aliments through the digestive tract. [...] Pathological states are characterized by obstructed or excessive flows and perturbations of this sort may signify illness, diminished fertility, or death.

[...]

Popular Medicine

During my fieldwork in Rwanda in the 1980s, I found that illnesses were often characterized by perceived irregularities in fluid flows and that these tended to have an alimentary or reproductive symptomatic focus. Concern with ordered flows and their proper embodiment was not just implicated in illness, however; it was also implicated in health. From the very moment when a human being enters this world, these metaphors figure prominently in the cultural construction of the person. Practices associated with childbirth, for example, focus upon certain portions of the child's anatomy. Rural Rwandans that I interviewed both in northern and southern Rwanda during the 1980s recounted versions of the following practices.

After giving birth a new mother is secluded for a period of eight days (today this period is often shorter). On the ninth day, the newborn child is presented to other members of the family and local community for the first time (*gusohora umwana*). This rite of passage can only be performed after the baby's body has been examined and found to be free of anal malformations. People at this occasion receive a meal, especially the children present, who are given favourite foods. These children in turn bestow a nickname on the new-born child, which will remain their name for the child. A few months later, the parents give the child another name, but the children continue to call the infant by their name. The meal given to the children is termed *kurya ubunyano*, which means 'to eat the baby's excrement', for Rwandans say that a tiny quantity of the baby's faecal matter is mixed with the food. This appellation celebrates the fact that the baby's body has been found to be an 'open conduit', an adequate vessel for perpetuating the process of 'flow'. In a sense, the baby's faeces are its first gift and the members of his age class are its first recipients. The children at the ceremony incorporate the child into their group by symbolically ingesting one of his bodily products. Their bestowal of a name upon the infant manifests their acceptance of the child as a social being.

The confirmation of the baby's body as an 'open conduit' is a socially and morally salient image. If the body were 'closed' at the anal end, the baby would still be able to ingest, though not to excrete. The baby would be able to receive, but unable to give up or pass on that which it had received. In effect, its body would be a 'blocked' conduit or pathway. In social terms, such a body would be unable to participate in reciprocity, for while it could receive, it could never give (see also Beidelman, 1982). That gift-giving and reciprocity are important aspects where Rwandan concepts of the moral person are concerned can be discerned

from the term for 'man' in Kinyarwanda –
unugabo – for it is derived from the verb, *kugaba*,
which means 'to give'. The construction of the
moral person among rural Rwandans is contingent
upon the social attestation that the person properly embodies the physiological attributes that
analogically evoke the capacity to reciprocate. This
entails the capacity to ingest and the capacity to
excrete, or, in socio-moral terms, the capacity to
receive and the capacity to give. Consequently,
two portions of the anatomy and their unobstructed connection are at issue: the mouth and
the anus. By analogical extension the concern with
unobstructed connection and unimpeded movement characterizes earlier Rwandan symbolic
thought about the topography of the land, its rivers, roads, and pathways in general.

Illnesses treated by Rwardan popular healers are
often said to be caused by the malevolent actions of
other human beings [...] Sorcerers act upon others
by arresting their flow of generative fluids; they
make women sterile and men impotent. They are
also vampirish, anthropophagic beings who para-
sitically and invisibly suck away the blood and other
vital fluids of their victims. In other instances sorcerers may induce fluids to leave the body in a tor-
rent causing symptoms such as haemorrhagic
menstruation, the vomiting of blood, projectile
vomiting, and violent diarrhoea. There are thus
two basic expressions to symptoms in this model:
'blocked flow' and 'haemorrhagic flow'.

[...]

Close to the southern Rwandan town of Butare,
I elicited the following illness narrative in 1984
from a woman named Verediana who had consulted a healer named Matthew. This narrative is
remarkable in that it illustrates the imagery of perturbed menstruation, perturbed lactation, reduced
fertility, and interruption during the course of a
journey. At the time, however, I had little idea that
the events related in this woman's story were connected in any other way than that which she persistently emphasized: these were persistent
misfortunes whose seriality proved that they were
due to the malevolent influence of sorcerers.

Verediana came to Matthew convinced that she
had been poisoned. This time she had been sick
since July 1983, approximately one year before I
met her. Her primary symptom consisted of

prolonged, abundant menstruation. Although she
had visited a hospital and received injections that
stopped her haemorrhagic periods, she still felt
intensely afraid. She often had trouble eating.
Recently she and her husband had separated.
Immediately after their separation her symptoms
improved, then they began to worsen anew.

According to Verediana, it was the older brother
of her husband and his wife who were her poison-
ers. She believed that this man afflicted others
through the use of malevolent spirits. In previous
years she had been suspicious of another brother
of her husband, a man who was suspected of sorcery and later killed by a group of his neighbours.
She also felt that her husband was in league with
his brothers all of whom were eager to have her
out of the way.

In recounting earlier misfortunes, Verediana
explained that her third pregnancy had been inter-
rupted by the baby's premature birth at eight and
a half months. Somehow the child managed to
survive despite her reduced lactation. Before this
occurrence, she had lost a child. During the troubled events of 1973 – revived tensions between
Hutu and Tutsi and the government's inability to
deal with the situation had led to a military coup –
she was being transported to the hospital in labour.
She recalls that there were numerous roadblocks
and barriers erected on the roads. Despite these
barriers, she finally arrived safely at the hospital.
Her child was born alive, but died the next day.
When I suggested to her that her difficulty in
reaching the hospital may have had more to do
with national events in Rwanda than with actions
of her persecutors, she replied, 'Yes, but why did I
go into labour at just such a time?'

Matthew's diagnosis was that Verediana was suffering from *amageza* affliction, a spirit illness that
can cause excessive blood flow from the vagina.

Notice that in this narrative, Verediana speaks of
disorderly bodily flows: haemorrhagic menstruation, premature birth, and diminished lactation.
She also mentions physical obstructions encountered while *en route* to the hospital in 1973. The
background to this incident, the political events of
1973, constitutes a moment when political relations between Rwanda's two most numerous ethnic groups, the Tutsi and the Hutu, had degenerated
into violence.

Many of the details that Verediana employs in her narrative are images of incompletion, partial arrest, or obstruction: difficulty in eating, diminished lactation, barriers on the roads, a child who dies soon after birth, or a baby who was born prematurely – that is, it left her womb before it had been completely formed by the process of intensified mixing of husband's semen and wife's blood that is supposed to occur during the final stages of pregnancy (*gukurakuza*). Other details are images of excessive flow: menstrual periods that are prolonged and haemorrhagic.

She implicates several domains of problematic social relations that merge together in her story: difficulties with her husband in the context of a polygynous household, relations with her affines, political conflict between Tutsi and Hutu during 1973. This woman's story is remarkable in touching so many levels at once. While the symptomatic focus is her body, an analogy is constantly being drawn between it and other domains of social life: her relationship with her husband, her relationship with her affines, even the relations between Tutsi and Hutu at the national level. Her narrative moves from her body, to the household, to the extended family, to the nation in a seamless series of symbolically logical leaps, for all are posed in terms of bodily and social processes whose movement or obstruction are causes for concern.

[…]

Ritual, Power, and Genocide

Issues of personhood and the body, all of which are generally implicated in nationalistic expressions of violence, do not follow a universal logic. Likewise, this logic is not limited to the common exigency to eliminate as many of the regime's adversaries as possible. State-promoted violence persistently defies the state's attempts to 'rationalize' and 'routinize' it. The psychologically detached, dispassionate torturer does not exist; the acultural torturer who acts independently of the *habitus* that he or she embodies does not exist. Nor can the interposition of killing machines or technology efface what Kafka so perceptively recognized in *The Penal Colony* – that societies 'write' their signatures onto the bodies of their sacrificial victims. As Foucault shows, power constructs human subjects and a certain

homology obtains between the quotidian disciplinary practices employed by social institutions like the army or the school to produce 'decile bodies', and the more coercive measures employed against criminals and enemies of the state (1979). Taking this observation further, one might ask: why the French once used the guillotine, the Spanish the garrotte, the English the rope, while Americans electrocute, gas, or lethally inject those in its midst whom it wishes to obliterate from the moral community? Among the numerous forms of state cruelty that Edward Peters examines in *Torture*, he notes that 'there seem to be culturally-favoured forms of torture in different societies' (1996: 171). Not all methods are used everywhere. In Greece, for example, there appears to be a preference for *falanga* (the beating of the soles of the feet), a torture that is absent from Latin America and where electrical shock predominates. In Rwanda of 1994, torturers manifested a certain proclivity to employ violent methods with specific forms. These forms betrayed a preoccupation with the movement of persons and substances and with the canals, arteries, and conduits along which persons and substances flow: rivers, roadways, pathways, and even the conduits of the human body such as the reproductive and digestive systems.

Controlling Flows

Rivers

In other work I have analysed the ritual and symbolic importance of Rwanda's rivers in light of the generative scheme of flow versus blockage. In the kingship ritual known as the 'path of the watering', for example, the Nyabugogo and Nybarongo Rivers served to revivify the magico-religious potency of the dynasty by recycling and reintegrating the ancestral benevolence of deceased kings (Taylor, 1988). While in the post-colonial Rwandan state these rivers appear to have lost their previous ritual significance, Rwanda's rivers were conscripted into the genocide. This is apparent in statements made by one of the leading proponents of Hutu extremism, Leon Mugesera.

Well in advance of the genocide, Rwandan politicians made statements indicating that elements in the President's entourage were contemplating large-scale massacres of Tutsi. One of the baldest pronouncements in this regard came from the Mugesera, an MRND party leader from the northern prefecture of Gisenyi. On 22 November 1992, Mugesera spoke to party faithful there. It was no accident that a venue in Gisenyi prefecture had been chosen for such an inflammatory speech, because this was the regime's home turf. Gisenyi solidly backed the Rwandan government and its president. For following Habyarimana's coup d'état in 1973, the region always received more than its allotted share of state jobs, secondary school placements, and so forth. Mugesera's words were not falling on deaf ears:

> The opposition parties have plotted with the enemy to make Byumba prefecture fall to the *Inyenzi*. [...] They have plotted to undermine our armed forces. [...] The law is quite clear on this point: 'Any person who is guilty of acts aiming at sapping the morale of the armed forces will be condemned to death.' What are we waiting for? [...] And what about those accomplices (*ibyilso*) here who are sending their children to the RPF? Why are we waiting to get rid of these families? [...] We have to take responsibility into our own hands and wipe out these hoodlums. [...] The fatal mistake we made in 1959 was to let them [the Tutsis] get out. [...] They belong in Ethiopia and we are going to find them a shortcut to get there by throwing them into the Nyabarongo river [which flows northwards]. I must insist on this point. We have to act. Wipe them all out! (Text cited from Prunier, 1995: 171–2)

Shortly after this occurrence, Mugesera repeated the same speech in other Rwandan venues and several violent incidents in which Tutsi were killed can be directly traced to its instigation. Although the then Minister of Justice, Stanislas Mbonampeka, charged Mugesera with inciting racial hatred and gave orders to have him arrested. Mugesera took refuge at an army base where police dared not enter (Prunier, 1995).

In this speech there are several important elements, some of which are more apparent and others less so. That Mugesera is calling for the extermination of all enemies of the regime and especially Tutsi seems clear. The old theme of Tutsi as originators from Ethiopia or 'invaders from Ethiopia' has also resurfaced in this speech.

The theme of Ethiopian origins, used during the late colonial era by apologists of Tutsi domination (cf. Kagame, 1959) has become in the hands of Hutu extremists, a means of denying Tutsi any share in the patrimony of Rwanda. Yet also present in this speech is the first explicit post-colonial reference that I know of, to the Nyabarongo River as a geographic entity with symbolic and political significance. In this speech the Nyabarongo has become the means by which Tutsi shall be removed from Rwanda and retransported to their presumed land of origin. Here, it should be emphasized, the river is again to play an important restorative and purifying role – that of sanitizing the nation of its internal 'foreign' minority. In the months of June, July, and August of 1994, when allegations of a massive genocide in Rwanda were just beginning to be taken seriously in the international media, thousands of bodies began washing up on the shores of Lale Victoria; bodies that had been carried there by the Nybarongo and then the Akagera Rivers.

Rwanda's rivers became part of the genocide by acting as the body politic's organs of elimination, in a sense 'excreting' its hated internal other. It is not much of a leap to infer that Tutsi were thought of as excrement by their persecutors. Other evidence of this is apparent in the fact that many Tutsi were stuffed into latrines after their deaths. Some were even thrown while still alive into latrines; a few of them actually managed to survive and to extricate themselves.

Gusiba Inzira, 'Blocking the path'

Among the accounts of Rwandan refugees that I interviewed in Kenya during the late spring and early summer of 1994, there was persistent mention of barriers and roadblocks. Like Nazi shower rooms in the concentration camps, these were the most frequent loci of execution for Rwanda's Tutsi and Hutu opponents of the regime. Barriers were erected almost ubiquitously and by many different groups. There were roadblocks manned by Rwandan Government Forces, roadblocks of the dreaded *Interahamwe* militia, Rwandan communal police roadblocks, roadblocks set up by neighbourhood protection groups, opportunistic roadblocks erected by groups of criminals, and even occasional roadblocks manned by the Rwandan

Patriotic Front in areas under their control. For people attempting to flee Rwanda, evading these roadblocks was virtually impossible. Moreover, during the genocide, participation in a team manning a roadblock was often a duty imposed upon people by local Rwandan government or military officials.

Several Hutu informants who escaped Rwanda via an overland route explained to me that they had had to traverse hundreds of roadblocks. One informant estimated that he had encountered one barrier per hundred metres in a certain area. Another counted forty-three roadblocks in a ten kilometre stretch on the paved road between Kigali and Gitarama.

Leaving major highways was no solution, for one would encounter barriers erected across dirt reads and footpaths manned by local peasants. At every barrier fleeing people were forced to show their national identity card. Since the ID card bore mention of one's ethnicity, distinguishing Tutsi from Hutu was no problem and almost always, fleeing Tutsi, said to be *ibyitso* or 'traitors', were robbed and killed. When a refugee claimed to have lost the ID card, his or her physical features were relied upon as ethnic identification. It was to one's advantage to look Hutu (to be of moderate height and to have a wide nose).

In order to traverse these barriers, even as a Hutu, it was often necessary to bribe those who were in control. One prosperous Hutu businessman that I had known in Kigali and who surely would have been killed because of his political affiliation (PSD) had he been recognized, told me that he had paid a total of over five thousand dollars in bribes.

Barriers were ritual and liminal spaces where 'obstructing beings' were to be obstructed in their turn and cast out of the nation. The roadblocks were the space both of ritual and of transgression, following an ambivalent logic that Bourdieu underlines, 'the most fundamental ritual actions are in fact denied transgression' (1990: 212). There were scenes of inordinate cruelty. Often the condemned had to pay for the quick death of a bullet, whereas the less fortunate were slashed with machetes or bludgeoned to death with nail-studded clubs. In many cases victims were intentionally maimed but not fully dispatched. Beside the line of motionless corpses awaiting pickup and disposal lay the mortally injured, exposed to the sun and still writhing, as their persecutors sat by calmly, drinking beer.

One refugee who had made it to Kenya by the circuitous route of fleeing southward to Burundi, told me that he and everyone else in his company had been forced to pay an unusual toll at one barrier. Each had been forced to bludgeon a captured Tutsi with a hammer before being allowed to move on. Some in the party had even been made to repeat their blows a second or third time for lack of initial enthusiasm. The reasoning behind this can be clarified by considering the logic of sacrifice and the stigma that inevitably accrues to the sacrificer, the person who actually spills the victim's blood. As Bourdieu puts it:

> The magical protections that are set to work whenever the reproduction of the vital order requires transgression of the limits that are the foundation of that order, especially whenever it is necessary to cut or kill, in short, to interrupt the normal course of life, include a number of ambivalent figures who are all equally despised and feared. (Bourdieu, 1990: 213)

Requiring those who were being spared at the roadblocks to kill a hapless captive may seem unnecessary and purely sadistic, yet it served a useful psychological function from the point of view of the genocide's perpetrators: that of removing the ambivalence of the sacrificial act and the stigma of the sacrificer/executioner by passing these on to everyone. The ritual obfuscated the boundary between 'genocidaires' and those who were otherwise innocent Hutu. Not only were Tutsi and Hutu 'traitors' being killed at the barriers – innocent Hutu were being forced to become morally complicit in the genocide by becoming both 'sacrificer' and 'sacrifier' (Hubert and Mauss, 1964) and shedding Tutsi blood.

[...]

Although the barriers that fleeing Rwandans had to contend with were effective as a means of robbing and killing many of them, roadblocks were next to useless as a means of halting the slow but inexorable RPF advance. In fact, the barriers defied military logic. Proliferated in all directions, they were counterproductive in any tactical sense, for they diverted manpower that could have been deployed in the field and they decentralized resistance to the RPF. Rwandan Government Forces and their associated *Interahamwe* militias were like a headless tentacular beast expending its rage against Tutsi civilians and Hutu moderates while doing little to confront its real adversary. Even from the point of view of the military and militia who controlled the barriers, their utility defied ordinary logic. With roadblocks so closely placed to one another – as close as one hundred meters in some instances – most were clearly redundant. Downstream barriers had little hope of catching people who had not already been stopped and fleeced of their money and belongings.

[…]

If the movement of people could be obstructed with barriers, it could also be hindered by directly attacking the body. The parts of the body most frequently targeted to induce immobility were the legs, feet, and Achilles' tendons. Thousands of corpses discovered after the violence showed evidence of one or both tendons sectioned by machete blows. Other victims later found alive in parts of Rwanda where humanitarian organizations were able to intervene had also sustained this injury. Medecins Sans Frontieres, when it entered eastern Rwanda in late June of 1994, declared in presentations to televised media that this injury was the one most frequently encountered in their area. While MSF managed to save many lives among those so injured, the organization warned that in practically every case, costly surgery would be needed to restore some capability of movement to the foot. This injury, known in medieval France as the 'coup de Jarnac', has sometimes been attributed to the influence of French troops and their alleged training of *Interahamwe* militia members (Braeckman, 1994). I have no evidence to refute this in this specific instance, but Braeckman's assertion does not explain why the technique was used before in Rwanda during the violence of 1959–64 and in 1973. Moreover, in previous episodes of violence as well as in 1994, assailants also mutilated cattle belonging to Tutsi by cutting the leg tendons. Although many cattle in 1994 were killed outright and eaten, and others were stolen, a large number were immobilized and left to die slowly in the field.

This technique of cruelty has a certain logic to it where human beings are concerned. In the presence of a large number of potential victims, too many to kill at once, *Interahamwe* might immobilize fleeing victims by a quick blow to one or both of the Achilles' tendons. Then the killers could return at their leisure and complete their work. This makes sense, yet it does not explain why many who sustained this injury were children too young to walk, elderly people, people who were crippled or infirm, and people in hospital beds incapable of running away. It is here that the pragmatic logic of immobilizing one's enemies and the symbolic logic of 'blocking the path', which are not contradictory in many cases, are in conflict. Why obstruct the immobile? As with barriers on paths and roadways, there is a deeper generative scheme that subtends both the killers' intentionality and the message inscribed on the bodies of their victims, even though these techniques of cruelty also involve a degree of improvisation. Power in this instance, in symbolic terms, derives from the capacity to obstruct. The persecutor 'blocks the path' of human beings and impedes the movement of the material symbolic capital necessary to the social reproduction of human beings – cattle. Even when it is apparently unnecessary to arrest the movement of the already immobile, the assertion of the capacity to obstruct is none the less the claim and assertion of power.

The Body as Conduit

In addition to the imagery of obstruction, numerous instances of the body as conduit can be discerned in the Rwandan violence of 1994.

[…]

The image of the body as conduit was […] seen in the techniques of cruelty used by the perpetrators of violence. Perhaps the most vivid example of this during the genocide was the practice of impalement. Recalling Malkki's observation above concerning the 1972 violence against Hutu in Burundi, Rwandan Tutsi men in 1994 were also impaled from anus to mouth with wooden or bamboo poles and metal spears. Tutsi women were often impaled from vagina to mouth. Although none of the refugees that I interviewed in Nairobi spoke of having witnessed impalement, it was reported in Kenyan newspapers that I read during the summer of 1994. More recently it has been cited in an African Rights report entitled 'Rwanda: Killing the Evidence' as a means by which perpetrators of the genocide still living on Rwandan soil terrorize surviving witnesses (Omaar and De Waal, 1996). For example, the report cites the case of a certain Makasi, a resident of the Kicukiro suburb of Kigali, who several months after the genocide found a leaflet shoved under his door threatening his life and that of several others:

> You, Makasi are going to die no matter what. And it will not only be you. It will be Byllngiro as well. Let your wife know that she will be killed with a pole that will run from her legs right up to her mouth. As for Charles' wife, her legs and arms will be cut off. (Omaar and De Waal, 1996: 15)

[...]

In pre-colonial and early colonial times Rwandans impaled cattle thieves. The executioners inserted a wooden stake into the thief's anus and then pushed it through the body, causing it to exit at the neck or the mouth. The pole with its agonizing charge was then erected, stuck into the earth, and left standing for several days. Dramatically gruesome and public, this punishment carried a clear and obvious normative message intended to deter cattle thievery. In a more subtle way, the message can be interpreted symbolically. Because cattle exchanges accompany, legitimize, and commemorate the most significant social transitions and relationships, most notably, patron–client relations, blood brotherhood, and marriage, obviating the possibility of such exchanges or subverting those which have already occurred by stealing cattle removes all tangible mnemonic evidence of the attendant social relationships. Diverting socially appropriate flows of cattle by means of thievery is a way of *gusiba inzira*, or 'blocking the path' between individuals and groups united through matrimonial alliance, blood brotherhood, or patron–client ties. It is symbolically appropriate, therefore, that people who obstruct the conduits of social exchange, have the conduit that is the body obstructed with a pole or spear.

Quite obviously between the pre- and early colonial times, where Rwandan executioners impaled cattle thieves and 1994 when genocidal murderers impaled Tutsi men and women, many things have changed. Clearly the more recent victims of the practice were no cattle thieves. Were they in some sense like cattle thieves in the minds of those committing the atrocities? My feeling is that they were, although the more recent terms used in Hutu extremist discourse to describe Tutsi only occasionally make reference to actual actions of which they might be guilty, such as theft. Instead 'Tutsi are invaders from Ethiopia', 'cockroaches', 'eaters of our sweat', or 'weight upon our back'. The Tutsi, much like the archetypal *agakeecuru* discussed above, exert their malevolent influence on the social group not so much by what they do, than by inherent qualities which they supposedly embody. In that sense they approach 'blocking beings', the mythical nemeses of Rwandan tradition – the *agakeecuru*, *impenebere*, or *impa* – and like these figures, they possess fearful powers. In this case they were obstructers of the cosmic unity of the nation as this unity was imagined by the Hutu extremist élite: a purified nation with a purified, reified 'Hutu culture' expunged of all elements of 'Tutsi culture' and rid of all who would resist the encompassing powers of the state. The torturers not only killed their victims – they transformed their bodies into powerful signs which resonated with a Rwandan *habitus* even as they improvised upon it and enlarged the original semantic domain of associated meanings to depict an entire ethnic group as enemies of the Hutu state.

[...]

The Rwandan Genocide and Historical Transformation

Although I believe that the imagery of flow and obstruction was pervasive during the genocide, it would be wrong to conclude from the above argument that Rwandan culture is simply a 'machine a tropes' constantly replicating the same structures and hermetically sealed off from all influences arising from within or beyond its borders. As Bourdieu maintains, people tend to reproduce the 'structured and structuring logic' of the *habitus*. Nevertheless, although older generations subtly inculcate this logic to their juniors, the socialization process is never perfect nor complete (1977, 1990). Transformed objective circumstances always influence socialization. The tendency to reproduce a structured logic thus should not be seen as simple and volitionless replication. There is always improvisation and innovation even if many of the basic patterns retain their saliency.

In the Rwandan instance, colonialism and concomitant transformations in economic and political conditions influenced the perception and depiction of evil. Because of these changes, the symbolism of malevolent obstruction could be applied to an entire ethnic group. This was a radical departure from the past. During pre-colonial times the image of the menacing 'blocking being' was confined to a limited number of individuals. These included: *impa* - women who had reached childbearing age and had never menstruated; *impenebere* - women who had reached childbearing age and had not developed breasts; individual enemies of the Rwandan king, and sorcerers. All these malevolent beings were mythically presaged in the legend about the *agakeecuru* and the origin of death. Occasionally, in the rituals associated with sacred kingship, such individuals were publicly sacrificed to rid the polity of their potentially nefarious influence.

It was not until Tutsi and Hutu ethnic identities had become substantialized under colonialism and then privileges awarded by the colonial rulers on the basis of these identities, that an entire group of people could be thought of as a source of obstruction to the polity as a whole. Tutsi could be easily assimilated to the category of 'invaders' because of their alliance with German, then Belgian, outsiders and the colonialists' reliance on Hamitic theories. When Belgians quickly shifted their allegiance to Hutu in the late 1950s, supporting the 'Hutu revolution', Tutsi were left to fend for themselves while retaining their substantialized identity. Tutsi assimilation to the imagery of malevolent others, 'blocked' or 'blocking beings', was facilitated by the fact that a minority among them had indeed been favoured socially and economically under the colonial regime. Where once there had been a sacred king whose actions were thought to assure a religious and material redistributive function – the downward flow of celestial beneficence, wealth, and prosperity – under colonialism popular credence in the ritual and pragmatic functions of kingship was undermined.

In its place a privileged class of Tutsi, Tutsi administrators in the colonial state apparatus, were perceived by other Rwandans to have become rich by subverting the redistribution process, or, in a symbolic sense, by impeding the flow of *imaana*. The 1959–62 revolution in Rwanda was not anti-colonial; Belgians were not endangered or forced to flee the country – Tutsi were. Nor were Belgian economic and cultural interests seriously threatened in the country. Belgians continued to enjoy privileged status in Rwanda until some time after 1990 when Belgium withdrew its military support for the Habyarimana regime. The symbolism of obstruction is indeed pre-colonial in origin, but its application to an entire group of people is a thoroughly recent, modern application reflecting transformed consciousness of the polity and of the people comprising it.

Secondly, many of the actual and symbolic forms of violence became syncretized to Euro-American or transnational forms. This is apparent in the cartoon depicting Melchior Ndadaye's death, and in other juxtapositions of transnational images and those of local vintage. Clearly the violent imaginary looks for inspiration to all possible sources. According to Jean-Pierre Chretien in *Rwanda: Les médias du genocide* (1995) Nazi symbols were attributed to the RPF by Hutu extremists. The French government's habit of referring to the RPF as 'Khmers noirs' followed in this pattern and echoed their Hutu extremist allies. Nevertheless, it was Hutu extremists who were more Nazi-like and Khmer Rouge-like in actual practice.

[…]

The Rwandan atrocities would then seem to have followed an empirical, rationalist logic centred on maximizing the number of one's enemies killed, or maximizing the psychological effect by the sheer horror of atrocity. Such an explanation might concur with what the authors of the atrocities themselves might claim was the reasoning behind their acts. Although such an explanation is accurate, it is incomplete. It cannot explain the depth of passion that clearly lay behind the Rwandan violence, nor the fact that it assumed specific forms. But one type of logic to the cruelty does not preclude all others;

pragmatism and symbolism in a general way are not necessarily conflictual (cf. Sperber, 1975). Killing one's adversaries while communicating powerful messages about them and oneself are not mutually exclusive. Pragmatic explanations alone, however, cannot account for the sheer number of roadblocks that refugees reported to me that they encountered. There was certainly a point of diminishing returns where adding new barriers was concerned, and it would appear that this point had been more than surpassed. Nor was impalement the only way of making one's victims endure atrocious and exemplary suffering. Did it make sense to sever the Achilles' tendons of those who had very little chance of running away? Did it make sense to castrate pre-pubescent boys? Did it make sense to cut the leg tendons of cattle rather than killing them outright?

This is where pragmatic logic alone does not fully explain the Rwandan violence. Many forms of the violence encountered here were enracinated in Rwandan ways of bodily experience and bodily predispositions lurking beneath the level of verbalization and rational calculation. Although these predispositions were political in the sense that they influenced thought and action where power was concerned, they were certainly not political in the ordinary and instrumental sense of symbols consciously used by one group to advance its claims in opposition to another group and its symbols. This symbolism was logically prior to its instantiation in a political form and not the other way around.

[...]

While the proclivity to see the genocide as purely ethnic in nature is understandable and is in part justified by local Rwandan social realities, we risk falling into the trap of extremist ideology (whether Hutu or Tutsi) if this is all we can see. Both Hutu and Tutsi extremists believe and would have others believe, that the conflicts in Rwanda and Burundi are purely racial in nature. Understanding only the ethnic dimension, however, blinds us to other social imbalances and inequities that cannot be amended by concentrating on ethnicity alone.

Where gender is concerned, this is a glaring oversight.

[...]

Gender on the Warpath

[...]

The genocide aimed at reasserting the cosmic order of the Hutu state as this was imagined through an idealized, nostalgic image of the 1959 Hutu revolution which brought an end to the Tutsi monarchy and to Tutsi dominance. The only perceived blemish of the revolution, repeated frequently in the days leading up to the genocide, was its failure to purify the country entirely. Extremists regretted that they had not gone far enough in 1959, that the revolution had failed to rid Rwanda of its polluting internal other once and for all. As a corollary to this image, though less overtly stated, extremists aimed at reclaiming the lost ground of patriarchy and re-asserting a male dominance that had probably never existed in Rwanda's actual history. [...] Tutsi women were pivotal enemies in the extremists' struggle to reclaim both patriarchy and the Hutu revolution, because in many respects they were socially positioned at the permeable boundary between the two ethnic groups. It was much more common in pre-genocide Rwanda, for example, to find Tutsi women married to Hutu men than to find Hutu women married to Tutsi men. As official ethnic identity (marked on everyone's national identity card) was determined by the father in pre-genocide Rwanda, [...] a Hutu man married to a Tutsi women produced offspring who were legally Hutu. Intermarriage between Hutu men and Tutsi women thus conferred the full benefits of Hutu citizenship to progeny who were perceived by many as racially impure.

As the social dichotomization process advanced during the 1990s, ambiguous ethnic identities became less and less tolerated. This applied not only to the progeny of Hutu–Tutsi unions but also to the progeny of European–Rwandan and Asian–Rwandan unions, as many such people told me. The negative portrayal of Tutsi women in Hutu extremist literature owed much to the fact that Tutsi women were potential mothers of ethnically anomalous children, for more Tutsi women than Hutu women married men of other ethnicities. As the ideology of Hutu extremism developed, racial purity came to be seen as a necessary component of Hutu identity. Miscegenation between Hutu men and Tutsi women began to be viewed with hostility.

Yet, at the same time, many Hutu men, including some who were extremists, either had Tutsi wives or Tutsi mistresses with whom they had sired children. Clearly a great deal of psychological and social ambivalence characterized the relation between Hutu men and Tutsi women before the genocide. In order to understand it and its consequences, we need to understand the history of inter-ethnic marriages in Rwanda and the colonial ideology of Hamitism, which depicted Tutsi as racially (and intellectually) superior to Hutu, and Tutsi women as more beautiful than Hutu women. Conjugal unions between Hutu men and Tutsi women were not all that uncommon in the 1970s and 1980s, even if they were not the norm, but by the 1990s the negative perception of such unions had become much more pronounced. During the genocide itself, Hutu men with Tutsi wives were often forced to kill their spouses themselves in order to prevent their own deaths and a more gruesome death for their wives.

As the dichotomization process intensified in the years leading up to the genocide, Tutsi women came to occupy a socially liminal position. As 'liminoid beings' (Turner, 1977), Tutsi women were capable of undermining the categories 'Hutu' and 'Tutsi' altogether, although it is doubtful that most individual Tutsi women possessed much cognizance of this fact. In marriages or long-term sexual liaisons with Hutu men, they were giving birth to children who were *de jure* Hutu but *de facto* 50 per cent Tutsi. By logical extension, the perpetuation and proliferation of Hutu–Tutsi unions threatened the categorical boundary between Hutu and Tutsi. In many cases children of mixed marriages could have typically Tutsi physiognomies, but yet be officially classified as Hutu on their national identity cards. One such woman, whose father was Hutu and whose mother was Tutsi, told me that in March 1992 the bush taxi that she was travelling in was stopped at a military roadblock. The soldier examined everyone's identity card; when he got to hers, he scoffed at the fact that the category 'Hutu' had been checkmarked. With an insult he threw the card onto the roadway where she was forced to pick it up.

It is here that we need to examine the role of women as symbols and to consider the nature of the representations that were associated with them. These representations, discernible in Hutu extremist literature, foreshadowed the degree of sadism perpetrated by extremists on the bodies of their victims. To many Rwandans gender relations in the 1980s and 1990s were falling into a state of decadence as more women attained positions of prominence in economic and public life, and as more of them exercised their personal preferences in their private lives. Complex sexual politics preceded the genocide and were manifest in it. Many of the bitter ironies and contradictions of ethnicity were played out in sex and gender terms.

Women as Symbols

[...]

Going further back into the past, to pre-colonial and early colonial times, taking a Tutsi wife was often perceived as a sign of social advancement on the part of a Hutu man. In order to obtain such a wife, one had to become wealthy in bovine capital. The children of such unions were usually considered Tutsi. (This, by the way, was in sharp contrast with the late colonial and post-colonial era where the father determined ethnicity.) In effect it was possible, as a Hutu in the late nineteenth and early twentieth centuries, to have one's descendants become Tutsi by acquiring wealth in cattle and intermarrying with Tutsi. Tutsi hypogamy was justified on their part for they would often absorb rich Hutu into their lineages in this way. Practices such as these occurred often enough to justify a word in Kinyarwanda, *kwihutura*, meaning 'to cease being Hutu, to become Tutsi'. When the Rwandan monarchy and the system of Tutsi dominance that had characterized the colonial era came to an end with the Hutu revolution of 1959–62, it would have been logical for such intermarriages to decline in frequency. As Tutsi in general were now relegated to second-class status, there could be little advantage in establishing matrimonial alliances with them. Nevertheless, the practice continued.

[...]

[During the genocide], Hutu extremists appear to be attempting to purge their ambivalence toward Tutsi women via symbolic violence, even as they project their own erotic fantasies upon them. At one level they were certainly aware that to preserve the racial purity of Hutu, they had to categorically renounce Tutsi women as objects of desire. At the same time they also knew that they themselves were not free of the forbidden desire. They were not impervious to the allure of Tutsi women and indeed they knew that many of the most prominent among then had succumbed to the temptation. If the choice between Hutu and Tutsi women were non-problematic for Hutu extremists, narratives to the effect that Tutsi use the beauty of their women to ensnare Hutu would be unnecessary. One can only speculate about the possible cognitive dissonance in the minds of many Hutu extremists where the question of Tutsi women was concerned. What is most important for our purposes is the fact that these sentiments received social expression.

For example, in December 1990 the Hutu extremist magazine, Kangura, printed what is perhaps the most succinct statement of Hutu extremist ideology - the infamous 'Hutu Ten Commandments'. Although this document has been quoted often and widely discussed by scholars who have written about the genocide (Prunier, 1995; Chretien, 1995), no one to my knowledge has pointed out that gender preoccupations were clearly very much on the minds of the extremists. Hutu extremists had to have accorded high priority to the question of relations between Hutu men and Tutsi women, for the first three of the Ten Commandments concern this subject and this subject alone.

Here are the first three commandments:

1. Every Muhutu [Hutu male] should know that wherever he finds Umututsikazi [a female Tutsi] she is working for her Tutsi ethnic group. As a result every Muhutu who marries a Mututsikazi, or who takes a Mututsikazi for a mistress, or employs her as a secretary or a protégée is a traitor.
2. Every Muhutu should know that our Bahutukazi [female Hutu] are more worthy of, and conscious of their roles as woman, spouse, and mother. Are they not pretty, good secretaries, and more honest!
3. Bahutukazi [Hutu women], be vigilant and bring your husbands, brothers, and sons back to the path of reason. (Chretien, 1995: 141 [my translation])

Would it have been necessary to recall all Hutu men to order in this way, if the women of the opponents' group had not exerted such compelling attraction? Why was it necessary for the extremists to assert that Hutu women are pretty, unless there were doubts to the contrary? The third commandment is also very telling: Hutu men cannot be expected to resist the attractions of Tutsi women alone; they need their Hutu wives, sisters, and mothers to call them back to reason!

Another commandment, the seventh, declared that the Rwandan Army must remain Hutu, but added to that an additional warning against Tutsi women. Apparently Hutu extremists were so preoccupied by this issue that no amount of redundancy or overemphasis could ever be deemed excessive.

7. The Rwandan Armed Forces must be exclusively Hutu. The experience of the October 1990 war teaches us this. No soldier should marry a Mututsikazi. (Chretien, 1995: 142 [my translation])

Beneath this ambivalence one cannot help but sense lurking Hamitic imagery - a tragic yet unacknowledgeable sense on the part of the extremists that, when all was said and done, early Europeans had indeed been correct in depicting Tutsi as 'golden-red beauties' and Hutu as inferior (and less attractive) negroids.

[...]

As Prunier points out in a footnote in his book, such evidence of a lingering inferiority complex may partly account for the degree of sadism unleashed by Hutu death squads against Tutsi.

Indeed, special measures of terrorism were reserved for Tutsi women by the extremists. Many Tutsi women suffered breast oblation, or were raped before being killed. Others were impaled with spears from vagina to mouth. Many were forced to commit incest with a male family member before being killed. Pregnant women were often eviscerated. Yet other Tutsi women were spared and taken as 'wives' by their persecutors and brought into the refugee camps of eastern Zaire. There they became sexual slaves to their captors. In the events that transpired in eastern Zaire during the last days of the Mobutu regime, some of these women managed to escape and to return to Rwanda pregnant and to seek abortion in a Catholic country that prohibits it.

Conclusion

The Rwandan genocide cannot be understood solely in ethnic terms. Although recent theoretical contributions to the study of ethno-nationalism are obviously of great importance in comprehending this tragedy, they tend to accord little weight to gender, if they deal with it all. Gender issues interacted with ethnic ones in complex ways involving the demarcation of social boundaries and local notions of racial purity.

[...]

References

Beidelman, T.O., *Colonial Evangelism: A Socio-Historical Study of an East African Mission at the Grassroots*, Bloomington, Indiana University Press, 1982.

Beidelman, T., *Moral Imagination in Kaguru Modes of Thought, Bloomington*, Indiana University Press, 1986.

Bourdieu, P., *Outline of a Theory of Practice*, Cambridge, Cambridge University Press, 1977.

Bourdieu, P., *The Logic of Practice*, Stanford, Stanford University Press, 1990.

Braeckman, C., *Rwanda, Histoire d'un genocide*, Paris, Fayard, 1994.

Chretien, J.-P., *Rwanda: les médias du genocide*, Paris, Editions Karthala, 1995.

Clastres, P., *La société contra l'état: recherches d'anthropologie politique*, Paris, Editions de Minuit, 1974.

Foucault, M., "On Governmentality." *Ideology and Consciousness* 6, 1979: pp. 5–22.

Goldhagen, D., *Hitler's Willing Executioners: Ordinary Germans and the Holocaust*, New York, Knopf, 1996.

Hubert, H., and Mauss, M., *Sacrifice: Its Nature and Functions*, Chicago, University of Chicago Press, 1981 [1964].

Kafka, Franz, *The Penal Colony: Stories and Short Pieces*. Trans. by Ian Johnston, 1914.

Kagame, A., *Inganji Karnga*, 2 vols., Kabgayi (Rwanda), 1959.

Kapferer, B., *Legends of People. Myths of State*, Washington DC, Smithsonian Institution Press, 1988.

Oniaar, R., and De Waal, A., (eds) *Rwanda: Killing the Evidence*, London, African Rights, April, 1996.

Peters, E., *Torture*, Philadelphia, University of Pennsylvania Press, 1996.

Prunier, G., *The Rwanda Crisis*, New York, Columbia University Press, 1995.

Sperber, D., *Le symbolisme en general*, Paris, Hermann, 1975.

Taylor, C., *Milk, Honey and Money*, Washington DC, Smithsonian Institution Press, 1992.

Turner, V., *The Ritual Process*, Ithaca NY, Cornell University Press, 1977.

40

Where to Be an Ancestor?

Reconstituting Socio-spiritual Worlds among Displaced Mozambicans

Stephen Lubkemann

[…]

Throughout the twentieth century Machazian subsistence strategies revolved around a social division of labour between female subsistence agriculture confined to Machaze and male migration to Southern Rhodesia (later Zimbabwe) and South Africa in pursuit of wage-labour. Most Machazian men spent long migratory careers working in South Africa, returning after years abroad for stays of several months in Machaze – a pattern often repeated for decades before final retirement in Machaze. In contrast, Machazian women rarely migrated and engaged almost exclusively in subsistence agriculture (Lubkemann 2000a, 2000d). Thus, Machazian 'social worlds' were not enacted entirely within delimited territorial boundaries but actually depended upon migratory processes and social networks that continuously spanned international borders and linked several rural and peri-urban environments.

It is also important to understand that Machazians perceived their social worlds to span not only spatial boundaries but spiritual ones as well. Machazians believed that social interaction occurred not only among the living but also between the living and the spirits of the dead. Foremost among these spirits were the *vadzimu*, one's own deceased ancestors. The *vadzimu* were believed to intervene in the lives of the living in order to correct moral failings or simply not to be forgotten, usually by causing minor illnesses (rather than grievous harm). This type of *vadzimu* admonishment was believed to occur if the living neglected to perform rituals of respect. However, Machazians also believed that ancestral reproach could easily be 'triggered' by contentious relationships among the living. The mere existence of feelings of ill will between social actors was believed to motivate *vadzimu* to act, particularly in defence of the rights of older and senior kin, whose age and social rank conferred on them a status that was 'closer to the ancestors'. Within this belief system social duties and obligations towards others were often fulfilled to avoid provoking ancestral resentment and not only out of fear that the living offended party might exercise material sanctions directly.

The spirits of the dead were also believed to be potentially the source of more grievous forms of harm, usually through the vehicle of witchcraft (*uloi*). Among Machazians, as among many other

From Stephen Lubkemann, "Where to Be an Ancestor? Reconstituting Socio-spiritual Worlds among Displaced Mozambicans," *Journal of Refugee Studies*, Vol. 15, No. 2, 2002, Oxford University Press (2002), pp. Lub. 3–18, Lub. 20–4.

Shona-speakers (Bourdillon 1991), all serious illnesses, misfortune, and death were attributed to *uloi*. Such misfortune was believed to be caused by a *mfukwa*,[1] a particular type or state of spirit motivated to cause death, in conjunction with a specific living actor who either intentionally or unintentionally directed or facilitated the *mfukwa*'s activity. Although *uloi* could be produced through the intentional intervention of ritual specialists, it was also believed that the mere existence of jealousy or intense hostility could open up a path for a *mfukwa* to act. Sometimes a person could unknowingly facilitate *mfukwa* action against another by harbouring hostile sentiments against that person. Alternatively, a *mfukwa* could even pursue his (or his kin's) own interests rather than those of an inadvertent facilitator. Thus, before the war the spirits of particularly powerful dead chiefs were believed to pursue their own lineages' interests after death as *mfukwas*. Similarly, during the war those wrongly slain and improperly buried, or the spirits of slain soldiers who were outsiders, were believed to be motivated by reason of their own 'violent deaths' to kill, by taking advantage of the 'paths opened up' by the hostile sentiments among the living, even if not intentionally summoned to do so.

Machazians consulted *nyangas* and *nyamossolos*, [...] two types of 'traditional' local healers and diviners, as well as local church *profetas* (prophets) in order to diagnose the sources of social conflict that gave rise to acrimonious socio-spiritual interaction. These specialists were believed capable of identifying which specific spiritual actors caused an illness, of interpreting their intentions and demands vis-à-vis the living, and of interceding with them for resolution. Local chiefs and church pastors also played important roles in mediating social interaction between spiritual and living members of the Machazian social world. At a community level, a loose and historically shifting hierarchy of local chiefs were charged with annual rain and grave cleaning ceremonies held to curry favour with the spirits of dead chiefs – believed to be the 'genuine owners' of the land – in order to assure crop prosperity. In the chronically drought ridden area of Machaze this has long been an important role. Meanwhile, pastors played a significant if highly variable role in ensuring the protective activity of the Holy Spirit in the lives of their parishioners. [...] All of these institutions reflect the degree to which Machazians perceived themselves to inhabit a space of social interaction that can be described as a 'socio-spiritual world'. Machazian coping strategies during and after the war were consequently responsive to the perceived effects of wartime violence, migration, and social change on the entire array of social relationships within this socio-spiritual world.

The Socio-Spiritual Spiral of Wartime Violence

Shortly after Mozambique achieved independence from Portugal in 1975, hostile neighbouring apartheid regimes instigated a civil war that lasted almost fifteen years. Machaze was one of the earliest settings for this conflict. By late 1979 the area was fully embroiled in the war between the Rhodesian (and later South African) supported anti-government faction (RENAMO) and the government forces (FRELIMO). Estimates suggest that between 40 per cent and 70 per cent of the population were forced out of the district and migrated to South Africa or Zimbabwe, or were internally displaced within Mozambique during the conflict (GTZ 1993, 1996; CARE 1994; Wenzel and Bannerman 1995). Those who remained within the district were displaced from their homesteads, forced to choose between moving into FRELIMO's fortified communal villages or fleeing deep into the 'bush', nominally under RENAMO's control.

Choices to move into either FRELIMO or RENAMO areas were more often than not unrelated to political sympathies with either of these parties. Rather they reflected the ways in which forms of local social conflict permeated and centrally shaped the military activity of both armed factions in the Machaze area. Both FRELIMO and RENAMO troops and commanders unfamiliar with the area relied on locals to guide them and to identify enemy cadres or collaborators. Machazians became adept at using this type of accusation in order to further private agendas founded in local forms of social strife unrelated to the political agendas of the warring parties – such as jealousy over differential success in labour migration or suspicions of witchcraft. In Machaze, local social divisions tended to occur primarily within kinship groups – often even within households – in part because of cultural beliefs that identify social intimates as the most likely source of rivalry. In contrast to Machaze, elsewhere in Mozambique, ethnicity (Roesch 1992; Geffray 1989), socio-economic class and urban/rural divides (O'Laughlin 1992; Geffray 1989; McGregor 1998; Manning 1998), and intra-community political rivalry among elites (Alexander 1994) played a more prominent role in shaping wartime violence and political alignments. [...]

As the war intensified in Machaze, more and more people took flight in reaction to accusations of political collaboration even though these allegations were mostly spurious. Moreover, many pre-emptively moved in the opposite direction taken by social rivals in fear of being identified to soldiers in the areas to which the rivals had moved as supporters of the opposition. Thus from the war's outset local social agendas cast in culturally-specific terms strongly influenced the deployment of violence by FRELIMO and RENAMO, and directed it in the service of local micro-political rather than national macro-political ends. Wartime violence in Machaze was thus primarily understood and reacted to as a product of locally generated and defined social conflicts, rather than as a product of political affiliation with RENAMO or FRELIMO *per se*. While a small minority of local FRELIMO cadres and early RENAMO mobilizers may have been motivated by the political projects of the contenders for national power, most residents of Machaze reacted to the way in which that power itself could be manipulated in the service of micro-political projects generated in the cultural logic of local social relations.

Wartime violence in Machaze was further aggravated by the ways in which religious beliefs amplified local social antagonism. Machazians believed that those who suffered violent deaths were likely to become *mfukwas*. The death of soldiers who were 'outsiders' raised the spectre of a proliferation of dangerous unknown *mfukwas* who could randomly intervene to cause death. A more predictable, yet also more constant threat was posed by the intimate relative whose violent death was believed to provoke them to take on a *mfukwa* state. Although wrongful death obligated the living to seek redress,

the culturally prescribed institutions for doing so had been enfeebled by targeted post-colonial government repression. Moreover, the impossibility of interacting with the guilty parties (often unknown or else unreachable in the opposing force's area of control) made the negotiation of a settlement with the *mfukwa* all the more difficult if not impossible. Sometimes even proper burials were not viable – another ritual failure thought likely to provoke ancestral virulence. Not only could an irate *mfukwa* threaten its own family members, but its 'presence' placed a family's relationships in the broader community at risk since the *mfukwa* became part of the 'package of actors' brought into social interactions of all forms with other parties. Any form of conflict with a family with a *mfukwa* was believed to be particularly dangerous.

Lacking the possibility for redress, revenge was upheld as the very lowest level of action believed capable of deflecting the ancestral wrath of those violently slain in war. This belief in conjunction with the crippling of 'peaceful' forms of resolution thus led many Machazians to perpetrate radically violent actions of revenge themselves in what amounted in part to a form of 'socio-spiritual defence'. Each act of violence inevitably gave motive for responses of at least the same magnitude, thus multiplying the number of accusations and violent deaths in a viciously escalating and ever more socially inclusive spiral. During the war Machazians perceived a violent radicalization of the terms of interaction throughout the socio-spiritual world. The war, thus, not only represented a dangerous transformation of social relations among the living, but was seen by the Machazians as a perilous change in relations between the living and the dead.

The Socio-spiritual Effects of Wartime Migration and Social Change

Wartime migration decisions were also responsive to other social processes that ultimately produced highly gender- and age-specific patterns of wartime population distribution and significantly reconfigured power and social relations within Machazian households. Throughout the war almost twice as many women as men remained in Machaze or in neighbouring rural districts

(GTZ 1993, 1996; CARE 1994; Lubkemann 2000a, 2000b, 2000d). By contrast, most adult Machazian men were forced out of the district to the peri-urban areas in South Africa during the first few years of the conflict.

The fact that men were targeted for forced recruitment, and were more likely to be killed played a part in this engendered population re-distribution. However, this pattern also reflected an attempt by both men and women to engage in long-established strategies of socio-economic reproduc-tion in a new wartime environment. The patterns of predominantly male migration to South Africa early in the conflict represented the continuation of long-established coping strategies similar to those employed historically during cycles of intensified colonial labour recruitment (Lubkemann 2000a: 90–5, 100–15, 127–31). Similarly, Machazian wom-en's relocation within the district reflected their preference for rural destinations that allowed them to re-establish some form of subsistence agricul-ture. Few Machazian women had the desire in the early days of the conflict to join male relatives migrating out of the district.

However, as explored in detail elsewhere (Lubkemann 2000c), attempts at minimizing dis-ruption to established life-strategies were not equally successful for men and women. The war's persistence for almost a decade and a half had far more disruptive effects on agricultural subsistence within Mozambique than it did on wage-labour employment in South Africa. Moreover, the war's intensification and successive droughts throughout the 1980s, which further restricted the possibilities for subsistence, forced more people out of the dis-trict. A large population of predominantly women, children, and elderly men[2] eventually fled to Zimbabwe and settled in UNHCR refugee camps.

As the war progressed Machazian men facing prolonged stays in South Africa began to establish conjugal unions with South African women. Although some of these men essentially aban-doned their Mozambican marriages, a majority sought to retain their marital rights with both South African and Mozambican spouses, despite maintaining minimal (if any) contact with the lat-ter, sometimes for well over a decade. This new strategy of 'transnational polygyny' (Lubkemann 2000a, 2000d) allowed Machazian men to have

families and children who could contribute to their old age care, while retaining the option of eventual post-conflict return. However, after the war ended in 1992 interest in transnational poly-gyny continued to grow. Of 200 Machazian men whom I surveyed in South Africa in 1998, 65 per cent were involved in ongoing conjugal relation-ships in South Africa. Twenty-six per cent had marital relationships only in South Africa, while 23 per cent were involved in marital relationships only in Mozambique (Lubkemann 2000a, 2000d). The wartime devastation of Mozambique and its uncertain political stability reinforced the long-established importance of employment in South Africa after the war. Moreover, during the war men had increasingly established other important social, legal, and economic ties to South Africa: 72 per cent of those 200 surveyed planned to keep a house in South Africa, and 79 per cent a busi-ness, while 47 per cent reported they were enrolled in a pension plan that had to be regularly collected in person in South Africa (Lubkemann 2000d). Many of these men thus began to see South Africa as more than merely a place of employment, but rather a site in which to pursue a social life that paralleled, rather than simply contributed to, their social lives back in Machaze.

By maintaining households in both countries, transnationally polygynous men diversified their risks – an important 'improvement' to many in light of different insecurities faced in Mozambique and South Africa. On one hand, inadequate social and medical services, perceived political volatility, and drought represented significant risks faced in Mozambique (Lubkemann 2000a). Yet, in South Africa Machazian men faced rising violence, crime, and xenophobia in the townships. Their illegal sta-tus made them particularly vulnerable to crime since it was known they would not report it to authorities, and to widespread extortion by corrupt local officials. The high cost of living and rising unemployment also made township life difficult. In contrast, Machaze afforded much lower living cost options if and when money became tight.

While Machazian men benefited from develop-ing new social and economic options in South Africa through the transnationalization of polygyny, these wartime changes reconfigured the balance of power and the meaning of social relationships within marriages and extended kinship groups in detrimental ways for several other categories of Machazians. In particular, the development of relationships between Machazian men and South African women eroded what benefits women in Machaze had once experienced from polygyny, while accentuating many of the problems experienced because of it. Before the war, polygyny realized solely within Machaze represented an ambiguous combination of potential gains and losses for Machazian women. Whereas a co-wife was often regarded as a rival and potential source of *uloi*, she could also help ease heavy domestic labour requirements. Consequently many women reported suggesting and participating in the selection of an additional wife for their spouse. In a polygynous configuration in which both wives remained in Machaze, a junior wife provided free labour and enhanced the status of a senior wife. Additionally, she often released the first wife from the responsibilities of assisting a mother-in-law, thus affording her greater independence.

In contrast, transnational polygyny afforded no labour relief or enhanced autonomy to Machazian women because transnational co-wives were not physically present in Machaze. Moreover, Machazian wives in these marriages often received a reduced share of resources from husbands, since South African wives had the advantage in pressing their claims because money was earned in South Africa and men spent more time there. The distribution of benefits among co-wives could also no longer be monitored by Machazian wives in particular, who had to settle for 'leftovers'. While Machazian women remained dependent on migrant husbands for cash, their husbands were now less dependent on them. Accordingly, power within Machazian marriages was redistributed to men's advantage. Whereas Machazian women still had to fulfil the obligations required by marriage (such as assisting mothers-in-law), and these obligations were made more difficult without co-resident co-wives, they lost much of the leverage they once had in enforcing a husband's fulfilment of reciprocal obligations.

South African marriages, in which parents played no part, also significantly reduced the leverage parents exercised over sons and further transformed the meaning of marriage itself. Local kinship alliance imperatives in which senior kin largely dictated the interests at stake did not factor into South African marriages. Moreover, the drain of resources in favour of South African social interests made it a more difficult job to manage extended households that often included wives and children left behind. Heightened dissatisfaction of neglected wives placed marriages at greater risk of failure and consequently threatened the loss of a daughter-in-law's labour. These factors fed parents' ultimate fear that children would neglect their old-age support.

After the conflict, these wartime changes introduced new forms of tension into everyday forms of Machazian social interaction at the domestic and community level. Ultimately, the development of new South African options for men and of transnational polygyny, repositioned migration and marriage in the struggle for power in the Machazian domestic sphere. In transnationally polygynous marriages men and women, and men and their parents, increasingly evidenced mutually exclusive expectations about what marriage should 'mean' – that is, what rights and obligations should the relationship imply. In many ways there was a zero-sum relationship between contesting views, as men's desire to practise transnational polygyny violated the expectations held by Machazian women about marriage. Furthermore, women and parents' desires to maintain Machaze as the sole point of migrant men's socio-economic reference and investment threatened the risk diversification strategies these men sought to pursue. Marriages became sites of intensified social strife and Machazian men who had developed stronger ties to South Africa were particularly concerned with the socio-spiritual effects of these exacerbated social tensions.

Drawing on this understanding of how wartime changes affected social strife and of how Machazians perceived the relationship between social contention and socio-spiritual interaction, the second half of this article examines how different post-conflict resettlement options presented Machazians with particular socio-spiritual dilemmas. First, a typology of responses to these socio-spiritual dilemmas is established. This typology is then used to categorize the mechanisms that different categories of Machazian social actors used to cope with the socio-spiritual dilemmas implied by their resettlement choices. Finally comes an analysis of the ways in which gendered (and other) differences in social power allowed some actors to pursue a broader range of strategies that often preserved or enhanced power gains, while forcing others to pursue riskier and more drastic strategies, that at best minimized power loss. I do not undertake a social psychology of return decision-making *per se* – i.e. I do not attempt to identify the range of social and psychological factors that led some Machazians to believe one thing and others to believe another. I do not identify how beliefs influenced particular resettlement choices either. Rather, I start my discussion describing resettlement choices that were made and analyse how these choices were negotiated between decision-makers and social others – a range of interpretive practices that drew upon a set of common symbolic referents and in a context in which differences in social power influenced whose interpretive practices were socially legitimized and whose were not. Thus, the analysis focuses less on what people 'really believed' and how beliefs influenced action, and more on how presentations of belief justified particular courses of action and what factored into the social legitimization of some presentations over others.

A Typology of Machazian Responses to Post-conflict Socio-spiritual Dilemmas: The 'Loyalty to Voice Continuum'

In his classic analysis of response to decline in organizations, Hirschman (1970) proposed three possible categories of reaction to dissatisfaction with the terms of interaction in associational life: 'loyalty', 'voice', and 'exit'. Loyalty strategies are attempts to realize objectives within the current terms of interaction – to abide by the rules of the game. In contrast, 'voice' strategies are attempts to realize objectives by modifying the terms of interaction itself – i.e. by changing the rules of the game. Finally, 'exit' strategies are attempts to realize objectives by leaving one milieu of social interaction (or organization) for another with entirely different terms of interaction altogether – i.e. leaving one type of game to play in an altogether different type of game.

It is useful to adapt Hirschman's analytical typology so that 'loyalty' and 'voice' are seen as ends on

a continuum rather than categorically dichotomous options. With this typology, modification responses are not seen as *either* 'voice' or 'loyalty' options but as all having *both* voice and loyalty aspects, that vary in their relative weight to each other depending on where the response is located between the two poles of the continuum. Thus, a response located closer to the 'loyalty' pole will involve fewer or more superficial challenges to the terms of interaction, whereas those located closer to the 'voice' pole will propose more fundamental epistemological shifts in the current terms of interpretation and interaction. Machazian strategies for coping with the socio-spiritual dilemmas posed by particular resettlement options can be analysed as ranging across the entirety of this continuum.

Negotiating return

Examined within this framework, those who returned to Machaze 'outright' without retaining social investments in South African marriages can be thought of as pursuing options closer to the 'loyalty' end of the continuum. Their strategies resembled those long practised by Machazian labour migrants. Throughout the twentieth century Machazian migrants professed a strong belief in the importance of maintaining connections not only with living relatives but also with their ancestral spirits in Machaze. The fact that ancestors were buried in Machaze also provided it with a form of 'place-specific utility' that played a role in encouraging ultimate permanent settlement in Machaze upon retirement. Throughout their migrant careers Machazian men remained attentive to their obligations vis-à-vis ancestors, believing that illness or misfortune during migration was often a sign that ritual gestures of respect due to ancestral spirits were overdue and necessitated a return. Such ritual obligations included cleaning graves and building or repairing 'houses' built specially for ancestral spirits. They also implied a physical return to Machaze itself. The transformation in status of important social others (such as a father) through death, provided particularly strong motivation for immediate return to Machaze. Many men reported leaving hard won jobs in order to return to Machaze for a funeral that would ensure good socio-spiritual relations with a new ancestor.

Moreover, in contrast to religious beliefs that draw a sharp boundary between worlds of living and spiritual interaction. Machazians believed their ultimate destiny was to continue to interact in death within the same social world they had been active in during their lifetime, albeit from a transformed and more powerful social position as ancestral spirits themselves. The realization of this destiny required preserving physical connections with ancestors[3] that translated into a strong desire to be buried in Machaze. It is difficult to overestimate the importance of this factor in motivating Machazian migrants to return to Machaze, a factor reported widely in other African societies as well (e.g. Caldwell 1969; Gugler 1975; Bourdillon 1991).

While a desire to retain connections with ancestors strongly motivated post-conflict return to Machaze, it is important to acknowledge that a whole range of different socio-spiritual dilemmas motivated returnees, often in conflicting ways that affected timing and destination decisions. Many individuals returned to the district but not to the exact localities they had lived in before the war so as to avoid others whose wartime activity had adversely affected them (or vice versa). Thus, in one post-conflict locality over 60 per cent of the village 'elders' (*madodas*) had lived elsewhere in the district before the war. Returnees were also concerned with the 'loose' *mfukwas* produced by the violent deaths and non-burial of soldiers. Local communities and churches often organized rituals to capture and 'send home' these spirits whose origin outside of Machazian socio-spiritual worlds made them particularly dangerous because they had no living ancestors and thus no potential and positive vested interests in Machaze. Finally, many Machazians waited to return until rain ceremonies that were disallowed by the pre-war regime[4] were successfully re-instated by local headman. Ultimately, many returnees to Machaze believed the potential consequences of offending ancestors outweighed other risks (water scarcity, chronic drought, and landmines in particular) that return entailed.

Investing in 'token return'

Prolonged absence from Machaze and consequent failures to perform necessary rituals during the war were often described in interviews as 'excused' by the spirits in light of the war's exigent circumstances. However, when return became possible Machazian men in South Africa faced greater challenges justifying to others (and even to themselves) any further deferral of these obligations or of return. In particular, men with South African wives feared that discontented spouses and elderly parents back in Machaze might trigger ancestral sanctions from *vadzimu* or more grievous harm via *mfukwas*.

In contrast to those who returned to Machaze outright after the war, those who desired to maintain socio-economic investments made in South Africa were forced to explore options further from the 'loyalty' end of the continuum. They thus faced a greater challenge in having their choices acknowledged as legitimate realizations (rather than violations) of the recognized socio-moral order. Two specific strategies – of 'token return' and of 'deferred contingent return' – represented attempts to justify maintaining socio-economic investments in South Africa in what were primarily 'loyalty' terms – i.e. not as challenges to the fundamental rules of the socio-moral order but as novel ways of realizing it. Most importantly, both of these strategies acknowledged the non-negotiability of Machaze as the primary point of socio-spiritual symbolic reference, but proposed novel interpretations of what ongoing investments in South African signalled about their ultimate investment in and attachment to Machaze itself.

Transnationally polygynous men contested claims that a zero–sum game relationship existed between their investments in Machaze and those in South Africa. It is important to realize that the distribution of investment between Machazian and South African poles did vary considerably among these men. Whereas some invested as much or even more heavily in Machaze than they did in South Africa, the strategies of those who invested primarily in South Africa are of primary interest to this analysis. Some men returned briefly to Machaze in order to obtain a wife in Machaze to live with their elderly parents, before returning to South Africa where they focused most of their interests, energies, and time. Through such 'marriages,' men essentially absent from Machaze were able to fulfil many of their prescribed duties towards mothers and ancestors.

In one case a Machazian man had briefly returned and rebuilt three huts on his deceased father's homestead – one for his mother, one for a new wife whom he brought to live with and help his mother, and a third for himself. Although he had not returned since this visit five years previously, he had sent money to his mother and wife and for a brother to build a ritual house for their father's spirit because of reported 'spiritual problems'. His primary concern was that his wife, who felt abandoned, might have to be sent home to her parents because her discontent was stirring up spiritual activity, thus leaving his mother without assistance and likely to become unhappy herself. With two adult, married sons living in South Africa, with two South African wives living with him in his home with plumbing and electricity, and with his own car and taxi business, he admitted the low likelihood of ever returning to actually live in 'his' hut in Machaze. Instead, he hoped to counter the emerging spiritual problem occasioned by his continued absence by sending more money to use as *lobola* in obtaining another wife in Machaze to live with their mother. Transnational polygyny allowed such men to simultaneously remain in South Africa while responding to critical moral imperatives, through what amounted to 'token returns'.

Narrating 'deferred/contingent return'

Other men with considerable investment in South Africa pursued strategies of 'deferred/ contingent' return, by reframing their continued presence in South Africa as delays in, rather than a definitive break with, social investment back in Machaze. One migrant interviewed in South Africa who pursued this strategy felt that his poor health signalled a need to return to Machaze in order to appease ancestral spirits. He elaborated highly detailed and concrete plans for his future post-return life in Machaze (constructing houses, starting a grinding mill and chicken raising business, drilling a well) that contrasted sharply with his vagueness about when exactly that return would occur. Interestingly, return was always stated as an imperative that was attached to indeterminate conditionality in its timing: 'of course I *must* return … *but* I must make sure I have enough money for the trip and for drilling (the well) … I *will* go soon … *but* my son *must*

first be well established in his work so all is well here …' Another man claimed to be postponing his return to Machaze because he lacked money for the trip. However, he lived in one of the better houses in the township with internal plumbing, five rooms, a stereo and a colour TV. He had a job that allowed him to play the lottery every day and was proud of the support he received from his son whom he described as working in Johannesburg as a medical technician. Although he clearly could afford to go back he seemed uninterested in doing so soon or in making significant investments back in Machaze.

Frequently such 'narratives of intended return' (Lubkemann 2000d) reframed delay not as a matter of reluctance to return, but as a desire to ensure the quality and success of that return, sometimes even emphasizing the responsibility that returnees had towards others and the need to remain abroad in order to save enough money to fulfil these responsibilities. These performances were structured to emphasize the inevitability and desirability of 'return' as an end while simultaneously emphasizing conditionality and indeterminacy in defining means to that end. Thus, 'narratives of intended return' were performance devices that paradoxically affirmed a connection to Machaze while justifying an ongoing absence from Machaze and continued social investment elsewhere. These performances thus effectively negotiated the socio-spiritual dilemmas created by the growth of wartime socio-economic investment in South Africa. Such 'narratives of intended return' might be seen above all as claims about moral positioning in a socio-spiritual world, rather than clear expressions of intentions to return or actual return. More than expressing intentions to go back to Machaze, narratives of 'intended return' were always public claims about the way social relations 'should be' and about how current activity met socio-spiritual obligations. On one hand, these presentations legitimized the continued participation of 'non-returnees' in a community in which those who retained active investments in affairs back in Mozambique constituted a 'moral majority'.

As explained elsewhere (Lubkemann 2000d), there were significant reasons why Machazian migrants primarily oriented towards South Africa wanted to remain within the Machazian community – i.e. to continue interact with other Machazians in

South Africa. In a competitive labour market, ethnic networks were critical for securing jobs or assistance during unemployment. In responding to growing xenophobia and crime in South Africa, these networks also provided the only alternative for illegal immigrants unable to avail themselves of legal recourse. A more complex set of issues involved new domestic strategies. In cases of marital dispute or dissolution, South African spouses sometimes used their Mozambican husband's illegal status as leverage. After the war some men replaced South African wives with women brought from Machaze (who had neither supporting kinship networks nor legal status in South Africa) in order to solve this problem. Despite their disinterest in Machaze, these men hoped to confine the social interaction of Machazian wives and children to Machazian social circles in order to counter the influence of what they perceived as a moral laxity in South African society that threatened their patriarchal authority. Migrant men thus participated in the Machazian community not only as an economic network but also as a socio-moral mechanism for reproducing power configurations and defining terms of social interaction that served their interests. Maintaining Machazian identity and community was paradoxically a way for men disinterested in Machaze itself to deal with various South African-specific problems entailed by their permanent residence in the townships.

However, it is also critical to realize that Machazian 'narratives of intended return' were presentations of self (Goffman 1974) performed not only for those living in the Machazian community but also to its spiritual inhabitants, in many ways regarded as the 'box seat' occupants for these performances. As such, they were claims made to the full audience of those perceived to exercise important forms of sanction over one's fortune in life. In fact, such narratives were performed in a variety of ways that redefined roles in Machazian religious institutions and transformed the marketplace of religious organizations. The business of negotiating postponements of return to Machaze was a booming cottage industry in South Africa in 1997–8. Whereas Machazian '*nyangas*' and '*nhamossoros*' were reported as rarely if ever active in South Africa before the war, their services in negotiating postponements of return with ancestral spirits were in high demand after the conflict. Moreover, after the war church *profetas* became increasingly active in such mediation roles whereas they had shunned such involvement before it.

Both strategies of 'token return' and 'deferred/ contingent return' represent a move further away from the 'loyalty' pole on the 'loyalty–voice' continuum of strategies for coping with the socio-spiritual dilemmas implied by post-conflict resettlement choices. Nevertheless, both these strategies justified change within already existent terms of interaction, in a sense casting aspects of 'voice' in 'loyalty' terms. As with strategies of 'token return', practices of social disinvestments from Machaze were interpreted as affirmations of, rather than challenges to the non-negotiability of Machaze's monopoly on centrality in the socio-spiritual world.

Voicing strategies of 're-place-ment'

In contrast, the strategies deployed to cope with socio-spiritual dilemmas by the minority of Machazian men (under 15 per cent) who openly sought to constitute post-conflict lives solely in South Africa without any return or investment back in Machaze, evidenced stronger elements of 'voice.' Many of these men actually brought their Machazian wives to live with them in South Africa after the war. What distinguished these men from the majority of other migrants was their affirmation that they did not suffer sanctions from spirits as a result of their decisions to remain permanently in South Africa, and that their ancestors had accepted this relocation as permanent.

The spirits' tolerance of this choice was explained with reference to historical events. Specifically, the Machazian origin myth that narrates original migration from Eastern Zimbabwe into the Machazian lowlands, and the historically documented migration of Machazians to Bilene in southern Mozambique under the pre-colonial ruler Gugunhanna (in the 1880s) were invoked as parallels to the wartime forced migration and resettlement of Machazians in South Africa. Both of these historical migrations involved permanent resettlement away from 'original' ancestral graves. This exegesis posited that historical occasions of permanent resettlement had avoided spiritual repercussions because they originated in exigent circumstances and involved respectful consultation with the ancestors. In particular, ancestors had been notified about their descendants' new whereabouts so they could 'find' and continue to interact with the living, thus reconstituting the socio-spiritual world. Key leaders among those who had decided to re-settle permanently in South Africa claimed to have successfully engaged in similar notifications, which legitimized their own permanent relocation. As one respondent put it 'When I die I will be an ancestor here (in South Africa) no, I will not make my children go back to Machaze, but rather they must come back here.'

While still clearly drawing on fundamental epistemological elements of Machazian religious beliefs, such narratives proposed a profound re-ordering of those elements. In particular, they challenged the notion of Machaze as the central and single stable referent for organizing the socio-spiritual world and socio-moral order, thus dislodging it from a non-negotiable position in socio-spiritual interaction. In fact, such narratives actually propose for South Africa a form of moral anchorage that was previously only attributed to Machaze through the claim that one's own spirit will compel children to remain oriented to the newly negotiated 'home' in South Africa.

Such 'narratives of re-place-ment' constituted far more radical infusions of 'voice' into strategies for coping with the perceived socio-spiritual challenges of displacement. Though these narratives were not uncontested and were only pursued by a minority, it is important to note that their public proposal was also not grounds for immediate marginalization by other Machazian community members in South Africa. In fact, far from being marginal members of the community, these men often played pivotal and powerful roles in its organization, as pastors and in other influential and respected capacities.

Exiting marginalization

Perhaps the most radical strategies for coping with the socio-spiritual dilemmas of post-conflict resettlement options were deployed by a small group of Machazian women whose extreme marginalized position was the product of wartime displacement. The same transnational strategies that allowed Machazian men to guard and enhance their life-

strategies, increasingly forced some Machazian wives to face extremely difficult and equally marginalizing choices related to the realization of their fertility.[5] Facing prolonged spousal separation[6] some women could only bear children – the critical element of future security – through culturally prohibited sexual unions with men other than their husbands. However, this option made divorce more likely and placed these women's children at risk in the case of divorce. Alternatively, women could remain faithful to absent husbands and risk having few or no children. The social organization of wartime displacement thus created a contradiction for women that could only be resolved by fulfilling one cultural prescription at the expense of the other.[7] For many women this dilemma became more acute as the war came to span more of their fertile years or robbed them of children already born.

Most women facing such choices opted to have children, even at the expense of doing so 'legitimately'. Some women who stayed in Machaze during the war bore children with soldiers. Others in UNHCR camps in Zimbabwe moved away from kin in order to bear children free from their social vigilance and disapproval. After the war, many of these women faced claims from husbands or affines on children produced in extra-marital wartime unions. Many women whose children were the product of non-consensual unions and wartime rape also faced similar threats of being divorced and losing children that had been borne as a result of their violent sexual exploitation during the conflict.

As examined in greater depth elsewhere (Lubkemann, 2000c), these women faced considerable disadvantages in pressing their claims to these children in the face of prevalent Machazian ideologies of kinship that privileged the rights of patrilineages who had paid *lobola*. Accordingly, many of these women opted not to return to Machaze after the war. Others in this predicament actually left Machaze for the first time *after* the war. Despite high costs of living that made subsistence a challenge, many of these women settled 200 kilometres to the north, in the peri-urban shanty towns around the provincial capital of Chimoio.

More than merely removing themselves from Machaze as a place, these women sought to extricate themselves entirely from the Machazian socio-spiritual world by minimizing their interaction with other Machazians in Chimoio.[8] Fearful not only that legal claims might be pressed against them, these women sought to counter the potential sanctions of reproachful Machazian spirits. By minimizing contact with other Machazians and in particular with kin whose reproach their residence in Chimoio was likely to invite, they believed they could lessen the chance of being found by these spirits and of being made both the targets of *uloi* and accused of causing it. 'My friends are from the church and the market' remarked one such woman in Chimoio, 'because there are fewer *complicoes* (complications) when they are not also from Machaze. When I worked near my (ex-) husband's wife she would tell her husband if I made more money. Then they said that I was making (spiritual) problems for her son. They wanted to take my children. That is why they have called me back to Machaze'. Another woman explained that despite a strong desire to find a husband who would support her and her children, she had refused the proposals of several Machazian suitors: 'I want nothing with them because they are from Machaze – I will marry anybody, *anybody except a man from Machaze.*' Such responses embody what can be thought of in terms of Hirschman's typology as strategies of 'exit' – attempts to realize objectives by leaving one 'game' to participate in another one rather than either abiding by its rules ('loyalty') or attempting to modify them ('voice').

Many of these women joined Protestant churches in Chimoio that were distinguished precisely by the fact that they had no sister congregations in Machaze itself. Virtually all the congregations in which migrant men in South Africa participated had counterparts back in Machaze. The strong popularity among these women of the Igreja Universal do Reino de Deus (Universal Kingdom of God Church) and the Igreja Evangelica Cristo Vive (Jesus Lives Evangelic Church) constituted alternative social support networks for them. Indeed, it also allowed them to interact with other Machazian women like themselves without the threat of spiritual sanctions, by re-casting these women in the role of 'church sisters' rather than 'Machazian women'.

The focus in these churches' teachings also struck a noteworthy contrast to the emphasis of teachings in churches attended by Machazians in South Africa and in Machaze itself. As others have also noted (Chingono 1995), the charismatic Protestant churches attended by these women emphasize the importance of the nuclear family – and in particular the mutual rights of spouses – rather than extended kinship obligations, reflecting their recent Western source (the Igreja Universal do Reino de Deus is Brazilian in origin and has large congregations in the USA and Portugal). The emphasis on nuclear family obligations ratified the sense of injustice these women felt as a result of wartime spousal abandonment and justified their own actions, while the emphasis in these charismatic congregations on 'holy spirit power' promised strong protection against ancestral spirits de-legitimized by being re-cast as 'demons'. In contrast, the Zionist denominations in Machaze that had been brought back by Machazians from the mines decades prior to the war tended to emphasize extended kinship obligations and to realize and work within, rather than challenge, the terms of the established socio-moral order (Lubkemann 2000a). Only within the terms of the new socio-spiritual worlds afforded by the Charismatic movements in Chimoio were radically marginalized Machazian women empowered to re-establish new networks with the living and ward off the unwanted sanction of spirits.

Conclusion: Social Power in Reconstituting Socio-spiritual Worlds

Anthropologists have long been attentive to the complex ways in which religious beliefs can serve to define social identities by delimiting the membership of 'moral communities', by assigning social actors particular positions within them, and by providing interpretations of the moral value of activity (Evans-Pritchard 1956; Barth 1969; Dumont 1970; Bloch 1986; Werbner 1989; Geschiere 1997). However, the ways in which religious beliefs authorize inclusion or exclusion or structure behaviour is not simply a matter of enacting self-evident and uncontested meanings. Precisely because they carry the 'symbolic power' (Bourdieu 1991) to authorize action and demarcate community, religious beliefs are critical resources whose meanings are constantly contested.

Other forms of power – symbolic and material – are mobilized in these contests in an attempt to shape the terms of authorization themselves. In conclusion, this analysis focuses on the ways in which other forms of social power bear on which authorizing claims are socially legitimized and which are not, and thus ultimately on the degree to which 'voice', 'loyalty', and 'exit' options are available to different categories of social actors.

The strategies reviewed in this article represented the attempts by a range of social actors with very different levels of social power to reconstitute socio-spiritual worlds that could preserve or enhance their own social positions. Which strategies were available to social actors in their attempts to authorize post-conflict resettlement options whose meanings were subject to being contested by other Machazian community members, was highly dependent on the very different levels and forms of social power available to different categories of Machazians.

[…]

Notes

1   In Machaze *mfukwa* referred not to an essentialized category of spirit but to a state into which a spirit entered because of violent death, being wronged in the extreme, or having grievously transgressed the socio-moral order in life. Thus particularly powerful and/or oppressive chiefs (suspected of using *uloi* themselves to become powerful) were often believed to reappear as *mfukwas* after death. Those who committed suicide were also feared as potential *mfukwas*. People reported that during the war their own relatives who perished violently assumed this state. This appears to have been a wartime shift in beliefs, since it was reported that prior to the war the dead only acted as *vadzimu* vis-à-vis their own kin, a report confirmed by scholarly accounts of Ndau beliefs earlier in the century (Curtis 1920; Rennie 1973). Historically, the distinction between *vadzimu* and *mfukwa* may have been categorical, although the evidence is unclear (Lubkemann 2000a).

2   Those men who did not migrate to South Africa during the war usually fell into one of three categories: those recruited by the military; young men who had not yet undertaken a migratory labour trip abroad; and older men who had retired from migratory careers. As the war progressed younger and older men tended to move in patterns similar to those of Machazian women (and frequently in their company), with the exception that once in Zimbabwe, younger men sought (illegally) work outside the refugee camps on farms or in other wage labour opportunities while retaining contact and mutual support with camp-settled relatives.

3   In Machazian religious beliefs spirits need physical connections to lead them to the living with whom they interact. Thus in *uloi* it is believed that a victim's hair or nails, or touching a common object, or crossing a victim's path, allow *mfukwas* to find their victims. Despite being powerful, spirits are seen to have human-like frailties such as the ability to get lost, become confused, or even be tricked. Thus for example, oral accounts focus on the importance of physical letters in assisting ancestral spirits to 'find' migrants who worked outside known mine areas (Lubkemann 2000a).

4   Many Machazians identified the post-independence government's policy of prohibiting rain ceremonies and desecrating the graves of chiefs as a primary cause for the war itself (Lubkemann 2000a).

5   Polygyny allowed men to obtain old-age support through marriages to younger women as well as from children. Women, however, were more likely to have a spouse die before they did and less likely to remarry after being widowed. Consequently, children provided the only source of old-age support for older Machazian women, making fertility more critical to their old age security than it was for men.

6   Strategies of transnational polygyny depended on the ability of Machazian men to keep their Mozambican spouses from joining them in South Africa. Machazian men often engaged in misinformation tactics or in attempts to indefinitely defer assistance to wives who did attempt to join them (Lubkemann 2000d).

7   Within Machazian cultural prescriptions fertility was a far more 'time-embedded' (Malmberg 1997) project – in the sense that it had to be realized within more narrowly prescribed temporal parameters for women than it was for men. Thanks to culturally prescribed polygyny and biology an adult man's fertility could span most of his lifetime. By contrast, Machazian women's fertility was biologically more time-restricted and culturally limited to children they alone gave birth to.

8   Chimoio was an internal migration destination from Machaze before the war. It garnered a large internally

displaced population from Machaze during the war. Many who returned from there to Machaze after the war retained houses and social or economic interests in Chimoio as well.

References

Alexander, J. (1994) 'Terra e Autoridade Politica no Pos-Guerra em Mocambique: O Caso da Provincia de Manica', *Arquivo* 16: 5–95.

Barth, F. (1969) *Ethnic Groups and Boundaries: The Social Organization of Cultural Differences*, Boston, Little Brown and Co.

Bloch, M. (1986) *From Blessing to Violence: History and Ideology in the Circumcision Ritual of the Merina of Madagascar*, Cambridge, Cambridge University Press.

Bourdieu, P. (1991) *Language and Symbolic Power*, Cambridge, Massachusetts, Harvard University Press.

Bourdillon, M. (1991) *The Shona Peoples*, Gweru, Zimbabwe: Mambo Press.

Caldwell, J. (1969) *African Rural–Urban Migration: The Movement to Ghana's Towns*, New York, Columbia University Press.

Care (1994) *Baseline Nutritional Survey: Machaze District (March, 1994)*, Maputo, Mozambique: CARE International Report.

Chingono, M. (1995) *The State Violence and Development*, Aldershot, United Kingdom, Avebury Press.

Curtis, N. (1920) *Songs and Tales from the Dark Continent Recorded from the Singing and the Sayings of C. Kamba Simango, Ndau Tribe, Portuguese East Africa*, New York, Shirmer Press.

Dumont, L. (1970) *Homo Hierarchicus*, London, Weidenfeld and Nicolson.

Evans-Pritchard, E. E. (1956) *Nuer Religion*, London, Oxford University Press.

Geffray, C. (1989) *A Causa Das Armas: Antropologia da Guerra Contemporanea em Mocambique*, Lisbon, Portugal, Editora Afrontamento.

Geschiere, P. (1997) *The Modernity of Witchcraft: Politics and the Occult in Post-Colonial Africa*, Charlottesville, Virginia, University of Virginia Press.

Goffman, E. (1974) *Frame Analysis: An Essay on the Organization of Experience*, Cambridge, Harvard University Press.

GTZ (1993) *Projecto de Reintegração, Reassentamento e Reconstrução do Distrito de Mossurize*, Chimoio, Mozambique, GTZ-MAARP.

GTZ (1996) *Conflict Driven Migration, Post-Conflict Reintegration, and Rehabilitation 1984–1996*, Chimoio, Mozambique, GTZ-MAARP.

Gugler, J. (1975) 'Migration and Ethnicity in Sub-Saharan Africa: Affinity, Rural Interests, and Urban Alignments', in H. I. Safa and B. M. du Toit (eds.) *Migration and Development: Implications for Ethnic Identity and Political Conflict*, Paris, Mouton, pp. 295–309.

Hirschman, A. O. (1970) *Exit, Voice and Loyalty: Responses to Decline in Firms, Organizations and States*, Cambridge, Harvard University Press.

Lubkemann, S. (2000a) 'Situating Wartime Migration in Central Mozambique: Gendered Social Struggle and the Transnationalization of Polygyny', Providence, Rhode Island, unpublished PhD dissertation for the Department of Anthropology, Brown University.

Lubkemann, S. (2000b) 'Sociocultural Factors Shaping the Mozambican Repatriation Process', in S. Lubkemann, L. Minear and T. G. Weiss (eds.) *Humanitarion Action: Social Science Connections*, Providence, Rhode Island: Thomas Watson Jr. Institute for International Studies.

Lubkemann, S. (2000c) 'Other Motives, Other Struggles: Gender Politics and the Shaping of Wartime Migration in Mozambique', in E. M. Gozdziak and D.J. Shandy (eds.) *Rethinking Refuge and Displacement: Selected Papers on Refugees and Immigrants Vol. VIII, 2000*, Arlington, Virginia: American Anthropological Association, pp. 343–368.

Lubkemann, S. (2000d) 'The Transformation of Transnationality Among Mozambican Migrants in South Africa', *Canadian Journal of African Studies*, 34(1): 41–63.

Manning, C. (1998) 'Constructing Opposition in Mozambique: RENAMO as Political Party', *Journal of Southern African Studies* 24(1): 161–189.

McGregor, J. (1998) 'Violence and Social Change in a Border Economy: War in the Maputo Hinterland, 1984–1992', *Journal of Southern African Studies* 24(1): 37–60.

O'Laughlin, B. (1992) 'Interpretations Matter: Evaluating the War in Mozambique', *Southern Africa Report*, January, pp. 22–33.

Rennie, J. K. (1973) 'Christianity, Colonialism and the Origins of Nationalism Among the Ndau of Southern Rhodesia 1890–1935', unpublished PhD Dissertation, Chicago, Northwestern University Department of History.

Roesch, O. (1992) 'RENAMO and the Peasantry in Southern Mozambique: A View from Gaza Province', *Canadian Journal of African Studies* 26(3).

Werbner, R. (1989) *Ritual Passage, Sacred Journey: The Process and Organization of Religious Movement*, Washington DC, Smithsonian Institution Press.

Part XII

Development, Governance, and Globalization

Introduction

"Development," "Governance," "Globalization" – three notions that refer to a broad range of partially overlapping ideas, practices, and dimensions of experience – have all served at one time or another as master narratives around which international engagement with postcolonial Africa has been imagined and mobilized. Within the international community these notions have generally been invoked to suggest something that Africa's postcolonial societies "lack," indicators of "deficits" requiring external intervention to remedy. Africa's postcolonial period of "independence" has thus been one in which former colonial rulers and contesting global powers – recast as "donors" and "aid providers" – have formulated and reformulated blueprints for socio-economic and political change and wielded their considerable power to influence the direction of economic policies and political practice.

Arguably no policy idea or practice has held greater sway for a longer period of time, or had more pervasive, consequential, and contradictory effects on social existence in postcolonial Africa than "development." At the dawn of independence "development" was touted by many African leaders as the primary means by which to achieve material progress and political rights that the social exclusions and economic predations of colonial rule had denied most Africans. Visionary postcolonial leaders such as Kwame Nkrumah (of Ghana), Julius Nyerere (of Tanzania), and Samora Moisés Machel (of Mozambique) believed that development should involve dramatic and comprehensive transformation not only in economic activity but also in social relations in order to engender national self-reliance and social justice, and not only material progress. This transformation would require shedding the economic subservience of colonial rule as well as what some political elites derided as "obscurantist tradition."

In the context of the global ideological and political struggle of the Cold War, this powerful modernization narrative had both its Marxist and Liberal variants, which, despite their differences, shared a common faith that African societies would replicate the social and economic steps that had been followed by nations in the already industrial world. In this narrative, urbanization and a shift from agricultural subsistence to industrial production and mechanized agriculture would signal progress and engender higher standards of living. However, for the vast majority of ordinary Africans most elements of this modernization vision remain unrealized. In fact, as James Ferguson has shown in Zambia (Chapter 41 in this volume) and in Lesotho (1994), Peter Uvin in Rwanda (Chapter 42 in this volume), James Howard Smith (2008) in Kenya, Donald Donham (1999) in Ethiopia, and many others elsewhere, the record of development policies across the continent has been a dismal one – whether measured in terms of improved living standards, or even with the more lenient and less socially attentive metrics used to gauge macroeconomic growth.

The reasons for this failure have been the subject of extensive debate and analysis to which entire volumes of readings have been hard pressed to do justice. Instead the readings here were selected because they focus on some of the most consequential social and cultural effects of development and its failure. In no small part, those social effects have been particularly profound because development has actually been highly successful as a social myth that charters the expectations and aspirations of ordinary Africans despite its failure to deliver on its promises. Thus, as Ferguson (Chapter 41 in this volume), Richards (Chapter 38 in this volume), J.H. Smith (2008), Comaroff and Comaroff (1993, 2001), Moran (2006), and others have all explained, the vision of material progress proffered by development has become an eminently "African" vision in which the "mythology of modernization" weighs heavily.

The material success that development policies have failed to produce – and the actual downturn in standards of living to which some of its orthodoxies (such as structural adjustment) directly contributed – have been a wellspring of such great frustration precisely because the way things actually are stands in stark contrast to what the cosmological blueprint of modernization suggests they should be. The gap between development-driven expectations and development-generated experiences – variously labeled as "abjection" (Ferguson, this volume) or as "structural violence" (Uvin, this volume) – has thus underwritten political action and even a great deal of the political violence that has plagued Africa throughout its relatively short postcolonial tenure (see also Lubkemann, Chapter 40 and Richards, Chapter 38 in this volume).

Development has nourished this frustration not only as a broadly subscribed set of unrealizable ideals or as a set of policies whose failures have often accentuated the challenges of basic subsistence, but also as a social presence – an effect that has been rarely noted by most analysts. Development practitioners are a pervasive and seemingly permanent social presence throughout much of the continent. As Uvin contends in Chapter 42 in this volume, the effects of the "development tribe's" presence can significantly accentuate perceptions of injustice and inequality, sometimes with the profoundest of consequences.

While analysts such as Immanuel Wallerststein (1974), Andre Gunder Frank (1991), and Walter Rodney (Chapter 30 in this volume) have noted how historical and global forces have been essential to the production and perpetuation of Africa's underdevelopment, many other analysts and international donors in particular have tended towards emphasizing "internalist"explanations for African development failures. Whereas earlier iterations of development ideology (such as modernization theory) identified forms of culture and modes of social organization as the primary impediments to development, the notion of a "crisis of governance" has gained greater sway as an explanation over the last two decades. In emphasizing the need to drastically shrink the public sector, the structural adjustment policies of the 1980s already foreshadowed international skepticism about the African state, that has since given rise to a far more explicit critique that emphasizes Africa's need for "good governance" and identifies the lack of the same for most of its development woes and much of its political volatility.

Neo-patrimonial forms of political organization have been singled out most specifically for such criticism and often as a particularly "African" political form – a view that Bayart in this volume challenges and turns on its head in arguing that it is rather the Weberian bureaucratic model prevalent in the West that is the historical and sociological exception. Bayart's general analysis of neo-patrimonial governance synthesizes and builds upon a distinction made by many others previously (e.g. Berry, 1993) and since (Richards, 1996; Ashforth, 2005; Moran, 2006; West, Chapter 45 in this volume) that emphasizes the importance of patronage networks in establishing and maintaining political power. In a context in which followers have been both a far scarcer and relatively more generative resource in sub-Saharan Africa than alternatives that may hold that pride of place elsewhere (such as land has in Europe) patrimonial systems have developed as mechanisms for building "wealth in people" rather than "wealth in things." In such systems power and wealth are therefore a function of a ruler's ability to attract and maintain subordinates.

While culturally prescribed expectations have played a role in sustaining this mode of political organization, Bayart (Chapter 44 in this volume) along with many others such as Smith (Chapter 43), van de Walle (2001), and Chabal and Daloz (1999) point out that international interests have been particularly well served by this mode of governance as well and that the reproduction of this system has also depended upon their active and powerful collusion. Moreover, as both Bayart (this volume) and West (Chapter 45 in this volume) point out, the latest "silver bullet" in the arsenal of the good governance evangelists – "democracy" – has often significantly reinforced the hand of predatory elites who have most benefitted from neo-patrimonialism. At the same time it has also undermined the benefits that clients once gleaned from such systems. Unsurprisingly enough these corrosive effects have meant that democracy has not always been held in the same high regard that its proponents assume it would or should have.

West reminds us that democratization in the postcolonial African context has never been merely about the institutionalization of competitive electoral politics, but has generally involved a package deal that has bundled together a variety of economic austerity measures, privatization and market liberalization, administrative decentralization, and the promotion of civil and individual rights (largely as conceived of in terms of Western values). West joins others such as Mary Moran (2006) and Adam Ashforth (2005) in pointing out how crucial it is to understand that when Africans have evaluated and reacted to "democracy" it has been to this full range of policies and their ramifying effects rather than to the more narrow notion of the term that hones in on political participation or elections alone. Moreover, these analysts along with Daniel Smith, Stephen Lubkemann, Ralph Austen (all in this volume), Donald Donham (1999), Jean and John Comaroff (1993, 1999, 2001), James Howard Smith (2009), and others, have shown that historically forged cultural understandings about power and legitimate governance have remained highly relevant in the constitution of these, often quite critical, evaluations.

Globalization – both in the more precise senses of greater integration in markets and improved access to communication technology, or the more vague notions of fuller immersion in globally circulating ideological currents and trends (such as democratization) – has arguably been the latest "remedy" touted for that which ails Africa (Ferguson, 2006). Yet as all the pieces in this section point out, Africa's ailments have not stemmed from any lack of "connectedness" with the rest of the world, but rather from the quality of the connections it has. Subordination is not in the final instance a matter of disconnection but a form of connection.

Even more so than "development," globalization is a term that has come to mean many things. In the pieces we have selected for this volume we have placed emphasis on some of the culturally shaped and transformative forms of social interaction that are among the most immediate embodiments of globalization. These include the social interaction with development practitioners, virtual interaction with e-mail scam victims on the internet, and interactions with kin members who have extended the coordinates of African social worlds through a relatively new and still growing second wave of diasporization.

In what he terms an "ethnography of decline," James Ferguson in the first article in this part, examines the social and cultural consequences of the failure of development policies to sustain economic prosperity in Zambia, even as the myths of development continued to capture the Zambian imagination. In the four decades that followed World War II and spanned the transition to postcolonial independence, Zambia experienced massive urbanization and rapid industrialization that gave many social scientists – and most importantly most Zambians themselves – reason to believe the country was poised to become a "developed nation," much in the mold of the Western nations on whose path to modernity it seemed to be so closely and successfully following.

Declining terms of trade for copper in the wake of the global oil crisis of the mid-1970s reversed Zambia's fortunes, starkly revealing the lack of diversification in an economy whose growth had depended almost solely on mining – a sector that began to shed jobs at a socially calamitous rate. Throughout the two decades that followed the international development apparatus' remedies of public austerity, the elimination of food subsidies, and the shrinkage of the public sector – all classic elements of "structural adjustment" in its heyday – added further to the woes of the growing number of unemployed Zambians who experienced a precipitous decline in their standards of living. In a context of rising costs and reduced employment opportunity a wave of unemployed urban wage earners was compelled to negotiate the economic and social challenges of return to rural areas of origin to which many maintained only the most tenuous forms of social attachment and affinity.

To most Zambians the accoutrements of modernity (as modeled in the West) at their fingertips – cars, air travel, higher education – seemed suddenly and inexplicably to be yanked from their grasp and placed far out of reach. Zambia's de-industrialization, its re-ruralization, and the shrinking of incomes and buying power seemed to everyday Zambians as a form of uninvited and undesired march away from modernity. This sense of "history running in reverse" stemmed from the fact that the charter myths of development had secured a firm grasp on the Zambian imagination of what the future ultimately *should* be about, despite the actual failure of development to sustain the economic prosperity it had once started to deliver. It is in the dissonance between development as a myth that charters social aspirations, and the lived experience of economic decline experienced under structural adjustment and because of a subordinate and vulnerable form of commodity-driven industrialization, that Ferguson locates the primary socio-cultural effects of development – a sentiment he labels "abjection."

Abjection, he suggests, is a particularly humiliating and profound sense of social exclusion, engendered by the experience of being excluded from conditions that have already been enjoyed at one time rather than merely from conditions imagined but never realized. In abjection Ferguson identifies a particularly volatile – and thus potentially politically generative and explosive form of social exclusion, in which deep frustration and despair well up and give rise to a sense that entitlement has been short-changed. It is precisely this experience of expulsion from the "garden of modernity" that has underwritten a great deal of the outrage and violent political mobilization in many other contemporary African settings, ranging from Mozambique (see Lubkemann, Chapter 40 in this volume), to Sierra Leone, and Liberia (see Richards, Chapter 38 in this volume; see also Ellis, 2001; Moran, 2006).

Far from being "unmodern," or in a condition that requires the amelioration of "development" and greater "global connectivity" (to markets, ideas, etc.), Ferguson pointedly establishes that the rural Zambian's conundrum – often as an unemployed former miner and urban resident – is in fact the product of development as it is realized in an economically subordinate corner of the global political and economic order. His or her experience as a simultaneous cognitive captive of the development myth and of the economic conditions that make that myth impossible to realize is an eminent –and perhaps in Africa, widely prevalent – form of "modernity." This experience of abjection is not in the final instance a result of global disconnection, but is the product of a particular quality of global connection that represents what Ferguson describes as the "underbelly of globalization."

Peter Uvin further extends Ferguson's critique of the contradictory effects of development as a myth that charters aspirations but also a set of policies that renders those aspirations largely unrealizable for most ordinary Africans. In "Development Aid and Structural Violence: The Case of Rwanda" he argues that the international development industry not only ignored the impending signs of the Rwandan genocide and thus did little to prevent it, but actually contributed to the social conditions that made genocidal violence possible. On the eve of genocide Rwanda was considered to be a model of development success as measured by macroeconomic indicators and the institution of donor-approved free market reforms. However, the lived reality of most Rwandans was one of growing income and asset inequality, in which over half of all households could not even meet basic nutritional requirements. The development enterprise contributed directly to both the extreme economic disparity in Rwandan society and the absolute poverty of its rural majority by reinforcing the power and economic position of predatory elites. Development projects populated their staff with these elites, and allowed jobs and projects themselves to be assigned according to patrimonial logics rather than on the basis of merit and in the process thus reinforced a predatory patrimonial logic that benefited only a very few. Moreover, by ignoring how "big men" used development projects to sequester large tracts of rural land in Africa's most densely populated country, the development apparatus contributed directly to making even basic subsistence less tenable for most rural Rwandans.

Even as development projects contributed in these ways to reducing the life chances of ordinary Rwandans the enterprise simultaneously contributed to raising their expectations. On the one hand, it did this through the explicit message it conveyed to rural residents: namely that their lives were lacking and required change – supposedly of the type that development projects could provide. On the other hand, and perhaps most consequently, it raised the expectations of rural youth through the implicit messages that were conveyed by the heavy social footprint of the international development community in Rwandan society. Thus, the socio-economically privileged international development technicians and their elite local collaborators continuously conveyed an image that shaped the aspirations and nourished the desperation and frustration of ordinary, and especially young, Rwandans. Uvin describes a sense of deep frustration that emerged among starving and impoverished Rwandans in the face of a constant and flagrant display of power and economic privilege by elites and international development professionals – who were driven around in cars most Rwandans could not even ride in let alone dream of owning, who led what were wildly opulent lifestyles by local standards, and who often treated everyday people with blatant condescension. Uvin traces the origin of the profound fury that a regime in crisis was able to harness for purposes of genocidal violence, back to the profound humiliation and desperation engendered by development's policies and social effects. His perspective is particularly unique in examining development as a socializing presence.

If Uvin's development practitioners and projects represent globalization's visceral social reach into and influence within Africa, Dan Smith looks at how young Nigerians use the internet to react to globalization by using e-mail scams to reach out to, and renegotiate their own position within, a highly unequal world. On the one hand Smith reveals how the discursive content of Nigerian e-mail scams reveals a critique by Nigerian youth of the national and international actors whose collusion they believe to be the driving force behind Nigeria's rampant corruption. "Corruption" as defined in this cultural context is revealed to be about the perceived erosion of traditional mechanisms of patron-clientism and the distortion of the moral economy that informs it because of collusion with foreign interests. Paradoxically, these same youth simultaneously use e-mail scams in an effort to renegotiate personal fortunes and constrained socio-economic opportunities that have been shaped by the global inequalities and corrupt collusions that they critique.

The issue of corruption is also at the heart of Jean-François Bayart's effort to produce a more general description of the neo-patrimonial forms of national governance that have predominated throughout postcolonial Africa. In his discussion of the "politics of the belly," Bayart draws on a wide range of African cases to demonstrate the importance of patronage networks in establishing and maintaining political power, and to explain its broader political and social effects. In his view, neither colonial nor postcolonial regimes ever proved capable of overwriting longer-standing and still operative logics for mobilizing and maintaining the personal networks that underwrite political power throughout so much of Africa. In fact both colonial indirect rule policies and the neo-colonial and geo-strategic interests of international partners during and since the Cold War have arguably reinforced patrimonial political systems organized around and by "big men."

Bayart first lays out the basic logic and concerns that drive neo-patrimonial political systems. In contradistinction to systems that organize groups around economic class, patrimonial social networks extend the principles of kinship – including both paternalistic hierarchy and filial responsibility and loyalty – to organize larger social networks that ultimately create personal bonds between leaders and followers. Governance in this mode becomes first and foremost a matter of cultivating these personal social networks often through the exercise of public power and by accessing public resources.

While the interests of external political and economic actors has been well served by this form of political organization, Bayart also argues that long-standing and deeply ingrained ideas about power and expectations about how it should be used by those who have it and their subordinates alike has also played a role in reproducing this type of system within contemporary African state politics. Thus, the pressure that subordinates exert on their leaders to use their power to gain access to resources which can be redistributed to their followers plays at least as much of a role in the "criminalization of the state" as do the personal ambitions of leaders or the foreign interests with which they collude.

As Bayart explains it, "big men" confront two major challenges in gaining and maintaining political power, and their strategies for contending with these are the drivers of neo-patrimonial political systems in Africa. They must cultivate followers – which must be done by using their power to gain access to (public) resources that can then be redistributed through private patronage networks; and they must maintain control over the resource distribution process by pre-empting the emergence of potential rivals within their own factions as well as from rival ones. Ranging across a variety of cases Bayart explains how these two imperatives have forged a political culture in which the state becomes a resource whose capture is hotly – and often violently – contested in order to nourish personalized social networks rather than realize publicly defined roles and responsibilities. Bayart's insights into the use to which rulers have put austerity measures and democratic elections – in particular to pre-empt rival claimants, provides a very different and critical perspective on the role of democracy and development policy in facilitating neo-patrimonial modes of governance throughout Africa.

In "Democracy and Carnage" Harry West hones in on a more specific case study of what has become since the early 1990s the standard donor prescription for Africa's "governance crisis": "democratization." Focusing on a country that has largely been regarded by donors and outside analysts as one of Africa's "triumphs in democracy," West reveals how ordinary Mozambicans from the Mueda region have come to view the democratic and decentralization reforms that have been instituted since the end of the civil war (1992) as a source of danger and disorder rather than welcoming it as a form of local empowerment. He focuses specifically on how historically forged understandings about the nature of political power and expectations about how it should be legitimately exercised have shaped local interpretations of the meaning of elections, the effects of privatization policies, and the expansion of individual rights and civil liberties.

Even though the efforts by Portuguese colonial rulers to control labor migration were often resisted, as were also the compulsory villagization and communal labor initiatives of the socialist postcolonial state prior to and during the civil war, both of these regimes were viewed as operating through a logic of governance that was fundamentally akin to those of precolonial rulers in terms of the central focus on maintaining wealth in people. Effective governance in this mode required constant negotiation with subjects who had considerable power to resist (or simply leave), through the provision of social and spiritual security – a task that required access to extra-local power and authority, initially in the spiritual world, but increasingly also in the form of access to and leverage with the state itself. West describes how Muedan skepticism about the election of local officials – a cornerstone of Mozambique's democratization and decentralization program – stems from their doubts that the state would listen to officials it had not had any role in appointing. Elections were thus seen as cutting such officials off from the resources of the state, and by extension as an expression of the national government's abdication from the redistributive obligations expected of legitimate governance.

Drastic reductions in social services and the rapid privatization of industrial and agro-business concerns (both the result of the liberal democratic and economic reform package) have only reinforced this suspicion and overall skepticism about "democracy." Privatization in particular allowed many local government officials to rapidly acquire a great deal of wealth. This new source of wealth has reduced their dependence upon and responsiveness to local people, and, no longer needing people these officials fail to redistribute their new found wealth. In this sense democracy is blamed for a rupturing of the long-standing compact between the governed and those who govern. Moreover, in a context in which self-enrichment without accompanying social largesse has long been characterized as illegitimate and designated as malevolent sorcery, democracy came to be blamed for an alarming rise in spiritual malfeasance and accompanying social disorder.

Official collusion in what is actually termed "government sorcery" has been further reinforced by the refusal of state officials to intervene against accused sorcerers. Whereas the government and its international backers believe this non-interference is an expression of civil liberties and religious tolerance, Muedans view this as an abrogation of the most fundamental responsibilities of governance: that of wielding power against the inevitable actions of those who seek personal advantage at the community's expense through the utilization of malevolent spiritual power. Only sorcerers can benefit from this new state of affairs, many Muedans reason, and those most obviously benefiting are rapacious local officials. Ironically enough, elections themselves are seen as further accentuating the general climate of insecurity in which sorcery flourishes. By institutionalizing the competition for political power, rather than definitively resolving it, elections are viewed as making permanent and far more prominent the forms of public contention that are most likely to invite recourse to sorcery. Ultimately, West's careful case study reveals how local languages of power are used to read, evaluate, and react to "democracy" in terms that differ significantly from those that shape liberal enthusiasm for the "global march towards democracy."

In the final chapter in this part, Diana Shandy explores an intriguing particular instance of a fairly recent facet of Africa's experience with globalization: its historically second, and still surging, wave of diasporization. In the seven decades since Evans-Pritchard (Chapter 5 in this volume) first described their customs, social structure, and subsistence strategies, the Nuer have weathered the effects of chronically resurgent civil wars and massive displacement (see Hutchinson, Chapter 10 in this volume). As a result of displacement, the Nuer social world now spans countries and continents, including economic migrants and the internally displaced in Khartoum, refugee camp communities in neighboring Kenya and Uganda, and growing communities as far afield as Minneapolis, MN in the United States. It is in this last, seemingly improbable corner of the Nuer social world that Shandy pursues her ethnography of a new African transnationalism that is increasingly vital to subsistence strategies in southern Sudan itself, even as it is also a site for the renegotiation of social relations and cultural meanings.

Unlike the historical first wave of African diasporization that was realized through the slave trade, the Nuer like the many other millions of Africa's new emigrants are able to maintain social ties with kin and community back on their continent of origin. As Shandy explains, through their remittances and other transnational social and economic investments and involvements, the Nuer in Minneapolis play a vital role in the economic survival of their relatives living back in Sudan or in displacement in neighboring nations. Culturally prescribed obligations and social expectations thus continue to carry great weight in shaping the behavior of Nuer diasporans, often burdening them with heavy duties that they struggle to fulfill. At the same time their greater access to resources has recalibrated the balance of power between those in diaspora and those who remain behind in Africa, and afforded women in particular with greater latitude for renegotiating the meaning and structure of gender relations. Cultural meaning is at the very center of these renegotiations – both as a resource deployed in some instances to invoke, constrain, or otherwise mold desired behavior, and as a system of moral prescription whose tenets are being actively contested and reformulated. While completing a fascinating trilogy that traces social transformation among the Nuer throughout the last century (see also Evans-Pritchard, Chapter 5 and Hutchinson, Chapter 10 in this volume), the transformative process of transnationalism that Shandy describes is increasingly relevant to a growing number of other postcolonial societies, as attested to by a rapidly growing list of recent studies such as those by Stoller (2002) of Senegalese in New York City, by Matsuoka and Sorenson (2001) of Eritreans and Ethiopians in Toronto, by Janet MacGaffey and Remy Bazenguissa-Ganga (2000) of Congolese in Paris, and by Stephen Lubkemann (2008) of Liberians in the United States.

References

Ashforth, Adam, 2005. *Witchcraft, Violence and Democracy in South Africa*. Chicago: University of Chicago Press.

Berry, Sara S. 1993. *No Condition Is Permanent: The Social Dynamics of Agrarian Change in Sub-Saharan Africa*. Madison: University of Wisconsin Press.

Chabal, Patrick, and Jean-Pascal Daloz. 1999. *Africa Works: Disorder as Political Instrument*. Oxford: James Currey.

Comaroff, John L., and Jean Comaroff, eds. 1993. *Modernity and its Malcontents*. Chicago: University of Chicago Press.

Comaroff, John L., and Jean Comaroff. 1999. *Civil Society and the Political Imagination in Africa: Critical Perspectives*. Chicago: University of Chicago Press.

Comaroff, John L., and Jean Comaroff. 2001. *Millennial Capitalism and the Culture of Neoliberalism*. Durham, NC: Duke University Press.

Donham, Donald, L. 1999. *Marxist Modern: An Ethnographic History of the Ethiopian Revolution*. Berkeley: University of California Press.

Ellis, Stephen. 2001. *The Mask of Anarchy: The Destruction of Liberia and the Religious Dimension of an African Civil War*. New York: New York University Press.

Ferguson, James. 1994. *The Anti-Politics Machine: "Development", Depoliticization, and Bureaucratic Power in Lesotho*. Minneapolis, MN: University of Minnesota Press.

Ferguson, James. 2006. *Global Shadows: Africa in the Neo-liberal World Order*. Durham, NC: Duke University Press.

Frank, Andre G. 1991. "The Development of Underdevelopment." *Scandinavian Journal of Development Alternatives*, 10(3): 5–72.

Lubkemann, Stephen. 2008. "Liberian Remittance Relief and Not-Only-for-Profit Entrepreneurship: The Liberian Case." In Jennifer Brinkerhoff, ed., *Diasporas and International Development: Exploring the Potential*. Boulder, CO: Lynne Rienner Press.

MacGaffey, Janet and Remy Bazenguissa-Ganga, 2000. *Congo-Paris: Transnational Traders on the Margins of the Law*. Bloomington, IN: Indiana University Press.

Matsuoka, Atsuoko, and John Sorenson. 2001. *Ghosts and Shadows: Construction of Identity and Community in an African Diaspora*. Toronto: University of Toronto Press.

Moran, Mary H. 2006. *Liberia: The Violence of Democracy*. Philadelphia, PA: University of Pennsylvania Press.

Richards, Paul. 1996. *Fighting for the Rainforest: War, Youth and Resources in Sierra Leone*. Portsmouth, NH: Heinemann.

Smith, James H. 2008. *Bewitching Development: Witchcraft and the Reinvention of Development in Neoliberal Kenya*. Chicago: University of Chicago Press.

Stoller, Paul. 2002. *Money Has No Smell: The Africanization of New York City*. Chicago: University of Chicago Press.

van de Walle, Nicolas. 2001. *African Economies and the Politics of Permanent Crisis, 1979–1999*. Cambridge: Cambridge University Press.

Wallerstein, Immanuel, 1974. *The Modern World System: Capitalist Agriculture and the Origins of the European World Economy in the Sixteenth Century*. New York: Academic Press.

Suggested Reading

Argenti, Nicolas. 2007. *The Intestines of the State: Youth, Violence, and Belated Histories in the Cameroon Grassfields*. Chicago: University of Chicago Press.

Bayart, Jean François. 1993. *The State in Africa: The Politics of the Belly*. London: Longmans.

Bayart, Jean-François, Stephen Ellis, and Beatrice Hibou. 1999. *The Criminalization of the State in Africa*. Oxford: James Currey.

Berman, Bruce, Dickson Eyoh and Will Kymlicka, eds. 2004. *Ethnicity and Democracy in Africa*. Oxford: James Currey.

Elyachar, Julia. 2005. *Markets of Dispossession: NGOs, Economic Development, and the State in Cairo*. Durham, NC: Duke University Press.

Ferguson, James. 1999. *Expectations of Modernity: Myths and Meanings of Urban Life on the Zambian Copperbelt*. Berkeley: University of California Press.

Ferme, Marianne C. 2001. *The Underneath of Things: Violence, History and the Everyday in Sierra Leone*. Berkeley: University of California Press.

Hart, Gillian. 2002. *Disabling Globalization: Places of Power in Post-Apartheid South Africa*. Pietermaritzburg, South Africa: University of Natal Press.

Kaarsholm, Preben K. ed. 2006. *Violence, Political Culture and Development in Africa*. Oxford: James Currey.

Mamdani, Mahmood. 1996. *Citizen and Subject: Contemporary Africa and the Legacy of Late Colonialism*. Princeton, NJ: Princeton University Press.

Membe, Achille. 2001. *On the Postcolony*. Berkeley, CA: University of California Press.

Piot, Charles. 1999. *Remotely Global: Village Modernity in West Africa*. Chicago: University of Chicago Press.

Reno, William. 1998. *Warlord Politics and African States*. Boulder, CO: Lynne Rienner.

Shandy, Dianna. 2007. *Nuer American Passages: Globalizing Sudanese Migration*. Gainesville, FL: University Press of Florida.

Uvin, Peter. 1998. *Aiding Violence: The Development Enterprise in Rwanda*. Bloomfield, CT: Kumarian Press.

West, Harry. 2005. *Kupilikula: Governance and the Invisible Realm in Mozambique*. Chicago: University of Chicago Press.

41

Expectations of Modernity
Myths and Meanings of Urban Life on the Zambian Copperbelt

James Ferguson

From "Emerging Africa" to the Ethnography of Decline

In the mid-1960s, everyone knew, Africa was "emerging." And no place was emerging faster or more hopefully than Zambia, the newly independent nation that had previously been known as Northern Rhodesia. The initiation of large-scale copper mining in the late 1920s had set off a burst of industrial development that had utterly transformed the country; by the time of Independence in 1964, that industrial growth seemed sure to propel the new nation rapidly along the path of what was called "modernization." From being a purely rural agricultural territory at the time of its takeover by Cecil Rhodes's British South Africa Company in the 1890s, the modern nation-state of Zambia had by 1969 arrived at an urban population of over 1 million (nearly 30 percent of the population), with total waged employment of over 750,000 (of a total population of just over 4 million) (Zambia 1973, 1:1), and a vibrant industrial economy that made it one of the richest and most promising of the new African states.

Observers from early on were stunned by the rapidity and scale of the social transformation that had taken place along the urban, industrial "line of rail" that ran from Livingstone in the south all the way to the Copperbelt in the north [...]. Within a few short years following the development of commercial copper mining, mining towns sprang up all along the Copperbelt [...]. European colonists settled the new towns in numbers, while "natives" came by the thousands to seek work in the mines and other new industries. Africa was having its "Industrial Revolution," thought the missionary Sandilands, at a brutal and blinding speed; the process had "something of the suddenness and ruthlessness and irresistibility, on the social plane, of what, on the military plane, we have become familiar with as the German 'blitzkrieg'" (Sandilands 1948, ix). The social anthropologist J. C. Mitchell concurred: "We in Northern Rhodesia to-day are living in a revolution, the intensity of which, as far as we can judge, has not been equalled in thousands of years" (1951, 20).

Already in 1941 Godfrey Wilson had sensed an epochal transformation:

From James Ferguson, *Expectations of Modernity: Myths and Meanings of Urban Life on the Zambian Copperbelt*, 1st edition (1999), pp. 1–7, 9–13, 234–47, © 1999. Reprinted by permission of University of California Press.

Over the heart of a poor and primitive continent civilization has laid a finger of steel; it has stirred a hundred tribes together; it has brought them new wealth, new ambitions, new knowledge, new interests, new faiths and new problems. (Wilson 1941, 9)

Thirty-five years later, Robert Bates remained equally impressed:

Less than a century ago, Zambia was exclusively agrarian; in the present era, it is a society dependent upon large-scale industry. Once characterized by village society, the territory that is now Zambia contains a score of cities of 100,000 or more persons, and these cities contain over 40 percent of its population. Where but a little over fifty years ago forests once stood, there now stand copper mines; and the marketed produce from these mines makes Zambia one of the world's leading exporters of this mineral. (Bates 1976, 1)

There was already something a little off here. Wilson's dramatic vision of "small-scale society" being suddenly replaced by "large-scale" industrialism ignored both the shallowness of "the industrial revolution" (which was largely confined to mining) as well as the way that Africans in the region had been bound up in large-scale political structures and long-distance trade for centuries before. Nor was wage labor so new in the 1920s and 1930s as it appeared – Africans from Northern Rhodesia had already been migrating in numbers to work in the mines in Katanga across the border with the Belgian Congo for at least twenty years, and some had gone as far as Rhodesia and South Africa even earlier (Perrings 1979, 14–23; Parpart 1983, 31–2; Meebelo 1986, 19). Bates's "score of cities of 100,000 or more persons," meanwhile, turned out on inspection to be only five. [...] The overdramatic and exaggerated narration of the rise of industrialism and urbanism here reflected the extent to which the Zambian experience captured something in the modernist imagination and came not only to exemplify but to epitomize the revolution that was understood to be taking place in Africa.

It was neither rapid change nor the existence of mineral wealth alone that made Zambia and its industrial core, the Copperbelt, such a good symbol of "emerging Africa." Africa, after all, had seen plenty of both in the past. Instead, it was the particular character of the social and economic transformation that captured the imagination. Zambia at its 1964 Independence was a highly urbanized nation, and newly so. The mining towns that had sprung up on the Copperbelt symbolized newness in a way that older cities could not. Here, unlike many other parts of Africa, the very idea of cities was a "modern" one. [...] And "urbanization" was understood to involve not simply a movement in space but an epochal leap in evolutionary time. Cooper has explained:

As Africans flocked into cities in ever greater numbers in the 1950s, the dualist approach to urbanization suggested that they were entering the mainstream of history. The key word in the urban anthropology of those years was "adaptation," and studies stressed how organizations from ethnic associations to trade unions eased the – inevitable – movement into an urban way of life. The liberal affirmation that the African was becoming an urbanite was an affirmation of modernity. (Cooper 1983, 12)

Urbanization, then, seemed to be a teleological process, a movement toward a known end point that would be nothing less than a Western-style industrial modernity. An urbanizing Africa was a modernizing one, and there was no place urbanizing faster than Zambia. What is more, the expanding mining economy that was driving the urbanization process was a stereotypically industrial one, whose noisy smelting plants and sooty miners seemed to reiterate a well-known chapter in the usual narratives of the West's own rise to modernity, evoking particularly the iconic images of the early period of British industrialization. And everyone knew where *that* had led. A certain convergence with a familiar Western model thus seemed to be no speculation; it was directly observable in the smokestacks that dramatically appeared on the horizon as a traveler approached the Copperbelt from the south.

What was happening along the line of rail, as Max Gluckman and others insisted, was nothing less than "the African Industrial Revolution" (Gluckman 1961; Moore and Sandilands 1948).

Until recently, this vision seemed to many a convincing and straightforwardly descriptive account of what was happening in Zambia. Throughout the 1960s and most of the 1970s, we must remember, Zambia was not reckoned an African "basket case," but a "middle-income country," with excellent prospects for "full" industrialization and even ultimate admission to the ranks of the "developed" world. In 1969 its per capita gross domestic product (GDP) was not only one of the highest in Africa (more than three times that of Kenya, and twice that of Egypt, for instance), it was also significantly higher than that of such "up-and-coming" middle-income nations as Brazil, Malaysia, South Korea, and Turkey. Indeed, with what appeared to be a rapidly rising per capita GDP of $431, it did not seem unreasonable to suppose that Zambia might soon reach the ranks of at least the poorer European nations such as Portugal, with a 1969 per capita GDP of just $568, or Spain, with $867 (United Nations 1973, 627–9). Even as late as 1979, Zambia was still being reckoned a "middle-income country," whose GNP justified a ranking above such countries as the Philippines, Thailand, or Egypt (World Bank 1979, 126). [...]

Somewhere along the way, though, "the African Industrial Revolution" slipped off the track. The script of Zambian "emergence" via industrialization and urbanization has been confounded by more than two decades of steep economic decline. According to the World Bank, per capita income in Zambia fell by more than 50 percent from 1974 to 1994 (World Bank 1996, 562). GNP per capita, meanwhile, shrunk by an average of 3.1 percent per year from 1980 to 1993, by which time the figure amounted to only $380, leaving Zambia near the bottom of the World Bank's hierarchy of "developing nations" (only 25 countries ranked lower) (World Bank 1995, 162). As of 1991, the bank reports, about 68 percent of Zambians were living in households with expenditures below a level sufficient to provide "basic needs," and 55 percent did not have sufficient income even to meet basic nutritional needs (World Bank 1996, 563).

Many causes could be cited for this precipitous decline. Probably the most important is the simplest: a steady decline in the buying power of Zambia's copper on the world market. Copper is the overwhelmingly dominant feature of the export-dependent Zambian economy and has historically accounted for some 90 percent of its exports. And in the years following the oil shock of the mid-1970s, the terms of trade for copper exporters declined sharply. [...] The market value (per unit) of Zambian exports fluctuated but remained mostly flat. The decline came about chiefly in relation to the goods that those exports could purchase, the cost of which rose markedly against copper, making exports effectively worth much less. To put the matter concretely, where in 1970 a ton of Zambian exports would have bought a certain quantity of imported goods, by the mid-1980s it would have taken more than *three* tons to buy the same quantity of goods. Since the volume of Zambia's copper exports also declined over the period, the buying power of the nation's exports declined even more rapidly than did the terms of trade. [...]

Not only the terms of trade but copper production itself declined through the period. Average annual production in the decade following Independence (1965–74) was some 672,000 tons (Daniel 1979, 87), but by 1995 several mines had closed, and the others were mostly showing declining yields. Production had dwindled to 327,000 tons and looked likely to decline even further (World Bank 1996, 562). There is no doubt that this drop in production reflected substantial operating inefficiencies, as has often been charged, as well as a declining copper content in the ore being mined (as is typical of aging mines). But, as Jamal and Weeks have pointed out, it is not surprising to see output decline while external prices are dramatically declining – indeed, this is just what classical economic theory would predict, though such obvious external factors have often been ignored by the proponents of a simplistic "African mismanagement" explanation for recent economic contraction (Jamal and Weeks 1993, 15, 84; see also Brown and Tiffen 1992).

Equally important to Zambia's hard times of late has been the burden of external debt, which continued to grow as the economy contracted, with disastrous results. At the end of 1995 Zambia's total debt amounted to $6.7 billion, and debt servicing took 41 cents of every dollar earned by exports (World Bank 1996, 562, 565). Long-term external debt in 1995 amounted to a staggering $650 per capita – this in a country whose 1995 GNP per capita was only $370 (the 1994 per capita GNP of the United States, for purposes of comparison, was $25,880) (World Bank 1995, 1996). The extreme burden of debt has left the country little choice but to yield to the demands made by lenders (via the International Monetary Fund [IMF] and World Bank) for measures of "structural adjustment" of the economy. Implemented on an on-again, off-again basis throughout the 1980s by a government that alternated between capitulation and defiance and carried through more consistently since the election of the Chiluba government in 1991, these measures have included devaluation of the currency and deregulation of foreign exchange, the removal of subsidies and price controls for food and other essential goods, the abandonment of government-guaranteed entitlements in the fields of health care and education, and the privatization of the major parastatal corporations, culminating in the selling off of the mines (underway at the time of writing). The aim has been to reduce the government's role in the economy, to establish "free markets" and a secure environment for capital, and to reduce urban consumption that is understood to have distorted rural–urban terms of trade and inhibited agricultural development.

It is important to note that these imposed policies of structural adjustment deliberately aimed to reduce urban living standards, in the belief that "high" urban wages and food subsidies had produced an "urban bias" that had "distorted" the economy. Jamal and Weeks have presented a detailed refutation of this argument, showing that the so-called rural–urban gap was largely illusory and had in any case been closed *before* the harsh austerity measures were applied to "correct" it (Jamal and Weeks 1993; see also Potts 1995). As Potts has put it, "Unfortunately for Africa's urban populations the IMF programmes were only too efficacious in decimating their incomes; even more unfortunately for them, their supposed privileged starting point was largely exaggerated" (Potts 1995, 247). The evidence is overwhelming, she goes on to say, "not only that

urban poor have become much poorer in many countries, but that their lives have become an almost incredible struggle." Nowhere is this outcome more evident than on the Copperbelt.

Between the declining mining economy and the IMF measures to reduce urban consumption, the lives of the Copperbelt's inhabitants have been "adjusted" to the point where hunger and malnutrition have become commonplace. The World Bank itself reports that the prevalence of urban poverty in Zambia increased from 4 percent in 1975 to just under 50 percent in 1994 (World Bank 1996). Jamal and Weeks, more concretely, cite a study showing that the rise in cost of a simple family food budget from 1980 to 1988 was more than 650 percent; wages did not keep up, so the monthly supplies that cost 64 percent of an unskilled worker's wage in 1980 cost 88 percent of it by 1988 (Jamal and Weeks 1993, 82). It is easy to understand, given these raw economic realities, why Copperbelt residents rioted so fiercely to protest a "structural adjustment" rise in the price of maize meal in 1987; for the urban poor, the price of food had become an issue of bare survival. Indeed, even many fully employed workers, as I found out in the course of my fieldwork in Kitwe in the late 1980s, were simply skipping meals to make it through the month. The majority who lacked formal employment were almost certainly having an even harder time. The following figures on life expectancy and child mortality, taken from the 1990 census, give an idea of the terrible consequences of such catastrophic economic contraction (Table 41.1). [...]

Economic decline is not the only cause of these demographic trends; surely the AIDS epidemic, which has hit Zambia hard, had a part in them as

Table 41.1   Life expectancy and child mortality of urban Copperbelt residents, 1980–1990

	1980	1990
Life expectancy at birth (in years)	55.3	50.3
Infant mortality rate (deaths < age 1 per 1,000 births)	84.5	107.3
Under-five mortality rate (deaths < age 5 per 1,000 births)	94.5	129.3

Source: Zambia 1995, 2:105.

well, though it is very difficult to say how large that part may be. [...] But the dramatic economic downturn has been paralleled quite closely by an equally dramatic downturn in life itself, a downturn so shattering as to shave a full five years off an average life within the span of a single decade.

Given such hardships, it is not surprising to find that the historically rapid growth of the Copperbelt towns, long fed by rural–urban migration, has dramatically slowed. In fact, the 1990 census showed that the rate of population growth for the Copperbelt cities from 1980 to 1990 was just 1.7 percent, while the national rate of population growth was 2.7 percent, meaning that the towns of the Copperbelt were actually shrinking as a proportion of the total population (almost certainly through urban–rural migration) (Zambia 1995, 2:23). This is a trend that Potts has also documented for other African cities undergoing "adjustment," which she terms "counter-urbanization" (Potts 1995; cf. Bayart 1993, 12; Berry 1976; Champion 1989).

Old linearities here seem strangely reversed. Urbanization has given way to "counter-urbanization." Industrialization has been replaced by "de-industrialization." The apparently inevitable processes of rural–urban migration and proletarianization are now replaced by mass layoffs and "back to the land" exercises. And now, with the privatization of the state-held mining company (Zambia Consolidated Copper Mines [ZCCM]), it seems that even "Zambianization" (the long-established policy of independent Zambia to seek the gradual replacement of white expatriate management with qualified black Zambians) is to become "de-Zambianization." [...] Such, at least, was the term applied in a recent newspaper article to describe the new policy of rehiring white expatriate executives to manage the mines before they go on the auction block for sale to private investors. [...]

It is not my purpose to explain the broad economic pattern I have sketched here, which many better-qualified scholars have already set out to do, [...] but rather to trace some of its effects on people's modes of conduct and ways of understanding their lives. For the circumstances of economic decline have affected not only national income figures and infant mortality rates but also urban cultural forms, modes of social interaction, configurations of identity and solidarity, and even the very meanings people are able to give to their own lives and fortunes. In a total of fourteen months of fieldwork in Zambia in the late 1980s, chiefly in the Copperbelt town of Kitwe (and the adjacent Nkana copper mine [formerly Rhokana]), I explored how the economic crisis was affecting the lives of mineworkers and others. [...] Everywhere, I found an overwhelming sense of decline and despair. Mineworkers in tattered clothes who were struggling to feed their families had to remind me that there was a time, not so long ago, when they could not only afford to eat meat regularly but could even buy tailored suits mail-ordered from London – a time, indeed, when a better-off mineworker could own a car. And what had been lost with the passing of this era, it seemed, was not simply the material comforts and satisfactions that it provided but the sense of legitimate expectation that had come with them – a certain ethos of hopefulness, self-respect, and optimism that, many seemed sure, was now (like the cars) simply "gone, gone never to return again."

I was struck by this sense of an irrecoverable loss of standing, of a demotion in the worldwide ranking of things, as I spoke with a young officer of the mineworkers' union, who was expressing his dismay at how difficult it had become to find neckties of decent quality. Soon, we were talking about the two main retail shopping districts in Kitwe, one located in what had once been in colonial days the "European" town center, the other in the former "location" reserved for "Africans." What struck me was that these two shopping districts were still called (as they had been in colonial days) "First Class" and "Second Class," respectively. Why, I wondered, did people continue this usage? Wasn't this an embarrassing holdover of colonial thinking, and of the idea of second-class status for Africans? Well, my companion replied, nobody really thought of it that way – it was just what the areas were called. "Anyway," he blurted out with a bitter, convulsive laugh, "now it's all 'second-class,' isn't it?"

The [...] faith in a country and people "going forward" seemed, in the Kitwe of the late 1980s, both absent and, in its very absence, somehow present. Like a dream, the idea of Zambians moving proudly into the ranks of the first class was both vividly remembered and manifestly unreal. The signs and symbols of modernity – within the reach of ordinary workers, for a few brief years – had been abruptly yanked away. Access to the "first-class" things of the world – cars, suits, fine clothes, a decent necktie – was not something to look forward to in an anticipated future but something to remember from a prosperous past – a past now "gone, gone never to return again." What was most striking here was the pervasive sense of enduring decline – not just a temporary patch of hard times but a durable and perhaps irreversible trend. As one man expressed it, "From now on, it's just down, down, down ..."

The mythology of modernization weighs heavily here. Since the story of urban Africa has for so long been narrated in terms of linear progressions and optimistic teleologies, it is hard to see the last twenty years on the Copperbelt as anything other than slipping backward: history, as it were, running in reverse. How else to account for life expectancies and incomes shrinking instead of growing, people becoming less educated instead of more, and migrants moving from urban centers to remote villages instead of vice versa? This is modernization through the looking-glass, where modernity is the object of nostalgic reverie, and "backwardness" the anticipated (or dreaded) future.

[...]

Global Disconnect: *Abjection and the Aftermath of Modernism*

When Godfrey Wilson published his "Essay on the Economics of Detribalization in Northern Rhodesia" in 1941, he considered that the Africans of Northern Rhodesia had just entered into an economically and culturally interconnected "world society," a "huge world-wide community" within which they would soon find a place for themselves as something more than peasants and unskilled workers (Wilson 1941, 12–13). The "civilized" clothing and manners to which so many urban Africans attached such importance, he argued, amounted to a claim to full membership in that worldwide community. Indeed, Wilson suggested, it was for this very reason that many white settlers resented and feared the well-dressed African who politely doffed his hat in the street, prefer-

ring to see all Africans in suitably humble rags. Fine formal evening wear, ballroom dancing, European-style handshaking – these, Wilson argued, were not inauthentic cultural mimicry but expressed "the Africans' claim to be respected by the Europeans and by one another as civilized, if humble, men, *members of the new world society*" (Wilson 1942, 19–20, emphasis added). [...]

That claim to full membership in "the new world society," of course, was refused in a racist colonial society. The color bar explicitly distinguished between "first-class" whites, who held the privileges of such membership, and "second-class" natives, who did not [...]. But nationalism promised to change all that, by overturning the colonial system and banishing forever the insulting idea that Zambians should be second-class citizens in their own land. The early years of Zambia's independence seemed on the verge of delivering on that promise. The color bar dropped as educated black Zambians took unprecedented positions of power and responsibility; a booming economy and strong labor unions meanwhile helped even ordinary workers to enjoy a new level of comfort and prosperity. As an "emerging new nation," Zambia appeared poised to enter the world of the "first class." It would be like other modern nations – right down to its state-of-the-art national airline, complete with up-to-date attractive airline hostesses [...]. Zambia was no exception. With a rising standard of living, bustling urban centers, and such symbols of modern status as suits made in London and a national airline, membership in the "new world society" seemed finally to be at hand.

It was the faltering of the "industrial revolution" that changed all that. For no sooner had the "blitzkrieg" of industrialization turned the world upside down for millions of Central Africans than rapid industrial decline set in motion another, even more devastating blitz. The economic hardships this has entailed have been staggering [...]. But equally important, if harder to measure, has been the sense of a loss of membership in that "world society" of which Wilson spoke, Zambia, in the good times, had been on the map – a country among others in the "modern world." It was, older mineworkers reminded me, a place regularly visited by internationally known musical acts conducting world tours. One man recalled an early 1960s concert by the American country-Western star Jim Reeves, for instance, and asked me with great feeling why such American acts no longer came to Zambia. But it is not just country-Western acts that have stopped coming to Zambia. In the 1970s, international airlines like British Caledonian, UTA, Lufthansa, and Alitalia connected Lusaka via direct flights to Frankfurt, Rome, London, and other European centers; British Caledonian even offered a flight to Manchester. Zambia's own national airline, Zambia Airways, also flew an impressive fleet of planes, proudly piloted by black Zambian pilots, to international destinations both expected (London, Frankfurt, New York) and surprising (Belgrade, Bombay, Larnaca). But as the economic situation deteriorated, the European carriers one by one dropped Zambia from their routes. Finally, in 1996 it was announced that Zambia Airways itself would be liquidated. Like the "industrial revolution," it had all apparently been a big mistake. Efficiency required that it be shut down. Today, a thrice-weekly British Airways plane to London is the only flight leaving Zambia for a non-African destination.

For many Zambians, then, as these details suggest, recent history has been experienced not – as the modernization plot led one to expect – as a process of moving forward or joining up with the world but as a process that has pushed them out of the place in the world that they once occupied. The only term I have found to capture this sense of humiliating expulsion is abjection (which I adapt from Kristeva [1982]; see also Borneman [1996]). *Abjection* refers to a process of being thrown aside, expelled, or discarded. But its literal meaning also implies not just being thrown out but being thrown *down* – thus expulsion but also debasement and humiliation. This complex of meanings, sad to report, captures quite precisely the sense I found among the Copperbelt mineworkers – a sense that the promises of modernization had been betrayed, and that they were being thrown out of the circle of full humanity, thrown back into the ranks of the "second class," cast outward and downward into the world of rags and huts where the color bar had always told "Africans" they belonged.

With much talk today of globalization, of new forms of worldwide interconnection, and of yet another "emerging" "new world society," it is useful to consider briefly where Zambia fits in all of this, and what the story I have told here of decline and abjection might have to say about the nature of this "new world order." The meaning of the Zambian case, I suggest, is not simply that it illustrates a gloomy process of decline and disconnection that has had no place in many of the rosier accounts of the new global economy. Beyond simply illustrating the down side of global capitalism, what has happened in Zambia reveals something more fundamental about the mechanisms of membership, exclusion, and abjection upon which the contemporary system of spatialized global inequality depends.

When the color bar cut across colonial Africa, it fell with a special force upon the "Westernized Africans" – those polished, well-dressed, educated urbanites who blurred the lines between a "civilized," first-class white world, and a supposedly "primitive," second-class black one. It was they – the "not quite/not white" (Bhabha 1997) – whose uncanny presence destabilized and menaced the racial hierarchy of the colonial social order. And it was they who felt the sting not just of exclusion but of abjection – of being pushed back across a boundary that they had been led to believe they might successfully cross (see Cooper and Stoler [1997] on the colonial dialectic of membership and exclusion). In a similar way, when the juncture between Africa and the industrialized world that had been presented as a global stairway (leading from the "developing" world to the "developed") revealed itself instead as a wall (separating the "first world" from the "third"), it was the Copperbelt and places like it – proud examples of just how modern, urban, and prosperous an emerging Africa could be – that experienced this boundary-fixing process most acutely, as a kind of abjection. The experience of abjection here was not a matter of being merely *excluded* from a status to which one had never had a claim but of being *expelled*, cast out-and-down from that status by the formation of a new (or newly impermeable) boundary. It is an experience that has left in its wake both a profound feeling of loss as well as the gnawing sense of a continuing affective attachment to that which lies on the other side of the boundary. When Copperbelt workers of an older generation spoke to me with such feeling of having once, long ago, owned a fine tuxedo or attended a concert by the Ink Spots or eaten T-bone steak at a restaurant, they were registering a connection to the "first class" that they had lost many years before but still felt, like the phantom pains from a limb long ago amputated.

When the Copperbelt mineworkers expressed their sense of abjection from an imagined modern world "out there," then, they were not simply lamenting a lack of connection but articulating a specific experience of *disconnection*, just as they inevitably described their material poverty not simply as a lack but as a loss. When we think about the fact that Zambia is today disconnected and excluded in so many ways from the mainstream of the global economy, it is useful to remember that disconnection, like connection, implies a relation and not the absence of a relation. Dependency theorists once usefully distinguished between a state of being undeveloped (an original condition) and a state of being underdeveloped (the historical result of an active process of underdevelopment). In a parallel fashion, we might usefully distinguish between being unconnected (an original condition) and being disconnected (the historical result of an active process of disconnection). Just as being hung up on is not the same thing as never having had a phone, the economic and social disconnection that Zambians experience today is quite distinct from a simple lack of connection. Disconnection, like abjection, implies an active relation, and the state of having been disconnected requires to be understood as the product of specific *structures and processes of disconnection*. What the Zambian case shows about globalization is just how important disconnection is to a "new world order" that insistently presents itself as a phenomenon of pure connection.

Global Redlining and the Neoliberal New World Order: Zambia Is no Exception?

The industrial complex is a new thing, and for all they know may disappear as quickly as it came. (William Watson, *Tribal Cohesion in a Money Economy: A Study of the Mambwe People of Zambia* (1958, 8))

On the verge of Zambian Independence, in 1963, Dudley Seers, one of the leading development economists of the period, felt it necessary to dispose of certain fallacies about industrial development that continued to linger in some minds. The first set of fallacies was what Seers called the "classical fallacies." His treatment of these was very brief and worth quoting in full.

[The classical fallacies] can be quickly disposed of. In the strict *laissez-faire* tradition, the best of all possible worlds is one in which every country specializes in the lines of production in which it has a "comparative advantage." This does not have to be worked out; it will automatically be demonstrated by the free play of market forces, provided that no tariffs, quotas, or exchange controls are imposed.

From the point of view of under-developed countries, this doctrine has one enormous drawback. Without protection from industries established overseas, new producers will find life extremely difficult (except for cases like cement, where a local producer has a natural advantage). Consequently, it means in effect that rich countries ought to stay rich and poor countries ought to stay poor. It is a doctrine which has always appealed to those in a strong competitive position; those who were relatively poor never embraced very enthusiastically the prospect of permanent poverty.

(I write about it in the present tense, because like many relics of Victoriana, it is of course still with us – especially among non-economists. We all cherish the heirlooms we inherit from our grandparents, partly out of sentimentality and partly because taste changes more slowly in ideas than in *objets d'art*.) (Seers 1963, 461–2)

The passage shows nicely not only how much the "development" world has changed since 1963 but also how malleable are even the most authoritatively expressed certainties of the discipline of economics. For leading development economists today pronounce with equally self-assured and superior intonations (albeit with far less elegance and grace) dogmas that are exactly opposite in every detail to those articulated by Seers in 1963.

For nearly two decades now, economists have insisted that the new African nations' attempts at industrialization were a foolhardy error flying in the face of basic economic laws. Exponents of what we might call "the African industrial counter-revolution" have railed against "protectionism" and "inefficient" state-subsidized industries and demanded "free markets" as a panacea for African economic ills. An industrialization that had once seemed to be a self-evidently necessary step on the road to a new nation's economic progress is now claimed to have been just a big mistake. The World Bank's influential Berg Report (World Bank 1982), for instance, explained that the only way forward for Africa was to open up its markets to the world and seek an export-led development based on the production of the products for which it had a comparative advantage – chiefly primary agricultural commodities. If Zambia was having trouble with a declining mineral export industry, it was explained, it was time to take up promising agricultural exports like coffee instead.

Thanks largely to the debt crisis and the IMF-World Bank practice of conditional lending, such wisdom came to inform national-level policy-making in Zambia, as in other parts of Africa. As outlined in chapter 1, this development led to attempts to "correct" a perceived urban bias by eliminating food subsidies and cutting real urban wages, along with privatizing state-held companies and closing down "inefficient" industries. For those declared "redundant" (laid off) or priced out of the urban market, the answer was clear: unproductive urbanites were to go "back to the land," where an agricultural future awaited them.

But now the high priests of economics may be changing their message yet again. No less a figure than Jeffrey Sachs (director of the Harvard Institute for International Development and chief guru of Eastern Europe's "transition") has recently suggested that the whole idea of an agriculture-led development strategy for African economies may have been a mistake. With the same cavalier disregard for economic history displayed by his predecessors, Sachs reduces the variation in global patterns of economic growth to four "factors": initial conditions, physical geography, government policy, and demographic change. Of these four, it is physical geography, he suggests, that turns out to be decisively important for tropical regions like sub-Saharan Africa. Permanently "penalized" by the disadvantages of its tropical climate, Africa may

never reach the income levels of temperate regions no matter what policies are followed. What is more, he claims, the virtues of agriculture-led growth may have been oversold. "Nowhere has tropical agriculture led the escape from poverty," he declares. "Sustained agriculture-led development, whether in the United States, Australia, Denmark or Argentina, has always been a temperate-zone affair" (Sachs 1997, 22). The better alternative, he suggests, may be "to accept as normal a situation in which Africa and other tropical regions are fed by temperate-zone exports, and in which the tropics earn their way in the world through manufacturing and service exports rather than primary commodity exports" (Sachs 1997, 22). "The advice of the World Bank," he adds in passing, "may also have to be rethought." Many former Copperbelt workers – recently forced against their will into a risky agricultural existence made wretched by the "disease, poor soil, unreliable rainfall, pests, and other tropical ills" that Sachs (1997, 22) seems just to have noticed – might agree. Did we say Back to the Land? Sorry, that was supposed to be Back to the Factory! All a big mistake.

In fact, it is not clear that there is any place for Africa at all in the new global economy being designed by Sachs and his associates, beyond its historic role as an open field for pillaging mineral wealth and a possible new one as a dumping ground for the industrial world's toxic waste (Ferguson 1995). As Jane Guyer has pointed out, a recent 35-page feature in *The Economist* on "The Global Economy," made almost no reference to Africa at all, making only a passing note of the "threat" to rich countries that may be posed by "the 500m or so people, most of them in Africa, who risk being left out of the global boom." The article continues, Guyer notes, "without a backward glance to the startling intellectual – not to mention political and moral – challenge of a theory of global economic growth that does not even address such a massive anomaly" (Guyer 1996, 83).

As Neil Smith has recently argued, in spite of aggressive "structural adjustment" and a rhetorical celebration of "free-market capitalism," "what is remarkable about the last two decades [in Africa] is its virtual systematic expulsion from capitalism" (1997, 180). With private ventures in the continent falling by 25 percent in the 1980s, and even further in the 1990s, Africa "has been treated to a crash course in the most vicious aspects of free-market capitalism while being largely denied any of the benefits" (Smith 1997, 180, 181; cf. Castells 1998, 90). Effectively "redlined" in global financial markets, and increasingly cut off from governmental aid flows as well, sub-Saharan Africa today functions as "a veritable ghetto of global capital" (1997, 179) – a zone of economic abjection that also makes a convenient object lesson for third-world governments in other regions that might, without the specter of "Africanization" hanging over them, be tempted to challenge capital's regime of "economic correctness" (Smith 1997; Ferguson 1995).

The very possibility of "redlining" on such a massive scale reveals that the much-vaunted flexibility of the new forms of global economy involves not simply new forms of connection but new forms of disconnection as well. With increasing international wage competition and pressure on state welfare provisions, as Smith (1997, 187) notes, "the global economy is ever more efficient at writing off redundant spaces of accumulation: the flexibility of investment and market options is matched by a wholly new flexibility in disinvestment and abandonment." It is precisely this "flexibility" that makes global redlining possible, and that makes Zambia's recent deindustrialization just as integral a part of globalization as the appearance of Mexican car factories or Shanghai skyscrapers.

To speak of expulsion and abandonment here is not to suggest that Zambia is today somehow outside the world capitalist system (and thus needs to be brought back into it). The mining industry, though shrunken, continues to dominate the Zambian economy, and may even (if the current plan for full privatization brings the new capital for exploration and development that its boosters promise) expand again in years to come; capitalists continue to profit from Zambia's copper. Other forms of capitalist production of course remain important as well. But the more fundamental point here is that the abjected, redlined spaces of decline and disinvestment in the contemporary global economy are as much a part of the geography of capitalism as the booming zones of enterprise and prosperity – they reveal less the outside of the system than its underbelly (cf. Castells 1998, 91). Expulsion and abandonment (in Smith's terms),

disconnection and abjection (in my own), occur within capitalism, not outside it. They refer to processes through which global capitalism constitutes its categories of social and geographical membership and privilege by constructing and maintaining a category of absolute non-membership: a holding tank for those turned away at the "development" door; a residuum of the economically discarded, disallowed, and disconnected – to put it plainly, a global "Second Class."

In its "Industrial Revolution" era, it was copper that connected Zambia to the world. The world needed Zambia's copper, and it was copper that put the new nation on the economic world map, while bringing in the export earnings that financed everything from cars for urban workers to state prestige projects like Zambia Airways. But copper not only connected Zambia economically, it also provided a vivid symbol of a specifically modern form of world connection. The copper wire bars produced by Zambian refineries literally did connect the world, via telephone and power cables that were forming a rapidly ramifying net across the globe. From the Soviet rural electrification program, to the United States' model Tennessee Valley Authority project, to the new South Africa's township electricity programs, electrification has provided the twentieth century with perhaps its most vivid symbol of modernization and development. Fusing a powerful image of universal connection in a national grid with the classical Enlightenment motif of illumination of the darkness, electrification has been an irresistible piece of symbolism for the modernist state (expressed perhaps most vividly in Lenin's suggestion that the "backward" Soviet peasantry be uplifted by melting enough church bells into copper wire to permit the placing of a light bulb in every village [Coopersmith 1992, 154–5]). […] It was no different in Zambia, where the electrification of the townships was a compelling symbol of inclusion, a sign that Africans, too, were to be hooked up with the "new world society." In the new Zambia, electricity (like those other primary goods of modern life, education and health care) would link all of the country's citizens in a universal, national grid of modernity.

Today, the Copperbelt mine townships are still wired for electricity. But the service is intermittent, as equipment often breaks down, and the copper power cables are from time to time stolen for sale as scrap. What is more, few township residents can afford to pay the monthly charges for the use of electricity, so electric appliances go unused as women huddle around charcoal fires preparing the daily meals and the township's skies fill with gray smoke each morning.

Nowadays, global interconnection does not depend so much on copper. The development of fiber optics and satellite communications technology, for instance, means that there is today much less need for copper-wired telephone cables. This "advance" in global connectivity is actually one of the causes of Zambia's drastic economic marginalization; the world "out there" can increasingly connect itself without relying on Zambia's copper (Mikesell 1988, 40). [...] Ironically, then, the communication revolution that is generally thought of as "connecting the globe" is playing a small but significant part in disconnecting Zambia.

There is a fundamental point suggested in this small detail. What we have come to call globalization is not simply a process that links together the world but also one that differentiates it. It creates new inequalities even as it brings into being new commonalities and lines of communication. And it creates new, up-to-date ways not only of connecting places but of bypassing and ignoring them (cf. Castells 1998).

Most Zambians, let us remember, have never made a telephone call in their lives. [...] With new technologies, will telecommunications now become more equally distributed, or even truly universal? One wonders. According to one recent report, at least, cellular telephone technology promises not to "hook up" the African masses but rather to make obsolete the very idea that they need to be "hooked up": many of the poorest parts of the world, the article claims, may now *never* be wired for phone service (*Economist* 1993). For cellular technology allows businesses and elites to ignore their limited and often malfunctioning national telephone systems and do their business via state-of-the-art satellite connectivity, bypassing altogether the idea of a universal copper grid providing service to all.

Wilson's "new world society," for all its faults, implied a promise of universality and even ulti-mate equality that is strikingly absent from the current visions of the "new world order." In the plotline of modernization, some countries were "behind," it is true, but they were all supposed to have the means to "catch up" in the end. And Zambia [...] was no exception. "Second-class" countries could and (the story promised) surely would eventually rise to the ranks of the "first class." Today, this promise is still mouthed by the ideologists of development here and there. But it is without much conviction. More characteristic is *The Economist*'s casual casting aside of that troublesome 500 million "or so" who have inexplicably missed the bandwagon of global growth. In the neoliberal "new world order," apparently, Zambia (along with most of the rest of Africa) *is* to be an exception.

Many of the people I spoke with on the Copperbelt understood this very well – understood that "Africa," in the new global dispensation, was becoming a category of objection. I noticed that whenever people were trying to convey their problems – to describe their suffering, to appeal for help, to explain the humiliation of their circumstances – they described themselves not as Zambians but as Africans. On the one hand, the term evoked all the images associated with Africa in contemporary international media discourse – pictures of poverty, starvation, and war; refugees, chaos, and charity. On the other, of course, it evoked the old colonial usage of African as a stigmatized race category. Putting the two connotations together suggested (tragically, if accurately) a reimposition of the old, despised "second-class" status but within a new macropolitical order. As one old man put it, at the end of a wrenching narration of his country's downward slide: "We are just poor Africans, now" (see also Ferguson 1997).

The End of Development?

A number of recent critical analysts have heralded the end of the "age of development." [...] For Wolfgang Sachs, editor of the influential critical work *The Development Dictionary* (1992), the whole project of development today "stands like a ruin in the intellectual landscape," a disastrous failure now made "obsolete," "outdated by history" (1992, 1, 2). It is not only that development has failed to deliver the economic growth and sociocultural modernization that it promised; more fundamentally, the whole ideal of development can no longer carry any conviction. Economically, Sachs argues, the very idea of the whole planet consuming at first-world levels presents an ecological disaster if not an impossibility, while socially and culturally, development offers only a thinly veiled Westernization, a colonizing global monoculture that must choke out the "traditional" world's wealth of diverse local modes of life. To the extent that third-world people have themselves sought development, in this view, they have been misguided; the schemas of development have provided only "the cognitive base for [a] pathetic self-pity" (1992, 2), which has been self-defeating, and which must continue no longer.

Esteva argues in similar fashion that development has led third-world peoples "to be enslaved to others' experience and dreams" (Esteva 1992, 7). When United States president Harry Truman labeled two billion people as "underdeveloped" in 1949,

> they ceased being what they were, in all their diversity, and were transmogrified into an inverted mirror of others' reality: a mirror that belittles them and sends them off to the end of the queue, a mirror that defines their identity, which is really that of a heterogeneous and diverse majority, simply in the terms of a homogenizing and narrow minority. (Esteva 1992, 7)

According to Esteva, the world would be well advised to do without such a concept (which is in any case "doomed to extinction" [1992, 7]) and proceed to emulate the "marginals" at the fringes of the capitalist economy who are rejecting the "needs"

imposed by the economic world-view of development and reinventing a world without scarcity (much like Sahlins's "original affluent society" of hunters and gatherers) (Esteva 1992, 19–22). [...]

There is reason to be doubtful of such sweeping claims for the end of development. Most obviously, it is clear that ideas of development (often remarkably unreconstructed ones at that) hold great sway in many parts of the world today, perhaps especially in areas (notably, many parts of East and Southeast Asia) that have enjoyed recent rapid economic expansion (though the recent "crash" that has stricken many countries in the region may yet shake that developmentalist faith). More theoretically, we might well be suspicious of criticisms of inevitable linear teleologies and progressive successions of epochs that proceed by constructing their own inevitable linear teleologies and progressive successions of epochs, as so many contemporary "post-" and "end of ..." narratives seem to do. [...] But it remains true that something has happened in recent years to the taken-for-granted faith in development as a universal prescription for poverty and inequality. For Africa, at least, as for some other parts of the world, there is a real break with the certainties and expectations that made a development era possible. The "rolling back" of the state, the abandonment of the goal of industrialization, the commitment to what are euphemistically called "market forces" and "private enterprise," and the shattering of expectations for economic convergence with the West, all come together to create a very real end, at least at the level of perceptions and expectations, of at least the grander versions of the development project in Africa.

[...]

References

Bates, Robert H. 1976.
  Rural Responses to Industrialization: A Study of Village Zambia. New Haven: Yale University Press.
Bayart, Jean-François
  1993. *The State in Africa: The Politics of the Belly*. London: Longman.
Berry, Brian J. L., ed.
  1976. *Urbanization and Counter-Urbanization*. Beverly Hills: Sage Publications.

Bhabha, Homi K.
  1997. Of Mimicry and Man: The Ambivalence of Colonial Discourse. In *Tensions of Empire: Colonial Cultures in a Bourgeois World*. Frederick Cooper and Ann Laura Stoler, eds. Berkeley: University of California Press.
Borneman, John
  1996. Until Death Do Us Part: Marriage/Death in Anthropological Discourse. *American Ethnologist* 23, no. 2:215–235.

Brown, Michael Barratt, and Pauline Tiffen
1992. *Short Changed: Africa and World Trade*. London: Pluto Press.

Castells, Manuel
1998. *The Information Age: Economy, Society and Culture*, vol. 3. *End of Millennium*. Malden, MA: Blackwell.

Champion, A. G., ed.
1989. *Counterurbanization: The Changing Pace and Nature of Population Deconcentration*. London: Edward Arnold.

Cooper, Frederick
1983. Urban Space, Industrial Time, and Wage Labor in Africa. In *Struggle for the City: Migrant Labor, Capital, and the State in Urban Africa*. Frederick Cooper, ed. Beverly Hills: Sage Publications.

Cooper, Frederick, and Ann Laura Stoler, eds.
1997. *Tensions of Empire: Colonial Cultures in a Bourgeois World*. Berkeley: University of California Press.

Coopersmith, Jonathan
1992. *The Electrification of Russia, 1880–1926*. Ithaca: Cornell University Press.

Daniel, Philip
1979. *Africanisation, Nationalisation, and Inequality: Mining Labour and the Copperbelt in Zambian Development*. New York: Cambridge University Press.

Economist, The
1993. Telecommunications Survey. *The Economist* 329, no. 7834:68ff (supplement).

Esteva, Gustavo
1992. Development. In *The Development Dictionary: A Guide to Knowledge as Power*. W. Sachs, ed. London: Zed Books.

Ferguson, James
1995. From African Socialism to Scientific Capitalism: Reflections on the Legitimation Crisis in IMF-ruled Africa. In *Debating Development Discourse: Institutional and Popular Perspectives*. D. B. Moore and G. J. Schmitz, eds. New York: St. Martin's Press.

Gluckman, Max
1961. Anthropological Problems Arising from the African Industrial Revolution. In *Social Change in Modern Africa*. A. Southall, ed. London: Oxford University Press.

Guyer, Jane I., with the help of Akbar Virmani and Amanda Kemp
1996. *African Studies in the United States: A Perspective*. Atlanta, GA: African Studies Association.

Harvey, David
1990. *The Condition of Postmodernity: An Enquiry into the Origins of Cultural Change*. Cambridge, MA: Blackwell.

Jamal, Vali, and John Weeks
1993. *Africa Misunderstood, or Whatever Happened to the Rural–Urban Gap?* London: Macmillan Press.

Kristeva, Julia
1982. *Power of Horror: An Essay on Abjection*. New York: Columbia University Press.

Meebelo, Henry S.
1986. *African Proletarians and Colonial Capitalism: The Origins, Growth and Struggles of the Zambian Labour Movement to 1964*. Lusaka: Kenneth Kaunda Foundation.

Mikesell, Raymond F.
1988. *The Global Copper Industry: Problems and Prospects*. London: Croom Helm.

Mitchell, J. Clyde
1951. A Note on the Urbanization of Africans on the Copperbelt. *Human Problems in British Central Africa* 12:20–27.

Moore, Reginald John Beagarie, and A. Sandilands
1948. *These African Copper Miners: A Study of The Industrial Revolution in Northern Rhodesia, with Principal Reference to the Copper Mining Industry*. London: Livingstone Press.

Parpart, Jane L.
1983. *Labor and Capital on the African Copperbelt*. Philadelphia: Temple University Press.

Perrings, Charles 1979.
Black Mineworkers in Central Africa. London: Heinemann.

Potts, Deborah
1995. Shall We Go Home? Increasing Urban Poverty in African Cities and Migration Processes. *The Geographical Journal* 161, no. 3:245–264.

Sachs, Jeffrey
1997. The Limits of Convergence: Nature, Nurture, and Growth. *The Economist*, June 14, pp. 19–22.

Sachs, Wolfgang, ed.
1992. *The Development Dictionary: A Guide to Knowledge as Power*. London: Zed Books.

Sandilands, A.
1948. Preface, In *These African Copper Miners*. R. J. B. Moore, ed. London: Livingstone Press.

Seers, Dudley
1963. The Role of Industry in Development: Some Fallacies. *Journal of Modern African Studies* 1, no. 4:461–465.

Smith, Neil
1997. The Satanic Geographics of Globalization: Uneven Development in the 1990s. *Public Culture* 10, no. 1:169–189.

United Nations
1973. *Statistical Yearbook 1972*. New York: Statistical Office of the United Nations, Dept. of Economic and Social Affairs.

Watson, William

1958. *Tribal Cohesion in a Money Economy: A Study of the Mambwe People of Northern Rhodesia*. Manchester: Manchester University Press.

Wilson, Godfrey

1941. *An Essay on the Economics of Detribalization in Northern Rhodesia* (part 1). Rhodes Livingstone Paper No. 5. Livingstone, Northern Rhodesia: Rhodes-Livingstone Institute.

1942. *An Essay on the Economics of Detribalization in Northern Rhodesia* (part 2). Rhodes-Livingstone Paper No. 6. Livingstone, Northern Rhodesia: Rhodes-Livingstone Institute.

World Bank

1979. *World Development Report 1979*. New York: Oxford University Press.

1982. *Accelerated Development in Sub-Saharan Africa: An Agenda for Action*. Washington, DC.

1995. *World Development Report 1995: Workers in an Integrating World*. New York: Oxford University Press.

1996. *Trends in Developing Economics 1996*. Washington, DC.

Zambia, Republic of

1973. *Census of Population and Housing 1969: Final Report*. Lusaka: Central Statistical Office.

42

Development Aid and Structural Violence

The Case of Rwanda

Peter Uvin

Introduction

Development practitioners and academics increasingly face unanswered questions about the role of the aid enterprise. Questions relate to aid's weakness in promoting genuine improvements in the quality of living of the vast majority of the poor; its top-down, external, and often unsustainable nature; and its interaction with the forces of exclusion, oppression, and powerlessness that are the root causes of continued poverty and disempowerment. The 'game' of development, played out in an almost ritualistic manner between governments, bilateral agencies, and international organizations (with increasing NGO participation), often contributes to exclusion, inequality, frustration, cynicism, and a potential for conflict.

The case of Rwanda is extreme, both because of the horrific nature of the violence, and because of the fact that, almost up to the last day, Rwanda was considered by most people in the development community to be a model developing country, at least by African standards. What does 'development' mean if a country that is seemingly succeeding so well at it can descend so rapidly into such

tragedy? And, on a different, more operational, level; how did development aid, as well as the presence of an expensive battalion of technical assistants and experts interact with the processes that led to genocide?

Structural Violence

Almost three decades ago, Johan Galtung (1969: 167–91) wrote about the condition of structural violence, in which the poor are denied decent and dignified lives because their basic physical and mental capacities are constrained by hunger, poverty, inequality, and exclusion. Galtung defined violence as 'those factors that cause people's actual physical and mental realizations to be below their potential realizations'. As such, violence of this type can be built into the structure of a society, 'showing up as ... unequal life chances'. One example:

> in a society where life expectancy is twice as high in the upper class as in the lower classes, violence is exercised even if there are no concrete actors one can point to directly attacking others, as when one person kills another (Galtung 1969:169–71).

From Peter Uvin, "Development Aid and Structural Violence: The Case of Rwanda," *Development*, vol. 42, No. 3 (September 1999), pp. 49–56.

According to Khan (1978:834–57), structural violence can take four forms:

- classical, or direct, violence;
- poverty – deprivation of basic material needs;
- repression – deprivation of human rights;
- alienation – of higher needs.

The latter category includes such intangibles as mental and emotional harm, denial of dignity and integrity, and the 'destruction of the individual in a psychological or spiritual sense'.

Human needs theorists have long agreed that violence against basic non-material needs for identity/recognition, security, and autonomy/self-determination can be built into the structure of society, and may well be the foremost cause of acute violence in this world (Burton, 1997). And Paul Farmer (1996:261) writes about 'insidious assaults on dignity, such as institutionalized racism and sexism', adding that 'for many [Haitians], life choices are structured by racism, sexism, political violence, and grinding poverty'.

Here as we define it, structural violence consists of the combination of extreme inequality, social exclusion, and humiliation/assaults on people's dignity. The concept thus includes attention to the more social and spiritual dimension of people's lives, unlike the one of development, which has too often been reduced to the economic or physical aspects of life. It tries to capture in a holistic manner the meaningfulness and dignity of life as seen by people themselves.

Structural Violence in Rwanda

Notwithstanding positive macro-economic indicators, Rwanda has been characterized for decades by a high degree of structural violence; during the years prior to the genocide, this structural violence greatly intensified. This reality contrasted greatly with the dominant image of Rwanda, shared by donors and government officials alike, of a country in which development was proceeding nicely, under the capable leadership of a free-market oriented government.

Contrary to appearances, Rwanda was characterized by great inequality of both assets and income. According to the 1984 National Agricultural Survey, approximately 15 percent of the farmers own 50 percent of the land; at the same time, 26 percent of the population has become landless; most of the farmers in the middle live below subsistence. Although Rwanda has a policy that forbids the purchase of land by those with three or more hectares, farmers have been able to circumvent that through long-term leases, or by buying in black markets. Data from André and Platteau (1995:22) for a particularly densely populated region show that land sales constitute approximately 30 percent of all land owned by households; up to 65 percent of these sales are distress sales.

Like elsewhere in Africa, the majority of these land purchases are not by small farmers who through sheer hard work manage to buy a few acres more, but by 'big men' with money earned outside agriculture in government and aid agency wages or commerce. Erny and many others describe the population as 'extremely unhappy with the accumulation of land by the privileged of the regime and the constitution of large pastoral domains' (1994:80). The situation in Rwanda, where almost all the poor depend on agriculture and where public policy renders migration to the city or employment in the informal sector nearly impossible, leaves people with little hope for the future, and with no possibilities of escaping extreme poverty.

Income inequality has grown faster, and is higher, than asset inequality. Data by Maton (1994) suggest that the income share of the richest decile in Rwanda has increased from 22 percent in 1982 to 52 percent in 1994. And according to Marysse and his colleagues (1993), in a rural region of the Province of Butare, the 20 percent richest earned 66 percent of all income in 1992. At the same time, 43 percent of the households spent nothing on education, while one-fifth had nothing left for health care. The same holds for salaries in the formal sector. According to 1988 Ministry of the Plan data, the lowest paid 65 percent of all public employees earned less than 4 percent of all salaries, while the share of the top 1 percent was 45.8 percent. These data do not include the well-known salaries and lifestyles of technical assistants and consultants, which are significantly higher still than those of top civil servants, and hundreds of times higher than those of farmers. They also do not include, by definition, illegal earnings from smuggling, corruption, and the like, accruing to the major dignitaries of the regime.

All in all, approximately half of all Rwandans are ultra-poor, i.e. incapable of feeding themselves decently or investing productively. Up to 40 percent more are poor, 9 percent non-poor, and maybe 1 percent positively rich. The latter consist of a few thousands of mostly foreign technical assistants and experts as well as a small elite of local 'big men' using their state and aid connections for rapid enrichment. It is this latter observation that brings us to the next element of structural violence, i.e. social exclusion.

Social exclusion can be defined as a property of societies in which 'the rules which enable and constrain access and entitlements to goods, services, activities and resources are unjust in the sense that certain categories of people are denied opportunities which are open to other persons who are comparable. Social exclusion is a property of society if racial, sexual, and other forms of discrimination are present, if the markets through which people earn a livelihood are segmented, or if public goods, which in theory should be available to everyone, are semi-public' (ILO/UNDP 1996:11). In Rwanda, like elsewhere in Africa, social exclusion was deeply embedded in the functioning of society. In Rwanda, this exclusion was foremost of a social and regional nature, with ethnicity coming a distant third. Such social exclusion processes can be seen at work in development projects, as witnessed in studies by Lemarchand (1982) and myself (1998).

Clientelism, corruption, and abuse of power constantly intervene in project execution, determining much of their impact on poverty, inequality, and exclusion. This starts at the drawing board of the project, when decisions are made on where to locate projects. According to some data, from 1982 to 1984, nine-tenths of all public investments – the main proportion of it financed by development aid – was in the four provinces of Kigali, Ruhengeri, Gisenyi, and Cyangugu (the first is the capital, the others are provinces in the North), while Gitarama, the most populous province after Kigali, received 0.16 percent and Kibuye 0.84 percent. This is the same pattern of regional inequality observed by Reyntjens (1994:33), who writes that more than a third of the 85 most important government positions, as well as the quasi-totality of direction functions in the army and the security apparatus, were held by people from Gisenyi, the president's native province.

The wheels of the machinery of social exclusion are further oiled when project-related jobs are allocated to the well-connected; when project employees use project cars, buildings, and work time for personal purposes; when farmers are required to pay kickbacks to get credits and when these credits go to the family members and friends of the project employees; and when significant proportions of improved or reclaimed lands end up in the hands of local administrators, political cadres, provincial civil servants, military men or traders, etc. The wheels turn further when, even if such abuses are discovered, no sanction follows. The number of corrupt administrators promoted to better jobs and unprofessional or unethical managers protected against all evidence and eventually given better paid positions, for example, is much larger than the number of those who receive punishment.

In this respect, it is instructive to look at the population's attitude toward development projects. Anyone who has worked in Rwanda will agree that distrust is probably the predominant attitude, combined with lack of involvement, if not outright resistance. Thus a team of World Bank experts (1987:12–13, 27) writes with a straight face:

> the local population does not, in general, question the nature of the projects to be carried out, provided,
>
> - they participate as paid labor (thereby earning extra cash income),
> - land developments do not affect their farm holdings (requisition of land or encroachment for infrastructure or other works);
> - the works can be reversed (erosion control measures); and
> - most of all the projects do not involve compulsory participation in the form of labor or result in heavy financial charges.

This paragraph should provoke some very serious thinking: it states quite correctly that most poor people manage to live with/survive development projects and the associated administration as long as these projects do not hurt them or force them to participate. The main merit of projects for poor people seems to reside in the fact that they create a plethora of (temporary) salaried jobs. This is a far cry from the original intentions of the development mission.

On occasion, people's sense of alienation and discontent with the way the development system works goes beyond passivity and distrust to move into active resistance. Indeed, there are many documented cases of farmers destroying project realizations supposed to benefit them, such as wells, electricity generators, reforestation areas, and other project-created infrastructures. Other documents report farmers invading uncultivated lands owned by churches or dignitaries of the regime. Some technical assistants have told me of stones repeatedly thrown on their vehicles by angry farmers. As a former Rwandan student of mine wrote,

> this resistance denotes a sense of disapproval, of indignation by people against the humiliation that is inflicted upon them in the treatment of 'their problems' and in the satisfaction of 'their needs' – and denounces the derailment of the integrated rural development programmes.

From the moment, in mid-1990, that multipartyism was allowed and the control by the single party relaxed, peasants increased their acts of vandalism, defiantly pulling out coffee plants, destroying anti-erosive structures on their own lands, and invading communal and project demonstration areas as well as reforestation areas. As a 1992 USAID report notes:

> in the last 2 years, ... people have attacked local authorities for launching development projects that brought little or no benefit to the community, for being personally corrupt, and for being inaccessible to and scornful of citizens in general. ... Those who felt themselves injured by past communal decisions on such matters as land-holding are taking matters into their own hands to reclaim their rights. People are refusing to do compulsory community labor and to pay taxes. They are refusing to listen to the burgomaster and even lock him out of his office or block the road so that he cannot get there. (USAID, 1992).

During the chaotic months of the genocide, there was further vandalism, including the complete and systematic destruction of most development project housing complexes, offices, storage places, and experimentation fields.

The latter quote's mention of officials' scornful attitude to farmers brings us to the third element of structural violence, i.e. humiliation. Prejudice existed in Rwanda not in one but two forms. One was the official, racist 'Hutu' ideology, designating all Tutsi as evil, dangerous, cunning, and intent on power; this racism, in its most radical form, constituted the moral basis for the genocide. The other is the prejudice of what are locally called the *evolués* – the urban, educated, modern, 'developed' people – versus their backward, rural, illiterate, 'underdeveloped' brothers. Some observers have written about a 'fourth ethnic group', that incorporates all those who have acquired an education and a European knowledge and who tend to denigrate the rural way of living. This group has a lifestyle that is radically different from the majority of the population. It is their lifestyle, culture, language, and dress code that is upheld as the only desirable, modern one. For the few who have acquired it, it accompanies an often extremely condescending, rude, and manipulative attitude toward the masses. Even family members are treated as inferior and their habits often ridiculed. As Ntamahungiro writes,

> A bad habit has installed itself in our mores, in which the rich, the powerful, the civil servant, the educated person always has priority over the poor, the weak, the non-educated, the 'non-civil servant'. This can be observed in court, at the doctor, in the administration and even in taxis. (...) This lack of respect towards peasants manifests itself amongst others in the way they are addressed. They are spoken to in a commandeering tone, often with disdain. They are required to behave as inferiors, to make themselves very small. (Ntamahungiro, 1988).

A large part of the population has internalized these values, accepting this lifestyle as the only 'good' one, and judging its own fate as primitive, inferior, and extremely undesirable. Little is left of the 'traditional' pride of the African farmer in his culture, in Rwanda as elsewhere. Most farmers, especially the young, consider the need to farm a demonstration of failure and lowness, and would give up farming immediately to become a simple sentry, cook, or, especially, driver, in any development project, and to live in the city.

In addition, relations between the administrative and technical state system and the population in Rwanda were vertical and authoritarian, making it almost impossible for ordinary people's voices to be heard. State personnel, whether agricultural extension agents, health personnel, livestock officers, etc. tend to be ill-trained and largely incapable of doing more than relaying messages from above. They, like their superiors, typically display condescending attitudes toward most farmers, if they do not seek to avoid meeting them at all. This is typical for Africa, but, given the omnipresence of the state and the development machinery in Rwanda – much more so than in other African countries – it led to an almost military style development approach, an 'encadrement' on the verge of forced labour.

From Structural to Acute Violence

Structural violence promotes explosions of acute, physical violence, whether in its organized communal/nationalistic forms, or in its more diffuse, individualistic criminality/domestic abuse manifestations. There are a number of processes that do so, and here we will focus on those that facilitate communal violence. All components of structural violence promote despair and cynicism. Social exclusion undermines the moral fabric of society through impunity on the one hand, and loss of credibility and legitimacy on the other. Humiliation creates a need for regaining self-respect, often done through scapegoating and prejudice.

If there is only one point that almost all people in Rwanda are willing to agree upon, it is probably that impunity was, and is, one of the key underlying problems in society. There were two types of impunity in Rwanda, and each contributed to violence in different ways. One was the well known and oft-discussed impunity enjoyed by the perpetrators of violence. Before 1994, the organizers and perpetrators of violence were basically never punished – not surprisingly as they usually worked closely with the powers-that-be. It is widely felt that if this kind of impunity for grave human rights

violations does not end, the cycle of violence in Rwanda will continue, for unpunished violence provokes further violence. This is the main reason for significant donor investment in the judicial sector in post-genocide Rwanda.

But there existed in Rwanda as in many countries, a second kind of impunity, which was a matter of daily life and worked hand-in-hand with the process of exclusion. Where judicial procedures often see the highest bidder prevail; where entry into secondary and tertiary education is the result of money and influence rather than knowledge and perseverance; when the best jobs are allocated not on the basis of competency but connections; and when cases of manifest incompetence or abuse of power often end in promotion of their perpetrators, people lose their faith in the system, become cynical, and are easily tempted to break laws themselves.

Social exclusion leads to an accumulation of anger and cynicism directed at the institutions and ideologies of the state and the aid system, for it is they who embody the development discourse that has lost its meaning, who transmit the humiliation, and who benefit from the processes of exclusion. As a former technical assistant from the ILO in Kigali admits with rare candor:

> our projects tell the farmers and artisans that if they organize and work hard, they will develop. But what is for these people the real-life model of success? (...) Who is the person that becomes wealthier fast? (...) Most of the time, the person who becomes richer did not have to join cooperatives, did not have to attend training sessions, did not need project credit. He became richer very fast because he had 'friends' in the right places, and because a little present given can always lead to a little present received. In that case, with our development model that takes so much time and effort, do we have any credibility at all?

In addition, when people are treated in a humiliating and prejudicial manner, when they are made to lose their self-respect, the result is frustration and anger, as well as a strong need to regain self-respect and dignity. Recourse to ethnic identity, scapegoating, and the projection of hostility onto weaker groups constitute important effects of structural violence. As Staub explains elsewhere:

For many people, the hatred of 'the Other' served to combat the low selfesteem due to chronic unemployment and squelched aspirations; these young, frustrated men were the ones most vulnerable to the kind of ethnic appeals that led to genocide. (Staub, 1990:47–64).

In guise of conclusion, the notion of structural violence allows us to understand the little people who execute the acute violence – the adolescents who everywhere, from Rwanda to Liberia, are the first ones to do the killing and to be killed; the ordinary farmers who take up arms against their neighbours; the women who betray other women. Structural violence, defined as the constant and humiliating reduction in the physical, intellectual and social life chances of people, tells us about how daily life becomes characterized by constraint and force – not of the gun (although that is usually never too far behind), but of biased structures and practices. It makes us understand how people's sense of self-respect is reduced, their acceptance of the rules of decency and good society put into question, their knowledge base reduced to slogans. In many ways, structural violence thus lays the groundwork for acute violence.

Furthermore, structural violence lowers the barriers against the use of violence. As the norms of society lose legitimacy; as people's knowledge base is reduced to slogans; as progress becomes a meaningless concept; as communities are riveted by conflict and jealousy; as people's sense of self-respect is reduced; and as segments of society show their contempt for the rules of decency as well as for farmers, people become increasingly unhampered by constraints on the use of violence to deal with problems.

In the specific case of Rwanda, genocidal violence emanated from a racist/genocidal ideology that, in turn, fed on two basic structural processes, one emanating from the top, and one from the bottom. For decades, anti-Tutsi racism had served as a deliberately maintained strategy of legitimization of the powers-that-be, and was kept alive through a systematic public structure of discrimination, in which the 'Tutsi problem' was never allowed to be forgotten. Under threat by political and economic processes, parts of the elite increased their use of the old strategy and effectively managed to spread it throughout society.

At the same time, racist prejudice was a means for ordinary people, subject to structural violence, to make sense of their predicament, to explain their ever-growing misery through projection and scapegoating. State-supplied racism provided poor Hutu a sense of value, as well as an 'explanation' for the mal-development they faced daily in their lives. As Simpson and Yinger stated in their seminal work on prejudice:

> the designation of inferior groups comes from those on top – an expression of their right to rule – as well as from frustrated persons often near the bottom, as an expression of their need for security. (Simpson and Yinger, 1953:83).

In Rwanda in the 1990s, the interaction between structural violence and racism created the conditions necessary for genocidal manipulation by the elites to be successful. It is the unique combination of these three factors that explains the Rwandan genocide. Structural violence is what provoked a need for scapegoating among ordinary people; the existence of longstanding racism is what allowed parts of the elite to build a genocidal movement on the basis of his need. Without long-standing racism, we would have found not genocide but 'ordinary' communal violence in Rwanda (as in so many other places in Africa). Without elite manipulation, structural violence could have led to more diffuse, anomic, modes of violence such as petty criminality, sorcery, domestic abuse – all of them also increasingly widespread in Africa.

The Role of the Aid Enterprise

What is the role of development aid in this? This question is not easy to answer. One can begin by observing that the development aid system still neglects most of the non-economic aspects of development in favour of a narrow economic-technical approach. It does not include addressing human rights violations, income inequality, authoritarianism, humiliation, fear, or persistent impunity in daily life to be part of its core mandate. There are little or no working relations between the development aid system and organizations dealing with these issues, such as political movements, human rights organizations, or unions. Even in the 1990s, when these issues became very visible in Rwanda, the development aid community by and large continued its own trajectory, unable to rethink its mission. Of course, this willful ignorance does not make these issues disappear, nor does it limit their impact on development, even narrowly defined. Rather, it allows the processes of exclusion and humiliation to continued unabated, if not to become strengthened, to the greater pleasure of those benefiting from them. Hence, much development aid helps to lay the groundwork for further inequality and mal-development, as well as structural, and, eventually, acute, violence.

Rhetoric notwithstanding, most of the development aid system also continues to function along top-down, externally defined, lines, bypassing people's own creativity, capacities, histories, and sense of value. At the same time, development aid greatly contributes to social inequality, both directly, by its own spending patterns which very largely favour the wealthier strata of society, and indirectly, through its support of mechanisms of exclusion and clientelism. All this goes hand in hand with the functioning of the state system that, for political and ideological reasons, is highly top-down, authoritarian, inequality promoting, and ignorant of local dynamics. Thus the ideological tenets of the 'developers' and the political dynamics of the powers-that-be join in defining development largely without people's input, without much respect for poor people, and often without much benefit to them.

References

André, C. and J.Ph. Platteau (1995) *Land Tenure under Unendurable Stress: Rwanda Caught in the Malthusian Trap*. Namur: Centre de Recherche en Economie du Développement, Faculty of Economics, University of Namur.

Burton, J.W. (1997) *Violence Explained: The Sources of Conflict, Violence and Crime and their Prevention*. Manchester: Manchester University Press.

Erny, P. (1994) *Rwanda 1994*. Paris: L'Harmattan.

Farmer, P. (1996) 'On Suffering and Structural Violence – A View from Below', *Daedalus*, 125.

Galtung, J. (1969) 'Violence, Peace, and Peace Research', *Journal of Peace Research*, 6.1.

Khan, R. (1978) 'Violence and socio-economic development', *International Social Science Journal* XXX(4).

ILO/UNDP (1996) *Overcoming Social Exclusion. A Contribution to the World Summit for Social Development*. Geneva: ILO.

Lemarchand, R. (1982) *The World Bank in Rwanda. The Case of the Office de Valorisation Agricole et Pastorale de Mutara (OVAPAM)*. Bloomington: University of Indiana, African Studies Programme.

Marysse, S. et al. (1993) *Appauvrissement de la population rurale et ajustement structurel: causalité au coincidence? Le cas de Kirarambogo (Rwanda)*. Antwerp: Centre for Development Studies.

Maton, J. (1994) *Développement économique et social au Rwanda entre 1980 et 1993. Le dixieme décile en face de l'Apocalypse*. Ghent: Faculty of Economics, Unit for Development Research and Teaching, State University of Ghent.

Ntamahungiro, J. (1988) 'Eloge du paysan rwandais', *Dialogue*, Sept.-Oct. 130.

Reyntjens, F. (1994) *L'Afrique des Grands Lacs en crise. Rwanda, Burundi: 1988–1994*. Paris: Karthala.

Simpson, G.E. and J.M. Yinger (1953) *Racial and Cultural Minorities: an Analysis of Prejudice and Discrimination*. Third edition. New York: Harper and Row.

Staub, E. (1990) 'Moral Exclusion, Personal Goal Theory and Extreme Destructiveness', *Journal of Social Issues* 46.1.

USAID (1992) *Democratic Initiatives and Governance Project*. Washington, DC: USAID.

Uvin, P. (1998) *Aiding Violence. The Development Enterprise in Rwanda*. West Hartford: Kumarian Press.

World Bank (1987) *Rwanda. The Role of the Communes in Socio-Economic Development*. Washington, DC: South, Central and Indian Ocean Department.

43

Nigerian Scams as Political Critique
Globalization, Inequality and 419

Daniel Jordan Smith

Nigeria is a country infamous for corruption. Perhaps the most potent international symbol of Nigerian corruption is the notorious fraudulent e-mail scam. Prior to the creation of more sophisticated spam-blocking software, many people using e-mail in the English-speaking world received a regular deluge of messages from Nigerians purporting to be in position to transfer millions of dollars into the bank accounts of willing foreign collaborators. The writers claim to be high government officials, senior military officers, oil industry executives, bank managers, politicians, and even widows of dead dictators. The scam letters are classic confidence tricks, wherein the writers attempt to lure the recipients into advancing money and bank account information against the promise of much larger payoffs.

Nigerian e-mail scams are certainly emblematic of the country's worldwide reputation for corruption. However, perhaps the most deceiving aspect of the e-mail scams is the tendency to see them only as a mode of Nigerian corruption. They are certainly that. But they are much better understood if they are also seen as a form of interpretation, and a Nigerian response to larger systems of inequality and corruption. When one knows, as I will explain, that the authors and senders of most of these e-mails are rather ordinary young Nigerians, most of whom have some secondary school or university education, then the style, content, and context of these letters and the motives of the authors must be read differently. The top figures in Nigerian networks of fraud are, no doubt, rightly considered kingpins of international crime. They are criminals by almost any definition, and they should probably be lumped with military strongmen, corrupt politicians, venal banking and oil executives, and all of their assorted international collaborators as the chief culprits in Nigeria's continued poverty, inequality, and instability. But an analysis of the history, social organization, and content of Nigerian e-mail scams suggests that these schemes reveal much more about Nigerian corruption and its relationship to systems of global inequality than is apparent in stereotypical understandings. The young men and women in Nigeria's burgeoning cybercafés who write, reproduce, and

From Daniel Jordan Smith, *A Culture of Corruption: Everyday Deception and Popular Discontent in Nigeria*, Princeton University Press (2008), pp. 28–52. © Princeton University Press. Reprinted by permission of Princeton University Press.

recreate the many genres of scam letters that appear in e-mail in-boxes around the world are creating cultural objects that illuminate the authors' interpretations and critical understandings of inequality and corruption, not only in Nigeria, but in the larger world system.

The History of Nigerian Advanced Fee Fraud

Though familiar in law enforcement circles for two decades, Nigerian fraud catapulted to global prominence over the past decade, as the internet grew into a principal means of international communication. The current notoriety of Nigerian e-mail scams makes it easy to forget that confidence men and their tricks have been an important part of the histories of many societies (Halttunen 1982; Rebhorn 1988). The perpetration of fraud through which somebody obtains something of value by first gaining the trust of the victim and then betraying that person is an ancient game. Further, confidence tricks have by no means disappeared as a means of making money for people in many countries around the world. Nigerians are not the only players in the multiple versions of international financial fraud, many of which continue to depend on some sort of confidence scheme. But at the beginning of the new millennium, Nigerian e-mail fraud is perhaps the most notorious of contemporary confidence tricks.

Nigerian advance fee fraud, known in Nigeria, and now internationally, as "419," first emerged as a worldwide phenomenon in the 1980s, following the dramatic decline in oil prices that left Nigeria's national economy reeling (Watts 1984; Apter 1999, 2005). The 1980s were also a period in which Nigeria's military retook and retained control of the government through coups, establishing a period of more than 15 years of uninterrupted military rule. The declining economy and the military's entrenched power contributed to the growth of Nigerian advance fee fraud in a number of ways. First, the oil boom of the 1970s resulted in vastly increased access to education for Nigeria's huge population, meaning that by the 1980s the country had larger numbers of young people with higher expectations for their futures than at any time in the past. By the late 1980s, approximately half of

Nigeria's then nearly 100 million people were less than 15 years old. The subsequent economic crash and the return of the military created a situation where this increasingly educated and ambitious young population was frustrated in its attempts to secure gainful employment or other legitimate economic opportunities.

Second, the military governments of the 1980s and 1990s were brazenly corrupt, and they created a climate where ordinary citizens believed that they would have to resort to any means available to achieve their own economic aspirations (Maier 2000; Bayart 1993). Indeed, some of the mechanisms used by Nigeria's longest serving military ruler, General Ibrahim Babangida (1985–93), to enrich himself and his cronies, presaged the kinds of schemes proposed by the 419 letter writers (Apter 1999). Many of the scam writers' seemingly preposterous stories of huge sums of money somehow siphoned from Nigeria's coffers are in fact reminiscent of the actual methods corrupt Nigerian elites have used to steal the country's wealth for years. Indeed, both international agencies and internal Nigerian critics have suggested that the Babangida administration not only served as a model for numerous 419 activities,[1] but that it also facilitated them (Apter 1999, 2005; Bayart, Ellis, and Hibou 1999).

Regardless of the actual levels of collusion between the ruling military elite and the kingpins of advance fee fraud, the record of the military's extensive corruption in 1980s and 1990s, and the fact that Nigerian officialdom has long been open to all kinds of shady deals, contributed to the evolution of Nigeria's advance fee fraud enterprises. Indeed, the reality of official corruption in Nigeria is one reason why at least some of the people targeted in these confidence tricks take the bait.

Babangida had earned a reputation for skillfully spreading the tentacles of corruption to every sector within the reach of government for the ultimate benefit of himself and his cronies. When General Sani Abacha took the reins of power in 1993 he promised, like every other new Nigerian leader before and after him, to root out corruption. A couple of years into the Abacha administration, many Nigerians joked that his strategy to clean up corruption was to make sure that only he and his very closest cronies profited from it. Abacha was notorious for clamping down on smaller-scale corruption even as he set up mechanisms to transfer the country's wealth directly to himself. For example, in the mid-1990s, Abacha ordered the closing down of all business centers, ostensibly in an effort to stamp out 419 that was perpetuated using fax and phone services in these establishments. While Abacha justified the new ban as a measure to fight 419, human rights activists in Nigeria criticized the move as a ploy to stifle Nigerian communication with the outside world during a regime that became increasingly brutal in its suppression of dissent. It is not clear what effect Abacha's crackdown on business centers had on the level of 419 scam activity in the mid-1990s. Some of it surely continued on phone and fax lines that could still be obtained with bribes paid to the right people. Other scams moved abroad, handled by Nigerian expatriates who had easier access to phone and fax service in other countries.

Advance fee fraud certainly did not suffer a fatal blow in Abacha's crackdown on business centers, and the transition to democracy in 1999 was followed swiftly by the proliferation of internet and cellular phone technology in Nigeria. By 2002, ordinary Nigerians in urban areas experienced remarkably improved access to international communication. Cybercafés and mobile phone call centers replaced, and ultimately far surpassed, the business centers of the early 1990s as the most common form of communications-related small enterprise in Nigeria. With expanding web access and growing numbers of young people who were internet and e-mail savvy, the worldwide web quickly became the primary means for disseminating 419 scam letters. E-mail technology multiplied exponentially the numbers of potential dupes who could be contacted at very little cost. It also opened up the possibility that much larger numbers of young Nigerians could try their hands at 419. While many of the promised dividends of democracy have yet to be realized by ordinary Nigerians, the democratization of 419 has been dramatic; almost anyone who wants to participate can try.

The United States Secret Service Agency estimates that these scams yield the perpetrators hundreds of millions of dollars each year, and that in the 1990s total losses associated with Nigerian 419 schemes amounted to five billion dollars

(Smith, Holmes, and Kaufman 1999; Edelson 2003). A recent article in the *United States Attorneys' Bulletin* (Buchanan and Grant 2001) describes several successful prosecutions of Nigerian 419 fraudsters in the US, with two of the three primary cases centered in Texas. The preeminence of Texas in these fraud stories is not coincidental. Texas has one of the largest populations of Nigerian immigrants in the United States and the literature suggests that Nigeria-based scam artists frequently have Nigerian expatriate partners who further develop the scam scenarios and hook potential dupes in places like Texas (Smith, Holmes, and Kaufman 1999; Buchanan and Grant 2001; Edelson 2003). In addition, Texas is the hub of the U.S. oil industry, and actual deals between Texas-based American companies and the Nigerian government are common. Sometimes even the official deals are plagued by allegations of corruption. For example, recent contracts between the Nigerian government and firms like Enron and Halliburton have come under scrutiny for alleged fraud.[2]

A Serpent without a Head: The Social Organization of E-mail Fraud

Over the past few years I have been a regular customer at cybercafés in Nigeria, which are now numerous in every city and major town. In Umuahia, a town of perhaps 200,000 people, for example, the number of internet cafés multiplied from just a handful in 2002 to more than 40 in 2004. The sizes of the cafés range from those with just four or five computer terminals to one café with almost 40 machines. It costs less than a dollar for an hour of access. In addition, at all the major cafés, customers could pay the equivalent of about two dollars for the privilege of "night browsing," meaning that one could stay on the internet uninterrupted from 10 p.m. until 7 a.m. for one low fee.

Through inadvertent glancing over the shoulders of the hundreds of Nigerian cybercafé customers sitting in neighboring terminals, through deliberate efforts to walk around cafés to see what customers were doing on the internet, and through interviews with cybercafé proprietors and a few scam letter senders who agreed to talk, I began to put together an emerging picture of the social organization of Nigerian e-mail scams, at least at the lowest levels of the 419 hierarchy. I have never been able to interview anyone at the higher levels of these scam operations, though I was told stories about the 419 bosses by some of the young people who send scam letters.

The Western criminology literature offers a somewhat limited picture of Nigerian fraud, and I think it is fair to say that very little scholarship has been able to penetrate 419 organizations in ways that have generated reliable descriptions and analyses. What I collected is partial at best; it is most empirically valid at the lowest rungs of the enterprise. My main interest, and the material about which I have the most information, is the wider popular Nigerian perception of 419, reflecting ordinary Nigerians' critical collective awareness about corruption. Before proceeding to analyze e-mail scam letters as texts that illuminate widespread Nigerian understandings and critiques of corruption, I describe what I have been able to learn about the social organization of 419 e-mail scams.

At almost any hour of the day Nigerian cybercafés in Owerri are busy, with peak patronage in the late afternoon and evening. The bigger operations often have televisions with satellite service mounted high on the walls at each end of the café, typically broadcasting CNN or MTV – making it all the less surprising that e-mail scam letters have evolved to include ruses based on the Iraq War, the Asian Tsunami, the U.S. financial crisis, and other recent current events. The scam writers compose their letters in response to real-time information about global events, observing and taking advantage of numerous worldwide crises that are rife with corruption, and which therefore make ideal fodder for scam letters.

The typical clientele ranges between ages 15 and 35, with those 18 to 25 years old being by far the most numerous. In addition to personal e-mail and chatting, other common uses of the internet in Nigerian cybercafés are searching for work, school, and visa opportunities outside Nigeria, viewing on-line pornography, doing research for a school assignment, reading the latest news or sports, and, of course, 419.

Despite the fact that in nearly every internet café I have visited in Nigeria large signs are posted warning customers against using the internet

for 419, on any given visit several customers are typically writing and sending scam letters. Most writers looked to be between the ages of 20 and 30. Although I did not do any scientific measurement, and although the proportion of customers sending 419 e-mails varied considerably each time I consciously tried to observe it, I think it is reasonably accurate to say that in an internet café of 20–25 active terminals, at any one time at least 5–6 terminals were being used to send scam letters. Over the course of my longest recent fieldwork in Nigeria – when I went to internet cafés in Umuahia about every other day – I was able to identify three young men and one young woman at three different cafés who were frequent internet café customers regularly sending 419 messages. I eventually approached each of them and asked if they would talk to me.

In each case, the scam writers initially denied they were involved in 419. They were afraid that I was in some way connected with law enforcement. Indeed, I recall numerous instances over the past few years when young people obviously sending scam letters would switch screens when I passed or stood behind them, no doubt concerned about being observed. But just as common were scam writers who seemed absolutely oblivious to my presence, or to any possibility that they might be caught or prosecuted for sending 419 e-mails. Eventually, I managed to convince each of the four scam writers to talk to me. I explained that I was an anthropologist, that I was interested in understanding how 419 actually worked, and that I was not interested in prosecuting anyone. I assured them that I didn't even need to know their names. As was always the case, when I told them about myself, and particularly the fact that my wife was Nigerian and Igbo, and that I had lived on and off in Nigeria for the past 15 years, it changed the whole way they viewed me. Instead of being a foreigner suspected of possible ties to the law I was seen first and foremost as an in-law, and thus I am fairly confident that what these young people told me is true.

All four young people said they got started sending 419 e-mails after having been internet café regulars for other reasons. Two of the young men had learned about computers and internet technology in previous jobs at cybercafés, and it was through those jobs that they became familiar with and eventually part of the somewhat loosely organized bottom tier of Nigeria's e-mail scam industry. The other two, a male and a female, had spent time at cafés doing ordinary e-mail, chatting on-line, and browsing the web. Other acquaintances in the cafés who were involved in sending 419 messages introduced them to the enterprise. My questions about where they got the e-mail addresses to send the messages produced predictable answers. Massive numbers of e-mail addresses can be accessed from on-line company directories, chat rooms, electronic bulletin boards, and personal ad sites. In addition, one can apparently purchase lists of tens of thousands of e-mail addresses on the internet for as little as a few dollars, though my informants said that only the bigger players did that, as it requires access to a credit card. All four said that they sometimes shared and received lists of e-mail addresses from friends who were also sending 419 messages. Two of the four worked directly with either the proprietor or the manager of the internet café where they wrote and sent most of their messages. The other two worked more independently, almost like freelancers, and were much more loosely connected to a larger organization. The two who worked with their manager or proprietor had regular access to free internet time at the cafés where they sent the messages, though they said that the managers or proprietors asked them to work mainly when legitimate business volume was low, especially during the all-night browsing hours. In only one case was it obvious that the café proprietor was directly aware of and involved in 419. In another case it seemed as if other employees managing the café may have been facilitating the activity behind the back of the proprietor, or perhaps they engaged in 419 with the proprietor's awareness, but the proprietor was not involved in any contact with the scam writers.

The fact that millions of 419 e-mails in in-boxes around the world fall into a few basic genres is a product of how the scam enterprises are organized. The people sending the e-mails usually begin with copies of other e-mails that have been used in the past. Their themes are directly related to the structure of real fraud and corruption in Nigeria, to the ways in which the biggest forms of Nigerian corruption occur at the nexus between the state and the global economy, and to the unfolding of current events. Those working directly within the loose organizational hierarchy send most of their e-mails based on the previously successful prototypes. Those working freelance also begin with the prototypes, but are more likely to try stories that could generate a direct transfer of money, since the freelancers obviously don't have the resources to concoct the elaborate scenarios that could produce the biggest payoffs.

When a 419 e-mail gets a reply, the scam writers may follow up with a few more communications in order to further hook the respondent. They are particularly interested in getting personal information like phone numbers, addresses, and, of course, bank account numbers. The two writers working freelance said that their first aim was to try to get the recipients to send them money – either by Western Union or by wire transfer to a bank. If that did not work, they could pass on information about a potential dupe to someone in the more organized sector of the business for a small fee. Those who worked more directly within the structure said that they were supposed to pass all responses to their bosses. However, one young man admitted that he sometimes tried to solicit direct transfers of money to himself and that he also sent his own scam e-mails that were somewhat different from the typical inflated contract, dead expatriate, and dictator's widow letters that are the staple of the more organized efforts. He and the two more independent scammers described some of their more creative e-mails, where the writer sometimes presented him or herself as a victim of persecution for reasons of religion, gender, or disability, or as a young person in need of assistance with education, health, or family problems. Sometimes they simply sent new versions of the more typical advance fee themes. None of my informants had ever actually received any money directly from a dupe, but they had all received some money from people higher up the hierarchy to whom they passed recipient responses. The two young men who worked directly in the loose organization received fairly regular money. None said they could really support themselves from the effort, though they all repeated stories they had heard about people who had received money directly from a scam victim. The dream of a big payoff seemed to be as much of a motive as the small income they actually earned.

I was curious how they viewed what they were doing, especially in light of the widespread awareness in Nigeria that the country's international reputation was dominated by the stigma of 419. All four expressed a certain amount of ambivalence. Each said they would prefer gainful employment to sending 419 letters. Each blamed the larger system of corruption in Nigeria for leaving them with no choice but to find any means to survive. One said he regretted any harm to the victims of these scams, but the other three said that anyone who would fall for the 419 scams was both greedy and rich enough so that there was no need to feel very sorry. The words of one of the young men in the loose 419 organization capture some of the common sentiment:

> For me, I am just struggling. I could not finish university because my parents did not have the money and our government does not care about the people. Obasanjo [then Nigeria's president] and his boys are stealing so much money while the rest of the society is falling apart. That's the real 419. What I am doing is just trying to survive. I would not be here sending these e-mails looking for rich, greedy foreigners if there were opportunities in Nigeria. How much do I really get from this anyway? The people getting rich from this are the same people at the top who are stealing our money. I am just a struggle-man.

The large volume and typical styles of the e-mails in Western in-boxes suggests that much of what we associate with Nigerian 419 begins with ordinary young Nigerians like my informants. A friend who owns a small cybercafé in Umuahia, and who denies any involvement in 419, says he knows many cybercafé businesses that either participate in or tolerate the 419 scams. He confirmed much of what my scam-writer informants revealed about the loose organizational structure of 419, particularly at the lower levels. Once a writer snags a potential dupe, the information gets passed up a hierarchy, eventually reaching those at the higher levels who are able to employ significant resources in order to make the scam more believable and eventually extract large sums of money from a few victims. When tens of thousands of e-mails are being sent every day by thousands of small-time

scammers like my informants, the success rate need not be very high to make it worthwhile for those who run these operations.

Western government criminal investigations, the criminology literature, and the little research that has been done in the traditional social sciences suggest that, even at the top, the networks of Nigerian fraud are loosely organized. Nigerian criminal networks purportedly manage these multi-million dollar illegal schemes using ties of kinship, place of origin, ethnicity, and patron–client relationships that cut across the government and the private sector and link Nigerians at home to the large Nigerian diaspora. Criminologists suggest that the same networks that run the higher echelons of the 419 e-mail scams are also involved in numerous other criminal activities, including identity theft, bank fraud, and drug trafficking. Although I am not in a position to verify the extent of government involvement in Nigeria's infamous 419 activities, it is undoubtedly the case that the whole 419 enterprise depends upon the perception that Nigerians at the highest levels of government, banking, and the oil industry are corrupt. This is certainly the reputation of Nigeria abroad, and it is also the view that most ordinary Nigerians have of their government and their leaders. Nigeria's global reputation for corruption and local Nigerian interpretations of corruption in their society are reflected in the content of the e-mail messages. As I suggest below, the scam letter writers depend on (and of course contribute to) the global dissemination of stereotypes about Nigerian fraud in order to engage it themselves.

Scam Letters as Political Critique and Cultural Commentary

Once one recognizes that the majority of Nigerian scam letters are written and sent by fairly ordinary young people rather than a few kingpins of fraud, it is clear why analyzing them as popular cultural texts might be a fruitful endeavor. In 2002, I began saving e-mail scam letters that I received on my university e-mail account. In addition, when they remembered, three colleagues, two at my own university, and one at another university, forwarded me their scam letters. I saved approximately 100 scam letters over three years and my colleagues sent me another 60. Several days of looking through the many humorous and anti-419 websites revealed a diversity of scam letter stories that is wider than my own collection, but also convinced me that my sample is representative of the main genres.[3] I use the letters I have received to show how Nigerian scam letters can be productively analyzed as a form of popular interpretation and critical cultural commentary.

I use letters that have Nigeria itself as the location where the 419 plot unfolds because I am interested particularly in what the letters reveal about the Nigerian writers' understandings of corruption in their own society. However, almost half of the letters I received have other countries as their focus. The increasing prevalence of non-Nigerian scam stories is partly due to the fact that con artists in other countries are imitating the Nigerian schemes, but research by information technology specialists who analyze e-mail headers that can reveal the actual place of origin of the e-mails suggests that upwards of two-thirds of scam letters in which stories focus on non-Nigerian locations originate in Nigeria (Edelson 2003). Changing the stories to non-Nigerian settings reflects a growing recognition on the part of the scammers that global awareness of the Nigerian scams has become so widespread that letters focused on Nigerian opportunities to make quick money might be less effective. While Nigeria's reputation for corruption is essential for successful scams, the increasing association of 419 e-mail scams with Nigeria is perceived to inhibit dupes from falling for these confidence tricks. The expanding portfolio of countries where the millions of ill-gotten gains are said to be available also reflects the long-standing capacity of scam letter writers to incorporate current events into their narratives. Nonetheless, Nigeria itself remains a staple location for, and international symbol of, the scam stories, in part, no doubt, because the premise of most scams still depends on the presumption of large-scale corruption in the place where the easy money is available. In the examples below, I show how the kinds of corruption stories utilized in these scam letters reveal Nigerians' critical understandings of corruption in their society and of the profound connections of Nigerian corruption to the country's place in the global economy.

Over-invoiced Contracts

One of the most common Nigerian scam scenarios builds on the supposed availability of funds from an inflated or over-invoiced contract, typically involving the petroleum industry. The writer usually portrays himself as a government bureaucrat, a national petroleum corporation executive, or a bank official who can gain access to the extra millions, but only with the aid of the recipient who will provide a much needed advance fee and a foreign bank account. Note that in many scam letters, such as this one, there is no attempt to solicit an advance fee immediately. This usually comes after the potential dupe has responded and expressed interest. This e-mail received September 20, 2002 with the subject heading "CONFIDENTIAL" is representative of the over-invoiced contract genre:

> From: Dr. Abubakar Usman
> Attn: Director/CEO;
>
> Sir,
> I am Dr. Abubakar Usman, a top management staff in the Nigerian National Petroleum Corporation (NNPC). I came to know of you in my search for a reliable and reputable person to handle a very confidential transaction that involves the transfer of a huge sum of money to a foreign account. There were series of contracts executed by a consortium Multinationals in the oil industry in favour of NNPC.
>
> The original value of these contracts was deliberately over invoiced in the sum of THIRTY EIGHT MILLION SIX HUNDRED THOUSAND UNITED STATES DOLLARS (38.6M) which has now been approved and is now ready to be transferred since the Companies that actually executed these contracts have been paid and the projects officially commissioned. Consequently, my colleagues and I are willing to transfer the total amount to your account for subsequent disbursement, since we as civil servants are prohibited by the Code of Conduct Bureau (Civil Service Laws) from opening and/or operating foreign accounts in our names. Needless to say, the trust reposed on you at this juncture is enormous. In return, we have agreed to offer

you 30% of the transferred sum, while 10% shall be set aside for incidental expenses (internal and external) between the parties in the course of the transaction. You will be mandated to remit the balance 60% to other accounts in due course. You must however NOTE that this transaction is subject to the following terms and conditions:

Our conviction of your transparent honesty and diligence. That you would treat this transaction with utmost secrecy and confidentiality. That as a foreign partner, you will follow our instructions to the letter. Provide the account required, and competent to assist us on profitable investment areas in your Country in an advisory capacity. Furthermore, Modalities have been worked out at the highest levels of the Ministry of Finance and the Central Bank of Nigeria for the immediate transfer of the funds within 14 working days subject to your satisfaction of the above stated terms. Our assurance is that your role is risk free. To accord this transaction the legality it deserves and for mutual security of the fund, the whole approval procedures will be officially and legally processed with your name of any Company you may nominate as the Bonafide beneficiary. Once more, I want you to understand that having put in over 26 years in the service of my country, I am averse to having my image and career dented. This matter should therefore be treated with utmost secrecy and urgency.

Kindly expedite action as we are behind schedule to enable us include this transfer in the first quarter of this financial year. Please acknowledge the receipt of this message via Fax No: 234-1-7592604; Tel No: 234-1-7744044. NOTE: PLEASE FURNISH ME WITH YOUR TEL/FAX# SO THAT I COULD SEND ACROSS DETAILS OF THE TRANSFER AND OTHER RELEVANT DOCUMENTS FOR YOUR ENDORSEMENT TO ENABLE US TRANSFER THE FUNDS TO YOUR PROVIDED ACCOUNT. I AWAIT YOUR IMMEDIATE RESPONSE.

Yours Sincerely,
Dr. Abubakar Usman.

The fact that over-invoiced contracts are one of the most common scam narratives reflects a widespread perception in Nigeria that inflated and bogus contracts are one of the principal means by which government officials and their private sector cronies loot the state. Official corruption is so taken-for-granted by the Nigerian public that many popular debates about the ethics of corruption focus not on whether money was skimmed from a government project for private gain, but on whether the contractor carried out the project at all, and, if so, whether the work was completed at anything near a professional standard. Many Nigerians are so cynical about official corruption that their primary plea is that at least some of the money should be used for the intended purposes. Countless friends and informants have said about government officials and their contractor collaborators, "let them eat their share, but let them not eat everything!" The assurances in Dr Usman's letter that the original contractors had been paid and that the project had been completed are meant to reassure the recipients that the money is not completely tainted. This concern may not even be apparent to a potential dupe, most of whom would be unaware of the nuances of moral assessments about degrees of corruption that are normal among Nigerians, but its prominence in the text reflects the extent to which scam letters are revealing cultural texts.

Perhaps even more illuminating than the nuances of Nigerian assessments regarding degrees of corruption is the fact that it is a government contract associated with the oil industry that is typically portrayed as the source of the millions. Nigerians are keenly aware that government contracts are the main mechanism by which elites divert national resources into personal wealth. The scam letter writers' focus on oil-industry contracts reflects widespread popular recognition that the biggest forms of national looting occur at the nexus of Nigeria's relationship to the world economy, particularly in the transactions between the government, the NNPC and multinational oil companies. A second popular scam story also highlights international connections.

Dead Expatriates' Bank Accounts

This second common scam scenario typically involves millions of dollars left unclaimed in a

Nigerian bank because of the death of an expatriate account holder, who is usually said to have worked in the oil industry, or perhaps for a development donor agency. In most cases he is reported to have died in a "ghastly" motor vehicle accident on one of Nigeria's highways. The letters almost always explain that extensive efforts have been made to locate the dead man's kin to no avail – indeed, the description of the car accident often includes the death of the expatriate's wife and children to help buttress the claim that all efforts to locate heirs have been futile. Several letters I received included suggestions that if the money was not quickly transferred from its current limbo, unscrupulous elites would channel it to the military for nefarious purposes. This e-mail, received on July 17, 2003, is fairly typical of the "dead expatriate" genre.

Attn: sir,
Permit me to introduce myself to you. My name is Johnson Elendu. I am one of the Senior Managers in the bank I work for (Union Bank, Nigeria PLC) and I work under the Director of Foreign Exchange Operations (International Remittance). I am contacting You presently because I need your urgent assistance in a business transaction that will be of immense benefit to both of us.

I have the immediate need to transfer some money that has long been declared "UNCLAIMED" by the chairman and some members of the board of directors of our bank. The money is the closing balance of one of our best customers ever, Late Engr. CHAW, I was his personal account officer just before he died in the ADC plane crash of 1996 in Nigeria.

Engr. CHAW an American citizen was a contractor with the Federal Government of Nigeria, he supplied and installed equipment and his company Creekland Contractors completed some of the best construction contracts in the country. His closing balance in the Bank, Union Bank of Nigeria PLC (US$40.Million) has been tagged Unclaimed because no relative of Engr. CHAW has come forward to make a statement of claim. We have no knowledge of a next of kin. At this point I trust you can picture what the situation is like. We have strong proof that the chairman and the board of directors

will keep most of the money for themselves and donate the remainder to a discredited military trust here in Nigeria. This invariably is an attempt to infuse more money into the acquisition of military equipment (arms and ammunition) for use in an already prostrate Africa.

This of course, is senseless, hence my mission.

My colleagues and my self have made several attempts at locating persons that could be remotely related to Engr. CHAW and we have been doing this for about 4 years now. Right now I am almost alone in this enterprise and I have presently decided on moving the money to a foreign account. I am hereby soliciting your assistance and I will be very grateful if you will be willing to help in this regard.

We have access to most of what it will take to transfer the money. The only thing we do not have is a safe account. We will provide you with answers to all the security questions, which you will have to answer to move the process towards completion. We will also provide you answers to questions that only a person related to him will know. You may however not need to make any appearance; every thing will be concluded on phone and email between you and the bank [UNION BANK NIGERIA PLC, LAGOS] for your participation you will get 30%, 5% has been earmarked for the expenses that may be incurred on both ends. 65% shall be for my colleague and I.

I make this proposal in trust and in good faith, therefore, if you are interested and you agree to assist me then contact me immediately you receive this email, there is a lot more to talk about. If you are not interested, then, please, do get rid of this email and please forgive me if this message has upset you in any way.

Thank you and best regards.
Mr. JOHNSON ELENDU

While this scam writer goes to great lengths to assure the recipient that Mr. Chaw's contract work in Nigeria was legitimate – his company "completed some of the best construction contracts in the country" – many other dead expatriates stories simply tie the deceased to the oil or development industry and presume that this connection is sufficient to explain why he would have tens of millions of dollars in a personal account. The scam writers thus represent the widely-held Nigerian assumption that expatriates working in the oil industry or with development agencies are getting fabulously rich. Widespread awareness of the exclusive enclaves in which expatriates live, rumors about their large salaries, and the fact that big scandals involving foreign oil companies are sometimes exposed in the international and national media all feed public perceptions that expatriates in Nigeria are making millions. The use of acronyms and a "legalese" rhetorical style indicates the degree to which ordinary Nigerians associate this sort of official language and posturing with the mechanisms of corruption that operate at the level of the relationship between the state and powerful global institutions. By using this language the scam writers both hope to participate in this form of corruption and also implicitly condemn it. The prevalence of the dead expatriate genre reflects a growing understanding among Nigeria's young population that corruption in Nigeria is intertwined with larger global systems of inequality. Some of the ambivalence ordinary Nigerians feel about the 419 scams is related to a perception that Nigeria in particular, and Africa in general, is often the victim of much larger mechanisms of resource redistribution in which Westerners are the primary winners and Africans are the primary losers; as the scam letter points out, Africa is "already prostrate."

A Deceased Dictator's Desperate Widow

A third common genre reflects scam letter writers' knowledge that Nigeria's stolen billions are frequently expatriated to Western countries, highlighting popular awareness that Nigeria's history of military dictatorship was in many ways tolerated, and even facilitated, by rich countries whose primary interest was access to Nigeria's oil. In conjunction with popular discontent over the country's stolen billions, the name employed more frequently than any other in recent Nigerian e-mail scam scenarios is that of Mrs Maryam Abacha, the widow of the late dictator, General Sani Abacha. When General Abacha died suddenly in July 1998, it was widely reported in both

national and international media that he had looted several billion dollars during his five-year reign. Much of the money was believed to have been hidden away in foreign bank accounts. Since Nigeria's return to democracy in 1999, the civilian government has made efforts to recover some of the Abacha loot. Further, Abacha's son, Mohammed, was imprisoned for several years accused of various crimes. Negotiations between the Abacha family and the government at one point reportedly included an agreement whereby the Abachas could keep $100 million in exchange for facilitating the return to the government of $1 billion. After considerable media scrutiny, the deal fell through. In late February, 2005 the Nigerian government reached a final arrangement with Swiss banks to repatriate almost half a billion dollars of Abacha's money that Swiss authorities determined was criminally obtained. Forty million dollars was reportedly left out of the deal because it could not be conclusively proven that it was dirty money. Those accounts remain indefinitely frozen.

The Abacha family fought the Nigerian government's attempts to repatriate the late dictator's stolen millions, and the Nigerian media carried extensive accounts of the whole process. While the predominant popular opinion seemed to favor the repatriation of as much Abacha loot as possible, there were also media stories and some public discourse that portrayed Abacha's widow as a victim of a vendetta by then president, Olusegun Obasanjo, who had been imprisoned by Abacha for two years for allegedly participating in a coup plot. Whatever public sympathy existed for Mrs Abacha was related, in part, to the common refrain that plenty of other dictators have been allowed to keep their money. Ordinary citizens also expressed cynicism about what would happen to the Abacha loot if it were returned, the suspicion being that it would simply further enrich the current president and his cronies.

All of this plays into a common scam story in which Mrs Abacha writes to appeal for help in transferring millions of dollars that have somehow escaped the hungry eyes of Nigeria's rapacious rulers. The example below, received August 9, 2003, contains many of the characteristic features of the Mrs Abacha genre.

Attention:

I am Mrs marriam Abacha, the wife to the late Head of State, of the federal Republic of Nigeria from 1993 -1998 - General Sani Abacha.

My late husband made a lot of money as the Head of state of Nigeria for 5 years. He has different accounts in many banks of the world. He has not left any stone unturned in accruing riches for his family. The present democratic government of Nigeria led by President (Gen. (Rtd)) Olusegun Obasanjo has not find favour with my family since their inception. This may be as a result of his hatred for my late husband who kept him in jail for over two years for a coup attempt, before the death of my father. He was released immediately my husband died and he was later made the present President.

He has confiscated and frozen all my family account in Nigeria and some other American, Europe and Asian continents. It has been in both the local and international news. Presently my son mohammed Abacha has been languishing in different prison centers in Nigeria for a case against his father which he knows nothing about.

Now, my purpose of all these introduction and proposal is just seeking for your candid assistance in saving this sum of $30.8.000,000.00 USD THIRTY.EIGHT MILLION.DOLLARS] which my late husband had hidden from the Nigerian govt. during his regime, and which is presently somewhere in a financial and security company outside the entire Nigeria and West African region. This is a huge sum of money, I cannot trust much on most saboteur friends of my family in Nigeria who could not be trusted.

I got your contact through our trade mission. I deemed it necessary to contact you for this trustworthy transaction. All whom I needed is a sincere, honest, trustworthy and God-fearing individuals whom my mind will absolve to help me in this deal. If you have feelings about my situation, don't hesitate to stand for me.

If my proposal is sudden to you, all I need now is for you to stand as the Beneficiary of this money to claim it and save for me. There is no difficulty, I will send your name as the recipient as well as the beneficiary of the money. On your identification and confirmation from me, the fund will be handle to you. all i need is your confirmention of willingness and i will give you the full details. You will be compensated with 25% of the total fund for all your efforts in this transaction, provided this fund is save for me for your account in your country.

Please this is a very serious matter, it is a save my soul request from you and I will be delighted too much to receive a positive response from you in order to move into action. I will give you details on request from you.

THANKS YOURS FAITHFULLY

MRS M ABACHA

Although the primary conscious strategy of the writer is to convince the recipient that the said millions are available for the taking, the Mrs Abacha scam is instructive in what it reveals about ordinary Nigerians' assumptions regarding the workings of corruption in their society. In the Mrs Abacha genre, scam writers assume that the recipients will be aware of the large amounts of money the late dictator allegedly looted, as well as the efforts of President Obasanjo's government to recover it. Most Nigerians also assume that no matter how much money the government recovers, Mrs Abacha and her family will be able to keep millions that are somehow hidden from the inquisitors, or that they will be allowed keep millions in exchange for large bribes to the authorities. 419 scam letters frequently allude to instances of corruption and to local current events that ordinary Nigerians take for granted, but that many Western recipients are unaware of. One variation of the Mrs Abacha genre, an e-mail I received on October 15, 2004, explains the origin of the available money as "a result of a payback contract deal between my husband and a Russian firm in our country's multi-billion dollar Ajaokuta steel plant." However plausible or implausible such a scenario sounds to ordinary Western readers, millions of literate Nigerians know that over a period of more than 20 years the Nigerian government sank over $8 billion into a steel plant that never produced even one sheet of steel. The primary technical consultants for the project have, in fact, been Russian. To many Nigerians, including this particular scam writer, the Ajaokuta steel plant is a national symbol of official graft. Ordinary Nigerians recognize that corruption is most profitable when it involves an international dimension, and Nigerians are widely aware that their leaders depend on these international connections for their most lucrative looting of national resources.

Scam Letters, Corruption, and Global Inequality

The scam letters analyzed here are a tiny sample of a huge body of texts through which one segment of Nigeria's population produces cultural objects that convey popular conceptions of corruption. My analysis has focused both on what these e-mails reveal about Nigerians' assumptions and understandings regarding corruption in their own society, and on how they illustrate Nigerians' awareness that corruption in Nigeria is intertwined with larger systems of inequality that link public and private economic spheres in the era of globalization. It is no coincidence that the oil industry, expatriate contractors, development projects, and Swiss bank accounts are central figures in the scam stories. If one broadens the lens to include an analysis of the growing numbers of scam letters that focus on settings other than Nigeria, it is clear that the scam writers recognize that corruption is intertwined with the larger machinery for producing and maintaining global inequality. Scam stories that focus on reconstruction contracts in Iraq, arms deals for Angola, refugee assistance in the Sudan, emergency aid in Indonesia, diamond deals in the Democratic Republic of Congo, or the pilfered millions of Charles Taylor, Mobutu Sese Seko, Gnassingbe Eyadema, and other dead or deposed African dictators demonstrate how attuned the scam writers are to the ubiquity of corruption and its links to larger structures of inequality.

Nigerian scam letters are evidence that the young Nigerians who write and send these e-mails are aware of the importance of what Bayart (2000) has called "a history of extraversion" in explaining patterns of inequality in African societies. Bayart argues that rather than seeing Africa's relative poverty as evidence of the continent's marginalization or exclusion from the world economy, we need to understand how profoundly Africa has been integrated in the global economy throughout history, in ways that deepen poverty and inequality. Bayart suggests that the structures of extraversion not only impoverish ordinary African peoples, they also create the mechanisms by which African elites accumulate wealth and amass power. The most common genres of Nigerian scam letters also express, and indeed depend upon, mechanisms of extraversion for their success.

While Nigerian 419 scam letters are an expression of critical awareness of these mechanisms of extraversion, the scams themselves are, of course, also an effort to participate in and benefit from these forms of corruption. But those who are actually getting rich from the hundreds of millions of dollars that are reportedly lost to Nigerian 419 scams are not the thousands of young people writing scam letters in the internet cafés across Nigeria's cities and towns. The young people at the bottom of the social hierarchy who participate in 419 commonly reap little or nothing, and they participate with considerable ambivalence. On the one hand, they believe that those at the very top of the Nigerian political economy are corrupt to the core. Corruption frustrates the scam letter writers, as it does most Nigerians. In an ideal world, almost all of these young people would prefer to do something different. In the abstract, Nigerians, including the scam writers I interviewed, know that 419 is inimical to their interests and the interests of their country. On the other hand, they are extremely cynical about the prospects for success without participating in the larger system of corruption, whether it is in scam letter writing or some other arena of Nigerian society. Though the numbers of young people who write e-mail scam letters has multiplied with the advent of the internet and the relative freedoms of democracy, scam writers still represent a tiny fraction of the population. But many other Nigerians participate in one way or another in the social reproduction of corruption, even as they simultaneously lament and condemn it.

Notes

1 419 was the section of the Nigerian criminal code that referred to crimes of fraud (Smith, 2007:2).

2 For examples of media coverage see: "Halliburton's $2.4 Million Bribe Revisited," *Vanguard* (Nigeria),

February 3, 2004; "Halliburton Seeks Distance Between Itself and Inquiry," Simon Romero, *The New York Times,* section c, p.9, June 14, 2004; "Halliburton Severs Link With 2 Over Nigeria Inquiry," Simon Romero, *The New York Times,* section C, p.1, June 19, 2004; "Two More Enron Executives Charged In Nigerian Energy Deal," Hector Igbikiowubo, *Vanguard* (Nigeria), October 21, 2003; and "Six Accused Over Enron Sham Sale," Laurel Brubaker Calkins, *National Post's Financial Post and FP Investing* (Canada), p. FP11, September 22, 2004; "Halliburton and KBR to Pay Record Fine," *The Wall Street Journal,* February 11, 2009.

3 Examples of anti-419 and humorous 419 websites can be found at: http://home.rica.net/alphae/419coal/fighters.htm, and http://www.scamorama.com.

References

Apter, Andrew. 1999. "IBB = 419: Nigerian Democracy and the Politics of Illusion." In *Civil Society and the Political Imagination in Africa: Critical Perspectives,* edited by John Comaroff and Jean Comaroff. Chicago: University of Chicago Press.

Apter, Andrew. 2005. *The Pan-African Nation: Oil and the Spectacle of Culture in Nigeria.* Chicago: University of Chicago Press.

Bayart, Jean-François. 1993. *The State in Africa: The Politics of the Belly.* London: Longman.

Bayart, Jean-François. 1999. "The 'Social Capital' of the Felonious State or the Ruses of Political Intelligence." In *The Criminalization of the African State,* edited by Jean-Francois Bayart, Stephen Ellis and Beatrice Hibou. Bloomington: Indiana University Press.

Bayart, Jean-François. 2000. "Africa in the World: A History of Extraversion." *African Affairs* 99(395): 217-267.

Bayart, Jean-François, Stephen Ellis, and Béatrice Hibou. 1999. *The Criminalization of the State in Africa.* Bloomington: Indiana University Press.

Buchanan, Jim and Grant, Alex J. 2001. Investigating and Prosecuting Nigerian Fraud. *United States Attorneys' Bulletin:* 39-47.

Edelson, Eve. 2003. The 419 Scam: Information Warfare on the Spam Front and a Proposal for Local Filtering. *Computers and Security* 22(5):392-402.

Halttunen, Karen. 1982. *Confidence Men and Painted Women: A Study of Middle-Class Culture in America, 1830–1870.* New Haven: Yale University Press.

Maier, Karl. 2000. *This House Has Fallen: Nigeria in Crisis.* Boulder, CO: Westview Press.

Rebhorn, Wayne A. 1988. *Foxes and Lions: Machiavelli's Confidence Men.* Ithaca, N.Y.: Cornell University Press.

Smith, Russell G., Holmes, Michael N. and Kaufmann, Philip. 1999. "Nigerian Advance Fee Fraud, No. 121." In *Trends and Issues in Crime and Criminal Justice.* Canberra: Australian Institute of Criminology.

Watts, Michael. 1984. "State, Oil and Accumulation: From Boom to Bust." *Society and Space* 2:402–428.

44

The State in Africa
The Politics of the Belly

Jean-François Bayart

South of the Sahara, class relations are in no way the primary source of conflict, despite the acuteness of social inequality. [...] In Ghana, for example, it has been remarked that factional or local struggles have dominated over 'class politics' in the decades following the proclamation of independence. This remark can be applied to the continent as a whole.

The unloosing of the highly personalised antagonisms, within the institutions of the postcolonial State, appears increasingly to be one of its primary modalities. [...] Whether of 'socialist' or 'capitalist' persuasion, dominated by a party or by the army, pluralist or monolithic, all these constitutional formulae – whose attributes are furthermore uncertain and changeable – rest upon one common denominator: at bottom, the actors organise themselves in factions in order to win or conserve power at the various echelons of the social pyramid, and this competition is the very stuff of political life.

Léopold Senghor stigmatised this state of affairs (from which he benefited and in which he showed an unrivalled talent) by speaking of 'politicking' (*politique politicienne*) and 'Senegalitis'. An eloquent neologism. In Senegal, factional struggles, known as 'clan' struggles, have beset the institutions. [...] Political debate, at the national level, has always opposed two personalities, conforming to the bipolar configuration which is characteristic of all factional arenas. The duel between Blaise Diagne and Galandou Diouf during the inter-war years was succeeded by Senghor's battles first against Lamine Gueye (1951–57), then against his Prime Minister, Mamadou Dia (1962–63) and finally against Abdoulaye Wade (at the end of the 1970s). The latter then became Abdou Diouf's challenger. Nevertheless, these combats between leaders reflected a more general reality. Even though Abdou Diouf straightaway announced his intention of putting an end to the 'clan politics', and Moustapha Kâ, the coordinator of the *Groupe d'études et de recherches* of the *Parti Socialiste* (PS), felt able to mention in 1984 that there had been 'a reduction of the phenomenon at the regional level' thanks to the policy of rotating the post of secretary-general of the regional unions between

From Jean-François Bayart, *The State in Africa: The Politics of the Belly*, 1993, pp. 211–27, 231–43, 268–9. Copyright © Longman Group UK Limited, 1993.

the different secretaries-general of coordination,[1] all the evidence shows that the factional dimension has continued to predominate. [...]

In truth, the recurrence of factionalism can only be explained by its deep-rootedness in Senegambian history. Donal Cruise O'Brien discerns in it a 'bizarre but effective' synthesis between the Islamic culture of the *zawiya* and the electoral experience of the 'Four Communes' under the Third Republic.[2] Far from being the result of obscure manipulations of dominant groups or of foreign imperialism, as was long believed, the permanence of factionalism is an expression of a consensus on the part of the social actors.

[...]

The current saying, 'do politics' (*faire de la politique*), is simply a translation of the Wolof *ngurgi* or the Pular *laamunga*, which both mean to be a devotee of a leader or a faction, and work actively in their interests. 'It means that a whole body of relationships, which are not obviously political, are located in the parties,' quickly adds an anthropologist, emphasising that politics in Senegal are not to be situated in the two-dimensional arena of political representations.[3] On the one hand, all institutions in society – the Islamic brotherhoods or the trade unions, for example – are subjected to the same type of action, and the development planners start to take stock of the integrationist force of the factional networks, resigning themselves to making their peace with them rather than trying to bypass or confront them. [...] On the other hand, the 'clan' struggles are a reflection of the contradictions of the segmentary order of the family, and more particularly of competition between agnatic brothers, in relation to which the differentiation of political and religious arenas may be debatable. [...]

The Senegalese example – a textbook case – is not unique. [...] In Zambia, Sierra Leone, Ghana and Somalia, keen personal rivalries suck the life out of the State.[4] Does this mean that this model is distinct from another, better organised, type of political organisation? Not at all. In countries such as Tanzania and Cameroon, where the mediation of the party, administration and ideology seems undeniable and autonomous, the power of networks, the acuteness of 'struggles for influence' are

more hidden and inhibited than truly exorcised.[5] In the same way, in the Ivory Coast, the preeminence of Félix Houphouët-Boigny presides over the unending conflicts which destabilise the PDCI and which necessitate the regular convocation of meetings of 'reconciliation', sometimes in the provinces, under the wing of special delegations sent by the Political Bureau to the four corners of the country, sometimes even in Yamoussoukro itself, the regime's home base. The return to competitive elections in 1980 was marked by a proliferation of settling of scores between candidates, both successful and unsuccessful. At the time of the 'Yamoussoukro days' of May 1982, Mr Alliali, the Keeper of the Seals, explained in a speech, which could be anthologised as part of the discourse of the reciprocal assimilation of elites:

> The head of the Party's wager to put the train of democracy back on the rails has been won, but for the train to progress it is necessary for the wagons of all the activists of the PDCI, winners and losers, to be coupled to it. Fed by tenacious opposition, unsoothed rancours, unhealed wounds and above all by a thirst for revenge, divisions can only hinder the progress of the train and delay its arrival. This is why the Political Bureau, on the instructions of the president of the Party, busied itself in searching everywhere for the reconciliation of divided cadres and activists. It did not, however, succeed in dissipating all incomprehension and misunderstandings. Here and there islands of resistance held out, necessitating a meeting under the authority of the president of our Party.

After several days of 'dialogue' there followed one of those deceptively good-natured exhortations of which Houphouët-Boigny is the master. It is such a good example of the true texture of political action south of the Sahara that it, too, deserves to be quoted at length. Once the customary congratulations had been offered ('Comrade activists, I should like once again to offer you my thanks and congratulations. You have come to Yamoussoukro where the accommodation is not as good as in our capital, Abidjan.[6] You have kept your seats for five continuous days. Etc.'), and after the audience had been reminded of the institutional generalities, the head of State proceeded to review the six regions where factional struggles still prevented 'divided comrade militants from working together, as reconciled brothers'. Thus, for example, speaking about Korhogo in the north of the country:

We do not agree with those who propose the separation of family problems from political problems. If it was only a question of families we would not be here. In the traditional family, hierarchy is a golden rule which no one would dream of transgressing. There are the father, the brothers, the nephews. The purely family problems should be sorted out by family members and by nobody else. But because of the influence which the Gon family still exercises in Senoufo country, arguments between the members of this family on political matters have always had unfortunate consequences throughout the region. The traditional chiefdoms have been abolished in several African countries, including Upper Volta and Guinea. In the Ivory Coast we have retained certain chiefdoms, including that of Korhogo. The children of this family are in the process of destroying it by their behaviour. These arguments, these fratricidal struggles, prejudice the peace necessary for the development of this region, which is so full of human and material potential. The trusty Senoufo peasants, and the numerous cadres of the region deserve better than this. I should like to remind the Gon family, whom I consider as my own, that, as with nobility, honour is in our blood. A nobleman neither insults nor is insulted. We should put an end to this sad state of affairs by forcing uncle Gon and nephew Gon to bury their differences, which have lasted too long already. The prefect of the *département* of Korhogo is delegated by the government to guarantee public order. Anything which might disturb the public order should be rooted out. I solemnly call upon these two political officers to inform their followers publicly that they have once and for all buried their fratricidal struggles which, I repeat, do no service to the cause of peace in Senoufo country. This country which is so dear to me.[7]

One should not have any illusions about the capacity of the centre to pacify the periphery of the political system. One of the regional officers of the PDCI in 1985 did not disguise the fact that 'reconciliation missions [...] sent to put out the fires at the time of the various election campaigns

of 1980' had frequently been no more than 'free opportunities to play act whilst sealing a fictitious reconciliation': 'the many embraces in front of the television and photographers' cameras were mere camouflages, to put the Party officials off their guard. As soon as the missions returned to Abidjan, the protagonists lost no time in unearthing the hatchet and returning with renewed bitterness to their internecine struggles'.[8]

Better than any abstruse academic lecture on development, these long extracts illustrate the daily reality of politics in Africa: the bad-tempered froth of factional conflicts and their uneasy resolution within the framework of the State according to the logic of the reciprocal assimilation of elites. In the end, no institution, however 'massive' or 'bureaucratic' it might be, escapes from the pernicious miasmas of personal rivalries. The phenomenon has been apparent since the time of the nationalist struggles. In 1957–58, a cadre of the *Parti démocratique de Guinée* was already remarking that his colleagues 'were killing each other in an implacable struggle for places'.[9] The observation could just as easily have been made of the Kenya African Union, the Kikuyu Central Association, the Convention People's Party or of the *Union des populations du Cameroun*.[10] Indeed, in neutralising the common appeal of the anti-colonial ideal, the achievement of independence left the way wide open for the exacerbation of factional cleavages. Today, the party, the administration, the revolutionary movement, the opposition in exile, are all prey to the demons of division. [...] Ideology has nothing to do with it: the personal attacks in avowedly Marxist-Leninist systems simply clothe themselves in the finery of respect for dogma, the vulgate of the 'party line' revealing itself to be singularly well-adapted to the task of setting individuals apart. [...]

Furthermore, the insertion of African societies in the international system (or, if one prefers, their articulation within the historical postcolonial bloc) is also filtered through this factional dimension. The 'Gabonese clan' is not a curiosity, uniquely typical of the favourite sphere of French influence south of the Sahara. [...] The pivotal role of a Bruce Mackenzie or a 'Tiny' Rowland in Eastern and Southern Africa, or of a Maurice Tempelsman in Zaïre or of a Jamil Said Mohammed in Sierra Leone, have been or still are

similar.[11] The para-judicial investigation of the
Njonjo case in Kenya, in 1983–84, showed how a
'machine', controlling a good part of the wheels
of the State and the national economy, firmly
established in a Kikuyu constituency, making
remarkably good use of electoral and parliamentary divisions, was able to benefit from tapping
into the 'Asiatic', Arab, British and South African
networks.[12] Daniel arap Moi did not overlook this
tradition for long.[13]

There is nothing innately surprising in this
supremacy of the factional dimension. The legal
rational model beloved of Max Weber is an historical aberration which, moreover, has been modified by various detours and practices of sociability.
[...] Outside the narrow time-space – the western
industrial societies – of Weber's model the logic of
factional struggles is predominant. One is entitled
to wonder about the heuristic utility of a concept
which is applied to historical contexts in societies
as varied as those of the Melanesia of the 'big
men', of the Iran of the *dowré*, of the Mexico of the
caciques and the Thailand of cliques, of the China
of the great campaigns of political rectification or
of the Japan of the *habatsu*. [...]

It is clearly not enough just to cite the evidence
of factions. It is important to restore the specific
historical background against which the factional
struggle is played out. Without prejudging either
the unity of the phenomenon across the continent,
or on the contrary its particularity from one sub-
Saharan society to another, we will simply observe
that the structuring of African political societies
around factional networks derives from historical
continuities and recurrent sociological realities. In
former times, the circulation of power and wealth
followed similar modalities, so much so that long-
distance commerce or the intrigues of the old
kingdoms are in the eyes of the political scientist
not without similarities to more contemporary
facts. In particular, what we today, in a somewhat
confusing way, call ethnicity, implying the intervention of interregional chains of political and
economic transactions, is equivalent to this 'articulation of internal and external networks of
exchange' through which the integration of the
continent and its docking to various world economies was undertaken. [...]

Here is a constant, or rather a line of concatena-
tion, which deserves further thought. Implicit in it
we find the social processes which we have already
encountered: conflicts appearing to feed off 'tribalism'; 'straddling' procedures between the private
and public sector and the personal accumulation
of capital; the frequent recourse to proxies in the
world of business; subtle and ambivalent coupling
of official political hierarchies and discrete local
hierarchies; the vigorous support of 'civil society'
for the architecture of the State; the jumbling up
of varied positions underlying the project of the
dominant class or of the historical postcolonial
bloc; and, finally, the attribution of status depending upon context along an axis of elders–juniors,
and big men–small boys. To a greater or lesser
extent all these mechanisms derive from the universe of networks. They all echo a global organisation of African societies to which a growing
number of studies devoted to trade, the salaried
class, migrations and family relations all bear witness. And as such they suppose that political
entrepreneurs exercise their talent, weaving the
web of constant wheeling and dealing, capable of
rationally managing their material and symbolic
resources in their own best interests and in the
interests of the community which has given them
fame and influence, able to mobilise the forces of
the Word, of passion and anxiety, even in the nocturnal world of the invisible, and, finally, educated
in the knowledge of the white man to which the
contemporary State claims kinship. In the absence
of a true structuring of social classes, the predominance of the big men at the head of networks continues to be circumstantial and in large measure
dependent upon the accomplishment of individual
performances.

An immediate paradox emerges, therefore, from
the fact that one of the most visible continuities
between former polities and the postcolonial State
is ensured by such volatile procedures and agencies. The networks are not invariables which provide us with the thread of continuity. They are
constructed and as such are very flexible. In the
contemporary world they reflect the inherent fissi-
parity of lineage societies. In no sense do they rest
upon fixed identities which can, without too much
alteration, be simply translated across time and

space. In particular, family bonds and ethnicity, which appear to be consubstantial with networks, are above all instrumental arguments, idioms at the service of actors. This is not a new phenomenon, and its existence in the past has been demonstrated. [...] But the change of scale associated with the colonial era, the intensification of trade and the creation of new communities in urban areas, has systematised this cobbling together of identities.

Thus, in the new town of Pikine on the outskirts of Dakar, the struggle for control over the health committees certainly takes on an ethnic dimension which results in 'disguising individual power conflicts with more noble and motivating appearances'. One report revealed that in January 1982 in the medical centre of D., 'racism divided the Toucouleur and Wolof' and that 'lots of wrangling prevented the correct execution of the tasks assigned to each member of the office'. The account of the head of the centre bears this view out: 'It is the Toucouleur who gave us problems.' However, analysis of the vote, which brought about the eviction of the Wolof president in favour of his Toucouleur opponent, contradicts this explanation. On his own admission, the outgoing president won five Toucouleur votes (56 per cent of his supporters), three Wolof votes (33 per cent) and one Serer vote (11 per cent). The new president claimed a different pattern of voting with eight delegates from the Toucouleur quarter (54 per cent), five Wolof (33 per cent) and two Serer (13 per cent) voting for him, and two Toucouleur (67 per cent) and one Wolof (33 per cent) for his unfortunate adversary. In both calculations, the Wolof loser did not receive more Wolof votes, and the Toucouleur winner did not collect more Toucouleur votes. Each one of them only invoked the ethnic factor in their analysis of the vote because it was advantageous for 'clan politics'.

For the elected president, there are obvious advantages in ethnicising his rivalry with his predecessor in quarters with a majority of his own ethnic group, the Toucouleur, to increase the number of those who support him. For the outgoing president, blaming his personal defeat on collective, even demographic factors, softens the blow of his own fall.[14]

Whatever echo they may find and whatever the passions they arouse around their respective *habitus*, these identities constructed from family relations, ethnicity, religion or locality are unable to hide the extreme social heterogeneity of the networks. The task of the big men amounts precisely to the achievement of a synthesis of composite influence, whilst assuming multiple roles in various functions. [...]

A second paradox now becomes apparent: the political integration of contemporary African societies follows in the first instance from the segmentary and compartmentalised nature of this network.

The central dynamic of the reciprocal assimilation of elites rests on a more common incorporation of subordinate social groups in the mesh of networks. B. Joinet has estimated, for example, that 80 per cent of the Tanzanian population and 99 per cent of its leaders belong to one or more of the horizontal chains of solidarity which emerged in response to the economic crises and poverty of the 1970s.[15] Similar estimates have been made for West Africa. [...] But networks are also stretched along a vertical axis within the framework of the unequal exchange of goods and services. They transcend, without nullifying them, the divisions of status, income and power. They link the 'lowest of the low' with the 'highest of the high' through the agencies of continuous news, requests, gifts and far from disinterested symbolic celebrations. The integration of African societies is all the more effective because, as we know, their populations are small. Freely described in terms of family relationships, the personal knowledge that individuals have of one another is the rule rather than the exception. The practice of 'dash' is a consequence of this personalisation of institutional relationships, particularly in the civil service. [...] The force and speed of social communication which results is sometimes disconcerting.

What can be observed in matters of daily sociability can be verified in the strictly political sphere. Even though one cannot, of course, accept without questioning the news bulletins on the 'Pavement Radio' (*Radio Trottoir*), the 'small men' are frequently up-to-date with the stratagems of the 'big men'. They follow these with sceptical attention, and demonstrate an undeniable civic knowledge which contrasts strongly with the poverty of the media. [...] Family celebrations, village reunions, the circulation of women and mistresses and the tangle of bars and popular eating places are sources of much of this knowledge. Furthermore, access to the 'boss', even if he is a minister, is much easier than in western industrial societies. With representations of witchcraft a factor, a notable cannot evade with impunity the 'courtesy visits' of his clients and his 'country' and deny them access to his verandah.[16]

In these conditions, as A. Cohen has shown in his work on the Creoles of Sierra Leone, the extreme personalisation of power relationships is not necessarily diametrically opposed to political institutionalisation.[17] In Senegal and in Kenya the vitality of the party (or parties) system has tended to be in proportion to that of the factional struggles which it shelters. In Tanzania, the integrationist potency of networks coincides with the crystallisation of a political society strongly welded around a far from insignificant socialist ideology.[18] It is even necessary to accept the hypothesis, advanced long ago by Ibn Khaldun, that factional struggle is a mode of political production, not of disintegration. At the price of a clearly alarming human cost, the rotation which makes competing entrepreneurs and political cliques succeed each other in power legitimises the statist framework inherited from the colonial era, in the image of a bloody alternation. In doing so, it contributes towards its reproduction. The fact that no Chadian or Ugandan thought seriously about secession, in ten or fifteen years of appalling civil war, speaks volumes. In its cruelty, the contradiction is only superficial because this model has the weight of the *longue durée*. In the past, power was distributed in this way, often to the advantage of 'men with neither fire nor hearth'.[19] Jan Vansina's notes on the former kingdom of San Salvador take on a decidedly modern significance:

The kingdom was reduced to nothing and royalty was no more than a symbol. Nevertheless, the possession of the title of knight and other titles of nobility retained a fascinating prestige, and the infantes who had broken the kingdom continued to act as if this was still the imposing State that it had been in the 16th century. [...] Clearly, the

processes of fragmentation which around 1900 were seen in a two hundred-year-old structure cannot simply be thought of as a 'decadence' but as a way of life, a structural socio-political system.[20]

In less extreme cases, political centralisation in the form of the progressive 'presidentialisation' of the regimes has been effected through the agency of liege men or locally influential personalities who have negotiated and presided over the incorporation of regions into the bosom of the State. In Nigeria, for example, the Sardauna, in order to federate the composite North in a 'united front', relied upon representatives whom he had delegated to the various emirates and minorities of the Middle Belt, and who acted as gatekeepers to these groups; he also made use of family ties, age classes and school friendships, and excelled in the ritual joking relationships which traditionally united members of the diverse communities of the region.[21] Other leaders, such as Kwame Nkrumah, Félix Houphouët-Boigny, Ahmadou Ahidjo and Field-Marshal Mobutu ruled in the same way. [...] Nguesso made use of his family in order to secure the Congolese system: in 1984, the ambassador in Paris was an uncle, the head of the cabinet and several other ministers were also relatives and, last but not least, the political Commissar of Hydro-Congo, the national oil company, was mother.[22]

In short, the postcolonial State operates as a rhizome rather than a root system. Although it is endowed with its own historicity, it is not one-dimensional, formed around a single genetic trunk, like a majestic oak tree whose roots are spread deep into the soil of history. It is rather an infinitely variable multiplicity of networks whose underground branches join together the scattered points of society. In order to understand it, we must do more than examine the institutional buds above ground and look instead at its adventitious roots in order to analyse the bulbs and tubers from which it secretly extracts its nourishment and its vivacity. [...]

It is indeed through the medium of these rhizomatic networks that the retroactive belt linking African societies to postcolonial institutions is formed. [...] In the absence of almost any revolutionary threat south of the Sahara these factional struggles represent the principal agencies of change in government. [...] But, whatever the Africanist orthodoxy tells us, the precariousness of national political equilibria is not a manifestation of the organic inadequacy of the State, nor even a supplementary proof of its extraneity. On the contrary, it reveals its narrow symbiosis with the grassroots that sustain it.

In other words, factional struggle does not belong to the periphery of political systems; it is not the opposite of the centralising and presidentialist principle which has come to dominate under the cover of the single party or military regimes. It is the mainspring of this evolution and reverberates at the heart of the State of which it is the true dynamic. In many cases conflicts for influence within the nationalist movements before independence prepared the way for the construction of the postcolonial political order, in such a way that it consisted of the autonomisation of a presidential network among the competing factions.

In a few cases, the holder of supreme power acquired an absolute preponderance by politically and physically eliminating his rivals and turning his back on the logic of the reciprocal assimilation of elites. With massive recourse to coercion, the presidential network – one is tempted to say, mob – appropriated all the resources of the State and absorbed the political arena for its own profit, even with a veneer of sometimes delinquent ideological logomania. Ahmed Sékou Touré was the person who came most quickly and closely to this model. From 'plot' to 'plot', his 'family clan', which formed 'the narrow circle of primary beneficiaries of the regime', brutally rid him of any of the inclinations of restraint which were still held by the other segments of the political class, the former members of the *Parti démocratique de Guinée*, or more recent converts who had been caught up in the fever of the 'No' vote delivered to General de Gaulle at the time of the constitutional referendum of 1958. This network was flanked by two half-brothers of the head of State, Amara and Ismaël Touré, by his half-sister Fatima Touré, his paternal cousin Mamourou Touré, another cousin (or, on some days, nephew) Siaka Touré, and by a whole line-up of other personalities more or less closely related to him.[23]

Nevertheless, the mob's monopoly is not always perfect. When its monopoly does become closer to perfection the mob soon becomes divided. In Guinea, for example, the trauma of the Portuguese raid on Conakry in November 1970 encouraged the wife of Sékou Touré, Andrée, née Keita, to throw her lot in with her family: her half-brothers Seydou and Mamadi Keita, the husband of her younger half-sister Moussa Diakité, and Nfanly Sangaré, the husband of another half-sister.[24] Moreover, some other influential networks survived, including that of the Prime Minister, Louis Lansana Beavogui. As all opposition to the inner circle of the regime had disappeared, political life was restricted to a 'struggle to the death fought out between clans who ripped power out of each others' hands' and who 'fought their battles through proxies, directors, deputy directors, women of high and low estate [*de grand et petit milieu*]'.[25] The sinister character of the Guinean case lay in the fact that this pitiless rivalry, knowingly regulated by the head of State, extended to the precincts of the Boiro detention centre through obtaining, under torture, crazy confessions designed to 'take' one or the other of these enemy groups. [...] After the death of the old dictator in 1984, the incapacity of the factional components of the regime to overcome their animosities and to agree on the succession finally opened the way to the intervention of the army. The saga of the Tourés and Keitas came to an end several months later with their massacre in prison.

[...]

However, for most of the time political competition has, despite appearances, remained relatively open, and the autonomisation of the presidential faction has been relative. Even the most prestigious leaders have seen their primacy, which had been dearly bought, being permanently threatened by the manoeuvres of competing networks, possible rivals or dauphins in a hurry. [...]

As with elders in lineage societies, or heads of networks in a suburban district, presidential preeminence is also circumstantial and depends upon the individual performance of the holder. It is earned week after week in this hard world of intrigue and 'court politics'. [...]

[T]he president attempts to limit the possibilities for political and economic accumulation open to competing networks and diverse other political forces and institutions. Certainly, the constitutional and administrative evolution since independence – which is too well known for us to need to rehearse it here – has gradually responded to this demand by ensuring the presidentialisation and centralisation of regimes. But other, perhaps more decisive, procedures have also contributed towards the necessary autonomisation of the head of State.

Firstly, factional and ethnic conflicts have proved themselves useful in this respect, even if they have been constantly criticised by the official ideologues. They have confirmed the presidents of the Republics in their role of 'Elder' or *Mzee* – to borrow the surnames of, respectively, Félix Houphouët-Boigny and Jomo Kenyatta – lifted above the political scrum and assuming the function of supreme arbiter. To this extent, struggles for influence have frequently been a necessary ingredient for political stability and not the reverse. Draped in the noble cloth of conflicts about 'principles' ('liberalism' versus 'statism' or 'nationalism', 'continuity' versus 'change', and so on) they have acted as points of equilibrium for the regimes by safeguarding the autonomy of the presidential power, however able the holder might be at playing off one 'clan' against another. [...]

More or less manipulated either before or after elections, universal suffrage – or, as one high-ranking municipal administrator in Cameroon confused it in a phrase which was more accurate than he knew, *chiffrage universel* ('universal counting') – is in this sense a priceless instrument for eroding the positions occupied by the 'barons', in other words (and sticking to our botanical metaphor), a first-class rhizome-killer. Furthermore, it is not the case that the freer the elections the worse they are at this particular job. The 'democratisation' of the Ivoirian systems and of Cameroon's single party have given the base of the system the task of carrying out purges, which would have been difficult to undertake from the top. [...]

Secondly, the economic austerity programmes made inescapable in the 1980s by worsening balances of payments and pressure from creditors have also in their turn been used to advantage. Many commentators have failed to understand this. The dismantling of the public sector which the international financial institutions demanded need not condemn the regimes in power. By drying up the principal channels of autonomous accumulation without creating a true market, it suits the hand of the president who finds himself restored to his posi-

tion of principal distributor of sinecures. Abdou Diouf (in closing down ONCAD, the unofficial cashbox of the 'barons' of the *Parti socialiste*), Sassou Nguesso (in launching a 'structural adjustment plan') and Houphouët-Boigny (in dissolving the State companies, in abolishing the posts of directors-general, in accepting the demand of the World Bank for separating the functions of management and accounting in the civil service and in attaching the Department of Public Works to the Presidency of the Republic) have all three recovered their freedom of action with regard to a political class and a bureaucracy which had cut loose financially from the centre, and they have regained their control over a patrimonial machine which had run out of hand at the expense of a wild and runaway foreign debt.[26] The policies of structural adjustment are thus not so very different from the policies of nationalisation during the two previous decades. By different means they both pursued the same ends.

[...]

Thirdly, 'moralisation' campaigns which were launched from the very first days of independence were aimed much less at the general level of corruption than at restraining the growing power of the groups of 'nizers' which had a hold on the apparatus of the State. They indicate the desire of a network to confiscate prebendal currents for its own purpose or the wish of a president to gain control over the process of exploiting public institutions in order to regulate them.

[...]

Thus there is no real paradox in seeing all new presidents start off their terms of office with a severe critique of corruption, only to allow their own factions to help themselves to wealth before even their first term is up. Faced with the manoeuvres of the 'Royal Family' of Jomo Kenyatta or of the partisans of Ahidjo, did Messrs arap Moi and Biya have any choice? [...]

At first sight the ferocity of the factional struggles south of the Sahara seems out of all proportion to the real powers invested in the posts for which the political entrepreneurs are allowed to compete. Was it reasonable, for example, in the Ivory Coast in 1985 to resort to poison and the forces of the invisible or to buy up the entire petrol reserves of a constituency in order to deprive one's rival, all for the sake of the simple hope of winning a seat in an Assembly crushed by the preeminence of the President? Apparently yes; and in the middle of a period of economic crisis the Ivoirian political class, taken in its totality, did not flinch from sacrificing huge sums of money to the electoral rite, equivalent, according to some estimates, to the revenue of exporting 40,000 tonnes of cocoa. ... In cultures which attach value to the 'wealth of men' and which submit to this objective 'fortune in money' (in Hausa *arzikin mutane* and *arzikin kud'i*) the constitution of what Malinowski called 'resources of power' is valorised in itself. The Congolese 'partisans' offered this explanation in 1964–65:

> The struggle for influence consists essentially in making use of all means available to build up one's prestige and authority at the expense of others and in contempt of truth and justice. In political organisations, the administration, etc. one pursues the struggle for influence in order either to achieve or maintain oneself in positions of responsibility or to install or consolidate one's personal power.[27]

Positions won in combat, even if relatively subordinate, permit a minimal accumulation of wealth which can then be redistributed according to the dictates of 'strategies of offering' in order to satisfy and increase one's clientele. [...]

In any case, one should not make too much of the principle of reciprocity – whether symbolic or concrete – institutionalised by the personalisation of social and political relations within networks. Malinowski went so far as to argue that 'the primitive state is not tyrannical for its own subjects' since 'everyone is linked, in reality or in fiction, to everybody else' through kinship, clan membership or through age groups.[28] We cannot allow ourselves such an idealised conclusion as far as African societies are concerned. Their intimate character is in no sense the opposite to, nor even necessarily a reduction of, domination and inequality. [...]

It was certainly not through any generosity of spirit that Léon Mba ruled Gabon 'in the manner of a village chief', giving up an impressive amount of his time to sort out himself the many 'small personal problems', such as the notorious divorce between the butcher and the secretary.[29] In this respect the small population of most African States

is a major advantage. It enables a leader in power for one or two decades to acquire direct knowledge of every individual with money or influence. Sékou Touré took surveillance of the social elite to extremes. He made a point of personally receiving not just students returning to Guinea after studying abroad but also political prisoners released from detention who were obliged to pay him 'wholehearted homage' at the risk of appearing 'to bear a grudge'. He also decided on 'the distribution of the income from bauxite exports and from the thirty-four factories which he pompously called his 'heavy industry' and on the allocation of foreign exchange from the Central Bank: 'Nothing is done without his order. No operation is undertaken unless he has ordained it. The President of Guinea has become the Papa Bondieu giving out thousands of francs CFA here, sheets of metal, a sack of cement, a motorbike or a bag of sugar there.'[30] In some ways, far from being a threat to the regime, economic stagnation and hardship have made this method of regulating political society easier.

Redistribution of sinecures and other benefits of power must be treated carefully. It is certainly not unheard of for a 'big man', influenced by the ethos of munificence, to make a point of honour of doing so. [...] However, it is more common for it to be imposed upon him by meetings of collective savings societies in his home town or village and by the continuous stream of beggars, masters either of the language of kinship and flattery or, more disturbingly, of the accusation of witchcraft: a man who manages 'to make good' without ensuring that his network shares in his prosperity brings 'shame' upon himself and acquires the reputation of 'eating' others in the invisible world: social disapproval and ostracism and, in extreme cases, a death sentence may in time be his reward. This is not enough to ensure that the redistribution of wealth always takes place: far from it. The personal relationship on which redistribution is supposed to depend is by definition highly inegalitarian and hierarchical. [...] The personal nature of the system makes the communication of grievances increasingly difficult as social stratifications become petrified and as the *habitus* (to borrow Pierre Bourdieu's concept for the world and culture of the dominant class) become more detached from society and as the dominant actors start to reproduce. As a railway worker from Sekondi-Takoradi told Richard Jeffries: 'Have you ever seen a wealthy man stop his Mercedes to get out and dash [give money to] a poor man? Not at all. It is we workers who have to look after our jobless brothers and friends.'[31]

The object of factional struggles is equally not just the distribution of status and power. They also resemble the distribution of wealth, or more accurately, the distribution of the possibilities of realising a primitive accumulation, in the strict sense of the concept, by the confiscation of the means of production and of trade. [...] And because they take place against a double backdrop of material scarcity and political precariousness, the combats are ruthless. [...] When the GNP is low and when the conservation of a position of power depends solely upon the good humour of the Prince, the temptation to exploit 'the situation' as quickly and as fully as possible is enormous: hence the unbridled predatoriness and violence of political entrepreneurs.

[...]

In reality, many regimes on the continent operate as *kleptocracies*. [...] With the material stakes so high no holds are barred in the competition between the chiefs of the network, however violent they may be: homicides, arbitrary imprisonment, forced displacement of whole communities or (simply) burning down buildings which contain evidence of malpractice.

'Goats Eat Where They Are Tethered'

We are now able to think of 'corruption' as well as conflicts inaccurately dubbed as 'ethnic' as being no more than the simple manifestation of the 'politics of the belly'. In other words, the social struggles which make up the quest for hegemony and the production of the State bear the hallmarks of the rush for spoils in which all actors – rich and poor – participate in the world of networks. 'I chop, you chop' was the promise of a Nigerian party. Whilst one cannot deny this, one has to stress that not everybody 'eats' equally. We recall the Cameroonian proverb 'Goats eat where they are tethered'. [...] Reality is often stranger than fiction. According to the testimony of one of its own junior officers, Zaïre's Air Force (FAZA) was actually cleared out

as a result of the looting of its personnel. The pilots and other air crew first of all transformed it into an air transport company, undercutting the rates of the official national airway Air Zaïre by more than a half: 'With the money they got from this they bought produce in the interior of the country which they sold at three times the price on their return to Kinshasa where the cost of living was much higher. With this new system of commerce the crews hit upon a goldmine.' However, the ground-based maintenance staff took a dim view of these profits from which they were excluded, and took less and less care of the aircraft, 'which caused numerous accidents and deaths amongst the military flight staff':

> Finally, in view of so much uncertainty and the fear of flying on board such perilous machines, some air captains took stock of the seriousness of the situation which was deteriorating all the time, and began to offer the ground staff the possibility of finding passengers of their own to enable them to earn a modest daily income. Consequently, several flights a day took off from Kinshasa with clandestine passengers on board (approximately two out of five!). Indeed, to alleviate the poverty which affected all levels of society it was necessary for everybody to find a solution by exploiting their profession or their workplace and thereby inadvertently bringing about the ruin of the nation. Those who had a right to fly on board the military planes were no longer sure of finding a place or, if they did, they were obliged, like civilians, to pay a fee, albeit smaller than usual in recognition of their military status. (...) This new life for the air force had one important side-effect: a dramatic reduction in the number of accidents, thanks to the solidarity between ground and air staff cemented by their mutual search for an improvement in the harsh conditions of life imposed on them by the ruling minority.

Alas! This 'solid solidarity between ground and air' aroused the jealousy of the fighter pilots, *de facto* excluded from 'the alliance which existed between the transporters'. Out of spite, the fighter pilots, swiftly followed by the rest of FAZA, began to sell the spare parts of the planes. Only the C-130 of the 'Guide' was spared. As a result of this 'thoroughgoing campaign of pillage' the entire fleet was soon grounded. Chaos ensued within FAZA as it was deprived so suddenly of its supplementary income. The 'discovery of another system of compensation' became a priority.

This was quickly done. Every morning pilots and mechanics arrived at the base and towed two planes to the fuel pump of Air Zaïre for a complete refuelling. As soon as they had been filled up they were towed back to the hangars where their fuel tanks were emptied. The first clients of this little operation were the wives of the soldiers based at the CETA training camp, who bought the petrol at half price, then proceeded to resell it in Masina, Kimbaseke and especially Kisangani. It was not long before the sale of air-force fuel became semi-official, as no attempt was made to hide what was happening: every day a flood of empty barrels, big oil drums and all kinds of receptacles passed though the main entry gate to Ndjili airbase under the watchful eye of guards who, had they been above corruption, would never have allowed so many customers to pass through, let alone help them carry their barrels to and from the hangar.

This account is interesting for reasons other than its humorous detail. It is a good illustration of how 'corruption' is a method of social struggle, in the full sense of the term, and how much it rests squarely upon a lively political consciousness of inequality:

Whilst all these operations were going on there was always plenty of gossip, directed principally against the dishonesty of the established authority which stubbornly refused to treat its subjects decently. Everybody mumbled: 'It isn't possible to live with that great jackal, he must go and give way to somebody who might do a better job'; 'It's not possible for us soldiers to live in our own country. Our families are so badly treated even though the rest of the country thinks we are the righthand men of Mobutu.' These sentiments were heard in military circles throughout the country, even amongst the most illiterate of the soldiers who were sick of the Guide, but above all by veterans of the colonial army who were nostalgic for the colonial period and by those who had started off in the ranks of the ANC until that unfortunate day of 24 November 1965 when

Mobutu became the guide of our nation. Under Monsieur Joseph Kasa-Vubu, our first President of the Republic, everybody in the army was treated fairly, as they were in other sectors, both public and private, whilst now the child of Mademoiselle Yemo has the lion's share and holds the rest of his people hostage.[32]

[…]

Activity within the informal economy is closely tied to official State practice: the two spheres are indivisible. Furthermore, the strategies adopted by the great majority of the population for survival are identical to the ones adopted by the leaders to accumulate wealth and power. The line dividing these two categories of actors is a thin one. The hazards of the economic climate or the dealings of competing networks under the pretext of cleaning up politics or respect of the law which everybody ignores, can bring ruin at any time – as, for example, Malinké traders in Guinea discovered in 1985 when their shops were sacked following an unsuccessful coup attempt.[33]

Contrary to the popular image of the innocent masses, corruption and predatoriness are not found exclusively amongst the powerful. […] Rather, they are modes of social and political behaviour shared by a plurality of actors on more or less a great scale. The longest overhead power line in the world joining the dams at Inga and Shaba serves as a perfect symbol of this truth: the corner irons of the pylons have been appropriated by villagers living underneath to make beds, shovels and other tools. The daily cannibalisation of the line is a modest and popular counterpoint to the huge profits made by foreign civil engineers and Zaïrois decision-makers as a result of the construction of this grandiose and useless project.[34] The celebration of the 'cargo cult' of the postcolonial State, which is by definition inegalitarian, affords the dominant actors the means of vociferously defending their material interests whilst at the same time laying claim to the highest ideals of development and public order. In this sense the 'politics of the belly' is truly a matter of life and death. Life – if one succeeds in taking one's part of the 'national cake' without being taken oneself. Death – if one is forced to make do with a hypothetical salary that will only feed the family for the first three days of the month; if one doesn't take one's chances; if one is ambushed and beaten by opponents no matter that they are dressed up in the tawdry finery of legitimacy and coercion. Such was the sad fate in Zaïre in July 1979 of the diamond miners of Katekelayi and Luamuela who were fired upon by soldiers under direct orders from central government and MIBA, the Bakwanga Mining Company. The majority of the miners were already paying fees to the traditional authorities as well as the local police force, and thought they were doing things by the book:

When the soldiers arrived they placed themselves with their backs to the hills in such a way as to allow us only one possible escape route – across the river Mbuji-Mayi. Then they ordered us to give ourselves up one by one and hand in to the commandants the stones we had dug. We didn't move. We were forced to react by the very same soldiers who dug for diamonds for the colonel, the commandant of the regional gendarmerie who made us pay for mining permits, who claimed they were there to protect us and took diamonds from us in return. We didn't move. As time passed the order was given to fire into the crowd. The order was carried out and some were killed. In the ensuing panic the survivors divided into two groups: one lot flung themselves into the river and attempted to swim across, whilst the others tried to make their way through the line of soldiers. That's when the shooting increased. Men fell like flies. Policemen stripped the bodies to steal the precious stones. [...] In eastern Kasaï it has become the norm for policemen to shoot clandestine diggers and in a cowardly fashion massacre the young and the unemployed who have no other means of supporting themselves in a town where the only industry is MIBA. [...] The situation was all the more serious because we genuinely believed that we were digging legitimately for diamonds. In fact, the Zaïrois army was receiving a duty of 5 Z from the clandestine diggers and 20 Z from the smugglers. On top of that the soldiers took turns on the mines and demanded diamonds from us to allow us to continue. Then to our great surprise as we thought that all the soldiers were following orders from the same boss, when the relief teams arrived they came into conflict with the departing teams of soldiers. Imagine our surprise when, with

the arrival of the shock forces (soldiers plus MIBA agents), the soldiers who were surrounding us and who were digging in the mines belonging to the commandant of the gendarmerie began to hide or run away or pack up.[35]

The significance of this account can only be fully appreciated if one remembers that Mobutu, along with his family and the politico-military hierarchy of the regime, were all personally involved in the diamond trade.[36] Within these sorts of contexts social struggle is a zero sum game where the only prize is the accumulation of power. [...]

The social frustrations caused by the economy of survival force many 'little men' to make radical choices: either allow oneself to sink into dementia, like the unemployed man in Douala who cut off his penis because he 'never had enough money to merit a woman',[37] or to seize by force that which society denies them.

The 'highest of the high' are very much aware of this and increasingly live in a siege mentality, protected by their personal guards. They perceive banditry as a political threat to their absolute seniority, a threat which derives in the main from the 'youth', the 'juniors' and the 'little men'. [...]

The 'politics of the belly' is firmly located in the continuity of the conflicts of the past. Today as yesterday, what is being fought for is the exclusive right to the riches claimed by the holders of 'absolute seniority'. The young challenge this claim. What is perhaps more revealing is that women are no more willing to accept the claim than the youth and that they are waging an authentic 'sex war' against the men.[38] Once again morality is not necessarily the victor: in order to achieve emancipation and economic advancement, young women are forced to sell their bodies as well as engage in other commercial activities or work in industry or on the land. [...] With the spread of sexually transmissible disease – and the tragic consequences of one of these diseases in particular – we see further proof of our proposition that south of the Sahara 'to eat' is a matter of life and death. All the same, we need to verify that in the end it is still a political question, albeit in a somewhat less than rigorous use of the epithet.

The Emergence of a Political Space

We do not intend to succumb – as too often happens – to the temptation of reducing African social actors to no more than glutinous enzymes, motivated by the sole desire of stuffing themselves as quickly as possible with the fruits of western modernism. The expression 'politics of the belly' must be understood in the totality of its meaning. It refers not just to the 'belly' but also to 'politics'. This 'African way of politics' furthermore suggests an ethic which is more complicated than that of lucre. A man of power who is able to amass and redistribute wealth becomes a 'man of honour' (*samba linguer* in Wolof).[39] In this context, material prosperity is one of the chief political virtues rather than being an object of disapproval. President Houphouët-Boigny, for example, once attempted to discredit a political opponent by describing him as a man who 'didn't own anything, not even a bicycle'.[40] The Ivoirian President was proud of having been the first person to import a Cadillac into the country, to the great annoyance of Governor Péchoux. He brought the full weight of his wealth to bear in a speech of epic proportions delivered to striking students: 'People are sometimes surprised that I like gold. It's because I was born in it.'[41] [...]

Other politicians – Nnamdi Azikiwe in Nigeria or Major-General Mobutu in Zaïre, for example – confirm that fortune is an attribute of a true chief, sometimes because it helps presumably to discourage the abuse of power. [...] It may be a good thing that physical corpulence is a sign of a true chief, and from this point of view as well the expression 'politics of the belly' carries a much richer symbolic meaning than its polemical connotation might at first suggest. In short, wealth is a potential sign of being at one with the forces of the cosmos. [...]

Social phenomena which western common sense interprets as 'corruption' of the State or 'political decay' lie right at the heart of our understanding of the State. They shed light on its social struggles, its relative indetermination and, finally, its moral culture, which condemns (and sometimes prevents) the monopolising of power, nourishes a certain idea of liberty and, at the same time, makes some forms of social injustice illegitimate. In other words, they flesh out the generic concepts of democracy, authoritarianism, totalitarianism or the State with a single truth which can be applied south of the Sahara – namely, that which is produced by history and which is drawn by the long-term trajectory. [...]

[This] analysis must then move towards the intelligence of this mode of 'government', in the sense that the word was understood in the sixteenth century, that is, the 'way in which the conduct of individuals or of groups might be directed'. 'To govern [...] is to structure the possible field of action of others.'[42] In order to designate this mode of 'government' – or, as Foucault would say, 'governmentality' – we have made use of the Cameroonian expression 'politics of the belly'. [...] Plantu, the caricaturist of the *Cameroon Tribune* whose cartoon of the infamous goat saying, 'I graze, therefore I am', suggests very precisely the contours of what is politically thinkable in postcolonial African societies.[43] This is not to say that this form of 'governmentality' belongs to a traditional culture whose contours cannot possibly be avoided, nor that it avoids the critique of a growing number of African citizens, and nor finally that it covers the totality of the continent's political 'ideo-logic'. But it has crushed most of the strategies and institutions, in particular the Christian churches, the nationalist parties and the civil services, which have worked for the advent of a modern Africa. The experiences of governments which attempted to break free from their grip have either not lasted a long time or have in their turn been absorbed by its practices.

Africa does not, however, 'eat' in a uniform way. The regimes of political manducation vary from the Nigerian or Zaïrois *bulimina* to the Tanzanian or Nigerien slimmers' diet, from the prophetic appetite of an Ahmed Sékou Touré or a Macias Nguema to the schizophrenic greed of Marxist-Leninist leaders, or from the redeeming austerity of a Jerry Rawlings or a Murtala Mohammed to the voluptuous appetite of a Félix Houphouët-Boigny or a Jomo Kenyatta. One must be aware of these variations rather than pontificate upon an eternal Africa. The study of sequences of events, ideological sedimentations, judicial codifications, institutional formalisations, structures for creating or redistributing wealth, political alliances and social exclusions and of the geographic and demographic morphology of each country should enable us to differentiate the national trajectories of politics, pursue comparisons and – perhaps – draw up a typology of the State south of the Sahara. [...]

Africa, furthermore, holds no monopoly in matters of the belly, nor of escape. For proof we need look no further than the increase in academic works dedicated to the description of 'corruption', 'clientelism' and 'migrations'. Assuming that such commonly found phenomena should not be taken as simply morbid, we are forced to admit that the analysis of politics in Africa opens the door to a wider reflection on the nature of politics. Yes, banal Africa – exoticism be damned! – leads us to some general lessons of methodology. If the majority of phenomena which it has allowed us to see and which taken together serve to typify it, are also found under other skies without none the less being seen as distinctive characteristics of systems of power in Asia, America or Europe, it is perhaps more a matter of degree or proportion. Let us first of all establish whether strategies of 'straddling', for example, are more or less decisive in Abidjan or Lagos than in Moscow, Beijing, Singapore, Washington or Paris! [...] The condescending perplexity of the observer faced with the political practices south of the Sahara derives less from the fact that these are in themselves astonishing than that such an observer is unable (or unwilling) to reconstruct the subjectivity of the African actors and remains instead a complacent hostage to the paradigm of the yoke. [...]

Notes

1   Parti socialiste du Sénégal, Groupe d'études et de recherches, *Séminaire sur le thème: les tendances et les clans*, Dakar, 1 Dec. 1984, p. 7; *Le Soleil* (Dakar), 3 Dec. 1984 and *Muntu-Dimanche* (Dakar), 19, Dec. 1986, p. 2.

2   D.B. Cruise O'Brien, 'Senegal' in J. Dunn, ed., *West African States. Failure and Promise. A Study in Comparative Politics*, Cambridge, Cambridge University Press, 1978, pp. 187–8.

3   J. Schmitz, 'Un politologue chez les marabouts', *Cahiers d'études africaines*, 91, XXIII (3), 1983, pp. 332 and 335.

4   M. Szeftel, 'The political process in post-colonial Zambia: the structural bases of factional conflict' in Centre of African Studies, *The Evolving Structure of Zambia Society*, Edinburgh, University of Edinburgh, 1980, multigr., pp. 64–95; R. Tangri, *Politics in sub-saharan Africa*, London, James Currey, Portsmouth, Heinemann, 1985, chap. ii; N. Chazan, *An Anatomy of Ghanaian Politics. Managing Political Recession. 1969–1982*, Boulder, Westview Press, 1983, pp. 95 ff.; and on Somalia *Africa Confidential*, 27 (12), 4 Jun. 1986 and 27 (22), 29 Oct. 1986.

5   D.-C. Martin, *Tanzanie: l'invention d'une culture politique*, Paris, Presses de la Fondation nationale des sciences politiques, Karthala, 1988, chap. xiv; J.-F. Bayart, *L'État au Cameroun*, Paris, Presses de la Fondation nationale des sciences politiques, 1979, *passim*.

6   A typical manifestation of courtesy. The transfer of the capital dates back only to 1984.

7   PDCI, 'Séminaires d'information et de formation des secrétaires généraux. Yamoussoukro: 3–7 mai 1982. Abidjan: 10–11 décembre 1982. Yamoussoukro: 27–29 décembre 1983' Abidjan, Fraternité-Hebdo, 1985, pp. 8–10 and 11–14. See also A. Bonnal, 'L'administration et le parti face aux tensions', *Politique africaine*, 24, Dec. 1986, pp. 20–8.

8   F. Amani Goly, Party inspector for the Centre West area, 'Entraves internes et externes à la bonne marche des sections' in PDCI, *Le Quatrième Séminaire des secrétaires généraux, Yamoussoukro: 7, 8 et 9 mars 1985*, Abidjan, Fraternité-Hebdo, 1985, p. 17.

9   Declaration of Ansoumane Magassouba, quoted in I. Baba Kaké, *Sékou Touré, le héros et le tyran*, Paris, Jeune Afrique, 1987, p. 60.

10 J. Spencer, *KAU. The Kenya African Union*, London, KPI, 1985; R. Um Nyobé, *Le Problème national kamerunais. Présenté par J.A. Mbembé*, Paris, L'Harmattan, 1984; N. Chazan, *An Anatomy of Ghanaian Politics*, pp. 95 ff.; R. Rathbone, 'Businessmen in politics: party struggle in Ghana, 1949–1957', *Journal of Development Studies*, 9 (3) April 1973, pp. 391–401; D.E. Apter, *Ghana in Transition*, Princeton, Princeton University Press, 1972.

11 M. Mamdani, *Imperialism and Fascism in Uganda*, Nairobi, Heinemann, 1983, pp. 98–9; J.-C. Willame, *Zaïre. L'épopée d'Inga. Chronique d'une prédation industrielle*, Paris, L'Harmattan, 1986, pp. 137–8; N. Swainson, *The Development of Corporate Capitalism in Kenya. 1918–1977*, London, Heinemann, 1980, pp. 274–6; C. Young, T. Turner,

The Rise and Decline of the Zaïrian State, Madison, The University of Wisconsin Press, 1985, pp. 171 and 176; Africa Confidential, 1984–1988.

12 Dossier 140/221, 'Élites politiques: Charles Njonjo', Nairobi, CREDU, 1983–1984; Weekly Review (Nairobi), 1983–1984; Republic of Kenya, Report of Judicial Commission Appointed to Inquire into Allegations Involving Charles Mugane Njonjo (Former Minister for Constitutional Affairs and Member of Parliament for Kikuyu Constituency), Nairobi, The Commissions of Inquiry Act, 1984.

13 Africa Confidential, 28 (13), 24 Jun. 1987.

14 D. Fassin et al., 'Les enjeux sociaux de la participation communautaire', pp. 217–18.

15 B. Joinet, Tanzanie, manger d'abord, Paris, Karthala, 1981, pp. 189–91.

16 E. Terray, 'Le climatiseur et la véranda' in Afrique plurielle, Afrique actuelle. Hommage à Georges Balandier, Paris, Karthala, 1986, pp. 37–44.

17 A. Cohen, The Politics of Elite Culture, Los Angeles, University of California at Los Angeles Press, 1981.

18 D.-C. Martin, Tanzanie; D. Martin, G. Dauch, L'Héritage de Kenyatta; J.-D. Barkan, 'The electoral process and peasant-state relations in Kenya' in F.M. Hayward, ed., Elections in Independent Africa, pp. 213–37; D. Bourmaud, 'Les élections au Kenya: tous derrière et Moi devant...' and B. Smith, 'Les élections au Kenya: du passé faisons table rase!', Politique africaine, 31, Oct. 1988, pp. 85–92; D.B. Cruise O'Brien, Saints and Politicians.

19 J. Bazin, 'Guerre et servitude à Ségou' in C. Meillassoux, ed., L'Esclavage en période précoloniale, Paris, Maspero, 1975, pp. 135–81.

20 J. Vansina, Les Anciens Royaumes de la savane, p. 149.

21 J.N. Paden, Ahmadu Bello, Sardauna of Sokoto. Values and Leadership in Nigeria, London, Hodder and Stoughton, 1986, pp. 202 ff. and p. 313 ff.

22 Africa Confidential, 17 Oct. 1984.

23 I. Baba Kaké, Sékou Touré, pp. 168 ff.

24 Ibid., pp. 171–2 and 179.

25 A. Diallo, La Mort de Diallo Telli, premier secrétaire général de l'OUA, Paris, Karthala, 1983, p. 19. Cf. also M. Selhami, 'Un seul gouvernement: la famille', Jeune Afrique plus, 8, June 1984, pp. 18–21.

26 Africa Confidential, 28 (10), 13 May 1987; Marchés tropicaux et méditerranéens, 7 March 1986, pp. 577–80;

ibid., 28 March 1986, pp. 857–8; ibid., 19 Sept. 1986, pp. 2375–6; ibid., 31 Oct. 1986. p. 2750; N. Casswell, 'Autopsie de l'ONCAD. La politique arachidière au Sénégal, 1966–1980', Politique africaine, 14, June 1984, pp. 66 ff.

27 Les Cahiers de Gamboma. Instructions politiques et militaires des partisans congolais (1964–1965), Brussels, CRISP, 1965, p. 57.

28 B. Malinowski, Freedom and Civilization, London, Allen and Unwin, 1947, pp. 266 and 253.

29 C. and A. Darlington, African Betrayal, New York, David McKay, 1968, p. 121.

30 A. Diallo, La Mort de Diallo Telli, pp. 18, 106 and 118.

31 R. Jeffries, Class, Power and Ideology in Ghana: the Railwaymen of Sekondi, Cambridge, Cambridge University Press, 1978, p. 182.

32 Anon., 'La Vie dans les forces aériennes zaïroises', n.d.

33 A. Morice, 'Guinée 1985', pp. 108–36; F. Gaulme, 'La Guinée à l'heure des réformes', Marchés tropicaux et méditerranéens, 13 Jun. 1986, pp. 1565 ff.; ibid., 2 Aug. 1985, pp. 1939–40.

34 J.-C. Willame, Zaïre: l'épopée d'Inga. Chronique d'une prédation industrielle, Paris, L'Harmattan, 1986, p. 128.

35 'Les massacres de Katekelayi et de Luamuela (Kasaï oriental)', Politique africaine, 6, May 1982, pp. 82–83.

36 C. Young, T. Turner, The Rise and Decline of the Zaïrian State, Madison, University of Wisconsin Press, 1985, pp. 181 and pp. 452–3, note 27.

37 La Gazette de la nation (Douala), 2 Aug. 1984.

38 C. Vidal, 'Guerre des sexes à; Abidjan. Masculin, féminin, CFA' in 'Des femmes sur l'Afrique des femmes', Cahiers d'études africaines, 65, XVII-1, 1977, pp. 121–53.

39 C. Coulon, 'Elections, factions et idéologies au Sénégal' in CEAN, CERI, Aux urnes l'Afrique!, p. 160.

40 L. Gbagbo, Côte-d'Ivoire. Pour une alternative démocratique, Paris, L'Harmattan, 1983, p. 80.

41 Fraternité-Matin (Abidjan), 29 April 1983, p. 16.

42 M. Foucault, 'Le pouvoir, comment s'exerce-t-il?' in H.L. Dreyfus, P. Rabinow, Michel Foucault, un parcours philosophique, Paris, Gallimard, 1984, pp. 313–14.

43 Cameroon Tribune (Yaoundé), 8–9 May 1988.

45

"Govern Yourselves!"
Democracy and Carnage in Northern Mozambique

Harry G. West

The killings in Muidumbe district began in the second half of the year 2002. In some cases, attacks were witnessed; in others, mauled bodies alone told grisly stories. It was by no means unheard of in the area for a lion to kill a person. But this was different. These lions – by collective reckoning, seven – lingered in and around villages and agricultural camps on the southeastern edge of the Mueda Plateau for months on end, taking victims one after another. Afraid to venture outside their homes, area residents abandoned their fields at the peak of the agricultural season. As the preceding year's stores ran out and the current year's crops rotted in the fields, many went hungry. Women fetched water from sources outside the village only en masse, escorted by men armed with bow and arrow. Bathing became almost impossible. Schools ended classes early so that students could return home while the sun was still high in the sky. Well before dark, makeshift chamber pots were placed inside as villagers made ready for another long night behind barricaded doors and boarded-up windows.

Hopes that the government would resolve the crisis went unmet. Muidumbe district administra-tor Pedro Seguro later asserted that provincial authorities failed to respond to his requisition for hunting rifles and ammunition. Villagers wondered whether any petition was even made. As far as they remembered, no word to that effect was ever issued from the administrator's office, nor was any other action taken to put an end to the carnage. As the death toll mounted, villagers took matters into their own hands, killing several lions by laying traps in the village or hunting them down with bow and arrow. They also began lynching fellow villag-ers whom they accused of making, or transforming into, lions to feed upon neighbors and kin. When mobs pulled the accused from their homes, bound and beat them, doused them with petrol, and set them alight, those attempting to intervene became the objects of potentially lethal popular suspicion (Israel n.d.; Limbombo 2003). [...]

For generations, Muedans have suspected a cer-tain few among them capable of making or trans-forming into lions. Sorcerers, by Muedan definition, perform astonishing acts through which they feed on the well-being of others. According to most people with whom we worked, such phenomena have greatly intensified in recent years, taking on alarming new dimensions. The reason? In a word, democracy. One elder put it succinctly: "In the past, sorcerers were regulated. Today, we have democracy. Anything is possible now. Everything is permitted." In pre-colonial times, individuals accused of sorcery were submitted to ordeals (Dias and Dias 1970:370). The failing of these tests indicated their guilt and often ended their lives. Colonial and post-colonial regimes prohibited anti-sorcery ordeals in Mueda and elsewhere in Mozambique, but these restrictions were interpreted by most as elements of a broader policy also prohibiting the practice of sorcery itself (West 2005). But this, no longer. When I asked the administrator of neighboring Mueda district, Ambrósio Vicente Bulasi, about a recent spate of lion attacks and vigilante justice there, he, too, linked such occurrences, in the present, to democracy. "Democracy," he stated, "means that each one has the right to believe what he believes." Personally, he did not "believe in sorcery": "Of course, people cannot make lions and send them to attack other people. These things arise out of conflicts between families." Nonetheless, democracy dictated that officials such as he remain uninvolved in these affairs. "It is essential not to get drawn into such matters," he told me. "If you try to adjudicate, you wind up taking sides. It is better to have [people] reach a resolution on their own," he concluded. "I tell them that they must sort these things out for themselves." According to residents of Muidumbe, this is precisely what their administrator did when lions besieged their villages in late 2002 and early 2003 (see Israel n.d.).

During a 1998 tour of Africa, US president Bill Clinton declared: "From Kampala to Capetown, from Dakar to Dar es Salaam, Africans are being stirred by new hopes for democracy and peace and prosperity." In support of this, he pointed to the fact that "half of the forty-eight nations in sub-Saharan Africa [had] chose[n] their own governments" (Clinton 1998). By many accounts, Mozambique was a – if not *the* – model for democratization in Africa, having recently emerged from a protracted civil war and successfully staged multiparty national elections (Chan and Venâncio 1998; Manning 2001, 2002). Only a few years later, however, the Democratization Policy Institute declared:

Despite high hopes following the end of the Cold War, promises of an "African Renaissance" remain largely unfulfilled. Most of the countries chosen by President Clinton as examples of a new Africa are either outright dictatorships, like Rwanda and Eritrea, or quasi-democratic autocracies, like Uganda and Ethiopia. Most African countries that adhere to democratic governance (loosely defined) have shown some slippage, with democratically elected leaders attempting to remain in power by tweaking constitutions. [Democratization Policy Institute 2001]

Meanwhile, observers have reported rising levels of corruption in Maputo – punctuated by the failure of the criminal justice system to detain those responsible for the assassination of whistleblowers – and international observers have expressed grave concerns over irregularities in the 2004 Mozambican general elections (The Carter Center 2005; Clemens 2002; Hanlon 2004). By Western standards, Africa's new democracies, including Mozambique, have had limited success in consolidating regime transition.

But what of African standards? The Cameroonian historian Achille Mbembe has argued that the project of democratization in contemporary Africa depends not on the application of a Western model of power to African realities but, instead, upon the cultivation within Africa of "other languages of power" that express emergent African political ethics. (The same might be said of democratization, political realities, and languages of power in other regions of the world.) These languages, he asserts, "must emerge from the daily life of the people, [and] address everyday fears and nightmares, and the images with which people express or dream them" (Geschiere 1997:7). Elsewhere (West 2005). I have examined sorcery discourse as one such language of power spoken by Muedans; I have also suggested that, in speaking of political realities, Muedans are not limited to this one language. Like most peoples, Muedans draw on multiple languages of power that intertwine in complex fashion in the world they inhabit. The way in which they speak of political realities today has been shaped by historical encounters with various others and the languages of power they have spoken, whether slave traders, Catholic missionaries,

Portuguese colonial administrators, Tanganyikan plantation owners, FRELIMO nationalist guerrillas, or agents of post-independence state socialism. At the broadest level, the language of power contemporary Muedans speak comprises multiple languages. It is a linguistic mosaic produced and sustained by speakers who have gained varying degrees of fluency in other languages and woven them into their own – a system in constant flux. In accordance with the topic at hand, its speakers draw meaning from different experiential subsystems, geographical reference points, and historical strata. In the current moment, Muedans have even engaged with the language of power spoken by democratic reformers, adopting or adapting some terms and concepts from the democracy lexicon while dismissing or ignoring others.

In this chapter, I argue that the language of power Muedans have spoken in the midst of neoliberal transformation of the Mozambican economy and polity differs substantially from the language spoken by democratic reformers, notwithstanding points of convergence, as well as internal variations and dynamic complexities, in both these languages. Recognizing that, in the face of reform, Muedans have not spoken with one voice, nor have their ideas and actions derived from some hermetic indigenous logic, I nonetheless suggest that the language of power Muedans generally speak reflects and sustains different notions of contemporary political realities. In the disjuncture between their language and that of democratic reformers, I argue, Muedans have critically engaged with the ongoing process of democratization. Indeed, I suggest, they have articulated their own vision of, and for, the working of power in the world they inhabit. Before examining this in detail, I provide an historical overview of democratic reform in Mozambique.

The "Democratization" of Mozambique

The southern African nation of Mozambique was born of guerrilla war waged against Portuguese colonizers by the Mozambican Liberation Front (Frente de Libertação de Moçambique, or FRELIMO) from 1964 to 1974. From rear bases in the newly independent and socialist-oriented

Tanzania, FRELIMO established its central base early in the campaign on the Mueda Plateau amidst generally supportive Makonde populations. With military support from China, the Soviet Union, and other Eastern bloc countries, the Front expelled the Portuguese from substantial portions of the northern Mozambican provinces of Tete, Niassa, and Cabo Delgado (including most of the Mueda Plateau). In 1974, a military coup in Lisbon toppled António Salazar's appointed successor, Marcelo Caetano, and set the stage for FRELIMO to take power in 1975 over an independent Mozambique (Henriksen 1983; Munslow 1983). The party's official adoption of a Marxist-Leninist platform in 1977 consolidated FRELIMO's commitment to socialism (Munslow 1983). In coming years, however, brutal civil war undermined the realization of "socialist modernization" in Mozambique.

The Mozambican National Resistance (Resistência National Moçambicana, or RENAMO) was born in the late 1970s of counterinsurgency operations undertaken by the neighboring Rhodesian regime to harass Zimbabwean nationalist guerrillas based, with Mozambican consent, across the border in central Mozambique. After Zimbabwean independence, the South African apartheid regime extracted, trained, armed, and redeployed RENAMO fighters to "destabilize" a Mozambican state then harboring African National Congress (ANC) activists. By the late 1980s, RENAMO had put down roots in Mozambique – drawing malcontents and conscripts into its ranks – and was operating in all ten Mozambican provinces.

In some areas, the insurgency enjoyed considerable popular support. Not, however, in Mueda. Deeply invested in the historical construction of FRELIMO nationalism, Muedans fended off sporadic attacks and successfully denied the insurgency any foothold on the plateau. Throughout the country, however, nearly one million Mozambicans died, and up to six million were displaced from their homes as rival armies waged war for more than a decade and a half (Africa Watch 1992; Egerö 1987; Finnegan 1992; Hall 1990; Hanlon 1990; Minter 1994; Vines 1991). With the end of the Cold War and then the end of apartheid in the early 1990s, both sides lost external support, making possible a negotiated settlement in October 1992 stipulating that national elections be held in

October 1994 (Alden 1995; Alden and Simpson 1993; Chan and Venâncio 1998; Hume 1994; Mazula 1995). FRELIMO prevailed at the ballot box, taking the presidency and a majority of seats in the national assembly (Hanlon 1994), as it would again in 1999 and 2004.

The democratization of Mozambique has consisted of far more than the staging of regular national elections. In the shadow of Soviet perestroika and glasnost and the global ascendance of neoliberalism, the ruling FRELIMO party initiated comprehensive reforms from the late 1980s onward to liberalize the Mozambican economy and polity. In 1986, fiscal austerity measures were unilaterally adopted by the FRELIMO government, making possible an agreement with the IMF the following year for structural adjustment support (Hanlon 1991). In 1989, the FRELIMO party officially abandoned its commitment to Marxism-Leninism. In the ensuing years, government privatized a great many state enterprises (Myers 1994; Pitcher 2002; West and Myers 1996). A new constitution in 1990 established individual rights of person and property, including freedoms of religion and political expression, fostering foreign and domestic investment and leading rapidly to the emergence of multiple political parties and also a vibrant independent press (Africa Watch 1992). In 1997, government created a framework for state decentralization and for subsequently staged local elections in a number of cities and towns (Alves and Cossa 1997). Simultaneously, government explored means of incorporating civil leaders – including hereditary authorities – into processes of local governance, eventually issuing a decree on the matter in the year 2000 (Buur and Kyed 2003; Hanlon 2000). All of these measures were underwritten by Western donor nations, as well as supported by an array of international organizations.

Although the democratization of Mozambique has comprised these multiple, interconnected, political and economic reform processes, three aspects have been central to the Muedan experience of democracy, namely elections, state decentralization, and the establishment of individual rights of person, property, and free expression. In the remainder of this chapter I consider these components in turn, focusing on how Muedans have,

through their own language of power, understood and engaged with them rather differently than reformers might have hoped and expected.

Electoral Democracy, Perpetual War

Not only is the Mueda Plateau one of the most geographically remote regions in Mozambique, but also it is one of the most politically isolated. The region – often called "the cradle of the revolution" – has, in many ways, remained more loyal to FRELIMO socialism than has the party itself. Indeed, most Muedans took notice of democracy only in 1994. During that event-filled year, UN peacekeepers established camp in the town of Mueda to oversee the demobilization of soldiers. RENAMO set up offices in district seats. UN election observers arrived en masse to coordinate electoral registration and voter education. RENAMO leader Afonso Dhlakama and FRELIMO leader Joaquim Chissano each held campaign rallies on the plateau. Finally, in late October, Muedans voted.

In the context of the modern nation-state, multiparty elections are often the most celebrated component of democracy. Accordingly, great emphasis has been placed on the successful staging of elections in Mozambique. In the aftermath of the first national multiparty elections in 1994, one observer declared: "Peace in Mozambique first and foremost means that the political conflict fought out between FRELIMO and RENAMO in a bloody war has been civilized in the sense that both its theatre and instruments have changed: from the bush to parliament and from weapons to words, respectively" (Weimer 1996:43–4). Above all else, democratic reformers in Mozambique conceived of elections as a means of ending violent conflict and of rationalizing political contestation by rendering contestants and their respective politics directly accountable to the Mozambican people.

From the outset, however, Muedans looked upon elections – and democracy, more generally – rather differently. Many Muedans first heard the word *democracy* spoken on Radio Moçambique and associated with RENAMO leader Afonso Dhlakama, who proclaimed that he had fought for, and won, democracy for the Mozambican people (Manning 2002: 144–5). Muedans subsequently saw the word in print on RENAMO flags and T-shirts appearing in the region during the electoral campaign. To be sure, UN representatives in Mozambique, from Maputo to Mueda, also frequently deployed the term *democracy* in public discourse and in printed matter distributed before elections. Tellingly, most Muedans conceived of the United Nations Operation in Mozambique (UNOMOZ) as a "political party" that, like RENAMO, contested FRELIMO's historical right to govern the nation it had liberated from colonial rule. That many ranking UN military officers were Portuguese, owing to competence in the Mozambican national language, exacerbated suspicions that UNOMOZ constituted a stealth invasion force under the control of the former colonizer.

In the months before elections, UNOMOZ worked to demobilize both combatant armies. Because there were no RENAMO bases on the plateau, however, Muedans bore witness only to the disarmament of FRELIMO troops, whose return as civilians to Muedan villages signaled to them FRELIMO vulnerability or defeat. Meanwhile, UNOMOZ visibly safeguarded the establishment of RENAMO headquarters in Mueda town, where "foreign delegations" frequently appeared to celebrate democracy's arrival in Mozambique by bestowing largesse on those Muedans considered "bandits" and "murderers." In these early days, Muedans conceived of democracy as the ideology of "opposition," the slogan of ignoble enemies, past and present. Democracy's arrival in Mueda signaled the potential undoing of all that FRELIMO – and with it Muedans – had accomplished since taking up arms in 1964, including the achievement of national sovereignty.

When voter registration began, many Muedans declined participation. When asked why, many told me that they had no use for the identification cards issued by elections officials, for they "already belonged to a political party" (West 2003). When local FRELIMO leaders themselves spoke out in support of democracy and urged Muedans to register for the vote, many worried that FRELIMO was "growing tired."

With the start of the electoral campaign, rival political parties focused attention on potential voters. This was the moment in which, according to democratic reformers, parties would be required to attune themselves to the desires of constituents. What actually happened was rather different from this. Mozambicans everywhere uttered the proverb, "When buffalos fight, the grass gets trampled." Indeed, the campaign was defined less by "debate" than by contestants' activating networks of patronage and coercion. Voters ultimately "recognized" candidates who most convincingly exercised power in their midst, RENAMO generally winning in regions it had come to control during the war and FRELIMO in regions it had held. The campaign introduced new tensions – sometimes violent – into communities throughout the country, including Muedan villages. At the beginning of the campaign, FRELIMO leaders circulated in the Mueda region calling upon villagers to remain "vigilant" against the appearance of RENAMO in their midst. This term – which invoked memories of revolutionary wartime campaigns to detect and eliminate "enemies within" the ranks of the FRELIMO insurgency (that is, spies, saboteurs) – accentuated Muedan resentment against, and fear of, RENAMO in the very moment of democratic "consolidation of the peace." Suspected RENAMO sympathizers were identified and beaten. Several times, Muedans attacked RENAMO headquarters in Mueda town, tearing down the RENAMO flag and chasing RENAMO delegates out of town. When RENAMO leader Afonso Dhlakama came to the plateau to stage a rally, Muedans "stoned" him with green (hard, unripened) mangoes and then the helicopter in which he fled. By contrast, FRELIMO leader Joaquim Chissano was met on the Mueda airstrip by throngs of supporters, who carried him on a makeshift throne to his rally in the center of town. [...] Weeks later, Muedans cast their ballots, voting overwhelmingly in favor of Chissano and FRELIMO. [...]

After ballots had been cast and results tabulated, most Muedans with whom we spoke expected talk of democracy to end, for they, and the nation, had recognized "Papa Chissano" as their legitimate leader. To their surprise and indignation, the RENAMO flag continued to fly at party headquarters in district seats on the plateau. RENAMO delegates continued to lay claim to power as they prepared for future elections. To most Muedans, such "provocation" was unprecedented. Under socialism, the one-party state knew no contestants; within the ranks of the highly centralized party, power struggles were quickly – if sometimes violently – resolved. The colonial state, too, had admitted no rivals, within or without. FRELIMO's challenge to Portuguese rule produced protracted, violent conflict, after which only one of the two claimants to power remained in Mozambique, namely, FRELIMO.

The model of singular, uncontested power resonated even more deeply than this among Muedans. To be sure, in pre-colonial times, young men often challenged the authority of their elders – whether on the basis of descent from a founding elder, aptitude for leadership, or courage – giving rise to struggles over settlement headmanships. And such contests sometimes turned violent. In any case, such affairs were considered finished only when all parties recognized a victor or when parties refusing to do so abandoned the settlement (often in the company of their supporters). Until the uncontested authority of one man was recognized, the security of settlement residents vis-à-vis one another and neighboring settlements remained unsure. In contrast to these familiar models for dispute resolution, multiparty democracy, from the Muedan perspective, promised to sustain and even proliferate rival claims to power at the highest levels in the land, with dramatic implications for those living in every province, district, and village in the country. Under democracy, it seemed, no defeat was recognized, and, therefore, no war finished – a political reality to which Muedans have only slowly and partially acclimated themselves. [...]

Democratic Decentralization, State Abandonment

Simultaneous with the staging of national-level multiparty elections, democratic reformers in Mozambique have pursued a policy of democratic decentralization. Just weeks before the 1994 elections, government passed a law (no. 3/94) devolving responsibility for a variety of governmental functions to "municipalities," to be formed of urban and rural districts and administered by elected officials. In 1995, before the law took force, it was declared unconstitutional. A new law (no. 2/97), passed in 1997, established the framework for devolution to democratically elected local governments called "autarchies," to be established only in the thirty-three largest cities and towns in the country (Alves and Cossa 1997; Weimer and Fandrych 1999). Elsewhere, the government would continue to appoint officials, from the district administrator down to the village president and neighborhood secretary.

In parallel, reformers pressed FRELIMO to reverse post-independence policy that had abolished the chieftaincy. FRELIMO justification for banning hereditary authorities from any role in government lay in arguments that such figures had actively collaborated with Portuguese colonial rule (Monteiro 1989). Indeed, colonial administrators had used chiefs at the highest levels as tax collectors, labor recruiters, and agents of law enforcement – tasks for which these individuals received substantial rewards. FRELIMO therefore proclaimed the need to liberate rural Mozambicans not only from the Portuguese but also from the feudal hierarchies through which colonial rule was consolidated. The party did so by establishing party-based structures of authority that reached deep into every village, displacing hereditary authorities at levels where they had collaborated with the colonial regime (Hanlon 1990). Some Mozambicans celebrated the abolition of the chieftaincy. Others resented it as an attack on local autonomy and custom. Still others manifested ambivalence.

Over the course of the Mozambican civil war, RENAMO insurgents played on mixed sentiments, resuscitating and (re)inventing institutions of hereditary authority among populations in the areas it came to control and using them to extract information, food supplies, labor, and guerrilla conscripts (Alexander 1997). Notwithstanding compulsion in most instances, many communities (particularly in the central part of the country, from which key RENAMO leaders hailed) supported the insurgency, in part because of resentment of various FRELIMO policies, including, but not limited to, the abolition of the chieftaincy (Englund 2002; Geffray 1990). By war's end, democratic reformers had taken notice of this and had begun to advocate renewed recognition of "traditional authorities" by the Mozambican government itself. Reformers sometimes suggested that the institutions of "traditional authority" might serve rural Mozambican communities as forms of "civil society" where successive authoritarian regimes – slave-trading kingdoms (in some places), Portuguese colonialism, the FRELIMO guerrilla (in its "liberated zones"), a centralized socialist state, and the RENAMO insurgency (in some places) – had rendered impossible the emergence and maintenance of other collective social forms (Lubkemann 2001; see also Orvis 2001). Some suggested that, through traditional authorities, the will of the people might be powerfully expressed in the new democratic era (Lundin 1995).

In 1991, the Ford Foundation provided funding for the establishment of a research project on the issue of traditional authority, to be housed within the walls of the Mozambican Ministry of State Administration. In 1995, the United States Agency for International Development (USAID) financed the continuance of the project under the rubric of its broader "Democracy in Mozambique" project (Fry 1997). As project researchers toured the country, holding workshops with ex-chiefs (African American Institute 1997), FRELIMO officials in some places sought to improve relations with these figures, whose potential influence over the rural electorate they deemed significant. Before elections, FRELIMO officials in many parts of the country made substantial overtures to ex-chiefs, particularly where they believed that doing so might swing the balance of support away from RENAMO.

Elsewhere, FRELIMO cadres expressed grave concerns that hereditary authorities were not necessarily qualified to discharge the duties of modern state administration. Perhaps more important, state officials wondered what would become of them if the chiefs who had been displaced by the creation of their positions were once more recognized. Some FRELIMO leaders in Maputo wondered how FRELIMO would hold power if it abandoned loyal cadres in rural areas in favor of traditional authorities, most of whom had been marginalized by FRELIMO rule (West and Kloeck-Jenson 1999). Others, still committed to the socialist project, saw recognition of hereditary authorities as the reestablishment of feudal hierarchies.

Despite promises in the mid-1990s from the minister of state administration that a law officially reinstating hereditary authorities was imminent, no such law was ever passed. Government policy on the matter eventually took the form of a decree (no. 15/2000) issued by the Council of Ministers in the year 2000. [...] The decree mandated local government consultation and cooperation with "community authorities" in relation to various governmental functions, including tax collection, voter registration, policing, judicial proceedings, land distribution, oversight of public education and public health, environmental protection, road construction, and other developmental issues (Buur and Kyed 2003; Hanlon 2000). The decree granted community authorities the right to wear uniforms and to use "symbols of the Republic"; however, it neither stipulated that government was required to heed their counsel nor strictly delineated who they were. Included in the category of potential community authorities were not only traditional authorities but also "village or neighborhood secretaries" (historically, FRELIMO appointees) and "other legitimate leaders" (Buur and Kyed 2003; Santos 2003:83; Hanlon 2000; Meneses et al. 2003:358). According to the decree, such leaders had to be duly "recognized as such by their respective communities" (Hanlon 2000), but the decree specified neither what constituted a community nor the mechanism for recognition (Buur and Kyed 2003).

The Autarchies Law, as well as the Community Authorities Decree, ultimately left it to the discretion of local state officials to craft relationships with traditional authorities in their jurisdictions in accordance with their governing strategies and agendas. In some areas of the country – especially where RENAMO relations with traditional authorities undermined FRELIMO hegemony – local government officials organized ceremonies in which traditional authorities were formally recognized as community authorities (Buur and Kyed 2003; Institutions for Natural Resource Management n.d.), seemingly in attempts to deny RENAMO a point of political contention while rendering these figures more beholden to the ruling party. [...] Some administrators, in fact, began using these duly recognized community authorities as tax collectors, granting them subsidies for their services in accordance with the provisions of the decree (Buur and Kyed 2003).

Recognition of community authorities played out differently in Mueda. There, in pre-colonial times, dispersed settlements had sustained a high degree of autonomy, one from another. Settlement heads had generally exercised authority over very small numbers of people. In order to administer local populations through the intermediary of hereditary authorities, the Portuguese administration had been obliged to construct hierarchies among settlement heads where none had previously existed. Colonial administrators interacted only with the highest-ranking figures in this hierarchy – figures whose authority the vast majority of Muedans considered illegitimate. At independence, FRELIMO orchestrated the construction of communal villages on the plateau, where the former populations of several dozen settlements would live together. Former settlement heads were no longer officially recognized by FRELIMO-appointed village presidents and neighborhood secretaries, but Muedan matrilineages continued to recognize them in clandestine. In the post-socialist era, Muedans openly recognized these lineage heads. However, they demonstrated no interest in resuscitating the hierarchy of chiefs through which the Portuguese had governed in colonial times.

Surprisingly, FRELIMO officials themselves pressed for the recognition of community authorities in Muedan villages. Community authority in Mueda, however, would not look like it did elsewhere in Mozambique. District officials in the plateau region orchestrated processes whereby village presidents – who held FRELIMO-created offices, by FRELIMO appointment – would simply be renamed "community leaders." [...] Like reinstated chiefs elsewhere in the country, these village-presidents-turned-community-leaders were given uniforms to wear and Mozambican flags to plant in their yards, just as colonial-era chiefs had once been given. Elsewhere in the country, debates raged over whether it was appropriate to stage elections to identify legitimate claimants to the title of "community authority"; hereditary authorities themselves often resisted the idea that popular ballot could determine their status. In Mueda, FRELIMO officials decided to stage elections to legitimate office holders in the moment of renaming village presidents as "community authorities." Some polls took the form of

referenda, and others, multicandidate contests. In some villages, incumbents prevailed (because villagers had, or felt they had, no choice or because they truly respected incumbents); in others, challengers unseated them.

Notwithstanding FRELIMO high jinks, the process of recognizing community leaders provided Muedans the opportunity to choose those who would govern them at the most proximate level. Ironically, to the extent that the election of community leaders constituted a meaningful form of democratic decentralization, Muedans saw in it peril instead of promise. To be sure, many were displeased with the FRELIMO appointees who had long governed them. As we shall see in the next section, in the years following independence, FRELIMO rule had brought fewer and fewer benefits to the ruled and more and more to the rulers. Before village elections, however, most responded to the idea of *electing* local authorities with a simple question: "Who would rule us then?" Reading such statements as capitulation to FRELIMO authoritarianism would be a mistake, however. Muedans with whom we worked understood the dynamics of governance to be complex, echoing popular understandings elsewhere on the continent. Such understandings warrant close scrutiny.

Many scholars of African history have suggested that, by varied logics, power in Africa has long depended more on "wealth in people" than on "wealth in things" (Bledsoe 1980; Cooper 1979; Guyer 1995; Miers and Kopytoff 1977; Miller 1988; Vansina 1988), more on cultivating social relations than on cultivating lands (Berry 2002). African rulers, they suggest, have long sought to transform material wealth into loyal subjects, for such subjects have been considered both means to the (re)production of power and power's ultimate end. Power in Mueda has, indeed, long been measured in terms of one's ability to attract and sustain subordinates. In precolonial Mueda, warlords depended upon loyal and productive subjects to harvest goods – such as India rubber, gum copal, beeswax, and sesame seed – that could be traded at the coast for arms. With such arms, they not only defended themselves and their people but also mounted raids to capture slaves, many of whom were ultimately absorbed into the group as members with full rights and contributed to its strength like any others. Rulers who abused subordinates or failed to defend them, or to create a mutually beneficial environment in which they might live, faced the prospect that their subjects would abandon them. The Portuguese colonial regime mostly relied (with limited success) on coercive means to capture Mozambican subjects and their productive potential, issuing passbooks in which the required fulfillment of periodic labor contracts was to be recorded. Displeased subjects of colonial rule fled in vast numbers across borders where they found more favorable labor regimes. In the post-independence period, FRELIMO implored rural Mozambicans to produce in their fields in order to produce the nation itself (Machel 1978); the party also rounded up "unproductive" city dwellers and set them to work in reeducation camps (Africa Watch 1992). One after another, these successive regimes struggled through various means to secure "wealth in people."

Muedans with whom we worked were accustomed to the idea that the legitimacy of authority depended in such varied ways upon "cultivating people." They also recognized that the establishment of a prosperous domain was inextricably bound up with the exercise of superior force. Correspondingly, they considered a ruler's power commensurate with his ability to tap resources beyond the reach of others – resources to be deployed in the construction of a mutually beneficial order and in the maintenance of that order, whether by force or by the cultivation of consent. The authority of local officials, as they had experienced it in both socialist and colonial eras, derived from the state, in whose voice and with whose backing local officials spoke. Local power depended upon the resources of the state – indeed, depended upon the state *as* resource.

Such conceptions gave foundation to Muedan anxieties about democratic decentralization and elections at the local level. As long as anyone with whom we worked could remember, the state had appointed local officials who acted in its name. Muedans feared that an official of their own nomination would not speak for the state and therefore would not bring the force of the state to bear in the maintenance of local order and in the resolution of local problems. An official of their own choosing would speak only with their voice – a voice they

had no reason to believe the state would hear. Many saw local elections to the post of community leader as an ominous sign. A state that no longer cared who occupied such positions, they reasoned, was a state no longer interested in the domains over which these office holders exercised authority. A state that allowed them to appoint their own officials, they feared, was a state no longer prepared to bestow its largesse in the interest of cultivating consent, a state preparing to abdicate authority over people it no longer considered a source of wealth.

The dynamics of post-socialist reform dramatically confirmed Muedan suspicions. To secure support from the International Monetary Fund (IMF) and Western donor nations, the Mozambican government slashed state budgets from 1986 onward. State enterprises, which had provided a large proportion of employment opportunities nationwide (many of which were not economically viable), began to shut down. The Nguri agricultural scheme in the lowlands immediately southeast of the plateau, where large numbers of Muedans worked, was among these. Shrinking budgets also translated into declining social services. In the Mueda region, teachers abandoned schools and nurses left health clinics as real salaries declined precipitously. Only those schools and clinics enjoying the patronage of a nongovernmental organization (NGO) continued to provide quality services. For all intents and purposes, the state ceased to provide an environment in which Muedans might "produce the wealth of the nation."

In the neoliberal era, the state looked elsewhere for wealth. Government carved up state sector enterprises, auctioning off some of the nation's most valuable assets, or rights thereto, to foreign investors (Alden 2001; Pitcher 2002). High rates of economic growth yielded disappointing employment prospects for Mozambicans because new enterprises tended to hire expert foreign workers and use capital-intensive means of production. Muedans watched from the side of the road as foreign lumber companies trucked massive loads of hardwood from the plateau interior to the coast. As a result of such arrangements, state power was, to an unprecedented extent, delinked from the productivity of the Mozambican people. Needing nothing from the people, the state offered them nothing. Apart from periodic election campaigns, the state betrayed near total lack of interest in "cultivating people" and their productive power. [...] To Muedans, the state's devaluation of its citizenry – of people as wealth – was nowhere more clearly communicated than in the mandate given them under the rubric of democratic decentralization to "govern themselves."

Individual Freedom, Collective Danger

Also among the essential elements of democratic reform in Mozambique was the ratification of a new constitution for the republic (1990), giving foundation to a wide range of civil liberties. Article 74 of the new constitution established rights to freedom of political expression. The freedom to "pursue religious aims freely" was laid down in article 78. Article 86 delineated the right to ownership of property. Whereas the rights of the Mozambican people as a whole had been elevated over those of the individual in the socialist era, democratic reformers argued that, to secure prosperity in post-war Mozambique, it was essential to lift socialist-era constraints on individual creativity and entrepreneurship. The early 1990s witnessed the formation of more than a dozen political parties, the growth and proliferation of religious communities, and the emergence of a robust independent media. Businesses, large and small, appeared on the economic landscape. Investors, including nationals and foreigners, canvassed cities, towns, and rural districts throughout the country for investment opportunities. By the end of the decade, Mozambique was able to claim some of the highest annual economic-growth rates on the African continent (Fauvet 2000).

Notwithstanding dramatic political and economic transformations, marked continuities were also observable. The faces of power remained familiar. Such continuities were, in part, the product of the very processes defining transition. For example, state officials controlled and often personally benefited from state enterprise divestiture. Calls for bids – many of which were issued before the passage of legislation officially mandating and giving structure to divestiture – were often posted in inconspicuous places, such as bulletin boards

on state officials' office walls. Through what the Mozambican attorney general later sarcastically referred to as "silent privatizations" (Harrison 1999), officials at various levels privatized assets unto themselves, their cronies, and clients from whom they might extract rents (Myers 1994; West and Myers 1996). [...] Through such means, national-level military leaders from the plateau region took possession of military warehouses, garages, and machine shops in Mueda. Agricultural officials staked claims to large plots of land in the Nguri State Farm irrigation scheme.

Advocates of privatization generally suggested that, through market mechanisms, these valuable assets would eventually pass into the hands of those most capable of exploiting them, contributing to sustained economic growth and greater national prosperity. Indeed, those who first took possession of state assets often sold them at considerable profit to more capable investors. In other cases, they kept controlling interest over such assets; seeking manager-investors who might provide essential expertise in exchange for a share of the wealth to be generated by their exploitation.

Included among advocates of democratic reform were those who criticized such forms of opportunism. Participants in donor-sponsored workshops on the topic of corruption railed against the use of public office for the pursuit of private gain. People spoke openly in the independent media about the criminalization of the Mozambican state (Hanlon 2004); Mozambican officials themselves were among the most vociferous critics of corruption, some speaking out in earnest and some to cover their own behavior. Ironically, public furor over rising rates of corruption provided grist for the mill of neoliberal condemnation of the Mozambican state and reinforced donor and NGO tendencies to bypass the state in order to "work directly" with intended beneficiaries, further weakening the project of state governance.

Muedans, too, looked critically upon the behavior of the national elite. They, however, expressed criticism in a different language. The standards by which they condemned the powerful among them derived from various historical moments and models of power. Indeed, Muedan experiences with and expectations of power, in some ways, licensed privilege. In pre-colonial days, Muedans told us, settlement heads never went hungry. These figures of authority enjoyed the best and the most of everything available. According to Muedan parlance, they not only "ate well" but also "ate" their subordinates. Youngsters, when successful in the hunt, offered these elders the choicest cuts of meat. Men returning from coastal trade expeditions were obliged to give these elders the goods they had procured. The most powerful of these elders even "ate" potential rivals by forcing their neighbors to join their own settlements, thereby augmenting the number of people paying them tribute and defending them against potential attackers. Through feeding their own appetites, these elders expanded the social bodies of which they were heads. At the same time, they fed these social bodies and the individuals of which they were composed. Successful settlement heads spurred their subjects to produce the wealth of the group, which they used to ensure the well-being of those upon whom they depended. They demanded that subjects fill their plates but also used their plates to feed their subjects. The satisfaction of their expansive appetites thus gave foundation to their subordinates' sustenance.

The power of the settlement head was diminished under a colonial administration that required subjects to fill the state plate instead. Only those used by the Portuguese as administrative intermediaries "ate well." When FRELIMO initiated its guerrilla campaign in the plateau region, party "chairmen" displaced hereditary authorities altogether. But, like their predecessors, these figures of authority mobilized subordinates to fill the plate from which all were fed (Negrão 1984). Following independence, the FRELIMO-orchestrated project of collective production was reproduced on a national scale. Faced with the prospect of total economic collapse in the wake of the mass exodus of Portuguese colonials following independence, FRELIMO "intervened" in the management of abandoned plantations, farms, factories, and machine shops and eventually nationalized many of these properties (Hanlon 1990). The party coordinated production and, through the management of trade and the setting of prices, appropriated and redistributed the nation's produce. Like settlement heads before them, FRELIMO leaders fed their subjects from

the plate their subjects were required to fill. Of course, state officials never went hungry. Although the wealth of the nation purportedly belonged to the people, these officials enjoyed it most directly. Goods were sometimes scarce, but ranking officials had first dibs. Vehicles belonged to the state, but party bosses generally rode in them. To most Muedans, this was not particularly surprising.

The behavior of the post-socialist elite was another matter altogether. They ate well, according to Muedans, but failed to feed others. With profits generated in the exploitation of former state enterprises or with rents garnered from foreign investors to whom they served as godfathers, elites tightened their hold on power even as the state weakened. On the plateau and elsewhere, they built new homes surrounded by walls. They sent their children abroad to be educated. They manipulated and controlled banks and donor-funded credit schemes to acquire fleets of cars, trucks, and tractors with which they often provided "services" at a charge, consolidating control over local economic hierarchies. As we have seen, the enterprises and transactions over which they presided generated few jobs. All but the closest of family members were denied access to the plates they filled high to satisfy seemingly insatiable appetites.

From pre-colonial days, Muedans have associated insatiable appetites with sorcery. Whereas the fruits of one's own labor can satisfy the ordinary appetite, the sorcerer is sated only by feeding on the well-being – indeed, the very life substance, the flesh – of others. This, it is said, sorcerers undertake in clandestine, through the use of a medicinal substance called *shikupi*, which renders them invisible to ordinary people. Such illicit consumption, as well as the social carnage (literally, meat derived from slaughter) to which it gives rise, challenges the prerogatives of legitimate authority to measure appetites against one another and to nourish the social body as a whole. According to Muedans, legitimate authorities have met this challenge since pre-colonial times by following sorcerers into the invisible realm of sorcery, wherein they monitor sorcerers' activities and quash their appetites. The exercise of legitimate authority constitutes a form of sorcery, according to Muedan conceptions. Muedans have long distinguished between the "sorcery of self-advancement" or "sorcery of self-enrichment" (*uwavi wa kushunga*) practiced by common sorcerers and the "sorcery of self-defense" (*uwavi wa kulishungila*) practiced by responsible authority figures in behalf of the larger group. They have also recognized the fine line between these two forms of sorcery. In the socialist era, they were generally convinced that FRELIMO leaders practiced uwavi wa kulishungila. In the era of democracy, by contrast, most suspected that authorities practiced uwavi wa kushunga. Post-socialist elites were suspected of transforming kin into *mandandosha* (zombie slave laborers) to tend their fields, work in their factories, or guard their houses, cars, and other possessions. "How else could they get so rich?!" Muedans often asked rhetorically. "How else could they protect themselves?! How else could they protect their wealth?!"[…]

The idea that present-day elites act as malefi-cent instead of beneficent sorcerers arose from and reinforced Muedan understandings of the new regime of tolerance for political and religious expression as well. In the socialist era, FRELIMO authorities in Mueda had prohibited sorcery accusations, proclaiming belief in sorcery to be a reactionary form of "obscurantism" that jeopardized the emergence and consolidation of class consciousness and solidarity. Muedans, however, interpreted socialist-era condemnations of sorcery beliefs and practices as the enforcement of a ban on self-serving forms of sorcery – in other words, as the FRELIMO enactment of a beneficent form of (counter) sorcery. In the new democratic era, as we have seen, FRELIMO officials demonstrated "respect" for individual "beliefs" through tolerance of sorcery discourse. Muedans interpreted such tolerance as official acceptance of – even collusion with – maleficent forms of sorcery. Indeed, state tolerance of sorcery discourse confirmed popular suspicions regarding the elite's practice of sorcery of self-enrichment. Tellingly, Muedans sometimes referred to the new, more liberal regime as one of *uwavi wa shilikali* (government sorcery).

New constitutional freedoms of expression contributed to an environment in which Muedans heard daily evidence of sorcery's rise. Radio Moçambique reported incidents of sorcery. New independent churches – along with traditional healers plying their trade openly after years in clandestine – called attention to sorcery in the act of treating its ills. But to Muedans, freedom of expression not only meant that one could speak *of* sorcery but also meant that *sorcerers* could *speak*. Muedans referred euphemistically to sorcery when they lamented, "With democracy, anything can be said, and anything can be done." Where state officials refused to intervene as responsible figures of authority in sorcery-related disputes, sorcery ran wild at all levels of society, Muedans told me. Under cover of democracy, it was said, sorcerers formed political parties of their own. Their motto, "Each one for himself!" echoed new constitutional rights in a sinister register. In the shadow of suspicion and resentment of the new elite, accusations flew among villagers themselves. As the wealthy and powerful ate their fill, ordinary Muedans went hungry or worse still, many feared, satisfied their hunger by feeding on their neighbors and kin.

Democracy, Carnage

The same language of power through which Muedans had engaged with democratic reform over the preceding decade and a half gave shape to their understandings of and responses to the grizzly attacks taking place in Muidumbe in late 2002 and early 2003. That provincial authorities took nearly a year after the maulings to provide arms and ammunition with which to kill the menacing lions only confirmed suspicions that the FRELIMO state was weak and that local officials did not have its ear. […] Even more disturbing to Muedans was that district administrator Pedro Seguro never publicly condemned the sorcerers they knew to be responsible for the attacks. They assumed Seguro – a man of great authority – capable of seeing into the invisible realm of sorcery and practicing (counter) sorcery therein. But as the death toll mounted, Seguro remained "silent." […]

Where provincial- and district-level authorities failed to resolve the crisis, village authorities did what they could. Hunting parties were organized, and, in time, six lions were caught in traps or killed with bow and arrow. […] Meanwhile, the community leaders in some villages summoned councils of elders in attempts to discern who was responsible for the killings. "When the situation got bad,"

Namakandi community leader Pedro Agostinho told Radio Moçambique reporter Óscar Limbombo, "we put out word that if anyone knew who was making these lions, they had better say so" (Limbombo 2003). Some community leaders made public pronouncements that the attacks must cease. Through such acts, these village authorities attempted to play the part of beneficent sorcerers. But in the wake of democratic decentralization – meaning, in this case, elections confirming the community leaders' "legitimacy" at the ballot box – villagers perceived these figures as representatives not of some greater power who governed them all but rather only of those who had voted for them (generally, their matrilineage). As such, community leaders were deemed able to quash sorcery attacks within their own matrilineages but not on the grander scale on which these attacks were apparently taking place. Tellingly, the proclamations and accusations of some community leaders only fanned the flames of intermatrilineage suspicion and hostility. In the villages of Litapata and Mandava, community leaders themselves incited villagers to lynch their neighbors (Israel n.d.; Limbombo 2003).

District administrator Seguro expressed frustration that he was able to respond to vigilante killings only after crimes were committed and frenzied mobs dispersed (Limbombo 2003). Villagers blamed him more for failing to prevent the precipitating incidents – the attacks of sorcerers qualions. Rumors circulated that Seguro himself was behind the attacks (see also Israel n.d.). Others suggested that Seguro had "sold the district" for "three sacks of money" to "three whites" (reportedly including an Italian dental technician working at the Nang'ololo Catholic mission health clinic), meaning that he had granted permission to these foreigners (and, by most accounts, their local sorcerer colleagues) to attack people within a domain nominally under his protection. [...] That Seguro was both the ranking state official and the leading businessman in the district was interpreted by many residents as evidence that he practiced sorcery of self-advancement rather than sorcery of self-defense in behalf of his constituents. He was, by all accounts, the richest man in the district. Whereas reformers saw in Seguro an energetic entrepreneur bringing development to the district, villagers generally saw in him a man of expansive appetite who fed only himself. In Muidumbe, as in

his previous posts, his personal "development" projects cannibalized the infrastructure of the collapsed collective project of socialist modernization, creating jobs for only a few close family members (his wife, for example, ran a "restaurant" in the town marketplace that captured meticals spent by visitors to the district on official business). While Seguro "ate well" in late 2002 and early 2003, those under his charge went hungry (for fear of harvesting their meager crops) and, in some cases, were devoured by fellow villagers or literally eaten alive by lions. By the middle of 2003, lions had claimed the lives of forty-six men, women, and children and gravely injured another six. Eighteen villagers had been lynched.

In mid-2003, provincial authorities finally convened and provisioned a hunting party, headed by a man named Fernando Alves, and dispatched it to Muidumbe. Alves killed the fifth lion, after which villagers killed two more, bringing to an end the carnage that had beset the district for more than a year. Alves was a man of local legend long before he killed what Muidumbe residents identified as the most vicious of the pride that had stalked them. The son of mulatto parents, Alves lived in Pemba in the *bairro do cimento* (the "concrete neighborhood," composed mostly of houses built by Portuguese occupants in the colonial period) and earned a living as a self-employed mechanic. Like his father, he was an avid big-game hunter. According to Makonde trackers employed by Alves, he was adept at recovering *lyungo*, the life substance Makonde say a predatory animal, such as a lion vomits in the moments immediately before dying. Alves himself attributed his success as a hunter to his ability to find and ingest lyungo. Thus, the man who put an end to the carnage in Muidumbe came from outside the district as the bearer of superior force but acted in defense of the well-being of ordinary Muedans in a language they recognized.

That Muedans conceived of and engaged with events defining their world in the post-socialist era in a language of their own did not mean that they failed to recognize or to understand democracy's emergence in their midst. Indeed, I would argue, the language of power Muedans spoke in the course of these events and processes afforded them profound insights and allowed them to formulate a nuanced critique of democracy as they experienced it. Whereas neoliberal reformers suggested that democracy would rationalize political competition, render power more accountable to the people, and open greater space for individual contribution to a prosperous post-war environment, Muedans experienced democracy as a regime that promoted irresolvable conflict in their midst and provided cover for dominant political actors to forego the responsibilities of authority and to feed themselves at the expense of others. Muedan perspectives on democracy have resonated with the critical assessments offered in recent years by various commentators of deepening corruption and electoral fraud in Mozambique. Their skepticism regarding the true objectives of democratization has been validated by ongoing donor support (notwithstanding these disconcerting phenomena) so long as Mozambique has continued to adhere to IMF provisions and to sustain a friendly climate for foreign investment and trade.

Muedan conceptions of and reactions to democracy *do not* constitute a failure of understanding. *Neither* do they support the idea that Africa and Africans are ill suited for democracy. I would argue that, by critically engaging with democratization in a language that differs profoundly from the one spoken by democratic reformers, Muedans have, ironically, enacted democracy. After all, if democracy is conceived of as "government of the people, by the people, and for the people," following Lincoln's famous formulation, then democracy necessarily resides within the languages and terminologies used by "the people" to assess power's workings in their midst. Accordingly, regardless of

constitutional reform, the staging of elections, and the devolution of power to the local level, any regime failing to create a beneficial order, by the people's definition, can scarcely call itself a democracy. If democracy resides in the understandings, experiences, and expressions of the people, then Muedans have enacted it – to the best of their abilities, albeit with limited success even by their own evaluations – through critical assessment of what reformers have called democracy, through expression of "the will of the people" in an altogether different language. [...]

Alas, democratic reformers rarely entertain such possibilities. In the run-up to the 1994 elections, the international community invested considerable resources in civic education programs designed to teach Mozambicans about democracy. If the meanings and methods of democracy depend, by definition, upon the political subjects in question, then such initiatives betray unfounded conceit and also render democracy's actualization more difficult. One can only imagine what might have come of investing such considerable resources in attempts to discern what the Mozambican people had to teach policymakers about viable and desirable forms of governance. The notion reinforces the idea underlying this volume, namely, that anthropologists – through the dialogical methods of extended fieldwork and ethnographic writing – potentially have much to contribute to facilitating and strengthening democracy as variably defined by people in diverse locales around the globe.

References

Africa Watch
   1992 *Conspicuous Destruction: War, Famine, and the Reform Process in Mozambique.* New York: Human Rights Watch.
African American Institute
   1997 *Relatório sobre Círculos de Trabalho e'Discussão.* Maputo: African American Institute.
Alden, Chris
   1995 The UN and the Resolution of Conflict in Mozambique. *The Journal of Modern African Studies* 33(1):103–28.
   2001 *Mozambique and the Construction of the New African State: From Negotiations to Nation Building.* New York: Palgrave.

Alden, Chris, and Mark Simpson
   1993 Mozambique: A Delicate Peace. *The Journal of Modern African Studies* 31(1):109–30.
Alexander, Jocelyn
   1997 The Local State in Post-war Mozambique: Political Practice and Ideas about Authority. *Africa* 76(1):1–25.
Alves, Armando Teixeira, and Benedito Ruben Cossa
   1997 *Guião das Autarquias Locais.* Maputo: Ministério da Administração Estatal.
Berry, Sara
   2002 Debating the Land Question in Africa. *Comparative Studies in Society and History* 44(4):638–68.

Bledsoe, Caroline
1980 *Women and Marriage in Kpelle Society*. Palo Alto, CA: Stanford University Press.

Buur, Lars, and Helene Maria Kyed
2003 Implementation of Decree 15/2000 in Mozambique: The Consequences of State Recognition of Traditional Authority in Sussundenga. Copenhagen: Centre for Development Research.

The Carter Center
2005 Postelection Statement on Mozambique Elections. http://www.cartercenter.org/news/documents/doc1999.html, accessed January 2008.

Chan, Stephen, and Moisés Venâncio
1998 *War and Peace in Mozambique*. Houndsmills, UK: Macmillan Press Ltd.

Clemens, Dave
2002 Requiem for a Dream of Mozambique? Mozambican Journalist Carlos Cardoso's Suspected Killers on Trial. December 16. http://www.worldpress.org/Africa/864.cfm, accessed January 2008.

Clinton, William Jefferson
1998 Remarks to the People of Accra in Ghana. March 23, http://findarticles.com/p/articles/mi_m2889/is_n13_v34/ai_20969083, accessed January 2008.

Cooper, Frederick
1979 The Problem of Slavery in African Societies. *Journal of African History* 20(1):103–25.

Democratization Policy Institute
2001 Focus on Africa. Vol. 2005. Unpublished paper, Washington DC. http://www.anonime.com/dpinstitute/africa/index.htm, accessed January 2008.

Dias, António Jorge, and Margot Schmidt Dias
1970 *Os Macondes de Moçambique*, vol. III: *Vida Social e Ritual*. Lisboa: Centro de Estudos de Antropologia Cultural, Junta de Investigações do Ultramar.

Egerö, Bertil
1987 *Mozambique: A Dream Undone: The Political Economy of Democracy, 1975–84*. Uppsala: Scandinavian Institute of African Studies.

Englund, Harri
2002 *From War to Peace on the Mozambique–Malawi Borderland*. Edinburgh: Edinburgh University Press.

Finnegan, William
1992 *A Complicated War: The Harrowing of Mozambique*. Berkeley: University of California Press.

Fry, Peter
1997 Final Evaluation of the Decentralization/Traditional Authority Component of the African American Institute's Project "Democratic Development in Mozambique" (Cooperative Agreement #656-A00-4029-00). Maputo: USAID.

Geffray, Christian
1990 *La Cause des Armes au Mozambique: Anthropologie d'une Guerre Civile*. Paris: Karthala.

Geschiere, Peter
1997 *The Modernity of Witchcraft: Politics and the Occult in Postcolonial Africa*. Charlottesville: University Press of Virginia.

Guyer, Jane
1995 Wealth in People as Wealth in Knowledge: Accumulation and Composition in Equatorial Africa. *Journal of African History* 36(1):91–120.

Hall, Margaret
1990 The Mozambican National Resistance Movement (RENAMO): A Study in the Destruction of an African Country. *Africa* 60(1):39–68.

Hanlon, Joseph
1990 *Mozambique: The Revolution under Fire*. London: Zed Books.
1991 *Mozambique: Who Calls the Shots?* London: James Currey.
1994 *Report of AWEPA's Observation of the Mozambique Electoral Process, 1992–1994*. Amsterdam: African-European Institute.
2000 New Decree Recognises "Traditional Chiefs." AWEPA Mozambique Peace Process Bulletin (August):4–5.
2004 *How Northern Donors Promote Corruption: Tales from Mozambique*. Oldham, UK: The Corner House.

Harrison, Graham
1999 Corruption as "Boundary Politics": The State, Democratisation, and Mozambique's Unstable Liberalisation. *Third World Quarterly* 20(3):537–50.

Henriksen, Thomas H.
1983 *Revolution and Counter-revolution: Mozambique's War of Independence, 1964–1974*. Westport, CT: Greenwood Press.

Hume, Cameron
1994 *Ending Mozambique's War*. Washington, DC: United States Institute of Peace.

Institutions for Nature Resource Management
N.d. implementing CBNRM in M'punga, http://www.geog.sussex.ac.uk/research/development/marena/pdf/Mozambique/Moz09.pdf, accessed January 2008.

Israel, Paolo
N.d. The "War of the Lions": Lion-Killings and Witch Hunts in Muidumbe (Mozambique), 2002–2003. Unpublished ms.

Limbombo, Oscar
2003 Leões de Muidumbe. "Questão de Fundo" radio show. Pemba: Radio Moçambique, radio broadcast (date unknown).

Lubkemann, Stephen
2001 Rebuilding Local Capacities in Mozambique: The National Health System and Civil Society. In *Patronage or Partnership: Local Capacity Building in Humanitarian Crises*. Ian Smillie, ed. Pp. 77–106. Bloomfield, CT: Kumarian Press.

Lundin, Iraê Baptista
1995 A Pesquisa Piloto Sobre a Autoridade/Poder Tradicional em Moçambique – Um Somatório Comentado e Analisado. In *Autoridade e Poder Tradicional*, vol. I. Iraê Baptista Lundin and Francisco Jamisse Machava, eds. Pp. 7–32. Maputo: Ministério da Administração Estatal/ Núcleo de Desenvolvimento Administrativo.

Machel, Samore
1978 *Produzir e Aprender: Aprender para Produzir e Lutar Melhor*. Maputo: FRELIMO.

Manning, Carrie
2001 Competition and Accommodation in Post-conflict Democracy: The Case of Mozambique. *Democratization* 8(2):140–68.
2002 *The Politics of Peace in Mozambique: Post-conflict Democratization, 1992–2000*. Westport, CT: Praeger Publishers.

Mazula, Brazão
1995 *Moçambique: Eleições, Democracia e Desenvolvimento*. Maputo: Embassy of Holland.

Meneses, Maria Paula, Joaquim Fumo, Guilherme Mbilana, and Conceição Gomes
2003 As Autoridades Tradicionais no Contexto do Pluralismo Jurídico. In *Conflito e Transformação Social: Uma Paisagem das Justiças em Moçambique*, vol. II. Boaventura de Sousa Santos and João Carlos Trindade, eds. Pp. 341–420. Porto: Edições Afrontamento.

Miers, Suzanne, and Igor Kopytoff
1977 *Slavery in Africa: Historical and Anthropological Perspectives*. Madison: University of Wisconsin Press.

Miller, J.
1988 *Way of Death: Merchant Capitalism and the Angolan Slave Trade, 1730–1830*. Madison: University of Wisconsin Press.

Minter, William
1994 *Apartheid's Contras*. London: Zed Books.

Monteiro, José Oscar
1989 *Power and Democracy*. Maputo: People's Assembly.

Munslow, Barry
1983 *Mozambique: The Revolution and Its Origins*. London: Longman.

Myers, Gregory
1994 Competitive Rights, Competitive Claims: Land Access in Post-war Mozambique, *Journal of Southern African Studies* 20(4):603–32.

Negrão, José Guilherme
1984 *A Produção e o Comércio nas Antigas Zonas Libertadas*. Maputo: Arquivo Histórico de Moçambique.

Orvis, Stephen
2001 Civil Society in Africa or African Civil Society? In *A Decade of Democracy in Africa*. S. N. Ndegwa, ed. Pp. 17–38. Leiden: Brill.

Pitcher, M. Anne
2002 *Transforming Mozambique: The Politics of Privatization, 1975–2000*. Cambridge: Cambridge University Press.

Santos, Boaventura de Sousa
2003 O Estado Hetrogénio e o Pluralismo Jurídico. In *Conflito e Transformação Social: Uma Paisagem des Justiças em Moçambique*, vol. I. Boaventura de Sousa Santos and João Carlos Trindade, eds. Pp. 47–95. Porto: Edições Afrontamento.

Vansina, Jan
1988 *Paths in the Rainforest: Toward a History of Political Tradition in Equatorial Africa*. Madison: University of Wisconsin Press.

Vines, Alex
1991 *RENAMO: Terrorism in Mozambique*. London: James Currey.

Weimer, Bernhard
1996 Challenges for Democratization and Regional Development in Southern Africa: Focus on Mozambique. *Regional Development Dialogue* 17(2):32–59.

Weimer, Bernhard and Sabine Fandrych
Mozambique: Administrative Reform—A Contribution to Peace and Democracy. In Local Government Democratisation and Decentralisation: A Review of the Southern African Region; Purshottam S. Reddy, ed. Pp. 151–77. Kenwyn, South Africa. Juta and Co.

West, Harry G.
1997 Creative Destruction and Sorcery of Construction: Power, Hope and Suspicion in Post-war Mozambique. *Cahiers d'Études Africaines* 37(147):675–98.
2003 "Who Rules Us Now?" Identity Tokens, Sorcery, and Other Metaphors in the 1994 Mozambican Elections. In *Transparency and Conspiracy: Ethnographies of Suspicion in the New World Order*. Harry G. West and Todd Sanders, eds. Pp. 92–124. Durham, NC: Duke University Press.
2005 *Kupilikula: Governance and the Invisible Realm in Mozambique*. Chicago: The University of Chicago Press.

West, Harry G., and Gregory W. Myers
1996 A Piece of Land in a Land of Peace? State Farm Divestiture in Mozambique. *Journal of Modern African Studies* 34(1):27–51.

46

Nuer-American Passages

Dianna Shandy

The Transnational Sandwich Generation

Slipping off my shoes and rapping on the Nuer family's apartment door, I smiled in anticipation of being overrun by the couple's two boisterous young children. When Nyawal Chuol opened the door, I understood quickly that something was wrong. Compared to the usual din, the small, one-bedroom apartment that Nyawal shared with her husband Nyang Deng and their two children was subdued. Nyawal explained that during the night they had received a phone call from Ethiopia informing her that her mother's sister's daughter had been in a motor vehicle accident. Nyawal was very worried about her sister. Yet she also was concerned with the dilemmas she now faced in maintaining her family in the United States, sending enough money to Ethiopia to pay for her sister's medical care, and continuing to meet the existing obligations she and her husband had to his family. Nyawal's dilemma represents an important dynamic in the Nuer migration experience by underscoring the intersection of transnational linkages with gender and generational relations.

It also provides insights into the contentious realm of Nuer marriage in the United States.

In the transnationalization of Nuer marriage and courtship the renegotiation of gender roles and generational relations are key sites of contestation where African-based elders' authority is challenged yet still perpetuated by US-based Nuer men and women. Marital tensions linked to familial investment of remittances are a growing source of conflict for Nuer married couples in the United States. Here I seek to carve out some conceptual space to move beyond the superficial demonizing discourse some Nuer males use to disparage segments of the Nuer female population. In these cases, men refer to those women who do not conform to their version of Nuer society's gender-role expectations by refusing to "settle down" as tourist women. Migration, which often alters the demographic composition of social groups along gender and age lines, provides opportunities to reconfigure authority structures and social relationships. For resettled Sudanese in America, engagement with the refugee resettlement apparatus has resulted in a skewed demographic profile, where the population is predominantly male. Similarly, most Nuer in the United States are

From Dianna Shandy, *Nuer-American Passages: Globalizing Sudanese Migration*, University Press of Florida, 1st edition (2007), pp. 109–26. Reprinted with permission by the University Press of Florida.

relatively young. Absent from Nuer gender relations in the United States, therefore, is the proximate influence of traditional elders.

The experience of migration between Africa and the United States introduced a whole complement of new variables with which Nuer migrants have had to contend. The conditions under which the Nuer lived in Sudan are not, for the most part, replicable in the United States. Obvious changes include the nature of work, the economics of daily life, and living arrangements. These changes have precipitated ongoing shifts in other domains such as gender roles and generational interactions.

A fundamental shift in Nuer gender relations in the United States is women's increased access to education and income-generating opportunities on par with their husbands. In Africa, Nuer women are certainly not described as meek. However, processes of commoditization of land and labor, war-induced destabilization, and a truncation of kinship ties due to displacement and increased mortality rates elevate women's vulnerability in these settings. In contrast, even Nuer women with little or no formal schooling before arrival in the United States find themselves equipped to contribute to the maintenance of family in the United States and in Africa. What this signifies, I suggest, is a new, transnationalized version of the "sandwich" generation, where one cares for and supports one's family of origin on one continent and one's family of procreation on another.

Ways Elders Exert Control

One half of the transnational sandwich equation can be seen in the ways elders in Africa exert control and command resources from Nuer in America. The institution of marriage is the principal avenue through which African-based elders accomplish this. This control is seen most vividly through the transfer of bridewealth, the selection of marriage partners, and the naming of children.

Age still matters within Sudanese families. One man whose father was killed in Sudan spoke to me about the weighty responsibility of being head not only of the family residing in the United States but also of the remaining family members in Africa. In another setting in a living room full of men in their late twenties, a man in his late teens served us food and drinks. The men joked that since he was the youngest he would be the "woman," illustrating the complex interplay of gender and generation. The difference, however, was that in contrast to what Nuer women typically do, when he finished serving us he sat down and joined us rather than retiring to another room. This scenario of a young man preparing and serving food is reminiscent of settings in cattle camps in Sudan, where males would fend for themselves when away from mothers, wives, and sisters.

A divorced Nuer woman in her late teens with a two-year-old son, Nyajok, noted that her mother and siblings were in Sudan; she said that she had tried to get her mother to come to the United States, but she refused. After finishing high school, Nyajok hoped to return to Africa to visit her mother; however, she is not interested in returning to Africa to live because "there is no future there." And, she appreciates "the freedom in America." Since she came to the United States when she was fourteen, she has enjoyed significant autonomy from family control. Nyajok notes that if she were living in Africa, she would have "to do everything mother says." But here, she makes her own decisions, including divorcing her husband, who is in his early twenties and who cares for their son.

Selection of marriage partners

Those familiar with the Nuer as described by Evans-Pritchard (1940, 1951, 1956) are undoubtedly curious about the ways in which marital alliances are brokered among such celebrated cattle-keeping people in the seeming absence of cattle. While there are exceptions, Nuer men are marrying Nuer women. I have documented one case where a Nuer man in Georgia reportedly married a woman from Thailand. Some Nuer men married Ethiopian women while still in Africa and resettled with them in the United States. At numerous gatherings, I have observed a handful of young Nuer men with American girlfriends, black or white. Since these gatherings are, for the most part, segregated by sex – the women and children in one area and the men in another – the American girlfriends stand out as they sit with their boyfriends in the men's area.

Many Sudanese men reported being married and awaiting the arrival of their wives from Africa.

Marriage in this context could mean a consummated marriage, which resulted in children, or simply a girl who was promised to a particular man when she reached an appropriate age. Both types of marriage are legitimate for Nuer. However, the latter form of marriage is more difficult to document for immigration authorities.

Other men are single and will rely on family members to broker a marriage for them or will adopt the dominant practice in the United States and choose their own wife without the intervention of their parents or family members in Africa. Tut Jak, a single Gaajak man in his late twenties who has attended college in the United States, asserted,

> Marriage is a matter of decision. If we were in villages in the South, we would be married by now, but here we are free. There we are told, Don't marry girls who are Anuak or Dinka. We are encouraged to marry girls from Africa whose backgrounds they [parents in Africa] know well. We are very traditional. Me, I am the elder one. My family needs my services. If I marry someone who is not Nuer, she may control the money. Or she may be surprised [in the sense of looking down on them]. It's not that they hate others, but my wife is the one that must give them the services they need – clothes, cooking with them. We dominate women there. My brother did it. My father did it. I won't do it. I will teach my wife my own culture so she won't be surprised. I will alert her.

The geographic dispersal of the Sudanese in the United States adds an interesting and challenging dimension to courtship. Deng Kurjiok, an unmarried Gaajak man in his mid-twenties, lived in a total of six different states during his first four years in the United States. He said that traveling throughout the United States to live in various locales was important to his marriage strategy. In his words, "you have to find a friend before you can have a wife." There are very few unmarried or unbetrothed Nuer women in America. However, divorce, canceling the betrothal, and putting in a word for a girl not yet of marriageable age would all be ways of increasing the number of Nuer women in circulation. Another young man, John Thok, reportedly had the favor and consent of his future wife and his future wife's brother, but he did not have the blessing of his future wife's sister or her husband. To remedy this situation, John moved away from the state where his future wife lived to another state to live close to his future wife's sister, in order to impress upon her and her husband his fine qualities as a future affine by demonstrating that he was a hard worker and a decent person.

Transfer of bridewealth cattle

Even among Nuer in the United States, the transfer of cattle to recognize marriage endures as an important element in claiming paternity and custody of children. This extends to Nuer marriages that take place in the United States. This finding contrasts sharply with Holtzman's statement that "in the United States there are no bridewealth cattle to be returned in the event of divorce" (2000, 401). In my research, I found the use of cattle to recognize marriage alive and well. One Nuer couple who married in the United States, she a widow and he a divorcé, described receiving a call from Ethiopia letting them know that a celebration had taken place the night before to recognize their marriage. They had been married eighteen months earlier in a church in the United States, but it had taken this long to save and transfer enough money to Africa to pay a significant portion of the bridewealth and funds for the celebration. John Wal, a Gaajak man in his early twenties, gave the following detailed financial account of bridewealth reckoned in a transnational context, where the current rate is $3,900: "If you marry here and the girl's father is here, you will pay money by how much one cow will take in money – twenty-eight big cows, two small cows, and five bulls. One bull is $200. One cow is $100. Two little cows are $50 each. That's the way we marry here. That's not the way they do it here, but we will keep this. In our country, the girl cannot choose. We learn that here the girl chooses. In our country we had a law for the marriage." Another Gaajak man I interviewed while in Ethiopia gave a more general accounting of bridewealth, with a different scale for Africa-based and diaspora-based Nuer. "Rich Nuer," especially those based in the United States, are expected to pay twenty to twenty-five cows ($1,500–$2,000); Nuer in camps are expected to pay ten to fifteen cows ($700–$1,000).

A variation on this theme can be seen when males return to Africa to marry. Many men I interviewed were already betrothed to women in Africa, usually through a family intermediary's efforts, so in some cases travel to Africa was to fulfill immigration requirements. In one case, the young man's mother "recruited" a wife, but the young man knew her family. From his perspective, knowing her family was akin to knowing her. He liquidated most of his possessions to purchase a plane ticket. He said that he did not need to travel to Africa to marry according to what he called Nuer law, but he had to do this for official immigration purposes. In Ethiopia he participated in a Christian ceremony to obtain a marriage certificate and submitted paperwork for his new wife to join him in America. He returned to the United States to work to pay for costs associated with his wife's resettlement here, and she eventually joined him. Upon arrival, she was greeted with a celebration at the airport. After a few months, when the man had saved enough money to pay for a party, he pooled resources with another man in a similar situation and they held a joint marriage celebration with food, dancing, and speeches, with the brides clad in matching pale yellow suits.

Men are also linked to their families in Africa through virilocal, postmarital residence practices. Some men exploit the ambiguity associated with the African concept of marriage as process rather than an event. One man described his dilemma of having a wife (or prospective wife) who was living with his family in Africa and having met a non-Nuer African woman in the United States with whom he had had a romantic relationship. He confessed to being torn about what to do, as he was betrothed to this young woman who was living with his family in Ethiopia, but since he was not truly married according to US norms, there was a loophole that he was contemplating exploiting, especially in light of stepped-up demands from both his family and his future wife in Africa for financial support.

Some transformation from virilocal to neolocal residency practices may have been underway in refugee camp settings, particularly in Kenya, where young people were more likely to be separated from families that they left behind in Ethiopia or Sudan. However, evidence that virilo-cal residence was still dominant can be seen in the instances, like the one described above, where Nuer men in America who were betrothed or married speak of their wives living with the men's families in Sudan, Ethiopia, or even Kenya.

Therefore, another reason men seek wives in Africa and marry with cattle is to draw upon elders' authority to reinforce their own control over their US-based household. US-based Nuer grapple with managing the migration-induced shift from virilocal to neolocal residency practices. Economic and spatial realities of urban and suburban residence in the United States have played an important part in this shift, as refugees with limited resources must rely on access to low-cost public housing. Yet, even more than in other housing situations, there are strict controls over the definition of the domestic unit eligible to reside in that dwelling. To be eligible for this housing, Nuer refugees must at least appear to conform to US nuclear family-based definitions of domestic units (Ong 1996, 2003).

Nuer live in a range of kinds of dwellings from single-family homes to public housing complexes. In terms of home ownership, I met only one family, who were Anuak, who had taken out a mortgage to purchase their home. One Nuer man expressed regret that he had not followed the advice of the voluntary agency representative who had resettled him, who had recommended that he and his cohort attempt to pool their resources and purchase the house in which they were living. Most Nuer rent homes on the open market, qualify for state-run public housing, or rent homes from landlords willing to accept state subsidies. The quality of accommodation varied dramatically from state to state and even within states. Unlike the urban public housing towers I encountered when I lived on the edge of Harlem in New York City in graduate school, Nuer in places like St. Paul, Minnesota; Nashville, Tennessee; Des Moines, Iowa; and Omaha, Nebraska tend to reside in public or subsidized housing blocks of no more than eight units. In Omaha, for instance, I vividly recall visiting some Nuer who had just moved there from Tennessee to avail themselves of what they had heard was very inexpensive public housing. The squat building looked okay from the outside, but I was immediately overwhelmed by the potent odor of urine-soaked carpeting on the stairs upon entering the building. It was as if the buildings had been abandoned and used as a public toilet before being turned into accommodation. In another of the buildings someone had torn the carpet up and removed it, exposing the bare, worn floorboards. Aside from the stench and disrepair, the corridor was rather tidy; there was no debris on the floors. Entering the apartments from the corridors was a pleasant surprise and reminded me of coming in off the dusty, hectic streets in African cities like Addis Ababa or Nairobi to find soothing compounds, which led to individual well-maintained dwellings. Typical of many other apartments I visited in various states, this particular apartment had a kitchen, a bathroom, and a very large living room, branching off to three bedrooms out of sight. The living room was dominated by large, seemingly new, matching sectional sofas, decorated with purple-and-white hand-crocheted antimacassars. There was a television and a rather sophisticated looking stereo that blasted Arabic language music over the sound of the television. The walls had a picture of Tupac Shakur and several pictures of Jesus and were decorated at regular intervals along the top by crosses made from decorative wall border material. Perched on a shelf were a couple of sports trophies inscribed with a Sudanese name. The wall-to-wall carpeting, while not nearly as filthy as that in the corridor leading into the apartment, was unclean, and the Nuer family living there had covered it with throw rugs.

Residency practices influence other domains of Nuer life in important ways. Social service providers assert, based on anecdotal evidence, that the incidence of domestic violence among Sudanese refugees is increasing as a result of neolocal residence. A refugee services worker told of one such experience:

> One woman wanted to leave her husband because of domestic violence. The husband's family beat the crap out of her, kicking her in the stomach when she was six months pregnant. This happened virtually on the steps of the ORR [Office of Refugee Resettlement] office. She was rushed to the hospital. There is a significant amount of spouse abuse. At the same time, the women chase the men down the street with butcher knives.

It is argued that this housing arrangement shifts the focus from an alliance between families to a more intense relationship between two individuals who may have been only marginally involved in the choice of the selection of their spouse. Tensions arising from this arrangement are aggravated by such factors as long separations when one spouse is resettled before the other (and the potential incorporation of additional children from a genitor that is not the pater); the young age of the wife at marriage; the absence of kin networks in the United States; and stress associated with incorporation into life in the United States intensified by a context of poverty.

One Nuer man in his early thirties whose wife had divorced him in the United States said that he intended to marry a woman from Sudan. Ideally, she would be twenty-five or twenty-six years old and have at least a few years of formal schooling. He dismissed the available Nuer women in the United States: "They come here, and they claim their rights. They are crazy here. They are kids. They must be [are expected to be] mature, but instead they like nightclubs and clothes." In this way, Africa symbolizes a repository of gender purity where women are not corrupted by what men describe as "the unreasonable levels of freedom for women in America."

In addition to relying on elders to select marriage partners in Africa, US-based Nuer also draw upon elders' knowledge of kinship and lineage matters to ensure that a prospective marriage does not break incest taboos. One couple who was married in the United States wrote letters to elders living in camps in Ethiopia to ask for permission to marry because they risked breaking incest rules. They genuinely wanted official sanction of this marriage, in part because they believed, as Hutchinson (1996) documents in Sudan, that the health and well-being of their progeny depended on it.

And a final apparently noncontentious area where it is possible to see the active elaboration of transnational ties between elders in Africa and US-based Nuer is in the naming of children [...]. Many families whom I interviewed said that elder kin in Africa had chosen the names for their US born children.

Ways Women and Men in Diaspora Subvert Authority

Therefore, while there are significant and ongoing threads of continuity between life in Africa and the way things are done in the United States, there is also room for the subversion of authority and the renegotiation of roles. One of the dilemmas the Nuer population faces in enforcing social norms is the relative lack of proximate elders. Gender and generation vie with each other for explanatory power in these situations. In some cases, men appeal to elders' authority for reinforcement and operationalize generational authority structures to influence gender relations. Simon Wal, age nineteen, married Nyariek Deng, age fifteen, in a Kenyan camp. Simon's father, who was living in Ethiopia, paid three of the twenty-five cows their family owed Nyariek's family, who were also living in Ethiopia. The families had reached an understanding that Simon would send his father money to buy the remaining cows after he reached America. Simon, his wife, and a friend were resettled in Des Moines. Two months after arrival, according to Simon, Nyariek said, "I don't want to be married. I want to go to school. I want to divorce you. I don't want to be married. I don't want to be controlled, because to be married is to be controlled." Simon reported that he asked Nyariek to talk the matter over by phone with her parents in Ethiopia, but she refused. He also said, "Nuer people gathered in Des Moines to talk to her, and she refused to cooperate." (In particular, her only family member in the United States, her mother's brother, came to talk with her.) The third level of arbitration this couple sought was the state's department of human services. Simon recounted the following conversation between Nyariek, the department's representative, and himself:

> They asked Nyariek whether she wanted to be with [me]. And then they say to her, who can pay your money [the loan for transport to America]? When you came from Africa, you had money on credit, and that money was documented for the head of the family [Simon.] Do you want to pay part and have Simon pay part? And she said yes. And then they asked where she would live because she was fifteen years old. She said she had an uncle [mother's brother] in California. She would go live with him. So they said they wanted to talk to [her mother's brother] first. And I say to them, we have some culture [a Nuer way of doing things]. When we marry we pay something. My father pays something to her father. What can we do? And they say: NO WAY HERE IN AMERICA!! So, you can inform your parents there, and they can do what they want, but here – NOTHING! They said if Nyariek wants to marry again, we go to the court. If I want to marry some other girl, we go to the court first. Or, when I get a job I can go to the court and do the paperwork. She [the social worker] told me when I get a job to call her. So, I got a job, I called her, she got a lawyer, and I paid $660 to divorce.

Nyariek's story brings to mind what Ong describes as "the feminist fervor of many social workers [that] actually works to weaken or reconstitute the ... family" (1996, 743). The push of the state and the civil institutions work at times in tandem to create pressure that encourages refugees to adopt normative roles with regard to behavior, particularly gender roles. Pressure is exerted through legal, social service, and other channels to promote assimilation to US values. Annette Busby (1998) captures this dynamic in her study of gender relations among Kurdish refugees in Sweden, where she writes that Swedes made the following remark about the Kurdish immigrants: "the problem is their culture." Minnesota, another site that prides itself on its liberal values and has been home to a sizable Hmong refugee population from Southeast Asia for more than three decades, provides another example of this pervasive dynamic. In autumn 1998, in the wake of a terrible tragedy where a young Hmong mother murdered all six of her young children, a local newspaper editorial arrived at a conclusion similar to Busby's – the problem was Hmong cultural norms regarding "patriarchal control" within the family. In the Nuer situation described above, the woman used the fact that elders were at a distance to her advantage. She appealed to the department of human services to support her efforts to divorce, as she was a minor. Divorce is a vivid example of how Nuer refugee women wield power and subvert the authority of Nuer males in America and Nuer elders in Africa. The baseline data provided by the work of Evans-Pritchard and Hutchinson (1990) make this a fascinating phenomenon to follow over time. At present, it is only possible to speak to the situation of recently arrived refugees, most of whose marriages reportedly were recognized by the transfer of bridewealth cattle from the husband's family's kraal to that of the wife's family. Hutchinson (1996) has documented significant shifts in the transition from a cattle-based to a cash-based economy. It is unclear why Holtzman (2003, 401) did not encounter the issue of the transfer of bridewealth cattle, when it was such a pervasive theme in my research. The transfer of cattle remains an important element in claiming paternity and custody of children. In the five divorce cases I have documented in the United States – where children were involved and where the man's family reportedly had paid cattle – the young children went to live with the father. In the words of one Nuer man in his thirties, "If you have a child in Nuer law, you cannot leave your kid. If you divorce, the kid stays with the man. The women don't like to leave the kids, but that is the law." (See Hutchinson 1990.)

In one disputed case, where the man claimed to have paid cattle and other Nuer reported that he did not pay cattle, the child went to live with the mother. I have not recorded instances where the US court system was involved in decisions about Nuer child custody in the event of divorce. However, given the strong tendency in US court cases for mothers to be awarded child custody, and the challenge that would pose to Nuer practices, it is likely that this will emerge as an area of contention. In the two divorce cases that I have followed where cattle have been paid but no children were yet produced, Nuer informants report that the woman's family has returned cattle to the man's family. (I heard of the case of an Anuak single mother whose children had been taken into protective custody, but she, understandably, was unwilling to meet with me to discuss her experience.)

Six months after his divorce from Nyariek, Simon married Sarah Kuach, a young widow who had been recently resettled in the United States, in the Covenant Church. Other Nuer people had suggested that they meet one another. Simon and Sarah knew each other only from a distance in Sudan and the camps in Ethiopia. The cows that were transferred from Simon's family to Nyariek's family were not returned immediately to Simon's family in Ethiopia. It was only when, several

months later, Nyariek, while staying with her mother's brother, became pregnant by another man that the cows were returned. At this point members of the Sudanese community sided in favor of Simon and said that the man who had impregnated Nyariek should send money to her family to buy three cows to return to Simon's family. Simon and his second wife, Sarah, moved to South Dakota, where Simon finished his GED and got a job. Sarah enrolled in ESL classes and, pushed into the labor market by strict rules governing public assistance introduced with welfare reform, began working in a factory. Sarah and Simon alternate shifts so that one of them is always home to care for their three small children [...].

Divorce, child custody, and bridewealth are all areas of contestation and transformation. Pal Both, a Nuer man in his late twenties, noted changing sensibilities with respect to the economic realities of having children in the United States: "When they divorce, it is hard to say whether the children will go with the man or the woman. In USA you have to feed the children of another man. A woman has a hard time to marry if she has children." Many factors contribute to divorce and men's concern over the role of women in initiating dissolution of the conjugal union. An obvious factor is the three-to-one ratio of adult males to females resettled in the United States. Divorce and the keen interest men take in this issue can also be linked to changes in accepted practice with respect to adultery. Nuer men reported grave consequences in Sudan for men accused of adultery with another man's wife: "These women are married with cows. In Sudan, this man would be killed!" In contrast, in the United States, Nuer note that the law protects not only the wife from her husband's wrath but also the man who committed adultery. Furthermore, married Nuer men assert that it is the single men who have more resources to "seduce women" because they are not supporting a family.

Peter Buometet, a Gaajok man in his early thirties, whose wife was still in Ethiopia awaiting resettlement through family reunification channels, provided this perspective:

> Marriage is very important. If three girls out of one thousand divorce, it is too much. The reasons for divorce are: no food at home, no cow or money

at home, or he's not a good worker. But these are not reasons. In Sudan, the wife can go and grow crops or go to the relatives, so they don't care with the man. People share problems in Sudan. The people gather and challenge these things and the girl will go back home.

The inadvertent transgression of incest taboos (*ruaal*) is reportedly the only condition under which divorce is reportedly acceptable. Mat Wal, a Gaaguang man in his twenties who lived with his wife, summarized:

> It is okay to divorce if it is ruaal, if you didn't know and married a blood relation. We call it when an old man marries a young girl a stolen marriage. If the girl is not a good cook, no, no, no that is not in the Nuer law to divorce. We say the girl is *bach*. She is not a good cook. She does not work well.

Related Tensions in Nuer Gender Relations: "Dancing before the Drum?"

Many of my interviews with Nuer men elicited very strong and often negative views about certain Nuer women. As with the disproportionate attention divorce garners relative to the number of cases of divorce I tracked, this seems out of proportion to my observations of daily life in Nuer families. In light of material presented thus far, it bears noting that discourse surrounding gender relations is indicative of and related to other forms of social tensions associated with the leveling effects of migration. A Gaajok man in his thirties put it this way:

> There is a gap between the "knows" and the "don't knows" in Sudan. They become one group in the U.S. If you give advice, the rural dwellers say they already know. Now, they are in one basket, including the ones who jump from nowhere. Machar and Garang, for example, with Ph.D.s, would also be in the same class in America. In this situation, there are no people to lead or to be led. In this society, women feel like they have reached heaven. In our society, women and children are subordinate.

Therefore, men's anger directed toward women that engage in adulterous liaisons or other transgressions is also related to men's inability to exact compensation from the men involved in these relationships. Similarly, the loss of control over wives also signals current and anticipated tensions between fathers and children. Some Nuer parents are contending with generational tensions already; however, it is expected that this will be a more pressing topic as the children of the relatively young Nuer parents in their twenties are raised in the United States. While I did not encounter this among Nuer I interviewed, I did speak with one Somali mother who sent her troublesome teenage son back to Africa as a way of managing his delinquency and other behavioral problems.

Given the disproportionately high number of adult Nuer women relative to Nuer men, women who choose not to remain with their husband have multiple options in choosing eligible Nuer men. Sudanese women whom men perceive as less committed to their families are frequently called tourists. Men charge that the women in the United States have life much easier than their counterparts in Africa. Simon Deng, a Gaajak man in his late twenties summed up this sentiment: "Women in America are tourist women. They [may seem to] do whatever they like. They may change men, but they [still] do the kitchen work. These women are considered with low prestige – like a prostitute. We presume a high chance of a second divorce. There is not really a second marriage. The woman is just a concubine." Jok Jieng, a Gaajok man in his thirties, put it this way: "Women face criticism because women look at family, and men look at the well-being of the whole community and see the tensions between man and wife. Such a creature is useless because she cannot manage her husband and child. Women in the US have it easy. They don't have to share food, etc. They just please themselves."

These women, according to the men, travel from state to state visiting friends and relatives. From an analytical stance, one could argue that these women are maintaining and creating ties of kinship, friendship, and ethnicity, but this is not how Nuer men see it. According to some of my male informants, these were women who did not have jobs, were not caring for children, and were not pursuing educational opportunities. Indeed, Nuer arrangements for child custody – whereby children for whom bridewealth cattle had been paid remained with the father – facilitated the mobility of these women. The emergence of the pejorative moniker *tourist women* may reveal less about any reality of these women's lives and, in effect, be more a lashing out by men to compensate for their diminished capacity to control women.

In attempting to move beyond the he said–she said roadblock, it is worth exploring the other half of the transnational sandwich equation. In addition to the pull of family in Africa, Nuer families have the responsibility of raising their family in the United States. Nuer are struggling with the intersection of Nuer and American cultural ideals about family size and the economic realities of raising children in America. In light of this, Nyajal Chuol, a Nuer woman in her late twenties, explained that she and her husband planned to limit their family to the son and daughter that they already had. Two children, in her estimation, were expensive enough to raise in America. Women spoke to me about using Depo-Provera injections, condoms, and withdrawal before ejaculation for contraception. Conversely, other Nuer couples expressed a desire for six or more children.

Many Nuer couples assert that a key area of family tensions is related to remittances. Sarah Mahler observes, "while a common household economy is often assumed, spouses frequently send remittances independently and for different purposes" (2006, 8). Now that women are contributing significantly to family income, they are demanding control over the allocation of remittances to support their own kin in Africa, as illustrated in the introductory ethnographic description of the woman whose relative in Ethiopia needed money for medical care. Mahler goes on to point out that "when female migrants send remittances home they improve their social standing in their families" (ibid.). Given tensions in Nuer marriages, as well as prospects for a durable peace in Sudan, women remitting to their own kinship networks can be seen as a specific means of investing in their own future and that of their children, should their marriage dissolve or should they wish to return to Africa.

Nuer women's increased access to education and opportunities to generate income is central to shifts in other dimensions of social life. One Nuer man explained Nuer women's access to educational opportunities in Sudan: "Dinka women have more education than Nuer women because the Nuer take girls out of school to get married. We don't have secondary schools for girls that were close to the house. If girls go away to school, the people think that they make prostitution. So, they don't send them." (For a similar observation, see MacDermot 1972.) Yet, even Nuer women with little or no education before arriving in the United States find themselves capable of earning in a month more than their parents in Sudan, or in a camp in a neighboring country, might earn in an entire year.

This is not lost on the Nuer. Peter Buometet, the Gaajok man whose wife is still in Ethiopia, introduced earlier described how he thinks the system is biased toward women in the United States: "There is bias in the workplace against men toward women. It is easier for women to get a job with higher pay. They don't need the husband, so they divorce. The US government gives children to women. Sudanese women say, Ahhh, there are human rights for women. They start dancing before the drum [that is, they are getting ahead of themselves.]" While Peter's observation about gendered access to the workforce may appear to run counter to discrepancies with respect to the larger American workforce, his point may be valid for certain segments of the workforce, such as African Americans (Collins 1990).

Nuer themselves see gender relations as a problem area in need of a solution. Paul Atak, a Madi man from southern Sudan who aspires to hold a Mutual Assistance Association leadership role and serve as a liaison between Sudanese people and social service providers, addressed a mixed group of social service providers and Nuer men to highlight gender issues that Sudanese faced as a result of migration:

> There is a cultural element to accessing resources through the women. Married women expect their husbands to bring those things; it is their responsibility. How do we address the issue of the husband spending money on luxury items such as the VCR? Men go to the grocery store and buy all fresh food and don't pay attention to the cost. It's an education issue regarding priorities of putting kids' shoes before the VCR. Husbands will, however, become angry if confronted about these issues.

You need friends and relatives to convey the message through storytelling.

However, controversy does not characterize all Nuer marriages. William Jiech, a married Gaajak man in his mid-twenties who lives with his wife and two small children, provides a counterpoint to the notion that all Nuer marriages are disharmonious, illustrating the limitations in a monolithic characterization of gender relations among the Nuer in the diaspora:

> The women are good. The men are crazy. The women organize themselves. They organize the families. If a man marries, he has the right to control the family. If you move, you decide a month ago, but you don't tell her until the day before. And you say, we move. The wife cannot fight with him. I have a power. That is why I do that. It is very bad. We see when we come to this country that this is bad. Every member of the family has rights. We have to share life. It's not good to be a Nuer woman in Nuer law. We cannot leave American law and we cannot leave our mother law. We take the good parts of both. Nuer law is applied by agreement. People are punished by [do not benefit from] fighting.

While there do appear to be limits to how far Nuer women go in challenging Nuer forms of authority, they do exhibit a great deal of independence in terms of decision making and action, which is consistent with how they lived in Africa but exceeds that which might be expected among a group of recently arrived refugees given their low proficiency in English language and limited education. My research supports Heldenbrand's findings in a Shilluk family case study (1996) involving a mother who availed of the services of community domestic violence shelters to move to another state with her children and leave her husband behind. As in the example Ong (1996) presents where a Cambodian woman wields control over her domestic situation by using the women's shelter and the social service agencies against her husband, Nyariek (described earlier) and several other young women who arrived in the United States as minors made use of social services to divorce their husbands. One possibly surprising phenomenon, from a US perspective, is the willingness of women, for a variety of reasons, to migrate in

order to leave their husbands and, in the process, their children. The distance to be traveled or a lack of familiarity with a location does not appear to deter women who are contemplating a move. Yet, in contrast to men, women seem less likely to set out to a destination where they have no kin or other ties.

Women appear to pool resources in the form of reciprocal gifts to mark life cycle events, but they do not appear to use a formalized credit scheme to do so. Mary Gach, a mother in her early twenties, spent about $100 on food for people coming to her home to celebrate the first birthday of her daughter, Changkuoth. Consequently, she had no money to buy an American-style birthday cake to share at the ESL class she attended daily. Her friends in the class, she said, chipped in to buy the cake to share in class. She also told me that when her daughter was born, other Nuer "family and friends" came to visit her and the baby. Each visitor typically gave her $20 "to buy soft things for the baby." In addition to her nuclear family, Mary's kin in the United States includes her husband's father's brother's son and his wife and children; and Mary's mother's brother's daughter and her husband and children. Mary's friends include another Nuer couple and their children who live in their apartment complex, Nuer women whom she knew from Sudan or the camp in Ethiopia, and women she had met in her ESL class.

Mary Gach and other women do establish cooperative bonds. To a certain extent, they form reciprocal networks to assist one another with child care. But there were limitations to these relationships. In one case, two Gaajak women who appeared to be good friends lived in the same apartment building with their respective families. When I was visiting one, the other invariably came to visit. Their children played together. One day, when sitting and chatting with one woman, the other knocked and came in the door carrying a bowl of food and eating. She went immediately to the refrigerator, grabbed a spoon and a jar of Hellmann's mayonnaise and deposited a huge blob on top of her food, continued eating, and soon left. This event prompted me to ask the woman who lived in the apartment whether the women pooled resources and shared cooking. She quickly and definitively said that they do not. Nor did she seem disturbed by her neighbor's behavior. Parties are another matter; there people do share food.

Women and families take turns visiting one household on any given Saturday. People drop in and out of the hosts' home throughout the day. If people are hungry, they ask the woman hosting for food, or they go to the cupboard, get a bowl, which they rinse in the sink, and serve themselves from the pot on the stove. The hosts also have a large stock of soda pop for guests, which they distribute in a ritualistic manner. If supplies run out, the husband will go to the supermarket to buy more. Visitors also go to the refrigerator and fill children's bottles with whole milk or serve themselves a glass.

Only about ten Nuer women whom I met had even low levels of formal schooling before arriving in the United States; most had none. My sample is perhaps biased because many of the opportunities that I had to meet women were through the ESL class, which tended to cater to women with very low literacy and English-language skills.

Nyandit Lual, a particularly dynamic woman in her early twenties, took the recently arrived young wife, Esther Kier, of her male relative into her home to teach her about "things in America." Esther and her husband, Ruey Kui, had been officially married in Ethiopia, but she had been awaiting resettlement. Nyandit taught Esther many basics, such as how to use the gas stove and the appliances in the laundry room of the apartment building; how to substitute ingredients obtained from the Egyptian grocery for familiar recipes; how to use voice mail and call waiting; and what products were available in US stores for her hair. Nyandit also took off days from her work at a dry cleaner's to spend a few days at the home of Nyanpal Kuey, who had just given birth to a set of twins. Nyandit's husband and a Nuer woman who lived in their apartment building cared for their three small children during her absence.

That Nyandit's husband cares for their children in her absence suggests the ways in which fathers are involved in raising their children. Some couples struggle to adapt to their changing environment and US expectations for gender roles. Other couples seem to take the changes in stride, extracting what they find helpful from Nuer culture and incorporating US norms in other ways. This range of experiences and ways of managing change is consistent with what one would expect for an emerging diaspora population.

References

Busby, Annette. 1998. "The Problem Is Their Culture: The Integration of Kurdish Refugees in Sweden." Paper presented at the Society for Applied Anthropology, San Juan, Puerto Rico.

Collins, Patricia Hill. 1990. *Black Feminist Thought: Knowledge, Consciousness, and the Politics of Empowerment*. New York: Routledge.

Evans-Pritchard, E. E. 1951. *Kinship and Marriage among the Nuer*. Oxford: Clarendon.

Evans-Pritchard, E. E. 1956. *Nuer Religion*. Oxford: Clarendon.

Evans-Pritchard, E. E. 1940. *The Nuer: A Description of the Modes of Livelihood and Political Institutions of a Nilotic People*. Oxford: Clarendon.

Heldenbrand, Kathleen. 1996. "Unwitting Pioneers: Sudanese Refugees in the Midwest." In *Selected Papers on Refugee Issues IV*, ed. A Rynearson and J. Phillips, pp. 106–26. Washington, DC: American Anthropological Association.

Holtzman, Jon D. 2003. "Dialing 911 in Nuer: Gender Transformations and Domestic Violence in a Midwestern Sudanese Refugee Community." In *Immigration Research for a New Century*, ed. Nancy Foner, Roben Rumbaut, and Steven J. Gold, pp. 390–408. New York: Russell Sage Foundation.

Holtzman, Jon D. 2000. *Nuer Journeys, Nuer Lives: Sudanese Refugees in Minnesota*. Boston: Allyn and Bacon.

Hutchinson, Sharon. 1990 "Rising Divorce among the Nuer, 1936–1983." *Man*, n.s., 25: 393–411.

Hutchinson, Sharon. 1996. *Nuer Dilemmas: Coping with Money, War, and the State*. Berkeley: University of California Press.

MacDermot, Brian Hugh. 1972. *Cult of the Sacred Spear: The Story of the Nuer Tribe in Ethiopia*. London: R. Hale.

Mahler, Sarah. 2006. "Gender Matters." *ID21 Insights* (Institute of Development Studies, University of Sussex), no. 60 (January): 8.

Ong, Aihwa 1996. "Cultural Citizenship as Subject-Making." *Current Anthropology* 37 (5): 737–51.

Ong, Aihwa 2003. *Buddha Is Hiding: Refugees, Citizenship, the New America*. Berkeley: University of California Press.

Index